Meet the Authors

Mark Hirschey, Ph.D., is the Anderson W. Chandler Professor of Business at the University of Kansas, where he teaches undergraduate and graduate courses in investments and security analysis. Author of more than 85 academic research articles, scholarly books, and textbooks, Professor Hirschey has an international reputation for research leadership and accomplishments at the interface of finance, managerial economics, and accounting. Professor Hirschey has published articles in the *Journal of Financial Economics, Journal of Finance, American Economic Review, Financial Analysts Journal, Journal of Portfolio Management,* and other leading scholarly journals. His work on the valuation effects of advertising, research and development, and patent quality has helped establish the importance of intangible capital in the stock market's valuation of firms. Similarly, his research on the economic implications of corporate restructuring illustrates the importance of managerial incentives in the stock market's ongoing assessment of managerial effectiveness. Professor Hirschey has earned research awards for his studies on the effects of the Internet on investor behavior and market efficiency. He is founding president of the Association of Financial Economists and co-editor of *Advances in Financial Economics,* a scholarly research series published by Elsevier Science. He is advisory editor for the *Financial Review, Journal of Business Finance & Accounting,* and *Managerial & Decision Economics* and author of *Managerial Economics, 11th Edition* and *Fundamentals of Managerial Economics, 8th Edition.*

John Nofsinger, Ph.D., is an Associate Professor and the Lang Fellow at Washington State University where he teaches undergraduate, master's, and doctoral level investment courses. His research focuses on investor behavior, investments, and international finance. More than 25 of his articles have been published in academic journals such as the *Journal of Business, Journal of Finance, Journal of Financial and Quantitative Analysis, Financial Management,* and *Journal of Behavioral Finance,* and industry journals such as the *Financial Analysts Journal* and *Journal of Investing.* Professor Nofsinger has also conducted research for national organizations such as the New York Stock Exchange, the Association of Investment Management Research (of the CFA Institute), and the Joint Economic Committee of the U.S. Congress. As an expert in behavioral finance, he has often been quoted in the financial media, including *The Wall Street Journal, BusinessWeek, Fortune, Kiplinger's Personal Finance, Bloomberg,* and *CNBC,* and other media from *USA Today* to TheStreet.com. He has authored six books on investing and finance. His book on investor psychology is a "required reading" for candidates seeking the Chartered Financial Analyst designation. Professor Nofsinger is also a frequent speaker at national and international finance conferences, as well as at universities and investment organizations.

With the purchase of a New Book*

You Can Access the Real Financial Data that the Experts Use!

*If you purchased a used book, see other side for access information.

This card entitles the purchaser of a new textbook to a semester of access to the Educational Version of Standard & Poor's Market Insight®, a rich online resource featuring hundreds of the most often researched companies in the Market Insight database.

For 1,000 companies, this website provides you:

- Access to six years' worth of fundamental financial data from the renowned Standard & Poor's COMPUSTAT® database
- 12 Excel Analytics Reports, including balance sheets, income statements, ratio reports and cash flow statements; adjusted prices reports, and profitability; forecasted values and monthly valuation data reports
- Access to Financial Highlights Reports including key ratios
- S & P Stock Reports that offer fundamental, quantitative and technical analysis
- EDGAR reports updated throughout the day
- Industry Surveys, written by S & P's Equity analysts
- News feeds (updated hourly) for companies and industries.

STANDARD &POOR'S

McGraw-Hill Irwin

Exclusive partnership!

See other side for your unique site ID access code.

Welcome to the Educational Version of Market Insight!

www.mhhe.com/edumarketinsight

Check out your textbook's website for details on how this special offer enhances the value of your purchase!

1. To get started, use your web browser to go to **www.mhhe.com/edumarketinsight**

2. Enter your site ID exactly as it appears below.

3. You may be prompted to enter the site ID for future use—please keep this card.

Your site ID is:

va167349

STANDARD &POOR'S

ISBN: 978-0-07-331041-1
MHID: 0-07-331041-7

 **McGraw-Hill Irwin**

*If you purchased a used book, this site ID may have expired. For new password purchase, please go to www.mhhe.com/edumarketinsight. Password activation is good for a 6 month duration.

Investments

Analysis and Behavior

The McGraw-Hill/Irwin Series in Finance, Insurance and Real Estate

Stephen A. Ross, Consulting Editor
Franco Modigliani Professor of Finance and Economics
Sloan School of Management, Massachusetts Institute of Technology

FINANCIAL MANAGEMENT

Adair
Excel Applications for Corporate Finance
Second Edition

Benninga and Sarig
Corporate Finance: A Valuation Approach

Block and Hirt
Foundations of Financial Management
Twelfth Edition

Brealey, Myers, and Allen
Principles of Corporate Finance
Eighth Edition

Brealey, Myers, and Marcus
Fundamentals of Corporate Finance
Fifth Edition

Brooks
FinGame Online 4.0

Bruner
Case Studies in Finance: Managing for
Corporate Value Creation
Fifth Edition

Chew
The New Corporate Finance: Where Theory
Meets Practice
Third Edition

Chew and Gillan
Corporate Governance at the Crossroads: A
Book of Readings
First Edition

DeMello
Cases in Finance
Second Edition

Grinblatt and Titman
Financial Markets and Corporate Strategy
Second Edition

Helfert
Techniques of Financial Analysis: A Guide to
Value Creation
Eleventh Edition

Higgins
Analysis for Financial Management
Eighth Edition

Kester, Ruback, and Tufano
Case Problems in Finance
Twelfth Edition

Ross, Westerfield, and Jaffe
Corporate Finance
Eighth Edition

Ross, Westerfield, Jaffe, and Jordan
Corporate Finance: Core Principles and
Applications
First Edition

Ross, Westerfield, and Jordan
Essentials of Corporate Finance
Fifth Edition

Ross, Westerfield, and Jordan
Fundamentals of Corporate Finance
Eighth Edition

Shefrin
Behavioral Corporate Finance: Decisions That
Create Value
First Edition

Smith
The Modern Theory of Corporate Finance
Second Edition

White
Financial Analysis with an Electronic
Calculator
Sixth Edition

INVESTMENTS

Bodie, Kane, and Marcus
Essentials of Investments
Sixth Edition

Bodie, Kane, and Marcus
Investments
Seventh Edition

Cohen, Zinbarg, and Zeikel
Investment Analysis and Portfolio
Management
Fifth Edition

Hirschey and Nofsinger
Investments: Analysis and Behavior
First Edition

Hirt and Block
Fundamentals of Investment Management
Eighth Edition

Jordan and Miller
Fundamentals of Investments: Valuation and
Management
Fourth Edition

FINANCIAL INSTITUTIONS AND MARKETS

Cornett and Saunders
Fundamentals of Financial Institutions
Management

Rose and Hudgins
Bank Management and Financial Services
Seventh Edition

Rose and Marquis
Money and Capital Markets: Financial
Institutions and Instruments in a Global
Marketplace
Ninth Edition

Santomero and Babbel
Financial Markets, Instruments, and
Institutions
Second Edition

Saunders and Cornett
Financial Institutions Management: A Risk
Management Approach
Fifth Edition

Saunders and Cornett
Financial Markets and Institutions: An
Introduction to the Risk Management
Approach
Third Edition

INTERNATIONAL FINANCE

Beim and Calomiris
Emerging Financial Markets

Eun and Resnick
International Financial Management
Fourth Edition

Kuemmerle
Case Studies in International
Entrepreneurship: Managing and Financing
Ventures in the Global Economy
First Edition

Levich
International Financial Markets: Prices and
Policies
Second Edition

REAL ESTATE

Brueggeman and Fisher
Real Estate Finance and Investments
Thirteenth Edition

Corgel, Ling, and Smith
Real Estate Perspectives: An Introduction to
Real Estate
Fourth Edition

Ling and Archer
Real Estate Principles: A Value Approach
Second Edition

FINANCIAL PLANNING AND INSURANCE

Allen, Melone, Rosenbloom, and Mahoney
Pension Planning: Pension, Profit-Sharing, and
Other Deferred Compensation Plans
Ninth Edition

Altfest
Personal Financial Planning
First Edition

Crawford
Life and Health Insurance Law
Eighth Edition (LOMA)

Harrington and Niehaus
Risk Management and Insurance
Second Edition

Hirsch
Casualty Claim Practice
Sixth Edition

Kapoor, Dlabay, and Hughes
Focus on Personal Finance: An Active
Approach to Help You Develop Successful
Financial Skills
First Edition

Kapoor, Dlabay, and Hughes
Personal Finance
Eighth Edition

Investments

Analysis and Behavior

MARK HIRSCHEY
University of Kansas

JOHN NOFSINGER
Washington State University

McGraw-Hill
Irwin

Boston   Burr Ridge, IL   Dubuque, IA   New York   San Francisco   St. Louis
Bangkok   Bogotá   Caracas   Kuala Lumpur   Lisbon   London   Madrid   Mexico City
Milan   Montreal   New Delhi   Santiago   Seoul   Singapore   Sydney   Taipei   Toronto

INVESTMENTS: ANALYSIS AND BEHAVIOR
Published by McGraw-Hill/Irwin, a business unit of The McGraw-Hill Companies, Inc., 1221 Avenue of the Americas, New York, NY, 10020.

Some ancillaries, including electronic and print components, may not be available to customers outside the United States.

This book is printed on acid-free paper.

1 2 3 4 5 6 7 8 9 0 QPD/QPD 0 9 8 7 6

ISBN 978-0-07-353064-2

MHID 0-07-353064-6

Editorial director: *Brent Gordon*
Publisher: *Stephen M. Patterson*
Executive editor: *Michele Janicek*
Developmental editor II: *Christina Kouvelis*
Senior marketing manager: *Julie Phifer*
Media producer: *Jennifer Wilson*
Senior project manager: *Susanne Riedell*
Production supervisor: *Jason Huls*
Senior designer: *Kami Carter*
Lead media project manager: *Becky Szura*
Cover design: *Kami Carter*
Interior design: *Kami Carter*
Cover Image: *© Corbis Images*
Typeface: *10/12 Times Roman*
Compositor: *Carlisle Publishing Services*
Printer: *Quebecor World Dubuque Inc.*

Library of Congress Cataloging-in-Publication Data

Hirschey, Mark.
    Investments : analysis and behavior / Mark Hirschey, John Nofsinger.
      p. cm. — (The McGraw-Hill/Irwin series in finance, insurance and real estate)
    Includes index.
    ISBN-13: 978-0-07-353064-2 (alk. paper)
    ISBN-10: 0-07-353064-6 (alk. paper)
    1. Investments. I. Nofsinger, John R. II. Title.
HG4521.H5778 2008
332.6—dc22
                                   2006029214

www.mhhe.com

dedication

For Christine—I still do.

—Mark Hirschey

For Anna, my wife and best friend

—John Nofsinger

preface

A Note from the Authors ...

On Friday, March 24, 2006, the market went simply gaga over Google, Inc., the Mountain View, California–based provider of free Internet search and advertising services. At the open, Google soared a whopping $26.73 (7.8 percent). What favorable operating news would cause investors to pile into Google despite the fact that the company was trading at a stunning 75 times prior-year earnings? Interestingly, there was none.

Traders snapped up shares of Google on the news that the Internet-search company would be added to the Standard & Poor's 500 Index. Funds that track the S&P 500 needed to buy Google because a company's prominence in the index is determined by the value of shares available to the public. In the case of Google, a big chunk of shares aren't publicly available. Instead, they are held as a separate class by founders Larry Page and Sergey Brin and other insiders. The information S&P first provided on Google left many Wall Streeters thinking that the company would go into the S&P 500 Index as if all its shares—including the ones held by insiders—were freely floating. However, insider shares aren't counted. Instead of needing to buy about 28 million shares, index funds needed to add only 18.8 million shares. When S&P corrected the misimpression, a flurry of selling resulted and Google's share price backed off 1.2 percent. One week later, index-related buying had pushed Google's share price up 14.1 percent from the preannouncement level.

Such wild gyrations simply don't happen in a fully efficient market. Google cannot be described as a poorly covered, generally misunderstood, and thinly capitalized company. Google's business strategy and stock market valuation (a whopping $108.7 billion) have been front-page fodder for analysts and market pundits since the company went public in August 2004. Like the tech-stock bubble collapse of 2000–2004, Google's recent history proves that stock prices don't always reflect a sensible and rational evaluation of a company's long-term earnings power.

While Google's stock market history illustrates that investors are not always rational, it does not prove that the market is wildly inefficient, nor does it prove that all investors are crazy. In fact, it is very difficult to earn above-average returns. Over the past five years, S&P reports that the indexes have outperformed 65.4 percent of large-cap mutual funds, 81.3 percent of mid-cap funds, and 72.4 percent of small-cap funds. Talented, hardworking pros find it difficult to consistently beat the averages. When they do, it is often not by enough to cover management fees and transaction costs. For the typical investor, index investing is a prudent long-term investing strategy. Indexing is so easy and sensible for the average investor that one wonders why so many prefer high-cost and poorly performing mutual funds. In fact, the psychological biases of many small investors explain why they speculate on high-risk stocks like Google and also hire expensive financial advisors to help them choose among high-cost and poorly performing mutual funds in their retirement accounts. Similarly, psychological biases explain why naïve investors tend to favor index funds with excessive expenses and/or engage in foolish market timing strategies.

To understand the markets for stocks, bonds, real estate, and other assets, investors need to know more than the economic underpinnings of financial assets. They also need to be aware of investor psychology and know how biases can undermine investment success. *Investments: Analysis and Behavior* is the first textbook to integrate exciting new developments from the field of behavioral finance in a comprehensive and balanced introduction to the field of investments. We hope you like it!

Mark Hirschey   John Nofsinger

Structure of This Text

Objectives

This text should help you accomplish the following objectives:

- Develop a clear understanding of the practical implications of financial theory.

- Acquire a framework for understanding the returns on all financial assets, including stocks, bonds, and financial derivatives.

- Gain familiarity with the institutions and language of Wall Street so as to facilitate the development of an effective personal investment strategy.

- Understand and avoid the psychological biases that trip up many investors.

For students seeking a career on Wall Street, this text gives essential background in financial theory and practice. For all students, this text shows how financial theory and analysis can be used to gain understanding of financial markets and point toward the solution for crucial investment decision problems.

Throughout the text, the emphasis is on the *practical* application of financial theory to understand the field of investments. It is vitally important to avoid the all-too-common trap of focusing on knowable but unimportant facts. For example, a student might learn with precision the hours of operation of the New York Stock Exchange (NYSE), number of securities offered for sale on the NYSE, and intricate details of the NYSE specialist system but have no facility whatsoever about how to value individual securities. The knowledgeable student of investments is one who comes to appreciate *how* investments perform and *why* they perform as they do.

Topic Development

The test of financial theory, or any theory in business, lies in its ability to explain real-world behavior. This text highlights the complementary relation between financial theory and investment practice. Financial theory is used to understand the experience of seasoned and novice investors alike. The study of practical experience is also important because it leads to the development of better theory. Good theory explains and predicts successful practice. Concepts like compound interest, the risk-return relationship, and diversification have endured because they are useful.

Chapter 1, "Introduction," describes the basic tools of the investment trade. Investors need to know how theory leads to practical strategies that can protect and build wealth for themselves and for others. A practical understanding of investment theory includes an ability to recognize how human emotions and psychological biases sometimes lead to poor decisions.

Chapter 2, "Equity Markets," explains interesting institutional aspects of Wall Street, including the organization of securities markets and financial regulation. The use and interpretation of popular stock market indexes, such as the Dow Jones Industrial Average, are also covered.

More specific information on Wall Street products and processes is given in **Chapter 3**, "Buying and Selling Equities." Types of investor accounts and the procedures for buying and selling equity securities are discussed. Acquiring good information is important, but successful investors must have the theoretical framework to convert information into knowledge. Successful investors also need to understand and avoid human emotions and psychological biases that can cause investment mistakes.

Chapter 4, "Risk and Return," focuses on the fundamental idea that there is no "free lunch" on Wall Street. The price of higher expected return is greater anticipated volatility. This chapter shows how investment return and risk are measured, how they are related, and how these concepts are employed to create diversified portfolios. Pitfalls to be avoided include an irrational focus on short-term price movements and the failure to base investment decisions on sensible future expectations.

The idea that stocks are priced in a market environment where buyers and sellers rationally value the firm's future earnings prospects is explored in **Chapter 5**, "Asset Pricing Theory and Performance Evaluation." The conceptual framework provided by asset pricing theory gives the background necessary to fairly evaluate investment practice and portfolio performance. Interestingly, traditional pricing models sometimes fail to predict risk and return relationships. Consequently, these models have been expanded to incorporate behavioral finance theory to improve their usefulness.

The notion that financial markets are perfectly efficient is perhaps the most talked-about concept in the field of investments. It is also a controversial one. **Chapter 6**, "Efficient-Market Hypothesis," explores this fundamental idea. Evidence that supports the EMH is carefully explored, as is evidence that seems to refute it. On the whole, it is clear that while financial markets are vigorously competitive, they still involve elements of inefficiency and investor bias.

Chapter 7, "Market Anomalies," highlights interesting deviations from the predictions of conventional pricing theory and the efficient-market hypothesis. Information about stock market anomalies is useful because it clarifies both the strengths and the limitations of traditional theory and points the way toward better theory. Theory and evidence from the field of behavioral finance often help explain such anomalous real-world behavior.

Chapter 8, "Psychology and the Stock Market," describes how insights from psychology and the study of human emotions can help us better understand investor behavior. Theories from the field of behavioral finance, such as prospect theory, mental shortcuts, mental accounting, self-deception, and social influences, are explained and illuminated. This is a new, exciting, and rapidly evolving field in the study of investment analysis and behavior.

For many, common stock analysis is the most exciting topic covered in investments. **Chapter 9**, "Business Environment," presents a top-down approach that describes the macroeconomic setting and competitive environment of the firm. Indicators of investor and consumer sentiment are also discussed, as are a number of important topics in corporate governance.

Then **Chapter 10**, "Financial Statement Analysis," shows how the financial condition and operating performance of a company are assessed. Key measures of profitability, firm size, and growth are considered as useful indicators of fundamental value. The strengths of these measures combine to determine the economic value of the firm and the level of investor confidence.

In **Chapter 11**, "Value Stock Investing," the vital role played by basic economic considerations in common stock valuation is explored. Firm valuation is seen to depend on fundamental economic trends, earnings, dividends, and growth opportunities. Value investors follow a contrarian investment philosophy in which they look for bargains among unpopular stocks.

Chapter 12, "Growth Stock Investing," illustrates the characteristics of a growing business and examines the concept of "growth at a reasonable price." Investors are sometimes overly enthusiastic about growth stocks because they incorrectly extrapolate past performance into the future. Investment analysts also tend to favor growth stocks and can affect investors with their optimistic biases.

Investors sometimes try to gauge the direction of stock prices using technical indicators designed to measure short-term demand and supply conditions. **Chapter 13**, "Technical Analysis," describes this process. Technical analysis is a controversial subject in academia and on Wall Street because little empirical evidence exists to suggest that it is consistently profitable. Still, it is worth asking why investors are drawn to graphical analysis.

Fixed-income securities are the subject of **Chapter 14**, "Bond Instruments and Markets," and **Chapter 15**, "Bond Valuation." Too many investors know too little about fixed-income securities. The bond market rivals the stock market in size and economic importance, and it merits careful investor attention. Bond types, risk characteristics, and bond trading dynamics are important considerations for the knowledgeable investor. Informed investors are also familiar with important fixed-income concepts, such as duration and convexity.

Chapter 16, "Mutual Funds," covers the basics of mutual fund investing, including open-end and closed-end mutual funds, exchange-traded funds, and hedge funds. These managed investment portfolios offer long-term attractive ways for participating in stock and bond markets. Unfortunately, investors succumb to the same profit-reducing human emotions and psychological biases when choosing mutual funds as they do when choosing stocks. In addition, mutual fund managers have incentives and biases that can adversely impact their investment decisions.

Chapter 17, "Global Investing," discusses investment opportunities and investor strategies in the global economic environment. The growing importance of global risks and return opportunities and the explosion of tools available to access global investment opportunities merit special attention. As in domestic markets, behavioral finance offers insights that are useful when studying investor preferences and behavior in a global investment environment.

Finally, this text turns its attention to the fascinating world of financial derivatives and tangible investment opportunities. In **Chapter 18**, "Option Markets and Strategies," the development of option markets, option concepts, and trading methods are explored. The theoretical foundations of option pricing, notably the Black-Scholes option pricing model, are investigated as useful means for option pricing. **Chapter 19**, "Futures Markets," traces the development of financial derivative markets for agricultural commodities, natural resources, and financial instruments. Common economic features of financial derivatives, the law of one price, and the notions of hedging and speculation are carefully evaluated. Investors looking for a broad range of investment alternatives may also seek opportunities in real estate and other tangible assets, such as gold. **Chapter 20**, "Real Estate and Tangible Assets," gives an introduction to valuation and pricing dynamics in these asset classes.

Walkthrough

Pedagogical Features

Chapter Opening Vignettes

Each chapter begins with an interesting story that incorporates behavioral themes to introduce students to chapter concepts. A great way to engage the reader and spark classroom discussion!

Chapter Objectives

A listing of the chapter's objectives is featured at the beginning of each chapter. The objectives provide students with an overview of the concepts they should understand after reading the chapter.

Key Terms

Key terms are presented in bold and defined in the margin as they are introduced. They also appear in the Glossary at the back of the book.

---

7 chapter

Market Anomalies

An old Wall Street maxim exhorts investors to "sell in May and go away." Also called the "Halloween Indicator," this investment strategy is based on research showing that since 1950 the total return to investors has been very positive between October 31 and May 1 but not much more than zero the rest of the year. Is there any sound economic reason for why such a calendar-based investment strategy might work, or is it just a statistical oddity that will not persist?

Research in behavioral finance tells us that stock returns can be affected by custom and tradition. It is common for people to start the year off with a New Year's resolution and for investors to rebalance their portfolios at the turn of the year. Pension funds and mutual funds also see tax-motivated inflows and make important portfolio decisions just prior to key tax dates, like December 31 and April 15. Many investors and investment professionals take vacations during the summer, and vacant trading desks can contribute to summer malaise and boring returns on Wall Street.

Are these logical behavioral explanations for stock market seasonality, or are they examples of problems tied to what researchers call "data snooping"? Even in random stock return data, unusual patterns can be detected over brief periods. Over the 20th

---

CHAPTER OBJECTIVES

- Learn where and how securities are traded.
- Know how stock market performance is measured.
- Become familiar with sector, industry, and global market indexes.
- Understand relevant laws governing the investment industry.

One of the most common uses of cash reserves is to buy **Treasury bills**. Treasury bills are debt obligations of the U.S. Treasury that have maturities of one year or less. Another popular means for investing cash reserves is to buy bank savings deposits, which are accounts that pay interest, typically at very low levels, do not have any specific maturity, and usually can be withdrawn on demand. A bank certificate of deposit, or CD, is a bank savings deposit that has a specific time of maturity, cannot be withdrawn on demand, and therefore pays a somewhat higher rate of interest.

Treasury bills
Treasury obligations with maturities of one year or less.

Bonds

Bonds are interest-bearing debt obligations issued by corporations, the federal government and its agencies, states, and local governments. Bonds represent a loan to the issuer and provide income plus a promise to repay principal on maturity. Although bonds generally offer higher and steadier income than cash reserves, their principal value fluctuates as interest rates change. In general, when interest rates rise, bond prices decline; when interest rates decline, bond prices rise. One popular variety of debt securities is issued by the U.S. Department of the Treasury. **Treasury notes** are debt obligations of the U.S. Treasury that have maturities of more than 1 year but less than 10 years. **Treasury bonds** are Treasury obligations with maturities of 10 years or more. In addition to such Treasury securities, there exists a wide variety of U.S. government agency bonds. For example, the Federal Home Loan Mortgage Corporation, an affiliate of the Federal Home Loan Bank, creates a secondary money market in conventional residential loans by purchasing mortgage loans from banks. Corporate bonds are simply debt obligations issued by individual firms. Municipal bonds are interest-bearing securities issued by local governments that are typically free of federal income taxes.

Bonds
Interest-bearing debt obligations.

Treasury notes
Treasury obligations with maturities of more than 1 year but less than 10 years.

Treasury bonds
Treasury obligations with maturities of 10 years or more.

Stocks

A third important type of investment asset is **common stock**. Equity securities represent ownership interest in a corporation. Figure 1.2 shows a common stock certificate for entertainment firm Disney. Stocks offer the potential for current income from dividends and for capital appreciation resulting from an increase in value over time. Although common stocks offer the

Common stock
A proportionate ownership stake in a corporation.

Try It! Boxes

Provided in each chapter, these helpful exercises enable students to check their understanding as they read. Worked out solutions immediately follow each question.

Try It!

If the market is expected to increase by 9 percent and the risk-free rate is 4 percent, what is the expected return of assets with beta = 1.5, 0.75, 0.25, and -0.5?

Solution

The expected rates of return are:

Beta = 1.5: $E(R) = 4\% + 1.5 \times (9\% - 4\%) = 11.5\%$
Beta = 0.75: $E(R) = 4\% + 0.75 \times (9\% - 4\%) = 7.75\%$
Beta = 0.25: $E(R) = 4\% + 0.25 \times (9\% - 4\%) = 5.25\%$
Beta = -0.5: $E(R) = 4\% + -0.5 \times (9\% - 4\%) = 1.5\%$

Street Smarts Boxes

Exploring information found in recent publications and building on chapter concepts, these boxes work through real-world issues relevant to the surrounding material. Four Street Smarts are presented in each chapter, with one box focused on a research perspective.

Street Smarts 8.4

Research Perspective

Pitfalls in Investor Behavior

In the late 1990s, a nationwide discount stock brokerage provided stockholding data for 78,000 household accounts over the period 1991–1996 to researchers Brad Barber and Terrance Odean. In a continuing series of studies, Barber, Odean, and their colleagues have discovered the following:

Traders trade too much. The investment performance of investors who rarely trade was compared with the performance of investors who seem to be constantly buying and selling stocks. Hyperactive traders do measurably worse than careful investors who trade infrequently.

Traders sell winners to buy losers. Not only are active traders hurt by high commission costs, but they also tend to make bad decisions about what and when to sell. In an interesting study, Barber and Odean considered what happens after an investor sells one stock to purchase another. On average, the stock sold tends to outperform the stock purchased! Active traders would be better off standing pat, rather than continually adjusting and readjusting their portfolios.

Traders are reluctant to realize losses. On average, active traders are more likely to sell winners than losers. However,

being quick to take profits and slow to realize losses (and associated tax benefits) is no way to run an investment portfolio. Investment legend Peter Lynch calls this "watering the weeds."

Traders become overconfident online. When successful traders move to online trading accounts, trading activity tends to increase dramatically. Such traders also see deterioration in the performance of their brokerage accounts after they go online.

Traders like story stocks. With literally thousands of stocks to choose among, traders and small investors have a difficult time trying to decide which stocks to buy. In general, they like widely admired, fast-growing firms with terrific stock market performance during the prior three- to five-year period. However, such story stocks tend to perform poorly during subsequent periods

The record shows that many active traders are subject to psychological biases that undermine investment performance. When it comes to investing, beware of the common refrain "I have met the enemy, and he is us!"

See Brad M. Barber and Terrance Odean, "Online Investors: Do the Slow Die First?" *Review of Financial Studies,* vol. 15, no. 2 (March 2002), pp. 455–487.

Company Financial Statement Analysis

Balance Sheet

Balance sheet
"Snapshot" information about a company's financial well-being at a specific point in time.

Public companies are required to file quarterly and annual financial reports to shareholders and the Securities and Exchange Commission. These statements give snapshots of the firm's financial condition. Financial statement analysis begins with study of the firm's **balance sheet**. To see what is involved, consider the Microsoft Corporation balance sheet, including stockholders' equity data, shown in Table 10.1. Complete balance sheet information can be obtained from Microsoft's annual report to shareholders or from its annual 10K report to the SEC. As is typical, Microsoft's annual report is available for viewing at the company's Web site on the Internet. SEC reports for Microsoft and other publicly traded companies can be downloaded from the SEC's Web site at **www.sec.gov**.

Microsoft's balance sheet information gives a snapshot of the company's financial well-being at a specific point in time. In this case, fiscal year-end information for 2004 and 2005 is provided, so some idea of the rate of change in financial condition is also given. Of course, according to

Pertinent Web Site Addresses

Web site addresses are presented in bold as they appear in each chapter, providing a quick way to search for additional information on the Internet.

End-of-Chapter Material

Summary

This bulleted summary of the important ideas presented in the chapter helps the student review the key points and provides closure to the chapter.

Self-Test Problems

Two Self-Test Problems are featured at the end of each chapter. They review concepts illustrated within the chapter and enable students to determine whether the material has been understood prior to completing the questions and problems that follow. Detailed solutions to the Self-Test Problems immediately follow each problem.

Questions and Problems

Because solving problems is so critical to students' learning of investments, at least 20 problems are included for each chapter and are written for varied levels of difficulty.

Excel Problems

Selected end-of-chapter questions have been included that require the use of Excel and are denoted by an icon. Spreadsheet templates for the exhibits only are available on the book's Web site at **www.mhhe.com/hirschey1e**.

Summary

- The **bid** is the highest price that an investor is willing to pay. The **ask** is the lowest price that an investor will accept to sell. The **bid-ask spread** is simply the gap between the bid and ask prices. Stocks are assigned **ticker symbols** to facilitate transaction speed and accuracy. **Bid size** is the number of round lots, groups of 100 shares of stock, represented on the buy side of the market. Significant **market depth** exists when a large number of buyers and sellers are active in the market.

- A **market order** is an instruction to buy or sell at the current market price. In a **limit order**, the customer specifies a price at which to buy or sell. A **stop order** is a market order to buy or sell a certain quantity of a security if a specified price (the stop price) is reached or passed. A position is said to be **stopped out** when the position is liquidated through the execution of a stop order. A **buy stop order** is a buy order that is to be held until the market price rises to a specified stop price, at which point it becomes a market order. A **stop-loss order** is a stop order to sell a long position at a specified price that is below the current market price. A **stop-limit order** is an order to buy or sell a certain quantity of a security at a specified price or better but only after a specified price has been reached. A **day order** is an order to buy or sell during the present trading session. An **open order** stays active until it is executed or canceled by the investor. Another expression for an open order is a **good 'til canceled order**. **All or none** is a stipulation to a buy or sell order that instructs the broker to either fill the entire order or not fill it at all. **Fill-or-kill** orders must be filled immediately or canceled.

- Investor orders are electronically routed to the stock exchanges for execution. Market orders are executed on the trading floor, and limit orders are listed in the limit-order book. Large orders of at least 10,000 shares are handled outside the normal auction process as **block transactions**.

- **Dollar-cost averaging** is a simple investment strategy of investing a fixed amount in a particular security at regular intervals.

- Active stock trading fosters the emotions and psychological biases that influence investment decisions and cause mistakes. The **illusion of knowledge** fools investors into thinking that because they have access to much information, they must be making good decisions. However, it takes good training to convert information to knowledge. Trading online increases the **illusion of control**, which can cause investors to trade more actively and make more mistakes. The illusion of control is the belief that you have influence over the outcome of an uncontrollable event.

- A **margin account** is an investor account that holds securities purchased with a combination of cash and borrowed funds. **Margin debt** is the amount borrowed to buy or maintain a security investment. A **margin call** is a broker's formal demand for additional collateral because of adverse price movements. The **broker call rate** is the interest rate that banks and brokerage houses charge to finance margin loans to investors.

Self-Test Problems

ST6.1 A necessary condition for stock market efficiency is that changes in stock prices be random and unpredictable. Is this also a sufficient condition for stock market efficiency?

Solution

No. In the short term, theory and evidence tell us that stock prices are equally apt to rise or fall in an efficient market. However, in an efficient stock market, changes in stock prices are random. Stock prices are not random, as if simply affected by investor psychology, moon spots, or whatever. In an efficient stock market, the price for any given stock effectively represents the expected net present value of all future profits. In this calculation, profits are discounted by using a fair or risk-adjusted rate of return. If the stock market is to be perfectly efficient, there must be a large number of buyers and sellers of essential identical securities, information must be free and readily available, and entry and exit by market players must be uninhibited.

ST6.2 Market professionals are bombarded with real-time, historical, and descriptive data, analytics, and news on markets and securities. On what level(s) is the idea that such data can be used to identify superior investment opportunities a violation of the efficient-market hypothesis?

Solution

The idea that such data can be used to identify superior investment opportunities is a violation of the weak form and semistrong form of the efficient-market hypothesis.

The weak-form hypothesis involves the easiest or lowest hurdle that must be met for one to argue that the stock market is efficient. According to the weak-form hypothesis, stock and bond prices reflect all prior price and trading volume activity. As such, in an efficient stock market, it would not be possible to earn above-market returns by buying or selling stocks on the premise that they are going up on price momentum or are bound to rise on a quick reversal of "panic selling." In a market that is perfectly efficient, there is no such thing as panic sell-

---

Questions and Problems

12.1 Describe the general approach of a growth stock investor. How is growth stock investing different from value investing?

12.2 What are the essential features of a growth stock?

12.3 List five or more criteria identified by T. Rowe Price as important characteristics of investment opportunities.

12.4 Investors in growth stocks are subject to price risk. Describe this variety of risk, and explain why exposure to price risk is of particular concern to growth stock investors.

12.5 Explain the PEG ratio and the PEG ratio rule of thumb.

12.6 A fast-growing company paid a dividend this year of $1 per share and is expected to grow at 20 percent for three years. Afterward, the growth rate will be 7 percent. If the required rate is 9 percent, what is the value of this stock?

12.7 Pfizer Inc. is a major producer of pharmaceuticals and other health care products. If a typical P/E for Pfizer is 25 and present earnings per share of $2.15 are expected to grow over the next five years at a rate of 10 percent per year, what is Pfizer's projected stock price in five years?

12.8 The Home Depot, Inc. (HD), operates a chain of retail building-supply and home-improvement "warehouse" stores across the United States and Canada. It has a return on equity of 20 percent and is expected to earn $2.50 and pay a dividend of $0.35 per share during the coming year. Calculate the amount of internally funded growth anticipated for HD.

13.10 Compute and graph a four-day moving average of the following Nasdaq Composite: **eXcel**

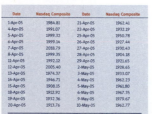

Date	Nasdaq Composite	Date	Nasdaq Composite
1-Apr-05	1984.81	21-Apr-05	1962.41
4-Apr-05	1991.07	22-Apr-05	1932.19
5-Apr-05	1999.32	25-Apr-05	1950.78
6-Apr-05	1999.14	26-Apr-05	1927.44
7-Apr-05	2018.79	27-Apr-05	1930.43
8-Apr-05	1999.35	28-Apr-05	1904.18
11-Apr-05	1992.12	29-Apr-05	1921.65
12-Apr-05	2005.40	2-May-05	1928.65
13-Apr-05	1974.37	3-May-05	1933.07
14-Apr-05	1946.71	4-May-05	1962.23
15-Apr-05	1908.15	5-May-05	1961.80
18-Apr-05	1912.92	6-May-05	1967.35
19-Apr-05	1932.36	9-May-05	1979.67
20-Apr-05	1913.76	10-May-05	1962.77

4.16 Which of the following statements about standard deviation is *true*? Standard deviation:

    a. Is the square of the variance
    b. Can be a positive or a negative number
    c. Is denominated in the same units as the original data
    d. Is the arithmetic mean of the squared deviations from the mean

4.17 A stock with a coefficient of variation of 0.50 has a(n):

    a. Variance equal to half the stock's expected return
    b. Expected return equal to half the stock's variance
    c. Expected return equal to half the stock's standard deviation
    d. Standard deviation equal to half the stock's expected return

4.18 Which of the following is *least likely* to affect the required rate of return on an investment?

    a. Real risk-free rate
    b. Asset risk premium
    c. Expected rate of inflation
    d. Investors' composite propensity to consume

4.19 The Markowitz efficient frontier is *best* described as the set of portfolios that has:

    a. The minimum risk for every level of return
    b. Proportionally equal units of risk and return
    c. The maximum excess rate of return for every given level of risk
    d. The highest return for each level of beta based on the capital asset pricing model

CFA Problems

Several questions from recent CFA exams are provided in applicable chapters and are denoted with an icon. These are the types of questions that professionals in the field believe are relevant. Appendix B lists each CFA question and the level and year of the CFA exam it was included in, for easy reference when students are studying for the exam.

11.14 Go to the Standard & Poor's Market Insight Web site at www.mhhe.com/edumarketinsight and enter the ticker "DOW" for Dow Chemical. From the information under "Financial Hlts." for Dow, obtain the current price, last year's dividend, and the dividend growth rate. Use these to compute the expected rate of return for Dow. Does this number seem reasonable? — STANDARD & POOR'S

11.15 Go to the Standard & Poor's Market Insight Web site at www.mhhe.com/edumarketinsight and enter the ticker "RBK" for Reebok International. Examine the information in S&P's "Stock Report" section for Reebok. Obtain the 12-month target price, the date the stock is expected to reach this price, and the annual dividend. From Yahoo! Finance, obtain the stock price one year before the expected target price is to occur. Using this information and the discounted present-value model, compute the implied required rate of return for RBK. What is the dividend yield and expected return from capital gain? — STANDARD & POOR'S

Standard & Poor's Problems

Included in each chapter are problems, denoted by an icon, directly incorporating the educational version of Market Insight, a service based on Standard & Poor's renowned Compustat database. These problems provide an easy way for students to incorporate current, real-world data into their learning.

 14.12 Suppose you are trying to decide whether to buy a municipal bond issued by the Massachusetts Health and Educational Facilities Authority (CUSIP: 57585J8P9) or a corporate bond issued by Dell Computer (CUSIP: 217025AE9). Compare the yields of these two bonds, both of which mature in 2028. If your marginal federal tax rate is 30 percent and the two bonds have the same risk, which bond is more attractive on an after-tax basis? (Note: Quotes may be found in the "Market Information" section of **http://bondmarket.com**.)

 14.13 Visit the US Treasury Department Web page at **www.ustreas.gov**. The Treasury's Office of Debt Management reports many actions and predictions of the Treasury Department. What is the auction schedule for new Treasury sales over the next month? What dollar values of Treasuries were sold last year?

 14.14 The U.S. Treasury Department allows individual investors to purchase Treasury securities directly through TreasuryDirect, at **www.treasurydirect.gov**. What securities can be purchased through TreasuryDirect?

Web Problems

Denoted by an icon, these Internet exercises weave the Web, real data, and practical applications with concepts found in the book.

Investment Applications

Featured at the end of each chapter, these integrative minicases allow students to apply their knowledge to relatively complex, practical problems and typical real-world scenarios. Questions at the end of each case require students to analyze and reflect on all of the material that they learned in the chapter.

INVESTMENT APPLICATION

Corporate Governance at Microsoft

Spectacular failures at companies such as Adelphia, Enron, and WorldCom have illustrated the importance of good corporate governance. Lawmakers focused on corporate governance issues and passed the Public Company Accounting Reform and Investor Protection Act of 2002 (also known as the Sarbanes-Oxley Act). The law set up a new oversight body to regulate auditors, created laws pertaining to corporate responsibility, and increased punishments for corporate white-collar crime. Good corporate governance is of particular importance to equity investors. Poor governance can lead to bankruptcy, as in the case of Adelphia, Enron, WorldCom, and others. The stockholders of bankrupt firms often lose their entire ownership position. Therefore, it is very important for stockholders to assess the level of corporate governance in any firm they are considering purchasing.

    Consider the governance characteristics of Microsoft Corporation. Incorporated in 1981, Microsoft develops, manufactures, licenses, and supports a wide range of software products. The company's software products include software for personal computers and intelligent devices, scalable operating systems for servers, server applications for client-server environments, software development tools, business solutions applications, and mobile and embedded devices. The company is best known for its Windows operating system and computer software products such as MS Office and Internet Explorer. The company also sells the Xbox video game console, along with games and peripherals. Its online businesses include the MSN network of Internet products and services. The company's seven product segments are Client, Server and Tools, Information Worker, Microsoft Business Solutions, MSN, Mobile and Embedded Devices, and Home and Entertainment.

Supplements

For The Instructor

Instructor's Resource CD (0073251704)

This comprehensive CD contains the following instructor supplements, *all* of which have been developed by the authors. We have compiled them in electronic format for easier access and convenience. Print copies are available through your McGraw-Hill representative.

- **Instructor's Manual:** This instructional tool includes sample syllabi, chapter overviews, video suggestions, and copies of the PowerPoint presentation for reference.

- **Solutions Manual:** This manual provides detailed solutions to the end-of-chapter problems. The solutions have been class tested by the authors to ensure accuracy.

- **Test Bank:** The Test Bank contains hundreds of questions that closely link with the text material and provides a variety of question formats (true/false, multiple-choice, and essay questions) and levels of difficulty to meet every instructor's testing needs.

- **Computerized Test Bank:** Utilizing McGraw-Hill's EZ Test testing software for Windows to quickly create customized exams, this user-friendly program allows instructors to sort questions by format; edit existing questions or add new ones; and scramble questions for multiple versions of the same test.

- **PowerPoint Presentation System:** The presentation slides contain chapter objectives, figures and tables from the text, key points, and summaries. They are presented in a four-color electronic format that you may customize for your own lectures.

DVD (0073294330)

McGraw-Hill/Irwin has produced a series of finance videos that present 10-minute case studies on financial markets, bonds, portfolio management, derivatives, foreign exchange, and other topics.

Online Support

Online Learning Center

A wealth of information is available online at **www.mhhe.com/hirschey1e**. Students will have *free* access to study materials specifically created for this text, such as:

- **Self-Study Software:** This tutorial software contains a self-study program, with questions written by the authors, to test students' understanding of the concepts in the text, as well as provide an infinite number of problems to solve with the random-number generator program. It also includes the glossary of terms, chapter concepts, and summaries.

- **Online Quizzes:** These quizzes offer a quick way to review concepts presented in the chapter. Ten multiple-choice questions are included for each chapter so that students can effectively practice solving problems related to specific chapter content.

- **Excel Templates:** Spreadsheets from the featured Excel Exhibits throughout the book, denoted by an Excel icon, will be available for students to refer to in order to familiarize themselves with this important tool.

- **Standard & Poor's Educational Version of Market Insight:** McGraw-Hill/Irwin is proud to partner with Standard & Poor's to offer access to the Educational Version of Market Insight free with the purchase of a new text. A pass-code card is provided, which will give students access to six years of financial data for over 1,000 top U.S. companies. See www.mhhe.com/edumarketinsight for details on this exclusive partnership.

- **Investments Online:** This exclusive Web tool from McGraw-Hill/Irwin provides 36 exercises for 18 different investment topics and allows students to complete challenging exercises and discussions drawn on recent articles, company reports, government data, and other Web-based resources. The "Finance Tutor Series" provides questions and problems that not only assess and improve students' understanding of the subject but also help students apply it to real-world contexts.

- **Finance Around the World:** This learning tool is an outstanding global financial resource for researching and exploring corporate finance and investments online. It includes country facts and daily coverage and analysis of financial markets and companies, as well as general finance and business news and articles for over 35 countries.

Instructors will have access to all of the material that students can view, but they will also have password-protected access to teaching supports such as electronic files of the ancillaries and other useful materials.

Packaging Options

Please contact your McGraw-Hill/Irwin sales representative to find out more about these exciting packaging options now available for your class:

- *BusinessWeek* **Package:** Your students can subscribe to *BusinessWeek* for a special rate of $8.25 in addition to the price of the text. Students will receive a pass-code card shrink-wrapped with their new text that will refer them to a registration site to receive their subscription. Subscriptions are available in print copy or digital format.

- *Wall Street Journal* **Package:** Your students can subscribe to *The Wall Street Journal* for 15 weeks at a special rate of $20 in addition to the price of the text. Students will receive a "How to Use the *WSJ*" handbook plus a subscription card shrink-wrapped with their new text. The subscription also gives students access to www.wsj.com.

- *Financial Times* **Package:** Your students can subscribe to the *Financial Times* for 15 weeks at a specially priced rate of $10 in addition to the price of the text. Students will receive a subscription card shrink-wrapped with their new text that will activate their subscriptions once they complete and submit the card. The subscription also provides access to http://FT.com.

- **Excel Applications for Investments:** This supplement, created by Troy Adair, University of North Carolina, can be packaged with *Investments: Analysis and Behavior* at a discounted price. It teaches students how to build financial models in Excel and shows students how to use these models to solve a variety of common corporate investment problems.

Acknowledgments

We would like to take this opportunity to thank all of those individuals who helped us prepare this first edition! We want to express our appreciation to those instructors whose insightful comments and suggestions were invaluable to us during the development of this text.

Clinton Andrews
Wayne State University

Bob Bear
Florida International University

Robert Eldridge
Southern Connecticut State University

Andrew Ellul
Indiana University

Richard Gritta
University of Portland

Bing Han
Ohio State University

Yvette Harman
Miami University

James Milanese
University of South Carolina at Greensboro

Lalatendru Misra
University of Texas at San Antonio

Ehsan Nikbakht
Hofstra University

Dan Oglevee
Ohio State University

Dev Prasad
University of Massachusetts at Lowell

Murli Rajan
University of Scranton

Philip Russel
Philadelphia University

Adam Schwartz
University of Mississippi

John Settle
Portland State University

John Teall
Pace University

Tommy Thompson
Lamar University

Joseph Vu
DePaul University

Allan Zebedee
San Diego State University

We are also grateful to the talented staff at McGraw-Hill/Irwin for their expertise and guidance, especially Steve Patterson, Publisher; Michele Janicek, Executive Editor; Christina Kouvelis, Development Editor II; Susanne Riedell, Senior Project Manager; Julie Phifer, Senior Marketing Manager; Kami Carter, Senior Designer; Jason Huls, Production Supervisor; Jennifer Wilson, Media Producer; Becky Szura, Media Project Manager; and Jennifer Jelinski, Marketing Specialist.

Mark Hirschey

John Nofsinger

brief contents

xvii

contents

1

Introduction

Warren E. Buffett, the celebrated chairman and chief executive officer of Omaha, Nebraska–based Berkshire Hathaway, Inc., started an investment partnership with $100 in 1956 and has gone on to accumulate a personal net worth in excess of $40 billion. The most successful stock market investor of all time, Buffett is adept at communicating the importance of basic investment concepts. In the winter of 2005, for example, Buffett was asked by a group of students if he thought the stock market is perfectly efficient. Buffett replied that most stock prices, most of the time, are appropriate. Buffett does not believe he could go line by line down the list of NYSE-listed firms and say that this one is a little high, this one is a little low, and so on. Prices are generally right most of the time, Buffett said, but not right all the time. If you know what you are doing, taking advantage of occasionally undervalued stocks can make you very rich.

Although stock prices are generally right most of the time, the occasionally overvalued stock can, and does, cause many novice investors to lose money. In fact, many otherwise levelheaded investors focus on foolish short-term speculation rather than sensible long-term investing. As a result, the average investor consistently underperforms the market averages, and many speculators consistently lose money. They tend to buy high and sell low, a surefire plan for losing money. The average investor needs a disciplined plan of regular investment for meeting long-term investment goals, such as providing for a comfortable retirement.

Investment analysis and behavior teaches us that the long-run performance of any investment is tied to the economic success of the underlying business. That's why it is so important to become familiar with common financial yardsticks of business performance and stock market valuation. Successful investors also need to avoid predictable psychological tendencies and mistakes in investor behavior that often lead to subpar investment results.[1]

---

[1] For details about Warren Buffett's investment philosophy, see the Berkshire Hathaway, Inc., Web site at **www.berkshirehathaway.com**. Buffett's letters to shareholders are especially insightful.

CHAPTER OBJECTIVES

- Learn the power of building wealth through investing over time.
- Understand the nature and performance of financial assets.
- Identify common objectives of investors.
- Practice obtaining important financial information.
- Become acquainted with job opportunities in the financial services sector.

Nature of Investing

Buy Low, Sell High

The investment process is much more complicated than this simple investing goal. Nevertheless, a successful investment program will see more stock and bond purchases at low prices and sales at high prices. Yet this simple objective is difficult to achieve. Consider the flow of money that individual investors invest in mutual funds. Figure 1.1 shows the net cash flow into stock mutual funds by month from September 1998 to January 2006 and the relationship with the S&P 500 Index. Notice that on average, investors poured money into stock funds near the peak of the bubble in March 2000. That is, they bought high. After three years of falling prices, investors started to abandon stock mutual funds in droves. They sold low.

Where did investors put the money they took out of equity funds? Investors poured $24 billion into bond funds in 2002 and nearly $65 billion during the first six months of 2003. This investment in the bond market coincides with a historic peak in bond prices (and the associated decline in interest rates). Did investors buy high again?

FIGURE 1.1	Monthly Net Flow into Equity Mutual Funds and the S&P 500 Index

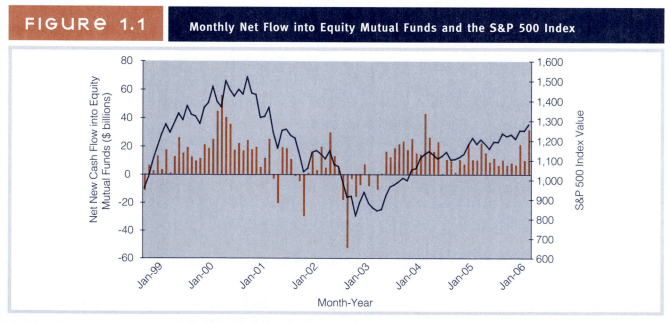

Source: Data from Investment Company Institute (**www.ici.org**).

This book explains the concepts and analytical tools that can be used to create a successful investment program. Most of these ideas have been available to investors for decades. Yet investors frequently make poor decisions caused by psychological biases and emotions. Investment theory is useful because it provides the framework necessary to aid investor understanding of asset pricing. Theories from related fields, such as psychology, are also useful because they help explain why investors sometimes make bad investment decisions. In a general sense, a careful understanding of these theories is essential because it allows for the understanding and prediction of the behavior of financial markets, investors, and investment professionals. Making good decisions and avoiding large mistakes induced by emotions allows an investor to build more wealth.

Building Wealth over Time

Building investment wealth takes time. The three most important factors are the investment rate of return, the amount of time the money will be invested, and the amount of money invested. More wealth can be built through a higher return and a longer investment horizon.

Consider how wealth is grown over time. In Table 1.1, notice how similar the amounts are that result from a $10,000 investment at 6, 9, and 12 percent when only one year of investment returns is considered. Starting from $10,000, a 6 percent rate of return in one year will result in a final investment value of $10,600. Similarly starting from $10,000, 9 and 12 percent rates of return generate ultimate investment values of $10,900 and $11,200, respectively. Over a single year, there is little difference between 6, 9, and 12 percent rates of return. What is intriguing is how different rates of interest compound to widely differing amounts over extended periods. By the way, if you feel a little rusty in the time-value-of-money concepts and computations, review Appendix A.

For example, over a 12-year period, 6 percent interest leads to a doubled amount of investment. If you look in Table 1.1 under the 6 percent column, you can see that over 12 years a $10,000 investment grows to $20,122, or roughly doubles. Over 24 years at 6 percent interest,

TABLE 1.1	**Compound Interest Leads to Amazing Growth** *Over a 24-year period, a 9 percent return leads to twice the wealth of a 6 percent return, and a 12 percent return almost quadruples the wealth generated by a 6 percent return.**

	Look What $10,000 Turns into with an Investment Return of:		
Number of Years	**6%**	**9%**	**12%**
1	$ 10,600	$ 10,900	$ 11,200
2	11,236	11,881	12,544
3	11,910	12,950	14,049
4	12,625	14,116	15,735
6	14,185	16,771	19,738
8	15,938	19,926	24,760
12	20,122	28,127	38,960
16	25,404	39,703	61,304
20	32,071	56,044	96,463
24	40,489	79,111	151,786
28	51,117	111,671	238,839
32	64,534	157,633	375,817
36	81,473	222,512	591,356
40	102,857	314,094	930,510

*Annual compounding is assumed.

an investment of $10,000 grows to $40,489, or roughly quadruples. Over 36 years, an investment of $10,000 at 6 percent interest grows to $81,473, or doubles roughly three times. Money growing at 6 percent roughly doubles in 12 years, doubles twice in 24 years, and doubles three times in 36 years.

What happens if the rate of return can be increased to 9 percent per year? An investment yielding 9 percent will roughly double every eight years. Notice from Table 1.1 that in eight years at 9 percent interest, money grows from $10,000 to $19,926. In an additional eight years, that money grows from $19,926 to $39,703, or roughly quadruples. In just another eight years, such an investment doubles once more to $79,111, or roughly $80,000. Note that a 9 percent return per year is 50 percent greater than a 6 percent return. Yet after 24 years earning a 9 percent return produces double the value of earning just 6 percent per year. Small differences in return lead to large differences in wealth over time!

The effect of differences in the rate of compound interest on the amount earned from investment becomes even clearer when one considers a 12 percent rate of return. Remember that over a one-year period, 12 percent returns simply twice the total amount earned on an investment earning 6 percent investment. Table 1.1 shows that over a period of 24 years, $10,000 grows by almost sixteen-fold to $151,786. It is impressive to recognize that over 24 years, 12 percent interest results in much more than simply twice the rate of return earned at 6 percent. Over an extended period, compound interest results in amazing growth. A 9 percent growth rate generates far more total return than does a 6 percent rate. The amount earned with 12 percent growth can become stunning over an extended period.

However, most people do not have a large amount of money with which to begin investing. Successful investors tend to start with a small amount and regularly invest over time. Consider that a young investor investing only $100 per month, or $1,200 per year, over a 40-year time horizon will accumulate $920,510 in a portfolio yielding 12 percent. Because of the advantage of time, this is achieved with a much lower investment than that required by a middle-aged investor seeking to accumulate a similar amount. Consider the middle-aged investor contributing $12,000 per year toward retirement, or 10 times as much as that contributed by the young investor. A middle-aged investor contributing $12,000 per year toward retirement in a common stock portfolio yielding 12 percent will accumulate $864,629. This means that, in investing for retirement, the advantage of a longer investment horizon gives the young investor more than 10 times the benefit earned by the middle-aged investor.

There is an old saying that rich people have three things in common: Rich people tend to be smart, lucky, and *old*.

As a student or novice investor, perhaps you don't have the advantage of a substantial amount to invest. Despite this limitation, the undeniable advantage enjoyed by all young investors is an extremely long investment horizon. The advantage of a long investment horizon can overcome the temporary disadvantage of not having a significant sum to invest. As shown in Table 1.2, an investment of as much as $1,000 per month over 40 years results in $9,205,097 in retirement wealth. This is a level of wealth seldom achieved in our economy. Building significant retirement wealth requires a significant sacrifice in terms of postponed spending.

How do people earn a 6 or 12 percent return over time? Investors must hold well-diversified portfolios that contain financial assets. These portfolios can contain different proportions of cash reserves, bonds, and stocks. The allocation of these assets determines the levels of risk and return likely to be experienced.

Types of Financial Assets

Cash Reserves

Cash reserves
Short-term money market instruments.

A major class of financial assets is generally referred to as **cash reserves**, or short-term money market instruments. The primary attraction of cash reserves is that they offer modest income with stability of principal. Although investing in cash reserves allows one to protect the initial value of an investment, there is a cost in that only meager rates of return are typically offered on cash reserves. The income generated from cash reserves rises and falls with short-term interest rates.

TABLE 1.2	Long-Term Payoff to Regular Investing Can Be Huge		
	Young investors can accumulate significant wealth through regular investing of modest amounts. The longer you wait to start investing, however, the greater the cost to building significant wealth.		

Amount Invested per Year	Number of Years	Wealth Created with an Investment Return of:		
		6%	9%	12%
Young Investor				
$ 300	40	$ 46,429	$ 101,365	$ 230,127
1,200	40	185,714	405,459	920,510
2,000	40	309,524	675,765	1,534,183
6,000	40	928,572	2,027,295	4,602,549
12,000	40	1,857,144	4,054,589	9,205,097
Middle-Aged investor				
$ 300	20	$ 11,036	$ 15,348	$ 21,616
1,200	20	44,143	61,392	86,463
2,000	20	73,571	102,320	144,105
6,000	20	220,714	306,961	432,315
12,000	20	441,427	613,921	864,629

One of the most common uses of cash reserves is to buy **Treasury bills**. Treasury bills are debt obligations of the U.S. Treasury that have maturities of one year or less. Another popular means for investing cash reserves is to buy bank savings deposits, which are accounts that pay interest, typically at very low levels, do not have any specific maturity, and usually can be withdrawn on demand. A bank certificate of deposit, or CD, is a bank savings deposit that has a specific time of maturity, cannot be withdrawn on demand, and therefore pays a somewhat higher rate of interest.

Treasury bills
Treasury obligations with maturities of one year or less.

Bonds

Bonds are interest-bearing debt obligations issued by corporations, the federal government and its agencies, states, and local governments. Bonds represent a loan to the issuer and provide income plus a promise to repay principal on maturity. Although bonds generally offer higher and steadier income than cash reserves, their principal value fluctuates as interest rates change. In general, when interest rates rise, bond prices decline; when interest rates decline, bond prices rise. One popular variety of debt securities is issued by the U.S. Department of the Treasury. **Treasury notes** are debt obligations of the U.S. Treasury that have maturities of more than 1 year but less than 10 years. **Treasury bonds** are Treasury obligations with maturities of 10 years or more. In addition to such Treasury securities, there exists a wide variety of U.S. government agency bonds. For example, the Federal Home Loan Mortgage Corporation, an affiliate of the Federal Home Loan Bank, creates a secondary money market in conventional residential loans by purchasing mortgage loans from banks. Corporate bonds are simply debt obligations issued by individual firms. Municipal bonds are interest-bearing securities issued by local governments that are typically free of federal income taxes.

Bonds
Interest-bearing debt obligations.

Treasury notes
Treasury obligations with maturities of more than 1 year but less than 10 years.

Treasury bonds
Treasury obligations with maturities of 10 years or more.

Stocks

A third important type of investment asset is **common stock**. Equity securities represent ownership interest in a corporation. Figure 1.2 shows a common stock certificate for entertainment firm Disney. Stocks offer the potential for current income from dividends and for capital appreciation resulting from an increase in value over time. Although common stocks offer the

Common stock
A proportionate ownership stake in a corporation.

FIGURE 1.2   **Stock Certificate of Walt Disney Company**

long-term potential for superior rates of return, stocks are susceptible to short-term price risks. Stock prices fluctuate over short time periods. At times, this volatility can be severe. Some companies, like Enron, can go bankrupt and lose all of their value.

Common stock represents ownership of a company. Ownership of common stock gives the stockholder a proportionate interest in the company's assets, profits, and dividends. In the event of a takeover, each individual shareholder is entitled to a proportionate share of the takeover purchase price. Over time, as some realized profits are reinvested in the business, the value of each shareholder's investment builds. At any point in time, the market value of a firm's common stock depends on many factors, including the company's current profitability, its growth prospects, interest rates, demand for the stock, and conditions in the overall stock market. Stocks appeal to long-term investors for their potential to provide competitive returns through dividends and capital gains. Over the long term, stocks have consistently offered investors the best opportunity to stay ahead of inflation and increase the value of their investment.

Historical Performance

The numbers shown in Tables 1.1 and 1.2 represent more than simple illustrations of the growth created by compound interest. These numbers fairly reflect investment returns that have been earned over time on stock and bond investments in the United States. Consider the data provided in Table 1.3. Note that the average annual stock market return over the period 1950–2005 was 13.3 percent as represented by the S&P 500 Index. U.S. Treasury bonds earned an average 6.4 percent return. The highest return in the stock market was in 1954, when it earned 52.6 percent. In that year, the bond market earned 7.19 percent. The worst year in the stock market was 1974, when it dove –26.5 percent. The bond market earned a 4.35 percent return that year. The best and worst years in the bond market were 1982 and 1967, when it earned 40.36 percent and –9.18 percent, respectively.

A 12 percent rate of return is commensurate with the rate of return earned on broadly diversified portfolios of stock market investments since World War II. In other words, a broadly diversified portfolio of common stocks could be expected over the long term to earn the investor a 12 percent rate of growth. At the other end of the spectrum, a 6 percent rate of return is a typical average for long-term bond investors. This means that over an extended period of time a broadly diversified portfolio of high-grade bonds could be expected to yield investors a rate of interest on the order of 6 percent. Between these two extremes of 6 and 12 percent is the 9 percent rate of return typically earned by mutual fund investors. Mutual funds typically own a blend of stocks and bonds and must pay the trading and management costs involved with running a mutual fund. As a result, they return investors about 9 percent, on average, or roughly

Are Investors Always Rational?

In the late 1950s and early 1960s, academics and practitioners changed their thinking about investor behavior. The framework in which investors were thought to behave in a "normal" manner became one in which investors were thought to behave in a "rational" manner at all times. This change in perception had profound impacts on the development of finance theory, education, practice, and regulatory policy over the next four decades.

Rational investors care only about the expected return and risk of their overall investment portfolios. They prefer more wealth to less wealth, and they are never confused about the present-value or future-value forms that money can take. This rational view of investors led to theories that stock market prices reflect stocks' actual economic values at all points in time, a concept generally referred to as the *efficient-market hypothesis*. It also became common to assume that investors seek to hold portfolios that minimize risk for an expected level of return and/or portfolios that maximize the expected rate of return for a given level of risk (modern portfolio theory). If in-

vestors are rational and prices are efficient, then government policy makers need to remember that it is always best to allow capital markets to operate free from onerous regulation.

During the past decade, there has been a growing recognition that "normal" investors sometimes behave in a manner that cannot be described as fully rational. Normal investors can become affected by cognitive biases and emotions. Such biases can cause investors to consider each of their stocks in isolation and somewhat distinct from their overall portfolio. Emotions such as hope, fear, and regret can also cause normal investors to differentiate between paper losses and realized losses, dividend gains and capital gains, and hard-earned money and a windfall. The returns expected by normal investors are sometimes influenced by more than anticipated risk levels.

Normal investors are not stupid. They simply behave in a manner that cannot always be described as fully rational.

See: Meir Statman, "Normal Investors, Then and Now," *Financial Analysts Journal*, vol. 61, no. 2 (March–April 2005), pp. 1–7.

TABLE 1.3

Returns on Common Stocks, Treasury Bonds, and Treasury Bills, 1950–2005 *In the long run, investor returns on common stocks have greatly outperformed the returns on long-term Treasury bonds and short-term Treasury bills.*

Year	Common Stocks (S&P 500)	Long-Term Treasury Bonds	U.S. Treasury Bills
1950	31.7%	0.06%	1.2%
1951	24.0	−3.93	1.6
1952	18.4	1.16	1.8
1953	−1.0	3.64	1.9
1954	52.6	7.19	1.0
1955	31.6	−1.29	1.8
1956	6.6	−5.59	2.7
1957	−10.8	7.46	3.3
1958	43.4	−6.09	1.8
1959	12.0	−2.26	3.4
1960	0.5	13.78	2.9
1961	26.9	0.97	2.4
1962	−8.7	6.89	2.8
1963	22.8	1.21	3.2
1964	16.5	3.51	3.5
1965	12.5	0.71	4.0
1966	−10.1	3.65	4.9
1967	24.0	−9.18	4.3
1968	11.1	−0.26	5.3
1969	−8.5	−5.07	6.7
1970	4.0	12.11	6.5
1971	14.3	13.23	4.3
1972	19.0	5.69	4.1

continues on next page

TABLE 1.3	Returns on Common Stocks, Treasury Bonds, and Treasury Bills, 1950–2005 *continued*

Year	Common Stocks (S&P 500)	Long-Term Treasury Bonds	U.S. Treasury Bills
1973	−14.7	−1.11	7.0
1974	−26.5	4.35	7.9
1975	37.2	9.20	5.8
1976	23.8	16.75	5.0
1977	−7.2	−0.69	5.3
1978	6.6	−1.18	7.2
1979	18.4	−1.23	10.0
1980	32.4	−3.95	11.5
1981	−4.9	1.86	14.0
1982	21.4	40.36	10.7
1983	22.5	0.65	8.6
1984	6.3	15.48	9.6
1985	32.2	30.97	7.5
1986	18.5	24.53	6.0
1987	5.2	−2.71	5.8
1988	16.8	9.67	6.7
1989	31.5	18.11	8.1
1990	−3.2	6.18	7.5
1991	30.6	19.30	5.4
1992	7.7	8.05	3.5
1993	10.0	18.24	3.0
1994	1.3	−7.77	4.3
1995	37.4	31.67	5.5
1996	23.1	−0.93	5.0
1997	33.4	15.08	5.1
1998	28.6	13.52	4.8
1999	21.0	−8.74	4.7
2000	−9.1	20.11	5.9
2001	−11.9	4.56	3.5
2002	−22.1	17.17	1.6
2003	28.7	2.06	1.0
2004	10.9	7.70	1.4
2005	4.9	3.05	3.1
Average	**13.3%**	**6.4%**	**4.9%**
Median	**15.4%**	**3.6%**	**4.7%**

Source: Council of Economic Advisors, *Economic Report of the President*, February 2006, and Lehman Brothers.

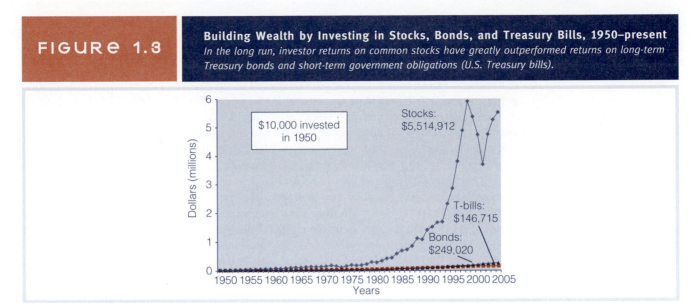

FIGURE 1.3

Building Wealth by Investing in Stocks, Bonds, and Treasury Bills, 1950–present
In the long run, investor returns on common stocks have greatly outperformed returns on long-term Treasury bonds and short-term government obligations (U.S. Treasury bills).

Source: Council of Economic Advisors, *Economic Report of the President*, February 2006, and Lehman Brothers.

3 percent below the return earned on broadly diversified portfolios of common stocks. Figure 1.3 shows the cumulative value of $10,000 invested in 1950 in stock, bonds, and T-bills.

Just because the performance shown in Figure 1.3 was available to investors does not mean that all investors achieved such returns. Many individual investors make decisions that are influenced by their emotions and psychological biases. They do not gain enough confidence in the stock market until after the market has risen for a long period. After investing, if the market declines for a while, many investors become discouraged and sell. These behaviors lead to buying high and selling low (see Figure 1.1). This is not the way to build wealth! In order to achieve the average 12 percent return, an investor needs to invest in equities and have the discipline to stay in the market even after it has fallen.

Simple illustrations of the amazing growth resulting from compound interest provide a helpful introduction to the nature of investing. It's not the whole story, but it's a useful beginning. Investing is about money. It is not just about accumulating money and helping it grow. It is about how people feel about money. Therefore, the theory of investing involves economics and psychology. Wall Street is a real place. It's an interesting place. It's a place well worth studying.

Investment Objectives

Investing for Retirement

By studying investment theory and behavior, it becomes possible to assess the returns needed and select the appropriate assets. Saving money for a down payment on a home is a perfect example. Using high-yield money market instruments, individual savers can often increase the interest earned over that from certificates of deposit offered by commercial banks or savings and loan institutions. Effective selection of stock and bond investments is an important consideration for all investors seeking to improve their chances for a satisfactory retirement income. Thirty years ago, it was common for individual companies to offer employees **defined-benefit retirement plans**. Under a defined-benefit retirement plan, employees are promised a fixed retirement income computed using a formula that includes the number of years employed multiplied by the last year's salary. In this plan, it is the employer's responsibility to fund the retirement program and invest the portfolio.

Over time, defined-benefit plans in the United States have been abandoned in favor of what are called **defined-contribution retirement plans**. Under a defined-contribution retirement

Defined-benefit retirement plan
Employer-funded retirement program in which the employer promises to pay the employee a fixed retirement income that depends on salary history and time employed.

Defined-contribution retirement plan
Employee-funded retirement program in which employees direct and contribute to their own retirement plans. Retirement income is dependent on employee success in investing.

plan, individual employee retirement income is determined by the amount the employee has accumulated in his or her retirement portfolio. Assume that an individual investor contributes $6,000 per year, or $500 per month, into her retirement plan with a major employer. If those funds are invested in bonds to earn a return of 6.4 percent per year, that employee would accumulate $230,443 over a 20-year period. Instead of investing in a broadly diversified bond portfolio earning 6.4 percent per year, consider the possibility of investing in common stocks yielding 13.3 percent. In common stocks returning 13.3 percent per year over a period of 20 years, a total retirement portfolio of $503,035 would accumulate. Having chosen common stocks rather than bonds, the employee would be able to fund a much higher level of retirement income than that afforded by the bond investment.

Since employees increasingly have defined-contribution retirement plans instead of defined-benefit plans, it is necessary that they themselves accept responsibility for the management of their retirement assets. Under a defined-contribution retirement plan, the employer accepts no responsibility for the amount accumulated in an individual employee's retirement account. If the individual employee fails to understand the fundamental relationships between risk and expected return, and the pluses and minuses of stock and bond investing in the long run, the individual is apt to pay a startling cost in terms of reduced retirement income.

Investing to Meet Other Financial Goals

Of course, the importance of learning about investing extends beyond the need for intelligent retirement planning. Many parents also wish to help children afford a quality college education. Carefully selected stock and bond investments can make an important contribution toward paying the costs of college education, especially when an extended investment horizon is possible.

For example, if parents of a newly born baby were to invest $10,000 in a common stock portfolio returning 12 percent over a 20-year period, this would accumulate to $96,463. This is an amount sufficient to carry a large share of the expected costs of a private college education in America today. Alternatively, if parents of a newborn child were to contribute $100 per month, or $1,200 per year, over a 20-year period into a common stock portfolio returning 12 percent per year, the portfolio would grow to $86,463. Again, this is an amount sufficient to pay a large share of the cost of an undergraduate education.

These simple examples illustrate that anytime an investor has a long-term financial goal, stock and bond investing can play a significant role in achieving that objective. From this standpoint, it is fair to say that all students have an important interest in learning as much as they can about investment theory and practice. Even small improvements in one's ability to manage a retirement portfolio, a college tuition portfolio, or any long-term investment can lead to significant rewards.

Investing Is Not a Game

Investors frequently behave as if investing were a game. Indeed, it often does seem like a competition. Investors compare their own returns to those they see on TV, read in the newspaper, and hear from their neighbors and friends. The media enhance this atmosphere by continually ranking the performance of investments (such as mutual funds, hedge funds, and individual stocks). This gamelike environment causes investors to focus on the short term and keep asking "How am I doing *now*?" Unfortunately, this short-term focus leads to psychological and emotional traps and investment blunders. The real challenge is that of achieving your financial goals. If you achieve the goals, you win! Yet how can you avoid being influenced by the gamelike environment? People who know how to use quantitative investment methods can use these techniques to make good decisions. People who do not know financial theory must rely on their psychological biases to help make decisions. Making decisions through sound financial theory and avoiding biases and emotions will set you on the road to investment success.

Stock Market Bubbles

The efficient-market hypothesis (EMH) states that every security at every point in time is fairly priced. Some would argue that a stock market bubble offers evidence against the EMH. A stock market bubble is said to occur when stock prices dramatically rise for a time and then seem to suddenly collapse.

Consider two modern stock market bubbles. One occurred in Japan, the other in the United States. The Japanese stock market experienced a dramatic rise in the 1980s. The Nikkei began 1984 near 10,000 and peaked in 1989 nearly four times higher. Then, in nine months, the Japanese market fell by roughly 50 percent to 21,000. More than a decade later, the Japanese stock market languished near 10,000, or down roughly 75 percent from the 1989 peak. Given subsequent performance, it seems improbable that the Japanese stock market was fairly valued in 1989.

The run-up and subsequent crash of technology stocks in the United States is another example of a stock market bubble. As early as December 1996, the Federal Reserve Bank chairman, Alan Greenspan, warned investors about "irrational exuberance." Yet the rally continued to accelerate. For example, the TSC Internet Index provided by **TheStreet.com** was at 569 on March 9, 1999. One year later, the index had risen 134 percent to 1,333. Then the index fell −81 percent to 249 on March 9, 2001, and it stood at 85 on March 10, 2003.

The dramatic rise and crash of Japanese equities and U.S. Internet stocks provide evidence that stock markets can be extremely volatile. From a financial perspective, stock market investors need to understand the source of such volatility. The EMH suggests that the underlying economic worth of such companies must have rapidly improved and later deteriorated. Critics of the EMH contend that such stock market volatility is simply too great to be fully explained by changes in economic fundamentals. According to the critics, stock prices deviate too much from fundamental values during "bubble" periods. Investor emotions, rather than economic fundamentals, may represent the driving force behind excessive stock market volatility during bubble periods.

See: Michael T. Darda, "Beyond the Bubble," *The Wall Street Journal Online*, December 1, 2005 (**http://online.wsj.com**).

Theory of Finance

Theory Provides a Road Map

Today, many novice investors are primarily concerned with two simple questions. First, how do you access investment information? The Internet and traditional financial publications offer today's investors a wealth of valuable investment information and analysis, often for free. A second common and important question is, How do you turn information into wisdom? This is where the theory of finance comes into play. Just as the effective practices of successful investors give clues about how to proceed, so too does investment theory provide a useful road map or context for analyzing investment problems. The road map provided by the theory of finance explains that economic forces determine the prices for stocks, bonds, and other assets such as real estate, art, collectibles, and so on. As demonstrated throughout this chapter, the first and most fundamental concept of investment is the idea of compound returns. Money grows over time according to economic fundamentals. Compound interest can create an astounding increase in the value of a company or investment over time.

Key Investment Concepts

In addition to the compound-interest concept, another key idea in investment theory is the concept of a **portfolio**. A portfolio is a diversified collection of stocks and bonds or other assets. An investor's intent in creating a portfolio of assets is to provide the basis for a stable rate of return. Portfolio theory tells us that diversification has the potential to reduce anticipated risk for a given expected return. Each individual firm has various influences that affect its risk. Firm-specific risk is tied to the chance that a key executive might leave the firm or die, important products might lose out to new competitors, or vital or brand names might be lost. Through an investment portfolio, firm-specific risks tend to cancel out.

A further fundamental investment theory is the idea that **risk** and **expected return** are related. The price of higher expected return is greater anticipated risk. This means that if low-risk U.S. Treasury bills yield 6 percent interest, bonds that yield more than 6 percent per year are, by definition, not Treasury bills. If you want to earn higher than risk-free rates of return,

Portfolio
Diversified collection of stocks, bonds, and other assets.

Risk
Chance of a loss of wealth or a failure to meet investment goals.

Expected return
Future return anticipated after analyzing the financial asset.

you must be willing to assume higher levels of risk. The importance of recognizing the relationship between risk and expected return is that, holding the length of the investment horizon constant, higher expected return is typically accompanied by greater volatility. The variation in annual stock returns compared to bond returns shown in Table 1.3 illustrates this point.

Efficient-market hypothesis
Idea that every security is correctly priced, not overvalued or undervalued.

Another key investment concept is the **efficient-market hypothesis**. The efficient-market hypothesis states that every security at every point in time is fairly priced. Prices are neither too low (undervalued) nor too high (overvalued). This is quite a controversial theory. Proponents of the hypothesis point to the fact that the average professional investor does not beat the market. Studies show that as many as 90 percent of professionally managed mutual funds and pension funds underperform the broad market averages over periods of time as short as 10 years. On the other hand, opponents of the theory point to the success of a few investment superstars. These investors have trounced the market over very long periods of time.

Analysis and Behavior

Investment Superstars

The typical investor cannot expect to beat the market averages. To consistently outperform, it takes a superstar. In the investment management business, it takes a superstar like Warren Buffett, Peter Lynch, or Sir John Templeton. In major-league baseball, it takes a superstar like Barry Bonds. Barry Bonds earns extraordinary compensation derived from his ability to hit home runs. The fact that Barry Bonds makes millions of dollars per year does not mean that it is easy to make millions playing baseball. His extraordinary returns reflect his extraordinary ability as a power hitter. Similarly, extraordinary returns for investment superstars, such as Warren Buffett, reflect superior ability to hit the ball out of the investment park.

Return on equity
Accounting net income divided by stockholders' equity, or book value per share.

Omaha-based Warren Buffett, chairman and chief executive officer of Berkshire Hathaway, looks for wonderful businesses selling at reasonable prices. A wonderful business is one that generates a high rate of profit for the amount of money committed to the enterprise. In terms of accounting information, the **return-on-equity** measure is the best available indicator of the firm's ability to profitably use operating and financial leverage. The return on equity is simply the ratio of net income divided by stockholders' equity, or book value per share. On average, return on equity falls in the range of 10 to12 percent per year for the broad cross section of businesses in the United States. Firms that consistently earn less than 10 to12 percent find that it becomes difficult to raise new funds for expansion and improvement. As a result, low-profit firms are forced to either improve their operations or shrink and retrench. In order to attract additional funds for expansion, firms must offer above-average rates of return. Because of competition, it is hard for a company to sustain a high return on equity for a long period of time. Thus, firms with a history of high profits tend to earn lower rates of return over time as more and more capital is committed to the enterprise. Alternatively, low-profit firms see their profit rate rise over time as investors redeploy funds to other more profitable uses. This recurring pattern, or tendency, of profit rates to return toward long-term industry and economywide averages is called **regression to the mean**.

Regression to the mean
Tendency of profit rates to return toward long-term industry and economywide averages.

When Buffett looks for wonderful businesses that are highly profitable, he is looking for companies that consistently earn 20 to 25 percent, or higher, rates of return on stockholders' equity. When Buffett says he is looking for stocks selling at reasonable prices, he is looking for companies whose price does not already reflect the company's superior profitability. A reasonable price is usually defined in terms of the **price-earnings (P/E) ratio** paid, where P/E is defined as the market value of the firm divided by net income. On a per-share basis, P/E is the company's stock price divided by earnings per share. A P/E of 20 means that the stock price is 20 times higher than each dollar of earnings per share. A P/E of 20 implies that the firm has five cents in earnings for each dollar of market value. Buffett finds these firms in the mundane and unglamorous industries, such as insurance, gas pipelines, and furniture retailers.

Price-earnings (P/E) ratio
Stock price divided by earnings per share.

Another legendary investor is Fidelity Investment's Peter Lynch. Lynch is credited with taking the Magellan Mutual Fund from a few million dollars in assets to $14 billion before his retirement in 1993. Lynch enjoyed fantastic results as the most successful mutual fund manager of our era by focusing on stocks that had rapid growth at a modest price, as measured by the firm's P/E ratio. When Lynch looked for outstanding growth, he was looking for firms that had the ability to grow earnings per share by 10, 15, or even 20 percent per year. Like Buffett, Lynch prefers bargains. However, he preferred high-growth companies with solid business models that sold for no more than the market-average P/E ratio.

A third legendary investor of recent years is Sir John Templeton of the Franklin-Templeton group of mutual funds. Templeton is known as the "father of global investing." He promotes searching far and wide for the best bargains available. In Templeton's opinion, the best stock market bargains are companies selling at low prices relative to their book value of tangible assets. This means that Templeton looks for companies that sell at a cheap price relative to the company's book value per share. Templeton's reasoning is that firms tend to grow earnings when book value grows, and as book value grows higher, share prices will follow.

In all three cases, Warren Buffett, Peter Lynch, and Sir John Templeton, successful investors have profited by considering stocks as part ownership in the company's underlying businesses. Notice that they don't think of stocks as a simple piece of paper; they don't use trading rules that favor stocks that are going up or stocks that are going down. Instead, they seek to develop an independent judgment of what a company is worth on the basis of its economic prospects compared with those of companies in general. In considering the development of their own stock-selection techniques, individual investors would be well advised to consider the underpinnings of the historical success enjoyed by these legendary investors.

Asset Valuation

How do investment superstars value stocks? While individual techniques vary slightly, a recurring theme is that investment superstars value stocks on an economic basis in terms of the prorated value of the underlying business.

Consider the example shown in Table 1.4. This example illustrates the economic rate of return and economic value of 1 acre of Iowa farmland. For simplicity, assume that such a parcel is able to generate 150 bushels of corn and that the price of a bushel of corn is $2.50. This means that $375 in revenue would be generated from corn raised on this 1 acre of Iowa farmland. Furthermore, assume that planting and tillage costs, seed and fertilizer costs, harvesting costs, taxes, and so on, total $225 per acre. This means that gross profit per acre is $150. In order to yield a 6 percent rate of return, an investor would pay no more than $2,500 per acre ($= \$150 \div 0.06$). This means that the economic value per acre of such land is $2,500. Of course, $2,500 is a very high price for farmland. It reflects the fact that Iowa farmland is among the most productive of all agricultural land in the world. If the land were less productive, it would sell at a much lower price.

TABLE 1.4	Economic Value of Iowa Farmland
Bushels of corn produced per acre	150
Price of corn per bushel	× $2.50
Total revenue per acre	$375
Planting, tillage costs	−75
Seed and fertilizer costs	−40
Harvesting costs	−90
Taxes, insurance, etc.	−20
Gross profit per acre	$150
Interest rate	6%
Economic value per acre	$2,500

Because of the high cropland productivity, investors who demand a 6 percent rate of return can pay up to $2,500 per acre. If an investor could buy such farmland for $1,000 per acre, he or she would scoop it up because it would then produce a 15 percent return (= $150 ÷ $1,000). That would be a heck of a deal. If someone came along, borrowed a bunch of cash, and bid up the price to $4,000 per acre, he or she would go broke. Such farmland will not support a price of $4,000 an acre for agricultural use. The simple fact is there is an economic value underpinning that farmland.

It is the same with stocks. Sometimes, inexperienced investors go out and bid up the price of some Internet stock figuring that revenues, earnings, and book values don't matter. For brief periods of time, sometimes they do not. This is especially true when there is a lot of uncertainty. However, in the long run, revenues, earnings, and book values matter a great deal. If earnings for very high-price biotech stocks absolutely explode to the upside over the next few years, their current stock prices will be justified. They may even rise. If earnings of those companies do not explode, those stocks are going to get crushed. In the long run, investors can do no better than the company in which they have invested. If the company prospers, so will its investors. If the company fails to generate above-average profits, its investors will not be able to earn above-average rates of return.

The fundamental point is that the value of a financial asset, such as farmland, is determined by economic considerations. This is the same for the value of stocks, bonds, and investments of all types. The value of any asset depends on how much profit is generated and the rate of interest demanded by the investor. The most successful investors of our time look at stocks and bonds in much the same way that a farmer would look at investing in real estate.

Behavior of Stock Market Participants

The stock market can be thought of as a system of human interaction. Every part of the investment process includes people interacting with one another. Investors exchange information and discuss stocks with neighbors, relatives, friends, and colleagues. Advice is sought from advisors, analysts, bankers, and planners. Buy and sell trades are communicated to brokers who send the trades to dealers, specialists, and traders at the stock exchanges.

Incentives
Financial reasons for inciting an action.

Differences between short-term and long-term objectives sometimes create conflicting **incentives**. For example, stockbrokers can have a long and successful career by providing good advice to clients and creating relationships built on trust. However, since a broker's pay derives from trading commissions, creating an environment where clients are induced to make many trades can increase the broker's short-term income. As a result, the clients' trading behavior can be influenced by the short-term incentives of the stockbroker. Similarly, consider the incentives of a mutual fund manager. Mutual fund investors flock to outperforming funds. The additional money invested in the fund increases the manager's salary. If a fund manager is underperforming in the first half of the year, the manager faces strong incentives to take on added risk and play "catch-up" during the latter half of the year. Alternatively, a manager who has beaten competitors during the first half of the year may become overly conservative so as not to risk a leadership position. As a result, short-term incentives can adversely affect mutual fund manager performance.

Investor psychology
The reasons, emotions, and perceptions of the human brain as they pertain to investments.

In addition to differences in personal incentives, investment decisions are also affected by **investor psychology**. Investors make investment decisions before outcomes are certain. Psychologists have found that as decisions become more difficult and involve higher levels of uncertainty, the decisions tend to be more greatly influenced by emotions and feelings. For example, investors are reluctant to sell a stock at a loss. They often want to hold a stock until it goes back up to the price they paid for it no matter how long it takes! Such a decision is based not so much on the opinion that the stock is a great investment opportunity but more on the desire to avoid that awful feeling associated with admitting a mistake.

Successful investors are able to understand and overcome these adverse psychological influences. This is especially true when crowd psychology influences the overall market, as was the case during the late-1990s Internet stock bubble in the United States and the Japanese stock market bubble of the late-1980s. Outbreaks of crowd behavior, typified by "extraordinary popular delusions and the madness of crowds," are occasionally observed in various markets—and are especially dangerous to investor wealth.

Are Debt Holders Myopic?

Since the end of World War II, major stock market averages have risen 10 to12 percent per year. However, a typical year is anything but average. Note from Table 1.2 that the annual return of the stock market is rarely near the overall average. It is common for the stock market to experience a return of 20 or 30 percent. It is also common for the stock market to rise much less than 10 percent or even decline. It is uncommon for the market to earn 10 to 12 percent in any given year. In the 1980s and 1990s, investor rates of return on common stocks averaged more than 15 percent per year. With inflation tamed, interest rates had plummeted, and the stock market soared.

On average, common stocks have returned roughly 6 percent more than the rate of inflation. This means that long-term stock investors have enjoyed a "real" increase of 6 percent per year in the amount of goods and services that they can buy with the proceeds from money set aside for investment in common stocks. To many it may seem surprising that common stocks grow 6 percent per year in real terms given that the overall economy, as measured by the gross domestic product, tends to grow at only 3 percent per year in real terms. For more than a century, real economic growth of 3 percent per year has been fueled by population growth of roughly 1 percent per year plus technological changes (productivity growth) of 2 percent per year. How can stocks grow at 6 percent in a world that is growing at 3 percent?

The answer is simple. Major corporations tend to be financed on almost a 50-50 basis with debt and equity. While common stocks have earned a real return of 6 percent per year for investors, bondholders have earned no net real return. In other words, the return to bondholders has just been enough, on average, to offset the effects of inflation. Another way of looking at it is to think of the 6 percent real rate of return earned by stockholders as the entire real return earned on investments financed by both debt and equity. Stock investors love bondholders!

See: Henny Sender, "Young Traders Thrive in the Stock/Bond Nexus," *The Wall Street Journal Online*, November 18, 2005 (**http://online.wsj.com**).

Information—A Key to Investment Success

Financial Information on the Web

The ability to obtain good information may be the most important determinant of investor success. After all, the quality of a decision is only as good as the quality of the information used in the decision-making process. **Stock quotes** in **real time**, for example, are often sought by investors several times during the trading day. When it comes to financial news and information, the Internet is a powerful tool.

Table 1.5 shows a number of leading Web sites for investment information. CBS MarketWatch, for example, is among the best at focused financial news and information. This Web site has excellent stock price and volume information, as well as pertinent financial data on individual companies, industries, and the overall economy. Late-breaking news tied to individual companies is offered on a real-time basis. This gives today's individual investors more detailed and timely information than Wall Street professionals enjoyed until recently.

The best free Web site for government reports filed by individual companies is called **EDGAR**. Experienced investors know that if you want complete details about SEC reports for an individual company, all you have to do is "ask EDGAR." EDGAR is an acronym for "Electronic Retrieval Analysis System" for SEC filings. It is a for-profit company that specializes in providing investor access to SEC reports and filings. For example, if you want the latest quarterly report on Microsoft Corporation, go to the EDGAR Web site and key in "MSFT," which is the four-letter **ticker symbol** for Microsoft. EDGAR will provide a plain text report of Microsoft's most recent quarterly accounting earnings information, or the Schedule **10Q report**. Other important bits of information available on EDGAR include the firm's Schedule **10K report**, or annual financial report, and the company's Schedule 14A **proxy statement**, or annual meeting announcement. The annual meeting announcement is a very interesting document because it includes information about the individuals in top management, the members of the board of directors, and other large investors in the firm. The proxy statement also tells how much company stock is owned by management and the board of directors.

Stock quotes
Offers to buy and sell shares at specific prices.

Real time
Up-to-the-minute, current stock quote.

EDGAR
Electronic Retrieval Analysis System for SEC filings.

Ticker symbol
Unique one-, two-, three-, or four-letter code for any company.

10Q report
Quarterly accounting information filed with the SEC.

10K report
Annual accounting information filed with the SEC.

Proxy statement
Annual meeting announcement and shareholder voting information.

TABLE 1.5	Where to Get Investment Information

Information Source	Internet Address	Description
Web-Based Sources		
Bloomberg.com	www.bloomberg.com	Concise reporting of news and information affecting stock and bond markets worldwide.
CBS Market Watch	www.cbs.marketwatch.com	Focused on financial news and information. Individual investors can find news, commentary, advice, and stock price information.
Daily Stocks	www.dailystocks.com	This site provides many tools used in technical analysis. Stocks can be found by sorting on momentum, daily highs and lows, etc. Price charts are available.
Morningstar.com	www.morningstar.com	Comprehensive mutual fund commentary and analysis.
The Motley Fool	www.fool.com	An online forum designed to "educate, amuse and enrich investors." A constant stream of witty investment advice spills over to active message boards.
MSN Money	http://moneycentral.msn.com/home.asp	Investing highlights for customized portfolios, market reports, mutual fund directory, retirement and wills, taxes, real estate, smart buying, insurance, etc.
Standard & Poors	www2.standardandpoors.com	This is the place to find information about S&P equity index methodology, fixed-income ratings, products, and services. View detailed information about the S&P indexes, including returns over various periods plus fundamental characteristics and sector weights, for any date back to index inception.
TheStreet.com	www.thestreet.com	A full menu of stock analysis, market commentary, and biting satire.
U.S. Securities and Exchange Commission	www.see.gov	This is the place to find free access to official SEC filings by individual companies, obtain information about individual brokers, or file a complaint about shady business practices.
ValueLine.com	www.valueline.com	Value Line publishes more than a dozen print and electronic products utilized by more than half-a-million investors. Best known for the Value Line Investment Survey, the most widely used independent investment service.
Yahoo! Finance	http://finance.yahoo.com	A terrific Web site with U.S. markets, world markets, quotes, financial news, message boards, chat, etc. Organize your news (life) with my.yahoo.com.
Newspapers		
Barron's	www.barrons.com	Biting market commentary once a week, portfolio analysis, and data bank.
Investor's Business Daily	www.investors.com	Founder William O'Neal dispenses stock picking, charting, and momentum strategies. Big on investor education.
The Wall Street Journal	online.wsj.com	*The* daily paper when it comes to financial news and information. Print subscribers get interactive access at a bargain price.
USA Today	www.usatoday.com/money/front.htm	Don't underestimate "McPaper's" Money Section when it comes to business, economic, and financial news. It's terrific!
Business Magazines		
Business Week	http://businessweek.com	Timely business news and analysis, tech center, and useful business school, career, and small business information.
The Economist	www.economist.com	Offers analysis and opinion on the business and political events of the week.
Forbes	http://forbes.com	Terrific commentary on economics and financial markets from an all-star stable of regular columnists. Stimulating reviews of companies and mutual funds.
Fortune	http://money.cnn.com/magazines/fortune	Famous for Fortune 500 company list. Interesting advice on career development.
Personal Finance Magazines		
Kiplinger's Personal Finance	www.kiplinger.com	Provides practical guidance on saving, investing, planning for retirement, and major purchases.
Money	http://money.cnn.com	Interesting market commentary, as well as company and mutual fund analysis aimed at novice investors. Lots of personal finance advice.
Smart Money	www.smartmoney.com	Serves the need for personal finance information for affluent, sophisticated, professional, and managerial Americans.

Schedule **13D** filings are made to the SEC within 10 days of an entity's attaining a 5 percent or more position in any class of a company's securities. Any subsequent change in holdings or intentions must be reported on an amended filing. SEC **Form 144** filings must be submitted by holders of restricted securities, sometimes called *letter stock*, who intend to sell shares. Note that 144 filings are only notices of intentions to sell shares; sometimes these shares aren't sold even though the owner has filed a Form 144. Small investors have easy access to this information on the SEC Web site (through EDGAR) and in leading financial publications such as *Barron's*.

13D
Filings made to the SEC within 10 days of an entity's attaining a 5 percent or more position in any class of a company's securities.

Form 144
Filings submitted to the SEC by holders of restricted stock who intend to sell shares.

Financial Newspapers

Another important source of financial news and information is the traditional financial press. Like many businesses, the financial press is quickly migrating to the Internet. In fact, the financial press is probably ahead of the curve, because magazine and newspaper publishers have witnessed firsthand the rapid growth of Internet portals like Yahoo!. Table 1.5 shows a number of important print media outlets for investment information.

Of course, the first and most important source of daily Wall Street information is *The Wall Street Journal*, published by Dow Jones, Inc. *The Wall Street Journal* is the stock and bond investor's daily newspaper when it comes to financial news and information. You can even get online access to *The Wall Street Journal* at a bargain price. On the Internet Web site for *The Wall Street Journal Online* you can read tomorrow's headlines for the print version. *The Wall Street Journal Online* is an extremely useful tool for news and information searches on individual companies. As you may already know, in each day's print version of *The Wall Street Journal*, typically on page B2, there's a company index that lists all firms mentioned in the news stories. If you want to find information about Intel, for example, you can quickly turn to the specific pages that contain news, articles, or other information pertinent to Intel investors. *The Wall Street Journal* is a "must read" for investment professionals.

⋯⋯⋯ Try It! ⋯⋯⋯

Using the *Wall Street Journal* index on page B2, find all the stories related to General Electric. If you have access to the *WSJ Online*, search for articles related to General Electric.

Financial Periodicals

Another source of useful investment information is *Barron's* financial weekly, also published by Dow Jones, Inc. It is a sister publication to *The Wall Street Journal*. *Barron's* is a financial weekly published on Saturdays, whereas *The Wall Street Journal* comes out on a daily basis. Because it is a weekly, *Barron's* focuses on market commentary and portfolio analysis, rather than company-specific news.

Barron's is a top source for information about trends in technology stocks, the mutual fund industry, or investing in general. Each week's issue features a wealth of market commentary about movements in interest rates and stock prices in the United States and in foreign markets, such as Asia, as well as industry-specific news and information. One of the most useful features of *Barron's* is its weekly "market laboratory" of investment statistics. This laboratory gives a host of financial statistics, data, and valuation ratios on stocks, bonds, credit conditions, and the economy.

BusinessWeek is another top source for financial news and information. *BusinessWeek* is a good source for timely business news and analysis and for technical information on individual sectors of the economy. It even has information about top business schools. For example, its once-a-year survey of business schools gives readers timely information about admission standards, quality, and strengths of various business schools around the country. *BusinessWeek* is also a top source of information about careers and small business opportunities.

Another favorite for financial news, analysis, and commentary is *Forbes* magazine. *Forbes* gives biweekly commentary on economics and the financial markets from an all-star stable of regular columnists. It also offers a stimulating review of individual companies, big and small business, and mutual funds. Portfolio strategy is a focus of financial columnists in every issue. Many who subscribe to *Forbes* for its financial news and information begin reading each issue in the back few pages, where financial columnists, such as portfolio manager David Dreman, give on-the-spot analysis of market trends.

Fortune magazine is another timely source of financial news and information. This biweekly publication is most famous for its Fortune 500 list of the 500 largest companies in the United States. The original list of 500 top industrials (according to sales) has been expanded. Today, *Fortune* covers the top 500 companies in America, along with the second 500, the so-called Fortune 1000. The magazine also covers global corporations. *Fortune* is an interesting source for information about career opportunities, as well as trends and strategies followed by the management of top corporations. *Money* and *Smart Money* are two quality personal finance magazines with full Web page support.

Becoming an Investment Professional

Financial Job Market Overview

Everyone has a practical interest in compiling sufficient wealth for a comfortable retirement, so investment is a practical subject for all students. In addition, many students seek to earn a productive and exciting living in the investment field. Employment opportunities in financial services are expected to grow rapidly in the years ahead. In addition, the amount of financial sophistication demanded of finance specialists and nonspecialists is also expected to rise. For example, corporate treasurers and chief financial officers must understand financial theory and practice if they are to efficiently finance firms' growth needs. This includes accessing the capital markets. Personnel and human resource heads also need to understand investment theory and practice in order to help employees with an increasingly complex array of retirement plans. In addition to such opportunities for improved job market prospects in financial and nonfinancial occupations, there are a growing number of career opportunities in the investment industry itself.

Table 1.6 shows a variety of employment opportunities in the financial services industry. Employment opportunities are most numerous with commercial banks, savings institutions, insurance carriers, and real estate companies. With respect to banks and savings institutions, many career opportunities in the investment field involve simple information processing. Nevertheless, many banks and savings institutions are moving toward offering financial planning and investment advice. Insurance companies offer a wide variety of career opportunities for executives interested in designing variable- and fixed-annuity products for sale to individual and institutional investors. Insurance companies hold large investment portfolios as reserves against potential disasters that require large benefit payouts. Investment professionals manage these portfolios.

Table 1.6

Career Opportunities in the Investment Field

Employment and career opportunities in the financial services industries are expected to grow rapidly in the years ahead. In addition, the amount of financial sophistication demanded of nonspecialists is also expected to rise. For example, personnel in human resource departments increasingly need to understand investment theory and practice in order to help employees with an increasingly complex array of deferred benefits, such as 401k plans, and retirement investment opportunities.

Kind of Business	No. of Establishments	No. of Employees	Payroll ($ billions)	Average Pay
Commercial banking	80,400	1,630,000	69.8	$ 42,822
Savings institutions	17,300	263,000	10.7	40,684
Credit unions	16,300	211,000	6.8	32,227
Nondepository credit institutions	53,000	662,000	37.1	56,042
Real estate credit	21,900	267,000	17.7	66,292
Credit intermediaries	28,800	234,000	11.5	49,145
Investment banking	7,100	165,000	27.7	167,879
Securities brokerage	32,800	443,000	47.2	106,546
Securities and commodities exchanges	200	7,000	0.7	100,000
Portfolio management	11,300	178,000	21	117,978
Direct life insurance carriers	9,800	478,000	24.9	52,092
Direct health and medical insurance carriers	2,900	320,000	16	50,000
Direct property and casualty insurance	13,000	602,000	31.4	52.159
Insurance agencies and brokerages	125,200	641,000	30	46,802
Mutual funds and trusts	3,500	34,000	2.4	70,588

Source: U.S. Census Bureau, *Statistical Abstract of the United States, 2006*, table 1155.

The real estate industry is also a prime employer of personnel with an investment background. Of course, most of the people employed in the real estate industry are directly involved with customers in terms of buying and selling homes or commercial properties. There are additional job opportunities for others involved in the administration end of the business. Lastly, even state and local governments hire investment professionals to run their public pension plans.

Brokerage Business

One of the most interesting areas in the financial services sector is the stock brokerage business. A **stockbroker**, sometimes referred to as an *account executive*, usually works with individual investors and institutions in advising and executing orders for individual common stocks or bonds. Although the broker may receive a base salary, it is common for the main part of a broker's compensation to come in the form of commission income.

In a typical arrangement, an individual broker might receive 35 to 50 percent of the total commissions generated. This means that if an individual broker generates gross commissions of $200,000 per year, he or she will receive a gross income of between $70,000 and $100,000.

Stockbroker
Financial agent who assists investors with buying and selling financial assets.

At Merrill Lynch, for example, a typical broker earns in excess of $100,000 a year. This means that the typical Merrill Lynch broker generates at least $200,000 to $285,000 in gross commissions per year. In an era when commission rates average 1 percent to one-half of 1 percent of the amount invested, this implies a tremendous amount of investment activity being administered by the account executive. To illustrate, consider the broker trying to earn that $100,000 income. If the gross commission generated is 1 percent of the amount traded, the broker would need to have customers generating a minimun of $20 million per year in buy or sell orders. Generating and maintaining the customer base necessary to provide $20 million per year in transactions is a daunting task indeed.

You can be sure that the typical brokerage account executive is not only highly educated, bright, and talented but also extremely hardworking. All top financial firms devote significant resources toward making individual account executives successful. The vast majority of successful stockbrokers can attribute their success to providing high-quality advice to their clients. However, the compensation structure of the commission system provides the incentive to stockbrokers to encourage trading, rather than a buy-and-hold strategy. Periodically, you may hear about a broker initiating many trades in clients' accounts, sometimes without their permission. This is called **churning** and is done for the sole purpose of generating commissions. The brokers that do this eventually get caught and get fired.

Churning
Illegal broker-initiated trading in client accounts to generate commission income.

Investment Management

The most sought-after jobs in the securities business include **security analysts** and **portfolio managers**. Analysts and portfolio managers work for mutual funds, pension funds, and hedge funds. However, relatively few persons are actively employed in these positions. Table 1.6 shows that the total number of securities brokers in the United States is over 440,000. At the same time, the total number of employees at mutual fund management companies is as few as 34,000. Moreover, most of the employees at mutual fund companies answer the phone. The number of mutual fund employees engaged in security analysis or portfolio management is a comparative handful.

Security analyst
Finance professional who analyzes and makes recommendations regarding stocks and other financial assets.

Portfolio manager
Finance professional in charge of making buy, sell, and hold decisions for a portfolio.

To get the top analyst and portfolio manager jobs, one usually must obtain the Certified Financial Analyst (CFA) designation. To do so, one must pass three rigorous exams that are given one per year. Therefore, it takes three years to obtain the CFA designation. For more information, see the sponsoring organization's Web site: **www.cfainstitute.org**.

Financial Planning

A relatively new field for students with backgrounds in investment is the financial planning business. This is a service business in which the planner gets to know the individual client and tries to match client risk and return preferences with a broad array of appropriate investment opportunities. The **Certified Financial Planner (CFP)** designation is earned by thousands of individuals who complete requirements set by the Certified Financial Planner Standards Board. These requirements involve ethics, education, an exam, and experience. To qualify as a CFP, the applicant must demonstrate proficiency in five areas through extensive training and testing: financial plan processing and insurance, investment planning, income tax planning, retirement planning and employee benefits, and estate planning.

Certified Financial Planner (CFP)
Finance professional who helps individuals identify and meet financial needs.

For information about the CFP program, visit the sponsoring organization's Web site at **www.cfp.net**, or write directly to the CFP Board. Information can also be obtained from colleges and universities that sponsor CFP classes and programs. The CFP designation in financial planning compares with the Certified Professional Accountant, or CPA, designation in the field of accounting.

Investment Banking

Investment banker
Finance professional who helps companies and government organizations acquire capital through the issuance of financial assets.

While the stockbroker and the financial planner deal mainly with individual investors, **investment bankers** deal mainly with institutional clients. Investment bankers are primarily

involved in raising capital for corporations by distributing the securities they issue to the general public.

Companies in need of capital hire the investment banker, who arranges to sell their debt or equity securities to the general public and acts as an intermediary between individual investors and the issuing corporations. Investment bankers also advise corporate clients on financial strategies, and they often help arrange mergers and acquisitions. Investment bankers tend to be talented, hardworking, and extremely aggressive. Investment banking is a "pressure cooker" occupation with enormous risk and staggering potential rewards. Individual investment bankers have been known to make tens of millions of dollars per year in total compensation. On the other hand, the penalty to failure can be extreme. Widespread layoffs during industry downturns are common.

This review of career opportunities in investments and the financial services industry is not meant to be exhaustive. Opportunities abound because financial services is a growth industry. Still, students are well advised to remember that compensation in the field of investments is performance-based. Rewards for success are substantial. Penalties for underperformance are swift.

Summary

■ A major class of financial assets is **cash reserves**, or short-term money market instruments. The primary attraction of cash reserves is that they offer modest income with stability of principal. A common use of cash reserves is to buy **Treasury bills**, which are debt obligations of the U.S. Treasury that have maturities of one year or less. **Treasury notes** are debt obligations of the U.S. Treasury that have maturities of more than 1 year but less than 10 years. **Treasury bonds** are Treasury obligations with maturities of 10 years or more. **Bonds** are an important class of investment assets and include interest-bearing debt obligations issued by corporations, the federal government and its agencies, and state and local governments. A third important type of investment asset is **common stock**. Ownership of common stock gives the owner a proportionate interest in the profits and dividends or other distributions of a corporation.

■ Under a **defined-benefit retirement plan**, the employer promises employees a fixed retirement income that depends on a formula that includes the number of years served times the last year's salary. Under a **defined-contribution retirement plan**, each employee's retirement income is determined by the amount of the employee's contributions and his or her success in investing the funds. When employees have defined-contribution retirement plans, they must accept responsibility for the management of their retirement assets.

■ A **portfolio** is a diversified collection of stocks and bonds or other assets. Portfolio theory tells us that diversification has the potential to reduce anticipated risk for a given expected return. **Risk** and **expected return** are related. The price of higher expected return is greater anticipated risk. Alternatively stated, the expected reward for taking more risk is a higher return.

■ The **efficient-market hypothesis** states that every security at every point in time is fairly priced. Prices are neither too low (undervalued) nor too high (overvalued).

■ In terms of accounting information, the **return-on-equity** measure is the best available indicator of the firm's ability to profitably use operating and financial leverage. The return on equity is simply the ratio of net income divided by stockholders' equity, or book value per share.

■ High-profit firms tend to earn lower rates of return over time as more and more capital is committed to the enterprise. At the same time, low-profit firms see their profit rate rise over time as investors redeploy funds to other, more profitable uses. This recurring pattern, or tendency, of profit rates to return toward long-term industry and economywide averages is called **regression to the mean**.

■ On a per-share basis, the **price-earnings ratio** is the company's stock price divided by earnings per share. A P/E of 20 means that the stock price is 20 times higher than each dollar of earnings per share. However, a P/E of 20 implies that the firm has five cents in earnings for each dollar of market value.

■ Investment decision making is influenced by the behavior of stock market participants. It is important to under-stand that both the **incentives** of others and **investor psychology** affect your decisions.

■ A wealth of stock market information is available on the Internet. Investors often seek **stock quotes**, or share prices, in **real time** several times during the trading day. **EDGAR** is an acronym for "Electronic Retrieval Analysis System" for SEC filings. Go to the EDGAR Web site and key in the **ticker symbol** for any company, and EDGAR will provide a plain-text report of the firm's most recent quarterly accounting earnings information, or the **10Q report**. Other important bits of information available on EDGAR include the firm's **10K report**, or annual financial report, and the company's **proxy statement**, or annual meeting announcement. Schedule **13D** filings are made to the SEC within 10 days of an entity's attaining a 5 percent or more position in any class of a company's securities. Holders of restricted securities, sometimes called *letter stock*, who intend to sell shares, must submit SEC **Form 144** filings.

■ One of the most interesting areas in the financial services sector is the stock brokerage business. A **stockbroker**, sometimes referred to as an *account executive*, usually works with individual investors and institutions in advising and executing orders for individual common stocks or bonds. Highly sought-after jobs in the securities business include **security analysts** and **portfolio managers**. Unfortunately, the number of persons actively employed in these positions is small.

■ The **Certified Financial Planner (CFP)** designation is earned by demonstrating proficiency in five areas through extensive training and testing: financial plan processing and insurance, investment planning, income tax planning, retirement planning and employee benefits, and estate planning. **Investment bankers** deal mainly with institutional clients. Investment bankers are primarily involved with the distribution of securities from issuing corporations to the general public.

Self-Test Problems

ST1.1   Individual investors typically pay management fees or brokerage "wrap" account fees, transactions costs tied to portfolio turnover, and marketing expenses for their mutual fund manager or broker. As a result, individual investors often pay an extra 3 percent per year in portfolio management costs when compared with low-cost index mutual funds designed to mimic the performance of the overall market. Assume an investor has $10,000 to invest for 30 years. If the portfolio earns 12 percent per year, but fees and expenses cut this return down to 9 percent, how much less money will be in the account because of the fees?

Solution

Using the future-value formula, the $10,000 would grow to FV = $10,000 \times (1.12)^{30} = $299,599 if it earned the full 12 percent per year. If the portfolio only nets 9 percent after fees, it will grow to FV = $10,000 \times (1.09)^{30} = $132,677.

Notice that the investment expense of 3 percent per year cuts the final portfolio value by nearly 56 percent over 30 years!

ST1.2 Show how the future value of a 12-year $100,000 investment growing at 6 percent differs when you use annual versus continuous compounding. Explain.

Solution

The future value of a 12-year $100,000 investment earning 6 percent interest with annual compounding can be easily calculated using the formula FV = $100,000 \times (1.06)^{12}$ = $201,220. Using continuous compounding, this value is FV = $100,000 \times e^{(0.06)(12)}$ = $205,443. Continuous compounding yields a larger result given more "interest on interest."

Questions and Problems

Many of these problems review some basic time-value-of-money concepts. See Appendix A for a refresher on these principles.

1.1 Suppose you want to buy a house. If you invest $17,500 in a bank account that pays 5 percent interest per year, how much will you have for a down payment in eight years?

1.2 Assume that you expect to inherit $100,000 in 12 years. What is the present value of that future $100,000 given a 6 percent annual interest rate compounded annually?

1.3 Almost all companies have an investor relations section on their corporate Web site. Harley-Davidson (**www.harley-davidson.com**) is a leading manufacturer of motorcycles. Go to its investor relations Web site and find information about its board of directors. What committees does the board have?

1.4 Go to the Standard & Poor's Market Insight Web site at **www.mhhe.com/ edumarketinsight** and enter the ticker (BAC) for Bank of America. Under the S&P Stock Reports heading, click on the Stock Report link. How does S&P rate Bank of America? What does the number of stars indicate? What is the 12-month target price?

1.5 Microsoft (MSFT) common stock made its Nasdaq debut on March 13, 1986, with an initial public offering (IPO) price of 21 per share. Nineteen years later, on March 13, 2005, MSFT closed at 25.11. During the intervening 19-year period, MSFT split its stock 288:1 in nine separate stock-split decisions. This means that an original share purchased for 21 had a split-adjusted price of $0.0729 some 19 years later. Use annual compounding to calculate the annual rate of capital appreciation earned by Microsoft shareholders over this period (before dividends).

1.6 According to the "Rule of 72" (see Appendix A), what rate of return is needed to double your investment in 12 years? Use both the annual and continuous methods for compounding interest to find the rate of return needed to double $5,000 in 12 years.

1.7 Detailed quotes for companies listed on major exchanges can be found at **http://finance.yahoo.com**. Use this site to find the most recent full-day trading volume for IBM.

1.8 Quarterly accounting information for Electronic Data Systems (EDS) is filed in 10Q reports, which can be found at **www.freerealtime.com**. What was the value of EDS's total assets during the most recent quarter?

1.9 At age 20, assume that you begin to invest $2,000 per year in common stocks earning 12 percent. If you stop contributing at age 40, but leave your investment to accumulate for an additional 25 years, how much will you have when you retire at 65? (Note: You can use Table 1.4 as a reference for this problem.)

1.10 MSN MoneyCentral is a good place to start company-specific research. Use **http://moneycentral.msn.com** to find the name of the institutions with the largest ownership interest in the Wm. Wrigley Jr. Company (WWY), a chewing gum manufacturer.

 1.11 Who is the chairman of the board of directors of Wal-Mart Stores, Inc. (WMT)? This information can be found in Wal-Mart's Schedule 14D on EDGAR online and can be accessed through the SEC filings section of **http://finance.yahoo.com**.

1.12 In late 2004, the Coca-Cola Company reported 2004 full-year earnings per share of $2, and the company's stock traded near a price of $41. What was the Coca-Cola Company's P/E ratio?

STANDARD &POOR'S **1.13** Go to Standard & Poor's Market Insight Web site at **www.mhhe.com/ edumarketinsight** and enter the ticker (K) for the Kellogg Company. Examine the "Stock Report" to find the most recent quarterly and annual earnings per share of Kellogg. What is the earnings trend?

 1.14 *Fortune* magazine's Fortune 500 list ranks the largest U.S. corporations by revenues at **http://money.cnn.com/magazines/fortune**. Name the top five companies on the Fortune 500 list.

1.15 Altria Group, Inc. (MO), is a leading consumer products manufacturer. Formerly known as Phillip Morris, MO is best known as the largest tobacco company in the world, with Marlboro, Benson & Hedges, Merit, and Virginia Slims. MO is also known as the producer of Post cereals and packaged foods such as Jell-O, Kool-Aid, Oscar Mayer, Kraft, Velveeta, and Miracle Whip. The company is known for paying stockholders a large and growing stream of dividend income over time. In 1995, MO paid a common stock dividend of $1.22 per share. By 2005, dividends per share had risen to $3.02. For this 10-year period, use annual compounding to calculate the annual rate of change in MO's dividend.

1.16 John Deere & Co. (DE) common stock sold for prices of $15.35 on December 31, 1994, and $74.40 on December 31, 2004. If the company paid an annual dividend rate of 5.4 percent, calculate the buy-and-hold investor's total return during this 10-year period. If an investor had a 20 percent required rate of return, was buying this stock a good decision?

 1.17 Go to the Web sites of the organizations that support the CFA and CFP designations (**www.cfainstitute.org** and **www.cfp.net**, respectively). Discuss minimum qualifications.

 1.18 An investor wants to have $1 million when she retires in 20 years. If she can earn a 10 percent annual return, compounded annually, on her investments, the lump-sum amount she would need to invest today to reach her goal is *closest to:*
a. $100,000
b. $117,459
c. $148,644
d. $161,506

 1.19 An individual deposits $10,000 at the beginning of each of the next 10 years, starting today, into an account paying 9 percent interest compounded annually. The amount of money in the account at the end of 10 years will be *closest to:*
a. $109,000
b. $143,200
c. $151,900
d. $165,600

1.20 The AIMR Code of Ethics specifically addresses all of the following *except:*
a. Competence
b. Integrity and dignity
c. Independent judgment
d. Importance of contractual obligations

investment application

Will You Be a Millionaire?

According to data available from *The Statistical Abstract of the United States, 2006*, per capita income in the United States is $32,907. Income before taxes for the median (or "middle") household is $43,318. There are presently about 112 million households in the United States. Roughly 26.1 percent earn household income of $75,000 or more per year. A total of 16.9 million households report income in excess of $100,000 per year. The cut-off point for the top 5 percent of U.S. families according to income before taxes is $170,082 per year.

All of these numbers relate to income, not to wealth. What does the distribution of wealth look like? The numbers may surprise you. For all families, the median level of wealth is only $86,100. This includes financial and nonfinancial assets, such as homes and cars, and adjusts for debt, such as mortgages. The median value of stocks and mutual funds is only $19,268. Among families earning between $100,000 and $250,000 per year, only 37.1 percent own stocks and mutual funds. It is perhaps surprising that high-income families accumulate relatively modest amounts of stock and mutual fund wealth.

How much wealth do you consider is necessary to qualify as rich? Is it more than $500,000? If so, fewer than 1 in 20 families in the United States command such a level of wealth. Similarly, if an income in excess of $170,000 per year is required before you would consider yourself rich, then only 1 in 20 families would enjoy a similar level of income in the United States. If the amount of wealth required exceeds $1 million, or the amount of income necessary exceeds $250,000, then you are well into the very narrow end of the wealth and income distribution in the overall population. For arguments sake, let's assume that $1 million is the amount of money required to be rich, although some might have a higher number in mind.

How do you build $1 million of wealth? As shown in Table 1.7, a retirement account investment of only $417 per year in a broadly diversified portfolio of common stocks has the potential to grow to $1 million over a 50-year period. This is only $34.75 per month! If the investment is not made in a tax-deferred retirement account, then you would have to increase the annual investment contributions to $1,227, or almost three times more. But most people are hoping that they will not have to work for and save for 50 years. If you have 40 years until your desired retirement date, it takes an annual retirement account stock investment of $1,304. Note that a fixed-income investment approach requires an annual retirement account investment of $6,462 in bonds or $8,278 in money market investments.

The reality is that $1 million isn't what it used to be. Due to inflation, it won't be nearly as valuable in 40 years. Over extended periods of time, taxes and inflation inhibit the building of real wealth.

a. Most investors do not contribute the same amount every year. Indeed, young investors usually earn less money and therefore have less to contribute. As a person ages, income rises because of job promotions and because of wage inflation. Using Table 1.7, determine how much money the following investor will have at retirement age. At age 25, the investor has 40 years until retirement. She opens a taxable stock brokerage account and contributes $1,480 per year for 40 years (note that this contribution is exactly half of the $2,960 shown in the table). At age 35, the investor gets a job with a defined-contribution plan and invests $4,144 per year in stocks for 30 years. At age 50, the investor has only 15 years left until retirement. Taking a fixed-income approach, the investor starts investing an additional $24,057 every year into a taxable bond account. How much money will this investor have at retirement?

b. Why do so few individuals accumulate a significant amount of retirement wealth? Will you? Use the data in Table 1.7 to show how.

TABLE 1.7	Annual Investment Needed to Become a Millionaire

Number of Investing Years	Stock Market Investments		Long-Term Bond Market Investments		Short-Term Money Market Investments	
	12% Before Taxes	9% After Taxes	6% Before Taxes	4.5% After Taxes	5% Before Taxes	3.75% After Taxes
1	$1,000,000	$1,000,000	$1,000,000	$1,000,000	$1,000,000	$1,000,000
2	471,698	478,469	485,437	488,998	487,805	490,798
3	296,349	305,055	314,110	318,773	317,209	321,140
4	209,234	218,669	228,591	233,744	232,012	236,369
5	157,410	167,092	177,396	182,792	180,975	185,552
6	123,226	132,920	143,363	148,878	147,017	151,712
7	99,118	108,691	119,135	124,701	122,820	127,574
8	81,303	90,674	101,036	106,610	104,722	109,498
9	67,679	76,799	87,022	92,574	90,690	95,465
10	56,984	65,820	75,868	81,379	79,505	84,261
11	48,415	56,947	66,793	72,248	70,389	75,115
12	41,437	49,651	59,277	64,666	62,825	67,512
13	35,677	43,567	52,960	58,275	56,456	61,096
14	30,871	38,433	47,585	52,820	51,024	55,613
15	26,824	34,059	42,963	48,114	46,342	50,876
20	13,879	19,546	27,185	31,876	30,243	34,462
25	7,500	11,806	18,227	22,439	20,952	24,832
30	4,144	7,336	12,649	16,392	15,051	18,588
35	2,317	4,636	8,974	12,270	11,072	14,273
40	1,304	2,960	6,462	9,343	8,278	11,159
45	736	1,902	4,700	7,202	6,262	8,841
50	417	1,227	3,444	5,602	4,777	7,074

Equity Markets

U.S. stock exchanges compete ferociously with each other and with foreign exchanges. What is the best business form for organized exchanges? Historically, the New York Stock Exchange (NYSE) was organized as a privately held partnership. However, new competitive pressures and the need to raise additional capital have forced the NYSE to follow Nasdaq's lead and become a publicly traded for-profit corporation. What is the best forum for organized trading? Is electronic trading better or worse than floor trading? Is some combination of electronic and floor trading best? These are the types of questions market makers and regulators must continually assess. Rapid change has occurred during the past decade, and the pace of that change is bound to accelerate.

In the late 1990s, the National Association of Securities Dealers (NASD) owned Nasdaq and acquired the American Stock Exchange and the Philadelphia Stock Exchange and attempted to fold them into Nasdaq. This attempt to align electronic markets with floor-trading markets was short-lived. In 2001 and 2002, the Nasdaq Stock Market separated from NASD by purchasing its ownership stake. It remained a privately held firm until 2002, when it went public, and it now trades under the ticker symbol NDAQ. Nasdaq has tried to compete globally by setting up electronic stock exchanges oversees. However, it has enjoyed only marginal success. Nasdaq opened Nasdaq Europe in June 2001 to trade all Euro securities. In 2002, Nasdaq changed to focus on trading stocks only in Germany. Nasdaq Japan opened in 2000 but ended in 2002. The exchange has refocused its efforts on U.S. trading in recent years. In 2004, the NASD gave control of the American Stock Exchange back to the Amex seat owners.

Long known for its floor-trading system, the NYSE has been working on its own electronic trading system since 2004. In 2005, the NYSE announced a merger with Archipelago, an electronic trading firm. This merger made the NYSE a publicly traded firm for the first time in its history. Change in the business of trading stocks, bonds, and other securities is not apt to slow down anytime soon.[1]

---

[1] Aaron Lucchetti, "A Big Exchange: NYSE Members Approve Deal; Vote Overwhelmingly Endorses Archipelago Plan, Public Listing; Closing In on 'the End of an Era,'" *The Wall Street Journal*, December 7, 2005, p. C1.

CHAPTER OBJECTIVES

- Learn where and how securities are traded.
- Know how stock market performance is measured.
- Become familiar with sector, industry, and global market indexes.
- Understand relevant laws governing the investment industry.

Major U.S. Securities Exchanges

Capital Markets

Capitalism is an economic system based on private enterprise. People and companies own land, farms, factories, and equipment, and they use those assets in an attempt to earn profits. Expansion into a large business usually requires additional money, or capital. Good access to capital is vitally important in this economic system.

Who has this capital? The citizens have their savings and a desire to invest these funds in a manner that allows them to participate in the profits of economic activities. Therefore, public corporations can raise money by issuing stocks and bonds to investors. Access to this capital causes entrepreneurs like Bill Gates of Microsoft, Steve Jobs of Apple, and Larry Ellison of Oracle to take their companies public so that their businesses can become corporations. Investors have earned much profit over the years from these firms. In addition, these companies have been terrific for the economy because they have produced important products and employed hundreds of thousands of people over the years.

If done properly, matching the capital of investors with the opportunities in the corporate world benefits everyone. But people will invest in corporate securities only when they know that they can convert those securities to cash at any time. This is where the capital markets come in. The stock and bond exchanges allow investors to buy and sell securities from and to other investors. It is this liquidity that gives people the confidence to invest. The most prestigious stock exchange is the New York Stock Exchange.

New York Stock Exchange

New York Stock Exchange (NYSE)
Largest stock market in terms of market capitalization.

Agency auction market
Market in which brokers represent buyers and sellers and prices are determined by supply and demand.

Specialist
Employee of a NYSE firm who manages the market for an individual stock.

After 213 years organized as a private partnership, the **New York Stock Exchange (NYSE)** purchased Archipelago, a publicly traded electronic trading firm, as a means of becoming the NYSE Group Inc., a public corporation. Big Board members approved the deal on December 6, 2005, and the new firm began trading in 2006. Located in New York City on the corner of Wall Street and Broad Street, the NYSE provides an auction market for common and preferred stocks. The NYSE is open for business daily from 9:30 a.m. to 4:00 p.m. EST, except on weekends and holidays, or about 252 to 254 days per year. The NYSE is what is called an **agency auction market**. Trading on the NYSE takes place in the form of bids and offers by exchange members, who are acting as agents for institutions or individual investors. Buy and sell orders meet directly on the trading floor, and prices are determined by the interplay of supply and demand. In contrast, within the over-the-counter (OTC) market, stock market prices are determined by a network of dealers who buy and sell from their own inventory of stock.

At the NYSE, each listed stock is assigned to a single post, where the **specialist** manages the auction process. NYSE members bring all orders for NYSE-listed stocks to the exchange floor electronically or by a floor broker. As a result, the flows of buy and sell orders for each stock are directed to a single location. This stream of diverse orders is one of the great strengths of the exchange. It provides liquidity—the ease with which securities can be bought and sold

TABLE 2.1	The NYSE: The Largest Equities Market in the World

	2005
NYSE average daily stock volume (millions)	1,604
NYSE annual turnover rate %	102%
NYSE average price per share traded	$34.93
NYSE average trade size per sale (in shares)	334
Number of NYSE non-U.S. stocks	453
NYSE dollar value of trading activity (billions of dollars)	$56.1
Average daily program volume on NYSE (millions)	913
Programs as % of total NYSE	56.9%
Dow Jones Industrial Average	10,718
S&P 500 Index	1,248.29
NYSE Composite Index	7,753.95
NYSE total annual bond volume (millions)	$1,291
NYSE average daily bond volume (millions)	$5.1
Companies listed on the NYSE	2,779

Source: The NYSE Group, **www.nyse.com**.

without wide price fluctuations. When an investor's transaction is completed, the best price will have been exposed to a wide range of would-be buyers and sellers. The NYSE is the largest U.S. securities market in terms of the value of companies listed and the dollar value of trading activity. The NYSE is the largest equities marketplace in the world and is home to 2,779 companies. While other exchanges may boast more companies listed, the largest companies in the world tend to list in New York. In 2005, the NYSE had, on average, 1.6 billion shares trade every day worth approximately $56.1 billion (see Table 2.1).

To be listed on the NYSE, both domestic and foreign-based firms are expected to meet certain governance and reporting standards. At a minimum, the company must be a going concern—or be the successor to a going concern. In determining eligibility for listing, particular attention is given to such qualifications as the degree of national interest in the company, its relative position and stability in the industry, and its business prospects.

NYSE listing requirements for domestic companies call for a minimum firm size and distribution of the company's shares within the United States. This distribution of shares can be accomplished through domestic public offerings, acquisitions made in the United States, or other similar means. As shown in Table 2.2, minimum quantitative listing standards for the NYSE start with a minimum total number of **round lot** holders, shareholders who own at least 100 shares, and a minimum level of trading volume. Listing companies must meet earnings, operating cash flow, or global market capitalization standards. Listing standards for foreign-based corporations are designed to enable major foreign corporations to list their shares on the NYSE. The principal criteria for foreign companies focus on worldwide liquidity rather than the U.S. distribution. Non-U.S. corporations may elect to qualify for listing under either the listing standards for non-U.S. corporations or the NYSE's domestic listing criteria. However, an applicant company must meet all the criteria within the standards under which it seeks to qualify for listing.

The NYSE is the most prestigious exchange in the world and generally has the highest listing standards. In addition, a listing firm must pay initial and continuing listing fees. Domestic corporations must pay an initial listing fee that includes a fixed charge and a sliding-scale amount tied to the number of outstanding shares. For example, the initial listing fee for a company with 5 million shares of common stock would consist of a one-time charge of $84,600.

Round lot
100 shares.

TABLE 2.2	NYSE Listing Standards

A. Standards for U.S. Corporations **Minimum Quantitative Standards:** **Distribution and Size Criteria**		**B. Standards for Non-U.S. Corporations**	
Round-lot holders (number of holders of a unit of trading—generally 100 shares)	2,000 U.S.	Round-lot holders (number of holders of a unit of trading—generally 100 shares)	5,000 worldwide
or:		Public shares	2.5 million worldwide
Total shareholders	2,200	Public market value	$100 million worldwide
. . . together with:			
Average monthly trading volume (for the most recent 6 months)	100,000 shares		
or:			
Total shareholders	500		
... together with:			
Average monthly trading volume (for the most recent 12 months)	1,000,000 shares		
Public shares	1,100,000 outstanding		
Market value of public shares:			
Public companies	$100,000,000		
IPOs, spin-offs, carve-outs	$60,000,000		
Minimum Quantitative Standards: **Financial Criteria Earnings**			
Aggregate pretax earnings over the last 3 years of $6,500,000		Pretax income	$100 million
achievable as:		Aggregate for the last 3 years	
Most recent year	$2,500,000	. . . together with	
Each of 2 preceding years	$2,000,000		
or:		Minimum in each of the 2 most recent years	$25 million
Most recent year (all 3 years must be profitable)	$4,500,000	or:	
or:			
Operating Cash Flow			
For companies with not less than $500 million in global market		For companies with not less than $500 million in global market capitalization	
Aggregate for the 3 years operating cash flow (each year must report a positive amount)	$25,000,000	Aggregate "Cash Flow" for last 3 years	$100 million
or:		. . . together with	
		Minimum in each of the 2 most recent years	$25 million
		or:	
Global Market Capitalization			
Revenues for the last fiscal year	$250,000,000		
Average global market capitalization	$1,000,000,000	Market capitalization	$1 billion
REITs (less than 3 years operating history)	$60,000,000	and	
Stockholders' equity			
Funds (less than 3 years operating history) Net assets	$60,000,000	Revenue (most recent fiscal year)	$100 million

Source: **www.nyse.com/listed/listed.html**, last modified in 1999.

FIGURΘ 2.1	The NYSE Web Site: A Valuable Resource for Investor Information

Source: The NYSE Group, **www.nyse.com** © 2006 New York Stock Exchange.

This company would then pay a continuing annual fee of $5,790. NYSE listing fees for non-U.S. corporations are determined in a similar manner. So, what benefits do NYSE-listing companies receive in return for these fees? In general, listed firms gain national and international visibility through exposure to the media and financial analysts. The investors of the firm gain a place to trade with high liquidity and low trading costs.

As shown in Figure 2.1, the NYSE sponsors an extraordinarily informative Web site. Investors can use the NYSE Web site to obtain stock quotes, get the latest information about listed companies, and learn more about how the NYSE and the investment community work. The site also has a wealth of valuable price and volume data for the overall market.

American Stock Exchange

The **American Stock Exchange (Amex)** is a specialist auction market like the NYSE. As the nation's second-largest floor-based stock auction exchange, the Amex has a significant presence in both listed equities and equity derivative securities. Today, the Amex is on the leading edge of exchanges worldwide in developing successful new investment products and innovative services for companies and investors.

> **American Stock Exchange (Amex)**
> Nation's second-largest stock exchange.

Regular financial guidelines for listing on the Amex include minimum pretax income of $750,000 in the latest fiscal year or in two of the most recent three years, a **public float** of $3 million, a stock price of $3, and stockholders' equity of $4 million. Public float includes shares not held by any officer or director of the issuer or by any person who is the beneficial owner of more than 10 percent of the total outstanding shares. In other words, public float is the market value of common stock held by unaffiliated institutional and individual investors. Less strenuous alternate financial guidelines include a public float of $15 million, a share price of $3, a three-year operating history, and stockholders' equity of $4 million. In all cases, companies listed on the Amex must have 500,000 to 1 million shares available to the public and 400 to 800 public shareholders.

> **Public float**
> Common stock held by unaffiliated institutional and individual investors.

NYSE History

In 1790, the federal government refinanced all federal and state Revolutionary War debt by issuing $80 million in bonds. These government bonds became the first major issues of publicly traded securities and marked the birth of the U.S. investment markets. Just two years later, in 1792, 24 prominent brokers and merchants gathered on Wall Street to sign the Buttonwood Agreement, agreeing to trade securities on a common commission basis. The New York Stock Exchange traces its beginnings to this historic pact. The Bank of New York was the first company listed and traded in this pact.

It wasn't until 25 years later, in 1817, that the New York brokers established a formal organization, the New York Stock & Exchange Board, and rented rooms for their trading activities at 40 Wall Street. In 1863, the New York Stock & Exchange Board adopted its present name. Two years later, the NYSE moved into its first permanent home, at 10-12 Broad Street, just south of Wall Street. This move established Wall and Broad as the center of securities trading in America. On April 22, 1903, the NYSE moved to 18 Broad Street, a facility that is still in use today.

Over its more than 200-year history, the NYSE has participated in many important events in history. When armed conflict engulfed Europe, securities exchanges around the world suspended operations to arrest plunging prices. The NYSE closed its doors on July 31, 1914, and didn't fully reopen for 4 1/2 months, the longest shutdown in Exchange history. Stock prices fell sharply on October 24, 1929, "Black Thursday." Five days later, the market crashed, ushering in the Great Depression. In 1945, victorious American troops were welcomed home with a ticker tape parade as the Exchange closed for business August 15 and 16 to celebrate VJ Day. On October 19, 1987, the Dow Jones Industrial Average experienced a one-day drop of 508 points, the first drop of more than 500 points in the DJIA in history. Volume surged to a then unprecedented 604 million shares.

Stock and bond trading has played a central role in the development of the American economy. It is a big part of American history.

See: The NYSE Group, **www.nyse.com**.

Over-the-Counter Markets

Nasdaq National Market

Nasdaq Stock Market
Largest organized equities market by trading volume and number of listed companies.

Trading on the **Nasdaq Stock Market**, the world's first electronic stock market, began in 1971. Today, Nasdaq is the fastest-growing stock market in the United States and features many of the fast-growing high-tech companies investors have come to crave. Just behind the NYSE, Nasdaq ranks second among the world's securities markets in terms of total dollar volume. Nasdaq lists more than 3,600 domestic and foreign companies. The market capitalization of Nasdaq-listed companies exceeds $6 trillion. Nasdaq's average daily share volume is around 1.5 billion shares. The electronic trading network manages over 5,000 transactions per second.

Table 2.3 shows a trading comparison of the three largest U.S. stock exchanges. Note that the highest trading volume is on Nasdaq, with the NYSE close behind. However, the average stock price is higher on the NYSE, so the value of all the shares traded is higher on the NYSE. The volume on the Amex is about 5 percent of that on Nasdaq.

What distinguishes Nasdaq is its use of computers and a vast telecommunications network to create an electronic trading system that allows market participants to meet over the computer rather than face-to-face. Since making its debut as the world's first electronic stock market, Nasdaq has been at the forefront of innovation, using technology to bring millions of investors together to trade some of the world's leading companies.

Negotiated market
Price determination through bargaining.

Market makers
Member firms that use their own capital to trade and hold an inventory of NASD stocks.

Another major distinguishing feature is Nasdaq's use of multiple financial intermediaries. Nasdaq is a **negotiated market** in which investors deal directly with **market makers**. Market makers are NASD member firms that use their own capital resources to compete with other dealers to buy and sell the stocks they represent. There are more than 500 member firms that act as Nasdaq market makers.

Customer order flow
Customer buy and sell activity.

Market maker spread
Difference between bid and ask prices.

One of the major differences between the Nasdaq Stock Market and the NYSE is Nasdaq's structure of competing market makers. Each market maker competes for **customer order flow** by displaying buy and sell quotations for a guaranteed number of shares. Once an order is received, the market maker will immediately purchase for or sell from its own inventory. All of this typically occurs in a matter of seconds. The difference between the price at which a market maker is willing to buy a security and the price at which the firm is willing to sell is called the **market-maker spread**. Each market maker positions itself to either buy or sell inventory at any given time; each individual market maker spread is not fully reflective of the market as

TABLE 2.3	Stock Market Diary for Wednesday, January 3, 2006		
	Latest Close	**Previous Close**	**Week Ago**
NYSE Market Diary			
Issues Traded	3,504	3,450	3,497
Advances	2,559	1,350	1,040
Declines	841	1,957	2,335
Unchanged	104	143	122
New Highs	221	44	127
New Lows	43	76	65
Advancing Volume	1,535,593,750	305,238,380	229,734,260
Declining Volume	364,725,620	762,270,640	894,127,890
Volume Traded	1,908,069,270	1,083,874,830	1,152,752,260
NASDAQ Market Diary			
Issues Traded	3,227	3,227	3,210
Advances	1,906	1,325	849
Declines	1,209	1,750	2,233
Unchanged	112	152	128
New Highs	94	33	87
New Lows	37	41	40
Advancing Volume	1,478,689,366	337,573,179	318,824,436
Declining Volume	472,067,125	894,290,211	910,184,410
Volume Traded	1,977,700,962	1,269,259,236	1,242,872,116
AMEX Market Diary			
Issues Traded	1,054	1,060	1,058
Advances	654	469	370
Declines	323	496	605
Unchanged	77	95	83
New Highs	56	32	46
New Lows	15	22	21
Advancing Volume	73,177,000	31,572,835	17,019,820
Declining Volume	12,497,458	33,817,899	42,716,878
Volume Traded	87,100,058	70,757,534	63,287,648

Source: *The Wall Street Journal Online,* 2006. © 2006 Dow Jones Co. Used with permission.

a whole. The **inside market** is the highest-bid and the lowest-offer prices among all competing market makers in a Nasdaq security. On Nasdaq, the typical stock has 10 market makers actively competing with one another for investor order flow.

Inside market
Highest bid and lowest offer prices.

Try It!

Want to be a dealer? Nasdaq has developed a dealer simulation game, called Nasdaq Head Trader. Go to the Web site at **www.nasdaqtrader.com**, read about the game, and then play it! How much money did you win or lose?

When a company submits an application for inclusion in the Nasdaq national market, it pays a one-time company listing fee of $5,000 plus a fee calculated on the basis of the total outstanding shares. For example, for companies with up to 1 million outstanding shares, the minimum Nasdaq listing fee is $34,525. For companies with more than 19 million outstanding shares, the Nasdaq listing fee is $90,000. Companies must also pay an annual fee calculated on the basis of the total shares outstanding for each issue. For up to 1 million outstanding shares, the minimum Nasdaq annual fee is $10,710. For companies with more than 100 million outstanding shares, Nasdaq's annual fee is $50,000. However, it is important to keep in mind that Nasdaq is in keen competition with the NYSE for company listings. To get or keep desired listings, the board of directors of the Nasdaq Stock Market may choose to defer or waive all or any part of the prescribed annual fees. As initial requirements, companies must have significant net tangible assets or operating income, a minimum public float of 500,000 shares, at least 400 shareholders, and a bid price of at least $5. The Nasdaq national market operates from 9:30 a.m. to 4:00 p.m. EST, with extended trading in SelectNet from 8:00 a.m. to 9:30 a.m. EST and from 4:00 p.m. to 5:15 p.m. EST. The Nasdaq International Service is an extension to the Nasdaq Stock Market's trading systems that allows early morning trading from 3:30 a.m. to 9:00 a.m. EST on each U.S. trading day. You can visit the Nasdaq at **www.nasdaq.com**.

Nasdaq SmallCap Market

Nasdaq SmallCap Market
Market for smaller companies that trade prior to full listing on the Nasdaq national market.

Penny stocks
Equities priced below $1.

The **Nasdaq SmallCap Market** comprises more than 800 companies that seek the sponsorship of Nasdaq market makers, have applied for listing, and meet specific financial requirements. Minimum criteria for listing on the Nasdaq SmallCap Market are far less strenuous than those for any other national market. The minimum bid price required for common and preferred stock is only $1. This $1 bid price requirement is meant to provide a safeguard against certain unscrupulous market activity associated with low-price **penny stocks** and enhances the credibility of the market. For initial listing, companies must have $4 million in net tangible assets, or $50 million in market capitalization, or $750,000 in net income in two of the past three fiscal years. Public float of at least 1 million shares worth at least $5 million, a $4 minimum bid price, three market makers, and 300 round-lot holders are also required. Listed companies are also required to meet minimum corporate governance requirements such as distribution of annual and interim reports, a minimum of two independent directors, and an accounting audit committee in which independent directors are a majority.

The Over-the-Counter Bulletin Board

OTC Bulletin Board (OTCBB)
Regulated quotation service for very small over-the-counter equity securities.

American Depositary Receipts (ADR)
Coupons that signify ownership of foreign stocks.

The **OTC Bulletin Board (OTCBB)** is a regulated quotation service that displays real-time quotes, last-sale prices, and volume information in (OTC) equity securities. An OTC equity security generally is any publicly traded equity that is not listed on Nasdaq or a national securities exchange. OTCBB securities include national, regional, and foreign equity issues, warrants, units, and **American Depositary Receipts (ADR)**.

In June 1990, the OTCBB began operation on a pilot basis, as part of important market structure reforms to improve efficiency in the OTC equity market. The Penny Stock Reform Act of 1990 mandated that the Securities and Exchange Commission (SEC) establish an electronic system that met the requirements of Section 17B of the Exchange Act. The system was designed to facilitate the widespread publication of quotation and last-sale information.

The OTCBB provides investors with access to more than 3,300 securities offered through more than 330 participating market makers. The OTCBB electronically transmits real-time quote and volume information and displays indications of interest and prior-day trading activity. The OTCBB is a quotation medium for subscribing members, not an issue-listing service. It should not be confused with the Nasdaq Stock Market. OTCBB securities are traded by a community of market makers that enter quotes and trade reports through a highly sophisticated computer network. The OTCBB is unlike the Nasdaq Stock Market in that it does not impose listing standards, provide automated trade executions, maintain relationships with quoted issuers, or have the same obligations for market makers.

The OTCBB is monitored by an online market surveillance system to help ensure compliance with the existing rules of the SEC and NASD. Nasdaq has no business relationship with the issuers quoted in the OTCBB. These companies do not have any filing or reporting requirements with the Nasdaq Stock Market, Inc., or NASD. However, issuers of securities are subject to periodic filing requirements with the SEC or other regulatory authorities.

For more detailed information about the OTCBB, see its Web site at **www.otcbb.com**.

Electronic Communications Networks

Large institutional investors often prefer to trade with one another directly because sending a large order to the floor of a stock exchange can impact the market price. A large buy order can cause the market price to rise; large sell orders can cause prices to fall. Sometimes, adverse price effects of large buy or sell orders can be mitigated when large institutional investors deal directly with other large institutions. One way they accomplish this is through *electronic communications networks, or ECNs*. ECNs are electronic trading systems that automatically match buy and sell orders at specified prices.

Institutional investors, broker-dealers, and market makers who subscribe to ECNs can place trades directly. ECNs post orders on their systems for other subscribers to view. The ECN will then automatically match orders for execution. If a subscriber wants to buy a stock through an ECN but there are no sell orders to match the buy order, the order can't be executed. If the order is placed through an ECN during regular trading hours, an ECN that cannot find a match may send the order to another ECN or a stock exchange for execution.

Beginning in 1997, the SEC allowed trading through ECNs to combat market abuses brought to light in several investigations of collusion among market makers in the 1990s. Instinet and Island ECN are the ECNs with the highest volume. All told, ECNs have captured about 35 to 40 percent of the Nasdaq-listed stock volume and constitute an important source of competition.

U.S. Large Company Stock Indexes

Dow Jones Industrial Average

In 1882, Charles H. Dow and Edward Davis Jones started Dow Jones & Co. From an unpainted basement office next to the NYSE, they published a tip sheet called the *Customer's Afternoon Letter*, a precursor to *The Wall Street Journal*. At that time, people on Wall Street found it difficult to discern whether stocks generally were rising, falling, or treading water. To remedy the problem, Dow invented the first stock average in 1884. He began with 11 stocks. Most of them were railroads. The mechanics of the first stock average were simple. Computing with paper and pencil, Dow simply added up 11 stock prices and divided by the number 11. The idea of using an index to differentiate short-term changes in individual stock prices from the market's long-term trends was unique. At the time, Dow compared his average with placing sticks in the sand to determine, wave after wave, whether the ocean tide was coming in or going out. If the average's peaks and troughs rose progressively higher, then a bull market prevailed. If peaks and troughs dropped lower and lower, a bear market was on.

At the turn of the century, railroads were the first major corporations. It is easy to see why investors were more interested in the progress of railroad stocks than in advancement of a fledgling industrial sector. After introducing his 11-stock railroad average, Dow decided to create separate indexes to track industrial and railroad stocks. On May 26, 1896, Dow began tracking a 12-stock industrial average.

At first, the Dow Jones & Co. stock averages were published irregularly, but daily publication in *The Wall Street Journal* began on October 7, 1896. In 1916, the industrial average was expanded to 20 stocks. That number was raised to 30 on October 1, 1928, where it remains today. Also in 1928, *Journal* editors began calculating index averages with special divisors, instead of the number of stocks, to avoid distortions caused by stock splits or company substitutions. The Dow Jones utility average came along in 1929, more than a quarter-century after Dow's death at age 51 in 1902. The railroad average was renamed the transportation average in 1970. Through tradition, Dow Jones & Co. indexes are commonly referred to as "averages" even though that description is technically incorrect.

Dow's simple invention has been an enduring hit. It provides a convenient benchmark for comparing individual stocks to the course of the market. It also gives a basis for comparing the market with other economic indicators. What is now referred to as the **Dow Jones Industrial Average (DJIA)** also gives investors a common focal point. Investors often ask, "How did the market do today?" The answers always seem to revolve around the DJIA.

Table 2.4 illustrates how the 30 stocks in the DJIA have changed since October 1, 1928. Changes in the composition of the DJIA, or any Dow Jones & Co. index, are made solely at

Dow Jones Industrial Average (DJIA)
Price-weighted index of 30 large, industry-leading stocks.

TABLE 2.4 Additions and Deletions in the Dow Jones Industrial Average since October 1, 1928*

Original DJIA Members 10/1/28	1929	1930s	1940s	1950s	1960s	1970s	1980s	1990s	Current DJIA Members
Postum Inc.	General Foods† ('29)								Altria Group† ('03)
Wright Aeronautical	Curtiss-Wright ('29)	Hudson Motor ('30) Coca-Cola ('32) National Steel ('35)		Aluminum Co. of America ('59)					Alcoa
North American		Johns-Manville ('30)					American Express ('82)		American Express
Victor Talking Machine	National Cash Register ('29)	IBM ('32) AT&T ('39)							American International Group ('04)
Union Carbide								SBC Communications ('99)	AT&T (New '06)
International Nickel						Inco Ltd.† ('76)	Boeing ('87)		Boeing
International Harvester							Navistar† ('86)	Caterpillar ('91)	Caterpillar
Westinghouse Electric								Traveler Group ('97) Citigroup† ('98)	Citigroup
Texas Gulf Sulphur		International Shoe ('32) United Aircraft ('33) National Distillers ('34)		Owens-Illinois ('59)			Coca-Cola ('87)		Coca-Cola
U.S. Steel							USX Corp.† ('86)	Disney (Walt) ('91)	Disney (Walt)
American Sugar		Borden ('30) Du Pont ('35)							Du Pont
Standard Oil (N.J.)						Exxon† ('72)			Exxon
General Electric									General Electric
General Motors									General Motors
Texas Corp.				Texaco† ('59)				Hewlett-Packard ('97)	Hewlett-Packard
Goodrich		Standard Oil (Calif) ('30)					Chevron† ('84)	Home Depot ('99)	Home Depot
Allied Chemical & Dye							Allied-Signal† ('85)	Honeywell† ('99)	Honeywell
Chrysler					IBM ('79)				IBM
Atlantic Refining		Goodyear ('30)						Intel ('99)	Intel

Original DJIA Members 10/1/28	1929	1930s	1940s	1950s	1960s	1970s	1980s	1990s	Current DJIA Members
American Can							Primerica† ('87)	J.P. Morgan ('91)	J.P. Morgan
Bethlehem Steel								Johnson & Johnson ('97)	Johnson & Johnson
General Railway Signal		Liggett & Myers ('30) / American Tobacco ('32)					McDonald's ('85)		McDonald's
Mack Trucks		Drug Inc. ('32) / Corn Products ('33)		Swift & Co. ('59)		Esmark† ('73) / Merk ('79)			Merck
Sears Roebuck								Microsoft ('99)	Microsoft
American Smelting				Anaconda ('59)		Minnesota Mining ('76)			Minnesota Mining
American Tobacco		Eastman Kodak ('30)							Pfizer ('04)
Nash Motors		United Air Trans. ('30) / Procter & Gamble ('32)							Procter & Gamble
Radio Corp.		Nash Motors ('32) / United Aircraft ('39)				United Tech.† ('75)			United Technologies
Paramount Publix		Loew's ('32)		International Paper ('56)					Verizon Communications ('04)
Woolworth								Wal-Mart Stores ('97)	Wal-Mart Stores

*Year of change shown in parentheses.

†Name change, sometimes following a takeover or merger.

Source: Dow Jones Indexes, **ww.djindexes.com**

the discretion of the editors of *The Wall Street Journal*. Neither the companies, the respective stock exchanges, nor any official agencies are consulted. Additions or deletions can be made at any time to achieve better representation of the broad market and of American industry. Each of the 30 stocks in the DJIA is a major factor in its industry, is listed on the NYSE or Nasdaq, and is widely held by individuals and institutional investors. In April 2004, three long-time components of the Dow (AT&T, Eastman Kodak, and International Paper) were replaced with American International Group, Pfizer, and Verizon Communications. While AT&T was dropped from the DJIA, two spin-offs from the company, SBC and Verizon, were included. Interestingly, SBC merged with the old AT&T and adopted that historic name in 2006. All members of the DJIA are also components of the S&P 500 Index.

Today, the 30 stocks in the DJIA represent roughly 30 percent of the approximately $12 trillion market capitalization of all U.S. equities. Because it is based on such large, frequently traded stocks, the DJIA can be measured with precision on a minute-by-minute basis during the trading day. This is not always true with indexes that contain less frequently traded stocks. The DJIA is the oldest continuous barometer of the U.S. stock market, and by far the most widely quoted indicator of U.S. stock market activity.

The DJIA is a price-weighted stock index. This means that the component stocks are accorded their relative weights based on share prices. Originally the DJIA was calculated by adding up stock prices of all 30 component stocks and then dividing by 30. Although that concept remains active today, the sum total of prices for all 30 stocks is now divided by a number called the **DJIA divisor**. The divisor has been decreased over the years to eliminate distortions caused by stock splits and company substitutions. Otherwise, a stock split would cause the DJIA to decline even though there has been no negative effect on the performance of the DJIA "basket" of stocks.

The formula used to determine the DJIA is simply

DJIA divisor
Adjustment factor used to account for stock splits.

$$DJIA_t = \frac{\sum_{i=1}^{30} P_{it}}{\text{DJIA divisor}}$$

(2.1)

where P is the stock price for the ith DJIA component company at any given point in time t.

The current value of the DJIA divisor is published daily on page C2 of *The Wall Street Journal* and on a weekly basis in *Barron's*. On January 1, 2006, for example, the divisor equaled 0.12493117. Because the DJIA divisor is less than 1, the DJIA rises or falls by more than 1 point with every $1 change in the value of any component stock. Using this divisor, a $1 rise in any component stock would cause the DJIA to rise by 8 points (= 1/DJIA divisor = 1/0.12493117).

Because the DJIA is a price-weighted index, a 10 percent change in the value of a high-price DJIA stock would have a much larger impact on the index than a similar percentage change in the value of a low-price component. For example, at the start of 2005, a 10 percent rise in a high-price DJIA stock selling for $88.20 (e.g., IBM) would cause an 8.82 climb in the stock price and a 65.8-point rise in the DJIA. A 10 percent rise in a low-price DJIA stock selling for $19.42 (e.g., GM) represented a $1.94 jump in the stock price and would cause a 15.54-point rise in the DJIA.

Dow Jones & Co. also publishes transport (20 stocks), utility (15 stocks), and composite (65 stocks) averages. Up-to-date information on all Dow Jones & Co. stock indexes and publications can be obtained on the Internet at **www.dowjones.com**.

Try It!

Consider a price-weighted index, like the DJIA, with only three stocks. If the stock prices are $40, $60, and $80 and the divisor is 2.5, what is the index level? Also, if the $80 stock does a 2-for-1 stock split to $40, what should the divisor be?

Solution

> The index would be (40 + 60 + 80) / 2.5 = 72.
> The new divisor would be 72 = (40 + 60 + 40) / x, solving for x = 1.9444.

Standard & Poor's 500 Index

The Standard & Poor's Corporation introduced a 90-stock average in 1928, but it was not until 1957 that it offered an expanded index of 500 stocks. Today, the **S&P 500 Index** is the most popular value-weighted market index. Companies included in the S&P 500 are chosen according to industry representation, liquidity, and stability criteria. Initially, the S&P 500 included 400 industrial, 40 utility, 40 financial, and 20 transportation stocks. In recent years, the composition of the S&P 500 has been changed periodically to maintain its reflection of the overall market. At the start of 2006, for example, the S&P 500 sector breakdown was 21.2 percent financial, 15.6 percent information technology, 12.8 percent health care, 11.3 percent industrial, 10.9 percent consumer discretionary, and the rest in consumer staples, energy, telecom services, utilities, and materials. Despite the fact that the S&P 500 is a large-cap index, it is important to recognize that stocks in the S&P 500 are not the 500 largest companies but an index designed to capture the returns of stocks from across the broad spectrum of the U.S. economy. Under float adjustment, the share counts used in calculating S&P indexes reflect only those shares that are available to investors, not all of a company's outstanding shares. Float adjustment excludes shares that are closely held by other publicly traded companies, control groups, or government agencies. With a float-adjusted index, the value of the index reflects the value available in the public markets.

In 2006, the float-adjusted market capitalization of the S&P 500 totaled $11.2 trillion and represented roughly 80 percent of the overall market. Each stock's weight in the S&P 500 Index is proportionate to the market capitalization of its public float, computed as stock price times the number of shares outstanding. The average capitalization was $23.4 billion for S&P 500 firms, but the median (or middle) firm size was $11.4 billion. This means that the average firm size is skewed upward by the truly enormous size of some firms. At the high end, the market capitalizations of the top 10 corporate giants included in the S&P 500 (General Electric, Exxon, Microsoft, etc.) typically account for more than one-fifth of the market cap of the overall index. At the low end, the market capitalization of small S&P 500 stocks typically runs in the range from $300 million to $400 million, or about 1 percent of the size of S&P 500 leaders.

The formula used to determine the S&P 500 is

$$\text{Value-weighted index} = \frac{\sum P_t Q_t}{\sum P_0 Q_0} \times \text{index base value}$$

(2.2)

where P is price and Q is number of outstanding shares. (Note: In 1941–1943, the index base of 10 was established.)

Companies selected for the S&P 500 represent a broad cross section from across the spectrum of the U.S. economy. Ownership of a company's outstanding common shares is also scrutinized to screen out closely held companies, like Berkshire Hathaway, Inc. Trading volume of a company's stock is measured on a daily, monthly, and annual basis to ensure ample liquidity and efficient share pricing. Companies in emerging industries and/or industry groups not fully represented in the index are obvious candidates for addition. From time to time, stocks are also removed from the index following mergers, bankruptcies, or other liquidations. In other instances, a company can be removed from the index because it no longer meets current criteria for inclusion or is no longer representative of its industry group.

As shown in Figure 2.2, despite obvious differences in the method of construction, the DJIA and the S&P 500 closely track each other over time. Both are attractive measures of short- and

S&P 500 Index
Popular value-weighted market index.

FIGURE 2.2

The DJIA and S&P 500 represent diversified portfolios of large-company stocks; the Nasdaq Composite Index tracks large-tech stocks

Equity benchmark
Performance standard to be evaluated against.

long-term trends in the prices of large-company stocks. Although the DJIA is a long-time favorite with individual investors, the S&P 500 is preferred as an investment **equity benchmark** by many institutional investors. S&P 500 performance is a standard against which performance is measured for 97 percent of U.S. money managers and pension plan sponsors.

Table 2.5 compares the S&P 500 Index with the three most popular Dow Jones averages. The S&P 500 had a higher P/E ratio than the DJIA, but recently the P/E ratios of the two indexes have become similar. The DJIA has a higher dividend yield than the S&P 500. Another important measure followed by investors is the ratio of market value to book value of the company. The DJIA has a higher market-to-book ratio. Current information on the S&P 500 can be obtained on the Internet at the S&P Web site, **www.spglobal.com**.

Try It!

Consider a market value-weighted index, like the S&P 500 Index, with only three stocks. The first stock's price is $40, with 300 shares outstanding. The second and third stocks sell for $60 and $80, with shares outstanding of 200 and 100, respectively. Each stock originally sold 100 shares at $30. If the base index value is 100, what is the value of the index? What happens when the $80 stock has a 2-for-1 stock split?

Solution

The index is

$$\frac{[(\$40 \times 300) + (\$60 \times 200) + (\$80 \times 100)]}{[(\$30 \times 100) + (\$30 \times 100) + (\$30 \times 100)]} \times 100 = 355.56$$

The index is unchanged if the $80 stock conducts a 2-for-1 stock split. The price becomes $40, and the shares outstanding become 200.

TABLE 2.5	Index P/E Ratio and Yields		
	Last Week	Previous Week	1 Year Ago
DJ Industrial Average	10717.5	10883.27	10783.01
P/E ratio	18.85	19.14	17.94
Earnings yield (%)	5.31	5.22	5.57
Earns $	568.59	568.59	601.02
Dividend yield (%)	2.31	2.28	2.21
Dividends ($)	247.74	247.74	238.66
Market to book	3.19	3.24	3.7
Book value ($)	3359.7	3359.7	2918.09
DJ Transporation Average	4196.03	4266.75	3798.05
P/E ratio	17.97	18.39	Nil
Earnings yield (%)	5.56	5.44	Nil
Earns ($)	233.48	232.03	−7.16
Dividend yield (%)	0.93	0.91	0.93
Dividends ($)	39.15	38.85	35.15
Market to book	3.87	3.93	3.02
Book value ($)	1085.11	1085.11	1257.15
DJ Utility Average	405.11	411.65	334.95
P/E ratio	18.25	18.55	19.78
Earnings yield (%)	5.48	5.39	5.05
Earns ($)	22.19	22.19	16.93
Dividend yield (%)	3.3	3.19	3.17
Dividends ($)	13.39	13.15	10.61
Market to book	2.54	2.58	2.31
Book value ($)	159.45	159.45	145.17
S&P 500 Index	1248.29	1268.66	1211.92
P/E ratio	18.7	19	20.99
Earnings yield (%)	5.35	5.26	4.77
Earns ($)	66.76	66.76	57.75
Dividend yield (%)	1.86	1.83	1.72
Dividends ($)	23.22	23.22	20.85
Market to book	3.01	3.06	3.3
Book value ($)	414.75	414.75	367.17

Source: *Barron's Online*, January 2, 2006. Copyright © 2006, Dow Jones Co. Used with permission.

Russell Large-Cap Indexes

Russell produces a family of 21 U.S. equity indexes. All Russell equity indexes are market-cap-weighted and include only common stocks incorporated in the United States and its territories. All these indexes are subsets of the Russell 3000 Index, which represents approximately 98 percent of the investable U.S. equity market.

The **Russell 3000 Index** measures the performance of the 3,000 largest U.S. companies based on total market capitalization, which represents approximately 98 percent of the investable U.S. equity market. Today, the dollar-weighted average market capitalization of Russell 3000 companies is approximately $75.3 billion. The median market capitalization is approximately $1 billion. The index has a market capitalization range from a high-end value of roughly $380 billion (for General Electric) to roughly $310 million for the smallest firm.

Russell 3000 Index
Market capitalization index for the 3,000 largest U.S. companies (98 percent of U.S. market cap).

Russell 1000 Index
Market capitalization index for the 1,000 largest U.S. companies (90 percent of U.S. market cap).

The **Russell 1000 Index** measures the performance of the 1,000 largest companies in the Russell 3000 Index. The Russell 1000 captures roughly 92 percent of the total market capitalization of publicly traded stocks in the United States. The dollar-weighted average market capitalization of Russell 1000 companies is about $82.5 billion. Information about Russell indexes are available at **www.russell.com**.

Wilshire (5000) Equity Index

Dow Jones Wilshire 5000 Composite Index
Total dollar value of the U.S. equity market (in billions of dollars).

The **Dow Jones Wilshire 5000 Composite Index** is the most comprehensive measure of the U.S. stock market. This market benchmark is designed to represent the performance of all U.S.-headquartered equity securities with readily available price data. Two versions of the index are calculated: one weighted by full market capitalization and the other weighted by float-adjusted market capitalization. The full-market-cap version is intended as a "wealth" measure, representing the total dollar value of funds entering or leaving the U.S. equity markets. The float-adjusted version is meant to be a more realistic benchmark, because it reflects the shares of securities that are actually available to investors. To be included in the index, a security must be the primary equity issue of a U.S. company. New issues must be traded on the New York Stock Exchange, American Stock Exchange, or Nasdaq Stock Market; newly issued bulletin board stocks are not added to the index.

Originally called the Wilshire 5000 Total Market Index, the Dow Jones Wilshire 5000 Composite Index was created in 1974 by the founder of Wilshire Associates and was named for the nearly 5,000 stocks it contained at the time. It now includes a variable number of companies reflecting changes in the number of U.S. securities. Dow Jones Indexes has assumed responsibility for calculating and maintaining the Dow Jones Wilshire 5000 and the other indexes under the Dow Jones Wilshire umbrella. The Dow Jones Wilshire 4500 Completion Index is a subset of the Dow Jones Wilshire 5000 and contains all stocks in the Dow Jones Wilshire 5000 except components of the S&P 500. It was created to allow investors who are using the S&P 500 already to track the remainder of the U.S. market.

At the start of 2006, the full-market-capitalization Dow Jones Wilshire 5000 Composite Index included 4,972 companies worth $15.5 trillion; the float-adjusted index included companies worth $14.2 billion. The mean market capitalization of component stocks was $2.8 billion, and the median market capitalization was $300 million. The range in firm size was from $380 billion (largest) to less than $100 million (smallest).

TABLE 2.6	Comparison of Dow Jones Wilshire and Other Broad Indexes				
Index	**Dow Jones Wilshire 5000 Composite**	**Dow Jones Wilshire 4500 Completion**	**DJIA**	**S&P 500**	**Nasdaq Composite**
Measurement objective	Broad market	Extended market	Broad market	Broad market	Nasdaq exchange
Number of stocks	5,400+	4,900+	30	500	7,400+
Distribution by market cap:					
NYSE	79.5%	60.3%	85.6%	84.6%	0.0%
Amex	0.6%	20.0%	0.0%	0.2%	0.0%
Nasdaq	19.9%	37.7%	14.4%	12.2%	100.0%
Weighting	Market cap	Market cap	Price	Market cap	Market cap
Established	Dec 1970	Dec 1983	May 1896	Jan 1928	Feb 1971
Style indexes	Yes	No	No	Yes	No
Percent of market	100%	21%	25%	79%	20%

Source: Wilshire Broad Market Index Comparison.

Is the Price Always Right?

Auction stock markets on the NYSE and Amex, and the negotiated Nasdaq market, are powerful price-setting mechanisms. Millions of buyers and sellers trade billions of shares every day, looking for mispriced stocks. With all of this attention, most stock prices tend to fairly reflect future business prospects. However, sometimes prices occur that are impossible to describe as accurate. Valuation errors made by individual investors, institutions, and analysts sometimes affect security prices.

Consider the case of 3Com's spin-off of its Palm subsidiary. One of the products 3Com developed in this subsidiary was the handheld computer known as the Palm Pilot. 3Com planned a two-part spin-off of Palm into a separate company. It would initially issue 4 percent of the shares of Palm in an initial public offering (IPO) and then distribute the remaining shares of Palm to 3Com stockholders in a ratio of 1.5 shares of Palm for every 1 share of 3Com owned. By the end of the IPO day, March 2, 2000, the newly issued shares of Palm traded at $95.06. Since 1 share of 3Com was scheduled to receive 1.5 shares of Palm, 3Com stock should have then been worth a minimum of $142.59 (=1.5 × $95.06) plus the value of 3Com's non-Palm operations. Amazingly, 3Com stock closed at only $81.81 per share on the day of the Palm IPO! Either 3Com stock was priced too low or Palm stock was priced too high. The pricing question for individual investors is simple: Can they add and subtract? The question for the overall market is similarly simple: Even if naïve individual investors make pricing errors, why are there insufficient savvy institutional investors to ensure pricing discipline?

The upshot is clear: At any point in time, stock market evidence suggests that market prices are usually right. However, glaring exceptions to this rule occur. An intelligent investor is one who can tell the difference between the current market price of a stock and a reasonable interpretation of what that part of the business is really worth—and takes advantage of any discrepancy.

See: Burton G. Malkiel, "The Efficient Market Hypothesis and Its Critics," *Journal of Economic Perspectives*, vol. 17, no. 1 (Winter 2003), pp. 59–82.

U.S. Medium-Sized Company Indexes

Nasdaq Composite Index

The **Nasdaq Composite Index** measures all common stocks listed on the Nasdaq Stock Market. The index is market value—weighted. It is calculated throughout the trading day. In 2006, the Nasdaq index incorporated 3,175 companies. Because it is so broad-based, the Nasdaq Composite Index is one of the most widely followed and quoted major market indexes. The Nasdaq Composite Index has been actively followed since 1971.

The rapid rate of price appreciation for the Nasdaq Composite Index during the 1990s is unprecedented for such a large and widely followed market index. The Nasdaq Composite rocketed from 457.90 to 4069.31, or 888.69 percent, during the 1990s. This represents a decade-long 24.4 percent annual rate of share price appreciation for Nasdaq stocks. During the most favorable market environment in history, capital gains on the Nasdaq far outstripped stellar capital gains of 411.24 percent for the DJIA (15.2 percent per year) and 410.28 percent for the S&P 500 (15.2 percent per year). As illustrated in Figure 2.2, this set up one of the most dramatic stock price declines in history, starting in March 2000. See **www.nasdaq.com** for details.

Nasdaq Composite Index
Market value—weighted index of all 5,000+ stocks listed on the Nasdaq Stock Market.

Nasdaq 100 Index

The **Nasdaq 100 Index** reflects Nasdaq's largest companies across major industry groups, including computer hardware and software, telecommunications, retail/wholesale trade, and biotechnology. Launched in January 1985, the Nasdaq 100 Index represents the largest and most active nonfinancial domestic and international issues listed on the Nasdaq national market. As of December 21, 1998, however, the Nasdaq 100 Index was rebalanced to a modified market-capitalization-weighted index. Such rebalancing is expected to retain the general economic attributes of capitalization weighting while providing enhanced diversification. To accomplish this, Nasdaq will review the composition of the Nasdaq 100 Index on a quarterly basis and will adjust component weights if certain preestablished distribution requirements are not met.

Eligibility criteria for the Nasdaq 100 Index includes a minimum average daily trading volume of 100,000 shares. Companies also must have been listed for a minimum of two years. If

Nasdaq 100 Index
Market-capitalization-weighted index of Nasdaq's largest companies.

a security would otherwise qualify to be among the top 25 percent of issuers included in the index by market capitalization, then a one-year seasoning criterion would apply. If the security represents a foreign entity, the company must have a worldwide market value of at least $10 billion, a U.S. market value of at least $4 billion, and an average trading volume of at least 200,000 shares per day. In addition, foreign securities must be eligible for listed-options trading. Component stocks are adjusted annually to reflect changes in market capitalization. Every 15 seconds during the trading day, the Nasdaq Stock Market calculates and disseminates the value of the Nasdaq 100 Index.

The large number of securities in the Nasdaq 100 Index makes it an effective vehicle for securities traders. In October 1993, the Nasdaq 100 Index options began trading on the Chicago Board Options Exchange (CBOE). On April 10, 1996, the Chicago Mercantile Exchange began trading futures and futures options on the Nasdaq 100 Index. As seen in Table 2.7, large technology stocks such as Microsoft, Intel Corp., Qualcomm, and Cisco Systems dominate the Nasdaq 100 Index. Although the Nasdaq 100 Index reflects Nasdaq's largest companies across major industry groups, it is clearly focused on the high-tech sector. Many investors take the performance of the Nasdaq 100 as a proxy for high-tech issues in general (see **www.nasdaq.com**).

Mid-Cap Indexes

S&P MidCap 400 Index
Market cap index for 400 medium-sized domestic stocks.

For a company to be considered a middle-capitalization, or mid-cap, stock, it generally must have a total market capitalization between $400 million and $15 billion. Whereas the stock price performance of the large-cap segment of the market is captured by the DJIA and the S&P 500, performance of mid-cap stocks is captured by a number of indexes, including the **S&P MidCap 400 Index**. This index consists of 400 domestic stocks chosen for market size, liquidity, and industry group representation, and it represents about 7 percent of the U.S. stock market. Like the S&P 500, the S&P MidCap 400 Index is a float-adjusted market value-weighted index and was the first benchmark of mid-cap stock price movement. It is an increasingly popular measure for the performance of the mid-sized company segment of the U.S. market.

Dow Jones Wilshire 4500 Completion Index
Mid-cap index of Dow Jones Wilshire (5000) Index companies minus the S&P 500.

The **Dow Jones Wilshire 4500 Completion Index** is the Dow Jones Wilshire 5000 minus the companies from the S&P 500 Index. As is the case with the Dow Jones Wilshire 5000, this index is misnamed. In 2006, there were 4,472 stocks represented in the Dow Jones Wilshire 4500, and about two-thirds of those stocks were mid-sized companies. In 2006, the market capitalization of the Dow Jones Wilshire 4500 was roughly one-fifth of the market capitalization of the Dow Jones Wilshire 5000 Index. Remember, the Wilshire 4500 is the Wilshire 5000 minus the S&P 500, and the S&P 500 accounts for roughly 80 percent of the market capitalization of the overall market.

U.S. Small Company Indexes

Russell 2000 Index

Russell 2000 Index
Small-company stock price index for the 2,000 smallest companies in the Russell 3000 Index.

Small-capitalization, or small-cap, stocks are generally described as publicly traded corporations with less than $5 billion in total market capitalization. The **Russell 2000 Index** measures the performance of the 2,000 smallest companies in the Russell 3000 Index, which represents approximately 6 percent of the total market capitalization of publicly traded equities. At the present time, the average market capitalization of Russell 2000 stocks is somewhat greater than $1 billion. The median market capitalization is approximately $598 million. The largest company in the index has a market capitalization of roughly $4 billion.

Unlike the case in most other indexes, the companies in the Russell 2000 change once a year. If a company gets taken over or delisted, it is not replaced until the next annual rebalancing of the index. Changes are announced on April 1 each year and implemented on May 1. See **www.russell.com** for details.

TaBLe 2.7	Top Holdings and Industry Makeup of Major Stock Market Indexes				
Top Ten Holdings	**Company Name**	**%**		**Industry Groups**	**%**
Dow Jones Industrial Average (DJIA)					
1	General Electric Co.	2.99		1 Financial	20.99
2	Exxon Mobil Corp.	2.68		2 Technology	14.59
3	Microsoft Corp.	2.20		3 Consumer, cyclical	14.35
4	Citigroup Inc.	1.85		4 Industrial	12.91
5	Pfizer Inc.	1.68		5 Health care	11.99
6	Bank of America Corp.	1.51		6 Consumer, noncyclical	8.34
7	Johnson & Johnson	1.43		7 Energy	7.54
8	International Business Machines	1.30		8 Utilities	3.30
9	American International Group Inc.	1.16		9 Telecommunications	2.98
10	Intel Corp.	1.15		10 Misc.	—
Total		**17.95**		**Total**	**96.99**
S&P 500					
1	General Electric Co.	3.42		1 Financial	20.42
2	Exxon Mobil Corp.	3.06		2 Information technology	16.24
3	Microsoft Corp.	2.67		3 Health care	12.47
4	Citigroup Inc.	2.12		4 Industrial	11.86
5	Wal-Mart Stores Inc.	2.02		5 Consumer discretionary	11.39
6	Pfizer Inc.	1.92		6 Consumer staples	10.49
7	Bank of America Corp.	1.72		7 Energy	7.50
8	Johnson & Johnson	1.64		8 Telecommunication services	3.30
9	American International Group Inc.	1.51		9 Materials	3.17
10	International Business Machines Corp.	1.45		10 Utilities	2.99
Total		**21.53**		**Total**	**99.83**
Nasdaq 100					
1	Microsoft Corp.	7.57		1 Information technology hardware	36.65
2	QUALCOMM Inc.	6.64		2 Computer software/services	19.74
3	Apple Computer, Inc.	5.82		3 Pharmaceuticals & biotechnology	12.77
4	Intel Corporation	4.22		4 Retail/wholesale trade	11.75
5	Amgen Inc.	3.45		5 Other services	10.77
6	eBay Inc.	3.35		6 Health	2.67
7	Cisco Systems, Inc.	2.97		7 Manufacturing	2.42
8	Starbucks Corp.	2.41		8 Telecommunications	1.10
9	Yahoo! Inc.	2.02		9 Consumer goods	1.08
10	Oracle Corporation	2.01		10. Misc.	—
Total		**40.46**		**Total**	**98.95**

Source: **www.nasdaq.com**.

S&P SmallCap 600 Index

The **S&P SmallCap 600 Index** comprises 600 domestic stocks chosen for market size, liquidity (bid-asked spread, ownership, share turnover, and number of no-trade days), and industry group representation. Like all major S&P indexes, the S&P SmallCap 600 Index is a float-adjusted market value-weighted index (stock price times the number of outstanding shares), with each stock's weight in the index proportionate to its market value.

S&P SmallCap 600 Index
Market-cap-weighted index of 600 small domestic stocks.

The average market capitalization of S&P SmallCap 600 Index stocks is roughly $600 million, and the median market capitalization is $500 million. The S&P SmallCap 600 Index is gaining acceptance as the preferred benchmark for both active and passive management due to its low turnover and fairly good liquidity. An increasing amount of assets is indexed to the S&P SmallCap 600 Index (see **www2.standardandpoors.com**).

Global Stock Indexes

Major Global Stock Market Indexes

Nikkei 225 Index
Leading measure of the Japanese stock market.

The second-largest national stock market in terms of market capitalization is the Japanese stock market. Japanese stock market performance is measured by the **Nikkei 225 Index** (see Figure 2.3). The Nikkei is a price-weighted average of 225 stocks from the first (most liquid) section of the Tokyo Stock Exchange. It was started on May 16, 1949.

FTSE-100
Capitalization-weighted index of the 100 top companies on the London Stock Exchange.

The world's third-largest equity market is in London. The U.K. market is widely followed by using the **FTSE-100**. The FTSE-100, or "footsie," is a market-capitalization-weighted index published by the *Financial Times* of the 100 top market-cap companies, from 27 industries, on the London Stock Exchange (LSE). FTSE-100 companies constitute roughly 70 percent of the market cap of all LSE companies.

TSE-35
Market basket of 35 blue-chip Canadian companies.

Canada features the second-largest national stock market in North America. Trading activity on the Toronto Stock Exchange is captured by the **TSE-35**, a market basket of 35 blue-chip Canadian companies. The TSE-35 accounts for roughly 45 percent of the total market cap of Canadian stocks.

Hang Seng Index
Market-cap-weighted measure of Hong Kong stocks.

The Hong Kong market is one of the most dynamic major stock markets in the world. This market is measured by the **Hang Seng Index**. Hang Seng companies must be among the top 90 percent of all Hong Kong stocks in terms of market cap and trading activity. Only the largest 33 companies from 10 industries are included, but the Hang Seng captures more than 80 percent of the market cap of all Hong Kong companies.

Morgan Stanley Capital International Indexes

Morgan Stanley Capital International (MSCI), Inc., is a subsidiary of Morgan Stanley, Inc., a global financial services firm and a market leader in securities, asset management, and credit services. MSCI has been an industry leader in providing global equity benchmark indexes for more than 30 years. MSCI indexes are the most widely used benchmarks for international portfolio managers. More than 1,200 institutional clients worldwide currently use MSCI benchmarks. In North America and Asia, more than 90 percent of institutional international equity assets are benchmarked to MSCI indexes. In Europe, more than one-half of Continental fund managers currently use MSCI indexes as their benchmark according to a recent Merrill Lynch/Gallup survey.

Europe, Australasia, Far East (EAFE) Index
Leading global stock index of stocks from 21 countries.

The **Europe, Australasia, Far East (EAFE) Index** is perhaps MSCI's most famous index. The EAFE stock index is designed to measure the investment returns of developed countries outside North America. When the index was first constructed in 1969, 14 countries were included. The index now includes stocks from 21 countries. The most recent addition was Portugal in 1997. The MSCI indexes are available at **www.mscibarra.com**.

Emerging market
Stock markets in developing nations.

There is no clear-cut set of characteristics to define an **emerging market**. The equity market develops in a country as economic growth accelerates and companies begin to raise capital in the public markets. As markets have evolved, MSCI has expanded its emerging markets' universe. These markets display gross domestic product (GDP) per capita that is substantially below the average for developed economies. For example, the average emerging market covered by MSCI has a GDP per capita that is roughly 15 percent of the GDP per capita in developed markets. The governments of emerging-market countries sometimes limit or ban foreign ownership in their public companies. Lax government regulation, irregular trading hours,

FIGURe 2.3   Global Stock Exchange Indexes

Americas | Asia/Pacific | **Europe** | Africa/Middle East

Symbol	Name	Last Trade	Change	Related Info
^ATX	ATX	3,763.89 11:33AM ET	⬆ 46.47 (1.25%)	Chart, More
^BFX	BEL-20	3,638.46 12:06PM ET	⬆ 34.52 (0.96%)	Chart, More
^OMXC20C	OMXC20C	399.91 11:21AM ET	⬆ 1.18 (0.30%)	Components, Chart, More
^FCHI	CAC 40	4,838.52 12:12PM ET	⬆ 61.54 (1.29%)	Chart, More
^GDAXI	DAX	5,523.62 11:45AM ET	⬆ 62.94 (1.15%)	Components, Chart, More
^AEX	AEX General	445.00 12:07PM ET	⬆ 3.07 (0.69%)	Chart, More
^OSEAX	OSE All Share	384.88 10:29AM ET	⬆ 3.01 (0.79%)	Components, Chart, More
^MIBTEL	MIBTel	27,317.0000 11:40AM ET	⬆ 204.0000 (0.75%)	Components, Chart, More
^IXX	ISE National-100	88.17 3:59PM ET	⬆ 0.34 (0.39%)	Chart, More
^SMSI	Madrid General	1,175.46 11:36AM ET	⬆ 8.68 (0.74%)	Components, Chart, More
^OMXSPI	Stockholm General	306.50 11:42AM ET	⬆ 1.70 (0.56%)	Chart, More
^SSMI	Swiss Market	7,723.71 11:31AM ET	⬆ 95.15 (1.25%)	Components, Chart, More
^FTSE	FTSE 100	5,714.60 11:36AM ET	⬆ 33.10 (0.58%)	Components, Chart, More

Americas | **Asia/Pacific** | Europe | Africa/Middle East

Symbol	Name	Last Trade	Change	Related Info
^AORD	All Ordinaries	4,765.100 12:17AM ET	0.000 (0.00%)	Components, Chart, More
^SSEC	Shanghai Composite	1,180.963 2:00AM ET	⬆ 19.906 (1.71%)	Components, Chart, More
^HSI	Hang Seng	15,200.06 4:59AM ET	⬆ 255.29 (1.71%)	Components, Chart, More
^BSESN	BSE 30	9,648.08 5:28AM ET	0.00 (0.00%)	Chart, More
^JKSE	Jakarta Composite	1,211.699 5:30AM ET	0 (0.00%)	Components, Chart, More
^KLSE	KLSE Composite	897.13 4:02AM ET	0.00 (0.00%)	Components, Chart, More
^N225	Nikkei 225	16,361.54 Jan 3	0.00 (0.00%)	Chart, More
^NZ50	NZSE 50	3,379.537 5:37PM ET	⬆ 5.073 (0.15%)	Components, Chart, More
^STI	Straits Times	2,384.14 4:05AM ET	0.00 (0.00%)	Components, Chart, More
^KS11	Seoul Composite	1,402.11 4:03AM ET	0 (0.00%)	Components, Chart, More
^SETI	SET	743.20 4:58AM ET	0.00 (0.00%)	Components, Chart, More
^TWII	Taiwan Weighted	6,616.44 12:46AM ET	0.00 (0.00%)	Components, Chart, More

Source: **http://finance.yahoo.com/intlindices?e-americas**. Reproduced by permission of Yahoo! Inc. Yahoo and the Yahoo! logo are trademarks of Yahoo! Inc.

and/or less sophisticated back-office operations, including clearing and settlement capabilities, are also common in emerging markets. Some emerging markets also feature restrictions on repatriation of initial capital, dividends, interest, and/or capital gains. All emerging markets involve companies with greater perceived investment risk than that of leading firms in a **developed market**.

Developed market
Stock markets in mature countries.

Securities Market Regulation

Important Legislation

The securities markets in the United States operate according to laws passed by Congress and the state legislatures. In Congress, the Senate Committee on Banking, Housing, and Urban Affairs and the House Committee on Commerce monitor the securities industry. Both committees measure the effectiveness of current laws and seek to determine the need for additional legislation.

The Securities Act of 1933 and the Securities Exchange Act of 1934 are the most significant laws for investors, issuers of securities, and broker-dealers. The 1933 act is primarily concerned with the issuance of new securities. It requires that companies going public register and supply financial and other material information concerning their securities offerings. The purpose is, of course, to enable investors to make informed decisions.

The Securities Exchange Act of 1934 focuses on securities trading. It authorized the creation of the SEC as the primary agency responsible for administering federal securities laws. The 1934 act also stipulated that the registration of securities offerings required by the 1933 act was to be done with the SEC. The 1934 act also authorizes the SEC to enforce federal securities statutes, rules, and regulations. SEC rules governing broker-dealers include mandatory registration with the SEC, financial responsibility requirements, restrictions on borrowing, and the prohibition of security price manipulation or deceptive sales or purchase practices. SEC rules governing issuers include ongoing disclosure requirements and regulation of the proxy solicitation and tender offer processes—both of which relate to shareholder voting.

Many other laws impacting the investment industry have been enacted over the years in response to various problems and scandals. The Investment Company Act and Investment Advisors Act, both in 1940, regulate investment companies (mainly mutual funds) and financial advisors. The Securities Investor Protection Act of 1970 was enacted to protect investors from broker fraud. Passed in 1988, the Insider Trading and Securities Fraud Enforcement Act beefed up the penalties for insider trading and investment fraud. This law was passed in response to the well-publicized insider-trading scandals involving junk-bond king Michael Milken and arbitrageur Ivan Boesky. In 2002, heightened public concerns with corporate wrongdoing led to passage of the **Sarbanes-Oxley Act**, formally referred to as the Public Company Accounting Reform and Investor Protection Act of 2002, the most dramatic change to U.S. securities laws in 70 years. Sarbanes-Oxley has radically redesigned federal regulation of corporate governance and corporate reporting obligations. It has also significantly tightened accountability standards for directors and officers, auditors, securities analysts, and legal counsel. Corporate audit committees must now comply with a new list of requirements affecting auditor appointment, compensation, and oversight. Each company must disclose current information about its financial condition, and the audit committee appointed by the board of directors must consist solely of independent directors. CEOs and chief financial officers (CFOs) must personally certify that corporate financial reports fully comply with SEC requirements and fairly represent the company's financial condition and operating results. Sarbanes-Oxley has also tightened regulations concerning personal financial dealings between top managers and their companies. Now, public companies can make personal loans to executive officers or directors only under very limited circumstances, and insider trading in company securities must be reported within two business days. The act has created several new crimes for securities violations, including destroying, altering, or falsifying records with the intent to impede or influence any federal investigation or bankruptcy proceeding; willful failure by an accountant to maintain all audit or work papers for five years; and executing a scheme to defraud investors in connection with any security.

Sarbanes-Oxley Act
Law instituting public accounting reforms and investor protections.

Does Psychology Influence Financial Regulation?

You may have heard about the business cycle, or the rhythmic change from economic growth to recession and back to expansion. You may have also heard people claim that stock prices rise and fall at various times of the year. Have you heard that stock market regulation also tends to be cyclical?

During bull markets, people tend to view business success with respect and appreciation. Legislators also enact laws that help business and reduce investor protection. Between 1925 and 1928, for example, the stock market rose over 200 percent. Toward the end of this bull market, the government made it possible for commercial banks to get into investment banking. Between 1991 and 1999, the Nasdaq stock index jumped nearly 900 percent. During that time, the U.S. government enacted the 1995 Private Securities Litigation Act, the 1998 Securities Litigation Uniform Standards Act, and the 1999 Financial Services Modernization Act. The first two laws limited damages available to investors suing for corporate fraud in both federal and state courts. The Modernization Act allowed for the combining of commercial and investment banking activities again.

Following severe bear markets, people tend to view business leaders with suspicion. In such an environment, legislators are eager to pass investor protection laws. After the stock market had lost 90 percent of its value following the 1929 crash, the 1933 Banking Act and the 1934 Securities Exchange Act separated commercial and investment banking activities and created the Securities and Exchange Commission. Other investor protection laws, like the Investment Company Act and the Investment Advisors Act in 1940, the Securities Investor Protection Act in 1970, and the Employee Retirement Income Security Act of 1974, followed vicious bear markets. The Insider Trading and Securities Fraud Enforcement Act came in 1988, after the crash of 1987. More recently, the Public Company Accounting Reform and Investor Protection Act was passed in 2002 after a 75 percent decline in the Nasdaq index. When investors are up in arms, lawmakers pass investor protection regulation.

Just as investor psychology influences the behavior of financial markets, psychology appears to influence politicians and stock market regulators.

See: Judith Burns, "Court Questions SEC Regulation for Hedge Funds," *The Wall Street Journal Online*, December 10, 2005 (**http://online.wsj.com**).

Try It!

The vast majority of people in the investment industry are ethical, hardworking, and competent. After all, you can make a good living in this industry. However, sometimes unscrupulous people try to take investors' money by committing fraud. Go to the SEC Web page and learn of the most recent scam being perpetrated. First, go to **www.sec.gov** and click on the Investor Information menu. Then click on Investor Alerts. Learn how to avoid being scammed!

Self-Regulatory Organizations

The SEC delegates regulatory authority to a number of securities industry organizations. Known as **self-regulatory organizations (SROs)**, these organizations oversee securities markets and participating member firms. The **National Association of Securities Dealers (NASD), Inc.,** is the largest SRO of the securities industry, with particular responsibility for the regulation of the Nasdaq Stock Market and the OTC markets. Other noteworthy SROs include the NYSE, Amex, CBOE, a number of regional stock and options exchanges, and the Municipal Securities Rulemaking Board.

When originally adopted, the 1934 Securities and Exchange Act empowered the SEC only to regulate the exchange markets. The Maloney Act of 1938 expanded the scope of the 1934 act by authorizing the registration of national securities associations to regulate the business of broker-dealer members in the OTC markets, subject to SEC supervision and authority. Although the NYSE, Amex, and regional stock and option markets are registered exchanges, the NASD is the only national securities association registered under the amended 1934 act. Any broker or dealer required to register with the SEC under the 1934 act must also become a member of the NASD

Self-regulatory organizations (SROs)
Industry group with oversight authority granted by the SEC.

National Association of Securities Dealers (NASD), Inc.
A self-regulatory organization of the securities industry.

unless its business is conducted only on a national exchange of which it is a member, such as the specialists on the NYSE and Amex. Thus, all broker-dealers registered in the United States that do business with the public are required to be members of the NASD and are regulated by it.

Responsibilities of the SROs include the formulation of rules governing business practices and markets. SROs must periodically review business practices to ensure fair dealing by members with their customers. Securities firms are examined for compliance with net capital and other financial and operational requirements. Market surveillance is carried out to ensure fair dealing and an absence of market manipulation. SROs also take enforcement actions when members or industry professionals violate the securities laws or SRO rules, and they are responsible for the imposition of disciplinary sanctions. Finally, SROs arbitrate disputes between investors and firms, as well as disputes between firms.

The SEC oversees SROs by using the authority granted by Congress. All SRO rules and regulations must be approved by the SEC before they can take effect. Because the SROs are self-regulatory in nature, they are fully funded by member and listed-company fees. No taxpayer money is used.

Because of the growing number of accounting scandals in the early 2000s, the SEC chairman called on SROs, the New York Stock Exchange, and the Nasdaq Stock Market to reexamine their corporate governance listing standards. The markets were challenged to develop and adopt governance listing standards. They developed new governance standards at the same time as the Sarbanes-Oxley Act was being debated in Congress. Therefore, it is not surprising that their new rules are very similar to the act's laws. However, there are a few differences that reflect the distinctive types of firms listed on the two exchanges. In November 2003, the SEC approved both the NYSE's and the Nasdaq's changes in listing standards.

Most of the new NYSE corporate governance rules have to do with the structure, function, and incentives of the board of directors. First, the NYSE mandates that companies have a majority of independent directors. A director is not independent if he or she (or immediate family) has worked for the company or its auditor within the past five years. Second, the NYSE requires that the auditing, nominating, and compensation committees of the board be composed entirely of independent directors. In addition, the audit committee members are to have necessary experience and expertise in finance and accounting. Third, the NYSE requires that shareholders approve all executive equity-based compensation plans.

The Nasdaq adopted rules in the same spirit as those adopted by the NYSE, but with differences intended to fit better with its listing firms. In general, the firms listing on the Nasdaq Stock Market tend to be smaller and are more likely associated with the technology industry than those listing on the NYSE. Since smaller firms have a smaller number of board members, the duties required of independent directors may overwhelm individuals serving on a small-firm board. So, instead of having a rule that an independent compensation committee must approve the executive's compensation, Nasdaq provides an alternative: The independent directors can approve the compensation directly without being members of a compensation committee.

Market Surveillance

Stock Watch
Computerized system that flags unusual volume or price changes.

Stock Watch is a key NYSE tool for protecting the integrity of the market in NYSE-listed securities. It is a computerized system that automatically flags unusual volume or price changes in any listed stock, helping the exchange guard against manipulation and insider trading.

Most large volume or price changes can be explained by company news, trends in the industry, or national economic factors. However, when no legitimate explanation is evident, the NYSE launches an investigation. The investigation begins by contacting the company to find out whether there are any pending announcements. At the same time, surveillance personnel draw on an electronic audit trail to reconstruct the details of every trade that takes place. Rebuilding the "time of execution" enables NYSE investigators to see whether any member firm stands out in the trading.

The next step is to contact the firm and obtain the names of the customers involved in questionable trades. These names are automatically matched against the names of officers, directors, and other corporate and noncorporate insiders to detect any possible connection or illicit flow of information. This task is performed by using the *Automated Search and Match (ASAM) system*, which contains the names of 800,000 executives, lawyers, bankers, and accountants, plus public profile data on officers and directors of approximately 80,000 public corporations and 30,000 corporate subsidiaries. Customer trading information is also analyzed for geographic concentrations and compared with names and chronological events provided by NYSE-listed companies and member firms.

No single regulator has complete oversight over all trading activity because stocks may be traded in multiple markets. With the advent of derivatives such as futures and options, trading activity in one market can be used to manipulate the price of the underlying security in another market. For this reason, the SROs formed the **Intermarket Surveillance Group** to share surveillance information and coordinate efforts to detect cross-market manipulative trading. Advanced computer-based surveillance systems are operated under NASD regulation to oversee activity in the Nasdaq Stock Market and other markets run by Nasdaq. Through the *StockWatch Automated Tracking (SWAT)* and *Research and Data Analysis Repository (RADAR)* systems, every bid and offer quotation and trade in every security on the Nasdaq market is subject to computerized scrutiny.

Intermarket Surveillance Group
Coordinated effort to detect cross-market manipulative trading.

If, after an investigation is completed, any suspicious trading practices are uncovered, an individual SRO can take disciplinary action and/or turn the information over to the SEC for further consideration.

Securities Arbitration

An interesting aspect of securities trading regulation is the extensive use of a unique private form of dispute resolution called **securities arbitration**.

Each day on the NYSE, more than 1 billion shares of stock change hands. Disputes sometimes arise. For more than 100 years, NYSE arbitration has been used to resolve disputes between brokers and investors. Arbitration is often viewed as an attractive alternative to lengthy and expensive litigation. In June 1987, the Supreme Court of the United States upheld the arbitration process as a fair, equitable, and efficient method for settling disputes within the securities industry.

Securities arbitration
Private form of dispute resolution with binding outcomes.

Arbitration enables a dispute to be resolved quickly and fairly by impartial persons—known as arbitrators—who are knowledgeable educators, lawyers, or other professionals. Claims involving the activities of stockbrokers may be arbitrated if the claim is filed within six years of the date of the event in dispute. A securities customer always has the right to require that a stockbroker submit to the arbitration process. In choosing arbitration as a means of resolution, all parties waive the right to pursue the matter through the courts.

The NYSE provides neutral arbitration panels to hear and decide disputes in more than 30 major cities throughout the United States. Typically, a panel for a case consists of one arbitrator with securities industry experience and two arbitrators who have no affiliation with the securities industry. At the hearing, parties present testimony and evidence to the arbitrators. Those who testify are subject to cross-examination by the opposing sides and to questions by the arbitrators. Both sides make opening statements, present their cases, and make concluding statements. Although legal representation is not required, it is advised. When the arbitrators reach their decision and have signed an award, copies are mailed to the parties involved. Generally, the arbitrators' decision is final and is subject to review by the courts only in rare circumstances.

Circuit Breakers and Curbs

Circuit breakers are rules for halting securities trading under certain circumstances. They are procedures that halt trading on the NYSE if prices have moved too much during the day. Circuit breakers are intended to allow for a cooling-off period during a severe market downturn. They represent an interesting example of securities market regulation that exemplifies the high level of cooperation between the SEC and the SROs. Under rules proposed by the various exchanges and approved by the SEC, all U.S. stock and futures exchanges halt trading to restore order when prices plummet. By calling a brief "time-out" during periods of panicky market

Circuit breakers
Rules for halting securities trading in volatile markets.

Can Securities Markets Regulate Themselves?

In addition to state and federal regulation, the securities markets are subject to self-regulation. Since 1934, the securities markets and their participants have regulated themselves via self-regulatory organizations (SROs). The job of the SROs is to protect the public investors by ensuring the markets have integrity. The two largest SROs are the National Association of Securities Dealers (NASD) and the New York Stock Exchange (NYSE). However, there are inherent conflicts of interest involved with the SRO approach.

In the 1990s, several Nasdaq dealers were found to be colluding in order to keep the bid-ask spread wide and highly profitable for market makers. This anticompetitive practice lined the pockets of the very NASD participants charged with self-regulation of the marketplace. More recently, state and federal regulators have accused Wall Street firms of a variety of unfair practices, such as rigging the allocation of initial public offering shares and publishing bogus stock research to win investment banking business.

Critics argue that the SROs must not be doing their jobs if government regulators such as the Securities and Exchange Commission and the New York attorney general must step in, investigate, and punish violators. Why didn't the NASD and the NYSE discover and stop illegal practices before they grew widespread and attracted government regulators? The answer may lie in the fact that malfeasance on Wall Street can be extraordinarily lucrative, and self-regulation by federal and state regulators is necessary to keep the markets fair and open for small and large investors.

To its credit, the NASD has recognized the inherent conflicts of a regulatory organization's actually owning a stock exchange. Over the past couple of years, the NASD has been trying to separate itself from the administration and ownership of Nasdaq and the American Exchange. So far, the NYSE has made no such admission and has failed to institute sufficient new safeguards to protect investors. Time will tell whether the industry will choose to heal itself or, instead, take the medicine of increasingly vigilant and aggressive outside regulators.

See: Susanne Craig, "Big Board and NASD Consider Merging Parts of Regulatory Units," *The Wall Street Journal Online,* November 11, 2005 (**http://online.wsj.com**).

turmoil, it is hoped that investors will refocus on investment opportunities and economic strengths and bring a halt to any tendency for contagious selling activity. This policy was first approved by the SEC for the NYSE following the October 1987 stock market crash. Circuit breakers subsequently were adopted by the other exchanges. This means that once trading is halted on the NYSE, trading is also halted on Nasdaq and all other U.S. stock, options, and futures exchanges.

Circuit breakers were tripped for the first time on October 27, 1997, when the Dow closed down 554 points. On that day, the NYSE and all other major securities markets stopped trading for 30 minutes after the Dow fell 350 points, and they closed early when the decline resumed. Whether the use of circuit breakers stemmed the market's decline on that day remains debatable. Some market participants complained that the speed and breadth of the market's decline actually worsened as panicked traders quickly exited the market. Others complained that the decline—which amounted to 7.2 percent—was too small to justify an early end to trading. These complaints led the investment community to propose changes that were approved by the SEC.

Under current rules, at the end of each calendar quarter, the NYSE figures the average daily closing value for the DJIA during the preceding month and multiplies that figure by 10, 20, and 30 percent. The resulting figures, rounded to the nearest 50, become the circuit breakers for the following quarter. For the first quarter of 2006, a decline of 10 percent (a 1,100-point drop in the DJIA) before 2 p.m. EST would have resulted in a one-hour trading halt. A decline of 10 percent at or after 2 p.m. EST but before 2:30 p.m. would have caused a 30-minute halt in trading. A two-hour trading interruption would have followed a 20 percent (2,150-point) decline before 1:00 p.m. If such a decline occurred after 1:00 p.m. but before 2:00 p.m., trading would have been halted for one hour. After 2:30 p.m., trading was scheduled to be halted after a 20 percent decline. If at any time during the trading day the DJIA was off 30 percent (3,150 points), trading was to be suspended for the rest of the day. These circuit breakers apply to the trading of not only stocks but also options on stocks and stock indexes, stock index futures, and options on stock index futures. Such restrictions are typically noted on CNBC with the "Curbs" sign.

The trading of individual securities can also be stopped. When a company has scheduled an important announcement during trading hours, the exchange often stops trading the company's stock before the announcement. Trading resumes after the announcement. This allows all interested investors to have the opportunity to learn the information. Exchanges will also temporarily stop trading a security if they believe trading on the basis of incomplete or perhaps erroneous information is detrimental to investors.

Investor Associations

American Association of Individual Investors

Investor associations are a popular way for novice investors to gain valuable investment education while they are gaining investment experience. One popular national group of investors is the *American Association of Individual Investors (AAII)*. This association specializes in providing education in stock investing, mutual funds, portfolio management, and retirement planning. It boasts 150,000 members. Some of the membership benefits of this not-for-profit organization are the *AAII Journal*, access to the association's Web site (**www.aaii.com**), and participation in local chapter activities. Many cities in the United States have a local AAII chapter. These local organizations schedule periodic gatherings at which speakers make presentations and investors can socialize. The association also sponsors national conferences that feature investor workshops and nationally known speakers.

Investment Clubs

One popular way to learn about investing is to form, or join, an **investment club**. A group of family members, friends, or colleagues band together by pooling their money to purchase stocks. The club meets periodically (usually monthly) to make trading decisions, learn about investing, and contribute additional money. More experienced members share with novice club members their knowledge of business and investing. These clubs can accumulate a significant amount of capital over time. Some clubs are all business in their approach to investing. Other clubs use the meetings as a chance to socialize. In other words, it can be fun too!

> **Investment clubs**
> A group formed to learn and invest. Members contribute money and investment ideas.

The association that supports investment clubs is the *National Association of Investors Corporation (NAIC)*, a nonprofit organization designed to help investors start or join investment clubs. The NAIC can provide groups with the organizational structure for a new club and helps all member clubs with education and useful investment and decision-making tools. Investors can belong to the NAIC (at **www.better-investing.org**) as individuals or as a club. The association has about 18,000 investment clubs registered with roughly 50,000 individual members. The NAIC is dedicated to collecting and delivering the resources that will enable individuals to become better investors. One benefit of being a member is the association's *Better Investing Magazine*.

Probably the most famous investment club in recent memory was the Beardstown Ladies Investment Club of Beardstown, Illinois. The club comprised elderly women who became media darlings when they claimed to have earned market-beating annual returns of more than 20 percent per year. After club members wrote several best-selling books describing how to beat the market, investigators for *The Wall Street Journal* discovered that the ladies had actually underperformed the market. As it turns out, they erroneously counted their monthly contributions as investment profits when computing their returns. Even in the feel-good world of investment clubs, investors need to be skeptical of market-beating strategies.

Try It!

Go to both the AAII and the NAIC Web sites, and list the membership benefits of belonging to each investor association.

Summary

■ Since 1817, the **New York Stock Exchange** has maintained an **agency auction market**. Trading at the NYSE takes place by open bids and offers by exchange members acting as agents for institutions or individual investors. Each listed stock is assigned to a single post where the **specialist** manages the auction process. Minimum listing standards for the NYSE start with a minimal number of **round-lot** holders, shareholders who own at least 100 shares.

■ The **National Association of Securities Dealers (NASD), Inc.,** is a self-regulatory organization of the securities industry. Guidelines for listing on the nation's second-largest stock exchange, the **American Stock Exchange (AMEX)**, include a **public float** of $3 million. Public float is the amount of common stock held by unaffiliated institutional and individual investors.

■ The **Nasdaq Stock Market** is a **negotiated market** in which investors deal directly with **market makers**. Market makers are NASD member firms that compete with one another to buy and sell the stocks they represent. Each market maker competes for **customer order flow**, or buy-sell business. The difference between the price at which a market maker is willing to buy a security and the price at which the firm is willing to sell is called the **market-maker spread**. The **inside market** is the highest-bid and lowest-offer prices among all competing market makers in a Nasdaq security.

■ The **Nasdaq SmallCap Market** is a national market with minimal listing criteria. A $1 bid price requirement rules out low-price **penny stocks** and enhances the credibility of the market. The **OTC Bulletin Board (OTCBB)** is a regulated quotation service that displays real-time quotes, last-sale prices, and volume information in over-the-counter (OTC) equity securities, which might include **American Depositary Receipts (ADRs)** or trading certificates that represent ownership of shares of foreign companies.

■ The **Dow Jones Industrial Average (DJIA)** is a price-weighted index calculated by adding the prices of 30 large industrial stocks and dividing by a number called the **DJIA divisor**. The DJIA divisor is an adjustment factor used to account for stock splits. The **S&P 500 Index** is the most popular value-weighted market index. The DJIA is a long-time favorite with individual investors; the S&P 500 is preferred as an investment **equity benchmark** to judge institutional investor performance. The **Russell 3000 Index** measures the performance of the 3,000 largest U.S. companies based on total market capitalization. The **Russell 1000 Index** measures the performance of the 1,000 largest companies in the Russell 3000 Index. The Russell 3000 captures approximately 98 percent of the total market capitalization of publicly traded stocks. The Russell 1000

Index accounts for 90 percent of the total market capitalization of publicly traded stocks in the United States. The **Dow Jones Wilshire 5000 Composite Index** approximates the total dollar value of the U.S. equity market.

■ In the United States, medium-sized company stock price performance is captured by the **Nasdaq Composite Index**, a market value-weighted index of all 5,000-plus stocks listed on the Nasdaq Stock Market. The **Nasdaq 100 Index** reflects Nasdaq's largest companies, such as Microsoft, Intel, and Dell Computer. The **S&P MidCap 400 Index** consists of 400 domestic stocks chosen for market size, liquidity, and industry group representation. The **Dow Jones Wilshire 4500 Completion Index** is the Dow Jones Wilshire 5000 minus the companies from the S&P 500.

■ The most popular U.S. small-company stock price index is the **Russell 2000 Index**, composed of the 2,000 smallest companies in the Russell 3000 Index. The **S&P SmallCap 600 Index** consists of 600 domestic stocks.

■ Major global stock market indexes include the United Kingdom's **FTSE-100**, Japan's **Nikkei 225 Index**, the **TSE-35**, and Hong Kong's **Hang Seng Index**. Global stock market performance is also tracked by a variety of indexes compiled by Morgan Stanley Capital International, a subsidiary of Morgan Stanley Dean Witter & Co. The **Europe, Australasia, Far East (EAFE) Index** is a value-weighted index of stocks from 21 countries. All **emerging markets** involve companies with greater perceived investment risk than that of leading firms in **developed markets**.

■ Industry **self-regulatory organizations (SROs)** oversee securities markets and participating member firms. Noteworthy SROs include the **NASD**, NYSE, Amex, CBOE, a number of regional stock and options exchanges, and the Municipal Securities Rulemaking Board. The **Sarbanes Oxley Act** was enacted in 2002 to improve public accounting and investor protections. **Stock Watch** is a computerized system that automatically flags unusual volume or price changes in any listed stock, thus helping the NYSE guard against manipulation and insider trading. The **Intermarket Surveillance Group** shares surveillance information and coordinates efforts to detect cross-market manipulative trading. **Securities arbitration** enables a dispute to be resolved quickly and fairly by impartial persons. **Circuit breakers** halt securities trading under certain circumstances.

■ Investor associations are a popular way for novice investors to gain valuable investment education while they are gaining investment experience. Another popular way to learn about investing is to form, or join, an **investment club**.

Self-Test Problems

ST2.1   Describe the important economic characteristics of the Standard & Poor's 500 Index.

Solution

Widely regarded as the best single gauge of the U.S. equities market, the S&P 500 Index is a market value-weighted index of 500 leading companies in leading industries of the U.S. economy. Although the S&P 500 focuses on the large-cap segment of the market, with over 80 percent coverage of U.S. equities, it is sometimes relied on as a proxy for the total market. In mid-2005, the market capitalization of the 500 companies contained in the index was $11.3 trillion, with an average company market capitalization of $22.6 billion (median of $10.6 billion) and a range in size from $750 million (smallest) to $386 billion (largest).

The S&P 500 is part of a series of S&P U.S. indexes maintained by a team of Standard & Poor's economists and index analysts who meet on a regular basis. The goal of the Index Committee is to ensure that the S&P 500 remains a leading indicator of U.S. equities, reflecting the risk and return characteristics of the broader large-cap universe on an ongoing basis. The Index Committee also monitors constituent liquidity to ensure efficient portfolio trading, while keeping index turnover at a minimum. The S&P Index Committee follows a set of published guidelines for maintaining the index. Complete details of these guidelines, including the criteria for index additions and removals, committee policy statements, and research papers are available on the Internet at **www.standardandpoors.com/indices**, under "Index Committee Policy."

ST2.2   On March 10, 2005, the DJIA closed at 10851.51, up 45.89 points. The value of the DJIA divisor on that date was 0.135. Calculate the average market price of DJIA component stocks, the cost of a round lot of all DJIA components, and the average price change (in dollars) on that date.

Solution

The DJIA = Σ prices/divisor, where Σ prices is the sum of stock prices for all 30 component stocks and the divisor is a constant calculated by Dow Jones. On March 10, 2005, DJIA = 10851.51 = Σ prices/0.135. Therefore, Σ prices = 10851.51 × 0.135 = $1,464.95. The average price of a component stock on that date was $48.83 = $1,464.95/30. A round lot is 100 shares of stock. The cost of a round lot of 100 shares of each component stock in the DJIA on March 10, 2005, was $146,495 = $1,464.95 × 100. Because the DJIA = Σ prices/divisor, ΔDJIA = $\Delta\Sigma$ prices/divisor. On March 10, 2005, ΔDJIA = 45.89 = $\Delta\Sigma$ prices/divisor = $\Delta\Sigma$ prices/0.135. Therefore, $\Delta\Sigma$ prices = 45.89 × 0.135 = $6.20. The average price change for a component stock on that date was $6.20/30 = $0.21, or 21 cents.

Questions and Problems

2.1   What is the difference between an agency auction market and an over-the-counter negotiated market? Include in your answer an example of both types of markets.

2.2   How does the Dow Jones Industrial Average (DJIA) differ from a simple average of the component stock prices?

2.3   Which companies have been added to the Dow Jones Industrial Average since 1990?

2.4   Suppose a given component of the DJIA is priced at $50 while another is priced at $90. If the divisor is 0.11, how much does the index decrease when the $50 stock loses 10 percent and when the $90 stock loses 10 percent?

2.5   Consider a price-weighted index like the DJIA with only three stocks. If the stock prices are $30, $50, and $70 and the divisor is 0.11, what is the index level? If the stocks change to $25, $53, and $76, what would the new index level be and what is the index return? If the $76 stock conducted a 2-for-1 stock split, what should the new divisor be?

2.6   Consider a market value-weighted index, like the S&P 500 Index, with only three stocks. The first stock's price is $50, with 300 shares outstanding. The second and third stocks sell for $65 and $90, with shares outstanding of 100 and 200, respectively. Each stock originally sold 100 shares at $30, $75, and $50, respectively. If the base index value is 100, what is the value of the index?

2.7   Describe the type of company included in the Russell 3000 Index, the Russell 1000 Index, and the Dow Jones Wilshire 5000 Composite Index. Approximately what percentage of the investable U.S. equity market does each of these three indexes capture?

2.8   Suppose that Microsoft represents a 5 percent weighting on a market value-weighted index. If the index is at 8,000 and Microsoft's stock price increases by 10 percent, how much will this cause the index to increase?

2.9   What is the purpose of NYSE trading curbs and circuit breakers?

2.10   What are the main securities laws passed by Congress to regulate the investment industry? What part of the industry does each law regulate?

2.11   Two stock indexes, one price-weighted average and one value-weighted index, are to be created from the following two stocks: Berkshire Hathaway (share price = $90,700, shares outstanding = 1.54 million) and Delta Air Lines (share price = $4.33, shares outstanding = 129.41 million).
a. If the divisor for the price-weighted average is 2, what is the index value?
b. If the beginning value of the value-weighted index is $103,880.26 million and the index base value is 100, what is the current value of this index?

2.12   Two stock indexes, one price-weighted average and one value-weighted index, are to be created from the following three stocks: Martha Stewart Living Omnimedia (share price = $24.15, shares outstanding = 20.67 million), McDonald's (share price = $32.75, shares outstanding = 1,272 million), and Apple Computer (share price = $39.83, shares outstanding = 817.17 million).
a. If the divisor for the price-weighted average is 0.9673, what is the index value?
b. If the beginning value of the value-weighted index is $74,705.06 million and the index base value is 100, what is the current value of this index?
c. If the prices of the three stocks change to Omnimedia = $30, McDonald's = $35, and Apple = $35, what is the value of the two indexes? Why are they different?

2.13   How could one create an investment portfolio that would exactly mimic the performance of the Dow Jones Industrial Average? Is the DJIA a good market index for investment purposes?

2.14.   Go to the CNN Money Web site at **money.cnn.com**. From the Markets & Stocks menu on the left, click on the World Markets option. Examine the performance of the world's stock markets. How much variation occurs in the daily percent change between the stock indexes? Why are there large differences?

2.15   In response to the market breaks in October 1987, the New York Stock Exchange instituted several circuit breakers to reduce market volatility and promote investor confidence. Go to the New York Stock Exchange Web Site at **www.nyse.com** to find a list and brief description of these circuit breakers, as well as their current levels. What are the circuit breakers used for and what are the current levels?

2.16 Compare the costs and benefits of membership in the AAII (**www.aaii.com**) and the NAIC (**www.better-investing.org**).

2.17 On January 1, 2006, DJIA = 10784.82 and the divisor was 0.12493117.
  a. Calculate the average market price of DJIA component stocks on that date.
  b. How much would it cost to buy 100 shares of all DJIA components on that date?

2.18 Go to Standard & Poor's Market Insight at **www.mhhe.com/edumarketinsight** and click on the Commentary link. Examine the most recent Investment Policy Committee (IPC) notes. The Standard & Poor's IPC is composed of 10 senior managers who meet weekly to oversee all investment-related activity done in Standard & Poor's name. What portion of your portfolio does the IPC recommend be invested in equities? What are the sector weights that make up the S&P 1500 Index?

2.19 An analyst gathered the following data about stocks J, K, and L, which together form a value-weighted index:

| Stock | Dec. 31, Year 1 | | Dec. 31, Year 2 | |
	Price	Shares Outstanding	Price	Shares Outstanding
J	$40	10,000	$50	10,000
K	30	6,000	20	12,000*
L	50	9,000	40	9,000

*2-for-1 stock split.

The ending value-weighted index (base index = 100) is *closest to:*
  a. 92.31
  b. 93.64
  c. 106.80
  d. 108.33

2.20 The divisor for the Dow Jones Industrial Average (DJIA) is *most likely* to decrease when a stock in the DJIA:
  a. Has a stock split
  b. Has a reverse split
  c. Pays a cash dividend
  d. Is removed and replaced

INVESTMENT APPLICATION

Buying Stocks without a Broker

A *dividend reinvestment plan (DRIP)* is an investment program offered by corporations for their shareholders. DRIPs allow shareholders participating in the plan to easily and cheaply reinvest cash dividends in additional shares of the company. Basically, DRIPs allow shareholders to buy further shares in their company at little or no commission cost in lieu of receiving cash dividends. Although there are some exceptions, fees associated with DRIPs are generally paid by the company offering the plan. Therefore, DRIPs allow shareholders to build on their investment in a company on a regular basis with little or no transactions costs.

A unique feature of DRIPs is that they typically allow plan participants to purchase and hold fractional shares. For example, suppose a shareholder who is enrolled in a DRIP owns 130 shares of stock in a company that pays a quarterly dividend of 30 cents per share. The total quarterly dividend income due to this shareholder would be $39 (= $0.30 × 130). Furthermore, assume that this company's common stock is selling for $45 on the New York Stock Exchange (NYSE). On the dividend payment date, the administrator of the company's DRIP would purchase on behalf of the shareholder 0.867 (= $39/$45) shares of stock in the company. Of course, 0.867 is actually the prorated number of shares to be purchased on behalf of this individual shareholder. In practice, on or about the dividend payment date, the plan administrator purchases the total amount of common stock that can be bought with the combined sum of dividend income to be reinvested by all DRIP participants. By pooling individual purchases through a DRIP, participants can minimize transaction costs and brokerage expenses. In some instances, sponsoring corporations use DRIPs as a cost-efficient means for raising new equity capital. In such cases, the corporation simply issues new shares to DRIP participants on the dividend payment date.

A very attractive feature of some DRIPs is that they offer a sizable discount on purchases of additional shares with reinvested dividends. Such discounts can be as much as 3 to 5 percent of the amount of reinvested dividend income. In its simplest terms, this means that shares purchased with reinvested dividends can sometimes be acquired by plan participants at only 97 or 95 percent of their actual market price. As a result, the DRIP participants sometimes have the opportunity to acquire 3 or 5 percent more shares than could be purchased in the absence of such a discount. Discount DRIPs are especially popular with utilities and other companies that have the reoccurring need to raise additional equity capital. For such companies, offering a discount on reinvested dividends is a cost-effective means for raising additional equity because it alleviates the need to pay investment banker fees, which can sometimes amount to 5 to 8 percent of the amount of new equity capital.

FIGURE 2.4   DRIP Central

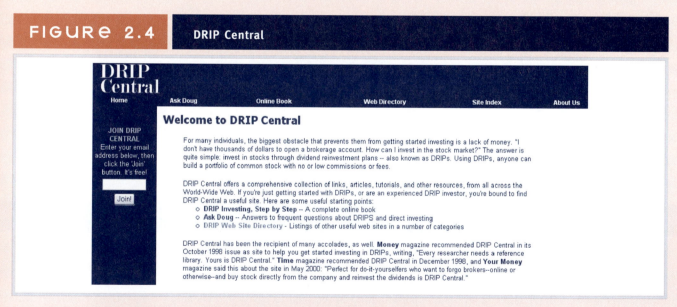

Source: DRIP Central, **www.dripcentral.com** © DRIP Central 2006. Used with permission.

In most instances, the minimum requirement for joining most DRIPs is that you have to be a registered shareholder. This typically means that you have to own at least one share of the company's stock. In general, such shares must be held in your own name—they cannot be held in your behalf by a broker. This initial share of stock must be purchased and delivered to you through a traditional broker or transferred to you from another shareholder. Once share ownership has been established, you should acquire the DRIP documentation of the company whose plan you are thinking of joining. This can be done by contacting either the company itself or its stock transfer agent. In many DRIP plans, companies have begun offering so-called no-load stock purchase programs to first-time investors. Companies such as General Electric, Home Depot, IBM, Lucent Technologies, Motorola, Nokia, Pfizer, SBC Communications, and Wal-Mart offer the most popular DRIP programs. Today, roughly one-half of the 1,000 companies with DRIPs allow open enrollment.

DRIP plan documentation, plus an enrollment/authorization form, can also be obtained from a number of Web sites on the Internet that specialize in DRIPs. One of the best of these Web sites is DRIP Central at **www.dripcentral.com**. Figure 2.4 is a screen shot of this useful site.

a. Explain why company management that fears an unfriendly takeover bid from an unwanted corporate suitor might favor a DRIP.

b. Can you think of any disadvantages faced by a small investor wanting to participate in a DRIP?

3

Buying and Selling Equities

Have you noticed that stock prices generally fall in a range from $20 to $40 per share for large publicly traded companies? Some "penny stocks" that trade for less than $5 per share are favored by speculators, but low-price stocks suffer from a general perception that they are from low-quality firms. Indeed, stock prices are often taken as a signal about investment quality. Some institutional investors and public pension funds are restricted from buying stocks with share prices that are lower than a specific price benchmark, say, $5. Such speculative penny stocks are simply not widely regarded as being of "investment grade" quality.

The levels of stock prices also matter for many individual investors who prefer low stock prices. Even with today's low commission rates, many small investors like to buy stocks in round lots of 100 shares each. When stock prices rise sharply, companies often conduct a stock split to maintain or enhance retail investor interest. Stock splits change the number of shares outstanding, and the price per share quickly adjusts. For example, a 2:1 split doubles the number of shares owned by every stockholder, and the stock price declines to one-half its presplit level. Note that the market value of each investor's holdings is unchanged—each stockholder ends up with twice the number of shares at half the price.

One company that has never conducted a stock split is Warren Buffett's Berkshire Hathaway. In 2006, for example, Berkshire stock was selling for more than $90,000 per share! Buffett has no interest in enhancing Berkshire's appeal among small retail investors and short-term speculators. Instead, Buffett seeks to attract investors who want to own quality businesses for very long periods of time. Ideally, Buffett would prefer that satisfied investors never sell a single share of Berkshire stock. It's fair to say that share price matters not only to institutional and small individual investors. Share price also matters to the savviest investor of all time![1]

[1] See Michael Santoli, "Charting the Market," *Barron's,* January 2, 2006. (See **http://online.barrons.com**.)

CHAPTER OBJECTIVES	■ Know the costs of trading securities.
	■ Be able to place a buy or sell order.
	■ Be able to compute margin debt and returns for long and short positions.
	■ Implement a dollar cost average strategy.
	■ Examine the initial public offer market.

Simple Buy-Sell Decisions

Bid-Ask Spreads

The quoted **bid** is the highest price that *market maker* is willing to pay to buy a security. Practically speaking, this is the highest currently available price at which an *investor* can sell shares of stock to the market maker. The quoted **ask** is the lowest price a market maker is willing to accept to sell a stock. This is the quoted offer at which an investor can presently buy shares of stock. The **bid-ask spread** is the gap between the bid price and the ask price. It is the price markup faced by investors and the profit margin earned by the exchange specialist or Nasdaq market maker.

To illustrate, consider the data shown in Table 3.1. On the date shown, International Business Machines had traded 3,643,600 shares by 12:01 p.m. EST on the NYSE. The last trade occurred at a price of $82.64. This price was $0.69 higher than the close on the previous trading day. Also notice that International Business Machines has been assigned the **ticker symbol** "IBM." Stocks listed on the NYSE are assigned unique one-, two-, or three-letter stock symbols to facilitate transaction speed and accuracy. Over-the-counter stocks are typically assigned unique four-letter symbols given the larger numbers of such companies.

Although much of the information contained in Table 3.1 is self-explanatory, **bid-size** and **ask-size** information may merit some explanation. Bid size is the number of round lots represented on the buy side of the market. A round lot is 100 shares of stock, so a bid size of 2 means that the bid of $82.60 for IBM is good for 200 shares worth $16,520. Ask size is the number of round lots represented on the sell side of the market, so an ask size of 11 means that the ask price of $82.66 for IBM is good for up to 1,100 shares worth $90,926. Note that buyers of IBM should expect to buy at $0.06 higher per share than the seller's price. This difference represents a cost of trading for investors. The bid and ask sizes, as well as the size at nearby quotes, are measures of the **market depth** of IBM. Because the bid size is somewhat larger than the ask size, demand could be somewhat greater than supply at the current bid-ask spread. This tends to place some upward pressure on IBM's stock price. If the ask size were somewhat larger than the bid size, demand would be somewhat lower than supply at the current bid-ask spread, and there would be some near-term upward pressure on IBM's stock price.

Consider the Nasdaq's Dell Computer quote. As shown in Table 3.1, part B, Dell has a bid for 200 shares at 30.71 and the ask is $30.72 for 8,200 shares. Notice that the market for Dell has more reported market depth than that for IBM. The bid-ask spread of Dell is only 1 cent, whereas the spread for IBM is 6 cents. In percentage terms, the Dell spread is 0.03 percent of the bid price, and the IBM spread is 0.07 percent of its bid price. A large market depth and small percentage spread are measures of high market liquidity. Liquidity is most important for larger, usually institutional, investors. But active and day traders value liquidity as well.

A top source of up-to-the-minute information about individual companies is the Web site freerealtime.com. On many different Web sites, it is possible to get stock quote information

Bid
Highest price an investor is willing to pay.

Ask
Lowest price an investor will accept to sell.

Bid-ask spread
Gap between the bid and ask prices that represents a cost to the investor.

Ticker symbols
Unique stock identifier with one to five letters.

Bid size
Number of shares sought by current buyers.

Ask size
Number of shares offered by current sellers.

Market depth
Number of active buyers and sellers.

TABLE 3.1 | Intrady Stock Quotes

A. NYSE-Listed IBM Stock Quote

INTERNATIONAL BUSINESS MACH—New York Stock Exchange: IBM

Last	Change(%)	Trade Time	Bid (size)	Ask (size)
82.64	▲0.69 (0.84)	12:01	82.60 (2)	82.66 (11)
Latest Ticks	Prev Close	Open	Low	High
-+-=	81.95	81.4	81	82.9
Day Volume	Avg Day Vol	VWAP	52 Wk Low	52 Wk High
3,643,600	6,307,900	82.2886	71.85	98.42
# of Trades	Last Size	Avg Trade Size	P/E Ratio	Market Cap (mil)
4,696	900	776	18	130,547

Thursday, January 5, 2006

B. Nasdaq-Listed Dell Stock Quote

DELL INC—Nasdaq National Market: DELL

Last	Change(%)	Trade Time	Bid (size)	Ask (size)
30.72	▼0.04 (0.13)	12:06	30.71 (2)	30.72(82)
Latest Ticks	Prey Close	Open	Low	High
====	30.76	30.96	30.59	30.98
Day Volume	Avg Day Vol	VWAP	52 Wk Low	52 Wk High
7,723,607	17,542,000	30.7783	28.62	41.99
# of Trades	Last Size	Avg Trade Size	P/E Ratio	Market Cap (mil)
21,605	300	357	24	72,277

Thursday, January 5, 2006

Source: Freerealtime.com (**quotes.freerealtime.com**).

Market order
Instruction to buy or sell at the current market price.

Limit order
Instruction to buy or sell at a specified price.

Stop order
Market order to buy or sell a certain quantity of a security if a specified price is reached or passed.

Stopped out
Position that is liquidated by the execution of a stop order.

Buy stop order
Buy order that is to be held until the market price rises to a specified stop price.

Stop-loss order
Stop order to sell a long position at a specified price that is below the current market price.

Stop-limit order
Order to buy or sell a certain quantity of a security at a specified price or better, but only after a specified price has been reached.

that is delayed by 15 or 20 minutes. Usually that's okay. In some fast-moving markets, however, delayed quotes can be different from up-to-the minute information. The freerealtime.com site offers up-to-the-minute, or real-time, stock quotes, news, and information.

Types of Orders

A **market order** is an instruction to immediately buy a security at the current ask price or to sell a security at the current bid price. This contrasts with a **limit order**, whereby the customer specifies a price at which to execute a buy or sell decision. A limit order can be executed only if the market price at least reaches the specified price target. With a buy limit order, securities are bought at or below the specified price target. With a limit order, an investor might instruct a broker to "buy 100 shares of Walt Disney at $35 or less." A sell limit order, which instructs a broker to "sell 100 shares of Walt Disney at $35 or better" specifies that securities are sold at or above the specified price target.

Wall Street investors use a wide variety of market and limit orders. A **stop order** is a market order to buy or sell a certain quantity of a security if a specified price (the *stop price*) is reached or passed. A position is said to be **stopped out** when the position is offset by the execution of a stop order. A **buy stop order** is a buy order that is to be held until the market price rises to a specified stop price, at which point it becomes a market order. Buy stop orders are often used by short sellers who wish to limit their risk exposure, but they are not permitted for over-the-counter trading. A **stop-loss order** is a stop order to sell a long position at a specified price that is below the current market price. A **stop-limit order** is an order to buy or sell a certain quan-

Story Stocks Are Bad Investments

There are literally thousands of stocks that investors might buy. How do they decide among the large number of available alternatives?

Brad M. Barber, Chip Heath, and Terrance Odean, three finance professors, recently studied 1 million stock trades and found that individual investors like to buy firms with "good reasons," or rationales, for investment. Generally speaking, investors like a good story. Unfortunately, good stories often lead to bad investment decisions. Investors tend to bid up the stock prices of companies with convincing investment rationales so that they represent no better than average investments for subsequent investors. Barber, Heath, and Odean found that the average number of stocks held in a typical brokerage account is only 4.3 companies. Apparently, individual investors tend to have only a modest amount of diversification in their brokerage accounts. Moreover, individual investors seem to like stocks that appear on *Fortune* magazine's "most-admired companies" list. These are firms with high past-sales growth and high prior-three-year returns. To individual investors, these are among the top characteristics considered attractive when making their investment decisions. Unfortunately, such glamorous stocks do not tend to produce high returns for subsequent investors. Barber, Heath, and Odean found that large, admired growth firms with strong prior-three-year stock returns and five-year sales growth earned poor returns for subsequent investors.

By identifying companies that have already experienced high growth and are enjoying media accolades, investors are pinpointing firms that have had their prices bid up by similarly enthusiastic investors. Buying such stocks results in paying high prices that are seldom justified by future performance. To earn above-normal returns, investors must select stocks with surprisingly good future performance, and glamour stocks seldom surprise to the upside. Individual investors tend to prefer growth stocks and usually overpay for them. When glamour begins to fade, subpar future returns often result.

Story stocks are bad investments.

See: Brad M. Barber, Chip Heath, and Terrance Odean, "Good Reasons Sell: Reason-Based Choice among Group and Individual Investors in the Stock Market," *Management Science*, vol. 49, no. 12 (December 2003), pp. 1636–1652.

---

tity of a security at a specified price or better, but only after that specified price has been reached. A stop-limit order can be thought of as a simple combination of a stop order and a limit order.

A **day order** is an order to buy or sell that automatically expires if it cannot be executed during the trading session in which it is entered. An **open order** is created when an investor places an offer to buy or sell a security at a price that differs from the current market price. An open order stays active until it is executed (filled) or canceled by the investor. In some instances, brokers set a time limit of 30 to 60 days on open orders. After such time has passed, an open order is sometimes automatically canceled unless the investor instructs the broker to keep it active. Another expression for an open order is a **good 'til canceled order.**

In most instances, investors are willing to accept partial executions. For example, if a day order is placed to sell 500 shares of Walt Disney at 35, most investors would be willing to sell 100, 200, or any fraction of 500 shares at that price. If this is not the case, different instructions must be communicated to the executing broker. **All or none** is a stipulation to a buy or sell order that instructs the broker to either fill the entire order or not fill it at all. With all-or-none orders, partial fulfillment of an order is not allowed. **Fill-or-kill** orders are a special type of all-or-none order. A fill-or-kill order must immediately be filled in its entirety or, if this is not possible, be completely canceled. All-or-none and fill-or-kill orders are used when investors are concerned about the potential for paying higher brokerage commissions on orders that are executed in piecemeal fashion.

Day order
Instruction to buy or sell during the present trading session.

Open order
A limit order that has yet to be executed.

Good 'til canceled order
A limit order that is open until executed or canceled by the investor.

All or none
Buy or sell instruction that must be filled exactly or not at all.

Fill or kill
All-or-none order that must be immediately filled or canceled.

Order Routing

Once an investor places an order with a stockbroker (personally, over the phone, or online), that order is routed to the proper stock exchange for execution. Orders for NYSE-listed stocks are electronically routed to the exchange. The exchange uses the SuperDot system to send market and limit orders directly to the proper trading post on the floor. Market orders are handled in the auction process at the post. Limit orders are listed on the specialist's limit-order book and also posted on the NYSE OpenBook for all interested people to observe. The specialist keeps an eye on the limit-order book and the prices in the auction. The specialist will execute the limit orders when they match bid and ask prices.

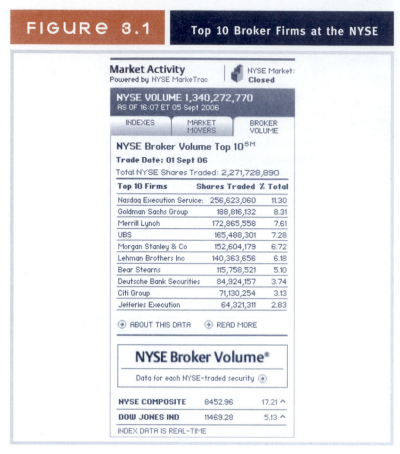

FIGURE 3.1 — Top 10 Broker Firms at the NYSE

Source: NYSE Group, **www.nyse.com**.

Block transactions
Transactions of at least 10,000 shares usually matched outside the auction process and then cleared through the exchange.

The system uses the same electronic circuit to send posttrade reports back to the brokerage firms. The firms routing the most trades are shown in Figure 3.1. Note that the amount of shares handled by these firms is measured in the hundreds of millions of shares per day. Although most stock trades at the NYSE are still done through the auction process, the exchange has been developing an electronic order match system, *NYSE Direct+*. More than 10 percent of the trades on the NYSE are now being conducted over this electronic system.

Large orders of 10,000 shares or more are called **block transactions**. They may be too large for specialists to handle on the floor without causing large price movements. Some finance firms work with large investors to match these block orders. After finding a seller for a block-sale order, they then send the matched order through the NYSE so that the trade is recognized by the NYSE. It is common for large block trades to occur every day.

Orders for stocks traded on the American Stock Exchange are electronically routed from the broker to the Amex. As the Amex is an auction market like the NYSE, its own computer systems function similarly to the SuperDot system at the NYSE. However, because the Amex also trades some securities other than common stock, such as options and exchange-traded funds, its systems must route orders to multiple trading mechanisms. The Nasdaq market is fully an electronic market. Brokers route buy and sell orders to the Nasdaq system to be executed by market-making dealers. Many stockbroker firms also conduct market-making functions, and thus a customer may end up trading directly with his or her broker firm. Such trades are cleared through the stock exchanges.

Trading Pitfalls

Hyperactive Trading

The allure of active trading is strong. People who believe that they have superior information or investment skills feel they should trade frequently in order to benefit from that advantage. However, studies show that active trading exacerbates psychological biases because of the constant focus on the market and stock price changes. This short-term focus causes investor decisions to be more influenced by emotions than does a long-term focus.

The actual trading performance of tens of thousands of investors at a national discount brokerage firm illustrates this point. Impatient investors trade actively; active trading also causes investors to be impatient. Consider the situation in which you learn of a stock you want to buy. Should you sell stocks you own and buy the new one, or should you just keep the stocks you already hold? In a recent study, the stocks that investors sold earned an average of 2.6 percent during the following four months, whereas the new stocks purchased earned only 0.11 percent. In the year following the trades, stocks that had been sold typically outperformed stocks purchased by 5.8 percent. On average, active trading causes investors to sell a good stock and purchase a poor one, thus making a bad investment decision.[2]

In addition, active trading is costly. Remember that the market maker captures the bid-ask spread as the profit for providing liquidity for investors. This means that investors are paying the spread, and thus it is a cost of trading. When investors think of trading costs, they typically think only of the commission costs. The commission fee from a full-service broker may be over $100 per trade. An online brokerage may charge less than $10 per trade. But the quality of the order fills has a large impact on the cost of trading. For example, consider an order to buy 1,000 shares of a company. If one brokerage fills the order at $15 per share and charges a $100 commission, the total cost of the shares is $15,100. Another broker may charge only $10 for the trade, but have the order filled at $15.10 per share. The total cost of this arrangement is $15,110. Note that receiving a low-quality order fill can be more expensive than paying a higher commission and receiving a high-quality fill.

Online Brokerage and Trading Activity

The last decade has seen a dramatic rise in online stock trading. In a traditional stock brokerage account, the investor places trades through a stockbroker. Trading in an online brokerage account allows investors to place trades without the interim step of talking to a stockbroker. However, in many cases, a stockbroker acts like a gatekeeper. The stockbroker can ask if the investment is suitable or can ask the reasons for the trade. Without this gatekeeper, many investors trade more actively and make more mistakes.

Consider the trading behavior of 1,607 investors who switched from a phone-based trading system to an Internet-based trading system at a discount brokerage firm. In the two years before these investors went online, the average portfolio turnover rate was about 70 percent per year. That is, these investors sold 70 percent of their stocks during the year, on average, and purchased new ones. After they went online, the trading of these investors immediately jumped to a turnover of 120 percent. Some of this increase was transitory, as the turnover returned to a 90 percent level two years after the investors had gone online. The switch to online trading also affected the performance of these investors. Before switching to the online trading service, these investors earned nearly 18 percent per year. This represented a return of 2.35 percent more than the general stock market return. After going online, the investors underperformed the market by 3.5 percent per year.[3]

Why does online trading have such a strong influence on one's psychological biases? Consider the characteristics of online brokerage. First, the low commission of trading makes transactions appear to have a low cost. But there is more cost to trading than just commissions. Investors must also bear the cost of making poor decisions. Second, the vast quantity of information on the Internet creates an illusion of knowledge that fosters trading.

The Illusion of Knowledge

The **illusion of knowledge** refers to the tendency of people to believe that the accuracy of their forecasts increases with more information. The more pieces of information you obtain, the better your stock picking will be, right?

The following simple example shows that access to information does not necessarily lead to knowledge, or even wisdom. What number do you think will come up when you roll a fair six-sided die? How sure are you that your number will come up? You have a one-sixth chance of being right with any number you pick between 1 and 6. Now consider that the last three rolls of the die have each produced the number 3. What number do you think will come up with the next roll of the die? What is your chance of being right? The numbers between 1 and 6 still have a one-sixth chance of being correct. The added information did nothing to increase your ability to forecast the

Illusion of knowledge
The illusion that more information creates more knowledge and better predictions.

---

[2] Terrance Odean, "Do Investors Trade Too Much?" *American Economic Review,* vol. 89, no. 5 (December 1999), pp. 1279–1298.

[3] Brad Barber and Terrance Odean, "Online Investors: Do the Slow Die First?" *Review of Financial Studies,* vol. 15, no. 2 (March 2002), pp. 455–487.

roll of the die. Yet many people would believe that the number 3 has a greater chance (than one-sixth) to be rolled again, while others would believe that it has a lower chance to be rolled again. The new information did not add any knowledge to the situation, yet people make different decisions because of that information and become more confident in their decisions even though their chances of being correct do not change. It is very common for naïve gamblers in games with number sequences (like the lottery, keno, roulette, and craps) to track past numbers and make decisions based on this history. This additional information gives them the illusion of knowledge.

Investors have access to vast quantities of information on the Internet. This information includes current information (e.g., real-time news, prices, and volume) as well as historical data (e.g., past prices, returns, and accounting performance). However, information itself does not lead to knowledge of what is happening or the wisdom to know how to profit from it. Ultimately, much of the information available does not give investors as much knowledge as they think because they do not have the training to interpret it properly.

In addition, one must be careful with some of the information on the Internet. Some of it, such as advice on stock message boards, is irrelevant noise. Other Internet information is fraudulent. While savvy investors do not base investment decisions on Internet chat, they do rely on wire services like Reuters and Dow Jones for news stories and company announcements. Recently, false stories have been planted and mistakenly circulated by reputable news services or made to appear as if they were circulated by reputable news services. Examples include a fake Bloomberg News announcement concerning a bogus takeover-bid announcement for PairGain Technologies. PairGain stock soared 30 percent as speculators snapped up shares in hopes of turning a quick profit. When PairGain officials debunked the false report, the stock price quickly dropped. In another case, stock manipulators planted false information claiming the CEO of Emulex had resigned amid an accounting scandal. The perpetrators had shorted the stock, and they profited when Emulex's stock price plunged 62 percent before the company could deny the hoax.

Good investment information is crucial to making solid investment decisions. Investors must also have the education and experience to make that information the basis for profitable investment decisions.

The Illusion of Control

Investors often believe that they have some influence, or control, over the outcome of uncontrollable events. For example, people tend to be more willing to bet on the flip of a coin if the coin has yet to be flipped. If the coin has already been flipped and the outcome is hidden, people are less likely to place a bet. Clearly, placing a bet before or after a coin flip has no influence on the outcome. Yet people behave as if they subconsciously believe that it does. The attributes that foster the **illusion of control** are prevalent in online brokerage services. These attributes are choice, active involvement, task familiarity, and information.[4]

Illusion of control
The belief that people have influence over the outcome of uncontrollable events.

Studies show that forcing decision makers to make an active choice induces their illusion of control. People who choose their own lottery numbers feel they have a better chance of winning than those who have numbers randomly given to them. Of course, the odds of winning the lottery are the same in both cases. Online brokers do not give investment advice. Therefore, investors must make their own choices. In addition, the greater one's participation in a particular task, the greater is one's feeling of being in control. Online investors have a high level of participation in the investment process. They must obtain and evaluate information, make trading decisions, and place trades. After some experience, online investors become familiar with the procedure of placing trades. The more familiar a person is with a task, the stronger the feeling of being in control. Lastly, the illusion of knowledge from a high level of information contributes to the illusion of control.

The illusion of control fostered by online brokerage services appears to give investors a false sense of confidence in their investment decisions. As a result, online investors tend to trade more actively, make more emotional and psychologically biased investment decisions, and ultimately experience reduced investment returns.

---

[4] Brad M. Barber and Terrance Odean, "The Internet and the Investor," *Journal of Economic Perspectives,* vol. 15, no. 1 (Winter 2001), pp. 41–54.

Buying on Margin

Margin Accounts

A **margin account** is an investment account that holds securities purchased with a combination of cash and borrowed funds. Brokerages earn a portion of their total profit by making such loans. The loan in the margin account is collateralized by stocks or bonds. If the value of these securities drops sufficiently, the owner will be asked to either put up more collateral or sell some of the securities held in the account.

Margin account
Account that holds securities purchased with a combination of cash and borrowed funds.

Minimum initial equity (called *initial margin*) for stock purchases in the United States is 50 percent of the total amount invested. This means that an investor can buy up to $10,000 worth of stock with only $5,000 of investment capital. The percentage amount of equity of a position is calculated by

$$\text{Percent equity} = \frac{\text{equity}}{\text{stock value}} = \frac{\text{stock value} - \text{margin debt}}{\text{stock value}} \qquad (3.1)$$

where the equity percentage is simply the market value of equities held in the account minus the amount of **margin debt** borrowed, all expressed as a percentage of the market value of equities held in the account. Note that investors who do not borrow money to invest will have an equity percentage of 100 percent. This means 100 percent of the value of a stock position is owned free and clear by the investor.

Margin debt
Amount borrowed to buy or maintain a security investment.

When a stock's value declines, the investor remains obligated to pay back the margin debt. Therefore, it is the equity portion of the stock position that declines with the stock's price. The broker will allow the equity of the position to decline only so far before demanding that the investor pay back some of the loan or sell the stock position. The Federal Reserve Board sets a minimum maintenance margin for common stocks of 25 percent equity, but most brokers have 30 percent minimum equity requirements. Consider the previously purchased stock position of $10,000. In that case, the stock was purchased with $5,000 equity and $5,000 margin debt. How far can the stock position decline before the account equity falls to 30 percent?

Solve for stock value in the margin equation:

$$0.30 = \frac{\text{stock value} - \$5,000}{\text{stock value}}$$
$$\text{Stock value} = \$7,143 \qquad (3.2)$$

This shows that the $10,000 stock position can decline 28.6 percent, to $7,143. At that point, the percentage equity in the account will be the typical brokerage minimum of 30 percent.

While the Federal Reserve Board federally regulates margin rules, margin requirements may vary above legal minimums for the customers of individual brokers and dealers. Many brokers require higher initial and maintenance margins for highly concentrated accounts that hold fewer than three securities and for accounts that hold especially volatile securities (e.g., tech stocks). Securities that exhibit lower price volatility, such as Treasury bonds, may have lower minimum initial and maintenance margin requirements. By using significant leverage, bond investors can transform these typically low-risk securities into very high-risk investments.

In Wall Street terminology, a **margin call** is a formal notification by one's broker, usually by telephone, demanding additional collateral because of adverse price movements. In the example discussed earlier, when the $10,000 stock value falls to $7,143, the investor's margin, or equity, falls to 30 percent. A phone call from the investor's broker will typically result, and the investor will be asked to increase the account's equity back to 50 percent within three business days or sell at least some of the stock position and pay down a portion of the margin debt. In this example, how much additional cash is required to bring the position back to a 50 percent margin? Again, use the percent equity equation:

Margin call
Broker's demand for additional collateral when the equity has declined below the maintenance margin level.

$$0.50 = \frac{\$7,143 - \text{new debt}}{\$7,143}$$
$$\text{New debt} = \$3,571.50 \qquad (3.3)$$

Broker call rate

Interest rate charged to investors using margin debt.

Since the new margin debt must be $3,571.50 and the current debt is $5,000, the investor must pay down the loan by $1,428.50 (= $5,000 – $3,571.50).

For lenders, margin debt represents a very low-risk loan. The **broker call rate**, or broker loan rate, is the interest rate that brokerage houses charge to finance margin loans to investors. It is one of the least expensive interest rates available to borrowers.

Margin Call Risk

Although margin accounts are a low-risk proposition for lenders, they entail substantial risks for margin account customers. Buying stocks with borrowed funds, called *buying on margin*, is risky for investors because they implicitly agree to sell in the event of a sharp downturn in

TABLE 3.2	**Leverage Increases Potential Gains and Losses** *An investment purchase using 50 percent initial margin will double with a 50 percent rise in price or get wiped out following a 50 percent fall in price. Such margin purchases trigger a margin call after a 28.6 percent price decline. A short sale using 50 percent initial margin will double with a 50 percent fall in price or get wiped out following a 50 percent rise in price. Such short sales trigger a margin call after only a 15.3 percent rise in price.*

Stock Price	Investor Equity	Required Equity with 30% Maintenance Margin	Excess Equity (deficiency)
Panel A: Buying on Margin.			
Investment results with an initial *purchase* of 1,000 shares at $10 using 50% initial margin			
$ 5	$ 0	$ 1,500	($1,500)
6	1,000	1,800	(800)
7	2,000	2,100	(100)
8	3,000	2,400	600
9	4,000	2,700	1,300
10	5,000	3,000	2,000
11	6,000	3,300	2,700
12	7,000	3,600	3,400
13	8,000	3,900	4,100
14	9,000	4,200	4,800
15	10,000	4,500	5,500
Panel B: Selling Short on Margin			
Investment results with an initial *short sale* of 1,000 shares at $10 using 50% initial margin			
$ 5	$10,000	$ 1,500	$ 8,500
6	9,000	1,800	7,200
7	8,000	2,100	5,900
8	7,000	2,400	4,600
9	6,000	2,700	3,300
10	5,000	3,000	2,000
11	4,000	3,300	700
12	3,000	3,600	(600)
13	2,000	3,900	(1,900)
14	1,000	4,200	(3,200)
15	0	4,500	(4,500)

the value of their portfolios. Temporary market downturns do no lasting damage to the stock portfolios of patient buy-and-hold investors. However, even a temporary market downturn can cause a margin call and force the liquidation of margin account securities at ruinously low prices. The use of margin account debt can greatly amplify the typical risks of stock and bond investors.

Table 3.2 illustrates how the use of margin debt increases the volatility of returns earned on investment. Part A of Table 3.2 shows how the use of 50 percent initial margin debt increases the volatility of returns earned on the purchase of 1,000 shares of stock at $10. Notice that this implies initial investor equity of $5,000 and initial margin debt of $5,000. The investor's equity will double from $5,000 to $10,000 with a 50 percent rise in the stock's price from 10 to 15 but get wiped out by a 50 percent decline in the stock's price from 10 to 5. In this example, the required maintenance margin is 30 percent. Notice that a margin call is triggered at a price between 7 and 8, specifically at $7.14. This means that the investor's broker will demand additional equity if the stock's price falls by 28.6 percent. If the investor is unable or unwilling to quickly provide additional equity, the broker will sell out the investor's position, and the investor will recognize a significant loss. In that event, the investor is unable to "weather the storm" of even a short-term decline in the stock's price. This makes stock purchases using margin debt risky. In making a margin purchase, the investor runs the risk of being forced to sell if the stock falls substantially for even a brief period of time. Even temporary downturns in the stock's price can lead to permanent losses for margin buyers.

The biggest problem with using leverage to buy stocks is simple: Margin calls come at the worst possible time. Brokers always want margin debt repaid at a time that is least convenient for the investor.

Try It!

You wish to purchase 500 shares of a $40-per-share stock using an equity percentage of 60 percent.

   a. How much cash do you need to buy the stock?
   b. How much do you need to borrow?
   c. If the maintenance margin is 25 percent, at what stock price would you receive a margin call?
   d. If the stock price rises to $60 per share, what is your return?

Solution

   a. 60 percent of $40 × 500 shares = 0.6 × 40 × 500 = $12,000 in cash
   b. $40 × 500 shares − $12,000 cash = $8,000 borrowed
   c. $0.25 = \dfrac{\text{stock value} - \$8,000}{\text{stock value}}$, solving for stock value = $10,667

   If stock value = $10,667 = P × 500 shares, then P = $21.33 per share would cause a margin call.
   d. Profit = ($60 − $40) × 500 shares = $10,000

   $$\text{Return} = \frac{\text{profit}}{\text{original equity}} = \frac{10,000}{12,000} = 83.33\%$$

Note: Implementing this strategy requires paying interest on the $8,000 borrowed. The interest rate and the time the money is borrowed are factors in the amount of interest owed.

Street Smarts 3.2

Margin Debt Fuels Speculation

Humorist Will Rogers used to joke that making money in the stock market was easy. "Buy a stock and sell it when it goes up. If it doesn't go up, don't buy it." Such circular logic makes for good humor but is tough to implement in practice. Even stock market billionaire Warren Buffett has argued that it's *easy* to figure out what will happen in the stock market but it is *impossible* to tell when. Successful margin account speculators need to know which stocks are going up, when they are going to rise, and how to avoid any sharp declines. Warren Buffett is not smart enough to do that, and few margin account speculators are either.

It is often relatively easy to cross a slow-moving river that is no more than 2 feet deep. On the other hand, variable currents and deep holes can make crossing treacherous for rivers that have an average depth of 2 feet. Buying stocks on margin is a bit like trying to cross a river that is, *on average*, no more than 2 feet deep. The impossibility of flawless market timing is what makes buying stocks on margin dangerous. If a long-term investor buys an attractively priced equity and it immediately plummets, the long-term investor can hold on and wait for better prices. Margin account speculators have no such luxury.

If a trader buys an equity security using 50 percent margin and it plummets 30 percent, the trader's equity falls below the minimum maintenance margin requirement. If the trader is unwilling or unable to quickly add funds, the brokerage firm will sell sufficient shares to restore the required minimum amount of investor capital, called *maintenance margin*. In a sharply correcting market, margin account customers can lose a bundle within a matter of days. In extreme circumstances, margin account customers hear their broker's margin call only after the broker has begun liquidating shares. Buying high and selling low is a prescription for disaster.

When it comes to margin buying, extreme caution is in order. For the overall market, a big increase in margin debt is a good sign of frothy short-term speculation.

See: Gaston F. Ceron, "Use of Margin Debt Rose in 3rd Quarter amid Rising Market," *The Wall Street Journal Online*, October 3, 2005 (**http://online.wsj.com**).

Other Problems with Leverage

Table 3.2 makes clear that margin buyers face exaggerated losses from even mild downturns in stock prices. It turns out that this is only the most obvious of many problems faced by investors who use leverage. The use of margin debt can also tempt investors to sell too soon following even a modest price increase. Because margin debt amplifies the investor's profit from an appreciating stock price, large changes in the value of a margin account can occur on a daily basis. This can tempt margin buyers to prematurely sell stocks bought at a bargain purchase price. Use of margin debt greatly increases the volatility of an investor's holdings and results in excessive trading activity and unreasonable transactions costs.

The ability to borrow can also cause margin account customers to buy too much of an individual security or otherwise neglect the importance of prudent diversification. This is illustrated by the behavior of investors in the late 1990s. As shown in Figure 3.2, the use of margin debt skyrocketed as the technology bubble expanded. As the bubble deflated, investors were forced to liquidate their stock positions to cover margin calls. In 2001 and 2002, margin debt returned to lower levels. Then, margin debt began rising again in the fall of 2003. Regulators were concerned about how such debt could magnify a second downturn if speculators were forced to sell again in a declining market. Exacerbating such risks is the fact that use of margin debt is highest among day traders and others who like fast-moving tech stocks. In considering the advantages and disadvantages of margin accounts, investors should consider the fact that none of the most successful stock investors of our time use leverage. Famously successful investors like Warren Buffett, Peter Lynch, and John Templeton do not advocate the use of financial leverage when buying stocks.

Selling Short

How to Profit from Falling Prices

Sometimes, investors identify a company with poor and deteriorating fundamentals. The stocks of such companies are obvious candidates for a sell decision, providing the stock is held in the investor's portfolio. In some cases, an investor does not presently own a com-

FIGURE 3.2   Use of Margin Debt at NYSE Member Firms

Source: NYSE Group, **www.nyse.com**.

pany with poor and deteriorating fundamentals but would still like to profit from the expected decline in the company's stock price. A **short sale** is one way to profit from the decline in a company's stock price. Normally, investors try to buy low and sell high. Selling short is trying to accomplish this strategy in the opposite order—sell high and buy back at a lower price. A short sale is the sale of borrowed stock. The borrower hopes to repurchase identical shares to return to the lender, or **cover the short**, at a lower price, thus making a profit. The brokerage firm is the lender in the short sale. The broker profits from client short selling through the net interest income derived from security borrowing and lending and from the brokerage commissions generated. If you borrow stock to sell short and the company pays a dividend, the short seller owes the dividend to the brokerage. Therefore, there is a holding cost for short positions that can be substantial in the case of high-dividend-paying stocks.

Although the purchase of stock on margin is risky, the short sale of stock is an inherently riskier proposition. If a stock is bought, the potential loss is limited to the amount invested. The potential gain from a stock purchase is unlimited. With a short sale, the potential gain is limited to the amount of proceeds obtained when the borrowed stock is sold short. If such a company went bankrupt, and its stock price went to zero, all sale proceeds could be kept by the short seller. Although the potential gain from a short-sale transaction is limited, the potential loss is unlimited. Short sellers lose enormous amounts of money when they are on the wrong side of an overpriced stock that continues to gallop skyward.

Short interest data are reported by brokers to the SEC on a once-a-month basis. A summary of this information is published in leading financial publications such as *Barron's* and *The Wall Street Journal*. The *Wall Street Journal Interactive Edition* and Yahoo! also show detailed short interest data on the Internet for most large companies. Table 3.3 shows short interest highlights for stocks traded on the NYSE.

Short interest in a particular stock is reported in two different ways. The number of shares sold short is a useful indicator of the level of bearish sentiment on a stock. When short interest is high, the market consensus is negative. The number of shares sold short relative to the average daily trading volume in a stock, called the **short interest ratio**, is another useful indicator of the relative amount of short interest. When either measure of short interest is high, bearish sentiment is significant. Usually, this portends negative future performance for the

Short sale
Sale of borrowed stock used to profit from a falling stock price.

Cover the short
Return borrowed shares.

Short interest
Number of shares sold short.

Short interest ratio
Short interest expressed in terms of an average day's trading volume.

TABLE 3.3	**Short Interest on the NYSE** *Short interest is the number of shares currently sold short. The short ratio is the number of days it would take to cover the short interest if trading continued at the average daily volume.*

Company	Short Interest July 2006	Short Interest June 2006	Average Daily Volume	Short Ratio
10 Largest Short Positions				
Lucent Technologies	117,000,000	109,900,000	55,714,000	2.1
Ford Motor Co.	108,900,000	124,100,000	25,929,000	4.2
AT&T Inc.	106,000,000	120,100,000	16,308,000	6.5
General Motors	76,900,000	67,500,000	10,253,000	7.5
Home Depot Inc.	65,800,000	32,000,000	27,417,000	2.4
Time Warner Inc.	57,300,000	47,000,000	27,286,000	2.1
Sprint Nxtel CP	55,700,000	60,500,000	21,423,000	2.6
Qwest Comm. Intl. I.	55,500,000	69,100,000	13,537,000	4.1
Pfizer Inc.	54,500,000	44,500,000	38,929,000	1.4
Hewlett Packard C.	50,200,000	51,100,000	12,550,000	4.0
10 Largest Increases in Shares Short				
Home Depot Inc.	65,800,000	32,000,000	27,417,000	2.4
Citigroup Inc.	36,900,000	25,100,000	21,706,000	1.7
Time Warner Inc.	57,300,000	47,000,000	27,286,000	2.1
Pfizer Inc.	54,500,000	44,500,000	38,929,000	1.4
General Motors	76,900,000	67,500,000	10,253,000	7.5
Bristol Myers SQI	47,900,000	40,600,000	17,107,000	2.8
Lucent Tech Inc.	117,000,000	109,900,000	55,714,000	2.1
Mittal Steel Co. N.	25,900,000	18,900,000	4,796,000	5.4
US Bancorp	25,500,000	19,300,000	7,727,000	3.3
Coca Cola Co The	13,800,000	9,000,000	9,200,000	1.5
10 Largest Short Interest Ratios				
Pre Paid Legal SV	5,400,000	5,300,000	53,000	101.2
T R C COS Inc.	1,100,000	1,100,000	1,800	62.5
Primedia Inc.	12,700,000	13,600,000	279,000	45.5
Amer. Ital. Pasta	7,300,000	7,400,000	171,000	42.6
Domtar Ltd.	6,900,000	5,900,000	164,000	42.2
Coachmen Ind. Inc.	1,800,000	1,700,000	4,600	38.9
Telkom Sa. Ltd. Ads.	120,000	130,000	3,500	36.5
Tim Hortons Inc.	12,300,000	14,300,000	339,000	36.3
Comptom Petroleum	2,500,000	2,700,000	69,000	36.3
Superior Ind. Intl.	11,000,000	10,300,000	307,000	35.8

Source: NYSE Group, **www.nyse.com**.

Short squeeze

Pressure on short sellers through margin calls caused by rapidly appreciating stock prices.

company and its stock price. At times, however, aggressive speculators regard the amount of short interest as latent buying interest because short sellers may be forced to buy the stock and cover their shorts in the event of a sharp upward spike in the stock price. Short covering can add dramatically to price volatility. When a volatile stock is pushed sharply higher by momentum players, the effect of frantic short covering can resemble throwing kerosene on a raging fire. If momentum investors jump into an appreciating stock, a **short squeeze** can result as buyers "squeeze" short sellers to cover their short positions at truly wild prices. Making matters worse for short sellers is the fact that widely published short interest data identify prime short-squeeze candidates. A successful short seller must master both the economics and the psychology of the situation.

To protect the stock market from short sellers pressuring the market with sell orders, the SEC limits when a short sale can be executed. Historically, the SEC required that the price of a stock had to trade up before a short sale could execute. This uptick rule required that the last stock price change was up. Table 3.1 shows the last four ticks for IBM and Dell. For IBM, the last two ticks were down and then neutral. A short sale had to wait. However, the decimalization of stock prices has caused prices to quickly change by 1 cent intervals, thus making difficult the detection of upticks and downticks. As a result, the SEC has enacted a new **bid test** rule. The bid test allows short sales to execute if the bid price is higher than the previous bid.

Bid test
SEC criterion that allows a short sale to occur if the current bid price is higher than the previous bid price.

Margin Call Risk for Short Sellers

Selling short is even more risky than purchasing a stock on margin because a rise in stock price both cuts the short seller's equity *and* increases the short seller's margin requirement. Consider the case where an investor sells short 1,000 shares of a stock at $10 per share. The sale nets $10,000 in proceeds, which is held by the broker. To enter this position, the investor must put some cash at risk as well. The investor can deposit cash of between 50 and 100 percent of the $10,000 position. Using a 50 percent initial margin, the investor would need $5,000 to establish the $10,000 short position. The broker would then hold the $10,000 proceeds of the sale and the $5,000 cash deposit. The equity percentage for a short seller is given by the expression

$$\text{Percentage equity} = \frac{\text{equity}}{\text{current stock value}} = \frac{\text{stock value when sold} + \text{cash} - \text{current stock value}}{\text{current stock value}}$$

(3.4)

If the price of the stock declines to $7 per share, then the equity of the position becomes $8,000 [= $10,000 + $5,000 − ($7 × 1,000)], for a profit of $3,000. This decline in the stock price increases the equity percentage to 1.14 (= $8,000/$7,000), or 114 percent. Part B of Table 3.3 shows the equity in the position for various stock price levels. Note that an increase in price to $15 per share completely wipes out the investor's equity.

Short sales with a 50 percent initial margin trigger a 30 percent maintenance margin call following only a 15.4 percent rise in price. To see this is the case, remember that margin debt for a short seller consists of two parts, initial margin debt plus any debt incurred from a *rising* stock price. Consider Equation 3.4 and the preceding example.

$$0.30 = \frac{\$10,000 + \$5,000 - 1,000 \times P}{1,000 \times P}$$

(3.5)

Solving for the price in Equation 3.5 yields $P = \$11.54$. Note that this represents a 15.4 percent increase over the original stock price of $10. A stock price increase of only 15.4 percent triggers a margin call. The investor will have to either add more cash to the margin account or buy back the shares and close the short position at a loss.

Compare the use of margin in buying versus selling short. In the case of a stock purchase with 50 percent margin debt, a typical 30 percent margin call occurs only when the stock price has fallen by at least 28.6 percent. In the case of a short-sale transaction with 50 percent margin debt, a similar margin call occurs when the stock price has risen by only 15.4 percent. Following adverse price moves, margin calls occur about twice as fast for short sellers as they do for stock buyers. The reason for this difference is simple: When a stock price falls, the margin buyer's equity and required margin both fall. When a stock price rises, the short seller's equity falls while the amount of required margin rises. This "squeezes" the short seller.

Try It!

You wish to sell short 500 shares of a $40-per-share stock using an initial equity percentage of 60 percent.

    a. How much cash do you need?

    b. If the maintenance margin is 25 percent, at what stock price would you receive a margin call?

    c. If the stock price falls to $20 per share, what is your return?

Solution

    a. 60% of $40 × 500 shares = 0.6 × 40 × 500 = $12,000 in cash

    b. $0.25 = \dfrac{\$20,000 + \$12,000 - 500 \times P}{500 \times P}$, solving for $P = \$51.20$

If the price rises to $51.20 per share, then margin would be at 25 percent.

    c. Profit = ($40 − $20) × 500 shares = $10,000

$$\text{Return} = \frac{\text{profit}}{\text{orriginal equity}} = \frac{10,000}{12,000} = 83.33\%$$

Simple Investment Strategies

Dollar-Cost Averaging

Every investor would love to have enough information to follow humorist Will Rogers' tongue-in-cheek advice: "Buy a stock. When it goes up, sell it. If it doesn't go up, don't buy it!" Of course, no investor knows for certain if an individual stock purchase will prove profitable. If the company is in a good business and the stock is held for a sufficiently long period of time, then chances are that a profit will be made following a purchase decision. However, there are no guarantees offered on Wall Street.

In a similar vein, one of the most famous maxims on Wall Street is to "buy low and sell high." That simple investment advice is as old as the market. Once again, however, such advice is much easier to give than to carry out. Over brief periods of time, financial markets are inherently unpredictable. It is not possible to consistently choose the best time to buy or sell. In addition, negative investor psychology inhibits many people from buying when stock prices have declined.

Dollar-cost averaging
Strategy of investing a fixed dollar amount in a security at regular intervals.

Fortunately, there is a simple mechanical means that allows investors to benefit from market volatility. This method is called **dollar-cost averaging**. Dollar-cost averaging is a simple investment strategy of investing a fixed amount in a particular security at regular intervals. Because the amount invested remains constant, the investor buys more shares when prices are low and fewer shares when prices are high. As a result, the average dollar amount paid, or the average cost per share, is always lower than the average price per share.

Table 3.4 offers a simple illustration of the dollar-cost-averaging concept. The example depicts a simple strategy of investing $400 per month, or $4,800 per year. Three different market environments are shown. A rising market is illustrated, along with a falling market and a directionless, but highly volatile, market. In each case, the average share price is $18. What is different about each market is the amount of volatility.

The example shows that relatively more shares will be purchased at low prices and relatively fewer shares will be bought at high prices. In a rising market, the attractiveness of dollar-cost averaging is evident in that the investor's average purchase price of $11.85 is less than the $18 average share price. Dollar-cost averaging also works to the investor's advantage in a

Anatomy of a Short Squeeze

In a rising market, short sellers become active momentum players. In the late 1990s, Internet and technology stocks such as Amazon.com, Lucent Technologies, and Yahoo! skyrocketed in price. These lofty prices attracted short sellers who thought the stocks were overvalued. However, momentum buyers continued to favor Internet and technology stocks, prices continued to advance, and short sellers became increasingly eager to end their private "nightmare" by "covering their shorts." As Internet stock prices skyrocketed, short sellers got killed. Short-squeeze episodes tend to end badly for buyers, too, because artificially high stock prices eventually collapse when demand from short covering is exhausted. This occurred during the 2000–2002 period.

Figure 3.3 illustrates how the stock-split-adjusted price of Amazon.com skyrocketed from $5 per share to nearly $90 per share in only 15 months. Along the way up, many short sellers believed the stock to be severely overvalued. Ultimately, they were correct. But if they sold short before the year 2000, they likely lost money. Successful short sellers must not only foretell a price collapse; they must pinpoint its timing. That's tough.

See: Peter A. McKay, "Short Interest Hits a Record as Stocks Rise," *The Wall Street Journal Online*, November 22, 2005 (**http://online.wsj.com**).

FIGURE 3.3 — Split-Adjusted Stock Price for Amazon.com from 1998 through 2002

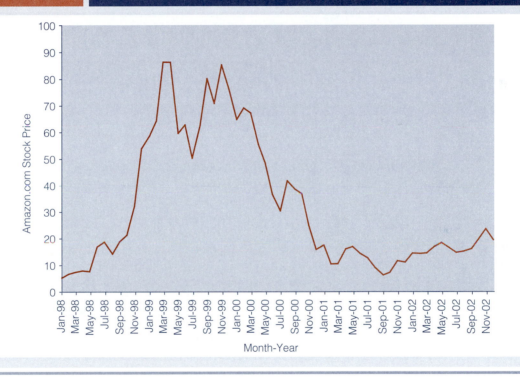

---

falling market. In this falling-market example, the investor's average cost is only $10.67 versus the average price of $18 per share. Keep in mind that the relative advantage enjoyed through dollar-cost averaging has nothing to do with the direction of change in the market. The benefit gained through dollar-cost averaging is in direct proportion to the amount of price volatility. The more volatile are prices, the greater the benefit that will be gained through dollar-cost averaging. In this example, the falling market is slightly more volatile than the rising market. If prices were completely stable, there would be no benefit at all gained through dollar-cost averaging.

To see the impact of price volatility on the advantage gained through dollar-cost averaging, look at the volatile-market illustration in Table 3.4. When share prices are most volatile, the investor is able to purchase 480 shares at an average price of only $10. When it comes to dollar-cost averaging, the more volatile the market, the better. It doesn't matter whether stock

TABLE 3.4	An Illustration of Dollar-Cost Averaging *When a fixed dollar amount is invested at regular intervals, the investor buys more shares when prices are low but fewer shares when prices are high. As a result, the average cost per share is always lower than the average price per share.*

	Monthly Investment	A Rising Market		A Failing Market		A Volatile Market	
		Share Price	Shares Purchased	Share Price	Shares Purchased	Share Price	Shares Purchased
	$400	4.00	100	$50.00	8	$40.00	10
	400	8.00	50	25.00	16	25.00	16
	400	8.00	50	25.00	16	16.00	25
	400	10.00	40	20.00	20	10.00	40
	400	12.50	32	20.00	20	8.00	50
	400	12.50	32	20.00	20	4.00	100
	400	16.00	25	16.00	25	4.00	100
	400	20.00	20	16.00	25	8.00	50
	400	20.00	20	10.00	40	10.00	40
	400	25.00	16	5.00	80	16.00	25
	400	40.00	10	5.00	80	25.00	16
	400	40.00	10	4.00	100	50.00	8
Total	$4,800	$216.00	405	$216.00	450	$216.00	480
Average Price		$18.00	$11.85	$18.00	$10.67	$18.00	$10.00
High Price		$40.00		$50.00		$50.00	
Low Price		$4.00		$4.00		$4.00	
Volatility (standard deviation)		$11.36		$12.04		$13.95	

prices are going up or down. Dollar-cost averaging will result in the greatest discount from the average share price in the most volatile market environments.

The example illustrated in Table 3.4 shows that dollar-cost averaging is an appropriate means for investing a stream of money over time. However, dollar-cost averaging does not guarantee an investment profit. The average cost of shares purchased by regular investors will always be lower than the average share price, but dollar-cost averaging does not eliminate the risks of investing in financial markets. It does not ensure a profit or protect against loss in declining markets. Neither will dollar-cost averaging prevent a loss if it is discontinued when the value of an account is less than its cost. On both economic and psychological grounds, it is often difficult to continue making periodic investment payments when stock prices are going down. The success of dollar-cost averaging depends on the investor's economic and psychological capacity for making regular purchases irrespective of market conditions.

It is also worth pointing out that there is no guarantee that dollar-cost averaging will always be the most efficient means for investing a given amount. Share prices tend to rise over time with growth in aggregate economic activity. As a result, it may be best to invest large lump-sum amounts as early as possible and thereby take advantage of long-term compound interest, rather than wait and engage in a program of dollar-cost averaging over time. Investors sometimes benefit if all their money is invested in one lump sum at the earliest moment in time. However, even in the case of investing a lump sum, dollar-cost averaging can reduce the risk of buying at the worst absolute time. Think of dollar-cost averaging as a "steady-as-you-go" investment strategy. Instead of trying to choose the right time to invest, dollar-cost averaging helps the investor reduce risk and build a significant investment portfolio over time.

Dollar-Cost Averaging for Retirement

Dollar-cost averaging is a good method for investing in company-sponsored defined-contribution retirement plans, such as 401(k) plans. Defined-contribution plans are the most common pension plans offered by employers. Under a defined-contribution pension plan, the employer is responsible for making specified contributions into the plan on behalf of qualifying participants. Sometimes, employer contributions are used to match additional voluntary contributions made by employees. Most often, the employee simply directs the employer to deduct a specific amount from each paycheck on a weekly or monthly basis. At the time of retirement, the amount of retirement income generated by a defined-contribution plan depends solely on the amount of income that can be generated from investments made possible by employer and employee contributions.

Dollar-cost averaging makes a defined-contribution retirement plan an effective tool for building significant retirement assets. In the same way, dollar-cost averaging is an appropriate means for investing in individual retirement accounts (IRAs) or other long-term investments. The longer an investment strategy is maintained, the more likely it is to help the investor cope effectively with market volatility. Individual investors can also enjoy the benefits of dollar-cost averaging by having their financial institution electronically transfer a fixed amount of money to their investment account on a monthly, bimonthly, or quarterly basis. Typically, such services allow investors to choose the date, the frequency, and the amount to be invested on a regular basis.

Buying Initial Public Offerings

Types of Security Offerings

When a corporation needs new capital to expand facilities, build inventories, and so on, it must issue debt or equity securities. Newly issued securities are sold in the **primary market**. All subsequent trading of those securities is done in the **secondary market**. Secondary markets involve the organized trading of outstanding securities on exchanges and over-the-counter markets. The NYSE, Nasdaq, and the bond markets are secondary markets.

Initial public offerings (IPOs) are a corporation's first sale of stock or bonds to the public. IPOs are offered by companies seeking outside equity capital and a public market for their securities. The Google, Inc., IPO in 2004, was one of the largest and most talked-about offerings in recent memory. Investors purchasing stock in an IPO must be prepared to accept large risks for the possibility of large gains.

A **seasoned issue** is the issuance of a security for which there is already an existing public market. For example, when IBM sells additional stock or bonds to the general public, such securities are seasoned issues. During 1998–1999, many companies offering IPOs quickly returned to the market to raise additional funds through seasoned offerings. Some of these firms where unable to find buyers for additional seasoned issues during the market downturn of 2000–2002 and were ultimately forced to file for bankruptcy. **Secondary offerings** are the public sale of previously issued securities held by large investors, corporations, or institutional investors. Corporate insiders are a typical source of secondary offerings when they sell large blocks of stock obtained through incentive compensation plans. The fundamental distinction between primary and secondary offerings is that the issuing corporation receives the proceeds of primary offerings but does not receive any sale proceeds in the event of a secondary offering. Many secondary offerings are handled informally by securities firms and are usually offered at a price related to the current market price of the stock.

Federal securities laws require that U.S. companies with more than 500 investors and $10 million in net assets must register with the SEC and file annual reports with audited financial statements. All companies that list their securities on the Nasdaq Stock Market or a

Primary market
Market for new securities sold to investors for the first time to raise capital for the issuer.

Secondary market
Stock exchange where investors trade stocks with each other.

Initial public offering (IPO)
Newly issued common stock in the primary market.

Seasoned issue
Issuance of a security to raise additional capital for which there is already an existing public market.

Secondary offerings
Public sale of previously issued securities held by large investors, corporations, or institutional investors.

major national stock exchange, such as the NYSE, also must file with the SEC. When investment securities are offered for sale to a small group of investors, generally under exemption of SEC and state securities registration requirements, the sale is referred to as a **private placement** or a *private offering*.

Some smaller companies do not have to register their securities or file reports on EDGAR. For example, companies raising less than $5 million in a 12-month period may be exempt from registering the transaction under a rule known as *Regulation A*. Instead, these companies must file an **offering circular** with the SEC containing financial statements and other information. Smaller companies raising less than $1 million do not have to register with the SEC, but they must file a Form D. Form D is a brief notice that includes the names and addresses of owners and stock promoters but little other information.

Underwriting Process

In most instances, corporations seeking additional investment capital hire an **investment bank**, or **underwriter**, to act in the role of advisor and distributor. Investment banking services include underwriting of debt and equity securities; advising on mergers, acquisitions, privatization, and restructuring; and participating in real estate, project finance, and leasing activities. Successful underwriters have a roster of regular customers, such as pension funds, mutual funds, and insurance companies, for new issues. Highly respected investment bankers must be sure to bring only high-quality IPOs to the attention of their regular institutional customers or risk the loss of potentially lucrative future business. At the same time, investment bankers are always on the prowl for more companies with securities to sell and for more institutional customers. As a result, an important part of the IPO process is the **road show** before institutional investors and the general public, in which an issuing company and its investment banker discuss the investment merits of the corporation's securities. This is a useful means of drumming up interest in the offering and determining investors' appetite for the firm's securities under different pricing scenarios. Throughout this process, the issuing corporation and the investment banker come to agreement on several things, including the amount of capital needed by the corporation, type of security to be issued, price of the security to be issued, and amount of compensation (or commission) paid by the firm to the investment banker. Table 3.5 shows a roster of leading investment bankers.

Private placement
Sale to a small group of investors, generally under exemption of SEC and state securities registration requirements.

Offering circular
Document filed with the SEC that describes a private placement.

Investment bank
Financial firm that helps other firms raise capital by selling securities to investors in the primary market.

Underwriter
Investment bank that endorses and sponsors a company's new securities.

Road show
Series of investment banker presentations to promote company securities being sold.

TABLE 3.5	Top Security Underwriters: Underwriting Revenue of Top Investment Banks (First Nine Months, 2005)

	Issue Amount (bilions)	2005 Market Share	2004 Market Share
J. P. Morgan	$3.09	7.1%	6.9%
Citigroup	3.09	7.1	7.4
Goldman Sachs	2.39	5.5	5.7
Deutsche Bank	2.36	5.4	4.9
Credit Suisse F.B.	2.22	5.1	5.4
Morgan Stanley	2.22	5.1	6.0
UBS	2.19	5.0	5.0
Merrill Lynch	2.04	4.7	4.5
Lehman Brothers	1.69	3.9	4.1
Banc of America Sec.	1.66	3.8	4.3
Top 10 total	**$22.93**	**52.7%**	**54.2%**
Industry total	**$43.48**	**100.0%**	**100.0%**

Source: Randall Smith, "Underwriting Fees Rise 4.3% on Resilient Market," *The Wall Street Journal,* October 3, 2005, p. C12. Copyright © 2005, Dow Jones Company. Used with permission.

There are two broad categories of agreements between investment bankers and issuing corporations. With a **firm-commitment underwriting**, the investment banker agrees to purchase the entire issue from the corporation and then reoffer the securities to the general public. Under this type of agreement, the investment banker guarantees to provide a certain sum of money to the corporation. Any risk associated with failing to resell securities to institutional investors and the general public falls entirely on the investment bank. If the investment banker fails in its bid to resell securities issued on a firm commitment, the corporation still receives the agreed-on amount, and the investment banker suffers a loss. In a second type of securities agreement, known as a **best-efforts underwriting**, the investment banker simply agrees to make its best effort at selling the agreed-on amount of debt and equity securities. If the investment banker fails in its bid to sell securities issued under a best-efforts offering at agreed-on prices, the corporation receives only the amount raised minus necessary commissions. When a best-efforts underwriting fails to raise the anticipated amount for debt and equity securities, the investment banker loses out on potential commission income but suffers no necessary capital loss. Best-efforts underwritings are called **all-or-none offerings** when the underwriter not only agrees to do its best to sell an entire issue by a certain date but also agrees that if all securities are not sold by that time, all money will be returned to purchasers and the issue will be canceled.

In a firm-commitment underwriting, the investment banker commits both its reputation and its investment capital to the success of the underwriting. With a best-efforts underwriting, the investment banker commits only its reputation. Therefore, a firm-commitment underwriting entails a greater level of risk for the investment banker. When a large and highly respected corporation, such as Procter & Gamble, seeks to offer debt or equity securities, the underwriting is almost always done on a firm-commitment basis. Investment bankers fight tooth and nail in the attempt to get a slice of such business. The result of such competition is very low commission rates of 1 to 2 percent of the amount of debt sold and 5 percent of the amount of new equity raised. IPOs by lesser-known companies, especially risky start-ups in high-tech or Internet-related businesses, are much more likely to be made on a best-efforts basis and typically entail a commission rate of 7 percent.

Many times, investment banks do not want to take on all the risk of an offering, so they form an **underwriting syndicate**, or group of underwriters who agree to participate in selling the issue. The lead investment bank, or **syndicate manager**, is responsible for determining the offering price, sets the timing of the issue, responds to any deficiency letters by the SEC, modifies selling commissions, and controls advertising and the amount of each **underwriter's allotment**. Finally, the syndicate manager has prime responsibility for the **dealer's agreement**, which specifies how securities dealers who are not part of the syndicate may contract to purchase some of the securities from the issue.

Figure 3.4 shows a **tombstone ad** for an IPO. Essential bits of information included in a tombstone ad consist of the name of the new issue, the number of shares offered, the offering price, and a list of the lead investment bankers and syndicate members. Lead investment bankers are usually identified by their prominent placement at the top of the list of participating firms. Syndicate members are usually arrayed from top to bottom according to the amount of participation in the offering.

Regulatory Requirements

Under the Securities Act of 1933, when a company makes a public offering, it must file a **registration statement** with the SEC. The day the investment bank submits the registration statement with the SEC is known as the **filing date**. Contained in this registration statement is a description of the company's main line of business, biographical material on officers and directors, and the amount of shares held by officers, directors, and other large shareholders owning more than 10 percent of the company (so-called insiders). Complete financial statements must also be submitted, along with information about how proceeds of the offering are going to be used. After the registration statement has been filed, the SEC requires a **cooling-off period** during which the issuing company and the investment banker try to drum up interest in the issue. They do this through a **preliminary prospectus**, which is sometimes referred to as

---

Firm-commitment underwriting
Security offering in which the investment banker underwrites or purchases the entire issue from the corporation and reoffers the securities to the general public.

Best-efforts underwriting
Security offering in which the investment banker simply agrees to make its best effort at selling the agreed-on amount of debt and equity securities.

All-or-none offering
Security offering in which a complete sale is required.

Underwriting syndicate
Group of underwriters who agree to participate in selling an issue.

Syndicate manager
Lead investment bank in a syndicate.

Underwriter's allotment
Investment banker's allocation of the new shares.

Dealer's agreement
Contractual obligation of syndicate members.

Tombstone ad
Advertisement announcing details of an upcoming security offering.

Registration statement
SEC document that describes an offering.

Filing date
Date the investment bank submits a registration statement with the SEC.

Cooling-off period
Period of time during which the SEC is examining the registration materials and the investment bankers are conducting marketing activities.

Preliminary prospectus
Preliminary statement of offering characteristics.

FIGURE 3.4 IPO Tombstone Ad

This announcement is under no circumstances to be construed as an offer to sell or as a solicitation of an offer to buy any of these securities.
The offering is made only by the Prospectus.

New Issue

February 13, 2006

18,000,000 Shares

MORGANS HOTEL GROUP

Common Stock
Initial Public Offering

Price $20 Per Share

The Nasdaq National Market symbol is MHGC

Copies of the Prospectus may be obtained in any State or jurisdiction in which this announcement is circulated from only such of the undersigned or other dealers or brokers as may lawfully offer these securities in such State or jurisdiction.

Morgan Stanley

Merrill Lynch & Co.

Citigroup

Banc of America Securities LLC

Thomas Weisel Partners LLC

Jefferies & Company

JMP Securities

Blaylock & Company, Inc. E*TRADE Securities LLC Susquehanna Financial Group, LLLP

a **red herring** because it has red print across the top and in the margins. Contained in the preliminary prospectus is much of the information from the registration statement. The public offering price and the effective date of the IPO are not contained in the red herring. The public offering price is determined on the effective date after investor interest in the issue has been determined. Securities are offered to institutional investors and the general public on the **effective date**. If the SEC does not approve a given issue, a **deficiency letter** is issued and the effective date is postponed.

During the cooling-off period, the issuing company and its investment banker may not provide any other information to the investment bank's clients beyond that which is contained in the preliminary prospectus. When a given institutional investor or other client of the investment banker expresses an indication of interest, such information is dutifully recorded as a useful indication of potential demand for the issue under a given set of pricing assumptions. Although no firm orders can yet be taken, indications of interest are a critical guide to the investment banker in its final pricing of the issue. Just prior to the effective date, the issuing corporation and its investment banker have a **due-diligence** meeting to ensure that no material changes have taken place between the filing date and the effective date. Once the effective date arrives, a **final prospectus** is issued, the security can be sold, and money is collected.

Morgan Stanley and Credit Suisse First Boston were co-lead underwriters for the Google IPO. Google offered 19.6 million shares at an offer price of $85 per share. In the original filing, Google announced that it intended to issue 25.7 million shares at a price between $108 and $135 per share. In the days before the issue, Google reduced the number of shares issued and the issue price. The first traded price for Google was $100. This represents a one-day return of 17.6 percent for investors who bought the Google IPO in the primary-market offering. It has not closed below $100 since. In fact, the price has skyrocketed. A year later, on September 13, 2005, Google offered another 14.2 million shares at $295 per share in a follow-on seasoned-equity offering. This raised another $4.18 billion in capital for the company.

Underwriters and dealers get paid out of the proceeds of the offering. The public offering price stated on the face of the prospectus is what the general public pays. However, the issuing corporation receives a lower price determined by the agreed-on spread. Any dealer or broker participating in the underwriting is compensated out of the spread, as specified in the underwriting agreement. The managing underwriter typically receives a manager's fee for each share sold. Each member of the underwriting syndicate is also entitled to an underwriting allowance to compensate for expenses and risks incurred. The selling group is also allocated a portion of the spread as a selling concession (or commission). A real-

Red herring
Nickname for the preliminary prospectus.

Effective date
Date securities are offered to institutional investors and the general public.

Deficiency letter
Disapproval notice issued by the SEC.

Due diligence
Required analysis of the security issuer by the underwriter.

Final prospectus
Final statement of offering.

FIGURE 3.5	Monthly Number of IPOs and Average First-Day Return

Source: Jay Ritter's Web site, **http://bear.cba.ufl.edu/ritter/ipodata.htm**. Data provided by Jay Ritter.

lowance is also paid to securities firms that contact members of the syndicate to purchase part of the issue to fill their own customer orders after the effective date. Because these firms have incurred no risk and made little effort in the underwriting, reallowance fees tend to be minimal.

IPO Market

Postissue Performance of IPOs

The line graph in Figure 3.5 gives a useful long-term perspective of IPO issuance. The strength of the late-1990s bull market in equities is forcefully reflected in the market for IPOs. The number of IPOs per month peaked in October 1996 with 106 firms going public, but IPO issuance continued strong until late 2001. As the stock market bubble collapsed, so did the market for IPOs. During several months in 2002 and 2003, no companies went public.

A **hot IPO** is an IPO for which demand is very high. Virtually every Internet IPO in the late 1990s qualified as a hot IPO. How should the underwriter price a hot IPO? IPO pricing poses an interesting dilemma for both issuing corporations and their investment bankers. On the one hand, the investment banker wants to offer securities for the issuing corporation at a high price to fairly compensate the company for giving up a significant ownership stake. On the other hand, the investment banker wants to price the IPO at an attractive level to offer its institutional clients a fair reward for the risk of investing in unseasoned securities. With too high an initial price, the offering fails, and the investment banker risks the loss of both customer goodwill and its own investment capital. With too low an initial price, the issuing corporation suffers a

Hot IPO
IPO with limited shares and high demand.

loss of potentially vital investment capital, investors reap exorbitant trading profits, and, again, the investment banker risks the loss of customer goodwill.

In a delicate balancing of conflicting interests, most IPOs are priced so that initial buyers can expect to see near-term gains that appear substantial on a percentage basis. That is, IPOs are typically underpriced so that they experience an initial first-day (and hopefully longer) positive return. In the United States, the average initial return of IPOs is 15 percent. It is the issuing company's hope that investors will be sufficiently impressed with their favorable experience in buying the company's securities that they will become willing buyers of future seasoned offerings. To mitigate the problem of short-term traders dumping their shares soon after the IPO, many investment bankers closely monitor how long buyers maintain their holdings. Short-term traders who quickly **flip** their shares of a hot IPO seldom have the opportunity to participate in future IPOs.

Flip

An IPO purchase in the primary market quickly followed by a sale on the stock exchange.

Understanding the IPO Market

When considering the postissue performance of IPOs, it is essential to keep in mind that the pricing of all IPOs is made within the context of ongoing business relationships among issuing corporations, investment bankers, institutional investors, and the general public. When one notices the first-day performance of high-demand IPOs, for example, it is easy to conclude that the market for IPOs is hopelessly inefficient. The first-day price increases of some IPOs of 100 percent, 200 percent, and more lead even the novice investor to conclude that huge excess profits await anyone who participates in the IPO market. This simply is not true.

The bar graph in Figure 3.5 shows the average first-day postissuance return of all IPOs during the month. Notice that the average first-day return is positive for every month during the period except one. On average, IPOs are underpriced in the primary market relative to the closing price of the first day of trading. But the averages do not necessarily bear out the risks. Consider the 9 IPOs from November 2005 shown in Table 3.6.

Under Armour, Inc., saw a large one-day return from the $13 issue price to the $31 first trade and the first-day closing price of $25.30. Four weeks later, its stock price was over $27. The other IPOs shown experienced modest gains or losses on the first day. Five of the nine firms experienced a positive return from the offer price several weeks later. Three firms, Actions Semiconductor, Vimicro, and Newkirk, saw their stock prices decline. While the average return is positive, the return of some IPOs is quite poor. This illustrates the high risk involved in purchasing securities issued by young firms going public.

TABLE 3.6	Performance of Some IPOs Issued in November of 2005			
Public Date	Name (Ticker)	Offer Price ($)	First-Day Open/ Close Price ($)	Price as of Dec. 15, 2005 ($)
30-Nov	Actions Semiconductor Co., Ltd. (ACTS)	8.00	7.90/8.00	7.30
22-Nov	Union Drilling, Inc. (UDRL)	14.00	13.61/14.41	14.48
22-Nov	Brookdale Senior Living Inc. (BKD)	19.00	23.10/25.43	28.52
18-Nov	Under Armour, Inc. (UARM)	13.00	31.00/25.30	27.39
18-Nov	Dover Saddlery, Inc. (DOVR)	10.00	10.06/10.25	10.00
15-Nov	Vimicro International Corp. (VIMC)	10.00	10.01/8.36	8.76
9-Nov	Saifun Semiconductors Ltd. (SFUN)	23.50	31.18/35.30	28.62
2-Nov	Newkirk Realty Trust, Inc. (NKT)	16.00	15.05/15.05	15.73
2-Nov	Cbeyond Communications, Inc. (CBEY)	12.00	12.00/12.00	12.07

Source: Hoovers Online, **www.hoovers.com**.

Street Smarts 3.4

IPO: "It's Probably Overpriced"

"There is no such thing as a free lunch" is a popular saying on Main Street; the same maxim applies on Wall Street too. That's worth remembering the next time you hear someone proclaim that participation in the initial public offering (IPO) market is a surefire way to investment success. IPOs represent the first sale of stock to the general public, and they represent something of a "baptism by fire" for new companies. Unfortunately, individual investors are seldom successful when they ask their brokers for shares of hard-to-buy "hot" IPOs. Instead, individual investors typically can get access to only tough-to-sell offerings, called "cold" IPOs. Why is that?

Investment bankers that underwrite initial and secondary stock offerings rely on the steady stream of business generated by big institutional investors. Big buyers mean big commissions on regular offerings of stocks and bonds. Investment bankers have big incentives to keep big institutions happy. It is also much easier to sell 200,000 shares of an IPO to mutual fund giant Fidelity Investments than it is to sell 500 shares each to 400 retail investors. Besides, Fidelity also buys other securities the bankers issue throughout the year. When IPO demand is strong, giant institutional investors get the lion's share. Individual investors get IPO allocations only when demand is tepid.

The bottom line on IPO investing for the small individual investor is simple: On Wall Street, the really good stuff is reserved for the investment banker's very best customers. If demand is robust, and a first-day pop in the IPO price seems likely, such shares are reserved for giant institutions that bring a recurring stream of revenue to the investment banker. If a small investor can get an IPO allotment, that's a strong signal of weak demand from the investment banker's best institutional customers.

The upshot: If an individual investor can get an IPO allocation, he or she probably doesn't want it. There is no such thing as a free lunch on Main Street or on Wall Street.

See: Lynn Cowan, "Suntech Power IPO Jumps 41%," *The Wall Street Journal Online*, December 15, 2005 (**http://online.wsj.com**).

Summary

■ The **bid** is the highest price that an investor is willing to pay. The **ask** is the lowest price that an investor will accept to sell. The **bid-ask spread** is simply the gap between the bid and ask prices. Stocks are assigned **ticker symbols** to facilitate transaction speed and accuracy. **Bid size** is the number of round lots, groups of 100 shares of stock, represented on the buy side of the market. Significant **market depth** exists when a large number of buyers and sellers are active in the market.

■ A **market order** is an instruction to buy or sell at the current market price. In a **limit order**, the customer specifies a price at which to buy or sell. A **stop order** is a market order to buy or sell a certain quantity of a security if a specified price (the stop price) is reached or passed. A position is said to be **stopped out** when the position is liquidated through the execution of a stop order. A **buy stop order** is a buy order that is to be held until the market price rises to a specified stop price, at which point it becomes a market order. A **stop-loss order** is a stop order to sell a long position at a specified price that is below the current market price. A **stop-limit order** is an order to buy or sell a certain quantity of a security at a specified price or better but only after a specified price has been reached. A **day order** is an order to buy or sell during the present trading session. An **open order** stays active until it is executed or canceled by the investor. Another expression for an open order is a **good 'til canceled order**. **All or none** is a stipulation to a buy or sell order that instructs the broker to either fill the entire order or not fill it at all. **Fill-or-kill** orders must be filled immediately or canceled.

■ Investor orders are electronically routed to the stock exchanges for execution. Market orders are executed on the trading floor, and limit orders are listed in the limit-order book. Large orders of at least 10,000 shares are handled outside the normal auction process as **block transactions**.

■ **Dollar-cost averaging** is a simple investment strategy of investing a fixed amount in a particular security at regular intervals.

■ Active stock trading fosters the emotions and psychological biases that influence investment decisions and cause mistakes. The **illusion of knowledge** fools investors into thinking that because they have access to much information, they must be making good decisions. However, it takes good training to convert information to knowledge. Trading online increases the **illusion of control**, which can cause investors to trade more actively and make more mistakes. The illusion of control is the belief that you have influence over the outcome of an uncontrollable event.

■ A **margin account** is an investor account that holds securities purchased with a combination of cash and borrowed funds. **Margin debt** is the amount borrowed to buy or maintain a security investment. A **margin call** is a broker's formal demand for additional collateral because of adverse price movements. The **broker call rate** is the interest rate that banks and brokerage houses charge to finance margin loans to investors.

- A **short sale** is the sale of borrowed stock. The borrower hopes to repurchase identical shares for return to the lender, or **cover the short**, at a lower price, thus making a profit. Notice that the amount of **short interest** in a particular stock is reported in two different ways. The number of shares sold short is presented as a useful overall indicator of the level of bearish sentiment on a stock. When short interest is high, the market consensus is negative. The number of shares sold short relative to the average daily trading volume in a stock, called the **short interest ratio**, is also provided as a useful indicator of the relative amount of short interest. If momentum investors jump into an appreciating stock, a **short squeeze** can result as buyers "squeeze" short sellers to cover their short positions at truly wild prices.

- The first buyer of a newly issued security buys that security in the **primary market**. All subsequent trading of securities is done in the **secondary market**. Primary markets are where new issues, called **initial public offerings (IPOs)**, are sold by corporations to raise new capital. An IPO is a corporation's first sale of stock or bonds to the public. A **seasoned issue** is the issuance of a security for which there is already an existing public market. **Secondary offerings** are the public sale of previously issued securities held by large investors, corporations, or institutional investors. When investments or businesses are offered for sale to a small group of investors, generally under exemption of SEC and state securities registration requirements, the offering is referred to as **private placement**, or a private offering. Such companies must file an **offering circular** with the SEC containing financial statements and other information. Corporations seeking additional investment capital hire an **investment bank**, or **underwriter**, to act in the role of advisor and distributor. An important part of the IPO process is the so-called **road show** for institutional investors and the general public in which the issuing company and its investment banker discuss the investment merits of the corporation's securities.

- With a **firm-commitment** offering, the investment banker agrees to underwrite or purchase the entire issue from the corporation and then reoffer the securities to the general public. In a **best-efforts** underwriting, the investment banker simply agrees to make its best effort at selling the agreed-on amount of debt and equity securities. A best-efforts underwriting is called an **all-or-none offering** when the underwriter agrees not only to do its best to sell an entire issue by a certain date but also agrees that if all securities are not sold by that time, all money will be returned to purchasers and the issue will be canceled.

- An **underwriting syndicate** is a group of underwriters who jointly agree to participate in selling the issue. The lead investment bank, or **syndicate manager**, determines the offering price, sets the timing of the issue, responds to any deficiency letters by the SEC, modifies selling commissions, and controls advertising and the amount of each **underwriter's allotment**. The syndicate manager has prime responsibility for the **dealer's agreement**, which specifies how securities dealers who are not part of the syndicate may contract to purchase some of the securities from the issue. Essential bits of information included in a **tombstone ad** include the name of the new issue, the number of shares offered, the offering price, and a list of the lead investment bankers and syndicate members.

- Under the Securities Act of 1933, when a company makes a public offering, it must file a **registration statement** with the SEC. The day the investment bank submits the registration statement with the SEC is known as the **filing date**. The SEC requires a **cooling-off period** during which the issuing company and the investment banker try to drum up interest in the issue. They do this through a **preliminary prospectus**, which is sometimes referred to as a **red herring** because it has red print across the top and in the margins. Securities are offered to institutional investors and the general public on the **effective date**. If the SEC does not approve a given issue, a **deficiency letter** is issued and the effective date is postponed. Just prior to the effective date, the issuing corporation and its investment banker have a **due-diligence** meeting to ensure that no material changes have taken place between the filing date and the effective date. Once the effective date arrives, a **final prospectus** is issued, the security can be sold, and money is collected.

- The public offering price stated on the face of the prospectus is the amount paid by institutional and individual investors who receive an allotment of the IPO. However, the issuing corporation receives a lower price determined by the agreed-on spread. A **hot IPO** is an IPO in which shares are limited and demand is high. Short-term traders who quickly **flip** their shares of a hot IPO seldom have the opportunity to participate in future offerings.

Self-Test Problems

ST3.1   Suppose an investor went long on JP Morgan Chase (JPM) at $36 using 50 percent margin. At what price would the investor face a 30 percent maintenance margin call?

Solution

$$0.30 = \frac{P_{call} \times shares - 0.5 \times \$36 \times shares}{P_{call} \times shares} = \frac{P_{call} - \$36}{P_{call}}, \text{ solving for } P_{call} = \$25.71$$

If the price falls to $25.71, the investor would get a margin call.

ST3.2   Assume an investor shorted 1,000 shares of JP Morgan Chase at $36 using 50 percent margin. Following a sharp rise in the stock to $43, the investor has received a maintenance margin call. At this point, the investor is required to wire sufficient funds to bring account equity back to 50 percent. How much in additional funds must be added to the account?

Solution

An investor who shorted 1,000 shares of JPM at 36 (worth $36,000) using 50 percent margin had an initial account equity value of $18,000 and initial margin debt of $18,000. Following a sharp rise in the stock to $43, the investor has an unrealized loss of $7 per share on 1,000 shares, or $7,000. This cuts the investor's account equity to $11,000 (= $18,000 - $7,000). At $43, the market value of the investor's short position is $43,000, and account equity must be brought up to $21,500 to achieve 50 percent account equity. Thus, the investor must wire an additional $10,500 (= $21,500 − $11,000) to bring account equity up to the required 50 percent.

Questions and Problems

3.1   Explain the meaning of market depth for a common stock.

3.2   What is the difference between a market order and a limit order? What is the advantage of a limit order?

3.3   How can investors benefit from dollar-cost averaging?

3.4   What is the difference between a primary offering and a secondary offering?

3.5   Detailed quotes for companies listed on major exchanges can be found at **www.freerealtime.com**. What is the bid, the ask, and the bid-ask spread for Sirius Satellite Radio (SIRI)? What is the market depth at these prices?

3.6   Verizon Communications (VZ) has a bid of 36.05, a bid size of 983, an ask of 36.07, and an ask size of 202. How much money is represented on the sell side of the market?

3.7   You place a limit order to buy 500 shares of Lucent Technologies (LU) at $2.51 per share or better. The next transaction prices (in order) are $2.52, $2.52, $2.50, $2.51. At what price do you buy the shares of LU? Why?

3.8   Suppose you have $15,000 to invest and want to buy as much stock in Amazon.com as is possible using margin debt. If your brokerage requires a 50 percent minimum initial margin and has a 35 percent minimum maintenance margin requirement, what percent decrease in Amazon.com's stock price will trigger a margin call? How much equity will you have after a 15 percent decline in Amazon.com's stock price?

3.9   Suppose you want to purchase $20,000 worth of stock trading at $40 per share. The broker allows you to borrow money with no less than 60 percent initial margin.
   a. How much money can you borrow, and how much of your own money must be used?
   b. What is the margin percentage if the stock increases to $50 per share?
   c. If the maintenance margin is 25 percent, at what price would the stock have to be for you to receive a margin call?

3.10   Suppose an investor decides to short-sell Amazon.com and has initial equity of $15,000. If the broker has a 50 percent initial minimum margin requirement and a 35 percent minimum maintenance margin requirement, what percent increase in Amazon.com's stock price will trigger a margin call? How much equity will the investor have after a 15 percent increase in Amazon's stock price? What is the investor's return if Amazon's stock price falls 10 percent?

3.11   You wish to sell short 400 shares of a $30 stock using an initial equity margin of 50 percent.
  a. How much of your money must you set aside to execute the transaction?
  b. If the stock price was to decline to $25, how much equity would you have in the position?
  c. What is your return if you cover the short position when the stock is at $25?

3.12   How does firm-commitment underwriting differ from best-efforts underwriting? Include in your explanation of each underwriting method a description of a firm that would typically use either a firm-commitment or a best-efforts underwriting.

3.13   Describe the illusion of knowledge, and explain how it can negatively impact investment performance.

3.14   In general, do IPOs outperform the market? What are so-called hot IPOs?

3.15   Visit the Hoovers Online Website at **www.hoovers.com**. Click on the IPO Central button. Use the IPO Filings link to identify firms that have recently filed their intentions to conduct an initial public offering. Use the IPO Calendar link to identify firms that recently conducted an IPO. Use the IPO Performance link to identify firms that sold their stock six months ago. Select one firm that recently filed for an IPO, one that recently went public, and one that went public six months ago. Report the company name, industry, managers, underwriters, offer price, and success of the issue (if applicable).

3.16   Go to the Standard & Poor's Market Insight Web site (**www.mhhe.com/edumarketinsight**) and enter the ticker (C) for the Citigroup Corp. Examine the information given in the Financial Hlts link. What was yesterday's closing price? How many Citigroup shares outstanding are there? How many shareholders?

3.17   An investor uses dollar-cost averaging by purchasing $300 worth of shares of the Boeing Company (BA) at the end of each month for two years. Below is the closing price each month. The investor can buy only whole shares of stock, so any cash left over every month should be saved. How many total shares are purchased, and how much profit (in dollars) has the investor made?

Date	Monthly Closing Price	Date	Monthly Closing Price
Mar 05	58.46	Mar 04	41.07
Feb 05	54.97	Feb 04	43.37
Jan 05	50.60	Jan 04	41.75
Dec 04	51.77	Dec 03	42.14
Nov 04	53.57	Nov 03	38.39
Oct 04	49.90	Oct 03	38.49
Sep 04	51.62	Sep 03	34.33
Aug 04	52.22	Aug 03	37.39
Jul 04	50.75	Jul 03	33.12
Jun 04	51.09	Jun 03	34.32
May 04	45.80	May 03	30.67
Apr 04	42.69	Apr 03	27.28

3.18   Which of the following statements about short selling is *true?*
  a. A short position may be hedged by writing call options.
  b. A short position may be hedged by purchasing put options.
  c. Short sellers may be subject to margin calls if the stock price increases.
  d. Stocks that pay large dividends should be sold short before the ex-dividend date and bought afterward to take advantage of the large price decline in a short time period.

3.19 When an AIMR member has a limited number of shares of an initial public offering to distribute, the member would *not* violate the AIMR Standards of Professional Conduct by:

a. Allocating the shares pro rata to all subscribers for which the issue is appropriate

b. First filling the orders of individual clients and then filling the orders of institutional clients

c. First filling the orders of clients who have generated the most commissions during the past year

d. First filling the orders of those who have been clients of the investment professional for the longest period of time

3.20 According to the AIMR *Standards of Practice Handbook,* which of the following statements about a member's use of clients' brokerage commission is *false?* Client brokerage commissions:

a. May be directed to pay for the investment manager's operating expenses

b. Should be used by the member to ensure that fairness to the client is maintained

c. Should be commensurate with the value of the brokerage and research services received

d. May be used by the member to pay for securities research used in managing the client's portfolio

invesTmenT aPPLiCaTiOn

Are Investors *Foolish*?

One of the most popular and interesting financial Web sites is *The Motley Fool*, run by brothers David and Tom Gardner. In July 1993, David Gardner, Tom Gardner, and Erik Rydholm launched *The Motley Fool* as an investment newsletter designed to "educate, enlighten and entertain investors." *The Motley Fool* name comes from Shakespeare's *As You Like It*. According to David Gardner, fools were the happy fellows paid to entertain the king and queen with self-effacing humor that instructed as it amused. In fact, fools were really the only members of their societies who could tell the truth to the king or queen without having their heads lopped off. After all, as David and Tom Gardner write, "The Wise would have you believe that 'A Fool and his money are soon parted.' But in a world where three quarters of all *professional* money managers lose to the market averages, year in and year out, how Wise should one aspire to be?"[5]

The newsletter version of *The Motley Fool* was a commercial failure. After attracting only 38 subscribers during its first month of operation, the Gardners made the momentous decision to take their "conversation" about stocks to cyberspace. *The Motley Fool* originally appeared on America Online on August 4, 1994. The Gardners are very enthusiastic and fun-loving entrepreneurs. Investors appreciated their anti-Wall Street attitude. Instead of the typical business suit seen on financial analysts, the Gardners would be interviewed on CNBC wearing brightly colored court jester hats. Their approach was refreshing. *The Motley Fool* Web site quickly became one of the most popular financial Web sites (**www.fool.com**).

It has been interesting watching the investment maturity of the Gardners and *The Motley Fool* grow over time. In the beginning, the young Gardners extolled the virtues of ignoring conventional investment wisdom on the premise that even novice individual investors know more than Wall Street professionals. They advocated following several naïve investment strategies, like the Rule Breaker portfolio introduced in 1994. Other portfolios included the Rule Maker, Drip, Boring, Retiree, and so on. Each portfolio strategy was purported to beat the market. None did. One by one, each portfolio was discontinued. By February 2003, all portfolios had been closed. Apparently beating the market is not as easy as they thought. With investment experience comes wisdom!

---

[5] See David Gardner and Tom Gardner, *The Motley Fool Investment Guide: How the Fool Beats Wall Street's Wise Men and How You Can Too* (Simon & Schuster, New York, 1996), p. 14.

The Gardners' most public lesson occurred with their Foolish Four strategy. In 1996, they wrote the book *The Motley Fool Investment Guide: How the Fools Beat Wall Street's Wise Men and How You Can Too*.[6] The Gardners reported an investment strategy that they claimed had an average annual return of 25.5 percent compared with 11.2 percent return on the Dow Jones Industrial Average during the same period. The Foolish Four strategy is derived from an investment strategy identified as the Dogs of the Dow in a 1991 book, *Beating the Dow*.[7] Michael O'Higgins and John Downes proposed buying stocks in the 10 companies found within the Dow Jones Industrial Average that had the highest dividend yield. The Dogs of the Dow portfolio was constructed by buying equal amounts of the 10 top dividend-yielding stocks in the DJIA on the first trading day of the year and then simply rebalancing the portfolio at year-end. Among the 10 top dividend-yielding DJIA stocks, the Gardners identified the five stocks with the lowest share prices, threw out the stock with the lowest share price, and doubled up on the stock with the second-lowest share price. Their Foolish Four strategy was to put 40 percent of the portfolio in the stock with the second-lowest price and 20 percent in each of the other three low-price Dow Dogs. Believe it or not, this convoluted Foolish Four stock picking was the focus of their best-selling investment guide.

At first, such a strategy might appear to have some validity as a contrarian approach or value investing strategy. However, the premise that such a simple analysis of publicly available information can lead to market-beating results is flawed. The market is not that inefficient. At the end of 2000, the Gardners discontinued their Foolish Four strategy because the strategy failed to produce consistent profits.

The Motley Fool is no longer a strong advocate of simply following historical price patterns. Most of the articles on the Web site and in the Gardners' syndicated newspaper columns have turned to more effective, but mundane, topics like diversification. The Gardners have learned a lot about investing. So have the investors who followed their money-losing advice.

a. Searching for patterns in historical return data is called *data mining*. How does one know the difference between a random pattern and a pattern that has the potential to make money?

b. How easy is it for investors to consistently beat the market? Why?

c. Why do you think investing on the basis of historical return patterns appeals to some investors?

---

[6] David Gardner and Tom Gardner, *The Motley Fool Investment Guide: How the Fool Beats Wall Street's Wise Men and How You Can Too* (Simon & Schuster, New York, 1996).

[7] Michael O'Higgins and John Downes, 1991, *Beating the Dow: A High-Return, Low-Risk Method for Investing in the Dow-Jones Industrial Stocks with as Little as $5,000* (HarperCollins, 1991).

Risk and Return

Conventional wisdom tells us that in order to have the opportunity to earn a high expected rate of return investors must be prepared to assume significant return volatility (or risk). If only very low-risk investments are made, only modest returns can be projected. Because the risks of various investments are usually gauged on the basis of historical experience, high expected returns are typically achieved only by making unconventional investments that can involve taking on high risks. However, when investors take on significant risk, they often experience heavy losses. According to an old adage, "If you keep betting the farm, eventually you lose the farm."

At least once every few months, *The Wall Street Journal* or *Barron's* runs a cover story describing how smart, talented, and sophisticated investors lost a substantial fortune because they forgot the simple fact that anticipated risk and expected return are related. Consider the Eifuku Master Fund, a $300 million hedge fund in Japan run by a former Lehman Brothers Tokyo-based trader. Established in 2000, the Eifuku fund rose 18 percent in 2001 and then rocketed 76 percent in 2002. These returns were from huge bets with borrowed money on a few positions. Such high returns suggest that big risks were being taken. In early 2003, Eifuku made massive wagers on three trades. Almost immediately the market started moving against the hedge fund's positions. Lenders demanded quick repayment of their loans, but low liquidity in the Japanese stock market prevented the fund from unwinding its positions in a timely manner. Eifuku experienced enormous losses. While hedge-fund losses are not unusual, the speed of Eifuku's demise was striking. In only seven days, Eifuku lost all of its capital.[1]

Why do intelligent professionals get caught in traps like this? Like small investors, they want to believe that astronomical risk-free returns are possible. Indeed, they view the achievement of high returns as a validation of their own ability. Be conscious of the fact that the consequence of risk-taking behavior has a tendency to reveal itself in dramatic and devastating ways.

---

[1] See Nikkei Net Interactive, "When Wall Street Sneezes, Tokyo Catches a Cold," *The Wall Street Journal Online*, November 4, 2005 (**http://online.wsj.com**).

CHAPTER OBJECTIVES

- Know the risk and return characteristics of different asset classes.
- Compute the impact of taxes on investment returns.
- Be able to compute the risk and return of a two-asset portfolio.
- Recognize the characteristics of optimal portfolios.
- Learn how gains and losses affect risk perceptions.

Financial Returns

Thinking about Returns

Investors evaluate the attractiveness of potential investments based on the anticipated trade-off between risk and expected return. Usually, the cost of higher expected return is the necessity of having to accept greater risk. In other words, finance theory stipulates that there be a positive relationship between risk and expected return. Required return consists of two main components.

The first component of required return can be thought of as the reward for postponing consumption. Because investors must forgo consumption to invest, they demand a monetary reward for waiting as part of their expected return. The reward for postponing consumption is the **nominal risk-free rate**, which consists of the **real risk-free rate of return** plus an amount equal to the expected rate of **inflation**. A second important component of required return is the **required risk premium**. This amount varies with the amount of risk entailed. High-risk investments involve a higher-risk premium. Low-risk investments involve a lower-risk premium. The expression for required return can be written

$$\text{Required return} = \text{nominal risk-free rate} + \text{required risk premium} \qquad \textbf{(4.1)}$$
$$= \text{real risk-free rate} + \text{expected inflation} + \text{required risk premium}$$

The greater volatility of common stocks implies a higher required return on equities than on either money market instruments or long-term bonds. In thinking about the return required in the future for taking some risk, investors commonly look at past returns. The returns investors see in the past influence the level of returns they expect in the future. Before the investment merit of stocks, bonds, and other asset classes can be determined, it is necessary to clearly and accurately measure investment returns.

Nominal risk-free rate
Monetary reward for postponing consumption (T-bill return).

Real risk-free rate of return
Return without chance of default or volatility.

Inflation
Increase in the cost of goods and services over time.

Required risk premium
Necessary compensation for risk taking.

⋯⋯⋯⋯⋯ Try It! ⋯⋯⋯⋯⋯

The return on T-bills is usually considered a proxy for the nominal risk-free rate. Consider the case where the T-bill is offering a 2.5 percent return and inflation is expected to be 1.8 percent. If the risk premium for the stock market is 5 percent, what is the required return to invest in the stock market?

Solution

Required return = 2.5% + 5% = 7.5%

Any measurement of past return must include both the impact of capital gains (or losses) and income received over a holding period. This **total return** is computed as

$$\text{Total return} = \frac{\text{ending price} - \text{beginning price} + \text{income}}{\text{beginning price}} \quad (4.2)$$

Total return
The sum of dividends, interest income, and capital gains or capital losses.

Equation 4.2 calculates the total return earned by a financial asset. The income input would include dividends from stock ownership and interest payments from bond ownership. For example, Boeing Company (BA) stock ended 2004 at $51.77 per share and rose to 70.24 by the end of 2005. During the year, BA made four quarterly dividend payments of 25 cents per share, for a total annual dividend of $1 per share. The one-year total return for BA investors during 2005 was 37.6 percent [= (70.24 + 1.00 − 51.77) ÷ 51.77]. For BA stockholders 2005 was a very good year. Long-term investors focus on the rate of return earned over multiple years, as is shown next.

Arithmetic Average versus Geometric Mean

Many fundamental mistakes made by investors stem from the common inability to accurately measure investment returns. Investors often wrongly focus on **arithmetic average return** when judging portfolio performance. The arithmetic average return is upward-biased and cannot be used to depict the return on investment over time.

Arithmetic average return
Sum of investment returns divided by number of periods or securities.

To see this, consider the formula for the arithmetic average return:

$$\text{Arithmetic average return} = \frac{\sum_{t=1}^{N} \text{return}_t}{N} \quad (4.3)$$

where Σ indicates summation, t is time (over N time periods), and *return* is the percentage total return during any given period (e.g., +50 percent or −25 percent).

The problem lies in the way investors see simple arithmetic average returns. If a stock appreciates by 100 percent and then falls by 50 percent, the arithmetic average return for two periods is 25 percent per year [= (100% − 50%)/2]. In fact, no net profit is made. If a $10 stock jumps to $20 (up 100 percent) and then falls back to $10 (declines by 50 percent), it has fallen back to its initial price. The actual investment return is 0 percent per year over the two-year holding period.

Accurate measurement of annual investment returns requires calculation of the **geometric mean return**. The geometric mean return is the appropriate measure of the compound rate of return earned on investment over time. The formula for geometric mean is

Geometric mean return
Compound rate of return earned on investment.

$$\text{Geometric mean return} = \left\{ \prod_{t=1}^{N} \left(1 + \frac{\text{return}_t}{100} \right) \right\}^{\frac{1}{N}} - 1 \quad (4.4)$$

where Π indicates the product and all other variables are as before.

If a $10 stock jumps to $20 (up 100 percent) and then falls back to $10 (declines by 50 percent), it has a geometric mean return of 0 percent [= $(2 \times 0.5)^{1/2} - 1$]. This is the same as the 0 percent actual investment return earned over the two-year holding period.

=========== **Try It!** ===========

Consider the following three annual returns: 25 percent, 25 percent, −50 percent. Compute the arithmetic average return and the geometric mean return. Would it matter if the −50 percent loss was first, i.e., does the order of returns matter?

(continued)

Solution

$$\text{Arithmetic average} = (\Sigma\ \text{return}_t)\ /\ N = (25 + 25 - 50)/3$$
$$=\quad 0.0\%$$

$$\text{Geometric mean} = (\textstyle\prod 1 + \text{return}_t)^{1/N} - 1 = (1.25 \times 1.25 \times 0.50)^{1/3} - 1$$
$$=\quad -7.9\%$$

The order of the returns does not matter.

Comparing Returns

Everybody loves a big winner. In investing, a big winner is a stock that absolutely crushes the market averages. Table 4.1 depicts a typical comparison.

During recent years, several aggressive investors have shown real preference for investing in Nasdaq high-tech stocks and emerging growth stocks. Not for the faint of heart, most Nasdaq stocks are appropriate only for investors who seek the significant return potential of high-tech stocks but also understand the high risks of technology stock investing. Literally hundreds of such high-risk/high-reward stock investments are commonly discussed in the print media, on television, and on popular stock message boards on the Internet.

Look at the performance of the Nasdaq Composite Index during a recent 12-year period. In 2005, Nasdaq had a very boring year with a return of 1.4 percent. It was certainly not the enviable return of 2003, +49.3 percent. Any investor would be happy with this type of performance. If you kept it up, you would become very rich indeed. Unfortunately, Nasdaq investors have experienced a real roller-coaster ride. In 1999, Nasdaq soared 89.6 percent, only to collapse −40.9 percent in 2000, another −20.6 percent in 2001, and yet another −31.5 percent in 2002. If you take a simple arithmetic average of Nasdaq annual rates of return over the 12-year 1994–2005 period, Nasdaq investors earned an enviable 14.8 percent per year. Based on arithmetic average returns, Nasdaq appears to have outperformed the DJIA before divi-

---

TABLE 4.1   Risk and Return in the Stock Market

	A	B	C	D	E	F	G	H	I	J	K
1											
2											
3						Blue Chips					
4		Tech Stocks		Blue Chips		With Dividends					
5	Year	(Nasdaq)		(DJIA)		DJIA With Dividends					
6	2005	1.4%	1.014	-0.6%	0.994	1.7%	1.017				
7	2004	8.6%	1.086	3.2%	1.032	5.4%	1.054				
8	2003	49.3%	1.493	25.3%	1.253	27.9%	1.279				
9	2002	-31.5%	0.685	-16.8%	0.832	-14.9%	0.851				
10	2001	-20.6%	0.794	-7.1%	0.929	-5.4%	0.946				
11	2000	-40.9%	0.591	-6.2%	0.938	-4.7%	0.953				
12	1999	89.6%	1.896	24.8%	1.248	27.1%	1.271				
13	1998	40.2%	1.402	16.5%	1.165	18.0%	1.180				
14	1997	21.8%	1.218	22.6%	1.226	24.8%	1.248				
15	1996	22.8%	1.228	26.0%	1.260	28.6%	1.286	←	To compute geometric returns,		
16	1995	40.1%	1.401	33.5%	1.335	36.5%	1.365	←	first add 1 to each return.		
17	1994	-2.9%	0.971	2.1%	1.021	5.0%	1.050				
18											
19	Arithmetic average:	14.8%		10.3%		12.5%					
20	Geometric mean:		9.2%		9.1%		11.3%	←	=GEOMEAN(G6:G17)-1		
21	Total return:	186.0%		185.6%		262.3%					
22	Initial investment:	$ 10,000.00		$ 10,000.00		$ 10,000.00					
23	Terminal value:	$ 28,599.99		$ 28,559.32		$ 36,226.04					
24											
25			=AVERAGE(B6:B17)		=((1+E20)^12)-1		=((1+G20)^12)*10000				

dends (10.3 percent) and with dividends reinvested (12.5 percent). However, looks can be deceiving. While the arithmetic average rate of return for Nasdaq is higher than similar returns for the DJIA, geometric-mean returns give a more accurate measure of how much money you will earn over time.

As shown in Table 4.1, Nasdaq's geometric-mean return is only 9.2 percent per year. Nasdaq's geometric return is similar to the DJIA before dividends (9.1 percent) and measurably lower than the DJIA with dividends reinvested (11.3 percent). The total compounded return over this 12-year holding period ranges from 186.0 percent for Nasdaq to 185.6 percent for the DJIA before dividends to 262.3 percent for the DJIA with dividends reinvested.

The reason why Nasdaq's overall performance is disappointing despite high average returns is simple: Tremendous upside rates of return are necessary to compensate for the harmful effects of portfolio losses. If you lose 50 percent of your portfolio, a 100 percent return is necessary to get back to even. In this case, Nasdaq's stunning performance during bull markets is insufficient to fully overcome the effects of devastating losses during market downturns. By avoiding serious losses, blue-chip investors are able to turn in superior long-term performance.

Like the fable "Tortoise and the Hare," Table 4.1 shows that "slow and steady" wins the investment race. The key to building significant wealth is not necessarily to pick an outstanding performer that will double or triple in one year. Building significant wealth often requires that investors avoid significant financial losses.

Historical Returns

Stocks versus Fixed-Income Securities

Which investment class (stocks, bonds, or cash reserves) has performed best over time? Historically, the answer has been common stocks. Common stocks have offered the highest average annual returns of the primary classes of investment assets. Table 4.2 shows annual rates of return from 1950 to 2005 for the Standard & Poor's (S&P) 500 Index, a good proxy for large-company stocks. Also shown are rates of return for long-term Treasury bonds, U.S. Treasury bills, and the rate of inflation as measured by the annual rate of change in the Consumer Price Index.

Total return is measured by the sum of dividends, interest income, and capital gains or capital losses. Since 1950, the before-tax geometric mean rate of return earned on the S&P 500 was 11.93 percent. Long-term government bonds had a total return of 5.92 percent, and U.S. Treasury bills paid an average interest income of 4.92 percent. These returns compare with an average annual rate of inflation of 3.85 percent.

However, mean returns do not explain stock returns very well. Only 4 of the 56 years experienced a return that was within 2 percent of the mean return. The S&P 500 Index usually earns much more, or much less, than the average return. Still, most years show a positive return. Common stock investors suffered losses during only 10 years since 1950. During the stock market bubble deflation of 2000, the S&P 500 Index lost only 9.1 percent. The bubble mostly occurred in Nasdaq technology and Internet stocks. By way of contrast, the Nasdaq Composite Index is very heavily weighted in technology companies and lost 40.9 percent during 2000.

Like common stock investors, investors in long-term Treasury bonds are prone to experience significant volatility. A dramatic downturn in interest rates leads to impressive capital gains for long-term bondholders. Similarly, any dramatic rise in interest rates can lead to significant capital losses. The usual culprit behind rising interest rates is an increase in inflation. During the past half-century, the highest annual rates of inflation were 13.31 percent (in 1979), 12.40 percent (in 1980), and 12.20 percent (in 1974). The lowest annual inflation rates were −0.50 percent (in 1954, when prices actually fell), 0.37 percent (in 1955), and 0.62 percent (in

		Long-Term	Short-Term	
Year	**Common Stocks**	**Treasury Bonds**	**Treasury Bills**	**Inflation Rate**
1950	31.71%	0.06%	1.20%	5.79%
1951	24.02	–3.93	1.49	5.87
1952	18.37	1.16	1.66	0.88
1953	–0.99	3.64	1.82	0.62
1954	52.62	7.19	0.86	–0.50
1955	31.56	–1.29	1.57	0.37
1956	6.56	–5.59	2.46	2.86
1957	–10.78	7.46	3.14	3.02
1958	43.36	–6.09	1.54	1.76
1959	11.96	–2.26	2.95	1.50
1960	0.47	13.78	2.66	1.48
1961	26.89	0.97	2.13	0.67
1962	–8.73	6.89	2.73	1.22
1963	22.80	1.21	3.12	1.65
1964	16.48	3.51	3.54	1.19
1965	12.45	0.71	3.93	1.92
1966	–10.06	3.65	4.76	3.35
1967	23.98	–9.18	4.21	3.04
1968	11.06	–0.26	5.21	4.72
1969	–8.50	–5.07	6.58	6.11
1970	4.01	12.11	6.52	5.49
1971	14.31	13.23	4.39	3.36
1972	18.98	5.69	3.84	3.41
1973	–14.66	–1.11	6.93	8.80
1974	–26.47	4.35	8.00	12.20
1975	37.20	9.20	5.80	7.01
1976	23.84	16.75	5.08	4.81
1977	–7.18	–0.69	5.12	6.77
1978	6.56	–1.18	7.18	9.03
1979	18.44	–1.23	10.38	13.31
1980	32.42	–3.95	11.24	12.40

TABLE 4.2 — Total Returns on Common Stocks and Government Bonds, 1950–2005

(continued on next page)

1953). Notice how an upsurge in inflation proves to be bad medicine for both stock and long-term bond investors, just as a fall in inflation proves to be a tonic for bull markets in both stocks and bonds. Also notice how interest rates on Treasury bills tend to track the rate of inflation. Investors in such money market instruments typically receive a rate of interest that is roughly equivalent to the rate of inflation.

Inflation Problem

Nominal return
Gross investment profit expressed as a percentage.

Real return
Investment return after inflation.

Investors face the ever-present danger that inflation, or a general increase in the cost of living, will reduce the value of any investment. If a particular investment earns a **nominal return** of 6 percent but the rate of inflation is 4 percent, the return after inflation, or **real return**, is only 2 percent. What makes the rate of inflation a particularly serious threat for investors is the fact that income taxes are paid on nominal returns. Thus, if an investor must pay a 35 percent marginal tax rate on a bond paying 6 percent interest, the after-tax rate of interest is only 3.9 percent. If inflation is averaging 4 percent per year, the bond investor is falling behind even if all

TABLE 4.2	Continued

Year	Common Stocks	Long-Term Treasury Bonds	Short-Term Treasury Bills	Inflation Rate
1981	−4.91	1.86	6.96	8.94
1982	21.41	40.36	11.59	3.87
1983	22.51	0.65	8.64	3.80
1984	6.27	15.48	10.20	3.95
1985	32.16	30.97	7.87	3.77
1986	18.47	24.53	6.41	1.13
1987	5.23	−2.71	6.37	4.41
1988	16.81	9.67	7.33	4.42
1989	31.49	18.11	9.15	4.65
1990	−3.17	6.18	8.07	6.11
1991	30.55	19.30	5.96	3.06
1992	7.67	8.05	3.68	2.90
1993	9.99	18.24	2.98	2.75
1994	1.31	−7.77	4.03	2.67
1995	37.43	31.67	5.77	2.54
1996	23.07	−0.93	5.24	3.32
1997	33.36	15.08	5.38	1.70
1998	28.58	13.52	5.31	1.61
1999	21.04	−8.74	4.94	2.68
2000	−9.10	20.11	5.97	3.44
2001	−11.90	4.56	3.45	1.49
2002	−22.10	17.17	1.79	2.48
2003	28.70	2.06	0.95	1.82
2004	10.90	7.70	2.18	2.97
2005	4.91	3.05	3.13	3.42
Arithmetic average	13.27%	6.39%	4.92%	3.89%
Median	15.40%	3.65%	4.85%	3.19%
Geometric mean	11.93%	5.92%	4.92%	3.85%
Standard deviation	17.24%	10.51%	2.71%	2.99%
Coefficent of variation	1.30	1.64	0.55	0.77

Source: The Federal Reserve.

after-tax interest income is reinvested. Bond investors typically find that the real value of their investment tends to erode over time given the dual threats posed by taxes and inflation.

Table 4.2 shows that inflation has consumed almost all the before-tax interest earned on money market instruments. On an after-tax basis, money market instruments are a losing proposition. Inflation has also consumed a large portion of the total return earned by investors in long-term bonds and large-company common stocks. After accounting for inflation, investors in large-company common stocks earn an average annual real rate of return of 8.08 percent (= 11.93% − 3.85%) before taxes. Before tax considerations, long-term Treasury bonds provide investors with a real long-term average annual return of only 2.07 percent (= 5.92% − 3.85%), just a bit ahead of the 1.07 percent (= 4.92% − 3.85%) real rate of return on Treasury bills. After accounting for both inflation and income taxes (at 35 percent), the real after-tax rate of return has been 3.90 percent {= [11.93% × (1 − 0.35)] − 3.85%} on common stocks, 0.00 percent {= [5.92% × (1 − 0.35)] − 3.85%} on Treasury bonds, and −0.65 percent {= [4.92% × (1 − 0.35) − 3.85%) on Treasury bills.

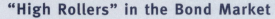

Street Smarts 4.1

"High Rollers" in the Bond Market

The success of state-run lotteries is convincing evidence that many "little" people display risk-seeking behavior, especially when small sums of money are involved. The profitability of state-run lotteries stems from the fact that ticket buyers are willing to pay $1 for a bet that has an expected return of less than $1. When only 50 percent of lottery-ticket revenues are paid out in the form of prizes, for example, each $1 ticket has an expected return of only 50 cents. The willingness to pay such a premium for the unlikely chance at a lottery payoff that might reach into the millions of dollars stems from the fact that such opportunities are rare. Many lottery-ticket buyers have no opportunity for hitting the jackpot in their careers. The lottery is their only chance, however remote, at a substantial sum of money. The success of state-run lottery promotions is noteworthy and occurs despite the fact that consumers typically display risk-averse behavior when making investments involving substantial sums of money.

Of course, not only little people are "high rollers" with an amazing appetite for risk. In 1998, for example, Myron S. Scholes and Robert C. Merton, who shared the Nobel Prize in economics for their work on options-pricing theory, lost *billions* of dollars of their own and other people's money in a high-risk bet on the differences in yield among various debt instruments. While computer models showed that the yield on various types of debt securities was attractive vis-à-vis that on U.S. Treasury bonds, global economic turmoil caused yield spreads to widen to historic levels. In the process, the heavily leveraged, and ironically named, Long-Term Capital Management (LTCM) hedge fund got slammed. The Federal Reserve became concerned that the fiasco would threaten other markets and institutions and organized a bailout.

Risk-assessment computer models like those employed by LTCM tend to ignore low-probability catastrophic events. It's too bad that LTCM investors couldn't do the same. Imagine trying to explain to your family that you lost your fortune, including the Nobel Prize money, speculating on bond interest rate spreads!

See Mark Whitehouse and Aaron Lucchetti, "Investors Bail Out of Refco's Bonds," *The Wall Street Journal Online*, October 14, 2005 (http://online.wsj.com/).

Because income taxes are paid on nominal rates of return, the modest returns earned on fixed-income investments are generally insufficient to offset the dual effects of inflation and taxes. Over the long term, common stocks have been the investment class with the highest real returns after taxes.

Cumulative Returns

For further perspective on the long-term advantage enjoyed by common stock investors, Figure 4.1 shows the cumulative value resulting from a $10,000 investment in 1950 in each respective asset class. The common stock investor commanded a portfolio with a total value of $5.5 million in 56 years. By contrast, the Treasury bond investor's portfolio grew to only $250,686 over this period. The Treasury bill investor's wealth increased to only $147,001. In tax-sheltered accounts, such as individual retirement accounts, fixed-income investors were able to achieve only a modest gain over the rate of inflation. However, common stock investors were able to build a significant amount of wealth over this period.

FIGURE 4.1	Cumulative Value of $10,000 Invested in Stocks and Bonds, 1950–2005

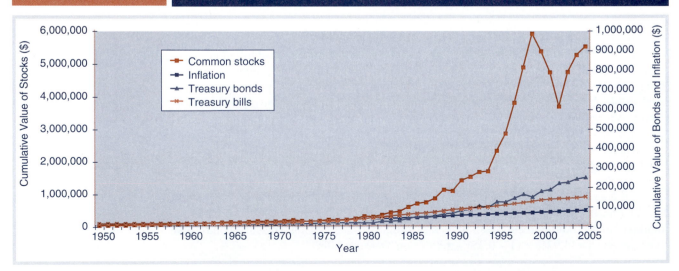

Source: The Federal Reserve.

TABLE 4.3	**Tax Deferral Benefits of IRAs Are Substantial**
	Tax deferral until the point of retirement results in meaningful tax savings. When income taxes are paid on an annual basis, the return on investment and the amount accumulated over time are cut dramatically.

A. Conventional Taxable Investment

After-Tax Value of $4,000 Invested Per Year
Earning 12% With Annual Income Taxes Paid at Rate of:

Number of Years	0%	30%	40%	50%
1	$4,000	$2,800	$2,400	$2,000
5	25,411	16,558	13,857	11,274
10	70,195	41,341	33,474	26,362
15	149,119	78,435	61,247	46,552
20	288,210	133,955	100,565	73,571
25	533,335	217,053	156,227	109,729
30	965,331	341,430	235,029	158,116

B. Tax-Deferred Benefits of Traditional IRA

After-Tax Value of $4,000 Invested Per Year
Earning 12% With Annual Income Taxes Paid at Rate of:

Number of Years	30%	40%	50%
1	$2,800	$2,400	$2,000
5	17,788	15,247	12,706
10	49,136	42,117	35,097
15	104,383	89,471	74,559
20	201,747	172,926	144,105
25	373,335	320,001	266,668
30	675,732	579,198	482,665

Taxes and Investment Returns

Tax Costs

Taxes have a dramatic impact on investor returns and wealth. Part A of Table 4.3 illustrates this point. Consider the person who earns $4,000 in income and wants to invest this amount for future consumption. At the 30 percent tax rate, $4,000 in income is reduced by income taxes of $1,200. Only $2,800 remains for investment. If the investment earns 12 percent each year, that profit is also taxed at the 30 percent rate. The need to pay income taxes on investment income clearly reduces the net after-tax amount of investment returns. Table 4.3 shows the future value of annual contributions of $4,000 to an investment account where taxes are due on an annual basis. Notice that, over a 30-year period, a person paying the 30 percent tax rate ends up with only about 35 percent of the wealth accumulated by someone contributing the same funds to a tax deferred account.

Capital Gains and Dividend Taxes

By themselves, tax considerations should never dictate investment decisions. From an investor's perspective, paying an income or capital gains tax may be only the second-worst thing that could happen following the sale of an investment. The worst outcome is having a net loss on the position! Still, practical portfolio management demands that tax considerations be carefully considered when making portfolio changes.

Since January 1, 1998, gains on securities held for more than a year are considered long term in nature. Net long-term capital gains are taxed at a maximum rate of 20 percent. Gains on securities held one year or less are considered short-term capital gains and are taxed as ordinary income. Of course, if appreciated securities are never sold, then capital gains taxes are never owed. Instead, after the investor dies, wealth (not gains) is taxed at the estate level.

The Jobs and Growth Tax Relief Reconciliation Act of 2003 reduced the tax rate on dividends to a flat 15 percent for most individuals, a decrease of approximately 57 percent from the top marginal rate of 35 percent. This change reduced the historical asymmetry in tax rates for dividend income and capital gains. Dividend income used to be taxed at the regular income tax rate while capital gains were taxed at a lower rate. Now, most investors will pay only 15 percent on dividend income and 20 percent on capital gains.

Tax Deferral Benefits

To increase the savings rate in the United States, the federal government created individual retirement accounts (IRAs) with enormous tax advantages. In a traditional IRA, eligible taxpayers can deduct contributions from gross income. A person with earned income who is not covered by an employer-sponsored retirement plan can deduct IRA contributions of up to $4,000 per year regardless of income. These limits increase to $5,000 in 2008. The money invested grows each year on a tax-deferred basis. Taxes are paid only when money is withdrawn from a traditional IRA. In a Roth IRA, tax is due on the income contributed into the retirement plan during the year in which it is contributed. However, no tax is levied on Roth IRA investment contributions or investment income at the time money is withdrawn. Limits for other popular tax-deferred investment plans, such as 401(k) plans for corporate employees and 403(b)(7) plans for employees of tax-exempt and charitable organizations and universities, recently rose to $15,000 per year. Some employees who are 50 years old or older can make an additional $500 contribution to their IRAs and an extra $1,000 to their retirement plans at work.

A simple illustration can be used to show the tax-deferral benefits of IRA investing. The basic message to be gained is that whenever legally possible, an investor should seek to shelter investment income from taxes. Part B of Table 4.3 shows the after-tax value of an annual investment of $4,000 earning 12 percent when the marginal income tax rate is 30 percent. Tax payments are deferred until retirement. If an investment of $4,000 per year is allowed to compound for 30 years at 12 percent, the before-tax value of the investment rises to $965,331. If 30 percent of the value of this investment is paid in taxes at the end of 30 years, the realized after-tax value is $675,732.

The $289,599 advantage gained through tax deferral is stunning. It stems from the fact that, over an investment horizon of 30 years, an annual investment compounding at 12 percent per year results in far more interest on interest than an investment earning an after-tax 8.4 percent [$= 12\% \times (1 - 0.3)$] per year. Even after paying a 30 percent tax at the end of 30 years, the after-tax proceeds from an investment compounding at 12 percent are sufficiently large to exceed the total proceeds earned on an investment earning 8.4 percent per year after taxes.

Risk Concepts and Measurement

Valuation Risk

The total return earned on common stocks and the risks associated with owning them depend on when such investments are made. The time-honored maxim "Buy low, sell high" is certainly an equation for stock market success, but near-term stock market performance is unpredictable. What is "low" and what is "high" are typically not known until it is too late to trade.

Long-term investors should be very skeptical about simpleminded projections of investment returns. This is especially true when recent rates of return are distinctly higher or sharply lower than long-term averages. In the short run of a few years, stock prices can and do race ahead of basic improvements in the firm's ability to increase earnings and dividends. This was clearly the case during the historic bull market of the late 1990s, when the ratio of stock mar-

Street Smarts 4.2

The Beardstown Ladies Myth

Portfolio managers like Legg Mason's Bill Miller beat the market become folk heroes. A more dubious example is the Beardstown Ladies, an investment club made up of 14 ladies from Beardstown, Illinois. The Ladies, who averaged 70 years in age, became famous when they reported 23.4 percent annual returns on their stock picks over a 10-year period. This is an outstanding rate of return considering that the S&P 500 earned 14.9 percent, and the average stock mutual fund earned 12.6 percent, during this same period. People loved the idea that such adorable little old ladies could beat the market and most professional money managers. If they could do it, anyone can. The Ladies became celebrities. They wrote five best-selling books on money management, sold about a million copies, starred in a video, and gave speeches on investment strategy all over the country.

Suddenly, the famous Beardstown Ladies lost their luster. *The Wall Street Journal* and other publications questioned the accuracy of the group's claims. By tracking stocks the Ladies had purchased, it was determined that it was not possible to earn such market-beating returns. Price Waterhouse audited the Ladies' actual portfolio performance and reported that their 23.4 percent annual return was really 9.1 percent per year. Rather than beating the market, the Ladies had actually underperformed the market and most mutual funds. Apparently, the Ladies didn't realize that measuring portfolio performance is different from monitoring change in the size of a portfolio over a given period. One must consider the exact starting dates of investments, and the timing and amount of all withdrawals, contributions, and dividends.

Unembarrassed by their gaff, and eager to satisfy the curiosity of a gullible investing public, the Ladies continue to produce best-selling investment guides. Their fifth book, *The Beardstown Ladies' Pocketbook Guide to Picking Stocks*, includes a chapter on how to use the Internet to pick stocks. That's an interesting concept. Internet-based stock-pickling advice from investors with a documented inability to match the market averages!

See Brad Barner and Terrance Odean, "Too Many Cooks Spoil the Profits: Investment Club Performance," *Financial Analysts Journal*, vol. 56, no. 1 (January–February 2000), pp. 17–25.

---

ket prices relative to earnings, called the *P/E ratio*, reached historic highs. Over this period, the ratio of dividends paid relative to stock market prices, called the *dividend yield*, reached historic lows. The protracted bear market of 1972–1974 saw a historic decline in stock prices despite growing earnings and dividends. At the market bottom in 1974, P/E ratios had reached historic lows and dividend yields jumped sharply.

At the start of the new millennium, and after having experienced one of the biggest bull markets in history, stock prices could no longer be considered "cheap" by historical standards. On January 1, 2000, the S&P 500 paid a dividend yield of only 1.14 percent, the lowest dividend yield on record, and traded at a stunning 33.4 times earning per share. Following such periods when stock prices have surged ahead of basic improvements in business, stock prices tend to "rest" while earnings and dividends "catch up" and justify higher prices. In some cases, stock prices correct sharply to lower levels, as they did during the 2000–2002 bear market.

Risk Measurement Concepts

In order to assess the level of risk in an investment, an investor needs a risk measurement device. How can risk be quantified? After the fact, investors view assets as risky if they lost money. But decisions must be made before the outcome is known. Therefore, financial theory suggests that investors look to the historical returns and determine the likelihood of a loss occurring. The likelihood of a loss depends on return volatility. In practical terms, the amount of stock market volatility is measured by the amount of "bounce" in stock prices. If a stock had a price of 30 and never varied, it would have zero volatility. There would be no chance of loss for investors. That's the good news. The bad news is that a stock permanently stuck at 30 would also have zero profit potential. What investors seek are investment opportunities that have a desirable trade-off between risk and expected return.

A common measure of return volatility is the **standard deviation** of investment returns. This number, measured in percentage terms, is calculated as the square root of the variance in the annual rate of return on investment. The formula for standard deviation is written

Standard deviation
A common risk measure.

$$\text{Standard deviation} = \sqrt{\frac{\sum_{t=1}^{N}(\text{return}_t - \text{average return})^2}{N-1}} \qquad (4.5)$$

The explanation for this somewhat complicated formula is actually simple: Volatility results from both upward and downward price movements. One avoids the problem of plus and minus deviations canceling each other out, and thus understating risk, by squaring the deviation from average returns and then taking the square root of that difference.

Students never have to go through the laborious process of calculating the standard deviation of annual returns by hand. Such calculations are easily made with statistical or spreadsheet software. To illustrate, look at Table 4.2 once again. Notice that the standard deviation of annual returns on common stocks is 17.24 percent and is higher than the standard deviation of 10.51 percent for long-term Treasury bonds. This means that stocks are riskier than bonds on an annual basis. Notice that the standard deviations for both common stocks and Treasury bonds are much higher than the 2.71 percent standard deviation for short-term Treasury bills. Both stocks and Treasury bonds are much riskier than Treasury bills.

Coefficient of variation
A common risk-reward measure.

Whereas the standard deviation is an absolute measure of risk, the **coefficient of variation** is a useful *relative* measure of the risk-reward relationship. The formula for the coefficient of variation is simply standard deviation divided by expected return:

$$\text{Coefficient of variation} = \frac{\text{standard deviation}}{\text{average return}} \qquad (4.6)$$

A smaller coefficient of variation denotes a better risk-reward relationship. When using the coefficient-of-variation measure of relative risk, it is important to recognize that this measure depends on the arithmetic average annual rate of return.

As shown in Table 4.2, the coefficient of variation, or risk-reward ratio, for common stock is 1.30 (= 17.24%/13.27%). When it comes to common stock investing, the "cost" of each percentage point of expected return is 1.3 percent in standard deviation (or risk). For Treasury bonds, the "cost" of each percentage point of expected return is 1.64 percent in standard deviation (or risk). Even though stocks are riskier than bonds because they have a higher standard deviation of annual returns, they involve a somewhat better risk-reward trade-off. Since 1950, stock investors have enjoyed a lower amount of risk for each percentage point of expected return than the risk-reward trade-off for Treasury bond investors.

Also notice in Table 4.2 that Treasury bills offer a very low risk-reward trade-off of only 0.55. This means that the "cost" of each percentage point of expected return is only 0.55 percent in standard deviation (or risk) for Treasury bill investors. However, it is worth pointing out that the very low risk associated with Treasury bill investing has a cost in terms of expected return. Before taxes, Treasury bill investors earn only a meager premium, at best, over the inflation rate.

Try It!

Consider the following returns: 10 percent, −8 percent, 15 percent. Compute the standard deviation and coefficient of variation of these returns.

Solution

To compute the standard deviation, the average must first be computed:

$$\text{Arithmetic average} = (\Sigma \text{ return}_t)/N = (10 - 8 + 15)/3 = 5.67\%$$

Now, the standard deviation can be computed:

$$\text{Standard deviation} = [(1/n - 1) \times \Sigma(\text{return}_t - \text{average return})^2]^{1/2}$$
$$= \{1/2 \times [(10 - 5.67)^2 + (-8 - 5.67)^2 + (15 - 5.67)^2]\}^{1/2} = 12.1\%$$

The coefficient of variation = standard deviation/average return = 12.1/5.67 = 2.12.

Remember that the lower the coefficient of variation, the better the risk-return trade-off.

Another risk concept is called *return comovement*. It measures the extent to which returns move up or down together. **Covariance** is an absolute measure of comovement that varies between plus and minus infinity, $+\infty$ and $-\infty$:

Covariance
An absolute measure of comovement that varies between plus and minus infinity, $+\infty$ and $-\infty$.

$$\text{Covariance}_{ij} = \frac{\sum_{t=1}^{N} [(\text{return}_{it} - \text{average return}_i) \times (\text{return}_{jt} - \text{average return}_j)]}{N} \tag{4.7}$$

where i and j are different individual securities or indexes. Related to covariance is the statistical concept of correlation. **Correlation**, ρ, is a relative measure of comovement that varies between -1 and $+1$

Correlation
A measure of comovement that varies between -1 and $+1$.

$$\text{Correlation}_{ij} = \rho_{ij} = \frac{\text{covariance}_{ij}}{\text{std. dev.}_i \times \text{std. dev.}_j} \tag{4.8}$$

Again, i and j are different individual securities or indexes.

Table 4.4 illustrates the correlations in total returns for common stocks, Treasury bonds, Treasury bills, and inflation from 1950 to the present. In terms of correlation, a value of -1 means that returns from two asset classes are perfectly inversely correlated. In that case, a positive return of 10 percent in one asset class would correspond with a negative return of -10 percent in some other asset class. A correlation value of $+1$ means that returns from two different asset classes are perfectly in sync. They move in lockstep fashion up and down together. Investors seeking diversification look for investments with high expected returns that tend to be inversely correlated.

Notice from Table 4.4 that the correlation in annual returns on common stocks and the inflation rate is -0.23. This means that an uptick in inflation is accompanied by a downturn in stock prices. Of course, the reason behind this inverse relation between stock returns and the inflation rate is that an uptick in inflation causes short-term interest rates to rise. The positive association between inflation and short-term interest rates is reflected in the positive 0.64 correlation between the inflation rate and interest rates on short-term Treasury bills. It is also interesting to note that both stock and Treasury bond investors benefit from a downturn in the rate of inflation. This stems from the fact that when interest rates fall, the present value of future dividends and interest payments tends to rise.

In practice, investors sometimes measure the risk of individual securities by contemplating the high-low range in stock prices over a 52-week period. For example, a stock priced at $40 with a 52-week high of $60 and low of $30 is obviously more volatile than one priced at $40 with a high of $45 and a low of $35. In most circumstances, the ratio of 52-week high-low stock prices is both easy to calculate and a useful method of risk measurement.

TABLE 4.4	Correlations in Total Returns for Stocks, Bonds, Bills, and Inflation, 1950–Present			
	Stocks	**Bonds**	**Bills**	**Inflation**
Stocks	1.00			
Bonds	0.11	1.00		
Bills	−0.06	0.31	1.00	
Inflation	−0.23	−0.17	0.64	1.00

Source: The Federal Reserve.

Try It!

The stock market earned the following returns: 10 percent, –8 percent, 15 percent. During the same period, gold earned returns of 5 percent, 10 percent, –3 percent. What is the covariance and correlation between the stock market and gold?

Solution

First compute the average and standard deviation for the stocks and for gold. The statistics for stock were computed in a Try It! earlier in this chapter (average = 5.67, standard deviation = 12.1 percent).

Gold's average return = $(5 + 10 - 3)/3 = 4\%$
Standard deviation = $\{(1/2) \times [(5 - 4)^2 + (10 - 4)^2 + (-3 - 4)^2]\}^{1/2} = 6.6\%$

Covariance = $(1/N)\Sigma$ [(stock return$_t$ – stock average) $\times$ (gold return$_t$ – gold average)]
= $(1/3)[(10 - 5.67) \times (5 - 1) + (-8 - 5.67) \times (10 - 6) + (15 - 5.67) \times (-3 - 4)] = -47.67$

Correlation = covariance/(standard deviation stock $\times$ standard deviation gold)
= $-47.67/(12.1 \times 6.6) = -0.60$

A negative correlation means that stocks and gold tend to move in opposite directions.

Spreadsheet Solution

◇	A	B	C	D	E	F
1						
2		Stocks	Gold			
3	Year 1 return	10%	5%			
4	Year 2 return	-8%	10%			
5	Year 3 return	15%	-3%			
6						
7	Average =	5.7%	4.0%			
8	Standard Deviation =	12.10%	6.56%			
9				=STDEV(C3:C5)		
10	Covariance =	-0.477%				
11	Correlation =	-0.60		=AVERAGE(B3:B5)		
12						
13		=B10/(B8*C8)		=COVAR(B3:B5,C3:C5)		
14						
15						

Holding-Period Returns

Although common stocks have consistently provided the highest average annual rate of return to long-term investors, it is important to keep in mind that this average involves a substantial amount of year-to-year variation. Similarly, the typically lower rates of return earned on bonds and money market instruments involve a meaningful amount of return volatility. For long-term investors, the simplest way to "smooth out" the effects of year-to-year volatility in the rates of return on common stocks and long-term bonds is to adopt an extended **investment horizon**, or holding period, as shown in Table 4.5.

Investment horizon
Holding period.

Table 4.5 shows compound annual rates of returns on stocks, bonds, and money market instruments for holding periods of 5, 10, and 20 years in length. During the five-year period ended December 31, 2005, for example, the S&P 500 returned an average 0.55 percent per year. This was one of the worst five-year periods for common stock investing since 1950. During the

TABLE 4.5	Total Returns on Common Stocks and Goverment Bonds for Overlapping Holding Periods of 5, 10, and 20 Years, 1950–2005								

Terminal Year	Common Stocks			Long-term Treasury Bonds			Short-term Treasury Bills		
	5 Years	10 Years	20 Years	5 Years	10 Years	20 Years	5 Years	10 Years	20 Years
1954	23.92%			1.56%			1.41%		
1955	23.89			1.28			1.48		
1956	20.18			0.93			1.67		
1957	13.58			2.16			1.97		
1958	22.30			0.16			1.91		
1959	14.96	19.35%		−1.67	−0.07%		2.33	1.87%	
1960	8.92	16.16		1.16	1.22		2.55	2.01	
1961	12.79	16.43		2.53	1.73		2.48	2.08	
1962	13.31	13.44		2.42	2.29		2.40	2.18	
1963	9.85	15.91		3.97	2.05		2.72	2.31	
1964	10.73	12.82		5.17	1.69		2.83	2.58	
1965	13.25	11.06		2.63	1.89		3.09	2.82	
1966	5.72	9.20		3.17	2.85		3.61	3.05	
1967	12.39	12.85		−0.14	1.13		3.91	3.15	
1968	10.16	10.01		−0.43	1.75		4.33	3.52	
1969	4.97	7.81	13.43%	−2.14	1.45	0.69%	4.93	3.88	2.87%
1970	3.34	8.18	12.10	−0.02	1.30	1.26	5.45	4.26	3.13
1971	8.42	7.06	11.65	1.77	2.47	2.10	5.38	4.49	3.28
1972	7.53	9.93	11.67	4.90	2.35	2.32	5.30	4.60	3.39
1973	2.01	6.01	10.85	4.72	2.11	2.08	5.64	4.98	3.64
1974	−2.35	1.24	6.87	6.72	2.20	1.94	5.92	5.43	4.00
1975	3.21	3.27	7.10	6.16	3.03	2.46	5.78	5.62	4.21
1976	4.87	6.63	7.91	6.81	4.26	3.55	5.92	5.65	4.34
1977	−0.21	3.59	8.12	5.49	5.20	3.15	6.18	5.74	4.44
1978	4.32	3.16	6.53	5.48	5.10	3.41	6.23	5.94	4.72
1979	14.76	5.86	6.83	4.33	5.52	3.46	6.69	6.31	5.09
1980	13.95	8.44	8.31	1.68	3.90	2.59	7.77	6.77	5.51
1981	8.08	6.47	6.76	−1.06	2.80	2.64	9.68	7.78	6.12
1982	14.05	6.68	8.30	6.03	5.76	4.04	10.78	8.46	6.51
1983	17.27	10.61	8.28	6.42	5.95	4.01	11.12	8.65	6.80
1984	14.76	14.76	7.79	−9.80	7.03	4.59	11.01	8.83	7.12
1985	14.71	14.33	−8.66	16.83	8.99	5.97	10.30	9.03	7.31
1986	19.87	13.82	10.17	21.62	9.70	6.94	8.60	9.14	7.38
1987	16.49	15.26	9.27	13.02	9.47	7.31	7.59	9.17	7.44
1988	15.38	16.33	9.55	14.98	10.62	7.82	7.10	9.09	7.50
1989	20.40	17.55	11.55	15.50	12.61	9.01	6.81	8.89	7.59
1990	13.14	13.93	11.15	10.75	13.75	8.71	6.83	8.55	7.66
1991	15.36	17.59	11.89	9.81	15.56	9.00	6.71	7.65	7.72
1992	15.89	16.19	11.33	12.13	12.58	9.12	6.31	6.95	7.70
1993	14.51	14.94	12.76	13.83	14.41	10.10	5.62	6.35	7.49
1994	8.69	14.40	14.58	8.34	11.86	9.42	4.73	5.76	7.29
1995	16.57	14.84	14.59	13.10	11.92	10.45	4.30	5.55	7.28
1996	15.20	15.28	14.55	8.98	9.39	9.54	4.22	5.46	7.28
1997	20.24	18.05	16.65	10.51	11.32	10.39	4.57	5.44	7.29
1998	24.06	19.18	17.75	9.61	11.70	11.16	5.05	5.33	7.20
1999	28.55	18.20	17.87	9.38	8.86	10.72	5.26	5.00	6.92

(continued on next page)

| TABLE 4.5 | Total Returns on Common Stocks and Goverment Bonds for Overlapping Holding Periods of 5, 10, and 20 Years, 1950–2005 *continued* | | | | | | | | |

	Common Stocks			Long-term Treasury Bonds			Short-term Treasury Bills		
Terminal Year	5 Years	10 Years	20 Years	5 Years	10 Years	20 Years	5 Years	10 Years	20 Years
2000	18.35	17.46	15.68	7.39	10.21	11.97	5.34	4.82	6.67
2001	10.70	12.93	15.24	8.55	8.76	12.11	4.98	4.60	6.12
2002	-0.59	9.33	12.71	8.80	9.65	11.10	4.28	4.42	5.68
2003	-0.57	11.06	12.99	6.51	8.05	11.18	3.40	4.23	5.28
2004	-2.29	12.07	13.23	10.09	9.74	10.79	2.85	4.05	4.90
2005	0.55	9.09	11.93	6.77	7.08	9.47	2.30	3.81	4.68
Arithmetic average	11.93%	11.89%	11.26%	6.32%	6.45%	6.66%	5.19%	5.45%	5.93%
Median	13.28%	12.85%	11.55%	6.10%	5.76%	7.31%	5.16%	5.43%	6.51%
Geometric mean	11.68%	11.79%	11.21%	6.19%	6.36%	6.60%	5.16%	5.43%	5.99%
Standard deviation	7.44%	4.75%	3.22%	5.23%	4.39%	3.72%	2.51%	2.20%	1.59%
Coefficient of variation	0.62	0.40	0.29%	0.83	0.68	0.56	0.48	0.40	0.27

Source: The Federal Reserve

10-year period ended December 31, 2005, the S&P 500 returned an average 9.09 percent per year. Stock investors earned 11.93 percent per year during the 20-year period ending in 2005.

The best way for protecting against a sharp downward correction in stock prices is to maintain a broadly diversified portfolio of common stocks for an extended period of time. Since 1950, negative returns have been earned by common stock investors during only 5 of 52 rolling five-year periods. Also since 1950, positive returns have been earned during each rolling 10-year and 20-year period. There is no way to eliminate investment risk during any given period without also eliminating the potential for profits higher than the risk-free returns earned by Treasury bill investors. However, over the long run, investors in stocks and long-term bonds can mitigate risk by maintaining their investments for an extended period of time.

Sources of Volatility

Company Risk

For long-term investors seeking maximum potential rewards, stocks are the most attractive asset class. However, for most investors, investment return is only one-half of the equation that needs to be considered when creating an investment portfolio. Although stocks and bonds offer higher expected returns than do money market instruments, they also involve greater volatility. Volatility can undermine the potential of long-term investments if investors are scared or forced out of equity investments during vicious bear markets. Finding an appropriate risk-reward trade-off is key.

Firm-specific risk
Chance that problems with an individual company will reduce the value of investment.

By owning individual stocks and bonds, the investor is exposed to **firm-specific risk**, or the chance that problems with an individual company will reduce the investment value. Firm-specific risk can be eliminated through diversification. Broad diversification across several stocks and bonds greatly diminishes the adverse impact associated with an unfavorable outcome following investment in any single stock or bond. Studies in financial economics show that firm-specific factors such as the quality of management, operating and financial leverage, and changes in product quality are responsible for slightly less than one-half of the total volatility in company stock returns.

Unanticipated changes in the growth of aggregate economic activity (as measured by the gross domestic product), changes in interest rates, or fluctuations in the value of the dollar all cause stock market volatility. Such changes in the overall economic environment cause about one-third of the volatility in common stock returns. Sector-related factors account for roughly 15 percent of stock price volatility. For example, an increase in the price of oil would drive up costs for the airline industry but have little impact on the software industry. Industry-related factors are also important. Surprising variation in the level of competition from domestic and foreign competitors, changes in the method or scope of regulation, or fluctuations in the cost of inputs and raw materials are all important. Such factors cause roughly 5–10 percent of stock price volatility. It is crucial for investors to remember that although company fortunes rise or fall based on the success of management's efforts, success is not fully within the control of company management.

Stock Market Risk

Although diversification reduces the risk of loss from a single investment, there remains **market risk** tied to the chance that the overall stock or bond markets will decline in value. The overall stock market is influenced by actual and anticipated changes in economic growth, the pace of inflation, interest rates, and so on. The two most severe bear markets since World War II occurred in 1973–1974 and 2000–2002. During those two periods, it was common for broadly diversified portfolios of common stocks to decline by as much as 35 to 50 percent. At such times, stock and bond investors must remember that time has a moderating effect on market risk. The longer an investor holds a broadly diversified portfolio of stock or bond investments, the lower is the chance of losing money and the greater are the odds of earning a return close to the long-term average.

Market risk
General fluctuation in stock and bond prices.

The overall stock market fluctuates from day to day and year to year with changes in the business climate and investor perceptions. In the short run, stock returns are volatile because they are driven by changing investor expectations. Most investors are aware that widely followed stock market averages, such as the DJIA or the S&P 500, can routinely vary by 0 to 3 percent per day. Long-run returns on equity investments are determined by fundamental economic factors such as dividend yield and the rate of growth in dividends and earnings. Although common stocks have considerable short-term price volatility, price swings tend to even out over time and become tolerable for long-term investors. For investors thinking about truly long-term goals, such as providing for retirement income, bond and money market investments have little day-to-day price volatility but scant chance of keeping pace with inflation, especially after taxes are considered.

The most popular measure of investor expectations and market valuation risk is given by price-earnings (P/E) ratios. High P/E ratios usually signify high risk. Low P/E ratios typically signal low valuation risk. However, P/E ratios can be distorted during recessions when massive write-offs cause index earnings to collapse and the DJIA P/E ratio to soar. In 1981, for example, the DJIA P/E ratio soared to 114.4 because of a collapse in earnings caused by massive write-offs following a deep recession. Similar peaks of 64.3 times earnings in 1991 and 47.3 times earnings in 1933 were caused by significant earnings shortfalls at a few DJIA companies. To get a clear picture of conventional DJIA P/E ratios during typical operating conditions, it is necessary to control for periods of dramatic earnings shortfalls. Figure 4.2 illustrates the actual DJIA P/E ratio data after index earnings have been normalized for three brief periods (1931–1935, 1982–1983, 1991–1992) in which index earnings plummeted by 50 percent or more. In those three instances, prior-year earnings were used instead of depressed current-year earnings.

After adjustment, it is easy to see in Figure 4.2, Panel A, that P/E ratios for the DJIA usually fall within a band from 8 to 20. At the start of 2006, a 19 P/E ratio for the DJIA was higher than the long-term median of 15. What makes an elevated P/E ratio for the DJIA worrisome in 2006 is that it remained high after the bear market of 2000–2002.

A similar picture of high investor expectations and high valuation risk in the market is given when one considers dividend yield information, as shown in Figure 4.2, Panel B. High dividend yields reflect investor caution and concern about future business prospects. Low dividend yields

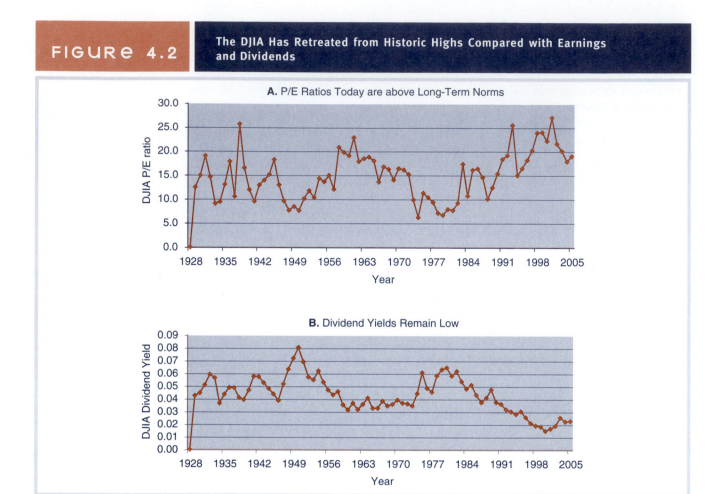

FIGURE 4.2 The DJIA Has Retreated from Historic Highs Compared with Earnings and Dividends

Note: P/E ratios in 1931–1935, 1982–1983, and 1991–1992 have been adjusted for massive losses at component firms.
Source: Dow Jones & Company

reflect investor optimism and enthusiasm for future business prospects. Historically, investment returns have been best when investors have bought stocks during periods of high dividend yields and sold stocks during periods of low dividend yields—hence, the time-tested admonition to "buy fear, sell greed." Although some contend that dividends are unimportant for growth-stock investors, it is worth remembering that roughly 40 percent of the total return earned by common stock investors comes in the form of dividend income. Over the long run, dividends matter.

Given historically high P/E ratios and historic lows for dividend yields, common stock investors have faced a significant amount of **valuation risk** in the new millennium. Robust periods of economic expansion are typically accompanied by rising stock prices and growing investor enthusiasm. Such robust periods often give way to subsequent periods of more tepid economic growth (or recession) and relatively lackluster market environments. Conversely, periods of anemic economic growth are typically accompanied by stagnant or falling stock prices and deepening investor pessimism. Such lackluster periods often give way to subsequent periods of more rapid economic growth and typically bullish market environments. This process, often described as **reversion to the mean**, is an inherent characteristic of economic and stock market environments.

Valuation risk
Chance of loss due to relatively high stock prices.

Reversion to the mean
Tendency of stock and bond returns to return toward long-term averages.

Bond Market Risk

Like the stock market, the bond market is influenced by economic expectations. Credit problems tend to be more severe during economic downturns, whereas rapid economic growth boosts the demand for credit. During economic expansions, surges in the demand for credit to finance new plant and equipment cause higher interest rates and adversely affect the value of outstanding bonds.

Although the bond market is typically less scary than the stock market, there are times when bonds are as risky as stocks. As seen in Table 4.2, bond market volatility can be significant. Bonds are linked to prevailing interest rates in the economy. As interest rates rise, bond prices fall. When rates fall, bond prices rise. The price volatility of a bond depends on its term to maturity. The longer the time to maturity for a bond, the greater its sensitivity to interest rates.

Interest rate risk is the chance of loss in the value of fixed-income investments following a rise in interest rates. Rapid increases in prevailing interest rates can have a devastating effect on the value of long-term Treasury bonds. Smaller, but meaningful declines would be seen in 10-year Treasury bonds and 5-year Treasury notes. Long-term bonds are more risky than many investors realize. In addition to facing interest rate risk, bond investors are also subject to **credit risk**. Credit risk is the chance that an individual issuer of a bond will fail to make timely payments of principal and interest. Low-quality bonds have a greater risk of default and generally offer higher yields to help compensate investors. Government bonds offer the lowest yields, carry the highest credit ratings, and have the lowest risk of default. Money market instruments generally provide stable principal and only minimal credit risk. The effect of credit and interest rate risk on bond values is studied in detail in Chapters 14 and 15.

Interest rate risk
Chance of loss in the value of fixed-income investments following a rise in interest rates.

Credit risk
Chance of loss due to issuer default.

Portfolio Theory

Basic Assumptions

Working in the early 1950s, Nobel laureate Harry Markowitz was among the first to focus investor attention on the risks and returns of an **investment portfolio**. An investment portfolio is a collection of securities that together provide an investor with an attractive trade-off between risk and expected return. Unlike investment theorists before him, Markowitz argued that the volatilities of individual securities are not the most important concern for investors. Of most consequence is how the expected return and volatility characteristics of individual securities affect the expected return and volatility of the overall portfolio. For example, most stock and bond prices tend to fall with an increase in the expected rate of inflation. However, gold mining and natural resource stocks tend to rise with an increase in inflationary expectations. Therefore, the price volatility of the general stock market and gold-mining stocks is often inversely related. When inflationary expectations rise, gold stocks jump up while general stock prices decline. Thus, by adding volatile gold stocks to a broadly diversified investment portfolio, the price volatility of the overall portfolio can actually decline.

Portfolio theory is the simple concept of making security choices based on the expected return and risk of a collection of securities. **Expected return** is measured by the amount of profit anticipated over some relevant holding period. **Risk** is captured by return dispersion. Within this framework, investment alternatives are represented by the **probability distribution** of security returns over some future period. As reflected by the Standard & Poor's (S&P) 500 Index in Table 4.2, the mean annual rate of return earned on common stocks has been roughly 12 percent per year during the post–World War II period. The median, or "middle," annual rate of return earned on common stocks during this time frame has been roughly 16 percent per year. Notice that when the average and median rates of return are very close, as is the case here, the distribution of annual rates of return approximates a normal distribution, or a bell-shaped curve. Under such circumstances, the average or median annual rate of return can form a useful estimate for the anticipated or expected rate of return on common stocks.

A basic assumption of portfolio theory is that investors seek out investments with the potential to provide maximum benefits. They search for the highest expected rate of return for a given amount of risk or the lowest amount of risk for a given expected rate of return. Investors get positive benefit, or **utility**, out of an increase in the expected rate of return and suffer a psychic loss, or **disutility**, from an increase in the amount of risk. This means that investors tend to be **risk-averse**. In selecting their investments, investors seek out investments with the characteristic of

Investment portfolio
Collection of securities that together provide an investor with an attractive trade-off between risk and return.

Portfolio theory
Concept of making security choices based on portfolio expected returns and risks.

Expected return
Anticipated profit over some relevant holding period.

Risk
Return dispersion; usually measured by the standard deviation of returns.

Probability distribution
Apportionment of likely occurrences.

Utility
Positive benefit.

Disutility
Psychic loss.

Risk averse
Desire to avoid risk.

Street Smarts 4.3

Big Risk Takers

Investment banks earn billions of dollars per year using their own funds to help companies raise capital by issuing stock and bonds. Wall Street firms offer so-called bridge financing to provide client companies with necessary funds during the brief period between the time that a deal is struck to raise new capital and the time that the proceeds from new security sales become available. Brokerage subsidiaries of investment banks also use their own capital to facilitate clients' trading activities by holding big inventories of stocks and bonds.

Following the market meltdown of 2000–2002, increased competition and thin profit margins plagued the brokerage business. Interest and dividend income plunged. Initial public offerings and merger activity slowed to a trickle. To generate profits, the investment banks started taking increased risk with their own capital. In 2003, for example, Goldman Sachs made big bets on the direction of interest rates and the strength of the U.S. dollar. These bets paid off and drove Goldman earnings to record levels. Other firms such as Morgan Stanley and Citigroup also increased their appetite for taking risk during the same period.

Financial firms can make or lose millions when world markets change suddenly. Unfortunately, big bets sometimes go bad and lead to gigantic losses. Goldman lost more than $600 million in 1998 after Russia defaulted on its debt. Another famous example is provided by Nicholas Leeson, a derivatives trader in Singapore for Barings Bank, who lost over $1 billion and bankrupted his employer in 1995. Barings Bank was over 200 years old at the time; it had helped negotiate and finance the Louisiana Purchase in 1803. Unfortunately, the Barings Bank episode is not unique. Rogue traders have cost Daiwa Bank over $1 billion, and First Capital Strategies lost $137 million.

The upshot is simple: Even experienced and knowledgeable investment banks sometimes find extreme risk taking irresistible. In the securities trading business, only one thing is certain: Big players can make gigantic mistakes.

See Rob Cox, Hugo Dixon, and Christopher Hughes, "Morgan Stanley Might Need to Hone Risk-Management Skills," *The Wall Street Journal Online*, November 15, 2005 (**http://online.wsj.com/**).

---

providing the maximum expected rate of return for a given level of risk or the minimum anticipated volatility for a given expected rate of return.

The concept of an optimal portfolio is based on the assumption that all of the advantages of an investment portfolio can be summarized in terms of the expected rate of return. Similarly, the anticipated level of volatility summarizes all of the disadvantages tied to an investment portfolio. The sole motivation behind investment decisions is to maximize economic welfare. This contradicts the possibility that investors may be motivated to buy stocks in "socially conscious" corporations. Portfolio theory is based on the concept that only monetary considerations are relevant when an investor is making investment decisions.

To summarize, portfolio theory is based on three fundamental assertions:

- Investors seek to maximize utility.

- Investors are risk-averse: Utility rises with expected return and falls with an increase in volatility.

- The optimal portfolio has the highest expected return for a given level of risk or the lowest level of risk for a given expected return.

Portfolio Risk and Return

Investment alternatives involve distinct combinations of expected return and anticipated volatility. The relationship between the expected rate of return and risk can be depicted in a two-dimensional graph in which expected return is on the vertical axis and risk is on the horizontal axis, as shown in Figure 4.3. Risk is depicted using the standard-deviation measure of return volatility.

In Panel A, each investment alternative is depicted as a simple dot in expected-return–risk space. The desirability of each portfolio can be described as a simple combination of expected return and the standard deviation of returns. Because investors favor investments with higher levels of expected return and lower levels of risk, investment opportunities tend to be regarded more favorably when they offer a higher level of expected return for a given level of risk.

The expected rate of return for each portfolio is simply

$$E(R_P) = \sum_{i=1}^{N} W_i E(R_i)$$

(4.9)

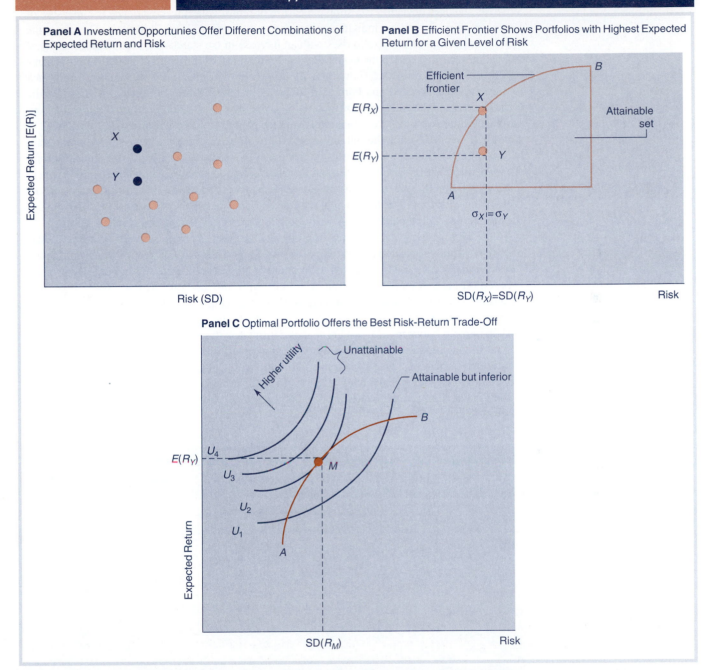

FIGURE 4.3   Expected Rate of Return and Risk Are Fundamental Economic Characteristics of Investment Opportunities

Panel A Investment Opportunies Offer Different Combinations of Expected Return and Risk

Panel B Efficient Frontier Shows Portfolios with Highest Expected Return for a Given Level of Risk

Panel C Optimal Portfolio Offers the Best Risk-Return Trade-Off

where W_i is the portfolio weight, or percentage, devoted to a given security i, and $E(R_i)$ is the expected rate of return on security i. For example, suppose an investor put 70 percent of a portfolio in a stock with an expected return of 12 percent and put 30 percent in a stock with an expected return of 15 percent. The expected rate of return on the overall portfolio is a simple weighted sum of the portfolio percentage times the anticipated return on each respective holding. In this case, the expected rate of return on the portfolio is 12.9 percent $[= 0.7(12\%) + 0.3(15\%)]$.

The standard deviation of a portfolio is calculated using the expression

$$\text{SD}(R_P) = \sqrt{\sum_{i=1}^{N} W_i^2 \times \text{VAR}(R_i) + \sum_{i=1}^{N} \sum_{\substack{j=1 \\ j \neq i}}^{N} W_i \times W_j \times \text{COV}\left(R_i R_j\right)} \qquad \textbf{(4.10)}$$

In this expression, SD(R_P) is the portfolio standard deviation; W is the portfolio weight in securities i and j, respectively; VAR(R_i) is the variance of returns for individual securities [and SD(R_i) = VAR(R_i)$^{1/2}$]; and COV(R_iR_j) is the covariance between the returns on securities i and j. Whereas standard deviation is a simple measure of return volatility, covariance is a measure of how rates of return on two individual securities vary together versus separately. Therefore, the standard deviation of a portfolio rises with an increase in the standard deviation or volatility of individual securities and to the extent these securities have high covariance or covary together.

The example in Table 4.6 shows how monthly returns for leading auto manufacturers such as General Motors (GM) and Ford tend to move together. During the period in question, the covariance of monthly returns for these two competitors was 0.66 percent. High positive covariance diminishes the diversification advantage gained from combining these two stocks in a single portfolio. Notice the much lower level of stock return covariance for software giant Microsoft and financial powerhouse Citigroup. Unlike GM and Ford, Microsoft and Citigroup are in distinctly different businesses and have few common economic characteristics. As such, it is unsurprising that essentially no covariance exists between the monthly stock returns of Microsoft and Citigroup. The low level of return covariance between Microsoft and Citigroup has the effect of reducing portfolio risk when both stocks are combined in a single portfolio.

In the example shown, two different portfolios are formed on the assumption that one-half of each portfolio is invested in each pair of stocks. In portfolio A, 50 percent of the overall portfolio is initially invested in GM, and the remaining 50 percent is invested in Ford. Portfolio B is based on the assumption of an initial 50-50 split in the amount invested in Microsoft and Citigroup. Portfolio standard deviation depends on the weight, standard deviation, and covariance of individual asset returns. As shown in Table 4.6, the relatively high positive covariance of 0.66 percent between GM and Ford stock returns has the effect of limiting the diversification advantage of combining both stocks in a single portfolio. Low covariance implies a much greater diversification advantage from combining two or more securities in a given portfolio. Notice the risk-reducing advantage of including Microsoft and Citigroup in a single portfolio in the light of their return covariance of 0.06 percent.

TABLE 4.6	Portfolio Risk Increases with the Volatility of Individual Holdings and the Extent to Which Holdings Have High Covariance					
Month	GM	Ford	Portfolio A	Microsoft	Citigroup	Portfolio B
November	0.0%	−2.0%	−1.0%	2.9%	−1.7%	0.6%
December	22.8	2.3	12.1	−7.4	−6.6	−7.0
January	11.7	17.1	14.4	0.1	−0.6	−0.2
February	11.7	1.1	6.3	6.4	−3.8	1.2
March	6.2	7.7	6.9	−6.7	−0.6	−3.7
April	−7.7	−5.6	−6.6	−3.0	5.2	1.0
May	−7.3	−2.5	−4.9	3.9	1.9	2.9
June	−16.7	−8.7	−12.8	−2.3	−0.3	−1.3
July	10.2	23.0	16.4	−4.5	−5.2	−4.8
August	21.3	11.7	16.4	4.1	6.2	5.1
September	1.9	4.1	3.0	4.1	1.9	3.0
October	8.8	10	9.6	1.7	−1.8	0.0
Mean	4.62%	4.50%	4.56%	−0.16%	−0.52%	−0.34%
Standard deviation	11.81%	9.43%	9.61%	4.64%	3.84%	3.49%
Covariance		0.66%			0.06%	

Source: Data from Yahoo! Finance, **http://finance.yahoo.com** (November 1, 2004, to October 1, 2005).

It is important to keep in mind that an individual security's contribution to portfolio risk depends on the asset's weight in the portfolio, its standard deviation, and its covariance with other portfolio securities. An equal investment in two securities with the same expected return and standard deviation but a perfect inverse correlation, $\rho_{ij} = -1$, would yield a **zero-risk portfolio** in which $SD_P = 0$.

Zero-risk portfolio
A constant-return portfolio.

To understand how the correlation concept relates to portfolio risk, consider a simple example. Suppose an investor owns a portfolio containing only two stocks priced at $40 per share. If one rose by $1 while the second fell by $1, portfolio value would remain unchanged. For an equal investment in two securities with the same expected return and standard deviation, $\rho_{ij} = -1$ implies that the returns on one security are perfect mirror images of the returns on the other held in the portfolio. Thus, an equal investment in two securities with the same expected return and standard deviation, but a perfect inverse correlation, will have a constant value over time. This is what is meant by a zero-risk portfolio. It never changes in value. For risky portfolios, asset covariance helps determine portfolio risk when the number of portfolio holdings is large.

Try It!

Consider the following two stocks: Stock A has an expected return of 15 percent and a standard deviation of 45 percent; stock B has an expected return of 10 percent and a standard deviation of 30 percent. Stocks A and B have a covariance of 225 percent. If a portfolio is made with 30 percent stock A and 70 percent stock B, find the expected return and standard deviation of the portfolio.

Solution

For two stocks, the expected-return equation (4.9) becomes

$$E(R_P) = \sum_{i=1}^{N} W_i E(R_i) = W_A E(R_A) + W_B E(R_B) = 0.30 \times 15\% + 0.70 \times 10\% = 11.5\%$$

The standard-deviation equation (4.10) is

$$SD(R_P) = \sqrt{W_A^2 \times VAR(R_A) + W_B^2 \times VAR(R_B) + 2 \times W_A \times W_B \times COV(R_A, R_B)} =$$
$$= \sqrt{0.3^2 \times 45^2 + 0.7^2 \times 30^2 + 2 \times 0.3 \times 0.7 \times 225} = \sqrt{717.75} = 26.8\%$$

The portfolio has an expected return of 11.5 percent and a standard deviation of 26.8 percent.

Optimal Portfolio Choice

An **efficient portfolio** is one that provides maximum expected return for a given level of risk or minimum risk for a given expected return. In Figure 4.3, Panel A, it is important to keep in mind that the expected rate of return on a stock is calculated as the ratio of expected future cash flows divided by the investor's purchase price per share. If a given company is expected to generate $4 per share in future cash flows per year, an investor paying $40 would enjoy a 10 percent annual rate of return ($10\% = \$4/\$40$). An investor who paid a price of $50 per share would have an expected rate of return of only 8 percent per year ($8\% = \$4/\$50$).

Efficient portfolio
Portfolio with maximum expected return for a given level of risk or with minimum risk for a given expected return.

Consider portfolios X and Y depicted in Figure 4.3(A) and 4.3(B). Suppose that they have the exact same level of risk, $SD(R_X) = SD(R_Y)$, but that the expected rate of return on X is greater than that on Y, or $E(R_X) > E(R_Y)$. In the real world, this would be an impossible situation. Under such circumstances, investors would naturally favor X over Y. They would sell Y and use the proceeds to buy X. This would cause the price of Y to decline until such point that

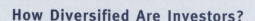
How Diversified Are Investors?

Holding a diversified portfolio of financial assets allows investors to eliminate firm-specific risk and minimize chance fluctuations. As a result, a traditional perspective has been that investors should seek to create portfolios that minimize the anticipated amount of risk for a given level of expected return. In order to accomplish appropriate diversification, investors must view their investment portfolios as a whole. However, there is evidence that investors do not adopt such a unified view of their financial portfolios. Instead, people seem to focus on the individual assets and make buy, hold, and sell decisions on the characteristics of each security alone. The results are surprising.

Every three years, the Board of Governors of the Federal Reserve System sponsors the Survey of Consumer Finances (SCF). About 4,500 families are surveyed to gather information on their finances. Examining the portfolios of these U.S. households sheds some light on the degree to which investors actually diversify. Survey results show that investors are often poorly diversified. Over the years, 10 to 16 percent of households that have over $10,000 in financial assets own no stock

equity. This includes direct stock ownership as well as indirect ownership through mutual funds and pension funds. Even families with over $1 million in assets frequently hold no common stocks. In households that own stocks, the median number of stocks owned by households with $100,000 to $1 million in wealth was only four stocks in 2001. About 40 percent of stockholders own only one stock; 70 percent of stockholders own five or fewer stocks. These stocks represent about 20 percent of the value of the entire portfolio.

Interestingly, investors who self-reported their propensity to take risks tend to have less diversified portfolios. Investors in general also appear to understand that they are taking greater risks when they hold underdiversified portfolios. While diversification does appear to increase with investor characteristics such as income and age, most investors appear to be influenced by behavioral biases that cause them to hold relatively concentrated portfolios.

See Valery Polkovnichenko, "Household Portfolio Diversification: A Case for Rank-Dependent Preferences," *Review of Financial Studies*, vol. 18, no. 4 (Winter 2005), pp. 1467–1502.

---

it would offer investors the same exact rate of return on investment as does X. Remember, assuming future cash flows are constant, the expected rate of return on a security rises with a fall in the purchase price. In fact, the prices of X and Y will continue to adjust until $E(R_X) = E(R_Y)$ and each offers investors an expected rate of return commensurate with its level of risk.

Efficient frontier
Collection of all efficient portfolios.

The **efficient frontier** is the complete set of efficient portfolios. The efficient frontier includes all efficient portfolios that provide maximum expected return for a given level of risk. Alternatively, the efficient frontier depicts all efficient portfolios that entail minimum risk for a given expected return. It is shown by a curved line that is upward-sloping to the right from A to B in Figure 4.3. Portfolio A consists of auto stocks and offers a relatively low expected rate of return with modest risk; portfolio B is made up of biotech stocks and offers a relatively high expected rate of return with greater risk. Both represent efficient portfolios. The shape of the efficient frontier implies that there are diminishing returns to risk taking in the investment world. To gain ever-higher expected rates of return, investors must be willing to take on ever-increasing amounts of risk. Relatively few investment opportunities in the economy offer investors the possibility of stupendous rates of return, and such opportunities entail equally stupendous amounts of risk.

Optimal portfolio
Collection of securities that provides an investor with the highest level of expected utility.

The **optimal portfolio** is one that provides an investor with the highest level of expected utility. To be sure, optimal portfolio choice depends on individual risk preferences. A very risk-averse individual may prefer a portfolio consisting of auto stocks, given their solid dividend income and high degree of price stability. An adventuresome investor may prefer a portfolio containing biotech stocks, given their enticing growth opportunities and potential for rapid price appreciation. Neither investor is wrong in making such choices. Each choice is appropriate given differences in individual risk preferences.

Market portfolio
The current value of all assets.

As shown in Figure 4.3, optimal portfolio choice involves a trade-off between that which is available, the efficient frontier, and that which is favored, as determined by investor preferences. A key concept in portfolio theory is that the **market portfolio** is an efficient portfolio, as depicted by portfolio M in Figure 4.3(C). This means that the market portfolio, as represented by the S&P 500 Index, for example, reflects an appropriate trade-off between risk and the expected rate of return.

Investor Perceptions of Risk

Choosing Financial Assets

The "modern portfolio theory" just described was developed in the 1950s and 1960s. It is based on the assumption that investors care only about the expected return and risk (as measured by volatility) of their portfolios. When making decisions on what new assets to buy, investors are assumed to be interested only in the new asset's interaction with the existing portfolio. How will portfolio expected return and risk change if the new stock or bond is purchased?

This traditional characterization does not describe how all people actually make investment decisions. Investors sometimes care about other characteristics of their investments and investment portfolios. For example, some investors want the companies they invest in to behave in ways that match their own values and beliefs. Socially responsible investors may favor stocks of companies that protect the environment or use alternative energy sources. They often shun companies that produce alcohol, weapons, or tobacco. American investors have also expressed patriotism through their investment choices. During World War I, for example, U.S. investors lined up to buy Liberty Bonds. In the cold war following World War II, Americans were asked to buy stocks to defend capitalism from communism. Similarly, after the 9/11 terrorist attacks in New York City and Washington, D.C., some Americans thought it was patriotic to buy stocks.

Investment history also illustrates periods in which investors appear to have been smitten with certain types of stocks. In the early 1990s, investors focused on consumer product stocks. In the late 1990s, investors focused on Internet stocks. As a result, investors sometimes form suboptimal portfolios. They could reduce risk for a given level of expected return, or increase expected return for a given level of risk, if they picked financial assets in the manner advocated by modern portfolio theory.

Making Decisions after Gains and Losses

So how do investors actually view risk? Interestingly, many investors tend to make a **myopic** assessment of risk. After experiencing three years of losses, investors with long-term horizons suddenly have three-year horizons—and they want out! Recent experience tends to have a disproportionate influence on investment decisions. For example, when offered a wager on a coin toss (heads you win $50, tails you lose $50), few are willing to take such a gamble. However, studies show that some people are more likely to take such a wager if they had just lost $50. Another coin toss gives them the chance to break even. Some people seem more willing to take on greater risk when seeking to get back to even.

Another interesting risk attitude is the **house money effect**—a change in behavior that sometimes occurs when people have experienced an unusual gain that makes them willing to take on more risk. Gamblers refer to this feeling as "playing with the house's money." After winning a big profit, some amateur gamblers do not fully consider the new money as their own. They act as if they are betting with the casino's money. The house money effect predicts that investors are more likely to enter into risky stocks after closing out successful positions. After locking in a big gain by selling a risky stock at a profit, some investors indeed appear more willing to buy even riskier stocks. Such behavior was widespread during the late 1990s. As investors gained wealth from a rapidly expanding bull market, many shifted their portfolios into even-higher-risk investments.

When the stock market bubble began to collapse in 2000, many high-tech investors suffered massive losses. As technology stocks collapsed, many high-tech investors bought even-riskier stocks and used margin debt to leverage their positions. Like gamblers down on their luck, these investors appeared to be looking for a "double or nothing" toss of the coin. In so doing, they made a very bad situation even worse. Short-term losses became permanent when the investors were unable to meet margin calls. Many were forced to liquidate positions at ruinously low prices.

Myopic
Short-term focus.

House money effect
The propensity to take risky gambles after winning some money.

TABLE 4.7	Monthly Retirement Income Provided by Three Different Investment Options during Good and Bad Market Conditions		
A	**Option A**	**Option B**	**Option C**
Good market conditions (50% chance)	$900	$1,100	$1,260
Bad market conditions (50% chance)	900	800	700
B	**Program 1**	**Program 2**	**Program 3**
Good market conditions (50% chance)	$1,100	$1,260	$1,380
Bad market conditions (50% chance)	800	700	600

Source: Shlomo Benartzi and Richard H. Thaler, "How Much Is Investor Autonomy Worth?" *Journal of Finance*, vol. 57, no. 4 (August 2002), pp. 1593–1616. Copyright © 2002. Used with permission.

Comparing Risky Investments

Some people find risk assessment difficult, and they can be influenced or tricked by how questions concerning risk are posed. When asked the same question in different ways, people sometimes give different answers. For example, employees must make asset allocation decisions in their retirement plans. Different investment options like stocks, bonds, and T-bills offer different levels of expected return and risk. How do investors decide to make their allocation among low-risk, medium-risk, and high-risk investments?

In a recent study, employees were asked to rank the investment options shown in Part A of Table 4.7 as the first, second, and third desired choices for their retirement plans.[2] Note that the options are ordered from the least amount of risk to the highest amount of risk. As more risk is taken, higher rewards become possible. However, high risk is also associated with a greater chance for a bad outcome if the stock market does not perform well. In the study, most participants selected the medium-risk option (option B). Only 29 percent thought the high-risk investment (option C) was better than the medium-risk investment. For most people, option C seemed too extreme.

Employees were also asked to rank-order the investment programs in Part B of Table 4.7. Notice that option B in Part A is the same as program 1 in Part B. When option C is repositioned as program 2 in Part B, it no longer looks as extreme as it did in Part A because another investment option is included that is even more extreme. Looking at the array of programs in Part B, nearly 54 percent of the employees ranked program 2 (option C) higher than program 1 (option B). When options B and C are characterized as the medium- and high-risk choices, investors prefer B. When they are characterized as the low- and medium-risk choices, investors prefer C.

Therefore, some people's assessment of investment risk is not absolute but appears to be relative. In other words, people sometimes compare available choices relative to each other instead of comparing them to personal needs or absolute preferences. In the investments world, when faced with many stock choices and fewer bond choices, investors sometimes end up choosing portfolios that are too heavily weighted toward stocks. When faced with few stock choices and many bond choices, investors sometimes select portfolios overly concentrated in bonds.

Mental Accounting

Mental accounting

Thinking about money and investing using individual categories instead of a unified perspective.

Accounting systems categorize and track the flow of money. In a similar manner, people sometimes use **mental accounting** to keep their financial affairs in order. For many of us, the brain uses a mental accounting system that is similar to a file cabinet. When you buy a new stock, a

---

[2] See Shlomo Benartzi and Richard H. Thaler, "How Much Is Investor Autonomy Worth?" *Journal of Finance*, vol. 57, no. 4 (August 2002), pp. 1593–1616.

new folder is opened to follow its progress. Each decision, action, and outcome about that stock is placed in the file folder. Each investment has its own file folder. Once an outcome is assigned a mental folder, it is difficult to view that outcome in another way. When interactions among assets in different folders are overlooked, this mental process can adversely affect investor wealth.

Ignoring interaction among mental accounts can adversely affect investment decisions. Modern portfolio theory shows how the combination of different assets in a portfolio of securities can reduce the volatility that comes with investing in any single security. If one class of equities (utility stocks) tends to fall when another group of equities (oil stocks) tends to rise, the volatility or risk of the investor's portfolio can be reduced by combining such assets into a single portfolio. Utility stocks get hit when oil prices rise because such companies are often unable to quickly recoup the costs of rising fuel prices. At the same time, rising oil prices tend to boost the profits and share prices of oil companies. If investors want to profit from rising oil prices, they buy oil stocks and avoid heavy energy users, such as public utilities. If investors want to avoid betting on trends in the price of oil altogether, they might construct an investment portfolio that includes well-managed public utilities and oil companies. Anytime an investor contemplates buying or selling a given security, it is how returns on that security interact with returns on the investor's overall portfolio that matters. Unfortunately, investors sometimes encounter difficulty evaluating interactions among various securities because of mental accounting errors.

Summary

■ The reward for postponing consumption is the **nominal risk-free rate**, which consists of the **risk-free rate of return** plus an amount equal to the expected rate of **inflation**. A second important component of required return is the **required risk premium**. High-risk investments involve a higher-risk premium; low-risk investments involve a lower-risk premium.

■ Investors often wrongly focus on **arithmetic average returns** when judging portfolio performance, and the arithmetic average is upward-biased. It cannot be used to accurately depict the compound rate of return earned on an investment over time. The **geometric mean return** is the appropriate measure of the compound rate of return earned on an investment over time. **Total return** is measured by the sum of dividends, interest income, and capital gains or capital losses.

■ Investors face the ever-present danger that inflation, or a general increase in the cost of living, will reduce the value of any investment. If a particular investment earns a **nominal return** of 6 percent but the rate of inflation is 4 percent, the return after inflation, or **real return**, is only 2 percent.

■ A common measure of return volatility is the **standard deviation** of investment returns. This is the square root of the variance of the annual rate of return on investment. The standard deviation is an absolute measure of risk. The **coefficient of variation** is a useful *relative* measure of the risk-reward relationship. The formula for the coefficient of variation is simply the standard deviation divided by the expected return. **Covariance** is an absolute measure of

comovement that varies between plus and minus infinity, $+\infty$ and $-\infty$. **Correlation** is a relative measure of comovement that varies between -1 and $+1$. For investors, the simplest way to "smooth out" the effects of year-to-year volatility in rates of return is to adopt an extended **investment horizon**, or holding period.

■ By owning individual stocks and bonds, the investor is exposed to **firm-specific risk**, or the chance that problems with an individual company will reduce the value of investment dramatically. Firm-specific risk can be mitigated through diversification. Although diversification reduces the risk of loss from a single investment, there remains **market risk** tied to the chance that the overall stock or bond markets will decline in value. Given historically high P/E ratios and historic lows for dividend yields, common stock investors have faced a significant amount of **valuation risk** in the new millennium. Economic expansion is typically accompanied by rising stock prices and growing investor enthusiasm. Anemic economic growth is typically accompanied by stagnant or falling stock prices and deepening investor pessimism. This process of fluctuating returns, described as **reversion to the mean**, is an inherent characteristic of economic and stock market environments.

■ Like the stock market, the bond market is influenced by economic expectations. **Interest rate risk** is the chance of loss in the value of fixed-income investments following a rise in interest rates. In addition to facing interest rate risk, bond investors are also subject to **credit risk**. Credit risk is the chance that an individual issuer of a bond will fail to make timely payments of principal and interest.

■ An **investment portfolio** is a collection of securities that together provide an investor with an attractive trade-off between risk and return. **Portfolio theory** is the simple concept of making security choices based on portfolio expected returns and risks. **Expected return** is measured by the amount of profit anticipated over some relevant holding period. **Risk** is captured by return dispersion. Within this framework, investment alternatives are represented by the **probability distribution** of security returns over some future period. Investors get positive benefit, or **utility**, out of an increase in the expected rate of return and suffer a psychic loss, or **disutility**, from an increase in the amount of risk, or return volatility. This means that investors tend to be **risk-averse**.

■ An equal investment in two securities with the same expected return and standard deviation but a perfect inverse correlation would create a constant return, or **zero-risk portfolio**. An **efficient portfolio** provides maximum expected return for a given level of risk. Alternatively, an efficient portfolio provides minimum risk for a given expected return. The **efficient frontier** includes all efficient portfolios that provide maximum expected return for a given level of risk. Alternatively, the efficient frontier depicts all efficient portfolios that entail minimum risk for a given expected return. The **optimal portfolio** provides an investor with the highest level of expected utility. A key concept in portfolio theory is that the **market portfolio** is an efficient portfolio.

■ Some investors are **myopic** in considering the risk in investments. Their investment choices are influenced by relative risk and reward comparisons. People succumb to the **house money effect** by increasing the level of risk in their portfolios after making a profit. After losing money, people feel desperate to break even and will accept risky gambles that they would not ordinarily take. Many investors use **mental accounting** to keep track of investment choices. Each investment has its own file, and interactions among the assets in different folders are often overlooked.

Self-Test Problems

ST4.1 Calculate and briefly describe any differences between the arithmetic versus geometric mean return for a stock with five-year annual returns of −10, 100, 15, 50, and −50 percent.

Solution

Arithmetic average = (−10% + 100% + 15% + 50% − 50%)/5 = 21%

Geometric mean = $(0.9 \times 2.0 \times 1.15 \times 1.5 \times 0.5)^{1/5} - 1 = 9.2\%$

Notice that the arithmetic average of 21 percent per year substantially exceeds the geometric mean of 9.2 percent per year (true return) over this period. The arithmetic average is biased upward in the case of highly volatile returns because it fails to account for the fact that downside volatility is limited to −100 percent but the upside is unlimited. If you buy a stock for 10 and it doubles to 20 (+100 percent) and then falls by 50 percent to 10, you are making *no* money despite the fact that the arithmetic average rate of return is a whopping 25 percent [= (100% − 50%)/2] per year. Many individual investors fail to appreciate the importance of avoiding losses when seeking to build a significant investment portfolio. Perhaps this is why investment billionaire Warren Buffett says that Rule 1 in investing is to not lose money. Rule 2, according to Buffett, is to not forget Rule 1.

 ST4.2 Use a spreadsheet to compute the portfolio expected return and standard deviation of a portfolio consisting of Williams Cos., Toys 'R' Us, and Advanced Micro Devices. Compute risk and return for each of the five portfolios made of the following weights:

Williams Cos.	Toy 'R' Us	Advanced Micro Devices
0.50	0.25	0.25
0.25	0.50	0.25
0.80	0.1	0.1
0.33	0.33	0.33
0.15	0.15	0.70

Use the following 24 monthly returns for each company:

	A	B	C	D	E	F
1						
2			1 Month Total Return (%)			
3						
4		Date	Williams Cos.	Toys R Us	Advanced Micro Devices	
5		Mar05	0.16	12.64	-7.62	
6		Feb05	12.02	6.62	10.44	
7		Jan05	3.19	4.79	-28.25	
8		Dec04	-1.98	5.84	3.48	
9		Nov04	33.25	7.39	26.52	
10		Oct04	3.39	1.52	29.39	
11		Sep04	1.77	9.24	13.74	
12		Aug04	-2.06	-1.34	-8.49	
13		Jul04	2.10	3.33	-21.45	
14		Jun04	0.00	1.34	2.25	
15		May04	15.63	1.75	9.35	
16		Apr04	7.63	-8.04	-12.38	
17		Mar04	1.16	7.01	8.20	
18		Feb04	-6.61	11.19	0.94	
19		Jan04	3.26	11.71	-0.27	
20		Dec03	4.80	7.67	-17.08	
21		Nov03	-8.04	-9.69	18.22	
22		Oct03	8.28	8.06	36.81	
23		Sep03	3.18	-11.67	-1.59	
24		Aug03	43.94	22.15	54.66	
25		Jul03	-19.62	-8.00	13.89	
26		Jun03	0.00	4.12	-11.95	
27		May03	13.81	13.56	-2.15	
28		Apr03	51.75	22.46	20.39	
29						

Solution

Use the average return as the expected return for each firm.

	A	B	C	D	E	F	G	H	I
30			Williams Cos.	Toys R Us	Advanced Micro Devices				
31		Average =	7.13	5.15	5.71		=AVERAGE(E5:E28)		
32		Standard De	15.85	8.78	19.25		=STDEV(E5:E28)		
33									
34			Covariance (Williams, Toys) =		85.16		=COVAR(C5:C28,D5:D28)		
35			Covariance (Williams, AMD) =		137.86				
36			Covariance (AMD, Toys) =		47.09				
37						Portfolio	Portfolio		
38						Expected Return	Standard Deviation		
39		Weights	0.50	0.25	0.25	6.28	12.35		
40			0.25	0.50	0.25	5.78	10.41		
41			0.80	0.10	0.10	6.79	14.21		
42			0.33	0.33	0.33	6.00	11.73		
43			0.15	0.15	0.70	5.84	15.22		
44									
45			=C43*$C$31+D43*$D$31+E43*$E$31						
46		=SQRT((C43^2*$C$32^2+D43^2*$D$32^2+E43^2*$E$32^2)+2*(C43*D43*$E$34+C43*E43*$E$35+D43*E43*$E$36))							
47									

An investor who forms a portfolio of 50 percent Williams, 25 percent Toys 'R' Us, and 25 percent AMD should expect a 6.28 percent return with a standard deviation of 12.35 percent. Note that an investor would not want to own AMD alone. By combining it with Williams and Toys 'R' Us, the investor can increase the expected return *and* decrease the risk. Of these five portfolios, the one consisting of 25 percent Williams, 50 percent Toys 'R' Us, and 25 percent AMD has the lowest coefficient of variation and thus has the best risk-return relationship.

Questions and Problems

4.1 Suppose that the return you require for investing in eBay Inc.'s corporate debt is 8 percent. If the nominal risk-free rate of return is 4.5 percent, what is the required risk premium?

4.2 Suppose the percentage change in a company's stock price was –10.0 percent in 2002, 79.4 percent in 2003, –9.4 percent in 2004, and 4.5 percent in 2005. What was the geometric mean return over the 2002–2005 period?

4.3 Calculate the 2002–2005 standard deviation of annual investment returns for a common stock that returned –10.0 percent in 2002, 79.4 percent in 2003, –9.4 percent in 2004, and 4.5 percent in 2005.

4.4 Use your answers from Questions 4.2 and 4.3 to find the coefficient of variation for the common stock in question over the 2002–2005 period.

4.5 What were the geometric mean returns of common stocks, long-term Treasury bonds, and short-term Treasury bills from January 2002 to December 2004? (Note: The annual returns for these three investment classes can be found in Table 4.2.)

4.6 Explain the characteristics of firm-specific risk. How might an investor limit his or her exposure to this type of risk?

4.7 What is valuation risk? Did P/E ratios at the start of 2000 signify high valuation risk?

4.8 How does interest rate risk differ from credit risk?

4.9 How do traditional IRAs and Roth IRAs allow investors to defer taxes? Use Table 4.3 to discuss the tax deferral benefits that can be derived from either type of IRA.

4.10 Consider the following risk and return measures for four firms:

	Average Return	Standard Deviation
Exxon	10%	14%
Proctor & Gamble	8	12
Verizon Communications	12	30
Weyerhauser	7	14

Rank-order the firms (best to worst) by their risk and return attractiveness using the coefficient of variation.

4.11 Investors seem to rank retirement plan investment alternatives relative to each other instead of relative to their risk and return needs. Give an example of how this happens. Why might investors do this?

 4.12 MSN Money has created a risk-return measure that it calls *StockScouter Rating*. This rating is meant to measure a stock's potential for outperforming the market given its level of risk. Go to the MSN Money site (**http://moneycentral.msn.com**) and enter the ticker for Coca-Cola (KO). Click the Stock Rating link on the left menu. What is Coke's rating and what does it mean? How are the ratings computed?

4.13 Suppose an investor wishes to combine a T-bill, which offers the risk-free rate of 3.5 percent, and Exxon Mobil Corp. (XOM). XOM has an expected return of 12 percent and a standard deviation of 25 percent. The portfolio is to consist of a 50-50 split between the T-bill and XOM. If the covariance between returns on the T-bill and XOM is zero, calculate the portfolio expected return and standard deviation.

STANDARD & POOR'S

4.14 Go to the Standard & Poor's Market Insight Web site at **www.mhhe.com/edumarketinsight** and enter the ticker (OSI) for Outback Steakhouse Inc. Examine the information given in the Mthly. Adj. Prices link in the "Excel Analytics" section. Using the monthly returns for Outback and for the S&P 500 Index, compute the average monthly return, geometric mean, standard deviation, and coefficient of variation. Compare these measures for Outback and the S&P 500.

4.15 Studies show that investors often hold only three or four stocks. In addition, they tend to be either highly weighted in the stock market or not invested in equities at all. Why might these investors fail to diversify?

4.16 Which of the following statements about standard deviation is *true*? Standard deviation:

a. Is the square of the variance
b. Can be a positive or a negative number
c. Is denominated in the same units as the original data
d. Is the arithmetic mean of the squared deviations from the mean

4.17 A stock with a coefficient of variation of 0.50 has a(n):

a. Variance equal to half the stock's expected return
b. Expected return equal to half the stock's variance
c. Expected return equal to half the stock's standard deviation
d. Standard deviation equal to half the stock's expected return

4.18 Which of the following is *least likely* to affect the required rate of return on an investment?

a. Real risk-free rate
b. Asset risk premium
c. Expected rate of inflation
d. Investors' composite propensity to consume

4.19 The Markowitz efficient frontier is *best* described as the set of portfolios that has:

a. The minimum risk for every level of return
b. Proportionally equal units of risk and return
c. The maximum excess rate of return for every given level of risk
d. The highest return for each level of beta based on the capital asset pricing model

4.20 An investor is considering adding another investment to a portfolio. To achieve the maximum diversification benefits, the investor should add an investment that has a correlation coefficient with the existing portfolio *closest to:*

a. −1.0
b. −0.5
c. 0.0
d. +1.0

INVESTMENT APPLICATION

Investing for Retirement

Most of us were not born into significant wealth. We do not have the opportunity to begin our investment careers with $100,000, $10,000, or even $1,000. Many investors start accumulating their retirement wealth with as little as $30 per month. If setting aside a portion of your monthly income is the only viable means for accumulating a retirement nest egg, a basic question must be addressed: How much must be set aside to build a satisfactory retirement income?

Table 4.8 provides information that can be used to help determine that amount. The first step in this process is to calculate the amount of investment wealth generated by various savings plans during one's working years. Then it is necessary to calculate the amount of retirement income that can be provided by that wealth.

For simplicity, let's look at retirement wealth and retirement income in real terms, after accounting for the effects of inflation. Long-term bonds generate real returns for investors on the order of 1 to 2 percent per year. Common stock investors have enjoyed real returns of as much as 5 to 6 percent per year during the post-World War II period. Although nominal rates of return on long-term bonds and common stock vary widely from year to year, these real returns have been quite stable. Real returns of 1 to 2 percent for long-term bond investors and 5 to 6 percent for common stock investors represent a reasonable expectation of future returns.

TABLE 4.8   Retirement Income Provided by a 10 Percent Savings Plan

	A. Cumulative Value of Savings as Last-Year-Salary Percentage—Funding Percentage: 100%							B. Wealth Requirement Necessary to Fund 100% of Final Salary					
Working Years	Retirement Fund Real Rate of Return						Retirement Years	Retirement Fund Real Rate of Return					
	10%	20%	30%	40%	50%	60%		10%	20%	30%	40%	50%	60%
1	0.1000	0.1000	0.1000	0.1000	0.1000	0.1000	1	0.9901	0.9804	0.9709	0.9615	0.9524	0.9434
2	0.2010	0.2020	0.2030	0.2040	0.2050	0.2060	2	1.9704	1.9416	1.9135	1.8861	1.8594	1.8334
3	0.3030	0.3060	0.3091	0.3122	0.3153	0.3184	3	2.9410	2.8839	2.8286	2.7751	2.7232	2.6730
4	0.4060	0.4122	0.4184	0.4246	0.4310	0.4375	4	3.9020	3.8077	3.7171	3.6299	3.5460	3.4651
5	0.5101	0.5204	0.5309	0.5416	0.5526	0.5637	5	4.8534	4.7135	4.5797	4.4518	4.3295	4.2124
10	1.0462	1.0950	1.1464	1.2006	1.2578	1.3181	10	9.4713	8.9826	8.5302	8.1109	7.7217	7.3601
15	1.6097	1.7293	1.8599	2.0024	2.1579	2.3276	15	13.8651	12.8493	11.9379	11.1184	10.3797	9.7122
20	2.2019	2.4297	2.6870	2.9778	3.3066	3.6786	20	18.0456	16.3514	14.8775	13.5903	12.4622	11.4699
25	2.8243	3.2030	3.6459	4.1646	4.7727	5.4865	25	22.0232	19.5235	17.4131	15.6221	14.0939	12.7834
30	3.4785	4.0568	4.7575	5.6085	6.6439	7.9058	30	25.8077	22.3965	19.6004	17.2920	15.3725	13.7648
35	4.1660	4.9994	6.0462	7.3652	9.0320	11.1435	35	29.4086	24.9986	21.4872	18.6646	16.3742	14.4982
40	4.8886	6.0402	7.5401	9.5026	12.0800	15.4762	40	32.8347	27.3555	23.1148	19.7928	17.1591	15.0463

For purposes of illustration, a 6 percent real return is a very reasonable expectation for a broadly diversified portfolio of common stocks. If you look at the 6 percent column of Part A in Table 4.8 and go to the 40 row, you will see the number 15.4762, which has a very practical interpretation. Suppose a young woman graduates from college at 25 years of age with a bachelor's degree in business administration. Let's assume that she takes a job with an accounting firm at a starting salary of $50,000 per year. For simplicity, let's also assume that raises received during her working career as a manager are just sufficient to offset the rising cost of living. If she saves 10 percent of her income each year of her working life and invests the proceeds at a real return of 6 percent, the cumulative value of her wealth at retirement will be $773,810 (= $50,000 × 15.4762). To avoid taxes, such an accumulation of wealth must take place within a tax-sheltered retirement plan, such as an individual retirement account (IRA) or a 401(k) plan. To be sure, the amount accumulated for retirement will actually be more than $773,810. The actual amount will be boosted in nominal terms by the effects of inflation. It is also important to recognize that the $773,810 amount has a simple interpretation in the light of a starting salary of $50,000 per year. This amount is 15.4762 times her starting salary of $50,000 per year.

The number 15.4762 is interesting because it has a very simple interpretation in terms of the amount of retirement income it can generate. Part B of Table 4.8 illustrates the retirement wealth necessary to fund 100 percent of one's final salary at various interest rates. Whereas Part A shows the amount of cumulative investment generated from a given investment per period, Part B shows the stream of annuity payments that can be generated by various levels of wealth. At the time of retirement, the retiree switches to an annuity payment mode. Look at the 6 percent column and the 40 years of retirement income row. Notice the number 15.0463. What this number means is, again, simple. If a retiree has wealth at the point of retirement equal to 15.0463 times his or her last year's salary and invests the funds at a real rate of interest of 6 percent, such wealth would be sufficient to fund a retirement income equal to his or her last year's pay for 40 years. In the present example, the manager has accumulated a retirement wealth of 15.4762 times her salary, which is more than enough to fund a full salary during a retirement of as long as 40 years. Even if she is healthy and makes it to retirement at 65, chances are not good that she will live past 105. Thus, a 40-year 10 percent savings plan generates more wealth than necessary to provide a retirement income equal to 100 percent of your last year's pay for the rest of your natural life.

This simple illustration explains why it has been a common rule of thumb in investing to advise employees to save at least 10 percent of their income for retirement. It is only one of many possible scenarios. If a comfortable retirement at less than 100 percent of one's final salary is feasible, a lower level of retirement savings or a shorter working career becomes possible. As illustrated in Table 4.8, there is an obvious trade-off involved between the amount saved for retirement, the real return on investment, the number of working years, and the number of retirement years. Notice the wonderful advantage gained by workers who begin saving for retirement early during their working careers. For example, 10 percent of income invested at 6 percent accumulates to only 3.6786 times final salary for a worker with only 20 years until retirement. Such a worker would have to set aside a whopping 42.1 percent (= 15.4762/3.6786 × 10%) of his or her salary to accumulate a retirement wealth equal to 15.4762 times the worker's final salary over an investment horizon of 20 years.

a. Suppose you are 45 years old, have no retirement savings, and wish to retire at 70 percent of your final salary in 15 years. How much of your income needs to be set aside to fund a retirement income for 30 years?

b. Now assume that such a high level of savings simply is not feasible. How much saving is required if you extend your working career to 65 years of age?

c. Is the assumption of retiring at 100 percent of final salary necessary to fund an adequate retirement lifestyle? Why?

5

chapter

Asset Pricing Theory and Performance Evaluation

Modern portfolio theory has made a compelling contribution to our understanding of financial markets. Models of market efficiency help academics understand the subtleties of risk-reward relationships, and they facilitate the construction of optimal portfolios by investment professionals. When success is measured in terms of market acceptance, modern portfolio theory has been enormously successful. Beta is an accepted measure of stock market risk at research seminars, on the pages of financial publications, and in the boardrooms of corporate America. The concept of risk-adjusted performance is also broadly accepted. Portfolio managers and investors everywhere seek to earn the largest possible return, given a specified level of risk, or the lowest level of risk, given a specified required return.

Hedge funds and investment banks often employ "rocket scientists" who use complex pricing models to assess relative risks and return opportunities among assets and asset classes. Some of these investors have earned outstanding returns for extended periods. In other notable instances, the limitations of modern portfolio theory have become obvious to academics and practitioners alike. Famous hedge funds, like Long Term Capital Management, have "blown up" in spectacular fashion when investment professionals forgot that asset pricing models describe behavior under idealized conditions that are seldom met in "messy" real-world markets. Conventional risk-reward relationships have a tendency to become distinctly unconventional when stock market volatility soars. As a result, even the most elegant asset pricing models leave ample room for improvement.[1]

On an overall basis, it is important to keep in mind that asset pricing theory is useful only when it helps investors understand and predict the performance of real-world markets for stocks, bonds, and related assets. Investors should not reject the

---

[1]Gregory Zuckerman, "Pros Say They Weren't Wrong—Just Early," *The Wall Street Journal Online*, December 18, 2005 (**http://online.wsj.com/**).

validity of the market efficiency concept just because a single characterization of that concept, such as the capital asset pricing model, has flaws and limitations. "The sun rises in the east" is a useful concept despite the fact that during the course of the year the timing and location of sunrise varies. Alternative versions of the market efficiency concept are similarly useful despite obvious limitations. Wise investors understand how models can help with investment decision making without pushing their use beyond reason and experience.

CHAPTER OBJECTIVES

- Become acquainted with CAPM theory and application.
- Learn about multifactor pricing models.
- Assess portfolio performance.
- Compute alpha, Sharpe ratio, and Treynor Index measures.
- Realize the limitations of asset pricing models.

Asset Pricing

Traditional Theory

A traditional tenet of investment theory is that expected returns are positively related to the amount of risk assumed. Anyone who wants to avoid all short-term investment risk can simply buy money market securities, such as T-bills, and earn the risk-free rate. Investors who want a higher than risk-free rate of return must be willing to take on some investment risk. How much risk must be taken in the attempt to achieve the expected return desired? What is the exact relationship between expected return and risk? The exploration of these questions lies at the heart of asset pricing theory. Formal asset pricing models reflect the attempt to determine an exact equation or set of equations that can be used to tell investors about the exact form of the relation between the expected rate of return and risk.

Asset pricing models can be used to predict the return that should be earned on various investments. If the anticipated amount of investment risk can be accurately measured, then traditional asset pricing models can be used to determine the predicted return. In fulfilling this function, asset pricing models become very useful and important to professional and individual investors alike. Asset pricing models can also be used as tools to help evaluate the historical performance of portfolios and answer questions such as, How good is a mutual fund manager? This chapter examines traditional asset pricing models commonly used to predict investment returns and evaluate portfolio manager performance.

New Behavioral Approaches

The design of asset pricing models began using theories of rational investor behavior. Rational investors are generally thought to be risk-averse, can fully exploit all available information, and do not suffer from psychological biases. In these models, the expected rate of return on investment for a given portfolio is solely a function of the economic risks faced. These economic risks might be things such as unexpected changes in inflation, interest rates, productivity growth, and employment, to name just a few. In fact, many economic risks have been explored and understanding has grown about how they help predict future returns. Nevertheless, traditional asset pricing models have demonstrated only limited ability to predict future returns.

Because the empirical performance and usefulness of traditional asset pricing models still leave a lot to be desired, finance scholars have begun to look beyond the traditional bounds of economic analysis for answers to important riddles in the investments field. Are investors always rational? What happens to typically rational investors when they interact as members of a crowd? Do lessons from the fields of personal psychology and social psychology have the potential to help us better understand investment behavior? An important aspect of recent developments in asset pricing theory is the ongoing effort to broaden our awareness of the role of investment behavior in asset pricing. With the growth of the behavioral finance literature, asset pricing models are now being created that reflect behavioral influences.

Capital Asset Pricing Model

History

Capital asset pricing model (CAPM)

Method for predicting how investment returns are determined in an efficient capital market.

In the mid-1960s, William Sharpe and John Lintner invented the **capital asset pricing model (CAPM)**, resulting in a Nobel Prize for Sharpe in 1990. Four decades later, the CAPM is widely used in investment applications, such as asset pricing, risk evaluation, and performance assessment of managed portfolios.

The attraction of the CAPM is that it offers powerful and intuitively pleasing predictions about risk measurement and the relation between expected return and risk. Unfortunately, the empirical record of the model is poor. The CAPM's empirical problems probably reflect both its theoretical failings, due to many simplifying assumptions, and the difficulties in its implementation. Nevertheless, a thorough understanding of the model is important for two reasons. First, the CAPM is commonly used in practice. Therefore, it is advantageous to know its strengths and weaknesses. And second, it is the theoretical foundation on which other asset pricing theories are built.

Basic Assumptions

The CAPM is an elaborate attempt to provide a complete description of how investment returns are determined. It is a method for predicting how investment returns are generated in a capital market.

The CAPM entails a number of important underlying assumptions. These basic assumptions are:

- Investors hold efficient portfolios—higher expected returns involve higher risk.
- Unlimited borrowing and lending is possible at the risk-free rate.
- Investors have homogenous expectations.
- There is a one-period time horizon.
- Investments are infinitely divisible.
- No taxes or transaction costs exist.
- Inflation is fully anticipated.
- Capital markets are in equilibrium.

Some criticize the CAPM for such a restrictive set of underlying assumptions. After all, taxes and transaction costs exist in the real world. However, it is worth pointing out that a model can be a useful predictive device even if its underlying assumptions fail to be met. If a model such as the CAPM can predict stock returns with a high degree of accuracy, then the restrictiveness of its underlying assumptions is a moot point.

Lending and Borrowing

An important underlying assumption of the CAPM is that investors have the opportunity to lend or borrow at the risk-free rate. Lending occurs if a portion of the investor's portfolio is held in a risk-free asset. For example, an individual investor is lending at the risk-free rate when Treasury bills constitute an important part of the investor's portfolio. Borrowing is used when more than 100 percent of the investor's portfolio is invested in risky assets. Margin account customers do, in fact, have the opportunity to leverage their stock investments by borrowing at the broker loan rate. The broker loan rate is often the most attractive interest rate available to individual borrowers and is seldom much above the three-month Treasury bill rate. Presently, U.S. investors are able to purchase equity securities with an initial margin requirement of 50 percent. This means that investors with $10,000 of capital can buy as much as $20,000 worth of equity securities.

Figure 5.1 shows the efficient frontier as developed from modern portfolio theory and illustrated in Chapter 4. Remember, the efficient frontier is the set of portfolios of risky assets that maximize expected return for any desired level of risk. The CAPM is based on modern portfolio theory.

In Figure 5.1(A), a straight line is drawn from the risk-free rate R_F to the market return R_M on the efficient frontier. At R_F, 100 percent of the investor's portfolio is invested in T-bills. At R_M, 100 percent of the investor's portfolio is invested in the market index. Between R_F and R_M, the investor's portfolio is invested in both. The closer to the vertical axis and R_F, the more that will be invested in T-bills. The closer to R_M, the more that will be invested in the market portfolio. At the midpoint of the line from R_F to R_M, the investor's portfolio is split 50-50 between T-bills and the market index. Indeed, it is interesting to see how an infinite variety of expected-return profiles can be constructed by simply varying the amount of an entire investment portfolio that is held in the risk-free asset and the market portfolio.

Note how a portfolio of risky assets with lending or borrowing at the risk-free rate can dominate many real-world investment alternatives. Notice how the expected return $E(R_{A*})$ on a portfolio containing the market index plus risk-free lending is higher than the expected return $E(R_A)$ on a portfolio of low-risk auto stocks. With the same level of risk $SD(R_A)$, the lending portfolio will be preferred by low-risk investors. Now observe how an investor can own the portfolio B*. An investor must use a margin account to borrow money and invest it all in the market portfolio. This leveraged portfolio has an expected return, $E(R_{B*})$, that is higher than the expected return $E(R_B)$ on a portfolio of high-risk biotech stocks. With the same level of risk $SD(R_B)$, the leveraged portfolio will be preferred by investors seeking a high level of risk.

FIGURE 5.1   **Efficient Frontier Becomes a Straight Line When Risk-Free Lending and Borrowing Are Possible**

A. Expected Return with Lending Beats the Low-Risk Portfolio, $E(R_{A*}) > E(R_A)$; Expected Return with Borrowing Beats the High-Risk Portfolio, $E(R_{B*}) > E(R_B)$

B. Lending Is Preferable to Low-Risk U_1 Investors; Borrowing Is Preferable to High-Risk U_1 Investors

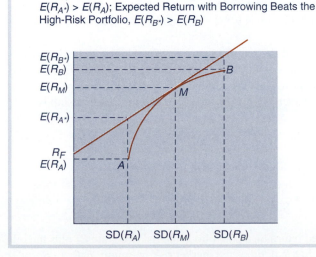
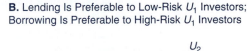
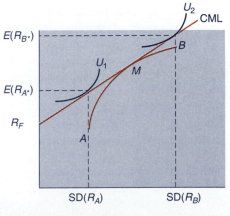

Street Smarts 5.1

Dear Abby (Joseph Cohen)

Abby Joseph Cohen is one of Wall Street's most respected and influential stock market analysts. Cohen is managing director and chair of the Investment Policy Committee of Goldman, Sachs & Co., where she is responsible for the firm's U.S. portfolio strategy. Born in 1952 in Queens, New York, Cohen obtained a BA in economics and computer science in 1973 from Cornell University. She earned an MS degree in economics from George Washington University in 1976. In an industry where chauffeured stretch limousines are the rule, the unpretentious and unassuming Cohen rises at 5 a.m. each workday and takes the city bus to work. Still, she logs more than 125,000 airline miles per year meeting with Goldman Sachs clients, and she gives more than 150 speeches per year to clients and other investors.

Cohen makes numerous television appearances and is frequently quoted in the financial press. If every bull market has its sage, the 1990s surely belonged to Cohen. She has been the bull market's most ardent supporter, explaining its every move to traders and urging them to believe it would continue its run. As stock prices continued to soar in the 1990s, she won more followers. When a rumor spread that she had turned bearish, stocks plummeted. In the summer of 1998, when valuations became stretched, Cohen declared that stocks had become "fairly valued." She became bullish once again in the fall of 1998 after stocks turned lower, or "corrected," by more than 10 percent. Cohen turned bearish on technology stocks in late March 2000, and thereby called the Nasdaq peak.

Cohen's long-term bullish view on the stock market has been based on her perception of continuous improvement in the overall economy. Cohen's success at forecasting the market's direction has convinced many investors that macroeconomic theory and analysis are vital tools for investment research. Unlike the case with once-famous but now-discredited security analysts, such as Henry Blodget and Jack Grubman, Cohen's reliance on solid economic analysis has allowed her to build and maintain a sterling reputation.

See Matthew Boyle, "Our Best and Worst Calls of '05," *Fortune*, December 12, 2005, p. 182.

The opportunity for risk-free lending and borrowing changes the efficient frontier from that derived in Chapter 4 into the straight-line capital market line (CML) shown in Figure 5.1(B). As shown, depending on their risk preferences, investors choose individually optimal locations along the CML. Low-risk investors choose to invest in low-risk portfolios consisting of both T-bills and the market portfolio. High-risk investors choose to invest in high-risk portfolios combining the use of leverage with the market portfolio.

Expected Return and Risk

Capital Market Line

Capital market line (CML)
Linear risk-return trade-off for all investment portfolios.

The CAPM describes three distinct relations between the expected rate of return and risk. The first of these is called the **capital market line (CML)**. The CML shows the linear risk-return trade-off for all investment portfolios. Figure 5.2 shows the CML redrawn from Figure 5.1(B) without the efficient frontier. It is useful to characterize the CML in its equation form. Remember that the mathematical equation for a line is simply $y = b + mx$, where b is the y-intercept and m is the slope of the line. In Figure 5.2, the y axis is the expected return, while the x axis is the risk, measured in standard deviation.

The y-intercept in Figure 5.2 occurs at the risk-free rate, R_F. The slope can be denoted as rise over run between two points. It is convenient to use the two points for the risk-free rate and the market portfolio. The rise is $E(R_M) - R_F$, and the run is $SD(R_M) - 0$. So the slope is $[E(R_M) - R_F]/SD(R_M)$. Therefore, the CML characterization of the risk and return relationship is

$$E(R_p) = R_F + \frac{E(R_M) - R_F}{SD(R_M)} SD(R_P) \tag{5.1}$$

Rearranging gives

$$= R_F + \frac{SD(R_P)}{SD(R_M)} [E(R_M) - R_F]$$

The CML asserts that the expected return on a portfolio is the risk-free rate R_F plus the relative risk of the portfolio, $SD(R_P) \div SD(R_M)$, times the market risk premium, $E(R_M) - R_F$.

FIGURE 5.2	Capital Market Line (CML) Shows the Straight-Line Relation for Portfolio Expected Return and Risk

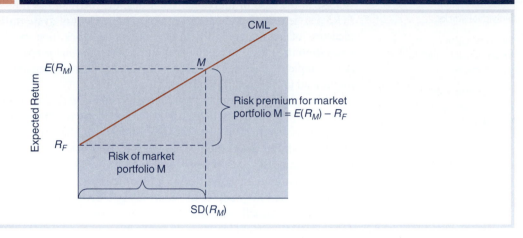

During the post-World War II period, the expected rate of return on the U.S. market has been roughly 12 percent per year and the risk-free rate roughly 5 percent. This implies that the market risk premium is 7 percent (= 12% - 5%). The CML identifies "reward for waiting" plus "reward for risk taking" components of expected return. In an overall market in which the expected rate of return is 12 percent per year, the risk-free rate of 5 percent can be thought of as the reward-for-waiting component of total return. The market risk premium of 7 percent can be thought of as the investor's reward for risk taking. The expected rate of return of 12 percent on the market portfolio represents both a reward for waiting and a reward for risk taking.

Market risk, as measured by the standard deviation of annual returns, falls in a range near 17 percent per year. According to the CML, a portfolio with twice the market risk level would need to provide investors with twice the standard risk premium of 7 percent per year. Therefore, a portfolio with $SD(R_P)$ = 34 percent would have an expected return of 19 percent [= 5% + (34%/17%) × (12% - 5%)]. A portfolio with one-half the market risk level would need to provide investors with one-half the standard risk premium of 7 percent per year. Thus, a portfolio with $SD(R_P)$ = 8.5 percent would have an expected return of 8.5 percent [= 5% + (8.5%/17%) × (12% - 5%)].

Thus, the CML depicts a linear risk-reward trade-off for all portfolios.

Try It!

Consider a situation in which Treasury bills offer a 3.5 percent yield and the market portfolio is expected to provide a 9 percent return with a 20 percent standard deviation. If you own a portfolio that consists of 20 percent Treasury bills and 80 percent stocks whose risk level is 15 percent, what is the expected return on the portfolio?

Solution

First compute the standard deviation of the portfolio. Note that the standard deviation of returns for T-bills is zero. Therefore,

$$SD(R_P) = \sqrt{0.2^2 \times 0^2 + 0.8^2 \times 15^2 + 2 \times 0.2 \times 0.8 \times 0} = 12\%$$

Now use Equation 5.1 to compute the expected return of the portfolio:

$$E(R_P) = 3.5\% + (12\% / 20\%) \times (9\% - 3.5\%) = 6.8\%$$

The expected return of this portfolio is 6.8 percent.

Security Market Line

Security market line (SML)
Linear risk-return trade-off for individual stocks.

Systematic risk
Return volatility tied to the overall market.

Unsystematic risk
Return volatility specific to an individual company.

Diversifiable risk
Another term for unsystematic risk.

Nondiversifiable risk
Another term for systematic risk.

Beta
The sensitivity of a security's returns to the systematic market risk factor.

The **security market line (SML)** characterizes a linear risk-return trade-off for individual stocks. In the case of individual securities, the SML shows how the expected rate of return $E(R_i)$ can be seen as a simple function of the amount of **systematic risk**. Systematic risk is a measure of return volatility in an individual stock that is tied to the overall market. **Unsystematic risk** is the amount of return volatility that is specific to an individual company. An example of unsystematic risk is the chance that a company's excessive use of leverage might lead to financial difficulties or bankruptcy.

Although both systematic risk and unsystematic risk contribute to the total amount of volatility experienced by investors, only systematic risk has a favorable influence on the expected rate of return. Investors cannot demand higher rates of expected return for unsystematic risk because such risk can be eliminated through judicious diversification. Unsystematic risk is also known as *firm-specific risk* or **diversifiable risk**. Figure 5.3 shows that the total amount of portfolio risk declines with an increase in the number of portfolio holdings. When the number of securities in a diversified portfolio approaches roughly 30, investors can virtually eliminate unsystematic risk. Remember that the Dow Jones Industrial Average (DJIA) includes 30 leading stocks, and the DJIA is often taken as a useful proxy for the overall market. However, even after unsystematic risk is eliminated through diversification, substantial systematic risk, or **nondiversifiable risk**, remains. Because systematic risk cannot be eliminated through diversification, the risk-return relationship dictates that investors be rewarded for any increase in systematic risk to justify their investment in a particular stock or market sector.

Systematic risk is the amount of unavoidable volatility that is directly tied to the overall market. For an individual stock or investment portfolio, systematic risk is measured by **beta**. Statisticians use the Greek letter beta, β, to signify the slope coefficient in a linear relation. Financial economists use the same Greek letter to signify systematic risk because stock price betas are the slope coefficients in the linear SML. The SML relation can be written as

$$E(R_i) = R_F + \frac{R_M - R_F}{\text{VAR}(R_M)} \times \text{COV}(R_i R_M) \tag{5.2}$$

$$= R_F + \frac{\text{COV}(R_i R_M)}{\text{VAR}(R_M)} \times (R_M - R_F)$$

$$= R_F + \beta_i (R_M - R_F)$$

FIGURE 5.3	Unsystematic Risk Can Be Eliminated through Diversification

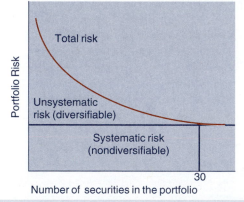

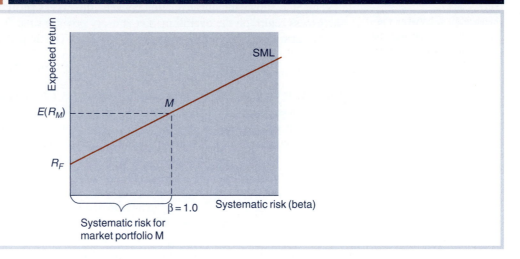

FIGURE 5.4   Security Market Line (SML) Shows the Straight-Line Relation between the Expected Rate of Return and Systematic Risk for an Individual Security

As shown in Figure 5.4, the SML depicts the straight-line relation between the expected rate of return and systematic risk for an individual security. In the SML, the expected rate of return is the risk-free rate plus relative risk, measured by β, multiplied by the market risk premium. Like the CML, the SML shows the reward for waiting and the reward for risk-taking parts of expected return. The difference lies in the fact that the CML deals with portfolios whereas the SML deals with individual securities.

Beta is a measure of relative risk, in which $\beta = 1$ for the overall market, $\beta = 2$ for a security with twice the systematic risk of the overall market, and $\beta = 0.5$ for a security with one-half the systematic risk of the market. As in the case of the CML, a fair estimate of the risk-free rate is 5 percent, and the expected rate of return on the market is 12 percent. This means that an individual security with $\beta = 2$ has an expected rate of return of 19 percent ($= 5\% + 2 \times 7\%$). An individual security with $\beta = 0.5$ has an expected rate of return of 8.5 percent ($= 5\% + 0.5 \times 7\%$).

Try It!

If the market is expected to increase by 9 percent and the risk-free rate is 4 percent, what is the expected return of assets with beta = 1.5, 0.75, 0.25, and -0.5?

Solution

The expected rates of return are:

Beta = 1.5: $E(R) = 4\% + 1.5 \times (9\% - 4\%) = 11.5\%$
Beta = 0.75: $E(R) = 4\% + 0.75 \times (9\% - 4\%) = 7.75\%$
Beta = 0.25: $E(R) = 4\% + 0.25 \times (9\% - 4\%) = 5.25\%$
Beta = -0.5: $E(R) = 4\% + -0.5 \times (9\% - 4\%) = 1.5\%$

Security Characteristic Line

The CML characterizes the relationship between the expected rate of return and risk for portfolios. It builds a link between the CAPM and traditional portfolio theory. The SML depicts the relationship between the expected rate of return and systematic risk for individual securities.

Security characteristic line (SCL)

Linear relation between the return on individual securities and the overall market at every point in time.

Excess return

A security or portfolio return less the risk-free rate.

Because it deals with individual securities, as opposed to well-diversified portfolios, the SML is somewhat more useful than the CML. The CAPM's third linear relationship between risk and return is called the **security characteristic line (SCL)**.

The SCL shows the linear relation between the **excess return** on individual securities and the excess return on the overall market at every point in time. The excess return is the return on the security less the return on the risk-free asset. The SCL is written

$$R_{it} - R_{Ft} = \alpha_i + \beta_i(R_{Mt} - R_{Ft}) + \varepsilon_i \qquad (5.3)$$

where R_{it} is the rate of return on an individual security i during period t, R_{Ft} is the return on the risk-free asset during period t, the intercept term is described by the Greek letter α (alpha), the slope coefficient is the Greek letter β (beta) and signifies systematic risk (as before), and the random disturbance or error term is depicted by the Greek letter ε (epsilon). At any point in time, the random disturbance term ε has an expected value of zero. This means that the expected return on an individual stock is determined by α, β, and the expected rate of return on the overall market because $R_{it} = \alpha_i + \beta_i R_{Mt} + \varepsilon_i$.

The slope coefficient β shows the anticipated effect on an individual security's rate of excess return following a 1 percent change in the market's excess return. If $\beta = 1.5$, then a 1 percent rise in the market would lead to a 1.5 percent hike in the stock, a 2 percent boost in the market would lead to a 3 percent jump in the stock, and so on. If $\beta = 0$, then the rate of return on an individual stock is totally unrelated to the overall market.

Positive abnormal returns

Above-average returns that cannot be explained as compensation for added risk.

Negative abnormal returns

Below-average returns that cannot be explained by below-market risk.

The intercept term α shows the anticipated rate of return when either $\beta = 0$ or $R_M = R_F$. When $\alpha > 0$, investors enjoy **positive abnormal returns**. When $\alpha < 0$, investors suffer **negative abnormal returns**. Investors would celebrate a portfolio manager whose portfolio consistently generated positive abnormal returns ($\alpha > 0$). They would fire managers with portfolios that consistently suffered negative abnormal returns ($\alpha < 0$). In a capital market where rates of return are solely determined by systematic risk, the CAPM asserts that both alpha and epsilon would equal zero, $\alpha = \varepsilon = 0$.

The SCL also lays out in precise detail how the total risk for an individual security consists of systematic (market-related) risk and unsystematic (firm-specific) risk. When $R_{it} - R_{Ft} = \alpha_i + \beta_i(R_{Mt} - R_{Ft}) + \varepsilon_i$, statisticians tell us that

$$\text{VAR}(R_i - R_F) = \text{VAR}(\alpha_i + \beta_i R_M - \beta_i R_F + \varepsilon_i) \qquad (5.4)$$
$$\text{VAR}(R_i) = \text{VAR}(\alpha_i) + \text{VAR}(\beta_i R_M - \beta_i R_F) + \text{VAR}(\varepsilon_i)$$
$$= 0 + \beta_i^2 \text{VAR}(R_M) + \text{VAR}(\varepsilon_i)$$

Since the random disturbance term is independent of the market return, Equation 5.4 implies that

$$\text{Total risk} = \text{systematic risk} + \text{unsystematic risk}$$
$$\text{SD}(R_i) = \beta_i \text{SD}(R_M) + \text{SD}(\varepsilon_i) \qquad (5.5)$$

Try It!

Clear Channel Communications (CCU) is a media company whose primary business is radio broadcasting. How much of its return volatility is due to systematic risk, and how much is due to unsystematic risk?

Solution

The company's beta can be found on Standard & Poors' Market Insight Web site. The beta is 1.614. Market Insight also provides monthly returns for CCU and for the S&P 500 Index over the past four years. The analysis is:

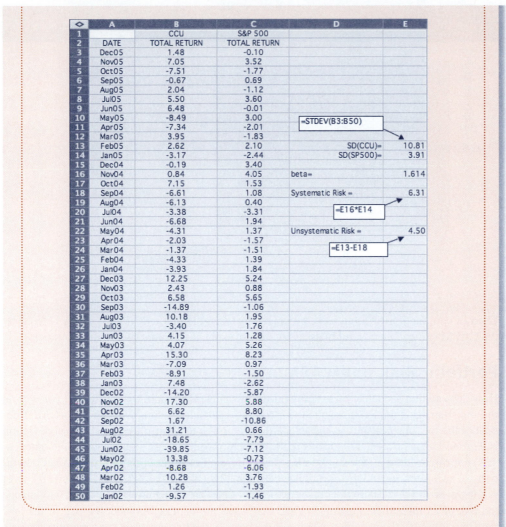

◇	A	B	C	D	E
1		CCU	S&P 500		
2	DATE	TOTAL RETURN	TOTAL RETURN		
3	Dec05	1.48	-0.10		
4	Nov05	7.05	3.52		
5	Oct05	-7.51	-1.77		
6	Sep05	-0.67	0.69		
7	Aug05	2.04	-1.12		
8	Jul05	5.50	3.60		
9	Jun05	6.48	-0.01		
10	May05	-8.49	3.00	=STDEV(B3:B50)	
11	Apr05	-7.34	-2.01		
12	Mar05	3.95	-1.83		
13	Feb05	2.62	2.10	SD(CCU)=	10.81
14	Jan05	-3.17	-2.44	SD(SP500)=	3.91
15	Dec04	-0.19	3.40		
16	Nov04	0.84	4.05	beta=	1.614
17	Oct04	7.15	1.53		
18	Sep04	-6.61	1.08	Systematic Risk =	6.31
19	Aug04	-6.13	0.40		
20	Jul04	-3.38	-3.31	=E16*E14	
21	Jun04	-6.68	1.94		
22	May04	-4.31	1.37	Unsystematic Risk =	4.50
23	Apr04	-2.03	-1.57		
24	Mar04	-1.37	-1.51	=E13-E18	
25	Feb04	-4.33	1.39		
26	Jan04	-3.93	1.84		
27	Dec03	12.25	5.24		
28	Nov03	2.43	0.88		
29	Oct03	6.58	5.65		
30	Sep03	-14.89	-1.06		
31	Aug03	10.18	1.95		
32	Jul03	-3.40	1.76		
33	Jun03	4.15	1.28		
34	May03	4.07	5.26		
35	Apr03	15.30	8.23		
36	Mar03	-7.09	0.97		
37	Feb03	-8.91	-1.50		
38	Jan03	7.48	-2.62		
39	Dec02	-14.20	-5.87		
40	Nov02	17.30	5.88		
41	Oct02	6.62	8.80		
42	Sep02	1.67	-10.86		
43	Aug02	31.21	0.66		
44	Jul02	-18.65	-7.79		
45	Jun02	-39.85	-7.12		
46	May02	13.38	-0.73		
47	Apr02	-8.68	-6.06		
48	Mar02	10.28	3.76		
49	Feb02	1.26	-1.93		
50	Jan02	-9.57	-1.46		

Note that a substantial amount of the total risk in Clear Channel is from unsystematic risk. This type of risk is not rewarded in the CAPM framework.

Using CAPM to Find Undervalued Stocks

The CAPM is best suited to helping determine what return to expect for a given level of systematic risk. Of course, investors might be interested in the extent to which the CAPM can be used to determine whether stocks are undervalued or overvalued. As a basic level, keep in mind that the idea of an undervalued or overvalued stock is inconsistent with the CAPM. Under CAPM, all stocks are fairly valued at all points in time. If an investor believes that an undervalued stock has been discovered, it would have an expected rate of return above that predicted by the CAPM. The expected-return and risk combination seen by the investor would therefore lie above the CAPM's SCL. If an investor believes that an overvalued stock has been discovered, it would have an expected rate of return below that predicted by the CAPM. The expected-return and risk combination seen by the investor would therefore lie below the CAPM's SCL.

Consider the case in which an investor has determined that company A will earn a high return, as shown in Figure 5.5. Note that CAPM shows what return, $E(R_A)$, should be expected given a beta of 0.9. Since the investor believes that company A will provide a return higher than that predicted by CAPM, that investor must believe this stock is undervalued. In addition, if company Z is thought to earn the return indicated in the figure, then it is thought to be overvalued. This is because it is thought to earn a return that is less than that predicted by CAPM.

FIGURE 5.5   **Use the Security Market Line (SML) to Identify Over- and Undervalued Stocks**

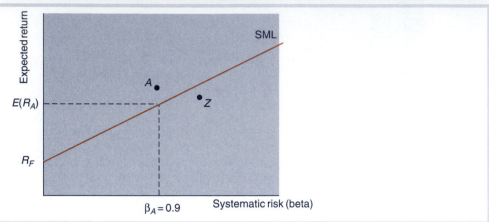

Used in conjunction with intensive company analysis, the theoretical perspective offered by the CAPM can become useful in assessing the investment potential of a particular stock.

Portfolio Risk and CAPM

How does adding a stock to an existing portfolio change the risk of that portfolio? Answering this question using modern portfolio theory requires substantial computational effort. MPT describes the risk of a portfolio as the standard deviation of the portfolio. The standard deviation is determined by how each security's return in the portfolio covaries with each of the other assets' returns. Adding a new stock to the portfolio requires computing all the standard deviations of each security and the covariance between all the securities. That can be quite a chore!

However, the CAPM provides an easy framework for assessing how a new stock will change the risk of an investment portfolio. When two assets are being combined, the risk of the new portfolio is simply the weighted average of the betas of the two assets. More generally, the beta of a portfolio is

$$\beta_P = \sum_{i=1}^{n} w_i \times \beta_i \qquad (5.6)$$

where w_i is the proportional weight of asset i in the portfolio. So consider an existing portfolio that has a beta of 1.1 and a new stock with a beta of 1.5. A new portfolio consisting of 90 percent of the old portfolio and 10 percent of the new stock will have a beta of 1.14 $(= 0.9 \times 1.1 + 0.1 \times 1.5)$.

Try It!

An investor wishes to invest $10,000 in the stock of Hewlett-Packard (beta = 0.655) and $15,000 in Time Warner, Inc. (beta = 2.186). What is the beta of the two-stock portfolio?

Solution

First compute the weights of each stock in the portfolio:

Portion in HP = $10,000 / ($10,000 + $15,000) = 40%
Portion in TWX = $15,000 / ($10,000 + $15,000) = 60%
The portfolio beta = (0.4 × 0.655) + (0.6 × 2.186) = 1.574

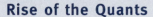
Rise of the Quants

"Quants" use economic models to measure the attractiveness of the overall market and individual stocks in light of earnings growth expectations, interest rates, and so on. Data on earnings, dividends, interest rates, and risk are all used to derive a "fair value" for many different types of assets. A "pure" quant shop is one that crunches numbers and selects investments according to model outcomes. Computers decide what to buy and sell. You might say they take the "I" out of investor.

The essence of quantitative investing is crunching numbers to determine whether a proposed investment or portfolio configuration is worthwhile. Anything and everything that can go into a digital computer is fair input. The central theme of quantitative approaches to investment is that history reveals enduring patterns of price behavior that can be discovered by statistical techniques. A big attraction is low cost. All the cost is involved with setting up the initial framework for analysis. Alternative "what if" scenarios can be run at virtually zero cost.

Quants do not meet with company management or swap stories with analysts. Instead, they estimate factors that they hope will have predictive ability and invest in companies where those factors are present. Quantitative analysts usually screen for features such as money flow, momentum in stock prices, or revisions in Wall Street earnings estimates. Some quants work at the proprietary trading desks of leading Wall Street firms where they worry about the price of active stocks three minutes from now. Others examine minute-by-minute differences in prices between stocks traded in U.S. and foreign markets.

Many of these Wall Street rocket scientists trade debt, mortgage-backed securities, and other exotic financial derivatives. Such assets fit comfortably into their mathematical models. However, as more and more quant shops discover the same pricing factors, competition tends to drive away profit-making opportunities. Nevertheless, institutional investors remain eager to try these new and innovative "black box" approaches to making money in the stock and bond markets.

See Henny Sender, "For Hedge Funds, the Money Spigot Flows Both Ways," *The Wall Street Journal Online*, December 22, 2005 (**http://online.wsj.com/**).

Empirical Estimation of Beta

Model Specification Problems

A telling criticism of beta as a standard risk measure is that the CAPM provides only an incomplete description of return volatility. On a theoretical level, the SCL asserts that volatility in stock returns can be usefully described in terms of the volatility of the overall market. However, obvious problems emerge in empirical work that attempts to confirm or deny the hypothesis that the SCL offers a compelling method for describing and predicting return volatility.

An important problem is that return volatility for the overall market is difficult to measure. On the nightly news, when commentators talk about the market being up or down, they often refer to moves in the DJIA. However, the DJIA includes only 30 component stocks representing roughly 30 percent of the value of all stocks traded on the New York Stock Exchange (NYSE), Nasdaq, and the American Stock Exchange. Although the DJIA offers good insight concerning changes in the prices of large blue-chip companies, it offers little insight concerning volatility in the returns earned by investors in smaller, high-tech stocks. From the perspective of many investors, the S&P 500 Index gives superior perspective concerning moves in the overall market. The Nasdaq and Russell 2000 indexes are popular measures of high-tech and smaller stock returns; they are much less informative about changes in the overall market.

As shown in Figure 5.6, beta can be estimated for individual stocks by using a simple ordinary least-squares regression model. Although there is a high degree of correlation in rates of return earned on the S&P 500 and Russell 2000 indexes, slight differences can have meaningful effects on beta estimates. **Market index bias** is the distortion to beta estimates caused by the fact that market indexes are only imperfect proxies for the overall market. To illustrate the problem posed by imprecise proxies for rates of return earned by the overall market, four alternative stock price beta estimates are shown for Internet bellwether Yahoo! over a one-year period. Yahoo!'s stock price beta is estimated as $\beta = 1.19$ when weekly rates of return on the S&P 500 are used as a proxy for rates of return on the overall market. When $\beta = 1.19$, the systematic risk of a stock is estimated to be 19 percent higher than that of the overall market. By way of contrast, Yahoo!'s stock price beta is estimated as $\beta = 0.55$ when the Russell 2000 is used as a market index. Thus, the relative risk borne by Yahoo! shareholders is estimated to be anywhere from nearly half as risky as the overall market to almost 20 percent riskier than the overall market, depending on the market index used, *during the same one-year period!*

Market index bias

Distortion to beta estimates caused by the fact that market indexes are only imperfect proxies for the overall market.

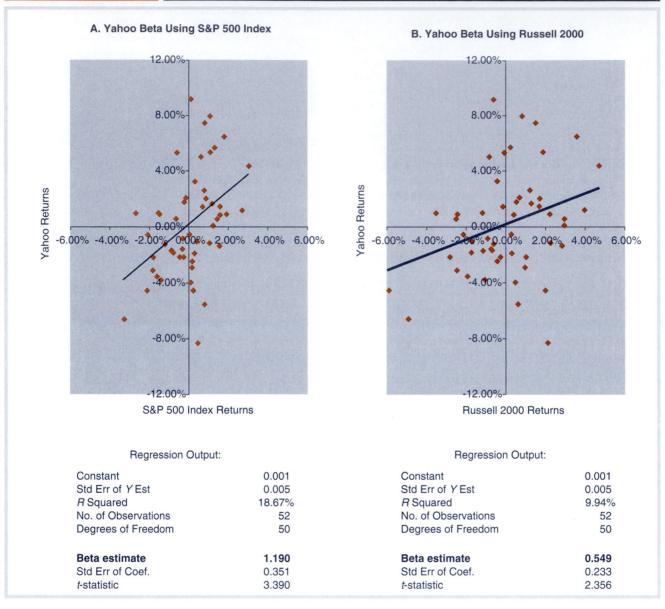

Regression Output:

Constant	0.001
Std Err of Y Est	0.005
R Squared	18.67%
No. of Observations	52
Degrees of Freedom	50
Beta estimate	**1.190**
Std Err of Coef.	0.351
t-statistic	3.390

Regression Output:

Constant	0.001
Std Err of Y Est	0.005
R Squared	9.94%
No. of Observations	52
Degrees of Freedom	50
Beta estimate	**0.549**
Std Err of Coef.	0.233
t-statistic	2.356

Source: Yahoo! Finance, **http://finance.yahoo.com**.

The presence of market index bias makes it imperative that beta comparisons among individual companies reflect identical and appropriate market benchmarks. From a theoretical perspective, the most appropriate benchmark would be a market index that included *all* capital assets—stocks, bonds, real estate, collectibles, and so on. Unfortunately, no such market index is available.

Beta estimate variability is caused not only by underlying differences in each respective proxy for the overall market. It is also caused by the fact that other important but unmeasured sources of common stock volatility are at work. **Model specification bias** distorts beta estimates because the SCL fails to include other important systematic influences on stock market volatility. In the case of Yahoo!, for example, R^2 information shown in Figure 5.6 indicates that only 9.9 to 18.7 percent of the total variation in Yahoo returns can be explained by variation in the overall market. This means that between 81.3 and 90.1 percent of the variation in the weekly returns for Yahoo! stock is unexplained by such a simple regression model.

Model specification bias
Distortion to beta estimates because the SCL fails to include other important systematic influences on stock market volatility.

FIGURE 5.7   Beta Estimates Will Vary with Choice of Estimation Time Interval

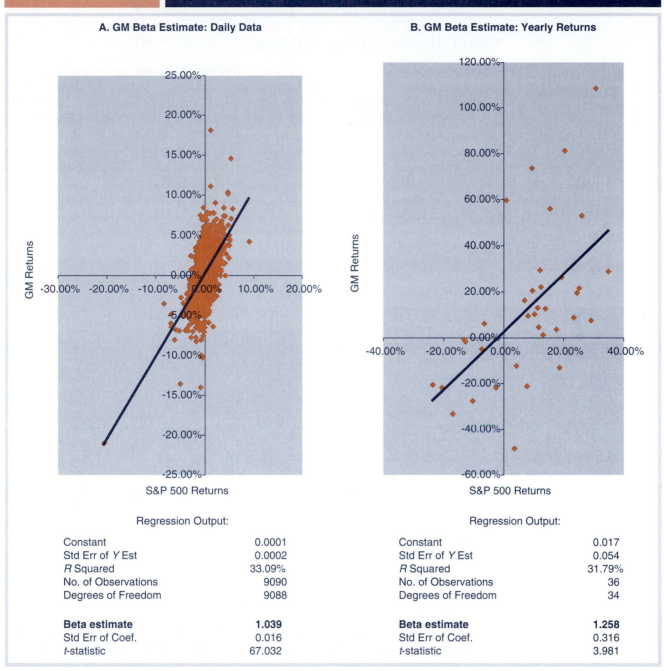

A. GM Beta Estimate: Daily Data

B. GM Beta Estimate: Yearly Returns

Regression Output:

Constant	0.0001
Std Err of Y Est	0.0002
R Squared	33.09%
No. of Observations	9090
Degrees of Freedom	9088
Beta estimate	**1.039**
Std Err of Coef.	0.016
t-statistic	67.032

Regression Output:

Constant	0.017
Std Err of Y Est	0.054
R Squared	31.79%
No. of Observations	36
Degrees of Freedom	34
Beta estimate	**1.258**
Std Err of Coef.	0.316
t-statistic	3.981

Source: Yahoo! Finance, **http://finance.yahoo.com**.

Data Interval Problems

Another problem faced in obtaining consistent and reliable beta estimates is the fact that these data are subject to estimation problems stemming from the length of time analyzed. **Time interval bias** exists because beta estimates are sensitive to the length of time over which stock return data are measured.

Figure 5.7 shows beta estimates derived for General Motors over the 1970-2005 period. For both estimates, returns on the S&P 500 Index were used as a proxy for the overall market. Using return data for 9,090 daily trading periods, β = 1.039. This daily-return beta estimate is less than

Time interval bias
Beta estimation problem derived from the fact that beta estimates depend on the data interval studied.

the estimate arrived at by analyzing annual return data over the same 36-year period, $\beta = 1.258$. Because beta estimates differ according to the time interval analyzed, the usefulness of beta as a consistent measure of risk is greatly diminished.

Nonstationary Beta Problem

An ideal measure of stock market risk would be stationary from one year to another. With an ideal risk measure, investors are able to control the risk exposure faced during volatile markets with well-targeted and well-timed investment buy-sell decisions. Suppose an elderly investor wants to maintain exposure to the equity markets during retirement but wants to limit the possibility of devastating losses. With an ideal risk measure, this retired investor could precisely tilt portfolio allocation toward securities with low risk. Alternatively, if an investor anticipated a surge in stock prices following a decline in interest rates, precise risk measures could help this investor tilt his or her investment portfolio toward more volatile stocks.

The usefulness of stock market risk indicators diminishes to the extent that they fail to provide accurate and consistent measures of risk exposure from one year to another. In fact, an important limitation of risk estimators derived from the CAPM is that they vary from one period to another in unpredictable ways. Table 5.1 shows alpha and beta estimates and R^2 information for the 30 stocks that together comprise the DJIA. These SCL-based estimates were derived over a one-year period by using 251 observations of daily returns and the S&P 500 Index as an indicator of the overall market.

Notice how the estimated average for alpha of 0.002 is very close to zero, as predicted for a perfectly competitive market by the CAPM. The average beta estimate of 0.953 means that a typical DJIA stock has risk characteristics that are representative of the overall market. As you recall, the overall market has a beta of 1. Although the magnitude of these alpha and beta estimates for DJIA stocks is not surprising, it is unfortunate that the average $R^2 = 29.2$ percent when the SCL is estimated for DJIA stocks. This means that volatility in the overall market explains roughly one-quarter (29.2 percent) of the volatility in individual DJIA stocks, and thus roughly three-quarters (70.8 percent) of this volatility is left unexplained by a simple SCL regression model.

Unfortunately, the beta you estimate today differs from the one you will estimate next year. This is the **nonstationary beta problem**. When betas vary from one year to another in ways that are essentially random and unpredictable, betas fail to provide investors with a risk assessment tool that can be used to effectively manage portfolio risk. Random changes in beta over time reduce the usefulness of CAPM as a practical risk assessment tool that can be used to effectively manage portfolio risk.

Nonstationary beta problem
Difficulty tied to the fact that betas are inherently unstable.

Multifactor Models

Multifactor CAPM or APT Approaches

In the traditional CAPM approach, the difference between the expected return on a portfolio and the risk-free rate $[E(R_i) - R_f]$ is explained by the return on a broad market portfolio in excess of the risk-free rate $[E(R_m) - R_f]$. Unfortunately, information provided in Table 5.1 and Figure 5.6 and 5.7 documents the fact that CAPM betas explain relatively little of the variation in average returns, diverge according to the market index chosen, and vary over time (the nonstationary β problem). These findings are consistent with results from a series of studies on the subject, by Professors Eugene Fama from the University of Chicago and Kenneth French from Dartmouth University, which demonstrate that there is no simple relation between average returns and CAPM betas. Contrary to the predictions of the CAPM, β alone cannot explain expected return.

The traditional CAPM assumes that a single market risk factor β is all that is required to measure the systematic risk of individual securities. Assuming that asset pricing is rational, average-return anomalies detected by using the CAPM may suggest that a **multifactor CAPM** model is more appropriate. Market betas might represent only one of the firm's many risk factors. For example, firm size might represent a second risk factor, price-book ratios a third, and

Multifactor CAPM
Asset pricing model that assumes portfolio risk is tied to market risk and other factors, such as firm size and P/B ratios.

TABLE 5.1

Beta Estimation Using the SCL for 30 Industrial Leaders That Comprise the DJIA (January 2005–December 2005)

Company Name (Ticker Symbol)	Alpha Estimate	t-Statistic	Beta Estimate	t-Statistic	R^2
Altria Group (MO)	0.091	1.47	0.867	9.01	24.5%
Aluminum Co. of America (AA)	-0.023	-0.32	1.182	10.79	31.8
American Express Co. (AXP)	0.012	0.22	1.032	12.29	37.7
American International Group (AIG)	0.014	0.18	1.006	8.35	21.8
AT&T (T)	-0.005	-0.12	0.672	10.11	29.0
Boeing Company (BA)	0.123	1.63	0.973	8.27	21.5
Caterpillar Inc. (CAT)	0.068	0.82	1.418	11.09	33.0
Citigroup Inc. (C)	0.011	0.29	0.713	12.13	37.0
Coca-Cola Company (KO)	-0.009	-0.22	0.650	10.68	31.3
E. I. du Pont de Nemours and Company (DD)	-0.052	-0.85	1.096	11.61	35.0
Exxon Mobil Corp. (XOM)	0.035	0.49	1.424	12.85	39.8
General Electric Company (GE)	-0.014	-0.36	0.891	14.47	45.6
General Motors Corporation (GM)	-0.246	-1.54	1.387	5.61	11.2
Hewlett-Packard Company (HPQ)	0.133	1.27	0.731	4.53	7.6
Home Depot (HD)	-0.028	-0.48	1.329	14.79	46.7
Honeywell International (HON)	0.022	0.33	1.043	10.15	29.2
Intel Corp. (INTC)	0.023	0.35	1.185	11.59	35.0
International Business Machines Corporation (IBM)	-0.074	-1.23	0.889	9.55	26.7
J.P. Morgan & Co. Incorporated (JPM)	0.013	0.34	0.927	15.63	49.4
Johnson & Johnson (JNJ)	-0.018	-0.37	0.598	7.84	19.8
McDonald's Corporation (MCD)	0.023	0.28	1.167	9.39	26.1
Merck & Co., Inc. (MRK)	0.210	0.20	0.712	4.40	7.2
Microsoft Corp. (MSFT)	-0.011	-0.22	0.787	10.76	31.6
Minnesota Mining and Manufacturing Company (MMM)	-0.021	-0.37	0.860	9.96	28.4
Pfizer, Inc. (PFE)	-0.046	-0.54	0.826	6.34	13.9
Procter & Gamble Company (PG)	0.021	0.43	0.782	10.43	30.3
United Technologies Corporation (UTX)	0.029	0.58	1.071	14.00	44.0
Verizon Communications (VZ)	-0.105	-2.21	0.711	9.62	27.0
Wal-Mart Stores, Inc. (WMT)	-0.049	-0.96	0.772	9.76	27.6
Walt Disney Company (DIS)	-0.061	-1.02	0.893	9.69	27.3
Average	**0.002**	**-0.06**	**0.953**	**10.19**	**29.2%**

so on. In that case, an asset pricing model that is capable of reflecting multiple aspects of risk would be preferable to the traditional single-factor CAPM.

On a theoretical level, the multiple-risk-factor approach, sometimes called **arbitrage pricing theory (APT)**, has the potential to provide a superior description of average returns. **Arbitrage** is simply the simultaneous buying and selling of the same asset. According to APT, a market is perfectly efficient if it is not possible to earn a risk-free arbitrage profit by simultaneously buying and selling the same asset. APT is a very simple model of security pricing. Its sole underlying assumption is that investors prefer more wealth to less wealth.

Whereas CAPM posits that excess returns on a portfolio are systematically affected by a single market risk factor β, APT suggests that the difference between the expected return on a portfolio and the risk-free rate $[E(R_i - R_f]$ is explained by the portfolio's return sensitivity to a variety of N risk factors, and therefore

Arbitrage pricing theory (APT)
Multifactor asset pricing model that allows market betas to represent only one of the firm's many risk factors.

Arbitrage
The simultaneous buying and selling of the same asset at different prices to capture a mispricing.

$$R_i - R_f = a_i + b_{1i}F_1 + b_{2i}F_2 + \cdots + b_{Ni}F_N + \varepsilon_i \qquad (5.7)$$

where F_N common risk factors affect security returns and b_i represents the return sensitivity to a given risk factor. Notice the similarity of this equation to the SCL from the traditional CAPM. The sole difference is that this multifactor approach allows for an unspecified number of important risk factors. These factors can include the CAPM's market β, but it does not necessarily need to be one of the factors. This is because the CAPM and APT are two independent theories. Two problems exist with the implementation of an APT model. First, this multifactor approach fails to specify the source of the risk factors. What are the risk factors? Second, the theory does not state the number of unknown risk factors. These limitations cause each user of the APT framework to specify his or her own unique model.

An investor using an APT model is never sure whether all the relevant risks are being accounted for. Yet the APT can still be very useful in identifying what risks a firm is sensitive to. For example, the stock return of a company may be affected by changes in the price of oil. Most transportation companies, such as the airlines or trucking firms, would have a negative sensitivity to a "change in oil price" factor. By examining the factor sensitivities in Equation 5.7, savvy investors will more thoroughly understand the risks of the stocks and bonds that they own.

Try It!

An investor specifies an APT model with three factors: the CAPM beta (F_1), unexpected inflation (F_2), and the risk yield spread (F_3). Unexpected inflation is the actual annual inflation less the amount that was expected by analysts and economists. The risk yield spread is the difference in the yield on high-risk bonds less the yield on low-risk bonds. This spread measures the premium for risk offered in the bond market. A company being analyzed has risk-factor sensitivities of $b_1 = 1.2$, $b_2 = -2.2$, and $b_3 = 0.1$. The intercept, α, of Equation 5.7 is 3.5 percent. If the risk premium on the market is 5 percent, unexpected inflation turns out to be +2 percent, and the yield spread is 4 percent, what risk premium should the company earn?

Solution

Notice that this firm's market risk is greater than 1. From the systematic risk perspective, this firm is riskier than the overall market. However, the firm is negatively and significantly affected by unexpected inflation. Lastly, this firm does not appear to have a large sensitivity to the yield spread. Given the level of risk of this firm and under these conditions, the firm's risk premium should be

$$R_i - R_f = 3.5\% + 1.2(5\%) - 2.2(2\%) + 0.1(4\%) = 5.5\%$$

Fama-French Three-Factor Model

Empirical studies show that average returns on common stocks are systematically related to firm characteristics such as size, P/E, cash flow/price, book-to-market equity, past sales growth, long-term past return (long-term momentum), and short-term past return (short-term momentum). Because these inexplicable patterns in average returns are not explained by the traditional one-factor CAPM, they are called *anomalies*. However, except for short-term momentum, these average-return anomalies largely disappear when a three-factor model is employed. In the standard multifactor CAPM approach, the difference between the expected return on a portfolio and the risk-free rate $[E(R_i) - R_f]$ is explained by the portfolio's return sensitivity to (1) the return on a broad market portfolio in excess of the risk-free rate $[E(R_m) - R_f]$; (2) the difference between the return on a portfolio of small stocks and that on a portfolio of large stocks (SMB, or small minus big); and (3) the difference between the return on a portfolio of low-book-to-market stocks and the return on a portfolio of high-book-to-market stocks (HML, or high minus low). In the multifactor CAPM approach, the market sensitivity or sys-

Investment Choices and Trading in Retirement Plans

Do people use asset pricing theory to allocate investments in their retirement accounts? To answer this important question, financial economists examine the decisions made by employees enrolled in various retirement plans. In one such study, nearly 7,000 employees in a 401(k) pension plan were studied over a five-year period. Several investment choices were available to these employees: a bond fund, a large-company stock fund, a small-/mid-cap stock fund, and an international stock fund. Alternatively, employees could choose one of four funds that offered a mix of bonds and stocks.

Researchers were interested in learning the mix of investment assets selected by employees and the extent to which employees tended to change the mix of retirement assets over time. Surprisingly, almost one-half of the employees allocated nothing to stocks. These people had all of their retirement money invested in bonds. Given the low real rate of return bonds have offered investors after inflation, such investors are not building much wealth. At the other end of the spectrum, about one-quarter of the employees had their entire retire-ment plan assets in equities. Taken together, about 70 per-cent of the retirement plan participants were not diversified with a mix of stocks and bonds. Because almost everyone participates in the Social Security system, a plan that promises bondlike returns, it is not surprising that many investors emphasize stocks in their retirement plans. Given Social Security plan participation, it is perhaps surprising that so many retirement plan participants emphasize bonds in their retirement plan investments.

In contrast with the broad predictions of asset pricing theory, many retirement plan participants do not adopt a broadly diversified perspective when it comes to retirement planning. In fact, many employees don't seem to do any retirement planning at all. Most retirement plan administrators hear from employees only twice: when they get hired and when they retire. Most employees tend to adopt a fixed allocation of pension assets to either stocks, bonds, or a mix of both and simply maintain that allocation over time.

See Julie Agnew, Pierluigi Balduzzi, and Annika Sunden, "Portfolio Choice and Trading in a Large 401(k) Plan," *American Economic Review*, vol. 93, no. 1 (March 2003), pp. 193–215.

tematic risk of a given portfolio is estimated using the following multiple-regression model over a time series of data:

$$R_i - R_f = a_i + b_{1i}(R_m - R_f) + b_{2i}\text{SMB} + b_{3i}\text{HML} + \varepsilon_i \qquad (5.8)$$

On an empirical level, the evidence seems to suggest that a three-factor CAPM model is superior to the traditional one-factor CAPM approach. Unfortunately, just like the volatile returns attributable to market β, returns attributable to small stocks (SMB) and low-P/B stocks (HML) tend to be unstable. Like the one-factor CAPM, even three-factor CAPM models explain very little of the variation in average returns. Therefore, although theory and evidence confirm that risk and return *are* related, neither single-factor nor multifactor CAPM approaches give investors a precise tool for risk assessment and management. Data for the Fama-French factors are available on Kenneth French's Web site at Dartmouth College, **http://mba.tuck.dartmouth.edu/pages/faculty/ken.french/data_library.html**.

Behavioral Influences

Empirical estimation problems suffered by the traditional CAPM are also problems for the newer multifactor CAPM and APT approaches. Because these approaches are not able to adequately describe the relationship between the expected rate of return on a portfolio and risk, other behavioral influences are now being considered.

When many investors suffer from similar biases at the same points in time, market prices can behave in ways that are not captured by traditional asset pricing models. Today, some finance scholars are studying the potential importance of behavioral risk factors like the reluctance to realize losses, overconfidence, and momentum. Studies of investor behavior show that the more stocks go up, the more novice investors think that they will continue to rise. For a time, **momentum**-based investment strategies can become a self-fulfilling prophecy, especially when crowd psychology is involved. The massive demand for tech stocks, especially Internet stocks, during the mid- to late 1990s is a good example of this tendency.

The traditional argument against the possibility of momentum in stock and bond markets is that predominantly rational investors focus on future expectations in their determination of current prices. Historical trends in prices and returns are irrelevant in this

Momentum
The belief that stocks with high prior returns will continue to achieve high returns in the future. Stocks with low prior returns are believed to continue earning low returns.

Noise traders
Investors who make systematic errors when they assess the characteristics of companies and expected stock returns.

process. Even if some naïve investors, or **noise traders**, incorrectly focus on historical trends, a sufficient number of rational professional investors are always available to recognize when prices get out of whack with economic reality. By instantaneously correcting situations where stocks or bonds become overvalued or undervalued, savvy professional investors capture profits from naïve investors pursuing momentum-based strategies. However, empirical research now suggests that professional investors trade with the crowd, not against it. Since many institutional and professional investors have a short-term focus, they would rather try to benefit from crowd psychology that moves prices up or down than bet against the crowd and try to force a reversal. As a result, the emotional forces that can propel stock prices ahead of economic fundamentals can also cause stocks to overshoot on the downside. In the 2000–2002 market crash, for example, panicky professional and individual investors sold tech stocks at ruinously low prices.

How might this aspect of investor behavior be captured in an asset pricing model? In fact, the answer is quite simple: It is now common to add a fourth momentum factor to the three-factor Fama-French model:

$$R_i - R_f = a_i + b_{1i}(R_m - R_f) + b_{2i}\text{SMB} + b_{3i}\text{HML} + b_{4i}\text{UMD} + \varepsilon_i \qquad \textbf{(5.9)}$$

The UMD (up-minus-down) momentum factor is the return on a portfolio of the best-performing stocks minus the portfolio return for the worst stocks during the preceding 12-month period. As the importance of other behavioral influences on stock returns becomes better recognized, the potential exists for more detailed and more useful asset pricing models that more fully reflect economic and behavioral influences.

Assessing Portfolio Performance

Portfolio Characteristics

In the evaluation of a portfolio, performance is always the bottom line. However, it is important to view performance in relative terms. Performance must always be viewed relative to an appropriate **benchmark** and against other portfolios that have similar objectives and policies. For example, a portfolio with a strategy of investing in large-cap stocks produced a 10 percent annual rate of return in 2006. However, this might be considered inadequate if the S&P 500 Index earned 12 percent. Did the portfolio lag the benchmark because it was overweighted in a market sector that faltered? Did a long-term bond portfolio fare well because interest rates declined? Analyzing these characteristics is important in assessing the performance of a portfolio.

Benchmark
A diversified portfolio of similar risk or investment style used as a comparison.

It is also important to consider long time periods. For example, it is never enough to consider performance over just the most recent few months or even one or two years. Extraordinary one-year performance often occurs. Investment managers should be evaluated over a longer time. Five-, ten-, and even twenty-year performance allows for a much better assessment of a manager's ability. Of course, historical performance is a useful guide to expected risk and return only if the investment manager's investment philosophy has not changed.

Alpha and Beta

On a theoretical basis, remember that the security market line posits a simple straight-line relation between the expected rate of return on a security and systematic risk, as in Equation 5.2. Written as the expected return on a portfolio, the equation is $E(R_P) = R_F + \beta_P(R_M - R_F)$. The risk premium earned by a given portfolio is expected to be proportional to the risk premium earned on the overall market.

On average, the risk premium earned by the portfolio should be β_P times as great as the market risk premium, where β_P is the beta measure of portfolio systematic risk. It shows the systematic relation between the risk premium earned by the portfolio and that on the overall market. If $\beta_P = 1.5$, the portfolio is one and one-half times as risky as the overall market. In that case, investors should anticipate earning an annual rate of return equal to the risk-free rate plus one and one-half times the market risk premium. If $\beta_P = 0.5$, the portfolio is only one-half times as risky as the overall market, and investors should anticipate earning an annual rate of return equal to the risk-free rate plus one-half the market risk premium. During the past 55 years in the United States, a fair estimate is that the risk-free rate has been 5 percent, and the expected rate of return on the market has been roughly 12 percent. This means that a portfolio with $\beta_P = 2$ has an expected rate of return of 19 percent $(= 5\% + 2 \times 7\%)$. But what can we say about the portfolio if it earned less than 19 percent. What can we say if it earned more than 19 percent?

Equation 5.10 can be used to identify any abnormal risk-adjusted performance; the Greek letter **alpha** (α_P) is used to signify the amount of annual return on the portfolio that cannot be tied to volatility in the overall market.

> **Alpha**
> Abnormal return measured from the CAPM required rate of return.

$$E(R_P) - R_F = \alpha_P + \beta_P(R_M - R_F) \qquad (5.10)$$

If $\alpha_P > 0$ and statistically significant, a portfolio has returned positive risk-adjusted performance to its owners. In this case, superior historical portfolio manager performance (or good luck) is indicated. If $\alpha_P < 0$ and significant, the portfolio has underperformed the market on a risk-adjusted basis, and inferior historical performance (or bad luck) is demonstrated.

When $\alpha_P > 0$, portfolio performance is better than the theoretical expectation derived from the CAPM. Superior portfolio performance can be due to **selectivity**, or the selection of stocks with exceptionally good risk-reward characteristics. This is the hallmark of a good stock picker. Although few portfolio managers have demonstrated good stock-picking ability that has stood the test of time, there are some notable exceptions. Warren Buffett, Fidelity's Peter Lynch, and global investor John Templeton are some examples. Outstanding portfolio performance can also be due to astute risk management through careful **market timing**. Over the years, few have demonstrated superior stock market timing.

> **Selectivity**
> Ability to pick stocks that outperform the overall stock market.

When $\alpha_P < 0$, portfolio performance is worse than the theoretical expectation. In the case of inferior performance, bad stock picking or bad market timing is sometimes to blame. Most often, inferior portfolio performance has a simpler explanation. Excessive operating expenses tied with extravagant portfolio manager compensation or unreasonably high portfolio turnover are often blamed for subpar results, especially in the mutual fund industry.

> **Market timing**
> Investment style that attempts to buy into the stock market before a bull market move and sell before a bear market move.

Despite well-known problems with CAPM, it is now standard to include α and β as measures of mutual fund abnormal performance and risk, respectively, derived from modern portfolio theory. Morningstar, the popular mutual fund information Web site (**www.morningstar.com**), reports estimates of α and β for the mutual funds it follows. It reports an α and β computed using three years of data and the S&P 500 Index as the market portfolio proxy. In addition, Morningstar also reports α and β estimates using the fund's benchmark as the proxy for the market portfolio and three years of returns. For example, in January 2006, the Oppenheimer Equity mutual fund was reported to have an alpha of 2.36 percent (and beta of 0.90) using the S&P 500 Index and an alpha of −1.00 percent (and beta of 0.72) using the Morningstar Midcap TR Index.

Is Alpha and Beta Information Useful?

Unfortunately, the usefulness of α and β are diminished because the CAPM fails to accurately depict the risk-reward relationship for mutual funds over time. Alpha and beta tend to be unstable when estimated for individual stocks such as the 30 stocks in the Dow Jones Industrial Average (DJIA). Table 5.2 suggests that the same seems to hold true when alpha and beta estimates for 10 of the largest common stock funds are considered. These SCL-based estimates were derived over a one-year period by using 251 observations of daily returns and the S&P 500 Index as an indicator of the overall market.

| TABLE 5.2 | Beta Estimation for 10 Large Mutual Funds Using the S&P 500 as a Market Index |

Mutual Fund	Ticker	Alpha Estimate	t-Statistic	Beta Estimate	t-Statistic	R^2
American Century Ultra	TWCUX	−0.004	−0.26	0.982	46.96	89.8%
Fidelity Advisors Growth Opportunity	FAGOX	0.020	1.34	1.111	49.15	90.6
Fidelity Contrafund	FCNTX	0.042	2.15	0.922	30.42	78.7
Fidelity Magellan Fund	FMAGX	−0.001	−0.02	0.993	41.13	87.1
Fidelity Puritan	FPURX	0.005	0.67	0.617	50.88	91.2
Investment Co. of America (American Funds)	AIVSX	0.004	0.26	0.759	32.43	80.8
Janus Fund	JANSX	0.004	0.28	0.988	47.54	90.0
Vanguard 500 Index	VFINX	0.005	2.22	1.000	303.80	99.7
Vanguard Wellington	VWELX	0.003	0.16	0.626	22.83	67.6
Washington Mutual (American Fund)	AWSHX	−0.004	−0.46	0.923	62.70	94.0
Average		**0.007**	**0.634**	**0.892**	**68.784**	**87.0%**

Source: Yahoo! Finance, **http://finance.yahoo.com** (2005 data).

Notice how the estimated average for alpha of 0.007 is very close to zero, as predicted for a perfectly competitive market by the CAPM. The average beta estimate of 0.892 means that a typical large-stock-fund stock has risk characteristics that are fairly representative of the overall market. As you recall, the overall market has a $\beta = 1$.

Risk-Adjusted Performance

Sharpe Ratio

Sharpe Ratio
Risk premium earned relative to total risk.

Nobel laureate William Sharpe developed a measure of risk-adjusted performance for portfolios called the **Sharpe Ratio**. This reward-to-variability measure can be used to provide a ranking of portfolios by the risk premium earned per unit of total systematic plus unsystematic risk. In other words, the Sharpe ratio considers the ex-post-risk premium earned per unit of *total risk*:

$$\text{Sharpe Ratio} = \frac{\bar{R}_P - \bar{R}_F}{\text{SD}(R_P)} = \frac{\text{excess return on portfolio } P}{\text{total risk for portfolio } P} \qquad (5.11)$$

$\bar{R}_P$ is the average rate of return on portfolio P during period t, $\bar{R}_F$ is the average risk-free rate of return, and $\text{SD}(R_P)$ is the portfolio standard deviation during period t. Poor relative performance exists if the Sharpe ratio < 0 or positive but small. Very good relative performance is indicated if the Sharpe ratio is positive and large in magnitude.

Treynor Index

Treynor Index
Risk premium earned relative to systematic risk.

Financial economist Jack Treynor developed an alternative measure for risk-adjusted performance that is now called the **Treynor Index**. This reward-to-volatility measure ranks portfolios by risk premium per unit of *systematic risk*. An increase in the Treynor Index is preferred by all investors, regardless of risk preferences, where

$$\text{Treynor Index} = \frac{\bar{R}_P - \bar{R}_F}{\beta_P} = \frac{\text{excess return on portfolio } P}{\text{systematic risk for portfolio } P} \qquad (5.12)$$

As before, $\bar{R}_P$ is the average rate of return on portfolio P during period t, and $\bar{R}_F$ is the average risk-free rate of return. In Equation 5.12, β_P is the beta measure of systematic risk for the investment portfolio. Poor relative performance exists if the Treynor Index < 0 or if the Treynor Index > 0 and is small. Good relative performance is indicated if the Treynor Index > 0 and large.

Comparing the Sharpe Ratio and Treynor Index

When comparing the Sharpe Ratio and Treynor Index, it is important to recognize that they differ only in terms of the risk measure used. The Sharpe Ratio ranks portfolios according to the risk premium earned relative to total risk using $SD(R_P)$, whereas the Treynor Index ranks portfolios according to the risk premium earned relative to systematic risk using β_P. Rank orderings of various portfolios are often similar. Getting back to the Oppenheimer Equity mutual fund, over the past three years Oppenheimer had a Sharpe Ratio of 1.19, meaning that an annual risk premium of 1.19 percent was earned for each 1 percent of portfolio SD. The positive value is indicative of good performance. Similarly, Oppenheimer had a Treynor Index of 12.7 over the past three years, meaning that a risk premium of 12.7 percent was earned for each unit of systematic risk as measured by β_P.

However, the Sharpe and Treynor risk-adjusted measures should be used less as absolute indictors of performance and more for comparison purposes. If the stock market was down during the period, it is likely that any stock portfolio will have a negative return. Therefore, its Sharpe Ratio and Treynor Index will also be negative. Consider a pension fund that earned an average -3 percent per year for the past three years. The risk-adjusted measures will be negative. In absolute terms, one would say that the portfolio manager did a poor job. However, if the S&P 500 Index was down an average -6 percent per year during the same period, one might conclude that the manager did fairly well after all. To assess portfolio manager performance, it is better to compare the pension fund's Sharpe and Treynor measures with those of the overall market or other portfolios. Portfolio alpha is a good absolute measure of performance, while the Sharpe and Treynor measures are good relative measures of performance.

Try It!

A pension fund's average monthly return for the year was 0.9 percent, and the standard deviation was 0.5 percent. The fund uses an aggressive strategy as indicated by its beta of 1.7. If the market averaged 0.7 percent, with a standard deviation of 0.3 percent, how did the pension fund perform relative to the market? The monthly risk-free rate was 0.2 percent.

Solution

Compute and compare the Sharpe and Treynor measures of the fund and market. For the pension fund:

$$\text{Sharpe Ratio} = \frac{\overline{R}_P - \overline{R}_F}{SD(R_P)} = \frac{0.9\% - 0.2\%}{0.5\%} = 1.4$$

$$\text{Treynor Index} = \frac{\overline{R}_P - \overline{R}_F}{\beta_P} = \frac{0.9\% - 0.2\%}{1.7} = 0.41$$

For the market:

$$\text{Sharpe Ratio} = \frac{0.7\% - 0.2\%}{0.3\%} = 1.67$$

$$\text{Treynor Index} = \frac{0.7\% - 0.2\%}{1.0} = 0.50$$

Both the Sharpe Ratio and the Treynor Index are greater for the market than for the mutual fund. Therefore, the mutual fund underperformed the market.

Street Smarts 5.4

Tactical and Analytical Skill

Institutional investors such as pension funds, university endowment funds, and foundations establish a strategic allocation of their investment portfolios across major asset classes. *Strategic asset allocation* among stocks, bonds, cash, real estate, and other assets is an important aspect of the institutional investor's long-term investment policy. Strategic asset allocation helps determine the amount of risk incorporated in the institutional investor's portfolio and helps the institutional investor meet long-term funding goals and spending commitments. Institutional investors also engage in tactical asset allocation. *Tactical asset allocation* is the purposeful shifting among asset categories with the goal in mind of earning extra returns. In other words, tactical asset allocation is an important part of the institutional investor's attempt to earn higher alphas, defined as above-market returns that cannot be explained by greater risk-taking behavior.

There are two basic ways in which positive or negative alphas can be earned. To earn above-market returns, investors must either engage in superior asset allocation among asset categories (display superior tactical skill) or engage in superior asset allocation within asset categories (display superior analytical skill). Remember, an index fund is an investment portfolio designed to mimic the returns of the overall market through an asset allocation that mimics the overall market. In the stock market, an S&P 500 index fund would mimic the asset allocation and overall returns of large-cap stocks. For example, an institutional investor with superior tactical skill might be adept at portfolio allocation among stocks, bonds, and real estate. An institutional investor with superior analytical skill might be adept at stock picking and know, for example, that Microsoft Corporation represents superior investment value compared to Google, Inc. A portfolio of undervalued stocks that earn above-market risk-adjusted returns will earn a positive alpha. Similarly, an investment portfolio that goes to cash when the stock market is overvalued and back into stocks when equities are undervalued will earn a positive alpha.

In practice, few portfolio managers display the superior tactical and analytical skill necessary to outperform the market (earn positive alphas) on a long-term basis.

See Karen Damato, "Mutual Funds Try to Play Hedge Game by Offering Investors 'Absolute' Gains," *The Wall Street Journal Online*, October 7, 2005 (**http://online.wsj.com/**).

Summary

■ The most detailed model or construct used to describe the efficient pricing of investment securities is called the **capital asset pricing model (CAPM)**. The CAPM is a method for predicting how investment returns are determined in an efficient capital market.

■ The CAPM describes three distinct relations between the expected rate of return and risk. The **capital market line (CML)** shows the linear risk-return trade-off for all investment portfolios. The **security market line (SML)** characterizes a linear risk-return trade-off for individual stocks.

■ The SML shows how the expected rate of return can be seen as a simple function of the amount of **systematic risk**. Systematic risk is a measure of return volatility in an individual stock that is tied to the overall market. **Unsystematic risk** is the amount of return volatility that is specific to an individual company. Unsystematic risk is synonymous with **diversifiable risk**. Even after unsystematic risk is eliminated through diversification, substantial systematic risk, or **nondiversifiable risk**, remains. Because systematic risk cannot be eliminated through diversification, investors must be rewarded for any increase in systematic risk to justify their investment in a particular stock or market sector. Financial economists use the Greek letter **beta** (β) to signify systematic risk.

■ The CAPM's third linear relationship between risk and return is called the **security characteristic line (SCL)**. The SCL shows the linear relation between the **excess return** on individual securities and the overall market at every point in time. The intercept term α shows the anticipated rate of return when either $\beta = 0$ or $R_M = 0$. When $\alpha > 0$, investors enjoy **positive abnormal returns**. When $\alpha < 0$, investors suffer **negative abnormal returns**. Investors would celebrate a mutual fund manager whose portfolio consistently generated positive abnormal returns ($\alpha > 0$). They would fire managers of portfolios that consistently suffered negative abnormal returns ($\alpha < 0$). A beta greater than 1 signifies above-market risk; a beta less than 1 signifies below-market risk.

■ One of the most telling criticisms of beta as a standard risk measure is that the CAPM provides only an incomplete description of return volatility. **Market index bias** is the distortion to beta estimates caused by the fact that market indexes are only imperfect proxies for the overall market. Beta estimate variability is caused by underlying differences in each respective proxy for the overall market. It is also caused by the fact that other important but unmeasured sources of common stock volatility are at work. **Model specification bias** distorts beta estimates because the SCL fails to include other important systematic influences on stock market volatility. **Time interval bias** exists because beta estimates are sensitive to the length of time over which stock return data are measured. The fact that betas are inherently unstable from one year to another is a further problem for the CAPM. This is the **nonstationary beta problem**.

■ When the CAPM fails to precisely describe or predict portfolio returns, model specification bias may be present. The traditional CAPM assumes that a single market risk factor β is all that is required to measure the systematic risk of individual securities. Assuming that asset pricing is rational, empirical research suggests that a **multifactor CAPM** model is more appropriate. Market betas might represent only one of the firm's many risk factors. For example, firm size might represent a second risk factor, price-book ratios a third, and so on.

■ On a theoretical level, the multifactor CAPM approach, sometimes called **arbitrage pricing theory (APT)**, has the potential to provide a superior description of average returns. **Arbitrage** is simply the simultaneous buying and selling of the same asset. Traditional finance theory suggests that risk and return *are* related, but neither the traditional one-factor CAPM nor multifactor CAPM approaches give investors a precise tool for risk assessment and management. This may be due to the existence of **noise traders** in the market who do not behave in the ways assumed by these traditional asset pricing models. As a result, models that incorporate behavioral attributes such as **momentum** factors are being used.

■ When **alpha** is positive ($\alpha_P > 0$), portfolio performance is better than the theoretical expectation derived from the CAPM. Superior portfolio performance can be due to **selectivity**, or the selection of stocks with exceptionally good risk-reward characteristics. This is the hallmark of a good stock picker. Outstanding portfolio performance can also be due to astute risk management through careful **market timing**.

■ Nobel laureate William Sharpe developed a measure of risk-adjusted performance for portfolios called the **Sharpe Ratio**. Financial economist Jack Treynor developed an alternative measure of risk-adjusted performance called the **Treynor Index**. The Sharpe Ratio ranks portfolios according to the risk premium earned relative to total risk using $SD(R_P)$, whereas the Treynor Index ranks portfolios according to the risk premium earned relative to systematic risk using β_P. Rank orderings of various portfolios are often similar under the two methods.

Self-Test Problems

ST5.1   The T. Rowe Price Growth Fund is known for its high returns. Using monthly returns over the past two years for the fund and the S&P 500 Index, compute the fund's beta.

Solution

Monthly prices can be obtained from the Yahoo! Finance Web site at **http://finance.yahoo.com**.
After acquiring the prices, compute monthly returns for both the T. Rowe Price Growth Fund (ticker: PRGFX) and the S&P 500 Index. Lastly, run a regression to determine beta. The results are shown below.

◇	A	B	C	D	E	F	G
1		T. Rowe			S&P500		
2	Date	Price	S&P 500	Price Return	Return		
3	1-Dec-05	28.4	1248.29	0.14%	-0.10%		
4	1-Nov-05	28.36	1249.48	4.38%	3.52%		
5	3-Oct-05	27.17	1207.01	-0.40%	-1.77%		
6	1-Sep-05	27.28	1228.81	0.66%	0.69%		
7	1-Aug-05	27.1	1220.33	-1.45%	-1.12%		
8	1-Jul-05	27.5	1234.18	4.32%	3.60%		
9	1-Jun-05	26.36	1191.33	0.57%	-0.01%		
10	2-May-05	26.21	1191.5	5.09%	3.00%		
11	1-Apr-05	24.94	1156.85	-1.89%	-2.01%		
12	1-Mar-05	25.42	1180.59	-2.23%	-1.91%		
13	1-Feb-05	26	1203.6	0.31%	1.89%		
14	3-Jan-05	25.92	1181.27	-2.81%	-2.53%		
15	1-Dec-04	26.67	1211.92	3.90%	3.25%		
16	1-Nov-04	25.67	1173.82	5.03%	3.86%		
17	1-Oct-04	24.44	1130.2	1.75%	1.40%		
18	1-Sep-04	24.02	1114.58	1.95%	0.94%		
19	2-Aug-04	23.56	1104.24	-0.21%	0.23%		
20	1-Jul-04	23.61	1101.72	-4.84%	-3.43%		
21	1-Jun-04	24.81	1140.84	1.47%	1.80%		
22	3-May-04	24.45	1120.68	1.62%	1.21%		
23	1-Apr-04	24.06	1107.3	-2.04%	-1.68%		
24	1-Mar-04	24.56	1126.21	-1.17%	-1.64%		
25	2-Feb-04	24.85	1144.94	0.89%	1.22%		
26	2-Jan-04	24.63	1131.13		=(B25-B26)/B26		
27							
28			Slope Coefficent =	1.17			
29				=SLOPE(D3:D25,E3:E25)			
30							

The beta of the T. Rowe Price Growth Fund is 1.17.

ST5.2   Using the returns from ST 5.1, assess the performance of the T. Rowe Price Growth Fund by computing its alpha, Sharpe Ratio, and Treynor Index measures. The average annual yield on the Treasury bill during this period was 2.8 percent.

Solution

The data are in monthly returns, so the risk-free rate (as denoted by the T-bill yield) should also be used as a monthly rate, 0.23 percent (= 2.8%/12). Average return and standard deviation also need to be computed:

	Price Return	S&P500 Return
Average =	0.65%	0.45%
Standard Deviation =	2.66%	2.17%
	=STDEV(D3:D25)	=AVERAGE(D3:D25)

The T. Rowe Price Growth Fund appears to have earned a slightly higher return than the index. However, it has done that with more risk. Therefore, examining the risk-adjusted measures will be helpful.

For alpha, use Equation 5.10:

$$\alpha = (R_{RTP} - R_F) - \beta_{TRP}(R_M - R_F) = (0.65\% - 0.23\%) - 1.17(0.45\% - 0.23\%) = 0.42\% - 0.26 = 0.16\%$$

Note that the fund's alpha is positive.

The Sharpe and Treynor measures for the T. Rowe Price Growth Fund are

$$\text{Sharpe} = \frac{\bar{R}_P - \bar{R}_F}{SD(R_P)} = \frac{0.65\% - 0.23\%}{2.66\%} = 0.158 \quad \text{Treynor} = \frac{\bar{R}_P - \bar{R}_F}{\beta_P} = \frac{0.65\% - 0.23\%}{1.17} = 0.359$$

To properly assess the performance of the fund, the Sharpe and Treynor measures should be compared to those of other portfolios, like the S&P 500 Index. The measures are

$$\text{Sharpe} = \frac{\bar{R}_P - \bar{R}_F}{SD(R_P)} = \frac{0.45\% - 0.23\%}{2.17\%} = 0.101 \quad \text{Treynor} = \frac{\bar{R}_P - \bar{R}_F}{\beta_P} = \frac{0.45\% - 0.23\%}{1.0} = 0.220$$

Note that the fund has outperformed the index in both the Sharpe Ratio and the Treynor Index measures. This means that the fund outperformed the market on a risk-adjusted basis.

Questions and Problems

5.1   The expected market risk premium and the risk-free rate are 4.5 percent and 3.5 percent, respectively. What is the expected rate of return for Abbot Labs and Black & Decker, which have betas of 1.3 and 0.7, respectively?

5.2   General Electric has a beta of 1, and Wendys' International has a beta of 0.5. The market return is expected to be 10 percent, and the risk free rate is 4 percent. Calculate the expected return for a portfolio with 50 percent invested in GE and 50 percent invested in Wendy's.

5.3   Describe the Sharpe Ratio.

5.4   Suppose an investor has identified three risk factors in the stock market. Those factors are expected to be $F_1 = 5$, $F_2 = 7$, and $F_3 = 2$. If the risk-free rate is 3 percent and the four stocks have the following factor sensitivities, what is the expected return of those stocks? (Assume that the APT model intercept for each stock is zero.)

	F_1	F_2	F_3
A	1	0.5	0.3
B	1.5	1	0
C	0.5	0.5	-0.5
D	0	2	0

5.5 Consider that Qualcomm Inc. has a beta of 1.22 and SMB and HML factor sensitivities of -0.2 and -0.9, respectively. Since 1980, the average annual equity risk premium has been 8.5 percent, average annual SMB has been 2.2 percent, and HML has been 4.6 percent. If the risk-free rate is expected to be 3.5 percent, what is the expected return for Qualcomm? (Assume that the 3-factor model intercept for Qualcomm is zero.)

5.6 Consider the following information:

Your Portfolio		**The Market**	
Return	15%	S&P 500 return	14%
Standard deviation	13%	Standard deviation	12%
Beta	1.3	Risk-free rate	5%

Calculate the Sharpe Ratio and the Treynor Index for both your portfolio and the market and compare them.

5.7 A portfolio manager manages a portfolio of assets that have a beta of 1.4. If the return on the fund is 11 percent, the return on the market is 9 percent, and the risk-free rate is 4 percent, what is the alpha of the portfolio? On a risk-adjusted basis, did the manager beat the market?

5.8 Redhook Ale Brewery has a beta of 0.406. Its monthly return standard deviation over the past four years has been 11.61 percent during a period when the S&P 500 has seen a standard deviation of 4.46 percent. What portion of Redhook's total risk is systematic risk?

5.9 Which investment benchmark is most commonly used to judge the investment performance of stock portfolios? Explain the concept and how it is employed.

5.10 An investor wishes to invest $15,000 in the stock of Sun Microsystems (beta = 3.106), $20,000 in WM Wrigley (beta = -0.087), and $25,000 in Wal-Mart Stores (beta = 0.403). What is the beta of this three-stock portfolio?

5.11 List some of the common empirical criticisms of the CAPM.

5.12 Popular financial Web sites frequently report a company's beta. Visit the "Company Info" section of Quote.com (**http://quote.com**) and the "Company Report" section of MSN Money (**http://moneycentral.msn.com**) to locate the beta for Saks, Inc., ticker SKS. Are the beta estimates the same? What might cause differences?

5.13 Go to the Standard & Poor's Market Insight Web site at **ww.mhhe.com/ edumarketinsight** and enter the ticker (LLY) for Eli Lilly. In the "Excel Analytics" section, click the Mthly. Val. Data link and examine the information given. What was the beta estimate for Eli Lilly in each of the past seven months? Why has the beta been changing?

5.14 Go to the Standard & Poor's Market Insight Web site at **www.mhhe.com/ edumarketinsight** and enter the ticker (PIR) for Pier 1 Imports Inc. In the "Excel Analytics" section, click the Mthly. Adj. Prices link and examine the information given. Using the total monthly returns for Pier 1 and for the S&P 500 Index, compute the CAPM beta for Pier 1.

5.15 Kenneth French maintains a Web site where you can obtain historical values of the Fama-French factors. Go to his site, at **mba.tuck.dartmouth.edu/pages/ faculty/ken.french/data_library.html**. What are the most recent market risk premium, SMB, and HML factors?

5.16 The Fama-French factors and the annual risk premiums for Microsoft are shown below. Compute Microsoft's sensitivity to the factors using regression analysis.

	A	B Rm-Rf	C SMB	D HML	E MSFT-Rf
1		Rm-Rf	SMB	HML	MSFT-Rf
2	1987	-3.51	-10.39	-2.54	49.75
3	1988	11.55	6.72	13.78	2.12
4	1989	20.5	-12.01	-5.65	45.95
5	1990	-13.84	-14.4	-10.6	103.03
6	1991	29.1	16.5	-15.08	78.77
7	1992	6.41	7.78	23.05	4.64
8	1993	8.36	7.48	16.95	-4.67
9	1994	-4.11	0.39	-0.08	35.27
10	1995	31.04	-6.94	-3.46	50.29
11	1996	16.25	-1.86	0.23	115.55
12	1997	26.07	-3.73	11.14	41.22
13	1998	19.42	-23.29	-15.04	130.77
14	1999	20.2	11.66	-39.41	7.14
15	2000	-16.71	-5.69	21.39	-43.51
16	2001	-14.78	28.41	27.25	0.83
17	2002	-22.91	4.36	3.72	-26.81
18	2003	30.74	28.08	15.14	17.2
19	2004	10.69	6.32	13.21	17.65

5.17 In the context of the security market line (SML), which of the following statements *best* characterizes the relationship between risk and the required rate of return for an investment?
  a. The slope of the SML indicates the risk per unit of return for a given individual investor.
  b. A parallel shift in the SML occurs in response to a change in the attitudes of investors toward risk.
  c. A movement along the SML shows a change in the risk characteristics of a specific investment, such as a change in its business risk or financial risk.
  d. A change in the slope of the SML reflects a change in market conditions, such as ease or tightness of monetary policy or a change in the expected rate of inflation.

5.18 Arbitrage pricing theory (APT) and the capital asset pricing model (CAPM) are *most* similar with respect to their assumption that
  a. Security returns are normally distributed.
  b. A mean-variance efficient-market portfolio exists and contains all risky assets.
  c. An asset's price is primarily determined by its covariance with one dominant factor.
  d. Unique risk factors are independent and will be diversified away in a large portfolio.

5.19 In the context of capital market theory, unsystematic risk
  a. Is described as unique risk
  b. Refers to nondiversifiable risk
  c. Remains in the market portfolio
  d. Refers to the variability in all risky assets caused by macroeconomic and other aggregate market-related variables

5.20 After several years, the board of trustees of the Glover Scholastic Aid Foundation has decided to allocate 12 percent of Glover's total portfolio to international equities.

The board is considering three alternative international equity managers: Highlands Investments, Coastal Asset Management, and Valley Advisors. Portfolio statistics for Glover's current total portfolio and each of the three alternative equity managers are given in Exhibit 1. Exhibit 2 gives portfolio statistics for Glover's current total portfolio combined with Coastal and Valley, respectively. The appropriate risk-free rate of return is 3.82 percent. All returns are U.S.-dollar-based.

EXHIBIT 1 — Glover Scholastic Aid Foundation: Portfolio Statistics

	Glover's Current Total Portfolio	Highlands Investments	Coastal Asset Management	Valley Advisors
Return prior 5 years	2.10%	-2.60%	-3.50%	-0.50%
Correlation prior 5 years with current Glover portfolio	—	0.83	0.80	0.87
Expected return	8.50%	8.50%	9.75%	10.50%
Expected standard deviation	13.50%	27.00%	18.50%	32.00%
Expected covariance with current Glover portfolio	—	309.80	162.34	367.20
Expected correlation with current Glover portfolio	—	0.85	0.65	0.85

EXHIBIT 2 — Glover Scholastic Aid Foundation: Combined Portfolio Statistics

	Highlands and Glover Portfolio Combined	Coastal and Glover Portfolio Combined	Valley and Glover Portfolio Combined
Return prior 5 years		1.43%	1.79%
Expected return		8.65	8.74
Expected standard deviation		13.43	15.28

a. Recommend *one* of the three alternative international equity managers being considered by Glover's board of trustees. Justify your response with reference to the portfolio statistics for all three managers.

The board has asked a consultant about possible determinants of the long-term performance of Glover's international equity investments. The consultant makes the following statements:
- "Because Glover's portfolio has a long-term time horizon, currency risk makes a much larger contribution to total risk than would be the case for an investor with a short-term time horizon."
- "So-called correlation breakdowns present Glover with an opportunity to enhance portfolio diversification."
- "Glover can expect to realize superior long-term returns by identifying and investing in international economies that have consistently offered superior performance over time."

b. Indicate whether *each* of the consultant's three statements is correct or incorrect. If incorrect, give *one* reason why the statement is incorrect.

INVESTMENT APPLICATION

Long-Term Capital Management: How Do You Say "Oops"?

The best-seller *Liar's Poker* chronicled the exploits of John Meriwether, a pioneer of fixed-income arbitrage at investment bank Salomon Brothers. Meriwether made bond trading a huge money maker by using enormous leverage to exploit small price differences in various bond markets. When forced to resign from Salomon following a Treasury bond bid-rigging scandal in 1991, Meriwether assembled an all-star lineup to form a new firm, called Long-Term Capital Management (LTCM).

Meriwether's group of heavy hitters included David Mullins, former Harvard Business School professor and vice chairman of the Federal Reserve Board, and Nobel laureates Myron Scholes, from Stanford University, and Robert Merton, from MIT. Scholes and Merton won the 1997 Nobel Prize in economics for their pathbreaking work on how financial options are priced. At LTCM, Scholes and Merton hoped to capture above-average returns for investors by exploiting tiny inefficiencies in world capital markets.

In the early to mid-1990s, LTCM's traders, economists, and mathematicians used computers to detect suspected mispricings, or anomalies, in the value of bonds and financial derivatives. In presentations before potential investors, Scholes, among others, described the firm's investment philosophy as "scouring world capital markets, looking for loose nickels." Even small mispricings in debt and equity securities could lead to big profits for LTCM if sufficient leverage was brought to bear. In the case of Scholes and his colleagues, enormous leverage was not to be feared. It was simply viewed as a tool that could be used to magnify gains. Unfortunately, just as massive leverage can magnify gains on the upside, it can exaggerate losses on the downside.

In U.S. equity markets, investors are limited by Federal Reserve regulations to using no more than 50 percent leverage. This means that $10 million worth of stock can be bought with as little as $5 million in equity. This implies a 2:1 leverage ratio because twice as much equity can be purchased relative to the amount of investment capital used. Because normally liquid U.S. Treasury securities enjoy the full faith and credit backing of the U.S. government, investors are able to buy them using anywhere from 10:1 to 20:1 leverage. In the case of LTCM, higher than typical leverage could be brought to bear because the firm made extensive use of options and other complicated financial derivatives. In the firm's heyday, published reports asserted that LTCM may have used financial leverage as high as 40:1 or 50:1. Notice that when 50:1 leverage is used, a 1 percent increase in the value of an investment security will lead to a 50 percent increase in the investor's capital. Conversely, when 50:1 leverage is used, a 2 percent decrease in the value will cause investors to get wiped out.

In August 1998, LTCM made a gigantic bet that the interest rate difference would narrow between U.S. Treasury bonds and riskier Danish mortgage securities. Instead, interest rate spreads widened, and LTCM lost—big time. To avert a wide-scale financial panic, Federal Reserve Board Chairman Allan Greenspan helped engineer a $3.6 billion bailout led by 14 major Wall Street securities firms and banks. Although financial panic was averted, terms of the bailout effectively wiped out more than 90 percent of the value of the ownership interest held by Meriwether and his colleagues.

a. Many criticized the Federal Reserve's role in the LTCM bailout as a troubling signal to the capital markets. What do you think?

b. To the extent that the bailout averted even steeper losses for LTCM investors, should taxpayers share in such benefits?

Efficient-Market Hypothesis

Internet Web sites give periodic buy-sell advice, provide timely financial news and information, and offer venues for investor message boards and chat rooms. One of the most popular of these is *The Motley Fool* (TMF), found at **www.fool.com**. Headquartered in Old Town Alexandria, Virginia, TMF was founded in 1993 by brothers David and Tom Gardner. Its name derives from Elizabethan drama where only the court jester (the "fool") could tell the king the truth without getting his head lopped off. For more than a decade, TMF has been dedicated to "educating, amusing, and enriching" individual investors. TMF has recently become active in the print and broadcast media as well. It appears in roughly 160 newspapers in the United States and Canada. TMF radio is heard in a three-hour program on more than 100 stations on Saturday or Sunday.

Investors can learn useful information at TMF and on other such sites. For example, TMF correctly points out that roughly three-quarters of all managed mutual funds underperform the stock market during a typical year. If investors want marketlike returns with very low transaction costs, index mutual funds typically represent a better bet than managed mutual funds. Similarly, TMF points out that nobody has ever demonstrated an ability to precisely time the market's occasional dips. History shows that the best long-term investment strategy is to simply buy and hold a broadly diversified portfolio of stocks for capital appreciation and dividend income.

Unfortunately, investors sometimes run into trouble when seeking investment advice on the Internet and in the traditional print and broadcast media. Too many succumb to the allure of "can't miss" investments that promise easy profits without risk. They don't exist. There are no $100 bills lying around on Wall Street, or on the Internet, just waiting for you to pick them up and put them in your pocket. Beware the investment advisor who suggests otherwise. On the Internet and on Main Street, a "fool" and his money are quickly parted.[1]

---

[1]See *The Motley Fool* on the Internet at **www.fool.com**.

CHAPTER OBJECTIVES

- Understand the role of randomness and luck in investment performance.

- Identify the levels of market efficiency.

- Characterize the time series of stock returns.

- Avoid the gambler's fallacy and data-snooping problems.

- Recognize how bubbles and fraud challenge the efficient-market concept.

Efficient-Market Concept

Treatise on Coin Flipping

Millions of stock market investors, and tens of thousands of professional money managers and security analysts, around the globe seek stock market bargains in a 24-hour trading day. Knowledgeable professional and individual investors comb through reams of widely available financial information looking for clues about how much to pay for what and when to do so. Enterprising professionals and amateurs alike look for valuable unpublished information that "The Street" does not already know. The daily level of activity is feverish. It seems like serious business because it is. Any edge, ever so slight, can lead to enormous profits when sufficient leverage is used. In a world filled with millions of investors hungry for stock market profits, enormous leverage will be brought to bear whenever valuable new information is discovered.

If anyone approaches investing as anything less than serious, millions of global investors stand ready to take his or her money, and they will. Nobody should ever compare long-term investing in the stock market with less serious pursuits such as gambling. In the long run, the expected rate of return on common stocks falls in a range from 10 to 12 percent per year. These returns are tied to economic growth and the overall rate of inflation. In buying stocks, long-term investors are participating in the process of raising and committing capital to productive investment. Without equity and fixed-income investors, capital raising and our economic system would flounder.

Coin-flipping contest
Investment metaphor for gambling.

Short-term speculation in the stock and bond markets is another thing altogether. Imagine a global **coin-flipping contest**. Have 6 billion people in the world pay $1 to stand up and flip a coin. If the coin comes up heads, the coin flipper gets to remain standing and keep playing. If it comes up tails, the coin flipper is out of the game and sits down. Everyone's dollar gets contributed to a pot to be won by those lucky enough or able enough to keep flipping heads. The game ends whenever all remaining players agree to stop playing or when only one player remains standing, whichever comes first.

After round one, 3 billion players remain standing. After 10 rounds, about 6 million coin flippers remain standing. These are among the luckiest coin flippers ever seen. They have flipped heads an astounding 10 times in a row. At this point, the good fortune enjoyed by the lucky coin flippers begins to give way to the perception that these folks are talented coin flippers. Among the crowd, the reasoning goes that these individuals must be unusually adept at coin flipping. Some players will even begin to fashion themselves as "experts" in the art and science of coin flipping.

After 10 more rounds, the elite circle of successful coin flippers has shrunk to roughly 6,000 persons worldwide. These people have flipped heads an unbelievable 20 times in a row. Local notoriety has given way to large and growing regional reputations. Nevertheless, half of these amazing success stories falter and fade on the next round, when half of the coin flippers inexplicably toss tails. After 25 rounds, only about 180 global coin flippers remain standing. If the game stopped now, each of these coin flippers would earn $33.3 million for their "efforts." For the first time, discussion begins among the winning coin flippers about whether they should call off the game, let each player collect his or her winnings, and go home. Conservatives get hooted down by more aggressive players. After all, these are among the most talented coin flippers of our generation. Books get written about them. Of course, the winners vote to continue playing the game. Why stop now? After all, these players are *good* at flipping coins.

It takes only 32 tosses to reduce the 6 billion flippers to a single, solitary coin flipper. With a 50-50 chance of flipping heads, the chance of flipping heads 32 times in a row is roughly 1 in 6 billion. Thus, after about 32 tosses of a coin, a single solitary coin flipper, the one who has never flipped tails, walks off with a cool $6 billion.

Efficient Markets

It is intriguing to compare coin flippers with stock market speculators. There are literally millions of speculators and stock pickers trying to beat the market on a daily basis. Based on the laws of probability, many will be successful in significantly outperforming the market. The relevant question is, Are successful stock pickers equivalent to lucky coin flippers?

An important point to realize is that a long run of strong investment performance does not necessarily signify skill. This is especially true when it comes to the feverishly quick in and out trading typical of day traders and other short-term speculators. There are tens of thousands of money managers, mutual funds, and other professional market "players" constantly trying to beat the market. Investors who ignore mathematical probabilities run the risk of investing on the basis of previous successes that are the result of nothing more than random chance. A "hot" mutual fund manager may be nothing more than lucky. It is human nature to believe that when you buy a stock and it goes up, the source of the success is your own skill. When you buy a stock and it goes down, the source is attributed to luck—all bad. This is a dangerous pattern of beliefs to fall into. In fact, an investor can be judged neither correct nor incorrect on the basis of whether the market agrees with him or her over the short term.

In the short term, theory and evidence tell us that stock prices are equally apt to rise or fall in an **efficient market**. In an efficient stock market, the price for any given stock effectively represents the expected net present value of all future profits. In this calculation, profits are discounted by using a fair or risk-adjusted rate of return. If the stock market is to be perfectly efficient, there must be a large number of buyers and sellers of essentially identical securities, information must be free and readily available, and entry and exit by market players must be uninhibited.

> **Efficient market**
> Stock market in which the price for any given stock effectively represents the expected net present value of all future profits.

On an overall basis, basic criteria for an efficient market seem easily met by the stock market. In the United States, there are literally thousands of actively traded securities that promise investors a wide array of capital gain and dividend-income-producing opportunities. For any given risk class, there are dozens of common stocks with essentially identical economic characteristics. Moreover, financial and nonfinancial stock market information is widely disseminated to individual investors on the Internet, television and radio, and in the financial press. Hard-to-find information that was sought and prized by professional investors only a decade ago is now instantly published and available to all on the Internet. And finally, not only are millions of eager investors available to bid up the prices of attractive securities, but the supply of available securities quickly adjusts to meet investor demand. When investor demand is high, new supply is created in the form of initial public offerings and seasoned-equity offerings.

At any point in time, prices in an efficient market reflect the interplay of demand and supply. Investors seeking bargains bid up the price of attractive securities. Companies with quickly deteriorating economic fundamentals see their stock prices collapse as investors desert in droves. At any point in time, the price for any stock or bond reflects the collective wisdom of market buyers and sellers regarding the company's future economic prospects. As such, the market price for a stock is the best available estimate of the company's future economic

Street Smarts 6.1

The Once-in-a-Lifetime Event

Most of the time, annual, monthly, and daily stock market returns follow a normal distribution with easy-to-measure means and standard deviations. The DJIA has not lost more than 10 percent of its value in one day since 1995 (see Table 6.3). Could the DJIA lose 20 percent tomorrow? The answer is yes, though it is very unlikely. There have been about 20,000 trading days since October 1, 1928, when the DJIA was expanded to 28 companies. The DJIA has collapsed by more than 20 percent only on one trading day, October 19, 1987, when it fell 22.61 percent. It has fallen by more than 10 percent on only three other trading days since 1928. Nevertheless, investors need to keep in mind the devastation that can occur when that adverse "once-in-a-lifetime event" actually happens.

Studying historical data often does not adequately prepare investors for the very occasional "rare event." Investors sometimes get fooled by long-term price stability and begin to think that market volatility has been tamed. Stable markets suggest steady and predictable returns. This can entice naïve investors to borrow money and leverage positions to magnify expected returns. Then, one day, the market does the unexpected and prices plummet. In such circumstances, highly leveraged investors can get wiped out.

In the 1990s, hedge funds bet heavily on continued growth in emerging markets such as Mexico. Beginning in 1994 and continuing through 1995, the "Mexican miracle" became the "Mexican peso crisis" as the peso fell 50 percent against the dollar. Historically steady currencies and rapid economic growth also attracted big players to speculate in Malaysia, Indonesia, and Thailand. When early bets paid off, they were doubled and tripled in size. Then Asian currencies collapsed in 1997. Known as the "Asian flu," this rare event blew up many hedge funds. Similarly, the Russian ruble collapsed by 97 percent against the dollar in the summer of 1998. Major currency devaluations also occurred in Brazil during 1999 and in Turkey during 2001.

Emerging market risks can be brutal for equity and bond investors and for currency speculators. Just like the proverbial 30-year flood, adverse once-in-a-lifetime financial events seem to occur much more often than advertised.

See E. S. Browning, Greg Ip, and Mark Whitehouse, "Sharp Decline in Stocks Reflects Investors' Greater Aversion to Risk," *The Wall Street Journal*, April 18, 2005, p. A1.

---

prospects given all that is presently known in the market. This makes it tough for professionals and amateurs alike to beat the market.

The Efficient-Market Hypothesis

Basic Premise

Efficient-market hypothesis (EMH)

Theory stating that security prices fully reflect all available information.

The **efficient-market hypothesis (EMH)** states that security prices fully reflect all available information. The implications of this simple idea are profound.

Individual and professional investors buy and sell stocks under the assumption that they have discovered a divergence between intrinsic value and the market price. When the market price is below perceived intrinsic value, buyers aggressively acquire and bid up the price of such securities. When the market price is above perceived intrinsic value, sellers aggressively abandon such securities and prices fall.

It is worth remembering that every transaction involves both buyers and sellers. Through their market activity, each buyer and seller is behaving in such a way as to imply that he or she somehow knows more than the person acting on the other side of the transaction. If stock and bond markets are perfectly efficient and current prices fully reflect all available information, then neither buyers nor sellers have an informational advantage. In an efficient market, both buyers and sellers have the same information.

Within this context, important characteristics of a perfectly competitive securities market include the following:

- New information arrives at the marketplace in an independent and random fashion.

- Current stock prices reflect all relevant risk and return information.

- Investors rapidly adjust stock prices to reflect unexpected new information.

The EMH can be viewed as a simple statement of the effectiveness with which stocks and bonds are priced. It implies that with the near-perfect distribution of financial information that is typical of our electronic society, stock prices accurately reflect everything that is known. Stock prices change when new information comes to the market, but new information cannot be anticipated and there is no way for the average investor to gain an edge.

Levels of Market Efficiency

Like any theory, the EMH is useful to the extent that it can describe or predict real-world behavior. To the extent that the EMH accurately explains securities prices, it can be useful in helping investors and others understand the price formation process. If the EMH does not yield useful insight concerning the security price formation process, it represents bad theory and should be abandoned.

Because real-world securities markets are fraught with uncertainty, obtaining convincing evidence regarding the EMH is difficult. As a result, stock market analysts and financial economists have settled on three basic definitions, or forms, of market efficiency that can be studied in an effort to learn the extent to which the EMH is a useful concept. These alternative forms of the EMH can be described as:

- **Weak-form hypothesis:** Current prices reflect all **stock market information**. Trading rules based on past stock market returns and trading volume are futile.

- **Semistrong-form hypothesis:** Current prices reflect all **public information**. All trading rules based on public information are ineffective.

- **Strong-form hypothesis:** Current prices reflect all public information and **nonpublic information**. All trading rules are pointless.

Notice how each form of the EMH involves slightly different assumptions regarding the level of information that is incorporated in security prices at any point in time. If none of the various forms of the EMH can be supported by the empirical evidence, then the market must be judged inefficient.

The weak-form hypothesis involves the easiest or lowest hurdle that must be met for one to argue that the stock market is efficient. According to the weak-form hypothesis, stock and bond prices reflect all price and trading volume activity. In an efficient stock market, it would not be possible to earn above-market returns by buying or selling stocks on the premise that they should continue to rise on price momentum or are bound to experience a quick reversal of "panic selling." In a perfectly efficient market there is no such thing as panic selling, or panic buying for that matter. Buyers and sellers are fully informed and act rationally on the basis of accurate assessments of future prospects.

The semistrong-form hypothesis is more stringent than the weak-form hypothesis. According to the semistrong-form hypothesis, no investor can earn excess returns buying or selling stocks on the basis of publicly available information. Historical returns and trading volume activity are only a small part of publicly available information. Whenever new and unpredictable quarterly earnings information is released, stock prices quickly and accurately readjust so that subsequent investors earn only a risk-adjusted normal rate of return on their investment. Similarly, the moment a favorable report is issued by Merrill Lynch or another leading Wall Street investment banker, stock prices rise or fall to fully reflect that information. According to the semistrong-form hypothesis, everything read in the newspaper, heard on television, or seen on the Internet is already reflected in stock and bond prices.

For example, after the stock market closed on Monday, April 18, 2005, Texas Instruments announced that it beat analyst earnings expectations for the first quarter of 2005. Figure 6.1 shows that the stock price traded up $1.59 per share at the opening the next day but traded in a tight range the rest of the day. This figure is consistent with the semistrong-form hypothesis. The strong-form hypothesis is the highest hurdle that must be met for the stock market to be regarded as perfectly efficient. It encompasses the information considered by the weak-form and semistrong-form hypotheses and more. The securities market is perfectly efficient only if all relevant information is accurately and instantaneously reflected in security prices. For example, to the extent that CEOs and other insiders earn above-normal rates of return on their stock market investments, the market would not be judged perfectly efficient according to the strong-form hypothesis. If insiders do, in fact, earn above-normal rates of return, one might conclude that they have profited by virtue of their access to superior or **insider information**.

Notice how it might be possible to reject the notion of strong-form efficiency in favor of some weaker criterion such as semistrong-form efficiency. For example, if company insiders

Weak-form hypothesis
Premise that current prices reflect all stock market information.

Stock market information
Stock price and trading volume information.

Semistrong-form hypothesis
Premise that stock prices reflect all public information.

Public information
Freely shared knowledge.

Strong-form hypothesis
Premise that stock prices reflect all public information and nonpublic information.

Nonpublic information
Proprietary data.

Insider information
Proprietary data within the firm.

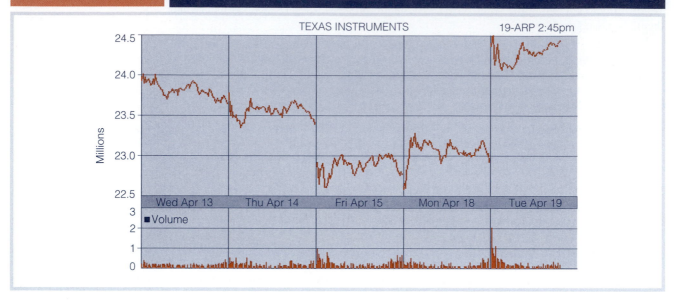

FIGURE 6.1

Stock Price Reaction to Texas Instruments' Announcement *After the close of the stock market on Monday, April 18, 2005, Texas Instruments announced that it beat Wall Street's expectations for the first quarter of 2005 and posted a profit of $411 million, which is 12 percent more than its profit in the year-ago quarter. TI had been expected to post single-digit profit growth.*

Source: Yahoo! Finance, **http://finance.yahoo.com**. Reproduced with permission of Yahoo! Inc. © 2005 by Yahoo! Inc. Yahoo! and the Yahoo! logo are trademarks of Yahoo! Inc.

consistently earn above-average rates of return, the concept of strong-form efficiency would be rejected. However, semistrong-form efficiency could still be maintained if investors fail to earn excess returns when they mimic insiders by basing buy and sell decisions on published reports of inside-trading activity.

Try It!

Consider the following observations. What does each one imply about market efficiency?

a. An investor looks for companies that have increased in price during each of the past five trading days. Suppose the investor consistently earns positive abnormal returns after buying such stocks and then selling them after a brief three-day holding period.

b. Another investor spends hours pouring over company annual reports to ferret out bargains with unusually low price-earnings ratios. This investor enjoys portfolio performance similar to that of the S&P 500 Index.

c. A stock market analyst discovers that company CEOs, on average, tend to sell their shares prior to periods of poor stock return performance.

Solution

a. If an investor is able to earn abnormal profits through a price momentum trading strategy, the weak form of the EMH would be violated.

b. An inability to earn extra profits by carefully analyzing public information is consistent with the semistrong form of the EMH.

c. If CEOs are able to benefit from inside information, the strong form of the EMH would be discredited.

Time Series of Stock Prices

Indexes Are Correlated over Time

The EMH has implications for the movement of stock prices. Over time, significant price movements should occur only when unexpected information is revealed to the market. By definition, unexpected information can be bad or good. Therefore, if the arrival of new information is random in the short run, the movement of stock prices should also be random in the short run. To explore this issue, consider the **time series** of stock prices.

Time series
Data points over time.

Most investors are well aware of the fact that stock market indexes move together over extended time frames. The nine-year period from April 19, 1996, to April 18, 2005, experienced a full market cycle (both a bull and bear market). The DJIA went on an unprecedented run from 5,571.2 (on April 19, 1996) to 11,908.5 (on January 14, 2000) and then back down to 7,181.5 (on October 10, 2002) before rebounding. The change in the S&P 500 was less dramatic. The S&P 500 went on a run from 643.6 (on April 19, 1996) to 1,553.1 (on March 24, 2000) and then back down to 768.6 (on October 10, 2002) before recovering. Nasdaq was the most volatile of all the major indexes over this period. The Nasdaq jumped from 1,141.99 (on April 19, 1996) to 5,132.5 (on March 10, 2000) and then went back down to 1,108.5 (on October 10, 2002) before rebounding.

As shown in Figure 6.2, the DJIA, S&P 500, and Nasdaq indexes moved together over this time frame. Market indexes typically move up or down together, though not with the same magnitude. In statistical terms, these measures of overall market performance are correlated over time. Whenever the movement of stock prices over time is being analyzed, the data are described as a time series of market data. Correlation is said to be high and positive when large values of one index set are associated with large values of another index. A correlation coefficient of +1 indicates perfect positive correlation. Correlation is said to be high and negative when large values of one index set are associated with small values of another index. A correlation coefficient of −1 indicates perfect negative, or inverse, correlation. When the values of market indexes are unrelated to one another, their correlation is near zero. A correlation coefficient of zero indicates that two sets of data have no relation.

Over this time frame, the correlation coefficient between daily returns for the DJIA and the S&P 500 is 0.93 (Table 6.1). These two indexes closely capture movement among large-cap stocks and are similarly influenced by changes in interest rates and economic

FIGURE 6.2   Market Indexes Move Together over Time

<table>
<tr><td rowspan="2"></td><td colspan="4">**TABLE 6.1**   The Degree of Correlation Shows How Stock Market Indexes Move Together*</td></tr>
</table>

	DJIA	S&P 500	Nasdaq
DJIA	1.00		
S&P 500	0.93	1.00	
Nasdaq	0.70	0.83	1.00

*Data are for the nine-year period from April 19, 1996, to April 18, 2005.
Source: Data from Yahoo! Finance, **http://finance.yahoo.com**.

conditions. The correlation coefficient between daily returns for the DJIA and the Nasdaq is only 0.70. This is consistent with the observation that over this period the DJIA and the Nasdaq indexes captured somewhat different aspects of the long-term advance in stock prices. The DJIA and the S&P 500 are dominated by established and diversified firms that represent a broad cross section of U.S. industry. The Nasdaq is dominated by large high-tech stocks such as Microsoft Corp., Intel Corp., and Cisco Systems, Inc. All 30 DJIA stocks are included in the S&P 500, but Microsoft and Intel are the only Nasdaq stocks included in the DJIA. Thus, it should come as no surprise that the correlation of 0.83 between the S&P 500 and the Nasdaq is somewhat greater than the 0.70 correlation between the DJIA and Nasdaq.

Daily Returns

In any given year, the expected rate of return on a diversified portfolio of common stocks is roughly 10 to 12 percent, the long-term average rate of return. This means that market indexes, such as the DJIA and the S&P 500, can be expected to advance at low double-digit rates. There are good economic reasons why stocks typically go up in price. Because stocks represent part ownership in real businesses, they benefit from economic growth made possible by technical progress and a growing population.

Although stocks can be counted on to advance over long periods of time, it is important to recognize that day-to-day changes in stock prices occur in an irregular and unpredictable pattern. Figure 6.3 shows the pattern of daily returns for the DJIA, S&P 500, and Nasdaq indexes over the nine-year April 19, 1996, to April 18, 2005, period. Notice how closely centered these daily returns are around zero. In fact, the average daily return on the DJIA over this period was a scant 0.03 percent. During the same period, the average daily return on the S&P 500 was 0.03 percent and on the Nasdaq index was 0.04 percent.

It is useful to note how often negative-return days occur. With respect to the DJIA, for example, Table 6.2 shows that 1,165 of 2,262 trading days were positive-return days, and 1,094 return days were negative. The DJIA experienced a downtick on 48.4 percent of all trading days. Significant volatility in the daily returns of the S&P 500 and the Nasdaq index are also evident over this period. The S&P 500 experienced negative returns on 1,090, or 48.2 percent, of all trading days, whereas the Nasdaq index went down on 1,058, or 46.8 percent, of all trading days.

Dispersion
Variation from the average.

As depicted in Figure 6.3 and Table 6.2, there is significant day-to-day volatility in stock market returns. This means that there is a significant amount of **dispersion** around the average daily return. During this nine-year time frame, the standard deviation of daily returns averaged more than 1.16 percent. This means that the typical daily deviation in stock market returns tends to be far greater than the average daily return. No wonder day traders and

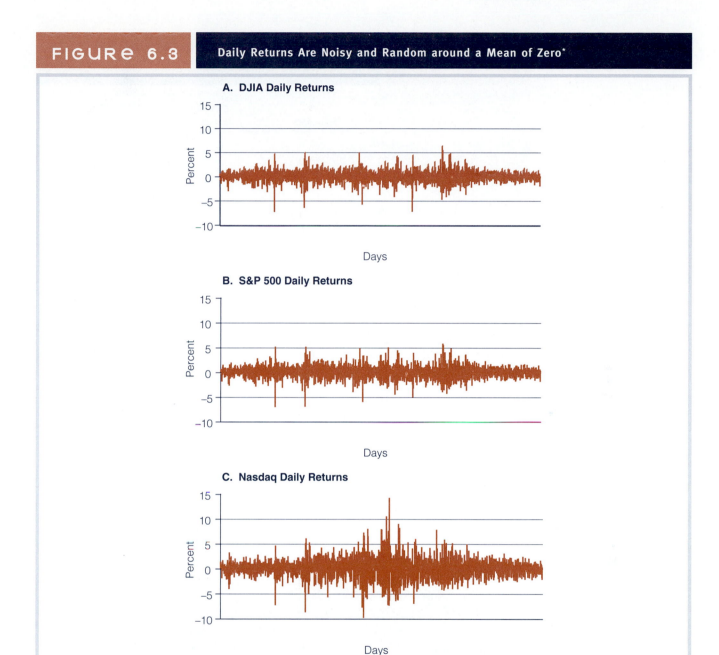

| FIGURE 6.3 | Daily Returns Are Noisy and Random around a Mean of Zero* |

*Data are for the nine-year period from April 19, 1996, to April 18, 2005.
Source: Yahoo! Finance, **http://finance.yahoo.com.**

other short-term speculators face a difficult task in deciphering the short-term direction of the market! Up-days are often followed by down-days. The day-to-day pattern in stock returns is essentially chaotic.

As shown in Table 6.2, daily returns are clearly centered in the region around zero, with small positive daily returns on the order of –0.25 to 0.25 percent most common. From a statistical perspective, the distribution of daily returns closely resembles a **normal distribution**, or bell-shaped curve, with an average daily return around zero. The normal distribution is a continuous probability description of possible investment returns. It has useful statistical properties. For example, assuming a normal return distribution, 68.3 percent of all returns will lie within one standard deviation of the average. All but 4.5 percent of the returns fall within two standard deviations from the average.

Normal distribution
Bell-shaped probability curve.

TABLE 6.2	Daily Market Returns Fluctuate around a Mean of Roughly 0 Percent*		
Bin	DJIA Frequency	S&P 500 Frequency	Nasdaq Frequency
−10.00%	0	0	0
−7.50	0	0	3
−5.00	4	3	20
−4.00	5	3	23
−3.00	11	16	70
−2.50	18	22	70
−2.00	51	51	94
−1.50	85	105	123
−1.25	70	73	74
−1.00	97	84	82
−0.75	133	141	92
−0.50	164	162	117
−0.25	212	196	141
0.00	244	234	149
0.25	245	237	164
0.50	217	216	159
0.75	183	194	158
1.00	144	142	140
1.25	116	111	117
1.50	81	79	83
2.00	95	95	127
2.50	42	47	95
3.00	18	20	52
4.00	16	20	58
5.00	9	6	22
7.50	2	5	20
10.00	0	0	7
More	0	0	2
Average	0.03%	0.03%	0.04%
Standard deviation	1.16%	1.19%	1.91%
Positive	1,165	1,170	1,204
Negative	1,094	1,090	1,058
Unchanged	3	2	0
Total days	2,262	2,262	2,262

*Data are for the nine-year period from April 19, 1996, to April 18, 2005.
Source: Yahoo! Finance, **http://finance.yahoo.com**.

Booms and Busts

During recent years, investors have become increasingly interested in abruptly changing stock prices. In an Internet era of instant communication and low-cost stock trading, investor sentiment on the market can change suddenly and lead to sharp upswings or quick downturns in the

TABLE 6.3	Short-Term Price Changes in the Market Are Random and Unpredictable*

Date	Open	High	Low	Close	Change	Percentage	Prior Day	Following Day
A. Dow Jones Industrial Average Big Up-Days								
24-Jul-02	7698.5	8243.1	7489.5	8191.3	489.0	6.35%	–1.06%	–0.06%
29-Jul-02	8268.0	8749.1	8268.0	8711.9	447.5	5.41	0.95	–0.37
8-Sep-98	7964.9	8103.7	7779.0	8020.8	380.5	4.98	–0.55	–1.94
16-Mar-00	10139.6	10716.2	10139.6	10630.6	499.2	4.93	3.26	–0.33
15-Oct-02	7883.2	8304.6	7883.2	8255.7	151.4	4.80	0.35	–2.66
28-Oct-97	7190.9	7553.6	6933.0	7498.3	337.1	4.71	–7.18	0.11
1-Oct-02	7593.0	7964.2	7558.4	7938.8	346.9	4.57	–1.42	–2.31
24-Sep-01	8242.3	8733.4	8242.3	8603.9	368.1	4.47	–1.68	0.65
5-Apr-01	9527.2	9969.9	9527.2	9918.1	402.6	4.23	0.31	–1.28
11-Oct-02	7540.7	7919.6	7540.7	7850.3	316.3	4.20	3.40	0.35
Average						4.86%	–0.36%	–0.78%
B. Dow Jones Industrial Average Big Down-Days								
27-Oct-97	7608.3	7717.4	7150.1	7161.2	–554.2	–7.18%	–1.69%	4.71%
17-Sep-01	9294.6	9294.6	8755.5	8920.7	–684.8	–7.13	0.00	–0.19
31-Aug-98	8079.0	8149.0	7517.7	7539.1	–512.6	–6.37	–1.40	3.82
14-Apr-00	10922.9	10922.9	10173.9	10305.8	–617.8	–5.66	–1.81	2.69
19-Jul-02	8356.7	8356.7	7940.8	8019.3	–390.2	–4.64	–1.56	–2.93
20-Sep-01	8375.7	8711.4	8304.5	8376.2	–382.8	–4.37	–1.62	–1.68
27-Aug-98	8377.9	8448.7	8062.2	8166.0	–357.4	–4.19	–0.92	–1.40
12-Mar-01	10638.52	10638.63	10138.9	10208.25	–436.4	–4.10	–1.97	0.81
3-Sep-02	8659.3	8659.3	8282.9	8308.1	–355.4	–4.10	–0.09	1.41
27-Sep-00	7996.0	7997.1	7664.9	7701.5	–295.7	–3.70	1.98	–1.42
Average						–5.14%	–0.91%	0.58%

*Data are for the nine-year period from January 1, 1997, to December 31, 2005.

Source: Yahoo! Finance, **http://finance.yahoo.com**.

market. Table 6.3 shows the 10 biggest up-days and the 10 biggest down-days in the DJIA over the nine-year period from January 1, 1997, to December 31, 2005.

Notice how often a big up-day for each respective market index was preceded by a day on which the index suffered negative returns. In the case of the DJIA, for example, 5 of 10 big up-days were preceded by negative-return days. In fact, the average rate of return on the day prior to a big up-day for the DJIA was –0.36 percent. Negative-return days just prior to big up-days may reflect a simple manifestation of the reversion-to-the-mean concept. During this time frame, big up-days for the DJIA averaged 4.86 percent. The day following this big up move turned out to be down in 7 of the 10 days.

A study of returns on the day just prior to and on the day just following big down-days in the overall market yields similar conclusions. In Table 6.3, notice how often the average down-day for each respective market index was preceded by a day on which the index also suffered negative returns. In the case of the DJIA, for example, 8 of 10 big down-days were preceded by negative-return days. However, the average rate of return on the day prior to a big down-day in the DJIA was only –0.91 percent. Interestingly, the market experienced modest up-days on the day following big down-days.

Random Walk Theory

Random Walk Concept

Random walk
Irregular pattern of numbers that defies prediction.

Random walk theory
Concept that stock price movements do not follow any patterns or trends.

Fair game
Even bet, or 50-50 chance.

A **random walk** is an irregular pattern of numbers that defies prediction. With respect to the stock market, **random walk theory** asserts that stock price movements do not follow any pattern or trend. As a result, past price action cannot be used to predict future price movements. All price changes represent arbitrary departures from previous prices.

Random walk theory can be traced back to a French mathematician named Louis Bachelier, who wrote a famous PhD dissertation titled "The Theory of Speculation" in 1900. A century ago, Bachelier came to the conclusion that the mathematical expectation of the speculator's profit is zero when stock prices follow a random walk. He described the market as a **fair game** in which the professional and the novice alike face the exact same chance for success. Unfortunately, Bachelier's insights were so far ahead of the times that they went largely unnoticed for more than 50 years, until his work was rediscovered and eventually translated into English.

The reasoning behind the random walk concept as it applies to the stock market is disarmingly simple: Securities markets are flooded with tens of thousands of intelligent, well-paid, and well-educated professional investors and security analysts. Millions of similarly capable individual investors are also standing by. All such market participants are constantly seeking undervalued securities to buy and overvalued securities to sell. The more contestants in the market, the faster the dissemination of relevant information and thus the more efficient the market becomes.

When information arises about a stock or the market as a whole, news spreads very rapidly and tends to be quickly reflected in security prices. The logic of the random walk idea is not that market prices are erratic. It is simply that when the flow of information is unimpeded, all of today's news is reflected in today's stock prices. Tomorrow's price changes reflect only tomorrow's news. By definition, news is unpredictable and random. Price changes that result when news is released must also be unpredictable and random.

Random walk with drift
Slight upward bias to inherently unpredictable daily stock prices.

Although stocks can be expected to advance over long periods of time, day-to-day rates of return in the stock market can be expected to exhibit what might be called a **random walk with drift**. Daily rates of return on common stocks have a slight upward bias, or upward drift, given the long-term positive expectation for investor rates of return. Still, random walk theory asserts that the overwhelming characteristic of short-term rates of return in the stock market is their unpredictability.

Patterns and the Gambler's Fallacy

Charting
Predicting the future direction of stock prices from graphs of previous prices.

Generally speaking, short-run stock returns tend to behave in random, unpredictable ways. Nevertheless, scores of investors and speculators sort through millions of bits of stock price and volume information on a daily basis looking for clues about future prices. This process, called **charting**, is based on the premise that future prices can be predicted on the basis of historical patterns. Charting experts, often called "chartists," frequently appear as commentators on popular financial shows on television.

Despite the popularity of charting, and the popular fascination with charts and graphs, it is worth emphasizing that there are no dependable patterns that can be used to predict the future course of randomly generated data. Investors sometimes "see" patterns in random stock return data and make predictions about the future based on those perceived patterns. A fair coin will show equal numbers of heads and tails, on average, provided that a large number of tosses are completed. With only five tosses, four heads and one tails is not unusual. Similarly, it's not uncommon to toss four tails and one heads in five tosses. A fair coin has a 50-50 chance of turning up heads or tails, but this probability may become obvious only after a large number of tosses, say, 30 or 40 coin flips. Importantly, a fair coin flip will have a 50-50 chance of coming up heads or tails irrespective of what has turned up in the past. In the unlikely event that a

Pyramid Schemes

Charles Ponzi, a Boston immigrant from Italy, embarked on a legendary investment fraud in 1920. Ponzi promised investors that he could double their money in a matter of months. When an early depositor cashed out, Ponzi used the money deposited by subsequent investors to pay withdrawals and phantom profits for early investors and enormous profits for himself. Ponzi's so-called pyramid scheme worked as long as the number of new investors continued to grow. Once the pyramid stopped growing, however, there was insufficient means to pay withdrawals and phantom profits. Investors began to clamor for the return of their funds along with hoped-for profits. When everyone wanted out, Ponzi's pyramid scheme collapsed and investors were left with enormous losses.

In a well-functioning and efficient market, investors should not be duped in large numbers by this type of fraud. Yet modern Ponzi schemes have flourished in eastern Europe and Russia. In Albania, for example, two-thirds of the population recently invested $1.5 billion in pyramid schemes perpetrated by companies that took consumer deposits. By the fall of 1996, pyramid schemes were offering to double depositors' money in two months or triple investors' money in three months (annualized returns of 6,300 percent and 8,000 percent, respectively). After the inevitable collapse, auditors found only $243 million in assets that could be distributed to depositors. Other recent pyramid schemes, like the Caritas pyramid in Romania and the MMM pyramid in Russia, have duped thousands of investors.

It is tempting to believe that pyramid schemes are a thing of the past for modern financial markets, but such scams are still perpetrated in the United States. A pyramid scheme that swept the United States recently was the "gift club," in which participants joined "clubs" by giving $2,000 to existing club members. Clubs commonly recruited groups of eight people, so each member hoped his or her $2,000 would turn into $16,000 as new members joined. Like all pyramid schemes, when new members failed to join, the pyramid collapsed and remaining members were left with enormous losses.

See Gregory Zuckerman, "SEC Charges Hedge-Fund HMC Principals of Fraud," *The Wall Street Journal Online*, December 22, 2005 (**http://online.wsj.com**).

---

fair coin flip has resulted in 10 straight heads (or tails), there is still a 50-50 chance that the next coin flip will come up heads (or tails).

The popular belief that there is an immediate self-correcting process in random events is known as the **gambler's fallacy**. It is wrong to presume that when a fair coin flip comes up heads it will be followed by tails, and vice versa. Similarly, it is wrong to observe a "trend" of heads and believe the trend will continue. It is interesting to note that books are sold that show bettors the frequency with which numbers come up in random state lottery drawings. Like some bettors, some stock market speculators appear to succumb to the gambler's fallacy by looking for patterns that don't exist in random numbers.

Gambler's fallacy
The belief that a short-term deviation from a "fair" gamble changes the odds of the next gamble.

Data-Snooping Problem

Deceptive patterns have a tendency to emerge in historical stock return data. This is true even when historical market returns resemble a table of random numbers. The reason for this **data-snooping problem** is quite simple: Given sufficient computer time, anyone is capable of finding some mechanical trading rule that would have provided superior historical returns. However, such **back testing**, or backward-looking analysis, is an unfair test of the EMH or the usefulness of any investment strategy. An investment strategy is useful only to the extent that it can be used to generate positive abnormal returns in the *future*. Using back testing to "prove" the usefulness of an investment strategy is like using the newspaper to predict yesterday's weather report.

Data-snooping problem
Reliance on chance observations in historical data as a guide to investment decision making.

Back testing
Backward-looking analysis.

For example, it is a well-known curiosity that the stock market has tended to perform well during years in which the winner of the Super Bowl comes from the old National Football League as opposed to the old American Football League. The reason for this statistical anomaly is simple. On average, the stock market tends to go up. Because there are more old NFL teams than old AFL teams, the probability of having a Super Bowl winner from the old NFL is higher than that of having a winner from the old AFL. Given the fact that most Super Bowl winners tend to come from the old NFL, and the fact that the stock market tends to rise, there will be a spurious historical correlation in observing an old NFL winner of the Super Bowl and a rising stock market. While some conclude that the Super Bowl winner can be used to predict the future direction of the stock market, the Super Bowl winner has nothing to do with the direction of the stock market.

Street Smarts 6.3

Research Perspective

Market Efficiency and Behavioral Finance

The efficient-market hypothesis provides a context for understanding financial markets based on the assumption that participants always exhibit rational behavior. According to the efficient-market hypothesis, when rational investors learn new information, they update their beliefs in an unbiased manner that is consistent with their views of expected returns and risk. The emerging field of behavioral finance seeks to understand financial markets in which participants do not always behave in a rational manner.

These two perspectives are very different. In an efficient market, stock prices always reflect the economic value represented by part ownership in the firm. Prices are always right. Behavioral finance adopts the perspective that prices can sometimes deviate from economic value because of irrational trading by investors. Traditionally, finance scholars assumed that there are sufficient smart traders to recognize and exploit inefficient price discrepancies. By buying undervalued assets and selling overvalued assets, smart traders can impose a type of discipline to ensure efficient prices. Unfortunately, fi-

nance scholars have learned during recent years that it sometimes becomes impossible to trade against irrational investors in a risk-free manner. For example, if irrational traders bid up a stock price to a level that is simply too high given the underlying economics of the situation, the smart investor may try to sell the stock short. If irrational momentum traders continue to buy, however, irrational stock prices can continue to rise to even more irrational levels. Betting against irrational momentum can be hazardous to your wealth. Just ask "smart traders" who shorted Google during its 2004–2006 meteoric rise.

When markets are populated by both rational and irrational investors, episodes occur that are inconsistent with perfectly efficient markets. As Warren Buffett, the most successful investor of all time, is known to say, the stock market is *very* efficient but cannot be described as *perfectly* efficient. Prices sometimes depart from a sensible economic valuation of the business, and it's the job of the intelligent investor to recognize and exploit such opportunities.

See Robert J. Shiller, "From Efficient Markets Theory to Behavioral Finance," *Journal of Economic Perspectives*, vol. 17, no. 1 (Winter 2003), pp. 83–104.

Investment Performance

Measuring Relative Performance

Investment benchmark
Investment standard to which portfolio performance is compared.

It is difficult to measure the success of professional investment management unless an appropriate **investment benchmark**, or investment standard, for expected investment risk and return is established. If the overall market rose 25 percent, the performance of an investment advisor would hardly be judged as spectacular if the advisor's portfolio returned a meager 15 percent rate of return. It would be cause for celebration if the overall market fell 10 percent and that same professional money manager earned 15 percent. One must consider investment performance relative to the overall market or an appropriate benchmark. It also is necessary to consider relative risk. For example, a professional investor who outperforms the overall market by taking on above-market risk might fail to provide superior risk-adjusted performance. Such an investor could scarcely be described as beating the market. Beating the market requires superior rates of return for the same level of risk or marketlike returns from a portfolio with below-market risk.

Traditionally, investors have tended to characterize stock portfolios as falling into one of four categories: large-company value, large-company growth, small-company value, and small-company growth. Company size is often an important risk consideration because larger companies typically have the diversification and financial strength necessary to fully exploit profitable opportunities and withstand severe economic hardship. Investment style is also an important risk consideration because growth-stock investors are typically more adventuresome than conservative-value investors.

As shown in Table 6.4, performance benchmarks are commonly selected from among the wide variety of available market indexes. The DJIA may be the index that leads the stock market report on the evening news, but few portfolio managers use the DJIA as a performance benchmark. The DJIA includes only 30 stocks, which together represent roughly 30 percent of the overall market's capitalization. By far the most commonly accepted investment benchmark, or reference point for investment performance, is the S&P 500 Index. As a value-weighted index of 500 major companies chosen as being broadly representative of U.S. industry, the S&P 500 satisfies the need for a widely understood and comprehensive standard for investment performance. Stocks in the S&P 500 represent about 70 to 80 percent of the market capitalization of the U.S.

Index	Key Facts
TABLE 6.4	**Major Indexes Make Useful Performance Benchmarks**
S&P 500	Market value-weighted index of 500 blue-chip stocks selected as to being broadly representative of overall market. Median market capitalization of roughly $65 billion.
Wilshire 4500	Mid-cap proxy comprising of the Wilshire 5000 Index minus the S&P 500. Market-value weighted with a median market capitalization of roughly $1.8 billion.
Russell 2000	Small-cap proxy comprising of the smallest 2000 stocks in Russell 3000. Market valued-weighted with a median market capitalization of roughly $725 million.
MSCI EAFE	Foreign-stock market proxy. Market value-weighted index that includes major stock markets of Europe, Asia, and the Far East.
Lehman Brothers Aggregate Bond Index	Bond market proxy composed of roughly 6,000 government, corporate, mortgage, and asset-backed securities. Average maturity tends to be less than 10 years; average duration is less than 5 years.

equity market. The S&P 500 has a decidedly large-cap bias. The Russell 3000 Index measures the performance of the 3,000 largest U.S. companies based on total market capitalization, and it represents approximately 98 percent of the U.S. equity market.

To measure the relative performance of portfolio managers that invest in the stocks of smaller companies, a number of more specialized market indexes have been used as investment benchmarks. For mid-cap stocks, the Wilshire 4500 is often used, as measured by the Wilshire 5000 total stock market index minus the large-cap S&P 500. A frequently used investment benchmark for small-cap stocks is the Russell 2000. The Russell 2000 consists of the 3,000 largest market-cap stocks (the Russell 3000) minus the largest 1,000 companies. When venturing outside the domestic U.S. equity market, the S&P 500 becomes even less relevant. For international equity investors, a commonly relied on investment benchmark is the Morgan Stanley Capital International, Inc., Europe, Asia, and Far East (EAFE) Index. Bond investment performance is typically judged relative to the performance of the Lehman Brothers Aggregate Bond Index.

To judge portfolio performance, both risk and return must be considered. Superior portfolio performance can be accomplished in one of two ways. Exceptional performance often involves beating the market in terms of earning above-market investment returns with marketlike risk. Alternatively, superior performance might involve earning marketlike returns from a portfolio with below-market risk.

The Loser's Game

Folklore has it that two investment professionals were walking down the street when one spotted a $100 bill on the sidewalk. When made aware of the anomaly, the companion said, "It must not be a real $100 bill or someone would have already picked it up." This fable illustrates the love-hate relationship between EMH proponents in financial economics and Wall Street professionals.

Proponents of the EMH believe that active portfolio management is a loser's game. Portfolio management is not costless, because it typically involves management fees, operating expenses, transaction costs composed of brokerage commissions and bid-ask spreads, and marketing expenses, such as mutual fund load charges. After these costs, investors in managed investment portfolios are bound to underperform conventional market indexes. On the other hand, it is active trading by institutions that creates an efficient market.

One of the strongest bits of evidence in support of the EMH is the fact that professional investors, on average, don't beat the market. After expenses, professional investors underperform benchmark indexes. For example, Morningstar, a mutual fund industry watchdog, reports that the average large-capitalization equity mutual fund earned a cumulative return of 0.62 percent for the five-year period ending January 6, 2006. During the same time frame, a low-cost index fund tied to the S&P 500 with annual expenses of 0.18 percent per year earned a cumulative return of 1.36 percent. The S&P 500 Index earned 1.47 percent per year. The average managed portfolio underperforms the market. Over more extended periods of a decade and more, the performance gap tends to widen to roughly 3 percent per year, on average.

Stock analysts make a very good living analyzing companies and making investor recommendations. Regrettably, studies show that most analysts tend to be uniformly bullish and the stocks they recommend most strongly tend to underperform the market averages. Results are no better when the recommendations of investment strategists and money managers are considered. Especially popular with investors are annual investment recommendations published in leading investment magazines. For example, at the turn of the year, *Barron's* invites a dozen or more mutual fund managers, stock analysts, and investment strategists to its annual roundtable discussion of investment picks and recommendations. Only experts with established reputations and prominent names are invited. *Barron's* panelists have included legendary mutual fund managers Peter Lynch, John Neff, and Mario Gabelli and prominent investment strategists Barton Biggs and Abby Joseph Cohen, to name just a few. Panelists typically meet during the first week of January for a question-and-answer session and then make their recommendations. A week or two later, *Barron's* publishes the discussion. Unfortunately, such popular investment advice seldom proves profitable for readers. Studies have shown that, after trading costs, the picks by roundtable panelists tend to underperform the market.

Investment newsletters
Subscription services that deliver periodic investing advice.

Similarly fruitless is the advice provided in **investment newsletters**. The newsletter writer offers investment advice about which stocks to purchase and whether to invest in stocks, bonds, or cash. Such newsletters may come in the mail every week or once a month. Some of the advice is delivered through e-mail, Web sites, and phone bulletin boards. Popular examples include *Investech Portfolio Strategy, Outstanding Investor Digest, The Prudent Speculator*, and *The Value Line Investment Survey*. Is this investment advice useful to investors? Depending on the newsletter, the cost can be anywhere from $50 to thousands of dollars per year. Again, the investment results suggest that this form of professional investment advice is a poor bargain. Overall, newsletter portfolios underperform the stock market averages.

Consistent underperformance by investment professionals constitutes strong evidence in favor of the EMH.

Role of Investment Professionals

Security analysts use different tools to determine the investment potential of stocks and bonds. Many use fundamental analysis to determine whether a given stock is undervalued or overvalued. Others use technical analysis to determine which stocks to buy. If the market is weak-form efficient, stock prices fully reflect historical price and volume information and the charting activities of technical analysts are useless. Fundamental analysis of competitive conditions, profit trends, and dividend information could still be profitable in a weak-form efficient market. However, fundamental analysis would not be profitable if the market were semistrong-form efficient because all public information would already be reflected in stock prices and be useless as a tool for discovering undervalued or overvalued stocks. In order to find undervalued stocks in a semistrong-form efficient market, an analyst would need to discover valuable nonpublic (private) information. In a strong-form efficient market, no amount of effort would be able to capture above-market returns because all stocks would be fairly priced all the time. In short, all forms of security analyst activity is fruitless in a perfectly efficient market. In a perfectly efficient market, above-normal or below-normal performance is a matter of luck, not skill.

Given empirical evidence that suggests the stock market is quite efficient, serious questions arise for investment professionals. What role do they play in the market? For what service can they demand compensation? For those who accept the logic and evidence in support of the EMH, the primary role of a portfolio manager consists of analyzing and making investment decisions based on an appropriate evaluation of tax considerations and investor risk preferences. Optimal portfolios for individual investors will vary according to factors such as age,

tax bracket, risk aversion, and employment status. The role of the portfolio manager in an efficient market is simply to tailor investment portfolios to investor needs, rather than to beat the market.

From the perspective of the EMH, investment professionals and the financial media provide an extremely valuable public service. Markets become more efficient when active investors, portfolio managers, and research analysts are on a constant search for market-beating investment strategies. The paradox of the efficient-market concept is that markets are efficient only if a sufficiently large number of market participants believe they are capable of finding and exploiting profit-making opportunities. If every investor believed the market was perfectly efficient, no one would analyze individual securities and the market would cease to be efficient. Therein lies a paradox: Efficient markets depend on the efforts of a large number of market participants who believe that the market is inefficient and actively attempt to beat the market.

Challeges to the EMH

Excess Volatility

For more than a decade, a debate has raged among scholars and Wall Street practitioners concerning the magnitude and interpretation of stock market volatility. Some contend that the amount of volatility seen on Wall Street simply reflects the amount of risk inherent in an efficiently functioning stock market. Others contend that the amount of observed volatility in stock prices is too high given the documented amount of volatility in dividends and other indicators of fundamental value. Under the EMH, deviations from fundamental value should not be systematic or predictable. Critics of the EMH contend that efficient forecasts of changes in fundamental value given by changes in stock prices should be no more volatile than the underlying changes in fundamental value, perhaps as reflected by changes in dividends. Otherwise, optimistic forecasts indicated by high stock prices would reflect positive forecast errors. Pessimistic forecasts indicated by low stock prices would reflect negative forecast errors. In both cases, the predictability of forecast errors gives rise to the opportunity for trading profits and is inconsistent with a perfectly efficient market. In a perfectly efficient market, **stock market volatility** should be no higher than the underlying volatility in fundamental value. In fact, indicators of fundamental value, such as dividends, change very slowly but stock prices change

Stock market volatility
Large increases and decreases in prices over time.

very quickly. This has led critics of the EMH to contend that stock prices are too volatile given the low level of observed volatility in dividends.

Excess volatility in the stock market can be seen in Figure 6.4, which compares real stock prices with estimates of fundamental values. Fundamental value is estimated as the present value of future dividends. The thickest line in Figure 6.4 shows the trend in the Standard & Poor 500 Index over time. Three other lines show the present value of future dividends under different discounting assumptions: a constant discount rate, a constant risk premium, and the presumed marginal rate of substitution in consumption for a risk-averse individual. No matter how fundamental value is computed, real stock prices appear much more volatile than underlying fundamental values. This is not consistent with the EMH. There appear to be periods when the stock market is severely overvalued or undervalued.

With millions of investors watching for profit-making opportunities, how can the stock market become overvalued or undervalued? Yale economist Robert Shiller blames mistakes in investor sentiment. In his best-selling book, *Irrational Exuberance*, Shiller argues that **investor mood** can strongly impact valuation by an investor who uses the dividend discount model. According to the dividend discount model (described in detail in Chapter 11), $PV = D_1/(k-g)$, where the present value of the firm, PV, equals expected dividends, D_1, divided by the required return, k, minus the future rate of growth in dividends, g. Given the influence of sentiment on risky and uncertain decisions, the expected value of the growth rate, $E(g)$, may become biased if investors become too optimistic or too pessimistic. These biases can affect market value expectations and trading behavior.

Suppose investors estimate expected market value as $E(P) = D_1/[k - E(g)]$. Estimation errors can lead to deviations from fundamental value. Consider the deviation of expected market value from the investor's notion of fundamental value:

$$\frac{E(P)}{PV} = \frac{D_1/[k-E(g)]}{D_1/(k-g)} \tag{6.1}$$

Rearranging Equation 6.1 produces

$$\frac{E(P)}{PV} = \frac{k-g}{k-E(g)} \tag{6.2}$$

Equation 6.2 illustrates how over- or undervalued expectations may develop. Consider an average annual return on the market of 11 percent and a long-term dividend growth rate of

Investor mood

Level of optimism or pessimism by investors; also called *sentiment*.

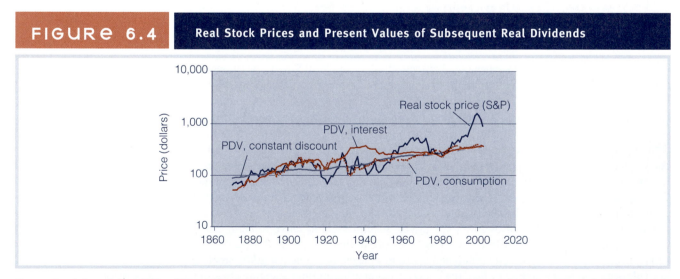

FIGURE 6.4 | **Real Stock Prices and Present Values of Subsequent Real Dividends**

Source: Graph from Robert Shiller, "From Efficient Market Theory to Behavioral Finance," *Journal of Economic Perspectives*, vol. 17, no. 1. Copyright © 2003 American Economic Association.

5 percent. When optimistic sentiment is high, market participants are being told through the media about a "new economy." In response, they overestimate the future growth rate as 7 percent. Equation 6.2 then shows that the market may become overvalued by as much as 50 percent because $E(P)/\text{PV} = 1.5$. On the other hand, if overly pessimistic sentiment occurs, investors may underestimate the future growth rate as 3 percent. This would lead to the stock market's being undervalued by 25 percent. If most investors are too optimistic or too pessimistic, prices can get pushed away from fundamental values and the market becomes inefficient.

Try It!

If the annual market return over a long period of time is expected to be 11 percent and the long-term expected growth rate of stock market firms is 4 percent, the Dow Jones Industrial Average is fairly valued at 10,000. If pessimistic investors believe the long-term growth rate is only 3 percent, how far would the DJIA be expected to fall?

Solution

Using Equation 6.2, the stock market should become undervalued as

$$\frac{E(P)}{PV} = \frac{k - g}{k - E(g)} = \frac{11 - 4}{11 - 3} = \frac{7}{8} = 0.875$$

The DJIA would be expected to fall to $0.875 \times 10{,}000 = 8{,}750$, a 12.5 percent decline.

Bubbles

According to the EMH, stock prices accurately reflects all information known about the firm and the business environment. If individual stocks are priced correctly, then the overall stock market is also priced correctly. A common criticism of the EMH is that the overall market sometimes seems too high or too low relative to fundamental value.

Market bubbles and subsequent crashes are good examples of market inefficiency. Market bubbles are identified after a tremendous inflation in prices is followed by a dramatic decline. History contains many colorful examples of stock, bond, and commodity markets in which rampant speculation caused a rapid boom in prices followed by a sudden collapse. Commodities are the asset class with the most bubbles in history, especially during the 19th century. From oil to grains like corn and wheat to precious metals like gold and silver, almost every commodity has seen bubbles. In 2006, some analysts forecast oil prices as high as $200 per barrel, while others cited such predictions as evidence of one of the biggest commodity bubbles in history. Noteworthy bubbles have also occurred in major stock markets during modern times. Remarkable examples include the U.S. stock market during the 1920s, the Japanese stock market of the 1980s, and the tech-stock bubble in the United States during the late 1990s.

As shown in Figure 6.5, the Nasdaq tech stocks soared during the 1990s, while Japan's Nikkei 225 Index crumbled. From a January 2, 1985, start at 11,543, the Nikkei soared to a closing high of 38,916 on December 29, 1989. This represents a gain of 237.1 percent in the Nikkei over a five-year period and a stunning 27.5 percent compound annual rate of return. Then the bubble burst and the bottom fell out of the Japanese equity market. In December 2004, fifteen years after the Japanese market peak, the Nikkei stood at 10,796. That's 72.3 percent below the December 1989 peak, and it's roughly in line with Japanese stock prices at the start of 1984.

The parallel between the rise and fall of the Japanese Nikkei and the performance of the Nasdaq tech stocks is striking. From a beginning split-adjusted level of 125 on January 31, 1985,

Market bubble
A significant overvaluation of economic fundamentals in the stock market.

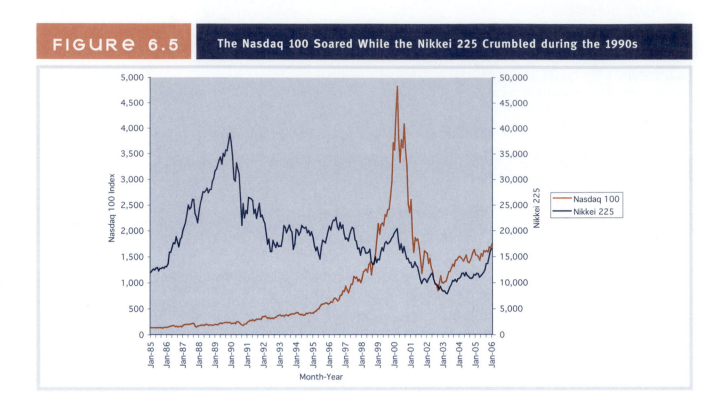

FIGURE 6.5   The Nasdaq 100 Soared While the Nikkei 225 Crumbled during the 1990s

the Nasdaq 100 soared to 4,816.35 on March 24, 2000. This represents a 15¼-year return of 3,753.3 percent and an amazing compound return of 27.1 percent per year. The Japanese stock market of 1989 and the Nasdaq stock market of 2000 were quite comparable with respect to the sustained above-average annual rates of return prior to important recent market peaks. They were also comparable with respect to total market capitalization, at roughly $6 trillion each. An important difference lies in the fact that the greater length of the Nasdaq bull market led to peak P/E ratios for Nasdaq and Nasdaq 100 companies that were far greater than the historic highs near 100 seen for the Nikkei in 1989. This suggests that the correction on Nasdaq may be as large as, if not greater than, the epic correction in Japanese stocks.

Figure 6.6 gives interesting perspective on what might lie in store for Nasdaq investors following the March 2000 bursting of the tech-stock bubble. If Nasdaq performance subsequent to the market top follows a pattern similar to that followed by the Nikkei, Nasdaq investors can expect to wait a very long time before tech stocks set new market highs. Based on the Japanese experience, it would not be unusual for Nasdaq stocks to trade below March 2000 peak levels for more than a decade.

Are asset price bubbles consistent with an efficient market? The answer to this question is debated in the context of whether bubbles represent rational or irrational behavior. **Rational bubbles** are defined as an inflation and subsequent decline in prices that can be reasonably explained by commensurate changes in the fundamental economics of the situation. That is, prices are efficient in a bubble if they reflect all available information. **Irrational bubbles** are defined as a stark deviation of prices from fundamental values. Irrational-bubble theory suggests that assets may go through periods of undervaluation and overvaluation due to episodes of widespread euphoric speculation and pervasive despairing panic. In stock markets, irrational bubbles can occur if investors are sometimes overly optimistic in evaluating the potential for future profits. Momentum investors may also display a tendency to buy stocks on the premise that rising prices will become a self-fulfilling prophecy, even when companies do not enjoy favorable business prospects. Stock market bubbles can be difficult to explain as rational and consistent with the market efficiency concept, especially when they occur in large, liquid markets such as Nasdaq in the late 1990s.

Rational bubbles
Extreme changes in financial asset values tied to changing economic fundamentals.

Irrational bubbles
Extreme changes in financial asset values that cannot be tied to changes in economic fundamentals.

| FIGURE 6.6 | Will Postcrash Nasdaq 100 Valuations Languish for a Decade or More? |

Investment Fraud

Microcap Fraud

A **microcap stock** is a company with a low or "micro" market capitalization, usually between $50 million and $250 million. Microcap companies typically have limited assets. In cases where the SEC has suspended trading in microcap stocks, the average company had only $6 million in net tangible assets and nearly half had less than $1.25 million. Microcap stocks tend to be priced below $5 per share. Microcap stocks also tend to experience volatile price movements and are subject to investment fraud. Reliable information about microcap stocks can be difficult to obtain because a company is not required to file reports with the SEC unless it has 500 or more investors *and* $10 million or more in assets or it is listed for trading on the NYSE, Amex, or Nasdaq. Many microcap stocks trade over the counter and are quoted on the OTC Bulletin Board or the **pink sheets**, a listing of price quotes for very small companies that trade in the over-the-counter market.

Most microcap companies are legitimate businesses with real products or services. However, the lack of reliable available information about some microcap stocks opens the door to fraud. It is far easier for stock promoters and con artists to manipulate a stock when there is little or no reliable public information about the company. Microcap, or **penny-stock**, fraud depends on spreading false information.

Stock con artists often issue press releases that contain exaggerations or outright lies about microcap-company sales, acquisitions, revenue projections, and new products or services. Some microcap companies also pay brokers and other stock promoters to recommend or "tout" their stocks in supposedly independent and unbiased investment newsletters and research reports or on radio and television shows. Federal securities laws require that newsletters disclose who paid them, the amount, and the type of payment. Many illegal stock promoters mislead investors into believing that they are receiving independent advice. Dishonest brokers and

Microcap stocks
Companies with very small stock market capitalizations.

Pink sheets
A listing of price quotes for microcap stocks that trade in the over-the-counter market.

Penny stocks
Stocks that trade at prices below $5.

Cold calls
Unrequested telephone solicitations.

stock promoters also assemble small armies of high-pressure salespeople to make literally hundreds of telephone **cold calls** to potential investors. For many businesses, including securities firms, random telephone solicitations serve as a legitimate way to reach potential customers. In the securities business, however, unwitting investors sometimes suffer financial losses when dishonest brokers pressure them to make unsuitable investments.

The best way for an individual investor to fight fraud is to become better armed with reliable information. Even when working with a broker or an investment advisor, investors should always obtain detailed written information about the company that they are investing in—its business plan, finances, and management. Company annual reports to shareholders often give a good overview of the company's historical performance and future prospects.

Affinity fraud
Investment scams that prey on members of identifiable groups, such as religious or ethnic communities, the elderly, or professional groups.

Periodically, the SEC warns investors about scams that it is investigating. The SEC posts such warnings on its Investor Education Web page at **www.sec.gov/investor.shtml**. The SEC has long been concerned about **affinity fraud**, wherein perpetrators enlist respected community or religious leaders to convince others that a fraudulent investment is legitimate and worthwhile. Many of these leaders become unwitting victims of the ruse. Such scams exploit the trust and friendship that exist in groups of people who have something in common. Because of the tight-knit structure of many groups, it can be difficult for regulators to detect an affinity scam. Victims often fail to notify authorities or pursue legal remedies and instead try to work things out within the group. Many affinity scams involve **Ponzi schemes**. This pyramid scheme uses funds contributed by new investors to pay outlandish rates of return to early investors and relies on an unending supply of new investors. When the supply of investors dries up, the whole scheme collapses and investors discover that most or all of their money is gone.

Ponzi scheme
Fraud in which new-investor money is used to make payments to earlier investors to give the false illusion of profitability (like a chain letter).

Fraud on the Internet

The Internet is a marvelous tool that allows investors to easily and inexpensively research investment opportunities. Unfortunately, the Internet is also an excellent tool for stock promoters and con artists. Increasingly, the Internet is a wild and woolly frontier for stock fraud and manipulation. The Internet enables individuals or companies to communicate with a large audience without spending a lot of time, effort, or money. Anyone can reach tens of thousands of people by building an Internet Web site, posting a message on an online bulletin board, entering a discussion in a live "chat" room, or sending mass e-mails. It is easy for con artists to make their messages look credible. At the same time, it is extremely difficult for investors to tell the difference between fact and fiction.

Online bulletin boards on the Internet and proprietary networks have become an increasingly popular forum for investors to share information. These bulletin boards typically feature "threads" of information focused on individual stocks or investment strategies. Although many messages reflect the sincere questions and opinions of individual investors, many are bogus and reflect the efforts of stock promoters and con artists who seek to use the Internet medium to widely spread false information. Fraudulent promoters sometimes pump up a company by pretending to reveal inside information about company management, new product announcements, mergers, acquisitions, or lucrative contracts. Determining the veracity of bulletin board information is made difficult by the fact that readers never know for certain with whom they are dealing. On bulletin boards it is easy for those posting messages to hide behind multiple aliases. Persons claiming to be unbiased investors who have carefully researched a company may actually be insiders, disgruntled employees, large shareholders, or paid promoters. A single individual can easily create the illusion of widespread interest in small, thinly traded stocks by posting a series of messages under various aliases.

Pump-and-dump scheme
Manipulation conspiracy in which promoters artificially inflate a stock price so that they can sell their own inventories to unwitting investors.

Stock fraud on the Internet is a big problem. The SEC investigates and prosecutes Internet fraud cases involving a range of illicit Internet conduct, including fraudulent spam, online newsletters, message board postings, and Web sites. The SEC's allegations include violations of the antifraud provisions and the antitouting provisions of federal securities laws. Suspected violations have included making misrepresentations about company operations or failing to disclose adequately the nature, source, and amount of compensation paid by the touted company. In a typical case, con artists sell their stock or exercise valuable call options immediately after causing it to rise through their fraudulent promotion. Artificially inflating, or "pumping up," a stock price and then selling the inflated stock to unwitting investors is called a **pump-and-dump** scheme.

Summary

- Short-term speculation in the stock and bond markets is akin to a **coin-flipping contest**. It is gambling, pure and simple. In the short term, theory and evidence tell us that stock prices are equally apt to rise or fall in an **efficient market**. In an efficient stock market, the price for any given stock effectively represents the expected net present value of all future profits. The **efficient-market hypothesis (EMH)** states that security prices fully reflect all available information. In an efficient market there is a 50-50 chance that the buyer will profit at the expense of the seller. Similarly, there is a 50-50 chance that the seller will profit at the expense of the buyer.

- Three alternative forms of the EMH exist. Under the **weak-form hypothesis**, current prices reflect all **stock market information**. Trading rules based on past stock market returns and trading volume are futile. The **semistrong-form hypothesis** asserts that prices reflect all **public information**. All trading rules based on public information are useless. The **strong-form hypothesis** posits that current prices reflect all public information and **nonpublic information**. In that case, all trading rules are pointless.

- To the extent that insiders such as the company chairperson and CEO earn above-normal rates of return on their stock market investments, the market would not be judged as perfectly efficient according to the strong-form hypothesis. If such insiders do, in fact, earn above-normal rates of return, one might conclude that they have profited by virtue of their access to superior or **insider information**.

- Whenever the movement of stock prices over time is being analyzed, the data are described as a **time series** of market data. A correlation coefficient of +100 percent indicates perfect positive correlation. A correlation coefficient of −100 percent indicates perfect negative, or inverse, correlation. A correlation coefficient of 0 percent indicates that two sets of data have no relation. From a statistical perspective, the distribution of daily returns closely resembles a **normal distribution**, or bell-shaped curve, with an average daily return around zero.

- A **random walk** is an irregular pattern of numbers that defies prediction. With respect to the stock market, **random walk theory** asserts that stock price movements do not follow any patterns or trends. The mathematical expectation of the speculator's profit is zero when stock prices follow a random walk. This market is a **fair game** in which the professional and the novice face the exact same chance for success. Although stocks can be expected to advance over long periods of time, day-to-day rates of return can be expected to exhibit what might be called a **random walk with drift**. Daily rates of return on commons stocks have a slight upward bias, or upward drift, given the long-term positive expectation for investor rates of return. Still, random walk theory asserts that the overwhelming characteristic of short-term rates of return in the stock market is their unpredictability.

- If stock prices do, indeed, follow a random walk, then there are no predictable patterns or trends in stock prices that can be exploited. Nevertheless, it is human nature to seek out patterns. Some investors graph out stock prices—a process called **charting**—to visualize patterns and make buy and sell decisions. However, when people see patterns in data that are random, they can make poor decisions because of the **gambler's fallacy**.

- Occasional "evidence" of investment merit for various technical trading rules is nothing more than the recurrent manifestation of the **data-snooping problem** in investment research. Given sufficient computer time, anyone is capable of finding some mechanical trading rule that would have provided superior investment returns over some historical time frame. This is true even when historical market returns resemble a table of random numbers. However, such **back testing**, or backward-looking analysis, is an unfair test of the usefulness of technical trading rules or any investment strategy. It is not surprising that there are inexplicable patterns in stock market returns over various historical time intervals. Historical patterns in stock market returns conflict with the EMH only when investors are able to exploit such regularities over some future time periods.

■ It is difficult to measure the success of professional investment management unless an appropriate **investment benchmark**, or investment standard, for expected investment risk and return is established. As a group, investment professionals do not seem to be able to outperform the market indexes. People who invest in equity mutual funds or try to follow the advice of financial analysts, superstar managers, or **investment newsletters** underperform the S&P 500 Index. Trading costs and investment fees are partly to blame. Nevertheless, the failure of professionals to outperform the market is strong evidence that the stock market is efficient.

■ Over time, the stock market sometimes appears inconsistent with the EMH. Excess **stock market volatility** suggests that the stock market does not always accurately reflect the underlying economic fundamentals. Markets sometimes appear to become overvalued or undervalued because of changes in **investor mood** from extreme optimism to excessive pessimism. Evidence of stock **market bubbles**, as given by the Japanese stock market of the 1980s and Nasdaq during the 1990s, undermines support for the notion that the stock market is always perfectly efficient. **Rational bubbles** can be explained by economic fundamentals; **irrational bubbles** defy easy explanation.

■ Dishonest brokers and stock promoters of small, **microcap stocks** sometimes assemble small armies of high-pressure salespeople to make literally hundreds of telephone **cold calls** to potential investors. Small companies sometimes pay the people who write online newsletters cash or securities to tout, or aggressively recommend, their stocks. In a typical case, con artists sold their stock or exercised their options immediately following their buy recommendations. A classic **pump-and-dump** scheme is one in which promoters attempt to pump up a stock price so that they can sell their own inventories to unwitting investors.

Self-Test Problems

ST6.1 A necessary condition for stock market efficiency is that changes in stock prices be random and unpredictable. Is this also a sufficient condition for market efficiency?

Solution

No. In the short term, theory and evidence tell us that stock prices are equally apt to rise or fall in an efficient market. However, in an efficient stock market, changes in stock prices are random. Stock prices are not random, as if simply affected by investor psychology, moon spots, or whatever. In an efficient stock market, the price for any given stock effectively represents the expected net present value of all future profits. In this calculation, profits are discounted by using a fair or risk-adjusted rate of return. If the stock market is to be perfectly efficient, there must be a large number of buyers and sellers of essential identical securities, information must be free and readily available, and entry and exit by market players must be uninhibited.

ST6.2 Market professionals are bombarded with real-time, historical, and descriptive data, analytics, and news on markets and securities. On what level(s) is the idea that such data can be used to identify superior investment opportunities a violation of the efficient-market hypothesis?

Solution

The idea that such data can be used to identify superior investment opportunities is a violation of the weak form and semistrong form of the efficient-market hypothesis.

The weak-form hypothesis involves the easiest or lowest hurdle that must be met for one to argue that the stock market is efficient. According to the weak-form hypothesis, stock and bond prices reflect all prior price and trading volume activity. As such, in an efficient stock market, it would not be possible to earn above-market returns by buying or selling stocks on the premise that they are going up on price momentum or are bound to rise on a quick reversal of "panic selling." In a market that is perfectly efficient, there is no such thing as panic selling, or panic buying for that matter. All buyers and sellers are fully informed and unbiased in their assessment of the intrinsic value of the company's future prospects.

The semistrong-form hypothesis is somewhat stricter than the weak-form hypothesis. According to the semistrong-form hypothesis, no investor can obtain an edge by buying or selling stocks on the basis of any publicly available information. Of course, past stock market returns and trading volume activity are only a small part of this publicly available information. For example, the moment unknown and unpredictable quarterly earnings information is released, stock prices quickly and accurately readjust so that subsequent investors earn only a risk-adjusted normal rate of return on their investment. Similarly, the moment a favorable report is issued by a leading Wall Street investment banker such as Merrill Lynch, stock prices react to incorporate that information. According to the semistrong-form hypothesis, anything you read in the newspaper, hear on television, or see on the Internet is already reflected in stock and bond prices.

Questions and Problems

6.1 Use the coin-flipping contest argument to determine how many of the 5,000 mutual funds you would expect to beat the market 10 years in a row by pure luck.

6.2 Give three essential characteristics of an efficient stock market.

6.3 Explain the efficient-market concept, and distinguish between weak-form efficiency, semistrong-form efficiency, and strong-form efficiency.

6.4 Suppose that a company CEO announces on CNBC that his firm has agreed to be acquired by another firm. The stock price of the CEO's company immediately increases $5 per share. What level of market efficiency predicts such a sequence of events?

6.5 An investor has noticed that Alcoa Inc., the aluminum producer, has traded in a range of $20 to $40 per share. Therefore, the investor implements a strategy of buying the stock when it is near $20 per share and selling it when it reaches $40. After the sale, the investor waits until the price falls to $20 in order to repurchase the stock. If this strategy works, what would this say about the level of market efficiency? Is it likely to work?

6.6 Describe the time series of daily returns in the stock market. Is this pattern consistent with the EMH?

6.7 Keno is a game with a board of numbers from 1 to 80. Gamblers pick some of these numbers, and then the casino randomly draws 15 numbers. If a high percentage of the numbers a given gambler picks is also selected by the casino, the gambler wins. A patron of the Big Bucks Casino in Las Vegas watched the Keno game for one hour and noticed that the number 28 was never randomly picked during the 10 games that hour. So this gambler bet on number 28 in the next game. What do you think of this strategy?

6.8 In the past few weeks, an aerospace company has made two negative announcements about business prospects. An investor believes that bad news always comes in threes. Therefore, the investor sells her stock in the company because she expects yet one more negative announcement. Is this belief consistent with the random walk theory? Why?

6.9 What is the data-snooping problem in investment research, and how does it relate to the back-testing concept?

6.10 The GO-GO mutual fund invests in high-risk tech stocks. Some of these firms have yet to earn a profit, and none of them pay a dividend. Last year's return was 13 percent. Given the information in the table below, determine how well the mutual fund performed.

Last Year's Return for:				
S&P 500	**Wilshire 4500**	**Russell 2000**	**MSCI EAFE**	**Small-Cap Value Funds**
10%	12%	14%	5%	16%
Small-Cap Growth Funds	**Mid-Cap Value Funds**	**Mid-Cap Growth Funds**	**High-Cap Value Funds**	**High-Cap Growth Funds**
12%	14%	10%	12%	8%

www.mhhe.com/hirschey1e

6.11 The long-term expected stock market return is about 10 percent per year, and the long-term growth rate of the economy has been 4 percent per year. Suppose undue investor pessimism is pricing stocks as if the long-term growth rate were only 2 percent. Calculate by how much this undue investor pessimism will cause the stock market to be undervalued.

6.12 Are stock market bubbles consistent with the efficient-market hypothesis? Why or why not?

 6.13 Go to the CNN Money Web site (**http://money.cnn.com**) and locate the "Mutual Funds" and then the "Winners & Losers" page. Notice the top 10 funds—year to date. What does the information shown about these funds tell you about market efficiency?

6.14 Explain how the pump-and-dump scheme operates. How can you avoid being a victim of the scheme?

 6.15 Go to the NASD Web site (**www.nasd.com**) and enter the "Investor Alerts" section. The NASD is the primary private-sector regulator of America's securities industry. Describe several of the investment scams the NASD is warning investors about.

 6.16 Go to the Yahoo! Finance Web site (**finance.yahoo.com**) and click on the Indices link in the "International" section. Do the international stock indexes appear to be correlated to a high degree or a low degree? Explain.

6.17 There were 21 trading days in April 2005. In five of those trading days, the Dow Jones Industrial Average was down over 100 points. In two days, the Dow increased over 100 points. One day it rose over 200 points. What does this volatility say about market efficiency?

6.18 Compare the following graph of gold prices in the early 1980s with the graph of the Japanese and Nasdaq stock markets in Figure 6.6. What features do the graphs share in common?

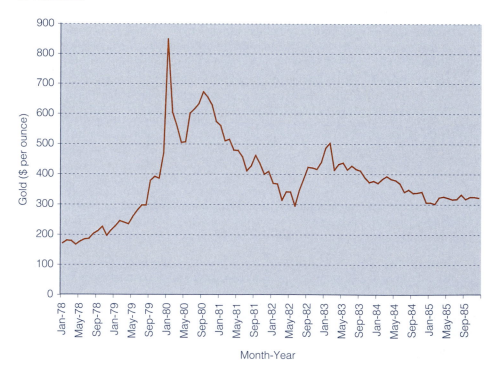

 6.19 A normal distribution would *least likely* be described as:
   a. Asymptotic
   b. A discrete probability distribution
   c. A symmetrical or bell-shaped distribution
   d. A curve that theoretically extends from negative infinity to positive infinity

6.20 An investment strategy has an expected return of 12 percent and a standard deviation of 10 percent. If investment returns are normally distributed, the probability of earning a return less than 2 percent is *closest to:*

a. 10 percent
b. 16 percent
c. 32 percent
d. 34 percent

INVESTMENT APPLICATION

How Much Is a Tulip Worth?[2]

During the 1600s, the Netherlands was a major sea power, accounting for roughly one-half of Europe's shipping trade. In 1602, Dutch firms trading with the East Indies combined to form the Dutch East India Company. The Dutch West India Company, founded in 1621, opened trade with the New World and western Africa. Expanding trade and the international influence of a great colonial empire made Amsterdam a major commercial city and gave the Dutch one of the highest standards of living in the world. It was during this "golden age" that tulips were introduced to The Netherlands.

Conrad Gesner is credited with bringing the first tulip bulbs from Constantinople to Holland and Germany in 1559, where they became much sought after among the rich and well-to-do. By 1634, the rage for possessing tulips had spread to the middle class of Dutch society. Merchants and shopkeepers began to vie with one another in the preposterous prices paid for simple tulip bulbs. Men became known for paying a fortune for a single bulb, not with the idea of reselling at a profit but simply for private admiration. Later, investors began to accumulate tulip bulbs for resale and trading profits.

Prices continued to rise until 1635, when persons were investing fortunes of as much as 100,000 florins in the purchase of 40 tulip bulbs. Various tulip bulbs fetched anywhere from 1,260 to 5,500 florins each. Of course, determining present-day values for 17th-century prices in florins, or in any early currency, is made difficult by changing price levels and monetary systems. However, a present-day equivalent of 17th-century Dutch tulip prices can be estimated because an early account of the craze by Charles Mackay gives an example in which the typical price paid is measured both in terms of florins and in terms of real goods received in trade.[3] This example, shown in Table 6.5, provides an opportunity to calculate a present-day equivalent price of the amount paid. Keep in mind throughout this example that one single tulip bulb was received in trade for *all* items listed.

The first item received in trade is two lasts of wheat. A last is a unit of weight or cubic measure that typically equals 4,000 pounds but can vary in different localities and for different loads.[4] Let's assume that 4,000 pounds is indeed the correct weight and that a bushel of wheat weighs 60 pounds, with the current price of wheat being roughly $3.30 per bushel. This gives a price of $440 for two lasts of wheat. Similarly, four lasts of rye at a price of $144.60 per ton, given 2,000 pounds per ton, are worth $1,152.

In 17th-century Holland, oxen were a valuable source of power in an agrarian economy. In present-day America, oxen have been replaced by a different kind of animal, *John Deere*. To measure the current value of the use of four fat oxen, one might reasonably measure the cost of a modest farm tractor or a commensurate value of four fat beef animals, say, white-faced Herefords. Four Herefords are cheaper than a modest *John Deere* tractor and thus represent a

[2] For further details, see Mark Hirschey, "How Much Is a Tulip Worth?" *Financial Analysts Journal*, vol. 54, no. 4 (July-August 1998), pp. 11–17.

[3] See Charles Mackay, *Memoirs of Extraordinary Popular Delusions and the Madness of Crowds* (Richard Bentley, London, 1841).

[4] *The World Book Dictionary*, Vol. 2 (Scott Fetzer, Chicago, 1994), p. 1182.

TABLE 6.5	How Much Is a Tulip Worth?

	Holland Price, 1635 (florins)	US Price, 2000 (dollars)
Two lasts of wheat	448	440
Four lasts of rye	558	1,152
Four fat oxen	480	3,476
Eight fat swine	240	1,134
Twelve fat sheep	120	702
Two hogsheads of wine	70	4,792
Four tuns of beer	32	7,571
Two tuns of butter	192	6,109
One thousand pounds of cheese	120	6,980
A complete bed	100	1,410
A suit of clothes	80	750
A silver drinking cup	60	68
Total	2,500	34,584

conservative measure of the value represented by four fat oxen. With a typical weight of 1,100 pounds and an on-the-hoof price of $0.79 per pound, a conservative estimate of the value of four fat Herefords is $3,476. Similarly, the value of eight fat swine with an average weight of 225 pounds and an on-the-hoof price of $0.63 per pound is $1,134. The value of 12 fat sheep with an average weight of 65 pounds and an on-the-hoof price of $0.90 per pound is $702. Likewise, all the products in Table 6.5 can be valued as shown.

In sum, a representative calculation of the present-day price paid for a single *Viceroy* tulip bulb during 1635, near the height of the tulip mania in Holland, totals a whopping $34,584. Therefore, Mackay's example of individual tulip bulbs fetching anywhere from 1,260 to 5,500 florins implies a present-day price range from $17,430 to $76,085 *each*.

It was during the early autumn of 1636 that the more prudent began to liquidate their tulip holdings. Tulip prices began to weaken, slowly at first but then more rapidly. Soon, confidence was destroyed, and panic seized the market. Within six weeks, tulip prices crashed by 90 percent or more; widespread defaults on purchase contracts and liens were experienced. At first, the Dutch government refused to interfere and advised tulip holders to agree among themselves to some plan for stabilizing tulip prices and restoring public credit. All such plans failed. After much bickering, assembled deputies in Amsterdam agreed to declare null and void all contracts made at the height of the mania, or prior to the month of November 1636. Tulip contracts entered into after that date were to be settled if buyers paid 10 percent of prices agreed upon previously. However, this decision gave no satisfaction as tulip prices continued to fall, and the Provincial Council in The Hague was asked to invent some measure to stabilize tulip prices and public credit. Again, all such efforts failed. Tulip prices plunged to less than the present-day equivalent of $1 each (or 10 guineas), and many of those who profited from the mania and the ensuing collapse apparently converted their gains into English or other funds to hide them from enraged countrymen. Commerce in Holland suffered a severe shock from which it took many years to recover.

a. Popular accounts of tulip bulb pricing in Holland during the 1634–1636 period refer to the word *mania* when describing that episode. What is a mania?

b. Explain how crowd behavior can affect asset pricing, and discuss its implications for the EMH.

Market Anomalies

An old Wall Street maxim exhorts investors to "sell in May and go away." Also called the "Halloween Indicator," this investment strategy is based on research showing that since 1950 the total return to investors has been very positive between October 31 and May 1 but not much more than zero the rest of the year. Is there any sound economic reason for why such a calendar-based investment strategy might work, or is it just a statistical oddity that will not persist?

Research in behavioral finance tells us that stock returns can be affected by custom and tradition. It is common for people to start the year off with a New Year's resolution and for investors to rebalance their portfolios at the turn of the year. Pension funds and mutual funds also see tax-motivated inflows and make important portfolio decisions just prior to key tax dates, like December 31 and April 15. Many investors and investment professionals take vacations during the summer, and vacant trading desks can contribute to summer malaise and boring returns on Wall Street.

Are these logical behavioral explanations for stock market seasonality, or are they examples of problems tied to what researchers call "data snooping"? Even in random stock return data, unusual patterns can be detected over brief periods. Over the 20th century in the United States, there have been notable periods of outstanding relative performance and various time periods of starkly inferior performance. Such variation may be within the realm of typical statistical variation in stock market return data. The same might be said of other unusual patterns of returns tied to firm-specific factors such as size, P/B ratios, or stock price momentum.

While inexplicable patterns in stock market returns attract lots of attention from researchers, savvy investors exercise caution before leaping to the conclusion that inexplicable patterns portend viable profit-making opportunities.[1]

---

[1] See Anjali Cordeiro and Karen Talley, "Small Stocks Enjoy 'January Effect,'" *The Wall Street Journal Online*, January 17, 2006. (**http://online.wsj.com**).

CHAPTER OBJECTIVES

- Understand the joint test problem.
- Recognize calendar anomalies.
- Know how to compute abnormal returns.
- Identify fundamental and news event anomalies.

Testing the EMH

Theory Is a Tool

The traditional one-factor capital asset pricing model (CAPM) and multifactor CAPM approaches, such as the Fama-French three-factor CAPM, can be used as tools to evaluate the efficient-market hypothesis (EMH). By isolating deviations from predicted returns, such models have the potential to help investors isolate instances in which the pricing of individual securities deviates from that predicted for a perfectly efficient capital market. Under such circumstances, portfolio managers might devise investment strategies to take advantage of unusual profit-making opportunities. In such situations, the CAPM-based approaches also offer investors and Wall Street professionals mechanisms that can be used to better understand the functioning of capital markets.

A basic criterion used to measure the usefulness of the CAPM, or any model for that matter, is the model's predictive capability. A fundamental test of the CAPM-based methods is their ability to explain and predict real-world behavior. It is never fair to say, "That may work well in theory, but it doesn't work in practice." If financial theory, such as the CAPM, does not predict security pricing in the real world, it must be rejected and the search must begin for better theory. When researchers or Wall Street professionals detect inexplicable patterns in historical stock market returns, such regularities represent a challenge to existing theory and to our understanding of market efficiency. For example, one must reject the EMH if tax-loss selling makes it possible for investors to buy stocks with depressed share prices in late December, only to sell them at a risk-free profit in early January. However, one could not reject the EMH if transaction costs and/or tax penalties eliminate the perceived advantage to buying beaten-down stocks during December and selling them in January.

Joint Test Problem

Return anomaly
An inexplicable pattern of abnormal stock market returns.

Whenever inexplicable patterns of abnormal stock market returns are detected in empirical studies of the stock market, a **return anomaly** is said to be found. Important stock market anomalies are regular, statistically significant, and persistent abnormal returns that have no ready explanation in financial theory. Economically meaningful stock market anomalies not only are statistically significant but also offer meaningful risk-adjusted economic rewards to investors. By definition, statistically significant stock market anomalies have yet-unknown economic and/or psychological explanations.

On the one hand, return anomalies may reflect some market inefficiency. For example, suppose stock prices tend to rise after widely anticipated stock-split announcements. Abnormal returns tied to such public information are inconsistent with the semistrong form of the EMH. Similarly, if corporate insiders regularly earn above-market returns on insider buy-sell transactions, such abnormal returns are inconsistent with the strong form of the EMH.

On the other hand, abnormal returns detected when using alternative forms of the CAPM as a measurement device may simply reflect the fact that these models fail to precisely capture the stock return generating process. In this case, abnormal returns reflect errors in the calculation of expected returns because some important determinant of stock market returns is left out of the analysis. When the CAPM or any model fails to precisely describe and predict stock market returns, model specification bias is present. If the amount of CAPM specification bias is substantial, abnormal returns detected by using such models shed little useful light on questions of market efficiency.

There is something of a "chicken-or-the-egg" problem when it comes to detailed tests of market efficiency. Suppose stock returns during late December and early January appear unusual given the predictions of the CAPM. This could mean that the stock market is in fact inefficient during the turn of the year. However, the CAPM may simply offer an incomplete picture of the stock return generating process. In other words, a **joint test problem** exists because anomalous evidence that is inconsistent with a perfectly efficient market could be an indication of either market inefficiency or a simple failure of CAPM precision.

Joint test problem
Situation in which anomalies can indicate market inefficiency or market model inaccuracy.

Practical Relevance

During recent years, the practical relevance of the joint test problem has become increasingly obvious. In the 1960s and 1970s, many stock market analysts and financial economists became convinced that the CAPM offered a precise view of highly liquid stock and bond markets. During the 1980s and 1990s, however, a number of inexplicable patterns in stock market returns emerged that caused some to actively question the appropriateness of CAPM-based approaches. A number of academic researchers and Wall Street professionals have come to reject the CAPM as a useful tool for predicting stock returns but retain the basic underlying premise offered by the EMH. Some others have come to reject both CAPM-based approaches and the underlying market efficiency concept.

At the same time, it is fascinating to observe that during the 1980s and 1990s many individual investors came to appreciate the diversification advantages of low-cost index funds. Tens of millions of investors now invest their retirement funds in indexed portfolios that seek to match the market without any active portfolio management whatsoever. As such, individual investors have entered their ringing endorsement for the simplest prescription of the EMH—broadly diversified buy-and-hold strategies work best in efficient stock and bond markets.

This apparent divergence of opinion about the EMH is noteworthy. It is also important to recognize that one can reject the CAPM but still maintain the validity of the EMH concept. CAPM-based approaches are only some of many possible descriptions of a perfectly efficient capital market. Although the market could be deemed perfectly efficient if the CAPM holds, the descriptive and predictive failures of the CAPM do not necessarily mean that the market is inefficient.

Fundamental Anomalies

Small-Cap Effect (or Myth?)

When publicly traded companies are formed into portfolios based on market capitalization (price times number of outstanding shares), empirical research in financial economics documents the fact that small firms consistently earn above-average rates of return. For example, James L. Davis, Eugene F. Fama, and Kenneth R. French estimate that the per-month rate of return of small-cap stocks was 0.2 percent higher than expected over the 1928-1993 period.[2] Therefore, small-cap stocks have tended to earn a 2.4 percent annual rate-of-return premium during much of the modern era on Wall Street.

In the eyes of some stock market participants, unusually large historical rates of return for small-cap stocks suggest a size-related market inefficiency. However, by characterizing the small-cap effect as an anomaly, stock market analysts and other researchers admit that these unusual patterns of abnormal returns remain unexplained.

---

[2] See James L. Davis, Eugene F. Fama, and Kenneth R. French, "Characteristics, Covariances, and Average Returns: 1928 to 1997," *Journal of Finance*, vol. 55, no. 1 (February 2000), pp. 389–406.

Beware the Internet News Hoax

Wise investors do not take seriously the rants commonly featured on Internet message boards and chat sites, but many rely on the late-breaking news published by traditional news services such as Bloomberg, Business Wire, Reuters, and *The Wall Street Journal Online*, among others. These services distribute market-moving news stories and company announcements. However, on the Internet a new type of dirty trick is being played on unsuspecting investors, the *Internet news hoax*. An Internet news hoax is a false story that is planted on the Internet and mistakenly circulated, or purported to be circulated, by reputable news services. Such stories are planted to cause big price moves that create profit-making opportunities for day traders and other speculators.

For example, in 2004 the British Broadcasting System (BBC) ran an interview with someone falsely claiming to be a Dow Chemical (DOW) official who said the company admitted responsibility for the 1984 disaster at Union Carbide's Bhopal facility and would set up a $12 billion fund to compensate victims. On the night of December 3, 1984, about 3,500 Bhopal residents were killed instantly when a cloud of methyl isocyanate gas from the nearby Union Carbide plant spread through the city—it was one of the worst industrial disasters ever. The overhang of the tragedy has been a major liability for DOW and a major drag on the company's stock price performance. Shares of DOW swung widely on the news. On the Frankfurt exchange, DOW fell to 35.50 euros per share before snapping back to close at 37.40 euros in thin trade. The BBC story was denied by DOW officials in Switzerland and New York and was retracted, with apologies, by the BBC. "There was no basis whatsoever for this report. BBC has been informed of this error and has pulled the erroneous story," DOW said in a statement posted on its Web site. BBC issued a statement admitting it had "fallen victim to an elaborate hoax timed to coincide with the twentieth anniversary of India's Bhopal chemical disaster."

The *New York Times* is famous for its motto, "All the news that's fit to print." Unfortunately, the same standards do not apply to what you read on the Internet.

See Gaston F. Ceron, "E*Trade to Offer Brokerage Clients Loss Protection for Online Fraud," *The Wall Street Journal Online*, January 18, 2006 (**http://online.wsj.com**).

Small-cap effect

Tendency for outperformance by small-capitalization stocks.

Table 7.1 gives interesting perspective on the **small-cap effect** phenomenon. Today, rates of return on small-cap stocks are typically measured by using the Russell 2000 Index. In 1984, the Russell Investment Group created the Russell family of stock indexes to help investors monitor the performance of investment managers across various market segments. The Russell 3000 Index measures the performance of the 3,000 largest U.S. companies based on total market capitalization, and it represents about 98 percent of the market capitalization of the U.S. equity market. In early 2006, the average market capitalization of companies included in the Russell 3000 was approximately $75.3 billion. The largest firm in the Russell 3000 had a market capitalization of approximately $378.8 billion. The Russell 2000 Index measures the performance of the 2,000 smallest companies in the Russell 3000 Index, and it captures about 8 percent of the total market capitalization of the Russell 3000 Index. In early 2006, the average market capitalization of Russell 2000 companies was approximately $1.1 billion. The largest company in the index had an approximate market capitalization of $4.1 billion. It is worth emphasizing that many small-cap stocks included within the Russell 2000 are apt to be underperforming "fallen angels," or companies with significant revenues and profitability that have fallen on hard times and seen their share prices collapse. Other firms in the index are young, up-and-coming companies.

As shown in Table 7.1, from 1980 to 2005, the annual rate of return on small-cap stocks was 12.13 percent per year. The typical level of risk (return standard deviation, or SD) for small-cap stocks was 18.36 percent per year. During this time frame, the annual rate of return on large-cap stocks, as captured by the Standard & Poor's 500, was 13.19 percent per year (and SD was 16.11 percent). Thus, during the past 26 years, the annual return *deficit* from investing in small-cap versus large-cap stocks was 1.48 percent per year. By focusing their attention on historical data from the 1940s, 1950s, 1960s, and 1970s, many market observers have failed to notice that less risky large-cap stocks have beaten small caps since 1980. The small-cap effect has gone away! In today's global economy, large-cap firms may be better equipped to compete with worldwide competitors. Alternatively, modern stock markets may simply be much more efficient than the stock markets of previous generations.

TABLE 7.1	Small Cap Outperformance May Be a Thing of the Past

Year	Russell 2000	S&P 500	Small-Cap Premium (+) Deficit (-)
1980	38.58%	32.42%	6.16%
1981	2.03	-4.91	6.94
1982	24.95	21.41	3.54
1983	29.13	22.51	6.62
1984	-7.30	6.27	-13.57
1985	31.05	32.16	-1.11
1986	5.68	18.47	-12.79
1987	-8.77	5.23	-14.00
1988	24.89	16.81	8.08
1989	16.24	31.49	-15.25
1990	-19.51	-3.17	-16.34
1991	46.05	30.55	15.50
1992	18.41	7.67	10.74
1993	18.91	9.99	8.92
1994	-1.82	1.31	-3.13
1995	28.44	37.43	-8.99
1996	16.49	23.07	-6.58
1997	22.36	33.36	-11.00
1998	-2.55	28.58	-31.13
1999	21.26	21.04	0.22
2000	-3.02	-9.10	6.08
2001	2.49	-11.90	14.39
2002	-20.48	-22.10	1.62
2003	47.25	28.70	18.55
2004	18.33	10.88	7.45
2005	4.55	4.91	-0.36
Mean	**12.13%**	**13.19%**	**-1.48%**
Standard deviation	**18.36%**	**16.11%**	**12.15%**

Source: Vanguard, **http://vanguard.com**.

Value Effects

The fact that firm size adds to the explanation of average returns provided by β is not the only problem faced by the CAPM. Several studies in financial economics document higher long-term rates of return for stocks with low price-earnings, price-cash flow, and price-book ratios and low historical sales growth. This value premium is typically measured in terms of the higher rate of return earned by firms with high accounting book value of stockholder's equity relative to the market value of common equity, or the book-to-market anomaly. As predicted by contrarian value-stock investors, such companies tend to be good candidates for benefiting from the reversion-to-the-mean phenomenon. However, although higher expected returns for beaten-down stocks make economic sense, the failure to reflect such influences in the CAPM reduces its practical value.

When publicly traded companies are formed into portfolios based on book-to-market ratios, Davis, Fama, and French estimate that firms with high book-to-market ratios earned a

0.5 percent-per-month rate-of-return premium over the 1928–1993 period.[3] High book-to-market stocks have tended to earn a 6.0 percent annual rate-of-return premium, or a premium more than twice as large as the small-cap effect. Despite lower risk, these stocks tended to outperform low book-to-market stocks over sustained periods up to the 1990s and since 2000. This **value effect** may be another manifestation of the small-cap effect. Beaten-down stocks have low prices and market values, by definition. As such, they also tend to have low price-earnings, price-cash flow, and price-book ratios. This is not to say that a value effect necessarily rules out a small-cap effect, or vice versa. Both can be present. Similarly, several Wall Street analysts have suggested superior performance for low price-sales ratio stocks, high dividend yield stocks, and neglected stocks that enjoy little coverage by Wall Street analysts. All such findings suggest that value stocks with low prices and low investor expectations tend to perform better than expected. Conversely, growth stocks with high prices reflecting optimistic investor expectations tend to underperform these high expectations.

> **Value effect**
> Tendency for outperformance by value stocks.

As in the case of the small-cap effect, traditional market models such as the one-factor CAPM may simply understate the higher risks associated with value stocks. In that event, superior rates of return would simply reflect the greater level of risk associated with value stocks, and no true value-effect anomaly would be present. The stock prices may be right, but popular asset pricing models may be wrong.

On the other hand, perhaps perceived advantages for value and growth stocks may be the sorts of inexplicable and reversible patterns in annual rates of return that will be observed from time to time. As shown in Figure 7.1, like all investment strategies, value and growth investment strategies go in and out of style at various points in time. Throughout the 1970s and 1980s, growth stocks were popular and contrarian strategies focusing on value stocks were profitable. During the 1990s, and after the sensibility of value-stock investing became generally accepted among investors, value strategies began to underperform growth. Since 2000, value has outperformed growth.

Experienced investors realize that you do not necessarily make above-average rates of return in the stock market by investing in companies with sterling historical performance. Investors make money by investing in companies that are better than the popular perception. Given the recent underperformance by small-cap and value stocks, a true contrarian strategy at the start of the new millennium would be to buy small-cap value stocks.

Calendar Anomalies

January Effect

Time-related patterns in stock prices and security returns are inconsistent with the market efficiency concept. No seasonality exists in an efficient stock market. Therefore, it is surprising that a variety of academic studies have documented an inexplicable pattern of abnormal returns tied to the turn of the year. A **January effect** has been documented in a number of studies that show unusually large positive rates of return for stocks during the first few trading days of the year. January seasonality has been noted in the rates of return tied to a variety of stock characteristics, including size, yield, and neglect. Small-cap stock performance is especially strong on the last trading day of the year and on the first four trading days of the new year. Such returns can be substantial.

> **January effect**
> Phenomenon of unusually large positive rates of return for stocks during the first few trading days of the year.

To illustrate the seasonal nature of monthly returns in the stock market, Figure 7.2 shows monthly average rates of return on the Dow Jones Industrial Average (DJIA) from 1900 to 2005. Roughly a century of stock market evidence shows that monthly rates of return tend to be highest in December (1.20 percent), July (1.16 percent), August (0.93 percent), and January (0.91 percent). Monthly rates of return tend to be lowest in September (-1.36 percent), February (-0.17 percent), and May (-0.17 percent). Notice that the monthly rate of return in January averages somewhat less than the monthly rates of return in July and December. The general perception of January as the most beneficial month for the stock mar-

---

[3] See James L. Davis, Eugene F. Fama, and Kenneth R. French, "Characteristics, Covariances, and Average Returns: 1928 to 1997," *Journal of Finance*, vol. 55, no. 1 (February 2000), pp. 389–406.

| FIGURE 7.1 | High B/M Outperforms Low B/M in Many Years |

*Through November

| FIGURE 7.2 | **Average Monthly Returns** *This figure presents the average returns for the Dow Jones Industrial Average from 1900 to 2005 by month. The figure suggests positive returns for all months except February, May, September, and October.* |

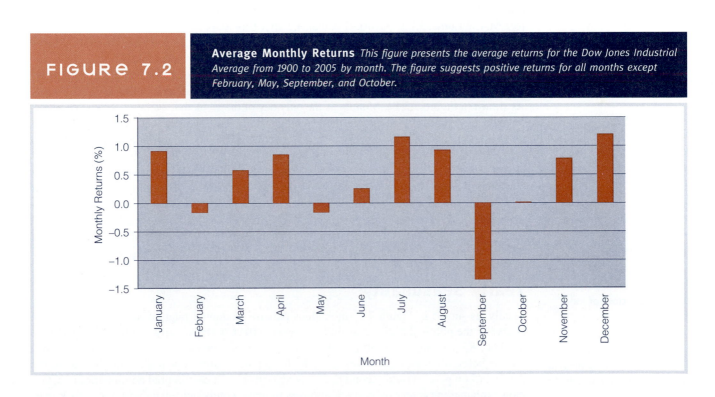

ket may stem from the fact that many researchers reported on the January-effect phenomenon during the 1980s, when January returns averaged 3.11 percent, the highest on record. During the 1990s, December (2.59 percent) and May (2.54 percent) rates of return were especially strong. From 2000 to 2005, October (3.35 percent) and November (2.79 percent) were the best months.

Because many top-performing small caps in January have poor prior-year performance, a bounce-back from tax-loss selling is an often-used explanation for the January effect. Individual stocks depressed near year-end are more likely to be sold for tax-loss recognition, whereas stocks that have run up are often held until after the new year begins so as to postpone capital gains taxes. However, this simplistic explanation defies equally simple logic. Suppose, for example, that there was indeed a dependable January effect. If investors knew that the stock market would rally in the first four trading days of the year, they would all rush to buy stocks during the last trading days of December and then rush to sell them at the end of the fourth trading day of the new year. If a large number of investors were involved, the market would rally strongly during late December. Similarly, it would drop sharply at the end of the fifth trading day of the new year. To beat the crowd, investors would be forced to buy earlier and earlier in December and sell earlier and earlier in January. Eventually, the January effect would self-destruct.

Interestingly, the January effect has been very weak to nonexistent during recent years. Some investors now believe the January effect has moved into November and December as a result of investor buying in anticipation of January gains. Strong monthly returns in November (2.07 percent) and December (2.59 percent) during the 1990s tend to support this inference. Institutional factors may also be at work. Mutual funds must now pay out capital gains distributions prior to the end of the calendar year, and they might sell losers before year-end to minimize the amount of taxable distributions that must be paid. In any event, the January-effect phenomenon remains a compelling riddle.

Day Effects

Holiday effects
Regularity of unusually good performance for stocks on the day prior to market-closing holidays.

By definition, all anomalies tend to be unpredictable. Patterns of returns that are inexplicable often arise or go away in an inexplicable fashion. This indeed appears to be the case with day effects. Unusually good performance for stocks on the day prior to market-closing holidays has been documented. Indeed, **holiday effects** have become an article of faith among practitioners. As shown in Figure 7.3(A), daily rates of return appear abnormally high on the day before Martin Luther King Day (0.91 percent), Labor Day (0.44 percent), the Fourth of July (0.34 percent), New Year's Day (0.32 percent), and Christmas Day (0.28 percent). However, Martin Luther King Day has been a national holiday only for a short period of time.

Monday effect
Regularity of Monday being the only day of the week that averages a negative rate of return.

Weekends are often bad for stocks, possibly because companies and governments tend to release bad news on the weekends. As a result, Monday is the worst-performing day of the week. As shown in Figure 7.3(B), Monday is the only day of the week that averages a negative rate of return. Daily returns on Monday average an abysmal -0.094 percent. This **Monday effect** has given rise to the refrain *"Don't sell stocks on (blue) Monday!"* Daily returns are especially strong on Wednesday (0.060 percent) and on Friday (0.068 percent), which is the best return day.

Beginning-of-day effect
Tendency of stock prices to rise during the first 45 minutes of the trading day.

Some researchers have also detected a **beginning-of-day effect** and an **end-of-day effect**. Tuesday through Friday, prices tend to rise during the first 45 minutes of the trading day and then trade flat until the last 15 minutes, at which point stocks tend to rally strongly to the close. Strong openings are usually attributed to the first few trades of the day. Strong closes are attributed to the last trade of the day. On Mondays, stocks tend to fall during the first 45 minutes of the trading day and then trade as on any other day of the week. There is little but conjecture to explain such patterns.

End-of-day effect
Tendency of stock prices to rise near the close of the trading day.

Yearly Seasonality

Political-cycle effect
Pattern of abnormally high annual returns during the third and last years of a presidential administration.

Finally, as shown in Figure 7.4, anomalous patterns in annual rates of return occur over the course of the political cycle. This **political-cycle effect** is statistically significant. During the third (12.85 percent) and fourth (9.99 percent) years of a presidential administration, annual returns before dividends are abnormally high. Annual returns appear abnormally low during the first (5.06 percent) and second (2.27 percent) years of a presidential administration. Common explanations center on political motives to make voters optimistic with high stock market returns in the period just prior to the next election. Nobody knows why voters and investors could be fooled by such a ruse, year after year, and from one administration to another.

Most inexplicable of all is why annual rates of return might be higher during years ending with the number 5, but they are. During years ending in "5," annual returns average a whop-

FIGURE 7.3

Daily Average Returns Preceding Holidays and by Days of the Week *Panel A presents the daily returns for the DJIA throughout the 20th century by days before holidays. The figure suggests that, on average, there are positive returns for each day preceding a holiday. Panel B presents the daily returns for the DJIA from 1900 to 1999 by days of the week. The figure suggests negative returns for Monday and positive returns for the other days of the week.*

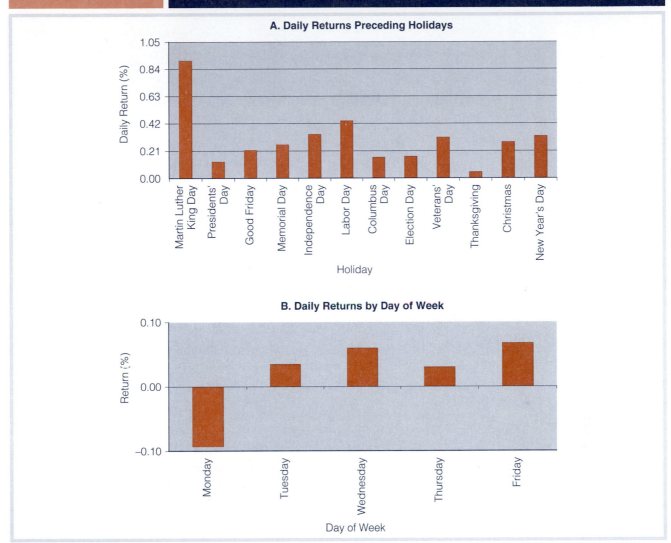

ping 28.96 percent before dividends. There is no rhyme or reason to explain such an impact. In all likelihood, it is simply the type of inexplicable regularity that occurs when enormous volumes of historical rate-of-return data are studied.

Event Studies

Announcement Effects

According to the semistrong-form EMH, current stock prices reflect all public information. The strong-form hypothesis posits that current stock prices incorporate all public information and nonpublic information. In both instances, new information is instantaneously reflected in stock prices, so subsequent investors are able to earn just a risk-adjusted normal rate of return. Thus, an interesting test of the EMH is to consider a firm's stock market returns in the few days

| FIGURE 7.4 | Annual Returns Are Unusually High during the Third and Last Years of a U.S. Presidential Administration and during Years Ending in "5" |

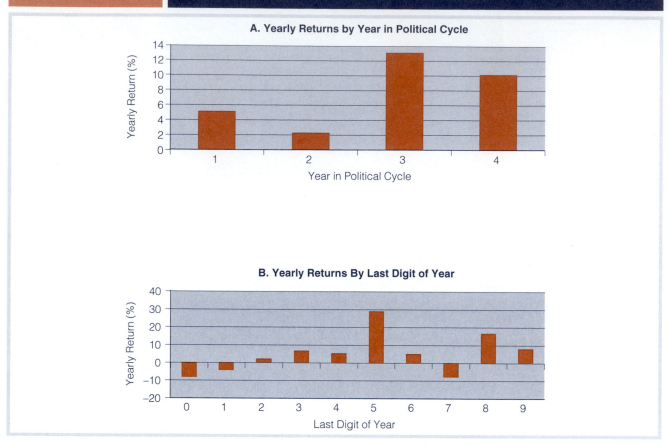

Source: NYSE Group, **www.nyse.com**.

Postannouncement drift
Predictable returns for a period after an announcement.

Economic event
Change in the underlying perceptions of investors.

Announcement period
Time frame during which an economic event occurs.

Event studies
Studies that measure abnormal returns surrounding significant news items that may have important economic consequences for the firm.

surrounding a cleanly identified date on which some important new information was communicated to the marketplace. In a perfectly efficient market, good news results in a sharp upward spike in shareholder returns on the announcement day. Bad news results in a downward spike in shareholder returns on the announcement day. In both instances, there should be no **postannouncement drift**, either positive or negative. In the postannouncement period, stock returns should be random.

In testing the importance of new information, it is important to keep in mind that several influences affect stock prices on any given day. Stocks go up or down for reasons tied to the overall market, the industry in which the firm competes, and other firm-specific influences. Whether a given stock goes up or down on a given day proves nothing about the importance of a given piece of news. For any news item to represent an important **economic event**, it must change the underlying perceptions of investors and result in an unusual movement in the stock's price during the **announcement period**. **Event studies** measure abnormal returns surrounding significant news items that may have important economic consequences for the firm, such as earnings announcements, mergers, and the death of a CEO. They are the primary means by which semistrong-form and strong-form versions of the EMH are investigated.

Many event studies begin with the simple underlying premise, or hypothesis, that stock market returns on individual companies can be usefully described by using the CAPM's SCL regression, in which

$$R_{jt} = \alpha_j + \beta_j R_{Mt} + \varepsilon_{jt}$$

(7.1)

In this model, R_{jt} is the rate of return on the common stock of the jth firm on day t and R_{Mt} is the market rate of return on day t. The market rate of return is typically described by the return on a broadly diversified market index, such as the S&P 500. Results from this SCL model are used to estimate **market-model abnormal returns**, AR, for the common stock of firm j on day t, such that

$$AR_{jt} = R_{jt} - (\alpha_j + \beta_j R_{Mt})$$ (7.2)

Market-model abnormal returns
Returns that cannot be explained by the CAPM.

Given the empirical limitations of the CAPM and SCL relation, abnormal returns are often also estimated by using alternative methods.

In a second common approach, **market-adjusted abnormal returns** are estimated by subtracting the return on the market index for day t, R_{Mt}, from the rate of return on the common stock of the jth firm on day t. Abnormal returns estimated by using market-adjusted returns are

$$AR_{jt} = R_{jt} - R_{Mt}$$ (7.3)

Market-adjusted abnormal returns
Returns different from the market return.

A third common approach involves estimating **mean-adjusted abnormal returns** by subtracting the arithmetic mean return of the common stock of the jth firm computed over the estimation period, from its return on day t:

$$AR_{jt} = R_{jt} - \bar{R}_j$$ (7.4)

Mean-adjusted abnormal returns
Returns different from the average return.

In all instances, the relation between firm and marketwide returns is established over a significant period of time before some newsworthy item. For example, it is common to consider a 255-day estimation period that begins 300 trading days before the event date, $t = -300$, and ends 45 trading days before the event date, $t = -45$. This estimation period corresponds to roughly one calendar year in length. The event date, $t = 0$, is typically assumed to be the day a particularly newsworthy item is broadly disseminated, such as when a company news item first appears in *The Wall Street Journal*.

Daily abnormal returns are averaged over a sample of N firms to yield average abnormal returns, AAR:

$$AAR_t = \frac{\sum_{j=1}^{N} AR_{jt}}{N}$$ (7.5)

Cumulative Abnormal Returns

To measure comprehensive influences, **cumulative abnormal returns (CAR)** are calculated over an event-interval period, typically of one, two, or three days:

$$CAR_{T_1,T_2} = \frac{\sum_{j=1}^{N} \sum_{t=T_1}^{T_2} AR_{jt}}{N}$$ (7.6)

Cumulative abnormal returns
The sum of abnormal returns over some event-interval period, typically of one, two, or three days.

The statistical significance of CARs is typically established by comparing their size and variability in so-called t-tests. When the CAR for an individual news event affecting a given stock is large relative to its underlying variability, it is said to be statistically significant and different from zero. This means that the pattern of stock prices surrounding a specific news item is indeed unusual, and the event has economic significance. When the CAR for an individual news event is small relative to its underlying variability, it is said to be insignificant and near zero. In this case, the pattern of stock prices surrounding a specific news item is typical, and the incident in question has no economic significance.

CARs can also be used to identify groups of stocks with unusually attractive or unusually unattractive performance characteristics. When the CARs for a group of securities are large

The "Other" January Effect

Wall Street professionals are always looking for profitable trading techniques. However, claims about such strategies often get picked up by the popular press and become part of "conventional wisdom" before they have undergone rigorous statistical analysis. As a result, some conventional wisdom on Wall Street is neither conventional nor wise.

For example, market historian Yale Hirsch coined the phrase, "As January goes, so goes the year." Between 1950 and 2004, in 44 out of 56 years, or about 80 percent of the time, the S&P 500's year-end finish mirrored how it fared during the first month of the year, says Hirsch's *Stock Trader's Almanac*. However, recent errors include 2001, when a 3.5 percent January gain was derailed by 9/11 and the market lost 13.0 percent; 2003, when there was a 26.4 percent gain despite a 2.7 percent January loss caused by angst due to the run-up to the Iraq war; and 2005, when a 3.3 percent January loss contrasted with a modest 4.9 percent gain in the overall market. Thus, January returns have failed to predict the market's direction during recent years.

More detailed statistical evidence suggests that there is indeed some tendency for January returns to predict the magnitude of positive returns throughout the rest of the year. Michael Cooper, John McConnell, and Alexei Ovtchinnikov recently discovered that January stock returns are a surprisingly robust predictor of market returns over the following 11 months. From 1940 to 2003, market returns over the next 11 months were much higher when January returns were positive as opposed to negative. This is a different phenomenon from the well-known "January effect," whereby small and low-priced stocks that have suffered price declines in the prior year tend to perform especially well during the following January.

The cause of the "January barometer" anomaly is not known. Some analysts say that stocks typically benefit from heavy cash inflows in January and that weak January returns have an adverse effect on market sentiment. Others are skeptical of its very existence. Stay tuned!

See Michael Cooper, John McConnell, and Alexei Ovtchinnikov, "The Other January Effect," *Journal of Financial Economics*, forthcoming in 2006.

relative to their underlying variability, such securities exhibit better-than-expected performance and represent historical bargains in the eyes of investors. Conversely, when CARs for a group of securities are small relative to their underlying variability, such securities exhibit typical performance and represent opportunities that offer no better than a risk-adjusted or normal rate of return.

Try It!

An investor wants to know if an announcement about a CEO's retirement is good or bad for the company. To investigate the announcement, he finds that the return on the company that day was 0.5 percent. The average return for the company over the past 6 months was 0.3 percent per day. On the announcement day, the S&P 500 Index rose 0.4 percent. The CAPM estimated coefficients for the firm are (α = −0.1 percent and β = 1.1. Did investors believe the announcement to be good or bad news?

Solution

Compute the abnormal return for the announcement.

Using the market model in Equation 7.2,

$$AR_{jt} = R_{jt} - (\alpha_j + \beta_j R_{Mt}) = 0.5 - (-0.1 + 1.1 \times 0.4) = 0.16\%$$

Using the market-adjusted model of Equation 7.3,

$$AR_{jt} = R_{jt} - R_{Mt} = 0.5\% - 0.4\% = 0.1\%$$

Lastly, using the mean-adjusted model of Equation 7.4 gives

$$AR_{jt} = R_{jt} - \bar{R}_j = 0.5\% - 0.3\% = 0.2\%$$

In all three cases, the abnormal return is positive. Therefore, the market reaction to the CEO retirement appears to mean that the announcement is good news.

Announcement Anomalies

Earnings Announcements

Event study methodology has been used to discover inexplicable patterns in stock prices following announcements of important firm-specific information. One of the most important of these patterns is tied to companies that report higher-than-expected earnings. Such companies are said to have a positive **earnings surprise**. Companies reporting better-than-expected earnings results typically see their stock prices move up briskly. Underperforming companies that report less-than-expected earnings often see their stock sell off sharply. Because earnings announcements represent important economic information, there is nothing inconsistent with the EMH when stock prices react strongly to earnings announcements. It would be inconsistent with the EMH if stock prices did not move when reported earnings differ greatly from the consensus earnings forecast. According to the semistrong-form EMH, current stock prices accurately reflect all public information. Good news should push stock prices up; bad news should cause stock prices to fall.

For example, any stock with earnings that plummet is a disaster for investors. This is especially true for companies with high price-earnings ratios stemming from a consensus expectation of spectacular earnings growth. Aware of high investor expectations, managements of some growth-stock companies have been known to stretch accounting conventions so as to place company earnings performance in a favorable light. When the fundamental operations of highly esteemed growth stocks begin to deteriorate, "creative accounting" has sometimes given way to outright fraud. Several companies whose earnings literally "fell off a cliff" were later found guilty of earnings manipulation, or outright fraud. Companies that report earnings later than usual or that report their earnings later than others in the industry often announce poor operating results. As a result, savvy investors often avoid companies with questionable reporting practices or ones that delay earnings reports. Remember, easy-to-predict earnings information is already reflected in the stock prices of companies set to report operating results. It is only the "news" component of current earnings information that affects stock prices in a perfectly efficient market.

On Wall Street, it is well known that analysts systematically overestimate good earnings and systematically understate poor earnings performance. However, as long as investors correctly discount the earnings forecast information provided, the optimistic bias of stock analysts has no necessary influence on market efficiency. What is inconsistent with the EMH is evidence of **post-earnings announcement drift**, whereby price movements tied to earnings announcements seem to continue for several weeks after the announcement. In such cases, investors have the potential to profit from previously disclosed public information by buying stocks in companies that report favorable results or by selling companies that report subpar results. In a perfectly efficient market, good and bad earnings information is instantaneously reflected in company stock prices, so subsequent investors earn only a risk-adjusted normal rate of return on their investment.

Before the stock market opened on Friday, May 7, 2004, Krispy Kreme Doughnuts Inc. warned that its quarterly and annual earnings would not meet analysts' estimates. The company reported that the increasing popularity of low-carb diets was beginning to hurt its business. As Figure 7.5 shows, Krispy's stock price fell $9.29 (29 percent) that day. Notice that the stock continued to fall another $2.21 on Monday, May 10. Post-earnings announcement drift can last many months. It remains a mystery as to why investors are so slow to react to significant news.

Stock-Split Announcements

An extensive body of research in financial economics agrees that, by themselves, stock-split announcements have no effect on the market value of the firm. On the face of it, stock splits appear to represent merely cosmetic changes because they increase the number of outstanding shares but do not directly affect the market value of the firm. With a 2:1 stock split, for example, the investor comes to own twice as many shares as before the split, but the postsplit

Earnings surprise
Earnings that differ from expected earnings.

Post-earnings announcement drift
Stock price movements tied to earnings announcements that continue after the announcement.

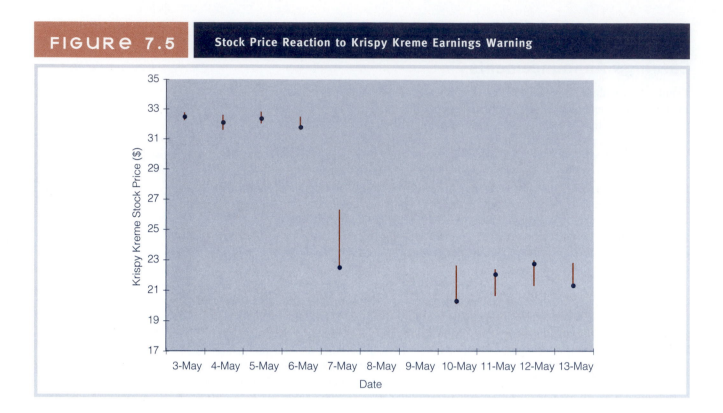

FIGURE 7.5 — Stock Price Reaction to Krispy Kreme Earnings Warning

Record date
Date on which a shareholder must be a registered owner in order to receive the benefit of a stock split (or other stockholder benefit).

Announcement date
News publication date.

Pay date
Date on which a split becomes effective.

Ex-split date
Date on which the stock begins trading at the new postsplit price.

Split ratio
Rate of increase in stock outstanding.

price falls by one-half. A traditional explanation for stock splits is that they increase the number of small shareholders. A possible reason for such an increase is that stocks with lower prices tend to have higher-percentage bid-ask spreads and give brokers more incentive to promote the stock.

For example, J&J Snack Foods made a 2:1 stock-split announcement on November 22, 2005. J&J manufactures and distributes nutritional snack foods. The **record date** of December 6 followed this **announcement date** by roughly two weeks, as is typical. Holders of record on December 6 received one additional share for every share owned on January 5, 2006, the **pay date**. In the case of stock splits, the **ex-split date** is the day following the pay date. This means that buyers of the stock would pay the presplit price all the way up through the pay date. Effective with the payday, the number of shares held by each J&J shareholder doubled but the share price split in one-half. In principle, J&J's stock split was a nonevent with no repercussions for the market value of the firm.

As shown in Table 7.2, 2:1 is the most common **split ratio**. Other popular ratios for stock splits are 3:1 and 3:2. Irrespective of the split ratio, the principle holds that the split has no impact on the market value of the firm. Following any stock split, the quantity of shares increases, and the share price declines by a commensurate amount so that the net effect on the value of the firm is zero.

Many investors are convinced that stock splits represent good news that tends to move the company's market value upward. Several investment newsletters and Web sites describe stock splits as one of the best marketing tools ever conceived by companies seeking to boost their market values. According to popular wisdom, stock splits create a positive feeling among shareholders. As the stock price drops as a result of a split, more retail investors jump on board. If retail investors are less easily shaken out on a downgrade or market downturn, stock splits can also moderate share price fluctuations. When a given market sector is hot, many stocks are setting new highs and become stock-split candidates. Indeed, the 90-day period prior to a stock-split announcement is one of the more profitable periods enjoyed by stocks. Many individual investors erroneously expect a stock to shoot higher on the announcement of a stock split than it did before the announcement.

TABLE 7.2	Stock Split Calendar for January 2006 *Notice that 2:1 stock splits are the most common.*

(Sorted by Ex-Date) Company	Ticker	Split	An-Date	Ex-Date	# Prior Splits	Price Month Prior to An-Date	Price Prior to An-Date	An-Date Price	Pay-Date Price
Charles & Colvard Ltd.	CTHR	5:4	Dec 21	Jan 31	0	28.05	31.11	21.47	?
Mercantile Bankshares Corp.	MRBK*	3:2	Jan 10	Jan 30	4	58.52	57.11	57.44	?
CVB Financial Corp.	CVBF	5:4	Dec 22	Jan 27	9	20.47	20.25	20.52	?
Balchem Corp.	BCP	3:2	Dec 15	Jan 23	2	28.95	27.25	28.00	?
TALX Corp.	TALX*	3:2	Nov 14	Jan 18	3	32.94	42.65	42.94	?
Papa John's International, Inc.	PZZA*	2:1	Dec 08	Jan 17	2	51.96	55.75	59.10	?
LKQ Corp.	LKQX	2:1	Dec 15	Jan 17	0	32.19	33.50	34.63	?
Coldwater Creek, Inc.	CWTR*	3:2	Dec 12	Jan 17	4	29.42	32.79	33.52	?
New River Pharmaceuticals Inc.	NRPH	2:1	Dec 20	Jan 13	0	53.30	50.63	52.67	?
Hi-Tech Pharmacal Co., Inc.	HITK	3:2	Dec 09	Jan 12	2	36.78	41.99	43.29	?
Psychiatric Solutions Inc.	PSYS	2:1	Nov 02	Jan 10	0	53.40	55.90	56.67	63.68
Cerner Corp.	CERN*	2:1	Dec 14	Jan 10	3	89.00	93.08	83.95	97.769
Panhandle Royalty Co.	PHX	2:1	Dec 14	Jan 10	2	29.75	35.50	38.50	40.80
Par Technology Corp.	PTC	3:2	Nov 15	Jan 09	0	21.07	28.72	30.26	31.50
J&J Snack Foods Corp.	JJSF	2:1	Nov 22	Jan 06	0	54.81	58.73	60.79	63.57
Espey Mfg. & Electronics Corp.	ESP	2:1	Nov 21	Jan 03	0	34.62	38.58	40.50	36.80
Brightpoint, Inc.	CELL*	3:2	Dec 05	Jan 03	7	21.57	28.81	30.00	27.73
Sierra Health Services, Inc.	SIE*	2:1	Dec 07	Jan 03	2	75.87	77.24	78.90	79.96
Old Republic International Corp.	ORI*	5:4	Dec 08	Jan 03	4	24.94	25.91	26.42	26.26

* = optionable.

Note: "An-Date" is the date the company announced the stock split. "Ex-Date" is the date that the stock price is adjusted to reflect the issuance of new shares due to the stock split. Thus, the "Price Month Prior To An-Date" is the stock's price about one month prior to its stock-split announcement; the "Price Prior to An-Date" is the last closing price prior to the stock-split announcement and the "An-Date Price" is the closing price the first trading date after the stock split is announced (which is generally the day after the "Price Prior to An-Date"). The "Pay Date" is the last day that the stock trades prior to the stock price being adjusted for the split.

Source: Stock Splits, **www.stocksplits.net**. © stocksplits.net, 2006. Used with permission.

The popular perception that stock splits cause stocks to shoot higher is fallacious. Stocks tend to split *after* their share price has surged, not before. Companies that split their stock tend to do somewhat better than the overall market during the presplit period but perform in line with the overall market during the postsplit period. It is not the stock split itself, or the expectation of a stock split, that causes the stock price to rise. Stock tends to rise with the announcement of a stock split only if other favorable fundamental news is issued at the same time as the stock-split announcement.

Companies sometimes announce **reverse stock splits**, in which the number of shares held by shareholders goes *down*. In a 1:3 reverse stock split, investors receive one share of stock for every three shares of stock held previously. Reverse stock splits are most common among companies with deteriorating fundamentals and a crumbling share price. To be sure, just as a stock split does not cause superior prior performance, reverse stock splits do not cause inferior prior performance.

Finally, there is a type of anomaly associated with stock splits, called the **spin-off anomaly**. A spin-off is the separation of a business from a diversified corporation by distributing stock in the new entity to current shareholders. Spin-offs of smaller companies from larger organizations often lead to favorable stock market performance. Among spin-offs, the best stock market performers tend to be companies that dramatically improve their operating performance by more tightly focusing on core operations. In the first three years on their own, these newly minted companies tend to earn an average return of 30 to 35 percent per year. Analysts

Reverse stock split
Stock split that reduces the number of shares outstanding.

Spin-off anomaly
Tendency of spin-offs of smaller companies from larger organizations to lead to favorable stock market performance.

argue that before the spin-off, smaller companies do not get as much executive attention as necessary. After the spin-off, management of the smaller company tends to be much better focused and has the right incentives to maximize shareholder value, and the stock tends to move up substantially. What is not understood is why investors do not fully realize the operating and financial advantages of these small independent operations and fail to bid up parent stock prices before the spin-off announcement becomes effective.

S&P 500 Listing

The S&P 500 is the most widely used benchmark for judging professional money managers. At the start of 2006, the S&P 500 included companies with a total market capitalization of $11 trillion, and about 65 percent of that amount was held by institutional investors. Roughly $1 trillion was directly linked to the S&P 500 through index funds. Portfolio managers of S&P 500 index funds must time their purchases and sales decisions to ensure a close correspondence between fund and index performance. Other fund managers whose performance is measured by the S&P 500 must also be sensitive to differences between the makeup of their portfolios and the S&P 500. As a result, S&P 500 additions and deletions have direct portfolio management implications that have given rise to an **index effect**. The index effect is the tendency of stocks to jump when S&P announces that they are about to be added to the S&P 500.

On the announcement that a stock is being added to the S&P 500, the stock tends to go up in price by 4.75 percent, on average, from the time the announcement is made to the time the change takes place. Many stocks subsequently give back some of this gain in the 10 days after the effective date. The average stock being added to the S&P 500 declines about 2 percent from the effective date to 10 days later, for a net gain of roughly 2.75 percent from the announcement date to 10 days after the effective date. However, these unadjusted returns fail to take into account general market conditions and thus contain an upward bias during a typically rising market environment. Adjusting for general market movements, being added to the S&P 500 means an immediate boost in share price of about 5 percent plus another increase of around 4 percent over the following year.

Table 7.3 shows a handful of recent S&P 500 additions. Of course, S&P does not want to move the market with its index change decisions. Several years ago, in an effort to reduce potential market impact, S&P began making index change announcements a few days in advance. Index addition and deletion decisions are made by the S&P Index Committee. Neither companies nor any other S&P clients play a role in the decision-making process. The

Index effect
Tendency of stocks to jump when Standard & Poor's announces that they are about to be added to the S&P 500.

TABLE 7.3	Stocks Added to the S&P 500 Often Experience a Price Jump*						
Company	Ticker	Date Announced	Announcement Closing Price	Next-Day Closing Price	Percent Change	Date Added to S&P 500	Date Added to S&P 500 Closing Price	Percent Change
Estee Lauder	EL	1/3/2006	33.34	35.00	4.98%	1/4/2006	35.00	4.98%
Whole Foods Market	WFMI	12/28/2005	75.43	79.10	4.87	12/30/2005	77.39	2.60
Genworth Financial Inc.	GNW	11/29/2005	34.00	34.45	1.32	12/1/2005	34.26	0.76
Amazon.com	AMZN	11/14/2005	42.34	44.45	4.98	11/18/2005	47.98	13.32
Patterson Companies Inc.	PDCO	10/7/2005	38.01	39.96	5.13	10/10/2005	39.96	5.13
Lennar Corp.	LEN	9/30/2005	59.76	61.70	3.25	10/3/2005	61.70	3.25
Coventry Health Care Inc.	CVH	8/28/2005	75.29	78.66	4.48	8/29/2005	78.66	4.48
Public Storage	PSA	8/15/2005	63.03	65.53	3.97	8/18/2005	66.24	5.09
Murphy Oil	MUR	8/9/2005	54.20	55.38	2.18	8/12/2005	55.88	3.10
Average price change					**3.91%**			**4.75%**
Median price change					**4.48%**			**4.48%**
Percent Positive					**87.5%**			**75.0%**

*All announcements are made after the market close, and percent change is from the announcement-date share price.

index is viewed as a collection of the leading companies in leading industries and an over-all reflection of the U.S. stock market. Only U.S. companies are eligible for addition to the index. Turnover among S&P 500 companies averages roughly 25 to 50 firms per year, representing roughly 5 percent of the market capitalization of the index. Closely held stocks, in which a small group has control of a company, will often be excluded from consideration. Finally, a rigorous fundamental analysis is performed. S&P seeks to add only relatively stable stocks to the S&P 500. Normally, announcements are made at about 5:15 p.m. New York time and are released to the public by the major wire services and posted on the S&P Index Services Web site (**www.spglobal.com**). Only after the public is informed does S&P notify its own clients and the companies involved.

The S&P 500 index addition effect can be explained as consistent with the EMH to the extent that it merely reflects the implicit endorsement of a company's future economic prospects by the Standard & Poor's Corp. However, the S&P 500 index effect is inconsistent with the EMH to the extent that it suggests stock prices move for reasons that have nothing to do with the fundamental economic prospects of the companies involved.

Try It!

National Oilwell Varco (NOV) designs and manufactures products used in oil and gas drilling and production. On March 7, 2005, Standard & Poor's announced that it was adding NOV to the S&P 500 Index. The addition would occur at the end of the day on March 11, 2005. Given the daily prices of NOV and the S&P 500 Index shown below, compute the market-adjusted abnormal returns for NOV around the announcement.

	A	B	C
1			
2	Date	NOV	S&P500
3	22-Feb-05	41.00	1184.16
4	23-Feb-05	42.00	1190.80
5	24-Feb-05	43.46	1200.20
6	25-Feb-05	44.72	1211.37
7	28-Feb-05	45.34	1203.60
8	1-Mar-05	43.81	1210.41
9	2-Mar-05	44.46	1210.08
10	3-Mar-05	46.21	1210.47
11	4-Mar-05	47.34	1222.12
12	7-Mar-05	48.13	1225.31
13	8-Mar-05	48.45	1219.43
14	9-Mar-05	48.02	1207.01
15	10-Mar-05	47.61	1209.25
16	11-Mar-05	48.85	1200.08
17	14-Mar-05	50.21	1206.83
18	15-Mar-05	49.31	1197.75
19	16-Mar-05	48.70	1188.07
20	17-Mar-05	49.75	1190.21
21	18-Mar-05	49.32	1189.65
22	21-Mar-05	48.88	1183.78
23	22-Mar-05	48.39	1171.71
24	23-Mar-05	46.94	1172.53
25	24-Mar-05	47.08	1171.42

(continued on the next page)

Solution

First compute daily returns for NOV and for the S&P 500 Index. Then use these returns to compute the market-adjusted abnormal returns.

	A	B	C	D	E	F	G	H	I
1								Market Adjusted	
2	Date	NOV	S&P500		NOV	S&P500		Abnormal Return	
3	22-Feb-05	41.00	1184.16						
4	23-Feb-05	42.00	1190.80		2.44%	0.56%		1.88%	
5	24-Feb-05	43.46	1200.20		3.48%	0.79%		2.69%	
6	25-Feb-05	44.72	1211.37		2.90%	0.93%		1.97%	
7	28-Feb-05	45.34	1203.60		1.39%	-0.64%		2.03%	
8	1-Mar-05	43.81	1210.41		-3.37%	0.57%		-3.94%	
9	2-Mar-05	44.46	1210.08		1.48%	-0.03%		1.51%	
10	3-Mar-05	46.21	1210.47		3.94%	0.03%		3.90%	
11	4-Mar-05	47.34	1222.12		2.45%	0.96%		1.48%	
12	7-Mar-05	48.13	1225.31		1.67%	0.26%		1.41%	
13	8-Mar-05	48.45	1219.43		0.66%	-0.48%		1.14%	
14	9-Mar-05	48.02	1207.01		-0.89%	-1.02%		0.13%	
15	10-Mar-05	47.61	1209.25		-0.85%	0.19%		-1.04%	
16	11-Mar-05	48.85	1200.08		2.60%	-0.76%		3.36%	
17	14-Mar-05	50.21	1206.83		2.78%	0.56%		2.22%	
18	15-Mar-05	49.31	1197.75		-1.79%	-0.75%		-1.04%	
19	16-Mar-05	48.70	1188.07		-1.24%	-0.81%		-0.43%	
20	17-Mar-05	49.75	1190.21		2.16%	0.18%		1.98%	
21	18-Mar-05	49.32	1189.65		-0.86%	-0.05%		-0.82%	
22	21-Mar-05	48.88	1183.78		-0.89%	-0.49%		-0.40%	
23	22-Mar-05	48.39	1171.71		-1.00%	-1.02%		0.02%	
24	23-Mar-05	46.94	1172.53		-3.00%	0.07%		-3.07%	
25	24-Mar-05	47.08	1171.42		0.30%	-0.09%		0.39%	
26									
27			=(B25-B24)/B24			=E25-F25			
28									

Notice that an investor who heard about the addition on March 8 could have still invested in NOV and outperformed the market for several days. However, when assessing this type of strategy, remember that there are trading costs that can substantially reduce profits!

Is the EMH Valid?

What Are the Riddles?

By the late 1970s, most financial economists had come to believe that the U.S. stock market was very efficient and that, apart from the long-term uptrend, changes in stock prices were essentially random and unpredictable. However, during the 1980s and 1990s, a large body of academic literature emerged that uncovered shortcomings in the CAPM and caused some observers to question the EMH. Such questioning began with several reputable studies that suggested anomalous patterns in stock market returns, such as the small-firm effect and the January effect. In fact, stocks in general and small-cap stocks in particular seem to do very well during the first few trading days of the new year. However, before rushing out to buy small stocks in late December, keep in mind that much of the apparent advantage of such bargain hunting can be offset by market volatility and transactions costs. The nonrandom positive effect on small-cap stocks at the turn of the year is quite small, on the order of 5 to 6 percent during the month of January, and can be overwhelmed by market volatility on the order of 7 to 8 percent per month. Round-trip transaction costs of 1 to 2 percent can dramatically reduce the attractiveness of turn-of-the-year speculation on small-cap stocks and can undermine the profitability of careful trading strategies. Similarly, investors trying to exploit fundamental or announcement-related anomalies must be sensitive to problems tied to risk estimation. Small-company stocks tend to be riskier than large-company stocks, for example, and should give investors a greater reward. In addition, the dependability of inex-

Believing Is Seeing

Skeptical investors study the facts before making an investment decision. When it comes to "story" stocks, there is often a really good story circulated about a company's future potential but little in the way of revenue, cash flow, or profits to back up the optimistic projections. "Seeing is believing" is the motto of the skeptical investor. Unfortunately, naïve investors are sometimes willing to believe incredible projections of future business opportunities because they desperately want to believe in their own potential for stock market riches. For gullible investors, a "believing is seeing" problem exists. They are victims of what psychologists call a "suspension of disbelief."

To invest wisely and avoid investing in companies with dubious prospects, be skeptical. Make sure you understand the company's business. Read Securities and Exchange Commission (SEC) reports carefully, and pay attention to financial statements, particularly if they are not audited or not certified by an accountant. If the company is small and does not file reports with the SEC, be sure to ask your broker for what's called the "Rule 15c2-11 file" on the company. That file will contain important information about the company. Check out the people running the company with state securities regulators, and find out if they've ever made money for investors. Also ask if company officers had run-ins with the regulators or other investors. Finally, make sure the broker you deal with is registered with the SEC and licensed to do business in your state. Don't be reluctant to ask the state securities regulator whether your broker and the broker's firm have ever been disciplined or have complaints against them.

Investment frauds and Internet scams are not merely an industry problem of unscrupulous promoters. While fraudulent promotions are a big problem, they are only effective because they reflect a basic problem with human nature. It's the believing-is-seeing problem. Savvy investors have a simple rule for assessing the validity of any stock promoter's claim: "If it sounds too good to be true, it probably is."

For detailed information on how to properly investigate company information and avoid investment scams, see the SEC website at **www.sec.gov**.

---

plicable return anomalies is notoriously poor. Just about the time investors recognize the potential for market-beating results, conditions change and profit-making opportunities tend to evaporate.

Researchers have used event study methodology for more than a generation to produce useful knowledge about how stock prices respond to new information. This approach works especially well when used to study ramifications of hard-to-anticipate economic events over brief periods of time. The underlying assumption is that stock prices should respond quickly and accurately to firm-specific information that is harmful or helpful. Any lag in the stock price response to important economic events should be short-lived. Long-lived price responses give investors the opportunity to profit from such information and thus are inconsistent with the EMH. The semistrong-form of the EMH is supported by studies that document the absence of postannouncement abnormal returns tied to public announcements of important new information. Despite this, event study methodology has identified at least a dozen different types of important economic events for which there appears to be sustained underreaction or long-term overreaction. As shown in Table 7.4, the evidence in favor of semistrong-form and strong-form EMH is somewhat mixed and controversial.[4]

In an efficient market, apparent underreaction will be about as frequent as apparent overreaction. If purported anomalies split about evenly between underreaction and overreaction, then, taken as a whole, they are generally consistent with market efficiency. When analyzed one by one, stock market anomalies seem to give damning evidence about the reliability of the EMH. When viewed on an overall basis, the event study literature seems to provide evidence of return anomalies that can reasonably be attributed to chance.

Evidence in support of the strong form of the EMH is fairly weak. In favor of the strong-form EMH lies evidence that the overwhelming majority of professional money managers fail to beat a buy-and-hold strategy. Insider-based trading rules also do not work. On the other hand, some superstar money managers like Berkshire Hathaway's Warren Buffett and Legg Mason's Bill Miller consistently beat a buy-and-hold strategy. Insiders such as corporate officers, board members, and 10 percent equity holders also appear to consistently earn positive abnormal returns. Stock exchange specialists also earn

---

[4] See Eugene F. Fama, "Market Efficiency, Long-Term Returns, and Behavioral Finance," *Journal of Financial Economics*, vol. 49, no. 3 (September 1998), pp. 283–306.

TABLE 7.4	Event Studies Give Evidence That Is Reasonably Split between Underreaction and Overreation		
Event	**Long-Term Preevent Return**	**Announcement Return**	**Long-Term Postevent Return**
Earnings announcements	Not available	Positive	Positive
Dividend initiations	Positive	Positive	Positive
Dividend omissions	Negative	Negative	Negative
Initial public offerings (IPOs)	Not available	Positive	Negative
Mergers (acquiring firm)	Positive	Zero	Negative
New exchange listings	Positive	Positive	Negative
Proxy fights	Negative	Positive	Negative (or zero)
Seasoned-equity offerings	Positive	Negative	Negative
Share repurchases (open market)	Zero	Positive	Positive
Share repurchases (tenders)	Zero	Positive	Positive
Stock spin-offs	Positive	Positive	Positive (or zero)
Stock splits	Positive	Positive	Positive

abnormal stock market returns based on their access to buy-sell information. Although technical analysis is not productive, fundamental analysis may have modest potential for discovering bargains among small, low price-earnings, and neglected stocks. Still, such findings remain tenuous.

The implications from the last half-century of stock market evidence are that a simple buy-and-hold strategy often is the most successful technique. Although some regular patterns appear in the stock market from time to time, they are not dependable. Some, such as the size effect, may simply reflect a better way of measuring risk than can be found with traditional measures. Others, such as popular calendar-related anomalies, come and go with unpredictable timing. Many so-called patterns in the stock market tend to self-destruct, as would be true in an efficient market.

Perspectives from Behavioral Finance

In the years ahead, an important challenge for academics and Wall Street professionals is the need to explore new and innovative means for testing the EMH. New theory, with input from the new and emerging field of behavioral finance, is sure to yield new insights that can be used to understand anomalies and other departures from accepted financial theory. Behavioral finance has the potential to offer new and useful perspectives on the ways markets actually work and to help us understand why many individual investors actually lose money in the stock market. In an efficient stock market, 50 percent of all investors will outperform the market averages, and 50 percent of all investors will underperform the averages. This is true *before* expenses. Because professional investment advisors charge mutual fund shareholders and other clients management fees of as much as 3 percent per year, it is not surprising that the average mutual fund underperforms the market averages. *After* expenses, the typical mutual fund underperforms the market averages. That's why many savvy investors know that low-cost index funds outperform the typical managed portfolio. Left unexplained by traditional financial theory is why many individual investors apparently do much worse than the professionals. Research in behavioral finance has discovered that psychological tendencies cause many investors to adopt money-losing investment strategies. They trade too much, buy high and sell low, and so on. Studies show that people do not always act in a rational and efficient manner. Indeed, cognitive errors

Soros

George Soros is famous for taking highly leveraged positions in stock, bond, and currency markets. In one of the most remarkably successful currency speculations of all time, Soros is reported to have made $1 billion by betting that Great Britain's pound sterling would fall in value relative to the dollar during September 1992.

Soros has outlined his theory of investing in two books, *The Alchemy of Finance* and *Soros on Soros: Staying Ahead of the Curve*. Soros' theory of reflexivity posits that the perceptions of market participants are often at conflict with market fundamentals. Most of the time, this conflict is small and the markets are "near equilibrium." Every now and then, a boom-bust cycle occurs that moves markets into "far-from-equilibrium" conditions. In an *initial phase*, incorrect investor perceptions survive some exogenous test. This strengthens wrongheaded investor perceptions, and general acceptance of incorrect views enters a *period of acceleration*. Misguided investor perceptions continue to deviate greatly from the economic fundamentals until a *moment of truth*. At that time, some market participants recognize their bias and attempt to take corrective action. However, trading momentum causes markets to remain in far-from-equilibrium conditions for an extended period, called the *twilight period*. Finally, the perceptions of market participants converge on the economic fundamentals, and markets collapse in a *crash*. For Soros, these are profit-making opportunities.

For example, investors overvalued the worth of Web site hits to young Internet companies in the mid-1990s. As a result, Internet stocks became overvalued. Because of investor demand, Internet firms issued more and more stock and used this capital to increase the number of free Web site visitors. This process reinforced the perception of growing Web traffic, and Internet stocks became more and more overvalued. The perception of Internet firm fundamentals became very different from business fundamentals until economic reality became obvious to all and the prices of wildly inflated Internet stocks collapsed. Of course, the trick is to recognize and profit from wide disparity between investor perceptions and market fundamentals.

See Merissa Marr, "Paramount May Sell Dream Works Library to Soros," *The Wall Street Journal Online*, January 7, 2006 (**http://online.wsj.com**).

---

that are commonly recognized in the psychology field can explain some stock market behaviors.

Consider two well-known psychological biases: **conservatism** and the **representativeness bias**. People are slow to change their views. When people are faced with new information that is contrary to prior beliefs, conservatism causes a slow update of those beliefs. (Note that psychological conservatism is not related to political conservatism.) Another bias that impacts an investor's beliefs is the representativness bias. This is a bias of stereotypes. With representativeness bias, the characteristics of something that we know are projected onto something that we do not know. For example, companies that have performed well for many years are projected to continue to do well. This assumption is made even though top companies seldom remain on top forever.

Ponder the situation in which investors commonly believe a company will continue to perform poorly. Suddenly, the firm reports earnings that exceed popular expectations, and the firm's stock price increases on this surprise. Investors may underreact to the news of a turnaround in operations because of conservatism. They do not believe that this poor company has really turned around. Therefore, investors are surprised again the next quarter when the same firm again exceeds earnings expectations. The slow updating of beliefs about the company has the potential to cause a prolonged underreaction by the market in general. Only when investors correctly perceive that the company has established a dependable history of strong performance will the firm be properly valued.

On the other hand, investors sometimes display a tendency to incorrectly project a company's past record of success into the future. In such situations, representativeness bias can lead investors to have an overly optimistic view of the future and bid stock prices too high. In such situations, investors overreact to the good prior long-term performance of the firm. Some scholars in behavioral finance have come to believe that stock prices tend to underreact to short-term news and information but overreact in the long term. Observing both short-term underreaction and long-term overreaction in the stock market does not mean that, on average, stock prices are efficient. It reflects the fact that investors can systematically fail to value companies in an appropriate manner.

Conservatism

A slow updating of opinions when new information is available.

Representativeness bias

A mental shortcut by which some known characteristics represent what is to be expected for other, unknown characteristics.

Proponents of the EMH commonly mention two empirical facts in support of the market efficiency concept. First, the typical investor appears unable to outperform the market index. Second, many hard-to-explain market anomalies, such as those found during the 1980s and early 1990s, seem transitory and hard to predict. These important points are worth remembering. Stock market evidence on the persistent failure of managed portfolios to beat the market, and the recent popularity of low-cost index funds, is consistent with the hypothesis that the market is generally efficient. At the same time, evidence concerning the susceptibility of investors to cognitive failures and psychological biases suggests that the market is not *perfectly* efficient. There is a big difference between a mostly efficient market and a perfectly efficient market. It is true that a change in price is impossible to predict in a rational and efficient market. However, the converse is not true. Just ask any Internet stock investor from the late-1990s if any impossible-to-predict change in price is also a rational change in price! In a mostly efficient market, bubbles and other pricing errors emerge from time to time. That's what makes recent advances from the field of behavioral finance exciting. Behavioral theories help us recognize and explain markets that are sometimes irrational and anomalies that would otherwise be left unexplained.

Summary

■ Whenever inexplicable patterns of abnormal stock market returns are detected in empirical studies of the stock market, a **return anomaly** is said to be found. A **joint test problem** exists because anomalous evidence that is inconsistent with a perfectly efficient market could be an indication of either market inefficiency or a simple failure of CAPM or APT accuracy.

■ On an annual rate-of-return basis, large-cap stocks have tended to earn annual rates of return significantly below those of small-cap stocks during much of the modern era on Wall Street. This **small-cap effect** phenomenon relates to companies listed on the New York Stock Exchange that rank in the bottom 20 percent in terms of market capitalization and to unlisted companies of comparable size.

■ Despite lower risk, value stocks tended to outperform growth stocks over sustained periods until the 1990s. This **value effect** may be another manifestation of the small-cap effect.

■ A **January effect** has been documented in several studies that show unusually large positive rates of return for stocks during the first few trading days of the year. Unusually good performance for stocks on the day prior to market-closing holidays has also been documented. Such **holiday effects** have become an article of faith among practitioners. Monday is the only day of the week that averages a negative rate of return. This **Monday effect** has given rise to the refrain "*Do not sell stocks on (blue) Monday!*" Some researchers have also detected a **beginning-of-day effect** and an **end-of-day effect**. Anomalous patterns in annual rates of return also occur over the course of the political cycle. This **political-cycle effect** is statistically significant. During the third and fourth years of a presidential administration, annual returns before dividends are abnormally high.

■ In a perfectly efficient market, good news results in a sharp upward spike in shareholder returns on an announcement day. Bad news results in a downward spike in shareholder returns on the announcement day. In both instances, there should be no **postannouncement drift**. In the postannouncement period, stock returns should be random. For any news item to represent an important **economic even**, it must change the underlying perceptions of investors and result in an unusual movement in the stock's price during the **announcement period**. **Event studies** measure abnormal returns surrounding significant news items that may have important economic consequences for the firm. In event studies, the SCL is used to estimate **market-model abnormal returns**, or returns that cannot be explained by the CAPM. **Market-adjusted abnormal returns** are also estimated by subtracting the return on the market index from the rate of return on a given stock for a given day. A third common approach involves estimating **mean-adjusted abnormal returns** by subtracting the arithmetic mean return on a common stock from its daily return. **Cumulative abnormal returns** are the sum of abnormal returns over some event interval period, typically of one, two, or three days.

■ Event study methodology has been used to discover inexplicable patterns in stock prices following announcements of important firm-specific information. One of the most important of these patterns is tied to companies that report higher-than-expected earnings, or a positive **earnings surprise.** Inconsistent with the EMH is evidence of a **post-earnings announcement drift**, whereby price movements tied to earnings announcements can continue for several weeks after the announcement.

■ Stock splits are merely cosmetic changes that increase the number of outstanding shares but have no direct effect on the market value of the firm. The **record date** is the date on which a shareholder must be a registered owner to receive the benefit of a stock split. This day follows the **announcement date** by roughly two weeks. The **pay date** is the date a split becomes effective. The **ex-split date** is the day following the pay date and marks the day on which the stock begins trading at the new postsplit price. Although 2:1 is the most common **split ratio**, other popular ratios for stock splits are 3:1 and 3:2. Companies sometimes announce **reverse stock splits**, in which the number of shares held by shareholders goes *down*. In a 1:3 reverse stock split, investors receive one share of stock for every three shares of stock held previously.

■ There is a type of anomaly associated with stock splits, called the **spin-off anomaly**. A spin-off is the separation of a business from a diversified corporation by distributing stock in the new entity to current shareholders. Spin-offs of smaller companies from larger organizations often lead to favorable stock market performance. The **index effect** is the tendency of stocks to jump when Standard & Poor's announces that they are about to be added to the S&P 500.

■ Decades of testing the EMH indicate that the theory has some cracks. Many market anomalies have been found. Some anomalies have persisted through time, while others have not. Also, stock prices seem to underreact to news at some times and overreact at other times. Behavioral finance offers some possible explanations. **Conservatism** causes investors to underreact to news, and the **representativeness bias** may cause long-term overreaction. Proponents of behavioral finance are attempting to provide an alternative theory to the EMH.

Self-Test Problems

ST7.1 Empirical research has uncovered a series of rate-of-return anomalies related to calendar-year events. Identify some of the most noteworthy calendar return anomalies.

Solution

During recent years, a number of calendar-year anomalies have been discovered. At various noteworthy points in time, at least some classes of common stocks seem to enjoy above-average rates of return that cannot be explained by the traditional CAPM and APT models of asset pricing. Abnormal rates of return have been observed and described as the:

- **January effect:** At the turn of the year, common stocks, especially small common stocks, enjoy significant abnormal returns. Such abnormal returns tend to be concentrated during the period from the last trading day of the year through the first four trading days of the new year.

- **Turn-of-the-month effect:** While not as dramatic as the January effect, turn-of-the-month returns alone fully account for the positive returns generated by stock market investments. Here, *turn of the month* is defined as the last trading day of the month through the first three days of the new month.

- **Day-of-the-week effect:** The "blue Monday" effect is alleged because Monday is the only day of the week on which returns are consistently negative. Conversely, returns on Friday are significantly higher than those earned on any other day.

- **Holiday effect:** The average preholiday return dwarfs the average daily rate of return. Returns are especially high before Labor Day, Memorial Day, and Thanksgiving. However, this effect is observed only when a market closure coincides with the holiday celebration.

- **Time-of-day effect:** Stock returns display intraday as well as interday patterns. Returns are typically high at the opening and immediately preceding the close. On Mondays, negative returns bottom out near 11 a.m.

No simple explanation exists for these patterns, but the upshot is clear: "Buy around 3 p.m. on the Thursday preceding Labor Day, and never sell on Monday!"

ST7.2 The Try It earlier in this chapter computed the market-adjusted abnormal returns around the announcement of National Oilwell Varco's addition to the S&P 500 Index. A few months earlier, four more companies were added to the S&P 500 (see Table 7.3). Using average abnormal return and cumulative abnormal returns, assess the strategy of buying stocks at the end of the day following index addition announcements.

Solution

Daily stock prices for each firm and for the S&P 500 Index need to be obtained around the announcement dates, as in the Try It example. Then compute abnormal daily returns. Average and cumulative abnormal returns are shown:

	N	O	P	Q	R	S	T	U	V
1		Market Adjusted Abnormal Returns							
2	Day	NOV	XTO	CBSS	ASN	NWS		AAR	CAR
3									
4	0	1.41%	1.14%	0.22%	-0.40%	-2.22%		0.03%	
5	1	1.14%	0.78%	2.99%	2.99%	-0.37%		1.51%	
6	2	0.13%	0.95%	-0.71%	-0.22%	1.92%		0.41%	0.41%
7	3	-1.04%	-1.35%	-0.23%	-1.56%	0.16%		-0.80%	-0.39%
8	4	3.36%	0.09%	-0.56%	-1.47%	-0.72%		0.14%	-0.25%
9	5	2.22%	0.89%	-0.34%	1.70%	2.91%		1.47%	1.23%
10	6	-1.04%	-0.42%	0.38%	0.73%	0.15%		-0.04%	1.18%
11	7	-0.43%	0.78%	1.54%	2.84%	1.82%		1.31%	2.50%
12	8	1.98%	-5.91%	0.05%	-1.21%	0.55%		-0.91%	1.59%
13	9	-0.82%	0.76%	0.11%	0.28%	-0.43%		-0.02%	1.57%
14	10	-0.40%	-2.52%	-0.30%	-0.18%	-0.66%		-0.81%	0.76%
15	11	0.02%	1.32%	0.27%	-0.90%	0.11%		0.16%	0.92%
16	12	-3.07%	-0.56%	-0.09%	-0.35%	0.69%		-0.67%	0.25%
17	13	0.39%	2.19%	-0.08%	-0.26%	0.18%		0.48%	0.73%
18									
19									
20					=AVERAGE(O17:S17)			=V16+U17	
21									

If an investor buys the stock at the end of the day following the announcement (day = 1) then the cumulative abnormal returns (CARs) shown in the last column would be achieved. It appears from this analysis that the high performance for index additions occurs for approximately seven trading days after the announcement.

Questions and Problems

7.1 Describe the joint test problem in investigating a return anomaly.

7.2 Is there a small-firm return anomaly? Describe the evidence that supports your point of view.

7.3 What are the day-effect return anomalies? Can an investor profit from them?

7.4 What is the January effect?

7.5 One day there were two important pieces of news for a company. The first was an announcement that the company had made a bid to acquire a smaller rival. Also, macroeconomic news showed that inflation was picking up. The day of the two announcements, the firm's return was -0.55 percent, and the market's return was 0.48. The daily CAPM model coefficients for the firm are $\alpha = 0.05$ and $\beta = 0.8$. Using the market model and the market-adjusted model, determine the abnormal return for the firm and assess whether the acquisition was good or bad news for the firm.

7.6 Suppose Big Tech announces a bid to acquire another firm, Little Tech. The daily single-factor CAPM model coefficients for Big Tech are $\alpha = -0.05$ and $\beta = 0.7$, and for Little Tech they are $\alpha = 0.15$ and $\beta = 1.6$. The day's returns for Big Tech and Little Tech were -0.7 percent and 1.4 percent, respectively. The market return for the day was 0.6 percent. Using the market model, determine the abnormal return for Big Tech and Little Tech. Did investors like the acquisition announcement?

7.7 Assume Hewlett-Packard, Inc., surprised analysts by earning $0.45 per share for the quarter when the consensus estimate was only $0.35 per share. The returns for Intercontinental over the next three months were 1.1, 0.3, and -0.2 percent. The S&P 500 Index earned 0.8, -0.2, and -0.7 percent during the same months. Using the market-adjusted model, compute the monthly and total abnormal returns for HP. Is this an example of a return anomaly? If so, which one?

7.8 Three companies have announced stock splits. Stock A announced a 2-for-1 split. Stock B announced a 5-for-3 split. Stock C announced a 1-for-3 reverse split. If the stock prices of A, B, and C are $80, $75, and $10 per share, respectively, before the ex-split date, what are the expected stock prices on the ex-split date?

7.9 Consider the information given in Problem 7.8. If an investor owns 300 shares of each stock before the splits, how many shares are owned after the splits? Is there any change in the market value of the investor's holding simply due to the splits?

7.10 After the stock market close, Standard & Poor's announced that two companies would be deleted from the S&P 500 Index and two other companies would be added. What do you expect will happen to these stocks' prices tomorrow? Explain.

7.11 Go to the Standard & Poor's Web site at **www.mhhe.com/edumarketinsight** and locate the Index Changes tab in the "S&P 500 Index" section. Which companies were recently added and deleted to the index? When did the additions replace the deletions?

STANDARD &POOR'S

7.12 You can obtain monthly values of major stock indexes at Yahoo! Finance (**finance.yahoo.com**). Get the values and compute returns for the last 12 months for the S&P 500 (SPX) and the Russell 2000 (RUT). Have small stocks been outperforming large stocks, or vice versa?

7.13 Go to any financial or news Web site and locate a firm that recently announced its quarterly earnings. Did they meet expectations? What happened to the stock price?

7.14 An investor has discovered that after a stock is added to a particular index, it earns a return of 1.5 percent over the next few days. If it costs the investor $10 per trade and 0.5 percent in the bid-ask spread, how much money must be invested to make a profit on the trade?

7.15 An investor has $5,000 invested in a diversified mutual fund that emulates the S&P 500 Index return. A company the investor closely follows announced that earnings beat analysts' expectations. The investor believes that the company will earn an abnormal return of 2.0 percent over the next couple of days. It costs the investor $20 to move the money from the mutual fund to the stock and another $20 to get back into the fund. If the investor also loses 0.5 percent on the bid-ask spread of the stock, how much profit can the investor achieve by the short-term trade? Should the investor do it?

STANDARD &POOR'S

7.16 If additions to the S&P 500 Index earn positive abnormal returns, it might be a profitable strategy to determine which companies are likely to be added next and purchase them before the addition. The companies added to the S&P 500 Index are likely to be the largest companies on the S&P MidCap 400 Index. What are currently the largest firms on the S&P MidCap 400 Index? One place you can find this information is the Standard & Poor's Web site at **www.mhhe.com/edumarketinsight**.

eXcel

7.17 On February 24, Staples announced it would conduct a 3-for-2 stock split. The split would be effective on April 18. Some investors believe that a split announcement is good news and buy companies that split their stock. Using the company (split-adjusted) stock price and the S&P 500 Index value, compute the daily market-adjusted abnormal return for Staples. Was the announcement good news?

◇	A	B	C
1	Date	SPLS	S&P 500
2	18-Feb-05	20.73	1201.59
3	22-Feb-05	20.54	1184.16
4	23-Feb-05	20.94	1190.8
5	24-Feb-05	21.27	1200.2
6	25-Feb-05	21.13	1211.37
7	28-Feb-05	20.75	1203.6
8	1-Mar-05	20.84	1210.41
9	2-Mar-05	20.81	1210.08
10	3-Mar-05	20.68	1210.47
11	4-Mar-05	20.94	1222.12
12	7-Mar-05	21.17	1225.31
13	8-Mar-05	21.52	1219.43
14	9-Mar-05	21.51	1207.01
15	10-Mar-05	21.49	1209.25
16	11-Mar-05	21.17	1200.08
17	14-Mar-05	21.35	1206.83
18	15-Mar-05	21.15	1197.75
19	16-Mar-05	20.3	1188.07
20	17-Mar-05	19.63	1190.21
21	18-Mar-05	20.09	1189.65
22	21-Mar-05	20.02	1183.78
23	22-Mar-05	19.93	1171.71
24	23-Mar-05	20.75	1172.53
25	24-Mar-05	20.66	1171.42
26	28-Mar-05	20.63	1174.28

◇	A	B	C
27	29-Mar-05	20.69	1165.36
28	30-Mar-05	20.77	1181.41
29	31-Mar-05	20.95	1180.59
30	1-Apr-05	20.3	1172.92
31	4-Apr-05	21.07	1176.12
32	5-Apr-05	21.1	1181.39
33	6-Apr-05	21.1	1184.07
34	7-Apr-05	21.07	1191.14
35	8-Apr-05	20.57	1181.2
36	11-Apr-05	20.73	1181.21
37	12-Apr-05	20.79	1187.76
38	13-Apr-05	20.54	1173.79
39	14-Apr-05	20.44	1162.05
40	15-Apr-05	19.5	1142.62
41	18-Apr-05	19.57	1145.98
42	19-Apr-05	19.25	1152.78
43	20-Apr-05	18.64	1137.5
44	21-Apr-05	19.95	1159.95
45	22-Apr-05	19.49	1152.12
46	25-Apr-05	19.84	1162.1
47	26-Apr-05	19.5	1151.83
48	27-Apr-05	19.57	1156.38
49	28-Apr-05	19.07	1143.22
50	29-Apr-05	19.07	1156.85
51	2-May-05	19.16	1162.16
52	3-May-05	19.88	1161.17

eXcel

7.18 Given the results of Problem 7.17, compute the cumulative abnormal return for the following periods: (a) between the announcement and the effective date (inclusive), (b) from the day after the announcement for 10 days, (c) after the effective date.

CFA® PROBLEMS

7.19 A market anomaly refers to:
   a. An exogenous shock to the market that is sharp but not persistent
   b. A price or volume event that is inconsistent with historical price or volume trends
   c. A trading or pricing structure that interferes with efficient buying and selling of securities
   d. Price behavior that differs from the behavior predicted by the efficient market hypothesis

CFA® PROBLEMS

7.20 Which of the following statements *best* reflects the importance of the asset allocation decision to the investment process? The asset allocation decision:
   a. Helps the investor decide on realistic investment goals
   b. Identifies the specific securities to include in a portfolio
   c. Determines most of the portfolio's returns and volatility over time
   d. Creates a standard by which to establish an appropriate investment time horizon

investment application

The "Dogs of the Dow" Myth[5]

During August 1988, a fascinating article titled "Study of Industrial Averages Finds Stocks with High Dividends Are Big Winners" appeared in *The Wall Street Journal*.[6] In that article, analyst John Slatter, then of Prescott, Ball & Turben, Inc., in Cleveland, Ohio, proposed a simple and intuitively appealing investment approach. Later dubbed the "Dogs of the Dow" investment strategy, Slatter suggested that investors confine their stock market selections to the 10 top-yielding stocks found among the 30 industrial giants included within the Dow Jones Industrial Average (DJIA). According to Slatter, these "dogs" provide anything but doglike returns. He offered evidence that a portfolio of high-yielding Dow stocks outperforms the DJIA by an eye-popping 7.59 percent per year (see Table 7.5)!

Over the years, the Dogs approach has generated significant interest among both institutional and individual investors. The only calculation required is to compute the current dividend yield for all 30 DJIA components on the first trading day of the year. Then rank the 30 DJIA stocks in descending order by dividend yield, buy the top 10 yielding stocks, and maintain these holdings until the first trading day of the next year. At that point, this simple selection process is repeated. With an elementary dividend yield criterion, anyone can adopt the strategy. With only once-a-year rebalancing, transaction costs tied to brokerage commissions and capital gains taxes are kept at a minimum. Because membership on the list of high-yielding DJIA stocks tends to be stable, low portfolio turnover rates and modest transaction costs can be expected.

Given the promise of huge excess returns, and its appeal as a simple-to-execute "contrarian" investment philosophy, the wide and still-growing popularity of the Dogs strategy is easy to understand. A number of best-selling books extolling the virtues of the approach have also served to speed its acceptance, for example, Michael O'Higgins and John Downs' *Beating the Dow* (1991), Harvey C. Knowles III and Damon H. Petty's *The Dividend Investor* (1992), and, most important, David and Tom Gardner's *The Motley Fool Investment Guide* (1996). The Gardners have also been instrumental in extending the popularity of the Dow Dog strategy beyond the print media and into cyberspace. In 1991, Merrill Lynch launched the Defined Asset Funds: Select Ten Portfolio to buy Dogs and attracted more than *$10 billion* in assets.

Companies included within the DJIA are among the largest, most liquid, and most heavily analyzed on Wall Street. Moreover, the Dow Dog method is a very simple investment strategy that uses widely scrutinized public data. In short, the popular press suggests an *unbelievable* level of excess returns for the Dow Dog approach. How could the market be so inefficient?

A simple check of figures used in prior studies suggests that data errors, rather than market inefficiency, may provide at least a partial explanation for the perceived advantage of Dow Dogs. For example, Slatter shows a total return of 44.4 percent for the DJIA in 1974. This is plainly incorrect. The market did not go up in 1974; returns were negative as the market concluded a long and painful bear market. If numbers such as these are wrong, perhaps other, less easily checked numbers are incorrect as well. There is troubling inconsistency in published estimates of Dow Dog returns for *identical time periods*. For example, Slatter's 27.3 percent annual rate of return for 1979 contrasts sharply with 1979 returns of 12.37, 9.67, 12.99, and 8.24 percent reported elsewhere (see Table 7.6).[7] In 1987, Slatter's 17.3 percent conflicts with 0.61, 6.89, 6.97, and 9.09 percent reported in other studies. These are not small differences

[5] For a complete review of this study, see Mark Hirschey, "The 'Dogs of the Dow' Myth," *Financial Review*, vol. 35, no. 2 (May 2000), pp. 1–16.

[6] John R. Dorfman, "Study of Industrial Averages Finds Stocks with High Dividends Are Big Winners," *The Wall Street Journal*, August 11, 1988, p. 29.

[7] See John R. Dorfman, p. 29; Michael O'Higgins and John Downs, pp. 191–192, as updated in Andrew Barry, "Canny Canines," *Barron's*, December 13, 1993, p. 14, and Andrew Barry, "Faithful Friends," *Barron's*, December 26, 1994, p. 14; Harvey C. Knowles III and Damon H. Petty, p. 30; Merrill Lynch, *Defined Asset Funds: Select Ten Portfolio, 1999*, promotional material; and **www.dogsofthedow.com/dogyrs.htm**.

www.mhhe.com/hirschey1e

TABLE 7.5

Previously Estimated Annual Rates of Return for Equally Weighted Portfolios of "Dow Dogs" and the DJIA, 1961–1998 *Prior studies suggest above-market returns from an investment strategy that focuses on the 10 highest-yield components of the DJIA. However, data errors, rather than market inefficiency, may provide a partial explanation. Transaction costs, like brokerage commissions and bid-ask spreads, and higher tax consequences tied to the technique are more than enough to overcome any perceived advantage, especially during recent years.*

Year	Slatter 10 High-Yield	Slatter DJIA	O'Higgins & Downs (as updated in *Barron's*) 10 High-Yield	O'Higgins & Downs DJIA	Knowles & Pretty 10 High-Yield	Knowles & Pretty DJIA	Merrill Lynch 10 High-Yield	Merrill Lynch DJIA	The Motley Fool 10 High-Yield	The Motley Fool Dow 30
1961									26.91%	22.74%
1962									-0.14%	-7.37
1963									19.57	23.03
1964									20.28	19.64
1965									18.26	17.32
1966									-13.92	-15.10
1967									25.81	21.95
1968									14.47	10.04
1969									-14.41	-8.91
1970									2.01	4.82
1971									6.20	9.01
1972	3.30%	-14.40%			23.85%	18.10%	23.26%	18.21%	23.90	16.72
1973	-2.90	-23.40	3.94%	-13.12%	3.88	-13.40	-4.08	-13.12	3.89	-10.86
1974	58.90	44.40	-1.28	-23.14	1.02	-23.40	-2.40	-23.14	1.04	-15.68
1975	35.60	22.30	55.87	44.40	53.23	44.40	55.65	44.40	50.99	44.24
1976	1.10	-13.20	34.81	22.72	33.21	22.30	33.25	22.72	33.24	29.20
1977	3.30	2.40	0.93	-12.71	-1.03	-13.20	-2.90	-12.71	1.17	12.41
1978	12.70	10.20	-0.13	2.69	2.40	2.40	-1.91	2.69	2.55	2.52
1979	27.30	21.00	12.37	10.52	9.67	10.20	10.48	10.52	8.24	11.34
1980	6.30	-3.60	27.23	21.41	27.53	21.00	24.69	21.41	31.23	25.31
1981	24.50	26.00	5.02	-3.40	2.68	-3.60	5.51	-3.40	4.25	-3.26
1982	41.10	25.50	23.58	25.79	20.68	26.00	23.79	25.79	20.85	19.59
1983	9.00	9.00	38.73	25.65	39.22	25.50	36.93	25.68	39.22	35.63
1984	23.30	27.80	7.64	1.08	6.27	0.71	5.41	1.06	6.36	0.51
1985	27.20	26.60	29.48	32.78	31.20	31.14	27.00	32.78	30.50	29.77
1986	6.30	5.80	32.08	26.92	28.12	26.60	32.96	26.91	26.20	21.69
1987	17.30	6.40	0.61	6.02	6.89	5.80	5.06	6.02	9.09	11.96
1988			26.14	15.95	18.22	15.55	22.44	15.95	17.96	14.64
1989			26.53	31.71	27.37	30.75	25.65	31.71	29.68	31.97
1990			-7.58	-0.40	-10.01	-3.36	-10.14	-0.57	-10.01	-9.17
1991			34.25	23.91			31.81	23.93	43.95	31.48
1992			7.86	7.44			6.44	7.34	6.24	10.96
1993			27.30	16.80			25.30	16.72	23.68	17.96
1994			4.10	4.90			1.95	4.95	2.43	3.73
1995			36.50	36.40			34.97	36.48	37.16	36.66
1996			27.90	28.60			26.34	28.57	27.47	24.33
1997			21.90	24.90			19.92	24.78	20.39	22.32
1998			10.70	17.75			8.55	18.00	11.66	13.51
Average	**18.39%**	**10.80%**	**18.71%**	**14.45%**	**17.07%**	**11.76%**	**17.26%**	**14.58%**	**16.01%**	**13.21%**
Standard deviation	**16.92%**	**18.36%**	**15.91%**	**16.67%**	**16.41%**	**18.06%**	**15.98%**	**16.38%**	**15.63%**	**15.67%**

The Motley Fool compares Dow Dog performance with returns for an equally weighted portfolio of DJIA stocks (the "Dow 30" portfolio).

Source: Mark Hirschey, "The 'Dogs of the Dow' Myth," *Financial Review*, vol. 35, no. 2 (May 2000): p. 1–16. Copyright © 2000 Blackwell Publishers.

TABLE 7.6

Total Returns for the DJIA and "Dow Dog" Portfolios, 1961–1998 *One cannot outperform a simple buy-and-hold strategy by focusing on high-yield stocks included within the DJIA. Much of the false impression of market outperformance by Dow Dogs is created by prior mistakes in rate-of-return calculations and by the common failure to accurately reflect transaction costs and taxes.*

Year	DJIA Total Return (from *Barron's*)	"Dow Dogs" Total Return	DD Advantage before Transaction Costs		
			Annual	5-Year Periods	10-Year Periods
1961	21.82%	26.06	4.24		
1962	-7.24	-2.48	4.76		
1963	20.07	19.03	-1.04		
1964	18.14	19.23	1.09		
1965	13.83	16.64	2.81		
1966	-14.88	-14.22	0.66		
1967	18.53	24.22	5.69		
1968	7.59	13.78	6.19	3.26%	
1969	-10.95	-15.92	-4.97		
1970	8.58	0.57	-8.01		
1971	9.58	4.88	-4.70		
1972	17.74	22.70	4.96		
1973	-12.43	0.32	12.75	-0.28	
1974	-21.45	-2.95	18.50		
1975	42.71	47.28	4.57		
1976	21.98	32.97	10.99		
1977	-11.76	0.97	12.73		
1978	2.88	1.15	-1.73	8.79	4.15%
1979	10.27	6.40	-3.87		
1980	20.57	28.41	7.84		
1981	-2.81	2.21	5.02		
1982	24.77	17.66	-7.11		
1983	24.74	37.97	13.23	2.75	
1984	1.26	4.85	3.59		
1985	31.67	27.72	-3.95		
1986	26.12	24.73	-1.39		
1987	5.93	7.45	1.52		
1988	15.52	17.71	2.19	0.36	1.54
1989	30.70	27.62	-3.08		
1990	-0.40	-12.95	-12.55		
1991	23.32	34.34	11.02		
1992	7.22	2.94	-4.28		
1993	16.37	22.80	6.43	-0.84	
1994	4.89	0.73	-4.16		
1995	35.75	35.17	-0.58		
1996	28.04	27.25	-0.79		
1997	24.36	19.80	-4.56		
1998	17.75	10.97	-6.78	-3.40	-2.13
Arithmetic average	**12.39%**	**14.16%**	**1.77%**		
Geometric mean	**11.35%**	**13.13%**	**1.55%**		
Standard deviation	**15.10%**	**15.33%**	**6.87%**		

Source: Mark Hirschey, "The 'Dogs of the Dow' Myth," *Financial Review*, vol. 35, no. 2 (May 2000): p. 1–16. Copyright © 2000 Blackwell Publishers.

www.mhhe.com/hirschey1e

in a market that averages 10.27 percent (1979) and 5.93 percent (1987), as measured by *Barron's* estimate of the annual rate of return for the DJIA (see Table 7.6). It is troubling when estimated returns for such an easily implemented strategy deviate wildly.[8]

Results from prior studies are also suspect because they fail to reflect transaction costs. The Dow Dog strategy involves picking stocks with higher-than-typical dividend yields, by definition. Like any high-yield approach, the method will necessarily involve higher-than-average income taxes on dividends, and therefore higher taxes on total realized returns. Such a high-yield approach will also involve annual portfolio rebalancing and brokerage commissions, bid-ask spread costs, and capital gains taxes that could be avoided if a simple buy-and-hold investment strategy were used.

To conduct a fair test of the Dow Dog investment strategy, individual stocks were "purchased" without commissions on the first trading day of the year—January 2, 3, or 4—and formed into portfolios of 10 stocks each. The high-yield portfolio consists of the 10 highest-yielding DJIA stocks. Dividends paid throughout the year, including extra or special dividends, are added to the year-end price, and then this total is divided by the initial price to calculate total returns as $R_{it} = [(P_{t+1} + D_t)/P_t] - 1]$. Stock dividends increase the number of shares sold at the end of the year. Spin-offs are recorded as if held from the time they were issued until the end of the year. Spun-off stocks are treated as if sold on the first trading day of the following year.

For the 38-year 1961–1998 time frame, Table 7.6 shows arithmetic and geometric total returns for the DJIA, as reported in *Barron's*,[9] and for the Dow Dog portfolios. Before transactions costs, the geometric mean return for the Dow Dogs is 13.13 percent, or only 1.55 percent per year greater than the 11.35 percent annual return on the DJIA.[10] Notice that this very modest 1.55 percent excess return, calculated before taxes and transaction costs, is sharply lower than the Dow Dog return premium suggested in earlier studies (see Table 7.5). Much of the popularly perceived premium to Dow Dog investing appears to be due to data coding errors and to the bias of arithmetic averages.

For the moment, consider the possibilities facing tax-efficient and transaction cost-efficient institutional investors. A potential annual excess return of 1.55 percent could make the Dow Dog investment strategy worth pursuing if such advantages were stable and predictable. Unfortunately, they are not. As shown in Table 7.6, Dow Dogs outperformed the DJIA portfolio in only 21 of 38 years during the 1961–1998 period. Dow Dogs outperformed the DJIA during only three of seven 5-year periods and exhibited an edge during two of three 10-year periods. This return pattern is typical of equally performing comparison portfolios. Interestingly, positive above-average returns for the Dow Dog strategy seem to be a thing of the past. During the most recent decade, for example, a total return penalty of 2.13 percent to Dow Dog investing was operative.

    a. A fair test of the Dow Dog strategy would consider both transaction costs and tax penalties tied to its implementation. Could such expenses explain the perceived advantage of Dow Dog investing?

    b. It is conceivable that the high-yield characteristic of Dow Dog stocks might make such an investment strategy perceptibly less risky than the DJIA portfolio. Use the evidence in Table 7.6 and simple logic to support or refute this assertion.

---

[8] Grant McQueen and Steven Thorley, "Mining Fool's Gold," *Financial Analysts Journal*, vol. 55, no. 2 (March-April 1999), pp. 61–72, discuss similar data errors in the "Foolish Four" investment strategy, which is based on a subset of the highest-yielding stocks in the DJIA.

[9] See *Barron's*, January 2, 1995, MW 95, plus updates from recent issues.

[10] Here the geometric mean of the difference between Dow Dog returns and the DJIA is 1.55 percent per year, whereas the simple difference between the geometric mean returns for the Dow Dogs and the DJIA is 1.78 percent per year. Because of compounding, the geometric mean of the differences is less than the difference of the geometric means.

8 chapter

Psychology and the Stock Market

Why do sensible and generally rational people sometimes make foolish and irrational decisions when it comes to investing? That question not only perplexes researchers in financial economics; it has baffled social commentators for centuries. For example, in 1634–1636, near the height of the "tulip mania" in Holland, the market price for a single tulip bulb approached $35,000 in present-day dollars. Then the bubble burst and tulip prices quickly plunged to less than the present-day equivalent of $1 each. Today, it is safe to characterize a $35,000 tulip price as "crazy." Not only is there 350 years of historical proof in the form of tulips selling for less than $1 each, but no living persons have any financial or emotional capital invested in the notion that it is wise to pay $35,000 for a single tulip bulb.

While it is now safe to characterize the behavior of anonymous investors as "crazy" during the Dutch tulip mania, look at the extreme prices paid for computer ("tronics") stocks in the 1960s, "nifty fifty" companies in the 1970s, U.S. oil companies and Japanese stocks during the 1980s, and Nasdaq tech stocks during the late 1990s. Prices for commodities such as gold, silver, corn, and oil have also skyrocketed during recent years, only to collapse back toward long-term norms. In retrospect, investment analysts have come to characterize such prices as more than simply very, very high—they look "crazy." Irrational bubblelike prices are not confined to tulips and the 17th century in Holland. Just ask Internet stock investors to relate their experience if you want a 20th-century perspective on bubbles.

This chapter shows how psychological influences can help explain market behavior when investor perceptions influence markets and how the market action influences participant perceptions. Concepts from the field of psychology can be useful in describing the traps that often ensnarl investors and can help investors make more reasonable investment decisions.[1]

---

[1] See Michael T. Darda, "Beyond the Bubble," *The Wall Street Journal Online*, December 1, 2005 (**http://online.wsj.com**).

CHAPTER OBJECTIVES

- Find out about the new field of behavioral finance.

- Understand how mental shortcuts impact investment decisions.

- Avoid the gambler's fallacy.

- Learn the social and emotional influences on investment behavior.

- Use rules of thumb to improve investment decisions.

Behavioral Finance

New Perspective

For more than 50 years, the field of finance has largely focused on the development and testing of sophisticated asset pricing models, like the capital asset pricing model, the Black-Scholes option price model, and so on. Such theories are based on the premise that investors behave rationally and that stock and bond markets are perfectly efficient. Because people value wealth, the presumption is that investors act carefully and objectively when making financial decisions. At the same time financial economists were assuming that people behaved rationally when making financial decisions, researchers in psychology were discovering that people often behave in odd ways when money is involved. Psychologists have found that economic decisions are often made in a seemingly irrational manner. Cognitive errors and extreme emotions can cause investors to make bad investment decisions. Over the past decade, the field of **behavioral finance** has evolved to consider how personal and social psychology influence financial decisions and the behavior of financial markets.

Behavioral finance
A study of cognitive errors and emotions in financial decisions.

Early proponents of behavioral finance are considered by some to be visionaries. For them, the awarding of the 2002 Nobel Prize in economics to psychologist Daniel Kahneman and experimental economist Vernon Smith vindicated the field. That was the first time that a psychologist won the top scientific award in economics. Now, mainstream financial economists realize that investors can behave irrationally. The thinking process does not work like a computer. Instead, the human brain often processes information using shortcuts and emotional filters. Sometimes people make investment decisions as if they were looking through rose-colored glasses. At other times, everything looks gloomy. This chapter describes a variety of **psychological biases** that savvy investors must learn to avoid.

Psychological biases
Predictable tendencies caused by cognitive errors.

Cognitive Errors

Information is critically important in the investment world. Because investors must be forward-looking in their analysis, investment choices usually need to be made on the basis of information that is incomplete, at best, and may even be biased and inaccurate. A common mistake made by investors is to overestimate the precision of their understanding. Not only do people make mistakes, but they make predictable mistakes.

For example, consider the 10 questions from history, science, art, and popular culture shown in Table 8.1. These questions were picked because few people would know every answer. However, to complete this quiz correctly, you do not need to know each correct answer. Instead, simply specify a range so that you are 90 percent certain that the correct answer lies

TABLE 8.1	Ten Questions From History, Science, Art, And Popular Culture *Enter the range (minimum and maximum) that you are 90 percent certain the answer lies within.*		

	Min	Max
1. How long (in miles) is the Grand Canyon?		
2. In what year did Michelangelo finish painting the ceiling of the Sistine Chapel?		
3. How many countries were members of the United Nations in 2004?		
4. How many species of spiders have been identified in the world?		
5. How many hair follicles are on an average adult human?		
6. In what year was the Great Pyramid of Giza built?		
7. How many new copyrights were registered at the U.S. Copyright Office in 2003?		
8. How many planets the size of the Earth would fit into the sun?		
9. On average, how many magnitude 3.0 and higher earthquakes are located worldwide annually by the U.S. Geological Survey?		
10. What was the 2000 census estimate for the U.S. population?		

between your low estimate and your high estimate. Do not make your range so wide that it is guaranteed to be right, but also do not make your range too narrow. Try to choose ranges so that you expect to get 9 of the 10 questions correct. Take the quiz now.

Given the diverse nature of the questions asked, many people will have no idea about some of the correct answers. If that is the case, then the specified range for such questions should be broad. When it is possible to make a good, educated guess, the specified range can be quite narrow. Here are the answers: (1) 277 miles, (2) 1512, (3) 191 countries, (4) 38,432 species, (5) 5 million hairs, (6) 2560 BC, (7) 514,121, (8) 1.3 million, (9) 14,000 earthquakes per year, and (10) 280 million people. Count your response correct if the right answer lies between your low and high guesses. Did you get 9 out of 10 correct?

Most people miss five or more questions on such a quiz. The reason that people miss so many questions is that they are overconfident in their own level of knowledge, even when they have very little information or knowledge about a topic. Intelligence and education do not influence this cognitive bias. Many finance professors will also miss at least five of the questions shown in Table 8.1! Seldom does anyone answer 9 out of 10 correctly. Interestingly, most wrong answers are predictably wrong. In many instances, the numbers given as an upper bound are not high enough. People tend to underestimate extreme values.

Now that you see the problem, try one more question. This one is about investing:

On October 1, 1928, the "modern era" began for the Dow Jones Industrial Average (DJIA) when the component list was expanded from 20 to 30 stocks and several substitutions were made. A divisor was also introduced to adjust for the effect of stock splits, stock distributions, and stock substitutions. In 1929, the year began with the DJIA at 300. At the end of 2005, the DJIA was at 10,717.5. The DJIA is a price-weighted average. Dividends are omitted from the index. What would the DJIA be at the end of 2005 *if dividends were reinvested each year?*

Notice that Table 8.1 has room at the bottom for your DJIA minimum-maximum range. Again, you should be 90 percent sure that the correct value lies within the range you choose. Write down your range.

Because you are 90 percent sure that the correct value lies within the range that you have chosen, you should get this one correct. If dividends were reinvested in the DJIA, the average would have been 262,846 at the end of 2005![2] Is this a surprise? For many it is. Even after learning that most people set their confidence ranges too narrowly, and experiencing the problem firsthand, most people continue to do so.

This example also illustrates another aspect of investor psychology called **anchoring**. When you read the question regarding the DJIA, there is a tendency to focus on the DJIA price level of 10,717.5. That is, readers tend to anchor their thinking to 10,717.5. Most make their guess regarding a level for the DJIA with dividends reinvested by starting at the 10,717.5 anchor and then trying to add an appropriate amount to compensate for dividends. Similarly, when trying to value individual common stocks, investors often make mistakes by incorrectly anchoring on past stock prices.

Anchoring
A strong mental attachment to a particular price.

Prospect Theory

The traditional view of human behavior assumes that people are always "rational" when it comes to financial decisions. This **normative** approach tells how people should behave in order to maximize their wealth. This useful perspective has provided the tools necessary to develop portfolio theory, the capital asset pricing model, arbitrage theory, and option pricing theory. In contrast to this traditional perspective, the emphasis of behavioral finance is on the **positive** description of human behavior. It studies how people actually behave in a financial setting.

Normative
A description of what people should do.

Positive
A description of what people actually do.

In the evaluation of decision making, Kahneman and Amos Tversky illustrate through a series of experiments how investor behavior tends to differ from the prescriptions of traditional normative theories. For example, would you rather have $5, or a gamble with a 0.1 percent chance to win $5,000 and a 99.9 percent chance to win $0? The expected value of the gamble is $5 (= 0.001 × $5,000), which is also the value of the sure thing. The normative approach tells us that people are risk-averse. With a choice between two alternatives with equal expected value, people should pick the riskless one—the $5. Yet Kahneman and Tversky found that 72 percent of the people in their experiment picked the gamble and thus preferred the more risky alternative.[3] Actually, people frequently exhibit this behavior by buying lottery tickets and playing slot machines in casinos. Interestingly, people behaved differently when Kahneman and Tversky's gamble was described differently: Would you either *pay* $5 or face a gamble with a 0.1 percent chance of paying $5,000? In this case, 82 percent of the people wanted to pay the $5 instead of facing the game. In this case, people preferred the less risky option. Such behavior is typical when people pay their car insurance premiums.

Prospect theory
A positive description of how people frame and value a decision involving uncertainty.

Kahneman and Tversky describe how people make decisions through **prospect theory**, the most developed theory in behavioral finance. Prospect theory describes the way people often frame and value decisions involving financial uncertainty. In many situations, investors tend to frame investment choices in terms of potential gains and losses relative to specific reference points. Although investors may anchor on various reference points, the investor's original purchase price appears to be one of the most important anchor points. Investors often value the gains and losses according to an S-shaped function, as shown in Figure 8.1.

Notice several things about the value function in Figure 8.1. First, the function is concave to the origin for gains. Investors feel better (i.e., have higher utility) when they make a $1,000 gain. The level of utility, or personal satisfaction level, is denoted as X in the figure. Investors feel better when they make a $2,000 gain, measured as Y. However, Y is not twice the level of X even though $2,000 is twice as much as $1,000. In other words, a doubling in

---

[2] During the 1929–2005 period, the 11.0 percent average total return per year on the DJIA was comprised of 6.7 percent in capital gains and 4.3 percent in dividend income. Notice that $262,846 = 10,717.5 \times (1.043)^{76}$.

[3] Technically speaking, the subjects in Kahneman and Tversky's experiment displayed risk-neutral behavior because they preferred a risky expected return of $5 rather than a certain sum of $5.

| FIGURE 8.1 | Investor Appreciation and Pain Tied to Gains and Losses |

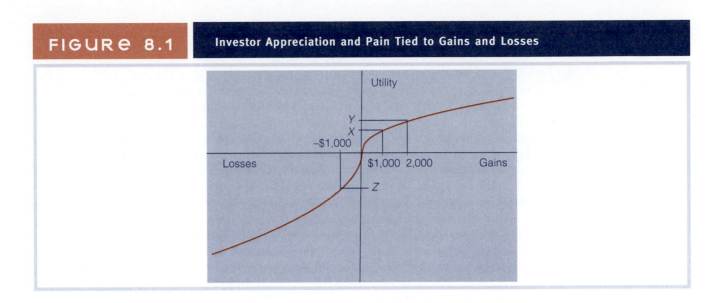

wealth does not typically lead to a doubling in investor well-being. Also notice that the function depicted in Figure 8.1 is convex to the origin when the investor takes a loss. This means that investors feel bad when they realize an investment loss, but twice as large a monetary loss does not make the typical investor feel twice as bad. Finally, notice that the utility-of-wealth function is steeper for investment losses than for investment gains. The asymmetry that exists between gains and losses leads to different investor reactions when dealing with winning and losing positions. The magnitude of the reduction in investor well-being tied to a $1,000 loss, measured at Z, is larger than the magnitude of the well-being attached to gaining $1,000. This makes many investors especially averse to taking investment losses. As a result, investors sometimes hold on to losing positions because recovering a loss is "worth more" in terms of investor utility than making a similar gain in another security. Unfortunately, when investors are especially averse to taking investment losses, they can hold on to losing positions for too long. Peter Lynch, one of the most successful mutual fund managers of all time, says that selling stock market winners and holding onto losers is like "watering the weeds." A skillful gardener prunes the weeds so that plants and flowers can flourish. Similarly, a skillful investor minimizes investment mistakes so that on-target selections can grow and flourish.

Because behavioral finance is a relatively new field, it has not yet produced an integrated theory or model of investor behavior. Much of what is known in behavioral finance comes from attributing investor behavior to the mental resource limitations and human emotions studied by psychologists. The rest of this chapter discusses some of the problems caused by mental limitations, the tendency to deceive ourselves to make us feel better, and the role of emotions in the investment decision-making process. Successful investors avoid these biases.

Mental Shortcuts

Familiarity Bias

The human brain uses shortcuts to reduce the complexity of analyzing information. This **heuristic simplification** allows the brain to generate an estimate of the best course of action to be followed in an uncertain situation. Even when access to adequate information is available, decisions often must be made before one has the opportunity to fully digest all relevant information. Mental shortcuts allow the brain to organize and quickly process large amounts

Heuristic simplification
Mental shortcuts used by the brain to make quicker decisions and choices with uncertain outcomes.

of information. Investors constantly rely on these shortcuts to make investment decisions. However, these shortcuts sometimes make it hard for investors to correctly analyze new information and can lead to bad investment decisions.

Consider the fact that there are literally tens of thousands of stocks available for investors to purchase. However, most people do not have the cognitive resources to analyze such a large number of firms. Instead of trying to gather and analyze information on hundreds of companies, most investors tend to stick with companies making familiar products. People prefer familiar companies because they require less learning and involve lower search costs. When investors have a relatively high comfort level with familiar stocks, they sometimes believe that such investments have lower risks and higher expected returns than warranted. In short, a **familiarity bias** can lead investors to wrongly believe that familiar companies tend to represent better investments than less familiar companies.

Familiarity bias
A mental shortcut that treats familiar things as better than less familiar things.

For example, several decades ago, the American Telephone and Telegraph Company dominated the local and long-distance telecommunications business in the United States. As a means for settling costly antitrust litigation brought by the federal government, AT&T divested the local-phone-service parts of the business on January 1, 1984. The Regional Bell Operating Companies (RBOCs), or "Baby Bells," were created when AT&T shareholders received shares of stock in the "new" AT&T, which retained the long-distance part of the business, and each of seven RBOCs.[4] At the time of the spin-off, a rational investor might be expected to carefully analyze the future business prospects of AT&T and each RBOC before deciding which, if any, should be retained for long-term capital appreciation and dividend income. Instead, studies show that in the 12 years following the breakup of AT&T most investors simply retained shares of stock in the RBOC with local-phone-service operations in the investor's own local-service area. Even better-managed RBOCs operating in more dynamically growing areas were sold, while shares in the local phone company were retained. The behavior of investors following the breakup of AT&T gives evidence of how familiarity bias can hurt investment returns. Investment returns for many investors were obviously hurt by staying with the familiar local phone company rather than fully investigating opportunities for local phone companies in other areas.

Another example of familiarity bias is provided by the fact that many investors hold a disproportionately large amount of their investment portfolios in the stock of their employer. On the one hand, employee stock ownership plans (ESOPs) make good sense. When employees have a significant ownership interest in the publicly traded stock of their employer, employees have a real financial incentive to work productively on behalf of shareholders. Indeed, a key aspect of enlightened corporate governance is to ensure that top-management compensation is closely tied to company stock price performance. Such incentive compensation plans give management and other employees the incentives necessary to ensure that they will all strive to maximize the market value of the firm and shareholder wealth. On the other hand, while employee stock ownership can provide beneficial incentives for productive efficiency, employees can face a dire diversification problem when a disproportionate share of their total wealth is tied up in the publicly traded stock of their employer. Imagine investing in an employer that is generally considered among the best in the industry, with frequent press coverage and widely heralded top management. Employees of Microsoft, Intel, General Electric, and other industry stalwarts have profited mightily as the value of company stock in their 401(k) plans has soared. Conversely, bankruptcies by former telecommunications kingpin Worldcom, energy goliath Enron, or retailing giant Kmart resulted in massive layoffs and devastating losses for employee stock ownership plans. When Enron imploded, for example, many employees not only lost their jobs but also saw the value of their retirement assets wiped out.

---

[4] Today, only four of the original seven RBOCs remain independent companies: BellSouth Corporation, Qwest Communications International, the "new" AT&T (formerly SBC Corporation), and Verizon Communications, Inc. In 1996, the "old" AT&T divested its equipment manufacturing business into Lucent Technologies, Inc.

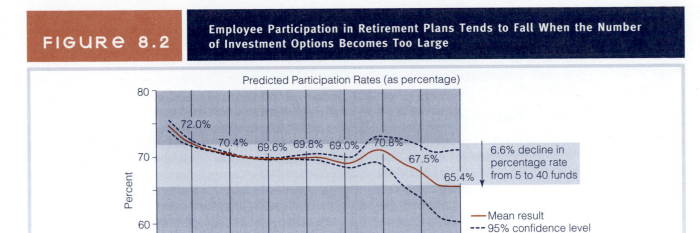

FIGURE 8.2   Employee Participation in Retirement Plans Tends to Fall When the Number of Investment Options Becomes Too Large

Source: "Can There Be Too Much Choice in a Retirement Savings Plan?" The Vanguard Center for Retirement Research, June 2003 (**https://institutional5.vanguard.com**). Also see Sheena S. Iyengar, Wei Jiang, and Gur Huberman, "How Much Choice Is Too Much? Determinants of Individual Contributions in 401(k) Retirement Plans," working paper presented at the Wharton Pension Research Council (April 2003).

In many large companies, it is common for roughly 10 to 15 percent of retirement plan assets to be invested in the employer's common stock. Many employees put 50 percent and more of their retirement assets in company stock. In many cases, these shares are awarded to employees as part of a profit-sharing plan and cannot be sold by the employee for a specified period of time. Employers like high employee stock ownership because they feel it makes for more highly motivated workers. Many employees also like investing in their employer's publicly traded common stock because the company is familiar to them. However, both employers and employees must keep firmly in mind the fact that a lack of proper diversification in employee retirement portfolios can become highly counterproductive. That's why most retirement plans offer employees a range of investment options, including broadly diversified common stock and fixed-income portfolios. Both employers and employees must be aware of the fact that familiarity bias can lead employees to wrongly underestimate the risk involved with undue concentration of retirement plan assets in the employer's common stock.

Familiarity bias explains why many investors resist the call for international diversification. The domestic capital market is typically more familiar than foreign markets. Familiarity bias also explains support for what is called the **choice overload hypothesis**. Researchers in behavioral finance have found that the probability that an employee will join an employer-sponsored retirement plan decreases as the number of investment options increases. The Vanguard Group of Investment Companies, a major force in the mutual fund industry, has found that as the number of investment options increases from 5 to 40 mutual funds, the predicted employee participation rate tends to decrease by roughly 6.6 percent, on average (see Figure 8.2). Aware of this problem, many leading employer-sponsored retirement plans have moved to restrict the number of investment options to a manageable number, say, 5 to 10 maximum.

However, when only a few investment options are available, investors tend to make choices governed by the **1/n heuristic**. That is, they invest equal portions in each of the alternatives. When 401(k) retirement plans were first introduced, many offered one safe,

Choice overload hypothesis
Theory that excessive options can limit participation because decision makers generally prefer a manageable number of decision alternatives.

1/n heuristic
Employees contribute equal amounts into each investment option offered in a pension plan.

money market-type instrument, one bond fund, and one stock fund. The most common contribution allocation was one-third of the contribution to each of these. The choice overload hypothesis and the $1/n$ heuristic show that when employees are uncertain of what to do with their retirement plan contributions, they tend to either do nothing or do a little of everything.

Representativeness Bias

Another bias that impacts an investor's perception of risk and return is representativeness bias. Representativeness bias is a bias of stereotypes. With representativeness bias, the characteristics of something that we know are projected onto something that we do not know. For example, consider the following description of Advanced Micro Devices, Inc.:

> Advanced Micro Devices, Inc., incorporated in 1969, is a semiconductor manufacturer with manufacturing facilities in the United States, Europe, and Asia and sales offices throughout the world. The company designs, manufactures, and markets digital integrated circuits that are used in desktop and mobile personal computers, workstations, servers, communications equipment, and automotive and consumer electronics. Intel Corp. is a major competitor.

If asked, "Which is more likely?" how would you respond: (1) is AMD a high-tech company or (2) is AMD a successful high-tech company like Intel? Many people would answer (2) because it seems to represent our mental image of high-tech companies. However, notice that (2) is a subset of (1). Only a subset of all high-tech companies is financially successful. Since (2) is a subset of (1), it cannot be more likely. Being a high-tech company is more likely than being a successful high-tech company.

Representativeness bias can lead consumers to wrongly infer that a generic box of tissues is just as good as Kleenex or that a mundane sports car is just as good as a BMW. Representativeness bias can lead investors to wrongly believe that an ordinary mutual fund manager is just as good as Legg Mason's superstar Bill Miller or that a run-of-the-mill stock picker is just as wise as Warren Buffett. Representativeness bias can also cause investors to wrongly infer that good employers or companies that produce high-quality products are also good investments. Good companies produce products that customers crave, have solid management, and enjoy steady growth in revenues, earnings, and cash flows. However, such characteristics may be fully recognized by investors and already be reflected in high share prices. As a result, good businesses sometimes represent mundane investment opportunities. On the other hand, mundane businesses with share prices that have been unfairly punished by emotional investors can represent investment bargains. When evaluating investment opportunities, investors must focus on risk and future expected return. Past investment success is not often a good indication of future prospects. A simpleminded extrapolation of past success or failure is seldom sufficient for evaluating investment opportunities.

Evidence of representativeness bias can be found by looking at the asset allocation decisions of retirement plan participants (see Figure 8.3). During the sharp market correction from 2000 to 2002, the percentage of retirement plan assets devoted to equity investments declined from 77 percent (in 2000) to 64 percent (in 2002). This is understandable. During bear markets, the value of stocks goes down. What is intriguing about the information in Figure 8.3 is that the percentage of retirement plan contributions devoted to equities also declined, from 78 percent (in 2000) to 71 percent (in 2002) during this period. After a sharp market correction, investors got scared and began to favor bonds rather than stocks for their retirement plan contributions. Backward-looking investors continued to fear an unrelenting market correction and cut their percentage of retirement plan contributions devoted to equities to 67 percent in 2003. It was not until the strong stock market return of nearly 29 percent in 2003 that people were convinced to start contributing more to equities again (71 percent) in 2004. Instead of cutting back equity exposure after a severe bear market, less emotional investors would have been increasing their equity exposure. After all, an important part of any plan for investment success is to buy *low*.

The time to sell stocks is before, not after, a severe market correction. Rational investors focus on future expected returns. Historical returns often provide useful insight concerning the

FIGURE 8.8

Representativeness Bias Caused Retirement Plan Investors to Cut Back on Equity Investments during the Postbubble Correction

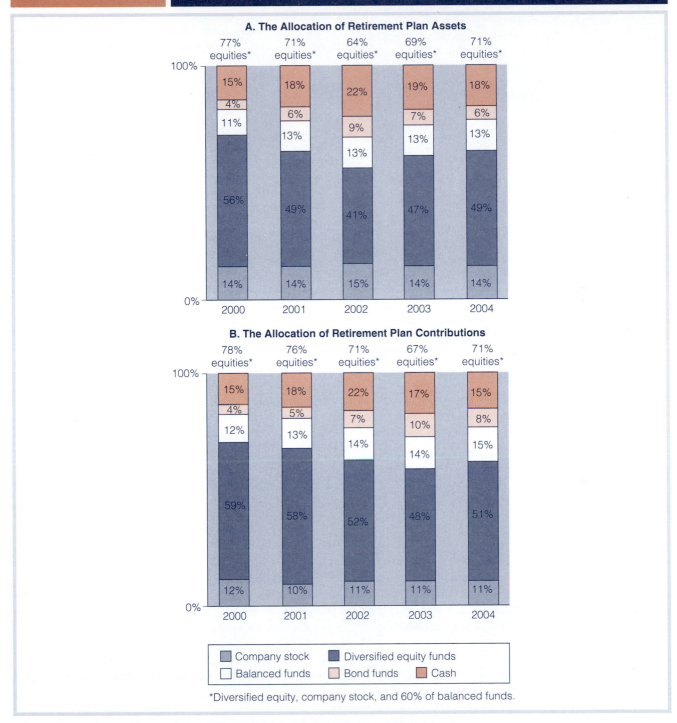

A. The Allocation of Retirement Plan Assets

	77% equities*	71% equities*	64% equities*	69% equities*	71% equities*
Cash	15%	18%	22%	19%	18%
Bond funds	4%	6%	9%	7%	6%
Balanced funds	11%	13%	13%	13%	13%
Diversified equity funds	56%	49%	41%	47%	49%
Company stock	14%	14%	15%	14%	14%
	2000	2001	2002	2003	2004

B. The Allocation of Retirement Plan Contributions

	78% equities*	76% equities*	71% equities*	67% equities*	71% equities*
Cash	15%	18%	22%	17%	15%
Bond funds	4%	5%	7%	10%	8%
Balanced funds	12%	13%	14%	14%	15%
Diversified equity funds	59%	58%	52%	48%	51%
Company stock	12%	10%	11%	11%	11%
	2000	2001	2002	2003	2004

Legend: Company stock ■ | Diversified equity funds ■ | Balanced funds ☐ | Bond funds ■ | Cash ■

*Diversified equity, company stock, and 60% of balanced funds.

Source: The Vanguard Group, "How America Saves, 2005," (**https://institutional5.vanguard.com**).

future, but no rational investor assumes the future will be a simpleminded extrapolation of the past. Nevertheless, many investors blindly maintain a **status quo** bias. When investors lack the courage to act, they often procrastinate and do nothing. Rather than being a sign of strength, such procrastination is a sign of weakness, like paralyzing fear. Times change, and successful investors change with the times.

Status quo
The tendency to do nothing.

The Psychology of Pension Investing

Defined-contribution pension plans, such as 401(k)s, are popular with employees because they are portable from one employer to another. They are also popular with employers because they eliminate the possibility of unfunded pension liabilities. In defined-contribution pension plans, employees and employers contribute to a separate account for each employee. The amount of retirement assets generated depends on the investment performance of each employee's account over time.

A crucial determinant of investment performance for pension plans is the amount devoted to stocks versus bonds. Over long retirement investment planning horizons, pension plans that focus on stocks as opposed to bonds tend to do best. This is especially true for younger investors, who have a significant period of time for plan assets to accumulate. Unfortunately, most employees have no formal training in finance and little investing experience. When people have modest knowledge or experience about a subject, they tend to fall back on psychological biases to help them make decisions.

The naïve approach is to simply split the pension plan allocation among the options given. Suppose an employer has three investment options: a money market account, a bond fund, and a stock fund. Naïve investors will use the 1/*n* approach and allocate one-third of their contribution to the money market fund, one-third to bonds, and one-third to stocks. This results in an asset allocation of 33 percent in stocks for a typical employee. Another employer may offer an additional two stock funds, one specializing in small companies and the other in technology firms. With five investment alternatives, the 1/*n* approach would put 20 percent of the pension plan contribution into each option. Since there are three stock options, the typical employee ends up with a 60 percent allocation in stocks.

The upshot is simple: Bad retirement planning can occur when employees make different asset allocations in their retirement plans simply because of differences in the number of investment options offered by their employer's pension plan.

See Ellen E. Schultz and Theo Francis, "How Safe Is Your Pension?" *The Wall Street Journal*, January 12, 2006, p. D1.

Gambler's Fallacy and Mental Accounting

Gambler's Fallacy

The human brain is very good at detecting patterns and using such information to make appropriate decisions. Much of what people do is based on prior experience. In everyday life, savvy shoppers avoid the last-minute rush at closing time, and careful drivers avoid rainy or snowy driving conditions. In the business world, experienced investors use their knowledge of economic relationships to make profitable investment decisions. While pattern recognition is an essential part of everyday life, investors can run into trouble when they imagine patterns in data that are essentially random in nature.

For example, you may recall that a fair coin toss will show an equal number of heads and tails, on average. Do not overlook the use of the word *average* in this sentence. A fair coin toss will actually show a 50-50 split between heads and tails only after a large number of tosses. For a fair coin toss, the occurrence of heads or tails is essentially random and does not depend on the result of prior tosses. Sometimes, gamblers believe in "lucky" numbers, streaks, or reversal patterns in data that are essentially random. This mistaken belief is called the **gambler's fallacy**. If a coin toss is fair, the probability of heads or tails on any toss is 50 percent regardless of what has happened during prior tosses. This point is so basic that it may appear trivial. However, best-selling books are sold that show the frequency with which random numbers are selected for winners of state-run lotteries. Why? People often succumb to the gambler's fallacy and make gambling decisions based on it. Picking lucky numbers in the lottery is silly, but popular.

In the sports world, the myth of the "hot hand" is a particular manifestation of the gambler's fallacy. Basketball fans often believe that a player is more likely to make a shot after having made several previous shots. "Feed the player with a hot hand" is a common refrain. To be sure, players have good nights and bad nights. However, the overriding consideration is that the probability of making a basket depends on a given player's career shooting percentage. Fluctuations around that average tend to be random and unpredictable. In professional basketball, for example, the percentage of shots made from the floor (field shooting percentage) hovers around 50 percent, on average. There is no evidence to support the notion that the probability of making a basket is increased or decreased based on what happened in prior shots. The notion that players with "hot hands" shoot in streaks is a myth.

Gambler's fallacy
The erroneous belief that there is a self-correcting process in a set of fair gambles.

Investors and speculators get into trouble when they base their decisions on the premise that they have identified patterns in return data that are essentially random. Day traders get crushed when they speculate that stocks with up or down moves at the market open are likely to continue that trend throughout the trading day. Long-term investors also get into trouble when they wrongly take past price movements as a fair representation of what to expect in the future. In the late 1990s, for example, the gambler's fallacy caused tech-stock investors to expect Microsoft, Intel, and Cisco Systems to continue to grow at 20 percent per year during the new millennium as they had during the prior decade. However, elephants seldom run like gazelles, and growth rates for tech-stock titans inevitably slow down.

Consequences of Mental Accounting

In Chapter 4, the concept of mental accounting was introduced. The brain uses a mental accounting system that is similar to a file cabinet. For each new stock purchased, a new mental account is opened to follow its progress. All actions and outcomes about that stock are placed in the account. Once an outcome is assigned a mental folder, it is difficult to view that outcome in any other way. Interactions among assets in different accounts tend to be overlooked, and this mental process can adversely affect investor wealth.

Ignoring the interaction among mental accounts can adversely affect investment decisions. Modern portfolio theory shows that the combination of different assets into a portfolio of securities can reduce the volatility that comes with investing in any single security. If stocks tend to fall when bonds tend to rise, the volatility or risk of the investor's portfolio can be reduced by combining both stocks and bonds into a single portfolio. Anytime an investor contemplates buying or selling a given security, it is how returns on that security interact with returns on the investor's overall portfolio that matters. Unfortunately, investors sometimes encounter difficulty evaluating interactions among various securities because of mental accounting errors.

Consider a purchase of Chevron stock for $49.82 per share that quickly trades for $60.59 (see Figure 8.4). Suppose an investor decides to keep Chevron based on optimistic expectations that fail to materialize, and the stock quickly slumps to $55.50, at which point it is sold. The profit of $5.68 per share (on a $49.82 stock) over a short time frame is a good return, but it is only half the profit that would have been made had the stock been sold at the peak earlier.

FIGURE 8.4	Reference Points Determine How Investors React to Chevron Stock Price Movements

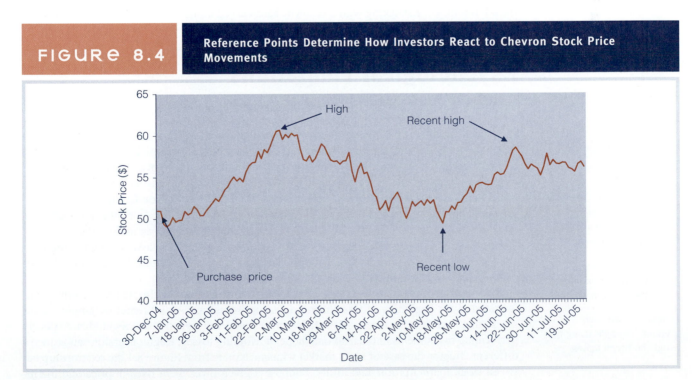

Source: Yahoo! Finance, **http://finance.yahoo.com**.

Reference points
Prices that investors remember and use for comparison with the current price.

How will the investor feel about such an experience? The answer depends on the investor's **reference point**. If the investor's reference point is the $49.82 purchase price, a quick sale at $55.50 will be favorably regarded and considered a big success. If the investor's reference point is the $60.59 peak price, a sale at $55.50 is apt to be disappointing. Knowledge about mental accounting and reference points is important for investors because it helps them avoid making investment mistakes based on psychological bias.

For many investors, the strongest reference point relating to any investment is the purchase price. Investors seem to set a strong anchor to this price. If a stock is bought and quickly plunges in price, many investors grimly hold on until the original purchase price is recouped and then sell irrespective of the company's future prospects. This is why trading volume tends to dry up when prices fall and tends to jump when prices rise toward recent highs. Investors seem to forget that share prices have no memory. If a stock is bought and quickly plunges in price, savvy investors buy more if their analysis of the fundamental value of the firm indicates a bargain price. Similarly, a rising stock price is no reason to sell, provided that the company's earnings, dividends, and growth prospects continue to improve.

Investment errors tied to reference points are common. If the purchase was made long ago, investors tend to use recently determined reference points, like the 200-day high or 200-day low price. If the price pattern of a stock plays out as in Figure 8.4, investors often feel as if they have missed a good opportunity to sell after the price has fallen below a recent high. If the stock then climbs back to this recent high, many investors quickly sell irrespective of the company's future prospects. This is a common and costly mistake.

House-money effect
Failure to mentally integrate new winnings as personal wealth.

Mental accounting errors can also be associated with highly profitable investments because investors and speculators can take on more than a prudent amount of risk following large gains. After a big win, gamblers often tip lavishly and take on excessive risk because a **house-money effect** makes them feel as if they are spending and betting with the casino's money. In such cases, mental accounting causes gamblers to separately consider bets made with their own money and those made with casino winnings. In such instances, lavish spending and excessive risk taking often causes gamblers to quickly give back to the casino the amount won and more. At the other extreme, gamblers are often willing to take on excessive risks in the effort to recoup losses. Casinos attribute much of their business success to the propensity of gamblers to take extreme chances (unfair bets) when enormous gains or losses have been incurred. In the stock market, investors sometimes succumb to similar mental accounting errors when they separately consider the advisability of risk taking with their own "hard-earned dollars" versus risk taking with stock market profits. On Wall Street, there is no such thing as "funny money," at least not for long.

Psychological Limitations

Regret Aversion

People avoid actions that cause regret. Regret is the emotional pain that comes with realizing that a previous decision has bad consequences. Consider the case of buying lottery tickets. Why do regular lottery-ticket buyers use the same numbers over and over? The probability that a regular set of "lucky" numbers might win the lottery is the same as the likelihood that any set of numbers might win. Regular players feel the **regret of omission** (disappointment from not taking an action) if they stick with the regular set of numbers and some other numbers win. They suffer the **regret of commission** (disappointment from taking an action) if they switch to a new set of numbers and their regular set of numbers wins. For most people, the regret of commission is more painful than the regret of omission. Thus, regular lottery-ticket buyers rarely switch to new numbers.

Regret of omission
Disappointment from not taking an action that would have had a good result.

Regret of commission
Disappointment from taking an action that had a bad result.

Myopic loss aversion
Irrational focus on trying to avoid short-term losses.

The concept of regret aversion is also relevant in the investing world. As prospect theory illustrated at the beginning of this chapter, investors sometimes avoid regret by holding on to stocks that have become losers. **Myopic loss aversion** results when investors hold on to poorly performing investments in the irrational hope of avoiding losses. Regret aversion can induce a different effect in the case of stock market winners. Notice from Figure 8.1 the relationship between stock market profits and utility. Suppose a given investment rises in price and the investor has an opportunity to realize a quick $1,000 profit. The increase in good feeling (utility)

	Stock A	Stock B
TABLE 8.2 — Proceeds from the Sale of Two Stocks		
Sale proceeds	$10,000	$10,000
Tax basis	8,000	12,500
Taxable gain (loss)	$ 2,000	($ 2,500)
Tax (credit) at 30%	$ 600	($ 750)
After-tax proceeds	$ 9,400	$10,750

tied to a further $1,000 rise in value is less than the regret (disutility) associated with a $1,000 loss in investment value (denoted by X). This causes many investors to quickly liquidate profitable investments and turn potential gains into realized profits. Regret aversion and pride-seeking behavior can cause investors to be predisposed to selling winners too early and riding losers too long. This is called the **disposition effect**.

Consider the example shown in Table 8.2. Suppose that for liquidity reasons an investor must sell stock A or stock B. Stock A has earned a 25 percent return, whereas stock B has lost 20 percent. Selling stock A validates the investor's good decision to make a purchase in the first place. Selling stock B at a loss requires that the investor admit that the purchase was a mistake and involves the obvious pain of regret. The disposition effect predicts that the typical investor will sell stock A and thereby trigger a feeling of pride and avoid the regret associated with selling stock B. From a psychological perspective this may be the correct choice, but it's a bad choice from an economic perspective.

On Wall Street, there is an old adage, "Cut your losses and let your profits run." Because capital gains taxes are paid only on realized gains, it is typically better to sell losers and hold on to stock market winners. Selling winners leads to the realization of a capital gain and the payment of taxes. Selling losers results in tax savings. In Table 8.2, selling either stock A or stock B provides $10,000 in gross receipts, but tax considerations impact net receipts. If the positions in stocks A and B are each valued at $10,000, then the original purchase price of stock A must have been $8,000 to have earned a 25 percent return. The purchase price of stock B must have been $12,500 to result in a 20 percent loss. When the capital gains tax rate is 30 percent, the net after-tax proceeds from selling stock A total $9,400, having been reduced by the necessity of paying $600 in capital gains taxes. Net after-tax proceeds from selling stock B total $10,750, having been increased with tax benefits of $750 tied to selling a loss-producing asset. If the investor's marginal state plus federal income tax rate is higher than 30 percent, as is often the case when capital gains are realized within one year of the original purchase, then the after-tax advantage associated with selling losers is even greater. Given the current tax code, investors maximize the after-tax performance of their portfolios when they cut their losses and let their profits run. However, studies of trading behavior show that investors are 50 percent more likely to sell a winner than to sell a loser. Too often, the disposition effect causes investors to sell winners too early and hold losers too long. These are not wealth-maximizing strategies.

Disposition effect
The predisposition to sell winners and hold losers.

Try It!

Consider the following quote from Eric Tyson's column in the *Seattle Post-Intelligencer* in July 2001. One investor asked what to do with his Conexant Systems stockholdings:

I invested quite a bit of money ($26,000) in Conexant stock. Of course, like most technology stocks, it has been struggling, and on paper I'm in trouble. Do you think it will ever reach the $80 that I paid for it? I really hate to cash it in for such a big loss, and I don't trust it enough to buy in at the low price ($8) it is now trading for. I feel like the company shows promise, but I am certainly not astute on such matters—I'm a dentist.

What psychological biases does the investor exhibit?

(continued)

Solution

The investor is anchored on the purchase price. The investor is not asking if the stock price will increase 10 percent, or even 100 percent. The investor is asking if the price will rise 1,000 percent to a specific reference point. The stock has not been sold yet because the investor is trying to avoid the regret tied to buying the stock in the first place. As the disposition effect predicts, the investor continues to hold a losing position despite a lack of confidence that the stock remains a good investment.

Behavioral Portfolios

The psychological limitations and tendencies of investors often cause them to think of their portfolios as a pyramid of assets (see Figure 8.5). Each layer in the investment pyramid is created to meet a specific goal, and progress toward each goal is managed within a separate mental account. To administer the process, investors pick investment themes or asset classes that match specific goals.

A basic safety net is provided by a range of wealth-preserving assets such as bank CDs (insured by the FDIC or FSLIC), low-risk money market mutual funds, Treasury bills, and insurance. Once this basic safety net is in place, many investors feel they are emotionally and financially able to take on higher levels of risk in the pursuit of higher expected rates of return. Wealth-building investment categories with the potential for higher rates of return include Treasury bonds, investment-grade corporate bonds, broad-market index funds, high-yield common stocks, and so on. Once the wealth-building goal is adequately funded, the typical investor feels ready to take on greater amounts of risk in the pursuit of even-higher

FIGURE 8.5   Behavioral Portfolios Involve a Variety of Mental Accounts

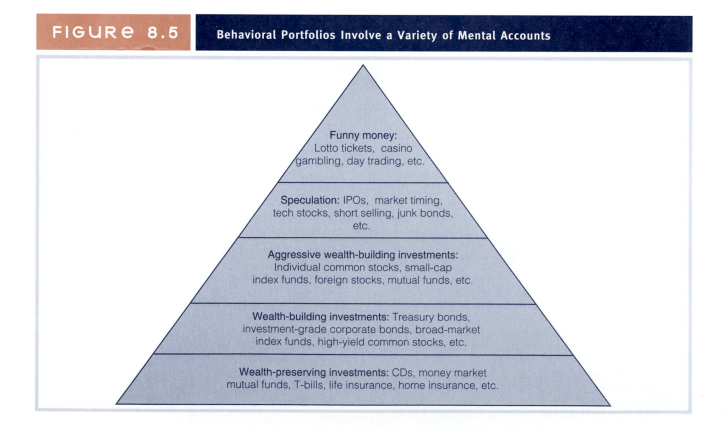

Funny money: Lotto tickets, casino gambling, day trading, etc.

Speculation: IPOs, market timing, tech stocks, short selling, junk bonds, etc.

Aggressive wealth-building investments: Individual common stocks, small-cap index funds, foreign stocks, mutual funds, etc.

Wealth-building investments: Treasury bonds, investment-grade corporate bonds, broad-market index funds, high-yield common stocks, etc.

Wealth-preserving investments: CDs, money market mutual funds, T-bills, life insurance, home insurance, etc.

Representativeness Bias among Professors

Ivo Welch, a professor at Yale University, has conducted several surveys of professors in financial economics over the years. The first such surveys were performed from 1997 through 1999, a period characterized as a rip-roaring bull market. During the 1997–1999 period, large-cap stocks as measured by the S&P 500 Index roughly doubled, and tech stocks as measured by the Nasdaq 100 Index approximately quadrupled. When Professor Welch asked finance professors for their estimate of the expected equity risk premium over the next 30 years, the mean response was 7.2 percent per year. In other words, in the midst of one of the most vigorous bull markets in history, finance professors thought it was reasonable to expect stocks to earn 7.2 percent per year more than risk-free Treasury bills. In response to another question, finance professors expressed their belief that stock market returns revert to long-term averages over time. In other words, they know that robust stock market returns are often followed by periods of below-average performance. Poor stock market performance tends to precede bull markets.

Professor Welch again surveyed the finance professors in 2001. This time, the survey was conducted during a period of falling stock prices. Both the S&P 500 and the Nasdaq 100 were then in the process of a sharp correction from highs reached during March 2000. The mean 30-year equity risk premium estimate from this latter survey was only 5.5 percent per year. Against a backdrop of falling stock prices, the professors had become more conservative (bearish)! Their collective forecast of a lower equity risk during a period of falling stock prices was inconsistent with their belief in mean reversion over time. Instead, their response was consistent with the notion that the stock market forecasts of finance professors are influenced by representativeness bias.

During the runaway bull market of the late 1990s, the finance professors forecast high equity risk premiums. During a sharp market correction, the same professors forecast lower equity risk premiums. Let's hope they were not making portfolio decisions on the basis of their forecasts!

See Edward Hadas, Simon Nixon, and Mike Verdin, "Economists See Modest Shifts in Trends They Missed in 2005," *The Wall Street Journal Online*, January 4, 2006 (**http://online.wsj.com**).

levels of wealth creation. Aggressive wealth-building investments include individual common stocks, small-cap index funds, foreign stocks, managed mutual funds, and so on. When this goal is adequately funded, the investor is emotionally and financially prepared to undertake a range of speculative investments that might entail the significant chance of loss. Common forms of speculation include investments in untried companies with initial public offerings (IPOs) of common stock, technical analysis and various market timing strategies, speculation in turnaround situations and tech stocks, short selling, and so on. Finally, some investors have what they call "funny money" accounts, whereby small amounts of money or prior winnings are bet with the full realization that complete loss is possible, if not probable. Wasting money on such "get-rich quick" schemes is often thought to be a form of recreation and not harmful to the investor's long-term emotional and financial well-being. While this may be true, a distressingly large number of investors appear to let rank speculation and gambling play too large a role in their investment strategies.

Notice that investment portfolios like the one depicted in Figure 8.5 are not necessarily designed from the standpoint of minimizing risk and maximizing expected return through optimal diversification across asset categories. Instead, the number of mental accounts and the amount of money funding each mental account determines the size and allocation of the investor's portfolio. **Behavioral portfolios** are determined by the distribution of investment goals and associated mental accounts. Diversification comes from investment goal diversification rather than from purposeful asset diversification. From an economic perspective, this means that many investors end up taking on more risk than necessary for the level of expected return they are getting.

Behavioral portfolios
The formation of a portfolio through the funding of individual goals.

Self-Deception

Overconfidence

Lake Wobegon is a fictitious community created by Minnesota radio personality and writer Garrison Keillor. According to Keillor, the people in this town have remarkable qualities: The women are all strong, the men are all good-looking, and the children are all of above-average intelligence. All kidding aside, Keillor has hit upon a common human characteristic. People generally believe that they are better than average. Obviously, we cannot all be above average in desirable characteristics such as kindness, intelligence, and strength. Nevertheless, it is common for people to retain strong memories of success and weak recollections of failure. As a result, most people believe they are better than they actually are.

Overconfidence

People overestimate their knowledge and ability.

Investors typically remember pleasing stock market gains more vividly than they recall disappointing stock market losses. This tends to make investors more confident than they should be. **Overconfidence** causes investors to overestimate their knowledge, underestimate risks, and exaggerate their ability to control events. As a simple illustration, consider the following question:

How good an investor are you? Compared with the broad-market averages, are you above average, average, or below average?

What is your answer? If overconfidence were not an issue, approximately one-third of all investors would answer above average; one-third, average; and one-third, below average. Generally, three-quarters of all people claim to be above average, and the rest claim to be just average. Few believe they are below-average investors. Obviously, many people are simply mistaken when it comes to judging their own investing abilities. People are mistaken because they are overconfident about their skill. Interestingly, it does not matter much whether this question is asked of a group of professional money managers or a collection of individual investors. Professionals and nonprofessionals alike tend to be overconfident in their ability to earn an above-average return.

In general, overconfidence causes investors to misinterpret the accuracy of information and overestimate their skill in analyzing it. This leads to excessive trading, unwarranted risk taking, and, ultimately, financial losses. Overconfident investors trade too much because they believe more strongly in their own valuation of a stock and concern themselves less about market movements and the beliefs of others. Overconfidence affects risk because overconfident investors tend to hold risky positions in smaller and newer companies and tend to focus on few industries. The level of investor overconfidence tends to become stronger after experiencing success. If a given investment decision makes money, it is human nature to attribute such success to skill. Money-losing outcomes are usually attributed to bad luck. During bull markets, overconfident investors attribute too much of their success to their own abilities and not enough to luck. As a result, rapid trading activity and escalating risk-taking behavior tend to become more pronounced during the late stages of bull markets, as in the late 1990s. During bear markets, investor confidence tends to diminish, trading activity slows down, and investors become more risk-averse.

Cognitive Dissonance

Cognitive dissonance

The mental discord that arises when the memory of an event conflicts with a positive self-perception.

A form of self-deception stems from the fact that people seek consistency. For example, most people want to view themselves as "smart and nice." However, everyone has at least one memory of some past action that was neither smart nor nice. It is common to feel uncomfortable with such a contradiction. Psychologists call this feeling **cognitive dissonance**. Cognitive dissonance results from the human brain's struggling with a conflict between perception and reality. To avoid psychological pain (guilt), people sometimes reject, ignore, or minimize information that conflicts with a positive self-image. Memories fade or change altogether to avoid conflict.

Investors can reduce psychological pain from investment decisions by adjusting their beliefs about the success of past decisions. Suppose an investor buys stock in Intel Corporation. Over time, business and stock price information will either confirm or question the wisdom of investing in Intel. To reduce cognitive dissonance, it is common for the investor to filter out negative information and focus on the positive. Therefore, investors tend to remember investment successes more so than investment failures. Past performance is remembered as being better than it really was.

Figure 8.6 shows the recollections of two types of investors. The first group consists of architects—highly educated professionals who may or may not be knowledgeable about investing. The second group comprises members of the American Association of Individual Investors (AAII), an association that provides education, information, and service to individual investors. The members of each group were asked two questions about the rate of return on their mutual fund investments: (1) What was your return last year? (2) By how much did you

FIGURE 8.6	Recollections of Investment Performance Tends to Be Flattering

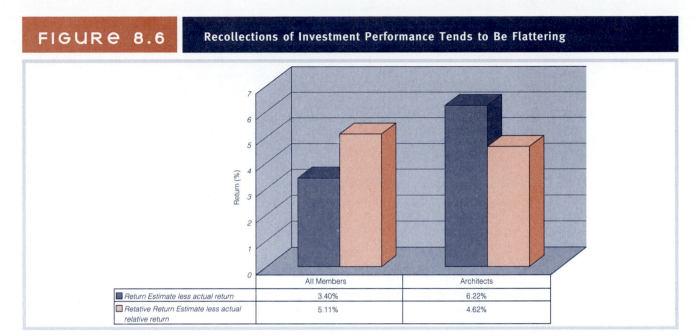

	All Members	Architects
▮ Return Estimate less actual return	3.40%	6.22%
▮ Relative Return Estimate less actual relative return	5.11%	4.62%

Source: William Goetzmann and Nadav Peles, "Cognitive Dissonance and Mutual Fund Investors," *Journal of Financial Research*, vol. 20, no. 2 (1997), pp. 145–158.

beat the market? Notice that one of these questions asks about actual performance while the other asks about performance relative to the overall market. If investors are not biased by cognitive dissonance, investor recollections should equal actual performance, on average.

On average, the architects recalled an investment performance that was 6.22 percent per year higher than their actual performance. These professionals remembered doing much better than they actually did. The architects also tended to overestimate by 4.62 percent the annual rate of return on their mutual fund investments relative to market benchmarks. The AAII investors also overestimated past returns, by 3.40 percent per year, and relative performance, by 5.11 percent per year, on average. This simple experiment shows that both highly educated professionals and experienced investors can tend to be overly optimistic in recalling past returns. In general, investors want to believe that they make sound investment decisions because doing so makes them feel good about themselves. This makes it difficult to objectively evaluate investment performance when personal recollections of past performance are biased.

Try It!

Las Vegas casinos offer many games. All games favor the casino. The size and elegance of the buildings reflect how much money the casinos make—and how much gamblers lose. Still, hoards of bettors pack the gaming tables and slot machines for hours on end. Over time, bettors inevitably lose money. Then they come back the following year. What biases might perpetuate this cycle?

Solution

People are overconfident in their abilities. While an individual gambler may recognize that average and below-average gamblers lose money, some people do make money. It must be the above-average gamblers who profit. To reduce cognitive dissonance, the gambler's brain minimizes his or her memory of losing and focuses on the jackpots that were won along the way. Gamblers tend to remember great events and a general feeling of success even when they have lost more money than they have won over the years.

Street Smarts 8.3

Smart Traders?

Broadcast media have a vested interest in convincing investors that staying abreast of late-breaking news is essential to their success. CNBC, for example, prides itself on turning up the latest in investment news and information on *Power Lunch* (from 12 to 2 p.m. EST), *Street Signs* (from 2 to 3 p.m. EST), and *Closing Bell* (from 3 to 5 p.m. EST). If you don't "stay tuned" 24/7, the risk of missing crucial investment information is daunting.

Is there in fact a compelling need for speed when it comes to investing? The simple answer is no. Warren Buffett, the most successful investor of our time, is on the Internet all the time—playing bridge with his friends. Buffett seldom uses the Internet to research companies or to obtain stock quotes. Making split-second investment decisions after listening to news reports is not investing; it is gambling. Gambling fosters strong emotional responses and can cause expensive mistakes.

Consider the kinds of mistakes that occur when traders make split-second decisions. In 1997, London's *Financial Times* reported that the Czech Value Fund, a closed-end mutual fund, was facing enormous losses. As the news reached the United States, the stock with ticker symbol CVF fell by 32 percent on high volume. The problem was that CVF is the ticker for the Castle Convertible Fund, not the Czech Value Fund. By the end of the day, the Castle Fund market price had recovered most of its early loss, but investors who sold at the bottom lost a lot of money. Similarly, in 1998, AT&T agreed to purchase Tele-Communications, Inc., for $45.8 billion, and the stock with ticker symbol TCI jumped nearly 5 percent on the news on heavy volume. Unfortunately for quick-moving speculators, TCI is the ticker symbol for Transcontinental Realty Investors Inc., not Tele-Communications, Inc.

Before you assume that such egregious mistakes are confined to naïve individual investors, conduct an Internet Google search on "trading losses." You'll be amazed at the types of mistakes, frauds, and scams that also claim smart professionals as victims.

See Peter A. Thatcher, "Mega-Leveraged Trades Have Inherent Risks," *The Wall Street Journal*, October 7, 2005, p. A17.

Misattribution bias
Tendency to attribute an unrelated feeling to the decision at hand.

Feelings can also influence financial decisions in more subtle ways through **misattribution bias**. Specifically, people can misattribute the mood they are in to the financial decision at hand. If an investor is in a good mood, he or she is more likely to be optimistic in evaluating an investment. Bad moods lead to more pessimism in evaluating investments. A prominent example is the way people misattribute the good feelings that stem from sunny days. Psychologists know that the degree of sunshine affects a person's frame of mind. A lack of sunlight has been linked to depression; when the sun is shinning, people feel good. When people are in a good mood, they tend to be more optimistic. This may explain why researchers have discovered that the stock market tends to rise more on sunny days than on cloudy days! The effect is small, to be sure, but it does suggest that investor emotions play a role in determining asset prices.

Social Influences

Social Interaction and Investing

Social norms
The informal opinions, rules, and procedures of a group.

People often learn by interacting with others, and everybody enjoys good conversation. Increasingly, the conversation is turning to investing. The **social norms** of investment conversation have dramatically changed over the past several decades. Not long ago, people avoided talking about investing. Until recently, it was thought to be impolite to talk about money. Asking someone about the performance of his or her portfolio was considered rude. Now, talk about money and investing seems to be everywhere. Financial shows on CNBC, CNN, and FOX pepper the airwaves. Message boards such as Raging Bull, Yahoo! Finance, Motley Fool, and the valueinvestorsclub.com are enormously popular on the Internet. Dozens of syndicated radio shows are devoted to investing. The more investors talk and listen to others talk about investing, the more they invest. Conversation is not only a tool investors use to exchange information but a method for sharing investment opinions and expressing emotions.

Investment bankers talk to security analysts, security analysts talk to stockbrokers, and brokers talk to institutional and individual investors. Business leaders, regulators, and the news media chime in with their own opinions. This is a social process that can and does influence the investment process. Of course, investors are better able to make informed investment decisions when there is a free flow of investment information. At the same time, emotional and poorly informed investors can be greatly harmed when they act on the basis of bogus information that is spread by stock manipulators and other crooks. It is imperative that all investors keep their emotions in check and independently verify all investment information before acting on it.

Herding

Both professional and individual investors often look to the actions of others to validate what they are doing. As investors learn what others think about various investments, a social consensus forms. When several people act at the same time on this consensus, a herd forms. **Investor herding** is the concerted movement of large groups of investors into or out of a stock or industry group at the same point in time. Studies show that investors like the validation given by many others making the same buy and sell decisions. When things go wrong and investors lose money, there is comfort in knowing that others are in the same predicament. Misery loves company.

Investor herding
The movement of large groups of investors into or out of a stock or industry of companies.

But there are problems with moving with the herd. Investors at the head of the herd enjoy profits when the rest of the herding investors drive up the price. Investors in the middle or at the end of the herd get stuck with artificially high prices that are poised to fall when herding demand wanes. Herding also magnifies psychological biases. Herding can cause investors to make decisions based on the "feel" of the herd instead of the rigor of independent fundamental analysis.

There are also problems with trying to move against the herd. If you determine that a stock is overvalued, you can avoid it or short it. Aggressive investors who short overvalued firms that have been run up by the herd can get run over. The herd can keep piling into the stock and driving the price higher, making it more overvalued. An investor going against the herd must be right about the direction and the timing of the stock price. Because the investor herd can be so unpredictable, the savvy investor avoids stocks being impacted by the herd.

The irrational exuberance of herding into Internet companies in the late 1990s shows how markets can be impacted. Crowd-following investors pushed the prices of Internet stocks to absurd valuations. For example, while the historical average price-earnings (P/E) ratio of the market is around 15, in the late 1990s companies like Yahoo! and eBay had P/E ratios of 1,300 and 3,300, respectively. Most Internet companies did not even have a P/E ratio because they did not have any earnings! A typical example was the valuation of eToys, an online toy retailer that went public in 1999. Shortly after its initial public offering, eToys had a market capitalization of $8 billion despite negative earnings of $28.6 million and total sales revenue of only $30 million. Compare eToys to Toys 'R' Us, the leading toy retailer. At that time, even though Toys 'R' Us had profits of $376 million per year, it had a market capitalization of $6 billion, or a whopping $2 billion less than eToys! Toys 'R' Us had a lower market valuation than did eToys even though it earned 12 times more in *profits* than eToys earned in *sales*. In fact, eToys never made a profit and eventually filed for bankruptcy. Instead of warning investors that the valuations in the Internet industry were ridiculous, many Wall Street analysts and some financial economists invented new valuation metrics to try to justify and prolong the irrational herding.

How to Avoid Investment Pitfalls

Investment Rules of Thumb

There is truth in the old Wall Street adage "Fear and greed rule the market." Emotions play an important role in investor decisions. The challenge for investors is to recognize and learn to avoid psychological biases that make rational decision making difficult. The problem is that such biases are subtle and hard to recognize. Many successful investors use **investment rules**

Investment rules of thumb
Simple procedures created in advance to help investors make good decisions.

Pitfalls in Investor Behavior

In the late 1990s, a nationwide discount stock brokerage provided stockholding data for 78,000 household accounts over the period 1991–1996 to researchers Brad Barber and Terrance Odean. In a continuing series of studies, Barber, Odean, and their colleagues have discovered the following:

Traders trade too much. The investment performance of investors who rarely trade was compared with the performance of investors who seem to be constantly buying and selling stocks. Hyperactive traders do measurably worse than careful investors who trade infrequently.

Traders sell winners to buy losers. Not only are active traders hurt by high commission costs, but they also tend to make bad decisions about what and when to sell. In an interesting study, Barber and Odean considered what happens after an investor sells one stock to purchase another. On average, the stock sold tends to outperform the stock purchased! Active traders would be better off standing pat, rather than continually adjusting and readjusting their portfolios.

Traders are reluctant to realize losses. On average, active traders are more likely to sell winners than losers. However, being quick to take profits and slow to realize losses (and associated tax benefits) is no way to run an investment portfolio. Investment legend Peter Lynch calls this "watering the weeds."

Traders become overconfident online. When successful traders move to online trading accounts, trading activity tends to increase dramatically. Such traders also see deterioration in the performance of their brokerage accounts after they go online.

Traders like story stocks. With literally thousands of stocks to choose among, traders and small investors have a difficult time trying to decide which stocks to buy. In general, they like widely admired, fast-growing firms with terrific stock market performance during the prior three- to five-year period. However, such story stocks tend to perform poorly during subsequent periods

The record shows that many active traders are subject to psychological biases that undermine investment performance. When it comes to investing, beware of the common refrain "I have met the enemy, and he is us!"

See Brad M. Barber and Terrance Odean, "Online Investors: Do the Slow Die First?" *Review of Financial Studies*, vol. 15, no. 2 (March 2002), pp. 455–487.

---

of thumb to help guide their investment decision making and guard against irrational behavior. Here are some common rules of thumb in the investing world:

- **Stay the course.** Maintain a long-term perspective, and seek to build significant wealth with regular contributions to your investment portfolio.

- **Long-run returns reflect fundamental business prospects.** Don't be surprised when pigs don't fly. Animals that fly are called *birds*. In the long run, you will do as well as the businesses you invest in.

- **Dumb money ceases to be dumb when it realizes its limitations.** Low-cost stock and bond index investing is best for almost everyone. Fewer than one in ten professionals consistently beat the market. Most active speculators *lose* money.

- **Don't confuse luck with brains.** Most investors think they are smart if the stocks they buy go up and think they are merely unlucky when their stocks go down.

- **Cut your losses, and let your profits run.** Admit when you are wrong. Be willing to make small mistakes. Being wrong and stubborn is expensive.

- **Bulls make money; bears can make money; hogs get slaughtered.** Beware of oversized positions in risky companies.

- **Be skeptical of buy-sell recommendations.** Assume that buy recommendations are made by investors with stock to sell and that sell recommendations are made by those wishing to buy at a cheaper price or those who need to cover a short position.

- **Market professionals tend to be articulate, bright, and well trained and to make a very good living for *themselves*.** Few market professionals help investors make money. Warren Buffett and Charlie Munger are the exceptional exception.

- **If everyone were right, everyone would be rich.** Since the average investor often has a poor investment performance, the herd isn't usually right.

- **Significant capital accumulation requires time *and* money.** The wealthy tend to be smart, lucky, and *old*.

These investment rules of thumb help investors make sound investment decisions and avoid emotional responses that can undermine investment success.

Plan for Investment Success

One of the best things an investor can do to control the psychological biases that often lead to poor investment decisions is to plan for investment success. Most institutional investors (pension funds, mutual funds, financial advisors, etc.) are required by law to have an investment plan. Few individual investors have one. Most investors do not have realistic investment goals, and they lack the concrete plans necessary to achieve them. The lack of a detailed financial plan allows investors to be swayed by social and emotional influences. Only disciplined investment strategies can help investors avoid the serious blunders that can undermine their financial well-being.

Successful investors develop specific and realistic financial goals. This keeps them focused on the long term and helps them avoid many of the psychological and emotional problems that can arise from a short-term focus. Successful investors also identify an appropriate asset allocation strategy that will help them achieve their financial goals. They also identify time-tested quantitative and qualitative criteria to select attractive stocks and other desirable investments. Such criteria do not have to be complicated. Simple value-stock filters can be used, like low P/E ratio or dividend yield criteria for stock investments. The discipline of checking prospective investments against time-tested investment criteria helps investors avoid falling into the trap of making decisions based on emotions, psychological biases, or the social forces of the financial media. And, finally, successful investors monitor progress toward their financial goals and make necessary asset allocation adjustments through periodic **portfolio rebalancing**. Rebalancing a portfolio involves reducing the allocation to an asset class that has done extraordinarily well and increasing the allocation to underperforming asset classes. Constructive portfolio rebalancing allows investors to sell high and buy low, and it can help reduce overall volatility.

Portfolio rebalancing
Adjusting a portfolio to a target asset allocation.

Of course, periodic decisions to rebalance a stock or bond portfolio must be made in light of the fundamental business prospects of individual companies. Nobody wants to eliminate healthy, prosperous, and growing companies from an investment portfolio simply in order to devote more funds to cheaper stocks or bonds in companies that may be sick or dying. In many cases, poorly performing stocks and bonds reflect operating problems in companies that eventually wither and die. Rational investors focus on the underlying business and buy stocks and bonds in companies enjoying a fundamental improvement in revenues, cash flows, and profits. If company revenues, cash flows, and earnings rise over time, stock and bond prices also tend to rise.

Summary

■ A traditional view of finance assumes that people make rational decisions to maximize wealth for a given level of risk or to minimize risk for a given level of wealth. This **normative** approach tells how investors should behave. **Behavioral finance** takes a different approach. Behavioral finance recognizes that cognitive errors and emotions often influence financial decision makers and cause them to make bad decisions. The emphasis of behavioral finance is on a **positive** description of human behavior. It studies how people actually behave in a financial setting. Specific **psychological biases** have been shown to affect investors.

■ **Prospect theory** describes how people frame and value decisions involving uncertainty. Investors often frame choices in terms of potential gains and losses relative to a specific reference point. Investors also tend to value gains and losses according to an S-shaped function that is concave for gains and convex for losses. This means that investors feel bad when they incur losses, but twice the loss does not make them feel twice as bad. Investors also do not feel twice as good when gains are doubled. For many investors, the utility-of-wealth function is steeper for losses than for gains.

■ The human brain uses shortcuts to reduce the complexity of analyzing information. **Heuristic simplification** allows the brain to generate an estimate of the best course of action to be followed in an uncertain situation. One shortcut, **familiarity bias**, leads investors to believe that the things they are familiar with are better than unfamiliar alternatives. Familiar investments are believed to be of lower risk and higher expected return. People frequently allocate too much of their retirement plans to the stock of their employer because it is the most familiar company. Too many choices cause employees to have **choice overload** and often end up not investing at all. When faced with fewer options, employees simply invest equal amounts in each one, an application of the **1/n heuristic**. Another shortcut, representativeness bias, leads investors to wrongly conclude that good companies are good investments and that good past performers will be good future performers. Without a strong conviction to act, investors continue the **status quo** by doing nothing.

■ When people know the distribution of payoffs from a gamble, and recent outcomes appear skewed, they often believe that there is some self-correcting process in the other direction. This incorrect assumption is known as the **gambler's fallacy**. Before the fact, investors cannot know future investment returns. So naïve investors tend to simply project the recent past into the future.

■ Many investors use **mental accounting** to keep track of investment choices. Each investment has its own file, and interactions among the assets in different folders are often overlooked. Investors also tend to use various **reference points** to gauge how they should feel after price changes. The purchase price is a particularly strong **anchor**. Mental accounting can lead to irrational investment behavior. The **house-money effect** often induces gamblers to recklessly bet prior winnings, and thus it can lead gamblers to quickly lose prior winnings. Similarly, stock market investors who recklessly speculate with prior stock market gains often face steep losses.

■ Regret is the emotional pain that comes with realizing that a previous decision has turned out badly. People avoid actions that cause the feeling of regret. The **regret of commission** (taking an action) tends to be more painful than the **regret of omission** (not changing). **Myopic loss aversion** causes people to be particularly sensitive to short-term losses. Avoiding regret and pride-seeking behavior causes many investors to be predisposed to selling winners too early and riding losers too long. This is called the **disposition effect**.

■ In many instances, investors focus on investment goal diversification rather than on purposeful asset diversification. The outcome is that **behavioral portfolios** are inefficiently formed and changed based on the distribution of investment goals and associated mental accounts. As a consequence, many investors take on more risk than is necessary for the level of expected return they achieve.

■ People generally believe that they are better than average. The human brain facilitates this self-deception by giving strong memories of success and weak recollections of failure.

One self-deception, **overconfidence**, causes people to overestimate their investment knowledge, underestimate risks, and exaggerate their ability to control events. Overconfident investors trade too much and take on too much risk. Overconfidence also tends to become stronger after experiencing success. During bull markets, individual investors tend to attribute too much of their success to their own ability and not enough to luck. As a consequence, overconfident behavior is more pronounced during bull markets than in bear markets.

■ A common form of self-deception is caused by **cognitive dissonance**, or psychological discomfort felt over the discrepancy between new information and what one already knows or believes. To avoid such psychological pain, many individuals ignore, reject, or minimize disconfirming information.

■ **Misattribution bias** can cause investors to attribute the mood they are in to the financial decision at hand. If an investor is in a good mood, he or she is more likely to be optimistic in evaluating investments. Bad moods lead to more pessimism in assessing investments.

■ People often learn by interacting with others. While everybody enjoys positive social interaction, investors must be aware of how their investment decisions can be affected by **social norms**. As investors learn what others think about various investments, a social consensus forms. When many people act on this consensus, a herd forms. **Investor herding** is the coordinated movement of large groups of investors into or out of a stock or industry group. While it seems safer to move with the herd, the end of herding in overpriced stocks can cause prices to collapse.

■ **Investment rules of thumb** can be used to avoid being influenced by emotions when making investment decisions. One of the best things an investor can do to control psychological biases is to have an investment plan that involves monitoring progress toward financial goals and making necessary asset allocation adjustments through **portfolio rebalancing**.

Self-Test Problems

ST8.1 Over 1,000 subscribers to Morningstar.com completed an online survey[5] that included the following three questions:[6]

a. How would you rate the return on the stock of your employing firm over the LAST five years versus the return of the overall stock market?

b. What is your best estimate of the future return on the stock of your employing firm over the *next* five years versus the return of the overall stock market?

c. In your opinion, is the stock of your employing firm more or less likely than the overall stock market to lose half of its value over the *next* five years?

[5] See Shlomo Benartzi, "Excessive Extrapolation and the Allocation of 401(k) Accounts to Company Stock," *Journal of Finance*, vol. 56, no. 5 (2001), pp. 1747–1764.

[6] © Morningstar®, 2006. Used with permission.

The responses show that the answers to Questions **a** and **b** are highly and positively correlated. For Question **c**, 83.6 percent of the respondents believed that their employing firm's stock price had the same or less chance of losing half of its value compared to the overall market.

What psychological biases do these responses demonstrate?

Solution

The responses to Questions **a** and **b** demonstrate that investors use the representativeness bias by extrapolating past performance into the future. People whose employing firm outperformed the market in the past are predicting it will do so again in the future. Firms that underperformed are predicted to continue underperforming.

The belief that their firm is safer than a diversified portfolio exhibits overconfidence. This overconfidence in their firm is probably caused by the familiarity bias. These investors believe that what is familiar to them (their company's stock) is better and less risky than things that are not as familiar (other stocks). However, a large amount of firm-specific risk is diversified away in a portfolio, making the overall market far less risky than one individual stock. Only 16.4 percent of the respondents seem to have realized this.

The representativeness bias and familiarity bias often influence employees to invest heavily in their employing firm's stock when that stock has exhibited high returns in the past. This can be a disastrous mistake.

ST8.2 Understanding investment psychology is very useful for helping an investor make better decisions. However, many people want to know how to earn high rates of return by benefiting from the folly of others. What investment strategies might benefit from the way large groups of investors behave, or herd?

Solution

A current mutual fund manager superstar is Bill Miller, who runs the Legg Mason Value Trust fund. He is the only mutual fund manager who has beaten the S&P 500 Index return every year for the past 15 years. Miller believes that the only sustainable market anomalies are the ones that arise from the way investors function psychologically. He looks for the cognitive and emotional errors that stem from the way people process and react to information. What errors are predictable? He mentions that the more a stock drops, the less inclined investors are to buy it. Investors buy what is in the news. So Miller looks for undervalued, neglected firms. That is, he looks for firms that are being ignored by the news and by investors. These firms typically have low valuations. Miller buys these firms and waits for the herd to eventually find them and bid up the prices. In other words, he does the opposite of what the investor masses are doing. Or, as Warren Buffett has said, "Be fearful when others are greedy and greedy when others are fearful."

Questions and Problems

8.1 What are three main characteristics of the value-of-money or -wealth function according to prospect theory?

8.2 Charles Prestwood retired from Enron in October 2000 with a $1.3 million retirement portfolio made up entirely of Enron stock. Just over a year later, Enron was bankrupt and Prestwood's portfolio was decimated. What psychological biases might have led Prestwood to invest his entire retirement portfolio in Enron stock?

8.3 Keno is a game where 10 numbers are drawn from 1 to 80. Gamblers get paid depending on how many numbers they pick that match the game's draw. Suppose a given gambler has noticed that the numbers 17, 24, 39, and 45 have not been drawn in the last 20 turns. If the gambler decides to bet heavily on those numbers being drawn on the next turn, is this a wise move? Why or why not?

www.mhhe.com/hirschey1e

8.4   Every mutual fund prospectus states, "Past performance may not be indicative of future results." But investors do use past performance to make decisions. The funds in the top 20 percent of performance receive most of the new investment money. Why do investors use past performance to pick mutual funds?

8.5   An investor purchased a stock 10 years ago for $15 per share. The price gradually increased each year until it peaked last year at $80 per share. This year, the price fell to $25 per share, and the investor sold the stock. Do you think the investor feels good or bad about this investment? Why?

8.6   The Steadman Funds is a mutual fund family with four equity funds. It is known as the "Rodney Dangerfield family" of mutual funds. The Steadman funds have ranked near or at the bottom of all mutual fund categories over the past 5-, 10-, and 15-year periods. In addition to poor stock picking and excessive turnover, exorbitant management fees have led to horrible investment performance. In the 1990s, the Steadman funds actually lost money during one of the 20th century's strongest bull markets. How can you explain the fact that 21,000 investors have maintained their accounts in these funds after such atrocious performance?

8.7   Suppose a gambler wins a very big pot playing no-limit Texas Hold'em (a poker game). In the next hand, the gambler bets heavily on a hand that is of only average quality. What bias might have caused this bet?

8.8   Assume that a gambler loses a very big pot playing no-limit Texas Hold'em (a poker game). In the next hand, the gambler bets heavily on a hand that is of only average quality. What bias might have caused this bet?

8.9   Why might people in a bad mood be better investors than those in a good mood?

8.10   What behaviors would be expected from an overconfident investor?

 8.11   Examine several stock message boards on the Raging Bull site (**ragingbull.quote. com**). Which companies have the most active message boards? Does the amount of discussion make sense for these firms?

 8.12   Warren Buffett is a strong believer that most investors are negatively influenced by emotions and psychological biases. He also believes that the biases of investors affect stock prices. Obtain an annual letter to Berkshire Hathaway shareholders written by Warren Buffett (**www.berkshirehathaway.com**). What comments in the letter express Buffett's thinking on investor psychology?

8.13   Each year, Merrill Lynch surveys investment fund managers from around the world. Typically, managers from Japan predict that the Japanese stock market will outperform foreign stock markets. Managers from the United Kingdom predict the U.K. market will outperform. Indeed, managers from each region predict their region's stock market will be the high performer. What mental shortcut explains this result?

8.14   A defined-contribution pension plan is offered to three employees who each can contribute $1,000 per month. Five investment options are provided: a money market fund, a government bond fund, a small-cap stock fund, a medium-cap stock fund, and a large-cap fund. Employee A desires an asset allocation of 50 percent bonds and 50 percent stocks; employee B suffers from the $1/n$ heuristic; and employee C suffers from choice overload. What asset allocations do you expect from the three employees?

8.15   What is portfolio rebalancing, and how can it control behavioral biases?

8.16   How is a portfolio built according to the behavioral portfolio theory?

8.17   An investor has a $40,000 portfolio (not in a retirement plan) consisting of two stocks, Texas Instruments (TI) and Intel. TI stock recently declined in price, and the investor's position is at a loss. Intel recently increased in price, and this position has a profit. Assume that TI and Intel have similar future prospects for capital appreciation and dividend income. If the investor wants to sell a stock and purchase a third stock, Cisco, which should be sold? Which will be the most likely one sold? Why?

8.18 In thinking about what changes to make in your portfolio, how does cognitive dissonance influence the decision-making process?

8.19 Louise and Christopher Maclin live in London, England, and currently rent an apartment in the metropolitan area. During an initial discussion of the Maclins' financial plans, Christopher Maclin makes the following statements to the Maclins' financial advisor, Grant Webb:

- "I have used the Internet extensively to research the outlook for the housing market over the next five years, and I believe now is the best time to buy a house."
- "I do not want to sell any bond in my portfolio for a lower price than I paid for the bond."
- "I will not sell any of my company stock because I know my company and I believe it has excellent prospects for the future."

Identify the behavioral finance concept *most* directly exhibited in *each* of Maclin's three statements. Explain how *each* behavioral finance concept is affecting Maclin's investment decision making.

8.20 In his recent professional reading, Mesa has become aware of three behavioral finance phenomena that he believes could be important in his work with the Smiths. These are:

- Mental accounting
- The representativeness heuristic
- Reference dependence

Describe *each* of the three behavioral finance phenomena identified by Mesa.

INVESTMENT APPLICATION

Combating Psychological Biases to Help Investors

Can knowledge about psychological biases be used to help investors? In fact, administrators of tax-deferred retirement plans believe that knowledge about psychological biases can be used to facilitate better retirement planning decisions. They have discovered that by reorganizing the investment process, the harmful effects of some biases can be avoided. For example, most 401(k) retirement plans are set up so that biases work against the employee. When employees become eligible for the retirement plan, they must act to start their contributions. They must decide how to allocate their investments and fill out all the paperwork. A status quo bias causes employees to procrastinate in making their retirement plan decisions. Many procrastinate so long that they never participate in their employer's retirement plan. It is in the best interest of these employees to invest for their future retirement, but their bias to procrastinate harms their long-term wealth. Such procrastination also hurts employers. Every employer wants employees who are free from long-term worry about their financial situation.

How can 401(k) plans be set up to overcome psychological biases? In some instances, the answer is surprisingly simple. Instead of having new employees take action to enroll in the plan, many employers now automatically enroll all employees. Those wishing not to participate must make the effort *not* to enroll (or must disenroll). In this manner, procrastination works in favor of the employee's long-term benefit. Studies show that automatic enrollment policies for 401(k) retirement savings plans cause a substantial increase in the number of employees who choose to participate. In such instances, employee procrastination can also cause another problem. Most employees choose to simply maintain the default level of contributions and a fixed asset allocation mix. Under most employer-sponsored plans, the default contribution level is typically set at a level that is much lower than the maximum allowed contribution. Default asset allocations also tend to be highly conservative, such as allocating 100 percent of plan assets to a money market account.

Two economists, Richard Thaler and Shlomo Benartzi, propose a four-step approach that they call Save More Tomorrow (SMT) to help employers and employees deal with the complexity of retirement planning.[7] The SMT plan overcomes psychological biases that often limit retirement plan participation. Their plan addresses those employees who are not contributing to their 401(k) plans. They can begin to do so by agreeing to the following: First, the employee is asked to agree to the plan a long time in advance so that the decision does not have any immediate ramifications. Second, the employee's contributions begin at the employee's next pay raise with a small amount, such as 1 to 2 percent of total pay. By combining pay raises with increases in the amount contributed to the employee's retirement plan, employees can begin retirement plan contributions in a relatively painless manner. Third, employees are asked to agree to a predictable increase in the contribution rate at the time of each subsequent pay raise. And, finally, employees are allowed to opt out of the plan at any time. Although plan sponsors hope that employees will not choose to opt out of the employer-sponsored retirement plan, an ability to opt out at any time tends to increase initial participation by making employees more comfortable about joining the plan. In such plans, status quo bias works in favor of plan participation because employees must act to avoid automatic participation.

This SMT plan was tested at a midsize manufacturing company with employees who generally failed to participate in the employer-sponsored retirement plan. Before changes in the employer's plan were implemented, the company's 315 employees had an average savings rate equal to 4.4 percent of average earnings. All employees were asked to increase their retirement plan contributions to 5 percent of total earnings, and those who were unwilling to do so were offered participation in the SMT program. On an overall basis, 162 employees agreed to join the SMT plan. Before implementation of the SMT program, these employees had a very low savings rate of 3.5 percent, on average. The effect of joining the SMT plan was dramatic. Those who joined the SMT plan increased their retirement savings rate from 3.5 to 11.6 percent of annual earnings after only three subsequent pay raises. Such a dramatic increase in employee retirement savings can be directly attributed to the careful design of default options.

The challenge for the financial industry is to develop more such programs that help investors overcome psychological biases that hinder good investment decision making.

a. Why does the SMT procedure help employees save for the future?

b. What rules of thumb can be used to avoid making decisions based on psychological biases?

[7] Richard H. Thaler and Shlomo Bernartzi, "Save More Tomorrow: Using Behavorial Economics to Increase Employee Savings," *Journal of Political Economy*, vol. 112, no. 1 (February 2004): pp. S164–S187. Copyright © 2004. Used with permission.

Business Environment

As the chairman of the Board of Governors for the Federal Reserve System walks to an important meeting in Washington, D.C., the scene is often shown live on CNBC's *Squawk Box*. The show's host, Mark Haines, tries to predict the Fed's actions by the thickness of the briefcase the chairman is carrying. If a thin briefcase is being carried, for example, an economic tightening may be in the works. This odd "Fed watching" is a national pastime for the global media. It's no wonder why. The Fed sets U.S. monetary policy to influence the availability and cost of money and credit. The Fed's actions can trigger a chain of events that affect short-term and long-term interest rates, foreign exchange rates, and, ultimately, a range of economic variables, including employment, output, and inflation.

The three main tools used by the Fed are open-market operations, the discount rate, and reserve requirements. The Federal Open Market Committee (FOMC) attempts to control interest rates by adding supply or demand in the securities market. The Fed frequently buys or sells large amounts of U.S. Treasuries or agency bonds. It may also try to influence the value of the dollar relative to foreign money by trading in the currency market.

The FOMC consists of 12 members—the 7 members of the Board of Governors of the Federal Reserve System; the president of the Federal Reserve Bank of New York; and 4 of the remaining 11 Reserve Bank presidents. The FOMC holds eight regularly scheduled meetings per year. At these meetings, the committee reviews economic and financial conditions, determines the appropriate stance of monetary policy, and assesses the risks to its long-run goals of price stability and sustainable economic growth. Therefore, it should come as no surprise that the media, economists, and investors rush to read FOMC pronouncements. While the Fed's actions eventually change the direction of the overall economy, they immediately affect bond, stock, and currency markets.[1]

---

[1] Greg Ip, "Fed Lifts Rate by Quarter Point," *The Wall Street Journal Online,* February 1, 2006 (**http://online.wsj.com**).

CHAPTER OBJECTIVES

- Know the major forces driving economic growth.
- Define the economic environment.
- Understand the importance of industry competition.
- Learn the impact of regulation.
- Analyze the level of corporate governance in a firm.

Dimensions of the Economy

Macroeconomic Environment

Macroeconomics
Study of aggregate measures of economic activity.

Macroeconomics is the study of aggregate measures of economic activity at the international, national, regional, or state level. Predictions of changes in the gross domestic product (GDP), unemployment, and interest rates by business economists are examples of macroeconomic forecasts that capture the attention of national media, business, government, and investors on a daily basis. GDP measures the final market value of goods and services produced by all labor and property located in the United States. As such, GDP is a measure of aggregate business activity during a given period by both domestic and foreign-owned enterprises.

Other macroeconomic forecasts commonly reported in the press include predictions of consumer spending, business investment, homebuilding, exports, imports, federal purchases, state and local government spending, and so on. Macroeconomic predictions are important because businesses and individuals use them to make day-to-day and long-term investment decisions. If interest rates are projected to rise, homeowners rush to refinance fixed-rate mortgages, while businesses float new bond and stock offerings to refinance existing debt or take advantage of investment opportunities. When such predictions are accurate, significant cost savings or revenue gains become possible. When such predictions are inaccurate, higher costs and lost marketing oppurtunities occur.

Despite the obvious potential for significant benefits from accurate macroeconomic forecasts, obstacles limit their usefulness. The accuracy of any forecast is subject to the influence of controllable and uncontrollable factors. In the case of macroeconomic forecasting, uncontrollable factors loom large. Take interest rate forecasting, for example. The demand for credit and short-term interest rates rise if businesses seek to build inventories or expand plant and equipment or if consumers wish to increase installment credit. The supply of credit rises and short-term interest rates fall if the Federal Reserve System acts to increase the money supply or if consumers cut back on spending to increase savings rates. Interest rate forecasting is made difficult by the fact that business decisions to build inventory, for example, are largely based on the expected pace of overall economic activity—which itself depends on interest rate expectations. The macroeconomic environment is interrelated in ways that are unstable and cannot be easily predicted. Even policy decisions are hard to predict. This is why "Fed watching" is a favorite pastime of business economists.

Microeconomic Environment

Microeconomics
Study of economic data at the industry, firm, plant, or product level.

Microeconomics is the study of economic data at the industry, firm, plant, or product level. Unlike predictions of GDP growth, which are widely followed in the press, the general public often ignores microeconomic forecasts of scrap prices for aluminum, the demand for new cars, or the production cost for *Crest* toothpaste. It is unlikely that the *CBS Evening News* will ever be interrupted to discuss an upward trend in used-car prices, even though these data are excel-

Beware the "New Economy"

In the late 1990s it was common to hear that we were transitioning from an "old economy" based on natural resources, production, and innovation to a "new economy" based on the seamless flow of information. To be sure, computers, the Internet, and automation have allowed even old-style companies to become more productive with fewer employees. The economy is in a constant process of dynamic change and revitalization. Companies have to keep up, or they risk becoming obsolete.

However, in the late 1990s many used the new-economy excuse to claim that basic economic principles were no longer valid or that traditional valuation techniques no longer worked. Such talk is typical of periods characterized by stock market bubbles. Pundits said this about railroads in the 1850s, the creation of the Federal Reserve System in the 1920s, the nifty-fifty era of the early 1970s, and the Internet bubble of the late 1990s.

To illustrate this point, take the behavior of Morgan Stanley's superstar analyst, Mary Meeker. Her frequent appearance on financial television, like CNBC, and her relentlessly bullish recommendations on Internet firms caused her to be dubbed the "Queen of the Internet." By 1998, stock prices for such companies far exceeded any rational valuation, so she invented new valuation methods. When profits can't justify a stock price, switch to sales or sales potential. When sales potential cannot be used to justify the price, switch to the number of "eyeballs" that might view the Web page of an upstart Internet firm. Instead of valuation based on price-earnings ratios, Internet stock valuations were based on price-eyeballs ratios! Unfortunately for Internet stock investors, eyeballs are seldom a secure source of predictable profits.

Every period is marked by the creative destruction of capitalism. There will always be new winners that produce desired goods and services cheaper, faster, or better than the competition. This presents opportunities for investors. However, investors must be very cautious when the new-economy excuse is used to justify irrational valuations. Beware when stock promoters argue "This time, it's different." It's not.

See Frederick Kempe, "The Google Economy," *The Wall Street Journal Online*, January 18, 2006 (**http://online.wsj.com**).

---

lent predictors of new-car demand. When used-car prices surge, new-car demand often grows rapidly. When used-car prices sag, new-car demand typically drops. The fact that used-car prices and new-car demand are closely related is not surprising given the strong substitute-good relation that exists between used cars and new cars.

Trained and experienced analysts often find it easier to accurately forecast microeconomic trends, such as the demand for new cars, than macroeconomic trends, such as GDP growth. With specialized knowledge about changes in new-car prices, car import tariffs, car loan rates, and used-car prices, among other factors, it is possible to focus on the fairly narrow range of important factors that influence new-car demand. In contrast, a similarly precise model of aggregate demand in the overall economy might involve literally thousands of economic variables and hundreds of functional relationships.

Major Forces Driving the Economy

Demographics

The **baby-boom generation** has had a huge impact on the financial fortunes of America over the last half-century. Sociologists define this group as those born between 1946 and 1964 (inclusive). A worldwide phenomenon, it began when men returned home from fighting in World War II. For the next 15-plus years, after the restraint of the Great Depression and the war, they were suddenly relatively affluent. The birthrate soared.

Figure 9.1 shows the age distribution of all Americans in 2005. The baby-boom generation is denoted by the 40-to-59-year-old groupings. There are about 76 million baby boomers. Note how much larger this generation is than older generations. It is also larger than the ones that came afterward.

Baby-boom generation
People born between 1946 and 1964.

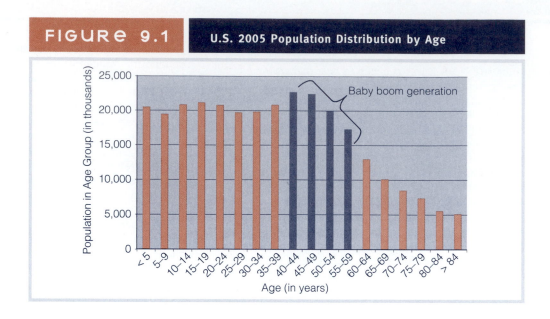

FIGURE 9.1 **U.S. 2005 Population Distribution by Age**

At every age, the baby boomers have had a significant impact on society. When they started going to school, for example, many new school buildings were built. Many of these buildings, 40 to 50 years old now, are still the backbone of the education system in older communities. The leading edge of the baby boomers became adults in the 1960s. They came of age by experimenting with drugs, adopting a more open attitude toward sexuality, and taking up vigorous involvement in the political process. They also had a tremendous impact on the American culture. As baby boomers married and had families, they spurred a massive housing boom. Real estate prices where driven up, and millions of new houses were constructed.

The baby-boom generation has now entered its peak earning years. During the past two decades, its members have been spending their earnings and expanding the economy. They have also been saving for their retirement. Through their personal investments, the baby boomers are largely responsible for pouring $4.3 trillion into the capital markets over the past 20 years. This demand is unprecedented in American history.

What will happen to the economy and the capital markets as baby boomers age? At every stage in their lives, they have changed society. Imagine how they might impact the health care system and the notion of retirement as they become "senior" citizens. By the year 2030, the nation's baby boomers will range in age from 66 to 84. Some stock market prognosticators have raised concerns that a demographic "time bomb" is set to explode. Some have sounded an alarm that the aging of baby boomers will cause an economic collapse and a stock market crash as they reduce spending and dump stocks and bonds to finance their retirement.

Indeed, the U.S. government faces difficulty in paying for social promises made to baby boomers. They have been promised Social Security income in retirement, starting at age 62, along with costly Medicare benefits. When Social Security and Medicare were created, there were many more workers compared to the relatively few senior citizens claiming benefits. Figure 9.2 shows that in 1950, 57.5 percent of the population was in their working years and only 8.2 percent in their retired years. This means that there were about seven workers to pay for the benefits of each retiree. By 2030, according to U.S. Census Bureau predictions, the portion of the population in retirement will increase to 19.7 percent. The ratio of working people to retired people will decline to nearly 3.5 to 1. That's half the ratio seen in 1950. How will we deal with this problem? Will we have to significantly raise taxes, eliminate or drastically reduce promised benefits? Whichever approach we take, the economy and capital markets will be impacted.

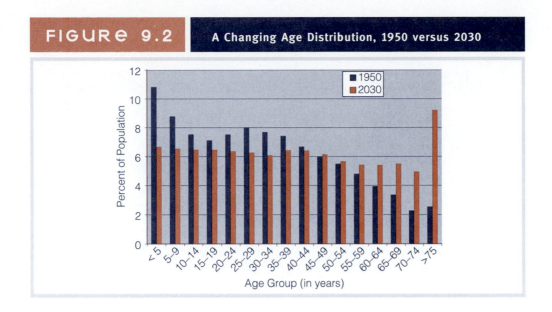

FIGURE 9.2   A Changing Age Distribution, 1950 versus 2030

Investors will be closely watching the behavior of the baby-boomer generation to see if these dire predictions come true. They may not. Baby boomers may continue to work beyond age 65, fueling economic growth and delaying the onset of retirement benefits from Social Security and Medicare. For many, the plan to keep working is a "default option" that reflects poor financial planning. These baby boomers have set aside far too little to fund a comfortable retirement. Many others plan to continue working because they enjoy successful careers. In any event, savvy investors position their investment portfolios to benefit from these demographic trends. Improving health care may allow baby boomers to be more active and to live longer in their "golden years." Older and more prosperous workers also tend to buy lots of distinctive financial services, like investment advice, tax planning, and mutual funds. As such, health care and financial services are favorite sectors for investors focused on demographic trends toward an older and more prosperous population.

Productivity

One of the most important drivers of economic growth is the pace of betterment in production, or **productivity growth**. Productivity growth is the rate of increase in output per unit of input. For example, if the amount of output produced in the economy were to grow by 5 percent following only a 2 percent increase in the quantity of inputs employed, then the overall rate of productivity growth would be roughly 3 percent. When productivity growth is robust in the overall economy, economic welfare per capita rises quickly. When productivity growth is sluggish, economic welfare improves slowly. If productivity growth is robust for individual companies, or within specific industry groups, superior efficiency is suggested and exceptional profitability often ensues. Thus, the rate of productivity growth is important both for managers and investors in individual companies and for decision makers in the public sector.

To provide detailed productivity data and other economic statistics on the location, activities, and products of U.S. manufacturers, the U.S. Commerce Department conducts mandatory annual surveys. Coverage is comprehensive in the *Annual Survey of Manufacturers*. Basic data obtained include the kind of business, location, ownership, value of shipments, payroll, and employment. Also collected are data on the cost of materials, inventories, new capital expenditures, fuel and energy costs, hours worked, and payroll supplements.

These survey data have many uses. The Bureau of Labor Statistics uses this information to calculate annual productivity series, update producer price indexes, and calculate weights for new index components. The Federal Reserve Board uses the data to prepare the Index of Industrial Production. The Bureau of Economic Analysis uses the data to prepare annual gross domestic product updates and weights for GDP deflators. The Department of Commerce's

Productivity growth
The change in output of a worker, a machine, or an entire national economy in the creation of goods and services.

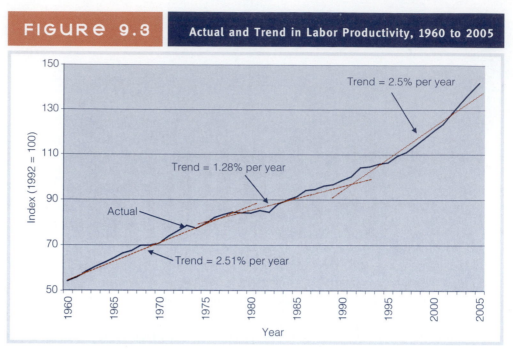

FIGURE 9.3 | Actual and Trend in Labor Productivity, 1960 to 2005

Source: U.S. Bureau of Labor Statistics.

International Trade Administration uses export data to evaluate and forecast industrial activity. State and local agencies use such data to design trade and economic policies. Private industry and trade associations use them to plan operations, analyze markets, and make investment and production decisions.

Figure 9.3 shows that productivity growth was quite robust in the United States, at 2.51 percent per year, from 1960 to the mid-1970s. Growth in productivity slowed to 1.28 percent from the mid-1970s through the 1980s. Productivity growth increased again to 2.5 percent through the 1990s to 2005.

Almost the entire recent productivity slowdown in the United States was attributable to a decrease in the efficiency with which capital and labor were used. During the 1950s and 1960s, rapid productivity growth stemmed from the civilian use of government-funded innovation inspired by the World War II effort. Important examples include the digital computer, advances in electronics, and nuclear energy. The recent increase in the trend of productivity growth has been a reward for the nation's increased investment in science. Innovations such as the Internet and communications technology have done wonders for productivity growth.

International Trade

In 1900, the United States was one of many countries with an abundance of natural resources, skilled workers, and a political system that encouraged economic expansion. Other countries now have these benefits, including China, Japan, Russia, and many countries in Europe. As events played out during the 20th century, the geographic isolation of the United States helped it avoid many of the world's problems. During the first half of the 20th century, Europe's economic infrastructure was devastated by two world wars. World War II was particularly disastrous as factories, warehouses, buildings, roads, and bridges were destroyed all over Europe, Russia, and Japan. Economic infrastructure in countries such as China and Russia not only suffered during World War II but were also ravaged by civil war and the turmoil created by extreme political change. Unlike the case with other world economic powers, the physical and economic infrastructure in the United States was not harmed by either world war. In fact, U.S. industrial capability increased through the invention of new, faster, and more efficient meth-

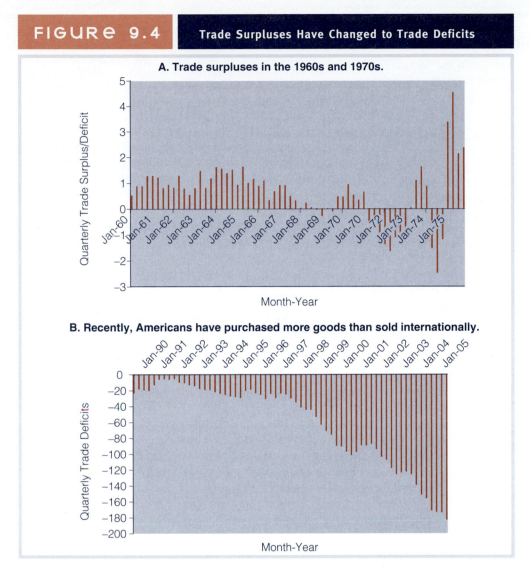

FIGURe 9.4 — Trade Surpluses Have Changed to Trade Deficits

Source: U.S. Department of Commerce, Bureau of Economic Analysis.

ods of production that were needed for wartime manufacturing. By the end of World War II, the United States was the only country left in the world with the economic capability to help rebuild Japan and Europe.

High relative productivity allowed the United States to **export** more goods and services than it **imported** for many years. Even in the 1960s and early 1970s, the U.S. economy produced many goods and services that were sold all over the world. Panel A of Figure 9.4 shows that from 1960 to 1975, the United States exported goods and services worth billions of dollars per year more than the value of what it imported. When a country exports more than it imports, domestic consumption is relatively low and the economy can grow faster than one might expect given its population and productivity growth.

Trade deficits occur when a country imports more goods and services than it exports. For the past two decades the United States has been running a large trade deficit. Panel B of the figure shows that the U.S. trade deficit is getting worse. In the mid-1990s, the trade deficit averaged $25 billion per quarter ($100 billion per year). By 2005, the U.S. deficit had grown to $175 billion per quarter ($700 billion per year). Economists and investors alike wonder how long the United States can continue such trade deficits without harming the economy. To this point, our growing trade deficits have been financed by foreign investors and foreign governments willing to hold dollars in return for goods and services sold to the American consumer.

Export
The amount of domestic goods and services sold internationally.

Import
The amount of foreign goods and services purchased domestically.

Trade deficit
Excess value of imports over exports.

Here Come China and India

Between 1870 and 1915, Germany and the United States emerged as giants in the global economy. By 1975, Japan had also materialized as a decisive force in the global economy. As the new millennium is getting under way, experts project that China will become the fourth example of a large, rapidly growing export economy being integrated into the international economic system. India may be next.

According to the World Bank, the top five economic powers are the United States, with a gross domestic product of $11.7 trillion, Japan ($4.6 trillion), Germany ($2.7 trillion), the United Kingdom ($2.1 trillion), and France ($2 trillion). Together, these global economic powerhouses account for roughly 58 percent of the total global GDP of $40 trillion. China is the world's seventh-largest economy, with GDP of $1.6 trillion; India is tenth, with GDP of $700 billion. (All figures are in 2004 dollars.) A different ranking occurs when countries are classified according to population, and hence economic potential, rather than current economic might. In terms of population, the top five countries are China, 1,297

million; India, 1,080 million; the United States, 294 million; Indonesia, 218 million; and Brazil, 179 million. Japan is the tenth-most-populous country, with 128 million people. Germany is thirteenth, with 83 million people. France is twentieth, with a population of 60 million; the United Kingdom is twenty-first, with 59 million people. The world's population is about 6.4 billion people.

Economists predict rapid economic development for China and India on the basis of their large and growing populations, commitment to education, and substantial investments in economic infrastructure such as roads, bridges, shipyards, and electric power. In both countries, factories are popping up all over to facilitate rapid growth in domestic and foreign trade. When one takes a broad historical perspective, the scale, speed, and global impact of China's and India's economic emergence is a big positive for global prosperity. Both will make a big contribution in the 21st century.

For access to interesting global economic data and information, consult the World Bank Web site at **http://web.worldbank.org**.

So far, so good. However, when such foreigners become reluctant to continue to hold U.S. dollars, those dollars will come home to America, cause inflation, and reduce the amount of goods and services available for domestic consumption.

Macroeconomic Forecasting

Business Cycles

The prime advantage gained from common stock investing is that it gives investors the opportunity to share in the benefits provided by economic growth. The profit and sales performance of all companies depends to a greater or lesser extent on the vigor of the overall economy. Business activity in the United States expanded at roughly 3.3 percent per year during the past decade when measured in terms of GDP. With inflation averaging 2.7 percent per year during the same period, business activity has expanded at a rate of roughly 0.6 percent per year when measured in terms of inflation-adjusted, or real, dollars. During robust expansions, the pace of growth in real GDP can increase to an annual rate of 4 to 5 percent or more for brief periods. During especially severe recessions, real GDP can actually decline for an extended period. In the case of firms that use significant financial and operating leverage, a difference of a few percentage points in the pace of overall economic activity can make the difference between vigorous expansion and gut-wrenching contraction.

Business cycle
Rhythmic pattern of contraction and expansion in the overall economy.

Contraction
A sustained period of declining economic activity.

Expansion
A sustained period of rising economic activity.

One of the most important economywide considerations for investors is the **business cycle**, or rhythmic pattern of **contraction** and **expansion** observed in the overall economy. Table 9.1 shows the pattern of business-cycle expansion and contraction that has been experienced in the United States since 1919. Between October 1919 and November 2001, there have been 16 complete business cycles. The economic expansion that started in November 2001 was continuing into 2006. Since 1945, the average duration of each cyclical contraction has been 10 months, with duration measured from the previous cyclical peak to the low point or trough of the subsequent business contraction. The average duration of each cyclical expansion has been 57 months, as measured by the amount of time from the previous cyclical trough to the peak of the following business expansion. Clearly, periods of economic expansion predominate, which indicates a healthy and growing economy.

TABLE 9.1	Business-Cycle Expansions and Contractions

Business Cycle Reference Dates		Duration in Months			
Peak	**Trough**	**Contraction**	**Expansion**	**Cycle**	
Quarterly Dates are in Parentheses		Peak to Trough	Previous Trough to this Peak	Trough from Previous Trough	Peak from Previous Peak
	March 1919(I)	—	—	—	—
January 1920(I)	July 1921(III)	18	10	28	17
May 1923(II)	July 1924(III)	14	22	36	40
October 1926(III)	November 1927(IV)	13	27	40	41
August 1929(III)	March 1933(I)	43	21	64	34
May 1937(II)	June 1938(II)	13	50	63	93
February 1945(I)	October 1945(IV)	8	80	88	93
November 1948(IV)	October 1949(IV)	11	37	48	45
July 1953(II)	May 1954(II)	10	45	55	56
August 1957(III)	April 1958(II)	8	39	47	49
April 1960(II)	February 1961(I)	10	24	34	32
December 1959(IV)	November 1970(IV)	11	106	117	116
November 1973(IV)	March 1975(I)	16	36	52	47
January 1980(I)	July 1980(III)	6	58	64	74
July 1981(III)	November 1982(IV)	16	12	28	18
July 1990(III)	March 1991(I)	8	92	100	108
March 2001(I)	November 2001(IV)	8	120	128	128
Average, all cycles:					
1854–2001 (32 cycles)		17	38	55	56
1854–1919 (16 cycles)		22	27	48	49
1919–1945 (6 cycles)		18	35	53	53
1945–2001 (10 cycles)		10	57	67	67
Average, peacetime cycles:					
1854–2001 (27 cycles)		18	33	51	52
1854–1919 (14 cycles)		22	24	46	47
1915–1945 (5 cycles)		20	26	46	45
1945–2001 (8 cycles)		10	52	63	63

Source: National Bureau of Economic Research. © NBER 2006. Used with permission.

On any given business day, a wide variety of news reports, press releases, and analyst comments can be found concerning the current state and future direction of the overall economy. The reason for intense interest is obvious: Whether the current economy is in a state of boom, moderate expansion, moderate contraction, or outright **recession**, there is sure to be widespread disagreement among analysts concerning current or future business prospects. This reflects the fact that, despite intense interest and widespread news coverage, the causes of economic contractions and expansions remain something of a mystery. *How* such shifts can be predicted and controlled is still largely beyond our knowledge.

Recession
Severe economic contraction.

Economic Indicators

Government and private institutions, like the National Bureau of Economic Research (NBER), collect and report a wide variety of **economic indicators** to describe the pattern of projected, current, or past economic activity. Some of the most readily available economic information is published regularly on the Internet and in leading business newspapers, such as *Barron's* "market laboratory." Table 9.2 lists a sampling of the types of economic measures available. Many

Economic indicators
Data series that successfully describe the pattern of projected, current, or past economic activity.

TABLE 9.2	Pulse of the Economy—Selected Economic Indicators, January 9, 2006			
	Latest Date	Latest Data	Preceding Period	Year Ago
Economic Growth and Investment				
Gross domestic product	3rd qtr	4.1	3.3	4.0
Industrial output *	Nov	109.0	r108.2	116.8
Manufacturing (NAICS) *	Nov	111.8	r111.4	119.9
Personal income (bil. $)	Nov	10,443	r10,413	9,837
Production				
Steel (thous. tons)	Dec 31	2,020	1,988	2,030
Utilities *	Nov	104.8	r104.5	114.4
Consumption and Distribution				
Consumer spending (bil. $)	Nov	8,894	r8,868	8,407
Retail store sales (bil. $)	Nov	353.87	r352.96	344.88
Inventories				
Factory inventories (bil. $)	Nov	467.14	r466.41	470.88
Wholesale inventories (mil. $)	Oct	356,993	r356,354	334,739
Orders				
Durable goods (bil. $)	Nov	223.0	r213.7	199.1
Purchasing management index	Dec	54.2	58.1	57.3
Trade				
Balance of payments (including services) (mil $)	3rd qtr	-195.8	r-197.8	167.0
Exports	3rd qtr	1,202.7	1,195.4	1,125.0
Imports	3rd qtr	1,820.2	1,809.2	1,731.5
Inflation				
Consumer price index † (unadjusted)	Nov	197.6	199.2	191.0
Producer price index (finished goods) ‡	Nov	158.9	160.0	151.8
Rate of inflation, % (annual, unadjusted)	Nov	3.5	4.3	3.5
Employment				
Initial jobless claims	Dec 31	291,000	r326,000	364,000
Unemployment rate, %	Dec	4.9	5.0	5.4
Construction				
Construction spending (bil. $)	Nov	1,146.4	r1,144.2	1,027.6
New housing starts (thous. units)	Nov	2,123	r2,017	1,805
Monthly Money Supply				
M1	Nov	1372.7	1367.7	1362.7
M2	Nov	6652.9	6627.2	6379.9
M3	Nov	10098.9	10058.2	9369.2
Other Indicators				
Index of coincident indicators	Nov	121.1	120.7	118.5
Index of lagging indicators	Nov	122.0	121.2	98.3
Index of leading indicators	Nov	138.8	137.9	115.2

Source: Barron's. Copyright © 2006, Dow Jones Company. Used with permission.

"r" denotes a revised number from previous report. * 1997 equals 100. † 1982–1984 equals 100.
‡ 1982 equals 100.

economic activity measures cover the pace of production for goods and services. In this regard, economists are interested in the production of power, steel, lumber, and the status of inventories. Other measures of economic activity view the economy from a consumption perspective. Important consumption figures include orders for materials and goods, retail store sales, consumer spending, and construction spending. Money supply and current levels of employment, inflation, gross domestic product, and interest rates are often used to characterize the current condition of the economy. Historical values of these economic measures (and many more) are available for free downloading at the Federal Reserve Bank of St. Louis Web site, **http://research.stlouisfed.org/fred2**.

Leading indicators are used to predict the level of future economic activity. Other measures, called **lagging indicators**, seem to follow trends in economic activity. Table 9.3 shows the economic data used by the Conference Board in creating its composite index of indicators. The basis for some of these lead and lag relationships is obvious. For example, building permits precede housing starts, and orders for plant and equipment lead production in durable goods industries. Each of these indicators directly reflects plans or commitments for the activity that follows. Other barometers are not directly related to the economic variables they

Leading indicators
An economic index that changes before the economy begins to follow a particular trend.

Lagging indicators
An economic index that changes after the economy has already begun to follow a particular trend.

Table 9.3

Leading Economic Indicators and Related Composite Indexes   *Composite indexes of leading, coincident, and lagging indicators are summary statistics for the U.S. economy. They are constructed by averaging individual components to smooth out the volatility of the individual series. Cyclical turning points in the leading index traditionally occur before those in aggregate economic activity. Cyclical turning points in the coincident index tend to occur at about the same time as those in aggregate economic activity, and cyclical turning points in the lagging index generally occur after those in the aggregate economic activity.*

	Standardization Factors
Leading Index (10 indicators)	
Average weekly hours, manufacturing	.2542
Average weekly initial claims for unemployment insurance	.0333
Manufacturers' new orders, consumer goods and materials	.0753
Vendor performance, slower deliveries diffusion index	.0698
Manufacturers' new orders, nondefense capital goods	.0186
Building permits, new private housing units	.0266
Stock prices, 500 common stocks	.0377
Money supply, M2	.3535
Interest rate spread, 10-year Treasury bonds less federal funds	.1019
Index of consumer expectations	.0291
Coincident Index (4 indicators)	
Employees on nonagricultural payrolls	.5293
Personal income less transfer payments	.2077
Industrial production	.1469
Manufacturing and trade sales	.1161
Lagging Index (7 indicators)	
Average duration of unemployment	.0373
Inventories to sales ratio, manufacturing and trade in 1992 dollars	.1221
Labor cost per unit of output, manufacturing	.0623
Average prime rate	.2777
Commercial and industrial loans	.1137
Consumer installment credit to personal income ratio	.1931
Consumer price index for services	.1937

Source: The Conference Board. Check **www.conference-board.org** for the latest updates on this information. © 2006, The Conference Board.

forecast. An index of common stock prices is a good leading indicator of general business activity. Although the causal linkage may not be readily apparent, stock prices reflect aggregate profit expectations by investors and thus give a consensus view of the likely course of future business conditions. At any point in time, stock prices both reflect and anticipate changes in aggregate economic conditions. All of this makes macroeconomic forecasting particularly nettlesome for investors. A great source of current and historical economic data is the St. Louis Fed Web site (**http://research.stlouisfed.org/fred2**).

Sentiment Surveys

Sentiment
General level of optimism or pessimism.

Investors want to know the direction of the economy so that they can make both asset allocation and stock-picking decisions. Because future economic activity depends on what people plan to do, **sentiment** surveys simply ask leaders in business and consumers to reveal their business outlook and future plans. Table 9.4 lists several common sentiment surveys. Part A shows surveys that focus on consumer expectations about spending and the "comfort level" of consumers. Rising sentiment often bodes well for the economy, while decreasing sentiment signals a possible decline in economic activity. Part B shows a number of surveys that focus on investors and investor expectations. If investors believe the stock market is going to increase, they are more likely to buy stocks, and rising stock prices become a self-fulfilling prophecy. If investors are cautious and do not intend to buy stocks, this signals dwindling demand for stocks and a possible decline in prices. Sentiment measures are widely followed and reported in the financial press. However, their interpretation is not always consistent among analysts. Some analysts believe that very high sentiment measures signal strong confidence, a strong economy, and rising stock prices. Other analysts take a contrarian perspective and believe that high sentiment readings are a sign of extreme optimism and irrational exuberance. They would argue that high sentiment readings signal a stock market top.

Changing Expectations

A subtle problem that bedevils both macroeconomic and microeconomic forecasting is the problem of changing expectations. If business purchasing agents are optimistic about future trends in the economy and boost inventories in anticipation of surging customer demand, the

---

TABLE 9.4	Survey Measures of Sentiment		
Survey	**Description**	**Frequency**	**Began**
A. Consumer Surveys			
Consumer Confidence Index	Sponsored by the Confidence Board. Surveys 5,000 households about their expectations in spending.	Monthly	February 1967
Index of Consumer Sentiment	Sponsored by the University of Michigan. Asks consumers about personal finances, business conditions, and buying conditions.	Monthly	Quarterly data: November 1952 Monthly data: January 1978
Consumer Comfort Index	Sponsored by ABC News/*Money Magazine*. Asks people for their view on the economy and the buying climate and about their personal finances.	Weekly	December 1985
B. Investor Surveys			
AAII Investor Sentiment Survey	Sponsored by the American Association of Individual Investors. Asks member investors about stock market expectations.	Weekly	July 1987
Stock Market Confidence Indices	Sponsored by the Yale School of Management. Asks investors about expectations of stock market valuation and crash probability.	Monthly	Semiannual data: 1989 Monthly data: July 2001

resulting inventory buildup can itself contribute to economic growth. Conversely, if purchasing agents fear an economic recession and cut back on orders and inventory growth, they themselves can be main contributors to any resulting economic downturn. The expectations of purchasing agents and other managers can become a self-fulfilling prophecy because the macroeconomic environment represents the sum of the investment and spending decisions of business, government, and the public. Indeed, the link between expectations and realizations has the potential to create an optimistic bias in government-reported statistics.

Government economists are sometimes criticized for being overly optimistic about the rate of growth in the overall economy, the future path of interest rates, or the magnitude of the federal deficit. As users of economic statistics, investors must realize that it can pay for government economists or politically motivated economists to be optimistic. If business leaders can be led to make appropriate decisions for a growing economy, their decisions can in fact help lead to a growing economy. Unlike many business economists from the private sector, government-employed and/or politically motivated economists often actively seek to manage the economic expectations of business leaders and the general public.

It is vital for investors to appreciate the link between economic expectations and realizations and to be wary of the potential for forecast bias.

Industries and Sectors

Industry Classification

In the United States, industries are classified using the **North American Industry Classification System (NAICS)**. The NAICS categorizes establishments by the principal activity in which they are engaged. The NAICS, developed in cooperation with Canada and Mexico, classifies North America's economic activities at 2-, 3-, 4-, and 5-digit levels of detail. The U.S. version of NAICS further defines some industries to a more precise sixth digit of detail. Table 9.5 illustrates how the entire scope of economic activity is subdivided into sectors described by two-digit classifications. Below the two-digit major group, or sector level, the NAICS system proceeds to desegregated levels of increasingly narrowly defined activity.

There are also other classification systems that categorize firms by broad economic sectors. For example, Standard & Poor's subdivides its S&P 500 Index into 10 sector indexes. Table 9.6 shows a breakdown of the 500 firms in the index as assigned to sectors such as energy, materials, industrials, and consumer discretionary. Financial firms make up the largest sector in the S&P 500 Index, consisting of 21 percent of the index. The Information Technology and Health Care sectors are the next-largest sectors in the index. The Telecommunication Services and Materials sectors are the smallest. The Dow Jones Company subdivides its global Dow Jones Titans Index into eighteen sectors.

North American Industry Classification System (NAICS)
Method for categorizing establishments according to the economic activity in which they are engaged.

Competitive Environment

The firm's competitive environment is described by the **market structure** the firm faces. Market structure includes the number and size distribution of buyers and sellers, degree of product differentiation, amount and cost of information about product price and quality, and conditions of entry and exit. In a series of books, Michael Porter characterized the competitive environment of an industry in terms of five driving forces. These five forces describe the competitive environment, indicate the magnitude of profit opportunities, and help to determine the extent to which such profit opportunities are sustainable in the long run. The five forces are:

Market structure
Competitive environment.

1. **Rivalry among existing competitors:** Generally speaking, the greater the number of companies in an industry, the more likely the industry will be very competitive. Competitive industries are characterized by low prices, low profitability, and erratic sales growth.

2. **Threat of new entrants:** When an industry has low barriers to entry, other firms can easily enter and compete with existing firms. Low-entry-barrier industries exhibit low

| | TABLE 9.5 | NAICS Classification of Industries, 2002 |

Code	Industry
11	Agriculture, Forestry, Fishing, and Hunting
21	Mining
22	Utilities
23	Construction
31	Manufacturing
42	Wholesale Trade
44-45	Retail Trade
48-49	Transportation and Warehousing
51	Information
52	Finance and Insurance
53	Real Estate and Rental and Leasing
54	Professional, Scientific, and Technical Services
55	Management of Companies and Enterprises
56	Administrative and Support and Waste Management and Remediation Services
61	Educational Services
62	Health Care and Social Assistance
71	Arts, Entertainment, and Recreation
72	Accommodation and Food Services
81	Other Services (except Public Administration)
92	Public Administration

Source: U.S. Census Bureau.

| | TABLE 9.6 | Standard & Poor's Sector Indexes |

	No. of Firms	Market Capitalization	Index Level	Jan. 12, 2006 Change	Year to Date
S&P 500	500	11,611,195	1,286.06	−0.63%	3.03%
Energy	29	1,117,864	397.602	−0.86	6.67
Materials	31	338,664	188.458	−1.40	0.71
Industrials	53	1,287,661	292.93	−0.79	0.80
Consumer Discretionary	90	1,250,256	265.312	−0.83	2.68
Consumer Staples	39	1,086,843	241.934	−0.48	0.74
Health Care	57	1,537,800	376.394	−0.09	2.42
Financials	84	2,451,745	437.149	−0.68	2.52
Information Technology	77	1,806,166	352.043	−0.70	6.42
Telecommunications Services	8	349,787	119.508	−0.56	1.78
Utilities	32	384,409	162.186	−0.02	1.58

Source: Standard & Poor's. © 2006 Standard and Poor's. Used with permission.

profitability. Anytime profitability increases to an above-normal rate in low-entry-barrier industries, entry or expansion by established competitors occurs. Prices and profits are driven down until above-normal profits are eliminated. Internet retailers experience this phenomenon. On the other hand, industries that depend on intensive capital investment or special patents have high barriers to entry.

TABLE 9.7	Number of Firms and Concentration Ratios for a Representative Sample of Industries					
Industry	NAICS Code	Industry Sales ($ millions)	Top 4 Firms (CR$_4$)	Top 8 Firms (CR$_8$)	Top 20 Firms (CR$_{20}$)	Top 50 Firms (CR$_{50}$)
Electronic shopping and mail-order houses	4541	121,416	19.0	29.8	44.2	57.9
Amusement and theme parks	713110	8,310	69.2	84.9	90.6	94.4
Hospitals	622	46,002	9.0	12.3	18.8	28.6
Air transportation	481	17,973	18.7	29.4	44.4	61.9
Beer, wine, and distilled alcoholic beverage wholesalers	4248	7,911	81.7	95.3	100.0	100.0
Computer systems design	5415	175,068	17.5	21.7	27.6	34.7
Securities and commodity exchanges	5232	3,213	79.5	93.8	100.0	100.0
Motion picture and video production	51211	45,019	51.1	67.4	72.7	77.8
Newspaper publishers	51111	45,660	32.2	44.6	62.2	77.3

Source: U.S. Census Bureau, 2002 Economic Census.

3. **Pressure from substitute products:** When good substitutes are available, competition from related industries can be fierce. The availability of substitute products tends to limit profit margins because when prices and profit margins begin to rise, demand switches to substitute products.

4. **Bargaining power of customers:** The ability of producers to raise prices depends on the bargaining power of customers. When a few large customers buy a huge proportion of total output, producers face great difficulty in controlling prices. If several customers buy a small proportion of total output, buyer power is minimal.

5. **Bargaining power of suppliers:** Profitability is often highly dependent on input costs. Thus, firms must be concerned with who controls the costs of supplies and raw materials. Sometimes, industries with a few large suppliers find themselves at a bargaining disadvantage and profits suffer.

Every industry has a different market structure, and the importance of the five factors listed above tends to vary. For example, manufacturers of consumer goods must face the buying power of big-box retailers like Wal-Mart. At the same time, Wal-Mart needs to stock distinctive consumer products offered by the Procter & Gamble (P&G) Company, such as *Charmin* tissue, *Gillette* razors, and *Tide* detergent. When Wal-Mart and P&G meet, the buying power of Wal-Mart collides with the selling power of P&G. Consumers benefit from the compromises that result. Of course, many other factors in addition to those listed above can help shape the firm's competitive environment, especially in the short run. Short-term changes in available production capacity, inventory, and currency exchange rates can all be important.

Most industries and lines of business offer some blend of vigorous competition and **monopoly**. They represent business opportunities in imperfectly competitive markets. Developing and implementing an effective investment strategy in imperfectly competitive markets involves a never-ending search for uniquely attractive products. Not all industries offer the same potential for sustained profitability.

Monopoly
A single seller in the industry.

Table 9.7 shows census information on the industry sales and leading-firm market share data for a small sample of industries. Industries that contain a large number of firms of roughly equal size are generally regarded as vigorously competitive. Questions about the intensity of competition sometimes arise when only a limited number of competitors are present or when only a handful of large firms dominates the industry.

Investors need to know how the level of competition within an industry can be quantitatively measured. As shown in Table 9.7, the Census Bureau describes the degree of competitor size

Concentration ratios (CRs)
Percentage market share held by a group of leading firms.

inequality within an industry using sales information for various clusters of top firms. These group market share data are called **concentration ratios (CRs)** because they measure the percentage market share concentrated in (or held by) an industry's top 4 (CR_4), 8 (CR_8), 20 (CR_{20}), or 50 (CR_{50}) firms. Thus, the concentration ratio for a group of n leading firms is defined in percentage terms as:

$$CR_n = \frac{\sum_{i=1}^{n} \text{firm sales}_i}{\text{industry sales}} \times 100 \qquad (9.1)$$

where i refers to an individual firm.

Concentration ratios can range from $CR_n = 0$ for an industry with a massive number of tiny competitors to $CR_1 = 100$ for an industry represented by a single monopolist. In the manufacturing sector, where concentration tends to be highest, four-firm concentration ratios tend to fall in a broad range between $CR_4 = 20$ and $CR_4 = 60$; eight-firm concentration ratios often lie in a range between $CR_8 = 30$ and $CR_8 = 70$. When concentration ratios are low, industries tend to include many firms and competition tends to be vigorous. Industries in which the four leading firms are responsible for less than 20 percent of total industry sales (i.e., $CR_4 < 20$) are highly competitive and approximate the perfect-competition model. On the other hand, when concentration ratios are high, leading firms dominate other firms in terms of size and may have more potential for pricing flexibility and economic profits. Industries in which the four leading firms control more than 80 percent of total industry sales (i.e., $CR_4 > 80$) are often described as highly concentrated. Industries with a $CR_4 < 20$ or $CR_4 > 80$, however, are quite rare. Three-quarters of all manufacturing activity takes place in hotly competitive industries with concentration ratios falling in the range between $20 \leq CR_4 \leq 80$.

Try It!

Consider a local industry with $1 million in sales. The largest firm in the industry has sales of $400,000, the second-largest firm has sales of $300,000, the third-largest firm has sales of $200,000, and the smallest firm has sales of $100,000. Calculate the CR_1, CR_2, CR_3, and CR_4 for this industry. Is this industry apt to be vigorously competitive?

Solution

From the formula for the CR_n:

$$CR_1 = \frac{400,000}{1,000,000} \times 100 = 40$$

$$CR_2 = \frac{400,000 + 300,000}{1,000,000} \times 100 = 70$$

$$CR_3 = \frac{400,000 + 300,000 + 200,000}{1,000,000} \times 100 = 90$$

$$CR_4 = \frac{400,000 + 300,000 + 200,000 + 100,000}{1,000,000} \times 100 = 100$$

These concentration ratios are high. They are indicative of an industry with few competitors and the level of price competition may be muted. However, competition among the few can be fierce.

By definition, concentration ratios rise with an increase in competitor size inequality within a given industry. Concentration ratios, however, are unaffected by the degree of size inequality within each respective group of leading firms. This can create problems because competition within industries featuring a handful of large competitors can be much more vigorous than in those where a single dominant firm faces no large adversaries. For example, while $CR_4 = 100$ would signal monopoly in the case of a single dominant firm, it might describe a vigorously competitive industry if each of the leading four firms enjoys a roughly equal market share of 25 percent. To capture all the effects of competitor size inequality, the **Herfindahl Hirschmann Index (HHI)** is used. Named after the economists who invented it, HHI is a measure of competitor size inequality that reflects size differences among large and small firms. Calculated in percentage terms, the HHI is the sum of the squared market shares for all n industry competitors:

Herfindahl Hirschmann Index (HHI)
Measure of size inequality among competitors.

$$\text{HHI} = \sum_{i=1}^{n} (\% \text{ industry market share}_i)^2 \qquad (9.2)$$

For example, a monopoly industry with a single dominant firm that has 100 percent of the market share has an $\text{HHI} = 100^2 = 10{,}000$. A moderately competitive industry where each of the leading four firms enjoys a market share of 25 percent features an $\text{HHI} = 25^2 + 25^2 + 25^2 + 25^2 = 2{,}500$. A vigorously competitive industry with 100 firms with 1 percent market share each has an $\text{HHI} = 100$. This measure of competitor size inequality is bounded by 0 and 10,000.

Investors use the HHI to find industries with low levels of competition (indicated with a high HHI) in hopes of finding firms in an environment conducive to achieving high profitability. However, it is the government's task to promote competition. In this regard, the U.S. Department of Justice uses the HHI for evaluating mergers for its antitrust function. Guidelines issued by the U.S. Department of Justice and the Federal Trade Commission illustrate that the government considers an industry with an HHI between 1,000 and 1,800 points to be moderately concentrated. Industries for which the HHI is in excess of 1,800 points are considered to be concentrated. Mergers that increase the HHI by more than 100 points in concentrated markets raise antitrust concerns.

It is always helpful to consider the number and size distribution of competitors, degree of product differentiation, level of information available in the marketplace, and conditions of entry when assessing the investment merits of a given company. Unfortunately, these and other readily obtained data are seldom definitive. For example, the HHI is a national measure and ignores international trade and local nuances. Japanese imports are a big factor in the auto industry, for example, and local newspapers have significant market power despite small overall size. When transportation costs are significant, as they are in construction materials, local firms can also enjoy significant market power. In addition, industry classifications themselves may be vague. Conditions of entry and exit are subtle and dynamic, as is the role of unseen potential entrants. All of this contributes to the difficulty of correctly assessing the profit potential of current products or prospective lines of business.

An effective investment strategy in imperfectly competitive markets must be based on the search for firms with a clear **competitive advantage**. A competitive advantage is a unique or rare ability to create, distribute, or service products valued by customers. Just as all industries are not alike in terms of their inherent profit potential, all firms are not alike in terms of their capacity to exploit available opportunities. In the business world, long-lasting above-normal rates of return require a sustainable competitive advantage that, by definition, cannot be easily duplicated. Although business and investor success is possible in hotly competitive markets, only difficult-to-enter monopoly and **oligopoly** markets hold the potential for long-lasting above-normal returns.

Competitive advantage
Unique ability to create, distribute, or service products.

Oligopoly
Few sellers in an industry.

Hotly competitive markets offer investors the potential for a normal risk-adjusted rate of return on investment during typical market conditions. If many capable competitors offer identical products, vigorous price competition tends to eliminate above-average profits. The only exception to this rule is that superior efficiency can sometimes lead to superior profits, even in perfectly competitive markets. Hamburger chain McDonald's and discount retailer Wal-Mart Stores, for example, have succeeded in providing investors with above-average rates of return in vigorously competitive industries. However, they are the exception. How many restaurant chains can you name that have achieved outstanding long-term success for investors? How many local and regional retailers has Wal-Mart put out of business?

Government-Guaranteed Oligopoly

The Federal National Mortgage Association (Fannie Mae) and the Federal Home Loan Mortgage Corporation (Freddie Mac) are publicly traded corporations that enjoy immense benefits as government-sponsored enterprises. Fannie and Freddie are potent competitors for banks, savings and loans, and other lenders because both have the implied guarantee of the federal government on their liabilities. This earns them the highest possible credit rating and allows Fannie and Freddie to attract institutional investors at the lowest possible interest rate. Fannie and Freddie purchase hundreds of billions of dollars in home mortgages from thrifts and other financial institutions every year. Most of these loans are packaged and resold to investors as mortgage-backed securities. Both Fannie and Freddie make a profit by selling their packages of home loans to investors at an interest rate that is roughly 1 percent per year lower than that on the underlying pool of mortgages. In so doing, they earn enormous and rapidly growing profits. Both often report an annual rate of return on stockholder's equity in excess of 20 percent, or nearly double the profit rate earned by financial institutions in general.

While the U.S. government charges nothing for its implied credit guarantee, Fannie and Freddie reap billions of dollars per year in profits. It should come as no surprise, therefore, that competing financial institutions are unhappy about continued Fannie and Freddie expansion. Competitors claim that Fannie and Freddie compete unfairly because of their implicit subsidy from the U.S. government. Competitors have a point. During the 1990s, total profits and earnings per share grew by more than 15 percent per year for both Fannie and Freddie. Recently, Congress has been pushing for stronger capital requirements for Fannie and Freddie, demanding more transparent accounting, and asking them to earmark more loans for low-income and moderate-income families. Congress also wants Fannie and Freddie to rein in future growth. Despite such limits, Fannie and Freddie are likely to continue to prosper. There are clearly tangible rewards to government-guaranteed oligopoly!

See Dawn Kopecki, "Greenspan Seeks to Recast Debate on Fannie and Freddie Portfolios," *The Wall Street Journal Online*, January 20, 2006 (**http://online.wsj.com**).

Try It!

Consider a local industry with $1 million in sales. The largest firm in the industry has sales of $400,000, the second-largest firm has sales of $300,000, the third-largest firm has sales of $200,000, and the smallest firm has sales of $100,000. Calculate the HHI for this industry. Is this industry highly concentrated?

Solution

From the formula for the HHI:

$$HHI = \Sigma\left[(\text{firm sales}_i / \text{industry sales}) \times 100\right]^2$$

$$= \left[(\$400,000/\$1,000,000) \times 100\right]^2 + \left[(\$300,000/\$1,000,000) \times 100\right]^2 +$$

$$\left[(\$200,000/\$1,000,000) \times 100\right]^2 + \left[(\$100,000/\$1,000,000) \times 100\right]^2$$

$$= 40^2 + 30^2 + 20^2 + 10^2$$

$$= 3,000$$

The HHI of 3,000 indicates that firms within this industry are operating in a highly concentrated environment.

Legal Environment

Regulation of the Competitive Environment

Regulation
Government control or influence.

Although all sectors of the U.S. economy are regulated to some degree, the method and scope of **regulation** vary widely. Most companies escape price and profit restraint, except during periods of general wage-price control, but they are subject to operating regulations governing pollution emissions, product packaging and labeling, worker safety and health, and so on.

Other firms, particularly in the financial and public utility sectors, must comply with financial regulation in addition to such operating controls. Banks and savings and loan institutions, for example, are subject to state and federal regulation of interest rates, fees, lending policies, and capital requirements. Unlike firms in the electric power and telecommunications industries, banks and savings and loans face no explicit limit on profitability.

Although the direct costs of regulation are immense, they may be less than indirect costs borne by consumers, employees, and investors. For example, extensive reporting requirements of the Occupational Safety and Health Administration (OSHA) drive up administrative costs and product prices. Consumers also bear the cost of auto emission standards mandated by the Environmental Protection Agency (EPA). Recent studies put direct and indirect expenses tied to federal regulation at roughly $2,500 per year for every man, woman, and child in the United States. Local and state regulations already cost consumers billions of dollars. New federal regulations on health care, worker safety, and the environment will add billions more. Investment success requires finding opportunities where the potential for debilitating regulatory costs can be avoided.

Antitrust Policy

The U.S. government seeks to promote competition. This task falls to the Bureau of Competition of the Federal Trade Commission (FTC) and the Antitrust Division of the Department of Justice (DOJ). These two government agencies conduct **antitrust policy**. Their main focus is on stemming anticompetitive business practices and ensuring a competitive environment.

In evaluating mergers, for example, enforcement agencies must strike a fine balance between the expected cost savings and the possible harm to competition. Both present-day and potential competitors must be considered. The impact on competition is particularly difficult to evaluate in industries experiencing rapid structural and technological change. Enforcement agencies must balance concerns about market power against the efficiencies mergers can make possible. Figure 9.5 shows the number of mergers announced each year and the number of challenges posed by either the FTC or the DOJ. Note that the number of mergers announced at the height of the stock market bubble was near 5,000 per year. The number of mergers significantly declined to 1,014 by 2003 and increased again in 2004. The FTC and DOJ challenge

Antitrust policy
Laws and rules designed to promote competition.

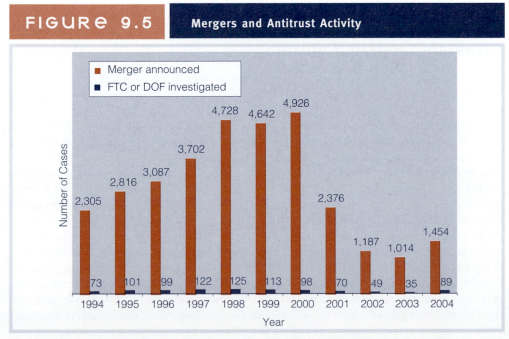

FIGURE 9.5 | **Mergers and Antitrust Activity**

Source: Federal Trace Commission and Department of Justice, 2005 Annual Report to Congress.

only a small fraction (2 to 4 percent) of announced mergers. A challenged merger typically ends in one of three outcomes. After further review, the FTC or DOJ may decide to consent to the merger. Alternatively, the companies involved may decide to abandon their merger proposal. Lastly, the merger may be restructured to resolve regulator concerns. For example, in March 2003 the FTC planned an injunction to block the $2.8 billion merger of Nestlé and Dreyers. The FTC was concerned about substantially lessened competition in the market for the sale of super-premium ice cream. Nestlé, Dreyers, and the FTC negotiated a remedy to the alleged anticompetitive effects of the merger. In June 2003, regulators approved a revised merger agreement that required the parties to **divest** the Dreamery and Godiva super-premium ice cream brands.

Divest
Sell a part of the business or a product line.

The FTC and DOJ also step in when they believe a firm is guilty of using anticompetitive practices to restrain competition. One fascinating case began in October 1997, when the DOJ sued Microsoft Corporation. DOJ alleged that Microsoft forced computer makers to install its Internet Explorer Web browser along with the Microsoft Windows operating system. In 1998, DOJ filed a comprehensive antitrust suit against the software giant, accusing it of having abused its Windows monopoly to crush Web browser competition, particularly the Netscape Web browser, and the Java programming language. In June 2000, U.S. District Judge Penfield Jackson ordered Microsoft to be split into two companies, one for applications software, such as MS-Word and Excel, and one for operating systems, such as Windows. Microsoft appealed that decision.

In June 2001, the appeals court unanimously ruled that Microsoft had indeed violated antitrust laws by illegally abusing its operating-system monopoly. However, the court rejected a breakup of the company and ordered that the parties negotiate a settlement. The settlement, approved in November 2002, sought to restore software competition by giving computer makers greater freedom to remove various features from Microsoft Windows and allowing computer manufacturers to install rival software, such as alternative Internet browsers or media programs. The settlement also required that Microsoft license software equitably to computer makers. It directed Microsoft to license communication protocols and share software interfaces that programmers use to write applications for Windows. Microsoft has also paid billions of dollars in fines and financial settlements with various competitors and suppliers. Antitrust litigation with the European Commission and the Korean Fair Trade Commission are ongoing.

As these examples illustrate, antitrust policy is a serious constraint to many business decisions, and antitrust considerations are an important aspect of the investment environment.

Corporate Governance

Ownership versus Control

Public corporations are legal entities. The biggest advantage of the corporate form of business is that it limits risk while allowing perhaps thousands of individual investors to pool economic resources. Investors would be reluctant to form a partnership with complete strangers because partnership liabilities are ultimately the responsibility of each individual partner. If a partnership lost millions of dollars on a failed project or an adverse legal judgment, for example, each individual partner could be held responsible for making good on that obligation. In a partnership arrangement, each partner faces unlimited liability. In a corporation, investor liability is limited to the amount invested in the corporation. The corporation can go broke, but individual investors with only a small investment in the bankrupt company can continue to prosper on the basis of their other investments.

By virtue of the fact that corporations are separate legal entities, some separation in ownership and control is typical. Especially in large companies, management tends to own a relatively small share of the corporation. In the S&P 500, for example, most top managers and members of the board of directors collectively own less than 1 to 2 percent of the corporation. In some circumstances, corporations suffer from serious governance problems in that self-serving managers pursue corporate policies that favor management, employees, or the firm's other stakeholders at the expense of shareholders. This is known as the *principal-agent problem,* or the firm's agency problem. It occurs when top management (the agent) hired by shareholders (the principal) acts in a manner that is inconsistent with the economic interests of shareholders. Resulting monitoring and enforcement expenses borne by shareholders are called *agency costs*.

Solutions to the firm's agency problem come about by providing management with proper incentives and carefully monitoring managerial performance. This system of incentives and monitoring devices is called the firm's **corporate governance** system.

Incentive Compensation

Companies try to align manager and shareholder interests through incentive-based pay. Company executives are compensated in many different ways. They receive a basic salary that typically includes standard pension contributions and various perquisites (company car, club memberships, etc.). Many top executives also receive a bonus that is linked to accounting or stock price performance through long-term incentive programs. Such incentive programs commonly include stock option rewards. Grants of restricted stock are another common form of long-term reward. A leading authority on executive compensation is the consulting firm Towers Perrin. In 2005, it reported that CEO pay in the United States came from basic salary (27 percent), **incentive pay** like stock options (62 percent), benefits (6 percent), and other perquisites (5 percent). Most CEO pay comes from incentive programs.

Executive stock options are the most common form of incentive-based pay. Stock options are contracts that allow executives to buy shares of company stock at a fixed price, called the exercise or strike price. At the time of issuance, the typical executive option contract sets a strike price equal to the prevailing stock price. The most common length of the option contract is 10 years. If the price of company stock rises above the strike price and the stock option is exercised, the executive will capture the difference between the strike price and the current stock price as ordinary income. Stock options give executives an incentive to manage the firm in such a way that the stock price will tend to increase. This is precisely what stockholders want. As a result, compensation experts believe that stock options align managerial and shareholder objectives.

Recent corporate scandals have caused companies to reassess the benefits of stock options. Stock options may have created improper incentives in some circumstances. Because the value of a stock option depends on the pace of stock price appreciation, some CEOs might have forgone reasonable increases in dividends in favor of risky leverage-increasing stock buybacks. Stock options also tend to reward top executives for normal stock price appreciation, rather than any abnormal returns tied to superior management efficiency. Also, stock options fail to provide necessary incentives if the stock price falls too far below the strike price. In such instances, stock options would be too far underwater to effectively motivate managers. Lastly, stock options can give harmful incentives to manage earnings and run the company in such a way so as to boost the perception of outstanding short-term performance, even at the cost of hurting long-term results.

Savvy investors carefully study information about incentive pay plans from the company's annual proxy statement, filed with the Securities and Exchange Commission. Table 9.8 shows the executive compensation for Microsoft managers. You may find it surprising that Bill Gates earns a company salary of less than $1 million per year as chairman of Microsoft. Don't feel too sorry for him; he owns over 1 billion shares of the firm's stock—that's worth over $27 billion!

Managerial Monitoring

Managerial performance is monitored inside the firm by the board of directors who hire and oversee management. Board members represent stockholder interests in frequent meetings with top management, as do representatives of large shareholders and institutional investors. Other outside monitors include independent auditors, security analysts, investment bankers, credit-rating agencies, and regulators.

People on the **board of directors** are elected by the shareholders to represent stockholder interests. The board is charged with four broad functions: (1) hire, evaluate, and perhaps even replace top management, (2) approve major operating proposals (large capital expenditures,

Corporate governance
Control system that helps corporations effectively administer economic resources.

Incentive pay
Compensation according to measurable performance.

Executive stock options
A compensation plan that pays the executive increasingly more as the price of the stock rises.

Board of directors
People elected by shareholders to hire management and monitor the firm.

TABLE 9.8	Executive Compensation at Microsoft Corp.					
			Annual Compensation		Long-Term Compensation Awards		
Name and Principal Position	Year	Salary	Bonus	Restricted Stock Award(s)	Securities Underlying Options (No.)	All Other Compensation
Steven A. Ballmer	2005	$600,000	$400,000	—	—	$　9,073
Chief Executive Officer; Director	2004	591,667	310,000	—	—	8,937
	2003	550,000	313,447	—	—	8,931
William H. Gates III	2005	600,000	400,000	—	—	2,469
Chairman; Chief Software Architect;	2004	591,667	310,000	—	—	2,787
Director	2003	550,000	313,447	—	—	2,931
James E. Allchin	2005	570,000	430,000	—	—	6,846
Co-President, Microsoft Platform Products &	2004	558,334	342,000	—	—	1,468,381
Service Division; Group Vice President	2003	504,168	350,000	383,840	1,300,000	6,207
Kevin R. Johnson	2005	502,386	550,000	—	—	8,983
Group Vice President,	2004	480,336	435,000	—	—	1,046,007
World Wide Sales, Marketing and Services	2003	379,125	300,000	$326,264	600,000	8,540
Jeffrey Raikes	2005	570,000	475,000	—	—	7,810
Group Vice President,	2004	562,500	400,000	—	—	7,758
Information Worker Business	2003	522,917	350,000	383,840 (6)	1,300,000	7,592

Source: Microsoft 2005 Proxy Statement, **www.microsoft.com/msft/sec.mspx**.

acquisitions, etc.), (3) approve major financial decisions (issuance of stocks and bonds, dividend payments, stock repurchases, etc.), and (4) offer expert operating and strategic advice to management. In executing these functions, members of the board of directors represent the interests of all shareholders.

Institutional investors

Mutual funds, pension funds, insurance companies, etc.

Institutional investors, such as pension funds, mutual funds, and insurance companies, face some restrictions about the types of securities that they can own. For example, some institutional investors are limited in the amount of their investment portfolios that can be invested in common stocks or are restricted from owning common stocks selling for less than $5 per share (penny stocks). Professional money managers often earn incentive compensation when the funds they manage exceed benchmark returns, so they face strong incentives to earn solid rates of return on their investment portfolios. As a result, many institutional investors actively encourage management to adopt policies that will increase stock market values, and they can become effective advocates for shareholder interests. Because institutional investors often hold a substantial stake in the firm, the potential benefits from their activism are often large enough to justify significant monitoring costs.

Auditors

Accountants hired by the board to validate the firm's financial statements.

Security analysts

People who investigate the value of firms for investors.

Investment banks

Banks that help companies acquire capital through the issuance of securities.

One of the most important outside monitors is the firm's independent auditor. The mission of **auditors**, who are hired by the board, is to examine the firm's accounting control system and give their opinion as to whether or not the firm's financial statements offer a fair representation of the firm's financial position. The independent auditor's fairness opinion letter is included in the firm's annual report to stockholders. **Security analysts** who follow the firm also conduct their own, independent evaluations of the company's business activities and report their findings to their employers or the overall investment community. When security analysts publish their opinions for the general investment community, they are supposed to give unbiased and expert assessments. Some security analysts are employed by **investment banks**, like the Goldman Sachs Group, that help companies raise capital. When obtaining additional capital from public investors, firms file various financial documents with regulators and seek

Does Corporate Governance Matter?

Research in financial economics has long focused on the operating implications and valuation effects of corporate governance. Some common examples of corporate governance mechanisms that weaken shareholder rights are: "poison pills," which make mergers or takeovers difficult; an insufficient number of independent board members, which can result in failure to discipline managers; and improperly aligned executive compensation. State laws and federal regulations are important when it comes to corporate governance. They set the tone for corporate governance by specifying basic shareholder rights and determining the form and timing of investor communications. In recent years, stronger guidelines on the method and scope of financial reporting by independent outside auditors have become increasingly important.

If a firm's governance rules are not strong, additional agency costs may be incurred by the firm. These additional agency costs may be reflected in reduced operating performance. Research shows that firms with weak shareholder rights tend to report relatively low profit margins, poor cash flow performance, and subpar revenue growth. Corporate management tends to do a relatively poor job when shareholders have a strictly limited ability to replace or otherwise discipline underperforming management. Moreover, when using analysts' earnings forecasts and returns around earnings announcements as proxies for investor expectations, researchers have found that analysts and investors are not surprised by substandard operating performance among firms with weak corporate governance. This means that the market knows that poor corporate governance leads to poor operating performance.

Relatively good operating performance for firms with strong shareholder rights suggests that the monitoring discipline provided by active shareholders can be beneficial. Indeed, one of the oldest remedies for an inefficient separation in ownership and control is to make top management and members of the board of directors become significant shareholders. Lots of empirical evidence suggests that owner-managers make better managers. Similarly, the evidence also suggests that strong corporate governance is better for everyone.

See John Core, Wayne Guay, and Tjomme Rusticus, "Does Weak Governance Cause Weak Returns? An Examination of Firm Operating Performance and Investors' Expectations," *Journal of Finance,* vol. 61, no. 2 (April 2006), pages 655–687.

---

the favorable independent opinion of a **credit-rating agency**, like Moody's Corporation. Moody's provides credit ratings and research analysis for debt instruments and other securities for global capital markets. These credit ratings assess the issuer's ability to make timely interest and principal payments and are a crucial determinant of an issuer's ability to effectively market debt securities.

The federal government also monitors business activities through the **Securities and Exchange Commission (SEC)** and the Internal Revenue Service (IRS). The SEC's mission is to regulate public firms for the protection of public investors. The commission has the power to make policy and punish violators in civil court. The IRS enforces the tax rules to ensure corporations pay taxes, just as it ensures that individual American citizens pay taxes. For criminal prosecution, regulators turn to the U.S. Department of Justice. In addition, the states exercise vigorous oversight through a variety of state agencies. In order to increase the effectiveness of federal and state regulation of corporate activities, the U.S. Congress passed the Sarbanes-Oxley Act in July 2002. It is the most dramatic federal law pertaining to corporate financial disclosure and corporate governance since the original securities laws of the 1930s. Overall, Sarbanes-Oxley created a new oversight body to regulate auditors, established rules pertaining to corporate responsibility (for both corporate boards and management), and increased punishment for corporate white-collar crime.

Credit-rating agencies
Companies that grade the quality of debt issues.

Securities and Exchange Commission (SEC)
Federal regulatory body charged with monitoring corporations and the investment industry.

Ownership Structure

Ownership structure is characterized by the amount of equity owned by managers, board members, institutional investors, and widely dispersed individual investors. Among these, the percentage of inside-equity financing receives the most attention. **Inside equity** is the share of stock closely held by the firm's chief executive officer (CEO), other corporate insiders including top managers, and members of the board of directors. Employees are another important source of inside-equity financing, perhaps as part of an employee stock ownership plan, or ESOP. The balance of equity financing is obtained from large single-party outside shareholders, mutual funds, insurance companies, pension funds, and the general public. Investors can easily obtain information about the amount of insider holdings from the company's annual proxy statement, filed with the SEC. This information is also commonly reported on popular financial Web sites such as Yahoo! Finance, MSN Money, and nasdaq.com.

Inside equity
Common stock held by management and other employees.

When the share of insider holdings is "large," a similarly substantial insider self-interest in the ongoing performance of the firm can be presumed. Managers with a significant ownership interest have an obvious incentive to run the firm in a value-maximizing manner. Similarly, when ownership is concentrated among a small group of large and vocal institutional shareholders, whose shares are called **institutional equity**, managers often have strong incentives to maximize corporate performance. On the other hand, when the amount of closely held stock is "small," and equity ownership is dispersed among a large number of small individual investors, top management can sometimes become insulated from the threat of stockholder sanctions following poor operating performance.

However, not all institutional owners are the same. Public pension funds and insurance companies tend to have a long-term view of their investments. Some public pension funds are outspoken in their efforts to spur management to increase shareholder value and improve corporate governance. Among the most publicly active institutional investors are the California Public Employees' Retirement System (CalPERS) and the Teachers Insurance and Annuity Association College Retirement Equities Fund (TIAA-CREF). Many institutional investors work with a coalition called the Council of Institutional Investors (CII) (see **www.cii.org**). On the other hand, many mutual fund portfolio managers tend to have a short-term focus. Many would rather sell their shares and move on to the next investment than fight with management to make substantial changes.

To get some direct insight on ownership structure among large firms, see Table 9.9, which shows insider and institutional stock ownership for S&P 500 companies. The chief executive officer, other members of top management, and members of the board of direc-

Institutuional equity

Common stock ownership by pension funds, mutual funds, and other large independent shareholders.

TABLE 9.9	Insider and Institutional Stock Ownership among S&P 500 Firms, January 2006			
Company Name	Ticker	Mkt. Cap. ($ billions)	Insider Holdings (%)	Institutional Holdings (%)
A. High Insider Holdings				
Estee Lauder Cos.	EL	7.518	67.2	47.5
Stryker Corp.	SYK	18.739	51.0	46.5
E. W. Scripps Class A.	SSP	8.083	48.4	53.0
Campbell Soup Co.	CPB	12.565	46.2	40.1
Chiron Corp.	CHIR	8.429	43.0	46.3
Metlife Inc.	MET	38.364	39.9	45.7
Reebok Intl.	RBK	3.503	38.0	89.0
Gap Inc.	GPS	15.201	37.6	65.3
Franklin Res Inc.	BEN	24.823	37.5	48.0
JCPenney Co. Holdings	JCP	13.182	35.9	88.1
B. High Institutional Holdings				
SLM Corp.	SLM	24.192	1.5	98.0
Ryder System Inc.	R	2.638	1.7	97.4
Health Management Assoc. A. stock	HMA	5.381	3.2	97.2
Eastman Kodak Co.	EK	7.154	0.3	97.2
Electronic Arts	ERTS	17.115	1.2	96.9
Tenet Healthcare Corp.	THC	3.624	0.2	96.5
Fluor Corp. (new)	FLR	7.122	1.1	96.3
Eog Resources Inc.	EOG	19.264	0.6	96.2
Millipore Corp.	MIL	3.542	0.3	95.9
Cummins Inc.	CMI	4.523	1.1	95.7
S&P 500 Average			**5.2**	**73.6**

Source: © 2006 Standard & Poor's. Used with permission.

tors together own an average 5.2 percent of the corporations they lead. Institutions own an average 73.6 percent of these companies. Some insider ownership is also included in the institutional ownership category because one company may own shares in another and have representatives on both boards of directors.

Data described in Table 9.9 reflect a well-established trend of increasing institutional investor ownership over time. The probability that investors will discover evidence of managerial inefficiency or malfeasance is increased when institutional ownership is substantial. Insider stock ownership and institutional stock ownership appear to represent alternative forms of ownership concentration that combine to form an effective method for ensuring that managers of large corporations are sensitive to investor interests.

Summary

■ **Macroeconomics** is the study of aggregate measures of economic activity at the international, national, regional, or state level. **Microeconomics** is the study of economic data at the industry, firm, plant, or product level.

■ Three major forces have driven the economy over the past decade: demographics, productivity growth, and international trade. The **baby-boom generation** has contributed to the economy with its spending and supported the stock and bond market with its investing. Boomers will soon enter their retirement years. **Productivity growth** is the rate of increase in output per unit of input. When productivity growth is robust, economic welfare rises quickly. International trade measures the **exports** and **imports** of each country. The United States has had increasing **trade deficits** for two decades.

■ One of the most important economywide considerations for investors is the **business cycle**, or rhythmic pattern of **contraction** and **expansion** observed in the overall economy. A **recession** is a sharp contraction. The Conference Board, a private research group, provides extensive data on a wide variety of **economic indicators**, or data series that successfully describe the pattern of projected, current, or past economic activity. Some indicators, like building permits, are known as **leading indicators** because they suggest where the economy is going. Other **lagging indicators** show where the economy has been. **Sentiment** surveys ask people their expectations about future purchases and investing.

■ **Market structure** is typically characterized on the basis of five forces of industry competitiveness: rivalry among existing firms, threat of new entrants, pressure from substitutes, bargaining power of customers, and bargaining power of suppliers.

■ An effective investment strategy in imperfectly competitive markets must be based on the search for firms with a clear **competitive advantage**. A competitive advantage is a unique ability to create, distribute, or service products valued by customers. Although business and investor success is possible in hotly competitive markets, only difficult-to-enter **monopoly** and **oligopoly** markets hold the potential for long-lasting above-normal returns.

■ Leading-firm market share data calculated from sales information for various clusters of top firms are called **concentration ratios (CRs)** because they measure the percentage market share concentrated in (or held by) an industry's top 4 (CR_4), 8 (CR_8), 20 (CR_{20}), or 50 (CR_{50}) firms. The **Herfindahl Hirschmann Index (HHI)**, named after the economists who invented it, is a popular measure of competitor size inequality that reflects size differences among large and small firms.

■ Although all sectors of the U.S. economy are regulated to some degree, the method and scope of **regulation** vary widely. Most companies escape price and profit restraint, except during periods of general wage-price control, but they are subject to operating regulations governing pollution emissions, product packaging and labeling, worker safety and health, and so on. A significant recent challenge for **antitrust policy** has been the dramatic rise in merger activity.

■ The separation between ownership and control in public firms causes the principal-agent problem between managers and shareholders. To monitor managers, firms have an elaborate **corporate governance** system. One aspect of this system is **incentive pay**, including the use of **executive stock options** to align the interests of managers and shareholders.

■ **Boards of directors** monitor the firm from within, and **institutional investors** have some influence on management as large shareholders. However, many people from outside the firm also attempt to monitor it. **Auditors** validate the financial statements, **investment analysts** give investors recommendations, **investment banks** conduct due diligence when issuing securities, and **credit-rating agencies** advise bondholders. Since the 1930s, the government regulates firms through the **Securities and Exchange Commission (SEC)**.

■ Ownership structure is characterized by the amount of equity owned by managers, board members, institutional investors, and widely dispersed individual investors. Among these, the percentage of **inside-equity** financing receives the most attention. Inside equity is the share of stock closely held by the firm's chief executive officer (CEO), other corporate insiders including top managers, and members of the board of directors. When ownership is concentrated among a small group of large and vocal institutional shareholders, called **institutional equity**, managers often have strong incentives to maximize corporate performance.

Self-Test Problems

ST9.1   The International Monetary Fund (IMF) gathers and reports global economic data. The following data on economic growth come from the "IMF World Economic Outlook," April 2005. Characterize the real GDP growth rate in advanced economies. Then examine and describe economic growth in emerging economies.

Country	1997	1998	1999	2000	2001	2002	2003	2004
Advances Economies Real GDP Growth								
Canada	4.2	4.1	5.5	5.2	1.8	3.4	2.0	2.8
France	1.9	3.6	3.2	4.2	2.1	1.1	0.5	2.3
Germany	1.4	2.0	2.0	2.9	0.8	0.1	−0.1	1.7
Italy	2.0	1.8	1.7	3.0	1.8	0.4	0.3	1.2
Japan	1.7	−1.1	0.0	2.4	0.2	−0.3	1.4	2.6
United Kingdom	3.3	3.1	2.9	3.9	2.3	1.8	2.2	3.1
United States	4.5	4.2	4.4	3.7	0.8	1.9	3.0	4.4
Emerging Economies Real GDP Growth								
Brazil	3.3	0.1	0.8	4.4	1.3	1.9	0.5	5.2
China	8.8	7.8	7.1	8.0	7.5	8.3	9.3	9.5
India	5.2	5.6	6.9	4.7	4.8	4.4	7.5	7.3
Mexico	6.8	5.0	3.6	6.6	0.0	0.6	1.6	4.4
Russia	1.4	−5.3	6.3	10.0	5.1	4.7	7.3	7.1

Solution

In general, the advanced economies appear to be fairly integrated. In other words, good economic years for some countries are also good economic years for most countries. For example, rapid economic growth for the United States was achieved in 1997, 1998, 1999, 2000, and 2004. These years were generally good for Canada, France, Germany, and the United Kingdom. The United States had slower growth in 2001 and 2002. These were also slower growth years for the other countries. Japan's economic growth has been much slower than that of the others, and it does not seem to be as strongly linked to the other advanced economies.

The pace of economic expansion has generally been higher in emerging economies than advanced economies. China and India have been experiencing particularly strong economic growth. However, the variation in economic growth is much lower in advanced economies than in emerging economies. Consider that the range of growth in advanced economies is -1.1 to 5.5 percent but the range in emerging economies is -5.3 to 10.0 percent.

www.mhhe.com/hirschey1e

ST9.2   On February 17, 2004, Cingular entered into an agreement to acquire AT&T Wireless. Cingular and AT&T Wireless are the second- and third-largest mobile wireless service providers in the United States, with approximately 24 and 22 million subscribers, respectively. They both provide mobile wireless services in many overlapping areas throughout the United States and are two of only six providers with a national presence. The 2002 Economic Census shows the cellular industry's total revenue was $97.1 billion. The largest four firms in the industry had combined revenues of $61.2 billion. The largest 8, 20, and 50 firms had combined revenues of $81.0, $88.8, and $92.9 billion, respectively. The Justice Department is concerned that the combination of Cingular's and AT&T Wireless's assets and businesses will likely result in substantially less competition for mobile wireless services. Should the Justice Department challenge the merger?

Solution

The concentration ratios for the cellular industry are

$$CR_4 = \frac{61.2}{97.1} \times 100 = 63.0 \qquad CR_8 = \frac{81.0}{97.1} \times 100 = 83.4$$

$$CR_{20} = \frac{88.8}{97.1} \times 100 = 91.4 \qquad CR_{50} = \frac{92.9}{97.1} \times 100 = 95.7$$

These concentration ratios suggest that the industry is highly concentrated on a national level. However, the industry may be even more concentrated in local markets. For example, some geographic locations may have only two or three cellular companies operating. Therefore, the Justice Department should compute HHI for various locations.

The level concentration, as measured by HHI, in various smaller markets range from approximately 2,600 to more than 5,300. This is well above the 1,800 threshold at which the Justice Department considers a market to be highly concentrated. After Cingular's proposed acquisition of AT&T Wireless is consummated, the HHIs in the relevant geographic markets would range from approximately 4,400 to more than 8,000. The increases in the HHI as a result of the merger would range from approximately 1,100 to more than 3,500. This is much higher than the threshold of 100 below which the Department considers a transaction unlikely to cause competitive harm.

The cellular industry is highly concentrated and the proposed merger is apt to be anticompetitive in many local markets. If so, the merger between Cingular and AT&T Wireless would substantially decrease competition and should be challenged by the Justice Department.

Questions and Problems

9.1   Describe the three major forces that have played an important role in shaping the U.S. economy for the past few decades, and speculate on their future impact.

9.2   Discuss factors that contribute to productivity growth. How do the factors needed to increase productivity in an emerging economy, like China, differ from those factors needed by a developed economy, such as the United States?

9.3   Why are business cycles important to investors? Why are cyclical economic expansions and contractions hard to predict?

9.4   What is an economic indicator? Include in your explanation a description of the relationship between leading, coincident, and lagging indicators.

www.mhhe.com/hirscheyle

9.5 Go to the Conference Board's Web page (**www.conference-board.org**) and click on the Economics menu. What are the up-to-date leading indicators for the United States and other countries? What do they suggest for economic growth?

9.6 How do business and consumer expectations affect economic fluctuations and forecasts?

9.7 Consider an industry with $1.2 million in sales and six firms. The largest firm in the industry has sales of $300,000, the second-largest firm has sales of $250,000, the third- and fourth-largest firms each have sales of $200,000, the fifth-largest firm has sales of $150,000, and the smallest firm has sales of $100,000. Calculate the concentration ratios CR_1 and CR_4 for the industry. Is this industry competitive?

9.8 Consider an industry with $1.2 million in sales and six firms. The largest firm in the industry has sales of $300,000, the second-largest firm has sales of $250,000, the third- and fourth-largest firms each have sales of $200,000, the fifth-largest firm has sales of $150,000, and the smallest firm has sales of $100,000. Calculate the HHI for this industry. Is this industry competitive?

9.9 One industry is made up of 25 different companies. The distribution of market share for these companies is listed below. What is the HHI for this industry? How competitive is the industry?

1 firm has 16 percent market share

2 firms have 12 percent market share each

3 firms have 8 percent market share each

4 firms have 4 percent market share each

5 firms have 2 percent market share each

10 firms have 1 percent market share each

9.10 Firms in imperfectly competitive monopoly and oligopoly markets have the potential to earn sustained above-normal profits. Such firms, however, will not always provide above-normal returns for investors. This can be true even if a firm exploits its potential to earn above-normal profits. How, then, does an investor earn above-average returns in monopoly and oligopoly markets?

9.11 What tactics do the FTC and Justice Department employ in order to prevent industry leaders from exerting undue market power following mergers?

9.12 Why do strong corporate governance mechanisms appeal to investors?

9.13 How do incentive pay plans and high levels of inside equity align the interests of management with those of shareholders?

9.14 Go to the Council of Institutional Investors Web page (**www.cii.org**) and view the most recent news. From the announcements, describe some of the causes the CII is actively pursuing.

9.15 Name and describe the different groups that monitor a firm.

STANDARD &POOR'S

9.16 Go to the Standard & Poor's Market Insight Web site at **www.mhhe.com/edumarketinsight** and click on the Commentary link. The Trends & Projections (T&P) report issued monthly by S&P provides an insightful economic analysis on various topics. Read the most recent T&P report. What is the topic of this report? What is the conclusion? The last table provides estimates for economic indicators. What GDP growth is predicted for next year? What is expected for the CPI?

STANDARD &POOR'S

9.17 Standard & Poor's Market Insight Web site at **www.mhhe.com/edumarketinsight** provides a great deal of information about industries. Click on the Industry link and then pick an industry in the pull-down menu. Explore the information provided. Give examples of firms in this industry. What does S&P say about the industry in its Industry Surveys? What is the environment? Is it very competitive?

9.18 An industry is currently growing at twice the rate of the overall economy. New competitors are entering the industry and the formerly high profit margins have begun to decline. The life-cycle stage that best characterizes this industry is:

a. Mature growth
b. Pioneering development
c. Rapid accelerating growth
d. Stabilization and market maturity

9.19 Which of the following is *least likely* to explain why government regulation is usually a suboptimal response to monopolistic markets?

a. Regulatory agencies often reflect the views of special interests.
b. Owners of regulated companies can lack the incentive to operate at a low cost.
c. Regulatory agencies may lack information about the true costs and profits of companies.
d. Regulatory agencies can typically enforce marginal cost pricing but not average cost pricing.

9.20 If the effects are fully anticipated, what impact is expansionary monetary policy *most likely* to have on real economic activity?

a. Little or no impact
b. Large expansionary impact
c. Moderate expansionary impact
d. Moderate contractionary impact

INVESTMENT APPLICATION

Corporate Governance at Microsoft

Spectacular failures at companies such as Adelphia, Enron, and WorldCom have illustrated the importance of good corporate governance. Lawmakers focused on corporate governance issues and passed the Public Company Accounting Reform and Investor Protection Act of 2002 (also known as the Sarbanes-Oxley Act). The law set up a new oversight body to regulate auditors, created laws pertaining to corporate responsibility, and increased punishments for corporate white-collar crime. Good corporate governance is of particular importance to equity investors. Poor governance can lead to bankruptcy, as in the case of Adelphia, Enron, World-Com, and others. The stockholders of bankrupt firms often lose their entire ownership position. Therefore, it is very important for stockholders to assess the level of corporate governance in any firm they are considering purchasing.

Consider the governance characteristics of Microsoft Corporation. Incorporated in 1981, Microsoft develops, manufactures, licenses, and supports a wide range of software products. The company's software products include software for personal computers and intelligent devices, scalable operating systems for servers, server applications for client-server environments, software development tools, business solutions applications, and mobile and embedded devices. The company is best known for its Windows operating system and computer software products such as MS Office and Internet Explorer. The company also sells the Xbox video game console, along with games and peripherals. Its online businesses include the MSN network of Internet products and services. The company's seven product segments are Client, Server and Tools, Information Worker, Microsoft Business Solutions, MSN, Mobile and Embedded Devices, and Home and Entertainment.

TABLE 9.10	Governance at Microsoft

A. Ownership Structure

Top Institutional Holders		Top Insiders		
Holder	**Shares**	**Holder**	**Position**	**Shares**
FMR Corp. (Fidelity Management & Research Corp).	440,573,874	Gates, William H., III	Chairman	1,057,499,336
Barclays Bank Plc.	412,758,081	Ballmer, Steven A.	CEO	409,977,990
State Street Corp.	312,027,594	Raikes, Jeffrey S.	Officer	4,633,000
Capital Research and Management Co.	267,406,480	Shirley, Jon A.	Director	2,030,894
Vanguard Group, Inc. (The)	232,234,981	Marquardt, David F.	Director	1,972,589
Axa	176,360,501			
Wellington Management Co., LLP	169,585,464	**Ownership Breakdown**		
Northern Trust Corp.	140,317,806	% of shares held by all insiders		14
Deutsche Bank Aktiengesellschaft	131,822,090	% of shares held by institutional & mutual funds		55
Citigroup Inc.	131,624,077	% of float held by institutional & mutual funds		63

Source: Yahoo! Finance.

B. Board of Directors

Member	History	Member		History
William H. Gates III	Chairman and Chief Software Architect, Microsoft Corporation	Ann McLaughlin Korologos	Com	Chairman, RAND Corporation; Chairman Emeritus, The Aspen Institute; Senior Advisor, Benedetto, Gartland & Co. Inc.
Steven A. Ballmer	Chief Executive Officer, Microsoft Corporation	David F. Marquardt		General Partner, August Capital
James I. Cash Jr., Ph.D — Aud	Former James E. Robison Professor, Harvard Business School	Charles H. Noski	Aud	Former Vice Chairman, AT&T Corporation
Dina Dublon — Aud	Former Chief Financial Officer, JPMorgan Chase	Helmut Panke	Com	Chairman of the Board of Management, BMW AG
Raymond V. Gilmartin	Chairman, President and Chief Executive Officer, Merck & Company, Inc.	Jon A. Shirley		Former President and Chief Operating Officer, Microsoft Corporation

(continued on next page)

Note: Aud = Audit Committee, Com = Compensation Committee.
Source: Microsoft 2004 Annual Report.

Microsoft has long been a highly profitable firm. In 2006, the company earned about $14 billion on $45 billion in revenue. Given its 10.2 billion shares outstanding, earnings per share were $1.30. During the year, Microsoft stock traded at a premium to the overall market, with a typical P/E of about 22. Table 9.10 shows the ownership structure, board structure, and executive compensation for Microsoft.

Microsoft also publishes its own corporate governance guidelines, which are available online at **www.microsoft.com/msft/governance/guidelines.mspx**.

www.mhhe.com/hirschey1e

TABLE 9.10	Governance at Microsoft *(continued)*

C. Executive Compensation

Name and Principal Position	Year	Salary	Bonus
Steven A. Ballmer	2004	$591,667	$310,000
Chief Executive Officer; Director	2003	550,000	313,447
	2002	545,833	205,810
William H. Gates III	2004	591,667	310,000
Chairman	2003	550,000	313,447
Chief Software Architect; Director	2002	545,833	205,810
James E. Allchin	2004	558,334	342,000
Group Vice President,	2003	504,168	400,000
Platforms Group	2002	493,750	400,000
Kevin R. Johnson	2004	480,336	435,000
Group Vice President,	2003	379,125	300,000
World Wide Sales, Marketing and Services	2002	340,959	243,100
Jeffrey S. Raikes	2004	562,500	400,000
Group Vice President,	2003	522,917	300,000
Information Worker Business	2002	493,749	250,000

Name and Principal Position	Year	Restricted Stock Award(s) ($)	Securities Underlying Options (No.)	All Other Compensation
Steven A. Ballmer	2004	—	—	$ 7,865
Chief Executive Officer; Director	2003	—	—	7,667
	2002	—	—	7,167
William H. Gates III	2004	—	—	1,715
Chairman;	2003	—	—	1,667
Chief Software Architect; Director	2002	—	—	1,667
James E. Allchin	2004	—	—	1,467,189
Group Vice President,	2003	$383,840	1,300,000	5,456
Platforms Group	2002	—	—	5,445
Kevin R. Johnson	2004	—	—	1,043,942
Group Vice President,	2003	326,264	600,000	7,036
World Wide Sales, Marketing and Services	2002	—	1,000,000	7,387
Jeffrey S. Raikes	2004	—	—	7,558
Group Vice President,	2003	383,840	1,300,000	7,392
Productivity and Business Services	2002	—	—	6,834

Source: Microsoft 2004 Proxy Statement.

a. Assess Microsoft's ownership structure. Is it conducive to good monitoring?

b. Assess the executive compensation package. Does it align manager and shareholder incentives?

c. Assess the structure and quality of the board of directors. Is this board capable of monitoring management?

10

chapter

Financial Statement Analysis

Many investors look forward to earnings season. Public companies report their performance and financial status four times per year (three quarterly reports and one annual report). Because most companies end their fiscal year on December 31, it is common for them to issue annual reports during January and quarterly reports in April, July, and October. On Wall Street, these months are known as "earnings season."

Corporate reports attract the attention of analysts, the media, and investors alike. Each report is closely examined to determine the company's profitability, growth, and financial health. How effective is management in using stockholders' money to earn profits? How efficient is the manufacturing process? How much financial risk is the firm taking? Investors can determine the answers to these important questions by carefully analyzing pertinent data from the firm's financial statements.

Accompanying this data about the past performance of the company are predictions about the future. Management often gives "guidance" about its expectations for profits and revenue growth for next year. This perspective is important because management knows the firm better than anyone else and has better information on which to base expectations. However, management may use this guidance to sway investors. Investors need to evaluate management expectations and determine whether these expectations are too optimistic or pessimistic.

The attractiveness of an individual common stock often depends on how successfully the company is competing in its industry. Investors often find it profitable to focus on the firm's effectiveness and efficiency in executing its business strategy. Companies that produce distinctive products, like Microsoft, are best prepared to defend their products and grab new opportunities. Savvy investors understand that Microsoft is successful because it makes life tough for competitors. How much would it cost to mount a successful competitive challenge to the Windows operating software? What are the odds that anybody will put a dent in Microsoft's dominant market position and rock-solid balance sheet during the next 10 years?[1]

CHAPTER OBJECTIVES

- Evaluate company profitability.
- Assess and interpret the return on equity.
- Determine a firm's financial liquidity.
- Compute valuation indicators.

Buying Part of a Business

Business Ownership

Holders of common stock are the actual owners of the issuing corporation. If an investor owns 1 percent of the total number of outstanding shares, he or she owns 1 percent of the company. When considering the advantages or disadvantage of share ownership, investors must keep firmly in mind the idea that they are buying or selling part of a real business. In the long run, the prospects for profiting from stock market investing are directly tied to the economic prospects of the underlying business. If an investor buys and holds stock in an attractive business with large and rapidly growing profits, long-term investment success will follow. If an investor buys and holds shares in companies with poor economic prospects, subpar investment returns are ensured. A company's prospects rely on the ability of management to run the business in a profitable manner and on the overall health of the economic environment. This chapter discusses financial statement analysis tools for measuring how well management is running the company.

Investment versus Speculation

Stock market investment is the process of buying and holding for dividend income and long-term capital appreciation the shares of companies with inherently attractive economic prospects. Investors seek to profit by sharing in the normal and predictable good fortune of such companies. **Stock market speculation** is the purchase or sale of securities on the expectation of capturing short-term trading profits from share price fluctuations that might be tied to the temporary good fortune of a given company. Speculators depend on favorable short-term trends in stock prices or on a dramatic positive change in the economic prospects facing a company.

Success in the investment process depends on a careful examination of the essential economic characteristics of business and stock market investing. Successful speculation depends on hard-to-predict changes in basic economic conditions, investor psychology, and luck. The focus of this chapter, indeed the focus of this entire book, is on the investment process. In the process of deciding the investment merit of a given company, investors must answer a number of questions tied to determining the investment merit of a given situation.

While every stock market investor must be concerned with company growth prospects, the first criterion that must be met by any attractive investment is a superior rate of profitability. An "all you can eat" diner with large portions but bad food is no bargain. Similarly, a rapidly growing

Stock market investment
Process of buying and holding stock for dividend income and long-term capital appreciation.

Stock market speculation
Purchase or sale of securities on the expectation of short-term trading profits from share price fluctuations tied to temporary good fortune.

---

[1] E. S. Browning, "Tech Stocks and Earnings Optimism Drive Major Indexes to 4½-Year Highs," *The Wall Street Journal*, January 12, 2006, p. C1.

Earnings Management

Over the past decade, the role of accounting has dramatically changed. Instead of just providing information to management, stockholders, and others regarding company performance, many corporate accounting departments have become profit centers. Instead of simply reporting profits, accounting departments are often asked how to increase profits through the use of innovative accounting methods. In some cases, ambiguity in Generally Accepted Accounting Principles (GAAP) allows for different sensible ways of accounting for the same transaction. Sometimes, ambiguity in GAAP leads to the abuse of accounting methods and outright fraud.

For example, General Electric (GE) takes advantage of legal accounting methods to help it achieve consistent earnings growth. For instance, GE's financing division, GE Capital, can reduce current earnings by using pessimistic loss estimates for problem loans. If a greater-than-expected number of troubled loans eventually get repaid, future profits will rise. By adjusting loan-loss reserve estimates, GE can manage current and future earnings. At fast-food giant McDonald's, weak operat-ing profits for a given quarter can be offset by profits from real estate transactions. McDonald's owns lots of its own restaurants and lets franchisees own and operate the rest. McDonald's enjoys significant unrealized appreciation on its real estate holdings, and it can carefully manage earnings in the volatile restaurant business by judiciously selling off property with large unrealized appreciation.

Recently, some corporate managers have used discretionary accruals to manipulate reported earnings. This form of accounting abuse appears to be more pronounced at firms where the chief executive officer's (CEO's) total compensation is closely tied to the value of stock and option holdings. During years of favorable accruals, CEOs tend to exercise unusually large numbers of options. At such times, CEOs and other insiders also tend to sell large quantities of shares. All of this makes judging the true economic performance of the firm difficult for shareholders and other outsiders. In some cases, earnings management is a big problem.

See Mohammed Hadi and Karen Talley, "Watch for Potholes as Earnings Roll In," *The Wall Street Journal Online*, January 8, 2006 (**http://online.wsj.com**).

company in a bad business is a poor investment choice. Investors must be able to discern prospects for business profits prior to making an appropriate investment decision. The most important question that must be answered by investors is disarmingly simple: Is this a good business?

Company Financial Statement Analysis

Balance Sheet

Balance sheet
"Snapshot" information about a company's financial well-being at a specific point in time.

Public companies are required to file quarterly and annual financial reports to shareholders and the Securities and Exchange Commission. These statements give snapshots of the firm's financial condition. Financial statement analysis begins with study of the firm's **balance sheet**. To see what is involved, consider the Microsoft Corporation balance sheet, including stockholders' equity data, shown in Table 10.1. Complete balance sheet information can be obtained from Microsoft's annual report to shareholders or from its annual 10K report to the SEC. As is typical, Microsoft's annual report is available for viewing at the company's Web site on the Internet. SEC reports for Microsoft and other publicly traded companies can be downloaded from the SEC's Web site at **www.sec.gov**.

Microsoft's balance sheet information gives a snapshot of the company's financial well-being at a specific point in time. In this case, fiscal year-end information for 2004 and 2005 is provided, so some idea of the rate of change in financial condition is also given. Of course, according to accounting convention, total assets equal the sum of total liabilities and stockholders' equity.

In terms of total assets, an important contribution from current assets, including cash and cash equivalents and inventories, can be detected. Total current assets account for more than two-thirds of Microsoft's total assets. Any rapid decline in cash or short-term investments might suggest problems with collections or accrual accounting problems with the estimation of operating expenses. Similarly, any rapid increase in accounts receivable would normally be cause for concern, especially if a buildup in older accounts receivable suggested collection problems. Any unwanted rapid buildup in finished-goods inventory might also be problematic. Such changes sometimes suggest softening product demand. However, no such problems are detected in the case of Microsoft. Microsoft has a very healthy balance sheet.

Also notice from Microsoft's balance sheet that stockholders' equity accounts for the bulk of company financing. Funds obtained from the sale of common stock and retained earnings account for more than 80 percent of total assets. Total liabilities, including accounts payable,

TABLE 10.1	Balance Sheet Information for Microsoft Corp.

MICROSOFT CORPORATION
Balance Sheet (in millions)

June 30	2004	2005
Assets		
Current assets:		
Cash and equivalents	$14,304	$ 4,851
Short-term investments	46,288	32,900
Total cash and short-term investments	60,592	37,751
Accounts receivable, net	5,890	7,180
Inventories	421	491
Deferred income taxes	2,097	1,701
Other	1,566	1,614
Total current assets	70,566	48,737
Property and equipment, net	2,326	2,346
Equity and other investments	12,210	11,004
Goodwill	3,115	3,309
Intangible assets, net	569	499
Deferred income taxes	3,808	3,621
Other long-term assets	1,774	1,299
Total assets	$94,368	$70,815
Liabilities and Stockholders' Equity		
Current liabilities:		
Accounts payable	$ 1,717	$ 2,086
Accrued compensation	1,339	1,662
Income taxes	3,478	2,020
Short-term unearned revenue	6,514	7,502
Other	1,921	3,607
Total current liabilities	14,969	16,877
Long-term unearned revenue	1,663	1,665
Other long-term liabilities	2,911	4,158
Commitments and contingencies		
Stockholders' equity:		
Common stock and paid-in capital—shares authorized 24,000; outstanding 10,862 and 10,710	56,396	60,413
Retained earnings (deficit), including accumulated other comprehensive income of $1,119 and $1,426	18,429	(12,298)
Total stockholders' equity	74,825	48,115
Total liabilities and stockholders' equity	$94,368	$70,815

Source: **www.microsoft.com/msft/ar05/flashversion/10k_fr_bal.html.**

accrued compensation, income taxes payable, and unearned revenue, were used to finance less than 20 percent of total assets. Microsoft makes very conservative use of financial leverage.[2]

Income and Cash Flow Statements

Whereas balance sheet information shows company financial well-being at a specific point in time, the company's **income statement** gives an ongoing view of dynamic change. If the balance

Income statement

Report of business inflows and outflows during a given period.

---

[2] In fiscal year 2005, retained earnings fell sharply because Microsoft paid a special $3 per share cash dividend.

Net income
Difference between revenues and expenses, often expressed on an after-tax basis.

Earnings per share
Net income divided by the number of shares outstanding

Diluted earnings per share
Net income divided by the number of shares outstanding after consideration of the possible conversion of stock options and convertible securities.

Basic earnings per share
Firm's earnings divided by number of shares outstanding.

Cash flow statement
Report that shows change in the company's cash position over a period of time.

sheet provides a snapshot of financial performance, then income and cash flow statements provide the "video." In the case of Microsoft, operating information is provided in Table 10.2 for the years 2003 to 2005. This is a standard format that gives investors an opportunity to judge the rate of change occurring in company operating performance.

The income statement begins with net revenues, typically defined as gross revenues minus returns, discounts, and allowances. Operating net income is the simple difference between net revenues and operating costs and expenses. In the case of Microsoft, major operating expense categories include research and development, sales and marketing, and general and administrative. Operating net income is affected by investment income and other minor adjustments to arrive at net income before taxes.

After taxes have been deducted, **net income** is divided by the number of shares outstanding to arrive at basic **earnings per share**. This is an important indication of earnings-per-share performance, but it can sometimes prove misleading when a company issues a significant number of stock options to top executives and other employees. In Microsoft's case, management and employee stock options are an important component of total compensation. As such, the potential dilution to the ownership position of current shareholders is significant. When the use of stock options is significant, investors focus their attention on **diluted earnings per share** numbers, rather than **basic earnings per share**.

Finally, while the income statement provides a vital measure of ongoing performance, accounting errors or bias sometimes reduces its value as a measure of economic performance. In such instances, investors often look to the **cash flow statement** for an interesting perspective

TABLE 10.2	Income Statement Information for Microsoft Corp.

MICROSOFT CORPORATION
INCOME STATEMENTS
(in millions, except earnings per share)

Year Ended June 30	2003	2004	2005
Revenue	$32,187	$36,835	$39,788
Operating expenses:			
Cost of revenue	6,059	6,716	6,200
Research and development	6,595	7,779	6,184
Sales and marketing	7,562	8,309	8,677
General and administrative	2,426	4,997	4,166
Total operating expenses	22,642	27,801	25,227
Operating income	9,545	9,034	14,561
Investment income and other	1,509	3,162	2,067
Income before income taxes	11,054	12,196	16,628
Provision for income taxes	3,523	4,028	4,374
Net income	$ 7,531	$ 8,168	$12,254
Earnings per share:			
Basic	$ 0.70	$ 0.76	$ 1.13
Diluted	$ 0.69	$ 0.75	$ 1.12
Weighted-average shares outstanding:			
Basic	10,723	10,803	10,839
Diluted	10,882	10,894	10,906
Cash dividends declared per share	$ 0.08	$ 0.16	$ 3.40

Source: **www.microsoft.com/msft/ar05/flashversion/10k_fr_inc.html.**

on change in the company's economic position. As shown in Table 10.3, cash flow has three primary sources. Net cash is provided by operating, financing, and investing activities. Operating cash flow is the change in company liquidity as captured by net income plus noncash charges, such as depreciation and amortization. Adjustments to reconcile net income to cash provided by operating activities also include various changes in assets and liabilities. Cash flows provided by or used for financing activities include transactions involving the purchase and/or sale of the company's own stocks and bonds. Cash flows provided by or used for

TABLE 10.3	Cash Flow Statement Information for Microsoft Corp.

MICROSOFT CORPORATION
CASH FLOWS STATEMENTS
(in millions)

Year Ended June 30	2003	2004	2005
Operations			
Net income	$ 7,531	$ 8,168	$ 12,254
Depreciation, amortization, and other noncash items	1,393	1,186	855
Stock-based compensation	3,749	5,734	2,448
Net recognized (gains)/losses on investments	380	(1,296)	(527)
Stock option income tax benefits	1,365	1,100	668
Deferred income taxes	(1,348)	(1,479)	(179)
Unearned revenue	12,519	11,777	13,831
Recognition of unearned revenue	(11,292)	(12,527)	(12,919)
Accounts receivable	187	(687)	(1,243)
Other current assets	412	478	(245)
Other long-term assets	(28)	34	21
Other current liabilities	35	1,529	396
Other long-term liabilities	894	609	1,245
Net cash from operations	15,797	14,626	16,605
Financing			
Common stock issued	2,120	2,748	3,109
Common stock repurchased	(6,486)	(3,383)	(8,057)
Common stock cash dividends	(857)	(1,729)	(36,112)
Other	—	—	(18)
Net cash used for financing	(5,223)	(2,364)	(41,078)
Investing			
Additions to property and equipment	(891)	(1,109)	(812)
Acquisition of companies, net of cash acquired	(1,063)	(4)	(207)
Purchases of investments	(91,869)	(95,005)	(68,045)
Maturities of investments	9,205	5,561	29,153
Sales of investments	77,123	87,215	54,938
Net cash from investing	(7,495)	(3,342)	15,027
Net change in cash and equivalents	3,079	8,920	(9,446)
Effect of exchange rates on cash and equivalents	61	27	(7)
Cash and equivalents, beginning of period	2,217	5,357	14,304
Cash and equivalents, end of period	$ 5,357	$ 14,304	$ 4,851

Source: **www.microsoft.com/msft/ar05/flashversion/10k_fr_cas.html.**

investing activities include additions to plant and equipment, changes in short-term investments, mergers, and acquisitions. Taken together with the income statement, the cash flow statement gives investors a clear view of the health of the company's ongoing operations.

Footnotes and Auditor Opinion

Footnotes
Additional disclosures and details of the firm's business activities.

The financial statements are a clear and concise summary report on the business activities of the firm. However, modern business activities sometimes need further clarification. **Footnotes** to the firm's financial statements are used to augment, clarify, and supplement line-item disclosures. Footnotes provide information about the accounting methods and assumptions used, discuss the status of pensions and taxes, and give details on a variety of off-balance sheet activities. The number of pages of footnotes in an annual report usually far exceeds the number of pages devoted to the financial statements.

While the annual report to stockholders usually begins with a discussion of management's rosy view of company performance, savvy investors know that the footnotes are where problems are sometimes hidden. For example, when UAL Corporation, parent of United Airlines, filed for Chapter 11 bankruptcy protection, the company's audited balance sheet showed $25.2 billion in assets and $22.2 billion in liabilities. However, this picture of financial health did not include $24.5 billion in noncancelable operating-lease commitments that were referred to as "off–balance sheet debt" in the footnotes. The company was insolvent because UAL's off–balance sheet debt and balance sheet liabilities exceeded total assets by a significant margin. To avoid such surprises, some shrewd investors actually *begin* their financial statement analysis by reading the footnotes.

Financial statement information is carefully inspected by the firm's independent auditor, who publishes a fairness opinion. The role of the auditor is to verify that the firm's financial statements conform to Generally Accepted Accounting Principles and that they provide a reasonable picture of the firm's financial well-being. Auditor reports are usually boilerplate in nature. Only when there is a substantial and irreconcilable disagreement between the auditor and top management will the auditor issue a qualified opinion. Investors typically react negatively to the issuance of qualified opinions because they raise uncertainty about the firm's operating performance and/or financial condition. In rare circumstances, substantial and irreconcilable disagreement between an auditor and top management results in auditor resignation or dismissal. Unscheduled changes in auditor-client relationships often lead to an adverse stock price reaction because they signal extreme uncertainty about the firm's operating performance and/or financial condition.

Problems with Accounting Information

Accounting information is compiled in a logical and consistent framework. Balance sheet data provide a historical record of the firm's past investment decisions and the financing decisions made to support those investments. Income statement information gives insight concerning the present flow of revenues and costs, as measured using GAAP. While such information is compiled in a coherent manner across firms and industries, relying on historical data rather than a forward-looking perspective can sometimes create problems for investors.

Historical cost
Actual cash cost for the asset.

Current cost
Amount that must be paid under prevailing market conditions.

When costs are calculated for a firm's income tax returns, the law requires use of the actual dollar amount spent to purchase labor, raw materials, and capital equipment used in production. For tax purposes, **historical cost**, or actual cash outlays, is the relevant cost. This is also generally true for annual 10K reports to the SEC and for reports to stockholders. Despite their usefulness, historical costs are not appropriate as the sole basis for many investment decisions. Current costs are typically more relevant. **Current cost** is the amount that must be paid under prevailing market conditions. Current cost is influenced by market conditions measured by the number of buyers and sellers, the present state of technology, inflation, and so on. For assets purchased recently, historical cost and current cost are often the same. For assets purchased several years ago, historical cost and current cost can be quite different. Since World War II, inflation has been an obvious source of large differences between current and historical costs throughout most of the world. With an inflation rate of roughly 5 percent per year, prices dou-

Bankruptcy

Federal bankruptcy laws govern how companies go out of business or recover from crippling debt. A bankrupt company, the "debtor," might use Chapter 11 of the Bankruptcy Code to "reorganize" its business and try to become profitable again. Management continues to run day-to-day business operations under Chapter 11, but important business decisions must be approved by the bankruptcy court. Under Chapter 7, a company stops all operations and goes out of business. A trustee is appointed to liquidate company assets, and the proceeds are used to pay off debts to creditors and bond investors.

Bankruptcy laws determine the order of payment as assets are liquidated. In general, investors who take on the least amount of risk are paid first. Secured creditors take on the least amount of risk because they extend credit that is usually backed by collateral, such as real estate or other assets. When a firm declares bankruptcy, bondholders also have some potential for recovering their losses because bonds represent a formal debt obligation of the company. Stockholders take on the greatest amount of risk when they invest, and they stand to lose the most in bankruptcy.

In most instances, companies that file under Chapter 11 of the Bankruptcy Code are unable to meet listing standards and are suspended from trading on Nasdaq or the New York Stock Exchange. However, even when a company is delisted, its shares may continue to trade on the OTCBB or the Pink Sheets. There is no federal law that prohibits trading of securities of bankrupt companies. Investors should be extremely cautious when buying common stock of bankrupt companies because the chance of loss is great. Even if a company successfully reorganizes in Chapter 11, bondholders and other creditors generally become the new owners of the company. In most instances, the company's plan of reorganization will cancel the existing equity, and former shareholders will get wiped out. Even when common stockholders share in the proceeds from asset liquidations, the value of their claims is usually subject to substantial dilution.

For detailed information on bankruptcy law and investor protection, consult the SEC Web site at **www.sec.gov/investor/pubs/bankrupt.htm**.

---

ble in less than 15 years and triple in roughly 22 years. Land purchased for $50,000 in 1970 often has a current cost in excess of $250,000. In California, Florida, Texas, and other rapidly growing areas, current costs run much higher. Just as no homeowner would sell his or her home for a low price based on low historical costs, no firm can afford to sell assets or products for less than current costs. Similarly, investors must be able to adjust historical accounting information to account for the presence of undervalued or overvalued assets on the firm's balance sheet. Just as investors must be on the lookout for hidden assets ("diamonds") on the company's balance sheet, care must be taken not to miss hidden liabilities ("lumps of coal").

Corporate restructuring often involves eliminating nonstrategic operations to redeploy assets and strengthen core lines of business. When nonessential assets are disposed of in a depressed market, there is typically no relation between low "fire sale" proceeds and book value or historical cost. Conversely, when assets are sold to others who can more effectively use such resources, sale proceeds can approximate replacement value and greatly exceed historical costs and book values. Even under normal circumstances, the link between economic and accounting values can be tenuous. Economic worth as determined by profit-generating capability, rather than accounting value, is always the most vital consideration when determining the investment value of specific assets.

Financial Ratios

Profit Measures

The most useful indicator of business quality is a consistently high level of profitability. More precisely, a good business consistently earns high profits relative to the amount of capital employed. To provide insight concerning business profit rates, investors rely on various measures of profitability. First among these is the rate of return on sales, or **net profit margin**, defined as accounting net income expressed as a percentage of sales revenue. Profit margins show the amount of profit earned per dollar of sales. In addition to considering net profit margin, analysts sometimes study gross profit margins or use cash flow rather than accounting income

Net profit margin
Profit earned per dollar of sales.

numbers in profit margin calculations. When profit margins are high, the company is operating at a high level of efficiency, competitive pressure is modest, or both.

$$\text{Net profit margin} = \frac{\text{net income}}{\text{total sales}} \tag{10.1}$$

Return on stockholders' equity (ROE)
Net income divided by the book value of stockholders' equity.

Business profit rates are also measured by the accounting rate of **return on stockholders' equity (ROE)**. The return on stockholders' equity is defined as net income divided by the book value of stockholders' equity. ROE tells how profitable a company is in terms of each dollar invested by shareholders. A limitation of ROE is that it can be distorted by share buybacks and other types of corporate restructuring. According to GAAP, the book value of stockholders' equity is simply the amount of money committed to the enterprise by stockholders. It is calculated as the sum of paid-in capital and retained earnings minus any amount paid for share repurchases. When "extraordinary" or "unusual" charges are significant, the book value of stockholders' equity is reduced and ROE can become inflated. Similarly, when share repurchases are at market prices that exceed the book value per share, book value per share falls and ROE rises.

$$\text{Return on equity} = \frac{\text{net income}}{\text{stockholders' equity}} \tag{10.2}$$

Return on assets (ROA)
Net income divided by the book value of total assets.

Given the difficulty of interpreting ROE for companies that have undergone significant restructuring, and for highly leveraged companies, some investors focus on the **return on assets (ROA)**, or net income divided by the book value of total assets. Like ROE, ROA captures the effects of managerial operating decisions. ROA tends to be less affected than ROE by the amount of financial leverage employed. As such, ROE has some advantages over ROA as a fundamental measure of business profits. As in the case of profit margin calculations, analysts sometimes use gross profits or cash flow numbers in the return-on-asset calculation. Irrespective of whether profit margin, ROE, ROA, or some other measure of business profits is employed, consistency requires using a common basis for between-firm comparisons.

$$\text{Return on assets} = \frac{\text{net income}}{\text{total assets}} \tag{10.3}$$

It is always appropriate to compare profitability measures among firms in the same industry. Because the firms in a given industry typically have similar economic opportunities, differences in profitability ratios are often interpreted as indicators of management efficiency. Differences in typical profitability measures across industries also give investors a useful indication of highly profitable market environments where fruitful investments are apt to be found versus mediocre market environments where finding productive investments is apt to be difficult.

Try It!

Using the financial statements in Tables 10.1 to 10.3, compute Microsoft's net profit margin, ROE, and ROA. Use the 2005 information on net cash flow from operations.

Solution

$$\text{Net profit margin} = \frac{\text{net income}}{\text{total sales}} = \frac{\$12,254}{\$39,788} = 0.3080 = 30.8\%$$

$$\text{Return on equity} = \frac{\text{net income}}{\text{stockholders' equity}} = \frac{\$12,254}{\$48,115} = 0.2547 = 25.5\%$$

$$\text{Return on assets} = \frac{\text{net cash from operations}}{\text{total assets}} = \frac{\$16,605}{\$70,815} = 0.2345 = 23.5\%$$

In 2005, Microsoft's profit margin was nearly 31 percent. This is very high compared to the average firm.

Elements of ROE

Despite its limitations, many investors continue to regard ROE as the best single indicator of corporate profitability because it reflects the company's use of both operating leverage and financial leverage. ROE can be seen as the simple product of three common accounting ratios. ROE equals the firm's profit margin multiplied by the total asset turnover ratio, all times the firm's leverage ratio. This equation is sometimes known as the Du Pont formula:

$$\text{ROE} = \text{profit margin} \times \text{asset turnover} \times \text{leverage ratio}$$

$$= \frac{\text{net income}}{\text{sales}} \times \frac{\text{sales}}{\text{assets}} \times \frac{\text{assets}}{\text{equity}} \qquad (10.4)$$

By looking at ROE as the product of the firm's profit margin, asset turnover, and leverage ratio, it becomes possible to focus on the source of the firms' profit performance. Generally speaking, firms with high and stable profit margins, like Microsoft, Coca-Cola, and Intel, have the best opportunity to report stellar ROE on a year-to-year basis. For such companies, management needs to know if ROE has increased due to higher margins, and therefore due to a better product mix. On the other hand, has better asset management, and hence higher total asset turnover, led to improved profitability? Alternatively, has ROE changed simply because the firm has altered its financial leverage? These are important questions that often lead to important operating and financial decisions.

Total asset turnover is sales revenue divided by the book value of total assets. When total asset turnover is high, the firm makes its investments work hard in the sense of generating a large amount of sales volume. Grocery and discount retailing are good examples of industries where high rates of total asset turnover can allow efficient firms to earn attractive rates of return on stockholders' equity despite modest profit margins. Wal-Mart is a standout performer in this regard. Despite razor-thin profit margins of 3.5 to 4 percent, Wal-Mart regularly earns a remarkable ROE in excess of 20 percent by virtue of diligent expense management, tight inventory control, and stellar total asset turnover.

Leverage is often defined as the book value of total assets divided by stockholders' equity. It reflects the extent to which debt and preferred stock are used in addition to common stock financing. Leverage is used to amplify firm profit rates over the business cycle. During economic booms, leverage can dramatically increase the firm's profit rate; during recessions and other economic contractions, leverage can just as dramatically decrease realized rates of return, if not lead to losses. However, it is worth remembering that a risky financial structure can lead to awe-inspiring profit rates during economic expansions, such as that experienced during the mid-1990s, but it can also lead to huge losses during economic contractions or recessions, such as that experienced during 1991. In the financial services sector, high rates of financial leverage can boost profits during periods of declining interest rates, but they cause financial distress during periods of rapidly fluctuating interest rates. For example, well-managed banks like Citigroup and JP Morgan-Chase report ROEs of 20 percent and higher during good times but can report significant losses during adverse market environments.

For large publicly traded companies in the United States, such as those found on the New York Stock Exchange and Nasdaq, ROE has fluctuated in a broad range between 8 and 16 percent during the post-World War II period. During economic recessions, many firms report operating losses, and the average ROE dives below 10 percent. During uninterrupted economic expansions, such as that experienced during the 1990s, the average ROE for publicly traded companies can soar above 20 percent for industry leaders and as high as 16 percent per year for all companies. For a typical year during the post-World War II period, the average ROE has tended to fall in a range between 12 and 14 percent.

Total asset turnover
Sales revenue divided by the book value of total assets.

Leverage
Total assets divided by stockholders' equity. It reflects the extent to which debt and preferred stock are used in addition to common stock financing.

Try It!

In 2004 and 2005, Microsoft's ROE was 10.9 percent and 25.5 percent, respectively. Why did Microsoft's ROE increase so dramatically over this period?

(continued on next page)

Solution

For 2004:

$$\text{ROE} = \frac{\text{net income}}{\text{sales}} \times \frac{\text{sales}}{\text{assets}} \times \frac{\text{assets}}{\text{equity}} = \frac{\$8,168}{\$36,835} \times \frac{\$36,835}{\$94,368} \times \frac{\$94,368}{\$74,825}$$

$$= 0.222 \times 0.388 \times 1.261 = 0.1086 = 10.9\%$$

For 2005:

$$\text{ROE} = \frac{\text{net income}}{\text{sales}} \times \frac{\text{sales}}{\text{assets}} \times \frac{\text{assets}}{\text{equity}} = \frac{\$12,254}{\$39,788} \times \frac{\$39,788}{\$70,815} \times \frac{\$70,815}{\$48,115}$$

$$= 0.308 \times 0.562 \times 1.472 = 0.2548 = 25.5\%$$

In comparing the profit margin, asset turnover, and leverage ratios for Microsoft in 2004 and 2005, it is obvious the dramatic increase in ROE can be traced to two things. First, Microsoft had a large increase in its profit margin. Second, Microsoft paid a big dividend in November 2004 (fiscal year 2005) to distribute excess cash to shareholders. This reduced the assets and equity in the firm, thereby magnifying its asset turnover ratio and leverage ratio.

Assessing Firm Performance

Operating Efficiency

Operating efficiency is a key determinant of profitability. Management needs to know if factories are running at or near capacity. Does the firm receive prompt payment from customers? Is the firm carrying too much inventory? These are questions of operating efficiency. Investors examine the asset turnover ratio to see how efficiently management is using assets to generate sales and profits. The higher the asset turnover, the more efficient the firm is at utilizing its assets. Other efficiency ratios include **receivables turnover** and **inventory turnover** ratios:

Receivables turnover
A measure that implies the speed at which receivables are collected.

$$\text{Receivables turnover} = \frac{\text{sales revenue}}{\text{receivables}} \qquad (10.5)$$

Inventory turnover
A measure of the amount of inventory needed to achieve the firm's sales.

$$\text{Inventory turnover} = \frac{\text{cost of goods sold}}{\text{inventory}} \qquad (10.6)$$

A high level of operating efficiency means that the firm is able to turn over its receivables and its inventory rapidly during the year. Because these turnover measures are highly variable across industries, comparisons are best done among firms within a given industry.

··········· Try It! ···········

Compute the 2005 receivables turnover and inventory turnover for Microsoft.

Solution

Use the information in Tables 10.1 and 10.2 with Equations 10.5 and 10.6:

$$\text{Receivables turnover} = \frac{\text{revenue}}{\text{accounts receivable}} = \frac{\$39,788}{\$7,180} = 5.54$$

$$\text{Inventory turnover} = \frac{\text{cost of revenue}}{\text{inventories}} = \frac{\$6,200}{\$491} = 12.63$$

Financial Leverage

A firm can magnify its business risk by borrowing money, thus adding financial risk. Consider a firm that wants to invest in an asset with a risky return of 10 or –10 percent. If the firm invests $50 of its own money, it will either gain or lose $5. Now suppose the firm borrows to invest an additional $50 paying a 6 percent interest rate, or financing costs of $3 per year. The firm will end up with a profit of $7 (= $10 gain – $3 interest) or a $13 loss (= –$10 loss – $3 interest). Using financial leverage, the firm has changed its profit-loss potential from $5 or –$5 to $7 or –$13. In other words, the use of financial leverage has increased the business risk of the investment.

Most companies use debt to increase the amount of funds available for investment. **Financial leverage** is measured using various debt ratios. Commonly employed are the debt-to-equity ratio and the debt-to-total-capital ratio:

$$\text{Debt to equity} = \frac{\text{long-term debt}}{\text{stockholder's equity}} \qquad (10.7)$$

$$\text{Debt to total capital} = \frac{\text{long-term debt}}{(\text{stockholder's equity} + \text{long-term debt})} \qquad (10.8)$$

Financial leverage
The amount of debt used. Its use magnifies the size of profits and losses, thus increasing the firm's risk.

Higher levels of debt do not imply that a firm is better or worse than others. It simply implies a riskier firm because more financial leverage is being used. Also, different industries tend to have different levels of debt. Industries with a high degree of real assets, such as manufacturing, tend to have higher debt levels. Firms in industries with intellectual assets, such as computer software, tend to use little or no debt.

A firm can also affect its business risk by its choice of **operating leverage**. High operating leverage is achieved when the firm uses production methods that employ high fixed costs and low variables costs. Examples are a company that operates a highly automated production facility and an airline that owns and operates a fleet of several large planes. Low operating leverage occurs when a firm's production is structured with low fixed costs and high variable costs. Examples are firms that outsource manufacturing to low-cost foreign suppliers and airlines that operate a fleet of leased aircraft. The degree of operating leverage is defined as the percentage change in profits generated from a change (in percent) in sales. What change in profit would you expect when sales increase 5 percent? If the firm has a high degree of operating leverage, profits will increase by much more than 5 percent. A firm with low operating leverage might see profits increase less the 5 percent. When operating leverage is high, profits soar with a robust expansion in sales. On the other hand, high operating leverage can lead to a sharp decline in profits when sales weaken.

Operating leverage
A measure of business risk taken through the use of fixed-cost production.

Financial Liquidity

Financial liquidity is always an important determinant of creditworthiness and investment merit. Key questions are, Does the firm have enough money to pay its short-term debts, and how comfortable is it in making required interest payments? These are questions of liquidity and solvency. Two common measures of liquidity are the current ratio and the quick ratio. The **current ratio** relates the amount of current assets of the firm to current liabilities:

$$\text{Current ratio} = \frac{\text{current assets}}{\text{current liabilities}} \qquad (10.9)$$

Current ratio
Liquidity measured by current assets divided by current liabilities.

A current ratio less than or equal to 1 often signals a potential problem. If the current ratio is less than 1, the firm doesn't have enough cash on hand to pay its upcoming bills. However, not all current assets are useful for paying bills. Inventory, for example, may be obsolete or otherwise not readily convertible into cash. Therefore, many investors prefer the **quick ratio** as an attractive measure of short-term liquidity:

$$\text{Quick ratio} = \frac{\text{cash} + \text{markable securities} + \text{receivables}}{\text{current liabilities}} \qquad (10.10)$$

Quick ratio
Cash and near-cash assets relative to current liabilities.

Interest coverage
A measure of the firm's ability to pay interest charges.

All leveraged firms face the regular need to make timely payments of principal and interest on debt. The larger the amount of debt, the more difficult it will be to make these payments. The firm's ability to make regular interest payments is measured with the **interest coverage** ratio:

$$\text{Interest coverage} = \frac{\text{EBIT}}{\text{debt interest charge}}$$

(10.11)

Remember, EBIT is earnings before interest and taxes; it is the amount of cash flow available to make interest payments. The higher the interest coverage ratio, the easier it becomes for the firm to make scheduled interest payments. Firms with higher interest coverage ratios are likely to be given higher debt ratings by credit rating agencies. When current and quick ratios and interest coverage begin to decline, however, investors often begin to worry about a firm's solvency.

Try It!

Compute the 2005 current and quick ratios for Microsoft.

Solution

Use the information in Table 10.1 and Equations 10.9 and 10.10:

$$\text{Current ratio} = \frac{\text{current assets}}{\text{current liabilities}} = \frac{\$48,737}{\$16,877} = 2.89$$

$$\text{Quick ratio} = \frac{\text{cash} + \text{marketable securities} + \text{receivables}}{\text{current liabilities}}$$

$$= \frac{\$4,851 + \$32,900 + \$7,180}{\$16,877} = 2.66$$

Microsoft's current and quick ratios are high because of the company's high short-term investments.

Relative Performance

Market Capitalization

Stocks are often grouped by industry or sector to describe companies that face a similar competitive environment. Classifying firms by their size is also common because academic research has documented that size is an important determinant of risk. The most common size measure is the total market capitalization of common stock, or **market cap** for short.

Market cap
Market value of the firm.

Large companies with market capitalization above $5 billion are generally considered less risky than mid-cap or small-cap stocks. This is because there is a large, liquid market for their shares and a longer history of earnings and dividend growth. Large companies have not only stood the test of time but also typically have a portfolio of different lines of business and operate in a variety of domestic and global markets. Many small-cap companies have one or only a few lines of business, operate in isolated regional markets, and have no meaningful global presence. Small-cap companies are often vulnerable to competitive pressure from larger, better-financed rivals.

While large companies tend to be rather predictable, investors must recognize that large size limits investor opportunities for above-average growth. For example, Microsoft first offered shares to the investment public for $21 per share on March 13, 1986. On that first trading day,

Microsoft opened at $25.50, traded as high as $29.25, and closed at $28. Between 1986 and 2006, Microsoft stock split on nine separate occasions, so one initial share purchased on March 13, 1986, grew to 288 shares of stock by 2006. Over that same period, the value of a $10,000 investment in Microsoft grew to $3.75 million, or by roughly 34.5 percent per year. Because of its enormous success during the 1980s and 1990s, there is simply no way that Microsoft can duplicate this feat. With its current market cap of roughly $300 billion, a 375:1 payoff over the next 20 years would imply a market cap for Microsoft of more than $112.5 trillion. This is roughly five times the current market cap of all companies traded on all global equity markets. With its enormous strengths, Microsoft may well enjoy notable success during the next 20 years, but it will never repeat the stock market success it enjoyed during the 1980s and 1990s. Elephants don't run like jackrabbits.

Industry Comparison

The capital structure and business operating characteristics of each industry are different. Therefore, it is common to compare a firm's financial performance with other companies in its own sector and industry or with sector and industry averages. Table 10.4 shows some financial ratios for Microsoft and for its sector (technology) and industry (application software). At $289 billion of market capitalization, Microsoft makes up over half of the application software industry. This means that the industry's averages will be skewed toward Microsoft's numbers. Nevertheless, the average profit margins in the technology sector and application software industry were 9.5 percent and 20.9 percent, respectively. These are considerably lower than Microsoft's profit margin of 30.8 percent, indicating that Microsoft has a dominant market position and is exploiting that position quite well. The table also shows the average financial ratios for several other industries in the technology sector: Internet software and services, Internet service providers, personal computers, and wireless communications. Within the technology sector there is a large range in performance. The profit margin of Internet service providers is negative (−1.4 percent), for example, suggesting that this is currently not a profitable business line.

The ROEs for the technology sector and the application software industry were 13.4 percent and 19.7 percent, respectively. Microsoft's ROE of 22.5 percent is high by comparison. The variation in the ROE shown for industries in the technology sector illustrates a low ROE of 0 percent in the Internet service provider industry and a high ROE of 34.6 percent in the personal computer industry. Many high-tech firms use little to no financial leverage. This is due to the fact that high-tech firms depend heavily on risky intangible capital derived from research and development, patents, and so on. Such risky assets have little collateral value and seldom offer the basis for bank loans or bond financing.

TABLE 10.4	**Comparison of Financial Ratios and Industry Averages**			
	Market Cap ($ billion)	**Net Profit Margin**	**ROE (%)**	**Debt to Equity**
Microsoft	289.43	30.8	22.5	0.000
Technology sector	5,059.60	9.5	13.4	0.017
Industry:				
Application software	495.05	20.9	19.7	0.000
Internet software and services	178.06	8.2	6.5	0.267
Internet service providers	7.07	−1.4	0.0	0.003
Personal computers	145.25	6.2	34.6	0.001
Wireless communications	562.10	2.4	1.8	0.007

Source: Data from Yahoo! Finance.

Pension Plan Underfunded— Stock Overvalued

Lots of major corporations, especially old industrial manufacturers, have traditional defined-benefit pension plans that promise employees a pension based on the number of years of service and employee age at retirement. In a defined-benefit pension plan, the payments promised to employees are a corporate liability to be covered by the value of pension plan assets. If corporate pension plan contributions fall short or pension plan assets fail to earn the expected rate of return, the pension plan is said to be underfunded and the corporation faces an underfunded pension plan liability. This liability does not show up on the company's balance sheet, but it is described in footnotes to the company's financial statements. It is a real off–balance sheet liability because companies must ultimately cover any underfunded pension plan liability with future payments to the company pension plan.

In a perfectly efficient stock market, investors appropriately value companies based on all available financial information. That includes tangible assets, like real estate, and both current and long-term liabilities. It also includes intangible assets, like brand names and patents, and off–balance sheet liabilities, like an underfunded pension plan. In a perfectly efficient stock market, pouring over financial statements to find undervalued bargains or overvalued stocks to avoid is thought to be fruitless on the premise that those statements have already been dissected. The efforts of every highly motivated and well-trained analyst are thought to be frustrated by the previous efforts of similarly well-trained and highly-motivated analysts.

Financial research now suggests that investors may not appropriately consider underfunded pension plan liabilities when making stock selections. Companies with the highest amount of underfunding earn low returns relative to companies with healthy defined-benefit plans. This relatively poor stock return performance is substantial (about 10 percent per year) and persists for years! Because investors are not paying close enough attention to the amount of pension plan underfunding, firms with significant underfunding appear to be overvalued. Contrary to the efficient-market hypothesis, careful financial statement analysis is worthwhile!

See Francesco Franzoni and José Marín, "Pension Plan Funding and Stock Market Efficiency," *Journal of Finance*, vol. 61, no. 2 (April 2006), pages 921–956.

Valuation Indicators

P/E Ratio

Price-earnings (P/E) ratio
Stock price divided by earnings per share.

Earnings yield
Earnings-price, or E/P, ratio.

The most common valuation yardstick used by investors to measure relative value is the **price-earnings (P/E) ratio**, or stock price divided by earnings per share. Major financial publications, like *The Wall Street Journal,* and most major daily newspapers report P/E ratio information alongside daily stock price quotes. The intuition behind the P/E ratio is disarmingly simple: A P/E ratio of 20:1 means that an investor buying at the current market price is paying $20 for $1 in earnings per share. Similarly, when a P/E ratio of 20:1 is paid, the **earnings yield**, or earnings-price (E/P) ratio, is 5 percent. Why would a present-day investor pay a P/E of 20:1, or settle for an earnings yield of only 5 percent on investment, in a market environment where risk-free short-term Treasury bills also pay roughly 5 percent? Obviously, it makes sense to pay a P/E of 20:1 only when underlying earnings per share are expected to grow rapidly. Just how rapidly earnings have to grow to justify paying a given P/E ratio depends on the amount of future earnings growth anticipated and the level of investor confidence.

Figure 10.1 shows the P/E ratio of the DJIA since 1940. Notice that there are large increases and large decreases over time. Such fluctuations occur because stock investors bid up prices during economic expansions and periods of investor optimism whereas investors become cautious and P/E ratios fall in advance of an expected economic downturn. P/E ratios can skyrocket during a severe economic recession, like the 1991 recession, because earnings tend to plummet about the same time investors begin to bid up prices in anticipation of the ensuing recovery. In 2006, the DJIA's P/E ratio remained near its long-term average of 18.

P/E ratios for individual companies can vary dramatically. For example, a typical P/E ratio for slow-growing energy giant Chevron is about 10, while investors accord a typical P/E ratio near 30 for faster-growing biotech titan Amgen. At the same time, investors accorded search engine juggernaut Google a P/E ratio of more than 75! In 2006, investors were betting heavily that Amgen would continue to develop and market a growing product line of human therapeutics based on advances in cellular and molecular biology. Google investors were betting that the company would be able to translate its lead in Internet search technology into a host of profitable and rapidly growing businesses.

| **FIGURE 10.1** | **P/E Ratio of the Dow Jones Industrial Average** |

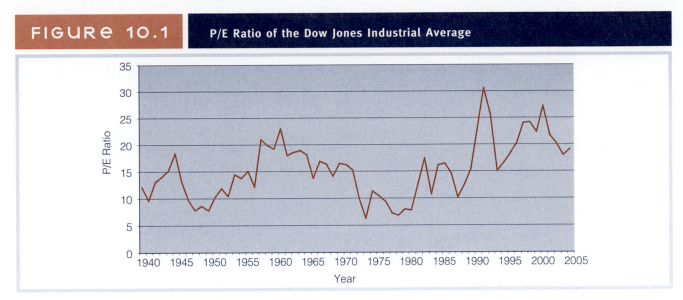

Source: Dow Jones and Company, **www.djindexes.com/jsp/index.jsp**.

Table 10.5 shows average P/E ratios and related information for firms in nine economic sectors. Price-earnings ratios tend to vary from the low end in the financial sector to the high end in the technology sector. Investors believe there is more growth potential in the technology sector than in the financial sector, and they are typically willing to pay high P/E ratios for rapidly growing tech stocks.

To help assess a firm's valuation over time, investors will compute the **relative P/E ratio**. This is simply the firm's P/E ratio divided by the P/E ratio of a benchmark industry or index. A relative P/E ratio greater than 1 (or 100 percent) indicates the firm is valued higher than the benchmark.

Relative P/E ratio
Firm's P/E ratio divided by an index P/E ratio.

P/B Ratio and Dividend Yield

Though much less popular than the P/E ratio, many investors judge whether or not a stock is expensive on the basis of its current market price relative to the accounting book value per share. The **price-book (P/B) ratio** shows the relationship between a stock's current price and its accounting net worth, where accounting book value per share is simply total assets minus total liabilities. Of course, accounting book values are historical measures of identifiable worth as mandated by GAAP. Despite compelling logic and consistency, GAAP book value numbers often fail to reflect important intangible assets like valuable brand names, copyrights, or patents. As a result, it is common to find that stock prices exceed accounting book values. P/B ratios typically exceed 1:1. As shown in Table 10.5, P/B ratios for various sectors average between roughly 2:1 to as high as 20:1. Rarely has the year-end P/B ratio for the DJIA fallen below 1:1. At such times, stock prices can be regarded as unusually cheap. It wasn't until the mid 1990s that year-end P/B ratios for the DJIA exceeded 3:1. At such times, stock prices must be regarded as unusually expensive. The negative P/B for the services industry is indicative of the large number of bankrupt airline firms. Because of P/B ratios variation over time, investors often examine a firm's relative P/B ratio, computed as the firm's P/B ratio divided by the P/B ratio of a benchmark industry or index.

Price-book (P/B) ratio
Stock price divided by accounting net worth.

Dividend yield is a third popular measure of relative valuation. This measure tells investors the amount of dividend income, where dividend income is expressed as a percentage of the amount paid for a stock. If a company's stock is selling for $40 per share and it pays a 25-cent quarterly dividend, or $1 per year, the dividend yield is 2.5 percent (= $1/$40) per year.

Dividend yield
Dividend income expressed as a percentage of the amount paid for a stock.

| | **Table 10.5** | | **Value Indicators for Sectors, January 13, 2006** | | | |

Sector	Market Cap ($ billions)	P/E	ROE (%)	Div. Yield (%)	Debt to Equity	Price to Book
Basic materials	4099.3	14.5	24.7	2.14	0.005	3.74
Conglomerates	670.0	19.4	15.5	2.34	0.021	11.72
Consumer goods	2335.4	28.9	19.3	2.36	0.015	19.01
Financial	5068.6	13.8	15.5	2.69	0.035	2.64
Health care	2596.6	19.5	12.7	1.54	0.005	12.10
Industrial goods	919.6	17.8	15.8	1.50	0.009	11.86
Services	2947.4	30.6	14.5	1.29	0.011	−7.50
Technology	5059.6	44.9	13.4	1.79	0.017	5.51
Utilities	832.0	17.9	13.8	3.46	0.022	2.84

Source: Yahoo! Finance. **http://finance.yahoo.com**.

Investors must not ignore the power of dividends in overall stock market performance because dividends play an important role in determining the investor's total return, where total return is the sum of dividend income plus capital appreciation. The compounding effect of dividends over time is also impressive. Over the long term, dividend income represents between one-third and one-half of the total return earned on common stocks. Since 1950, for example, DJIA companies have paid an average 4 percent dividend and provided capital appreciation of roughly 8 percent per year. This means that one-third of the long-term investor's total return has come from dividend income. To provide a competitive long-term rate of return, a riskier stock that paid no dividends would have to grow by 12 percent per year, or fully 50 percent faster than the 8 percent growth typical of the average DJIA stock.

Economic Value

Free cash flow
The cash that a company is able to generate after the expenses required to maintain or expand its asset base.

While many professional and individual investors focus on traditional accounting measures of profits and profitability (EPS, P/E, ROE, and profit margin), others also examine economic as opposed to accounting-based measures. Because accrual accounting information is imprecise and can be manipulated, some investors focus on the amount of cash being generated in the business. As an alternative to accounting net income, these investors focus on **free cash flow**. Free cash flow is the amount of cash flow the firm generates after allowing for necessary capital expenditures on plant and equipment. The cash flow statement reports cash flow from operations. This is a good place to start when calculating free cash flow. Starting with cash flow from operations, the calculation of free cash flow involves subtracting capital expenditures and adding back any incidental receipts, such as proceeds from dispositions of property:

$$\text{Free cash flow} = \text{cash flow from operations} - \text{capital expenditures} \qquad (10.12)$$

Free cash flow has become an especially important measure of economic profitability because it is perceived as being more difficult to manipulate than traditional accounting information. Instead of examining P/E ratios, some investors tend to focus on price–free cash flow ratios. Generating large amounts of free cash flow allows companies to pursue new business opportunities, pay dividends, engage in share buybacks, and reduce debt.

In addition to using the free cash flow measure of economic profits, some investors follow measures tied to the amount of wealth being added to the firm over time. Stockholders own the firm and are obviously interested in the amount of wealth being generated over time. Not only do stockholders want the firm to increase revenue, profits, and cash flows, but stockholders demand that the firm do so in a cost-efficient manner. Any 2 percent bank savings account will grow year in and year out. However, such an account represents a poor investment if no-risk 5 percent Treasury bills can be purchased. Similarly, a company growing at 5 percent per year represents a poor investment if it faces a 10 percent cost of capital. Economic wealth is created over time only if the firm generates a rate of return on invested capital that exceeds the firm's **cost of capital.**

The consulting firm Stern Stewart (**www.sternstewart.com**) defines one popular measure of **economic value added (EVA)** as

$$\text{EVA} = \text{net operating profit after taxes (NOPAT)} - (\text{capital of the firm} \times \text{cost of capital}) \quad \textbf{(10.13)}$$

Consider EVA for Microsoft. In 2005, Microsoft's NOPAT was $12.25 billion. It is an all-equity firm with market capitalization of about $300 billion. Assuming a cost of capital of 11.5 percent, the expected rate of growth in earnings per share over the next five years, Microsoft's EVA is –$22.25 billion (= $12.25 – $300 × 0.115). Even though Microsoft has an outstanding profit margin and ROE, it has not been generating enough wealth to fully compensate its stockholders for the amount of risk undertaken. This may be why Microsoft stock has languished within a range of $25 to $30 for several years. EVA analysis helps some investors identify attractive investment opportunities.

Can Financial Statements Be Trusted?

Accounting Fraud

Complex accounting standards sometimes make it difficult for investors to understand the financial condition and operating performance of firms. Investors have long relied on auditors and financial analysts to interpret financial statements and comment on the financial health of publicly traded companies. However, such experts examined the financial statements of firms such as Adelphia, Enron, and WorldCom and didn't predict their imminent bankruptcy. Auditor letters in the annual reports of literally hundreds of Internet firms seemed to validate their health, only to see the companies quickly implode. If analysts and auditors have trouble discovering problems by examining financial statements, what hope is there for the average investor?

Two common problems compound the issue: faking the numbers and changing the numbers. Since the 1990s, many companies have faced extreme pressure trying to keep pace with high Wall Street expectations. Instead of risking the sharp stock price decline associated with missing Wall Street expectations, some companies simply faked their financial performance. In conjunction with its establishment of offshore partnerships, energy trader Enron improperly booked increases in debt as revenue. Cable television behemoth Adelphia excluded hundreds of millions of dollars of debt from its financial statements. Telecom giant WorldCom inflated its earnings by $9 billion. Drugstore retailer Rite Aid used illegal accounting schemes to boost net income by more than $1 billion. Xerox accelerated revenue from leasing arrangements over a four-year period that increased revenue by $3 billion and net income by $1.5 billion. While the vast majority of public companies honestly report their financial performance, investors have a tough time finding out which ones are faking it. By the time they find out, it's often too late.

After a series of public accounting scandals during the late 1990s and early 2000s, government regulators became very concerned about the creation of a general lack of trust in financial statements. Congress created new laws governing the accounting and auditing industry. The most famous of the new regulations was the Sarbanes-Oxley Act of 2002. It aimed to toughen accounting rules and regulations in an effort to regain **investor confidence.** More specifically, Sarbanes-Oxley set up a new oversight body to regulate auditors, created laws pertaining to corporate responsibility, and increased punishments for corporate white-collar crime.

Cost of capital
The cost to the firm that is required by debt and equity holders.

Economic value added (EVA)
A measure of residual wealth calculated by deducting the cost of capital from operating profit.

Investor confidence
The level of the investing public's trust in corporate information and investment industry advice.

Shame on Adelphia

A corporation is a separate legal entity. If members of top management or of a founding family own 100 percent of a privately held company, they are entitled to do with it as they wish. Once common stock is sold to the general public, however, company resources belong to all the stockholders. If top management or a founding family owns a 50 percent controlling interest, one-half of corporate resources belong to the other shareholders. In this instance, if a member of top management used corporate resources for his or her own personal benefit, that would be stealing because 50 percent of that money belonged to the other shareholders. This simple investment concept was forgotten by top management at Adelphia Communications, Corporation, once the fifth-largest cable television provider in the United States. As a result, Adelphia's stock and bond investors got burned, badly.

In 2004, members of Adelphia's founding Rigas family were found guilty of conspiracy and securities fraud. Apparently, the Rigas family used Adelphia as a personal piggy bank. They had Adelphia pay for everything from personal real estate taxes to African safari vacations. Adelphia also built a golf course for the Rigas family and purchased the Buffalo Sabres hockey team for them. The Rigas family also borrowed and lost hundreds of millions of dollars of Adelphia's money in the stock market. Trading losses became permanent when Adelphia declared bankruptcy, thus wiping out common stockholders and the Rigas family fortune. In conjunction with criminal convictions handed down in 2004, the company asked a federal bankruptcy court to order the Rigas family to repay *$3.2 billion* it said they owed Adelphia.

How did this happen?

- Five of the nine members on Adelphia's board of directors were members of the Rigas family.
- Adelphia's accountants created fake documents to mislead independent board members about the commingling of family and firm money.
- Auditors Deloitte & Touche validated financial statements that were incomplete and misleading.
- Investment bankers failed to provide effective due diligence before marketing Adelphia's debt securities to an unsuspecting public.
- Credit-rating agencies missed obvious signs of Adelphia's deteriorating financial condition.

Nobody was looking out for the shareholders.

See Gregory Zuckerman and Peter Grant, "Adelphia Debt Stings Investors," *The Wall Street Journal Online*, December 23, 2005 (**http://online.wsj.com**).

Accounting Restatements

Since the enactment of Sarbanes-Oxley, accounting scandals at Freddie Mac, Fannie Mae, AIG Insurance, Delphi, and others have been splashed across the front pages of *The Wall Street Journal*. As Figure 10.2 shows, the number of companies restating their earnings has also soared. Restatements tend to occur when companies either change accounting methods or find errors in the numbers they already published. In principle, there is nothing wrong with

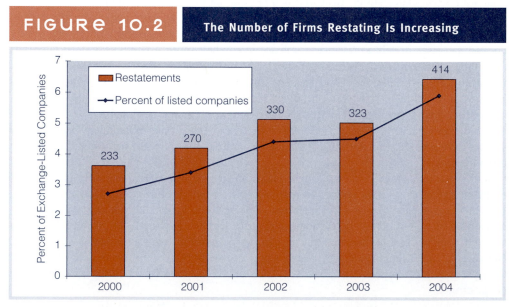

FIGURE 10.2 — The Number of Firms Restating Is Increasing

Source: Huron Consulting Group, 2004 Annual Review of Financial Reporting Matters.

accounting restatements made necessary by accounting changes. However, companies some-times try to hide a basic deterioration in economic performance by arguing that restatements are "merely" accounting changes that affect neither cash flows nor the company's basic oper-ations. Savvy investors know there is no such thing as an "immaterial" change in the published financial statements of publicly traded companies.

Little more than two years after the passage of Sarbanes-Oxley, a record number of com-panies were revising their financials statements. The number of firms restating increased from 270 in 2000 to 414 in 2004. Because the number of public firms listed on stock exchanges de-clined over the same period, the increase in the number of firms making financial restatements over time has been growing on a relative basis. Nearly 6 percent of stock exchange–listed firms restated their earnings in 2004. Unfortunately, much of this recent growth in restatements is due to firms correcting errors in previous financial statements.

The vast majority of public companies and their auditors work hard to provide sharehold-ers with a true picture of the financial health of the firm. Nevertheless, investors face a con-tinuing challenge to avoid the few firms that may be misstating the numbers.

Accounting restatements
Changes to balance sheet, income statement, and cash flow statement numbers published previously.

Summary

■ **Stock market investment** is the process of buying and holding for dividend income and long-term capital appreci-ation the shares of companies with inherently attractive economic prospects. Investors seek to profit by sharing in the normal and predictable good fortune of such compa-nies. **Stock market speculation** is the purchase or sale of securities on the expectation of capturing short-term trad-ing profits from share price fluctuations tied to the perhaps temporary good fortune of a given company. Speculators depend on a short-term or fundamental change in the eco-nomic prospects facing a company.

■ Whereas **balance sheet** information shows company fi-nancial well-being at a specific point in time, the com-pany's **income statement** gives an ongoing view of dynamic change. While the income statement provides a vi-tal measure of ongoing performance, accrual accounting errors (or bias) sometimes reduce its value as a measure of economic performance. In such instances, investors often look to the **cash flow statement** for an interesting perspec-tive on change in the company's economic position.

■ When evaluating business profits, many investors refer to the amount of **net income** generated, or **earnings per share**. Net income is simply the difference between rev-enues and expenses, often expressed on an after-tax basis. Earnings per share is simply net income divided by the number of shares outstanding, referred to as **basic earnings per share**, or the amount of net income divided by the num-ber of shares outstanding after consideration of the possible conversion of stock options, called **diluted earnings per share**. These details and other business activity disclosures are made in the **footnotes**.

■ In financial statements, firms use the actual dollar amount spent to purchase the labor, raw materials, and cap-ital equipment used in production. **Historical cost**, or ac-tual cash outlays, is the relevant cost. Despite their useful-ness, historical costs are not appropriate as the sole basis for many investment decisions. Current costs are typically much more relevant. **Current cost** is the amount that must be paid under prevailing market conditions.

■ **Net profit margins** show the amount of profit earned per dollar of sales. When profit margins are high, the com-pany is operating at a high level of efficiency, competitive pressure is modest, or both. The **return on stockholders' equity (ROE)** is defined as net income divided by the book value of stockholders' equity. ROE tells how profitable a company is in terms of each dollar invested by sharehold-ers. Some knowledgeable investors focus on the **return on assets (ROA)**, or net income divided by the book value of total assets.

■ **Total asset turnover** is sales revenue divided by the book value of total assets. When total asset turnover is high, the firm makes its investments work hard in the sense of gener-ating a large amount of sales volume. **Leverage** is often defined as the book value of total assets divided by stock-holders' equity. It reflects the extent to which debt and pre-ferred stock are used in addition to common stock financing. A firm increases its total risk when it uses **financial lever-age** by acquiring debt. A firm can also use **operating lever-age**, the proportion of costs attributable to fixed costs.

■ How profitable a firm becomes is partially determined by how well the firm is managed. When firms manage their assets and processes well, they will have high **receivables turnover** and high **inventory turnover** rela-tive to their competitors. Investors can examine a firm's liquidity by studying its **current ratio**, **quick ratio**, and **interest coverage ratio**.

■ Risk is sometimes measured by the size of a firm. Total market capitalization of common stock, or **market cap** for short, is calculated by multiplying the number of shares outstanding by the current stock price. When assessing risk, financial ratios should be compared with those of other firms in the industry as well as with sector and industry averages.

■ The most common valuation yardstick used to measure relative value is the **price-earnings (P/E) ratio**, or stock price divided by earnings per share. When a P/E ratio of 20:1 is paid, the **earnings yield**, or E/P ratio, is 5 percent. The **price-book (P/B) ratio** shows the relationship between a stock's current price and its accounting net worth, where accounting book value per share is simply total assets minus total liabilities. **Dividend yield** tells investors the amount of dividend income, where dividend income is expressed as a percentage of the amount paid for a stock. Dividends play an important role in determining the investor's total return. Investors also use economic-focused measures such as **free cash flow** and **economic value added** to assess the economic profits and wealth generated by a firm in excess of its **cost of capital**.

■ Two problems with relying on a company's financial statements are that unscrupulous firms may fake some of the numbers and that other managers faced with the extreme pressure of trying to keep pace with high Wall Street expectations may use aggressive accounting techniques. **Investor confidence** in these financial statements is important for a successful and efficient capital market. The use of aggressive accounting usually leads to **accounting restatements** to correct prior errors.

Self-Test Problems

ST10.1 The Fruit-Smoothie Company has $7,600 in sales, $6,400 in expenses, $9,000 in total assets, and $5,400 in total liabilities. All profits of the Fruit-Smoothie Company are subject to a 25 percent tax rate. Calculate net income, stockholders' equity, profit margin, total asset turnover, leverage, ROA, and ROE for the company.

Solution

Net income is the after-tax difference between revenues and expenses:

$$
\begin{aligned}
\text{Net income} &= (\text{sales} - \text{expenses}) - \text{taxes} \\
&= (\$7,600 - \$6,400) - .25 \times (\$7,600 - \$6,400) \\
&= \$900
\end{aligned}
$$

Stockholders' equity is the book value of total assets minus total liabilities:

$$
\begin{aligned}
\text{Equity} &= \text{total assets} - \text{total liabilities} \\
&= \$9,000 - \$5,400 \\
&= \$3,600
\end{aligned}
$$

To find the firm's profit margin, simply divide net income by sales:

$$
\begin{aligned}
\text{Profit margin} &= \text{net income/sales} \\
&= \$900/\$7,600 \\
&= 11.8\%
\end{aligned}
$$

Total asset turnover is an easily computed component of ROE:

$$
\begin{aligned}
\text{Total asset turnover} &= \text{sales/total assets} \\
&= \$7,600/\$9,000 \\
&= 0.844
\end{aligned}
$$

Similarly, leverage can be computed using a simple formula:

$$\text{Leverage} = \text{total assets/stockholders' equity}$$
$$= \$9,000/\$3,600$$
$$= 2.50$$

The Fruit-Smoothie Company's return on assets is its net income divided by the book value of total assets:

$$\text{ROA} = \text{net income/total assets}$$
$$= \$900/\$9,000$$
$$= 10\%$$

Finally, having computed the components of ROE, we can calculate this measure of profitability itself:

$$\text{ROE} = \text{profit margin} \times \text{total asset turnover} \times \text{leverage}$$
$$= 0.118 \times 0.844 \times 2.50$$
$$= 25\%$$

Alternatively,

$$\text{ROE} = \text{net income/equity}$$
$$= \$9,000/\$3,600$$
$$= 25\%$$

ST10.2 Dell Inc. sells personal computers, servers, printers, and personal digital assistants directly to customers. The table below shows performance ratios for Dell, its industry, and its sector. What do these recent numbers tell you about Dell's relative operating efficiency?

	Dell	Industry	Sector	S&P 500
Return on assets	15.53	8.32	5.96	6.43
Return on equity	47.89	29.77	11.96	18.77
Receivables turnover	13.91	7.36	7.66	9.77
Inventory turnover	105.06	21.02	9.63	10.54
Asset turnover	2.43	1.46	0.77	0.92

Solution

Dell's returns on assets and equity are much higher than those of its industry, its sector, and the market in general. This appears to be the result of Dell's effective asset management. Dell's receivables, inventory, and asset turnovers are all much higher than those of industry competitors, firms throughout the high-tech sector, and the overall market. This means that Dell achieves sales with fewer assets and inventory and gets its customers to pay much sooner than is typical in corporate America.

www.mhhe.com/hirschey1e

Questions and Problems

10.1 What is the basic difference between investment and speculation with common stocks?

10.2 Clarify how return-on-equity (ROE) numbers can become biased by share buybacks and corporate restructuring.

10.3 What is total asset turnover, and how does it contribute to profitability?

10.4 What is the difference between a company's return on assets and its return on stock-holders' equity? Why should investors be skeptical of seemingly extraordinary ROE?

10.5 Why is it important for firms to earn a business profit rate, or return on equity, of 12 percent or more per year?

10.6 Consider the Microsoft financial statements in Tables 10.1 to 10.3. Using the data for 2004, compute the asset, receivables, and inventory turnover ratios.

10.7 Using the Microsoft financial statements in Tables 10.1 to 10.3 for 2004, compute the current ratio and quick ratio.

10.8 Using the balance sheet information below for Dell, compute the leverage ratio, debt-to-equity ratio, and debt-to-capital ratio.

Total current assets	$10,633	Accounts payable	$ 7,316
Property/plant/equipment, total net	1,517	Accrued expenses	3,580
Long-term investments	6,770	Total current liabilities	10,896
Other long term assets, total	391	Total long-term debt	505
		Other liabilities, total	1,630
		Total liabilities	$13,031
		Total equity	6,280
Total assets	$19,311	Total liabilities and equity	$19,311

10.9 Use Dell's balance sheet information in Problem 10.8 and the income statement information shown below to compute ROE. If Dell were structured differently, it might have more debt and less equity. If total equity was only $3,140 and net income was only $2,525 (due to increased interest expense), what would ROE have been? What would shareholders think about this change?

Sales	$41,444
Cost of goods sold	33,892
EBIT	3,738
Net income	2,645

10.10 The table below shows the valuation ratios for Dell Inc. and its industry and sector. What do these numbers tell you about Dell's valuation and investor expectations?

Valuation Ratio	Dell Inc.	Comp. Industry	Tech. Sector	S&P 500
P/E ratio	35.28	28.39	35.65	24.71
Price to book	14.51	8.02	5.21	4.52

 10.11 Many financially oriented Web sites provide important financial ratio information. Go to the Yahoo! Finance Web site (**finance.yahoo.com**) and find these ratios for Procter

& Gamble (ticker PG) by clicking on the Key Statistics link. What ratios are provided? How well is Procter & Gamble's management running the firm?

10.12 Go to the Standard & Poor's Market Insight Web site at **www.mhhe.com/ edumarketinsight** and click on the Company link. Enter the ticker "KO " for Coca-Cola. Using annual report information from the most recent fiscal year, compute the following ratios for Coke (and show your calculations):

STANDARD &POOR'S

Net profit margin	Inventory turnover
Return on equity	Debt to equity
Return on assets	Debt to total capital
Total asset turnover	Current ratio
Leverage ratio	Quick ratio
Receivables turnover	Interest coverage

10.13 Go to the Standard & Poor's Market Insight Web site at **www.mhhe.com/ edumarketinsight** and click on the Company link. Enter the ticker "JCI" for Johnson Controls, Inc. Using Johnson Control's financial statements, compute its net profit margin, ROE, asset turnover, and leverage ratio using net cash flow from operations information for the most recent fiscal year. Using the DuPont formula, what is the source of Johnson Control's ROE? Show your work.

STANDARD &POOR'S

10.14 Consider the following partial balance sheet for Delta Airlines. Compute Delta's current ratio and quick ratio. Comment on Delta's liquidity.

Period Ending 31-Dec-04			
Assets		**Liabilities**	
Current assets:		Current liabilities:	
Cash and cash equivalents	$ 1,811,000	Accounts payable	$ 3,481,000
Short-term investments	336,000	Short-/current long-term debt	893,000
Net receivables	731,000	Other current liabilities	1,567,000
Inventory	203,000	Total current liabilities	$ 5,941,000
Other current assets	525,000	Long-term debt	13,005,000
Total current assets	$ 3,606,000	Other liabilities	7,843,000
Long-term investments	127,000	Deferred long-term liability charges	531,000
Property plant and equipment	16,556,000		
Goodwill	227,000		
Intangible assets	79,000		
Other assets	1,206,000		
Total assets	$21,801,000	Total liabilities	$27,597,000

10.15 Go to the Standard & Poor's Market Insight Web site at **www.mhhe.com/ edumarketinsight** and click on the Company link. Enter the ticker "MAT" for Mattel, Inc. Using Mattel's monthly valuation data in the "Excel Analysts" section, graph Mattel's relative P/E ratio. Is Mattel valued low or high compared to the benchmarks?

STANDARD &POOR'S

10.16 Go to the Standard & Poor's Market Insight Web site at **www.mhhe.com/ edumarketinsight** and click on the Company link. Click on the Population link and review the companies listed in "Market Insight." Choose a company whose name begins with the same letter as your last name. Read the stock report for this company in the "S&P Stock Reports" section. What does this company do? How is the firm performing, and what is its valuation? What does S&P recommend?

STANDARD &POOR'S

10.17 A company's current ratio is 2.0. If the company uses cash to retire notes payable that are due within one year, would this transaction *most likely* increase or decrease the current ratio and asset turnover ratio, respectively?

	Current Ratio	Asset Turnover Ratio
a.	Increase	Increase
b.	Increase	Decrease
c.	Decrease	Increase
d.	Decrease	Decrease

10.18 An analyst gathered the following information about a company whose fiscal year-end is December 31:
- Net income for the year was $10.5 million.
- Preferred stock dividends of $2 million were paid for the year.
- Common stock dividends of $3.5 million were paid for the year.
- 20 million shares of common stock were outstanding on January 1, 2001.
- The company issued 6 million new shares of common stock on April 1, 2001.
- The capital structure does not include any potentially dilutive convertible securities, options, warrants, or other contingent securities

The company's basic earnings per share for 2001 was *closest to:*
  a. $0.35
  b. $0.37
  c. $0.43
  d. $0.46

10.19 Two companies are identical except for substantially different dividend payout ratios. After several years, the company with the lower dividend payout ratio is *most likely* to have:
  a. Lower stock price
  b. Higher debt-equity ratio
  c. Less rapid growth of earnings per share
  d. More rapid growth of earnings per share

10.20 An analyst applied the DuPont system to the following data for a company:

Equity turnover	4.2
Net profit margin	5.5 percent
Total asset turnover	2.0
Dividend payout ratio	31.8 percent

The company's return on equity is *closest to:*
  a. 1.3 percent
  b. 11.0 percent
  c. 23.1 percent
  d. 63.6 percent

INVESTMENT APPLICATION

Is Coca-Cola a "Perfect" Business?

One of the most basic principles of investing is that, in the long run, investors can do no better than the businesses in which they invest. Common stock represents share ownership in the corporation and entitles the owner to a proportionate share of the company's earnings, dividends, and/or any proceeds in the event of a merger or dissolution. To make above-normal returns, investors must identify and invest in companies with above-normal business prospects. Moreover, these above-normal prospects must not be recognized in the marketplace and already factored into the company's stock price. Ideally, one would like to identify and purchase shares in a "perfect" business. Thus, a fundamental question for any investor is simply, "What does a perfect business look like?"

For Warren Buffett and his partner Charlie Munger, the chairman and vice-chairman of Berkshire Hathaway, Inc., respectively, Coca-Cola looks pretty close to perfect. To see why, imagine going back in time to 1885, to Atlanta, Georgia, and trying to invent something from scratch, a beverage perhaps, that would make you, your family, and all of your friends rich.

Your beverage would be nonalcoholic to ensure widespread appeal among both young and old alike. It would be cold rather than hot so as to provide relief from climatic effects. It must be ordered by name—a trademarked name. Nobody gets rich selling easy-to-imitate generic products. It must generate a lot of repeat business through what psychologists call *conditioned reflexes*. To get the desired positive conditioned reflex, you will want to make the beverage sweet, rather than bitter, with no aftertaste. Without any aftertaste, consumers will be able to drink as much of your product as they like. By adding sugar to make your beverage sweet, you increase its food value and give it a positive stimulant. To get extra-powerful combinatorial effects, you may want to add caffeine as an additional stimulant. Both sugar and caffeine work as stimulants; by combining them you get more than a double effect—you get what Munger calls a "lollapalooza" effect. Additional combinatorial effects can be realized if you design the product to appear exotic. Coffee is another popular product, so making your beverage dark in color seems like a safe bet. By adding carbonation, you add a little fizz to your beverage's appearance and its appeal.

To ensure enormous profits, you must have high profit margins and a high rate of return on invested capital. To ensure a high rate of return on sales, you must charge a price that is substantially above unit costs. Because consumers tend to be least price-sensitive for moderately priced items, you would like to have a modest "price point," say, roughly $1 to $2 per serving. This is a big problem for most beverages because water is a key ingredient, and water is very expensive to ship long distances. To get around this cost-of-delivery difficulty, you will want to sell not the beverage itself but a key ingredient, such as syrup, to local bottlers. By selling syrup to independent bottlers, your company can also better safeguard its "secret ingredients." It also avoids the problem of having to invest a substantial amount in bottling plants, machinery, delivery trucks, and so on. This minimizes capital requirements and boosts the rate of return on invested capital. If you correctly price the key syrup ingredient, you can ensure that the enormous profits generated by carefully developed lollapalooza effects accrue to your company and not to the bottlers. Of course, you want to offer independent bottlers the potential for highly satisfactory profits in order to provide the necessary incentive for them to push your product. You not only want to "leave something on the table" for the bottlers in terms of the bottlers' profit potential but also want to encourage them to "leave something on the table" for restaurant and other customers. This means that you must demand that bottlers deliver a consistently high-quality product at carefully specified prices if they are to maintain their valuable franchise to sell your beverage in the local area.

If you had indeed gone back to 1885, to Atlanta, Georgia, and followed all of these suggestions, you would have created what you and I know as the Coca-Cola Company. To be sure, there would have been surprises along the way. Take widespread refrigeration, for example. Early on, Coca-Cola management saw the fountain business as the primary driver in cold carbonated beverage sales. Management didn't foretell that widespread refrigeration would make grocery store sales and in-home consumption popular. Still, much of Coca-Cola's success has been achieved because its management had, and still has, a good grasp of both the economics and the psychology of the beverage business. By getting into rapidly growing foreign markets with a winning formula, the current management hopes to create local brand-name recognition, scale economies in distribution, and other "first mover" advantages like the ones its predecessors have nurtured in the United States for more than 100 years.

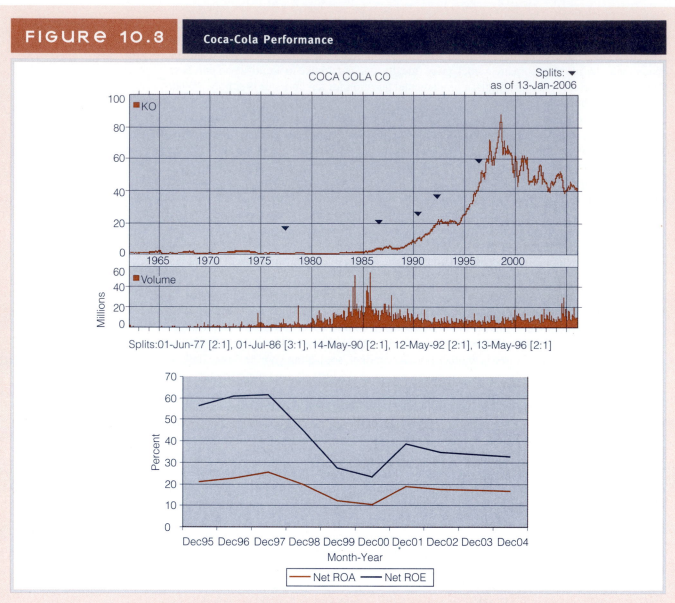

FIGURe 10.3 Coca-Cola Performance

Source: Yahoo! Finance (**http://finance.yahoo.com**) and Standard & Poor's Market Insight (**www.mhhe.com/edumarketinsight**). Reproduced with permission of Yahoo! Inc. © 2006 by Yahoo! Inc. Yahoo! and the Yahoo! logo are trademarks of Yahoo! Inc.

As shown in Figure 10.3, in a world where the typical company earns 12 to 14 percent rates of return on invested capital, Coca-Cola earns three times as much. Typical profit rates, let alone operating losses, are unheard of at Coca-Cola. It enjoys large and growing profits and requires practically no tangible capital investment. Almost its entire value results from brand equity derived from generations of advertising and carefully nurtured positive "lollapalooza" effects. On an overall basis, it is easy to see why Buffett and Munger regard Coca-Cola as a "perfect" business.

a. One of the most important skills to learn in investment is the ability to identify a good business. Discuss at least four characteristics of a wonderful business.

b. Identify at least four companies that you regard as having the wonderful characteristics you identified in Question **a**, above. Suppose you bought common stock in each of them. Three years from now, how would you know if your analysis was correct? What would convince you that your analysis was wrong?

Value Stock Investing

I n 1934, Benjamin Graham and David L. Dodd published a book with the modest title *Security Analysis*. At the time, Graham was a hedge fund manager and lecturer in finance at Columbia University, where Dodd was an associate professor. Together, Graham and Dodd laid down the essential standards for value investing, an investment approach aimed at identifying stock market bargains. More than 70 years later, the principles put down by Graham and Dodd have lasted the test of time, and *Security Analysis* remains one of the most influential books ever written on investments.

In Omaha, Nebraska, near the first Monday in May, Graham's most famous and successful student, Warren Buffett, preaches the gospel according to Ben at Berkshire Hathaway, Inc.'s annual meeting. As chairman and CEO of Berkshire, Buffett has amassed a personal fortune of over $40 billion and made scores of believers into multimillionaires. Over three-dozen books have been written about Buffett and his investing opinions and strategies. It is easy to see why literally thousands of well-heeled investors make the annual pilgrimage to Omaha to hear Buffett speak. Inevitably, the crowd roars as Buffett skewers commonly held beliefs about stock market speculation. Misguided financial theorists, momentum players, and day traders all feel his sharp tongue.

Buffett's annual letter to shareholders often uses humor to make his most damning points. Buffett describes abusive tax shelters as part of an "Alice in Wonderland" corporate environment. He calls derivatives "weapons of mass financial destruction." Buffett also suggests that investors "should try to be fearful when others are greedy and greedy only when others are fearful." In the light of Buffett's astounding success and enormous personal popularity, it is amazing that Buffett's sensible value approach and keen appreciation for the importance of understanding investor psychology is not shared by the overwhelming majority of investors. Value investing and a contrarian investment philosophy involve dedication and patience that is often missing among present-day investors.[1]

---

[1] Gene Colter, "He Gets Requests: College Crowd Kicks Tires for Buffett in Presentation of Buyout Plans," *The Wall Street Journal Online*, December 3, 2005 (**http://online.wsj.com**).

Value Stock Philosophy

Conservative Approach

Value investing Investment approach that concentrates on securities considered to be temporarily undervalued or unpopular.

Value investing involves focusing on securities considered to be undervalued or unpopular for various reasons. Another popular approach, **growth stock investing**, involves focusing on companies expected to have above-average rates of growth in sales and earnings. Growth stock investing techniques are detailed in Chapter 12. In both cases, investors seek bargains selling at prices below their actual **economic value**. In value investing, bargains are typically described in terms of a market price that is below the economic value of assets in place. In growth stock investing, bargains are defined in terms of securities selling for prices below the value of future growth opportunities.

Growth stock investing Investment approach that focuses on companies expected to have above-average rates of growth in sales and earnings.

Value investors like bargains. Whereas growth stock investors seek companies with the potential for above-average rates of growth in earnings and dividends, value investors seek companies whose stock prices have been unfairly beaten down in price. In both cases, investors seek bargains selling at prices below their real economic value, but differences in investment philosophy lead to distinctive investment decisions.

Economic value Value determined by business prospects.

In the case of value investing, bargains are often measured in terms of market prices that are below the estimated economic value of tangible and intangible assets. Most value investors focus on rather easily measured tangible assets such as plant, equipment, common stock or other financial holdings in subsidiaries or other companies, and real estate. A bargain is discovered when market prices are temporarily depressed below a conservative estimate of the current market value of tangible assets. When the gap between stock market prices and the market value of tangible assets is great, an attractive candidate for purchase is discovered.

Contrarian investment philosophy Investment strategy based on the premise that investors can profit by betting against the overly emotional crowd.

Value investors argue that overly emotional investors sometimes cause stock prices to be moved by "fear" and "greed" to levels that are too low or too high based on the economic fundamentals. As a result, value investors adopt a **contrarian investment philosophy** based on the premise that investors can profit by betting against the overly emotional crowd. To be successful, contrarian investors argue that one must "buy fear" and "sell greed."

What Is a Value Stock?

Value investors Investors who seek out-of-favor stocks selling at a discount to the overall market.

Traditional **value investors** seek out-of-favor stocks selling at a discount to the overall market. Such discounts are measured in terms of low P/E and low P/B ratios and/or high dividend yields. Value investors like to find companies with good businesses whose stock is priced so that its P/E ratio is lower than the market average (often < 10) or whose dividend yield is unusually high. These investment criteria often result in an investment preference for basic industry stocks, financial services companies, and utilities.

In judging the investment merit of the value approach, it is important to recognize that, by themselves, low stock prices do not necessarily signal attractive value any more than low prices signify attractive value at a department store or grocery store. No reasonable shopper would

	Value Stocks in the S&P 500 Typically Feature Low P/E and Attractive Dividend Yields
TABLE 11.1	

Symbol	Company	Current Dividend Yield	Current P/E Ratio
VZ	Verizon Communications	5.1	10.1
F	Ford Motor Co.	4.8	8.6
FHN	First Horizon National Corp.	4.6	11.6
BAC	Bank of America Corp.	4.4	10.9
WM	Washington Mutual Inc.	4.4	12.2
BLS	BellSouth Corp.	4.3	12.3
NCC	National City Corp.	4.2	8.9
AEP	American Electric Power	4.0	12.4
KEY	KeyCorp	3.9	13.1
ASO	AmSouth Bancorporation	3.9	13.3
CMA	Comerica Inc.	3.8	11.3
NFB	North Fork Bancorporation, Inc.	3.8	13.0
WB	Wachovia Corp.	3.8	13.1
C	Citigroup Inc.	3.6	11.0
PCG	PG&E Corp.	3.5	9.7
EMN	Eastman Chemical Co.	3.4	7.6
DOW	Dow Chemical	3.1	9.3
CVX	Chevron Corp.	2.9	9.8
CTB	Cooper Tire & Rubber Co.	2.6	9.2
CLX	Clorox Co.	2.0	9.4
FNM	Fannie Mae	1.9	7.0
COP	ConocoPhillips	1.9	7.4
LPX	Louisiana-Pacific Corp.	1.9	7.7
ASH	Ashland Inc.	1.7	2.4
OXY	Occidental Petroleum Corp.	1.6	7.7
	Average	3.4	10.0

Source: msnMoney, January 18, 2006 (**http://moneycentral.msn.com/investor/finder/customstocksdl.asp**).

go into a grocery store and restrict buying to items selling for less than $1, $5, or $10. Similarly, no reasonable value investor would restrict buying interest to stocks selling for less than $1, $5, or $10. Even sharply marked-down produce represents no real bargain when it is well past its prime and spoilage is at hand. A shrewd produce shopper looks for bargain prices on fruits and vegetables that are in the peak of condition. Similarly, a savvy value investor looks for quality companies selling at unusually attractive prices when compared with conventional P/E, P/B, and/or dividend yield criteria.

Table 11.1 shows a sample of firms in the S&P 500 Index that might be considered attractive by the value investor. You may not have heard of all of these firms even though they are among the largest firms in the nation. Value stocks are often firms that have had unusually negative media coverage. They are often in industries that many investors would not normally consider for investment.

Value investors look for companies selling at sharp discounts to the company's economic value, or **fundamental value**. This is like buying the company on sale. If a company is worth $40 per share, a market price of $25 represents an opportunity to buy an **undervalued** firm. Attractive stock market values can be created when an entire industry falls into disfavor. Companies that may be only temporarily affected by industry problems can become undervalued

Fundamental value
Underlying value based on the firm's assets and profit potential.

Undervalued
A stock priced below its true economic value.

in the marketplace. Some years ago, for example, investors turned their backs on the steel industry when big U.S. producers lost their ability to compete in world markets. Nevertheless, some small and highly efficient specialty steel mills proved to be excellent investments for discriminating investors. Radical changes facing the health care and financial services industries have also created opportunities for clever value investors able to identify bargains amid the general uncertainty over these businesses.

Although the basic principle of value investing is easy to grasp, identifying undervalued opportunities requires considerable know-how and investment research. Low prices alone do not indicate an undervalued asset. It is the comparison between market prices and fundamental value that is important. The next section discusses methods for assessing fundamental value.

Fundamental Value

Estimating Fundamental Value

Consider the simple case of valuing a stock to be held for one year. The fundamental value of such a stock, P_0, is the present value of the dividend to be received at the end of the first year, D_1, plus the present value of the expected sales price in one year, P_1. It is important for investors to keep in mind that the future stock price and future dividend payments cannot be known with certainty. Whenever investors deal with future stock prices and future dividend payments, they are dealing with **expected values**, not certain sums. The per-share value of a stock to be sold in one year is the present value of future dividends and the price to be received at the point of sale:

Expected values
Anticipated amounts.

$$P_0 = \frac{D_1 + P_1}{1 + k}$$

(11.1)

Risk-adjusted discount rate
Investor's required return.

In Equation 11.1, the **risk-adjusted discount rate** k, or required return, is the interest rate required to fairly compensate investors for risk.

Most companies hate to cut their dividends, so dividend estimation is seldom difficult. Thus, Equation 11.1 offers a useful means for estimating the true economic value of a stock, provided that the year-end stock price can be estimated with similar precision. To estimate the year-end stock price, P_1, Equation 11.1 again comes into play. Using the same logic as used to estimate P_0, the year-end value P_1 will be

$$P_1 = \frac{D_2 + P_2}{1 + k} \tag{11.2}$$

If investors can assume that the stock in question will be selling for its actual value next year, Equation 11.2 can be substituted into Equation 11.1 to yield

$$P_0 = \frac{D_1}{1 + k} + \frac{D_2 + P_2}{(1 + k)^2} \tag{11.3}$$

This equation gives the present value of the stock as the present value of dividends to be received over the next two years, plus the present value of the share price to be received at the end of two years. Notice that the expression beneath the second term on the right-hand side of Equation 11.3 is raised to the second power. This reflects the fact that two years will elapse before second-year dividends and stock sale proceeds will be received.

The logic evident in Equation 11.3 can be repeated for any number of years. For an expected holding period of t years, the fundamental value of a stock is measured by the present value of dividends over the t years and the ultimate sales price, P_t:

$$P_0 = \frac{D_1}{1 + k} + \frac{D_2}{(1 + k)^2} + \ldots + \frac{D_t + P_t}{(1 + k)^t} \tag{11.4}$$

This formula involves both future dividend payments and the future stock price. As such, it incorporates both dividend income and capital appreciation or loss. It involves full consideration of both major components of the investor's **total return** from investment.

Total return
Dividend income plus capital appreciation.

Try It!

Assume a stock is trading for $45 per share. You expect the firm to pay a dividend next year of $1.50, in year 2 of $1.60, and in year 3 of $1.75. If you expect the stock to sell for $60 in three years and the required rate is 9 percent, is this stock undervalued or overvalued?

Solution

Compare the present value of the dividends and future price to the current stock price. Using Equation 11.4,

$$P_0 = \frac{1.50}{1 + 0.09} + \frac{1.60}{(1 + 0.09)^2} + \frac{1.75 + 60}{(1 + 0.09)^3} = 1.37 + 1.347 + 47.682 = \$50.40$$

Since the value of the stock, $50.40, is greater than the current price, $45, the stock is undervalued.

Estimating Future Stock Prices

To calculate the fundamental value of a stock using Equation 11.4, a value investor would need to estimate the future stock price in year t. One common method for doing so is to use reasonable estimates of the firm's future P/E ratio and potential earnings per share. The expected share price is simply the relevant P/E ratio multiplied by expected earnings per share:

$$P_t = \left(\frac{P}{E}\right)_t \times E_t$$

$$= \left(\frac{P}{E}\right)_t \times E_0 \times (1 + g)^t \tag{11.5}$$

Mr. Market

Benjamin Graham is justly famous as the dean of fundamental analysis. The three pillars of Graham's fundamental approach to investing are (1) common stock values ultimately reflect their proportionate share of the economic net worth of the corporation, (2) it is prudent to build in a "margin of safety" in stock valuation, and (3) investors can make prudent assessments only if they ignore market sentiment.

Graham used a legendary "Mr. Market" parable to explain how the intelligent investor might deal with market sentiment. Graham's fable goes something like this: Think of yourself as being in partnership with a bright but irrational fellow named Mr. Market. The two of you have what is called a *buy-sell agreement*. If one party offers to buy the other out at a given price, then the offering party is obligated to sell out at that same price. Being neurotic, Mr. Market's mood fluctuates from normal behavior to incredible optimism to overwhelming depression.

On a good day, Mr. Market is buoyant and will offer to buy out your share of the business at an enormous, sky-high price. On a bad day, Mr. Market is gloomy and will offer to sell his share of the business at a very low, or rock-bottom, price. Mr. Market's judgment is formed more by mood swings than by rational thought. This gives you, the rational partner, multiple profit-making opportunities. If Mr. Market's buying price is unreasonably high, you can take advantage of the opportunity to sell. If Mr. Market's selling price is unreasonably low, you can take advantage of the opportunity to buy.

In the stock market, the intelligent investor's goal is to earn above-normal returns by making judgments that, on average, are more sensible than those reflected in sometimes irrational market prices. Graham wrote that the only importance of market prices is that they give the intelligent investor an opportunity to buy wisely when prices fall in an irrational fashion, and sell wisely when they advance irrationally. At other times, the intelligent investor does best to forget about day-to-day price fluctuations and focus on company operating results.

See Karen Richardson, "Berkshire Hathaway to Acquire News Distributor Business Wire," *The Wall Street Journal Online*, January 18, 2006 (**http://online.wsj.com**).

In many instances, the firm's typical P/E ratio over a 5- to 10-year period can be used as a useful proxy for the P/E ratio in year t. As the formula shows, assumptions about the growth rate of earnings can be used to estimate earnings in year t. Value investors often examine historical earning per share and historical earnings-per-share growth rates to gain insight concerning future possibilities. Historical growth rates are then adjusted to account for expected changes in profitability due to changing competition, new products, regulation changes, and so on. With an estimate of P_t, value investors can estimate the fundamental value of a stock at any prior point in time.

Try It!

Assume a firm has a current P/E ratio of 11 and its current EPS is $2.50. It has increased its earnings per share by 5 percent annually in the past and this rate is likely to continue for some time. If the P/E ratio is expected to increase to 14 in five years, what is the stock price expected to be in year 5?

Solution

Using Equation 11.5,

$$P_t = \left(\frac{P}{E}\right)_t \times E_t \times (1 + g)^t = 14 \times \$2.50 \times (1.05)^5 = \$44.67$$

The stock price is expected to be $44.67 in five years.

Dividend Discount Model

To a value investor, the fundamental value of a stock is the present value of all expected cash flows. When future cash flows are paid out in the form of future dividends, the fundamental value of a stock is the present value of all future dividends. If one continues to substitute for stock price in Equation 11.4, the fundamental value of a stock can be seen as the present value of all future dividends:

$$P_0 = \frac{D_1}{1+k} + \frac{D_2}{(1+k)^2} + \frac{D_3}{(1+k)^3} + \ldots$$ **(11.6)**

This formula is called the **dividend discount model**. It is easy to misinterpret this model as implying that capital gains are not important. Although the dividend discount model focuses exclusively on future dividend income, future stock prices at any point in time are determined by anticipated dividend income. Expected capital gains are implicitly incorporated in the dividend discount model, but their influence is captured in terms of anticipated future dividend income. The fact that only dividends appear in the dividend discount model does not imply that common stock investors should ignore capital gains in their buy-sell decisions. It simply means that capital gains will be determined by dividend forecasts made by other investors at the time the stock is sold. This is why stock prices at any point in time can be described as the present value of dividends plus the sale price over *any* investment horizon.

The dividend discount model is useful because it focuses investor attention on the importance of dividends as a fundamental determinant of share prices. For example, suppose a value investor knew that a company was operating in a business so bad that it could never afford to pay a single dividend. If a value investor knew for certain that the company could never pay a dividend, its stock would have zero fundamental value. The only potential for such a speculation is that a trader might hope to find some "greater fool" to sell the worthless shares to at some inflated price. However, that form of speculation has nothing to do with value investing, and it is a very tough way to make money in the stock market.

Dividend discount model
Stock valuation approach based on expected dividend income and risk considerations.

Constant-Growth Model

The dividend discount model shown in Equation 11.6 is difficult to apply because it requires a precise estimate of future dividends. To simplify matters, investors often make the assumption of a constant rate of dividend growth, g. Next year's dividend is simply this year's dividend growing at g, that is, $D_1 = D_0(1 + g)$. Assuming constant dividend growth, Equation 11.6 can be written

$$P_0 = \frac{D_0(1+g)}{1+k} + \frac{D_0(1+g)^2}{(1+k)^2} + \frac{D_0(1+g)^3}{(1+k)^3} + \ldots$$ **(11.7)**

This **constant-growth model** for stock valuation can be simplified to

$$P_0 = \frac{D_0(1+g)}{k-g} = \frac{D_1}{k-g}$$ **(11.8)**

Constant-growth model
Stock valuation method based on constantly growing future dividends and risk considerations.

This constant-growth model is sometimes referred to as the *Gordon growth model*, after financial economist Myron J. Gordon, who popularized its use. In this model, the required return, k, must exceed the dividend growth rate, g, to calculate a finite stock price. When $k > g$, the constant-growth model can derive useful valuation estimates. If $k \le g$, rapid growth would overwhelm the effect of discounting, and investors would theoretically be willing to pay an infinite price for the stock. Economically, this is a nonsensical result. In the long run, no stock can grow dividends at a pace that exceeds the nominal rate of growth in the overall economy, say 5 to 7 percent per year. When a typical 10 to 15 percent rate of discount is employed, the rate of discount will always exceed the constant rate of growth in dividends that can be achieved, and the constant-growth model can give sensible valuation estimates.

Try It!

A company paid a $0.75 per-share dividend this year, and it is expected to grow at 5 percent. If the required rate of return for this firm is 10 percent, what is its fundamental value?

Solution

Use Equation 11.8:

$$P_0 = \frac{D_0(1 + g)}{k - g} = \frac{\$0.75 \times (1 + 0.05)}{0.10 - 0.05} = \$15.75$$

Preferred stock

A class of stock with fixed dividends.

A special case of the constant-growth model is the valuation of **preferred stock**. The term *preferred* refers to the preference this stock is given over common stock in bankruptcy proceedings. Preferred stockholders receive more value than common stockholders when a firm files for bankruptcy protection. In addition, preferred stock is different from common stock in that it pays a constant dividend. Preferred stock is also different from bonds in that preferred stock typically does not have a maturity date. Preferred stock often pays a fixed dividend in perpetuity. Because the dividend rate never changes, the preferred stock dividend growth rate is typically zero. Therefore, investors can determine the fundamental value of a preferred stock simply as $P = D / k$.

When interest rates change in the economy over time, the risk-adjusted discount rate, k, also changes. When interest rates rise, risk-adjusted interest rates also tend to rise, and both common and preferred stock prices tend to fall. When interest rates fall, risk-adjusted interest rates also tend to fall, and both common and preferred stock prices tend to rise. Because the link between interest rates and preferred stock prices is especially close, many investors consider preferred stocks to be an example of **fixed-income securities**.

Fixed-income securities

A group of securities that include preferred stocks and bonds.

Estimating Required Return

The required rate of return k is a key ingredient in models used to determine fundamental values, Equations 11.1 to 11.8. From Equation 4.1 in Chapter 4, it is clear that the required rate of return includes two components: a nominal risk-free rate and a risk premium. Therefore, required-rate-of-return estimation requires estimating an appropriate nominal risk-free rate and the appropriate risk premium. In most instances, the nominal risk-free rate can be estimated as the rate of return on short-term Treasury bills. As obligations of the federal government, T-bills are free from default risk. Given a term to maturity of 90 days or less, T-bills are also free from holding-period risk.

While estimating the nominal risk-free rate using T-bill rates is straightforward, estimating an appropriate risk premium is more difficult. One popular approach for estimating the required return is the capital asset pricing model (CAPM) detailed in Chapter 5. However, there is controversy as to the validity of the CAPM, and many investors use several alternative methods to estimate k. Some investors estimate k using the average annual historical rate of return on the firm's common stock. A second method is to add today's risk-free rate to the average risk premium earned by investors in the firm over time. To compute the annual risk premium, one only needs to subtract the T-bill rate from the investor's realized rate of return per year. This annual risk premium can be averaged over time to determine a typical risk premium.

Sensitivity analysis

Computation of fundamental values in which small changes are made to the model's input data to determine how sensitive the results are to those variables.

Given investor uncertainty, a prudent **sensitivity analysis** computes fundamental values using alternative growth rate estimates and required rates of return. For example, consider a firm that is expected to pay a $1.50 dividend next year, and assume that dividend is expected to grow at 5 percent per year. If the required rate of return is 10 percent, then the fundamental value is $30 per share [= 1.5/(0.1 − 0.05)]. If the current stock price is $28 per share, then the company is undervalued. With an expected growth rate of 4 percent per year, the fundamental value of the company is $25 per share and the stock appears to be overvalued. Sensitivity analysis shows how sensitive buy-sell decisions are to reasonable changes in underlying assumptions.

In some cases, the constant-growth rate model can be used to derive market-based estimates of the required rate of return for individual common stocks. After manipulation, Equation 11.8 shows that the required rate of return k consists of dividend yield plus the rate of growth due to capital appreciation:

$$k = \frac{D_1}{P_0} + g = \text{dividend yield} + \text{capital gain}$$

(11.9)

For example, if a company is expected to pay a 2 percent dividend yield and security analysts expect that dividend to grow at 10 percent per year, a market-based estimate of the investor's required rate of return is 12 percent per year.

An Example of Fundamental Valuation

As an example, consider using fundamental analysis to value Chevron Corporation. Chevron is a $120 billion (market-cap) oil company with annual sales of more than $160 billion. With a P/E ratio of 9 and a dividend yield of 3.1 percent, it has the making of a value stock. However, its price increased 50 percent during the last two years. Is Chevron still undervalued, or is too late to buy?

Figure 11.1 shows that Chevron's dividend increased from $1.30 in 2000 to $1.75 in 2005. This represents a 6.1 percent rate of growth in dividends. Earnings per share increased from $3.61 to $6.96 during the same period, representing a 14 percent rate of annual gain. If it is reasonable to expect dividend growth to continue at 6.1 percent per year, then Chevron will be paying a $2.36 dividend in 2010. To calculate Chevron's fundamental value, a reasonable estimate of Chevron's future share price is needed. A reasonable Chevron share price for 2010 can be estimated using Equation 11.5. Even though Chevron has a current P/E ratio of 9, a future P/E ratio of 12 is chosen as reasonable because energy stocks are beginning to become more popular and their prices are being bid up. If earnings per share continue to grow at the 14 percent rate they have been growing at recently, then Chevron will be earning $13.42 per share in 2010. Figure 11.1 shows an estimated share price for Chevron in 2010 of $161 based on these assumptions.

FIGURe 11.1	Valuing Chevron

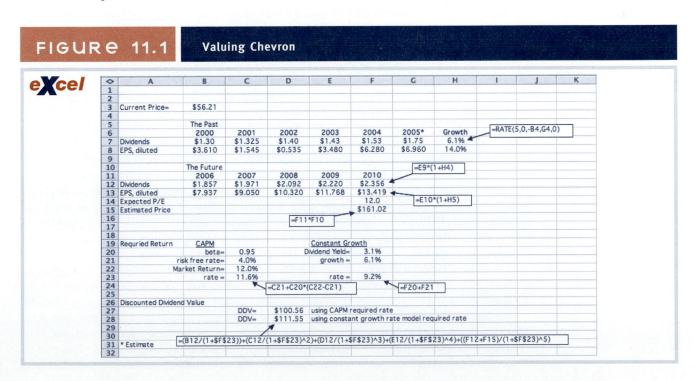

The last item needed to compute an appropriate fundamental valuation for Chevron is an estimate of the required rate of return for discounting future dividends and the 2010 share price. Figure 11.1 shows the effects of using alternative methods for computing the required rate of return. Using a beta of 0.95, a risk-free rate of 4 percent per year, and an expected market return of 12 percent, the single factor CAPM yields a required rate of 11.6 percent [= $R_F + \beta(R_M - R_F) = 4\% + 0.95(12\% - 4\%)$]. Based on a dividend yield of 3.1 percent and a dividend growth rate of 6.1 percent per year, the constant-growth model suggests a lower required rate of return of 9.2 percent per year. A lower (higher) present value will be indicated when a higher (lower) required rate of return is employed. It is more conservative to value Chevron using the higher required rate of return, so the 11.6 percent figure is used. If dividends to be paid from 2006 to 2010 and the estimated price in 2010 are discounted using an 11.6 percent required rate of return, the present value for Chevron is $100 per share. At the 2006 price of $56 per share, Chevron appears to be undervalued and to represent a real bargain.

Before buying the stock, however, it is helpful to do a sensitivity analysis. How do small but reasonable changes in input parameters affect the decision to buy the stock? What if there is reason to believe that earnings might grow at only a 10 percent rate? What if the expected P/E ratio should be the current P/E ratio of 9? If the expected earnings growth rate is changed to 10 percent, the present value of Chevron stock is $85. Alternatively, if the expected P/E ratio is changed to 9, the present value of Chevron stock becomes $77. If the expected growth rate is changed to 10 percent and the anticipated P/E ratio is lowered to 9, the present value of Chevron stock is $66. In all cases, the fundamental value for Chevron exceeds the current share price of $56. Chevron looks like a real bargain.

Graham and Dodd Approach

Benjamin Graham

For many investors, the value investing concept is synonymous with the name of Benjamin Graham. Graham started his Wall Street career in 1914 as a brokerage firm messenger for $12 per week. From that position, he quickly rose to writing research reports. In 1920, at the young age of 26, Graham took his place as a partner in the Wall Street firm of Newburger, Henderson & Loeb, having proved his ability to manage complex investment strategies. During the early 1920s, Graham developed a knack for finding companies with understated earnings and hidden assets. In 1923, Graham left Newburger to start his own firm. He started a hedge fund focused on buying deeply undervalued securities, shorting overvalued stocks, and taking advantage of profitable hedging opportunities. In 1928, to help formalize his theories about the market, Graham began teaching a night class, titled "Advanced Security Analysis," at Columbia University in New York. The course was an immediate hit with students and Wall Street professionals who sat in on the class to get valuable investment tips. By 1929, Graham was making $600,000 per year and was so confident of his future success that he turned down an offer to become partners with Wall Street legend Bernard M. Baruch.

As it turned out, the tide was about to turn for the worse for the overall market and for Graham. Between 1921 and 1929, the market had surged 450 percent. Stock price manipulation was widespread. Margin buying with only 10 percent down had fueled a meteoric and unsustainable rise. In the ensuing stock market crash, the DJIA fell a mind-numbing 89.1 percent, from 381.17 on September 3, 1929, to 41.22 on July 8, 1932. So complete was the devastation that it would be 25 years before the 1929 peak was surmounted. On a personal level, Graham's heavy reliance on financial leverage brought enormous losses. Despite savvy stock selections, Graham was ruined.

Although Graham's enormous stock market profits from the "Roaring 20s" were gone, he formed a legendary partnership with Jerome A. Newman. With the improving fortunes of the Graham-Newman partnership, Graham's financial situation began a long and steady rebound. Graham had learned that the true measure of stock market values comes not from short-term price movements but from earnings, dividends, asset values, and a conservative appraisal of future prospects. In May 1934, Graham teamed up with David. L. Dodd, an associate professor of finance at Columbia, to write and publish his thoughts in the investment classic, *Security*

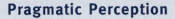
Pragmatic Perception

Bill Miller, celebrated portfolio manager of Legg Mason's Value Trust, put together an astonishing streak of beating the S&P 500 each year for 15 years in a row from 1991 to 2005. Miller is also famous for his incisive stock market analysis.

As a value investor, Miller avoids confusing business fundamentals with investment merit. According to Miller, a company with great management, an enviable rate of return on capital, wonderful products, and strong prospects can be a terrible investment if lofty expectations are embedded in the current stock price. On the other hand, a company with poor business fundamentals, mediocre management, and indifferent prospects can be a wonderful investment opportunity if the market is unduly pessimistic about the business. In other words, Miller looks for a mismatch between business fundamentals and market perceptions. Miller is a keen student of investor psychology.

Miller believes markets are pragmatically efficient, which means that it is very difficult to analyze and use publicly available information to outperform a relevant benchmark. According to Miller, systematic outperformance requires variant perception—one must believe something different from what the market believes, and one must be right. This usually involves weighting publicly available information differently from the market, either as to its magnitude or its duration. More simply, the market is either wrong about how important something is or wrong about when that something occurs, or both. Successful investors need to think independently and value things carefully.

Miller summarizes his investment philosophy as follows:

- Our analysis is based on valuation, not some short-term factor such as whether a company beats next quarter's earning's estimate, or whether guidance is raised or lowered.
- We average down relentlessly. No one can consistently buy at the low or sell at the high. Importantly, the lowest average cost wins.
- We practice creative inaction with annual turnover that has averaged in the 15 to 20 percent range, implying holding periods of more than five years. Successful investing involves anticipating change, not reacting to it.

Interesting investment commentary by Bill Miller and other Legg Mason portfolio managers can be found at **www.leggmason.com**.

Analysis. Because of this work, and another easy-to-read version titled *The Intelligent Investor*, published in 1949, Graham has come to be considered the "Dean of Financial Analysis." Value investors who follow Graham's conservative fundamental approach to stock picking are called **Graham and Dodd** investors.

Graham and Dodd
Coauthors of *Security Analysis*, the value investor's bible.

Margin of Safety

Like any investment philosophy, value investing cannot be easily summarized. Still, the most important idea for a value investor is the **margin-of-safety** concept. According to Graham and Dodd, the margin-of-safety idea becomes evident when applied to undervalued or bargain securities. When the economic value per share measurably exceeds the stock market price, buyers enjoy a favorable margin of safety to absorb the effects of miscalculations or bad luck. Bargain buyers place particular emphasis on the ability of a given investment to withstand adverse developments.

Margin of safety
Positive difference between price and appraised value.

The objective of security analysis is to obtain a true picture of the company as a going concern over a representative time period. Analysts search for an informed judgment of future profitability and growth and seek to arrive at company valuations that, on average, prove more reliable than the marketplace. The goal of enlightened analysis is to identify underpriced securities and to enjoy excess returns following the market's subsequent upward revaluation to a price consistent with **intrinsic value**, or fundamental value. Assets, earnings, dividends, sure prospects, and good management justify the intrinsic value of a stock. According to Graham and Dodd, intrinsic values and current market prices rarely coincide exactly because of the effects of investor pessimism and euphoria.

Intrinsic value
Real economic value.

Stock Selection Criteria

Graham and Dodd looked for stocks selling below **liquidation value**. They wanted to find stocks selling for less than the value that could be obtained from closing down operations, liquidating assets, paying off creditors, and giving the residual to stockholders. Remember, this

Liquidation value
Company worth measured in terms of scrap value.

was an investment philosophy born during the Great Depression. Stock prices had then fallen so low that many firms were selling at bargain-basement prices. However, even under the best of circumstances, implementing such a strategy is difficult. Liquidation values are often difficult to determine because assets are sold at market values but are carried on the balance sheets of publicly traded companies at values based on historical cost.

Finding stocks selling below liquidation value is very rare these days. Present-day Graham and Dodd investors often settle for finding bargain stocks that are cheap relative to tangible assets, earnings power, or future prospects. Table 11.2 shows samples of such firms. Among companies found within the S&P 500, General Motors shows up as one of the lowest P/B ratio stocks. In early 2006, GM was selling at a price equivalent to just 51 percent of the book value of its balance sheet assets. At that time, stock market investors were clearly betting that GM's balance sheet assets were severely overstated. On the other hand, value investors were attracted by the potential earnings power of GM's finance operation, General Motors Acceptance Corporation.

An attractive feature of focusing on stocks with low P/B ratios is that it allows value investors to systematically consider investing in companies that might presently be operating at a loss due to temporary bad fortune. A strict low P/E approach would eliminate such stocks from consideration. To avoid the negative earnings problem that makes a strict low P/E ratio approach to value investing difficult, some value investors search for stocks with low **price-to-sales (P/S)** ratios. Firms with low P/S ratios are often seen as attractive because they may have the potential for large future earnings and low P/E ratios once that future earnings potential has been realized. Similarly, companies with low **price-to-cash flow (P/CF)** ratios are often regarded as having the potential for large future earnings and low P/E ratios in the future. An advantage of the low P/S and low P/CF approaches is that they explicitly allow for the future earnings potential of firms with current earnings that are abnormally low or even negative. A risk tied to both methods is that they can cause investors to focus on companies that may be incapable of translating earnings potential into reported net income.

An important problem faced by Graham and Dodd investors is that some stocks that look cheap on a fundamental basis are no investment bargain. Some firms are cheaply priced because their business models are failing and they are on the brink of bankruptcy. It is of vital importance that value investors distinguish between bad companies that are fairly priced and good companies that are undervalued.

Buffettology

Warren Buffett is Graham's most famous and successful student. After running a spectacularly successful private partnership, Buffett gained control of textile manufacturer Berkshire Hathaway in 1965, at age 34. As chairman and CEO, Buffett has built Berkshire into a $135 billion holding company with an immense portfolio of publicly traded common stocks, including American Express, Coca-Cola, and Procter & Gamble, and a host of diverse and enormously successful operating companies. The most important of Berkshire's operating subsidiaries are in the property and casualty insurance business. Included among these is GEICO, the fifth-largest auto insurer in the United States; General Re, one of the four largest reinsurers in the world; and the Berkshire Hathaway Reinsurance Group. Numerous business activities are also conducted through Berkshire's noninsurance subsidiaries, including Shaw Industries, Benjamin Moore, Johns Manville, Nebraska Furniture Mart, R.C. Willey Home Furnishings, Star Furniture, Jordan's Furniture, Borsheim's, Helzberg Diamond Shops, Ben Bridge Jeweler, and International Dairy Queen.

During 40 years of Buffett's stewardship, Berkshire's net worth per share has compounded at more than 20 percent per year. In an era when median Fortune 500 companies count themselves lucky to earn half that much, Buffett's accomplishment can only be viewed as amazing—especially for a debt-free company. In addition to being uniquely capable as an investor and manager, Buffett has the uncommon ability to communicate his insights on management in a disarmingly modest and humorous fashion that is equally valuable for stock market investors and experienced business managers. Among the most important do's and don'ts learned by Buffett are the following 10 lessons:[2]

Price to sales (P/S)
Current stock price dividend by annual sales, or revenue.

Price to cash flow (P/CF)
Current stock price dividend by annual cash flow.

---

[2] Buffett's Top 10 Do's and Dont's © Warren Buffett. Used with permission of the author.

TABLE 11.2 | Value Stocks in the S&P 500 Sorted by Price-Sales, Price-Book, and Price–Cash Flow Ratios

Ticker	Company	Price	Price/Sales	Price/Book	Price/Cash Flow
A. Low Price-Book Value Stocks					
DCN	Dana Corp.	4.95	0.08	0.44	1.12
GM	General Motors	19.78	0.06	0.51	0.74
DDS	Dillard's Inc.	25.61	0.26	0.92	27.51
AMCC	Applied Micro	2.87	3.39	0.93	2.32
UNM	Unumprovident Corp.	22.60	0.65	0.95	17.97
CTB	Cooper Tire Rubber	16.18	0.46	1.03	2.22
SANM	Sanmina-Sci Corp.	4.61	0.20	1.05	2.17
OMX	Office Max Inc.	26.60	0.20	1.09	24.01
TAP	Molson Coors Co.	66.96	1.05	1.10	56.32
PNW	Pinnacle West Cap.	42.30	1.36	1.16	4.45
	Average	**23.25**	**0.77**	**0.92**	**13.88**
B. Low Price-Cash Flow Stocks					
CFC	Countrywide Fnl. Corp.	36.33	1.82	1.81	0.58
GM	General Motors	19.78	0.06	0.51	0.74
F	Ford Motor Co.	8.22	0.09	1.17	0.90
WB	Wachovia Corp.	53.63	3.29	1.79	0.90
FRE	Freddie Mac	67.39	16.61	1.71	0.96
HIG	Hartford Financial Svc.	86.51	1.03	1.72	1.05
DCN	Dana Corp.	4.95	0.08	0.44	1.12
PRU	Prudential Financial	74.65	1.22	1.62	1.36
LTR	Loews Corp.	99.38	1.17	1.46	1.64
CMA	Comerica Inc.	57.43	3.35	1.88	1.75
	Average	**50.83**	**2.87**	**1.41**	**1.10**
C. Low Price-Sales Stocks					
GM	General Motors	19.78	0.06	0.51	0.74
DCN	Dana Corp.	4.95	0.08	0.44	1.12
F	Ford Motor Co.	8.22	0.09	1.17	0.90
TWX	Time Warner Inc.	17.23	0.15	1.27	10.09
OMX	Office Max Inc.	26.60	0.20	1.09	24.01
SANM	Sanmina-Sci Corp.	4.61	0.20	1.05	2.17
ABS	Albertsons Inc.	22.84	0.21	1.51	33.05
SVU	Supervalu Inc.	32.59	0.22	1.68	7.80
DDS	Dillard's Inc.	25.61	0.26	0.92	27.51
AN	Autonation Inc.	22.20	0.29	1.29	20.98
	Average	**18.46**	**0.18**	**1.09**	**12.84**

Source: Yahoo! Finance, January 18, 2006 (**http://screen.finance.yahoo.com/newscreener.html**).

- **It is far better to buy a wonderful company at a fair price than a fair company at a wonderful price.** In a difficult business, no sooner is one problem solved than another surfaces. "There is never just one cockroach in the kitchen."

- **When a management with a reputation for brilliance tackles a business with a reputation for bad economics, it is the reputation of the business that remains intact.** According to Buffett, attractive economics include a 20 percent plus rate of return on capital without leverage or accounting gimmicks, high margins, high cash flow, low capital investment requirements, a lack of government regulation, and strong prospects for continuing growth. "Good jockeys do well on good horses," Buffett says, "but not on broken down old nags."

- **Management does better by avoiding dragons, not slaying them.** Buffett attributes his success to avoiding, rather than solving, tough business problems. As Buffett says, "We have been successful because we concentrated on identifying one-foot hurdles that we could step over, rather than because we acquired any ability to clear seven-footers."

- **As if governed by Newton's first law of motion, an institution will resist any change in its current direction.** Too often, the call for necessary change is blithely ignored.

- **Just as work expands to fill available time, corporate projects or acquisitions will materialize to soak up available funds.** Even when plainly called for, dividends or share buybacks are seldom seen as the best use of funds.

- **Any business craving of the leader, however foolish, will be quickly supported by detailed rate-of-return and strategic studies prepared by the troops.** Rationality frequently wilts when the institutional imperative comes into play.

- **The behavior of peer companies, whether they are expanding, acquiring, setting compensation, or whatever, will be mindlessly imitated.** Institutional dynamics often set management on a misguided course.

- **It is not a sin to miss a business opportunity outside one's area of expertise.** By inference, it is a sin to miss opportunities that you are fully capable of understanding.

- **If your actions are sensible, you are certain to get good results.** Leverage moves things along faster but at the unavoidable risk of anguish or default.

- **Do not join with managers who lack admirable qualities, no matter how attractive the prospects of their business.** When searching for businesses to buy, Buffett looks for first-class businesses accompanied by first-class management.

How well do these capital allocation rules work in practice? Consider that when Buffett gained control of Berkshire Hathaway in 1965 the company had a stock price of $12 per share. By 2006, Berkshire's stock price had risen to more than $90,000 per share, making Buffett's personal stake worth about *$40 billion*. All in all, not too shabby!

Dividends and Value Investing

Dividends Mitigate Risk

A hallmark of conservative stock portfolios is an emphasis on established companies with above-average dividend yields and dividend growth rates. Focusing on "cheap" stocks with secure dividends allows investors to participate in bull markets while minimizing the loss potential tied to inevitable market downturns. To value investors, limiting downside risk is a vital component of long-term value maximization.

When the dividend yield on an investor's portfolio is above average, the investor is guaranteed that at least one of the two components of investment return will be positive. The other, the change in portfolio market value, can be positive or negative. For example, a stock purchased at $40 per share that pays an annual dividend of $1 provides a 2.5 percent annual yield (= $1/$40). If the stock's price grows 7.5 percent, or $3, during the year, the total return to investors will equal 10 percent, or the dividend yield of 2.5 percent plus capital appreciation of 7.5 percent. If the share price declines 7.5 percent, a 2.5 percent dividend will offset one-third of the decline and cut the investor's overall loss to 5 percent. Because companies are extremely reluctant to cut dividends, dividend yields tend to be much more predictable than capital gains. They constitute an important steadying influence on investor returns. The advantage of having dividend income play a prominent role in an investor's stock selection strategy is that such an approach reduces the risk of overpaying for a stock. This tends to lower downside risk and increase upside potential.

As shown in Figure 11.2, dividend yields have been in a long-term decline across all major segments of the U.S. market. From a marketwide perspective, the long-term decline in divi-

FIGURE 11.2 **Dividend Yields over Time, 1977–2005**

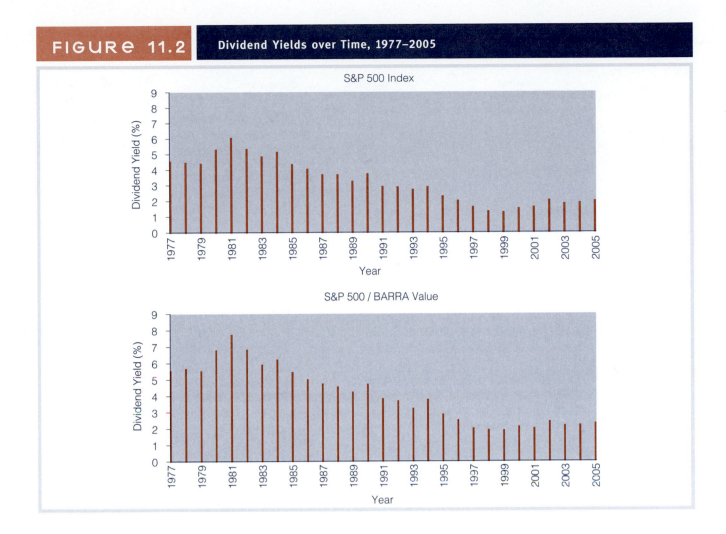

dend yields has reduced an important source of long-term returns on common stocks. During the 19th century, dividend yield constituted approximately 45 to 50 percent of the total rate of return earned by common stockholders. During the post-World War II period, dividend yield has accounted for approximately 25 percent of total returns. Historically, the best time to buy common stocks has been during periods when dividend yields were above average, as in 1982, when the dividend yield on the S&P 500 stood at roughly 6 percent. Below-average long-term rates of return typically follow periods of below-average dividend yields, as in 1972, when the dividend yield on the S&P 500 stood at roughly 3 percent. Even after the stock market decline of 2000–2002, dividend yields remained low. A dividend yield of only 2 percent on the S&P 500 seems to portend an anemic expected rate of return on common stocks over the next several years. However, value stocks have a tendency to have higher dividend yields. This helps reduce the risk to value stock investors from a stagnant stock market.

Dividend Growth

Dividend-paying stocks have the compelling virtue of offering income-motivated investors the opportunity for growing levels of dividend income over time. Dividend income for the S&P 500 has historically grown faster than the rate of inflation. Over time, rising dividend income on S&P 500 stocks has enabled investors to preserve and increase the buying power of their dividend income. If income-motivated investors are willing to accept some price fluctuation, owning stocks for dividend income is a viable long-term strategy.

For example, suppose an investor paid $50 per share for a stock that pays a current dividend of $1 per share. Under these circumstances, the investor's dividend yield is 2 percent. If the

TABLE 11.3	Dividend Growth Leads to a Rising Stream of Investment Income						
Year	Current Stock Price ($50 growing at 8%)	Current Dividend ($1 growing at 8%)	Dividend Yield	Dividend Yield on Original $50 Purchase Price	Cumulative Value of $50 Stock Investment (10% total return)	Bond Interest Income ($50 at 6%)	Cumulative Value of $50 Bond Investment (6% interest)
2006	$ 54.00	$1.08	2.0%	2.2%	$ 55.00	$3.00	$53.00
2007	58.32	1.17	2.0	2.3	60.50	3.00	56.18
2008	62.99	1.26	2.0	2.5	66.55	3.00	59.55
2009	68.02	1.36	2.0	2.7	73.21	3.00	63.12
2010	73.47	1.47	2.0	2.9	80.53	3.00	66.91
2011	79.34	1.59	2.0	3.2	88.58	3.00	70.93
2012	85.69	1.71	2.0	3.4	97.44	3.00	75.18
2013	92.55	1.85	2.0	3.7	107.18	3.00	79.69
2014	99.95	2.00	2.0	4.0	117.90	3.00	84.47
2015	107.95	2.16	2.0	4.3	129.69	3.00	89.54
2016	116.58	2.33	2.0	4.7	142.66	3.00	94.91
2017	125.91	2.52	2.0	5.0	156.92	3.00	100.61
2018	135.98	2.72	2.0	5.4	172.61	3.00	106.65
2019	146.86	2.94	2.0	5.9	189.87	3.00	113.05
2020	158.61	3.17	2.0	6.3	208.86	3.00	119.83
2021	171.30	3.43	2.0	6.9	229.75	3.00	127.02
2022	185.00	3.70	2.0	7.4	252.72	3.00	134.64
2023	199.80	4.00	2.0	8.0	278.00	3.00	142.72
2024	215.79	4.32	2.0	8.6	305.80	3.00	151.28
2025	233.05	4.66	2.0	9.3	336.37	3.00	160.36
2026	251.69	5.03	2.0	10.1	370.01	3.00	169.98
2027	271.83	5.44	2.0	10.9	407.01	3.00	180.18
2028	293.57	5.87	2.0	11.7	447.72	3.00	190.99
2029	317.06	6.34	2.0	12.7	492.49	3.00	202.45
2030	342.42	6.85	2.0	13.7	541.74	3.00	214.59
Total		$78.95				$75.00	

company prospers and continues to pay out a similar share of its rising income stream, the cash dividend paid to investors will increase steadily. Dividend growth will provide investors with ever-higher income on the original $50 investment. If dividend income grows by a modest 8 percent per year, which is the historical dividend growth rate for the S&P 500, the dividend paid will rise to $6.85 per share in 25 years. As shown in Table 11.3, investors would then earn a 2 percent annual dividend on a stock price that has appreciated in price to $342.42. The higher dividend in 25 years represents a dividend yield of 13.7 percent on the original amount invested.

Growth-and-income investors
Investors who seek a relative balance between the goals of high and stable income and long-term capital growth.

Notice how well **growth-and-income investors** fare when compared with the fixed-income investor. Even a below-average total return of 10 percent per year results in a substantial investment advantage over the 6 percent interest income earned by the fixed-income investor. In addition to the substantial capital gains, notice how the stock investor's dividend income exceeds the interest income earned by the fixed-income investor. Observe how modest dividend growth of 8 percent per year has allowed a modest initial dividend yield of 2 percent per year to overcome the substantial interest income advantage initially enjoyed by a 6 percent bond. Of course, in the present example, the fixed-income investor would have the modest advantage of having received greater investment income during the first few years after the initial investment was made. Going forward, the growth-and-income investor has the dual advantages of significant capital appreciation and vastly superior investment income.

FIGURE 11.3 **Reinvested Dividends Are a Big Part of Total Return for the S&P 500 (1976–2005)**

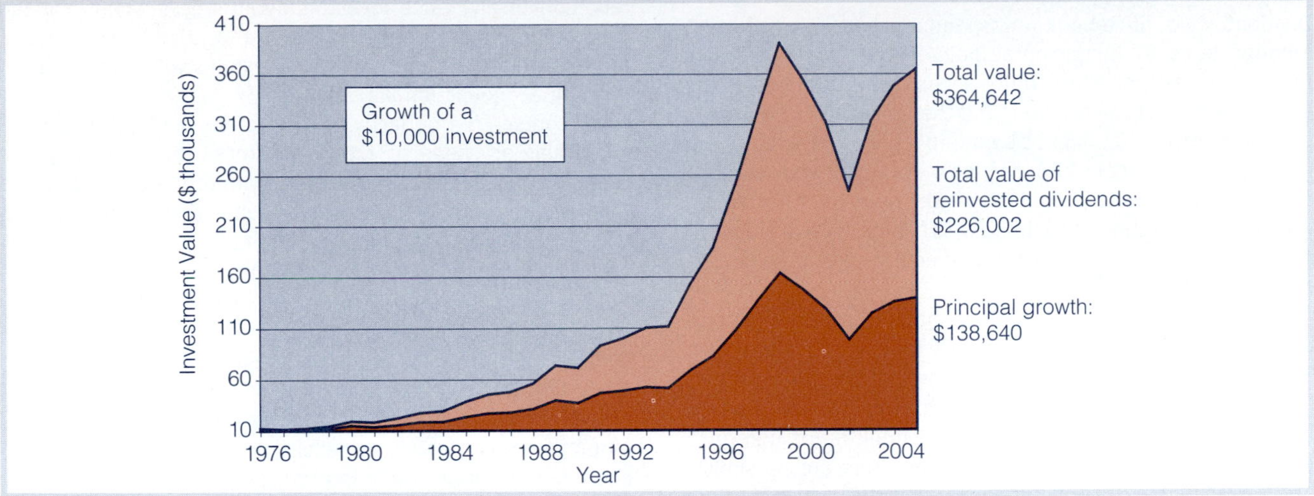

Source: MSCI Barra, **www.mscibarra.com**.

If dividends are reinvested, they can play a powerful role in helping investors build capital. Between 1976 and 2005, for example, if dividends were taken in cash, a $10,000 initial investment in the stocks constituting the S&P 500 Stock Index would have grown to $138,640. This $10,000 initial investment would have grown to $364,642 if all dividends were reinvested. Over this period, the total value of reinvested dividends was $226,002. As shown in Figure 11.3, reinvested dividend income accounts for more than one-half of the total return earned by long-term investors on the S&P 500 during this 30-year period.

Obviously, high and growing dividend income makes an important contribution to the long-term return achieved from common stock investments.

Dividends and Profitability

Dividends are also a useful indicator of corporate profitability. Corporations are not obligated to share earnings with stockholders. This makes voluntary cash dividends a useful indicator of the size and likely persistence of company profitability.

Obviously, cash dividends cannot be paid unless they are funded through current earnings, asset liquidations, or increased indebtedness. If a company is able to pay a $1 cash dividend without reducing assets or taking on additional debt, this cash dividend represents a conservative assessment of corporate profitability during the period. Only highly profitable companies are able to pay high dividends for extended periods of time. Because companies are very reluctant to cut their dividends, a corporate policy of paying high dividends also suggests that management has an optimistic view of the future. To the extent that rising dividends reflect rising profits, companies that consistently increase their dividends should enjoy rising share prices over time.

To be sure, dividend yields must be analyzed carefully. In assessing dividend yields, investors must be cautious to search for yields that are both comparatively high and relatively safe. Most industrial companies distribute less than 50 percent of earnings in the form of cash dividends. They reinvest the rest in plant and equipment to facilitate future growth. Some solid utilities with scant growth prospects may pay out as much as 60 to 70 percent of total earnings in the form of dividend income. When the dividend payout ratio is much higher than that, the culprit may be transient earnings problems. If a permanent deterioration in the fundamental earning power of the company is evident, then a dividend cut is likely. Investors seeking high dividend yields with moderate risk must take care to diversify their portfolios across several industries.

Predicting Market Returns with Value Ratios

Dividend yield, price-book ratios, and price-earnings ratios are among the useful fundamental indicators of investment value to value investors. These ratios incorporate both accounting and stock market information, and they are commonly used to highlight stocks that might be underpriced, and therefore represent real investment bargains, or overvalued, and represent stocks to avoid or sell. Dividend yields, price-book ratios, and price-earnings ratios tend to vary for firms within industries and economic sectors and for the overall market from one period to another period.

Generally speaking, when stock market investors are optimistic about growth opportunities for individual companies or the market in general, share prices rise relative to dividends, book values, and reported earnings. This causes dividend yields to fall and brings a rise in price-book ratios and price-earnings ratios. When stock market investors are pessimistic about individual companies or the market in general, share prices fall relative to dividends, book values, and reported earnings. This causes dividend yields to rise and brings a decline in price-book ratios and price-earnings ratios. Value investors prefer to buy when dividend yields are high and both price-book and price-earnings ratios are low because stocks are then "cheap" relative to underlying economic fundamentals. Conversely, value investors avoid stocks when dividend yields are low and both price-book and price-earnings ratios are high because stocks are then "expensive" relative to underlying economic fundamentals.

Of course, in a perfectly efficient stock market, there is no such thing as cheap or expensive stocks. In a perfectly efficient market, all stocks are always appropriately priced and the study of fundamental ratios is fruitless. Interestingly, academic research reports that fundamental analysis can be useful in predicting investment returns. Financial economist Jonathan Lewellen has found that low dividend yields are linked to low future rates of return for the overall market. Conversely, high dividend yields are associated with high future rates of return for stock market investors. A similar, but weaker, relationship holds for price-book ratios and price-earnings ratios. Overall, Lewellen concludes that these financial ratios do have power in predicting stock market returns. In the real world there are such things as cheap and expensive stocks!

See Jonathan Lewellen, "Predicting Returns with Financial Ratios," *Journal of Financial Economics*, vol. 74, no. 2 (February 2004), pp. 209–235.

Equity-income investors
Investors who stress income first and long-term capital growth second.

Dividend-growth investors
Investors who place primary emphasis on the potential for dividend growth in their stock selection strategy.

Equity-income investors stress income first and long-term capital growth second. Capital appreciation is typically expected to result as individual holdings move from undervalued to fairly valued following an improvement in investor sentiment. Equity-income portfolios typically have dividend yields considerably higher than the yield of the overall market. They have strong appeal for retired investors seeking added income. **Dividend-growth investors** place primary emphasis on the potential for dividend growth in their stock selection strategy. Consistent dividend growth is often associated with companies able to grow earnings faster than the overall rate of inflation. Although such companies tend to pay out a relatively small percentage of their earnings at any given point in time, earnings growth typically leads to higher dividend income over time. Chances are that company share prices will also rise with earnings growth and thereby create capital gains opportunities. Dividend-growth investors are typically satisfied with dividend yields that match or fall slightly below the dividend yield on the overall market. Although dividend-growth investors enjoy a greater potential for long-term capital appreciation than other value investors, such an investment philosophy involves the potential for relatively high share price volatility.

Value Investing Strategies

Focus on Bargains

Forward P/E ratio
Current stock price divided by expected next year's earnings per share.

The search for value almost always starts with a review of basic financial information, such as P/E and P/B ratios and dividend yields. **Forward P/E** multiples are frequently used. These multiples use the current stock price and the projected earnings per share over the next 12 months. Forward P/E ratios tend to be lower than traditional P/E ratios because next year's earnings are usually forecasted to be higher than last year's earnings. A stock with a P/E ratio that is significantly below that of its peers, the market as a whole, or its own historical norm may represent a relative bargain. Of course, careful research is necessary to determine whether a low P/E indicates fundamental business problems, temporary difficulties, or just a lack of knowledge about the company. P/E ratios are perhaps the most widely used value measure, where low P/E ratios signal relatively cheap stocks and high P/E ratios signal relatively expensive stocks.

Historically, the marketwide average for P/E ratios tends to fall between 10 and 20, with a typical average of roughly 15. In today's market, P/E ratios below 15 for individual stocks are relatively low, and P/E ratios above 30 are relatively high. *The Wall Street Journal* and most newspapers list P/E ratios for individual companies alongside daily stock quotations.

Value investors seek opportunities for mispriced equities among stocks with low P/E and P/B ratios. Real bargains also may be found among small and/or misunderstood stocks that have the potential to be temporarily underpriced. Unfortunately, companies with low P/E ratios often face a dramatic downturn in earnings or poor future growth prospects. Similarly, low P/B ratio companies often have assets with values that are difficult to realize during present market conditions. Retailers with obsolete inventory are a prime example. Value investors depend on their specialized expertise to separate the wheat from the chaff and uncover real bargains among low P/E and low P/B companies. In their view, a sound valuation will be *eventually* validated in the marketplace.

Some value investors focus on **free cash flow**. Free cash flow consists of earnings before interest, taxes, depreciation and amortization, sometimes referred to as **EBITDA**, minus necessary capital expenditures. Free cash flow is a basic measure of profitability that often foreshadows earnings improvement. Similar to the P/E ratio, the price-free cash flow ratio measures the relationship between a company's stock price and the amount of net cash generated by company operations. If a firm generates $10 per share in free cash flow and has a stock price of $50, it has a price-free cash flow ratio of 5 and a cash-to-price rate of return of 20 percent. Companies with low price-cash flow ratios may end up as takeover targets or restructuring candidates.

Table 11.4 summarizes the financial criteria commonly used to identify value stocks. A single value stock seldom embodies all such criteria, but most will fit the definition of a value stock on multiple dimensions.

Free cash flow
Earnings before depreciation, interest, taxes, and amortization, minus necessary capital expenditures.

EBITDA
Earnings before interest, taxes, depreciation and amortization.

Quality at a Reasonable Price

Determining a reasonable price to pay for any stock is always difficult. To deal effectively with the uncertainties involved, some value investors rely on a simple investment rule of thumb called the **value of ROE**, or VRE for short.

Value of ROE
ROE percentage divided by the P/E ratio.

TABLE 11.4	Common Criteria for Value Stocks

Ample cash reserves (cash > 10% of market cap).

Ample free cash flow to fund necessary investment (EBIDTA > capital spending).

Conservative dividend payout policy (dividend < 75% of EPS).

Conservative financial structure (debt < 50% of market cap).

Conservative issuance of common stock to managers and other employees (constant or falling number of shares outstanding).

Low price-book ratio relative to the market and a company's own history (P/B < 75% of S&P 500 average).

Low price-cash flow ratio relative to the market and a company's own history (P/CF < 75% of S&P 500 average).

Low price-earnings ratio relative to the market and a company's own history (P/E < 75% of S&P 500 average).

Negative investor sentiment as reflected in poor financial ratings (S&P rating of B– or worse).

Significant dividend income (yield > 150% of S&P 500 average).

The VRE ratio is simply the return on equity, or ROE, percentage divided by the P/E ratio. If a company is expected to enjoy an ROE of 20 percent and has a P/E ratio of 20, the company's VRE ratio would be 1. Generally speaking, according to value investors, a stock is fully valued if it sports a VRE ratio of less than 1. If the VRE ratio is greater than 1, the stock is worthy of investment consideration. The VRE ratio rule of thumb goes something like this:

- If VRE ≥ 1, the stock may be worthy of investment attention and possible purchase.
- If VRE ≥ 2, the stock is definitely worthy of investment attention and may represent a very attractive investment.
- If VRE ≥ 3, the stock is apt to represent an extraordinarily attractive investment opportunity.

Needless to say, the investment merit of a stock increases with an increase in the VRE ratio. Strict **quality-at-a-reasonable-price investors** seldom, if ever, buy value stocks with VRE ratios less than 1.

Quality-at-a-reasonable-price investors
Investors who seldom buy value stocks with VRE ratios less than 1.

Try It!

Use the value of ROE to determine the worthiness of each of the following stocks to a value investor:

Company	ROE	P/E
Intel	19.6%	20.0
Ford Motor	24.1	6.3
Procter & Gamble	40.2	20.9

Solution

Compute the value of ROE:

Company		VRE
Intel	19.6% / 20.0 =	0.98
Ford Motor	24.1% / 6.3 =	3.83
Procter & Gamble	40.2% / 20.9 =	1.92

With a VRE = 0.98, Intel is not a candidate for a quality-at-a-reasonable-price stock. Procter & Gamble may be worthy of further investigation. Since Ford Motor's VRE is greater than 3, it represents a very attractive possibility for a value investor.

Contrarian Investment Philosophy

While all stock, bond, and commodity market investors and traders embrace the motto "Buy low, sell high," few act accordingly. In practice, it is difficult to go against the crowd. Powerful psychological forces act against buying securities that are out of favor on Wall Street. It is similarly difficult to sell big winners that have become Wall Street darlings. As British economist John Maynard Keynes once suggested, it is often far safer to lose money conventionally than it is to take on risk by making an unpopular investment decision. Proponents of a **contrarian investment philosophy** hope to profit from hard-to-predict trend reversals and seek profits by betting against the overly emotional crowd.

Contrarian investment philosophy
Strategy to select unpopular stocks.

One of Wall Street's best-known and most articulate contrarians is David Dreman, a successful money manager, *Forbes* columnist, and the respected author of an investment classic, *Contrarian Investment Strategies*. Using recent research on investor psychology, Dreman gives insights on how to profit from the irrational fears or foolish enthusiasm of investors. In picking individual stocks, Dreman pays only cursory attention to a company's growth prospects. Instead, Dreman looks for cheap stocks trading at below-market multiples of per-share earnings, cash flow, and book value or those with attractive dividend yields. Dreman offers his own investment success as proof that cheap stocks tend to outperform the market averages, and he rejects the EMH concept. As a practical matter, Dreman seeks to make long-term investments in bargain-priced stocks trading at new 52-week lows and avoids stocks selling near recent 52-week highs. This is the antithesis of the trading approach favored by technical analysts.

Dreman is at the forefront of professional investors who make profitable use of findings from the field of cognitive psychology. Psychologists argue that people are woefully inadequate as intuitive statisticians. Logic dictates that after an extended economic expansion and exceptionally strong bull market, the future rates of economic growth and stock market gains are apt to regress toward long-term averages. Similarly, it is reasonable to expect that after a typically brief economic recession and sharp market correction, there will be a resumption of long-term economic growth and positive stock market gains. Too often, investors fall victim to representativeness bias and exaggerate the likelihood that current trends, either good or bad, will continue into the future. Representativeness bias explains why even Wall Street professionals were gloomiest about stocks after market crashes in 1987 and 2002. It also explains the irrational exuberance of stock market investors at market tops, like the 2000 peak. Dreman agrees with psychologists who maintain that the human brain is hard-wired to underperform the market because few investors can maintain a contrarian approach. Dreman likes to buy stocks when prices are falling; the worse the panic, the better. That contrarian approach requires overriding powerful psychological instincts.

The success of a contrarian investment strategy depends on the **regression-to-the-mean** concept illustrated in Figure 11.4. At any point in time, the rate of return on stockholders' equity varies among firms and industries. Over time, however, these profit rates tend to converge toward the overall average of 12 to 14 percent per year. Experienced investors know that competitor entry and growth in highly profitable industries causes above-normal profits to eventually

Regression to the mean
The concept that both past outperformers and past underperformers tend to become average in the future.

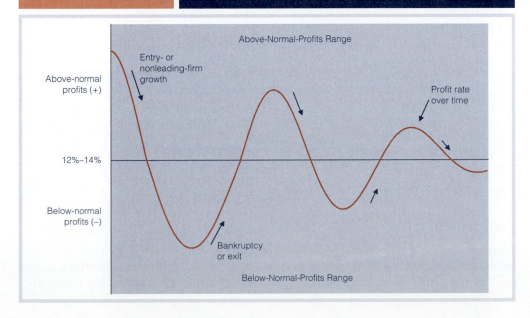

FIGURE 11.4

Profit Rates and Stock Returns Display a Regression to the Mean over Time. *Over time, entry- and nonleading-firm growth causes above-normal profits to regress toward the mean. Similarly, bankruptcy or exit by weak competitors boosts profits for depressed industries. As a result, firm profits and stock market returns converge toward the long-term average of 12 to 14 percent.*

Above-Normal-Profits Range

Above-normal profits (+)

Entry- or nonleading-firm growth

Profit rate over time

12%–14%

Below-normal profits (−)

Bankruptcy or exit

Below-Normal-Profits Range

TABLE 11.5	S&P 500 Operating Earnings Growth by Economic Sector						

	2002	2003	Percent Change	2004	Percent Change	2005	Percent Change
S&P 500	46.04	54.69	18.80	67.67	23.7	76.56	13.1
Consumer discretionary	9.53	10.53	10.56	13.63	29.5	13.03	−4.4
Consumer staples	11.91	11.79	−0.96	12.82	8.8	13.18	2.8
Energy	9.87	16.32	65.34	24.29	48.9	34.97	44.0
Financials	21.03	26.76	27.22	30.88	15.4	32.79	6.2
Health care	14.89	14.63	−1.73	17.20	17.5	18.61	8.2
Industrials	10.53	10.88	3.27	13.13	20.7	16.18	23.2
Information technology	3.36	8.04	139.23	12.60	56.7	14.83	17.7
Materials	4.48	5.32	18.66	10.10	90.0	11.77	16.5
Telecommunication services	6.86	6.81	−0.66	6.86	0.8	7.52	9.6
Utilities	9.69	8.77	−9.42	8.63	−1.6	9.50	10.1

Source: Standard & Poor's, **www2standardandpoors.com**. © 2006 Standard & Poor's. Used with permission.

fall as competition increases. Conversely, bankruptcy and exit allow the below-normal profits of depressed industries to rise.

For example, drugs, health care services, and medical supplies were among the most profitable industries during the 1990s as an aging population and U.S. government-sponsored health programs caused the demand for health care to skyrocket. During the next decade, however, a proliferation of new drug therapies, cost-containment measures, and government regulations may conspire to limit profit-making opportunities in health care. As a result, profit and sales growth in health care are expected to turn downward. Over the next decade, it is not likely that health care industry profits and stock gains will dramatically exceed all-industry averages. In that event, they will have regressed toward the mean profit level. Table 11.5 shows how the profitability of different economic sectors varies on a year-by-year basis. Among firms found in the S&P 500, notice how industries with the highest rate of earnings growth in one year tend to underperform in the following year. Conversely, industries and sectors that suffer through lean times in one year often bounce back during subsequent periods.

Noted value investors such as Benjamin Graham, David Dreman, and Sir John Templeton use investment selection criteria designed to identify "survivors" in industries undergoing extreme hardship. By withstanding extreme hardship that eliminates notable competitors, such companies are poised to enjoy a favorable reversal of fortune when industry conditions improve. At the same time, by avoiding high P/E stocks with ebullient expectations, value investors avoid the types of earnings and stock price disappointments tied to an emergence of competition in high-profit and high-profile industries.

Implementing a Value Strategy

Computer Stock Screens

Computer stock screen
A computerized sort of companies according to financial characteristics.

Investors can use stock screens available on the Internet to obtain lists of value stocks that meet fundamental criteria. Table 11.6 shows a list of free Web site **computer stock screen** engines and the types of screens available to the user. Figure 11.5 shows such a screen from

TABLE 11.6	Screening Stocks Online		

	Number of Search Fields	Categories
MSN Money http://moneycentral.msn.com/investor/finder/customstocksdl.asp	134	Company basics, investment returns, price ratios, management efficiency, financial condition, dividends, trading and volume, growth rates, stock price history, profit margins, current financials, analyst projections, advisor FYI, Stockscouter rating
Quicken http://screener.finance.yahoo.com/newscreener.html?quicken=2	41	Industry, valuation ratios, growth rates, analyst estimates, financial strength, stock return, and ownership information
Morningstar http://screen.morningstar.com/StockSelector.html	18	Stock basics, Morningstar grades, company performance, stock performance, valuation
Yahoo!Finance http://screen.yahoo.com/stocks.html	17	Industry, share data, performance, sales and profitability, valuation ratios, analyst estimates
CBS MarketWatch www2.marketwatch.com/tools/stockresearch/screener/default.asp	11	Price, volume, fundamentals, technicals, exchange and industry

Yahoo! Finance. Notice that investors can pick an industry and membership in an index, like the S&P 500, or search all industries. The "Share Data" section allows the investor to seek companies that have specific ranges in stock price, volume, firm size, and dividend yield. More ranges are available in the categories of performance, sales and profitability, valuation ratios, and analyst estimates.

A value investor might seek large, profitable companies that have good growth prospects but remain reasonably priced. In such a case, the investor might use the criteria of a minimum ROE of 15 percent, five-year average annual EPS growth of 10 percent, and anticipated EPS growth over the next five years of 10 percent. Maximum stock screen criteria might include a current P/E ratio no greater than 14 and a debt-to-equity ratio of no more than 0.5 (50 percent). Table 11.7 shows firms that met such criteria in January 2006. Broadening search screens by relaxing some criteria is often necessary to find more firms and more diverse firms for more detailed analysis.

Many of the search screen features offered by popular investing Web sites on the Internet have predefined screens. For example, the MSN Money Web site has a variety of valued-oriented screens that are labeled "Contrarian Strategy," "Dogs of the Dow," "Great Expectations," "Highest-Yielding S&P 500 Stocks," and so on. These searches highlight stocks that investors can further investigate.

Advantages and Limitations

Like all strategies, value investing has its advantages and limitations. A principal advantage is that careful stock selection should limit downside risk. When an investor buys stocks that are already cheap, they should be less vulnerable to market downdrafts than stocks that are richly valued. This is especially true when value stocks offer above-average dividend yields, as is the case for many large companies that fall within the value stock category. Because dividend income always makes a positive contribution to total return, large dividends tend to cushion falling stock prices.

A possible impediment to adopting a value investment philosophy is the difficulty involved with obtaining relevant information. Although good financial data are readily available, detailed knowledge of a company's business and market environment is needed to interpret those data correctly. For instance, does a low P/E ratio indicate that a company is temporarily undervalued or permanently impaired? Because many low P/E and low P/B stocks are neglected

FIGURE 11.5   Stock Screener at Yahoo! Finance

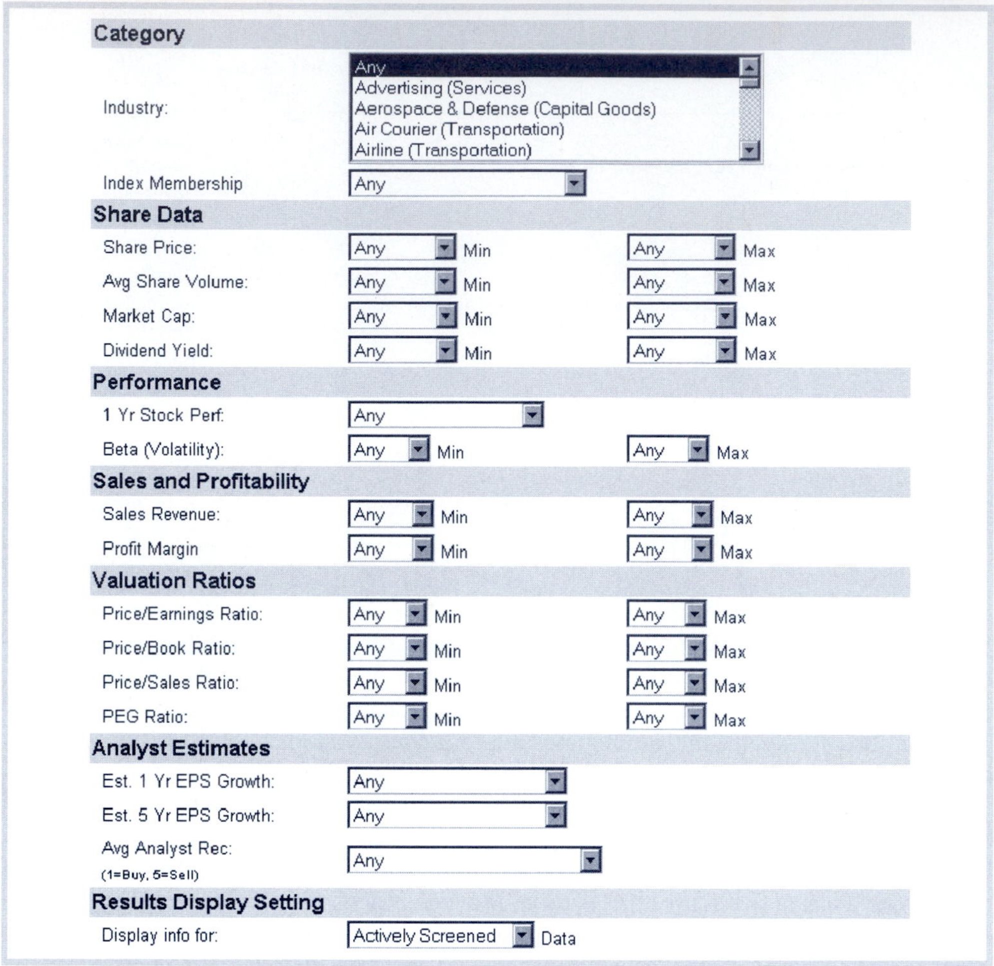

Category					
Industry:	Any / Advertising (Services) / Aerospace & Defense (Capital Goods) / Air Courier (Transportation) / Airline (Transportation)				
Index Membership	Any				
Share Data					
Share Price:	Any	Min	Any	Max	
Avg Share Volume:	Any	Min	Any	Max	
Market Cap:	Any	Min	Any	Max	
Dividend Yield:	Any	Min	Any	Max	
Performance					
1 Yr Stock Perf:	Any				
Beta (Volatility):	Any	Min	Any	Max	
Sales and Profitability					
Sales Revenue:	Any	Min	Any	Max	
Profit Margin	Any	Min	Any	Max	
Valuation Ratios					
Price/Earnings Ratio:	Any	Min	Any	Max	
Price/Book Ratio:	Any	Min	Any	Max	
Price/Sales Ratio:	Any	Min	Any	Max	
PEG Ratio:	Any	Min	Any	Max	
Analyst Estimates					
Est. 1 Yr EPS Growth:	Any				
Est. 5 Yr EPS Growth:	Any				
Avg Analyst Rec: (1=Buy, 5=Sell)	Any				
Results Display Setting					
Display info for:	Actively Screened	Data			

Source: Yahoo! Finance, **http://finance.yahoo.com**. Reproduced with permission of Yahoo! Inc. © 2006 by Yahoo! Inc. Yahoo and the Yahoo! logo are trademarks of Yahoo! Inc.

by Wall Street analysts, finding out about many value stocks is a time-consuming and arduous task. This is especially true for the stocks of small companies, in which investment information is often scarce.

Another potential disadvantage is that value investing is not necessarily a buy-and-hold strategy. It implies constant recycling of stocks through the portfolio as their value is recognized by the market. This means that value investors face the need for constant research and monitoring. Such vigilance may be difficult for an individual investor. Also bear in mind that the value approach involves buying unpopular stocks with a checkered operating and financial history. A successful value investor is a contrarian in the truest sense of the word. Buying a stock when the market is pessimistic and selling when the market is optimistic is a psychological challenge. All of us enjoy being popular, and buying stocks that are unpopular in the market is a sure way to invite criticism.

Finally, it is important to recognize the complex problem faced by simple investment strategy rules of thumb, such as the value of ROE and P/E measures. The usefulness of simple rules is apt to be frustrated by their own popularity. If low P/E stocks as a group tended to consistently outperform the market, such stocks would become popular with investors. They would then lose their bargain-basement status, and their P/E ratios would rise. In the world of investments, popular investment strategies *cannot* lead to superior profitability. If an investor

TABLE 11.7

Stock Screens Can Help Turn Up Stock Market Bargains *Minimum stock screen criteria: ROE, 15 percent; five-year EPS growth rate average, 10 percent; EPS growth next five years, 10 percent (analyst estimate). Maximum stock screen criteria: current P/E ratio, 14; debt-to-equity ratio, 0.5.*

Ticker	Company	Price	Market Cap	P/E	Earnings Growth Estimate, Next 5 Years	Return on Equity	Earnings Growth, Past 5 Years	Total Debt/Equity
GPS	Gap Inc.	17.17	14.931B	13.6	12.0	21.6	22.8	0.09
PH	Parker Hannifin Corp.	73.98	8.860B	13.5	11.0	17.1	11.6	0.27
AEOS	American Eagle Outfit	24.87	3.718B	13.6	14.5	31.1	12.0	0.00
NOVL	Novell Inc.	8.99	3.489B	10.2	10.0	31.6	27.9	0.43
NX	Quanex Corp.	60.26	1.535B	9.9	15.0	30.6	33.6	0.21
OFIX	Orthofix Intl. Nv	41.28	660.8M	8.9	14.0	23.5	15.3	0.15
ASFI	Asta Funding Inc.	29.75	404.4M	13.9	15.0	23.9	17.4	0.20
WSTL	Westell Tech. Class A	4.12	287.5M	7.9	20.0	31.1	44.5	0.00
CRMT	America's CarMart	18.40	218.2M	13.3	18.0	15.9	23.0	0.35

Source: Yahoo! Finance Stock screener.

chooses the same investment strategy as everyone else, that investor is bound to get the same rate of return as everyone else. Only by choosing a different investment strategy can an investor hope to obtain different returns. Only by choosing a superior but unpopular strategy can investors hope to obtain superior investment returns.

Summary

■ Typically, **growth stocks** are defined as the S&P 500 stocks with the highest (above-average) P/B ratios. **Value stocks** are the remaining S&P 500 stocks with relatively lower P/B ratios. Value investors adopt a **contrarian investment philosophy** based on the premise that investors can profit by betting against the overly emotional crowd. According to practitioners of contrarian investment strategies, investors can profit if they are able to withstand the peer group and psychological pressures tied to common stock investing. To be successful, contrarian investors argue that one must "buy fear" and "sell greed." Traditional **value investors** seek out-of-favor stocks selling at a discount to the overall market, in which such discounts are measured in terms of low P/E and P/B ratios and/or high dividend yields.

■ Value investors rely on a variety of tangible indicators of a stock's **fundamental value**. Fundamental value is the worth of a stock derived from a company's assets in place, sure prospects, durable strengths, and profit forecasts. Value investors seek **undervalued** stocks, which sell at a discount to their fundamental value.

■ The present value of a stock, or fundamental economic value of a company, is determined by prospects for future cash flows received by investors in the form of regular cash dividends or share repurchases. The **risk-adjusted discount rate**, or required return, is the interest rate required to fairly compensate investors for the risk involved with making their investment. Although the discounted present-value approach can be described as a type of dividend discount model, it involves full consideration of both major components of the investor's **total return** from investment, in which total return is dividend income plus capital appreciation.

■ The **dividend discount model** focuses exclusively on future dividend income, but future stock prices at any point in time will also be determined by anticipated dividend income. Expected capital gains are explicitly incorporated in the dividend discount model, but their influence is captured in terms of anticipated future dividend income. The **constant-growth model** for stock valuation gives investors a simple means for calculating the required rate of return as the sum of dividend income and growth (capital gains). A special case of the model is used for **preferred stock** because its dividends have zero growth. Because of its price dynamics, it is usually included in an asset class of **fixed-income securities**. It is useful to conduct a **sensitivity analysis** on the model's results to determine the most important parameters.

■ Value investors who follow the conservative stock-picking style of Benjamin Graham are called **Graham and Dodd** investors, in reference to Graham and his *Security Analysis* coauthor David L. Dodd. One of the most important ideas for a value investor is the **margin-of-safety** concept. By definition, bargains reflect a favorable difference between price and appraised value. That difference is the margin of safety. It is available for absorbing the effect of miscalculations or bad luck. The goal of enlightened stock analysis is to identify underpriced securities and to enjoy excess returns following the market's subsequent upward revaluation to a price consistent with **intrinsic value**. The intrinsic value of a stock is justified by assets, earnings, dividends, sure prospects, and management.

■ Graham and Dodd looked to find bargain-basement stocks selling at prices below **liquidation value**. Other important measures are the price-to-earnings ratio, the price-to-book ratio, the **price-to-sales (P/S)** ratio, and the **price-to-cash flow(P/CF)** ratio. One of the most important indicators of fundamental value is a company's **free cash flow.** Free cash flow consists of earnings before depreciation, interest, taxes, and amortization, sometimes referred to as **EBITDA**, minus necessary capital expenditures.

■ **Growth-and-income investors** seek a relative balance between the goals of high and stable income and long-term capital growth. **Equity-income investors** stress income first and long-term capital growth second. Such portfolios have few, if any, equity holdings that do not provide significant dividend income. **Dividend-growth investors** place primary emphasis on the potential for dividend growth in their stock selection strategy. Consistent dividend growth is often associated with companies able to grow earnings faster than the rate of inflation.

■ Some value investors rely on a simple investment rule of thumb called the **value of ROE**, or VRE for short. The VRE ratio is simply the return on equity or ROE percentage divided by the P/E ratio. The investment merit of a stock increases with an increase in the VRE ratio. Strict **quality-at-a-reasonable-price investors** seldom, if ever, buy value stocks with VRE ratios less than 1.

■ A **contrarian investment philosophy** focuses on looking for bargains among unpopular stocks. Investment success from adopting this approach depends on the **regression-to-the-mean** concept. Experienced investors know that competitor entry and growth in highly profitable industries causes above-normal profits to regress toward the mean. Conversely, bankruptcy and exit allow the below-normal profits of depressed industries to rise toward the mean. If both good news and bad news are already in stock prices, investors should buy downtrodden low P/E stocks of "reversal-of-fortune" companies.

■ Free Internet Web sites provide investors with powerful search tools by which they can easily use **computer stock screens** to find the firms that meet their value criteria. Careful stock selection using value strategies should limit downside risk. Since this is not a buy-and-hold strategy, value investors must continue to seek good information and monitor their investments.

Self-Test Problems

ST11.1 Freddie Mac (FRE, formally known as Federal Home Loan Mortgage Corporation) maintains a secondary market in residential mortgages, primarily by securitizing and guaranteeing such loans. FRE's debt enjoys favorable "government-agency" status, but is not explicitly backed by the full faith and credit of the U.S. government. The company also maintains a portfolio of residential mortgages for its own account. According to information obtained from Yahoo! Finance, FRE has a current price of $64 per share, an expected dividend per share of $1.40, expected EPS of $7.50, expected EPS growth of 6 percent per year, and a typical P/E ratio of 12. According to the present-value model, what is the expected rate of return on FRE over the next five years?

Solution

15.67 percent per year. Using Equation 11.5, the expected price for FRE in five years is

$$P_5 = (1 + g)^5 \times \text{EPS}_0 \times P/E = (1.06)^5 \times \$7.50 \times 12 = \$120.44$$

According to the model, with a present price of $64 and a price of $120.44 in five years, the expected rate of capital appreciation is

$$g = (I_t/I_0)^{1/t} - 1 = (\$120.44/\$64)^{1/5} - 1 = 1.1348 - 1 = 13.48\%$$

With an expected dividend of $1.40, the expected dividend yield is $1.40/$64 = 2.19%
Therefore, the expected total return is 13.48% + 2.19% = 15.67%

ST11.2 Alcoa (AA) is the world's largest aluminum producer. Important products include
alumina, chemicals, primary metals, flat-rolled products, engineered products, and
packaging. Given the highly cyclical nature of its business, AA typically sells at a
multiple of relatively stable cash flows rather than on the basis of highly volatile
earnings. According to information obtained from *The Value Line Investment
Survey* on March 13, 2005, AA then had a current price of $31 per share, an
expected dividend per share of $0.70, expected cash flow (CF) of $3.80, expected
CF growth of 10 percent per year, and a typical P/CF ratio of 12. To create an
expected price range for 2010, use CF growth estimates of 4 to 12 percent per year
in 2 percent increments. To create discounted present values, use a risk-adjusted
discount rate of 15 percent. For simplicity, you may assume that the current
dividend yield of 2.26 percent (= $0.70/$31) will be maintained over the
2005–2010 period. Based on these expectations, set up a spreadsheet to estimate a
typical range in price for AA in 2010 (five years hence). Was AA a buy, sell or hold
at a 2005 price of $31?

Solution

A spreadsheet analysis of AA is shown in the table below.

Discounting Dividends

(1) Intrinsic Economic Value of Stock, (6)/[1 + (8)⁵]	(2) Current CF	(3) Expected CF Growth	(4) Expected CF in 5 Years, CF [1 + (3)⁵]	(5) Expected P/CF ratio	(6) Expected Stock Price in 5 Years, (4) × (5)	(7) Risk-Adjusted Discount Rate, *k*	(8) Discount Rate— Dividend Yield, (7) − 2.26%
30.46	3.80	4.0%	4.62	12	$55.44	15.0%	12.74%
33.50	3.80	6.0	5.09	12	61.08	15.0	12.74
36.79	3.80	8.0	5.58	12	67.08	15.0	12.74
40.32	3.80	10.0	6.12	12	73.44	15.0	12.74
44.12	3.80	12.0	6.70	12	80.40	15.0	12.74

Based on the assumptions given, a typical price range for AA in 2010 is $55.44 to $80.40 and
a reasonable range for the 2005 value of AA is $30.46 to $44.12. Because the 2005 price of
$31 for AA was within the range specified for AA's intrinsic economic value, AA represented
a *hold* in 2005 and was expected to return roughly the 15 percent per year cost of capital over
the 2005–2010 time frame. Pull up a current price for AA on the Internet and see how shareholders who followed such an approach have fared since 2005.

Questions and Problems

11.1 What is the basic premise of value investing? What does it mean to buy "fear" and sell
"greed"?

11.2 Calculate the present value of a stock that you believe will have a market value of $15
in two years. Assume the stock pays a $0.25 annual dividend and the risk-adjusted
discount rate is 20 percent. If the stock is selling for $12 per share, should you buy it?

11.3 Consumer health care products giant Johnson & Johnson (JNJ) had a recent stock
price of $50, an expected dividend per share of $1.05, expected EPS of $3, expected

EPS growth of 12 percent per year, and a typical P/E ratio of 20. What is the expected price for JNJ in five years?

11.4 Consider a share of common stock that paid a cash dividend of $0.50 and grows by 13 percent each year. The risk-adjusted discount rate for this share of common stock is 15 percent. Use the constant-growth model to compute the stock's intrinsic economic value.

11.5 Consider a share of preferred stock that paid a cash dividend of $0.50. The risk-adjusted discount rate for this share of preferred stock is 12 percent. Use the constant-growth model to compute the stock's intrinsic economic value. Why is the value so different from your answer to Problem 11.4?

11.6 Pfizer, Inc. (PFE), is a major producer of pharmaceuticals, hospital products, consumer products, and animal health lines. According to *The Value Line Investment Survey,* dividends are expected to grow at a rate of 13 percent per year for the foreseeable future. If the stock presently sells for $28 per share and is expected to pay an $0.84 dividend next year, what is the expected rate of return to stockholders? Use the constant-growth model to calculate the rate. If the typical investor has a required rate of return of 12 percent per year, is the stock a bargain? Why or why not?

11.7 The Procter & Gamble Company (PG) makes detergents, soaps, toiletries, foods, paper, and industrial products. According to *The Value Line Investment Survey,* dividends are expected to grow at a rate of 9.5 percent per year for the foreseeable future. If the stock presently sells for $55 per share and is expected to pay a $1.10 dividend next year, what is the expected rate of return to stockholders? Use the constant growth model to calculate your answer. If the typical investor has a required rate of return of 12 percent per year, is the stock a bargain? Why or why not?

11.8 Explain the Graham and Dodd "margin-of-safety" concept.

11.9 Consider the ROE, price, and earnings per share of the three companies listed below. Compute the value of ROE (VRE) ratio, and determine which of the firms might interest a value investor.

	ROE	Price	EPS
Company A	20%	$13.25	$2
Company B	35	75	2
Company C	25	12.40	1

11.10 What are the advantages of buying stocks that pay dividends rather than stocks that pay no dividends?

 11.11 The Boeing Company (BA) is a leading manufacturer of commercial jet aircraft, fighter planes, cargo carriers, helicopters, submarine communicators, ground transportation systems, and the space station. According to information obtained from *The Value Line Investment Survey* on March 13, 2005, BA then had a current price of $57.46, an expected dividend per share of $1, expected cash flow (CF) of $4.25, expected CF growth of 7 percent per year, and a typical P/CF ratio of 12. To create an expected price range for 2010, use CF growth estimates of 6 to 10 percent per year in 1 percent increments. To create present values, use a risk-adjusted discount rate of 12 percent. For simplicity, you may assume that the current dividend yield of 1.74 percent (= $1/$57.46) will be maintained over the 2005–2010 period. Based on these expectations, set up a spreadsheet to estimate a typical range in price for BA in 2010 (five years hence). Was BA a buy, sell, or hold at a 2005 price of $57.46?

 11.12 Consider the commonly used value search screen criteria in Table 11.4. With these in mind, create search criteria of your own. Using one of the Internet search screens listed in Table 11.6, run your search. What is the result? How do the results change with small changes in the search criteria?

11.13 Some financial Web sites have preset screens for various strategies. Go to the Yahoo! Finance preset screens (**http://screen.finance.yahoo.com/presetscreens.html**) and run the Large Cap Value screen. What are the criteria used? Which firms meet these criteria?

11.14 Go to the Standard & Poor's Market Insight Web site at **www.mhhe.com/edumarketinsight** and enter the ticker "DOW" for Dow Chemical. From the information under "Financial Hlts." for Dow, obtain the current price, last year's dividend, and the dividend growth rate. Use these to compute the expected rate of return for Dow. Does this number seem reasonable?

11.15 Go to the Standard & Poor's Market Insight Web site at **www.mhhe.com/edumarketinsight** and enter the ticker "RBK" for Reebok International. Examine the information in S&P's "Stock Report" section for Reebok. Obtain the 12-month target price, the date the stock is expected to reach this price, and the annual dividend. From Yahoo! Finance, obtain the stock price one year before the expected target price is to occur. Using this information and the discounted present-value model, compute the implied required rate of return for RBK. What is the dividend yield and expected return from capital gain?

11.16 An investment promises to pay $100 one year from today, $200 two years from today, and $300 three years from today. If the required rate of return is 14 percent, compounded annually, the value of this investment today is *closest to:*

a. $404
b. $444
c. $462
d. $516

11.17 An analyst gathered the following information about a common stock:

Annual dividend per share	$2.10
Risk-free rate	7 percent
Risk premium for this stock	4 percent

If the annual dividend is expected to remain at $2.10, the value of the stock is *closest to:*

a. $19.09
b. $30.00
c. $52.50
d. $70.00

11.18 An analyst gathered the following information about a company:

2001 net sales	$10,000,000
2001 net profit margin	5.0 percent
2002 expected sales growth	−15.0 percent
2002 expected profit margin	5.4 percent
2002 expected common stock shares outstanding	120,000

The company's 2002 expected earnings per share is *closest to:*

a. $3.26
b. $3.72
c. $3.83
d. $4.17

11.19 Graham Industries has two separate divisions: the Farm Equipment Division and the Household Products Division. Each division accounts for about 50 percent of the company's revenues and assets. Managers now want to enter the toy industry. In assessing the attractiveness of investment projects in the toy industry, Graham should use a required rate of return based on:

a. A required return computed for the toy industry
b. The required rate of return on the market portfolio
c. Graham's current weighted-average cost of capital
d. A weighted-average required return computed for the farm equipment, household products, and toy industries

11.20 Dynamic Communication is a U.S. industrial company with several electronics divisions.

EXHIBIT 1.2	Dynamic Communication

Summary Statements of Income
Years Ended 31 December
(U.S. $ millions except for share data)

	2003	2002
Total revenues	$3,425	$3,300
Operating costs and expenses	2,379	2,319
Earnings before interest, taxes, depreciation, and amortization (EBITDA)	$1,046	$ 981
Depreciation and amortization	483	454
Operating income (EBIT)	$ 563	$ 527
Interest expense	104	107
Income before taxes	$ 459	$ 420
Taxes (40%)	184	168
Net income	$ 275	$ 252
Dividends	$ 80	$ 80
Change in retained earnings	$ 195	$ 172
Earnings per share	$ 2.75	$ 2.52
Dividends per share	$ 0.80	$ 0.80
Number of shares outstanding (millions)	100	100

Mike Brandreth, an analyst who specializes in the electronics industry, is preparing a research report on Dynamic Communication. A colleague suggests to Brandreth that he may be able to determine Dynamic's implied dividend growth rate from Dynamic's current common stock price, using the Gordon growth model. Brandreth believes that the appropriate required rate of return for Dynamic's equity is 8 percent.

a. Calculate, given a current common stock price of $58.49, Dynamic's implied dividend growth rate as of December 31, 2003, using the Gordon growth model. Show your calculations.

The management of Dynamic has indicated to Brandreth and other analysts that the company's current dividend policy will be continued.

b. Determine whether using the Gordon growth model to value Dynamic's common stock is appropriate or inappropriate. Justify your response with *one* reason based on the assumptions of the Gordon growth model.

INVESTMENT APPLICATION

Should You Buy Stock in a Mickey Mouse Organization?

The Walt Disney Company is a diversified worldwide entertainment company with operations in four business segments: media networks, parks and resorts, studio entertainment, and consumer products. The media networks segment consists of the company's television (ABC,

ESPN, and Discovery), cable/satellite and international broadcast operations, production and distribution of television programming, and Internet operations. The studio entertainment segment produces live-action and animated motion pictures, television animation programs, musical recordings, and live stage plays. The consumer products segment licenses the company's characters and other intellectual property to manufacturers, retailers, show promoters, and publishers. The company's family entertainment marketing strategy is so broad in its reach that Disney characters such as Mickey Mouse, Donald Duck, and Goofy have become an integral part of the American culture. Given its ability to turn whimsy into outstanding operating performance, the Walt Disney Company is one firm that doesn't mind being called a "Mickey Mouse organization."

Table 11.8 shows a variety of accounting operating statistics, including revenues, cash flow, capital spending, dividends, earnings, book value, and year-end share prices for the Walt Disney Company during the 1980–2003 period. All data are expressed in dollars per share to illustrate how individual shareholders have benefited from the company's growth. During this time frame, revenue per share grew at an annual rate of 14.5 percent per year, and earnings per share grew by 9.0 percent per year. These performance measures exceed industry and

TABLE 11.8	Operating Statistics for the Walt Disney Company (all data in dollars per share)						
Year	Revenues	Cash Flow	Capital Spending	Dividends	Earnings	Book Value	Year-End Stock Price[1]
1980	$0.59	$0.11	$0.10	$0.02	$0.09	$0.69	$1.07
1981	0.65	0.10	0.21	0.02	0.08	0.75	1.09
1982	0.64	0.09	0.38	0.03	0.06	0.80	1.32
1983	0.79	0.11	0.20	0.03	0.06	0.85	1.10
1984	1.02	0.13	0.12	0.03	0.06	0.71	1.25
1985	1.30	0.18	0.12	0.03	0.11	0.76	2.35
1986	1.58	0.24	0.11	0.03	0.15	0.90	3.59
1987	1.82	0.34	0.18	0.03	0.24	1.17	4.94
1988	2.15	0.42	0.37	0.03	0.32	1.48	5.48
1989	2.83	0.55	0.46	0.04	0.43	1.87	9.33
1990	3.70	0.65	0.45	0.05	0.50	2.21	8.46
1991	3.96	0.58	0.59	0.06	0.40	2.48	9.54
1992	4.77	0.72	0.35	0.07	0.51	2.99	14.33
1993	5.31	0.78	0.49	0.08	0.54	3.13	14.21
1994	6.40	0.97	0.65	0.10	0.68	3.50	15.33
1995	7.70	1.15	0.57	0.12	0.84	4.23	19.63
1996	10.50	1.32	0.86	0.14	0.74	7.96	23.25
1997	11.10	1.51	0.95	0.17	0.92	8.54	33.00
1998	11.21	1.52	1.13	0.20	0.90	9.46	30.00
1999	11.34	1.30	1.03	0.20	0.66	10.16	29.25
2000	12.09	1.98	1.02	0.21	0.90	11.65	28.44
2001	12.52	1.89	0.89	0.21	0.98	11.23	20.72
2002	12.40	1.06	0.53	0.21	0.55	11.48	16.31
2003	13.23	1.19	0.51	0.21	0.66	11.63	23.33
2007–2009[2]	18.10	2.25	0.45	0.21	1.65	17.55	

[1]Split-adjusted share prices.
[2]Value Line estimates.
Source: Company annual reports (various years), **www.valueline.com, http://yahoo.com**.

economywide norms. Disney employees, CEO Michael D. Eisner, and all stockholders profited greatly from the company's outstanding stock price performance during the 1980s and 1990s but have grown frustrated by stagnant results during recent years. Over the 1980–2003 period, Disney common stock exploded in price from $1.07 per share to $23.33, after adjusting for stock splits. This represents a 14.3 percent annual rate of return and illustrates that Disney has been an above-average stock market performer. However, the stock price has been flat since 1996, and stockholders are getting restless.

Investors want to know how the company will fare during coming years. Will the company be able to reassert itself and once again enjoy enviable growth, or, like many companies, will Disney find it impossible to maintain above-average performance? Given the many uncertainties faced by Disney and most major corporations, forecasts of operating performance are usually restricted to a fairly short time perspective. *The Value Line Investment Survey,* one of the most widely respected forecast services, focuses on a three- to five-year time horizon. For the 2007–2009 period, Value Line forecasts Disney revenues of $18.10, cash flow of $2.25, earnings of $1.65, dividends of $0.21, capital spending of $0.45, and book value per share of $17.55. Actual results will vary, but these assumptions offer a fruitful basis for measuring the relative growth potential of Disney.

The most interesting economic statistic for Disney stockholders is the stock price during some future period, say, 2007–2009. In economic terms, stock prices represent the net present value of future cash flows, discounted at an appropriate risk-adjusted rate of return. To forecast Disney's stock price during the 2007–2009 period, one might use any or all of the data in Table 11.8. Historical numbers for a recent period, such as 1980–2003, represent a useful context for projecting future stock prices. For example, Fidelity's legendary mutual fund investor Peter Lynch argues that stock prices are largely determined by future earnings per share. Stock prices rise following an increase in earnings per share and plunge when earnings per share plummet. Sir John Templeton, the father of global stock market investing, focuses on book value per share. Templeton contends that future earnings are closely related to the book value of the firm, or accounting net worth. "Bargains" can be found when stock can be purchased in companies that sell in the marketplace at a significant discount to book value or when book value per share is expected to rise dramatically. Both Lynch and Templeton have built a large following among investors who have profited mightily using their stock market selection techniques.

It will prove interesting to employ the data provided in Table 11.8 to forecast the average common stock price for the Walt Disney Company over the 2007–2009 period.

a. A simple regression model over the 1980–2003 period where the Y variable is the Disney year-end stock price and the X variable is Disney's earnings per share reads as follows (t-statistics in parentheses):

$$P_t = -\$1.661 + \$31.388\text{EPS}_t, R^2 = 86.8\%$$
$$(-1.13) \quad (12.03)$$

Use this model to forecast Disney's average stock price for the 2007–2009 period, using the Value Line estimate of Disney's average earnings per share for 2007–2009. Discuss this share price forecast.

b. A simple regression model over the 1980–2003 period where the Y variable is the Disney year-end stock price and the X variable is Disney's book value per share reads as follows (t-statistics in parentheses):

$$P_t = \$3.161 + \$2.182\text{BV}_t, R^2 = 76.9\%$$
$$(1.99) \quad (8.57)$$

Use this model to forecast Disney's average stock price for the 2007–2009 period, using the Value Line estimate of Disney's average book value per share for 2007–2009. Discuss this share price forecast.

c. A multiple regression model over the 1980–2003 period where the Y variable is the Disney year-end stock price and the X variables are Disney's earnings per share and book value per share reads as follows (t-statistics in parentheses):

$$P_t = -\$1.112 + \$21.777EPS_t + \$0.869BV_t, \quad R^2 = 90.9\%$$
$$(-0.88) \qquad (5.66) \qquad\quad (3.06)$$

d. Use this model to forecast Disney's average stock price for the 2007–2009 period, using the Value Line estimate of Disney's average earnings per share and book value per share for 2007–2009. Discuss this share price forecast.

A multiple regression model over the 1980–2003 period where the Y variable is the Disney year-end stock price and the X variables include the accounting operating statistics shown in Table 11.8 reads as follows (t-statistics in parentheses):

$$P_t = -\$2.453 + \$2.377REV_t + \$0.822CF_t + \$13.603CAPX_t +$$
$$(-1.75) \qquad (1.46) \qquad\quad (0.09) \qquad\qquad (2.84)$$

$$\$17.706DIV_t + \$0.437EPS_t - \$1.665BV_t, \quad R^2 = 94.3\%$$
$$(0.24) \qquad\qquad (0.3) \qquad\quad (-0.94)$$

Use this model and Value Line estimates to forecast Disney's average stock price for the 2007–2009 period. Discuss this share price forecast.

www.mhhe.com/hirschey1e

12
chapter

Growth Stock Investing

From March 1991 through March 2001, the longest uninterrupted economic expansion of the 20th century caused investors to favor providers of high-tech equipment like Cisco Systems, JDS Uniphase, and Qualcomm. Such "New Economy" companies richly rewarded investors. Cisco started March 26, 1990, at a split-adjusted price of $0.08 per share and ended the decade at $53.56. During the 1990s, investors would have earned 94.9 percent per year with a Cisco buy-and-hold strategy! Even huge firms that showed consistent earnings growth saw incredible gains. The stock of the General Electric Company, one of the world's largest corporations and an original member of the Dow Jones Industrial Average, generated total returns (capital gains plus dividends) of 56.2 percent per year in the 1990s.

Alas, the 1990s came to an end, and so too did the red-hot performance of growth stocks. Historically, it has been very tough to pinpoint "permanent winners" among rapidly evolving technology companies. After the peak of the "Nifty 50" era in 1972, so-called one-decision growth stocks crumbled by 70 to 90 percent in the ensuing market downturn. A generation later, the incredible rise of growth stocks in the 1990s led Federal Reserve Chairman Alan Greenspan to suggest that "irrational exuberance" had taken hold of investors by 1999. Growth stocks peaked just a few months later, and growth stock investors were decimated in the ensuing bear market. When the bubble burst, the tech-stock dominated Nasdaq index plummeted by more than 75 percent; the carnage was even worse for market leaders such as Cisco Systems (-86 percent), JDS Uniphase (-95 percent), and Qualcomm (-82 percent). Even GE dropped by more than 60 percent from its peak.

By late-2002, things couldn't get any worse and the overall market began to improve. Going forward, careful consideration of long-term growth prospects remains a key component of security analysis and company valuation. No doubt, the recent investment experience of growth stock investors will help them focus on prudent valuations based upon reasonable assessments of future prospects.[1]

---

[1] Jack Hough, "Bargain Growth Stocks," *The Wall Street Journal Online*, January 5, 2006 (**http://online.wsj.com**).

Growth Stocks

Forward-Looking Analysis

Value investors focus on the present. They look for bargains by comparing the value of assets in place to market prices. Growth investors look to the future. They look for companies that are apt to deliver ever-higher revenue, earnings, and dividends.

Different growth stock investors use different criteria to identify attractive candidates for purchase. Some look for companies with three or more consecutive years of above-average growth in both per-share earnings and revenues. Others look for firms with high profit margins and projected earnings increases of 10 to 15 percent (or more) for three to five years. Still others look for earnings growth at a rate that is at least twice that of the average company represented by the Standard & Poor's 500 Index. Growth stock investors also look beyond earnings-per-share numbers to gauge whether a company can prudently sustain rapid growth.

An important consideration is whether a growth company has sufficient financial resources to finance future growth internally or will need to borrow funds. Ideally, growth companies generate sufficient funds for above-average growth from retained earnings. In those instances in which growth companies cannot be self-financing, they are expected to have healthy balance sheets with adequate equity.

The quality of management is also a key concern to growth stock investors. Do managers have the experience and know-how to cope with rapid growth? Are management and employee compensation plans in place to provide appropriate incentives for high-margin growth? If the answers to these questions are yes, then a rapidly growing company may indeed be appropriate for investment consideration.

Seeking Opportunity

Growth stock investors favor aggressive companies that may sell at premium valuations when value is measured in terms of conventional P/E ratios. Dividend income is typically a secondary consideration, if relevant at all. Such investors may be willing to accept larger-than-typical levels of risk in the pursuit of above-average long-term investment results.

Many growth stock investors focus first on a company's external economic environment. Does the company operate in a fast-growing economic sector in which a "rising tide lifts all boats"? Alternatively, does the company occupy a lucrative niche in an otherwise slow-growth industry? Is the company's market niche expanding? If the company is in a market experiencing explosive growth, will new entrants diminish or eliminate future profit opportunities?

Pinpointing the source of recent and expected earnings growth is crucial. Ideally, rising sales and earnings growth should be accompanied by higher profit margins. When rapid earnings growth is accompanied by stagnant or falling profit margins, negative implications for future growth opportunities often emerge. For example, if rising earnings are due to higher unit sales only made possible by expanding the number of retail stores, established stores may be losing momentum in fully saturated markets. Alternatively, if sales growth is made possible only by steep price cuts, future earnings growth may be constrained by product market competition. Worse still is the situation in which earnings growth is achieved only by a one-shot boost, such as a well-timed merger or a dip in the company's effective tax rate.

Financial maneuvering is a poor substitute for economic growth and a common precursor to poor future results.

Growth Stock Characteristics

Essential Features

Growth stock investing focuses on well-managed companies whose revenue and earnings are expected to grow faster than the rate of inflation and the overall economy. In the late 1930s, Thomas Rowe Price, founder of Baltimore, Maryland-based mutual fund company T. Rowe Price and Associates, Inc., was a pioneer of the growth stock approach to investing. Price saw the test for a growth company as being its ability to sustain earnings momentum during economic slowdowns. He predicted that such companies would provide above-average long-term growth of earnings, dividends, and capital, thus preserving the investor's purchasing power against erosion from the effects of continuing inflation.

According to Price, growth stocks display a number of attractive economic characteristics. Growth stocks:

- Display high profit margins, an attractive return on total assets (ROA), and consistent earnings-per-share growth and use low levels of debt financing.

- Lack cutthroat competition.

- Have superior research to develop distinctive products and new markets.

- Have low overall labor costs but pay high wages to talented employees.

- Are immune from regulation.

At any point in time, it would be rare to find several growth stock investment opportunities that embody all these essential features. Still, prudence requires at least some diversification. Phillip Fisher, another famous early proponent of growth stock investing, was so focused on buying the best companies in the best industries that he often advocated an investment portfolio of as few as three to five well-chosen industry leaders. Although T. Rowe Price was also a fierce advocate of buying the best companies in the best industries, his investment approach advocated broader diversification and typically included as many as 20 to 25 individual positions.

A defining characteristic of growth stock investing is that it focuses first and foremost on the inherent economic quality of a given investment opportunity. Notice how none of Price's essential growth stock characteristics speak to the question of valuation. Little guidance is offered to help investors answer the question, How much is a growth stock worth? Growth stock investing is sometimes referred to as "one-decision" investing. Once the decision to buy has been made, a true growth stock investor is content to maintain a holding for years and years. Selling is contemplated only in the event of a rapid deterioration in the favorable economic characteristics of a given company. If a growth stock investor has done his or her homework, sell decisions should be rare. Portfolio turnover should be minimal.

Fertile Fields for Growth

From Price's growth stock selection criteria, it is clear that the first requirement for sustainable growth is that the company must be involved in an inherently appealing business. High profit margins and an above-average rate of return on total assets (ROA) are the most basic growth stock investment criteria. High profit margins signal relatively low levels of price competition in the company's main product lines and/or superior levels of operating efficiency. When either or both of these forces are at work, the groundwork is laid for superior long-term investment returns.

Dot.con

The power of brand-name advertising has long been measured in the traditional broadcast and print media. Brand names like *BMW, Budweiser, Coca-Cola, Marlboro*, and *Microsoft* are worth tens of millions of dollars each. Now, Google, eBay, America Online (AOL), and Yahoo! have made brand-name advertising a key competitive strategy in cyberspace. From irreverent advertising to the choice of their own monikers, companies like Google and Yahoo! seek to create the perception of carefree fun for the antiestablishment crowd, and on the Internet, who is not antiestablishment? Yahoo!.

The effect of brand-name advertising is sometimes so persuasive that it is almost too powerful. When words become unforgettably associated with innovative new products, the result can spell trouble. Aspirin, brassiere, cellophane, escalator, linoleum, yo-yo, and zipper are all products that lost distinctiveness because their trademarks fell into common usage. All suffered from *too much* success. Either the product was as new and innovative as its name, or the trademark seemed to be especially well suited to the underlying product. Owners of such modern-day trademarks as *Astroturf, Coke, Frisbee, Kleenex, Kitty Litter, Styrofoam, Walkman*, and *Xerox* employ

a veritable army of lawyers in an endless struggle against "generic" treatment.

In the late 1990s, company names related to the Internet came into vogue. From mid-1998 to mid-1999, scores of publicly traded companies changed to a new name with a "dot-com" orientation. Investors loved the change. In a matter of weeks following such name change announcements, stock prices soared for affected firms. Pure Internet companies beat the market by as much as 50 percent and more; firms with some Internet presence earned 30 to 40 percent more than the market. During the bubble period, Net-crazed speculators appeared willing to bid up almost anything that could be tied to the Internet.

Of course, what goes up can come down. In the case of Internet hype, the postbubble crash was stunning. Millions of dollars in dot-com market capitalization simply vanished as investors began to focus once again on companies with real sales revenues, cash flow, and earnings.

See Rebecca Buckman, "Google and Skype Join Backers of Spain's FON Web Start-Up," *The Wall Street Journal Online*, February 6, 2006 (**http://online.wsj.com**).

Sustainable above-average earnings growth is much more likely for distinctive industry leaders in fertile competitive environments with attractive revenue growth, lucrative profit margins, and significant barriers to entry. Only growth companies that produce unique products have the potential to create sustainable above-average profits for investors. To maintain above-average profits, imitation must be prevented through advertising, patents, copyrights, or other means. Although a few growth companies have been able to dominate large or rapidly growing markets, most have been able to maintain their superior investment status through the successful exploitation of a **market niche**. A market niche is a segment of a market that can be successfully exploited through the special capabilities of a given firm. To be durable, above-normal profits derived from a market niche must not be vulnerable to imitation by competitors.

Market niche
Market segment that can be successfully exploited through the special capabilities of a given firm.

Consider the financial services firm T. Rowe Price Group, the mutual fund giant founded by T. Rowe Price. People are familiar with growth stock mutual fund investing but seldom consider investing in mutual fund management companies. That's a mistake. Mutual fund management is an extremely lucrative business, and stockholders in the few publicly traded mutual fund companies have done extremely well over time. T. Rowe Price Group earns a 15 to 20 percent return on assets with very little financial leverage. T. Rowe Price Group is an example of a firm that enjoys tremendous success through market niche dominance.

Sales Growth

The most valuable overall indicator of change or **top-line growth** in the firm's business prospects is revenue growth. The first step in establishing a valuable business is to generate sales. Without sales revenue, no amount of judicious cost cutting or operating efficiency can be used to establish a valuable franchise.

Top-line growth
Growth in revenue (the top line of the income statement).

Table 12.1, Part A, shows 10 companies that have generated outstanding levels of revenue growth over the past five years. The list includes XM Satellite Radio and several biotech and technology companies. These firms have increased revenue over 1,200 percent per year for the past five years. While the long-term success of these companies and the other rapidly growing firms is far from ensured, all have taken important first steps toward developing valuable

TABLE 12.1 Historical Growth and Estimated Future Growth

Company	Symbol	Last Price	Market Capitalization (millions)	P/E Ratio, Current	5-Year Revenue Growth	EPS Growth Rate	EPS Growth, Next 5 Years	5-Year Dividend Growth
A. High 5-Year Revenue Growth								
Stonepath Group, Inc.	STG	0.74	32.3		3,081.26			
The Medicines Company	MDCO	19.00	944.7	633.3	2,484.04		35.7	
LaPolla Industries Inc.	LPA	0.61	30.9		1,348.10			
Zanett, Inc.	ZANE	3.44	99.4		1,030.83			
XM Satellite Radio Holdings Inc.	XMSR	27.54	6,119.6		911.57		17	
Spectrum Pharmaceuticals, Inc.	SPPI	4.35	101.7		843.19			
Silverstar Holdings Ltd.	SSTR	1.45	13.1	72.5	746.05			
Asconi Corp.	ASCD	0.42	4.5	5.3	638.41			
Bioenvision, Inc.	BIVN	7.76	316.3		628.78			
Fortune Diversified Industries, Inc.	FFI	3.93	41.5		576.39			
Average		**6.92**	**770.4**	**237.0**	**1,228.9**		**26.4**	
B. High Annual EPS Growth Rate								
The Progressive Corp.	PGR	108.13	21,328.7	14.3	17.70	131.36	10.5	4.25
Stewart Information Services Corp.	STC	51.10	927.1	9.3	21.08	123.92		
USA Truck, Inc.	USAK	29.50	336.1	20.2	12.12	108.88	31.6	
American Healthways, Inc.	AMHC	43.69	1,497.3	49.1	40.34	105.92	27.5	
Atlantis Plastics, Inc.	ATPL	9.00	74.3	10.8	9.21	104.31		
Bio-Reference Laboratories, Inc.	BRLI	16.00	207.7	27.6	19.39	98.01		
Schnitzer Steel Industries, Inc.	SCHN	30.01	914.7	6.4	25.19	90.80	7	−0.88
Lowrance Electronics, Inc.	LEIX	25.52	131.1	15.8	15.53	90.10		
Tarragon Corp.	TARR	20.33	584.4	5.8	32.64	89.93		
Makita Corp. (ADR)	MKTAY	25.28	3,633.4	11.6	6.97	88.66		
Average		**35.86**	**2,963.5**	**17.1**	**20.0**	**103.2**	**19.2**	**1.7**
C. High Expected 5-Year EPS Growth								
Newpark Resources, Inc.	NR	8.91	786.9	46.9	11.37		65.5	
8x8, Inc.	EGHT	1.89	101.8		−7.90		56	
Taleo Corp.	TLEO	12.21	144.0				54.5	
Pioneer Drilling Co.	PDC	21.26	989.5	32.2	36.64		54	
Goldcorp INC.	GG	24.76	8,366.1	39.9	43.51		54	
Baidu.com, Inc. (ADR)	BIDU	60.86	1,065.5	760.8			50.5	
True Religion Apparel, Inc.	TRLG	21.30	470.5	26.6			50	
Patterson-UTI Energy, Inc.	PTEN	37.47	6,474.9	22.7	27.76	26.53	50	
Basic Energy Services, Inc.	BAS	24.90	840.5	59.3			50	
Cutera, Inc.	CUTR	26.03	308.1	34.7			50	
Average		**23.96**	**1,954.8**	**127.9**	**22.3**		**53.5**	
D. High 5-Year Dividend Growth								
CBRL Group, Inc.	CBRL	34.99	1,636.0	14.6	6.75	21.56	12.4	119.23
Lennar Corp.	LEN	61.75	7,726.0	8.8	21.33	29.74	14.6	102.62
The St. Joe Co.	JOE	63.20	4,759.4	41.3	2.37	5.43	17	97.19
Burlington Coat Factory Warehouse Corp.	BCF	44.32	1,984.1	17.9	6.61	7.49		91.16
Fastenal Co.	FAST	38.37	5,796.0	34.9	15.05	17.35	22.5	85.86
Inter-Tel, Inc.	INTL	21.36	559.6	47.5	1.60		3.6	81.71
Kinder Morgan, Inc.	KMI	100.98	12,326.1	22.7	−10.14	23.70	12.8	78.48
Fidelity National Financial	FNF	37.68	6,538.5	6.5	29.53	38.16	12.3	77.41
Flagstar Bancorp, Inc.	FBC	14.22	887.0	11	13.60	26.73	8	75.18
Southern Copper Corp. (USA)	PCU	70.02	10,308.9	6.9	29.53	62.77		74.14
Average		48.69	5,252.2	21.2	11.6	25.9	12.9	88.3

Source: msnMoney, January 20, 2006 (**http://moneycentral.msn.com/investor/finder/customstocksdl.asp**).

franchises. However, the precarious operating performance history of these firms scares off lots of investors. None have built a record of sustained profitability or dividend-paying ability.

Until recently, the need to build sustainable revenue as a foundation for corporate success was taken for granted. However, during the late 1990s "dot-com mania," billions of dollars of market value were accorded to companies with little or no current revenues. Worse yet, many dot-com companies were valued in the billions of dollars despite having no ready prospects of ever generating significant revenues. Some, like Netscape Communications, now part of America Online, Inc., adopted a business model whereby they gave away products in the hope of building customer loyalty and "eventually" figuring out a way to charge customers. Even software giant Microsoft proudly points to widespread use of its products in China, where software piracy is rampant and little, if any, current revenues are generated. However, there is a big difference between products that are unable to generate much in the way of current revenues and products that have little or no hope of *ever* generating sales. If users of free computer software become loyal adopters and eager customers for product upgrades, it can be a prudent business plan to give away early versions, called "freeware." No matter how alluring the "story," it never makes sense to place a positive value on companies that have no hope of generating significant revenues, profits, and dividends.

EPS Growth

Because the value of the firm is the discounted net present value of all future profits, the rate of earnings growth is a vital determinant of the value of the firm. If long-term investors identify and hold companies with above-average **EPS growth**, above-average long-term rates of return may be anticipated. If long-term investors identify and purchase companies with below-average EPS growth, mediocre returns, at best, will be realized.

Table 12.1, Part B, shows 10 companies that have produced excellent EPS growth over the past five years. The list includes insurance holding-company heavyweight Progressive, whose earnings per share grew 131 percent per year for the past five years. The list also includes Japan's Makita Corporation, a power tool manufacturer that has listed its stock in the United States as an American Depository Receipt. The list of 10 firms is surprisingly diverse. Health care, manufacturing, insurance, information, transportation, and real estate are all represented. In all cases, notice that analysts expect future earnings growth to slow down substantially. The main focus of growth stock investing is to find firms that will grow revenue, profits, and dividends at a fast clip in the future. Rapid historical growth is a useful but often imperfect measure of future potential. Part C of Table 12.1 shows a sample of companies with high expected future EPS growth. This is also a diverse list of companies. High-tech, energy, mining, employee staffing, and retail companies are represented. While some industries are more likely to produce high-growth firms, top performers in stodgy industries can also experience rapid growth.

EPS growth
Growth in earnings per share; achieved by increasing earnings and/or decreasing the number of shares outstanding.

Dividend Growth

Rapid revenue and earnings growth are valuable to investors because they lay the foundation for high and rapidly growing dividends over time. Suppose a firm paid no current dividend and had no prospect of ever paying dividends. How much would such a firm be worth? The answer is zero. An investment with no prospect for any payoff is worth nothing. In contrast, companies that pay high and rapidly growing dividends over time are extremely valuable. Part D of Table 12.1 shows a sample of dividend-paying companies with high historical dividend growth. Again, this is a diverse list of companies. Outstanding performers from the slow-growing financial services and retailing sectors have been able to produce outstanding dividend growth rates over time. An interesting example is the Miami-based Lennar Corporation, a rapidly growing home builder. Its homebuilding operations include the sale and construction of single-family attached and detached homes. A key competitive advantage of the company is that its financial services subsidiaries provide mortgage financing, title insurance, closing services, and insurance for home buyers. This has been a winning competitive strategy for the company and a winning investment strategy for Lennar investors.

Conservative Financial Structure

An obvious advantage of investing in growth stocks with high profit margins and high ROA is that these companies are often able to finance investment projects with internally generated funds. An ongoing need to raise equity financing through the sale of common stock dilutes the ownership position of current equity holders and makes it much more difficult to achieve above-average EPS growth. Growth stock investors like Price are also leery of investing in companies that use extremely high levels of financial leverage. Proponents of using debt argue that it is an attractive means for magnifying investor returns from good investment decisions. The problem with debt financing is that, during times of financial distress, lenders tend to be inflexible. Bankers always seem to want their loans repaid at the least convenient time for borrowers.

Financial leverage

The use of debt to magnify the operating performance of the firm.

Debt-to-asset ratio

Long-term debt divided by total assets.

Table 12.2 shows the amount of **financial leverage** used by 15 firms that are commonly among the most profitable firms in the S&P 500 and the rate of profitability (ROA) for another sample of 15 S&P 500 firms with the highest levels of financial leverage. As is often the case, financial leverage is measured by the **debt-to-assets ratio**, which illustrates the firm's use of leverage as a permanent source of financing for new plant and equipment. When long-term debt plus short-term debt is substantial, debt as a percentage of total assets becomes high, and there is significant risk of financial distress in the event of an economic downturn.

It is perhaps startling to note the low levels of financial leverage used by some of the most profitable companies. S&P 500 firms with high ROA display an average debt load of only 2.8 percent of equity. Many such firms have little or no long-term debt. With a five-year average ROA of 20.4 percent, these are highly profitable firms. At the same time, they have attractive growth prospects. Analysts expect them to grow EPS at a 13.8 percent pace in the future. Notice how these conservatively financed, high-profit firms are able to exploit attractive long-term growth opportunities with internally generated funds.

It is natural for investors to ask why such well-run and highly profitable firms use such modest financial leverage. For example, why don't firms such as Forest Labs and Microsoft have *any* long-term debt? Surely, Microsoft could borrow as much as $100 billion to $250 billion at very attractive interest rates. Presumably, the rate of interest paid would reflect Microsoft's gilded reputation and compare favorably with the rate paid on Treasury securities with similar maturities. Even if Microsoft had no immediate investment need for the funds, it could use the proceeds from a debt issue to retire common stock and thereby leverage future returns for stockholders.

Financial engineering

Sophisticated manipulation of the balance sheet through use of exotic forms of debt and equity financing.

Only company insiders know the precise reason that Microsoft has chosen such a conservative financial structure. However, it appears that the company has chosen to focus on making new and exciting software products rather than be distracted by **financial engineering**. Microsoft has striven to dominate a business with the potential to generate huge amounts of cash flow with little need for investment in tangible plant and equipment. When software engineers and other key employees are paid in the form of stock options and other incentive-based compensation, Microsoft is able to tightly control out-of-pocket costs and generate astounding pretax profit margins.

Part B of Table 12.2 shows that S&P 500 firms with enormous financial leverage are only moderately profitable. The ROA for highly leveraged S&P 500 firms is actually a *negative* 1.6 percent, a big difference from the ROA earned by the most profitable firms. Highly leveraged firms also appear to have more modest growth opportunities. Analysts believe these firms will grow EPS at only 11.8 percent per year in the future. This is not to say that all firms with high leverage have low profitability. However, the data show that many firms that employ huge financial leverage have modest records for profitable performance.

The lesson for investors about the relationship between financial leverage and business quality seems simple: Enormous financial leverage cannot transform a mediocre business into a wonderful franchise. If a high degree of financial leverage is used in a wonderful business, the potential for leverage-induced benefits is obtained only at the risk of a harmful reduction in financial and operating decision flexibility. In a mediocre business, the use of financial leverage can magnify investor upside potential at the risk of a similar magnification of downside risk.

TaBLe 12.2	The Most Profitable S&P 500 Companies Have Low Financial Leverage

Company	Industry	Symbol	Price	Ratio: 5-Year Avg.	ROA: 5-Year Avg. (%)	Leverage Ratio	EPS Growth Next 5 Years (%)
A. Low Financial Leverage Is Typical among Highly Profitable Firms							
Moody's Corp.	Business Services	MCO	61.20	27.0	37.6	3.1	15.7
Federated Investors, Inc.	Asset Management	FII	38.15	19.1	25.8	1.9	11.3
Coach, Inc.	Textile - Apparel Footwear & Accessories	COH	31.75	30.3	25.6	1.3	19.1
Apollo Group, Inc.	Education & Training Services	APOL	54.51	55.1	21.4	2.1	19.8
Adobe Systems Inc.	Application Software	ADBE	38.43	40.3	21.3	1.3	13.2
Forest Laboratories, Inc.	Drug Manufacturers - Other	FRX	43.13	36.1	19.8	1.2	14.0
IMS Health, Inc.	Business Software & Services	RX	25.34	28.7	19.3	4.7	13.3
Oracle Corp.	Application Software	ORCL	12.29	26.3	19.1	1.6	12.0
William Wrigley Jr. Co.	Confectioners	WWY	65.79	31.1	18.3	2.0	10.8
Avon Products, Inc.	Personal Products	AVP	28.66	24.0	17.4	5.2	12.0
Colgate Palmolive	Personal Products	CL	53.70	27.0	16.7	8.3	9.0
Biomet, Inc.	Medical Appliances & Equipment	BMET	35.83	31.4	16.4	1.3	14.8
T. Rowe Price Group, Inc.	Asset Management	TROW	75.62	22.5	16.0	1.2	12.4
Merck and Co. Inc.	Drug Manufacturers - Major	MRK	33.25	18.6	15.8	2.5	17.3
Waters Corp.	Scientific & Technical Instruments	WAT	38.10	37.9	15.8	3.8	12.8
Average			**42.38**	**30.4**	**20.4**	**2.8**	**13.8**
B. Low Profitability Is Typical among Highly Leveraged Firms							
Amazon.com, Inc.	Internet Software & Services	AMZN	43.92		−13.4	472.0	22.7
Goodyear Tire & Rubber	Rubber & Plastics	GT	17.63		−2.7	54.9	
Fannie Mae	Credit Services	FNM	53.21	14.9	0.7	44.9	9.0
Lucent Technologies Inc.	Processing Systems & Products	LU	2.55		−26.5	43.7	7.9
Hercules Inc.	Synthetics	HPC	11.05		−0.6	38.4	
TXU Corp.	Electric Utilities	TXU	51.44		−0.7	31.4	14.9
The Bear Stearns Cos.	Investment Brokerage - National	BSC	119.55	10.1	0.5	29.9	10.7
Freddie Mac	Mortgage Investment	FRE	65.91	12.6	0.7	29.7	12.5
SLM Corp.	Credit Services	SLM	55.32	21.6	1.6	29.6	16.0
Goldman Sachs Group, Inc.	Investment Brokerage - National	GS	131.44	16.5	0.8	25.9	12.5
Lehman Brothers Holdings Inc.	Investment Brokerage - National	LEH	134.79	12.5	0.6	25.2	11.9
Merrill Lynch & Co., Inc.	Investment Brokerage - National	MER	70.80	30.1	0.6	21.0	12.0
The AES Corp.	Electric Utilities	AES	17.64		−1.4	20.9	12.7
General Motors	Auto Manufacturers - Major	GM	20.05	12.3	0.7	20.9	4.8
UST Inc.	Tobacco Products, Other	UST	40.45		15.4	20.3	6.3
Average			**55.72**	**16.3**	**−1.6**	**60.6**	**11.8**

Source: msnMoney, January 20, 2006 (**http://moneycentral.msn.com/investor/finder/customstocksdl.asp**).

Pitfalls to Growth

Customer Loyalty Risk

One of the most prized possessions of any successful company is a large and growing body of satisfied customers. Customer loyalty built through years of dedicated service is often a wellspring of future business opportunity for both established and new products. Stealing satisfied customers is never easy, but it is sometimes impossible for smaller competitors or start-ups. New entrants seeking a foothold by simply offering "me-too" products at a lower price are seldom successful against larger and more established competitors with deep pockets. Successful entry in stable or slow-growing markets with established competitors requires products and services that are substantially better, notably cheaper, or delivered much faster than the competition.

Entry into fast-growing markets is another matter, however. When new markets are undergoing explosive growth, few competitors need fear the problem of overcoming long-established customer loyalty. By definition, everything is up for grabs in new and rapidly growing markets. As a result, **customer loyalty risk** is high and market-share stability is low in new and rapidly growing markets. New and rapidly growing markets are filled with risk and opportunity for companies and their investors. Sometimes, early movers are able to achieve durable advantages over subsequent competitors. More often, however, quick and unpredictable changes in the marketplace leave both companies and their investors looking for answers. In the realm of desktop computers, for example, early winners such as Atari, Digital Equipment, and Apple have given way to Dell, Compaq, Hewlett-Packard, and an ever-changing roster of capable competitors.

Just as growth in mere size is no guarantee of growing EPS or growing stock value, growth that is simply tied to an expanding overall market is no guarantee of long-term success. In fact, rapid industry growth sometimes guarantees that new and highly capable competitors will quickly be attracted. In the early 1990s, for example, the Snapple Beverage Company caused quite a stir by inventing the "New Age" beverage industry with a range of healthful, noncola soft drinks. At first, Coca-Cola and PepsiCo seemed amused by this upstart's irreverence, and they shunned tea and fruit-flavored beverages as a mere fad. Once Snapple and a host of imitators demonstrated that significant market demand existed for such products, Coca-Cola and PepsiCo brought out their own offerings. The onslaught of competition nearly forced Snapple out of business. Today, Snapple limps along as a marginally profitable competitor in a fiercely competitive market.

Merger Risk

A true growth company is able to profitably supply distinctive products and services to a rapidly growing marketplace. A vital determinant of a growth company's long-term success is the extent to which the company is able to maintain its ability to produce distinctively appealing products and services. True growth is based on the creative capability demonstrated by the firm and the creative differences enjoyed by its customers. The creative capability that gives rise to true growth is inherent to the firm, or comes from within.

For example, Wal-Mart Stores, Inc., has enjoyed stunning success operating discount department stores (Wal-Marts), warehouse membership clubs (Sam's Clubs), and combination full-line supermarket and discount department stores (Wal-Mart Supercenters) in the United States and foreign markets. All Wal-Mart shoppers are aware of Sam Walton's legendary prowess as a merchandiser. Relatively few recognize that the company's amazing success is also due to a state-of-the-art internal communications network (intranet) that efficiently communicates buyer decisions to Wal-Mart's suppliers. Wal-Mart beats the competition because it precisely meets customer needs while minimizing inventory and merchandising costs. Although Kmart was among the first to popularize the discount-retailer concept, Wal-Mart used communications technology to perfect it. Wal-Mart has succeeded because of its innate ability to meet customer needs quicker and cheaper than the competition.

Customer loyalty risk
Chance of losing customers to established competitors or new entrants.

Although Wal-Mart has built its success on this ability to exploit communications technology, other growth companies have built their success on a variety of inherent capabilities. Coca-Cola's long-standing success as a growth stock is based on the company's legendary advertising capability and tremendous economies of scale in distribution. Computer microprocessor titan Intel and pharmaceutical giant Merck have built long-term success on the basis of remarkable research and development capability that helps produce an ongoing string of products and product lines that shape and reshape important industries. Notice that all these great growth companies have built from within. None are the result of an ongoing series of mergers or acquisitions. The reason for this is simple: Acquired companies often underperform as divisions of larger companies. Employees that flourish in the entrepreneurial environment of a start-up or smaller company often chafe in the more structured atmosphere of a larger company. Following settlement of major mergers, key employees often leave the acquirer to start anew. Lost key employees often form the basis for new and vibrant competitors. As a result, it is seldom true that growth through merger and acquisition leads to durable long-term business success or investor prosperity. More typical is the case in which companies fall victim to **merger risk** and suffer merger indigestion and investor disappointment.

On Wall Street, a **roll-up** is a company that grows through a constant acquisition binge. Fans view roll-ups as a way to bring economies of scale, management discipline, and superior access to low-cost capital into industries dominated by inefficient, undercapitalized, mom-and-pop operations. For example, Wayne Huizenga reached hero status on Wall Street as he built an empire consolidating local garbage haulers into Waste Management, Inc., and independent video stores into Blockbuster Entertainment. Others have rolled up everything from funeral homes to rental businesses to Internet service providers. Skeptics view roll-ups as a game of financial engineering. Using highly valued stock as cheap currency to buy smaller companies, roll-ups use an ongoing string of mergers to produce a continuing boost to earnings per share. However, critics contend that when roll-up companies stop the process of constant acquisition, they often fail to deliver operating efficiencies.

Houston-based Waste Management, Inc., provides a classic example. Waste Management offers a variety of integrated waste management services, including collection, transfer, disposal, recycling, and resource-recovery services. Until mid-1999, Waste Management was a Wall Street darling and showed stunning revenue and profit growth from acquisitions, internal growth, and lower general and administrative expenses. Investors prospered. As shown in Figure 12.1, Waste Management stock increased dramatically during the 1990s. In July 1999, the Waste Management story hit a speed bump. Hoped-for operating efficiencies failed to materialize, and the company began to strain under a daunting load of debt. Within weeks of the announcement of operating disappointments, the stock collapsed from near $60 to less than $20 per share, thus wiping out years of investor gains.

The lesson for investors is simple but important: Growth made possible by superior capability provides an attractive basis for sustainable above-average returns. When growth depends on a continuing series of beneficial mergers and acquisitions, the risk of eventual loss and investor disappointment is significant.

Merger risk
Economic loss stemming from failure to achieve merger benefits.

Roll-up
Company that grows through constant acquisition.

Regulation Risk

According to legendary growth stock investors like T. Rowe Price and Phil Fisher, it is necessary to seek out fertile fields for economic growth to succeed in common stock investing. Risk can be reduced, but not eliminated, when growth stock investors buy and hold for long-term appreciation and future income the best companies in the best industries. A host of important problems can also be avoided when investors seek to minimize **regulation risk**.

At the start of the new millennium, it is easy to predict that an aging population is apt to place increasing burdens on health care services. Over time, the demand for health care services, drugs, and medical supplies is sure to grow. Unfortunately, as demand skyrockets, so too does the demand for federal and state regulation to contain the upward spiral in health care costs. In the late 1990s, strong regulatory and cost containment efforts were directed at hospitals and health maintenance organizations (HMOs). Investors in hospital chains and HMOs

Regulation risk
Chance of investor loss due to burdensome government rules and regulations.

FIGURE 12.1 Growth through Acquisition Led to Problems at Waste Management, Inc.

have suffered accordingly. As the cost of prescription drugs continues to climb, some states are allowing citizens to buy subsidized drugs at cheaper prices from Canada and other countries. This pits federal government agencies such as the Food and Drug Administration against state governments. Like investors in public utilities, investors in important sectors of the health care industry have come to learn that booming revenues can lead to a profitless prosperity when the industry is subject to onerous regulation. It is no wonder that growth stock investors seek companies in industries that are not natural targets of regulation.

Price Risk

One of the most important potential pitfalls tied to growth stock investing is that the approach seldom offers clear guidance about how much is too much to pay for a stock with attractive growth prospects. The lack of a strict buying discipline leaves growth stock investors open to **price risk**, or the chance of overpaying for attractive companies, and the risk of suffering gut-wrenching devastation to their investment portfolios during temporary declines in the overall market. For example, one of the most successful and popular growth stock mutual funds during the 1990s bull market was the Janus Twenty Fund, Inc. The Janus Twenty Fund seeks capital appreciation by investing in a concentrated portfolio of between 20 and 30 common stocks. To select its investments, fund management evaluates profit margins, earnings, and unit growth to detect the fundamental investment value of the security.

Like most growth stock investors, the Janus Twenty Fund focuses on leading-edge companies in rapidly emerging high-tech industries, such as Genentech, and Internet firms like eBay (Figure 12.2). The concentration of the portfolio is obvious; 31.4 percent of the portfolio is held in only five stocks. The high-risk growth orientation has created some extremely volatile returns. During the end of the 1990s bull market, Janus had very high returns that outperformed other growth funds and the index. However, the following bear market severely affected the performance of the Janus Twenty Fund. During 2000-2002, this aggressive growth fund significantly underperformed other growth funds and the index. The fund rebounded in 2003 and 2004, along with the general stock market, and did well into 2006.

Price risk
Chance of overpaying for attractive companies.

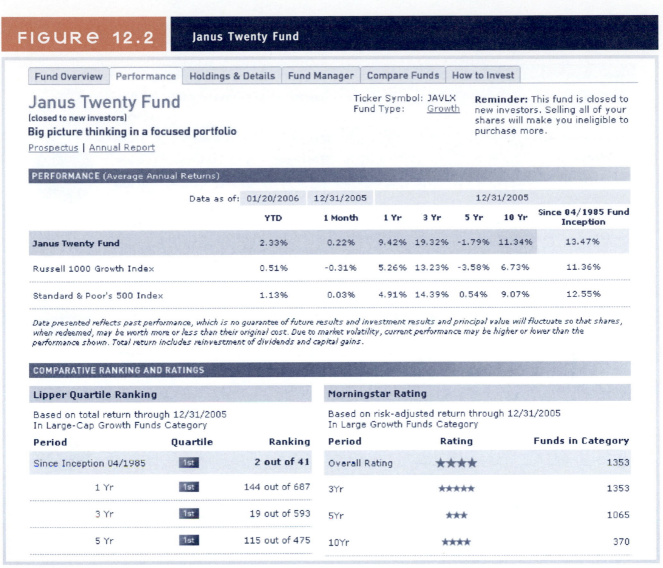

FIGURE 12.2 — Janus Twenty Fund

(continued on next page)

Valuing Growth

Variable-Growth Model

Growth companies are often difficult to value because they grow at a very fast rate. High growth rates might be sustainable for a few years but cannot continue indefinitely. In the previous chapter, the idea of regression to the mean was discussed. Companies that have experienced unusually high growth in the recent past tend to experience more typical rates of growth in the future. Consider the constant-growth model for stock valuation presented in Chapter 11, where the current stock price P_0 depends on the expected dividend per share D_1, the required return k, and the expected growth rate g.

$$P_0 = \frac{D_1}{k - g}$$

(12.1)

The problem with implementing this model for some growth stocks is that the expected growth rate, g, for the company can be greater than the required rate of return, k. The model is not valid for companies where $g > k$. The negative price that the model generates when $g > k$

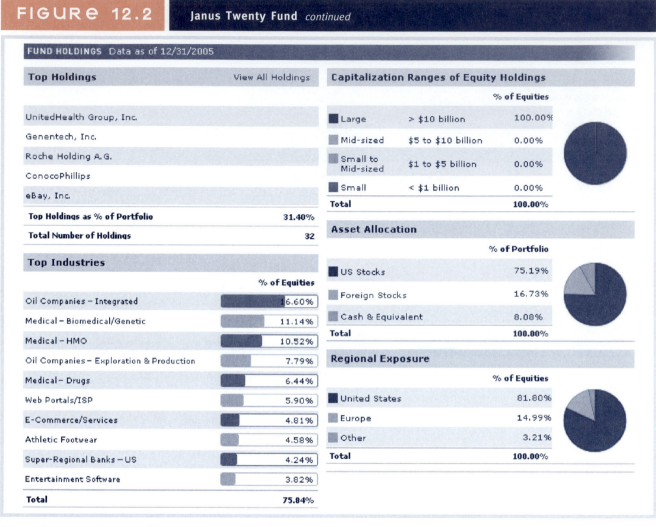

FIGURE 12.2	Janus Twenty Fund *continued*

FUND HOLDINGS Data as of 12/31/2005

Top Holdings   View All Holdings

UnitedHealth Group, Inc.

Genentech, Inc.

Roche Holding A.G.

ConocoPhillips

eBay, Inc.

Top Holdings as % of Portfolio	31.40%
Total Number of Holdings	32

Top Industries

	% of Equities
Oil Companies – Integrated	16.60%
Medical – Biomedical/Genetic	11.14%
Medical – HMO	10.52%
Oil Companies – Exploration & Production	7.79%
Medical – Drugs	6.44%
Web Portals/ISP	5.90%
E-Commerce/Services	4.81%
Athletic Footwear	4.58%
Super-Regional Banks – US	4.24%
Entertainment Software	3.82%
Total	**75.84%**

Capitalization Ranges of Equity Holdings

		% of Equities
Large	> $10 billion	100.00%
Mid-sized	$5 to $10 billion	0.00%
Small to Mid-sized	$1 to $5 billion	0.00%
Small	< $1 billion	0.00%
Total		**100.00%**

Asset Allocation

	% of Portfolio
US Stocks	75.19%
Foreign Stocks	16.73%
Cash & Equivalent	8.08%
Total	**100.00%**

Regional Exposure

	% of Equities
United States	81.80%
Europe	14.99%
Other	3.21%
Total	**100.00%**

Source: Janus, **www.janus.com** © Janus, Inc. Used with permission.

Variable growth rate
Model used when short-term growth rates are not expected to persist in the long run.

is a nonsensical result because such hypergrowth is not sustainable in practice. When growth rates vary, investors must use a **variable growth rate** model to price growth stocks. To implement the model, the investor must choose two different growth rates. The first growth rate, g_1, is the current high rate of growth. A few years into the future, this rate of growth will slow into a more sustainable rate, g_2. If this second growth rate begins in year $t + 1$, the dividend discount model can be written as:

$$P_0 = \frac{D_1}{1+k} + \frac{D_2}{(1+k)^2} + \ldots + \frac{D_t + P_t}{(1+k)^t}$$ **(12.2)**

Dividends paid during the next few years, D_1, D_2, and so on, can be expressed in terms of the current dividend, D_0, and the current above-average growth rate g_1. The terminal price, P_t, can be expressed in terms of the constant-growth rate model using the second stage of growth, g_2. Making these substitutions, Equation 12.2 becomes

$$P_0 = \frac{D_0(1+g_1)}{1+k} + \frac{D_0(1+g_1)^2}{(1+k)^2} + \frac{D_0(1+g_1)^3}{(1+k)^3} + \ldots + \frac{D_0(1+g_1)^t + \dfrac{D_0(1+g_1)^t(1+g_2)}{k-g_2}}{(1+k)^t}$$ **(12.3)**

The investor must decide how long the current growth rate will last before it declines to a more sustainable rate.

Try It!

A fast-growing company paid a dividend this year of $1.50 per share and is expected to grow at 25 percent for two years. Afterward, the growth rate will be 8 percent. If the required rate is 10 percent, what is the value of this stock?

Solution

Using Equation 12.3,

$$P_0 = \frac{1.50(1 + 0.25)}{1 + 0.10} + \frac{1.50(1 + 0.25)^2 + \dfrac{1.50(1 + 0.25)^2(1 + 0.08)}{0.10 - 0.08}}{(1+0.10)^2} =$$

$$\frac{1.875}{1.10} + \frac{2.344 + \dfrac{2.531}{0.02}}{1.21} = 1.705 + 106.534 = \$108.24$$

PEG: Growth at a Reasonable Price

Determining a reasonable price to pay for a growth stock is always difficult. To deal effectively with the uncertainties involved, growth stock investors have developed some straightforward valuation metrics. An **investment rule of thumb** is a simple guide to investment valuation that has served the test of time.

For example, legendary mutual fund investor Peter Lynch is famous for developing the so-called P/E-to-growth, or PEG, ratio. The **PEG ratio** is simply the P/E ratio divided by the expected EPS growth rate (in percent). If a company has a P/E of 20 and is expected to enjoy EPS growth of 20 percent per year, the company's PEG ratio would be 1 (= 20/20%). Generally speaking, a stock is fully valued if it sports a PEG ratio of 1 or more. If the PEG ratio is less than 1, the stock is worthy of investment consideration. The PEG ratio rule of thumb goes something like this:

- If PEG ≤ 1, the stock may be worthy of investment attention and possible purchase.

- If PEG ≤ 0.5, the stock is definitely worthy of investment attention and may represent a very attractive investment.

- If PEG ≤ 0.33, the stock is apt to represent an extraordinarily attractive investment opportunity.

Needless to say, the investment merit of a stock increases with a decrease in the PEG ratio. Strict **growth at-a-reasonable-price (GARP) investors** seldom, if ever, buy growth stocks with PEG ratios that are significantly greater than 1. Table 12.3 shows a list of companies in the S&P 500 Index that have a PEG ratio of less than1. These firms have high expected earnings growth but are selling for relatively modest valuations. Notice that most stocks that appear attractive according to the PEG criterion have P/E ratios that are well below marketwide P/E norms.

Investment rule of thumb
Simple guide to investment valuation that has served the test of time.

PEG ratio
P/E divided by the expected EPS growth rate.

Growth at-a-reasonable-price (GARP) investors
Disciplined growth stock investors who seldom buy growth stocks with PEG ratios greater than 1.

Try It!

Consider the price, earnings per share, and growth rate of the three companies listed below. Using the PEG ratio, determine which of the firms might interest a growth investor.

	Growth	Price	EPS
Company A	20%	$13.25	$2
Company B	35	75.00	2
Company C	25	12.40	1

(continued)

Solution

The PEG ratio is

$$PEG = P/E\ ratio/growth\ rate$$

For Company A, PEG = (13.25/2) / 20 = 0.33   Great opportunity!
For Company B, PEG = (75/2) / 35 = 1.07   Do not consider buying!
For Company C, PEG = (12.40/1) / 25 = 0.496   Consider buying.

To effectively use the PEG ratio approach, investors must come up with simple but effective means for predicting EPS growth. Many investors rely on the EPS growth estimates provided by security analysts, but others rely on their own EPS growth estimates derived from company financial information. In a common approach, growth stock investors focus on retained earnings as the primary source of internally generated funds for investment. Earnings

---

TABLE 12.3 Growth at-a-Reasonable-Price Investors Like Stocks with Moderate P/E Ratios and Attractive Growth Prospects

Company	Symbol	Industry	Current P/E	Analyst Estimate of EPS Growth, Next 5 Years (%)	Payout: 5-Year Avg. (%)	ROE: 5-Year Avg. (%)	PEG Ratio Based On Analysts' Estimates
Amerada Hess Corp.	AHC	Oil & Gas Refining & Market	14.7	35.1		13.9	0.42
Navistar International	NAV	Trucks & Other Vehicles	6.8	16.2			0.42
Nabors Industries Ltd.	NBR	Oil & Gas Drilling & Exploration	23.5	49.5		9.8	0.47
D.R. Horton Inc.	DHI	Residential Construction	8.3	15.8	7	23.5	0.53
KB Home	KBH	Residential Construction	9.3	17.3	6	23.8	0.54
Centex Corp.	CTX	Residential Construction	8.2	15.1	2	22.2	0.54
Lennar Corp.	LEN	Residential Construction	8.8	14.6	3	23.2	0.60
Pulte Homes, Inc.	PHM	Residential Construction	8.1	13.3	3	17.9	0.61
Cummins Inc.	CMI	Diversified Machinery	9.3	14.5		7.0	0.64
CSX Corp.	CSX	Railroads	12.1	16.6	55	4.7	0.73
Freeport-McMoRan Copper & Gold	FCX	Copper	15.9	21.7	31	380.9	0.73
SafeCo Corp.	SAFC	Property & Casualty Insurance	10.6	14.4		1.5	0.74
Paccar Inc.	PCAR	Trucks & Other Vehicles	11.4	14.5	48	17.2	0.79
Ambac Financial Group, Inc.	ABK	Surety & Title Insurance	11.2	13.7	8	13.9	0.82
Merck and Co. Inc.	MRK	Drug Manufacturers - Major	15.8	17.3	47	41.4	0.91
Yahoo! Inc.	YHOO	Internet Information Providers	26.4	28.6		6.6	0.92
Capital One Financial Corp.	COF	Credit Services	12.9	13.6	3	19.3	0.95
Average			**12.5**	**19.5**	**19**	**39.2**	**0.67**

Source: msnMoney, January 20, 2006 (**http://moneycentral.msn.com/investor/finder/customstocksdl.asp**).

retention refers to all earnings not paid out to stockholders in the form of dividends, with dividends broadly defined to include both regular and irregular cash dividends and stock repurchases. The **retention rate** is the share of earnings retained to fund investment:

$$\text{Retention rate} = 1 - \frac{\text{dividends}}{\text{net income}} \qquad (12.4)$$

Retention rate
Share of earnings retained to fund investment.

When retained earnings are the primary source of internally generated funds for investment, the amount of **internally sustainable growth** is given by the expression:

$$\text{Internally sustainable growth} = \text{retention rate} \times \text{ROE} \qquad (12.5)$$

Internally sustainable growth
Rate at which a firm can grow without obtaining more capital.

Whereas the retention rate is the share of earnings retained to fund investment, the **dividend payout ratio** is the percentage of income paid out in the form of dividends:

$$\text{Dividend payout ratio} = \frac{\text{dividends}}{\text{net income}} \qquad (12.6)$$

Dividend payout ratio
Percentage of income paid out in the form of dividends.

Obviously, a retention rate of 75 percent implies a payout ratio of 25 percent, and vice versa. Thus, the retention rate and ROE determine the rate of growth made possible by internally generated funds. This means that if a company earns a 20 percent rate of ROE and retains one-half of all earnings for future investment, the amount of book value growth that could be funded internally is 10 percent (= 20% × 0.5). If the company's P/E and P/B ratios remain constant over time, internally funded earnings and book value growth of 10 percent per year would also result in capital appreciation of 10 percent per year. Notice that there is a fairly high degree of consistency between PEG ratios based on security analyst estimates of EPS growth and such estimates based solely on company financial information.

Growth at-a-reasonable-price investors also rely on ROE and EPS growth information to help them decide on a reasonable P/E ratio to pay for growth stocks. Recall from the constant-growth rate model that $P_0 = D_1/(k - g)$. Equation 12.7 shows that growth $g = b \times ROE$, where the retention ratio $b = 1 - D_1/E_1$ (and $0 \le b \le 1$) and ROE is the rate of return on common equity. It follows that an appropriate P/E ratio for a given growth stock can be calculated as

$$\frac{P_0}{E_1} = \frac{D_1/E_1}{k - g} = \frac{1 - b}{k - b \times ROE} \qquad (12.7)$$

Holding all else equal, an appropriate P/E ratio will fall with a decrease in the retention rate b or a rise in the risk-adjusted required rate of return k. The appropriate P/E ratio will rise with an increase in the ROE. This equation also demonstrates the relationship between company growth and P/E ratio. Higher growth, g, can be used to justify paying a higher P/E ratio.

Try It!

Consider a company that earns $5 per share and pays a $1 dividend. The management expressed an expected growth rate of 25 percent. If the firm earns a 20 percent return on equity, can the firm grow with internal funds, or will it need additional capital?

Solution

Using Equation 12.7,

Internally sustainable growth = retention rate × ROE = (1 − $1/$5) × 20% = 16%

Since the expected growth of 25 percent is higher than would be possible with internally generated funds, the firm is likely to seek more capital or slow down the growth rate.

Street Smarts 12.2

Valuing Internet Stocks

Long-term investors seek to arrive at a sensible price to pay for a stock on the basis of a careful examination of expected cash flows, the degree of competition, and the overall market environment. Historical accounting data, market research, and competitor analysis all play important roles in the process.

In the late 1990s, investors turned their backs on such time-tested methods when it came to the valuation of Internet stocks. How do you value a firm with no revenue, let alone cash flow or profits? What is the potential market for free Internet search? Will customers that gladly use free Internet news and information ever be willing to pay the costs of doing business on the Internet? How do you define the borders of the competitive environment when it looks like an Internet free-for-all with competitors entering and exiting at the drop of a hat?

Investors faced such questions when trying to place a value on Internet stocks in the late 1990s. They turned to Morgan Stanley's superstar analyst, Mary Meeker, for advice. Meeker earned the nickname "Queen of the Internet" for her relentlessly bullish stance on Internet stocks in both the print and broadcast media. Stocks recommended by Meeker soared far beyond any levels that could be justified using discounted cash flow methods and the most generous underlying assumptions. When potential revenues, cash flows, or profits could not be used to justify Internet stock prices, Meeker blamed the shortcomings of traditional approaches. How can you justify highly inflated Internet stock prices when the numbers just do not add up? Meeker argued that the answer was disarmingly simple: Just ignore the traditional numbers—invent new ones. Meeker argued that Internet stocks needed to be valued on the basis of the number of potential viewers per Web page (or eyeballs).

Everybody now knows that throwing out traditional approaches in the valuation of Internet stocks during the late 1990s was a big mistake. Revenue, cash flow, and profits matter when it comes to valuing all stocks. Trying to base Internet stock valuation on flat-out guesses concerning the potential number of viewers per Web page is so silly as to be farcical. It should have been taken as a warning to investors when traditional methods could not be used to justify the prices paid for Internet stocks in the late 1990s. Traditional methods were fine; it was the Internet stock prices that were wrong.

Be wary of the stocks that "cannot be valued with traditional methods." In these cases, the problems are usually with the prices, not the methods!

See Loretta Chao, "Internet Onboard," *The Wall Street Journal Online*, January 12, 2006 (**http://online.wsj.com**).

Cash Flow Model

Fast-growing firms need capital to grow. As a result, many fast-growing firms do not pay a dividend. They reinvest the cash that could be used to pay a dividend into business opportunities. How can a discount model be used for companies that do not pay a dividend? Instead of valuing the dividend stream investors receive from owning the stock, investors can value the firm's business. Specifically, investors can value the free cash flows of the firm's business. The value of the business, V, is determined by

$$V = \sum_{t=1}^{n} \frac{CF_t}{(1+k)^t} \tag{12.8}$$

where CF_t is the free cash flow of the firm in year t. If the firm has acquired capital through debt, then the equity value of the firm, EV, is the total value, V, less the market value of the debt. To obtain a per-share-of-stock value, simply divide by the number of shares outstanding. The intrinsic value of a non-dividend-paying stock can be modeled as

$$P_0 = \frac{EV}{\text{no. of shares}} = \frac{\sum_{t=1}^{n} \frac{CF_t}{(1+k)^t} - \text{market value of debt}}{\text{no. of shares}} \tag{12.9}$$

This model is useful for valuing up-and-coming growth firms that do not pay dividends. Investors should be aware that the results of Equation 12.9 are very sensitive to expected future operating cash flows. Many young growth firms have very little (or even negative) operating cash flows but expect large cash flows in the future. The value of the company largely depends on the probability that the company survives long enough to realize those future cash flows. When news is released about the firm's progress, investors update the assumed probability that future cash flows will materialize. Small changes in future prospects create large changes in the firm's estimated value, P_0. Indeed, the stock prices of young growth companies are extremely volatile.

Try It!

A young and fast-growing company pays no dividends, and none are expected in the near future. The firm will earn \$3 million in net free cash flow next year. This cash flow is expected to grow at 20 percent during the next four years and then grow at 8 percent per year indefinitely. The firm has \$50 million in debt and 300,000 shares of common stock outstanding. Compute the intrinsic value of the stock using a 15 percent discount rate.

Solution

The cash flows in the next few years will be

$$CF_1 = 3,000,000$$

$$CF_2 = 3,000,000 \times 1.20 = 3,600,000$$

$$CF_3 = 3,000,000 \times (1.20)^2 = 4,320,000$$

$$CF_4 = 3,000,000 \times (1.20)^3 = 5,184,000$$

$$CF_5 = 3,000,000 \times (1.20)^4 = 6,220,800$$

The constant-growth rate model of Equation 12.1 is used to determine the terminal cash flow in year 5:

$$CF_{Year\ 5\ terminal\ value} = \frac{6,220,800 \times (1.08)}{0.15 - 0.08} = 95,978,057$$

Using Equation 12.5,

$$P_0 = \frac{EV}{no.\ of\ shares}$$

$$= \frac{\dfrac{3,000,000}{1.15} + \dfrac{3,600,000}{(1.15)^2} + \dfrac{4,320,000}{(1.15)^3} + \dfrac{5,184,000}{(1.15)^4} + \dfrac{6,220,800 + 95,978,057}{(1.15)^5} - 50,000,000}{300,000}$$

$$= \$39.82$$

Technology Stock Investing

Tech Stock Advantages

Many growth stock investors display asset category preferences reflecting strong underlying beliefs about where the best growth opportunities can be found. Since the 1990s, many such investors have come to display a strong preference for **technology stocks** at the vanguard of important new innovations in biotechnology, laptop computers, portable communications devices, cellular telephone technology, digital cameras and video disks, and the Internet. Companies expected to benefit from growth tied to the Internet have become a special focus. Important new areas for Internet-related growth include Internet infrastructure building and development (e.g., Cisco Systems), Internet access and content (e.g., Google and Yahoo!) and e-commerce (e.g., eBay and Amazon.com).

High-tech stocks can be found across a broad spectrum of industries. Basic, diversified, and specialized chemical companies devote an enormous amount of spending to research and development (R&D) and are responsible for a continuing stream of important new inventions and innovations. Some of the most profitable applications from such discoveries are found in related areas such as pharmaceutical drugs, toiletries, and cosmetics. The biotechnology industry, the focus of intense speculative interest in the early 1990s, is now coming into its own with a string of important new pharmaceutical therapies and other bioengineered products, such as

Technology stocks
Shares in companies at the vanguard of important new innovations.

disease-resistant crops. Spending on R&D is also significant across a broad range of industrial machinery and equipment industries, including computers, electronic devices, measuring instruments, medical devices, telecommunications, and transportation equipment. Of course, computer software and services are areas of large and growing importance for R&D.

The allure of technology stock investing is obvious. Technology stocks tend to do well during economic expansions as capital spending rises, and the U.S. economy grew rapidly throughout the 1990s. Fundamentally important new innovations during the 1990s have also contributed to the explosion of more recent interest in high-tech stocks. First, the advent of amazingly powerful microprocessors transformed the PC into a mighty tool for business calculations. Then the advent of the Internet and even more powerful microprocessors made it possible for the PC to become the focus of a communications industry revolution. What used to be called cameras, cellular phones, computers, copy machines, fax machines, printers, telephones, and televisions are quickly converging toward multicapability communications devices.

Tech Stock Risks

Huge potential rewards await those companies able to successfully navigate in a rapidly changing environment. Somewhat less understood are the equally enormous risks facing companies unable to successfully anticipate and adapt to such challenges. To illustrate, Table 12.4 shows the rapidly changing landscape for high-tech companies in the computer networking equipment and computer software industries. Notice how few industry giants have been able to stay

TABLE 12.4 — High Tech Market Capitalization Rankings Change Dramatically over Time ($ millions)

1980		1990		2000	
A. Computers and Peripheral Equipment					
1. IBM	$39,625.9	IBM	$64,567.2	Cisco Systems	$347,897.3
2. Computer Sciences Corp.	240.4	Computer Sciences Corp.	1,071.4	IBM	209,148.0
3. American Management Systems	53.9	American Management Systems	175.4	Dell Computer	127,437.4
4. CGA Computers Inc.	34.3	Computer Task Group Inc.	62.8	Sun Microsystems	111,242.8
5. Hadron Inc.	32.6	BRC Holdings Inc.	55.2	Hewlett-Packard	109,277.4
6. Computer Task Group Inc.	20.5	Data Transmission Network	39.1	EMC Corp.	104,803.0
7. Dyatron Corp.	17.1	Medstat Group Inc.	33.0	Compaq Computer	47,600.0
8. BRC Holdings Inc.	12.7	National Information Group	30.9	Gateway Inc.	18,042.5
9. Cerplex Group Inc.	6.3	Cerplex Group Inc.	21.0	Apple Computer	16,731.5
10. Auxton Computer Enterprises	5.7	Mpsi Systems Inc.	19.0	3Com Corp.	15,203.0
B. Computer Software And Services					
1. Computervision Corp.	$1,206.2	Microsoft Corp.	$8,641.1	Microsoft Corp.	$588,884.1
2. Wang Labs Inc.	875.0	Novell Inc.	1,742.7	Oracle Corp.	145,214.6
3. Cullinet Software Inc.	196.5	Computer Associates Intl. Inc.	1,615.4	Computer Associates	33,864.2
4. UCCEL Corp.	190.9	Autodesk Inc.	1,110.7	Veritas Software	32,736.7
5. Tyler Technologies Inc.	150.3	BMC Software Inc.	1,030.1	Automatic Data Processing	32,193.1
6. Banctec Inc.	78.8	Oracle Corp.	1,022.2	Electronic Data Systems	28,070.4
7. Intelligent System Corp.	51.3	Lotus Development Corp.	844.4	First Data Corp.	20,567.2
8. Informatics General Corp.	51.0	Inprise Corp.	807.9	Intuit Inc.	14,646.2
9. Comshare Inc.	45.7	Policy Management Systems Corp.	801.1	Siebel Systems	13,810.7
10. Continuum Inc.	37.7	Cadence Design Systems Inc.	713.0	Computer Sciences	13,778.9

Source: 1980 and 1990 data from Compustat PC+; 2000 data from Value Line Investment Survey for Windows, January 2000.

atop their competitors. Although IBM has been able to remain a force in the production of computers and peripheral equipment, no other company has been able to maintain a top 10 position in the industry for 20 years. Present-day giants, such as Cisco Systems, founded in 1984, have literally come out of nowhere. Similarly, Microsoft, founded in 1975, came out of nowhere to dominate the important computer software and services industry.

Rather than assume that Cisco and Microsoft, for example, will naturally dominate a quickly changing high tech landscape for the next 20 years, long-term investors may want to consider what will happen to their stock prices if (or when) they stumble. Similarly, consumers that love listening to music on their iPods need to think long and hard about emerging competition before buying stock in Apple Computer, Inc. Investors in other high tech leaders, like Qualcomm, Inc., and Amgen, Inc., also need to ponder the difficulty of staying on top of the quickly changing high tech landscape.

Whereas value stock investors seek good companies that are out of favor and selling at a bargain price, tech stock investors seek fast growing companies that may dominate their industry. History shows that tech stock investing can be profitable, but is risky. During the late-1990s, value investors found that conservative stock picking can lead to below-average rates of return during a rip-roaring bull market. In a period of uninterrupted economic expansion, **capital spending** rises, productivity gains are created, and technology spending booms. These basic economic trends favor tech stock investors and penalize investors in the basic industry stocks often considered most attractive by value investors. However, when the economy slows down and capital spending declines, as was true in the period following the market peak in March 2000, tech stocks get hit hard and value stocks tend to outperform.

Capital spending
When firms buy assets to increase efficiency or expand operations.

Growth versus Value

Growth and Value Stock Indexes

Until recently, growth and value stock performance benchmarks were identified using simple quantitative criteria, like P/B ratios. Because growth stocks tend to have high P/B ratios while value stocks tend to have low P/B ratios, a simple classification "growth" and "value" stocks according to P/B ratios was long deemed satisfactory. However, such simplistic quantitative approaches are imprecise, and in September 2005 the Standard & Poor's Corporation unveiled a new generation of style indices for growth and value investors. S&P is the best known provider of index benchmarks used by institutional investors, mutual funds, and individuals. S&P estimates over $4.0 trillion in assets are benchmarked to the S&P 500 alone, with indexed assets making up over $1.1 trillion of this total. This makes S&P benchmarks important when it comes to judging the relative performance of growth and value stocks.

S&P Pure Style benchmark indices for the large-cap S&P 500, S&P MidCap 400, and the S&P SmallCap 600 include only pure growth and pure value stocks as characterized by S&P criteria; there are no overlapping stocks. In the proprietary S&P methodology, stocks are assigned standardized value and growth scores based on four value factors and three growth factors. Within each parent index, stocks are then assigned growth and value ranks based on their growth score and value score, respectively. They are then sorted based on the ratio of their growth ranks and value ranks. Stocks comprising the top one-third of the market cap of an appropriate S&P parent index are allocated to the pure growth basket, whereas stocks comprising the bottom one-third of the market cap of the appropriate parent index are allotted to the pure value basket (see Figure 12.3). In S&P's Pure Style benchmark indices, stocks are weighted in proportion to their relative style attractiveness. Stocks in S&P's pure growth index are weighted according to their growth scores; stocks in S&P's pure value index are weighted according to their value scores. These S&P Pure Style benchmark indices avoid the size bias induced by market cap weighting, since stocks are weighted in proportion to their relative style attractiveness.

S&P Pure Style benchmark indices
Performance standards for growth and value stocks precisely identified using S&P criteria.

Alternative **S&P Style benchmark indices** for the large-cap S&P 500, S&P MidCap 400, and the S&P SmallCap 600 divide the market cap of each parent index approximately equally into value and growth indices. S&P Style benchmark indices cover all stocks in the parent index, and use a conventional market cap-weighting scheme. The S&P Style benchmark indices are created by dividing the complete market cap of each parent index into approximately equal

S&P Style benchmark indices
Performance standards for growth and value stock components of popular S&P Indices.

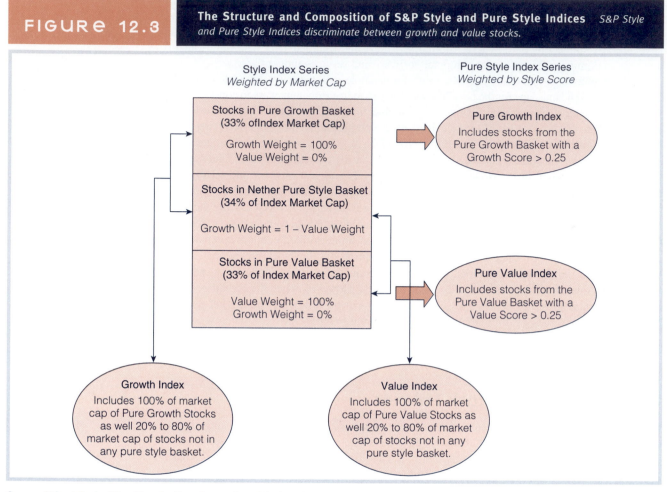

FIGURE 12.3

The Structure and Composition of S&P Style and Pure Style Indices *S&P Style and Pure Style Indices discriminate between growth and value stocks.*

growth and value index components using market cap weights. Because growth stocks tend to be bigger than value stocks, the S&P Growth Style index has fewer stocks than the S&P Value Style index. Stocks in the parent indices that do not fall into pure growth or pure value Style baskets have their market caps distributed between the growth and value indices. Because many companies share growth and value-stock characteristics, roughly one-third of each parent index market cap overlaps across the growth and value categories.

For the three-year period ending in 2005, 127 of the large-cap stocks in the S&P 500 were classified as pure growth stocks, 226 were pure value stocks, and 147 fell into the overlap category. For the S&P Midcap 400, 104 were classified as pure growth stocks, 163 were pure value stocks, and 133 fell into the overlap category. For the S&P Smallcap 600, 147 were classified as pure growth stocks, 250 were pure value stocks, and 203 were in the overlap category. S&P regularly publishes factor scores and portfolio weights for each component stock in the S&P Pure Style and Style Indices to make it easy for institutional investors and mutual funds to construct portfolios with matching risk and return characteristics. Turnover is rather modest at 10–25% per year, so matching benchmark index performance involves only modest transactions costs.

The key advantage of any style index series lies in its ability to discriminate between value and growth during market cycles where one style is favored over the other. Historical returns suggest that the S&P Pure Style benchmark indices differentiate in an exacting fashion between stocks with growth versus value attributes. For example, the eighteen-month period before March 2000 featured a robust upward move in the overall market that greatly favored growth stocks. After the bubble burst, the market crashed over the following eighteen-month period, and value stocks returned to favor. Figure 12.4 shows the perfor-

FIGURE 12.4

S&P 500 Style and Pure Style Indices Capture Market Cycles *Growth stocks do best in up markets. Value stocks offer protection during market downturns.*

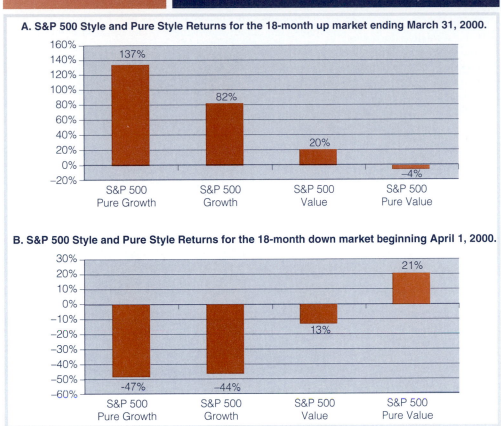

A. S&P 500 Style and Pure Style Returns for the 18-month up market ending March 31, 2000.

B. S&P 500 Style and Pure Style Returns for the 18-month down market beginning April 1, 2000.

Source: Sirkant Dash, "Unveiling the Next Generation of Style Indexing," Standard & Poor's, September 20, 2005. (**www2.standardandpoors.com/spf/pdf/index/style_nextgeneration_whiteppr.pdf**) © 2005 Standard & Poor's. Used with permission.

mance of the S&P 500 Style and Pure Style indices during the 18-month periods before and after the market peak on March 31, 2000. While both sets of S&P indices capture cycles in market performance by growth versus value stocks, the S&P Pure Style growth and values series provide the sharper contrast.

As Figure 12.4 illustrates, growth and value stocks can display distinctly different performance over the market cycle. Growth stocks tend to do best during robust bull markets, whereas value stocks do best during bear markets. Over a complete market cycle covering both bull and bear markets, baskets of value and growth stocks often give comparable risk-adjusted performance. For further information about S&P Style and Pure Style Indices, see: **www2.standardandpoors.com**.

Another important provider of growth and value style benchmarks for stocks of all sizes is the Russell Investment Group. Russell oversees a host of alternative U.S. benchmark indices, all of which are subsets of the large-cap Russell 3000. Remember, the Russell 3000 Index measures the performance of the 3,000 largest U.S. companies based on total market capitalization. The **Russell 3000 Growth Index** measures the performance of those Russell 3000 Index companies with higher price-book ratios and higher forecasted growth. The **Russell 3000 Value Index** measures the performance of those Russell 3000 Index companies with lower price-book ratios and lower forecasted growth. The small-cap Russell 2000 Index measures the performance of the 2,000 smallest companies in the Russell 3000 Index. The **Russell 2000 Growth Index** measures the performance of those Russell 2000 companies with higher price-book ratios and higher forecasted growth. The **Russell 2000 Value Index** measures the performance of those Russell 2000 companies with lower price-book ratios and lower forecasted growth. Russell estimates roughly

Russell 3000 Growth Index
Large-cap benchmark for growth stocks with relatively high price-book ratios and high forecasted growth.

Russell 3000 Value Index
Large-cap benchmark for value stocks with relatively low price-book ratios and low forecasted growth.

Russell 2000 Growth Index
Small-cap benchmark for growth stocks with relatively high price-book ratios and high forecasted growth.

Russell 2000 Value Index
Small-cap benchmark for value stocks with relatively low price-book ratios and low forecasted growth.

Is Value Riskier than Growth?

The long-term performance of value and growth stocks represents a quandary for efficient market enthusiasts. Since 1927, higher raw rates of return have been earned on stocks with relatively high accounting book values relative to market prices (value stocks). Despite general agreement that value stocks have outperformed growth stocks, various explanations have been offered to explain the phenomenon.

Efficient market enthusiasts argue that value strategies produce superior returns because they are fundamentally riskier than growth stocks. Consider one popular measure of risk, stock price beta. In the Fama-French three-factor capital asset pricing model framework, both the firm's size and the book-market ratio contribute to stock risk. Higher rates of return for both small-cap stocks and value stocks with high book-market ratios are thought to simply represent return premiums for riskier investments. According to this argument, both value stocks and growth stocks offer only a fair risk-adjusted rate of return.

The standard deviation of annual returns on value stocks tends to be lower than comparable rates of return for growth stocks. Value stocks also tend to perform better than growth stocks during economic recessions and bear markets. This suggests that value stocks are less risky than growth stocks. If value stocks are indeed less risky than growth stocks, higher rates of return for value stocks would be inconsistent with the efficient-market hypothesis. Research in behavioral finance has sought to better understand why less risky value stocks might actually outperform more risky growth stock portfolios. Recent results suggest that reverse S-shaped utility functions with risk aversion for losses and risk seeking for gains can explain such stock returns. Lower rates of return earned on large-cap stocks and growth stocks may reflect investors' twin desire for downside protection in bear markets and upside potential in bull markets.

At a minimum, such conflicts in recent research suggest that it is very difficult to square the stellar performance of value stocks with the efficient-market hypothesis.

See Thierry Post and Haim Levy, "Does Risk Seeking Drive Stock Prices? A Stochastic Dominance Analysis of Aggregate Investor Preferences and Beliefs," *Review of Financial Studies*, vol. 18, no. 3 (Fall 2005), pp. 925–953.

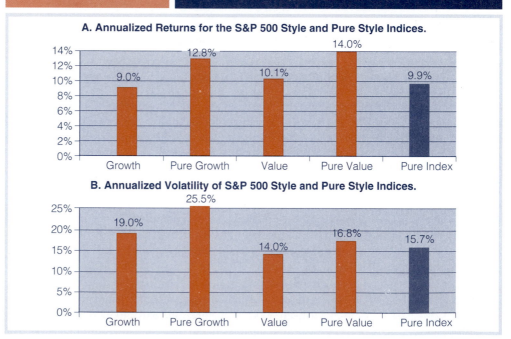

FIGURE 12.5

Risk and Return for S&P 500 Style and Pure Style Indices   *The higher returns observed for the S&P 500 Pure Style Indices come with higher volatility.*

A. Annualized Returns for the S&P 500 Style and Pure Style Indices.

Growth	Pure Growth	Value	Pure Value	Pure Index
9.0%	12.8%	10.1%	14.0%	9.9%

B. Annualized Volatility of S&P 500 Style and Pure Style Indices.

Growth	Pure Growth	Value	Pure Value	Pure Index
19.0%	25.5%	14.0%	16.8%	15.7%

Source: Sirkant Dash, "Unveiling the Next Generation of Style Indexing," Standard & Poor's, September 20, 2005. (**www2.standardandpoors.com/spf/pdf/index/style_nextgeneration_whitepppr.pdf**) © 2005 Standard & Poor's. Used with permission.

$3.8 trillion in benchmarked assets for the Russell family of U.S indices. Like the S&P Pure Style and Style Index benchmarks, Russell style benchmarks give investors an attractive means for judging the relative risk and reward characteristics of growth and value stocks. For further information about the wide variety of Russell style indices, see **www.russell.com**.

Growth Stocks Can Appear Too Attractive

Representativeness Bias

Psychology research shows that the human brain uses shortcuts to reduce the difficulty of analyzing complex information. Shortcuts allow the brain to organize and quickly process large amounts of information. These shortcuts allow us to estimate the correct answer before fully digesting all available information. Because investing is a difficult activity full of uncertainty, investors are apt to use shortcuts when analyzing investments information. However, these shortcuts can make it hard for investors to correctly analyze new information and can lead to inaccurate conclusions.

One flaw introduced by mental shortcuts, called representativeness bias, occurs when the brain makes the assumption that certain qualities of an item must imply other qualities for the same or a related item. For example, a clean used car is often thought to be well maintained and in good mechanical condition. The good quality of being clean causes used-car buyers to assume another attractive quality—good operating performance. **Representativeness bias** can affect investor conclusions by causing investors to confuse a good company with a good investment. Representativeness bias can also cause investors to wrongly extrapolate recent prices or historical returns into the future.

Good companies have high-quality management and generate strong earnings and revenue growth. Good investments are stocks that increase in price. However, all good companies do not necessarily represent good investments. For a stock to represent an attractive investment, it must increase in price as it meets and/or exceeds investor expectations concerning future performance. However, because outstanding financial performance tends to regress to the mean over time, firms with outstanding historical performance tend to have more mundane future performance. Popular firms with a history of consistent earnings tend to disappoint on an operating basis, and that disappointment can cause their share prices to fall and turn the firms into poor investments. Conversely, unpopular firms with a history of inconsistent earnings often surprise to the upside, and such surprises can cause their share prices to rise and turn the firms into good investments. Every investor knows that the objective is to buy low and sell high, but representativeness bias can cause people to do the opposite—buy after prices have risen and sell after large declines.

Representativeness bias
A perception that historical data will be repeated in the future.

Financial Analyst Bias

Financial analysts look at operating and financial market conditions, immediate and long-term prospects, management effectiveness, and industry outlook for the firms they evaluate. On the basis of this evaluation, analysts make earnings predictions and trading recommendations. Such predictions and recommendations can help investors decide to buy, hold, or sell the stock. Unfortunately, because of **financial analyst bias**, hold and sell recommendations are exceedingly rare on Wall Street. Analyst recommendations usually boil down to simple recommendations such as "accumulate," "buy," or "outperform."

For example, a summary of analyst recommendations for eBay is shown in Figure 12.6. Notice that 14 of the 28 analysts following eBay have a strong buy or a buy recommendation. Eleven analysts have issued a hold recommendation, and three have a sell or strong-sell recommendation. The relative lack of sell recommendations is not confined to just eBay. Wall Street analysts rarely issue sell recommendations. Only 0 to 5 percent of all stocks carry sell recommendations. Knowledgeable investors know that neutral or hold recommendations are about as negative as most analysts get.

Analysts hired by brokerage firms and investment banks are called **sell-side analysts** because their employers make money by selling stocks and bonds. Sell-side analysts publicize their earnings estimates and recommendations, get quoted in *The Wall Street Journal*, and appear on CNBC. Positive recommendations by sell-side analysts can help attract lucrative investment banking business. As a result, sell-side analysts face powerful incentives to maintain an optimistic bias in their buy, sell, and hold recommendations. In many cases, when an analyst really believes that a company has poor prospects, the analyst will simply drop coverage instead of publishing a sell rating.

Financial analyst bias
Tendency of Wall Street analysts to issue favorable recommendations.

Sell-side analysts
Analysts who work for brokerage firms or investments banks.

FIGURE 12.6 — Analyst Opinion for eBay, Inc.

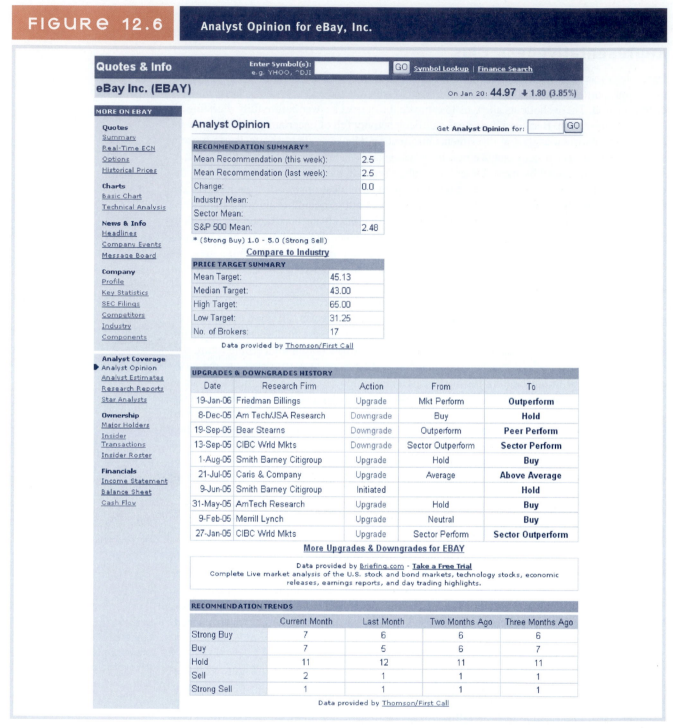

Source: Yahoo! Finance, **http://finance.yahoo.com**. Reproduced with permission of Yahoo! Inc. © 2006 by Yahoo! Inc. Yahoo and the Yahoo! logos are trademarks of Yahoo! Inc.

Buy-side analysts

Analysts who work for mutual funds and other institutions managing portfolios.

To avoid the optimistic bias of Wall Street analysts, pension funds and mutual funds often hire their own analysts to give them unbiased opinions. They are referred to as **buy-side analysts** because they are hired by investment firms that buy rather than sell stocks and bonds. Unfortunately, little buy-side research is made available to individual investors.

Expectations Management

Wall Street analysts offer consistently conservative earnings predictions. They make earnings predictions that end up being slightly lower than actual earnings. This might seem odd given that analysts are equally well known for being overly optimistic in making buy recommendations. (Buy recommendations swamp sell recommendations on Wall Street.) However, analysts need ready access to top management, and access is much easier to get when management regards a given analyst as friendly to management. Any company failure to meet analyst earnings expectations is typically viewed as a failure by top management. When companies exceed analyst earnings estimates, this is often viewed as an example of shrewd management. Therefore, analysts must be knowledgeable and have sufficient access to company operating information so as to be in a position to make sensible earnings forecasts. At the same time, analyst earnings forecasts must be sufficiently conservative so as to appeal to management and thus maintain analyst access to top management.

The best way to keep everybody happy in this ongoing game of expectations management is for analysts to provide earnings forecasts that are realistic enough to be only slightly exceeded. When management slightly exceeds analyst expectations, analysts get high marks for accuracy and management gets kudos for top performance. Management of large tech stocks, like Cisco Systems, Intel, and Oracle, are especially adept at earnings expectations management. At Cisco Systems, for example, the company was once known for exceeding quarterly earnings expectations by exactly one cent per share, quarter in and quarter out.

How does a company beat estimates when earnings take an unexpected downturn? The answer is simple: Just preannounce an earnings shortfall so that analysts can readjust their expectations to a lower and still beatable level. When companies preannounce bad news and analysts readjust downward their expectations, the company's stock price often takes a dive. However, when the official earnings announcement is made weeks later, the firm miraculously tends to beat the now-lowered estimate, and the company stock price begins its recovery.

Expectations management is alive and well on Wall Street!

See "Analysts React: GM Plan," *The Wall Street Journal Online*, February 7, 2006 (**http://online.wsj.com**).

Summary

■ Growth stocks are firms that investors believe will rapidly expand their operations over time. This expansion is measured by **top-line growth** and **EPS growth**. Few growth companies dominate large or rapidly growing markets. Most maintain their superior investment status through the successful exploitation of a **market niche**. A market niche is a segment of a market that can be successfully exploited through the firm's special capabilities. Few successful growth stocks achieve their status through the use of **financial leverage**, as measured by the **debt-to-assets ratio**. Highly successful companies focus on making new and exciting products. They are seldom distracted by **financial engineering**, or the sophisticated manipulation of the balance sheet through use of exotic forms of debt and equity financing.

■ Growth stock investors face important pitfalls to growth. **Customer loyalty risk** is high and market share stability is low in rapidly growing markets. Acquired companies often underperform as divisions of larger companies. Many rapidly growing companies fall victim to **merger risk** and suffer merger indigestion and investor disappointment. On Wall Street, a **roll-up** is a company that grows through constant acquisition. When roll-up companies stop the process of constant acquisition, they often fail to deliver operating efficiencies. Problems can also be avoided when investors seek to minimize **regulation risk**. The lack of a strict buying discipline leaves growth stock investors open to **price risk**, or the chance of overpaying for attractive companies.

■ Determining a reasonable price to pay for any growth stock is always difficult. Investors often use **variable-growth rate** valuation models. Growth stock investors rely on various simple valuation devices. An **investment rule of thumb** is a simple guide to investment valuation that has served the test of time. Legendary mutual fund investor Peter Lynch is famous for developing the so-called P/E-to-growth ratio, or **PEG ratio**. Generally speaking, a stock is fully valued if it sports a PEG ratio of 1 or more. **Growth at-a-reasonable-price (GARP) investors** seldom, if ever, buy growth stocks with PEG ratios greater than 1.

■ To effectively use the PEG ratio approach, investors must come up with simple but effective means for predicting EPS growth. In addition to using security analyst estimates, growth stock investors rely on financial information to estimate sustainable growth. The **retention rate** is the share of earnings retained to fund investment. The **internally sustainable growth** rate made possible by internally generated funds is calculated as the retention rate multiplied by ROE. Whereas the retention rate is the share of earnings retained to fund investment, the **dividend payout ratio** is the percentage of income paid out in the form of dividends. Holding all else equal, an appropriate P/E ratio will fall with an increase in the dividend payout ratio or a rise in the risk-adjusted required rate of return. The appropriate P/E ratio will rise with an increase in the ROE.

■ Many growth stock investors have a strong preference for **technology stocks** at the vanguard of important new innovations. Huge potential rewards await those companies able to successfully navigate in such a rapidly changing environment. Enormous risks face those companies unable to successfully anticipate and adapt to such challenges.

■ Growth stocks outperform value stocks during vigorous bull markets, but value stocks do better during bear markets. Over complete market cycles including both bull and bear markets, growth and value stocks have turned in very similar annual rates of return when measured using popular growth and value stock indices. **S&P Pure Style benchmark indices** are performance standards for growth and value stocks precisely identified using S&P criteria. **S&P Style benchmark indices** are performance standards for growth and value stock components of popular S&P Indices. The **Russell 3000 Growth Index** is a large-cap benchmark for growth stocks with relatively high price-book ratios and high forecasted growth. The **Russell 3000 Value Index** is a large-cap benchmark for value stocks with relatively low price-book ratios and low forecasted growth. The **Russell 2000 Growth Index** and the **Russell 2000 Value Index** are small-cap benchmarks for growth and value stocks, respectively. Investors are sometimes overly attracted to growth stocks because **representativeness bias** causes them to irrationally extrapolate recent prices or historical performance into the future. In fact, companies with outstanding historical financial performance can have subpar future performance. Conversely, companies with flawed operating histories sometimes turn in surprisingly good future performance. Simple extrapolation of past operating and stock market performance can lead investors to buy at high prices and sell at low prices. Because Wall Street analysts make money by encouraging individual and institutional investors to purchase stocks and bonds, **financial analyst bias** is present. Both hold and sell recommendations seldom issued by **sell-side analysts** are employed by brokers and investment bankers. **Buy-side analysts** are employed by mutual funds and other large institutional investors and tend to offer balanced assessments of company prospects to their employers.

Self-Test Problems

ST12.1 Can the companies listed below justify their P/E ratios? These dividend-paying stocks are all members of the S&P 500 Index. Yet they have very different P/E ratios. In April 2005, investors were willing to pay $48.20 to buy a dollar of Charles Schwab's earnings but would pay only $5.20 to buy a dollar of GM's earnings. Do Schwab's prospects justify this lofty valuation? Assess the expected return for each firm as implied by the P/E ratio.

Company	P/E Ratio	5-Year Avg. P/E Ratio	Payout Ratio (5-Year Avg.)	ROE (5-Year Avg.)	Analyst EPS Growth (Next 5 Years)
Charles Schwab Corp.	48.2	111.8	33	7.8	14.2
Stryker Corp.	40.6	41.9	6	21.1	20.0
Paychex, Inc.	37.1	51.7	53	29.1	15.9
Molex, Inc.	22.2	52.2	15	8.2	14.3
Intel Corp.	19.1	55.4	18	15.2	15.8
Pfizer Inc.	18.6	42.8	58	19.4	9.5
General Motors Corp.	5.2	12.3	54	12.2	5.2
Centex Corp.	7.7	6.4	3	21.2	15.4
Countrywide Financial Corp.	8.7	9.8	9	20.1	12.2
Pulte Homes, Inc.	9.0	8.2	3	17.9	13.9
Freddie Mac	9.1	12.0	15	28.5	11.8
The Bear Stearns Companies Inc.	9.7	10.1	11	15.5	10.3

Solution

Note that the current P/E ratios of these firms are not artifacts of temporary earnings and stock price fluctuations. The high P/E ratio firms have had high P/E ratios for the past five years.

Equation 12.7 shows the relationship between valuation, growth, payout ratios, and expected returns:

$$\frac{P}{E} = \frac{D/E}{k - g}$$

Rearranging gives

$$k = \frac{1 - b}{P/E} + g$$

What is the firm's anticipated growth rate? Expected return can be computed either by using the analyst forecast for growth or by computing the internally sustainable growth rate using the firm's ROE. At first glance, it appears that analysts believe that the high P/E ratio firms will grow at a faster rate than the low P/E ratio firms. However, the ROEs of the two groups appear similar. The following table shows the computed expected returns using analyst forecasts and also reports the internally sustainable growth rate.

Company	k, from Analyst Forecast	Sustainable Growth, from Payout and ROE
Charles Schwab Corp.	14.9%	7.3%
Stryker Corp.	20.1	9.9
Paychex, Inc.	17.3	24.7
Molex, Inc.	15.0	6.7
Intel Corp.	16.7	6.4
Pfizer Inc.	12.6	19.4
General Motors Corp.	15.6	11.8
Centex Corp.	15.8	19.3
Countrywide Financial Corp.	13.2	19.5
Pulte Homes, Inc.	14.2	15.2
Freddie Mac	13.4	25.4
The Bear Stearns Companies Inc.	11.4	15.5

Note that the high P/E ratio firms can internally fund a slower growth rate than the low P/E firms. Indeed, some of the highly valued firms may need to obtain additional capital in order to grow at the rates analysts are forecasting. The expected returns implied from the analyst forecasts are higher for the high P/E firms. Does this sound reasonable? Remember that while growth firms outperform value firms at times, value has outperformed growth over the long run. This analysis suggests that while their growth justifies higher P/E ratios, these highly valued firms may be valued just a little too high.

ST12.2 Apple Computer, Inc. (AAPL), is a major developer, manufacturer, and marketer of personal computers and peripheral and consumer products for sale primarily to the business, creative, education, government, and consumer markets. An especially popular item with consumers has been the Apple iPod, a pocket-sized ultralight device used to store and play music, videos, and computer games. Foreign sales account for about 40 percent of total revenues, and 5.9 percent of revenues are spent on research and development. According to information obtained from Yahoo! Finance, AAPL had a 2005 price of $39.87, expected EPS of $1.25, expected EPS growth of 20 percent per year, and a typical P/E ratio of 30. AAPL does not pay a dividend. To create an expected price range for 2010, use EPS growth estimates of

10 to 20 percent per year in 2.5 percent increments. To create discounted present values, use a risk-adjusted discount rate of 20 percent. Based on these expectations, set up a spreadsheet to estimate a typical range in price for AAPL in 2010 (five years hence). Was AAPL a buy, sell, or hold at a 2005 price of $39.87?

 Solution

A spreadsheet analysis of AAPL is shown below.

(1) Intrinsic Economic Value of Stock, $(6)/[1 + (8)^5]$	(2) Current EPS	(3) Expected EPS Growth	(4) Expected EPS in 5 Years, EPS $(1 + g)^5$	(5) Expected P/E ratio	(6) Expected Stock Price in 5 Years, (4) × (5)	(7) Risk-Adjusted Discount Rate, k	(8) Discount Rate – Dividend Yield (7) – 0.0%
24.27	1.25	10.0%	2.01	30.00	60.39	20.0%	20.00%
27.16	1.25	12.5	2.25	30.00	67.58	20.0	20.00
30.31	1.25	15.0	2.51	30.00	75.43	20.0	20.00
33.75	1.25	17.5	2.80	30.00	83.99	20.0	20.00
37.50	1.25	20.0	3.11	30.00	93.31	20.0	20.00

Based on the assumptions given, a typical price range for AAPL in 2010 is $60.39 to $93.31 and a reasonable range for the 2005 value of AAPL is $24.27 to $37.50. Because the 2005 price for AAPL of $39.87 was above the range specified for AAPL's intrinsic economic value, AAPL represented a *sell* in 2005 and was expected to return less than the 20 percent-per-year cost of capital over the 2005-2010 time frame. Pull up a current price for AAPL on the Internet and see how shareholders who followed such an approach have fared since 2005.

Questions and Problems

12.1 Describe the general approach of a growth stock investor. How is growth stock investing different from value investing?

12.2 What are the essential features of a growth stock?

12.3 List five or more criteria identified by T. Rowe Price as important characteristics of investment opportunities.

12.4 Investors in growth stocks are subject to price risk. Describe this variety of risk, and explain why exposure to price risk is of particular concern to growth stock investors.

12.5 Explain the PEG ratio and the PEG ratio rule of thumb.

12.6 A fast-growing company paid a dividend this year of $1 per share and is expected to grow at 20 percent for three years. Afterward, the growth rate will be 7 percent. If the required rate is 9 percent, what is the value of this stock?

12.7 Pfizer Inc. is a major producer of pharmaceuticals and other health care products. If a typical P/E for Pfizer is 25 and present earnings per share of $2.15 are expected to grow over the next five years at a rate of 10 percent per year, what is Pfizer's projected stock price in five years?

12.8 The Home Depot, Inc. (HD), operates a chain of retail building-supply and home-improvement "warehouse" stores across the United States and Canada. It has a return on equity of 20 percent and is expected to earn $2.50 and pay a dividend of $0.35 per share during the coming year. Calculate the amount of internally funded growth anticipated for HD.

12.9 Go to the Standard & Poor's Market Insight Web site at **www.mhhe.com/ edumarketinsight** and enter the ticker "EL" for Lauder Estee Companies. Obtain the profitability data in the "Excel Analytics" section. Using the net ROE and dividend payout ratio information, compute and graph the internally funded growth rate for the past nine years.

12.10 At the end of 2002, investors considered the past three years of returns for stocks and bonds. Stocks earned -9.1, -11.9, and -22.1 percent in 2000, 2001, and 2002, respectively. Long-term Treasury bonds earned 20.1, 4.6, and 17.2 percent, respectively. Given representativeness bias, how would investors be expected to reallocate their portfolios between stocks and bonds in 2003?

12.11 Suppose Merck & Company will earn $2.15 per share and pay a $0.68 dividend in the next 12 months. Merck will also earn a 20 percent return on shareholders' equity. If a reasonable risk-adjusted discount rate for Merck is 16 percent, what P/E ratio would growth-at-a-reasonable-price investors deem appropriate for Merck?

12.12 Intel Corporation (INTC) is a leading manufacturer of integrated circuits used in personal computers, communications, industrial automation, military, and other electronic equipment. INTC had a 2005 price of $24.36, an expected dividend per share of $0.32, expected EPS of $1.20, expected EPS growth of 19.5 percent per year, and a typical P/E ratio of 25. To create an expected price range for 2010, use EPS growth estimates of 10 to 20 percent per year in 2.5 percent increments. To create discounted present values, use a risk-adjusted discount rate of 15 percent. For simplicity, you may assume that the current dividend yield of 1.31 percent (= $0.32/$24.36) will be maintained over the 2005–2010 period. Based on these expectations, set up a spreadsheet to estimate a typical range in price for INTC in 2010 (five years hence). Was INTC a buy, sell, or hold at a 2005 price of $24.36?

12.13 The long-term performance of the S&P 500, value stocks, and growth stocks can be seen at the BARRA Web site (**www.mscibarra.com**). Click on the Research Indexes link and see how the performance of value stocks compared to the performance of growth stocks over the past quarter-century. Which type of environment is best for growth versus value stocks?

12.14 Some financial Web sites have preset screens for various strategies. Go to the Yahoo! Finance preset screens (**http://screen.finance.yahoo.com/presetscreens.html**) and run the "Large Cap Growth" screen. What are the criteria used? Which firms meet these criteria?

12.15 Go to the Standard & Poor's Market Insight Web site at **www.mhhe.com/ edumarketinsight** and enter the ticker "ORCL" for Oracle Corporation. In the S&P "Stock Report" section, click on the Wall St. Consen. link. Discuss the distribution of the analyst buy-sell opinions both currently and over time. Does there appear to be an analyst bias?

12.16 An industry is currently growing at twice the rate of the overall economy. New competitors are entering the industry, and the formerly high profit margins have begun to decline. The life-cycle stage that best characterizes this industry is:
a. Mature growth
b. Pioneering development
c. Rapid accelerating growth
d. Stabilization and market maturity

12.17 An analyst applied the DuPont equation to estimate ROE for a company with:

Equity turnover	4.2
Net profit margin	5.5 percent
Total asset turnover	2.0
Dividend payout ratio	31.8 percent

The company's return on equity is *closest to*:
a. 1.3 percent
b. 11.0 percent
c. 23.1 percent
d. 63.6 percent

12.18 Two companies are identical except for substantially different dividend payout ratios. After several years, the company with the lower dividend payout ratio is *most likely* to have:
a. Lower stock price
b. Higher debt-equity ratio
c. Less rapid growth of earnings per share
d. More rapid growth of earnings per share

12.19 Financial leverage differs from operating leverage because financial leverage accounts for a company's:
a. Use of debt
b. Variability in sales
c. Use of plant and equipment
d. Variability in fixed operating costs

12.20 A company's return on equity is greater than its required rate of return on equity. The earnings multiplier (FI/E) for that company's stock is *most likely* to be positively related to the:
a. Risk-free rate
b. Market risk premium
c. Earnings retention ratio
d. Stock's capital asset pricing model beta

INVESTMENT APPLICATION

The "Nifty 50"

Not since the early 1970s has a small group of favored stocks come close to dominating investor interest as "Cisco and the Kids" did during the late 1990s. Those were the days when stocks such as Coca-Cola, Disney, Eastman Kodak, McDonald's, and Philip Morris had price-earnings multiples as high as 95. All were visible components of the so-called Nifty 50.

The Nifty 50 was a group of 50 premier growth stocks that became stock market darlings during the early 1970s. At the market peak in 1972, the group of Nifty 50 stocks sold at a P/E ratio of 41.9, or more than double the market average of 18.1. Each of these stocks had proven growth in revenues, earnings, and dividends. Virtually none had experienced a dividend cut during the post-World War II period. All had sufficiently large market capitalizations to allow large institutional investors to buy as much of them as their portfolios could hold. They represented the ultimate in one-decision stock investing. An investor simply had to buy and hold. No matter how high Nifty 50 stock prices seemed relative to revenue, earnings, or any other fundamental factors, any perception of being overvalued was sure to be temporary. Superior rates of growth would bail out any buyer, no matter how high the price seemed at the time of purchase. Nifty 50 investors could not lose, or so the story went until the vicious bear market of 1972–1974.

From a bull market peak of 1,036.27 on December 11, 1972, the DJIA crashed to 577.60 on December 6, 1974. This bone-chilling drop of 44.3 percent for the market was relatively mild when compared with the devastation suffered by Nifty 50 darlings. Coca-Cola dove 66.9 percent, from 149¾ to 49⅝; Disney cascaded down 91.3 percent, from 236¾ to 20½; Eastman Kodak tumbled 58.9 percent, from 149¼ to 61¼; McDonald's plunged 63.2 percent, from 77⅜ to 28½; while Philip Morris plummeted 59.4 percent, from 118¼ to 45. The devastation experienced by stockholders of these Nifty 50 companies does not represent the worst of the story. Former Nifty 50 companies such as Burroughs, Digital Equipment, Joseph Schlitz Brewing, and MGIC Investment are gone. Their status as "bulletproof" growth stocks not only failed to protect them from disturbing volatility in a full-fledged bear market but also left them down and out.

The plunge in prices for the original Nifty 50 during the severe bear market correction of 1972–1974 has long been viewed as just punishment for absurdly valued stocks and the naïve investors willing to buy them. Until recently, no one rose to defend such excesses. No one, that is, until Jeremy Siegel, a professor of finance at the University of Pennsylvania's Wharton School, became part of the Nifty 50 story in 1994 when he published an eminently readable book on the stock market titled *Stocks for the Long Run*. In his book, Siegel laid out a bullish argument for Nifty 50 equity investing and calculated that an investor paying top dollar for the Nifty 50 in late 1972 would have earned nearly the same returns over the next 25 years as someone holding the S&P 500. Siegel calculated that the original Nifty 50 produced a 12.5 percent annualized return, only slightly behind the 12.7 percent for the S&P 500. "Good growth stocks are expensive, but they can be worth the price," said Siegel.

Siegel's book added fuel to the firestorm of controversy surrounding valuations of the 1990s version of the Nifty 50, the high-flying high-tech stocks, especially those tied to the Internet. When asked what he thought of the new Nifty 50, Siegel said the notion that good growth companies can be worth more than 50 times earnings has been proved by the facts. As presented in Table 12.5, Siegel showed the "warranted" P/E of the original Nifty 50, using a stock price then that would result in a return equal to the S&P 500 over the ensuing 25-plus years. Coca-Cola, for example, traded for a P/E of 46.4:1 in late 1972 but was actually worth a P/E of 82.3:1 given its market-beating results since then. That being said, it is clear that some of the best performances turned in by former Nifty 50 stocks have been generated by lower-multiple consumer products companies, such as Gillette, Pfizer, and Philip Morris. Nearly all the superhigh P/E stocks lagged behind, including Avon, International Flavor & Fragrances, and Polaroid. Siegel proclaims that only a handful of the best growth stocks in the past have been worth more than 70 times earnings. Microsoft is one stock that could well live up to its lofty P/E of 70, yet it is worth remembering that IBM was once thought to be invincible. Of course, that was when Microsoft was a baby.

a. Siegel's research shows that technology companies have had a tough time maintaining their edge over the long run. Why is that?

b. Back in 1972, the Nifty 50 represented an important group of stocks, but the market was dominated by non-Nifty industrials such as General Motors and Ford. In 2000, the market was dominated by the largest technology stocks, such as $450 billion market cap Microsoft Corporation (P/E = 65:1), $215 billion Cisco Systems, Inc. (P/E = 100:1), and $195 billion Lucent Technologies, Inc. (P/E = 75:1). Describe how the enormous size of these high-tech giants limits their future growth opportunities.

www.mhhe.com/hirschey1e

TABLE 12.5 — The Nifty 50: Were They Worth It?

Company	Annualized Return (%)	1972 P/E Ratio	1998 Warranted P/E Ratio
Philip Morris	18.8	24.0	68.5
Pfizer	18.1	28.4	72.3
Bristol-Myers	16.8	24.9	49.8
Gillette	16.8	24.3	45.4
Coca-Cola	16.2	46.4	82.3
Merck	15.9	43.0	76.3
Heublein	15.7	29.4	47.0
General Electric	15.7	23.4	37.8
Schering-Plough	15.7	48.1	79.8
Squibb	15.5	30.1	48.7
PepsiCo	15.0	27.6	41.1
Eli Lily	14.0	40.6	50.4
American Home Product	13.8	36.7	43.6
Procter & Gamble	13.2	29.8	32.4
Revlon	13.1	25.0	26.9
Johnson & Johnson	12.6	57.1	56.6
Anheuser-Busch	12.5	31.5	30.8
Chesebrough Ponds	12.5	39.1	38.2
McDonald's	12.1	71.0	63.2
First National City (Citigroup)	11.4	20.5	16.9
Walt Disney	11.3	71.2	53.6
American Express	10.8	37.7	28.0
Dow Chemical	10.6	24.1	17.7
American Hospital Supply	10.6	48.1	33.1
Schlumberger	10.2	45.6	28.6
Upjohn	10.0	38.8	25.3
AMP	9.7	42.9	25.0
Texas Instruments	9.1	39.5	20.2
3M	8.5	39.0	20.6
Baxter	8.1	71.4	29.6
ITT	8.0	15.4	8.6
IBM	7.7	35.5	17.1
J.C. Penney	7.3	31.5	14.8
Sears Roebuck	7.3	29.2	14.2
International Flavors & Fragrance	7.0	69.1	27.7
Jos. Schlitz Brewing	6.6	39.6	15.6
Xerox	6.5	45.8	19.4
Haliburton	6.3	35.5	12.7
Lubrizol	6.0	32.6	12.1
Eastman Kodak	5.5	43.5	16.1
Simplicity Patterns	5.3	50.0	8.7
Digital Equipment	5.2	56.2	9.7
Avon Products	5.0	61.2	24.2
Louisiana Land & Exploration	4.4	26.6	8.6
Black & Decker	2.8	47.8	10.5
Kresge (Kmart)	2.1	49.5	10.1
Burroughs	(0.4)	46.0	6.6
Polaroid	(0.1)	94.8	11.9
Emery Air Freight	(1.9)	55.3	8.0
MGIC Investments	(8.6)	68.5	4.8
Nifty Fifty	12.5	41.9	
S&P 500	12.7	18.9	

Source: Barron's, March 15, 1999, pp. 21–22. Copyright 1999 Dow Jones Inc. Used with permission.

Technical Analysis

Wall Street traders often look at price and volume trends to guide short-term buy and sell decisions. While contrarian traders might hold off on buying when a stock price has spiked up on heavy volume, momentum players look to buy stocks that go up on rising volume. The interpretation of key signals obviously differs, but many contrarian and momentum players pay close attention to price and volume information. Even long-term retail investors like to consult price and volume information. Both fundamental investors and growth-stock advocates often look to recent price and volume information to help guide their buy and sell decisions. Look at Yahoo! Finance or MSN Money and note the prominent role played by price and volume charts. The same is true in the print and broadcast media. Notice how *The Wall Street Journal* makes prominent use of price-volume charts; CNBC and other financial networks also make liberal use of splashy graphics. The graphical display of price-volume information has obvious and widespread appeal.

Despite the pervasive popularity of eye-catching displays of price-volume information, many academics remain skeptical about the usefulness of technical analysis. As a result, some mainstream academics regard technical analysis as antiquated and simply ignore it in their investments classes. We understand that perspective but believe that technical analysis is an interesting and useful part of a well-rounded study of investments for two reasons. First, part of becoming knowledgeable about investments involves becoming familiar with popular terms and methods of analysis. After all, technical analysis has a language of its own that is frequently used in the media. The analysis of price and volume information is certainly popular, and students need to know what the buzz is about. Second, even if the effectiveness of technical analysis is controversial, popular use of technical analysis is an interesting aspect of investor behavior. Why do investors consult charts? In light of skepticism about the usefulness of technical analysis, it is worth asking: Why does every brokerage report start with a price-volume chart?[1]

[1] Scott Patterson, "Fear and Loathing on Wall Street," *The Wall Street Journal Online*, January 20, 2006 (**http://online.wsj.com**).

CHAPTER OBJECTIVES

- Learn technical analysis tools.
- Identify stock price patterns.
- Know how trading volume relates to price patterns.
- Learn technical indicators for measuring market activity.
- Understand how investor sentiment is measured and used.

What Is Technical Analysis?

Supply-Demand Focus

Technical analysis
Study of historical price and volume information to forecast future prices.

Technicians
Technical analysts.

Chartists
Another name for technicians.

Technical analysis involves the study of price-volume information and is based on a simple premise. Technical analysts believe that changes in the short-run supply and demand for a stock cause prices to change. Instead of focusing on the intrinsic or economic value of a stock as fundamental analysts do, technical analysts try to understand, measure, and predict the forces of supply and demand. Technical analysts, typically referred to as **technicians**, are sometimes referred to as **chartists** because they frequently rely on charts for their analysis. Many profess to know nothing about the underlying assets depicted on their charts and graphs. Others see technical analysis merely as a means for identifying attractive purchase or sale prices and a useful supplement to fundamental analysis.

To value a company, fundamental analysts strive to understand the underlying business. What are the company's expected revenues, profits, and cash flows? What are its opportunities, threats, and growth potential? Such detailed company-specific operating and valuation information is of much less interest to the technical analyst. Indeed, some technical analysts consider company operating and valuation information irrelevant. For the dedicated technical analyst, all relevant information is contained in past share price and trading volume information. Technical analysts turn to the charts to tell them whether the optimism that drives buyer demand for a stock is mounting or fading. They also look to charts to examine whether the pessimism for a stock that fuels seller supply is mounting or diminishing.

Fundamental analysts treat the stock of each company as a unique asset. They seek to determine its intrinsic value, expected return, risk, and return correlation with other assets and groups of assets. Technicians treat the stock of each company like a commodity. In economic equilibrium, market prices are determined by the perfect balance of supply and demand under a specified set of market conditions. Technical analysts focus on understanding and predicting supply and demand relationships for stocks, bonds, and commodities by studying the dynamics of changing price and volume information and by assessing who is buying and selling.

Visual Approach

In the depiction of price movements, a basic question must be addressed: How can changes in supply and demand be measured, characterized, and evaluated? Lots of free and valuable low-cost information is available today about who is buying and who is selling in many different types of markets. This wasn't always the case. Early in the 20th century, such information was expensive and hard to come by. Until very recently, there was no Internet or even easy access to computer-generated and electronically stored information. Laws regulating the dissemination of vital information are also a relatively recent phenomenon. When companies were not required to disclose key financial information on a regular basis, and when standards were weak for what meager information they did divulge, there were big obstacles to the conduct of insightful fundamental analysis. Early in the 20th century, the information necessary for insightful fundamental analysis was not widely available. For several years, there was one current and reliable source of information for stock market investors—the stock market itself. The New York Stock Exchange has long collected and distributed stock price quotes and volume. Years ago, investors would literally sit at their local brokerage firms and watch stock price and volume information on what was referred to as the "ticker tape."

Ticker tape information is not useful for determining a firm's fundamental value, but might be helpful in assessing short-term supply and demand conditions for its stock. Because ticker tape price and volume information is a natural by-product of the trading process, it has been widely available since the start of organized trading. Therefore, technical analysis is a much older profession than fundamental analysis. Since the beginning, technicians have used market price-volume information to develop measures of market activity that go beyond just the reporting of market index levels and overall trading volume information. Technicians want to know more than just whether the stock market went up or down today. Technicians study how many companies rose in price versus how many declined during the trading period. If the number of firms rising in price tends to decline over time, this could lead to an interpretation that demand is weakening. That might indicate a market top is approaching. Conversely, if the number of firms falling in price tends to decline over time, this could mean that supply is drying up and that a market bottom is approaching. In the search for repeated patterns that might be used to accurately predict the future, technicians adopted a visual approach based on two-dimensional graphs of stock price and volume information. This process, called **charting**, is still the basis of much technical analysis.

Charting
Use of two-dimensional price and volume graphs to analyze market behavior and anticipate future price movements.

Modern proponents of technical analysis face the problem of having to efficiently condense and interpret widely available price-volume information. Examples of the types of data analyzed and methods employed can be found by going to various sites on the Internet (see Table 13.1) including the Market Technicians Association (MTA) Web site (Figure 13.1). The MTA is a national association for market professionals interested in technical analysis; it sponsors national conferences and oversees a certification program. Passing the three exams for the Chartered Market Technician (CMT) certification allows market professionals to signal clients that they have demonstrated proficiency in a broad range of technical analysis subjects.

TABLE 13.1 Popular Web Sites for Technical Analysis Information

Name	Site Address	Information Available
Big Charts	bigcharts.marketwatch.com	Free investment research Web site providing access to interactive charts, quotes, industry analysis, and intraday stock screeners, as well as market news and commentary.
Chartpatterns	www.chartpatterns.com	Specializes in recognizing price patterns in stocks and commodities; focuses on charting techniques.
DecisionPoint.com	www.decisionpoint.com	Over 500 unique charts and data sets.
InvesterTech	www.investertech.com	Extensive graphs and technical tools available; excellent ability to conduct analysis using moving averages, momentum, and many more graphing tools over long and short time periods.
StockCharts.com	http://stockcharts.com	Extensive graphical tools and a great educational Web site.
Stock Technical Analysis	www.stockta.com	Useful trend analysis with breakout levels and moving averages.

FIGURE 13.1   The Market Technician's Association Sponsors an Informative Web Site

©2005 Market Technicians Association, Inc.

Theory versus Practice

The study of technical analysis is interesting because it is an important part of investment behavior. Lots of traders seem to use technical trading rules to guide trading decisions. Lots of individual investors also appear interested in technical analysis. Whenever a stock analyst discusses an investment opportunity on television, the discussion seems to always be accompanied by a price chart that depicts recent price and volume information. Technical analysis is also interesting for what it says about investor behavior and the role of investor psychology in stock, bond, and commodity markets.

Technical analysis is a controversial subject in academia and on Wall Street. Many academics and Wall Street practitioners spent the last half of the 20th century working from an efficient-market hypothesis (EMH) perspective (see Chapter 6). According to the EMH, the current market price is the best available estimate of the intrinsic value of the firm. Moreover, short-run changes in price and volume information appear to be essentially random in nature. Trading rules based on historical price and volume information are fruitless in a perfectly efficient market. If markets are highly efficient, technical trading tools will not enable investors to earn positive abnormal returns. Of course, if markets are perfectly efficient, or even semi-strong-form efficient, most fundamental analysis would be fruitless as well. However, research has uncovered some limitations of the EMH in the past decade, thus emboldening dedicated technicians. If markets are not fully efficient, technical tools may have merit.

For several decades, many academics (including those who wrote textbooks) believed that markets were very efficient. They rarely taught their students about technical analysis. More recently, many scholars have started to question the EMH. The field of behavioral finance offers a variety of explanations as to why people may sometimes react irrationally and make irrational investment decisions. If irrational investor behavior sometimes moves prices, then technical analysis may offer tools to help visualize how stock prices are impacted. Indeed, some stock price movements over time are hard to reconcile with the EMH.

Technical Analysis of Commodities

Technical analysis is popular among some stock market speculators. It is even more fashionable among traders in fast-moving commodities markets. In commodities markets, short-term price swings depend on hard-to-predict changes in supply and demand conditions and market psychology. In a real economic sense, supply and demand conditions for all commodities depend on the actions of producers, consumers, and speculators. In some markets, speculative demand and supply play a vital role in determining prices in both the short and the long runs. In gold and silver markets, for example, changes in speculative demand and supply have an enormous influence. In all commodity markets, changes in market psychology can cause speculators to greatly exacerbate short-term price swings caused by fundamental factors.

In a real economic sense, commodity demand and supply conditions are determined by the pace of economic growth, rate of inflation, changes in weather, and a host of other hard-to-predict factors, such as the balance of imports and exports. While savvy stock pickers can focus on company valuation in light of hard-to-imitate competitive advantages, commodities have no special characteristics. By definition, commodities are perfect substitutes. This makes commodity prices extremely sensitive to slight changes in demand and supply conditions or to shifts in market psychology.

Consistently accurate prediction of short-term price changes is extraordinarily difficult, if not impossible. An unexpected drought in the Midwest can have a big negative effect on the corn crop; an unexpected freeze in Florida can devastate the orange crop. In either case, big price swings will result. However, if one cannot accurately forecast the weather, and nobody seems able to forecast the weather, how is it possible to accurately predict changes in commodity supply and demand conditions? The short answer is simple: You can't.

Lacking any special economic insight or forecasting ability, many commodity traders turn to technical trading rules based on hypothesized patterns in historical prices. This is a risky business. Trends in commodity prices can quickly reverse and cause enormous losses for trend-following speculators. Before speculating on the price of oil, for example, you might ask yourself a simple question: What do I know about oil that Exxon Mobil Corp. does not know?

See Ciara Linnane, "Crude Falls to 2006 Low," *The Wall Street Journal Online*, February 14, 2006 (**http://online.wsj.com**).

For example, on January 14, 2000, the Dow Jones Industrial Average hit an all-time intraday high of 11,908.5, traded as low as 11,506.43, and achieved a record close of 11,722.98. On that day, the difference between the daily trading high and the daily trading low for the DJIA was a remarkably high 3.43 percent. That's enormous volatility for a major stock market index on a day with little in the way of meaningful economic or political news. Moreover, the huge amount of volatility experienced on January 14, 2000, was typical of the first 10 trading days of January 2000, when the difference between the daily trading high and the daily trading low for the DJIA *averaged* a stunning 3.65 percent per day! In a U.S. stock market with an average annual total rate of return (including dividends) of roughly 12 percent per year, why should investors and traders shift so wildly from buying to selling and back to buying? Is it possible that conventional valuations are sometimes established on the basis of investor psychology and are thus prone to change violently as the result of a change in opinion that may have little to do with underlying economic values?

Consider the trading news five years to the day after the DJIA reached its peak. On January 14, 2005, *The Wall Street Journal* reported that traders blamed the market's tepid performance at the start of the year to gushing oil prices, disappointing unemployment reports, and uninspiring 2005 profit forecasts. Just as important, traders blamed investor nervousness. "It kind of snowballed" late in the day, said stock trader Michael Driscoll at New York brokerage firm Bear Stearns. "It is not one particular item that causes this undue pressure on the market; it is a series of one seemingly innocuous event after another, and suddenly you are down 112 points. A lot of people are watching for the early tone of the market to set the tone for the year, and it obviously isn't going the bulls' way."

In an imperfectly efficient stock market in which investor psychology plays an important role, fundamental valuation is not all that matters. In an imperfectly efficient stock market, how investors react matters. If investment news and information makes investors optimistic, they will put buying pressure on stocks and prices will rise. If investment news and information makes investors pessimistic, prices will fall.

Plotting the Market

Support and Resistance

A basic tenet of technical analysis is that trends in supply and demand tend to persist. Another core belief is that momentum is to be expected in terms of changes in supply and demand. From a profit-making standpoint, the trick is to identify and profitably follow the current trend while looking for signs that the current trend is ending and that a new trend is about to begin. When a change in trend is imminent, a change in strategy must occur. Technical analysis is a trading tool used to guide short-term buy and sell decisions.

Consider the recent stock history for the Federal National Mortgage (FNM) Association. Popularly referred to as "Fannie Mae," FNM is a source of financing for home mortgages in the United States. The company was chartered by Congress to provide liquidity in the secondary mortgage market to increase the availability and affordability of homeownership for low-, moderate-, and middle-income Americans. During late 2004, the stock came under pressure when federal regulators questioned the company's accounting for financial derivatives. In December 2004, the company's top management was forced to resign. A daily price chart for FNM is shown in Figure 13.2. Note that in 2005 the stock price continued to struggle. Also depicted is the 50-day price moving average (MA). Each point on a **50-day moving average** shows the average price over the previous 50 trading days (roughly two calendar months). Use of the **200-day moving average** is also popular among technicians; the points show average prices over roughly one year of trading activity. Notice that moving averages show much less volatility than the actual price graph. This makes it easier for technical analysts to surmise the underlying trend in prices. From a visual perspective, technical analysts see that the price trend is reversing itself when the actual price line crosses over an important moving average. When the actual price line crosses above its moving average, a bull trend has started and a buy signal is generated. As shown in Figure 13.2, FNM experienced a breakout to the upside in May 2005 and a severe breakout to the downside in July 2005. Technical analysts generally expect that after such breakouts the price will continue moving in the direction of the breakout.

In Figure 13.2, notice how the stock price for FNM fell below the 50-day moving average during July. Technical analysts regard this as bearish. The graph also depicts a **resistance line** and a **support line**. The resistance line represents price points at which selling pressure (supply) has emerged in the recent past and can therefore limit a stock's up-

50-day moving average
Average stock price over the previous 50 trading days (roughly two calendar months).

200-day moving average
Average stock price over 200 trading days (roughly one year).

Resistance line
Graphical depiction of price points at which selling pressure (supply) has emerged in the recent past.

Support line
Graphical depiction of price points at which additional demand for the stock has emerged in the past.

FIGURE 13.2   Technical Analysts Focus on Price Resistance and Support

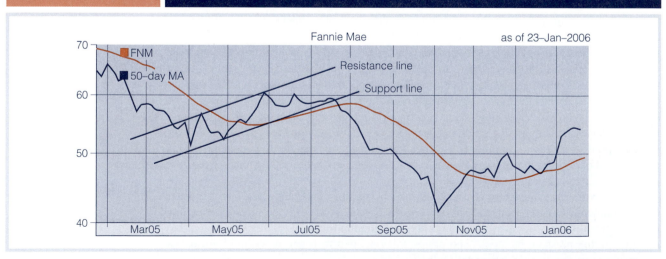

Fannie Mae   as of 23–Jan–2006

Source: Yahoo! Finance, **http://finance.yahoo.com**. Reproduced with permission of Yahoo! Inc. © 2006 by Yahoo! Inc. Yahoo and the Yahoo! logos are trademarks of Yahoo! Inc.

side potential. However, once the current stock price has risen through the resistance line, the price is predicted to continue rising. A price support line connects relatively low points on a stock price graph and represents prices at which additional demand for the stock has emerged in the past. The support line also represents price points at which buying pressure (demand) is expected to emerge in the future to limit a stock's downside risk. Technical analysts believe that as price increases to approach the resistance line, more investors want to sell, thereby increasing supply and limiting future price increases. On the other hand, as prices decline toward the support line, more investors want to buy, thereby increasing demand and limiting downside risk.

Taken together, the resistance line and the support line form a **channel** trend for the price. According to technical analysts, as prices bounce between the upper and the lower bounds of the channel, excess demand or supply will eventually get used up and the price will break out of the channel. A breakout through the support line is bearish, while a breakout to the upside of the resistance line is bullish. Whenever a channel breakout occurs, technical analysts say that a reversal of the historical trend is at hand. Notice that in July 2005, the price of FNM crossed both the 50-day moving average and the support line. This "double crossing" was followed by a severe price decline.

Channel
Area between resistance and support lines.

===== Try It! =====

Compute the 10-day moving average of Symantec's stock price.

Date	SYMC
16-Sep-05	$21.93
19-Sep-05	21.79
20-Sep-05	21.75
21-Sep-05	21.32
22-Sep-05	21.19
23-Sep-05	21.20
26-Sep-05	20.86
27-Sep-05	21.26
28-Sep-05	21.47
29-Sep-05	22.13
30-Sep-05	22.66
3-Oct-05	22.82
4-Oct-05	22.56
5-Oct-05	22.59
6-Oct-05	21.56
7-Oct-05	21.92
10-Oct-05	22.15
11-Oct-05	22.06
12-Oct-05	21.98
13-Oct-05	21.67
14-Oct-05	22.09
17-Oct-05	22.25
18-Oct-05	22.19
19-Oct-05	22.68
20-Oct-05	22.66

(continued)

Solution

e**X**cel

Using Excel,

◇	A	B	C	D
1	Date	SYMC	10-day MA	
2	16-Sep-05	$21.93		
3	19-Sep-05	$21.79		
4	20-Sep-05	$21.75		
5	21-Sep-05	$21.32		
6	22-Sep-05	$21.19		
7	23-Sep-05	$21.20	=AVERAGE(B2:B11)	
8	26-Sep-05	$20.86		
9	27-Sep-05	$21.26		
10	28-Sep-05	$21.47		
11	29-Sep-05	$22.13	$21.49	
12	30-Sep-05	$22.66	$21.56	
13	3-Oct-05	$22.82	$21.67	
14	4-Oct-05	$22.56	$21.75	
15	5-Oct-05	$22.59	$21.87	
16	6-Oct-05	$21.56	$21.91	
17	7-Oct-05	$21.92	$21.98	
18	10-Oct-05	$22.15	$22.11	
19	11-Oct-05	$22.06	$22.19	
20	12-Oct-05	$21.98	$22.24	
21	13-Oct-05	$21.67	$22.20	
22	14-Oct-05	$22.09	$22.14	
23	17-Oct-05	$22.25	$22.08	
24	18-Oct-05	$22.19	$22.05	
25	19-Oct-05	$22.68	$22.06	
26	20-Oct-05	$22.66	$22.17	

Transaction Cost Problem

High trading costs are a common impediment to the profitable use of technical analysis. When technical analysis is used to generate trading signals as prices bounce back and forth through 50-day or 200-day moving averages, excessive amounts of trading and burdensome trading costs can result.

For example, consider Figure 13.2 and the possibility of using the 50-day moving average as a trading guide. Traders in FNM got a buy signal in late October 2005 as the stock price fell below the 50-day moving average, only to receive an ambiguous signal when it touched the 50-day moving average a few weeks later. When buy and sell signals follow each other quickly, traders must reverse positions and incur transaction costs.

The profitable use of channels and moving averages requires that the stock price move in a convincingly new direction before a buy or sell signal is given. The problem for technically motivated traders is to define the word *convincingly*. The laws of physics say that an object in motion remains in motion until an opposing force affects it. An object at rest stays at rest until a force moves it. Traders who focus on **stock price trends** bet on the propensity for a stock that is rising in price to continue to rise until some new demand or supply force takes effect. A stock falling in price is expected to continue to go down until some force for change is exerted. Many technicians gauge stock price momentum using returns for a company relative to its industry or the overall market. Positive relative returns suggest upward momentum and constitute a buy signal. Negative relative returns suggest downward momentum and represent a sell signal.

Stock-price trend
Propensity for a stock that is rising in price to continue to rise or for one falling in price to continue to fall until some new demand or supply force takes effect.

Dow Theory

Importance of Investor Psychology

Dow Theory was developed in the late 1890s by Charles Dow, one of the founders of *The Wall Street Journal* and its first editor. From 1902 to 1929, William Hamilton, Dow's successor as editor, published over 250 stock market predictions using theories proposed by Dow. Dow's technical basis for stock market forecasts came to be known as Dow Theory, and it was articulated in a 1922 book called *The Stock Market Barometer*. Dow Theory proposes that the market moves in long bull and bear market trends that are hampered by short-term reversals. Hamilton wrote, "The pragmatic basis for the theory, a working hypothesis, if nothing more, lies in human nature itself. Prosperity will drive men to excess, and repentance for the consequences of those excesses will produce a corresponding depression." In other words, Hamilton believed that bull and bear markets are at least partially the result of investor psychology.

A main tenet of Dow Theory is that there are three levels of market trends: primary, secondary, and tertiary. Major, long-term movements are **primary trends**. They are known as bull and bear markets and can last anywhere from less than one year up to several years. Bull markets are thought to have three phases: the initial revival of confidence, response to improved economics, and then rampant speculation. The three phases of bear markets are thought to be the abandonment of speculation, selling due to declining economics, and then the distressed selling of sound stocks. **Secondary trends** are short-term moves in the market that run contrary to the primary trend and usually last from three weeks to three months. A secondary trend in a bull market is often referred to as a **market correction** and seen as a temporary decline in an ongoing bull market. A secondary trend in a bear market is typically referred to as a **bear trap** and is reflected by a temporary increase in prices followed by a further sharp decline in the market. Bear traps trick investors into buying too early by making them falsely believe that a new bull market has begun. Very short-term stock market trends that reflect minor price moves are called **tertiary trends** and have very little long-term forecasting value under Dow theory.

Dow Theory Doctrine

Proponents of Dow Theory argue that although the best strategy for many investors is a buy-and-hold approach, there is always value in knowing whether the market's primary trend is bullish or bearish. They assert that no market timing tool does a better job of keeping investors on the right side of the primary trend than the Dow Theory.

  Basic tenets of Dow Theory are:

- Only the DJIA and DJTA matter. Fluctuations in the daily closing prices of the DJIA and DJTA take into account all hopes, disappointments, and knowledge of market participants.

Dow Theory
Idea that market movements can be predicted by studying trends in the DJIA and DJTA.

Primary trends
Bull and bear markets that last anywhere from less than one year up to several years.

Secondary trends
Short-term moves in the market that run contrary to the primary trend and usually last from three weeks to three months.

Market correction
Temporary decline in an ongoing bull market.

Bear trap
Temporary increase in prices followed by a further sharp decline in the market.

Tertiary trends
Very short-term stock market trends that reflect minor price moves.

FIGURE 13.3 | **Dow Theory Focuses on Confirmatory Trends in the DJIA and DJTA** *The success of Dow Theory rises and falls on much more than the simple confirming nature of the transports and the industrials. Nevertheless, a simple graphical view can illustrate the pain inflicted as a result of ignoring a nonconfirmation signal such as existed in both March 2003 and January 2004.*

Source: The Dow Theory Project Website, **www.dowtheoryproject.com/fcharts.php.**

- Movements of the DJIA and DJTA should be considered together. Conclusions based on the movement of one average, unconfirmed by the movement of the other, are often erroneous.

- The primary trend remains intact until a change in that trend has been given by the theory. The last major signal remains in force until a new signal develops. While many believe that a bull market must always be moving to new highs, the market can undergo extended periods of sideways or lackluster trading. If the last major signal under the theory was bullish, the primary bull market trend remains in force until a bear market signal is given.

For many market participants, the simplicity of Dow Theory is a primary virtue. Figure 13.3 shows that a bullish indication occurs when rallies in both the DJIA and DJTA penetrate previous high points. A bull market has begun when both the DJIA and DJTA have moved to new highs. After a secondary market correction, if both the DJIA and the DJTA fail to move to new highs and instead fall to new lows, a bear market is signaled. The difficulty, of course, lies in knowing which points represent "significant" highs or lows for these major averages.

One reason for the popularity of Dow Theory is that, in addition to considering the role of market psychology, it rests on a simple economic premise. An uptick in economic activity can result in an uptick in stock prices for industrial companies as perhaps-bloated inventories are depleted. However, any sustainable economic expansion requires the shipment of newly manufactured goods to retailers and end users. A sustainable market advance is under way when investors see business improving for both industrial and transport companies. Dow Theory has also stood the test of time because it avoids the frequent "whipsawing" that occurs with many market timing models. Dow Theory signals are long-term in nature, usually lasting one year or longer.

Street Smarts 13.2

Super Bowl Superstition

The Green Bay Packers defeated the Kansas City Chiefs 35–10 in the first Super Bowl on January 15, 1967. The rest is stock market history because, according to Wall Street folklore, the direction of the stock market is predicted by the winner of the Super Bowl. According to the "Super Bowl indicator," a triumphant team from the old American Football League (now the American Football Conference, or AFC) foreshadows a down year for the Dow Jones Industrial Average, but a winner from the old NFL (now the National Football Conference, or NFC) means the bulls are coming to Wall Street.

Through 2005, the Super Bowl indicator has been on the money 31 out of 39 times, a success rate of 79.4 percent. Nevertheless, the recent record has been spotty. 2000 and 2001 wins by the NFC's St. Louis Rams and the AFC's Baltimore Ravens wrongly promised favorable years for the market. (The AFC Ravens count as an NFC team because the original Cleveland Browns were an NFL club.) The NFC's Tampa Bay Bucca-

neers won in 2003 and the DJIA rose, but the market went up despite a victory by the AFC's New England Patriots in 2004. In 2005, the Patriots won again, and the DJIA fell as predicted by the indicator. In 2006, both the Pittsburgh Steelers and the Seattle Seahawks counted as "bullish" teams. The Seahawks are in the NFC, and the Steelers are an original NFL team. That made the 2006 Super Bowl a win-win situation for investors!

The success of the Super Bowl indicator can be easily explained. Of the 24 teams that made up the postmerger NFL, 10 (41.6 percent) came from the AFL and 14 (58.3 percent) came from the old NFL. More often than not, a Super Bowl winner tends to come from the old NFL. Because stocks usually go up, it's not surprising to find a spurious positive correlation between old NFL winners of the Super Bowl and up markets. It is surprising that some superstitious investors actually believe the Super Bowl winner *causes* the market to rise or fall.

See Susanne Craig, "Heads I Win, Tails I Win: A Super Prediction for Stocks in '06," *The Wall Street Journal Online*, February 4, 2006 (**http://online.wsj.com**).

Chart Formations

Price Patterns

Technical analysts believe that specific price patterns tend to emerge when the forces of supply and demand change. Changes in trend are due to a shift in supply or demand. As these shifts sort themselves out over time, they create consistent patterns. Over the past hundred years, a variety of price patterns have been identified and categorized. Technical analysts look for these familiar patterns and use them to predict the future direction of price changes.

Perhaps the most popular chart price pattern is known as the **head and shoulders** (Figure 13.4). As its name implies, the head-and-shoulders pattern is made up of a left shoulder, neckline, head, and right shoulder. While still in an uptrend, the left shoulder forms a peak that marks the high point of the current trend. After making this peak, a decline ensues to complete the formation of the shoulder. The low of the decline usually remains above the trend line, keeping the uptrend intact. From the low of the left shoulder, an advance begins that exceeds the previous high and marks the top of the head. After peaking, the low of the subsequent decline marks the second point of the neckline. The low of the decline usually breaks the uptrend line, putting the uptrend in jeopardy. The right shoulder peak is lower than the head (a lower high) and usually in line with the high of the left shoulder. While symmetry is preferred, sometimes shoulders can be out of whack. The decline from the peak of the right shoulder should break the neckline. The neckline forms by connecting low points from the formation of each shoulder prior to the formation of the head. Depending on the relationship between the two low points, the neckline can slope up, slope down, or be horizontal. The slope of the neckline will affect the pattern's degree of bearishness—a downward slope is more bearish than an upward slope. During a bull market trend, the formation of the head-and-shoulders pattern signals a reversal to a bear market trend. A sell signal occurs when the price falls below the neckline after the right shoulder forms.

Head and shoulders
Popular price chart pattern that signals a reversal to a bear market trend.

While the head-and-shoulders price formation pattern is one of the most popular price formations studied by chartists, dozens of other price patterns also come under scrutiny. Examples of popular price patterns are shown in Figure 13.5. **Reversal patterns** that indicate an important change in trend include the bump and run, double top, double bottom, head and shoulders top, head and shoulders bottom, falling wedge, rising wedge, rounding bottom, triple top, and triple

Reversal pattern
Change in trend signal.

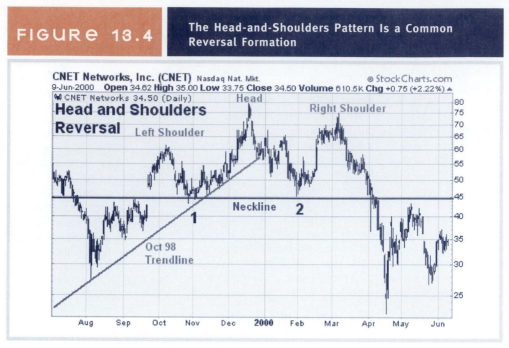

FIGURE 13.4 | The Head-and-Shoulders Pattern Is a Common Reversal Formation

Source: StockCharts.com, **http://stockcharts.com**

Continuation pattern
Persistence of the underlying bullish or bearish trend signal.

bottom. **Continuation patterns** that indicate a persistence of the underlying bullish or bearish trend include the cup with handle, flag, symmetrical triangle, ascending triangle, descending triangle, price channel, rectangle, measured bear move, and measured bull move. As their names suggest, the study of reversal and continuation patterns is an interesting and colorful aspect of stock market lore. For more details on charting, a number of Web sites can be consulted. StockCharts.com is an especially colorful and interesting source for such information. Chartists use price patterns to make future price predictions, but they do not take such predictions as literal truth. Instead, they think of such forecasts in terms of probabilities. *If* the bearish prediction of a head-and-shoulders pattern is correct 66.7 percent of the time, investors making decisions based on this pattern would be correct twice as often as they are wrong. When dealing with the uncertainty of the stock market, charting is one tool that technical analysts believe provides investors with methods for profitably assessing the underlying forces of supply and demand.

Try It!

Go to StockCharts.com, Yahoo! Finance, or some other quote service and check out the recent price history for CNET. Was technical analysis helpful in predicting the future in this case? In particular, note that once support is broken, technical analysts believe it is common for the same support level to turn into resistance. Sometimes, but certainly not always, the price will return to the support break and offer a second chance to sell. After breaking neckline support, the projected price decline is found by measuring the distance from the neckline to the top of the head. This distance is then subtracted from the neckline to reach a price target. Any price target should serve as a rough guide, and other factors should be considered as well.

Market Cycles

Economists frequently talk about the business cycle. For economic and other reasons that are only partially understood, the economy seems to move on a rhythmic cycle from boom to bust and back to boom again. Writing in the 1920s, a Russian economist, Nikolai Kondratieff, speculated that the

FIGURE 13.5 | Common Price Patterns and Predictions

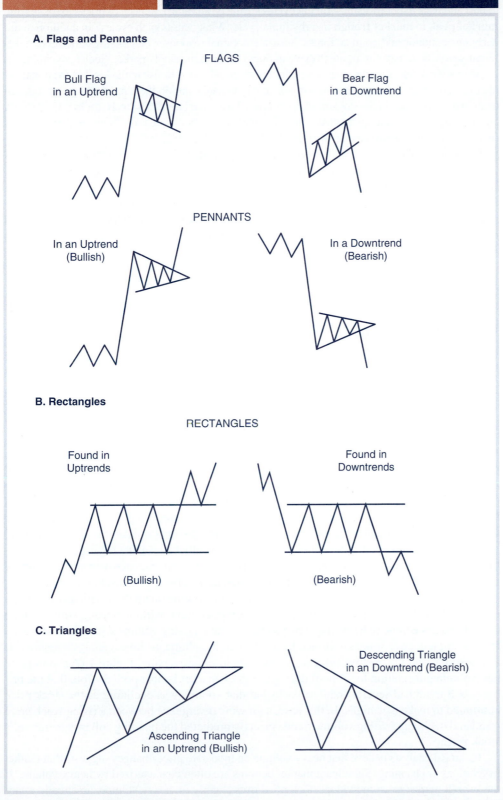

A. Flags and Pennants

FLAGS

Bull Flag
in an Uptrend

Bear Flag
in a Downtrend

PENNANTS

In an Uptrend
(Bullish)

In a Downtrend
(Bearish)

B. Rectangles

RECTANGLES

Found in
Uptrends

Found in
Downtrends

(Bullish)

(Bearish)

C. Triangles

Descending Triangle
in an Downtrend (Bearish)

Ascending Triangle
in an Uptrend (Bullish)

Source: Chartpatterns.com, **www.chartpatterns.com.**

Kondratieff wave
Long, 60-year economic cycle.

Market cycles
Observable tendency of prices to rotate.

Market peak
Price high point.

Market trough
Price low point.

world economy evolved in a 60-year cycle. Today, this is known as the **Kondratieff wave**, or K-wave. Many technicians believe that the stock market also moves in a rhythmic cycle from boom to bust and back to boom again. **Market cycles** are the observable tendency of prices to rotate from **market peak** to **market trough** in a rhythmic cycle. What causes such cycles? In addition to underlying economic and political forces, human emotional responses that manifest themselves differently over time may contribute to cyclical fluctuations in the stock market. Social psychologists know that it can take months, even years, for crowd psychology to rise to the level of irrational exuberance, decline to despondent pessimism, and then rise again. In the United States, episodes of irrational exuberance in the stock market occurred during the late 1960s (tech stocks), 1972 (Nifty 50 era), late 1980s (energy stocks), and late 1990s (tech stocks again). Stock market investors seemed unusually pessimistic at stock market lows in 1974, 1982, 1990, and 2002.

Investor interest in stock market cycles is also cyclical. The 1930s and 1940s saw lots of investor interest in stock market cycles as people sought an explanation for the 1929 stock market crash. By the 1960s, the study of cycles became passé. Cycles again came into vogue during the 1970s and 1980s as investors sought some explanation for the market's long-term malaise. When the stock market erupted on a long-term advance in 1982, investors appeared to lose interest in the study of stock market cycles. Why study cycles when the stock market seems to be going in a straight line and that line is up?

Volume

Volume Measures

While price information can be useful for identifying trends that are the consequence of changes in supply and demand, the volume of trading also has the potential to provide useful information. When investors are uncertain, they do nothing. That is why trading volume has a tendency to diminish during periods of sideways movement or near a market reversal. Trading volume information can give clues as to the possible future direction of prices by measuring the level of conviction among buyers and the sellers.

Technical analysts often interpret volume information in light of underlying price trends. For the primary trend to continue, volume should increase in the direction of that trend. Technical analysts believe that if the primary trend in prices is up, then volume should be higher on up days and lower on down days. Alternatively, if the primary price trend is down, volume should be higher on down days. It is often taken as a warning that the trend in place is losing steam and that a reversal could be ahead if volume starts to decline. In a bull market trend, when trading volume is higher on dips than on rallies, technicians typically believe that buying pressure is diminishing and sellers are becoming more aggressive. Any large divergence between the primary price trend and the trend in volume is typically taken as a warning of a pending reversal.

Technical analysts do more than simply contrast up volume on up days with down volume on down days. The most positive signal is a bullish price trend with increasing volume on up days. For a price trend to be bullish, price should climb on rising volume with minor setbacks. If a new high in price is not confirmed by a new high in volume, technical analysts regard this as a warning that the positive price trend may be close to reversing. Figure 13.6 shows price and volume information for Yahoo! during the stock market bubble period. Note that the primary bull trend had several small setbacks but that volume was declining as the stock price continued to make new highs. In this case, a growing divergence between a rising stock price trend and declining trading volume trend correctly predicted the pending collapse in Yahoo!'s stock price.

Technical analysts believe that heavy volume on moderate price changes suggests that market psychology is changing. Significant market bottoms are often characterized by heavy volume. If the overall market or an individual stock price rises slightly on heavy volume, an already established bear trend is thought to be in the process of reversing. A similar interpretation is given during bull trends. If a price trend seems to have stalled out in a long bull market, it is called a final **blow off** if volume continues to rise when prices have stalled. This is seen as a bearish signal.

Blow off
Spike in volume when prices have stalled.

FIGURE 13.6	Declining Trading Volume Was a Warning for Yahoo! Investers

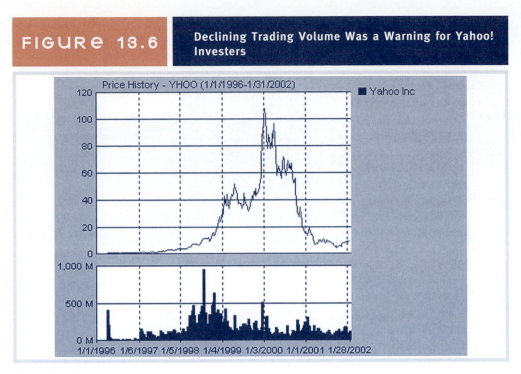

Source: MSN Money.

Money Flows

To measure the level of conviction among buyers and sellers, technical analysts keep a close eye on **money flow** indicators. Money flows measure the relative buying and selling pressure each day on share prices. Money flow data are used by many technical analysts and some fundamental analysts to discern what the "smart money" is doing and to determine whether price trends are sustainable. Table 13.2 compares the dollar value of uptick trading activity with the dollar value of downtick trading activity. An **uptick trade** is one at a higher price than the previous trade, while a **downtick trade** is one at a lower price than the previous trade. The money flow dollar value is computed by multiplying the price by the number of shares traded, and the net gain or decline at the end of the day is the money flow for that stock or groups of stock. The **up-down ratio** reflects the value of uptick trades relative to the value of downtick trades in millions of dollars. Percent changes are calculated from the prior day's 4 p.m., EST, closing price. Money flow data are also commonly reported for institutional **block trades** (trades of 10,000 shares or more) and nonblock trades for individual stocks and various major stock market indexes. Blocks reflect trading by institutional investors.

For example, suppose a stock has five trades in sequence at $20, $20 (no change), $21 (uptick), $19 (downtick), and $20 (uptick). It would end those trades unchanged in price. However, if 100 shares traded at $21, then 1,000 shares at $19, and then 100 shares at $20 at the close, the uptick money flow would be $4,100 and the downtick money flow would be $19,000. The net inflow for those trades would be $4,100 minus $19,000, or a net negative $14,900, indicating more activity at lower prices. This suggests that despite the flat price trend, sellers were acting with more conviction than buyers, and the outlook is thought to be negative for the stock's future price trend.

The intuition behind the use of money flow information is quite simple: For every buyer there is a seller, but they may not agree on price. It is the urgency of the purchase or sale that is the determining factor in terms of the market price. A greater volume of stock changing hands on an uptick indicates that buyers are being relatively more aggressive at accumulating stock than the sellers are at dumping it. Because more aggressive investors can be expected to carry the price trend over time, positive money flow figures are taken as bullish.

Money flow
The relative buying and selling pressure each day on share prices.

Uptick trade
Trade at a higher price than the previous trade.

Downtick trade
Trade at a lower price than the previous trade.

Up-down ratio
Value of uptick trades relative to value of downtick trades.

Block trades
Trades of 10,000 shares or more.

Daily money flows are calculated and widely reported for all 30 issues in the DJIA, the Dow Jones U.S. Total Market Index, the Standard & Poor's 500 Index, and the Russell 2000 Index, a measure of small-market-capitalization issues. Individual stocks with the largest net up or down money flow for each trading day are also tallied and reported on a daily basis in *The Wall Street Journal*.

TABLE 13.2	**Momentum Traders Keep a Close Watch on Money Flow Figures** *The table below gives money flow figures and the corresponding figures for block trades for the stocks with the largest net gains and losses in money flows on January 23, 2006. Money flows are calculated as the dollar value of composite uptick trades minus the dollar value of downtick trades. The up–down ratio reflects the value of uptick trades relative to the value of downtick trades (in $ millions). Percent change is calculated from the prior day's 4 p.m., EST, closing price.*

A. Money Flows—Top Gainers

Company	Exchange	Last Price	Percent Change	Money Flow	Uptick Volume	Downtick Volume	Ratio	Block Trades	Uptick Volume	Downtick Volume	Ratio
Citigroup	NYSE	46.12	0.12	126.27	182.51	56.23	3.25	116.01	136.41	20.40	6.69
SPDR	AMEX	126.68	0.26	108.21	645.32	537.10	1.20	117.69	475.88	358.19	1.33
MerLyn	NYSE	72.70	0.60	60.70	118.50	57.81	2.05	64.88	81.76	16.88	4.84
HewlettPk	NYSE	31.65	0.31	58.46	84.90	26.43	3.21	57.57	64.89	7.32	8.86
AmExpress	NYSE	52.37	0.93	55.04	87.34	32.30	2.70	54.90	65.43	10.53	6.21
Google	NASD	441.14	13.64	52.41	1,265.66	1,213.25	1.04	26.61	26.61	0	0
iShrRu2000	AMEX	70.86	0.45	35.77	93.49	57.72	1.62	34.00	59.20	25.20	2.35
Wal–Mart	NYSE	45.68	0.43	33.54	128.23	94.69	1.35	38.49	77.67	39.18	1.98
ChespkeEngy	NYSE	33.56	0.35	32.40	68.34	35.95	1.90	30.39	38.35	7.96	4.82
AppleCptr	NASD	77.79	0.12	30.72	255.84	225.12	1.14	29.47	56.74	27.27	2.08
SemiConHldrs	AMEX	37.49	0.15	29.38	85.66	56.28	1.52	28.67	57.55	28.88	1.99
ExxonMobil	NYSE	61.36	0.16	28.99	130.17	101.18	1.29	32.12	54.94	22.81	2.41
FedDeptStr	NYSE	70.95	0.55	27.95	43.66	15.71	2.78	19.10	19.10	0	0
RegBkHldrs	AMEX	138.61	0.32	25.57	40.02	14.46	2.77	24.53	28.55	4.01	7.11
Alcoa	NYSE	28.92	−0.26	24.03	37.88	13.85	2.74	26.19	27.85	1.66	16.78
Averages		**89.06**	**1.21**	**48.63**	**217.83**	**169.21**	**2.04**	**46.71**	**84.73**	**38.02**	**4.50**

B. Money Flows—Top Decliners

Company	Exchange	Last Price	Percent Change	Money Flow	Uptick Volume	Downtick Volume	Ratio	Block Trades	Uptick Volume	Downtick Volume	Ratio
GenElec	NYSE	33.00	−0.29	−99.90	116.00	215.90	0.54	−96.14	69.03	165.17	0.42
iShrSP600	NYSE	60.83	0.50	−87.85	6.63	94.48	0.07	−88.99	2.95	91.94	0.03
Disney	NYSE	26.01	0.49	−73.50	29.08	102.58	0.28	−74.28	16.17	90.45	0.18
Schlumbgr	NYSE	124.35	−1.65	−65.88	129.15	195.03	0.66	−56.85	31.68	88.52	0.36
Danaher	NYSE	54.48	0.13	−41.10	5.62	46.73	0.12	−41.46	0.81	42.27	0.02
CVS	NYSE	27.45	0.49	−30.08	15.71	45.80	0.34	−30.47	7.69	38.16	0.20
McAfee	NYSE	23.25	−4.38	−28.57	49.45	78.02	0.63	−22.76	30.87	53.63	0.58
EMC	NYSE	13.58	0.32	−27.08	35.13	62.21	0.56	−26.67	23.56	50.24	0.47
UtdHlthGp	NYSE	58.46	0.47	−24.13	53.01	77.15	0.69	−15.40	18.01	33.41	0.54
Amgen	NASD	75.04	0.14	−23.45	68.13	91.57	0.74	−25.85	20.33	46.18	0.44
GoldmanSachs	NYSE	133.45	0.58	−22.16	60.75	82.90	0.73	−7.05	6.09	13.14	0.46
DowChem	NYSE	42.51	0.08	−19.68	26.23	45.91	0.57	−20.07	8.96	29.04	0.31
SeagateTch	NYSE	26.19	0.62	−17.98	22.33	40.30	0.55	−18.48	6.72	25.20	0.27
HealthNet	NYSE	48.87	0.18	−17.23	3.60	20.83	0.17	−16.40	0	16.40	0
Viacom B	NYSE	43.12	−0.03	−17.06	14.52	31.58	0.46	−17.56	6.07	23.62	0.26
Average		**52.71**	**−0.16**	**−39.71**	**42.36**	**82.07**	**0.47**	**−37.23**	**16.60**	**53.82**	**0.30**

Source: The Wall Street Journal Online (**http://online.wsj.com**), January 23, 2006. Copyright © 2006. Dow Jones Co. Used with permission.

Technical Indicators

Market Breadth

Even during a rampant bull market, not all stocks rise in price. Individual stocks seldom rise in a straight line, and neither does the overall market. Some stocks and market sectors flourish during the early part of the business cycle (e.g., health care companies), while others do best while an economic recovery is well under way (e.g., capital equipment manufacturers). In order for the overall market to be classified as healthy, the bulk of stocks must be rising in price on rising volume. **Market breadth** measures how many issues are rising relative to the number of issues that are declining (see Table 13.3). In a healthy bull market, most companies are experiencing an increase in price on rising volume. Bear markets suffer from "bad" breadth because relatively few stocks are rising. If companies from only one sector of the market are driving the market higher, then such a rally also suffers from bad breadth. Unless breadth increases, technical analysts worry that the bull market is aging or nearing an end.

Some of the most widely used market breadth measures are based on advance-decline data. At the end of the trading day, each trading venue reports the number of stocks that advanced in value, declined, and remained unchanged. In Table 13.3, for example, 2,000 Nasdaq stocks advanced in price while 1,018 declined in price. Nasdaq's **advance-decline ratio** for that trading day is the number of firms that advanced in price divided by the number that declined, or 1.96 (= 2,000/1,018). The advance-decline ratio is considered by technical analysts as good measure of the overall market's direction. Technicians consider it bullish if the advance-decline ratio is greater than 1 and bearish if the ratio is less than 1.

The **advance-decline line** is the ongoing sum of the number of advancing stocks minus the number of declining stocks. Like the advance-decline ratio, it is used as a measure of market strength because a rising advance-decline line reflects the fact that there are more advancing issues than declining issues. If the advance-decline line moves lower, there are more declining issues than advancing issues. If the advance-decline line is rising, advancing issues are dominating declining issues and the market is then said to be healthy. If the advance-decline line is falling, then the market is said to be unhealthy. Most of the time, the advance-decline line and the overall market move higher and lower together. At times, however, the overall market can continue to move higher despite a drop in the advance-decline line. This is taken by technicians as a warning of a pending reversal in the underlying price trend.

Market breadth
Measure of how many issues are rising relative to the number of issues that are declining.

Advance-decline ratio
The number of firms that advanced in price divided by the number that declined on a given trading day.

Advance-decline line
Ongoing sum of the number of advancing stocks minus the number of declining stocks.

Market Imbalance

The advance-decline line gives technical analysts a useful broad measure of daily changes in supply and demand. A common indicator of market imbalance was developed by Richard Arms and

TABLE 13.3	Market Breadth Measures			
	NYSE	**Amex**	**Nasdaq**	**OTC BB**
Advancing issues	2,228	583	2,000	761
Declining issues	1,073	408	1,018	785
Unchanged issues	135	89	162	432
Total issues	**3,436**	**1,080**	**3,180**	**1,978**
New highs	248	62	189	161
New lows	36	20	34	155
Up volume	1,585,999,550	243,224,612	1,188,539,914	505,671,486
Down volume	875,383,650	106,015,090	805,549,381	554,470,602
Unchanged volume	41,660,370	31,142,100	72,784,810	794,041,622
Total volume	**2,503,043,570**	**380,381,802**	**2,066,874,105**	**1,854,183,710**

Source: Yahoo! Finance, **http://finance.yahoo.com/advances**, January 24, 2006.

TRIN (*trading index*) ratio
Common indicator of market imbalance.

Overbought
Insufficient future demand at market top.

Oversold
Insufficient future supply at market bottom.

is called the **TRIN (*trading index*) ratio** or the Arms index. The TRIN ratio is a indicator used to detect **overbought** and **oversold** levels in the market. The TRIN ratio combines advance and decline data with upside and downside volume information. The ratio is computed as

$$\text{TRIN} = \frac{\text{no. of advancing stocks/no. of declining stocks}}{\text{up volume/down volume}} \tag{13.1}$$

TRIN provides a look at the volume that is trading in the advancing and declining stocks. If the number of advancing issues equals the number of declining issues and total up volume equals total down volume, the TRIN ratio is 1.0. Ratios less than 1.0 are considered bullish; ratios over 1.0 are considered bearish. Generally speaking, technical analysts consider a TRIN < 0.65 as very bullish, 0.65 < TRIN < 0.90 as bullish, 0.90 < TRIN < 1.10 as neutral, 1.10 < TRIN < 1.35 as bearish, and a TRIN > 1.35 as very bearish. On the other hand, some technicians argue that TRIN ratios at the furthest extremes become contraindicative. A ratio of 1.80 might be argued as bullish because it indicates an extremely oversold condition. Most technical analysts use TRIN charts with 20-day moving averages as a short-term barometer for the market or individual stocks. Generally speaking, a rising TRIN is bearish, and a falling TRIN is bullish. Unusually large volume among advancing issues will create a low TRIN ratio and is a sign of intense buying demand. Heavy volume among declining issues causes a high TRIN ratio and suggests intense selling pressure.

Try It!

Compute and interpret the New York Stock Exchange TRIN ratio using the data in Table 13.3.

Solution

Substituting the data from Table 13.3 into Equation 13.1, the TRIN ratio is

$$\text{TRIN} = \frac{2{,}228/1{,}073}{1{,}585{,}999{,}550/875{,}383{,}650} = \frac{2.076}{1.812} = 1.15$$

This value gives a bearish reading.

Momentum

Momentum Indicators

Momentum
The rate of change, or velocity, of a price change.

Momentum strategies based on the technical analysis of price and volume information have become increasingly popular with both retail investors and professionals, like hedge funds. Momentum is typically measured by the speed of price change. Advocates of momentum strategies consider momentum to be a leading indicator of change in a stock's price trend. In the stock market, momentum players believe stock price and volume trends behave much like a pendulum. Drop a pendulum and it starts down slowly, picking up speed as gravity pulls it down. After the pendulum swings through its lowest point, its speed slows until it stops and reverses direction. A momentum investor buys a stock that is in an upward trend and follows various momentum indicators to assess whether the trend may be ending soon. Several different indicators have been developed to track momentum.

   Momentum indicators are designed to identify the relative enthusiasm of buyers and sellers. Some momentum indicators compare the change in price over a period of time, while others measure deviations from trend lines. The simplest momentum indicator is the *rate-of-change (ROC) indicator*. The ROC shows the amount prices have changed over the given time period, often over 10 to 12 days. A rising ROC indicates expanding momentum, a bullish signal, while a falling ROC is a bearish signal of declining momentum. The lower the ROC, the more undersold the market and the more likely is a recovery. An extremely high ROC suggests that the market is overbought. Figure 13.7A shows the stock price and ROC of Citigroup. Notice that the direction of the ROC started moving lower two months before the stock price peaked. ROC is interpreted as a leading indicator of a change in price trend.

One of the most popular momentum indicators is the *moving-average convergence-divergence (MACD) indicator*. It has two aspects. The first, called the *MACD line,* is calculated by subtracting the value of a 26-period exponential moving average from the value of a 12-period exponential moving average. The second is determined by calculating a 9-day exponential moving average of the MACD. The MACD trading rule is to sell when the MACD line falls below its 9-day moving average and to buy when the MACD line rises above the 9-day moving average. Traders sometimes

Momentum indicators
Measures of momentum. Popular indicators are the rate of change, MACD, and Relative Strength Index.

FIGURE 13.7 | **Technical Analysis of Citigroup**

A. An increase in Citigroup's Rate of Change Signals an Upcoming Change in the Upward Price Trend

B. Citigroup and the MACD Momentum Indictor

Source: Yahoo! Finance, (**http://finance.yahoo.com**) January 24, 2006. Reprinted with permission of Yahoo! Inc. © 2006 by Yahoo! Inc. Yahoo and the Yahoo! logos are trademarks of Yahoo! Inc.

Street Smarts 13.3

Quants

Lots of people with highly developed quantitative skills have moved to Wall Street. Engineers, physicists, computer programmers, and others who like to run reams of data through their computers have been attracted to the stock, bond, and commodity markets. They use Kalman filters, neural networks, models based on chaos theory, and "kitchen sink" models that include every variable imaginable to explain the movement of stock prices.

People with highly developed quantitative skills are called "quants" in the investment community. The number of hedge funds using quantitative strategies has increased dramatically during recent years. In 2005, there were roughly 8,000 hedge funds managing almost $1 trillion. Many hedge funds employ complex trading strategies devised by physics PhDs instead of the simple buy-and-hold approach favored by Warren Buffett. Small investors rarely get to meet such quants because they are notoriously bad at interacting with retail customers. Instead, they are kept alone in back rooms surrounded by computers and reams of data. Quants build sophisticated computer models that try to determine trends and complex associations among thousands of economic and financial variables.

Although many quantitative models and computer programs are elaborate, portfolio managers who rely on them run the risk of succumbing to the same problems that bedevil unsophisticated investors. Complex statistical models may be good at quantifying meaningless systematic trends in historical data, but they may have no documented advantage when it comes to discovering the path to future stock market profits. In many cases, the data-driven approach favored by quants has no theoretical underpinning. In other words, quants don't care why a given valuation model worked in the past. They just focus on what has worked in the past and hope it will work in the future. Sometimes, that approach produces profits in the stock market. More often, it does not.

When evaluating the sophistication of any quantitative model or stock-picking philosophy, it is important not to confuse the concept of statistical complexity with financial sophistication. An investment philosophy is sophisticated in the financial sense if it consistently leads to attractive long-term performance. Many quants have failed to meet this simple criterion.

See Gregory Zukerman and Henry Sender, "Hedge Funds Grow Popular with Investors," *The Wall Street Journal*, January 3, 2006, p. R12.

---

vary the calculation period of the moving average and may use different moving-average lengths in calculating the MACD, depending on the security and trading strategy. The MACD line and its 9-day moving average can be shown, or just the difference can be illustrated, as in Figure 13.7B. Sell signals occur when the MACD is negative; traders look to buy when the MACD is positive.

In addition to the ROC and MACD, common momentum indicators include stochastic momentum, Williams %R, the Relative Strength Index (RSI), the ultimate oscillator, and the price oscillator. There are different variations of each, as well as a host of others.

Momentum Interpretation

Divergence
A momemtum reversal within a continuing price trend.

Each momentum indicator has specific characteristics, but they all share a few common methods of interpretation. Most momentum indicators are used to generate overbought or oversold signals that warn of a price reversal to come. Sometimes, momentum indicators diverge from the underlying price trend, and thereby give warning of an upcoming price-trend reversal. When a trend in momentum reverses but the price trend does not, a **divergence** is said to have occurred. A divergence is a signal that the price trend is weakening and may soon reverse. According to momentum players, the longer a divergence is in effect, the more drastic the reversal is likely to be. However, when the trend in momentum reverses, the price trend does not always follow quickly. Not all divergences will lead to a reversal, and so supporting evidence is sought from other technical techniques, such as channel breakout, moving averages, price pattern recognition, and so on.

Sector Timing

Market-Cap Rotation

Some investors consider themselves value-stock investors. Other people prefer growth stocks. As illustrated in Chapter 12 and in Figure 13.8, value does not always outperform growth, nor does growth always outperform value. Indeed, they seem to take turns doing well. Some investors try to time the market by rotating between value and growth stocks in hopes of always owning the stocks that are performing well.

| FIGURE 13.8 | Growth and Value Stocks Take Turns Doing Well |

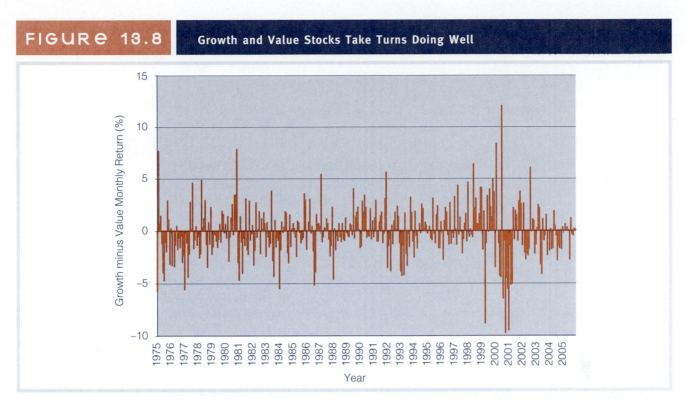

Just as some investors trade between growth and value stocks, the relative popularity of large-cap versus small-cap stocks can spur trading among firm size classifications. Starting in the mid-1970s, for example, small-cap growth stocks rebounded from a prolonged slump and significantly outperformed large-company growth stocks until mid-1983. During the 1984–1989 bull market, the situation was reversed. In late 1990 and 1991, however, small-cap stocks, especially small growth companies, staged an explosive rally and by year-end had surpassed their larger brethren. Small-cap stocks retained their lead until 1994. Large-caps led the market during the 1995–1999 period, but small caps outperformed their larger peers from 2000 to 2003, rebounding from record lows in terms of relative valuations.

In the United States, periods of strong performance for small-company growth stocks *as a group* have come in multiyear waves and have usually been followed by periods of stagnation or underperformance. To illustrate this cycle, Figure 13.9 shows the value of $10,000 invested in a small-cap index, such as the Russell 2000, and in a large-cap index, such as the S&P 500. Interestingly, after 18 years, the value of investing in small-cap stocks is nearly the same as the value of investing in large-caps stock. Nevertheless, there were periods when small caps beat large caps, and vice versa. Investors who rotated from one market cap to the other at the right times would have substantially increased their wealth. Those who rotated at the wrong times would have missed good returns.

Industry Group Rotation

Savvy market timers also tend to avoid industry groups where investor enthusiasm has pushed relative valuations to levels that are well above long term. Instead, they focus on industry groups with relatively low market valuations. Figure 13.10 shows the recent relative valuation of market sectors. In 1980, energy stocks were in vogue as investors sought to profit from permanent energy shortages and sky-high oil prices. Investor optimism was so rampant that energy stocks grew to approach 30 percent of the market capitalization of the S&P 500. Such enthusiasm for a single market sector was unprecedented, until the tech-stock bubble of 2000. In both cases, sector crashes of historic proportions ensued after the bubbles popped. Savvy

FIGURE 13.9 | Sometimes Large-Capitalization Stocks Outperform . . . Sometimes Small Caps Do

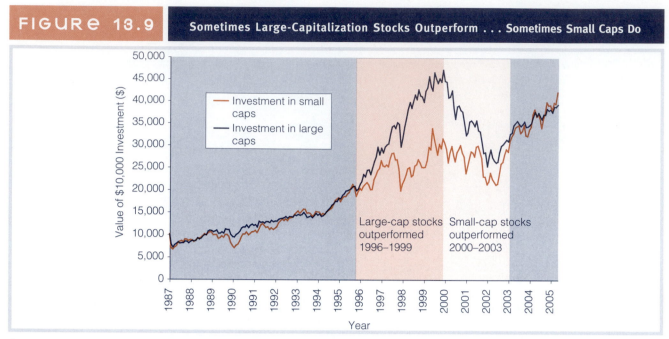

Large-cap stocks outperformed 1996–1999

Small-cap stocks outperformed 2000–2003

Source: Data from Yahoo! Finance.

FIGURE 13.10 | Relative Valuation of Market Sectors Reflects Enthusiasm or Pessimism

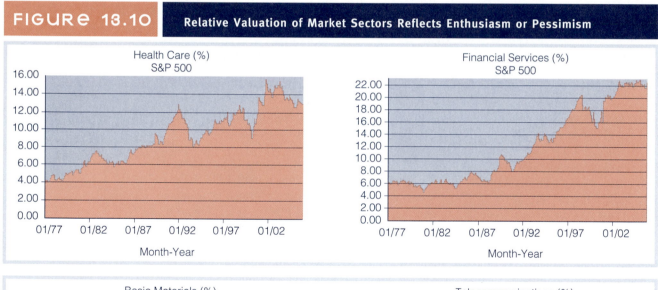

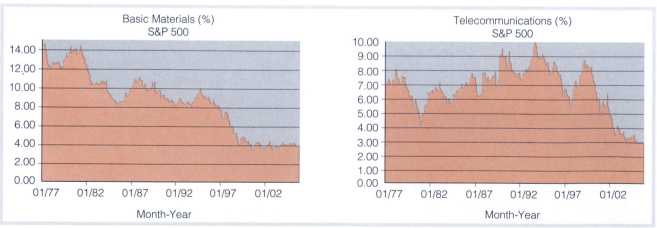

Source: Barra (**www.barra.com/Research/SectorWeightsCharts.aspx**). © Barra, Inc. The Barra data contained herein is the property of Barra, Inc. (Barra). Barra, its affiliates and information providers make no warranties with respect to any such data. The Barra data contained herein is used under license and may not be further used, distributed or disseminated without the express written consent of Barra.

investors dodged enormous losses by avoiding energy stocks and tech stocks during the period leading up to such important market peaks.

At present, neither energy stocks nor tech stocks appear unusually cheap, and they are not prominently featured in the investment portfolios of contrarian investors. Of the 13 market sectors in the S&P 500 Index, basic-materials stocks (DuPont, Dow Chemical, Alcoa, etc.) and telecom stocks (Bell South, SBC Communications, Verizon, etc.) are currently out of favor and apt to be focused on by contrarian investors.

Sentiment Indicators

Survey Indicators

Savvy traders become wary whenever the crowd on Wall Street becomes extremely optimistic or exceedingly bearish. To better track the mood of Wall Street investors, regular surveys of **investor sentiment** are published.

Investor sentiment
Investor mood of optimism or pessimism.

Among the more widely followed surveys used to gauge investor sentiment are the following:

- **AAII Investor Sentiment Survey:** The American Association of Individual Investors Sentiment Survey measures the percentage of individual investors who are bullish, bearish, and neutral on the stock market in the short term. Individuals are polled on a weekly basis from the AAII Web site (**www.aaii.com**).

- **Consumer Confidence Survey:** The Consumer Confidence Survey is based on a representative sample of 5,000 U.S. households. The monthly survey is conducted for the Conference Board by NFO WorldGroup.

- **University of Michigan Consumer Sentiment:** The Index of Consumer Sentiment (ICS) is based on consumer responses to each of five survey questions on spending plans.

- **ABC News/Money Magazine Consumer Comfort Index:** The Consumer Comfort Index is based on a rolling four-week sample of approximately 1,000 adults nationwide. Using a scale of +100 to −100, the index reflects ratings of the economy, buying climate, and personal finances.

- **International Strategy & Investment (ISI) Investor Survey:** Each week, ISI surveys a group of institutional bond managers to gauge the amount of bullishness or bearishness over the next 30 days for the 10-year U.S. Treasury note.

- **Investor's Intelligence:** The *Investor's Intelligence* newsletter (**www.investorsintelligence.com**) reviews other investment newsletters and reports the percentage that is bullish on a weekly basis.

- **Merrill Lynch Sell Side Indicator:** Published by the top Wall Street broker, this monthly indicator is based on a survey of Wall Street strategist asset allocation recommendations.

- **Robert Shiller's Stock Market Confidence Indexes:** Yale Professor Robert Shiller compiles four different indexes based on surveys of individual and institutional investors: One-Year Confidence Index, Buy on Dips Confidence Index, Crash Confidence Index, and Valuation Confidence Index (**icf.som.yale.edu/confidence.index**).

Statistical studies of investor sentiment and stock returns document that sentiment and stock prices tend to move together—that is, until sentiment gets too extreme. Then savvy investors use sentiment as a contrary indicator. Excessive optimism on the part of the public and market professionals almost always coincides with market tops. Acute pessimism tends to coincide with market bottoms.

Buy-Sell Indicators

An important difficulty with using surveys to measure investor sentiment is that people often say one thing and do another. Survey responses do not provide as much information about investor behavior as one might like. As an alternative means for judging investor sentiment, analysts often strive to measure actual investor behavior.

Odd-lot indicators
Gauges of small-investor buying and selling.

For example, some technical analysts follow various **odd-lot indicators**, Recall that in the stock market a round lot is 100 shares. While individual investors sometimes buy shares in odd lots, like 35 shares or 88 shares, institutional investors typically deal in terms of thousands of shares, or tens of thousands of shares, per trade. Analysts who want to track what individual investors are doing look at odd-lot trading volume. If odd-lot purchases are greater than odd-lot sales, then individual investors are buying. If odd-lot sales are greater than odd-lot purchases, then individual investors are selling. Most technicians believe institutional investors represent "smart money," whereas individual investors symbolize the overly emotional crowd.

Contrary indicator
A measure that assesses what others are doing and suggests you should do the opposite.

Therefore, odd lots are considered a **contrary indicator**, Measures that focus on individual investors and regular consumers are contrary indicators. Measures that are based on professional investors are not considered to be contrary indicators. Many technical analysts suggest that savvy investors do just the opposite of the individual investor: Sell in the face of net buying activity by odd-lot traders; buy in the face of net selling activity by odd-lot traders.

Mutual fund flow indicators
Mutual fund inflows, outflows, and credit balance information.

Brokerage account credit balance indicators
Gauges of buying power that resides in the account balances of Wall Street brokerage customers.

Other buy-sell indicators focus on mutual fund cash flows and brokerage account credit balances. Every month, the Investment Company Institute (**www.ici.org**) reports the amount of new money that is invested in equity and bond mutual funds. It also reports the amount of money that has been withdrawn from mutual funds. Because individual investors are the biggest investors in mutual funds, **mutual fund flow indicators** that show mutual fund inflows, outflows, and credit balance information illustrate the actions of individual investors. Similarly **brokerage account credit balance indicators** focus on the amount of buying power that resides in the account balances of Wall Street brokerage customers. Credit balance information is reported weekly in *Barron's* and other leading financial publications. Technical analysts regard high credit balances as bullish because they represent potential buying power. Low credit balances reflect a lack of potential buying power.

Confidence Index
Indicator of investor mood based on bond yields.

Technicians also look to the bond and option markets for insight concerning the future direction of stock prices. If a weak economy and weak stock prices are expected, bond traders favor high-quality bonds because financial stress and the risk of bankruptcy increase during recessions. Traders are more likely to favor lower-rated bond issues if robust economic growth and a positive stock market environment are expected. The **Confidence Index** (0 to 1) is measured by the ratio of the yield to maturity on top-grade corporate bonds to a large cross section of bonds. The bond market Confidence Index will be low if a weak economy and a poor stock market environment are expected and will be high if a robust economy and favorable stock market are anticipated. In the option market, technicians know that optimists buy call options while pessimists buy put options.

Put-call ratio
A ratio of the trading volume of put options to call options.

Put-option trading volume divided by call-option trading volume is the **put-call ratio** and a useful contrarian indicator. A high put-call ratio indicates that option traders are pessimistic; a low put-call ratio means that option traders are optimistic. Typically, this ratio falls in a range between 0.6 and 0.4. When the put-call ratio moves outside this range, technicians take notice.

Try It!

If the 10 highest-grade corporate bonds yield an average 6.0 percent and the Dow Jones Industrial Bond Average has a yield of 6.5 percent, what is the Confidence Index?

Solution

The Confidence Index is 6.0%/6.5% = 0.92. This is quite high and suggests that bond market participants expect the economy to be good. This is a bullish sign for the technical analyst.

Street Smarts 13.4

Research Perspective

Does Investor Sentiment Predict Returns?

When a subset of investors becomes overly optimistic or pessimistic about the stock market, are stock prices impacted? Two financial economists, Greg Brown and Michael Cliff, argue that investor sentiment does in fact move stock prices. As people become optimistic, their optimism can become reinforced and be driven to more extreme levels when other investors join the bandwagon. If such bandwagon effects lead to periods of overvaluation in the stock market, such periods of overvaluation may be followed by sustained periods of low returns.

Specifically, Brown and Cliff argue that overly optimistic investors can drive stock prices above fundamental values. Prices then revert back down to fundamental values over a multiyear time period. Similarly, overly pessimistic investors can drive prices below fundamental values, but this error is eventually reversed in the long run. As a result, the authors hypothesize that stock market returns will tend to follow changes in investor sentiment. If investor sentiment is optimistic, stock prices will be above fundamental values and subsequent returns will be below average. If investor sentiment is pessimistic, stock prices will be below fundamental values and subsequent returns will be above average.

Brown and Cliff study investment sentiment provided by Investor's Intelligence (II) and monthly stock returns from 1963 to 2000. Investor's Intelligence examines over 100 investment newsletter recommendations each week to determine whether each is bullish, bearish, or neutral on the stock market. The sentiment measure used is the bull-bear spread measured as the percentage of newsletters deemed to be bullish minus the percentage deemed to be bearish. A positive number represents general optimism; a large negative number is pessimistic. As anticipated, Brown and Cliff find that optimistic sentiment is followed by lower returns in the market. They conclude that optimistic investors can indeed affect asset prices and that investor sentiment indicators can be used to predict long-run returns in the stock market. In the long run, Brown and Cliff suggest that it pays to go against the crowd!

See Gregory Brown and Michael Cliff, "Investor Sentiment and Asset Valuation," *Journal of Business*, vol. 78, no. 2 (March 2005), pp. 405–440.

Is Technical Analysis Useful?

Useful in Application?

Some academics and Wall Street professionals doubt the practical value of technical analysis. Such skepticism stems from the lack of convincing evidence that the application of technical trading rules can be consistently profitable. Proponents of technical analysis lay the blame on a lack of empirical evidence on the methods used in such studies. Many academics say the fault lies in the failure of technical analysis to give precise trading rules. Can traders make money when they place short-term bets based on breakouts, oversold conditions, overbought conditions, or strong market trends? Even when profitable, it is difficult to ascertain if any such trading profits adequately compensate traders for the level of risk undertaken.

Given the skepticism of many academics toward the value of technical analysis, it may be surprising to see the enthusiasm with which technical analysis is embraced in the financial media. This is partially due to the obvious visual appeal of eye-catching graphics. It is also due to the natural tendency of people to make mistakes when learning by observation and induction. Psychologists know that people commonly use inductive reasoning based on limited observation because it is a useful tool for interacting with the natural world. Unfortunately, many naïve investors lose money because inductive reasoning based on limited observation can be harmful in the stock market. For example, suppose you eat an apple and get sick. You might believe that you will again get sick if you eat another apple. Such inductive reasoning works great when it identifies the outcome from an underlying process that is deterministic and always true. However, inductive reasoning based on limited experience can fail miserably when the underlying process is not deterministic. You might have gotten sick because of food you ate before eating the apple. You have an unfounded fear of eating an apple and getting sick because you incorrectly extrapolated from limited experience. Investors often make the same type of mistake. Suppose an investor buys a stock after its price completes a flag pattern and ends up making a profit. Using inductive reasoning based on limited experience, the investor might assume that a profit will be made every time he or she buys a stock that has displayed a flag pattern. However, because short-term changes in stock prices have a large random component, inferences based on such technical trading rules will often be wrong. Many investors make the mistake of thinking that the market is more deterministic than it really is. This causes them to look for patterns that they believe are meaningful and that will repeat. Too often, investors lose money when such patterns inexplicably change.

Useful for Framing Investment Decisions?

From a behavioral perspective, investors appear to like and use various elements of technical analysis when making buy and sell decisions. There is obviously a significant demand among investors for historical price and trading volume information displayed in a pleasing graphical format. Investors are literally bombarded with colorful displays and whiz-bang graphics of historical price and trading volume information when they tune in to their favorite investing programs on CNBC or visit the plethora of Internet Web sites devoted to investing. It is rare to see a Wall Street professional discuss the investment merits of a given stock, bond, or commodity without the television or computer screen flashing a chart displaying historical price and trading volume information. Investors not only want to hear the investment merits of a given situation discussed; they want to *see* what an investment bargain looks like.

Edward R. Tufte, professor emeritus of political science, computer science and statistics, and graphic design at Yale University and author of *The Visual Display of Quantitative Information* is famous for illustrating the role of graphical analysis in effective communication. According to Tufte, the problem with presenting quantitative information is that the world is multidimensional but visual displays tend to be two-dimensional. The quantitative thinking of investors often comes down to one question: Compared to what? If a stock is said to be cheap, the investor always wants to know if the recommended company has a current stock price that is cheap compared with recent prices. That is why investors tend to rely on charts that show historical price and volume information. Both analysts and investors strive very hard to show cause and effect. In graphical analysis, good design is clear thinking made visible. When a low stock price is compared with a higher 50-day moving average, it is easy for analysts and investors to argue that the price has *got* to go up. Look! It's a bargain!

Another reason that investors like graphical analysis and technical trading tools is that they support natural tendencies. People like to create order out of chaos. Stock price movements appear random to investors. Yet the brain often thinks it identifies patterns within random movements. The identification of repeatable patterns in stock price movements using technical analysis is a comfortable behavior for many investors. For many investors, technical analysis just feels right. However, such an appreciation for technical analysis does not necessarily make it a profitable activity.

Technical analysts have cheered the development of behavioral finance over the past decade. This enthusiasm stems from the fact that technicians believe that prices are driven by both rational and irrational behavior. However, while researchers in behavioral finance have identified how emotions can drive investment decisions, such irrational behavior has not yet been linked to specific price patterns identified by technical analysts. As a result, significant gaps exist in our understanding of the popularity of technical analysis.

Summary

■ **Technical analysis** is the study of past price movements and trading volume information to forecast future price movements in stock, bond, and commodity markets. Technical analysts, typically referred to as **technicians**, are sometimes referred to as **chartists** because they rely almost exclusively on charts for their analysis.

■ Technicians adopt a visual approach based on two-dimensional graphs of stock price and volume information.

This process, called **charting**, is the basis of technical analysis. Each point on a **50-day moving average** shows the average price over the previous 50 trading days (roughly two calendar months). Use of the **200-day moving average** is also popular among technicians and shows average prices over roughly one year of trading activity.

■ Technical analysts consider it extremely bullish whenever a stock price pushes through the price **resistance line** given by the 50-day or 200-day moving average. Resistance lines represent price points at which selling pressure (supply) has emerged in the recent past and can therefore limit a stock's upside potential. However, once the current stock price has risen through the 50-day or 200-day moving average, these moving averages are thought to offer support for future prices. A price **support line** connects relatively low points on a stock price graph and represents prices at which additional demand for the stock has emerged in the past. Taken together, the resistance line and the support line form a **channel** trend for the price. Traders who focus on **stock price trends** bet on the propensity for a stock that is rising in price to continue to rise until some new demand or supply force takes effect.

■ A main tenet of **Dow Theory** is that there are three levels of market trends: primary, secondary, and tertiary. Major, long-term movements are **primary trends**. They are known as bull and bear markets and can last anywhere from less than one year up to several years. **Secondary trends** are short-term moves in the market that run contrary to the primary trend and usually last from three weeks to three months. A secondary trend in a bull market is often referred to as a **market correction** and seen as a temporary decline in an ongoing bull market. The secondary trend in a bear market is typically referred to as a **bear trap** and is reflected by a temporary increase in prices followed by a further sharp decline in the market. Very short-term stock market trends that reflect minor price moves are called **tertiary trends**.

■ A popular chart price pattern is the **head and shoulders**. During a bull market trend, the formation of the head-and-shoulders pattern signals a trend reversal to a bear market trend. A variety of **reversal patterns** indicate an important change in trend, while **continuation patterns** indicate a persistence of the underlying bullish or bearish trend.

■ Writing in the 1920s, a Russian economist, Nikolai Kondratieff, speculated that the world economy evolved in a 60-year cycle. Today, this is known as the **Kondratieff wave**, or K-wave. **Market cycles** are the observable tendency of prices to rotate from **market peak** to **market trough** in a rhythmic cycle.

■ If a price trend seems to have stalled out in a long bull market, it is called a final **blow off** if volume continues to rise when prices have stalled. To measure the level of conviction among buyers and sellers, technical analysts keep a close eye on **money flow** indicators. Money flows measure the relative buying and selling pressure each day on share prices. An **uptick trade** is one at a higher price than the previous trade, while a **downtick trade** is one at a lower price than the previous trade. The **up-down ratio** reflects the value of uptick trades relative to the value of downtick trades (in millions of dollars). Money flow data are also commonly reported for institutional **block trades** (trades of 10,000 shares or more).

■ **Market breadth** measures how many issues are rising relative to the number of issues that are declining. The **advance-decline ratio** is the number of firms that advanced in price divided by the number that declined on a given trading day. The **advance-decline line** is the ongoing sum of the number of advancing stocks minus the number of declining stocks. Most of the time, the advance-decline line and the overall market move higher and lower together. At times, however, the overall market can continue to move higher despite a drop in the advance-decline line. This is taken by technicians as a warning of a pending reversal in the underlying price trend. A common indicator of market imbalance is the **TRIN (*tr*ading *in*dex) ratio**. The TRIN ratio combines advance and decline data with upside and downside volume information to signal overbought and oversold conditions in the market.

■ **Momentum** is the measure of the speed of price change. It is considered a leading indicator of the change in a stock's trend. There are many different indicators that have been developed to track momentum. **Momentum indicators** are designed to identify the relative enthusiasm of buyers and sellers involved in the price trend development. **Divergence** is a momentum reversal within a continuing price trend.

■ To better judge and track the mood of Wall Street investors, regular surveys of **investor sentiment** are published. Technical analysts follow various **odd-lot indicators**. Recall that in the stock market a round lot is 100 shares. Most technicians believe institutional investors represent "smart money," whereas individual investors symbolize the overly emotional crowd. Many technical analysts suggest that savvy investors take measures of individual trading as **contrary indicators** and do just the opposite of the individual investor.

■ Because individual investors are the biggest investors in mutual funds, **mutual fund flow indicators** that show mutual fund inflows, outflows, and credit balance information illustrate the actions of individual investors. Similarly, **brokerage account credit balance indicators** focus on the amount of buying power that resides in the account balances of Wall Street brokerage customers. Technical analysts regard high credit balances as bullish because they represent potential buying power. The bond market **Confidence Index** will be low if a weak economy and a poor stock market environment are expected and will be high if a robust economy and favorable stock market are anticipated.

■ Skepticism of technical analysis stems from the lack of convincing evidence that technical trading rules can be consistently profitable. Nevertheless, technical analysis is popular because investors naturally want to *see* what an investment bargain looks like.

Self-Test Problems

ST13.1   StockCharts.com and other technical analysis Web sites on the Internet offer stock screens and other tools that help investors locate stocks with buy or sell signals according to various technical indicators. Go to **http://stockcharts.com** and link to "Stock Scans" to generate a list of such buy and sell candidates.

Solution

The StockCharts.com link to "Stock Scans" provided the following information on May 11, 2005.

	Equities						Mutual
Technical Indicators	**Nasdaq**	**NYSE**	**Amex**	**TSE**	**CDNX**	**Total**	**Funds**
New 52-week highs	30	51	5	13	2	101	93
New 52-week lows	74	35	8	15	8	140	35
Strong volume gainers	38	8	3	16	6	71	
Strong volume decliners	37	14	2	6	12	71	
Bullish 50/200-day MA crossovers	3	0	0	0	1	4	2
Bearish 50/200-day MA crossovers	19	19	4	5	2	49	79
Bullish MACD crossovers	20	5	1	5	4	35	4
Bearish MACD crossovers	15	11	4	7	4	41	37
Improving Chaikin money flow	45	32	8	14	6	105	
Declining Chaikin money flow	39	14	1	5	8	67	
Stocks in a new uptrend (Aroon)	40	41	3	8	4	96	30
Stocks in a new downtrend (Aroon)	46	30	10	15	9	110	26

The three bullish moving-average crossovers in the Nasdaq market were ComGuard.com (CGUD), DataMEG Corporation (DTMG), and GPS Industries (GPSN). The five NYSE-listed stocks that moved to a positive momentum were Chiquita Brands (CQB), Interline Brands (IBI), Kohls (KSS), Meadowbrook Insurance Corporation (MIG), and Managed Muni Portfolio Inc. (MMU). How have these stocks done since May 2005?

ST13.2   Assess the technical condition of Nortel Networks (NT) using price movements, volume, and momentum indicators.

Solution

Examine the one-year chart for Nortel, from Standard & Poor's Market Insight, with support and resistance lines drawn. Note that volume and MACD are also illustrated.

The stock remains stuck in a down channel. It is a bad sign that volume tends to spike during the large down-days. The MACD histogram has not shown any strong buy or sell signals for many months. Given that the price is trending down and volume is more convincing on the downside, this does not appear to be the time to buy Nortel. In May 2005, technical analysts would describe NT's technical condition as poor. How has the stock done since May 2005?

Questions and Problems

13.1 Discuss the reasoning behind support levels.

13.2 Discuss what types of investor behavior are associated with each of the three phases of a bull market, according to the Dow Theory.

13.3 Go to Yahoo! Finance at **http://finance.yahoo.com** and create a stock price chart that shows current quotes for the S&P 500 Index plus 50-day and 200-day moving averages using the "Technical Analysis" charting tools. Explain what type of price movement causes the 50-day moving average to rise above the 200-day moving average.

13.4 Go to Yahoo! Finance at **http://finance.yahoo.com** and create a stock price chart that shows current quotes for the Nasdaq Composite plus 50-day and 200-day moving averages using the "Technical Analysis" charting tools. Explain what type of price movement causes the 50-day moving average to fall below the 200-day moving average.

13.5 Explain the economic intuition that underlies the Dow Theory.

13.6 Why do technical analysts consider a breakthrough of the neckline in a head-and-shoulders pattern to be a bear signal?

13.7 Briefly describe what is known as the rectangles chart formation. Is there any economic basis for this pattern to predict stock price movements?

13.8 What information can volume add to that of price information?

13.9 Money flow figures for important stocks are reported daily in *The Wall Street Journal* and in *The Wall Street Journal Online* (**http://online.wsj.com**). Go to today's paper and interpret the numbers found for "Money Flow—Top Gainers" and "Money Flows—Top Decliners."

13.10 Compute and graph a four-day moving average of the following Nasdaq Composite:

Date	Nasdaq Composite	Date	Nasdaq Composite
1-Apr-05	1984.81	21-Apr-05	1962.41
4-Apr-05	1991.07	22-Apr-05	1932.19
5-Apr-05	1999.32	25-Apr-05	1950.78
6-Apr-05	1999.14	26-Apr-05	1927.44
7-Apr-05	2018.79	27-Apr-05	1930.43
8-Apr-05	1999.35	28-Apr-05	1904.18
11-Apr-05	1992.12	29-Apr-05	1921.65
12-Apr-05	2005.40	2-May-05	1928.65
13-Apr-05	1974.37	3-May-05	1933.07
14-Apr-05	1946.71	4-May-05	1962.23
15-Apr-05	1908.15	5-May-05	1961.80
18-Apr-05	1912.92	6-May-05	1967.35
19-Apr-05	1932.36	9-May-05	1979.67
20-Apr-05	1913.76	10-May-05	1962.77

13.11 What buy and sell signals are given by the price crossing the moving average in Problem 13.10?

13.12 Why is an increase in credit balances in stock brokerage accounts considered bullish?

13.13 From the information given in Table 13.3, compute the advance-decline ratio and the ratio of new highs to new lows for the Amex Stock Exchange. Any conclusion from the answers?

13.14 From the information given in Table 13.3, compute the TRIN ratio for the Amex Stock Exchange and give an interpretation.

13.15 The table below shows the net new cash flow into stock mutual funds during each month and the level of the S&P 500 Index. What do technicians believe about this mutual fund flow and what would be an interpretation of this data?

Date	Net New Cash	S&P 500 Index
Mar-05	14986	1180.59
Feb-05	22180	1203.60
Jan-05	9965	1181.27
Dec-04	10246	1211.92
Nov-04	21406	1173.82
Oct-04	7203	1130.20
Sep-04	10218	1114.58
Aug-04	1160	1104.24
Jul-04	9368	1101.72
Jun-04	10397	1140.84
May-04	431	1120.68
Apr-04	22958	1107.30
Mar-04	15972	1126.21
Feb-04	26214	1144.94
Jan-04	42981	1131.13
Dec-03	14178	1111.92
Nov-03	14930	1058.20
Oct-03	25306	1050.71
Sep-03	17255	995.97
Aug-03	23397	1008.01
Jul-03	21448	990.31
Jun-03	18632	974.51

STANDARD &POOR'S

13.16 Go to the Standard & Poor's Market Insight Web site at **www.mhhe.com/ edumarketinsight** and enter the ticker "WEN" for Wendy's International. Load "Charting by Prophet" and insert the WEN ticker. There are many technical analysis tools in the "Technical Studies" section. Use the simple-moving-average tool in the "Moving-Average" section. What is the current signal for Wendy's?

STANDARD &POOR'S

13.17 Go to the Standard & Poor's Market Insight Web site at **www.mhhe.com/ edumarketinsight** and enter the ticker "JBX" for Jack in the Box Inc. Load "Charting by Prophet" and insert the JBX ticker. What does the MACD momentum indicator suggest for Jack in the Box? Use the MACD histogram option.

STANDARD &POOR'S

13.18 Go to the Standard & Poor's Market Insight Web site at **www.mhhe.com/ edumarketinsight** and enter the ticker "SLE" for Sara Lee Corporation. Load "Charting by Prophet" and insert the SLE ticker. Print the SLE price chart for the year. Draw the support and resistance lines on the chart. Also print the SLE chart for a five-year period, and draw in the support and resistance lines. Do the two charts give different perspectives?

13.19 Use the Dow Theory, technical indicators, and sentiment indicators to assess the current condition of the market. (This problem is similar to the assessment in Self-Test 13.1.)

13.20 Savvy investors compare the price-earnings multiple for the T. Rowe Price New Horizons Fund, which focuses on emerging growth stocks, to the price-earnings multiple on the large-cap S&P 500. The highly profitable and rapidly growing small-cap stocks held in the New Horizons Fund usually sell in a range of one to two times the S&P 500 multiple. When New Horizons' relative multiple is near the low end of this range, the fund is a buy. When the relative multiple drifts up toward two, it's a good time to avoid emerging growth stocks. The chart below plots the relative multiple on an inverted scale (on the left) and the subsequent five-year performance of the fund versus the S&P 500 (on the right). Does the convergence of the crests and troughs in this chart suggest investors should buy the New Horizon Fund when fund holdings are relatively cheap in P/E terms? What does the relative P/E indicator suggest to investors now? Explain why the volatility displayed in this graph may be diminishing over time.

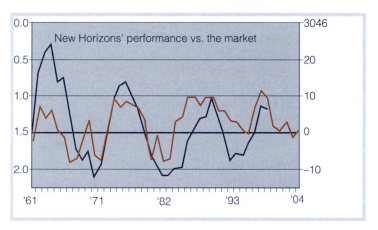

Source: T. Rowe Price.

INVESTMENT APPLICATION

Extreme Return Reversal in the Stock Market[2]

Since 1950, there have been 17 instances when the overall market, as measured by the S&P 500, suffered a sustained market correction of at least -10 percent in historical 12-month returns (see Table 13.4). On average, such corrections in the S&P 500 last five months and involve a decline of −14.4 percent. During the subsequent 12-month period, forward-looking investors consistently earn above-average market returns of 14.2 percent per year. Since 1950, there have been only eight periods when the overall market, as measured by the S&P 500, suffered a sustained bear market of at least −20 percent in 12-month returns. On average, such bear markets in the S&P 500 last only 2.63 months and involve a decline of −24.3 percent. During the subsequent 12-month period, forward-looking investors consistently earn above-average market returns of 16.7 percent per year.

---

[2] See Mark Hirschey, "Extreme Return Reversal in the Stock Market: Strong Support for Insightful Fundamental Analysis," *Journal of Portfolio Management*, vol. 29, no. 3 (Spring 2003), pp. 78–90.

www.mhhe.com/hirschey1e

TABLE 13.4 — Recent Bear Markets and Subsequent 12-Month Returns

Time Period	Duration (months)	Average Historical 12-Month Returns	Average Forward-looking 12-Month Returns	Time Period	Duration (months)	Average Historical 12-Month Returns	Average Forward-Looking 12-month Returns
S&P 500—10% 12-month Corrections (1950–2005)				**Nasdaq—10% 12-month Corrections (1971–2005)**			
December 1957	1	-14.3%	38.1%	April 1973–March 1975	24	-26.0%	-5.8%
May–December 1962	8	-13.7	22.7	March–July 1982	5	-18.6	70.7
August–December 1966	5	-13.0	20.2	April–December 1984	9	-17.2	22.4
November 1969–January 1970	3	-14.1	1.9	October–November 1987	2	-12.8	20.0
March–August 1970	6	-19.1	24.9	January–March 1988	3	-12.9	11.3
October 1970	1	-14.3	13.2	May 1988	1	-11.1	20.5
November 1973–March 1975	17	-21.5	7.7	September 1988	3	-13.6	21.3
October 1977	1	-10.3	0.9	August 1990–December 1990	5	-22.5	51.6
December 1977–February 1978	3	-12.3	7.9	November 2001–February 2002	16	-40.2	-24.1
November 1981	1	-10.1	9.6	April 2002–April 2003	13	-25.4	33.3
February–July 1982	6	-15.7	43.1				
March 1988	1	-11.2	13.9				
June–October 1988	4	-15.2	26.6				
September–October 1990	2	-11.5	27.9				
December 2000	1	-10.1	-13.0				
March 2001–February 2002	12	-17.7	-18.4				
April 2002–April 2003	13	-20.0	15.0				
Average	**5.00**	**-14.4%**	**14.2%**	**Average**	**8.10**	**-20.0%**	**22.1%**
S&P 500—20% 12–Month Bear Markets (1950–2005)				**Nasdaq—20% 12–Month Bear Markets (1971–2005)**			
April–June 1970	3	−24.3%	31.1%	May–June 1973	2	−22.5%	−23.3%
July 1974–January 1975	7	−29.7	25.4	November 1973–March 1974	5	−26.0	−27.0
August 1988	1	−20.7	34.4	May 1974–February 1975	10	−33.0	21.9
March 2001	1	−22.6	−1.1	May–July 1982	3	−20.5	80.2
August–October 2001	3	−26.2	−19.2	May–July 1984	3	−24.6	26.6
July 2002	1	−24.7	8.6	September–November 1990	3	−25.3	54.5
September 2002	1	−21.7	22.2	November 2000–January 2002	15	−41.5	−24.2
December 2002–March 2003	4	−24.4	31.9	April 2002–March 2003	12	−26.5	33.5
Average	**2.63**	**−24.3%**	**16.7%**	**Average**	**6.63**	**−27.5%**	**17.8%**

A similar pattern of extreme return reversal is even more obvious for the highly volatile Nasdaq. Since 1971 and the start of the Nasdaq index, there have been 10 unique instances when Nasdaq suffered a sustained market correction of at least –10 percent in historical 12-month returns. On average, Nasdaq corrections last 8.10 months and involve a decline of –20.0 percent. During the subsequent 12-month period, forward-looking Nasdaq investors consistently earn above-average market returns of 22.1 percent per year. Since 1971, there have been eight periods when Nasdaq suffered a sustained bear market of at least –20 percent in 12-month returns. Nasdaq bear markets average 6.63 months in duration and involve a decline of –27.5 percent. During the subsequent 12-month period, forward-looking Nasdaq investors earn above-average market returns of 17.8 percent per year.

Stock market evidence reported in Table 13.4 and behavioral finance research on overreaction are consistent with a predictable process of long-term return reversal in stock market returns. If investors systematically overweight recent bad news about negative market returns, investor fear can push stock prices far below fundamental economic values. Similarly, if investors systematically overweight recent good news about positive market returns, investor greed can push stock prices above fundamental economic values. In both instances, cognitive bias among investors can lead to predictable mispricing.

The high degree of negative autocorrelation evident in annual rates of return for the S&P 500 and Nasdaq suggest that long-term returns in the stock market are not random. Instead, this evidence is consistent with the notion that, in the short run, stock prices may in fact be susceptible to extraordinary swings driven by investor sentiments of greed and fear. In the long run, however, trends in stock prices mirror real changes in business prospects as measured by revenues, earnings, dividends, and so on. As a result, periods with extraordinary above-normal market returns tend to be followed by periods of subpar performance. Similarly, intervals of sharply below-normal market returns tend to be followed by stretches of above-normal performance.

a. Is evidence of extreme return reversal in the stock market consistent with the EMH? Why or why not?

b. Explain why investors might overreact to bad news in the stock market, and explain the practical usefulness of the overreaction concept for portfolio managers.

www.mhhe.com/hirschey1e

14
chapter

Bond Instruments and Markets

The U.S. bond market, with a market value of roughly $25 trillion, is among the largest and most liquid securities markets in the world (see **http://bondmarket.com**). Detailed information about credit market conditions and the credit quality of individual issuers is quickly and widely disseminated over the Internet and through proprietary electronic networks. As a result, the bond market quickly reflects changes in the credit quality of corporate and governmental issuers and changes in investor expectations tied to anticipated fluctuations in aggregate economic conditions. In the bond market, it's very difficult to find underpriced bargains. For large buyers and sellers of debt instruments, the bond market is very efficient.

At the same time, the secondary market for outstanding bonds tends to be relatively illiquid for buyers and sellers of less than a "round lot" of fixed-income securities. In the bond market, a round lot consists of $1 million in face amount or par value of bonds. For small buyers and sellers, transaction costs tend to average 3 to 4 percent of the principal amount. This means that brokerage commissions of $300 to $400 are typical for the sale or purchase of bonds with a face amount of $10,000. Contrast these high bond market trading costs with transaction costs in the stock market. A host of discount brokers on the Internet make it possible to buy or sell up to 5,000 shares of common stock for less than $10 per trade. For small investors, high transaction costs make the bond market a very expensive place to trade.

Against this backdrop, it is difficult to understand the lack of popularity for bond index funds. Low-cost index funds that passively track the bond market routinely produce top returns and soundly beat almost all the competition provided by bond mutual funds.[1] Strangely, bond investors are not buying. Bond index funds are getting passed up by investors, even though they boast the same low-cost, broad-diversification qualities that have made stock index funds a rip-roaring success.

---

[1] See Dave Kansas, "Bond Beginners, Here's the Gist," *The Wall Street Journal Online*, January 29, 2006 (**http://online.wsj.com**).

CHAPTER OBJECTIVES

- Be able to read bond quotes.
- Learn the characteristics of corporate bonds.
- Identify bonds with low credit risk.
- Understand Treasury, agency, and asset-backed instruments.
- Compute the tax advantages of municipal bonds.

Bond Market Overview

Amount of Public and Private Debt

The bond market matches corporations and government agencies that need to borrow money with investors that have money to lend. **Bond dealers** are securities firms and banks that act as financial intermediaries between **bond issuers** and **bond investors**. Bond issuers sell new bonds in the **primary bond market** to dealers, who then resell those bonds to investors in the **secondary bond market**. Once bonds have been issued and sold to individual and institutional investors, bond dealers use their capital to maintain active secondary markets. Dealers bid for bonds that investors seek to sell, and they offer bonds from their own inventory when investors want to buy.

As illustrated in Figure 14.1, at the start of 2006, the U.S. bond market represented roughly $24.7 trillion in outstanding debt obligations. By way of comparison, the 2006 market value of common and preferred stock in the United States was roughly $12.7 trillion, as captured by the Dow Jones Wilshire 5000 Equity Index. This makes the U.S. bond market one of the world's largest securities markets. Because of historically low interest rates in 2001 to 2005, the mortgage-backed security debt market exploded. Of the $24.7 trillion in U.S. debt obligations, the

Bond dealers
Securities firms and banks that act as financial intermediaries between bond issuers and investors.

Bond issuers
Entities that supply new bonds (supply source).

Bond investors
Individuals and institutions that purchase bonds for interest income and long-term capital gains.

Primary bond market
Market for new bonds; the issuer-to-investor market.

Secondary bond market
Market for previously issued bonds; an investor-to-investor market.

| **FIGURE 14.1** | **Outstanding Level of Public and Private Debt** |

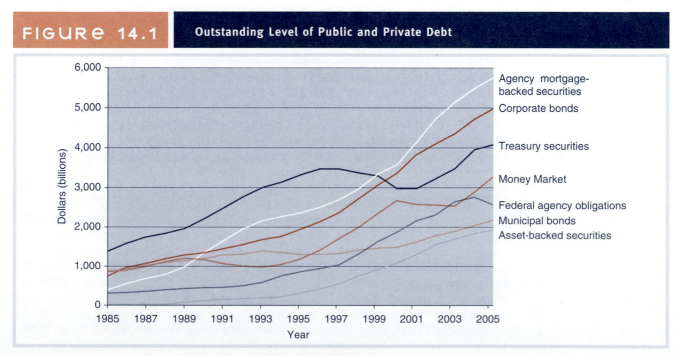

Source: Bond Market Association. © Bond Market Association. Used with permission.

largest share is accounted for by mortgage-backed securities. The total value of mortgage-backed obligations is on the order of $5.8 trillion and represents roughly one-quarter (23.3 percent) of the U.S. bond market. Corporate bonds are the second-largest debt category, at roughly $5.0 trillion, and represent 20.2 percent of the total. Historically, U.S. Treasury bills, notes, and bonds were among the largest segments of the bond market. However, federal budget surpluses during the late 1990s allowed some of this debt to be repaid. U.S. Treasury obligations of $4.1 trillion now represent 16.6 percent of the total bond market. Other major debt categories include money market securities ($3.3 trillion, or 13.2 percent), federal agency obligations ($2.6 trillion, or 10.5 percent), municipal bonds ($2.2 trillion, or 8.9 percent), and asset-backed securities ($1.9 trillion, or 7.7 percent).

As shown in Figure 14.2, comprehensive interest rate information for all major bond indexes is reported daily in *The Wall Street Journal* (both in print and online) and the financial press. Different indexes illustrate important segments of the bond market. Investors track bonds by type of issuer (federal government, corporation, local government, etc.) and time to maturity (short, intermediate, and long). Since mortgage-backed securities are such a large portion of the market, many different indexes are devoted to tracking this market segment.

The U.S. bond market has grown rapidly during recent years. In the private sector, there is the pressing need to fund plant and equipment investment for an expanding economy. In the public sector, an increasing level of debt financing has been used to fund a growing number of public programs. On an overall basis, the U.S. bond market grew from $4.5 trillion in 1985 to more than $24.7 trillion in 2005, an 8.9 percent compound annual rate of growth. Over this period, growth was especially rapid in the federal agency mortgage-backed securities market, in which the total value of bonds outstanding rose at a 14.2 percent annual rate. Much government-guaranteed debt financing is to fund housing and includes mortgage-backed securities issued by Ginnie Mae (Government National Mortgage Association), Fannie Mae (Federal National Mortgage Association), and Freddie Mac (Federal Home Loan Mortgage Corporation). The much smaller private-sector asset-backed bond market has grown at an even quicker pace of 39.7 percent per year over this period. Clearly, the bond market represents a growth industry, and the mortgage-backed and asset-backed securities parts of the business have enjoyed explosive development.

Tracking the Bond Market

Because the bond market includes a wide variety of debt securities with varying credit quality and other characteristics, no one price or yield index can be used to fully describe changes in the overall bond market. As shown in Figure 14.3, the trend in long-term interest rates is often summarized through reference to changes in the **current yield** for long-term Treasury bonds. These long-term bonds capture the **holding-period risk** typical of long-term bonds. Holding-period risk is the chance of loss incurred by bondholders that might be forced to liquidate bond holdings during periods of adverse changes in bond prices. Because all Treasury securities are backed by the full faith and credit of the U.S. government, they entail no **default risk**. As a result, Treasury bonds offer the lowest interest rates available on any long-term debt security. More adventuresome long-term bond investors can earn a slight risk premium, usually 1 to 2 percent per year, by investing in high-grade corporate bonds. Bond price and yield changes in such securities are captured by indexes maintained by Dow Jones and various brokerages, such as Merrill Lynch (shown in Figure 14.2). More than 5,000 taxable government, investment-grade corporate, and mortgage-backed securities are included in the Lehman Brothers Aggregate Bond Index. Because of the vast number of securities in this index, and because many of them are fairly illiquid, index funds use sampling techniques to track the Lehman index. Merrill Lynch Taxable Bond Indexes provide value-weighted total returns (coupon plus capital change) for a range of bond types. Price and yield trends for long-term tax-free municipal bonds are tracked by the Bond Buyer Municipal Bond Index.

Figure 14.3 also illustrates how bond yields depend on both the time to maturity and the credit quality. The yield curves pictured are unusually flat. It is more common for short-term bonds to earn a much lower yield than long-term bonds. The trend in interest rates for short-term

Current yield

Bond's promised interest payment divided by its current purchase price.

Holding-period risk

Chance of loss during periods of adverse changes in bond prices.

Default risk

Chance of nonpayment of interest or principal.

Major Indexes

For Close of February 03, 2006

High	Low	Index	Close	Chg.	%Chg.	12 Month Chg.	%Chg.	From 12/31 Chg.	%Chg.
U.S. Treasury Securities Lehman Brothers									
1356.50	131.15	Composite (Price)	1307.96	1.57	0.12	−39.49	−2.93	−9.98	−0.76
9154.12	8114.80	Composite (Total Return)	9062.94	11.95	0.13	127.05	1.42	−30.66	−0.34
1212.16	1173.74	Intermediate (Price)	1174.89	0.00	unch	−34.14	−2.82	−7.34	−0.62
7862.58	7615.11	Intermediate (Total Return)	7812.70	0.94	0.01	89.97	1.17	−17.97	−0.23
1861.93	1719.57	Long–Term (Price)	1756.49	8.71	0.50	−58.52	−3.22	−21.28	−1.20
13962.64	12737.95	Long–Term (Total Return)	13616.54	69.56	0.51	298.67	2.24	−93.48	−0.68
Broad Market Lehman Brothers									
1326.33	1266.47	U.S. Government/Credit	1313.07	2.37	0.17	15.61	1.59	−2.14	−0.15
1145.85	1096.43	U.S. Aggregate Bond	1137.88	1.61	0.13	17.88	1.84	−0.18	−0.01
U.S. Corporate Debt Issues Merrill Lynch									
1343.73	1251.97	10+ Year Maturities	1307.20	7.43	0.57	−6.96	−0.53	−3.10	−0.24
1101.36	1060.55	1–10 Year Maturities	1091.66	0.89	0.08	8.70	0.80	−0.96	−0.09
1563.96	1495.27	Corporate Master	1544.37	3.07	0.20	7.54	0.49	−1.92	−0.12
756.04	697.17	High Yield	755.89	−0.15	−0.02	28.54	3.92	12.31	1.66
1149.35	1089.50	Yankee Bonds	1140.59	1.84	0.16	23.84	2.13	−1.84	−0.16
Tax-Exempt Securities Bond Buyer Muni Index, from Dec. 22, 1999									
116.75	111.09	Bond Buyer 6% Muni	114.03	0.19	0.16	−1.50	−1.30	−0.28	−0.25
229.39	217.40	12–22 Year General Obligation	228.43	0.25	0.11	5.78	2.60	0.91	0.40
211.53	202.06	7–12 Year General Obligation	210.01	0.08	0.04	2.53	1.22	0.21	0.10
221.92	209.11	22+ Year Revenue	221.46	0.35	0.16	9.69	4.58	0.80	0.36
Mortgage-Backed Securities Current Coupon; Merrill Lynch: Dec. 31, 1986 = 100									
457.37	440.71	Fannie Mae (FNMA)	454.22	0.15	0.03	3.34	0.74	1.29	0.28
280.78	270.03	Freddie Mac (FHLMC)	278.84	0.22	0.08	2.31	0.84	0.83	0.30
465.30	442.93	Ginnie Mae (GNMA)	461.49	0.28	0.06	7.68	1.69	0.77	0.17
1181.29	1128.96	Lehman Bros. Fixed MBS	1173.46	0.94	0.07	26.40	2.33	2.85	0.22

Mortgage-Backed Securities, Friday, February 3, 2006

Indicative, not guaranteed; from Bear Stearns Cos./Street Software Technology Inc.

		Price (Pts-32ds)	Price Change (32ds)	Avg Life (Years)	Spread to Avg Life (Bps)	Spread Change	PSA (Prepay Spread)	Yield to Maturity*
30-Year								
FMAC GOLD	5.5%	98–27	+03	8.0	121	—	184	5.73
FMAC GOLD	6.0%	100–27	+01	6.3	134	1	239	5.84
FMAC GOLD	6.5%	102–09	—	4.3	134	—	342	5.85
FNMA	5.5%	98–25	+03	8.0	120	1	184	5.71
FNMA	6.0%	100–26	—	5.6	129	1	278	5.79
FNMA	6.5%	102–12	—	4.6	131	—	314	5.81
GNMA**	5.5%	100–09	+03	7.4	96	—	193	5.47
GNMA**	6.0%	102–10	+01	6.0	101	1	234	5.51
GNMA**	6.5%	104–12	—	4.4	77	—	314	5.27
15–Year								
FMAC GOLD	5.0%	98–19	+02	5.6	83	—	172	5.32
FNMA	5.0%	98–19	+02	5.6	80	1	173	5.29
GNMA**	5.0%	99–16	—	5.4	63	1	172	5.12

*Extrapolated from benchmarks based on projections from Bear Stearns prepayment model, assuming interest rates remain unchanged.

**Government guaranteed.

Source: WSJ online, **http://online.wsj.com/page/mdc/2_0500-majbondi-10.html**, February 3, 2006. Copyright © 2006, Dow Jones Co. Used with permission.

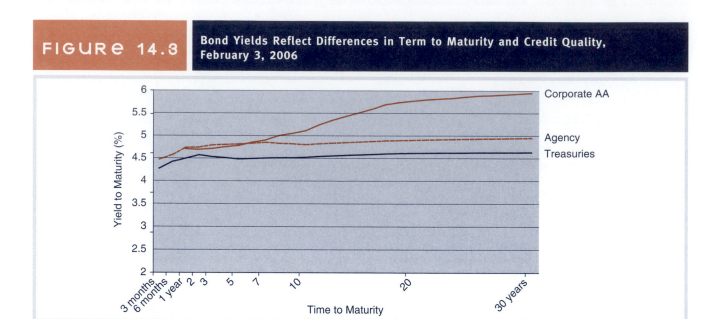

FIGURE 14.3   Bond Yields Reflect Differences in Term to Maturity and Credit Quality, February 3, 2006

Federal funds rate
Overnight bank lending rate.

Discount rate
Interest rate charged by the Federal Reserve to member banks.

Eurodollar
Dollar deposit in a European bank.

London Interbank Offered Rates (LIBOR)
London federal funds rate.

securities that involve no holding period or default risk is captured by changes in the yield on three-month Treasury bills. Also important in the short-term is the **federal funds rate**, the amount charged by member banks of the Federal Reserve System to other member banks that need funds to maintain required balances with the Federal Reserve. Member banks are required to keep a certain percentage of their assets on deposit with the Federal Reserve bank in their geographic region to provide collateral for savings and checking deposits. Although the fed funds rate is for bank-to-bank lending, the **discount rate** is the interest rate charged on loans made by the Federal Reserve itself. The discount rate changes infrequently according to Federal Reserve policy, but the fed funds rate changes on a daily basis according to credit market demand and supply conditions. Next to the 30-day Treasury bill rate, the federal funds rate is the lowest but most volatile of all money market rates. It is typically a bit lower than rates on bank certificates of deposit (CDs) and short-term corporate loans (commercial paper). Modestly higher than the fed funds rate are short-term rates in Europe for dollar-denominated loans, the **Eurodollar** market, and **London Interbank Offered Rates (LIBOR)**.

Trading Activity

The stock market has large and active exchange markets, such as the New York Stock Exchange (NYSE) and American Stock Exchange (Amex), plus active over-the-counter (OTC) markets such as Nasdaq. By contrast, the bond market functions largely as an OTC market. It has no primary physical location. This is despite the fact that a limited amount of bond trading takes place on the NYSE. In terms of relative market size, the NYSE is far more important for stock investors than for bond investors. The bond market largely functions as a sophisticated electronic information, communications, and processing network. It is through this network that debt securities are bought and sold from dealer to dealer and, in turn, are bought and sold by individual and institutional investors.

An interesting characteristic of the bond market is its relatively low average trading volume, at least when noninstitutional investors are considered. In the stock market, average trading volume measured in terms of the number of shares and value of shares traded is substantial. On the NYSE, for example, average trading volume in stocks is roughly 1.9 billion shares per day. The average dollar value of trading volume often exceeds $70 billion per day. The Nasdaq stock market trades another 2.1 billion shares per day valued at $54 billion. By way of contrast, trading activity in the $5 trillion corporate bond market is anemic. The **par value** of corporate bonds traded averages only $5 billion on a typical trading day.

Par value
Face amount, usually $1,000.

Historically, small investors have tended to buy and hold bond market investments for current income and long-term capital appreciation. Similarly, many pension funds and other long-term investors have turned to bonds as a durable component of a diversified portfolio. Much of the observed trading activity seen in the bond market, particularly in the Treasury securities market, is driven by hedge funds and other speculators seeking to profit from short-term movements in interest rates and currency markets. For many small investors, the bond market has historically been relatively illiquid. Bid-ask spreads in the bond market, in which a **round lot** is measured in terms of $1 million in par value, have simply been too wide to allow small investors to pursue short-term trading strategies. However, thanks to the Internet, bond market liquidity and efficiency are improving as standardized market practices and technology-based innovations increase the level of competition among both sellers and buyers.

Round lot

In the bond market, $1 million of par value.

How to Read Bond Tables

Bond Listings

For investors accustomed to reading stock listings, bond-pricing tables look somewhat different and can be hard to understand, at least initially (see Table 14.1). Once investors become familiar with bond-pricing terminology, bond tables become understandable and provide the information needed to make informed investment decisions.

In the stock tables published by *The Wall Street Journal*, investors can look up a specific company and see high, low, and last prices for the prior trading day. Such information is also available online for thousands of companies on a 15-minute delayed basis throughout the trading day. The reason that detailed stock price information is readily available is simple: Stock market investors tend to focus on the roughly 8,000 securities that are actively traded on the NYSE, Amex, and Nasdaq. Although this is an impressive number, there are far fewer stocks listed on the three major stock markets than there are bond issues outstanding. There are more than 50,000 different issues in the municipal bond market alone, and it is simply not possible for newspapers to list detailed quote information for every issue. Daily price information for the municipal bond market alone would take up to 100 pages in *The Wall Street Journal*. In addition, because widely followed common stocks are actively traded, current pricing information is easy to obtain for stocks.

TABLE 14.1	Sample Listings for Corporate, Treasury, and Municipal Bonds

A. Corporate Bond Listings

Bonds	Cur. Yield.	Vol.	Close	Net Chg.
Lucent 6.45s 29	7.46	170	86 1/2	+1 1/8
IBM 8 3/8 19	6.44	12	130 1/8	+ 7/8

B. Treasury Bond Listings

Rate	Maturity	Bid	Ask	Chg.
3.785	Jan. 09	105:30	105:31	+1
6¼	May 30	122:11	122:12	+5

C. Municipal Bond Listings

Issue	Coupon	Maturity	Price	Yield to Maturity
Orlando Orange Co Exprwy	5.00	7-01-35	107	4.67
Port of Seattle	5.00	9-01-24	104	4.48

Data Source: *Barron's Online*, December 15, 2005. Copyright © 2005 Barron's Inc. Reprinted with permission from Dow Jones Company, Inc.

Most retail investors buy bonds with the intent to receive regular interest income until **maturity**, or the specific future point in time at which the principal will be repaid in full. With only tepid trading activity, listing daily prices for bonds is neither necessary nor useful. Because only a small fraction of outstanding bonds trade on any given day, most bond listing services provide only a representative price or benchmark to gauge a current fair price. To find precise bid-ask information, bond market investors must supply their brokers with the bond's **CUSIP** number. This unique code numbering system was developed by the Committee on Uniform Security Identification Procedures as a method for identifying corporate, U.S. government, and municipal securities. Investors can use CUSIP numbers to obtain specific bond-pricing information on the Bond Market Association's Web site at **http://bondmarket.com**.

Corporate Bonds

Bond tables show basic information needed to compare prices for similar corporate, Treasury, municipal, and mortgage-backed bonds. When considering bond investments, investors need to know several pieces of information. Essential information includes the bond's coupon rate, term-to-maturity, call information, recent price, and current yield. All bond tables provide such basic information. Because corporate bonds are sometimes actively traded by institutional investors, corporate bond listings often show both the current yield and the volume traded. Table 14.2 shows a recent listing of the 25 most actively traded corporate bonds on the NYSE

TABLE 14.2	Most Active Bonds on NYSE, 2005	
Issue	**Characteristics**	**Par Value of Reported Volume (thousands)**
GENERAL MOTORS ACCEPTANCE	ZR CPN 6/15/15	$177,780
GENERAL MOTORS ACCEPTANCE	ZR CPN 12/1/12	$154,170
GENERAL MOTORS ACCEPTANCE	6% DEEP DISC 4/1/11	$76,775
GENERAL MOTORS ACCEPTANCE	6 1/8% NTS 1/22/08	$57,975
AT&T CORP	6.000% NTS 03/15/2009	$35,281
AMR CORP	9% DEBS 9/15/16	$33,344
FORD MOTOR CREDIT CORP	6 3/8% NTS 11/05/08	$29,664
AT&T CORP	6.500% NTS 03/15/2029	$21,066
AT&T CORP	6.50% NTS 03/15/2013	$20,117
LUCENT TECHNOLOGIES INC	6.45% DEB 03/15/2029	$17,736
SEA CONTAINERS LTD	7 7/8% NTS 02/15/2008	$16,254
LUCENT TECHNOLOGIES INC	7.25% NTS 07/15/2006	$14,859
LUCENT TECHNOLOGIES INC	6.50% DEB 01/15/2028	$14,304
AT&T CORP	8.35% DEB 01/15/25	$13,067
SEA CONTAINERS	10.500% NTS 5/15/2012	$12,659
DELPHI CORP	7 1/8% NTS 05/01/2029	$9,011
DELPHI CORP	6 1/2% NTS 05/01/2009	$8,716
TENET HEALTHCARE CORP	6 3/8% NTS 12/01/2011	$8,659
TENET HEALTHCARE CORP	6 7/8% NTS 11/15/2031	$8,497
INLAND FIBER GROUP	9.625% 11/15/07	$8,312
DELCO REMY INT'L	8.625% NTS 12/15/2007	$7,984
SILICON GRAPHICS INC	6.50% SR CV NTS 6/1/2009	$7,979
TENET HEALTHCARE CORP	6 1/2% NTS 06/01/2012	$7,923
AT&T CORP	7 1/2% NTS 06/01/06	$5,994
MBNA CAPITAL A	8.278% CAP SEC SER A 12/01/26	$5,798

Source: NYSE Stock Exchange. © 2005 New York Stock Exchange.

Bond Exchange. Notice that many companies, such as AT&T, Lucent, and General Motors, have several issues of bonds that are popular.

Table 14.1, Part A, shows corporate bond quotes for Lucent and IBM issues. The interest rate paid, the bond price, and the change in price are indicated as a percentage of $1,000, the bond's par value. The Lucent bond pays 6.45 percent interest on par value, or $64.50 per year, paid in two equal semiannual payments of $32.25. The small s in the Lucent listing simply separates the interest rate from the year the bond matures, 2029. The IBM bond pays 8 3/8 percent and matures in 2019.

Lucent's bond has a current yield of 7.46 percent based on its closing price of $865 per $1,000. Notice that this bond is selling for a price that is less than the $1,000 par value. This is called selling at a **discount to par**. The bond's volume traded on the NYSE the prior day amounted to $170,000 in face value, or 170 bonds, and the bond price was up $11.25. Similarly, the IBM bond had a volume of $12,000 and closed at $1,301.25, well over its par value of $1,000, up $8.75 for the day.

Discount to par
Markdown from par value.

Treasury Bonds

A typical listing for Treasury bonds is shown in Table 14.1, Part B. The first row shows that the Treasury bond indicated pays bondholders 3.785 percent interest income and is due to mature in January 2009. Prices in the bid and ask columns are expressed as percentages of the bond's **face amount** of $1,000, sometimes referred to as the **principal amount**. Numbers after the colons represent 32nds of 1 percent. A bid of 105:30 means that a buyer was willing to pay $1,059.375, compared with the seller's lowest asking price, 105:31, or $1,059.6875, a difference of only 31.25 cents per thousand dollars of face amount.

Face amount
Stated bond principal obligation (also par value).

Principal amount
Face amount or par value.

Looking at the bid and ask prices, notice that an investor who bought such a bond at par value would benefit from a principal gain of $59.375, or slightly more than 5.9 percent if it were sold at the present time. The reason for such a gain can be explained by the rate column. The Treasury note in question pays a higher interest rate than that paid on newly issued Treasury notes of similar maturity. It is more attractive than newly issued Treasury notes. As a result, current investors are willing to buy the January 9 bond at a **premium to par**.

Premium to par
Excess of market price over face amount.

The effect of falling interest rates on bond prices can also be illustrated in the case of long-term Treasury bonds. In the next row of Table 14.1, Part B, a long-term Treasury bond maturing in May 2030 is priced to yield 4.75 percent. Because current investors would pay a premium to purchase the existing Treasury bond, they bid up its current market price, and its yield to maturity fell to 4.75 percent. Obviously, interest rates had dramatically fallen from the 6¼ percent coupon rate paid when this Treasury bond was newly issued. Given this Treasury bond's relatively attractive coupon interest rate, it is presently selling in the secondary market for roughly 122:12, or $1,223.75.

Municipal Bond Market

The tax-exempt bond market is perhaps the most popular bond market sector for individual investors. About 30 percent of all outstanding municipal bonds are held by individuals. For that reason, it is particularly important that investors have an understanding of how to read municipal bond price information.

Table 14.1, Part C, shows two examples of municipal bonds. In the first row, the Orlando Orange County Expressway bond pays 5 percent interest and would provide a 4.67 percent yield to maturity. The bonds reach maturity in July 2035. The most recent price is shown as a percentage of face value, 107. Municipal bonds are frequently sold at $5,000 par value. In this case, the Orlando bond would cost $5,350. The bond is selling at a premium because prevailing interest rates are now lower on similar tax-exempt bonds than the 5 percent coupon offered on the bond. The second issue, offered by the Port of Seattle, has the same coupon of 5 percent and matures in September 2024. Just as in the Orlando bond example, sellers of the Seattle bond would receive more than the amount paid for the bond when it was originally issued.

Billionaire Bonds

Texas Billionaire Ross Perot has run for president of the United States a number of times. As such, he has had to file financial disclosure forms with the Federal Election Commission. These filings do not include exact dollar figures for the amount of candidate wealth but show candidate wealth in terms of the types of investment securities held and broad ranges for their value. They give interesting insight concerning the investment strategies employed by presidential candidates. Perot's 1992 disclosure had 123 pages and included 332 different types of income-producing assets. Several years later the number of income-producing assets increased to 595. His total wealth had been estimated to be anywhere from $1.5 billion to $3.3 billion.

Perot became a billionaire by building Electronic Data Systems, Inc., into an information processing juggernaut and then selling the company to General Motors in 1984 for $991 million in cash and over 5.6 million shares of GM stock. Two years later, GM bought Perot's stock for $701 million. Perot then acquired real estate, invested in Steve Jobs's Next, Inc., and founded Perot Systems Corporation, which he took public in 1999. Since becoming one of the richest men in America, Perot has also invested heavily in the bond market. Many of Perot's income-producing assets are municipal bonds, and many of these were issued by municipalities from Perot's home state of Texas. Interest income from low-yielding municipal bonds is free from federal income taxes; income from in-state issuers is also exempt from state income taxes. Critics contend that it is unfair for a billionaire like Perot to earn millions of dollars per year in nontaxable municipal bond interest, but they forget that the very low rate of interest paid on municipal bonds reflects their tax-exempt status. In addition, Perot's municipal bond investments have helped local communities build schools, dams, sewers, parks, hospitals, and highways.

Interestingly, bond investments have provided a substantial retirement income but have not allowed Perot to maintain his position among the most wealthy. Once the richest man in America, Perot now falls well down the list.

See Michael A. Pollock, "Muni-Bond Funds Gain Fresh Allure; Pros View Sector's Yields as Offering Sound Value vs. U.S. Government Issues," *The Wall Street Journal Online*, December 29, 2005 (**http://online.wsj.com**).

Corporate Bonds

Uses of Corporate Debt

Corporations raise capital to finance investments in inventory, plant and equipment, research and development, and general business expansion. In deciding how to raise capital, corporations can issue debt, equity, or a mixture of both. The driving force behind a corporation's financing strategy is the desire to minimize its cost of capital. In doing so, corporations take advantage of a wide variety of debt instruments that can be used to match financing requirements with investor needs.

By taking advantage of changing market conditions, corporate bond issuers can also lower borrowing costs. Most corporate debt securities offer bond investors predictable cash flows and rates of return. They are generally secure investments because, as creditors to the issuing corporation, bondholders have a significant claim on corporate cash flow and assets. Most corporate bonds are not issued directly by corporations but are instead purchased by underwriters, who then make them available to investors. Following their issuance, many corporate bonds trade in an efficient OTC market maintained by national and regional bond dealers. The corporate bond market is now valued in excess of $4.3 trillion.

Corporate Bond Characteristics

Indenture
Legal stipulation of bond agreement.

Bearer bonds
Bonds with ownership defined by possession.

Coupon bonds
Bonds with tangible interest vouchers.

Coupons
Interest vouchers.

Corporate bond obligations include the corporation's responsibility to pay back a given amount of money at a specific time and an agreed amount of interest to the bondholder. The precise terms of the legal agreement between the corporation and the bondholder are called the **indenture**. The indenture specifies the duties and obligations of the trustee (usually a bank or trust company hired by the corporation), how and when the principal will be repaid, the rate of interest, a description of any property to be pledged as collateral, callable features, and steps that the bondholder can take in the event of default. Interest on corporate bonds is usually paid twice a year.

Traditionally, many corporate bonds were sold as **bearer bonds**, or **coupon bonds**. Both feature **coupons** that are submitted twice a year to an authorized bank for the payment of interest. For example, a 20-year $1,000 bearer bond paying 8 percent interest would have 40 coupons for $40 each and one for the $1,000 principal. Coupon interest payments are made every six months. Such bonds are highly negotiable and can be used like cash. Although there are still many bearer bonds in circulation, they make tracking interest income difficult for the Internal Revenue Service, and the Tax Reform Act of 1982 ended the practice of issuing bearer bonds. Today, all fixed-income securities are sold as **registered bonds**. Bonds are now registered with the name of the bondholder, and interest income is paid twice a year in the form of a check. At bond maturity, the registered owner also receives a check for the principal. Like most bonds, corporate bonds today are typically issued in **book-entry form** only. Whereas common stocks feature a certificate that signifies ownership, a brokerage statement is typically the bondholder's only proof of ownership.

Although many municipal bonds are sold in denominations of $5,000, the face value of a corporate bond is always $1,000 unless specified otherwise. An **unsecured corporate bond** is backed only by the reputation and financial stability of the corporation. Unsecured bonds, sometimes referred to as **debentures**, are generally issued by the largest and most creditworthy corporations. A **senior bond** has prior claim to other, junior securities in the event of default or bankruptcy. Every debt security has priority, or senior claim, to preferred stock, which, in turn, has priority to common stock. **Mortgage bonds** or **equipment trust certificates** are often referred to as *senior bonds* because they are senior to any other type of debt instrument. A debenture that is **subordinated** comes behind every liability.

Equipment trust certificates are analogous to personal automobile loans. When a consumer borrows money for a car, a substantial down payment is followed by monthly installment payments. At no time throughout the life of the loan is the car worth less than the amount of the outstanding loan. Many transportation and computer leasing companies use this same type of financing. Usually, 20 to 50 percent of the purchase price is paid in the form of a down payment with the balance paid off over a term of 3 to 10 years. When the loan is fully paid, the company receives clear title from the trustee. If the company defaults on its loan, equipment is sold and the bondholders are paid off. Many equipment trust certificates are **serial bonds**. Each payment represents both interest and a partial repayment of principal.

The most junior corporate bonds are called **income bonds**. As their name implies, income bonds pay interest only to the extent that the issuing corporation has earned income. Income bonds are the only bond type in which failure to pay interest in a timely fashion does not lead to immediate default. Usually, income bonds are issued by the least creditworthy corporate borrowers or by companies already in bankruptcy.

Registered bonds
Bonds sold in book-entry form.

Book-entry form
Electronic record of bond ownership.

Unsecured corporate bond
Debt backed only by the reputation, credit record, and financial stability of the corporation.

Debenture
Unsecured debt.

Senior bond
Debt with prior claim to other, junior securities in the event of default.

Mortgage bond
Debt backed by a specific property lien.

Equipment trust certificate
Debt backed by a specific equipment lien.

Subordinated
Ranked as less important.

Serial bonds
A series of bonds to be retired in sequence.

Income bonds
Bonds with interest that must be paid only in the event of positive earnings.

Try It!

Calculate the dollar amount of interest payment and current market value of the following bonds:

AT&T Corp 8 1/8 24 quoted at 103 3/8

Treasury 3 May 10 quoted at 95:13

Solution

The AT&T Corp. bond pays annual interest of $81.25 in two semiannual payments of $40.62. The bond matures in 2024 and is valued at $1033.75 (= 103.375% of $1,000).

The Treasury bond has a 3.5 percent coupon, so it pays $35 per year, or $17.50 every six months, in interest. It matures in May 2010 and is valued at $954.06 (= 95 and 13/32 percent of $1,000).

Credit-Quality Risk

Bond Ratings

Bond rating
Measure of credit quality.

Credit-quality risk
Chance of loss due to the inability of a bond issuer to make timely interest and principal payments.

Below-investment-grade bonds
Junk bonds.

Junk bonds
Highly speculative debt securities.

High-yield bonds
Below-investment-grade bonds.

Yield spread
Difference in yield for bonds with the same term to maturity but different credit risks.

When a bond is issued, the issuer is responsible for providing details concerning its financial soundness. Still, it remains difficult for bond investors to know if a given company has the capability to make promised interest and principal payments 10, 20, or even 30 years from the date of issue. For this reason, independent **bond rating** agencies assess bond risk at the time of issue and monitor developments during the bond's lifetime. Securities firms and banks also maintain research staffs to monitor the creditworthiness of various issuers.

Credit-quality risk is the chance of investment loss due to the inability of a bond issuer to make timely interest and principal payments. Bond credit quality ranges from the highest-quality U.S. Treasury securities, backed by the full faith and credit of the U.S. government, to **below-investment-grade bonds**, or **junk bonds**, that are considered highly speculative. Because a long-term bond may not be redeemed or reach maturity for 10, 20, or even 30 years, credit quality is a prime consideration for bond investors. Prestigious bond credit rating agencies in the United States include Moody's Investors Service, Standard & Poor's Corporation, Fitch IBCA Inc., Dominion Bond Rating Service (DBRS), and A.M. Best Company. Each of these credit analysis firms assigns ratings based on a detailed analysis of the issuer's financial condition, general economic and credit market conditions, and the economic value of any underlying collateral. As shown in Table 14.3, the highest-credit-quality ratings are AAA (from S&P, Fitch, and DBRS), Aaa (from Moody's), and aaa (from A.M. Best). Bonds rated BBB or higher are generally considered investment grade with little chance of impairment in the ability of the issuer to make promised interest and principal payments. Bonds rated BB and below are considered junk bonds, or **high-yield bonds**.

Credit-quality assessment agencies signal they are considering a rating change by placing an individual bond, or all the bonds of a given issuer, on CreditWatch (S&P), under "review" (Moody's), or on "rating alert" (Fitch IBCA). Rating agencies make their ratings information available to the public through their ratings information desks. In addition to the agencies' published reports, their ratings are made available in many public libraries and over the Internet.

Because bond investors are subject to credit risk, many bonds are quoted in terms of their yield premium to the premium on higher-credit-quality bonds. **Yield spreads** show the differ-

| TABLE 14.3 | Bond Credit Ratings Distinguish Investment-Grade Bonds from High-Yield or "Junk" Bonds |

Credit Risk	Moody's	Standard & Poor's	Fitch	DBRS	A.M. Best
Investment Grade					
Highest quality	Aaa	AAA	AAA	AAA	aaa
High quality (very strong)	Aa	AA	AA	AA	aa
Upper medium grade (strong)	A	A	A	A	a
Medium grade	Baa	BBB	BBB	BBB	bbb
Below Investment Grade					
Somewhat speculative	Ba	BB	BB	BB	b
Speculative	B	B	B	B	b
Highly speculative	Caa	CCC	CCC	CCC	ccc
Most speculative	Ca	CC	CC	CC	c
Default	C	D	D	D	d

Source: Company Web pages.

| FIGURE 14.4 | Historical Yield of Corporate Bonds Rated Aaa to Baa |

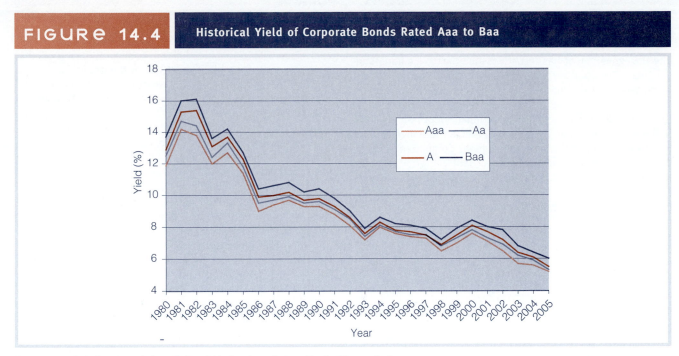

Source: Bond Market Association. © Bond Market Association. Used with permission.

ence in yield for bonds with the same term to maturity but different credit risks. Differences in default risk are a prime source of yield spreads between government and corporate bonds.

Figure 14.4 shows the 1980–2005 average annual yields for 20-year corporate bonds with credit ratings of Aaa, Aa, A, and Baa. Notice that riskier low-quality bonds always offer a higher yield than higher-quality bonds. The yield spreads between high- and low-quality bonds vary substantially. In 1982, the yield difference between Baa bonds and Aaa bonds was 2.3 percent. The difference was only 0.6 percent in the mid-1990s. Periodically, bond investors worry about low-credit-quality issuers (junk bonds, emerging markets, etc.) and sell these bonds to buy U.S. Treasuries. This is known as a "flight to quality" and creates a large yield spread between high- and low-quality credits.

High-Yield Bonds

Small, relatively new, or financially ailing corporations offer high-yield bonds, commonly referred to as "junk bonds," to compensate investors for the greater risks involved with buying their bonds. After all, corporate bond investors have a variety of safe but lower-yielding options. For example, safe but low-yield corporate bonds issued by the likes of International Business Machines or Citigroup are backed by the "full faith and credit" of some of the most creditworthy corporate bond issuers in the world.

Some junk bonds are issued from companies that are not financially strong. Other junk bonds started as investment-grade bonds issued by once-solid companies. Over time, those companies began to suffer some difficulties, and their bonds were downgraded to junk status. For example, General Motors bonds were considered of the highest quality from the 1950s through the 1980s. After the company encountered some financial difficulty in the early 1990s, GM bonds continued to enjoy investment-grade status from 1995 to 2005. Then, on May 9, 2005, Standard & Poor's downgraded GM bonds to junk status. Junk bonds that were originally issued at investment-grade status are often referred to as "fallen angels." High-yield bonds are commonly referred to as junk bonds because they carry a relatively high risk of default. When an issuer defaults, bond investors fail to receive timely interest and principal payments. In extreme circumstances, interest and principal payments are never paid. In the eyes of bond investors, the big question is whether or not the higher yield offered by junk bonds is sufficient to compensate for the higher risk of default.

The Selling of America

The U.S. government has recently issued massive amounts of new debt. The "borrow and spend" policies of the government increased the total amount of government debt to roughly $8.6 trillion by 2006. Given that there are about 300 million Americans, the total amount of government debt now exceeds $28,500 for every man, woman, and child in the United States. Projections from the U.S. Senate Budget Committee suggest that the total amount of government debt will grow to more than $15 trillion by 2014. With the recent rate of growth in government debt of more than $2 billion *per day*, those Senate projections are apt to be met, if not exceeded.

Who is buying all of this new debt? In many cases, the answer is foreign central banks and other foreign investors. In 2000, about 30 percent of U.S. government debt was held by foreigners. By 2006, that figure had risen to more than 50 percent. Big foreign holders of U.S. government debt include (in order) Japan, China, the United Kingdom, Korea, OPEC, Taiwan, Germany, Hong Kong, Switzerland, Canada, and Mexico.

History tells us that there will come a time when foreigners become less willing to hold dollar-denominated assets. If that happens, serious problems could be in the offing.

What happens if foreign investors panic? Suppose investors in a few foreign countries begin to sell U.S. bonds in order to diversify their dollar holdings. That would cause the value of the dollar to decline relative to the value of other foreign currencies, like the yen and euro. In a worst-case scenario, the decline in the dollar could snowball as other foreign investors rushed to sell their dollar holdings. With few buyers and many foreign sellers, the value of the dollar could fall sharply and cause a rapid rise in U.S. interest rates and inflation. While everybody hopes that this doomsday scenario is not likely, rapidly growing foreign holdings of U.S. debt clearly mean there is less domestic control over our own economic well-being.

See Campion Walsh, "Foreign Investors Shift to Bonds and Away from U.S. Stocks," *The Wall Street Journal Online*, January 19, 2006 (**http://online.wsj.com**).

Figure 14.5 shows the historical likelihood of rating changes or default, by rating, on corporate bonds as ranked by Moody's. For example, Figure 14.5 shows that, on average, 23.3 percent of all bonds rated Aaa were downgraded to Aa status over a five-year horizon. In addition, 1.6 percent of BaaB bonds defaulted within five years, compared to only 0.1 percent of Aaa bonds. Keep in mind that these are average default and downgrade rates. During periods of economic weakness, defaults and downgrades tend to be higher.

A vibrant economy provides an excellent environment for bond investors because it reduces the risk of default. In a good economic environment, some financially troubled companies regain a more solid foundation and get upgraded to investment-grade status. This causes their bonds to rise in price. In a weak economic environment, high-yield bonds lose their luster because the risk of default rises. To guard against hard-to-predict downturns in the overall economy, many junk-bond investors broadly diversify their junk-bond portfolios.

FIGURE 14.5   Moody's Corporate Bond Rating Changes and Defaults* (5-year periods over 1970–2001 time frame)

5–Year Corporate Bond Rating/Default Transition Rates 1970–2001

From Ratings	To Ratings									
	Aaa	Aa	A	Baa	Ba	B	Caa–C	Default	Withdrawn[†]	
Aaa	56.0	23.3	5.0	0.5	0.5	0.2	0.1	0.1	14.4	Investment Grade
Aa	4.5	52.0	23.3	3.6	0.9	0.3	0.0	1.3	15.1	Investment Grade
A	0.3	8.2	58.3	13.7	3.0	0.8	0.1	0.4	15.3	Investment Grade
Baa	0.2	1.6	15.8	47.1	9.6	2.4	0.3	1.6	21.4	Investment Grade
Ba	0.1	0.3	2.9	12.6	33.0	10.6	0.7	8.2	31.7	Noninvestment Grade
B	0.1	0.1	0.5	2.9	13.3	30.4	1.6	19.6	31.6	Noninvestment Grade
Caa–C	0.0	0.0	0.0	2.2	6.1	7.7	16.2	41.9	25.9	Noninvestment Grade

*All numbers are percentages.

[†]A bond that has been withdrawn may have matured, been called, or been brought private by the issuer. Ninety-nine percent of the withdrawn bonds could not be traced to a negative credit event.

Source: Moody's, 2002.

U.S. Treasury Securities

Treasury Securities Market

The Federal Reserve System, through its New York branch, uses the Treasury securities market to implement monetary policy. If the Fed wishes to increase the money supply, it simply buys Treasury securities, thereby injecting funds into the financial system, and reduces interest rates. If the Fed wishes to decrease the money supply, it simply sells Treasury securities, thereby withdrawing funds from the financial system, and increases interest rates. In this manner, the Fed tries to manage growth in the economy and tame the rate of inflation.

The Treasury securities market is also an efficient means for financing federal deficits at the lowest possible cost. Treasury securities carry the "full-faith-and-credit" backing of the U.S. government and have long been considered among the safest fixed-income investments in the world. Thus, U.S. Treasuries are not rated for levels of risk as corporate bonds are. Indeed, they are considered of the highest quality. Maintaining this reputation for safety and ensuring market liquidity and efficiency are of prime importance to U.S. taxpayers. An increase of only one-hundredth of 1 percent, or 1 basis point, in the interest rate on new U.S. government bonds could cost taxpayers hundreds of millions of dollars per year.

Figure 14.6 shows interest rate quotes provided for the Treasury securities market on a daily basis in *The Wall Street Journal Online;* similar data are provided by other leading financial publications. Notice the large number of Treasury securities and the very small bid-ask spreads that are typical of this market.

The Treasury issues securities through regularly scheduled public auctions. Key participants in these auctions are various investment bankers known as **primary dealers**. Primary dealers are obligated to bid at every auction for their own account and on behalf of customers and to make a continuous secondary market in Treasury securities. Once Treasury securities are issued, primary dealers provide bids and offers in the secondary market and maintain a working inventory of bonds. Primary dealers act in conjunction with bond brokers, who act as intermediaries between dealers and institutional and individual customers. Trading volume in the Treasury securities market averages an enormous $400 billion per day. The liquidity and efficiency of this market help maintain the value of the U.S. dollar in world trade and allow the dollar to remain the world's preeminent exchange currency. The U.S. Treasury is the largest issuer of debt securities in the world. More than $4 trillion in marketable Treasury securities is presently outstanding.

Primary dealers
Investment bankers that buy new Treasury securities.

T-Bills, T-Notes, and T-Bonds

Treasury securities are the safest bonds in circulation. They enjoy the full-faith-and-credit backing of the U.S. government and rely on the interest and principal paying might of the U.S. taxpayer.

At the initial point of issue, most Treasury bills have maturities of three months and six months. They are sold by government auction on a weekly basis. Once-a-month, nine-month and one-year Treasury bills are also auctioned. The face amount or par value of **T-bills** can vary from $1,000 to $5 million. All such T-bills are actively traded, highly liquid, direct short-term obligations of the U.S. government. T-bills do not pay interest. Instead, they are purchased by investors at a discount. For example, an investor might buy at auction a $10,000 three-month T-bill for $9,877.28. The investor would then receive a full $10,000 when the T-bill reached maturity in three months. Of the $10,000 to be received in three months time, $9,877.28 represents a repayment of principal and $122.72 represents a payment of taxable interest income. In this example, the compounded annual rate of return earned by the T-bill investor is approximately 5 percent per year.

T-bills are the only U. S. Treasury security issued at a discount without any stated interest rate. T-bill interest rates are determined at auction through the simple forces of supply and demand. If government borrowing rises, the supply of T-bills increases, T-bill prices fall, and the yield to maturity rises. Conversely, if the demand for T-bills rises, T-bill prices rise and the yield to maturity falls.

T-bills
Treasury bills (mature in less than one year).

FIGURE 14.6   Trading in Treasury Bonds, Notes, and Bills, February 3, 2006

U.S. Government Bonds and Notes

Colons in bond and note bid-and-asked quotes represent 32nds; 101:01 means 101 1/32. Net change in 32nds. n-Treasury Note. i-Inflation-indexed issue.

Rate	Maturity Mo./Yr.	Bid	Ask	Chg.	Asked Yield
9 3/8	Feb 06	100:02	100:03	−2	4.54
1 1/2	Mar 06 n	99:16	99:17	−1	4.39
2 1/4	Apr 06 n	99:13	99:14	−1	4.53
7	Jul 06 n	100:30	100:31	−2	4.63
2 5/8	Nov 06 n	98:11	98:12	−3	4.73
3 3/8	Jan 07 i	101:12	101:13	+1	1.86
3 1/8	Jan 07 n	98:12	98:13	−4	4.71
3 7/8	Jul 07 n	99:00	99:00	+1	4.58
4 1/4	Oct 07 n	99:12	99:13	−1	4.60
3	Nov 07 n	97:10	97:11	+1	4.56
3 5/8	Jan 08 i	103:11	103:12	+3	1.84
3 7/8	Jan 09 i	105:22	105:23	+3	1.86
3	Feb 09 n	95:19	95:20	−1	4.56
3	Jul 12 i	106:10	106:11	+7	1.95
4 3/8	Aug 12 n	99:00	99:01	+4	4.55
7	Nov 24	134:25	134:26	+33	4.69
2 3/8	Jan 25 i	106:15	106:16	+31	1.96
7 5/8	Feb 25	136:19	136:20	+33	4.69
5 3/8	Feb 31	110:28	110:29	+31	4.63
3 3/8	Apr 32 i	132:01	132:02	+51	1.83

Treasury bill quotes in hundredths, quoted in terms of a rate of discount.

Maturity	Days to Mat.	Bid	Ask	Chg.	Ask Yield
			Treasury Bills		
Feb 16 06	12	4.01	3.99	−0.03	4.05
Feb 23 06	19	4.18	4.18	+0.06	4.24
Mar 02 06	26	4.14	4.13	−0.11	4.20
Mar 09 06	33	4.19	4.18	...	4.25
Mar 16 06	40	4.20	4.18	+0.01	4.26
Mar 30 06	54	4.28	4.26	+0.03	4.34
Apr 06 06	61	4.29	4.27	+0.02	4.36
Apr 20 06	75	4.35	4.34	...	4.44
Apr 27 06	82	4.35	4.34	+0.01	4.45
May 04 06	89	4.36	4.36	...	4.46
May 25 06	110	4.43	4.41	+0.03	4.54
Jun 01 06	117	4.43	4.43	+0.05	4.55
Jun 08 06	124	4.40	4.39	...	4.52
Jul 20 06	166	4.45	4.43	+0.01	4.58
Aug 03 06	180	4.47	4.46	+0.02	4.62

Source: The Wall Street Journal Online. Copyright © 2006, Dow Jones Co. Used with permission.

Treasury notes are direct obligations of the U.S. government that have maturities ranging from 1 year to 10 years. **T-notes** pay interest on a semiannual basis and mature at par value, which may vary from $1,000 to $10,000 to $5 million. Different-length T-notes are auctioned at various periods throughout the year. Historically, the U. S. Treasury has also issued 30-year Treasury bonds. However, in 2001, the Treasury stopped issuing the 30-year **T-bond**. In 2006, the Treasury reversed course and began issuing the 30-year bond once again.

In 1997, the U.S. Treasury began issuing a new type of Treasury bond indexed to inflation. The **Treasury Inflation Protected Securities (TIPS)** have fixed coupon rates like traditional T-bonds. The difference is that the principal amount of the bond is adjusted for inflation. The par value of TIPS increases with the rate of inflation, as measured by the non-seasonally ad-justed Consumer Price Index (CPI) published monthly by the Bureau of Labor Statistics. As the par value of the bond changes over time, interest payments change. At maturity, the in-vestor is paid an inflation-adjusted principal amount, which may be substantially higher than the original $1,000 if inflation has been high. In Figure 14.6, the letter *i* denotes the quotes that are for TIPS.

For example, TIPS issued in January 2005 might have a coupon rate of 2 percent, paid semi-annually. In January 2005, the CPI was at 190.7. Bondholders received their first semiannual interest payment in July 2005, when the CPI stood at 195.4. At that time, the par value was ad-justed to $1,024.65 [=$1,000 × (195.4/190.7)], and an interest payment of $10.25 (= $1,024.65 × 2% × 1/2) was made. The investor profited from a $24.65 increase in the value of the bond and a $10.25 interest payment. Both sources of profit are treated as taxable income each year even though the bond investor does not realize any capital appreciation until the bond either is sold or matures. In the case of TIPS, the government assumes the risk of inflation. Since bond investors are not bearing this risk, TIPS offer a lower rate of return than T-bonds with similar maturities.

T-notes
Treasury notes (mature in 1 to 10 years).

T-bonds
Treasury bonds (mature in 10 to 30 years).

Treasury Inflation Protected Securities (TIPS)
Treasury bonds whose par value is adjusted semiannually for inflation, as measured by the CPI.

Try It!

Consider a TIPS note issued in January 1999 that has a coupon rate of 3 7/8 percent. The CPI was at 164.3 for this issue. By January 2005, the CPI had risen to 190.7. What was the par value of the TIPS note and the interest payment in January 2005?

Solution

The par value was adjusted to $1,000 × (190.7/164.3) = $1,160.68.
The interest payment was ½(3⅞% × $1,160.68) = $22.49

Agency and Asset-Backed Securities Markets

Agency Securities

Certain U.S. government agencies and **government-sponsored enterprises** issue debt securities to provide low-cost financing for desirable private-sector activities such as home ownership, farming, and education. The federal agency market includes debt securities issued by Fannie Mae, Freddie Mac, the Federal Farm Credit System, Federal Home Loan Banks, the Student Loan Marketing Association (Sallie Mae), and the Small Business Administration, among oth-ers. Although most agency securities do not carry the government's full-faith-and-credit guaran-tee, credit quality is enhanced and borrowing costs are lowered by their government-sponsored status. The agency securities market is smaller than the Treasury securities market, with roughly $2.6 trillion in outstanding debt.

Government-sponsored enterprises
Private corporations with a public purpose.

Mortgage-Backed Securities

Mortgage-backed securities are issued by government-sponsored enterprises and other large financial institutions. For example, Fannie Mae and Freddie Mac are often described as private corporations with a public purpose. Both started out as government-owned enterprises but were converted into privately held corporations in 1968 (for Fannie Mae) and 1970 (for Freddie Mac). Both Fannie Mae and Freddie Mac supply lenders with money by purchasing home mortgages in the secondary market. Fannie Mae and Freddie Mac assemble these mortgages into diversified packages or **pools** of such loans and then issue securities that represent a proportionate share in the interest and principal payments derived on that pool. This is sometimes referred to as **mortgage securitization**. As the underlying pool of mortgage loans is paid off by homeowners, investors receive monthly payments of interest and principal. Before the invention of mortgage-backed securities, people in some parts of the country found it hard to get mortgages simply because of limited access to funding sources. Lenders can now sell the mortgage loans that they generate and use the proceeds to make new mortgage loans. This results in a constant replenishment of the supply of mortgage funds and makes mortgages more affordable.

> **Pools**
> Diversified loan portfolios.
>
> **Mortgage securitization**
> Process of creating diversified loan portfolios and selling proportionate shares to investors.

Fannie Mae and Freddie Mac get their resources by selling securities to equity investors and by borrowing from both private investors and the Treasury Department. Both earn a profit because the amount of interest paid on mortgage-backed securities tends to be about 1 percent per year less than the amount earned on the underlying pool of mortgages. Competition limits the size of this profit rate and ensures that the benefits of an active secondary mortgage market are passed on to home buyers and renters in the form of lower housing costs. Fannie Mae and Freddie Mac have become so successful that together they purchase more than 50 percent of all residential loans originated during a given year.

When the government spun off Fannie Mae into a private corporation, it split Fannie Mae's historical mission into two parts. Ginnie Mae is the second part. Ginnie Mae is a government agency within the Department of Housing and Urban Development (HUD); it was created by Congress to ensure adequate funds for government loans insured by the Federal Housing Administration (FHA) and guaranteed by the Department of Veterans Affairs (VA) and Veterans Administration. Ginnie Mae issues modified pass-through certificates that represent an interest in a given pool of FHA and VA mortgages. As homeowners make their mortgage payments, a proportionate share passes through to the investor on a monthly basis. Each payment the investor receives is part interest and part repayment of principal. The minimum denomination is $25,000. Ginnie Mae bonds are backed by the full faith and credit of the U.S. government, but interest payments are subject to state and local taxes.

Another prime beneficiary of agency and asset-backed securities is the agricultural lending market. For example, the Farm Credit Association supervises loans made to farmers and ranchers. They are secured by mortgages made by federal land banks through the Federal Land Banks Association. These are considered moral obligations of the U.S. government. Interest received by investors is free from state and local taxes but not federal income tax. The Federal Intermediate Credit Bank (FICB) is a group of 12 banks authorized to make loans to farmers. The money is to be used for expenses, machinery, and livestock. The loans may not run for more than 10 years. Similarly, the Bank for Cooperatives makes loans to farm cooperatives. Interest received by investors is free from state and local taxes but not federal income tax.

Table 14.4 compares various mortgage-backed securities in terms of guarantee, minimum investment, and payment characteristics. Notice important differences between mortgage-backed securities issued by government-sponsored enterprises and those issued by various private institutions.

Other Asset-Backed Securities

The concept of creating diversified pools of loans and then issuing asset-backed securities to share in interest and principal payments has become popular and highly profitable during recent years. Transforming individual loans into diversified pools or related securities has been extended from home mortgages to a broad range of consumer and commercial debt. Typical

TaBLe 14.4	Comparison of Mortgage Securities

Security	Guarantee	Minimum Investment	Payment Date
Pass-Through Mortgage Securities			
Ginnie Mae I and II	Full and timely payment of principal and interest, backed by the full-faith-and-credit guarantee of the U.S. government.	$25,000 minimum; $1 increments	15th or the 20th of the month for Ginnie Mae I and II pools, respectively, following the record date and every month thereafter
Ginnie Mae Platinum	Full and timely payment of principal and interest, backed by the full-faith-and-credit guarantee of the U.S. government.	$25,000 minimum; $1 increments	15th or the 20th of the month for Ginnie Mae I and II pools, respectively, following the record date and every month thereafter
Fannie Mae Mortgage-backed Securities	Full and timely payment of principal and interest guaranteed by Fannie Mae.	$1,000 minimum; $1 increments	25th of the month following the record date and every month thereafter
Freddie Mac Participation Certificate (75-day PC)	Full and timely payment of interest and ultimate payment of principal guaranteed by Freddie Mac.	$1,000 minimum; $1 increments	15th of the second month following the record date and every month thereafter
Freddie Mac Gold PC	Full and timely payment of interest and scheduled principal guaranteed by Freddie Mac.	$1,000 minimum; $1 increments	15th of the month following the record date and every month thereafter
CMO/REMIC Mortgage Securities			
Ginnie Mae Real Estate Mortgage Investment Conduits (**REMIC**)	Full and timely payment of principal and interest, backed by the full-faith-and-credit guarantee of the U.S. government.	$1,000 minimum; $1 increments	16th or the 20th of the month for Ginnie Mae I and II collateral, respectively, following the record date and every month thereafter
Freddie Mac REMIC	Full and timely payment of interest and scheduled principal, guaranteed by Freddie Mac.	$1; $1 increments (Most dealers, however, require a minimum investment of $1,000 or more.)	15th of the month following the record date and every month thereafter
Fannie Mae REMIC	Full and timely payment of interest and scheduled principal guaranteed by Fannie Mae. (Collateral of Fannie Mae "G" series is also backed by the full faith and credit of the U.S. government.)	$1,000 minimum; $1 increments	18th or the 25th of the month following the record date and every month thereafter
Agency-Backed, Private-Label Collateralized Mortgage Obligation (CMO/REMIC)	Collateral guaranteed by Ginnie Mae, Fannie Mae, or Freddie Mac. Structure provides basis for AAA rating, but these securities carry no explicit government guarantee; they are the sole obligation of their issuer.	Varies	Varies; may be monthly, quarterly, or semiannually; with or without payment delay
Whole-Loan-Backed, Private-Label CMO/REMIC	Credit support provided by some combination of issuer or third-party guarantee, letter of credit, overcollateralization, pool insurance, and/or subordination; generally rated AA or AAA.	Varies	Varies; may be monthly, quarterly, or semiannually; with or without payment delay

Source: Bond Market Association. © Bond Market Association. Used with permission.

Bonds and Bankruptcy

Under Chapter 11 of the U.S. bankruptcy law, a failing firm can apply to the courts for protection against creditors while it is reorganized for ongoing operation. In this reorganization process, stockholders typically lose their ownership position. Various creditors, like bondholders, are typically given newly issued stock and become the owners of the newly reorganized firm. This makes bondholders important participants in the bankruptcy process.

Bankruptcy courts seek to prevent the unnecessary liquidation of firms that might become viable in the long run. The focus is on protecting the rights of current creditors and maintaining job opportunities for workers. Critics contend that the bankruptcy process is often too slow and thereby delays the liquidation of "basket cases," or firms that are simply not viable on an economic basis. Even when reorganization is viable, the bankruptcy code is thought to cause unnecessary and costly delay. Consider the bankruptcy case of UAL Corporation, the parent company of United Airlines. After incurring expenses of millions of dollars for legal and related fees, UAL finally emerged from Chapter 11 bankruptcy protection in Feb-

ruary 2006. The UAL restructuring had begun in 2002 and lasted a record 1,150 days! Critics contend that when a company pays legal and financial advisors as much as $500 to $700 per hour, the bankruptcy process tends to drag on for too long.

Studies show that successfully reorganized firms tend to be those with better prefiling operating performance (relative to their industry). They also tend to be firms that spend relatively little time in the bankruptcy process. Unfortunately, even after overly long protection from creditors, many firms that emerge from bankruptcy court do not prove to be viable. As many as 40 percent of the firms that emerge from Chapter 11 continue to experience operating losses. About one-third of all reorganized firms file a subsequent petition for bankruptcy protection. Firms that fail to achieve improvements in operating profitability while in bankruptcy and those from less profitable industries are more likely to have more financial difficulty within three years of their initial reorganization in bankruptcy court.

See Diane K. Denis and Kimberly J. Rodgers, "Chapter 11: Duration, Outcome, and Post-Reorganization Performance," *Journal of Financial and Quantitative Analysis* (forthcoming 2006).

examples include credit card debt, auto loans, home equity loans, and equipment leases. The asset-backed securities market not only provides a ready source of funds for lending to consumers and other borrowers but also facilitates specialization among financial services providers as it frees manufacturers from financing requirements.

Like mortgage-backed securities, asset-backed securities are underwritten by dealers and sold to investors around the world. As the underlying loans are repaid by borrowers, interest income and principal repayments are passed on to investors. In some instances, insurance or letters of credit are used to enhance the creditworthiness of asset-backed securities and increase their appeal among investors.

The asset-backed securities market is one of the fastest-growing areas in the financial services sector. At this point, the total value of outstanding asset-backed securities is more than $1.9 trillion.

Money Market

Market Characteristics

The money market is the market used for buying and selling short-term debt securities that can be quickly converted into cash. The buyer of a money market instrument is the lender; the seller of a money market instrument is the borrower. By definition, money market instruments have a term to maturity of one year or less. Most have a maturity that is much shorter, on the order of six months or less. As in the case of T-bills, the majority of money market instruments are issued at a discount from par or face value. For the most part, $100,000 is the minimum face amount traded in the money market. Obviously, this market is dominated by institutional investors. Smaller investors participate via money market mutual funds that have minimum investment requirements as low as $1,000.

Money market instruments are generally regarded as safe. Of course, some money market instruments are safer than others. Given very short maturities, both corporate and government-issued market instruments are free from interest rate risk. Despite the fact that only blue-chip private-sector issuers are able to participate in the money market, only government-issued money market instruments are considered free from default risk.

Money Market Instruments

In terms of dollar volume, the money market is dominated by trading in Treasury securities. In addition to T-bills, Treasury bonds and notes with one year or less to maturity are also traded. The outstanding volume of such securities gives great liquidity to the money market. Feverish trading activity ensures low dealer bid-ask spreads and low customer trading costs. Dealer spreads in the T-bill market, for example, often range as low as 6 to 8 **basis points**, or 0.06 to 0.08 percent. Dealer spreads in the market for privately issued money market instruments, called **commercial paper**, tend to be slightly higher.

Common forms of commercial paper include promissory notes issued by finance companies, such as General Electric Capital Corporation, in denominations that range from $100,000 to $5,000,000. The term to maturity is typically within 15 to 170 days. Industrial dealer paper includes the very short-term promissory notes of leading industrial firms used to finance inventories. Such obligations typically have maturities from 30 to 180 days. Most promissory notes have only a limited secondary market.

Bankers' acceptances are time drafts drawn on and accepted by banking institutions. Importers and exporters often rely on bankers' acceptances because it can be difficult for them to assess the credit quality of foreign companies. Bankers' acceptances typically range in denomination from $25,000 to $1,000,000 and can have a term to maturity that runs up to 270 days. They feature an active secondary market in which bid-ask spreads tend to be on the order of 50 basis points, or 0.5 percent, or less. **Negotiable certificates of deposit** are time deposits at commercial banks that range from $100,000 to $1,000,000 in denomination and feature an active secondary market.

The generally short maturities of money market instruments enable borrowers to have great flexibility in funding short-term cash needs. Money market instruments appeal to investors who seek protection from sometimes highly volatile interest rates. From the investor's perspective, money market instruments represent a liquid, low-risk investment that generally offers a higher yield than bank deposits. The rising popularity of money market mutual funds has been a major factor in the growing demand for money market instruments. The commercial paper market is roughly $1.6 trillion in size. The immense size and easy liquidity of the money market makes it an extraordinarily cost-effective source for corporate financing.

Municipal Bonds

Tax Advantages

State and local governments borrow money by issuing **municipal bonds**, or *muni bonds,* to build, repair, or improve schools, streets, highways, hospitals, sewer systems, and so on. Municipal bond issuers repay their debts in two ways. Projects that benefit the entire community, such as schools, courthouses, and municipal office buildings, are typically funded by general-obligation bonds repaid with tax revenues. Projects that benefit only certain users or user groups, such as utilities and toll roads, are typically funded by revenue bonds that are paid for with user fees.

When the federal income tax law was adopted in 1913, interest on municipal bonds was excluded from federal taxation. The underlying rationale is that it would be improper for the federal government to tax state and local operations. As a result, municipal bond investors are willing to accept lower yields than those they can obtain from taxable bonds. Generally speaking, after adjusting for risk, investors look to equate the after-tax interest income earned on taxable bonds with the tax-free return earned on municipal bonds. The appropriate tax rate is the highest *marginal* federal tax rate paid by the typical municipal bond investor. As a result, state and local governments are able to borrow at interest rates that are, on average, 30 to 40 percent lower than would otherwise be possible. Given the taxing authority of state and local governments, the municipal securities market is generally regarded as having relatively high quality, though credit quality varies among issuers.

Under present federal income tax law, the interest income received from investing in municipal bonds is free from federal income taxes. In most states, interest income received from securities

Basis points
1/100th of 1 percent (e.g., percent is 50 basis points.

Commercial paper
Money market instruments issued by private entities.

Bankers' acceptances
Time drafts drawn on and accepted by banking institutions.

Negotiable certificates of deposit
Time deposits at commercial banks.

Municipal bonds
Debt issued by state or local governments.

issued by government units within the state is also exempt from state and local taxes. In all 50 states, interest income from securities issued by U.S. territories and possessions is exempt from federal, state, and local income taxes. If a resident of New York City buys a municipal bond issued by the City of New York, resulting interest income is not subject to income taxes imposed by the federal government, New York State, or New York City. If that same investor bought a municipal bond issued by a city in Connecticut, state and local taxes would be payable on interest income. Keep in mind that any capital gains realized from the sale of municipal bonds are not exempt from tax.

One of the best ways to appreciate the tax-exempt advantages of municipal securities is to compare after-tax returns with similar bond investments that produce taxable interest income. Suppose an investor in the 35 percent marginal income tax bracket has $1 million to invest in corporate or municipal bonds. Which is better: earning a taxable $70,000 from 7 percent corporate bonds or $50,000 in nontaxable income from 5 percent municipal bonds? In this case, the 5 percent tax-free earnings on muni bonds exceeds the after-tax earnings on 7 percent corporate bonds. After taxes, the taxable corporate bond leaves the investor with $45,500 [= (1 − 0.35) × $70,000], whereas $50,000 in tax-free income is generated by the muni bond. Another simple way to analyze the situation is by converting the muni yield to a taxable equivalent yield, as shown in Equation 14.1. For the high-income investor in the 35 percent tax bracket, a 5 percent muni bond has an equivalent taxable yield of 7.69 percent [= 5%/(1 − .35)]. For a middle-income investor in the 28 percent tax bracket, the equivalent taxable yield is only 6.9 percent. Thus, it is easy to see why muni bonds are popular among high-income investors with substantial marginal tax rates.

$$\text{Equivalent taxable yield} = \frac{\text{muni yield}}{1 - \text{tax rate}} \quad \textbf{(14.1)}$$

Try It!

Between a corporate bond with a 7.5 percent coupon and a muni bond with a 5.5 percent coupon, which is more attractive for an investor in the 30 percent tax bracket? At what tax bracket would the investor be indifferent?

Solution

The equivalent taxable yield of the muni is 7.86 percent [= 5.5%/(1 − 0.3)]. This is greater than the 7.5 percent taxable bond, so the investor prefers the muni.

The investor is indifferent between the two at the tax rate that solves the equality 7.5% = 5.5% / (1 − tax rate). That tax rate is 26.67 percent.

Municipal Bond Types

General-obligation bonds
Municipal bonds backed by the full faith and credit of the issuer.

Revenue bonds
Bonds payable from the earnings of revenue-producing government agencies or public enterprises.

A wide variety of municipal bonds are issued by state and local governments to support general and specific financing needs. **General-obligation bonds** are backed by the full faith and credit of the issuer for prompt payment of principal and interest. Issued by cities, counties, and school districts, such bonds often enjoy added security because issuing authorities can raise property taxes to ensure payment. If sufficient tax revenues are not forthcoming, property and other assets can be sold to satisfy legal claims. As a result, general-obligation bonds are among the most creditworthy of all municipal bond instruments.

Revenue bonds are payable from the earnings of revenue-producing government agencies or public enterprises. Examples include water and sewer utilities, school districts, and airport authorities. Many such agencies have the ability to levy taxes, service charges, or fees (e.g., landing fees at the local airport). Revenue bonds can entail substantial risk because any shortfall in projected revenues will jeopardize interest and principal payments. For example, in the

Behavioral Mistakes by Bondholders

Similar to stock market investors, bond market investors must overcome a variety of behavioral biases in order to be successful. Chasing high prior returns, underestimating risk, displaying an inefficient reluctance to realize losses, and failing to adjust predictions with new information are common behavioral problems faced by bond market investors. For example, data from the mutual fund industry show that individual investors started selling bond mutual funds in 2000 after bonds had earned a poor relative rate of return during the late 1990s. Then, after strong relative performance by the bond market in 2001, individual investors started switching tens of billions of dollars from stock funds back into bond funds in 2002 and 2003. In other words, suffering from representativeness bias, individual investors sold bonds to buy stocks during the stock market peak of 2000. Then, after the stock market crash of 2000–2002, investors returned to bonds. That's called buying high and selling low, and it's no way to make money in the stock and bond markets.

Professional bond traders suffer from behavioral biases too. Consider the case of Toshihide Iguchi, an investment professional who spent eight years handling back-office bookkeeping and accounting operations for Daiwa Bank's government bond trading activities. When Iguchi was promoted to bond trader, the Daiwa operation was small and Iguchi both kept the books and traded U.S. government bills, notes, and bonds. Almost immediately, Iguchi incurred trading losses of $200,000. Instead of recognizing this relatively modest loss, Iguchi decided to hide it and try to recoup by taking increasingly larger and more risky trades. Amazingly, Iguchi's cover-up lasted 11 years. During that time, Iguchi made 30,000 unauthorized transactions and lost a total of $1.1 billion. This included $733 million in losses from Daiwa's capital account and $377 million from the unauthorized sale of customer securities.

Think of it. Iguchi lost more than a billion dollars trading plain-vanilla U.S. Treasury securities. Trading eight hours per day and five days per week for 11 years, Iguchi lost about $50,000 per hour!

See Nikkei Net Interactive, "Daiwa Securities SMBC Suffers Big Loss on Botched Sell Order," *The Wall Street Journal Online*, January 14, 2006 (**http://online.wsj.com**).

---

late 1950s, the city of Chicago built a new expressway and sold Chicago Skyway revenue bonds to be paid by tolls on the new road. Due to lower-than-expected use, the bonds defaulted in 1964 and remained in default for 30 years. By 1994, expressway usage had increased substantially, and the Chicago Skyway revenue bonds resumed making promised interest payments. Some revenue bonds default and never make investors whole. During the 1970s and 1980s, for example, the Washington Public Power Supply System (WPPSS) financed the construction of five nuclear power plants through the issuance of billions of dollars in municipal bonds. In 1983, construction on a couple of the plants was canceled and construction on the remaining plants seemed unlikely. Consequently, the revenue municipal bonds were eventually ruled void by the Washington Supreme Court. It's no wonder that municipal bond investors came to refer to the WPPSS bonds as "whoops bonds."

Finally, many communities issue **industrial revenue bonds** to develop industrial and/or commercial property for the benefit of private users. Money raised from this type of municipal bond is used to pay for the construction of new facilities, which are then leased to a corporate guarantor. The safety of industrial revenue bonds depends on the creditworthiness of the issuing municipality and the corporate guarantor. The yield on revenue bonds is generally somewhat higher than that on general obligation bonds because tax receipts tend to be more predictable than fee-based revenue streams.

Industrial revenue bonds
Bonds used to develop industrial and/or commercial property for the benefit of private users.

Bond Market Information and Innovation

Bond Information

If one is interested in buying or selling bonds, a good way to start is by comparing prices among similar securities. An easy place to check bond prices is in the financial media, such as *The Wall Street Journal, Investor's Business Daily,* or *Barron's*. Each of these publications has extensive tables showing representative bond prices. These publications also offer excellent running commentary about factors influencing the fixed-income securities market. Investors must recognize that bond prices and other information in printed financial publications represent historical snapshots. Current prices and trading information can and do vary based on current market conditions.

The Internet is another rich source for bond market information. Many sites provide comprehensive market data and descriptive information about bonds. Perhaps the best of these is maintained by the Bond Market Association. The association is a nonprofit organization headquartered in New York City and represents securities firms and banks that underwrite, trade, and sell debt securities. The Bond Market Association speaks for the bond industry and advocates its positions. It keeps members informed on relevant legislative, regulatory, and market practices, and it provides a forum through which the industry can review and respond to current issues. The association also strives to educate legislators, regulators, the press, and investors on the size and importance of the bond market. The association also compiles and tracks various industry-related statistics on a historical basis and disseminates the information through published research reports and on the Internet at **www.bondmarkets.com**.

Bond Innovations

New and innovative fixed-income products are always being introduced into the marketplace. Some new securities become popular, while others fade away. Some new bond types introduced in the last 50 years have grown into their own market segments. Mortgage-backed securities are the most impressive of these innovations. Started in the late 1960s, this innovation grew to the largest segment in the bond industry! Other successful innovations include other asset-backed securities, bonds with no coupon payments (zero-coupon bonds), and Brady bonds (foreign government bonds denominated in U.S. dollars).

Some recent innovations appear to be successful too. The U.S. Treasury's introduction of inflation-adjusted Treasury bonds seems to have been well received. Many other very interesting bonds have been issued. For example, in 1993, Disney issued bonds with 100 years to maturity. The industry has nicked them "Sleeping Beauty bonds." Also, insurance companies issue contingent-claim bonds that pay a high yield. If the company has a large loss due to a catastrophe (earthquake or hurricane, e.g.), the issuer's obligation to pay interest and/or repay the principal is either deferred or completely forgiven. The advantage of this bond for investors is that its pricing dynamics are unrelated to the normal business cycle. Therefore, it provides more diversification than other bonds. Time will tell how popular these innovations become!

Summary

■ **Bond dealers** are securities firms and banks that act as financial intermediaries between **bond issuers** and **bond investors**. Bond issuers sell newly minted bonds in the **primary bond market** to dealers who then resell those bonds to investors in the **secondary bond market**. Once bonds have been issued and sold to individual and institutional investors, bond dealers use their capital to maintain active secondary markets.

■ The long-term Treasury bond is a benchmark statistic for the **current yield** on long-term bonds and reflects the **holding-period risk** typical of long-term bonds, or the chance of loss during periods of adverse changes in bond prices. Because all Treasury securities are backed by the full faith and credit of the U.S. government, they entail no **default risk**. The **federal funds rate** is the amount charged to member banks of the Federal Reserve System that need funds to maintain required balances with the Federal Reserve. The **discount rate** is the interest rate charged on loans made by the Federal Reserve itself. Modestly higher than the fed funds rate are short-term

rates in Europe for dollar-denominated loans, the **Eurodollar** market, and **London Interbank Offered Rates (LIBOR)**.

■ Bonds are debt securities that pay a rate of interest based on the initial or **par value** of the bond. In the bond market, a **round lot** is measured in terms of $1 million in par value. Most debt securities carry an interest rate that remains fixed until **maturity**, or the specific future point in time at which principal and interest will be paid in full. For specific price-yield information, investors supply their brokers with the bond's **CUSIP** number. If a bond is trading for less than the face amount, it is trading at a **discount to par**. Bond interest rates are commonly expressed as a percentage of the **face amount** of the bond, sometimes referred to as its **principal amount**. If a bond is trading for more than the face amount (usually $1,000), it is trading at a **premium to par**.

■ The precise terms of the legal agreement between the corporation and the bondholder is called the **indenture**.

Bearer bonds, or **coupon bonds**, feature vouchers that are submitted twice a year to authorized banks for the payment of interest. Today, all fixed-income securities are sold as **registered bonds**. At maturity, the registered owner also receives a check for the principal. Like most bonds, corporate bonds today are typically issued in **book-entry form** only. The owner of book-entry bonds has no certificate. An **unsecured corporate bond** is backed only by the reputation, credit record, and financial stability of the corporation. Unsecured bonds, sometimes referred to as **debentures**, are generally issued by the largest and most creditworthy corporations.

■ A **senior bond** has prior claim to other, junior securities in the event of default. **Mortgage bonds** or **equipment trust certificates** are often referred to as senior bonds because they are senior to any other type of debt instrument. A debenture that is **subordinated** comes behind every other liability, but still ahead of preferred and common stock. **Serial bonds** are a series of bonds to be retired in sequence. The most junior grade of corporate bonds is called **income bonds**.

■ Independent **bond rating** agencies assess bond risk at the time of issue and monitor developments during the bond's lifetime. **Credit-quality risk** is the chance of investment loss due to the inability of a bond issuer to make timely interest and principal payments. Bond credit quality ranges from the highest-quality U.S. Treasury securities to **below-investment-grade bonds**, typically referred to as **junk bonds** or **high-yield bonds**. Because bond investors are subject to credit risk, many bonds are often quoted in terms of a **yield spread** to higher-credit-quality bonds.

■ The Treasury issues its securities through regularly scheduled public auctions using **primary dealers**. Short-term (one year or less) **T-bills** are very actively traded, highly liquid, direct short-term obligations of the U.S. government. T-bills do not pay interest and are purchased by investors at a discount. Intermediate-term (1- to 10-year) **T-notes** pay interest on a semiannual basis and always expire at par value, which may vary from $5,000 to $10,000 to $1 million. **T-bonds** mature in 10 to 30 years. Lastly, **Treasury Inflation Protected Securities (TIPS)** are T-bonds with a par value indexed to inflation.

■ Certain U.S. government agencies and **government-sponsored enterprises** issue debt to help finance desirable private-sector activities such as homeownership, farming, and education. Fannie Mae and Freddie Mac assemble these residential mortgages into diversified packages, or **pools**, of such loans and then issue securities that represent a proportionate share in the interest and principal payments derived on the pool. This is sometimes referred to as the **mortgage securitization process**. The Government National Mortgage Association (or Ginnie Mae) issues modified pass-through certificates, which represent an interest in a given pool of FHA and VA mortgages.

■ Bid-ask spreads in the money market are tiny and measured in **basis points**, or 1/100th of 1 percent. Money market instruments issued by private entities are called **commercial paper**. **Bankers' acceptances** are time drafts drawn on and accepted by banking institutions that substitute their credit for that of an importer or other buyer of merchandise. **Negotiable certificates of deposit** are time deposits at commercial banks that range from $100,000 to $1,000,000 in denomination and feature an active secondary market.

■ State and local governments and their agencies borrow money by issuing **municipal bonds**. The favorable tax treatment of municipal bond interest income creates a clientele effect whereby such securities are of primary appeal only to those investors with the highest taxable income. **General-obligation bonds** are backed by the full faith and credit of the issuer for prompt payment of principal and interest. **Revenue bonds** are payable from the earnings of revenue-producing government agencies or public enterprises. Many communities also issue **industrial revenue bonds** to develop commercial property for the benefit of private users.

Self-Test Problems

ST14.1 Detailed up-to-date information about the size of the bond market can be obtained on the Internet at BondMarkets.com. Go to **http://bondmarket.com** and click on the Outstanding Public and Private Bond Market Debt link to get information on the overall size of the bond market and its various components. How big is the U.S. bond market? Name the primary segments of the U.S. bond market.

Solution

In 2005, the total value of the U.S. bond market was about $24.7 trillion.

Outstanding Level of Public and Private Bond Market Debt 1985–2005 ($ billions)

	Municipal	U.S. Treasury[1]	Mortgage Related[2]	Corporate[3]	Fed Agencies	Money Market[4]	Asset Backed[3,5]	Total
1985	859.5	1,437.7	372.1	776.5	293.9	847.0	0.9	4,587.6
1986	920.4	1,619.0	534.4	959.6	307.4	877.0	7.2	5,225.0
1987	1,010.4	1,724.7	672.1	1,074.9	341.4	979.8	12.9	5,816.2
1988	1,082.3	1,821.3	772.4	1,195.7	381.5	1,108.5	29.3	6,391.0
1989	1,135.2	1,945.4	971.5	1,292.5	411.8	1,192.3	51.3	7,000.0
1990	1,184.4	2,195.8	1,333.4[6]	1,350.4	434.7	1,156.8	89.9	7,745.4
1991	1,272.2	2,471.6	1,636.9	1,454.7	442.8	1,054.3	129.9	8,462.4
1992	1,302.8	2,754.1	1,937.0	1,557.0	484.0	994.2	163.7	9,192.8
1993	1,377.5	2,989.5	2,144.7	1,674.7	570.7	971.8	199.9	9,928.8
1994	1,341.7	3,126.0	2,251.6	1,755.6	738.9	1,034.7	257.3	10,505.8
1995	1,293.5	3,307.2	2,352.1	1,937.5	844.6	1,177.3	316.3	11,228.5
1996	1,296.0	3,444.7	2,486.1	2,122.2	925.8	1,393.9	404.4	12,073.1
1997	1,318.7	3,441.8	2,680.2	2,359.0	1,022.6	1,692.8	535.8	13,050.9
1998	1,402.9	3,340.5	2,955.2	2,708.6	1,300.6	1,977.8	731.5	14,417.1
1999	1,457.2	3,266.0	3,334.2	3,046.5	1,620.0	2,338.8	900.8	15,963.5
2000	1,480.9	2,951.9	3,564.7	3,358.6	1,854.6	2,662.6	1,071.8	16,945.1
2001	1,603.7	2,967.5	4,125.5	3,835.4	2,149.6	2,566.8	1,281.1	18,529.9
2002	1,763.1	3,204.9	4,704.9	4,094.1	2,292.8	2,546.2	1,543.3	20,149.2
2003	1,898.2	3,574.9	5,309.1	4,462.0	2,636.7	2,526.3	1,693.7	22,101.2
2004	2,028.0	3,943.6	5,472.5	4,704.5	2,745.1	2,872.1	1,827.8	23,584.2
2005 Q3	2,171.8[3]	4,066.1	5,752.1	4,982.2	2,555.7	3,274.2	1,922.6	24,724.7

Source: U.S. Department of Treasury, Federal Reserve System, Federal National Mortgage Association, Government National Mortgage Association, and Federal Home Loan Mortgage Corporation.

[1] Interest-bearing marketable public debt.

[2] Includes GNMA, FNMA, and FHLMC mortgage-backed securities and CMOs and nonagency MBS/CMOs.

[3] Bond Market Association estimates.

[4] Includes commercial paper, banker's acceptances, and large time deposits.

[5] Includes public and private placements.

[6] Denotes break in series due to the inclusion of additional source data on nonagency MBS/CMOs.

ST14.2   Use a spreadsheet to analyze the data provided at the BondMarkets.com Web site (**http://bondmarket.com**), and describe the relative size of each major sector of the bond market. Which sectors are growing the fastest? Which sectors are shrinking in relative importance?

Solution

From the data provided at the BondMarket.com Web site (and displayed in ST14.1), it is clear that mortgage-related and asset-backed securities have grown rapidly in relative importance. Conversely, the relative importance of municipal and U.S. Treasury securities has shrunk.

	Municipal	U.S Treasury	Mortage Related	Corporate	Fed Agencies	Money Market	Asset Backed	Total
			Outstanding Level of Public and Private Bond Market Debt 1985–2005 (percent)					
1985	19.3	30.5	8.4	16.2	6.6	19.0	0.1	100
1986	17.8	30.3	10.4	18.5	6.0	17.0	0.1	100
1987	17.4	29.8	11.6	18.3	5.9	16.9	0.1	100
1988	17.0	28.7	12.2	18.6	6.0	17.4	0.1	100
1989	16.2	27.8	13.9	18.3	5.9	17.1	0.9	100
1990	15.3	28.4	17.2	17.2	5.6	14.9	1.3	100
1991	15.1	29.2	19.4	17.0	5.2	12.5	1.6	100
1992	14.2	30.0	21.1	16.8	5.3	10.8	1.7	100
1993	13.9	30.2	21.6	16.9	5.8	9.8	1.8	100
1994	12.8	29.9	21.5	16.8	7.1	9.9	2.0	100
1995	11.5	29.5	21.0	17.3	7.5	10.5	2.7	100
1996	10.7	28.6	20.6	17.6	7.7	11.5	3.3	100
1997	10.1	26.5	20.5	18.1	7.8	13.0	4.1	100
1998	9.7	23.3	20.5	18.8	9.0	13.7	5.1	100
1999	9.1	20.5	20.8	19.1	10.1	14.6	5.6	100
2000	8.7	17.5	21.0	19.8	10.9	15.7	6.3	100
2001	8.7	16.0	22.3	20.6	11.6	13.9	6.9	100
2002	8.8	15.9	23.4	20.3	11.4	12.7	7.7	100
2003	8.7	16.0	23.7	20.1	12.2	11.7	7.8	100
2004	8.6	16.7	23.2	19.9	11.6	12.2	7.8	100
2005	8.8	16.4	23.3	20.2	10.3	13.2	7.8	100

Questions and Problems

14.1 Detailed up-to-date information about the size of the bond market can be obtained on the Internet at BondMarket.com (**http://bondmarket.com**). Similar information about the size of the U.S. equities market can be obtained on the Dow Jones Wilshire 5000 Composite Index from the Dow Jones Indexes Web site (**www.djindexes.com/mdsidx**). Which is bigger, the stock or bond market?

14.2 What is the difference between the primary market and the secondary market for bonds?

14.3 Describe the meaning of each number in the following two bond quotes:

	Corporate Bonds				
Bonds	Current Yield	Volume	Close	Chg.
Ford 7.45s31	7.403	45	$100 \frac{5}{8}$	$-\frac{2}{8}$

	U.S. Treasury Notes and Bonds				
Rate	Maturity Mo./Yr.	Bid	Asked	Chg.	Asked Yield
$5 \frac{3}{4}$	Aug 2010n	115:13	115:14	−5	3.07

14.4   An investor in the 31 percent tax bracket is considering two bonds. One bond is a highly rated corporate bond that pays a coupon of 6.5 percent. The other bond is a tax-exempt muni offering a 4.4 percent coupon. Which bond offers a higher return to the investor?

14.5   Historically, why has the bond market been relatively illiquid for individual investors?

14.6   On June 4, 2003, corporate debt of General Electric Capital paying 6 percent interest and maturing on October 25, 2011, was quoted at a price of $1144.52. What premium to par were buyers willing to pay for this bond?

14.7   A 3 1/2 percent TIPS bond was issued in January 2002. The bond paid interest on the following three dates: July 2002, January 2003, and July 2003. The CPI was at 177.1, 180.1, 181.7, and 183.9 on the four dates, respectively. What was the interest payment at each of the three payment dates? What was the gain in the par value of the bond between January 2002 and July 2003?

14.8   Explain how the determination of T-bill interest rates differs from that for all other Treasury securities.

14.9   What is the mortgage securitization process?

14.10   Describe the characteristics of the money market.

14.11   Use the bond ratings below to rank the four bonds (a) by yield, highest to lowest, (b) by credit risk, lowest to highest, and (c) by status, as investment grade or junk bond.

Company	Moody's Rating
Bell South	A
Ford Motor Credit	Baa
Credit Suisse First Boston	Aaa
General Motors Acceptance	B

 14.12   Suppose you are trying to decide whether to buy a municipal bond issued by the Massachusetts Health and Educational Facilities Authority (CUSIP: 57585J8P9) or a corporate bond issued by Dell Computer (CUSIP: 247025AE9). Compare the yields of these two bonds, both of which mature in 2028. If your marginal federal tax rate is 30 percent and the two bonds have the same risk, which bond is more attractive on an after-tax basis. (Note: Quotes may be found in the "Market Information" section of **http://bondmarket.com**.)

 14.13   Visit the US Treasury Department Web page at **www.ustreas.gov**. The Treasury's Office of Debt Management reports many actions and predictions of the Treasury Department. What is the auction schedule for new Treasury sales over the next month? What dollar values of Treasuries were sold last year?

 14.14   The U.S. Treasury Department allows individual investors to purchase Treasury securities directly through TreasuryDirect, at **www.treasurydirect.gov**. What securities can be purchased through TreasuryDirect?

 14.15   Visit the Standard & Poor's Web page at **www2.standardandpoors.com** and click on the Credit Rating link. What credit rating actions has S&P taken lately? What will be the impact on the bonds of these companies?

14.16   Go to the Standard & Poor's Market Insight Web site at **www.mhhe.com/edumarketinsight** and enter the ticker "GM" for General Motors. In the "Financial Hlts." section, locate the credit rating that S&P has given General Motors. What is the rating? Is it investment grade or speculative grade? Also locate the credit rating for Toyota Motors (TM). These two firms are in the same industry; why are the ratings so different?

14.17 The supply and demand for U.S. Treasury securities are important factors for determining the long-term interest rates in the economy. Savvy investors can get an indication of future supply by examining U.S. budget deficit-surplus projections. Go to the Congressional Budget Office (CBO) Web site at **www.cbo.gov**. Examine the CBO's current budget projections. What does the CBO say about the future supply of Treasury bonds and long-term interest rates?

14.18 Omega Corporation has outstanding a $100 million, 9 percent coupon bond issue that is refund-protected until July 1, 2010. This issue:

   a. Is noncallable
   b. Is call-protected until July 1, 2010
   c. Currently may be redeemed with funds from general operations
   d. Currently may be redeemed but only if refunded by an issue with a lower cost

14.19 Which of the following *best* describes how issuing zero-coupon bonds affects a company's financial statements? The company's:

   a. Net income is overstated every year until maturity
   b. Cash flow from operations decreases for the life of the bond
   c. Cash flow from investing decreases during the year of maturity
   d. Cash flow from financing increases during the year of issuance

14.20 When the inflationary side effects of expansionary government macroeconomic policies are anticipated quickly, the *primary* impact of a demand stimulus is a(n):

   a. Increase in output
   b. Increase in the price level
   c. Decrease in unemployment
   d. Increase in aggregate supply

INVESTMENT APPLICATION

Bills, Notes, Bonds, and Inflation

Treasury securities are considered the safest of all debt instruments because they are legally backed by the "full faith and credit" of the U.S. government. This designation is the highest level of backing given on a U.S. government security. It means that the federal government pledges to use its full taxing and borrowing authority to make promised interest payments and to repay the full amount of borrowed principal, or face amount of the security. The federal government can also avoid default by simply printing more money. Notice that the cash in your pocket, called a Federal Reserve Note, is simply a non-interest-bearing certificate that enables the holder to demand payment of "one dollar" from the U.S. Treasury. Of course, there is a bit of circular reasoning at work here because the U.S. Treasury defines "one dollar" as one Federal Reserve Note. A demand at the Treasury for the payment of "one dollar" in exchange for one Federal Reserve Note will be met by the issuance of one new, crisp Federal Reserve Note. The advantage of holding T-bills or other Treasury securities over cash is that Treasury securities pay interest income but the cash held in your pocket earns a 0 percent rate of return. The advantage of cash over Treasury securities, of course, is that only cash is widely recognized as the currency of choice for the purchase of goods and services.

The price of Treasury securities at any point in time is simply set by the interplay of supply and demand. When bond investors project a marketwide decline in interest rates, they scramble to lock in current interest rates, thus bidding up bond prices, and yields begin to fall. In such instances, bond investors are simply trading cash for Treasury securities. When bond investors project a rise in interest rates, they dump bond portfolios, causing bond prices to fall, and yields begin to rise. This represents a simple trade of Treasury securities for cash. Remember, bond prices are just the terms of trade for bonds expressed in terms of cash. If the Treasury Department flooded the marketplace with an immense supply of new bonds, Treasury bond prices would plummet and interest rates would soar. Conversely, if a budget surplus cut borrowing needs and allowed the federal government to begin to buy back Treasury securities, the supply of new bonds would fall, Treasury bond prices would rise, and interest rates would drop.

Although many investors feel comfortable with the notion that bond prices and interest rates are determined by the forces of supply and demand, they feel less comfortable with the concept that the "price" of money is set in a similar fashion. Indeed, what is the "price" of money? The answer is simple: When a consumer buys a blouse for $40, the terms of trade are simply one blouse: $40. Not only is the blouse price $40, the "worth" of that same $40 is one blouse. If importers flooded the marketplace with an immense supply of new blouses, blouse prices would plummet and the value of cash would rise. Conversely, if an import embargo cut the supply of new blouses, blouse prices would rise and the value of cash would fall. The market for all goods and services works the same way. If the money supply rises faster than the pace of growth in the overall economy, prices rise and inflation occurs. If the money supply rises slower than the pace at which the overall economy grows, prices fall and deflation occurs. When the money supply and the overall economy grow at the same rate, price stability ensues. During the 20th century, the U.S. economy has been marked by persistent inflation that averages on the order of 3 to 4 percent per year. Falling prices, or deflation, is seldom seen, and has not been common in the United States since the 1930s and the Great Depression.

Given the enormous size of the Treasury securities market, a strong link is forged between bond prices, interest rates, and the rate of inflation. A rise in the rate of inflation causes a sharp decline in the value of future interest and principal payments and a downturn in bond prices. This is especially true in the case of T-bonds and other long-term debt securities. Because current market prices are determined on the basis of investor expectations, even the "whiff" of an uptick in inflation can throw a scare into bond investors and create bond market turmoil. However, if investors expect a downturn in inflation, the worth of future interest and principal payments rises and bond prices rise. Thus, it is important to recognize that although all federal government debt obligations are free from default risk, the value of long-term government obligations is subject to changes in market interest rates. The market prices of long-term T-bonds are not guaranteed and will fluctuate daily—just like the prices of any other long-term bonds.

As shown in Table 14.5, total rates of return earned by investors in Treasury securities can fluctuate widely. This is especially true in the case of long-term T-bonds. In 1999, for example, long-term T-bond investors suffered a loss of 8.74 percent in the value of their holdings during the course of a single year. The same portfolio earned 20 percent the following year. Although such losses are rare for T-bond investors, such investors experienced negative total returns (before taxes) during 17 years since 1950, or during 30 percent of the past 56 years. Investor rates of return on intermediate-term T-notes can also show disturbing volatility. T-note investors suffered a negative total return of −3.99 percent during 1999 and experienced losses during 7 of the past 56 years. Although T-bill investors earned a positive rate of return before taxes during each year since 1950, these total returns are often meager.

a. Notice from Table 14.5 that the rate of interest earned by T-bills was substantially in excess of the inflation rate during the early to mid-1980s. Why did investors demand such a high after-inflation or real return during this period?

b. Would holders of T-bonds prefer that a federal government surplus be used to reduce taxes or pay down the debt? Why?

Year	Long-Term Treasury Bonds (> 10 years)	Intermediate-Term Treasury Notes (< 10 years)	Short-term Treasury Bills (< 1 year)	Inflation Rate	T-Bill Real Return
1950	0.06%	0.70%	1.20%	5.79%	−4.59%
1951	−3.93	0.36	1.49	5.87	−4.38
1952	1.16	1.63	1.66	0.88	0.78
1953	3.64	3.23	1.82	0.62	1.20
1954	7.19	2.68	0.86	−0.50	1.36
1955	−1.29	−0.65	1.57	0.37	1.20
1956	−5.59	−0.42	2.46	2.86	−0.40
1957	7.46	7.84	3.14	3.02	0.12
1958	−6.09	−1.29	1.54	1.76	−0.22
1959	−2.26	−0.39	2.95	1.50	1.45
1960	13.78	11.76	2.66	1.48	1.18
1961	0.97	1.85	2.13	0.67	1.46
1962	6.89	5.56	2.73	1.22	1.51
1963	1.21	1.64	3.12	1.65	1.47
1964	3.51	4.04	3.54	1.19	2.35
1965	0.71	1.02	3.93	1.92	2.01
1966	3.65	4.69	4.76	3.35	1.41
1967	−9.18	1.01	4.21	3.04	1.17
1968	−0.26	4.54	5.21	4.72	0.49
1969	−5.07	−0.74	6.58	6.11	0.47
1970	12.11	16.86	6.52	5.49	1.03
1971	13.23	8.72	4.39	3.36	1.03
1972	5.69	5.16	3.84	3.41	0.43
1973	−1.11	4.61	6.93	8.80	−1.87
1974	4.35	5.69	8.00	12.20	−4.20
1975	9.20	7.83	5.80	7.01	−1.21
1976	16.75	12.87	5.08	4.81	0.27
1977	−0.69	1.14	5.12	6.77	−1.65
1978	−1.18	3.49	7.18	9.03	−1.85
1979	−1.23	4.09	10.38	13.31	−2.93
1980	−3.95	3.91	11.24	12.40	−1.16
1981	1.86	9.45	6.96	8.94	−1.98
1982	40.36	29.10	11.59	3.87	7.72
1983	0.65	7.41	8.64	3.80	4.84
1984	15.48	14.02	10.20	3.95	6.25
1985	30.97	20.33	7.87	3.77	4.10
1986	24.53	15.14	6.41	1.13	5.28
1987	−2.71	2.90	6.37	4.41	1.96
1988	9.67	6.10	7.33	4.42	2.91
1989	18.11	13.29	9.15	4.65	4.50
1990	6.18	9.73	8.07	6.11	1.96
1991	19.30	15.46	5.96	3.06	2.90
1992	8.05	7.19	3.68	2.90	0.78
1993	18.24	11.24	2.98	2.75	0.23
1994	−7.77	−5.14	4.03	2.67	1.36
1995	31.67	16.80	5.77	2.54	3.23
1996	−0.93	2.10	5.24	3.32	1.92
1997	15.08	8.38	5.38	1.70	3.68
1998	13.52	10.21	5.31	1.61	3.70
1999	−8.74	−3.99	4.94	2.30	2.64
2000	20.11	14.03	5.97	3.44	2.53
2001	4.56	7.27	4.06	1.49	2.57
2002	17.17	13.94	1.79	2.48	−0.69
2003	2.06	2.02	0.95	1.82	−0.87
2004	7.70	4.01	1.13	2.97	−1.84
2005	6.50	2.16	2.90	3.42	−0.52
Arithmetic average	6.45%	6.37%	4.91%	3.89%	1.02%
Median	4.00%	4.65%	4.85%	3.19%	1.19%
Geometric mean	5.97%	6.18%	4.87%	3.85%	0.99%
Standard deviation	10.40%	6.41%	2.70%	2.96%	2.45%
Coefficient of variation	1.61	1.01	0.55	0.76	2.40

15

chapter

Bond Valuation

The Federal Reserve System ("the Fed") is the central bank of the United States. The Federal Reserve was created by Congress in 1913, and its role has evolved and expanded over the years. Today, the Fed's responsibilities fall into four general areas: conducting the nation's monetary policy in pursuit of full employment and stable prices; supervising and regulating banking institutions to ensure the safety and soundness of the financial system; containing systemic risk in the financial markets; and providing financial services to the U.S. government, to the public, to financial institutions, and to foreign official institutions. When Fed Chairman Ben Bernanke speaks, bond markets around the world listen, and listen intently. Perhaps no other individual is credited (or blamed) with having such power to move the financial markets.

The price of money is the interest rate. As the supply and demand for money change, so too does the price of money, the interest rate. When the Fed increases the supply of money to spur economic growth, interest rates decrease. When the Fed wants to fight inflation, it will decrease the supply of money and interest rates will rise. Changing market interest rates can have a tremendous impact on bond prices and the value of bond portfolios. The value of long-term bonds can rise by 5 to 10 percent in a matter of days following a sharp decline in market interest rates, or it can plummet following a sharp uptick in interest rates. Bond portfolio managers often try to time moves in market interest rates and use leverage to amplify their bets. Because Fed actions can influence the direction of interest rates, these bond investors and speculators want to know what the Fed is thinking. Is Bernanke worried about anemic economic growth or more concerned about rising inflation? Market interest rates, the value of bond portfolios, and the jobs of bond portfolio managers are on the line every time Bernanke speaks. No wonder that Fed watching is a common pastime of both bond traders and fixed-income investors![1]

---

[1]Greg Ip, "Fed Lifts Rate by Quarter Point, Casts Doubt on More Increases," *The Wall Street Journal Online, February* 1, 2006 (**http://online.wsj.com**).

CHAPTER OBJECTIVES

- Calculate the value of a bond.

- Compute the yield offered by various types of bonds.

- Measure the interest rate risk of bonds using duration and convexity concepts.

- Discover the characteristics of convertible bonds.

- Learn how to implement bond investment strategies.

Bond Valuation Concepts

Economic Characteristics of Bonds

Bonds are debt securities that pay a rate of interest based on the face amount, or par value, of the bond. The interest rate can be fixed or variable. Most debt securities carry a fixed rate of interest. Usually, bond investors receive interest payments twice per year, or on a semiannual basis. For example, a $1,000 bond sold at par with a 5 percent interest rate pays interest of $50 per year, in $25 installments every six months. When a bond matures, typically in 10, 20, or 30 years, bond investors also receive the full face amount of the bond. Over time, interest rates in the economy change. If interest rates rise from 5 to 7 percent, a fixed-rate 5 percent bond still pays $50 per year. However, newly issued fixed-rate bonds with similar default risk would pay $70. The older bond paying $50 then becomes unattractive to investors, and its market price falls to a price that will offer subsequent buyers a competitive yield to maturity of 7 percent. Fixed-rate bond prices change over time when **market interest rates** change.

While fixed-rate bonds are most common, bond market participants sometimes prefer interest rates that are adjustable on a daily, monthly, or annual basis. This allows the interest rate paid on a given bond to closely track market interest rates. Interest rates on floating-rate bonds are reset periodically to keep them in line with changes in an underlying **benchmark interest rate**. Rates on short-term Treasury bills or 30-year Treasury bonds are popular interest rate benchmarks.

Another popular bond type, called **zero-coupon bonds ("zeros")**, makes no periodic interest payments. Instead of getting regular interest payments, the bond investor receives a single payment at the time of maturity that equals a return of the original purchase price (or principal) plus the total interest earned. Zero-coupon bonds are sold at an original price that is a substantial discount from their face amount. For example, a bond with a face amount of $1,000, maturing in 30 years, and priced to yield 6 percent might be purchased for about $174. At the end of 30 years, the bond investor will receive $1,000. The difference between $1,000 and $174 represents the interest income to be received, based on an interest rate of roughly 6 percent.

Zero-coupon bonds were introduced in 1982. They have become popular because issuers avoid the need to make periodic interest and principal payments. Long-term bond investors have also been attracted to zeros because they eliminate **interest reinvestment risk**, or the chance that a subsequent decline in interest rates will reduce the amount earned on reinvested interest income. Today, zero-coupon bonds are offered by the U.S. Treasury, corporations, and state and local governments. As with all types of bond issues, zeros issued by the Treasury are generally considered the safest because they are backed by the full faith and credit of the U.S. government. Municipal zeros also offer a high degree of safety and can generate attractive returns when calculated on a tax-equivalent basis. Zero-coupon bonds issued by a corporation or the U.S. Treasury generate taxable income even though bondholders receive no periodic cash payments. Each year, holders of zero-coupon bonds must pay taxes on a prorated share of the bond's expected appreciation between the time of purchase and the time of maturity.

Market interest rate
Prevailing rate of interest on essentially identical securities.

Benchmark interest rate
Interest rate standard.

Zero-coupon bonds ("zeros")
Discount bonds that pay no coupon interest.

Interest reinvestment risk
Chance of lost income on reinvested interest payments.

Present Value of a Bond

An interesting aspect of bond market tradition is that bond prices are conventionally quoted as a percentage of par, where par is typically $1,000. This means that a bond price of 98½ implies a bond market value of $985 (= 98.5% × $1,000). While the initial or par value of a bond is typically set by the issuer at $1,000, from that point until the time of maturity its price is set by the forces of supply and demand in the marketplace. Whereas newly issued bonds normally sell at or close to their face value or principal amount, prices for **seasoned bonds** can fluctuate widely.

Seasoned bonds
Bonds traded from one investor to another.

Prices for seasoned bonds depend on a number of factors, including prevailing market interest rates, the supply and demand for similar types of bonds, credit quality, term to maturity, and the tax status of individual bonds. In general, the economic value of a bond equals the present value of all expected interest and principal payments:

Present value of bond = present value of interest payments + present value of principal

$$= \sum_{t=1}^{T} \frac{\text{cash payment}_t}{(1 + \text{yield})^t} \tag{15.1}$$

where T is the number of years until maturity, when all promised interest and principal payments have been made, and *yield* is the market interest rate on securities with the same essential economic characteristics. Holding all else equal, a rise in prevailing interest rates has the effect of increasing the denominator of the above expression and reducing bond value. Whereas the value of a bond will fall with a rise in prevailing interest rates, the value of a bond will rise with a decline in interest rates.

Settlement date
Date on which the buyer takes effective possession of a security.

Bond Pricing

Maturity date
Date on which the security expires, or ceases to accrue interest.

To calculate the price for an individual bond, investors need information about the bond's settlement terms, maturity, coupon rate, yield, redemption value, frequency of interest payment, and day-count basis. A bond's **settlement date** is the date on which the buyer takes effective possession of the security. For an initial public offering, the settlement date is the day after the issue date. In most instances, bond transactions are governed by a one-day settlement period, so the settlement date typically follows the transaction date by one day. The **maturity date** is the date on which the security ceases to accrue interest. The time remaining until maturity is the simple difference between the maturity date and the settlement date. Another important component of bond valuation is the **bond coupon rate**, expressed as a percentage of par value. This interest rate often differs from the securities yield to maturity, which is closely determined by prevailing market interest rates. **Bond redemption value** is the amount to be received from the issuer on the maturity date. This amount is usually equal to par value and is typically $1,000. Most bonds pay **semiannual interest** in two equal installments. In the United States it is conventional to calculate bond interest rates on the **day-count basis** of 30 days per month and 360 days per year.

Bond coupon rate
Bond interest rate expressed as a percentage of par value.

Bond redemption value
Amount to be received from the issuer on the maturity date.

Semiannual interest
Interest paid in two equal installments per year.

The present value of interest payments and bond prices can be easily calculated using the formula for the present value of an annuity.[2] Thus, Equation 15.1 can be characterized as

Day-count basis
Method for calculating interest rates, usually 30 days per month and 360 days per year.

Bond price = PV of annuity (pmt, i, T) + PV (FV, i, T) (15.2)

---

[2]The exact solution to the bond equation is

$$\text{Price} = \left[\frac{\text{redemption value}}{\left(1 + \dfrac{\text{yield}}{\text{frequency}}\right)^{\left(T-1+\frac{\text{DSC}}{E}\right)}} \right] + \left[\sum_{k=1}^{T} \frac{100 \times \dfrac{\text{coupon rate}}{\text{frequency}}}{\left(1 + \dfrac{\text{yield}}{\text{frequency}}\right)^{\left(k-1+\frac{\text{DSC}}{E}\right)}} \right] - \left(100 \times \frac{\text{coupon rate}}{\text{frequency}} \times \frac{A}{E}\right)$$

where *DSC* is the number of days from settlement to the next coupon date, E is the number of days in the coupon period within which the settlement date falls, T is the number of coupons payable between the settlement date and the redemption date, and A is the number of days from the beginning of the coupon period to the settlement date.

| | TABLE 15.1 | | Bond Valuation Depends on Promised Cash Payments, the Maturity Date, and the Prevailing Interest Rate | | | | | | | | | eXcel |

	A	B	C	D	E	F	G	H	I	J	K
1											
2											
3											
4					Bond Type						
5			(1)	(2)	(3)	(4)	(5)				
6	Face amount		$1,000	$1,000	$1,000	$1,000	$1,000				
7											
8	Semi-annual interest		$27.50	$37.50	$25.00	$45.00	$35.00	=(G10*G6)/2			
9											
10	Coupon interest rate		5.50%	7.50%	5.00%	9.00%	7.00%				
11											
12	Yield (market interest rate)		5.75%	6.50%	7.00%	7.25%	7.25%				
13											
14	Issue date		1/26/78	2/16/91	4/9/99	11/6/87	10/12/06				
15											
16	Settlement date (purchase date)		1/26/07	2/16/07	1/14/07	7/16/06	10/13/06				
17											
18	Maturity date		1/26/08	2/16/12	4/9/20	11/6/28	10/13/36	=(G18-G16)/365			
19											
20	Term to maturity (years)		1.0	5.0	13.2	22.3	30.0				
21								=-0.1*PV(0.5*G12,2*G20,G8,G6,0)			
22	Bond price (% of par)		99.76	104.21	82.92	119.22	96.96				
23								=G22*10			
24	Bond valuation ($)		$ 997.60	$1,042.13	$ 829.15	$1,192.16	$ 969.58				
25											

In the annuity formula, *pmt* is the semiannual coupon payment, *i* is the discount interest rate, and *T* is the number of semiannual periods until maturity. The second present-value function in Equation 15.2 is the present value of the principal to be paid at maturity. Investors can easily calculate the price of a bond using present-value tables, present-value equations (see Appendix A), or, most commonly, business calculators. Bond investors can also use spreadsheet software programs, like Microsoft Excel, to quickly and easily calculate bond prices.

To illustrate, consider the bond pricing information given in Table 15.1. This table shows the present-value function available in Excel. As usual, all bonds shown have a face amount, or par value, of $1,000 and pay semiannual interest. In the case of the bond shown in column (1), the coupon interest rate is 5.5 percent of par, or $27.50 every six months. The yield to maturity, or market interest rate, for this security is 5.75 percent. This is also the market interest rate for securities of essentially the same payment terms and credit quality. The bond was issued on January 26, 1978, for a 30-year term that expires on January 26, 2008, and it was last purchased for investment on January 26, 2007. As of that purchase or settlement date, the bond had a remaining term to maturity of one year and a price of 99.76, where price is expressed as a percentage of par value. This implies an economic valuation as of January 26, 2007, of $997.60.

Notice from the bond pricing examples given in Table 15.1 that bond prices exceed the face amount of $1,000 when yield to maturity is less than the bond's coupon rate. Bond prices are less than par value when the market interest rate is higher than the bond's coupon yield.

Try It!

Consider the following bond that is between coupon interest payments. The bond pays $25 every six months, and there are three years and one month to maturity. The yield for the bond is 6 percent annually. What is the price of the bond?

Solution

Use a financial calculator or spreadsheet function to compute the answer. Four values are needed to compute the price of the bond. They are (1) the number of periods until maturity, (2) the bond's yield, (3) the dollar value of each interest payment, and (4) the redemption value of the bond.

(continued)

N (or T) = $2 \times 3\frac{1}{12}$ = 6.167 periods

I/Y (or i) = 6% / 2 = 3%

PMT = $25

FV = $1,000

Entering these values into a financial calculator or spreadsheet function produces a bond price of $972.23.

Yield to Maturity

Common Maturities

Bond maturities generally range from one day for overnight loans to 30 years for long-term obligations. In rare instances, corporate and government bonds have been issued for terms of up to 100 years! Bonds are often classified according to time to maturity using the following broad categories:

- Short-term notes have initial maturities of up to five years.

- Medium-term notes or bonds have initial maturities of 5 to 10 years.

- Long-term bonds generally have initial maturities of 11 or more years.

Average life
Typical period before refunding.

Some bonds, especially mortgage-backed securities, are typically priced and traded on the basis of the bond's expected **average life** rather than on the basis of any stated term to maturity. When mortgage rates decline, homeowners often move quickly to prepay their mortgages. This may reduce the expected average life of the bondholder's investment. When mortgage rates rise, the reverse tends to be true. Homeowners tend to be slow to prepay fixed-rate mortgages in the face of rising interest rates. Under such circumstances, bondholders often find that their principal remains committed for a longer-than-expected holding period.

The investor's choice of a preferred term to maturity depends on when principal repayment is required, what investment return is sought, and what the investor's risk tolerance is. Many bond investors prefer short-term bonds for their comparative stability of principal and interest payments. In turn, such investors are willing to accept the typically lower rates of return offered on short-term bonds. Bond investors seeking greater overall returns tend to favor long-term securities despite the fact that such bonds are more vulnerable to interest rate fluctuations and other market risks.

Expected-Yield Calculation

Yield to maturity
Investor return over the period from the settlement day to the security's expiration.

Bond yield is the investor's expected rate of return based on the price paid and the anticipated amount and timing of interest and principal payments. **Yield to maturity** is typically more meaningful than a simple current-yield calculation. Current yield is the bond interest amount divided by the current market price. It gives an approximation of the bond's quick cash-on-cash return. The yield-to-maturity calculation tells bond investors the total rate of return that might be expected if they were to buy and hold the bond until maturity.

The yield-to-maturity calculation is usually much more informative than the current-yield calculation because it enables investors to compare bonds with different maturity and coupon characteristics. Yield-to-maturity calculations involve computing the internal rate of return on a bond investment. This internal rate of return is the interest rate that equates the current purchase price of the bond with the economic value of all anticipated future interest and principal payments. Therefore, the yield to maturity equals all interest payments received from the time of purchase until the point of maturity plus any capital gain resulting from the purchase of a bond at a discount from par, or face, value. Alternatively, the yield to maturity equals all in-

Street Smarts 15.1

Who's Default Is It?

In 2001, WorldCom-MCI issued $11.9 billion in bonds. World-Com was then the second-largest long-distance phone company in the United States, and its debt offering was then the largest bond issue in American history. Nearly all of the money raised represented new borrowing; less than $2 billion was used to refund previously issued bonds. This massive new offering by WorldCom came with detailed analyses by investment bank underwriters and credit rating agencies. WorldCom's massive debt issue was given an investment-grade rating—A3 by Moody's and BBB+ by Standard & Poor's. Because of this high rating, many institutional investors, such as pension funds and insurance companies, purchased the securities.

Only one year later, the credit agencies downgraded World-Com debt to junk-bond status. The rationale behind the downgrade was that WorldCom's total debt of $40 billion was simply too high and was apt to make difficult the timely payment of interest and principal obligations. In fact, WorldCom's onerous financial obligations eventually led to the largest corporate bankruptcy in U.S. history. Given this subsequent turn of events, both individual investors and professional money managers have reason to wonder why the risks attached to WorldCom's massive debt issue were not obvious to underwriters and credit rating agencies at the time the bonds were issued. Shouldn't underwriters and bond credit rating agencies have been better able to predict the subsequent inability of WorldCom to meet its financial obligations?

Bond investors have every right to question why investment banks and credit rating agencies would actively promote a massive bond issue, and collect enormous fees for doing so, only to quickly reverse course when the risks attached to the debt became obvious to everyone. It seems incredible that investment bankers and credit rating agencies could get paid millions of dollars in fees to validate an enormous bond issue and then use the giant size of that same issue as a reason to downgrade the company within a matter of 12 months.

Irate bond investors were left with enormous losses and justifiable concerns about a lack of accountability on the part of both investment bankers and credit rating agencies.

See Charles Fleming and Carrick Mollenkamp, "Insurers, Banks Clash over Claims for Enron, WorldCom Settlements," *The Wall Street Journal Online*, December 23, 2005 (**http://online.wsj.com**).

---

terest payments received prior to the point of maturity minus any capital loss resulting from the purchase of a bond at a premium to par. It is important to remember that bond prices and bond yields are *inversely* related. As bond prices fall, yield to maturity increases. Rising bond prices portend falling yields.

For example, if a newly issued 30-year bond is bought for a purchase price of $1,000 (or par) and the promised interest rate is 7 percent ($70), then the current yield and the yield to maturity on the bond are both 7 percent (= $70/$1,000). If such a bond had a remaining term to maturity of 30 years and was purchased in the secondary market at a discount for $933, then, given the promised interest payments of $70 per year, the yield to maturity would equal roughly 7.57 percent (using a spreadsheet or business calculator). The bond would have a current yield of 7.50 percent (= $70/$933). If such a bond were purchased at a premium for $1,077, given interest payments of $70 per year, the yield to maturity would equal roughly 6.42 percent. The current yield would then be 6.50 percent (= $70/$1,077). Notice that yield to maturity is higher than current yield for discount bonds and lower than current yield for premium bonds.

After obtaining the price of a bond, bond coupon rate, and maturity date, an investor can compute the yield to maturity.[3] The yield to maturity is the discount rate that causes the present value of bond cash flows to exactly equal the current price of the bond. To calculate yield to maturity, investors must solve for the discount rate, i, in Equation 15.2 or solve for i in

$$\text{Bond price} = \text{PV of annuity (pmt, } i, T) + \text{PV (FV, } i, T)\qquad\qquad(15.3)$$

---

[3] The detailed formula for yield to maturity is

$$\text{Yield} = \left\{ \cfrac{\cfrac{\text{redemption value}}{100} + \cfrac{\text{coupon rate}}{\text{frequency}} - \left[\cfrac{\text{par}}{100} + \left(\cfrac{A}{E} \times \cfrac{\text{coupon rate}}{\text{frequency}}\right)\right]}{\cfrac{\text{par}}{100} + \left(\cfrac{A}{E} \times \cfrac{\text{coupon rate}}{\text{frequency}}\right)} \right\} \times \cfrac{\text{frequency} \times E}{\text{DSR}}$$

where A is the number of days from the beginning of the coupon period to the settlement day (accrued days), *DSR* is the number of days from the settlement date to the redemption date, and E is the number of days in the coupon period.

Investors commonly compute the yield to maturity using business calculators or spreadsheets.

To illustrate, consider the expected yield-to-maturity calculations shown in Table 15.2. The table also shows the Excel RATE function. As in Table 15.1, all the bonds have a face amount or par value of $1,000 and pay semiannual interest. For the bond example shown in column (1), the coupon interest rate is 4 percent of par, or $20 every six months. This is a 30-year bond issued on July 4, 1977, that expires on July 4, 2007, and it was last purchased for investment on July 4, 2006. As of that purchase or settlement date, the bond had a remaining term to maturity of one year and a price of 98.21, where price is expressed as a percentage of par value. This implies an economic value as of July 4, 2006, of $982.10.

Notice from the bond pricing examples given in Table 15.2 that yield to maturity exceeds the coupon rate when bond prices are less than the par value of $1,000. The yield to maturity is less than the bond's coupon rate when the current market price of the bond exceeds par value.

Try It!

Consider the following bond that is between coupon interest payments. The bond pays $25 every six months, and there are three years and one month to maturity. The price of the bond is $972.23. What is the bond's yield?

Solution

Use a financial calculator or spreadsheet function to compute the answer. The four values needed are (1) the number of periods until maturity, (2) the bond's price, (3) the dollar value of each interest payment, and (4) the redemption value of the bond.

$$N \text{ (or } T) = 2 \times 3\frac{1}{12} = 6.167 \text{ periods}$$

$$PV = \$972.23$$
$$PMT = \$25$$
$$FV = \$1{,}000$$

Note: To enter the cash flows into some financial calculators, the inflows and outflows must be of different signs. In this case, make the PV negative (–$972.23) because you must buy the bond to receive the cash flows. The calculator computes a yield of 3 percent. Note that this yield is for a six-month period. It is customary to report this as an annual yield, 2 × 3% = 6%.

This example (and the previous example) show that any of the five characteristics of a bond (periods to maturity, yield, price, interest payment, and redemption value) can easily be determined when the other four characteristics are known.

Call Provisions

Call provisions
Contractual authority that allows the issuer to redeem bonds prior to scheduled maturity.

Most bonds have **call provisions** that allow the issuer to repay the investor's principal early at a specified date and price and thereby redeem the bond prior to scheduled maturity. Bonds are commonly called by issuers following a significant drop in prevailing interest rates. It is common for issuers to pay bondholders the par value of the bond plus one year of interest payments when the bond is called. Bonds can also be called when issuer credit quality rises substantially following an upturn in business prospects or an increase in government agency tax receipts. If a bond is called, the call date is usually one of the two dates that semiannual interest is due. The reasons behind early bond redemptions are obvious. When interest rates fall or credit quality improves, new bonds can be

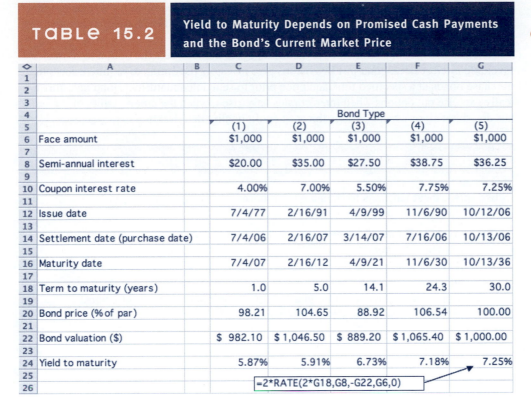

| TABLE 15.2 | Yield to Maturity Depends on Promised Cash Payments and the Bond's Current Market Price | | | | |

◇	A	B	C	D	E	F	G
1							
2							
3							
4					Bond Type		
5			(1)	(2)	(3)	(4)	(5)
6	Face amount		$1,000	$1,000	$1,000	$1,000	$1,000
7							
8	Semi-annual interest		$20.00	$35.00	$27.50	$38.75	$36.25
9							
10	Coupon interest rate		4.00%	7.00%	5.50%	7.75%	7.25%
11							
12	Issue date		7/4/77	2/16/91	4/9/99	11/6/90	10/12/06
13							
14	Settlement date (purchase date)		7/4/06	2/16/07	3/14/07	7/16/06	10/13/06
15							
16	Maturity date		7/4/07	2/16/12	4/9/21	11/6/30	10/13/36
17							
18	Term to maturity (years)		1.0	5.0	14.1	24.3	30.0
19							
20	Bond price (% of par)		98.21	104.65	88.92	106.54	100.00
21							
22	Bond valuation ($)		$ 982.10	$ 1,046.50	$ 889.20	$ 1,065.40	$ 1,000.00
23							
24	Yield to maturity		5.87%	5.91%	6.73%	7.18%	7.25%
25							
26				=2*RATE(2*G18,G8,-G22,G6,0)			

issued at lower interest rates. Companies want to refinance their debt just as homeowners do. Call provisions represent an important advantage for issuers because they represent a refinancing opportunity, like a call option. Call provisions entail no obligation to refinance on the part of the issuer. **Call protection** is the amount of time before a newly issued bond is callable.

Call provisions represent something of a double-edged sword for bond investors. If interest rates fall or credit quality improves, bonds are apt to be called prior to scheduled maturity. This denies bond investors the upward gain in bond prices that would otherwise follow such favorable developments. If interest rates rise or credit quality deteriorates, bond prices tumble and call provisions are not apt to be exercised. As a result, bond investors are only liable to have the opportunity to keep bonds to scheduled maturity in the event of adverse influences on bond prices. Call provisions, which must be explicitly detailed in the bond offering circular, must be fully considered by bond investors. Bonds with limited call protection usually have a higher expected return to compensate for the risk that the bonds might be called for early redemption.

Call provisions facilitate debt refinancing on terms favorable to the issuing entity. Other refinancing options also exist. Issuers are free to buy back their bonds in the open market at any time. For lightly traded issues, companies might publish a formal **bond tender offer** announcement in financial newspapers, such as *The Wall Street Journal*. In doing so, they might offer to repurchase part or all of a given issue at a slight premium to the current market price. If the offer is to buy only part of an issue, it will probably be on a first-come, first-served basis. This type of transaction is called a **refunding** and is designed to reduce financing costs or otherwise improve financial flexibility.

The **yield to call** is calculated the same way as yield to maturity, but it assumes that an investor will receive the face value of the bond and possibly a **call premium** at the call date. Call provisions are especially important for bonds trading in the secondary market at a significant

Call protection
Amount of time before a newly issued bond is callable.

Bond tender offer
Offer to buy an entire outstanding class of securities.

Refunding
Retirement of seasoned securities with proceeds from a new issue.

Yield to call
Investor return over the period from the settlement day to the security's repurchase by the issuer.

Call premium
The dollar amount over the par value of a callable bond that is paid to holders when the bond is called by the issuer.

premium because such bonds have a good chance of being called. Call provisions are much less important for bonds trading in the secondary market at a significant discount because such bonds are not apt to be called by issuers.

Whereas many bonds have call provisions that give bond issuers the option to refinance at favorable interest rates, bond **put provisions** give investors the option to require issuers to repurchase bonds at a specified time and price prior to scheduled maturity. Bond investors typically exercise put options when interest rates have risen, when the credit quality of the issuer has deteriorated, or when a serious threat of credit quality deterioration is present.

Put provisions
Contractual authority that allows investors to sell bonds back to the issuer prior to scheduled maturity.

Try It!

Use spreadsheet functions to compute bond prices and yields. A bond pays a coupon rate of 7.25 percent and matures on June 1, 2015.

a. Compute the bond's price if today is November 11, 2006, and market interest rates are at 6 percent.

b. If the bond's price has changed to 111.85 by March 18, 2007, what is the yield to maturity?

c. If the bond can be called on June 1, 2010, for par plus one year of interest payments, what is the yield to call on March 18, 2007?

Solution

	A	B	C	D	E	F
1	Bond Information					
2	Coupon Rate	7.25%				
3	Maturity Date	6/1/15	← =DATE(2015,6,1)			
4						
5	Question (A) Information					
6	Market Interest Rate	6.00%				
7	Settlement Date	11/11/06				
8			=PRICE(B7,B3,B2,B6,100,2,1)			
9	Quoted Price =	108.26	←			
10	Dollar Price =	$1,082.64	← =10*B9			
11						
12	Question (B) Information					
13	Bond's Price	111.85				
14	Settlement Date	3/18/07				
15						
16	Yield to Maturity =	5.44%	← =YIELD(B15,B4,B3,B14,100,2,1)			
17						
18	Question (C) Information					
19	Call Price	106.25				
20	Call Date	6/1/10				
21			=YIELD(B14,B20,B2,B13,B19,2,1)			
22	Yield to Call =	5.02%	←			
23						

If interest rates remain low, this bond is likely to be called on June 1, 2010.

Interest Rate Risk

Changing Market Conditions

From the time a bond is issued until it matures, its price in the secondary market fluctuates according to changes in general credit market conditions and issuer-specific changes in credit quality. Constant fluctuation of bond prices in the secondary market reflects evolving expectations as investors process information about likely changes in the overall economy. Because all long-term bonds are priced, at least in part, within the context of aggregate credit market conditions, all long-term bonds are sensitive to marketwide changes in interest rates. This is called **interest rate risk**.

When interest rates rise, newly issued bonds offer a promise to pay interest that is higher than that offered on older, seasoned bonds. As a result, when market interest rates rise, market prices for outstanding bonds fall to bring the yield to maturity for new buyers of seasoned bonds into line with higher-yield new issues. Similarly, when the prevailing rate of interest falls, market prices for outstanding bonds rise to bring the yield to maturity for new buyers of such seasoned bonds into line with lower-yield new issues. Bond investors must be aware that bond prices fluctuate on a day-to-day basis. If a bond investor sells a previously purchased bond, either capital gains or losses can be incurred. During periods of volatile interest rates, gains and losses experienced by bond investors can be substantial. While very short-term bonds issued by the most creditworthy institutions involve little or no risk, long-term bonds issued by even the highest-quality issuers involve substantial interest rate risk.

Table 15.3 illustrates interest rate risk for various Treasury securities that feature a 6 percent coupon and are sold with an initial par value of $1,000. These data illustrate how sensitive the value of various Treasury securities can be to rising and falling interest rates. Consider a hypothetical two-year Treasury note that promises to pay $60 per year in interest payments plus a return of the investor's initial $1,000 in 24 months. As shown in Table 15.3, the economic value and market price of a promise to pay $60 per year for two years plus an additional $1,000 at the end of that period is mildly sensitive to interest rates. Still, if interest rates rise, the market value of such a bond would fall to compete with newly issued bonds that pay higher interest. If interest rates fall, the value of such a bond would rise.

Many novice investors don't understand how price sensitive bonds can be to changing market conditions. If interest rates on newly issued two-year Treasury notes rise 1 percent, or from 6 to 7 percent, the value of older or seasoned notes must fall to provide subsequent investors with a competitive 7 percent yield to maturity. In the case of a two-year Treasury note, a 1 percent rise in rates causes a very modest 1.84 percent decline in the value of seasoned two-year Treasury notes. If interest rates rise by 3 percent, even very short-term two-year bonds suffer a meaningful 5.38 percent decline in market value.

The reaction of seasoned bond prices to changing interest rates becomes severe when longer-maturity bonds are considered. The market price for a 30-year Treasury bond with a 6 percent coupon selling at par would fall by 12.47 percent following a 1 percent rise in market interest rates from 6 to 7 percent. If interest rates rise by as much as 3 percent, or from 6 to 9 percent, the value of such a 30-year bond would fall by a whopping 30.96 percent! Of course, the volatility of long-term bonds can work to the advantage of bond investors when interest

Interest rate risk
Chance of bondholder loss due to marketwide fluctuation in interest rates.

TABLE 15.3	Illustration of Interest Rate Risk for Treasury Securities with a 6 Percent Coupon Selling at Par of $1,000					
Bond Type	Term to Maturity	Decline in Bond Value Following an Increase in Rates (%)			Rise in Bond Value Following an Decrease in Rates (%)		
		+1%	+2%	+3%	−1%	−2%	−3%
Treasury bill (money-market)	6 mo	0	0	0	0	0	0
Treasury note	2 yr	−1.84	−3.63	−5.38	1.88	3.81	5.78
Treasury note	5 yr	−4.16	−8.11	−11.87	4.38	8.98	13.83
Treasury note	10 yr	−7.11	−13.59	−19.51	7.79	16.35	25.75
Treasury bond	20 yr	−10.68	−19.79	−27.60	12.55	27.36	44.87
Treasury bond	30 yr	−12.47	−22.62	−30.96	15.45	34.76	59.07

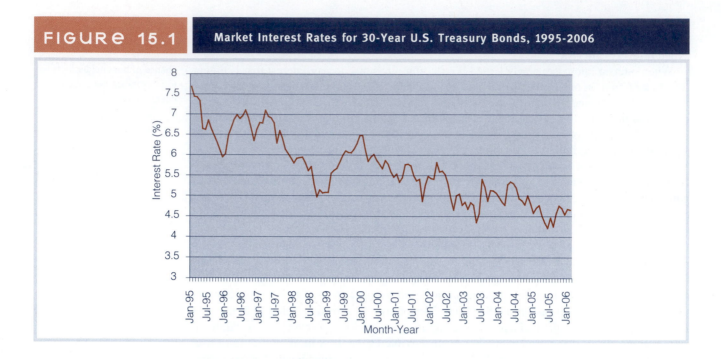

FIGURE 15.1   Market Interest Rates for 30-Year U.S. Treasury Bonds, 1995-2006

rates fall. If long-term interest rates fall by 1 percent from 6 to 5 percent, the value of a seasoned 6 percent bond selling at par would rise by 15.45 percent. The value of such a 30-year bond would rise a whopping 59.07 percent following a 3 percent fall in interest rates from 6 to 3 percent.

Notice that the percentage rise in bond value following a decline in rates is not symmetric with the percentage decline in bond value incurred following a rise in rates. This stems from the fact that while increases in bond prices are theoretically unlimited, no bond can decline by more than 100 percent in value. Remember: If the value of bond price declines by one-third, it takes a 50 percent rise in price to recoup your original investment.

While a 1 percent change in market interest rates isn't commonly seen on a daily or monthly basis, such a change is not unusual over the course of a year. As seen in Figure 15.1, 30-year Treasury bond yields rose nearly 1.5 percent in 1999. Over longer time frames, changes in long-term interest rates of as much as 2 to 3 percent are common. During periods of rapidly changing interest rates, long-term bonds can become extremely volatile assets.

Basis point
1/100th of 1 percent; e.g., 50 basis points = 0.5%.

Because changes in bond yields tend to be fairly small over daily, weekly, or monthly time frames, changes in bond yields are typically quoted in terms of **basis points**, where each basis point equals 1/100th of 1 percent. Thus, a 1.25 percent rise in rates translates into a rise of 125 basis points in yield. A 0.30 percent fall in yield represents a 30-basis-point decline in rates.

Factors That Change Prevailing Interest Rates

The most important cause of fluctuations in the bond market is a change in prevailing interest rates. Interest rates change in response to changes in the supply and demand for credit, Federal Reserve policy, fiscal policy, exchange rates, economic conditions, market psychology, and, most important for the bond market, expectations about inflation.

While the general public is often puzzled by the fact that bond prices typically react negatively to positive economic news, there is a simple explanation for this phenomenon. The bond market acts as a barometer for inflationary expectations. Bond investors fear an increase in inflation because it reduces the buying power of future interest and principal payments. An increase in the expected rate of inflation tends to increase the market rate of interest and lowers the value of outstanding bonds. Thus, any economic report that raises the possibility of robust economic growth and higher future inflation also raises interest rates and lowers bond prices. "Good" economic news, such as lower unemployment or higher retail sales, is typically "bad" for bonds and tends to weaken bond prices. On the other hand, "bad" economic news, such as

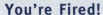
You're Fired!

Donald Trump, the New York real estate mogul, became a reality TV celebrity with the hit show *The Apprentice*. On the show, Trump interviewed a number of contestants seeking lucrative employment with Trump's New York real estate empire. Each week during the course of the TV season, the pool of contestants was reduced by one as Trump shouted "You're fired!" Ironically, it was Trump himself that faced ouster at the hands of irate investors and investment bank Credit Suisse First Boston (CFSB) following the bond market default of Trump Hotels & Casino Resorts.

Trump Hotels & Casino Resorts (including the Taj Mahal and Trump Marina in Atlantic City, New Jersey) was saddled with nearly $1.8 billion in debt and interest payments of $150 million per year. The debt issues carried onerous credit terms, 11.25 and 11.625 percent coupon rates. In 2004, Trump Hotels & Casino Resorts threatened bankruptcy. Investment bank Credit Suisse First Boston engineered a bailout prior to the formal declaration of bankruptcy, called a *prepackaged bankruptcy petition*, or "prepak." A much-needed infusion of $400 million, largely from a private-equity fund managed by

CFSB, helped stem the decline of Trump's once-attractive hotel and gaming properties in Atlantic City. Despite the cachet of the Trump name, the simple fact is that Trump Hotels & Casino Resorts had been a very poorly run business. Not only had profit margins at Trump gaming properties suffered from increased competition, but the buildings were in dire need of basic upgrades and refurbishments. After years of leaning on heavy media promotion and glitz, Trump Hotels & Casino Resorts needed fundamental improvements in basic operations.

In the bankruptcy court restructuring of the company, bondholders pushed to retain the cachet of the Trump name but increase operating controls. Trump's personal stake in the company was cut from 54.5 to 25 percent, and Trump was forced to cede operating control to more accomplished managers. Bondholders had to withstand Trump's famous negotiating tactics and overcome the enormous management fees and restructuring charges imposed by CFSB and its affiliates. Ah! The joys of junk-bond ownership!

See Nicolas Brulliard, "Morgan Stanley Puts Chips on Trump," *The Wall Street Journal Online*, January 11, 2006 (**http://online.wsj.com**).

---

higher unemployment or weak economic growth, tends to reduce inflationary expectations and is "good" for bonds. When inflationary expectations abate, bond prices tend to rise. Remember, bond prices and yields move in opposite directions. Because bond yields tend to move up during good economic conditions, a booming economy can be bad for bond prices. Since bond yields tend to move down during bad economic conditions, a poor economic environment is typically good for bond prices.

The Term Structure of Interest Rates

Widely regarded as the "bellwether" of the bond market, the yield on the 30-year Treasury bond is watched carefully by bond investors just as the Dow Jones Industrial Average is closely followed by stock market investors. Generally speaking, bond investors expect to be compensated for taking on the higher degree of interest rate risk tied to investments in long-term bonds. As a result, there is often a direct positive relation between the time to maturity (in years) and yield to maturity (in percent) for bonds of the same risk class. This link can best be seen by drawing a line connecting the yields offered on similar-risk bonds of different maturities, from shortest to longest. Such a line is called a **yield curve** and describes the **term structure of interest rates**.

Figure 15.2 illustrates the typically upward-sloping yield curve for Treasury securities, as was prevalent during March 2005. The yield curve had an even more positive slope one year earlier. In February 2006, the yield curve was unusually flat. While a yield curve could be drawn for any risk-class segment of the bond market, it is most commonly drawn for the U.S. Treasury market. The U.S. Treasury offers securities of virtually every maturity length, and all such issues enjoy the full-faith backing of the federal government and the highest credit ranking. By watching changes in the yield curve over time, bond investors gain a sense of where interest rates seem to be headed.

The term structure of interest rates displays the relation between yield to maturity and term to maturity for bonds of a given risk class. The **liquidity preference hypothesis** posits that the typically rising yield curve gives long-term bond investors a holding-period risk premium. This explanation of the prevailing term structure of interest rates is widely supported in academia and in the professional world. Another point of view, called the **segmented-market hypothesis**, suggests that yield curves reflect the hedging and maturity needs of institutional investors. It posits a strong clientele-effect explanation for the sometimes anomalous result

Yield curve
Line connecting the yields offered on similar-risk bonds of different maturities.

Term structure of interest rates
Interest rate relation among bonds with the same credit quality but different maturities.

Liquidity preference hypothesis
Theory that rising yield curves give long-term bond investors a holding-period risk premium.

Segmented-market hypothesis
Theory that yield curves reflect the hedging and maturity needs of institutional investors.

FIGURE 15.2   U.S. Treasury Yield Curve, March 21, 2005, and February 10, 2006

Source: Bond Market Association. © Bond Market Association. Used with permission.

that short-term bonds offer the same rate of interest as, or even higher rates of interest than, long-term bonds.

The generally upward-sloping nature of the yield curve reflects the fact that longer-term bonds are exposed to relatively greater interest rate risk, and bond investors typically require an interest rate premium to invest in long-term bonds. If the yield curve is said to be "steep," yields on short-term bonds are relatively low when compared with those on long-term bonds. A steep yield curve implies bond investors can obtain significantly increased income (yield) by buying longer as opposed to shorter maturities. If the yield curve is relatively "flat," the difference between short-term and long-term rates is relatively small. This means that the reward for extending maturities is relatively small, and relatively risk-averse bond investors often choose to stay at the short end of the maturity range. When yields on short-term bonds are higher than those on longer-term bonds, the yield curve is said to be "inverted." As in the case of a relatively flat yield curve, an inverted yield curve suggests that bond investors expect interest rates to decline. An inverted yield curve reflects a particularly aggressive expectation of declining rates and is sometimes considered a precursor to economic recession.

Duration and Convexity

Duration Concept

The term to maturity of a bond is the amount of time required before all promised interest and principal payments are paid in full. Holding all else equal, the longer the term to maturity, the more sensitive bond prices are to changes in prevailing interest rates. However, term to maturity is an imperfect measure of bond risk because it ignores the valuation effects of differences in interest coupon and principal payment schedules.

Consider the change in price for three different bonds when interest rates suddenly rise by 1 percent (or 100 basis points). The first bond is a 6 percent coupon bond (paid semiannually) that will mature in eight years. If the prevailing interest rate is 5 percent, then the bond should be priced at $1,065.28 (using a financial calculator with N (or T) = 16, I/Y (or i) = 2.5, PMT = 30, and FV = 1,000). If interest rates increase 1 percent, the price will change to $1,000. The decline in price of $65.28 represents a 6.1 percent decrease. The second bond is identical except that it matures in 15 years. This bond will sell for $1,104.65 before the interest rate change and $1,000 afterward. This bond's price decreases by 9.5 percent following a 1 percent rise in interest rates. Longer-term bonds are more price-sensitive, and thus more risky. The third bond is identical to the first except that it has a lower coupon of 3 percent (paid semiannually). Before the increase in interest rates, this bond sells for $869.45. After the interest rate change, the bond will be priced at $811.58. The change of

$57.87 represents a 6.7 percent decline in price following a 1 percent rise in interest rates. Like long-term bonds, bonds that pay lower coupon interest tend to be price-sensitive and risky.

It would be useful to combine bond maturity and coupon size into one measure in order to assess a bond's level of risk. To provide a more direct assessment of the risk to bondholders from changes in market interest rates, a financial economist by the name of Frederick R. Macaulay developed a measure called **duration**. Duration is an estimate of the economic life of a bond as measured by the weighted-average time to receipt of interest and principal payments. In the duration calculation, each cash payment is weighted by its present-value percentage of the bond's total market value. A bond's duration, measured in years, tells bondholders how sensitive the bond's price is to changes in prevailing interest rates. The shorter the duration, the less sensitive is a bond's price to fluctuations in market interest rates. The longer the duration, the more a bond's price will fluctuate when prevailing interest rates rise or fall. The formula that can be used to calculate duration, sometimes referred to as *Macaulay duration,* is

Duration
Economic life of a bond measured by the weighted-average time to receipt of interest and principal payments.

$$\text{Duration} = \frac{\displaystyle\sum_{t=1}^{T}\frac{t \times \text{cash payment}_t}{(1+\text{yield})^t}}{\displaystyle\sum_{t=1}^{T}\frac{\text{cash payment}_t}{(1+\text{yield})^t}} = \frac{\displaystyle\sum_{t=1}^{T}\frac{t \times \text{cash payment}_t}{(1+\text{yield})^t}}{\text{bond price}}$$

$$(15.4)$$

where t is the amount of time until receipt of the tth cash flow, and the amount of yield is for one time period. While this formula appears complicated, keep in mind that the numerator is simply the present value of cash flows weighted by (or multiplied by) their year of receipt. The denominator of this equation is the present value of the bond's future interest and principal payments. Therefore, the denominator also equals the bond's current market price.

Duration and Bond Prices

Duration is a way to compare the interest rate risk of bonds that differ in face amount, coupon, and/or term to maturity. Since maturity is only part of the duration equation, bonds with the same maturity but different coupons or call provisions will have different durations. For bondholders, risk from fluctuating prices and reinvestment rates is eliminated, or immunized, when duration equals the bond investor's investment horizon, or planning period. Banks and other financial institutions use this concept to match the durations of their financial assets and liabilities and lock in a profit margin on their loan portfolios. Thus, a prime use of the duration concept is for **risk immunization**.

Risk immunization
Elimination of interest rate risk by matching the durations of financial assets and liabilities.

From Equation 15.4, it is clear that the duration period depends on the bond's term to maturity, size of promised cash payments, and yield to maturity (or market interest rate). These relationships are illustrated further through examples provided in Table 15.4. As seen through these examples, longer maturities mean longer duration and, therefore, greater risk. The coupon rate on a bond helps determine duration because when greater interest income is received, the bond investor more quickly recoups the amount originally invested. Therefore, higher coupon rates shorten duration. All else being equal, callable bonds tend to have shorter duration than noncallable bonds. At the heart of the duration concept is a simple notion that the quicker a bond investor recoups the amount invested, the less risky is the investment.

As shown in Table 15.4, the duration of a bond that pays coupon interest is always less than its term to maturity. Duration typically increases with term to maturity but at a slower rate. For zero-coupon bonds, shown in columns (1) and (4), the bond investor receives no payment until maturity, and duration is exactly equal to the length of the term to maturity. If two bonds have the same coupon rate and yield, the bond with the greater term to maturity has the greater duration. If two bonds have the same yield and maturity, the bond with the lower coupon rate has the greater duration. Duration also decreases with an increase in coupon payments or in the yield to maturity.

TABLE 15.4	Duration Depends on the Bond's Term to Maturity, Size of Promised Cash Payments, and Yield to Maturity

	A	B	C	D	E	F	G	H	I
4					Bond Type				
5			(1)	(2)	(3)	(4)	(5)		
6	Face amount		$1,000	$1,000	$1,000	$1,000	$1,000		
8	Semiannual interest		$0.00	$37.50	$25.00	$0.00	$35.00		
10	Coupon interest rate		0.00%	7.50%	5.00%	0.00%	7.00%		
12	Yield (market interest rate)		6.00%	6.75%	7.00%	8.25%	7.50%		
14	Issue date		1/26/03	6/30/81	4/9/99	9/12/94	10/12/06		
16	Settlement date (purchase date)		1/26/07	6/30/06	1/1/07	7/21/06	10/13/06		
18	Maturity date		1/26/08	6/30/11	4/20/20	9/12/24	10/13/36		
20	Term to maturity (years)		1.0	5.0	13.3	18.2	30.0		
22	Bond price (% of par)		94.26	103.14	82.86	23.04	94.06		
24	Bond valuation ($)		$ 942.60	$1,031.40	$828.63	$ 230.38	$ 940.64		
26	Duration (years)		1.0	4.3	9.4	18.1	12.5		
28	Modified duration		1.0	4.1	9.1	17.4	12.0		

=DURATION(D16,D18,D10,D12,2,0)　　　　　=MDURATION(E16,E18,E10,E12,2,0)

The duration concept can be modified to measure the sensitivity of bond prices to changes in yield to maturity. **Modified duration** is simply duration divided by 1 plus the yield to maturity:

Modified duration

Percentage change in bond price for each percentage-point change in market interest rates.

$$\text{Modified duration} = \frac{\text{duration}}{1 + \left(\dfrac{\text{yield}}{\text{coupon payments per year}} \right)}$$

(15.5)

Modified duration gives an estimate of the percentage change in bond prices for a 1 percent change in market interest rates:

$$\text{Estimated \% change in bond price} = -1 \times \% \text{ yield change} \times \text{modified duration}$$　(15.6)

The negative sign in Equation 15.6 indicates that bond prices move in the opposite direction to interest rates. In the case of the bond depicted in column (4) of Table 15.4, for example, modified duration of 17.4 means that this zero-coupon bond's price would fall roughly 17.4 percent with a 1 percent rise in interest rates or would rise by a commensurate amount if prevailing rates fell by 1 percent. Bond investors able to understand the duration concept can assess the risk of fixed-income investments and take on as much risk as is appropriate for their situations.

Investors typically buy several different types of bonds. Instead of knowing how sensitive each bond is to changes in interest rates, bond investors want to know how the value of their entire bond portfolios might change when interest rates change. The duration of a bond portfolio can be found by taking a weighted average of the duration of each individual bond, where the appropriate weights are the value percentages represented by each bond. Consider a portfolio made up of one bond of type (1) shown in Table 15.4 and two bonds of type (2). The total value of this portfolio is $3,005.40 [= $942.60 + 2 ($1,031.40)]. The portion of portfolio value represented by bond (1) is 0.314 (= $942.60 / $3,005.40), and the share of portfolio value represented by bonds (2) is 0.686. Given the duration shown in Table 15.4 for these three bonds, the duration of the portfolio is 3.26 years [= 0.314(1.0) + 0.686(4.3)]. Using this approach, investors can compute modified duration and learn the interest rate sensitivity of their bond portfolios.

For individual bonds, duration calculations like those displayed in Table 15.4 can be made quickly and easily using financial formulas found in leading spreadsheet software programs, like Microsoft Excel. Fortunately for bond investors, it is seldom necessary to make the complex calculations required to derive duration for a large bond portfolio. Leading bond mutual fund families, like the Vanguard Group of Investment Companies, calculate and publish duration statistics for their bond mutual funds.   Other printed publications, including *Morningstar Mutual Funds* and *The Value Line Mutual Fund Survey*, also report bond fund duration information.

Try It!

Show the calculations for determining the duration of bond (2) in Table 15.4. If interest rates decline by 0.5 percent, how will the bond be affected?

Solution

The bond has five years left to maturity and thus has 10 interest payments of $37.50 and one principal payment of $1,000. The bond's price is $1,031.40, and it is priced to yield 6.75 percent. Using Equation 15.4, the duration is computed as

$$\text{Duration} = \left[\frac{0.5 \times \$37.50}{1.0675^{0.5}} + \frac{1 \times \$37.50}{1.0675^{1}} + \frac{1.5 \times \$37.50}{1.0675^{1.5}} + ... + \frac{4.5 \times \$37.50}{1.0675^{4.5}} + \frac{5 \times (\$37.50 + \$1,000)}{1.0675^{5}} \right]$$

$$\div \$1,031.40 = 4.3 \text{ years}$$

Then, using Equation 15.5, the modified duration is 4.3/1.0337 = 4.16.
A decline of 0.5 percent in yield will increase the price of the bond by – (–0.5%) × 4.16 = 2.08%. This is an increase of $21.45 (= 2.08% × $1,031.40).

Convexity

Modified duration measures the sensitivity of bond prices to changes in yield to maturity. **Convexity** measures the sensitivity of modified duration to changes in interest rates. If modified duration can be thought of as the "speed" of bond price changes due to yield changes, then convexity is the rate of "acceleration" in bond price changes tied to yield changes. The convexity concept can be seen in Table 15.5, which shows yield to maturity, bond price, and modified duration for two bonds over a range of interest rates. Data are given for a 30-year, 6 percent coupon bond and for a 5-year, 6 percent coupon bond. Notice how the price of the 30-year bond appears to be more sensitive to yield changes than is the price of the 5-year bond. Also see how modified duration for the 30-year bond appears to be more sensitive to yield changes than is the modified duration of the 5-year bond.

This relationship can also be shown graphically. In Figure 15.3, the *Y* axis is bond price, and the *X* axis is yield to maturity. Price-yield curves are shown for both the 30-year bond and the 5-year bond. Price-yield curves show the effects on bond prices of changes in the yield to maturity and are convex to (bend away from) the origin. The slope of the line at any point is the duration of the bond at that yield to maturity. The slope is higher for lower yields. Thus duration is higher at lower yields. The rate of change in the slope is convexity. Thus, the degree of convexity describes the degree of bend in the price-yield curve.

Convexity
Sensitivity of modified duration to changes in yield to maturity.

		TABLE 15.5	The Percentage Impact on Bond Prices from Yield Changes Depends on the Yield to Maturity		

	30-Year, 6% Bond		5-Year, 6% Bond	
Yield	Price	Modified Duration	Price	Modified Duration
1.00%	$2,293.14	19.42	$1,243.26	4.44
1.50	2,083.90	18.85	1,215.99	4.43
2.00	1,899.10	18.29	1,189.43	4.41
2.50	1,735.61	17.72	1,163.55	4.39
3.00	1,590.70	17.15	1,138.33	4.37
3.50	1,462.05	16.58	1,113.77	4.35
4.00	1,347.61	16.02	1,089.83	4.34
4.50	1,245.62	15.46	1,066.50	4.32
5.00	1,154.54	14.91	1,043.76	4.30
5.50	1,073.06	14.37	1,021.60	4.28
6.00	1,000.00	13.84	1,000.00	4.27
6.50	934.37	13.32	978.94	4.25
7.00	875.28	12.81	958.42	4.23
7.50	821.97	12.32	938.40	4.21
8.00	773.77	11.85	918.89	4.19
8.50	730.09	11.39	899.86	4.18
9.00	690.43	10.95	881.31	4.16
9.50	654.34	10.53	863.21	4.14
10.00	621.41	10.12	845.57	4.12

Relatively low convexity in the price-yield relationship for the short-term 5-year bond is reflected in a comparatively straight downward-sloping price-yield curve. High convexity in the price-yield relationship for the long-term 30-year bond is reflected in a more sharply curved downward-sloping price-yield curve. In this example, the long-term 30-year bond is said to be more convex than the short-term 5-year bond.

		FIGURE 15.3	The Price-Yield Curve for a 30-Year, 6 Percent Bond Is More Convex to the Origin Than Is the Price-Yield Curve for a 5-Year, 6 Percent Bond

The equation for computing convexity has many similarities with the duration computation. The equation is

$$\text{Convexity} = \frac{\sum_{t=1}^{T} \dfrac{\left(t^2 + t\right) \times \text{cash payment}_t}{(1+\text{yield})^t}}{\text{bond price} \times (1+\text{yield})^2} \tag{15.7}$$

The differences between the duration and convexity equations reflect the fact that for convexity cash payments are multiplied by $t^2 + t$ instead of just t and the denominator includes a function of the yield.

Convexity arises in the price-yield curve because, as yields change, the weights given to cash flow timing fluctuate more than yields. In general, convexity increases with a lower coupon, longer term to maturity, and lower yield. For very low-yield, long-term bonds, small changes in a low yield to maturity can lead to big changes in bond prices. For high-yield, short-term bonds, it can take a very big change in a high yield to maturity to measurably affect the bond's price.

Using both duration and convexity allows for more accurate estimation of how bond prices change when interest rates change. Adding the effects of convexity to the price change Equation 15.6, results in

$$\% \text{ bond in price change} = -1 \times \% \text{ yield change} \times \text{modified duration} \tag{15.8}$$
$$+ \tfrac{1}{2} \times \text{convexity} \times (\text{yield change})^2$$

Be sure to use the decimal form of the interest rate change in this equation. By including convexity, you can increase the accuracy of predictions about how bond prices will change following interest rate moves. Increased accuracy is important for large changes in interest rates.

Try It!

Compute the convexity of bond (2) in Table 15.4. The modified duration of this bond is 4.16. If interest rates decline by 0.5 percent, how will the bond's price be affected?

Solution

Use the information from the previous Try It! Using Equation 15.7, convexity is computed as

$$\text{Convexity} = \frac{\left[\dfrac{\left(0.5^2+0.5\right) \times \$37.50}{1.0675^{0.5}} + \dfrac{\left(1^2+1\right) \times \$37.50}{1.0675^1} + \dots + \dfrac{\left(4.5^2+4.5\right) \times \$37.50}{1.0675^{4.5}} + \dfrac{\left(5^2+5\right) \times (\$37.50+\$1{,}000)}{1.0675^5}\right]}{\$1{,}031.40 \times (1.0675)^2}$$

$$= 21.49$$

Using Equation 15.8, a decline of 0.5 percent in yield will increase the price of the bond by

$$-(-0.005) \times 4.16 + \tfrac{1}{2} \times 21.49 \times (-0.005)^2 = 2.11\%$$

This is an increase of $21.73 (= 2.11% × $1,031.40). Notice that this answer is 28 cents higher than the price computed by using duration alone (see the answer in the previous Try It!).

Squeezing Orange County

In December 1994, after suffering staggering losses in the financial markets, Orange County was forced to declare bankruptcy. Primarily at fault was the unsupervised investment activity of Bob Citron, the county treasurer, who was entrusted with a $7.5 billion portfolio of investment funds belonging to county schools, cities, special districts, and the county itself. Traditionally, municipal funds are invested conservatively to provide stable income for local governments. However, Citron committed the county to high-risk fixed-income strategies that promised higher earnings. Citron's investment bets promised to pay off big if interest rates stayed low but promised enormous losses if interest rates rose.

In 1994, Citron's risky investment strategy backfired. The Federal Reserve Board started a rapid series of interest rate hikes to fight inflation. This caused bond prices to fall, and Orange County suffered enormous losses. In early December, the county was unable to pay off a $1.2 billion loan that had become due to one of its Wall Street creditors. The creditor refused to continue the loan and began selling off the Orange County securities it was holding as collateral. Shortly thereafter, the county declared bankruptcy and liquidated its investment portfolio, taking a massive loss of $1.6 billion.

In retrospect, it is clear that Citron succumbed to a number of psychological biases. After years of outstanding returns, Citron was reluctant to get out of a small losing position. As a result, the loss kept growing. Overconfidence was clearly a problem, as Citron decided to fight the Fed and bet that interest rates would fall rather than increase as the Fed intended. Asked how he knew rates would not continue to rise, Citron said, "I am one of the largest investors in America. I know these things." In a final bid to recoup his losses, Citron actually increased his enormous bets on losing positions. Such "double or nothing" risk-seeking behavior is common among people trying to get back to even.

Remember the Orange County squeeze next time someone says municipal bonds are risk-free assets.

See Stan Rosenberg, "Orange County, Calif., Is Buying Own Note to Save on Pensions," *The Wall Street Journal Online*, January 28, 2006 (**http://online.wsj.com**).

Convertible bond
Debt that can be exchanged into more junior securities.

Indenture agreement
Bond contract.

Conversion ratio
Number of junior securities per bond after conversion.

Conversion price
Amount per unit of the junior security that the company is willing to accept in trade per bond.

Conversion value
Worth of a bond as a junior security if converted at the present time.

Common stock equivalent value
Worth of a bond as common stock if converted at the present time.

Premium to conversion
Percentage over conversion value at which a convertible bond trades.

Break-even time
Number of years over which the conversion premium can be recovered by the increased income of the senior security over the junior security.

Convertible Bonds

Convertible Bond Features

A **convertible bond** is a special type of corporate bond that can be exchanged under certain circumstances into a more junior grade of securities. Many convertible bonds are sold that can be converted into common stock. Terms of the conversion option are set forth in the **indenture agreement**, or bond contract, and may be exercised at the discretion of the bondholder. Convertible bonds involve a combination of a straight financial instrument *plus* an option. Convertibles are hybrid securities.

For example, the conversion option might specify that a $1,000 bond is convertible into 25 shares of stock. In this case, the **conversion ratio** is simply 25:1. The conversion option can also be specified in terms of a **conversion price**. The conversion price is the price per share that the company is willing to accept in trade for the bond. If the indenture states that the conversion price is $40 per share, a $1,000 bond is convertible into 25 (= $1,000/$40) shares of stock. This is equivalent to a 25:1 conversion ratio. In some instances, the convertible bond indenture might state that the conversion ratio changes over time. The conversion price might be $40 for the first five years, $50 for the next five years, and so on. The purpose behind such a sliding scale is to force quick conversion and thereby reduce interest expenses. To protect bondholders, convertible bonds typically have antidilution features. If the corporation were to split its stock 2:1, and the conversion ratio was 25:1 prior to the split, the postsplit conversion ratio would be adjusted to 50:1. Stock dividends have a similar effect on the conversion ratio or conversion price.

Conversion value is the worth of a convertible as a junior security if converted at the present time. For bonds convertible into common stock, conversion value is often expressed as the bond's **common stock equivalent** value. Because convertible bonds offer an income premium above the amount that would be earned on the junior security, they tend to sell in the marketplace at some premium to the common stock equivalent value. **Premium to conversion** is the percentage over conversion value at which the convertible trades. **Break-even time** is the number of years over which the conversion premium can be recovered by the increased income of the senior security over the junior security.

Convertible Bond Valuation

Suppose the common stock of XYZ, Inc., pays a 25-cent dividend and has a market price of $20 per share. Also assume that XYZ's 7 percent convertible bond sells at 80 (or $800), and is convertible into common at $40 per share. Bond prices are always quoted in terms of a percentage of par, so *80* implies a bond price of $800 (= 80% × $1,000). See Table 15.6 for details.

In this case, the conversion value is the number of equivalent common shares multiplied by the current share price, or $500 = ($1,000/$40) × $20. Alternatively, with a par of $1,000 and a conversion price of $40 per share, each convertible bond has a conversion ratio of 25:1 (= $1,000/$40). This means that each bond represents an ownership interest equivalent to 25 shares of common stock. With a common share price of $20, each bond has a common stock equivalent value of $500 (= 25 × $20).

Because the convertible bond offers superior interest income to an equivalent amount invested in the company's common stock, the convertible bond typically sells at a premium to its common stock equivalent value. Premium to conversion value is the percentage by which the current market value of the convertible bond exceeds the underlying common stock equivalent value. In this case, the market value of the bond is $800, or $300 more than the bond's $500 common stock equivalent value. This means that the bond's premium to conversion value is 60% [= ($800 − $500)/$500].

Break-even time is the number of years needed to recover the conversion premium with the convertible's higher income. In this case, a $20 stock paying a 25-cent dividend offers a 1.25 percent yield to common shareholders. On an $800 investment in the company's common stock, a stockholder would earn $10 (= 0.0125 × $800) of dividend income. In contrast, a holder of a convertible bond would earn $70 of interest income on a similar $800 investment in one bond. On an annual basis, the holder of the convertible bond earns $60 in additional income. With a conversion premium of $300, it would take the holder of the convertible five years to recoup the conversion premium. In this case, break-even time is five years (= $300/$60).

Convertible bonds appeal to patient, long-term investors. If an investor expects to buy and hold a given security for an extended period, convertible bonds can be a cost-effective investment. In the present example, if an investor wanted to buy and hold stock in XYZ for more than five years, buying the convertible bond would be preferable to buying the common stock. Purchasers of convertibles tend to hold the security to maturity and then convert to the stock. Converting earlier might make sense if anticipated dividend income exceeds expected interest income.

TABLE 15.6	Convertible Bond Pricing Example	
Bond par value		$1,000
Bond market value		$800
Conversion price		$40
Market price of XYZ common		$20
Common dividend per share		$0.25
Common dividend yield ($0.25 / $20)		1.25%
Conversion ratio = par value / conversion price = $1,000 / $40 = 25:1		
Conversion value = common stock equivalent × common price = 25 × $20 = $500		

$$\text{Premium to conversion} = \frac{\text{bond market value} - \text{conversion value}}{\text{conversion value}} = \frac{\$800 - \$500}{\$500} = 60\%$$

$$\text{Break-even time} = \frac{\$800 - \$500}{\$70 - (\$800 \times 1.25\%)} = 5 \text{ years}$$

Try It!

The common stock of MNO, Inc., pays a 35-cent dividend and has a market price of $55 per share. MNO also has a 6 percent convertible bond selling at 118 that is convertible into common at $50 per share. What are the conversion ratio, conversion value, and premium to convert? Should a holder of the convertible bond convert?

Solution

The conversion ratio is $1,000/$50 = 20:1.
The conversion value is 20 × $55 = $1,100.
The premium to convert is $1,180 − $1,100 = $80.

The convertible holder earns 6 percent in interest each year, or $60. A conversion to the 20 shares of stock would earn $7 per year in dividends. Holding the convertible allows the investor to earn higher annual cash flow and save the conversion premium. If the investor continues to view the company's prospects favorably, the convertible bond should be held and not converted.

Bond Investment Strategies

Why Invest in Bonds?

Bonds make attractive investments for two key reasons: stable income and diversification. Interest income earned by bonds is generally higher and more stable than the interest earned by investments such as money market funds, certificates of deposit, or bank passbook savings accounts. However, the added income potential of bonds comes with added risk. Unlike bonds, passbook savings accounts and bank CDs are guaranteed within limits by an agency of the federal government. Many investors, particularly retirees who need current income, use bonds for a substantial part of their investment portfolios. Many investors in the stock market also hold bonds to help smooth out inevitable fluctuations in the value of their overall investment portfolios. Although bond prices fluctuate in value, they do not always move in the same direction or to the same degree as stocks.

Most financial advisors recommend that investors maintain a diversified investment portfolio consisting of stocks, bonds, and cash reserves, depending on individual circumstances and objectives. Since bonds typically produce a predictable stream of interest and principal payments, many investors are attracted to them as a means of preserving capital and receiving dependable interest income. The broad diversity of fixed-income securities presents investors with a variety of choices to tailor investments to individual financial objectives.

Asset Allocation

Asset allocation
Process of diversifying an investment portfolio across various asset categories, such as stocks, bonds, and cash.

Because investment risk is inescapable, investors are best served by time-tested strategies for risk management. An important tool in managing risk is the knowledge that long-term returns are driven by economic fundamentals but that fear and greed can hold sway over brief periods. When emotion runs high during rampant bull markets, as in the late 1990s, an investor must maintain discipline by sticking to his or her **asset allocation** targets and not becoming overly aggressive. The successful long-term investor also avoids panic in the face of a sharp downturn in stock prices, as occurred during the 2000–2002 bear market. How would you react to a typical bear market decline of 20 to 25 percent? Would you be more inclined to buy or sell during such a period? It's best to ask such questions before the fact. To be forewarned is to be forearmed.

Figure 15.4 shows investment results for a series of asset allocation decisions that investors might make to balance the risk-reward trade-off among stocks, bonds, and cash investments. For the period from 1950 to the present, it shows the average annual return, the number of

FIGURE 15.4	Asset Allocation Can Help Achieve a Balance between Risk and Return, 1950–Present

	Annual Return	Risk (St. Dev.)	Risk-Reward (Coef. Var.)	How Often the Best Mix?	Years with Loss	Worst Loss (year)
Asset Allocation Aggressive Growth 100%	13.27%	17.24%	1.30	64.3%	23%	−26.47% (1974)
Growth 80% / 20%	11.90%	14.19%	1.19	0%	25%	−20.31% (1974)
Growth & Income 60% / 40%	10.52%	11.60%	1.10	7.1%	20%	−14.14% (1974)
Balanced Portfolio 40% / 40% / 20%	8.85%	8.55%	0.97	5.4%	18%	−7.25% (1974)
Income 20% / 20% / 60%	6.88%	4.70%	0.68	23.2%	0%	0.09% (2002)

Common stock (S&P 500)

Long-term Treasury bonds

Short-term Treasury bills

Data Source: Federal Reserve Bulletin.

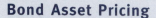
Bond Asset Pricing

Many people are familiar with asset pricing models used in the stock market to define the relationship between expected return and risk. Such models have undergone significant evolution over the decades from the "classic" one-factor CAPM to arbitrage pricing theory, the Fama-French three-factor model, the behavioral four-factor model (with momentum), and so on. Bond investors also seek attractive means for explaining expected returns and risk in the bond market.

Two primary risks in the corporate bond market are a bond's sensitivity to interest rate changes and the likelihood of default. Financial economists William Gebhardt, Soeren Hvidkjaer, and Bhaskaran Swaminathan have shown that two factors related to these risks do a good job of explaining returns in the bond market. One factor measures the term structure of interest rates, while a second factor measures the default risk premium as the difference between the long-term yield on investment-grade corporate bonds and the yield on long-term Treasury bonds. Individual bonds appear to have their own unique systematic risk–factor loadings just as stocks have their own unique betas.

In the stock market, company characteristics like firm size, the book-to-market ratio, and momentum appear to have a good deal of predictive power in explaining expected returns. These characteristics are not easily explained as reflections of systematic risk and may instead reveal some of the hard-to-measure influences of behavioral factors. Bond market investors want to know if similar behavioral factors influence bond pricing. In the bond market, duration and credit ratings have predictive power, but these risk factors are highly correlated with systematic risk tied to the term structure and default risk factors. Interestingly, bond market research shows that the yield to maturity gives bond risk information that is independent of systematic risk. Like firm size, the book-to-market ratio, and momentum in the stock market, yield to maturity may reflect some mispricing in the bond market caused by irrational investor behavior.

See William R. Gebhardt, Soeren Hvidkjaer, and Bhaskaran Swaminathan, "The Cross-Section of Expected Corporate Bond Returns: Betas or Characteristics?" *Journal of Financial Economics*, vol. 75, no. 1 (January 2005), pp. 85–114.

years with a loss, and the worst annual loss for various portfolios consisting of stocks, long-term Treasury bonds, and short-term Treasury bills. Annual returns on four different asset allocation portfolios are compared with an "aggressive growth" portfolio consisting solely of common stocks. In a "growth" portfolio, 80 percent is devoted to stocks and 20 percent to Treasury bonds. A "growth and income" portfolio contains 60 percent stocks and 40 percent Treasury bonds. The remaining two asset allocation portfolios are a "balanced portfolio," containing 40 percent stocks, 40 percent Treasury bonds, and 20 percent Treasury bills, and an "income" portfolio, consisting of 20 percent stocks, 20 percent Treasury bonds, and 60 percent Treasury bills.

In analyzing the effects of various asset allocation decisions, it is obvious that the prime benefit of asset allocation is measured in terms of risk reduction. When risk is captured by the volatility of annual returns, the income portfolio has roughly one-half of the annual return volatility experienced by the aggressive growth (all-stock) portfolio. Such an impressive reduction in risk is costly, however, in that the income portfolio has a mean annual rate of return that is also roughly one-half that of the aggressive-growth portfolio. Interestingly, a 100 percent allocation to common stocks gives the highest annual rate of return for all portfolios in 64 percent of the years since 1950. The income portfolio is the top-performing mix in 23 percent of the years studied. Investors interested in maximizing annual rates of return should obviously focus their long-term investment portfolios on common stocks. On the other hand, investors especially concerned about the potential for substantial year-to-year volatility might find an appropriate asset allocation that is similar to the income portfolio. Since 1950, the worst annual rate of return on common stocks was –26.47 percent, experienced in 1974. During that year, the income portfolio gained 0.38 percent. The worst year for the income portfolio was 2002, when a gain of only 0.09 percent was experienced.

An important lesson to be gained from the data presented in Figure 15.4 is that even a modest amount of diversification can sharply curtail portfolio risk. Another important lesson is that effective risk reduction entails widespread diversification within each specific asset type, such as common stocks, and among classes of investment assets. Which specific asset allocation is most appropriate depends on a number of factors: personal objectives, time horizon, risk tolerance, and financial circumstances. Finally, perhaps the best advice for mitigating investment risk is to remind the investor to be patient. Successful long-term investors have three things in common: They tend to be smart, lucky, and *old*.

Maturity-Based Strategies

A bond portfolio consisting solely of short-term securities would have a high degree of price stability but earn only a modest yield. Conversely, a bond portfolio exclusively invested in long-term securities would have a relatively high expected yield but be subject to volatile price swings. Bond investors seeking greater interest income with minimum price volatility can achieve both with a maturity-based strategy called **laddering**.

When an investor constructs a portfolio using bonds with a series of targeted maturities, and thus resembling a bond maturity "ladder," the risk of loss due to fluctuating interest rates can be reduced or eliminated. For example, suppose an investor has projected financial needs in 2, 4, 6, 8, and 10 years. A laddered portfolio could be constructed by buying an appropriate amount of bonds with identical 2-, 4-, 6-, 8-, and 10-year maturities. At the end of each two-year period, sufficient bonds would mature to take care of immediate financial needs. No bonds would ever need to be sold prior to maturity, and the risk of loss due to fluctuating market conditions would be eliminated. The advantages of bond laddering are obvious. The return on a laddered portfolio is higher than that on a portfolio consisting solely of short-term issues. Such a portfolio also entails less risk than one including only a single-maturity bond or long-term issues.

A **barbell strategy** also involves investing in securities of more than one maturity to limit the risk of fluctuating prices. Instead of dividing a portfolio into a series of bonds that mature over time, as with a laddered portfolio, a barbell strategy emphasizes portfolio concentration at both ends of the maturity spectrum. For example, a barbell strategy might involve portfolio concentration in six-month Treasury bills and 30-year Treasury bonds. Such a portfolio might have a weighted-average time to maturity of 8 to 10 years and entail relatively high interest income with moderate price volatility.

A **bond swap** involves the simultaneous sale and purchase of fixed-income securities. Bond swaps are sometimes motivated by an investor's desire to change the portfolio's average maturity, credit quality, or current income or achieve other objectives. A common motivation for bond swaps is to achieve tax savings. Any investor that owns bonds selling below their purchase price has suffered a paper loss that might be used to offset other capital gains or up to $3,000 per year in ordinary income on a joint return. In a bond swap transaction, such an investor might sell a bond that is worth less than the price paid and simultaneously purchase a similar bond at approximately the same price. By swapping such securities, the investor converts the paper loss into an actual loss, which can be used to offset capital gains and ordinary income. At the same time, the investor maintains a bond portfolio with the same essential expected return and risk characteristics.

Laddering
Portfolio allocation into bonds with a steplike sequence of maturity dates.

Barbell strategy
Bond portfolio concentration at both the short and the long ends of the maturity spectrum.

Bond swap
Simultaneous sale and purchase of fixed-income securities to achieve some investment purpose.

Summary

■ Economic characteristics of any bond include the bond's interest payment obligation, price, yield, maturity, redemption features, and credit quality. In combination with the level of the prevailing **market interest rate**, these factors determine bond value and determine the degree to which it matches the financial objectives of any given investor. Interest rates on floating-rate bonds are reset periodically to keep in line with changes in an underlying **benchmark interest rate**. Rates on short-term Treasury bills or 30-year Treasury bonds are popular interest rate benchmarks. For another popular bond type, called **zero-coupon bonds**, the bond investor receives one single payment at the time of maturity that equals a return of the original purchase price (or principal) plus the total interest earned. Zero-coupon bonds eliminate **interest reinvestment risk**. Prices for **seasoned bonds** depend on a number of factors, including prevailing market interest rates, the supply and demand for similar types of bonds, credit quality, and the term to maturity and tax status of individual bonds.

■ A bond's **settlement date** is the date on which the buyer takes effective possession of the security. The **maturity date** is the date on which the security ceases to accrue interest. Another important component of bond valuation is the **bond coupon rate**, expressed as a percentage of par value. **Bond redemption value** is the amount to be received from the issuer on the maturity date. This amount is usually equal to par value, which is typically $1,000. Most bonds pay **semiannual interest** in two equal installments. In the United States, it is conventional to calculate bond interest rates on the **day-count basis** of 30 days per month and 360 days per year. Some bonds, especially mortgage-backed securities, are typically priced and traded on the basis of an expected **average life** rather than on the basis of any stated term to maturity.

■ The most useful measure of bond yield is **yield to maturity**, or the total rate that would be earned if the bond is held until the date that the security ceases to accrue interest. Most bonds have **call provisions** that allow the issuer to redeem the bond prior to scheduled maturity. **Call protection** is the amount of time before a newly issued bond is callable. For lightly traded issues, the company might make a formal **bond tender offer** announcement in large financial newspapers. This type of transaction is called a **refunding** and is designed to reduce financing costs or improve financial flexibility.

■ **Yield-to-call** calculations tell bond investors the total rate of return that might be expected if the bond is held until it is expected to be called away by the issuer. On the date bonds are called for redemption, a **call premium** is typically offered. Some bond **put provisions** give investors the option of requiring that issuers repurchase bonds when interest rates have risen, when the credit quality of the issuer has deteriorated, or when a serious threat of credit quality deterioration is present.

■ Because all long-term bonds are priced, at least in part, within the context of aggregate credit market conditions, all long-term bonds are sensitive to marketwide changes in interest rates. This is called **interest rate risk**. Because changes in bond yields tend to be fairly small over daily, weekly, or monthly time frames, bond yield changes are typically quoted in terms of **basis points**, with each basis point equal to 1/100th of 1 percent.

■ A line connecting the yields offered on similar-risk bonds of different maturities, from shortest to longest, is called a **yield curve** and describes the **term structure of interest rates**. The **liquidity preference hypothesis** posits that the typically rising yield curve gives long-term bond investors a holding-period risk premium. This explanation of the prevailing term structure of interest rates is widely supported. Another point of view, called the **segmented-market hypothesis**, suggests that yield curves reflect the hedging and maturity needs of institutional investors. **Duration** is an estimate of the economic life of a bond as measured by the weighted-average time to receipt of interest and principal payments. The longer the duration, the more a bond's price will fluctuate when prevailing interest rates rise or fall. A prime use of the duration concept is for **risk immunization**. **Modified duration** is simply duration divided by 1 plus the yield to maturity. Modified duration is a direct estimate of the percentage change that will occur in a bond's market price for each percentage-point change in market interest rates. **Convexity** measures the sensitivity of modified duration to changes in yield to maturity.

■ A **convertible bond** is a special type of corporate bond that can be exchanged under certain circumstances into a junior grade of securities. Terms of the conversion option are set forth in the **indenture agreement**, or bond contract, and may be exercised at the discretion of the bondholder. For example, a $1,000 bond convertible into 25 shares of stock has a **conversion ratio** of 25:1. The **conversion price** is the price per share that the company is willing to accept in trade for the bond. The **conversion value** is the worth of a convertible as a junior security if converted at the present time. For bonds convertible into common stock, conversion value is often expressed as the bond's **common stock equivalent** value. **Premium to conversion** is the percentage over conversion value at which the convertible trades. **Break-even time** is the number of years over which the conversion premium can be recovered by the increased income of the senior security over the junior security.

■ **Asset allocation** decisions are made by investors to balance the risk-reward trade-off among stocks, bonds, and cash investments. Bond investors seeking greater interest income with minimum price volatility can do so with a maturity-based strategy called **laddering**. Instead of dividing a portfolio into a series of bonds that mature over time, as with a laddered portfolio, a **barbell strategy** emphasizes portfolio concentration at both ends of the maturity spectrum. A **bond swap** involves the simultaneous sale and purchase of fixed-income securities.

Self-Test Problems

ST15.1 A 30-year bond promises to pay interest of $30 every six months and repay principal of $1,000 at maturity in 30 years. Assume the market interest rate is 6 percent (3 percent per six-month period).

    a. How much of the value of the bond is represented by the present value of interest payments? How much is represented by the present value of the return of principal?

    b. If the market interest rate rises to 8 percent, how much of the value of the bond is represented by the present value of interest payments? How much is represented by the present value of the return of principal? What effect does a rise in interest rates have on the value of this bond?

Solution

    a. From the present value of a bond formula,

$$PV_{bond} = \text{present value}_{interest} + \text{present value}_{principal}$$

Using a financial calculator for the interest,

    N (or T) = 60, I/Y (or i) = 3, PMT = 30, FV = 0. Then PV = $830.27.

Using a financial calculator for the principal,

    N (or T) = 60, I/Y (or i) = 3, PMT = 0, FV = 1,000. Then PV = $169.73.

The portion of the bond's value represented by interest rates is $830.27, or 83 percent of the present value of the bond. The actual principal repayment represents very little of the bond's value, only $169.73. In this case, the 6 percent interest payments (3 percent per six-month period) represent most of the bond's value. Notice that when the bond pays a rate of interest equal to the market interest rate, the value of the bond is equal to the face amount.

    b. Using a financial calculator for the interest,

    N (or T) = 60, I/Y (or i) = 4, PMT = 30, FV = 0. Then PV = $678.70.

Using a financial calculator for the principal,

    N (or T) = 60, I/Y (or i) = 4, PMT = 0, FV = 1,000. Then PV = $95.06.

Interest payments now represent $678.70 out of the total bond value of $773.77. This is equivalent to about 88 percent of the bond's total present value. The repayment of principal now accounts for only $95.06, or about 12 percent, of the bond's total present value. The value of the bond falls dramatically after the increase in interest rates. After the rise in the market interest rate to 8 percent, the value of the bond paying 6 percent interest falls to $773.77. A 33 percent increase in interest rates, from 6 to 8 percent, results in a 23 percent decline in bond value. This affirms that rising interest rates result in declining bond values. Notice that when the bond's coupon rate is less than the market interest rate, the bond sells at a discount to par.

ST15.2 Use a spreadsheet to compute the duration and convexity for the bond in ST15.1.

Solution

In the table below, columns C and D are used to compute duration and columns E and F are used for computing convexity

	A	B	C	D	E	F	G
1	Yield =	6.0%					
2							
3	Period	Payment	t*Payment	PV of (t*Payment)	(t^2+t)*Payment	PV of (t^2+t)*Payment	
4	0.5	$30	$15	$14.57	$22.50	$21.85	
5	1.0	$30	$30	$28.30	$60.00	$56.60	
6	1.5	$30	$45	$41.23	$112.50	$103.08	
7	2.0	$30	$60	$53.40	$180.00	$160.20	
8	2.5	$30	$75	$64.83	$262.50	$226.92	
9	3.0	$30	$90	$75.57	$360.00	$302.26	
10	3.5	$30	$105	$85.63	$472.50	$385.33	
11	4.0	$30	$120	$95.05	$600.00	$475.26	
12	4.5	$30	$135	$103.86	$742.50	$571.24	
13	5.0	$30	$150	$112.09	$900.00	$672.53	
14	5.5	$30	$165	$119.76	$1,072.50	$778.42	
15	6.0	$30	$180	$126.89	$1,260.00	$888.25	
16	6.5	$30	$195	$133.52	$1,462.50	$1,001.40	
17	7.0	$30	$210	$139.66	$1,680.00	$1,117.30	
18	7.5	$30	$225	$145.34	$1,912.50	$1,235.40	
19	8.0	$30	$240	$150.58	$2,160.00	$1,355.21	
20	8.5	$30	$255	$155.40	$2,422.50	$1,476.26	
21	9.0	$30	$270	$159.81	$2,700.00	$1,598.13	
22	9.5	$30	$285	$163.85	$2,992.50	$1,720.40	
23	10.0	$30	$300	$167.52	$3,300.00	$1,842.70	
24	10.5	$30	$315	$170.84	$3,622.50	$1,964.70	
25	11.0	$30	$330	$173.84	$3,960.00	$2,086.08	
26	11.5	$30	$345	$176.52	$4,312.50	$2,206.54	
27	12.0	$30	$360	$178.91	$4,680.00	$2,325.82	
28	12.5	$30	$375	$181.01	$5,062.50	$2,443.67	
29	13.0	$30	$390	$182.85	$5,460.00	$2,559.86	
30	13.5	$30	$405	$184.43	$5,872.50	$2,674.20	
31	14.0	$30	$420	$185.77	$6,300.00	$2,786.50	
32	14.5	$30	$435	$186.88	$6,742.50	$2,896.58	
33	15.0	$30	$450	$187.77	$7,200.00	$3,004.31	
34	15.5	$30	$465	$188.46	$7,672.50	$3,109.54	
35	16.0	$30	$480	$188.95	$8,160.00	$3,212.15	
36	16.5	$30	$495	$189.26	$8,662.50	$3,312.05	
37	17.0	$30	$510	$189.40	$9,180.00	$3,409.13	
38	17.5	$30	$525	$189.37	$9,712.50	$3,503.31	
39	18.0	$30	$540	$189.19	$10,260.00	$3,594.53	
40	18.5	$30	$555	$188.86	$10,822.50	$3,682.72	
41	19.0	$30	$570	$188.39	$11,400.00	$3,767.85	
42	19.5	$30	$585	$187.80	$11,992.50	$3,849.86	
43	20.0	$30	$600	$187.08	$12,600.00	$3,928.74	
44	20.5	$30	$615	$186.25	$13,222.50	$4,004.45	
45	21.0	$30	$630	$185.32	$13,860.00	$4,076.99	
46	21.5	$30	$645	$184.28	$14,512.50	$4,146.35	
47	22.0	$30	$660	$183.15	$15,180.00	$4,212.53	
48	22.5	$30	$675	$181.94	$15,862.50	$4,275.53	
49	23.0	$30	$690	$180.64	$16,560.00	$4,335.36	
50	23.5	$30	$705	$179.27	$17,272.50	$4,392.05	
51	24.0	$30	$720	$177.82	$18,000.00	$4,445.61	
52	24.5	$30	$735	$176.32	$18,742.50	$4,496.08	
53	25.0	$30	$750	$174.75	$19,500.00	$4,543.47	
54	25.5	$30	$765	$173.13	$20,272.50	$4,587.83	
55	26.0	$30	$780	$171.45	$21,060.00	$4,629.20	
56	26.5	$30	$795	$169.73	$21,862.50	$4,667.61	
57	27.0	$30	$810	$167.97	$22,680.00	$4,703.11	
58	27.5	$30	$825	$166.17	$23,512.50	$4,735.74	
59	28.0	$30	$840	$164.33	$24,360.00	$4,765.55	
60	28.5	$30	$855	$162.46	$25,222.50	$4,792.60	
61	29.0	$30	$870	$160.56	$26,100.00	$4,816.93	
62	29.5	$30	$885	$158.64	$26,992.50	$4,838.60	
63	30.0	$1,030	$30,900	$5,380.00	$957,900.00	$166,780.09	
64	=C63/((1+$B$1)^A63)						
65			=(A63+A63^2)*B63		=E63/((1+$B$1)^A63)		
66							
67	=SUM(D4:D63)		sum =	$14,516.61	sum =	$328,552.57	
68							
69			Duration =	14.52	Convexity =	292.41	
70			=D67/1000		=F67/(1000*(1+B1)^2)		
71							
72							

The duration of this bond is 14.5 years, and the convexity is 292.4.

Questions and Problems

15.1   If the market interest rate falls to 4 percent, what effect does such a decline in interest rates have on the value of the bond described in ST15.1?

15.2   A 7 percent coupon bond with a maturity of 10 years is priced at $1,050. The bond can be called in three years at a call price of par plus one year of interest payments. What is the yield to call for the bond?

15.3   Calculate the yield to maturity for a bond selling at $1,205.16 that matures in six years at a par value of $1,000 and pays a 9 percent coupon in the form of two semi-annual interest payments per year.

15.4   Calculate the current market price of a seasoned zero-coupon bond that has a face amount of $1,000, matures in 18 years, and is priced to yield 12 percent.

15.5   How does the concept of bond maturity differ from the concepts of Macaulay duration and convexity?

15.6   An 8 percent coupon bond paying semiannual interest is bought on December 12, 2005. The bond will mature in exactly 10 years and has a yield to maturity of 11 percent. What is the duration of this bond?

15.7   Calculate the modified duration of the bond in Problem 15.6. What percentage change in the market price of this bond would you expect to see for every 1 percent change in market interest rates?

15.8   Consider the bonds listed in Table 15.4. Construct a bond portfolio comprised of one of each bond, or five bonds in total. What is the duration of the portfolio?

15.9   Calculate the convexity of the bond in Problem 15.6.

15.10   Using your modified-duration answer to Problem 15.8 and your convexity answer to Problem 15.9, compute the change in price of the bond in Problem 15.7 when interest rates decline 0.75 percent.

15.11   Explain why the yield curve that describes the term structure of interest rates typically has a positive slope.

15.12   Calculate the percentage change in price for a bond featuring modified duration of 3.5 following a 30-basis-point jump in interest rates.

15.13   Suppose the common stock of Next-Day Freight, Inc., pays a 90-cent dividend and has a market price of $45 per share. The company also has a 9 percent convertible bond selling at 75, which is convertible into common at $100 per share. If an investor bought the bond at the market price, what premium to conversion would be paid and how long would the bond have to be held to recoup this conversion premium?

15.14   Go to the Bond Market Association's Web page at **www.bondmarkets.com**. Examine the yield curve graphs. Is the yield curve for Treasuries upward-sloping? Has it changed much over the past year? What is the yield spread between different types of bonds (corporate, Treasury, and muni)? Has it changed over time?

15.15   Go to the Standard & Poor's Market Insight Web site at **www.mhhe.com/ edumarketinsight** and enter the "Commentary" section. The last page of the "Trends & Projections" report shows what Standard & Poor's analysts project for the next couple of years. What are these analysts projecting for future interest rates? What impact will this have on bond prices if it turns out to be correct?

15.16 A fixed-income manager wants to take advantage of a forecast decline in interest rates over the next several months. Which of the following combinations of maturity and coupon rate would *most likely* result in the largest increase in portfolio value?

	Maturity	Coupon Rate
A.	2015	10%
B.	2015	12
C.	2030	10
D.	2030	12

15.17 An analyst determines the following information about a semiannual coupon bond (par = $1,000):

Par value	$1,000
Modified duration	10
Current price	$800
Yield to maturity (YTM)	8 percent

If the YTM increases to 9 percent, the predicted decrease in price, using the duration concept, is *closest to:*

a. $80.00
b. $77.67
c. $76.92
d. $75.56

15.18 A newly issued 10-year option-free bond is valued at par on June 1, 2000. The bond has an annual coupon of 8.0 percent. On June 1, 2003, the bond has a yield to maturity of 7.1 percent. The first coupon is reinvested at 8.0 percent and the second coupon is reinvested at a yield to maturity of 7.0 percent. The future price of the bond on June 1, 2003, is *closest to:*

a. 100.0 percent of par
b. 102.5 percent of par
c. 104.8 percent of par
d. 105.4 percent of par

15.19 The interest rate risk of a noncallable bond is *most likely* to be positively related to the:

a. Risk-free rate
b. Bond's coupon rate
c. Bond's time to maturity
d. Bond's yield to maturity

15.20 Interest rate sensitivity for bonds with embedded options is *most accurately* measured by:

a. Convexity
b. Effective duration
c. Modified duration
d. Macaulay duration

INVESTMENT APPLICATION

How to Buy Bonds

Individual and institutional investors have an enormous variety of individual securities from among which they can make their bond investment selections. Most individual bonds are bought and sold in the over-the-counter (OTC) market, but some corporate bonds are also listed on the New York Stock Exchange. Like the OTC stock market, the OTC bond market includes hundreds of dealers who trade with individual and institutional investors by phone or electronically. Some bond dealers keep an inventory of bonds and make markets in them. Others act only as brokers and buy or sell to dealers in response to specific requests on behalf of customers.

There are a number of services to help investors compare current prices for bonds of various types. For municipal bond prices, benchmark yields are available on the Internet and in newspapers through the Bond Market Association/Bloomberg National Municipal Yield Table. For a nominal fee, investors can also obtain current dealer prices or evaluations by subscribing to a service provided by Standard & Poor's and the Bond Market Association. Rules issued by the Municipal Securities Rulemaking Board make prices of actively traded municipal bonds widely available, and these prices are sometimes reported in the financial press. For Treasury securities, corporate bonds, and other types of bonds, a number of media sources and vendors provide current pricing information. The Bond Market Association Web site provides links to multiple services providing price-yield information on all market segments. Bond investors can also compare prices for specific fixed-income securities by getting bids from several brokers and dealers. See www.bondmarkets.com.

Bond mutual funds offer small investors an efficient way to invest in the bond markets. Bond funds, like stock funds, offer professional selection and management of a diversified portfolio of securities. They allow bond investors to diversify risks across a broad range of issues, and they offer a number of other conveniences, such as the option of having interest payments reinvested. Bond funds tend to be actively managed, with securities added or eliminated from the portfolio in response to market conditions and investor demand. They have no specific maturity date. With conventional mutual funds, bond investors are able to buy or sell fund shares at any time. Because the market value of outstanding bonds fluctuates on a daily basis, bond fund values also change from day to day. As a result, when an investor chooses to sell shares in a bond fund, the value of such an investment may be higher or lower than it was at the time of purchase.

Most bond funds charge annual management fees averaging 1 percent. Some also impose initial sales charges of as much as 5 percent or impose fees when shares are sold. Because annual management fees and sales commissions lower investor returns, bond fund investors need to be aware of them when calculating expected returns. The minimum initial investment in bond mutual funds is usually between $1,000 and $2,500 for taxable accounts and $500 for retirement accounts.

Another alternative for bond investors is bond unit investment trusts, which have certain similarities to bond mutual funds. Bond unit investment trusts offer a fixed portfolio of investments in government, municipal, mortgage-backed, or corporate bonds, which are professionally selected and remain constant throughout the life of the trust. The benefit of a unit trust is that investors know exactly how interest income will be earned because the composition of the portfolio remains stable. Another advantage is that since unit trusts are not an actively managed pool of assets, there is usually no management fee. Investors can earn interest income during the life of the trust and recover their principal as securities within the trust are redeemed. The trust typically ends when the last investment matures. Investors pay sales charges plus a small annual fee to cover supervision, evaluation expenses, and trustee fees. The minimum initial investment in bond unit investment trusts is usually between $1,000 and $5,000.

www.mhhe.com/hirschey1e

For many small investors, U.S. Series EE savings bonds offer an attractive combination of safety, market-based yields, and tax benefits. Savings bonds can be purchased for small amounts. The minimum investment is only $25 for bonds bought through financial institutions. They are lower-risk than most investments since both principal and interest are guaranteed by the full faith and credit of the United States, and lost, stolen, or destroyed bonds can be replaced. They are also convenient. Savings bonds can be bought through most financial institutions and through payroll savings plans. There are no commissions or similar fees. Interest is exempt from state and local income tax and federal income taxation can be postponed until you cash your bond or until it stops earning interest in 30 years. Education savings bonds may provide further tax savings when used to finance higher education.

There are numerous sources of mutual fund and unit investment trust information available for bond investors, including *The Wall Street Journal* and *Barron's*. Major financial publications such as *Forbes, BusinessWeek*, and *Money* magazine also provide regular in-depth coverage. Well-known mutual fund research firms, such as Morningstar Inc. and Lipper Analytical Services, also provide detailed analyses by subscription and on the Internet. Investors interested in savings bonds should consult **www.publicdebt.treas.gov/indiv/products/products.htm**.

a. Under what circumstances might an investor prefer bond mutual funds to bond unit investment trusts?

b. Are savings bonds obsolete?

16

chapter

Mutual Funds

More than 92 million Americans own mutual funds worth more than $9 trillion. There are some 8,000 different funds available to U.S. investors that are managed by more than 600 diverse mutual fund companies. The Investment Company Institute reports that more than $18 trillion is invested in mutual funds on a global basis (www.ici.org). Because investors can easily transfer investments from one mutual fund to another, funds that do well can expect large inflows of cash from investors, rapidly growing investment management fees, and enormous profits for the fund management companies that run them.

Until recently, the mutual fund industry had a squeaky-clean image. However, a scandal erupted in the early 2000s when then New York attorney general, Eliott Spitzer, discovered instances of illegal late trading in mutual funds and favoritism for hedge funds and other large customers. Late trading involves orders placed after the market close. In certain instances, large mutual fund customers were allowed to trade after the market close at stale prices that failed to reflect late-breaking news. For example, illegal late trading could be highly profitable for buyers if the government announced favorable interest rate information after the close of business on Wall Street. Similarly, short sellers can profit from late trading by dumping stocks at stale prices when negative news comes out after the market close. Spitzer also discovered that some mutual funds were allowing favored customers to make short-term trades into and out of their funds. While such market timing is not illegal per se, it would constitute illegal favoritism if a mutual fund had a policy against the practice and then allowed certain investors to do it anyway.

Investor outrage over the mutual fund scandals led to massive outflows for offending fund management companies (such as Putnam Investments) and inflows for others with well-deserved reputations for honestly dealing with all investors (such as T. Rowe Price and Associates). Mutual fund companies have learned, or relearned, that fair dealing is an essential requirement of a trusted investment advisor. Investors have also learned, or relearned, that constant vigilance is an essential ingredient for investment success.[1]

CHAPTER OBJECTIVES

- Understand the structure and pricing of mutual funds.
- Know the advantages and disadvantages of buying mutual funds.
- Be able to assess mutual fund performance.
- Assess mutual fund manager incentives.
- Recognize the impact of taxable distributions on fund returns.

Mutual Fund Basics

What Is a Mutual Fund?

Mutual fund
Open-end investment company.

A **mutual fund** is an investment company that issues shares to the public. The money it receives from shareholders is pooled and invested in a wide range of stocks, bonds, or money market securities to meet specific investment objectives. The various investments included in a fund's portfolio are handled by professional money managers in line with the stated investment policy of the fund. Some funds invest primarily in securities offering long-term growth, others invest in securities providing current income, and still others focus on particular industries or classes of securities. Many strive to achieve a combination of objectives.

In a mutual fund, each investor shares proportionately in the income and investment gains and losses that the fund's investments produce. Similarly, each investor shares proportionately in the brokerage expenses, management fees, and other operating costs incurred by the fund. In the most common type of mutual fund, called **open-end funds**, investors can sell their shares or buy new shares any business day at the per-share value of the fund's cash holdings and stock or bond investments. The per-share value of a mutual fund's stock, bond, and cash reserve holdings is called the fund's **net asset value (NAV)**, as seen in Equation 16.1.

Open-end funds
Mutual funds that continuously offer to sell and buy shares.

Net asset value
Per-share value of a mutual fund's stock, bond, and cash reserve holdings.

$$NAV = \frac{\text{market value of assets} - \text{portfolio liabilities}}{\text{no. of shares outstanding}}$$

$$(16.1)$$

All mutual funds have a portfolio manager, or investment advisor, who directs the fund's investments according to explicit investment objectives. Common mutual fund objectives often include some combination of long-term growth, high current income, or stability of principal. Depending on its investment objective, a mutual fund may invest in common stocks, various types of taxable and nontaxable bonds, or money market investments.

Mutual funds have been in existence for more than 80 years. The oldest mutual funds have survived a wide variety of turbulent economic and political conditions, including the Great Depression and World War II. Over their long history, mutual funds have never been more popular than they are today. According to the Investment Company Institute, investors in the United States have entrusted their advisors with nearly $9 trillion in more than 8,000 mutual funds. Mu-

---

[1]Nisha Gopalan, "Global Funds Warm to China," *The Wall Street Journal Online*, February 24, 2006 (**http://online.wsj.com**).

tual fund assets account for roughly one-quarter of the total value of the stock and bond markets. General information about mutual funds can be obtained from the Investment Company Institute (**www.ici.org**), a national trade association representing mutual funds, unit investment trusts, and closed-end funds. ICI is a nonprofit organization supported primarily by its membership. The purpose of the ICI is to represent members and their shareholders in matters relating to mutual fund regulation, taxation, marketing, industry statistics, and market research.

Try It!

A mutual fund has $100 million in portfolio assets and $3 million in short-term liabilities. If there are 10.765 million shares outstanding, what is the NAV of the mutual fund? If the portfolio assets increase in value to $103 million, what does the NAV change to?

Solution

Using Equation 16.1,

$$NAV = \frac{\text{market value of assets} - \text{portfolio liabilities}}{\text{no. of shares outstanding}}$$

$$= \frac{\$100 \text{ million} - \$3 \text{ million}}{10.765 \text{ million}} = \$9.0107 \text{ per share}$$

After the assets increase in value, the NAV becomes

$$NAV = \frac{\$103 \text{ million} - \$3 \text{ million}}{10.765 \text{ million}} = \$9.2894 \text{ per share, or an increase by } 3.09\%$$

Mutual Fund Types

Investors have different objectives, so various types of mutual funds are needed to help them achieve their goals. As shown in Table 16.1, most funds fit into one of three basic categories: money market, bond, and stock mutual funds.

Money market mutual funds hold cash reserves, or short-term debt instruments issued by the government, corporations, or financial institutions. U.S. Treasury bills and bank certificates of deposit (CDs) that mature in 90 days or less are two popular types of cash investments. **Bond funds** invest in debt instruments issued by corporations or government agencies. Bond funds can be grouped according to short-term, intermediate-term, and long-term maturity and according to the credit quality or tax status of their holdings. **Stock funds** are one of the most popular types of mutual funds. They range from relatively conservative equity income funds to value funds, growth funds, aggressive growth funds, small-company funds, and international funds.

Money market mutual funds
Funds that invest in cash reserves, or short-term IOUs.

Bond funds
Funds that buy debt instruments.

Stock funds
Funds that make equity investments.

Sources of Information

Several print publications, including *Smart Money* and *Forbes*, offer intensive coverage of the mutual fund industry on a semiannual basis. *Barron's* gives weekly commentary about the industry and up-to-date information about fund performance, management strategies, industry trends, and so on.

Lipper Inc., together with its affiliated companies, compiles and tracks extensive performance data on the global mutual fund industry (see Table 16.2). In the United States, Lipper clients include 95 percent of the fund management groups. Lipper data are published in more than 100 newspapers, in various magazines, on the radio, and on TV. On the Internet at **www.lipperweb.com**, Lipper offers a multitude of useful tips and valuable information, including links to hundreds of useful mutual fund sites with information on mutual fund education, search tools, portfolio trackers, and asset allocation.

TABLE 16.1	Types of Mutual Funds				
Types of Mutual Funds	**Investor Objective**	**What These Funds Hold**	**Capital Growth Potential**	**Current Income Potential**	**Stability of Principal**
Money Market Funds					
Taxable money market	Current income, stability of principal	Cash investments	None	Moderate	Very high
Tax-exempt money market	Tax-free income, stability of principal	Municipal cash investments	None	Moderate	Very high
Bond Funds					
Taxable bond	Current income	Wide range of government and/or corporate bonds	None	Moderate to high	Low to moderate
Tax-exempt bond	Tax-free income	Wide range of municipal bonds	None	Moderate to high	Low to moderate
Common Stock Funds					
Balanced	Current income, capital growth	Stocks and bonds	Moderate	Moderate to high	Low to moderate
Equity income	Growing dividend income, low volatility	High-yielding stocks, convertible bonds	Moderate to high	Moderate	Low to moderate
Value funds	Low volatility, growth potential	Low P/E, P/B stocks	Moderate to high	Low to moderate	Low to moderate
Growth and income	Growing income and capital gains	Dividend-paying stocks	Moderate to high	Low to moderate	Low to moderate
Domestic growth	Capital growth	U.S. stocks with high potential for growth	High	Very low	Low
International growth	Diversified growth	Stocks of companies outside U.S.	High	Very low to low	Very low
Aggressive growth	Aggressive growth of capital	Stocks with very high potential for growth	Very high	Very low	Very low
Small cap	Diversified aggressive growth	Stocks of small companies	Very High	Very low	Very low
Specialized	Targeted aggressive growth	Stocks of industry sectors	High to very high	Very low to moderate	Very low to low

Chicago-based Morningstar.com is another leading provider of mutual fund information. Morningstar does not own, operate, or hold any interest in mutual funds, so investors have come to rely on Morningstar for unbiased data and analysis and candid editorial commentary. Financial planners and other investment professionals turn to Morningstar for tools that can help them analyze and support their investment ideas. Broadcast and cable television, newspapers, and magazines seek out Morningstar editors and analysts for authoritative commentary about breaking financial news on mutual funds. Morningstar was the first to track the performance of individual fund managers. Morningstar was also the first to calculate fund price-earnings and price-book ratios and the first to do fundamental analysis on the underlying stocks held by various funds.

Morningstar.com (**www.morningstar.com**) offers a unique blend of proprietary analysis, interactive tools, regular news updates, and market reports (see Figure 16.1). Of course, the Internet is a convenient source for timely information on individual mutual funds and mutual fund investing. Millions of investors rely on electronic media to obtain news and investment

TABLE 16.2	Lipper Mutual Fund Data Are Published in Many Places

Top 10 U.S. Domestic Funds Based on 3-Year Return

Fund Name: Classification	1 Mon.	YTD	1 Year	3 Year	5 Year	10 Year
Pacific Adv: Small Cp;A **PASMX** Small-Cap Value	16.8%	16.8%	27.8%	49.2%	19.3%	12.1%
ProFunds: UltraSm-Cap;Inv **UAPIX** Small-Cap Core	17.7	17.7	29.3	49.2	6.4	—
Pacific Adv. Small Cp;C **PGSCX** Small-Cap Value	16.6	16.6	26.7	48.0	18.0	—
ProFunds: UltraSm-Cap;Svc **UAPSX** Small-Cap Core	17.6	17.6	28.0	47.7	5.4	—
Schneider Sm Cap Val **SCMVX** Small-Cap Value	5.1	5.1	22.4	46.8	22.3	—
ProFunds: UltraMidCap;Inv **UMPIX** Mid-Cap Core	11.6	11.6	39.7	45.6	7.6	—
Hodges Fund **HDPMX** Multi-Cap Core	9.8	9.8	33.3	45.0	14.5	13.6
Fidelity Lvrgd Co Stk **FLVCX** Mid-Cap Core	6.9	6.9	26.1	44.4	22.4	—
ProFunds: UltraMidCap;Svc **UMPSX** Mid-Cap Core	11.5	11.5	38.2	44.1	6.6	—
Fidelity Adv Lev Co; Ins **FLVIX** Mid-Cap Value	6.7	6.7	25.4	43.3	22.6	—

Top 10 International Large-Cap Funds Based on 3-Year Return

Fund Name: Classification	1 Mon.	YTD	1 Year	3 Year	5 Year	10 Year
Harbor: Intl;Inst **HAINX** International Large-Cap Core	8.7%	8.7%	33.5%	32.0%	11.8%	12.3%
Harbor: Intl;Ret **HRINX** International Large-Cap Core	8.7	8.7	33.1	31.7	—	—
Harbor: Intl;Inv **HIINX** International Large-Cap Core	8.7	8.7	32.9	31.5	—	—
Elfun Intl Equity Fund **EGLBX** International Large-Cap Core	7.3	7.3	30.6	29.9	6.0	9.7
GE Instl: Intl Equity;Inv **GIEIX** International Large-Cap Core	7.3	7.3	30.2	29.4	5.6	—
GE Instl: Intl Equity;Svc International Large-Cap Core	7.2	7.2	29.8	29.0	5.3	—
Accessor: Intl Eqty;Adv **ACIEX** International Large-Cap Core	9.7	9.7	28.2	28.2	5.2	7.7
Northern Instl: In EI;A **BIEIX** International Large-Cap Core	5.8	5.8	22.2	28.1	5.8	—
Am Beacon: IE Index;Inst **AIIIX** International Large-Cap Core	6.1	6.1	22.6	28.0	5.7	—
Ivy: Intl Value;Adv **IVIVX** International Large-Cap Core	9.3	9.3	35.8	27.8	6.9	—

(continued on next page)

TABLE 16.2	Lipper Mutual Fund Data Are Published in Many Places *continued*

Top 10 U.S. Government Funds Based on 3-Year Return

Fund Name: Classification	1 Mon.	YTD	1 Year	3 Year	5 Year	10 Year
Wasatch: Hoisington Trs **WHOSX** General US Treasury	-1.6%	-1.6%	4.0%	6.8%	7.9%	8.3%
iShares: Lehm 20+ Trs **TLT** General US Treasury	-1.2	-1.2	3.5	6.0	—	—
Vanguard Lg-Tm Trs; Adm **VUSUX** General US Treasury	-0.9	-0.9	3.1	5.4	—	—
Vanguard Lg-Tm Trs; Inv **VUSTX** General US Treasury	-0.9	-0.9	3.0	5.3	7.1	7.0
Dreyfus US Treas Lng Trm **DRGBX** General US Treasury	-1.0	-1.0	2.8	4.5	5.2	5.7
T Rowe Price Treas: Long **PRULX** General US Treasury	-0.9	-0.9	2.2	4.3	6.1	6.4
iShares: Lehm 7-10 Trs **IEF** General US Treasury	-0.5	-0.5	1.0	3.0	—	—
ISI Total Ret Treas; ISI **TRUSX** General US Treasury	-0.5	-0.5	1.9	2.9	4.8	5.4
Vanguard Int-Tm Trs; Adm **VFIUX** General US Treasury	-0.3	-0.3	1.6	2.9	—	—
Vanguard Int-Tm Trs; Inv **VFITX** General US Treasury	0.3	-0.3	1.4	2.8	5.5	5.9

Source: Reuters.

FIGURE 16.1	Morningstar.com Is a Top Choice for Mutual Fund Investor Information

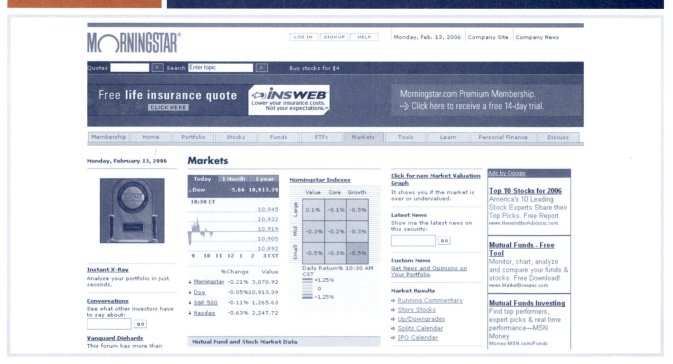

Source: © Morningstar® Mutual Fund Page, 2006. Used with permission.

		No. of funds investing in:				
Fund Group	Internet address	Stocks	Balanced	Fixed Income	Money Market	Comments
American Century	www.americancentury.com	33	13	19	6	Known for its aggressive growth funds.
Dreyfus	www.dreyfus.com	47	0	27	32	Good basic investor information.
Fidelity	www.fidelity.com	129	19	45	31	Known for the flagship fund Fidelity Magellan.
Janus	www.janus.com	19	5	4	3	Known for its stock funds.
Legg Mason	www.leggmason.com	38	25	34	22	Outstanding performance, behavioral focus.
Charles Schwab	www.schwab.com	24	8	14	21	Discount brokerage firm with mutual funds.
T. Rowe Price	www.troweprice.com	42	17	26	8	Excellent investor tools on Web site.
Vanguard	www.vanguard.com	47	16	28	10	Popularized the indexing strategy.

TABLE 16.3 Web Sites for the Largest Mutual Fund Groups Give Investors a Valuable Investment Tool

and account information. Some of the best sites for mutual fund investors are described in Table 16.3. Among these is **www.vanguard.com**, the investment Web site of the Vanguard Group of investment companies. Since its founding in 1974, Vanguard has emerged as a leader in the mutual fund industry by providing competitive investment performance, a diversity of fund alternatives, and the lowest operating expenses in the industry. Vanguard has also taken the industry lead in investor education.

Advantages and Disadvantages

Mutual Fund Advantages

Most mutual funds hold dozens of issues from a variety of asset categories. Diversified stock funds typically hold large-cap and small-cap stocks broadly spread across industries and economic sectors. Diversified bond funds hold a wide assortment of bonds issued by numerous issuers with an eclectic mix of maturity structures, coupon payments, and credit quality. By pooling their resources, shareholders in diversified stock and bond funds are able to achieve a level of diversification that few investors could achieve on their own. In the case of specialized stock and bond funds, portfolio holdings may be fairly uniform in terms of the general characteristics of issuing corporations, but a variety of issues is held to minimize the risk of adverse operating results at any single company. When investors hold a carefully selected mix of specialized mutual funds, they are able to spread their assets among many different securities and asset classes. This also sharply reduces the risk of loss from problems with any one company or asset class.

Another principal benefit enjoyed by mutual fund shareholders is the ability to retain professional investment management at a reasonable cost. Professional investment managers make decisions about which securities to buy and sell based on extensive company research, market information, and insight provided by skilled securities traders. Professional management is a valuable service because few investors have the time or expertise to carefully investigate the tens of thousands of individual stocks and bonds available in the financial markets. Similarly, few individual investors have the time or patience to manage their personal investments on a daily basis.

A further advantage of investing in mutual funds is investor convenience. At financial institutions offering a "family" of mutual funds, or **fund family**, money can also be moved easily from

Fund family
A mutual fund firm that offers many portfolio choices.

one fund to another as investor needs or investment priorities change. Automatically investing a fixed amount per month, or redeeming a fixed amount per month, is made easy by electronic transfers of funds between the investor's bank account and mutual fund account. At the investor's option, interest and dividend income can be paid directly to the mutual fund investor or automatically reinvested. Most mutual funds also provide extensive record-keeping services. This helps investors keep track of transactions, follow fund performance, and assist in completing tax returns. Fund performance can easily be monitored in daily newspapers, such as *The Wall Street Journal*, by telephone, or at a number of financial Web sites on the Internet.

Mutual Fund Disadvantages

Although mutual funds are extensively regulated by the Securities and Exchange Commission and state securities officials, such regulation is typically focused on the need for full and fair disclosure of relevant investment information. Mutual fund regulation does not eliminate the risk of losing money. Money invested in the stock and bond markets through mutual funds can be expected to vary on a day-to-day basis. At times, such volatility can be significant.

Although broad diversification reduces the risk of catastrophic loss from holding a single security that plummets in price, it also eliminates the potential for huge returns from a single holding that skyrockets in price. It is important to remember that diversification does not protect against the risk of loss from an overall decline in the financial markets. In particular, investors in focused or single-sector mutual funds can anticipate significant losses during some periods of the economic cycle.

A further, but avoidable, disadvantage of investing in some mutual funds is that many mutual funds feature high management fees and sales commission expenses. In most instances, mutual funds represent a low-cost way to buy stocks and bonds. However, as shown in Figure 16.2, mutual fund costs and taxes can sometimes greatly diminish portfolio wealth. A $100 investment earning 10 percent will become $4,526 after 40 years if no costs or taxes are owed. If gross returns are reduced by only 1 percent per year due to mutual fund management fees and related expenses, such a portfolio will grow to only $3,141 after 40 years. With capital gains taxes of 30 percent each year, the portfolio will grow to only $1,152 after 40 years. When funds are

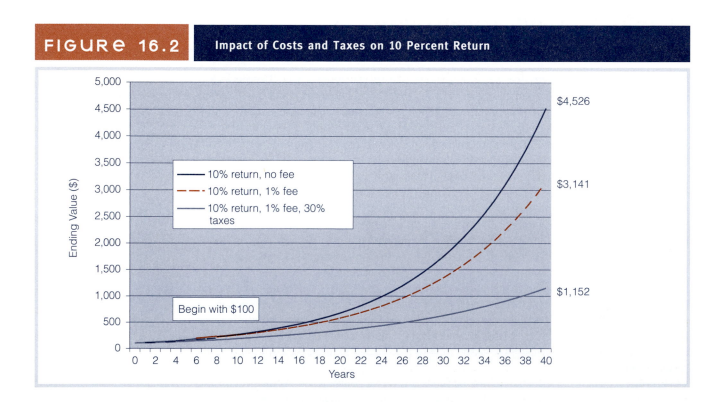

FIGURE 16.2   **Impact of Costs and Taxes on 10 Percent Return**

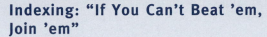
Indexing: "If You Can't Beat 'em, Join 'em"

On April 6, 2000, the Vanguard 500 Index Fund surpassed Fidelity Magellan as the world's largest mutual fund. This event marked an important signpost in the history of investment management. Long a recognized investment strategy among institutional pension fund managers, the indexing concept has clearly caught on with mutual fund investors. Standard & Poor's estimates that more than $4 trillion worth of equity investments is benchmarked to the S&P 500, and more than $1.1 trillion is indexed to match S&P Index performance. Much of this is managed in pension plans. In the mutual fund industry, index funds claim roughly $580 billion.

Like the Vanguard 500 Index Fund, most popular index funds are designed to mimic the Standard & Poor's 500 Index. However, indexing can be used to match the returns of any stock or bond market benchmark, or index. When an index strategy is employed, a computer staff simply attempts to replicate the investment results of the benchmark index by holding the index securities. Index funds make no attempt to use stock selection or traditional active management tech-

niques to beat the market. Similarly, index funds shun bets on individual stocks or narrow industry sectors in an attempt to outpace the overall market. Indexing can be described as a passive investment approach that emphasizes broad diversification and low portfolio trading activity.

The key advantage of index fund investing is relatively low cost. The average general equity fund has an annual expense ratio of about 1.4 percent of assets under management. Traditional equity fund managers with a typical portfolio turnover rate of 85 percent per year incur portfolio brokerage and trading costs of 0.5 to 1 percent annually. When selling commissions and other costs are considered, it's easy to see how the typical equity mutual fund underperforms the broad market averages by 3 to 4 percent per year. Index funds pay minimal advisory fees, if any, and minimize operating expenses and portfolio turnover.

In short, indexing is a time-tested investment strategy that offers long-term investors an efficient means for achieving market-matching results that typically beat professionally managed mutual funds.

See Ron Lieber, "Smackdown: Index Funds v. ETFs," *Wall Street Journal Online*, January 21, 2006 (**http://online.wsj.com**).

---

purchased through retail brokers and other investment professionals who charge sales commissions, such charges can dramatically cut the total return earned by mutual fund shareholders. By contrast, **no-load funds** are sold directly by mutual fund management companies to investors without commission expenses. It is vital that mutual fund shareholders carefully compare the total costs of various mutual fund alternatives to ensure a cost-effective selection.

No-load fund
Fund sold without sales commission.

Mutual Fund Performance

Sources of Investment Return

Mutual fund performance is best measured by the fund's **total return**, consisting of dividend and interest income and both realized and unrealized appreciation. A fund's total return is reflected by the change in investment value over time.

Mutual funds produce current income for shareholders from investments in interest-bearing securities, such as short-term and long-term bonds, and from dividends paid on common stocks owned by the fund. After expenses, all mutual fund income is paid out to fund shareholders in the form of **income distributions**. Depending on the type of fund, income distributions may be paid on a monthly basis for money market funds and short-term bond funds or on a quarterly, semiannual, or annual basis for stock and long-term bond funds. Fund shareholders can choose to receive income distributions in cash or to have their dividends reinvested in additional shares of the fund. Shareholders designate the method of dividend payment when an account is opened but may change their selection at any time.

When securities that a fund has purchased rise in value, the fund generates **unrealized capital gains**. Unrealized capital gains raise the net asset value (or market value) of a fund. If a fund sells securities at a profit, a taxable capital gain is realized. Realized capital gains are typically paid out to mutual fund shareholders in December in the form of a **capital gains distribution**. When a fund pays out realized capital gains, the fund's share price is reduced by the amount of the distribution. As in the case of income dividends, capital gains distributions may be received by a shareholder in cash or reinvested for further appreciation. Of course, stocks and bonds can also fall in value, and funds periodically incur capital losses that reduce the mar-

Total return
Dividend and interest income and realized and unrealized appreciation.

Income distribution
Payment of interest and dividends.

Unrealized capital gains
Increase in fund value caused by a rise in the value of fund investments.

Capital gains distribution
Payment of realized capital gains.

ket value of fund shares. Likewise, individual investors can suffer losses on their mutual fund investments by selling shares at a price lower than they paid for them.

Try It!

A mutual fund in which you own 276.3245 shares begins the last quarter of the year with a NAV of $34.597 per share. At the end of the quarter the fund declares an income distribution of $0.511 per share and a capital gains distribution of $1.245 per share. Before the distribution, the NAV of the fund is $38.109. If you want your distributions reinvested in more shares, how many shares will you have after the distribution?

Solution

The combined distribution of $1.756 per share comes to a total of $485.225 (= $1.756 × 276.3245). Immediately following the distribution, the NAV of the fund will be $36.353 (= $38.109 − $0.511 − $1.245). Automatic reinvesting yields 13.3476 new shares (= $485.225 / $36.353). After receiving the new shares, you own 289.6721 shares of the fund.

Mutual Fund Expenses

Mutual funds have operating expenses that are deducted from interest and dividend income. Only after such expenses have been paid is any remaining net income passed along to mutual fund shareholders in the form of dividends. Basic mutual fund operating expenses include investment advisory fees and the costs of legal and accounting services, postage, printing, and related services. The total of these costs expressed as a percentage of the fund's average net assets is called the fund's **operating expense ratio**.

Operating expense ratio
Operating expenses expressed as a percentage of fund assets.

Annual expense ratios typically range from a low of about 0.2 percent (or $20 per $10,000 in assets) to 2 percent ($200 per $10,000 in assets). Annual expense ratios are typically lowest for money market mutual funds and highest for international stock funds. A conventional operating expense charge for money market funds falls in the range of 0.5 percent per year. For stock funds, operating expenses of 1.5 percent per year are common. Operating expense ratios for bond funds typically fall somewhere between 0.5 and 1.5 percent, depending on fund size and investment philosophy. Operating expense ratios tend to be lowest for large funds that invest in the most actively traded (liquid) stocks and bonds. Operating expense ratios tend to be highest for small or specialized funds that invest in illiquid sectors of the market or in smaller and riskier foreign markets.

Regardless of the type of mutual fund, investors must be aware of how fees and expenses affect the fund's total return. Those costs are the most important source of any differences in yield observed among comparable money market and bond funds. Once bond fund investors have chosen an acceptable level of credit quality and average maturity, most funds will have a similar gross yield before expenses. High expenses have the potential to consume a substantial portion of this amount. For example, if a short-term corporate bond fund has a gross yield of 6.5 percent and an industry-average expense ratio of 0.86 percent, its net yield to the investor is only 5.64 percent. If a similar but cost-efficient fund has the same gross yield but an expense ratio of only 0.3 percent, the net yield to the investor would be 6.2 percent. The interest income received by an investor in the low-cost fund is roughly 10 percent greater than that received by an investor in the fund of average efficiency. Compounding the problem of high-cost funds is the tendency of high-cost fund managers to take on additional risk in the hope of receiving higher returns. Low-cost funds have the potential to provide competitive returns with a lower level of risk than other funds.

Many mutual fund investors also pay one-time sales commissions, or **load charges**. Sales commissions are often charged at the time of purchase as a simple percentage of the amounts invested. Such **front-end loads** typically range from 4 to 8.5 percent (or $400 to $850 per $10,000 invested). Funds that charge sales fees ranging from 1 to 3 percent (or $100 to $300 per $10,000 invested) are called **low-load funds**. Another form of sales charge is the **back-end load**, which is assessed when an investor sells fund shares. Back-end loads are sometimes called contingent deferred sales charges because their timing depends on the investor's sale decision. Back-end loads may be as high as 6 percent for redemptions that take place within one year of the original investment. These charges typically decline over time and may disappear by the seventh year after the original purchase of fund shares.

Some funds also charge investors an additional amount to cover marketing and distribution costs. These marketing charges are sometimes called **12b-1 fees**, after the 1980 U.S. SEC rule that permits this practice. According to SEC regulations, a fund is required to disclose a 12b-1 fee in its stated expense ratio. There is no legal limit to the 12b-1 fees that a fund may charge, but such fees normally run between 0.25 and 1 percent of the fund's average annual net assets. At 1 percent, the 12b-1 charge to the investor is $100 per $10,000 in fund assets per year. If a fund charges a 12b-1 fee in excess of 0.25 percent, it may not call itself a no-load fund even if it has no other sales charges. Funds that are sold without front-end or back-end load charges are called **no-load funds**.

Some mutual funds also charge a variety of miscellaneous fees. An **exchange fee** of $5 to $25 per transaction may be assessed when an investor exchanges shares from one fund to another within the same fund family. All funds allow switches based on the investor's written instructions. Many funds also allow switches using the fund's toll-free telephone number or a PC-based trading system on the Internet. In many cases, fees charged for Internet transactions are somewhat lower than those incurred using other mediums. Account **maintenance fees** of between $10 and $25 per year also may be assessed. Such charges are sometimes reserved for very small accounts having balances below a stated dollar level, such as $5,000 to $10,000 in assets. Maintenance charges are designed to fairly apportion fixed costs associated with maintaining individual accounts.

How Mutual Fund Costs Affect Returns

The best resource to help investors determine mutual fund costs is the fund's **prospectus**, which must be given to all investors at or before the time of purchase. The SEC requires that information about mutual fund sales charges and operating expenses be clearly spelled out in a table near the front of the prospectus. This information makes it easy to compare mutual fund costs and helps investors identify funds that can meet their investment objectives on a cost-efficient basis. This fee table includes all expenses that a hypothetical investor would pay assuming a 5 percent annual return on a $10,000 investment over investment horizons of 1, 3, 5, and 10 years. SEC regulations also make it easy for mutual fund shareholders to compare load charges and operating expense ratios across funds. Paying higher operating expenses or load charges might make sense if doing so leads to higher investor returns. Unfortunately, there is no evidence to suggest funds with higher expense ratios or load charges do better than cost-efficient no-load funds. To the contrary, simple logic confirms that cost-efficient no-load funds leave more dollars available to build long-term wealth for mutual fund investors.

Representative prospectus fee tables are shown in Table 16.4, Part A. This table shows all fees and expenses assessed by three hypothetical mutual funds. First indicated is whether or not the fund imposes load charges on the initial amount invested and on reinvested dividends. Any redemption and exchange fees must also be indicated. Important components of the funds' annual fund operating expenses are also noted. The "bottom line" is the fund's total operating expense. Although this percentage can seem rather small, small savings add up to important amounts over extended time periods. The savings realized from using a cost-efficient stock fund can be impressive over time, as illustrated in Table 16.4, Part B.

In the hypothetical examples illustrated, fund A is a typical cost-efficient **index fund** designed to mimic the performance of a broad market index such as the Standard & Poor's (S&P) 500. Fund B is a conventional no-load stock mutual fund with typical operating expenses. Fund

---

Load charges
Sales commissions.

Front-end loads
Commissions paid at the time of a fund purchase.

Low-load funds
Funds that charge sales fees ranging from 1 to 3 percent.

Back-end load
Commissions paid when a fund is sold.

12b-1 fees
Marketing expenses.

No-load funds
Funds sold on a commission-free basis.

Exchange fee
Charge assessed when an investor exchanges shares from one fund to another within the same fund family.

Maintenance fees
Bookeeping charges.

Prospectus
Offering circular.

Index fund
Mutual fund strategy designed to mimic the performance of some broad market benchmark.

	Fund A	Fund B	Fund C

TABLE 16.4

Mutual Fund Expenses Have a Dramatic Effect on Investor Returns. *This table illustrates all expenses and fees that a shareholder of three hypothetical mutual funds would incur. It also shows the expenses that investors would incur on a $10,000 investment over various time periods, assuming (1) a 5 percent annual rate of return and (2) redemptions at the end of each period.*

A. Typical Fee Tables in Mutual Fund Prospectuses

	Fund A	Fund B	Fund C
Shareholder transaction expenses:			
Sales load imposed on purchases	None	None	4.75%
Sales load imposed on reinvested dividends	None	None	4.75
Redemption fees	None	None	None
Exchange fees	None	None	None
Annual fund operating expenses:			
Management and administrative expenses	0.22%	0.60%	0.70%
Investment advisory expenses	0.02	—	—
12b-1 marketing fees	—	0.30	—
Marketing and distribution costs	0.02	—	—
Miscellaneous expenses	0.03	0.32	0.26
Total operating expenses	**0.29%**	**1.22%**	**0.96%**
Expenses on a $10,000 investment: *			
1 year	$ 30	$124	$587
3 years	93	387	823
5 years	163	670	1,077
10 years	368	1,477	1,805

B. The Impact of Equity Mutual Fund Costs on Long-Term Investor Returns

	Fund A	Fund B	Fund C
Initial investment	$ 10,000	$10,000	$10,000
Day 1	10,000	10,000	9,525
5 years	18,189	17,451	16,186
10 years	33,084	30,565	29,689
15 years	60,178	53,145	52,416
20 years	109,458	92,743	92,539
Gross return	13.00%	13.00%	13.00%
Operating expenses	0.29	1.22	0.96
Net return	**12.71%**	**11.78%**	**12.04%**

* Expenses are charged on the average investment throughout the year.
Source: Vanguard, **www.vanguard.com**.

C is a full-load stock mutual fund with less than typical annual operating expenses. For simplicity, each fund is assumed to earn the market average of 13 percent per year before expenses. From these three examples, it becomes clear that high mutual fund costs are a significant, but sometimes overlooked, limiting force on long-term investment performance. Before investing in a mutual fund with front-end or back-end load charges, the mutual fund investor must weigh such costs against the value of any investment advice received from the investment professional who helped with the transaction. Valuable professional service must also be rendered to justify investing in a fund that carries 12b-1 fees, as do about half the mutual funds tracked by Lipper Analytical Services, Inc. And, finally, all mutual fund investors should consider the merits of investing in funds that have low expense ratios. High marketing and operating expenses reduce the total return and can be justified only by valuable professional services.

Try It!

Examine the performance of three mutual funds. One fund has a load, the second has a back-end load, and the third is a no-load fund. Given the information below, determine for each fund (a) the number of shares purchased one year ago with $10,000 and (b) the total profit in dollars for the year.

Load		NAV 1 Year Ago	NAV Today
Fund A	Load of 3%	$10.23	$11.25
Fund B	Back-end load of 2%	23.45	25.79
Fund C	No load	44.22	48.64

Solution

a. Number of shares of fund A: $\dfrac{\$10,000}{10.23(1.03)} = 949.046$ shares

Number of shares of fund B: $\dfrac{\$10,000}{23.45} = 426.439$ shares

Number of shares of fund C: $\dfrac{\$10,000}{44.22} = 226.142$ shares

b. Fund A profit: $11.25 \times (949.046) - 10,000 = \$676.77$ profit

Fund B profit:

$25.79 \times (426.439) - 10,000 = \$997.86$ profit if the shares are not sold
$25.79 \times (1 - 0.02) \times (426.439) - 10,000 = \$777.90$ profit if the shares are sold

Fund C profit: $48.64 \times (226.142) - 10,000 = \$999.55$ profit

Note that all three funds earned a 10 percent return on their NAV. However, not all the investors earn 10 percent. The investor in fund A earns 6.77 percent because they paid a 3 percent load. The fund B investor earns 10 percent if the shares are not sold; if the shares are sold, then the back-end load must be paid and the investor earns only 7.78 percent. The no-load, fund C, investor earns 10 percent.

Style Boxes

Comparing the performance of mutual funds with different investment strategies and different levels of risk is difficult. Instead of comparing different funds, it is common to compare funds with similar characteristics. A **style box** is a simple means for characterizing portfolio risk according to market capitalization and value-growth orientation. Table 16.5 illustrates the style box concept by using a methodology articulated by Morningstar. Rather than go by each fund's self-proclaimed investment objective, Morningstar assesses the stocks each fund actually owns.

Characterizing mutual funds and investment portfolios by market capitalization is the first step. In the United States, the 5,000 largest companies together represent virtually the entire market capitalization of the stock market. Morningstar considers the top 250 companies by market capitalization to be "large cap." The next 750 are classified as "mid-cap." The remaining 4,000 companies are considered "small cap." Although these numbers may seem a bit lopsided, a relatively small number of big blue-chip stocks account for an overwhelming portion of the total amount of money invested in the market. The S&P 500 is an appropriate market benchmark for large-cap stocks. A common performance standard for mid-cap portfolios is the

Style box
Means of characterizing portfolio risk according to market capitalization and value-growth orientation. Morningstar classifies fund portfolio holdings into nine categories based on these characteristics.

TABLE 16.5	Morningstar's Innovative Nine-Part Style Boxes Allow Investors to Characterize Portfolio Risk and Return

	Value Strategy (score < 1.75)	Blend (1.75 ≤ score ≤ 2.25)	Growth Strategy (score > 2.25)
Large cap (top 5%)		S & P 500 Benchmark	
Mid-cap (next 15%)		Wilshire 4500 Benchmark	
Small cap (bottom 80%)		Russell 2000 Benchmark	

Dow Jones Wilshire 4500 Index, which is composed of the DJ Wilshire 5000 minus the S&P 500. The Russell 2000 is an appropriate benchmark for small-cap stocks.

To place funds along the horizontal axis of the style box, Morningstar determines how cheap or expensive portfolio holdings are relative to the overall market. Value stocks are typically defined as stocks that feature low price-earnings (P/E) and low price-book (P/B) ratios. Absolute figures are less telling than relative numbers. Morningstar looks at P/E and P/B ratios relative to each market-cap group. In other words, P/E and P/B ratios for a small-cap stock fund are compared with those for small-cap stocks in general and not against those of large blue-chip companies.

In the Morningstar style box system each portfolio holding receives a relative P/E and a relative P/B score. A score of 1.00 indicates that a P/E or P/B ratio is exactly in line with the market-cap group norm. For each mutual fund, Morningstar then calculates an average score using P/E and P/B ratios and adds these two results together. If a fund has a relative P/E score and relative P/B score that together exceed 2.25, it falls into the growth column of the style box. If the combined score falls below 1.75, the fund is considered a value fund. Anywhere in between, from 1.75 to 2.25, lands the fund in the blend column.

Armed with style box information, investors are capable of doing an effective assessment of portfolio manager performance. For example, performance of funds in the Large-Company Blend style box should be compared relative to the S&P 500 Index. The performance of large value-stock portfolios can be compared with a low P/B portfolio derived from the S&P 500. The performance of large growth-stock portfolios can be compared with a high P/B portfolio derived from the S&P 500. Funds and investment portfolios that find themselves in the Mid-Cap Blend style box are most effectively compared with the Wilshire 4500 Index. Wilshire value and growth components can be used to measure the performance of mid-cap value and growth portfolios. The Russell 2000 proxy for the small-cap segment of the market is an appropriate performance benchmark for funds and portfolios in the Small-Cap Blend style box. Similarly, value and growth components of the Russell 2000 can be used to measure the relative performance of small-cap value and growth portfolios.

Try It!

Visit the Morningstar Web site at **www.morningstar.com**. You can examine the performance and style of a mutual fund from the Fund menu link. For example, on February 13, 2006, the Dreyfus Appreciation mutual fund was categorized by Morningstar as a Large-Cap Value/Growth Blend fund. This fund outperformed this category in 2001 and 2002 by 0.5 percent and 4.6 percent, respectively. It underperformed the other funds in this category by -7.2 percent in 2003, -4.5 percent in 2004, and -1.6 percent in 2005. Morningstar also has a mutual fund screener that allows you to search for mutual funds in the style desired.

Evaluating Fund Performance

Tools that mutual fund investors use to evaluate the performance of a mutual fund fall into two categories. Investors can use various ranking tools that compare performance among funds with similar objectives. Investors can also use portfolio evaluation tools based on the CAPM (alpha, Sharpe ratio, and Treynor Index) described in Chapter 5.

Morningstar assigns each domestic equity mutual fund into one of 20 categories. Nine of these categories reflect the Morningstar style box combinations of firm size and value-growth orientation. Other categories include specialized groups of funds that focus on individual sectors (e.g., energy or health stocks), or special strategies (e.g., convertible securities). International stock mutual funds are assigned into 14 different categories. There are 12 and 17 categories for fixed-income and municipal bond funds, respectively. After assigning a fund to a category, Morningstar ranks the fund's performance versus its peers over various time periods. Figure 16.3 shows information provided by Yahoo! Finance on the popular Dreyfus Appreciation Fund. Morningstar categorizes the fund as a large blend fund. Notice that fund expenses are shown side-by-side with category averages. Dreyfus is a no-load fund with a low expense ratio relative to its peers.

Figure 16.4 shows how the fund's performance compares to that of its peers over various time periods. Dreyfus underperformed its peers and the S&P 500 Index during the past one and three years. The Dreyfus fund outperformed in the recent bear market and underperformed in the recent bull market. The figure also shows that a fund's rank within the category is shown by time period. Dreyfus has performed poorly recently and ranks 2,087 out of 2,174 funds year-to-date.

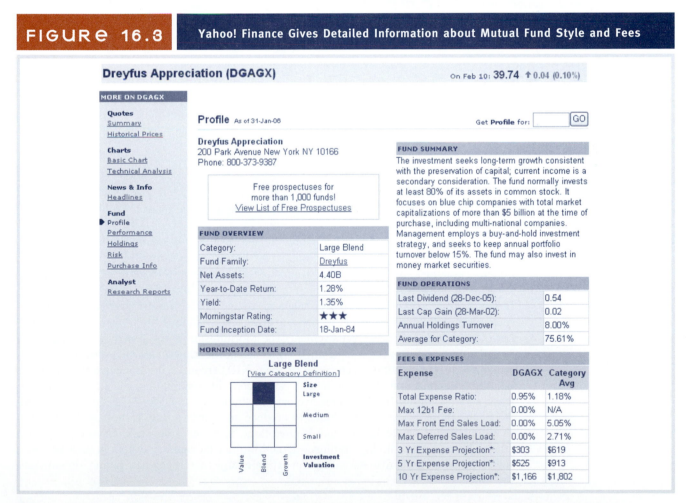

FIGURE 16.3   Yahoo! Finance Gives Detailed Information about Mutual Fund Style and Fees

FIGURE 16.4   Dreyfus Appreciation Fund Performance from Yahoo! Finance

Performance As of 31-Jan-06   Get **Performance** for: [   ] [GO]

PERFORMANCE OVERVIEW

Morningstar Return Rating:	Average
Year to Date Return:	1.28%
5-Year Average Return:	-0.07%
Number of Years Up:	18
Number of Years Down:	3
Best 1-Yr Total Return (1991):	38.43%
Worst 1-Yr Total Return (2002):	-17.14%
Best 3-Yr Total Return (1995-97):	30.36%
Worst 3-Yr Total Return (2000-2):	-9.03%

LOAD ADJUSTED RETURNS

1-Year:	No load
3-Year:	No load
5-Year:	No load
10-Year:	No load

TRAILING RETURNS (%) VS. BENCHMARKS

Return	DGAGX	Category	Diff	Index*	Diff
Year To Date	1.28	3.25	-1.97	4.91	-3.63
1-Month	1.28	3.25	-1.97	0.04	1.24
3-Month	3.21	7.54	-4.33	2.08	1.13
1-Year	6.69	11.64	-4.95	4.91	1.78
3-Year	11.54	16.16	-4.62	14.38	-2.84
5-Year	-0.07	0.59	-0.66	0.54	-0.61
Last Bull Market (28-Feb-03 to 31-Mar-04)	26.16	33.26	-7.1	33.61	-7.45
Last Bear Market (31-Mar-02 to 30-Apr-03)	-16.15	-17.48	1.33	-17.13	0.98

(continued on next page)

Source: Reproduced with permission of Yahoo! Inc., © 2006 by Yahoo! Inc. Yahoo and the Yahoo! logos are trademarks of Yahoo! Inc.

Mutual fund performance is commonly judged relative to peers and an appropriate performance benchmark. However, as Figure 16.4 illustrates, it can still be difficult to reach concrete conclusions. Is the Dreyfus Appreciation Fund an attractive investment? At times it seems to outperform the average fund in its category; at other times it underperforms. To help investors assess the past performance of mutual funds, Morningstar issues "achievement scores." Between one and five stars are given to each mutual fund, where a higher number of stars indicates better achievement. The Morningstar rating system is based on how well the fund performs (after adjusting for risk and accounting for all sales charges) in comparison to its peers. Within each category, the top 10 percent of funds receive five stars, the next 22.5 percent four stars, the middle 35 percent three stars, the next 22.5 percent two stars, and the bottom 10 percent receive one star. Funds are rated for 3-, 5-, and 10-year periods, and these ratings are combined to produce an overall rating. Note from Figure 16.3 that the Dreyfus Appreciation Fund is rated three stars. Investors seek out funds with five stars. Mutual funds with high ratings use the Morningstar ranking system in their advertising. A fund that has a five-star rating can expect a large increase in new money flowing into the fund.

FIGURE 16.4	Dreyfus Appreciation Fund Performance from Yahoo! Finance *continued*

ANNUAL TOTAL RETURN (%) HISTORY

Year		DGAGX	Category	Diff
2005		4.14	5.77	-1.63
2004		5.57	10.10	-4.53
2003		20.39	27.62	-7.23
2002		-17.14	-21.78	4.64
2001		-10.75	-11.20	0.45
2000		1.80	-3.51	5.31
1999		9.97	20.21	-10.24
1998		30.85	21.39	9.46
1997		27.85	27.63	0.22
1996		25.67	21.47	4.20

PAST QUARTERLY RETURNS (%) FOR DGAGX

	Q1	Q2	Q3	Q4
2005	-0.06	0.72	3.36	0.08
2004	0.69	1.39	-3.59	7.26
2003	-4.28	12.96	0.71	10.55
2002	2.60	-11.29	-14.34	6.27
2001	-10.83	3.79	-8.74	5.67
2000	0.65	2.94	-1.98	0.24
1999	3.12	3.64	-6.65	10.22
1998	15.69	4.54	-10.23	20.52
1997	3.52	16.35	4.45	1.63
1996	5.84	5.66	4.22	7.83

RANK IN CATEGORY (BY TOTAL RETURN)

Period	Rank	Funds in Category	% Rank
Year To Date	2087	2174	96.00
1-Month	2043	2174	93.97
3-Month	2106	2149	98.00
6-Month	1777	1975	89.97
1-Year	1424	1853	76.85
3-Year	1232	1498	82.24
5-Year	707	1153	61.32

Investors also use the portfolio evaluation measures described in Chapter 5. Remember that abnormal performance can be measured using a mutual fund's alpha. A positive alpha is better than the theoretical return expectation derived from the CAPM. In addition, common risk-adjusted performance measures compute the risk premium earned by a portfolio relative to the level of risk. The Sharpe ratio ranks portfolios according to the risk premium earned relative to total risk using $SD(R_P)$, whereas the Treynor Index ranks portfolios according to the risk premium earned relative to systematic risk using β_P. Morningstar reports portfolio evaluation

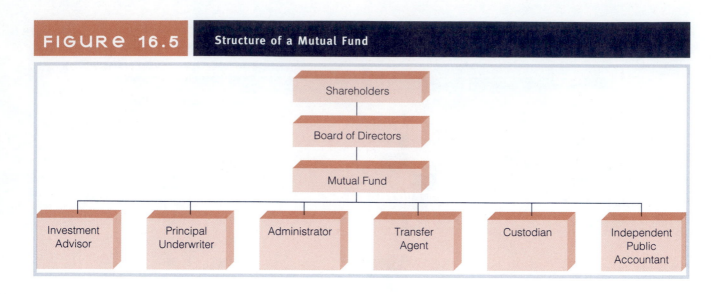

FIGURE 16.5   Structure of a Mutual Fund

measures in its "Risk Measures" section. In February 2006, Morningstar reported a –1.66 percent alpha over the past three years for the Dreyfus Appreciation Fund. The negative alpha indicates that this Dreyfus fund earned a negative abnormal return. Nevertheless, a Sharpe ratio of 1.19 is given for the Dreyfus Appreciation Fund. Since the Sharpe ratio of the S&P 500 Index was 0.46 during this period, this Dreyfus fund achieved a better return-risk relationship than the index over this period.

Mutual fund shareholders
Investors in the mutual fund portfolio.

Independent directors
Board directors with no business ties to the investment advisor.

Investment advisor
Firm that manages the fund's portfolio and policies.

Principal underwriter
Firm that sells the fund shares to the public.

Administrator
Person who oversees the services provided by other firms.

Transfer agent
Person or firm who executes shareholder transactions, maintains records, and issues account statements.

Custodian
Bank that holds portfolio securities.

Mutual Fund Organization

Governance Structure

Most mutual funds rely on other parties to provide many of the services demanded by shareholders. For example, many mutual fund management companies hire other firms to keep track of investor accounts, hold securities, and provide accounting services. Even marketing and investment advisory functions may be contracted out to third parties. Figure 16.5 shows the most common mutual fund structure.

Mutual fund shareholders are the investors who own shares in the portfolio of assets. Like shareholders of other companies, they have the right to vote on the board's directors and on material changes in the terms of the contract with the investment advisor. Shareholders also vote on any significant changes in the investment objectives of the fund, like a switch from a value focus to a growth focus.

The board of directors does not participate in the day-to-day operations of the fund, but it contracts with the investment advisor to determine the fees paid by shareholders. A majority of mutual fund board members must be **independent directors**, and they cannot have any significant relationship with the fund's advisor. The **investment advisor** dictates the makeup of the investment portfolio, either directly or through the retention of an independent professional money manager. The investment advisor typically hires a **principal underwriter** to sell the shares to the general public. The advisor may also be the **administrator**, who oversees all the services being provided. Or the advisor may hire someone else to do this. The **transfer agent**, usually a third party, executes shareholder transactions and maintains shareholder records. The **custodian** is a bank that holds portfolio securities and is required by law to be separate from the investment advisor. As in other public companies, the board of directors of a mutual fund hires an **independent public accountant** to audit the financial activities of the fund.

The investment advisor pays for all of these services from the revenue it generates from fees on the portfolio. Management fees, maintenance fees, transfer fees, and 12b-1 fees pay needed revenue.

Independent public accountant
Person or firm that audits the mutual fund's financial statements.

Mutual Funds as Tournaments

Mutual fund management companies earn their revenue as a portion of assets under management (AUM). A mutual fund with $100 million in assets will reap $1 million in revenue with a 1 percent management fee. This arrangement creates an incentive to maximize fund size. Investors also have a tendency to chase winning investment strategies and top-performing mutual funds. These related tendencies can create dangerous tournamentlike behavior among mutual fund managers.

To rapidly grow AUM and asset-based fees, mutual funds have an incentive to take on high-risk investment strategies. Such high risk-taking behavior may not be good for the mutual fund investor because the mutual fund is essentially gambling with the investor's money. If high-risk gambles pay off, the investor gets a high return and the mutual fund company receives enormous future rewards in terms of high management fees. However, if high-risk gambles fail to pay off, the investor can lose a significant amount of investment capital but the mutual fund's investment management company loses only a profit-making opportunity. From the investor's perspective, such "heads they win, tails I lose" gambles are most common in the hedge fund industry, where incentive-based compensation gives managers as much as 20 percent of investment gains but leaves investors responsible for absorbing all losses.

An unfortunate side effect of mutual fund performance rankings is that they create a **mutual fund tournament** atmosphere in which mutual fund management companies play for their own self-interest. Performance rankings also give incentives for "window dressing" and other costly portfolio strategies that hurt mutual fund investors in the long run.

Mutual fund tournament
Incentive-created behavior where funds increase portfolio risk to increase potential performance.

Do Winners Repeat?

In the never-ending quest for above-market performance, mutual fund investors often chase last year's winners. However, chasing last year's winners is a dangerous investment strategy. Mutual funds that earn atypically good or bad investment returns tend to have atypical investment portfolios. If a mutual fund concentrates its investments in a few stocks or industries, it is more likely to have a return that is very different from marketwide norms. Of course, it could be spectacularly good or spectacularly bad. Most mutual funds that show great performance in a given year lack broad diversification. Before leaping to buy top-performing funds, investors need to ask: Are mutual fund winners successful because of superior stock-picking skills, or were they just lucky?

One way to define winners is to examine Morningstar's five-star-rated mutual funds. All such funds performed very well before they received Morningstar's top ranking. On average, these funds beat the market by slightly less than 5 percent per year during the three-year period prior to receiving the five-star rating. However, after receiving Morningstar's top rating, studies show that such funds tend to underperform the overall market by roughly 5 percent per year. On average, mutual fund winners do not repeat! Unfortunately, the only performance consistency in the mutual fund industry appears to be among poor performers. Funds found among the poorest-performing Morningstar-rated funds tend to stay there because of their generally high management fees. The message for long-term investors seems clear: Be wary of chasing past performance, and be careful to focus on funds that keep expenses low.

Timing the Market

The stock market has seen tremendous bull markets and devastating bear markets. On average, stocks return about 10 percent per year. If an investor somehow figured out how to time the market and avoid bear markets while still participating in bull markets, total returns would skyrocket. Unfortunately, nobody knows how to do this consistently. Even the pros get it wrong when it comes to timing the market.

Consider the big market timing bet made by Jeffrey Vinik, manager of the colossal Fidelity Magellan Fund. In 1995 and 1996, the stock market was at record highs, and Vinik believed it to be overvalued. Vinik dumped stocks and bought bonds until bonds made up 19.2 percent of Magellan's assets in the first quarter of 1996. Taken together, bonds and cash accounted for nearly one-third of assets for the largest and most popular stock mutual funds. This was an extraordinarily risky market timing bet. If the market fell, bonds and cash would retain their value and allow Magellan to outperform its peers on a relative basis. If stocks continued to soar, such a big bet on bonds and cash

would be a drag on performance and Magellan would underperform its peers. As it turns out, the stock market continued to roar ahead, and Magellan's near-term performance started to lag. Shareholders grew restless as the fund returned just 2.4 percent on an annualized basis in the first four months of 1996, while the S&P 500 Index surged ahead 6.9 percent. Investors yanked $1 billion out of Magellan, and Magellan's parent, Fidelity Advisors, lost $10 million in revenue.

Before going into bonds and cash, Vinik had bested the competition with a strong performance record of 17.2 percent per year over nearly four years. However, one bad quarter at Fidelity's highly visible Magellan fund brought Vinik's Fidelity career to an end. In May 1996, Vinik announced his resignation, and Robert Stansky took over the leadership of the fund. Stansky immediately began selling the bonds and buying technology stocks. That's why few mutual fund managers try to time the market. The professional risks are simply too great.

See Arden Dale, "Investors Return to Japanese Funds," *Wall Street Journal Online*, February 8, 2006 (**http://online.wsj.com**).

Specialized Funds

Exchange-Traded Funds

Exchange-traded funds (ETFs)
Tradeable shares that represent proportional ownership in baskets of stocks.

Standard & Poor's Depository Receipts (SPDR)s
ETFs that track the price performance and dividend yield of the S&P 500 Index.

DIAMONDS
ETFs that track the price performance and dividend yield of the Dow Jones Industrial Average.

QQQQs
ETFs that track the price performance and dividend yield of the Nasdaq 100 Index.

Select sector SPDRs
ETFs that track the price performance and dividend yield of particular industry groups.

iShares
Index shares (ETFs) created by Barclays Global Investors.

The hottest new products to hit the mutual fund industry in decades are called **exchange-traded funds (ETFs)**. ETFs offer investors a convenient means for investing in baskets of stocks that closely track any one of a large number of market indexes. Exchange-traded funds are available that track the performance of broad market averages, such as the Standard and Poor's 500 Index; narrow market sectors, such as technology; or major stock markets from around the world, such as Japan. Unlike traditional mutual funds, which can be purchased or redeemed only at the end of the trading day, ETFs can be purchased or sold anytime the markets are open. Like stocks, ETFs can also be held for long-term capital appreciation. Exchange-traded funds pay quarterly cash dividends from interest and dividend income, less fees and expenses that average roughly .10 to .50 percent per year.

Among the most popular ETFs are **Standard & Poor's Depository Receipts (SPDRs)**, based on the S&P 500. Called "spiders" (ticker, SPY), SPDRs closely track the price performance and dividend yield of the S&P 500 Index. Using SPDRs, investors can buy or sell the entire S&P 500 portfolio as easily as buying or selling shares of a single stock. Exchange-traded funds have also been established to track the Dow Jones Industrial Average (they are called "**DIAMONDS**"; ticker, DIA), the Nasdaq 100 Index (ticker, **QQQQs**), and the S&P MidCap 400 Index (these are called "MidCap SPDRs"). Also popular are **select sector SPDRs** that reflect a particular market sector or group of industries within the S&P 500 Index. At the present time, select sector SPDRs are offered for basic industries, consumer services, consumer staples, cyclicals/transportation, energy, financial services, industrials, technology, utilities, and so on.

Barclays Global Investors has been among the most innovative companies in the development of ETFs and now offers more than 80 index portfolios called **iShares**, or index shares. Using iShares, investors are able to trade portfolios that are constructed according to various broad market indexes, investing styles, market sectors, industries, and regions around the globe. With iShares, it's easy to add exposure to a wide variety of equity investment opportunities. For example, iShares are available for growth and value investors who want to track the performance of all the major U.S. market indexes and sector indexes produced by Dow Jones,

TABLE 16.6   The Twenty-five Largest Exchange Traded Funds (ETFs)

Fund Name	Ticker	Category	Fund Family	Net Assets ($ bil.)	Expense Ratio	Annual Turnover Ratio	Inception Date
SPDRs	SPY	Large Blend	SPDR TRUST SERIES 1	57.04	0.10%	6%	January-03
iShares MSCI EAFE Index	EFA	Foreign Large Blend	iShares Trust	29.32	0.38%	8%	August-01
NASDAQ 100 Trust Shares	QQQQ	Large Growth	NASDAQ 100 TRUST SERIES	17.40	0.20%	15%	March-99
iShares S&P 500 Index	IVV	Large Blend	iShares Trust	16.86	0.10%	7%	May-00
iShares MSCI Japan Index	EWJ	Japan Stock	iShares Inc	13.49	0.57%	6%	March-96
iShares MSCI Emerg Mkts Index	EEM	Diversified Emerging Mkts	iShares Trust	12.00	0.77%	9%	April-03
iShares Russell 2000 Index	IWM	Small Blend	iShares Trust	10.31	0.20%	20%	May-00
MidCap SPDRs	MDY	Mid-Cap Blend	MIDCAP SPDR TRUST SERIE	8.59	0.25%	19%	May-95
streetTRACKS Gold Shares	GLD	Specialty-Precious Metals	streetTRACKS Gold Trust	7.82	N/A	N/A	November-04
iShares Russell 1000 Value Index	IWD	Large Value	iShares Trust	6.87	0.20%	7%	May-00
iShares Dow Jones Select Dividend Index	DVY	Mid-Cap Value	iShares Trust	6.41	0.40%	14%	November-03
DIAMONDS Trust, Series 1	DIA	Large Value	DIAMONDS TRUST SERIES I	6.30	0.18%	8%	January-98
Vanguard Total Stock Market VIPERs	VTI	Large Blend	Vanguard Index Funds	5.63	0.07%	16%	May-01
iShares Russell 1000 Growth Index	IWF	Large Growth	iShares Trust	5.40	0.20%	18%	May-00
iShares Lehman 1-3 Year Treasury Bond	SHY	Short Government	iShares Trust	4.91	0.15%	83%	July-02
iShares S&P SmallCap 600 Index	IJR	Small Blend	iShares Trust	4.70	0.20%	16%	May-00
Energy Select Sector SPDR	XLE	Specialty-Natural Res	Select Sector Spdr Trust	4.28	0.26%	10%	December-98
iShares Lehman TIPS Bond	TIP	N/A	iShares Trust	4.09	0.20%	13%	December-03
iShares S&P MidCap 400 Index	IJH	Mid-Cap Blend	iShares Trust	3.72	0.20%	9%	May-00
iShares Lehman Aggregate Bond	AGG	Intermediate-Term Bond	iShares Trust	3.72	0.20%	456%	September-03
iShares S&P 500 Value Index	IVE	Large Value	iShares Trust	3.40	0.18%	7%	May-00
iShares S&P 500 Growth Index	IVW	Large Growth	iShares Trust	3.38	0.18%	12%	May-00
iShares Russell 2000 Value Index	IWN	Small Value	iShares Trust	3.36	0.25%	14%	July-00
iShares FTSE/Xinhua China 25 Index	FXI	Pacific/Asia ex-Japan Stk	iShares Trust	2.93	0.74%	13%	October-04
Utilities Select Sector SPDR	XLU	Specially-Utilities	Select Sector Spdr Trust	2.68	0.26%	4%	December-98
Average				**9.78**	**0.27%**	**33%**	

Data source: Yahoo! Finance (August 21, 2006) (**http://finance.yahoo.com/ett/browser/op**). Reproduced with permission of Yahoo! Inc. © 2006 by Yahoo! Inc. Yahoo and the Yahoo! logos are trademarks of Yahoo! Inc.

Standard & Poor's, and the Russell Investment Group. They are also available to track the performance of global stock markets, as reflected in 24 regional iShares, as well as economic sector global indexes. Through iShares, investors can achieve broad geographic diversification with investments in developed global markets, such as Canada, Germany, and the United Kingdom, and in emerging markets, such as Hong Kong, Malaysia, and Mexico.

Over 180 ETFs trade on the American Stock Exchange. Exchange-traded funds are very popular. On Friday, February 10, 2006, the most traded security in the United States was the QQQQ (traded on Nasdaq) with 99 million shares in volume. The second-highest-volume stock was Intel, with a volume of 82 million shares. The S&P 500 ETF (SPY) had a volume of over 61 million shares. For long-term investors, ETFs and iShares represent valuable investment vehicles. See **www.amex.com** for details.

Closed-End Funds

Closed-end funds
Investment companies that issue a fixed number of shares at a given point in time.

A **closed-end fund** is a publicly traded investment company. The shares of closed-end funds trade on exchanges such as the New York Stock Exchange (NYSE) and the American Stock Exchange (AMEX) or on the Nasdaq stock market. Closed-end funds collect money from investors through an initial public offering (IPO) and use this money to invest in securities. The number of shares issued by the fund and the dollar value of assets under management are fixed at the time of the fund's IPO. Thereafter, total assets under management grow or decline depending on investment success. In some circumstances, closed-end fund assets can be increased following a secondary offering of shares to the general public.

Closed-end funds offer a wide array of investment alternatives. Broadly diversified domestic funds reflect the portfolio managers' investment philosophy in their stock selection methods. Among U.S. equity funds, there are those that emphasize growth, value, market timing, blue chips, and small caps. Many specialized closed-end funds focus on individual sectors such as banking and financial services, environmental, health care, media, and gold and natural resources. Other specialized closed-end funds focus on stocks in individual foreign countries such as Germany, India, Korea, Mexico, or Thailand. Some foreign closed-end funds focus on regions rather than individual countries. In addition to deciding which countries have particularly attractive investment environments, such funds also must decide how to allocate investments within each country. Examples include funds that focus on Africa, Asia, Europe, Latin America, and Africa. Other closed-end funds focus on emerging markets in general.

Premium
Percentage by which the market price per share for a closed-end fund exceeds net asset value.

Discount
Percentage by which the market price per share for a closed-end fund is less than net asset value.

As for any mutual fund, net asset value is the current net worth per share. Closed-end fund shares trade at prices that may exceed or fall short of net asset values. When the market price per share for a closed-end fund exceeds its net asset value, the fund is selling at a **premium**. Closed-end funds sell at a premium to net asset value when investors are unusually optimistic about the fund's investment prospects. When the market price per share for a closed-end fund is less than its net asset value, the fund is selling at a **discount**. If net asset value is $10 per share and the fund is selling on the NYSE for $12, the fund is selling at a 20 percent premium. If the same fund is selling for $8.50, the fund is selling at a 15 percent discount to NAV.

Closed-end mutual funds typically sell at a discount of 5 to 10 percent. Some of the discounts may be due to the relative obscurity in which closed-end funds operate. Although most investors have heard about traditional open-end mutual funds, very few have heard about closed-end funds. Conventional open-end mutual funds advertise extensively to attract new investors because fund managers receive a percentage of the total assets under management. For conventional mutual funds, a growing pool of assets under management leads to higher fee income for the investment advisor. Closed-end funds, except under very rare circumstances, operate with a stable pool of investment money.

Some investment advisors recommend that investors purchase closed-end funds that trade at a significant discount to NAV. Such discounts tend to grow during bear markets and fall during bull markets. Economic, social, or political developments can also affect the short-term outlook for various markets around the world as well as discounts and premiums. The introduction of new closed-end funds with similar investment philosophies or investment objectives can also limit premiums or increase discounts by drawing away money that would otherwise have been committed to established funds.

In sum, closed-end funds offer long-term investors an investment alternative that may be well suited to specialized investing in small or illiquid markets in which portfolio turnover is harmful to long-term results. However, conventional mutual funds offer many of these same advantages with more flexibility and at a lower cost.

Hedge Funds

Hedge funds are similar to conventional mutual funds, but there are important differences in investment philosophy, investor suitability, and regulation. Like mutual funds, hedge funds represent a means for groups of investors to pool financial resources to efficiently purchase various types of securities in the pursuit of a specific financial goal. In the United States, hedge funds are typically organized as partnership arrangements available to wealthy investors with more than $1 million in financial assets. Hedge funds also have the flexibility to use speculative investment techniques that are prohibited for mutual funds.

Hedge funds
Investment partnerships that employ speculative investment techniques, such as leverage and short selling, that are very risky and commonly prohibited for mutual funds.

Unlike mutual funds, which are extensively regulated by the SEC, hedge funds are subject to only limited oversight because they ostensibly serve only sophisticated investors. Not only must U.S. mutual funds register with the SEC, they are also subject to extensive reporting and operating requirements designed to protect investors. Virtually every aspect of mutual fund operations is subject to strict regulation. For example, mutual funds are strictly prohibited from investing more than 5 percent of fund assets in the securities of any single issuer. Mutual funds are also required to provide shareholders with regular information about fund investment strategies, performance, fees, and expenses. Because hedge funds are largely unregulated, there is little reliable information about their operations. The SEC estimates there are as many as 7,000 domestic and offshore hedge funds with more than $1.5 trillion in investor equity.

Table 16.7 shows important differences between hedge funds and traditional mutual funds. Notice that 91 million Americans own mutual fund shares. The only financial qualification for

TABLE 16.7	Hedge Funds Differ from Mutual Funds in a Number of Ways	
	Mutual Funds	**Hedge Funds**
Who invests	91 million Americans own mutual fund shares. The only qualification for investing is having the minimum investment to open an account with a fund company—often $1,000 or less.	Only sophisticated, high-net-worth investors are eligible to invest. The typical investor is a wealthy individual or an institution such as an endowment or foundation. A minimum investment of $1 million or more is required.
Fees	Mutual fund shareholders pay, on average, an annual expense ratio of roughly 1.5% of assets. Load charges can increase this to 2.5% to 5% per year. Funds must disclose fees and expenses in detail. Sales charges and other distribution fees are subject to regulatory limits.	Hedge fund investors often pay a portfolio management fee of 1% to 2% of net assets, plus a performance-based fee that can run as high as 10% per year, depending on performance. Fees are not subject to specific regulatory limits.
Investment practices	Securities laws restrict a mutual fund's ability to leverage, or borrow against, the value of securities in its portfolio. Funds that use options, futures, forward contracts, and short selling generally must "cover" their positions with cash reserves or other liquid securities. Investment policies must be fully disclosed to investors.	Leveraging strategies are hallmarks of hedge funds. Investment policies do not have to be disclosed, even to investors in the fund.
Pricing and liquidity	Mutual funds must value their portfolio securities and compute their share price daily. They generally must also allow shareholders to redeem shares on at least a daily basis.	There are no specific rules on valuation or pricing. As a result, hedge fund investors may be unable to determine the value of their investment at any given time. In addition, new investors typically must pledge to keep their money in a hedge fund for at least one year.

Source: Investment Company Institute.

Street Smarts 16.3

Research Perspective

Are Mutual Fund Investors Always Rational?

Every business day, money moves from stock funds to money market funds. It also moves among funds with similar assets, such as from small-cap value funds to large-cap growth funds. By examining mutual fund money flows, financial economists can identify what fund characteristics are desired by investors. Also studied is whether or not fund flows seem rational. Often they do not.

Consider the choice of a mutual fund indexed to the S&P 500. All such index funds are trying to replicate the same returns; they must hold the same stocks. This makes the top-performing S&P 500 index funds easy to spot in advance. Simply pick the S&P 500 index fund with the lowest expense ratio, and it will outperform those with higher expenses. Some S&P 500 index funds have minimal turnover and expense ratios as low as 0.1 percent of assets under management. Would rational and fully informed investors choose index funds with expense ratios over 1 percent, or 10 times higher than the most efficient S&P 500 funds? The simple answer is no. Nev-

ertheless, index funds with high expenses have seen rapid asset growth during recent years. This looks irrational to some informed observers.

Because of representativeness bias, mutual fund investors also tend to pour money into funds that have performed well over the previous year. This is called "chasing historical performance," and it seldom leads to market-beating returns. Investing based on last year's performance is a bit like driving down the highway by focusing on the rearview mirror and ignoring what appears through the windshield. Worse yet, because poorly performing funds typically see investors pull their money out in droves, some funds appear to fool investors by changing their names but not their portfolios. Some funds change their names to last year's "hot" style, thus fooling naïve investors. Unfortunately, those naïve investors tend to lose money on these name-changing funds.

Again, such naïve behavior looks irrational to informed observers

See Michael Cooper, Huseyin Gulen, and Raghavendra Rau, "Changing Names with Style: Mutual Fund Name Changes and Their Effects on Fund Flows," *Journal of Finance*, vol. 60, no. 6 (December 2005), pp. 2825–2858.

investing in a typical mutual fund is having the minimum investment to open an account. This is often $1,000 or less. In the case of hedge funds, only sophisticated, high-net-worth individuals are eligible to invest. A typical hedge fund investor is a wealthy individual or institution with a minimum of $1 million in financial assets. Annual expense ratios average 1.24 percent of net mutual fund assets, whereas hedge fund investors pay annual fees of 1 to 2 percent of net assets under management *plus* 20 percent or more of the total rate of return earned on investment. Securities laws restrict the ability of a mutual fund to use leverage or borrow against the value of securities in its portfolio, but hedge funds face no such limitation. Many hedge funds use aggressive investment techniques such as stock and index options, futures and forward contracts, and short selling. The aggressive use of leverage and other such speculative techniques is a distinguishing characteristic of hedge funds and explains why many of their operations remain secret, even to long-term investors.

Taxes

Taxes on Distributions

Mutual funds are not taxed on investment income or capital gains so long as those earnings are fully passed along to shareholders in the form of dividends. Once income dividends and capital gains distributions have been received by shareholders, shareholders must pay any taxes due when they file their personal income taxes with the Internal Revenue Service (IRS).

Income dividends are derived from all interest and dividend income earned from the fund's cash investments, bonds, and stock positions. The amount paid to shareholders is the fund's net income, after subtracting operating expenses. Capital gains distributions represent the net profit made during a given calendar year following sales of the fund's stocks and bonds. When such securities are sold at a price higher than the amount paid, the fund realizes a capital gain. When securities are sold at a lower price, the fund realizes a capital loss. If capital gains exceed capital losses, the fund has net realized capital gains that must be fully distributed to its shareholders. Net realized capital losses are retained by the fund and may be used to offset future capital gains.

All income and capital gains distributions are generally subject to local, state, and federal income taxes. Taxes must be paid on distributions regardless of whether they are received in cash or reinvested in additional shares. Exceptions to this rule include interest income derived from U.S. Treasury securities, which is exempt from state and local income taxes, and municipal bond interest income, which is exempt from federal taxes and is also typically exempt from state and local taxes for shareholders in the same tax jurisdiction as that of the issuing authority. California residents do not pay state and local income taxes on interest income derived from bonds issued by California municipalities, for example. Any capital gains on U.S. Treasury securities or municipal bond funds are generally taxable.

When a mutual fund pays a dividend or capital gains distribution, its share price and net asset value fall by the amount of the dividend or distribution. For example, the net asset value of a mutual fund that trades for $15 per share falls to $12.50 per share on the day its shareholders receive a distribution of $2.50, before accounting for any market activity on that day. Even if the entire amount is reinvested, the fund shareholder owes regular income or capital gains taxes on the entire $2.50 distribution. As a result, before purchasing a fund, the buyer needs to know when the fund plans to make its next distribution. If a shareholder owns shares on the fund's record date, a distribution will be received. Purchasing shares shortly before a distribution is made is called "buying the dividend" and exposes the buyer to taxes on the distribution. For fund shares purchased in an IRA, the timing of dividend payments is not relevant. For taxable accounts, the timing of dividends is a valid consideration.

Tax Efficiency

Successful mutual funds generate lots of investment income and capital gains. All else equal, it is obviously preferable to own a fund that generates profits. At the same time, it is desirable to invest in funds that achieve shareholder objectives with a minimum of deadweight loss due to taxes. Thus, it is important for all mutual fund investors to consider tax efficiency as a significant criterion in mutual fund selection.

Money market funds pay dividends on interest income that are fully taxable, except in the case of low-yield funds that invest in tax-exempt municipal bonds. Because money market funds are designed to maintain a constant net asset value of $1 per share, they do not ordinarily generate capital gains or losses. Bond funds also typically produce relatively high levels of taxable income. The exception is, again, those bond funds that invest in tax-exempt securities. Stock funds generate income from dividends paid by common stocks held in the portfolio and from capital gains on sales of stock. Over time, most of the return earned from owning a common stock mutual fund comes in the form of stock price appreciation. Given the much greater volatility of stocks versus bonds, mutual fund investors are much more likely to realize a capital gain or loss when selling shares of a stock mutual fund than when selling shares of bond funds or money market funds.

Because capital gains distributions result from the profitable sale of securities in the portfolio, frequent selling within a fund makes the fund more likely to produce taxable distributions than a fund that follows a "buy-and-hold" strategy. A common measure of a mutual fund's trading activity is the **turnover rate**, expressed as a percentage of the fund's average assets. According to Lipper Analytical Services, the industry-average turnover rate for U.S. stock mutual funds is 79 percent. This means that, over the course of a year, the typical stock fund sells and replaces securities with a value equal to 79 percent of the fund's average net assets. Another way of describing turnover of 79 percent is to say that the average fund holds a typical stock purchase for about 15 months (a 50 percent turnover rate implies a two-year holding period, and so on). Funds with high turnover seek to generate lots of short-term gains and incur relatively higher taxes for their shareholders. Funds with low turnover generate mostly long-term gains and lots of unrealized long-term appreciation. This can result in an important tax advantage for mutual fund shareholders because unrealized gains are allowed to compound on a tax-free basis. A compelling advantage of a simple buy-and-hold investment strategy is that it is a tax-efficient means of building shareholder wealth.

Turnover rate
A common measure of a mutual fund's trading activity.

Street Smarts 16.4

Do Hedge Funds Hedge?

Popular use of the term *hedge fund* dates back to a fund started by Alfred Winslow Jones in 1949. Jones sought a market-neutral position for his fund by holding both long and short positions in stocks. For example, a hedge fund manager might simultaneously buy stock in General Motors Corporation and short-sell stock in the Ford Motor Company. Such a position is hedged against industry effects and general market movements. It does not matter if the stock market goes up or down, the profitablility of a long-short position on Ford-GM depends solely on the relative performance of the two companies. If Ford management does a better job than GM, the business prospects of Ford will improve relative to those of GM and a long-short position in Ford-GM will prove profitable. Similarly a hedge fund might buy oil giant ExxonMobil while shorting Chevron or might buy pharmaceutical colossus Pfizer while shorting Merck.

Hedge funds trade stocks, bonds, currencies, and commodities in both long and short positions, but it is often difficult to know the extent to which individual funds actually hedge their positions. Hedge funds are not required to fully disclose holdings, trading costs, and investment strategies, as are mutual funds. It is often only when a hedge fund blows up in spectacular fashion that investors learn about flawed trading strategies or outright fraud. In October 2005, for example, Wood River Capital Management disclosed that it owned 40 percent (4.3 million shares) of Endwave Corporation, a wireless transceiver manufacturer. (A transceiver is a transmitter and receiver housed together in a single unit for portable or mobile use.) The hedge fund had bet more than 65 percent of its capital on a single risky tech stock and lost. Endwave's stock price plunged 74 percent between July and September. Hedge fund Bayou Management turned out to be a vehicle for its manager to squander money on bad trades and personal expenses; Lancer Group apparently manipulated pink-sheet stocks.

Too often, hedge fund investors have been victimized by fraud and by hedge fund promoters that pursue speculative trading strategies. In practice, many hedge funds don't live up to their names. Many hedge funds don't hedge. They should be called "*un*hedged funds."

See Kara Scannell, "Making Hedge Funds Less Secret," *Wall Street Journal Online*, February 3, 2006 (**http://online.wsj.com**).

Try It!

At the beginning of the year, an investor owns 316.206 shares of a mutual fund with a NAV of $57.22. At the end of the year, the mutual fund has an income distribution of $1.23 per share and a capital gains distribution of $2.84 per share—ending the year with a NAV of $59.84. If the investor elects to take all distributions in cash and pays a 20 percent tax on dividends and capital gains, what are the after-tax profit and return for the year?

Solution

The investor begins the year with an $18,093.31 (= $57.22 × 316.206) mutual fund investment. The investment is valued at $18,921.77 (= $59.84 × 316.206) at the end of the year, providing an $828.46 increase in value. The investor also received a cash payment of $1,286.96 [= ($1.23 + $2.84) × 316.206]. After paying the 20 percent tax, the investor keeps $1,029.57 (= $1,286.96 × 0.80) of the cash payment.

Therefore, the total after-tax profit is $1,858.03 (= $828.46 + $ 1,029.57), which is a 10.27 percent (= $1,858.03/$18,093.31) return.

Summary

■ A **mutual fund** is an investment company that issues its shares to the public. Money received from shareholders is pooled and invested in a wide range of stocks, bonds, or money market securities to meet specific investment objectives. The per-share value of a mutual fund's stock, bond, and cash reserve holdings is called the fund's **net asset value**. Most mutual funds are also called **open-end funds** because as investor demand grows, the number of shares issued by the fund and the dollar value of assets under management increases.

■ **Money market mutual funds** invest in cash reserves or short-term debt instruments issued by the government, corporations, or financial institutions. **Stock funds** are one of the most popular types of mutual funds and invest in the ownership of corporations. **Bond funds** invest in debt instruments issued by corporations or government agencies. A **fund family** may offer investors many different money market, stock, and bond portfolios.

■ Mutual funds have ongoing expenses that are deducted from interest and dividend income. The total of these costs expressed as a percentage of the fund's average net assets during the year is called the fund's **operating expense ratio**. Many mutual fund investors also pay one-time sales commissions, or **load charges**. Sales loads are often charged at the time of purchase as a simple percentage of the amounts invested. Such **front-end loads** typically range from 4 to 8.5 percent. Funds that charge sales fees ranging from 1 to 3 percent are called **low-load funds**. Another form of sales charge is the **back-end load**, which is assessed when an investor sells fund shares. Some funds also charge investors an additional amount to cover marketing and distribution costs. These marketing charges are called **12b-1 fees**. The term **level load** describes the portion of a 12b-1 fee used to compensate brokers and investment advisors for selling shares of the fund. A **load fund** is a mutual fund that charges significant sales commissions. If a fund charges a 12b-1 fee in excess of 0.25 percent, it may not call itself a **no-load fund** even if it has no other sales charges. Funds that are sold without front-end or back-end load charges are called no-load funds. An **exchange fee** of $5 to $25 per transaction may be assessed when an investor exchanges shares from one fund to another within the same fund family. Account **maintenance fees** of between $10 and $25 per year also may be assessed. The best resource to help investors determine mutual fund costs is the fund's **prospectus**, or offering circular, which must be given to all investors at or before the time of purchase.

■ Mutual fund performance is best measured by the fund's **total return**, which consists of **income distributions** and realized and unrealized appreciation. When securities that a fund has purchased rise in value, the fund generates an **unrealized capital gain**. This unrealized capital gain raises the net asset value (or market value) of the fund's shares. When the fund sells securities at a profit, a taxable capital gain is realized and paid out to shareholders in the form of a **capital gains distribution**.

■ An **index fund** is a mutual fund designed to mimic the performance of some broad market index. Investors can use a **style box** to characterize portfolio risk in terms of market capitalization and value-growth orientation.

■ Mutual funds are owned by the **mutual fund shareholders**, who elect the board of directors to oversee the fund's activities. By law, a majority of the directors must be **independent directors**. The fund is initially set up by the investment advisor, who manages day-to-day operations. The **principal underwriter**, **administrator**, **transfer agent**, **custodian**, and **independent public accountant** perform other important services. The compensation structure of mutual funds, and individual investors who chase funds with attractive historical performance, creates a **mutual fund tournament** atmosphere.

■ The hottest new products to hit the mutual fund industry in decades are called **exchange-traded funds (ETFs)**. They are tradeable shares in baskets of stocks that closely track broad market averages, market sectors, or major stock markets from around the world. Among the most popular ETFs are **Standard & Poor's Depository Receipts (SPDRs)** (called "spiders"), which closely track the price performance and dividend yield of the S&P 500 Index. Exchange-traded funds have also been established to track the Dow Jones Industrial Average (they are called "**DIAMONDS**), " Nasdaq 100 Index (these are called **QQQQs**), and the S&P MidCap 400 Index. Also popular are **select sector SPDRs** that give investors ownership in a particular market sector. Barclays Global Investors has been among the most innovative companies in the development of ETFs and offers more than 50 index portfolios called **iShares**, or index shares.

■ Closed-end funds issue a fixed number of shares at a given point in time. They collect money from investors through an initial public offering (IPO) and use this money to invest in securities. When the market price per share for a closed-end fund exceeds its net asset value, the fund is selling at a **premium**. When the market price per share for a closed-end fund is less than its net asset value, the fund is selling at a **discount**. **Hedge funds** are similar to traditional mutual funds, but there are important differences in investment philosophy, investor suitability, and regulation.

■ A common measure of mutual fund trading activity is the **turnover rate**, expressed as a percentage of the fund's average assets. Over the course of a year, the typical stock fund sells and replaces securities with a value equal to 79 percent of the fund's average net assets.

Self-Test Problems

ST16.1 Suppose an investor wishes to add a mid-cap growth mutual fund to their portfolio. An advisor has recommended three: the Franklin Aggressive Growth (FGRAX), Putnam Vista (PVTBX), and T. Rowe Price Mid-Cap Growth (RPMGX). Which fund should the investor choose?

Solution

This decision should be made on long-term risk-adjusted performance and factors that impact this performance. These factors are loads, fees, and portfolio turnover. Investigation of these funds using either the Morningstar (**www.morningstar.com**) or the Yahoo! Finance (**http://finance.yahoo.com**) mutual fund Web site reveals the following facts:

Fund	Load	Total Expense Ratio	Star Rating	Return Difference from Cat. 5 Year	Return Difference from Cat. 3 Year	5-Year Alpha	Turnover
Franklin Aggr.	5.75%	1.62%	*	−6.04%	−0.41%	−1.44%	115%
Putnam Vista	0	1.83	***	−4.77	−0.09	−3.74	78
TRP Mid-Cap	0	0.83	*****	10.31	4.69	8.41	30

The Franklin fund has a high load and high fees. This has probably led to its poor three- and five-year performance relative to other mid-cap growth funds and its low Morningstar rating. The high turnover will create more capital gains distributions, which will cause more tax liabilities. The Putnam fund is a no-load fund but still has high fees. This may be a contributor to its long-term underperformance. The T. Rowe Price Mid-Cap Growth fund has low fees, low turnover, and outstanding performance. The investor should pick the T. Rowe Price Mid-Cap Growth fund.

ST16.2 The investor in ST16.1 realizes that there are more mid-cap funds to choose from than just the three recommended. How can the investor research all the potential funds?

Solution

There are several good mutual fund Web screeners for this purpose. Yahoo! Finance's Mutual Fund Web page (**http://biz.yahoo.com/funds**) is a good example. Consider the criteria of mid-cap growth, Morningstar five stars, no load, < 1 percent expense ratio, and < 50 percent turnover. This search yields six funds to investigate:

Symbol	Fund Name	Category	Morningstar Rating	Turnover (%)	Front Load (%)	Exp. Ratio (%)
MGRFX	MassMutual Select Mid Cap Gr Eq II S	Mid-cap growth	★★★★★	42.0	0.00	0.85
MEFYX	MassMutual Select Mid Cap Gr Eq II Y	Mid-cap growth	★★★★★	42.0	0.00	0.94
MERDX	Meridian Growth	Mid-cap growth	★★★★★	19.0	0.00	0.88
PMEGX	T. Rowe Price Instl Mid-Cap Equity Gr	Mid-cap growth	★★★★★	40.0	0.00	0.64
RPMGX	T. Rowe Price Mid-Cap Growth	Mid-cap growth	★★★★★	30.0	0.00	0.83
VHCAX	Vanguard Capital Opportunity Adm	Mid-cap growth	★★★★★	10.0	0.00	0.41

Questions and Problems

16.1 Does effective diversification require one to invest in a large number of different mutual funds? How can an investor easily and cheaply achieve broad diversification?

16.2 What is the difference between no-load and load mutual funds?

16.3 What is the difference between an open-end mutual fund and an exchange-traded fund?

16.4 What are some investment activities that hedge funds can engage in that mutual funds are not allowed to do?

16.5 Which investment benchmark is most commonly used to judge the investment performance of mutual funds? Explain the benchmark concept and how it is employed.

16.6 How does a closed-end mutual fund differ from an open-end mutual fund? Which is more popular, and why?

16.7 Describe the important investment characteristics and composition of the QQQQs. What trading characteristics make the QQQQs a favorite tool of speculators?

16.8 Why do some investors describe ownership of mutual funds with low portfolio turnover rates as a tax-efficient investment strategy?

16.9 Suppose Select Mutual Fund presently owns only the four positions shown below and has no liabilities. The fund originated by selling $100,000 of fund shares at $10 per share. No shares have been sold or redeemed since then. What is the funds current NAV?

Stock	Shares	Price
W	2000	$12
X	2200	15
Y	2400	22
Z	1900	14

16.10 Suppose you own 43.158 shares of an equity mutual fund that has a NAV of $12.04 per share at the beginning of the year. During the year, you decided to reinvest all distributions in more shares. If you received an additional 2.667 shares from dividend reinvestment and the NAV of the fund is $15.12 per share at the end of the year, what was your total return?

16.11 A mutual fund has a 5 percent front-end load and a NAV of $15 per share. What is the load charge on a $2,000 investment? How many shares can be purchased for $2,000?

16.12 A closed-end fund has a NAV of $10 per share, but the fund is trading at a price of $8.50 per share. What is the percentage discount from net asset value? Assume you purchase the fund for $8.50 per share. What is your return if the NAV increases to $11 and the discount is eliminated?

16.13 Visit the Morningstar Web site (**www.morningstar.com**). Compare the loads and fees of the Vanguard 500 index fund with the Salomon Brothers Large-Cap Growth fund?

16.14 Visit the Lipper Web site (**www.lipperweb.com**). Choose "Funds" on the menu and then "Top Performing Funds." What are the best performing funds over the past five years?

16.15 Visit the American Stock Exchange Web site (**www.amex.com**). Select the ETF menu. What new ETFs have been listed?

16.16 Go to the Yahoo! Finance Web site (**http://finance.yahoo.com**) and enter the "Mutual Fund" section. Enter the ticker for the Legg Mason Value fund (LMVTX). What category is this fund in? What is its Morningstar rating? Use the Portfolio and Risk links to assess the fund's performance.

16.17 Examine the performance of two mutual funds. One fund has a load, and the other is a no-load fund. Given the information on loads and NAV below, determine for each fund (a) the number of shares purchased one year ago with $10,000 and (b) the total profit in dollars for the year.

	Load	NAV 1 Year Ago	NAV Today
Fund X	Load of 4%	$14.57	$16.03
Fund Z	No load	33.16	36.14

16.18 At the beginning of the year, an investor owns 213.554 shares of a mutual fund with a NAV of $67.92. At the end of the year, the mutual fund has an income distribution of $2.05 per share and a capital gains distribution of $0.75 per share—ending the year with a NAV of $66.84. If the investor elects to take all distributions in cash and pays a 20 percent tax on dividends and capital gains, what are the after-tax profit and return for the year?

16.19 Go to the Morningstar Web site (**www.morningstar.com**) and enter the "Funds" section. Use the mutual fund screener to find the funds that meet the following criteria: small blend, manager tenure ≥ 3 years, no load, expense ratio < 1 percent, 5 stars, turnover < 100 percent. What funds meet these criteria?

16.20 The structure of an investment company is *least likely* to be characterized by: CFA® PROBLEMS

 a. A corporate form of organization
 b. Investment of a pool of funds from many investors in a portfolio of investments
 c. An annual management fee ranging from 3 to 5 percent of the total value of the fund
 d. A board of directors that hires a separate investment management company to manage the portfolio of securities and to handle other administrative duties

www.mhhe.com/hirschey1e

INVESTMENT APPLICATION

Warren Buffett: The 5σ Investor

Statisticians like to use Greek letters to symbolize statistical concepts. For example, the Greek letter mu, or μ, is used to signify the mean, or the central tendency of a population. The Greek letter sigma, or σ, is used to represent standard deviation, or the degree of dispersion in the population. From a statistical point of view, portfolio returns that are as much as 5σ above the average market return (μ) are so rare as to be seldom, if ever, observed. On the basis of the evidence, Warren Buffett, chairman and CEO of Omaha-based Berkshire Hathaway, is a 5σ investor.

Buffett started an investment partnership with $100 in 1956 and has gone on to accumulate a personal net worth in excess of $40 billion. Today, Buffett runs Berkshire like a closed-end mutual fund. He combines a stable of wonderful operating businesses, such as Geico Insurance, with a handful of core investment holdings, such as stock in the Coca-Cola Company. As shown in Table 16.8, Buffett has earned 22.4 percent annual returns in a typical market environment of 11.7 percent per year. Moreover, the S&P 500 numbers are pretax, whereas the Berkshire numbers are after-tax. If a corporation such as Berkshire were simply to have owned the S&P 500 and accrued the appropriate taxes, its results would have lagged the S&P 500 in years when that index showed a positive return but would have exceeded the S&P in years when the index showed a negative return. Even before adjusting for the significant tax burden borne by Berkshire shareholders over the years, Buffett has *doubled* the overall market's annual rate of return over an investment career that stretches for more than *40 years*. In the world of investments, Buffett's performance is so outlandishly good as to defy description.

How does Buffett do it? Buffett's first rule is, Do not lose money. The second rule is, Don't forget the first rule. Buffett argues that it is not terribly important to have a big circle of competence but it is terribly important to know the boundaries of that circle. Buy only what you know. Buffett has also been known to say that it is better to buy a *wonderful* company at a *fair* price than a *fair* company at a *wonderful* price. Bargain purchases seldom turn out to be a steal. In a difficult business, no sooner is one problem solved than another surfaces. "Never is there just one cockroach in the kitchen." Although good jockeys will do well on good horses, nobody rides well on broken-down old nags. Buffett looks for first-class businesses and first-class management. "It is usually far more profitable to stick with the easy and obvious," says Buffett, "than it is to resolve the difficult."

Buffett looks for companies that enjoy strong franchises, pricing flexibility, high return on equity (ROE), high cash flow, owner-oriented management, and predictable earnings growth. Buffett also looks for companies that are not natural targets of regulation. The Coca-Cola Company, one of Berkshire's biggest and most successful holdings, typifies the concept of a wonderful business. Coca-Cola enjoys perhaps the world's strongest franchise, owner-oriented management, and both predictable and growing returns. Also, the company is not subject to price or profit regulation. From the standpoint of being a wonderful business, Coca-Cola is clearly the "real thing." Berkshire also holds a large stake in the American Express Company, a premier travel and financial services firm that is strategically positioned to benefit from aging baby boomers. Other fine companies such as Anheuser Busch, Inc., Wells Fargo & Company, Moody's Corporation, the Procter & Gamble Company, and the Washington Post Company enjoy immense economies of scale and dominating competitive advantages that fit Buffett's criteria for wonderful businesses.

TABLE 16.8	Berkshire Hathaway's Performance Has Been Outstanding Compared to the S&P 500			
	Berkshire's Book Value Growth (%)	S&P 500 Total Return (%)	Relative Performance (%)	Cumulative Value of $10,000 ($) Invested in Berkshire	Cumulative Value of $10,000 ($) Invested in the S&P 500
1965	23.8	10.0	13.8	12,380	11,000
1966	20.3	(11.7)	32.0	14,893	9,713
1967	11.0	30.9	(19.9)	16,531	12,714
1968	19.0	11.0	8.0	19,672	14,113
1969	16.2	(8.4)	24.6	22,859	12,927
1970	12.0	3.9	8.1	25,602	13,432
1971	16.4	14.6	1.8	29,801	15,393
1972	21.7	18.9	2.8	36,268	18,302
1973	4.7	(14.8)	19.5	37,973	15,593
1974	5.5	(26.4)	31.9	40,061	11,477
1975	21.9	37.2	(15.3)	48,835	15,746
1976	59.3	23.6	35.7	77,793	19,462
1977	31.9	(7.4)	39.3	102,609	18,022
1978	24.0	6.4	17.6	127,236	19,175
1979	35.7	18.2	17.5	172,659	22,665
1980	19.3	32.3	(13.0)	205,982	29,986
1981	31.4	(5.0)	36.4	270,660	28,486
1982	40.0	21.4	18.6	378,925	34,582
1983	32.3	22.4	9.9	501,317	42,329
1984	13.6	6.1	7.5	569,496	44,911
1985	48.2	31.6	16.6	843,993	59,103
1986	26.1	18.6	7.5	1,064,276	70,096
1987	19.5	5.1	14.4	1,271,810	73,671
1988	20.1	16.6	3.5	1,527,443	85,900
1989	44.4	31.7	12.7	2,205,628	113,131
1990	7.4	(3.1)	10.5	2,368,845	109,624
1991	39.6	30.5	9.1	3,306,907	143,059
1992	20.3	7.6	12.7	3,978,209	153,931
1993	14.3	10.1	4.2	4,547,093	169,478
1994	13.9	1.3	12.6	5,179,139	171,681
1995	43.1	37.6	5.5	7,411,348	236,234
1996	31.8	23.0	8.8	9,768,157	290,567
1997	34.1	33.4	0.7	13,099,098	387,617
1998	48.3	28.6	19.7	19,425,962	498,475
1999	0.5	21.0	(20.5)	19,523,092	603,155
2000	6.5	(9.1)	15.6	20,792,093	548,268
2001	(6.2)	(11.9)	5.7	19,502,983	483,024
2002	10.0	(22.1)	32.1	21,453,282	376,276
2003	21.0	28.7	(7.7)	25,958,471	484,267
2004	10.5	10.9	(0.4)	28,684,110	537,052
2005	6.4	4.9	1.5	30,519,893	563,368
Average	22.4	11.7	10.8		
Standard deviation	14.5	16.9	14.3		
Median	20.3	11.0	9.9		

Source: Berkshire Hathaway, **http://berkshirehathaway.com**. © 2006 Berkshire Hathaway. Used by permission of Warren Buffett.

www.mhhe.com/hirschey1e

To be sure, above-normal returns from investing in wonderful businesses are possible only to the extent that such advantages are not fully recognized by other investors. Buffett has profited by taking major positions in wonderful companies that suffer from some significant, but curable, malady. In 2003, for example, Buffett picked up a midwestern natural gas pipeline company that was liquidated in the fallout from the Enron failure. Buffett picked up a highly profitable operation cheap because its parent company was in financial trouble.

The fact that Buffett has compiled an enviable record by buying large and well-known public companies makes his astounding success even more remarkable. Moreover, each year on the first Monday in May, Buffett teaches his investment philosophy to a crowd of thousands at Berkshire's annual stockholders' meeting. By mixing classic Ben Graham with the growth-stock philosophies of T. Rowe Price and Phil Fisher, Buffett has achieved a level of investment success that has caused many to question the veracity of the efficient-market hypothesis (EMH).

a. Explain how Buffett's investment success can be interpreted within the context of the EMH.

b. Explain how Buffett's investment success might be described as a contradiction of the EMH.

Global Investing

If you are looking for evidence that world stock and bond markets are becoming fully integrated, consider the implications of recent decisions by Apple Computer, IBM, PepsiCo, and Procter & Gamble to delist their shares from major stock exchanges in Frankfurt, Tokyo, Vienna, and Zurich. Like some other gigantic global enterprises, these giant U.S. companies are reducing the number of exchanges that host trading of their stocks. In some instances, global investors have shunned local listings because they have been able to get better execution and lower transaction costs by trading in the large, centralized, and extraordinarily active U.S. marketplace. For example, roughly 90 percent of IBM stock trading occurs on the floor of the New York Stock Exchange, including the vast majority of orders coming from Japan and other foreign markets. Because companies pay annual fees to list their stocks and bonds on both foreign and domestic exchanges, they have strong financial incentives to consolidate trading activity on the NYSE when trading in much smaller foreign markets is light. When stock and bond trading in thousands of global corporations is spread across several different time zones, even a major blue chip like IBM may not see heavy-enough trading in foreign markets to justify worldwide listings. At the same time, recent research shows that stocks of foreign firms that cross-list their shares for sale in both the United States (on the NYSE or Nasdaq) and their home markets tend to have higher valuations than foreign stocks listed only in their home markets. When it comes to global stock trading, the world is converging toward the most active markets.

There is obvious value added when global companies are able to offer their shares for sale to the public on large, liquid, global exchanges. In 2005, the NYSE signed up 36 new foreign-based companies. Another popular stock exchange with foreign companies is the London Stock Exchange (LSE), which listed 19 new foreign stocks in 2005. Both the NYSE and the LSE are at the vanguard of the movement toward truly global stock exchanges.[1]

---

[1]See Jeongjin Lim, "Lotte's Dual Listing Is Approved," *The Wall Street Journal Online*, January 13, 2006 (**http://online.wsj.com**).

CHAPTER
OBJECTIVES
- Know the benefits of international diversification.
- Understand the risks of international investing.
- Track developed and emerging markets.
- Recognize the home bias.
- Be able to utilize the different tools of international investing.

Global Investing Benefits

Attractive Opportunities

Some of the largest and best-performing stocks in the world are located in the United States. As a result, some might ask, Why go abroad and invest in markets, companies, and currencies that you do not fully understand? Savvy investors know that attractive investment opportunities are available outside the United States. As shown in Table 17.1, the United States is the largest economy in the world, but other countries have very large economies too. Some of the

TABLE 17.1	Gross Domestic Product and GDP Growth in the Largest Economies around the World		
		Annualized GDP Growth (%)	
Country	2003 GDP ($ billions)	1980–1990	1990–2003
United States	10,949	3.5	3.3
Japan	4,301	4.1	1.2
Germany	2,403	2.3	1.5
United Kingdom	1,795	3.2	2.7
France	1,758	2.4	1.9
Italy	1,468	2.5	1.6
China	1,417	10.3	9.6
Canada	857	3.2	3.3
Spain	839	3.1	2.8
Mexico	626	1.1	3.0
South Korea	605	8.9	5.5
India	601	5.7	5.9
Australia	522	3.4	3.8
Netherlands	512	2.4	2.7
Brazil	492	2.7	2.6
Russia	433	na*	–1.8
Switzerland	320	2.0	1.2
Belguim	302	2.1	2.1
Sweden	302	2.5	2.3
Austria	253	2.3	2.1
Average	**1,538**	**3.6**	**2.9**

Source: World Bank, 2005 World Development Indicators.

*na means not available.

largest and best-performing stocks in the world are located outside the United States. In addition, notice that the U.S. economy grows at close to the average worldwide rate. Economic growth is much faster in several emerging markets than it is in the United States and in several other developed markets. Indeed, the table shows why there is so much interest in China recently. China has a big economy that is growing very rapidly. The economies of India and Korea have also experienced strong growth during recent years.

At times, foreign markets outperform U.S. stocks. Japan's Nikkei 225 Index outperformed the S&P 500 Index in the late 1980s, and Australia outperformed in the early 2000s, as shown in Figure 17.1. However, U.S. equities have done very well since 1985 relative to the Australia, Japan, and U.K. markets (and most others). While the U.S. equity market reached high relative valuations in the late 1990s, many foreign markets did as well. The decline in 2000–2003 impacted equity markets worldwide. Some equity markets did not fall as hard as the U.S. market; some fell harder.

Diversification Benefits

Diversification is an important consideration in any prudent investment program. In addition to providing global investors with more and perhaps better investment opportunities, added diversification is a prime benefit that can be derived through adoption of a global investment strategy. All global economies are directly affected by local economic conditions, and many experience economic cycles that differ from those experienced in the domestic market by U.S. investors. When the U.S. economy slows down or is in recession, some foreign economies may continue to grow and prosper. As a result, foreign equity markets generally do not move in lockstep fashion with the U.S. equity market. As U.S. stock prices rise or fall, foreign stocks can move in a different direction, as seen in Figure 17.1. **Global diversification** has the potential to cushion investor portfolios from downward fluctuations in domestic markets. Similarly, domestic portfolios can cushion the fall experienced in foreign stock portfolios.

Studies show that adding foreign stocks to a well-rounded portfolio may enhance total returns while reducing overall volatility. By moderating downward swings, a modest allocation

Global diversification
The addition of foreign investment assets to a portfolio, thereby decreasing the total risk.

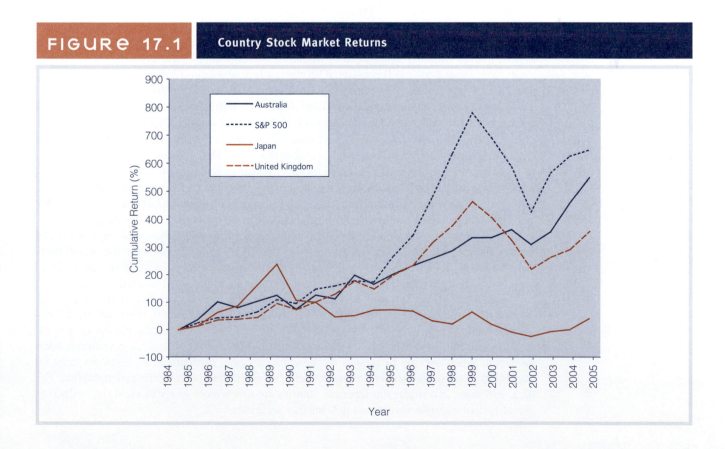

FIGURE 17.1   **Country Stock Market Returns**

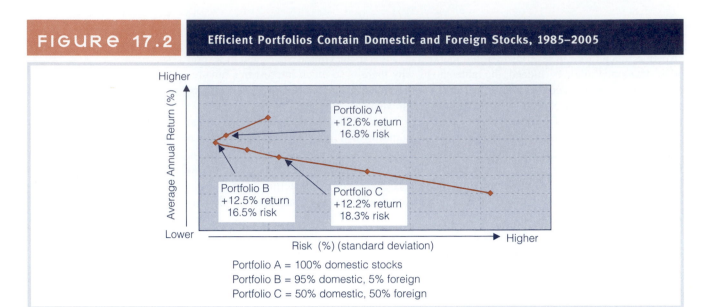

FIGURE 17.2 — Efficient Portfolios Contain Domestic and Foreign Stocks, 1985–2005

Portfolio A = 100% domestic stocks
Portfolio B = 95% domestic, 5% foreign
Portfolio C = 50% domestic, 50% foreign

Source: Vanguard, **www.vanguard.com**.

to foreign stocks can also make it easier for investors to ride out downturns in domestic markets. Given that foreign equity markets tend to be riskier than the U.S. market, it may not seem reasonable that adding international stocks to an investment portfolio could reduce overall risk. However, research shows that combinations of domestic and foreign equities often produce the lowest risk for a given expected level of return. Likewise, combinations of domestic and foreign equities often produce the highest expected rate of return for a given level of risk.

To illustrate the concept of an efficient portfolio with domestic and foreign stocks, Figure 17.2 plots both the expected rate of return and the level of risk for various combinations of domestic and foreign equities. Portfolio A is 100 percent invested in U.S. stocks as represented by the Wilshire 5000 Index. As shown in the figure, over the 21-year period ending December 31, 2005, such a portfolio produced a 12.6 percent average annual rate of return. Over this time frame, market volatility as captured by the standard deviation of annual returns was 16.8 percent. Notice that portfolio B consists of 95 percent U.S. stocks and 5 percent foreign stocks as measured by the Europe, Australasia, Far East Index. Such a globally diversified portfolio produced nearly the same average annual rate of return as portfolio A and involved a somewhat lower risk level with a standard deviation of 16.5 percent per year. Globally diversified portfolio C, invested 50 percent in U.S. stocks and 50 percent in foreign stocks, produced a lower, 12.2 percent annual rate of return with a higher risk level, 18.3 percent.

In short, the highest portfolio return for this 21-year period came from portfolio A, an entirely domestic portfolio. However, even during this period of unprecedented returns for U.S. investors, there were risk-reduction benefits to be had through global diversification. By adding 5 percent of the higher-risk foreign portfolio, the total risk of the diversified global portfolio was lower than that of the 100 percent domestic portfolio. This shows that an investor can reduce risk by adding a higher risk asset if that asset has a low correlation with the overall portfolio. Since U.S. equity markets and foreign markets do not always move in the same direction, there are diversification benefits to be gained from owning some of each asset class.

Around the globe, assorted developed and emerging markets exhibit varying economic growth and equity market performance. Certain markets, such as Canada, move almost in lockstep fashion with the United States. Other equity markets, such as Australia, display only weak positive correlation with the U.S. market. Some markets display an inverse correlation, such as Japan. When seeking to achieve the benefits of global diversification, investors must be careful to select investments in countries that offer significant potential for risk reduction. For U.S. investors, investments in Japanese equities are much more likely to yield risk-reduction benefits than a similar investment in Canadian securities.

Tracking Global Markets

Global Market Indexes

The stock market in each country has one or more indexes used to measure the performance of equities in that country. Most global investors are familiar with Japan's Nikkei 225, the United Kingdom's FTSE 100, Germany's DAX indexes, and others reported on Yahoo! Finance's Web site and shown in Table 17.2. Note the large differences among the daily changes. Yahoo! Finance also allows investors to see individual company components that make up each index. Obviously, there is much better information available today about foreign stock markets than ever before. Even novice investors can investigate global investment opportunities with a level of insight that was available only to the most sophisticated professional managers just a few years ago.

One problem with these local indexes is that they are generally not comparable across countries. Each index is computed in a local currency, and there are differences in the way each index is computed. Some are equally weighted, some are capitalization-weighted, and some are price-weighted, like the Dow Jones Industrial Average. Some add dividends back in, and some do not. To provide consistent information and benchmarking services to investors, Morgan

TaBLe 17.2 Yahoo! Finance Reports: World Equity Market Indexes (February 20, 2006)

Symbol	Name	Last Trade	Change	Related Info
Americans				
^MERV	MerVal	1,721.140 3:00PM ET	↑21.650 (1.27%)	Components, Chart, More
^GSPTSE	S&P TSX Composite	11,878.54 3:42PM ET	↑120.50 (1.02%)	Components, Chart, More
^MXX	IPC	18,549.199 3:36PM ET	↑68.420 (0.37%)	Components, Chart, More
^GSPC	500 Index	1,287.24 Feb 17	↓2.14 (0.17%)	Components, Chart, More
Asia/Pacific				
^AORD	All Ordinaries	4,788.100 12:17AM ET	0.000 (0.00%)	Components, Chart, More
^SSEC	Shanghai Composite	1,267.542 2:00AM ET	↑0.134 (0.01%)	Components, Chart, More
^JKSE	Jakarta Composite	1,247.4139 5:29AM ET	↑3.939 (0.32%)	Components, Chart, More
^N225	Nikkei 225	15,437.93 3:34AM ET	0.00 (0.00%)	Chart, More
^STI	Straits Times	2,431.77 4:05AM ET	↑0.43 (0.02%)	Components, Chart, More
^KS11	Seoul Composite	1,348.25 4:03AM ET	0 (0.00%)	Components, Chart, More
^TWII	Taiwan Weighted	6,686.55 12:46AM ET	↑12.80 (0.19%)	Components, Chart, More
Europe				
^OMXC20C	OMXC20C	391.96 11:21AM ET	↑1.03 (0.26%)	Components, Chart, More
^FCHI	CAC 40	4,979.94 12:10PM ET	↓20.06 (0.40%)	Chart, More
^GDAXI	DAX	5,793.95 11:45AM ET	↓1.53 (0.03%)	Components, Chart, More
^OSEAX	OSE All Share	415.83 10:29AM ET	↑7.11 (1.74%)	Components, Chart, More
^MIBTEL	MIBTel	28,649.0000 11:40AM ET	↑160.0000 (0.56%)	Components, Chart, More
^IXX	ISE National-100	87.99 Feb 17	0.00 (0.00%)	Chart, More
^SMSI	Madrid General	1,250.84 11:36AM ET	↑5.08 (0.41%)	Components, Chart, More
^SSMI	Swiss Market	7,950.22 11:31AM ET	↑33.10 (0.42%)	Components, Chart, More
^FTSE	FTSE 100	5,863.00 11:36AM ET	↑16.80 (0.29%)	Components, Chart, More
Africa/Middle East				
^CCSI	CMA	2,344.52 Feb 19	↑58.29 (2.55%)	Chart, More
^TA100	TA-100	813.58 10:55AM ET	↑7.20 (0.89%)	Components, Chart, More

Source: Reproduced with permission of Yahoo! Inc. © 2006 by Yahoo! Inc. Yahoo and the Yahoo! logos are trademarks of Yahoo! Inc.

Stanley Capital International (MSCI) Inc. applies the same company selection criteria and calculation methodology across all markets for all of its indexes. In fact, MSCI is the only provider of indexes that are consistently developed and applied across developed and emerging markets.

Morgan Stanley Capital International

Morgan Stanley Capital International is the leading provider of global stock market and bond market indexes. Its indexes are the most widely used benchmarks for measuring the performance of global portfolio managers. On the Internet, MSCI gives global investors an abundance of information about the global economic environment and the risk and return characteristics of global stock and bond markets (see **www.mscibarra.com**).

To get some feel for how interest in global investing has developed, consider the fact that it was not until 1969 that MSCI introduced generally accepted measures of stock market performance for **developed markets**. Eighteen years later, in 1987, MSCI responded to the growth of interest in newer stock markets in developing economies with measures designed to track **emerging markets**. In the 1990s, the pace of global benchmark index innovation quickened considerably. In 1995, MSCI introduced the All Country Series. In 1997, value indexes and growth indexes were added for developed and emerging markets. In 1998, small-cap, extended-market, and fixed-income indexes were added. In 1999, a variety of euro indexes were introduced, along with two Chinese indexes in 2000. All Country Sector indexes were created in 2001, and all the indexes began to be computed in real time in 2002.

In addition to providing individual country coverage, MSCI compiles regional and composite indexes for developed markets, emerging markets, and all countries by region as shown in Table 17.3. The MSCI World Index, the MSCI EAFE (Europe, Australasia, Far East) Index, and the MSCI Emerging Markets Free Index are the premier benchmarks used by investment managers to measure the performance of global stock markets. In addition, MSCI country indexes are commonly used to measure stock market investment performance in more than 50 countries around the world. Fixed-income indexes are also provided for more than 30 countries. The consistent construction methodology used for the various country indexes allows for simple aggregation of country indexes to form regional stock market indexes. Such regions are found within both developed and emerging markets. Investment-style indexes produced by MSCI include the MSCI Value and Growth Indexes and are available for developed and emerging markets.

All MSCI equity indexes are calculated using **full-market-capitalization weight** (price multiplied by the number of outstanding shares). MSCI covers more than 60 percent of the market cap of global equities in developed and emerging markets. Its objective in doing so is to create a series of indexes that together replicate the investment opportunities available in all equity markets around the world, a true global portfolio. Nevertheless, MSCI performance calculations incorporate sophisticated dividend reinvestment assumptions, which, although relevant throughout the developed world, may be problematic in high-inflation emerging markets. Because some money managers prefer to use alternative weighting schemes, MSCI calculates regional indexes by using GDP weighting for individual emerging markets.

Comparing the MSCI World Index, the World Index ex United States, and the U.S. equity markets shows (see Figure 17.3) a similar story to that shown in Figures 17.1 and 17.2. U.S. equity markets performed very well during the last decade compared to foreign equity markets. Notice that the 6.66 percent annual rate of return for the MSCI World Index compounded to earn a total 103.3 percent over the January 1995–December 2005 period. During this time frame, the 9.59 percent annual return earned by U.S. equities compounded to a total return of 173.8 percent—much more than the 4.86 percent annual return, and 68.6 percent total return, earned by global equities excluding the United States.

Such stunningly good performance by a major world equity market is seldom encountered. The last major world market to turn in such amazingly good relative performance was the Japanese stock market during the 1980s. That was a period in which "Japan, Inc." and "Japan's long-term investment perspective" became standard topical fare in business schools around the

Developed markets
Securities markets in countries with advanced economies.

Emerging markets
Securities markets in countries with rapidly evolving economies.

Full-market-capitalization weight
Price multiplied by the number of outstanding shares.

TABLE 17.3   MSCI Global Indexes

Developed Markets

International Indexes	National Indexes
EAFE	Australia
EMU	Austria
Euro	Belgium
Europe	Canada
Far East	Denmark
G7 Index	Finland
Nordic Countries	France
North America	Germany
Pacific	Greece
Pan-Euro	Hong Kong
The World Index	Ireland
Special Areas	Italy
EAFE + Canada	Japan
EAFE ex UK	Netherlands
EASEA Index (EAFE ex JAPAN)	New Zealand
Europe ex EMU	Norway
Europe ex Switzerland	Portugal
Europe ex UK	Singapore
Kokusai Index (World ex Japan)	Singapore Free
Pacific ex Japan	Spain
World ex Australia	Sweden
World ex EMU	Switzerland
World ex Europe	United Kingdom
World ex UK	Usa
World ex USA	

Emerging Markets

International Indexes	India
EM (Emerging Markets)	Indonesia
EM Asia	Israel
EM Eastern Europe	Jordan
EM EMEA	Korea
EM Europe	Malaysia
EM Europe & Middle East	Mexico
EM ex Asia	Morocco
EM Far East	Pakistan
EM Latin America	Peru
National Indexes	Philippines
Argentina	Poland
Brazil	Russia
Chile	South Africa
China	Sri Lanka
Colombia	Taiwan
Czech Republic	Thailand
Egypt	Turkey
Hungary	Venezuela

FIGURE 17.3   Global Equity Markets Soared during the Late 1990s and Then Collapsed

Source: MSCI Barra, **www.mscibarra.com**. © MSCI. The MSCI data contained herein is the property of Morgan Stanley Capital International Inc. (MSCI). MSCI, its affiliates and information providers make no warranties with respect to any such data. The MSCI data contained herein is used under license and may not be further used, distributed or disseminated without the express written consent of MSCI.

FIGURE 17.4   A Booming Japanese Stock Market in the 1980s Gave Way to a Stunning Collapse during the 1990s

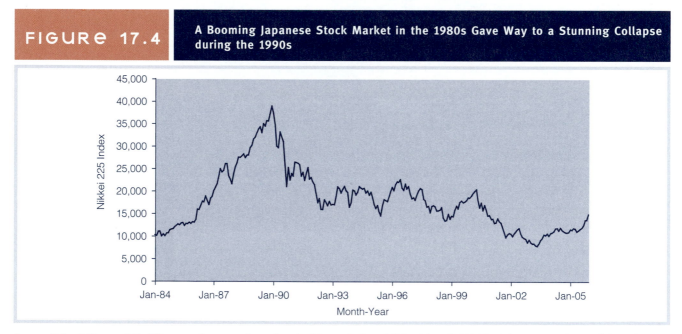

Source: Yahoo! Finance, **http://finance.yahoo.com**. Reproduced with permission of Yahoo! Inc. © 2006 by Yahoo! Inc. Yahoo and the Yahoo! logos are trademarks of Yahoo! Inc.

country. The superiority of Japanese technology and innovation also became taken for granted. In the 1980s, enthusiasm for all things Japanese helped fuel a historical rise in Japan's stock market. As shown in Figure 17.4, Japan's Nikkei 225 Index reached a stunning peak of 38,957 on December 29, 1989, or more than triple the 10,196 level of January 1, 1984. At that point, typical price-earnings (P/E) ratios for Japanese blue chips exceeded 100 times earnings. Then the bubble burst. It no longer seemed prudent to global investors to pay in excess of 100 times earnings for Japan's telecommunications giant NTT when America's telecommunications go-liath AT&T could be had for a mere 15 times earnings. At the beginning of 2006, the Nikkei 225 was at 16,400, nearly the same as it was two decades earlier!

The Japanese stock market shows that stock prices do not always quickly recover after a big decline. Seventeen years after the peak, the market is still less then one-half of that lofty level. Of course, you may consider parallels between the late 1990s technology bubble in the Nasdaq index and the bubble of Japanese equities a decade earlier. The Nasdaq peaked on March 10, 2000, at 5,132. Five years later (March 10, 2005) it closed at 2,060, only 40 percent of its peak value. How many years will it take to regain the 5,000 mark? Given that individual countries, or sectors, may experience cataclysmic collapse, global diversification has the potential to shield investors from harm.

Developed and Emerging Markets

Established global stock markets in the United States, Japan, United Kingdom, Germany, and other countries hold investment potential for a variety of industries and companies. The emerging markets of countries such as Brazil, Mexico, South Africa, and Taiwan, among others, hold speculative potential and offer investors the opportunity to participate in dynamically growing economies. From an investment perspective, there are no economic characteristics that definitively identify an emerging market, but emerging markets share a variety of common economic characteristics. Use of the word *emerging* describes equity and bond markets that are developing, unfolding, or maturing. It is important to recognize that countries with emerging markets may or may not be successful in translating immense economic opportunities into lasting economic success. Some emerging stock markets such as Argentina, for example, have long histories of economic progress punctuated by bouts of economic turmoil and depression. It is important to recognize that some emerging markets may never, in fact, emerge to join the ranks of developed markets.

One of the problems investors have with investing in emerging markets is the small amount of available investable assets. For example, global investors rushed into promising emerging markets like Thailand in the early and mid-1990s. Then, in 1998, Russia and other emerging markets showed signs of financial stress. Suddenly global investors rushed to withdraw their capital from these countries. Many economies collapsed as capital was sucked out of those countries. Emerging-market governments want foreign capital to help develop their economies, but they want it to remain invested. For example, China has its public companies funded with different classes of stock. One class of stock can be held only by Chinese investors, while another is held by Chinese financial institutions. A third class of stock was originally designed to be owned by foreign investors. Any flight out of China by global investors impacts only one class of stock, not the entire stock market. As a result, much of the equity in emerging markets is not available to foreign investors. In some emerging markets, MSCI designates **free indexes** and **nonfree indexes**. A free index is one in which all component securities are available without restriction to foreign investors. A nonfree index includes various securities that either are available only to domestic investors or are available to domestic investors on more favorable terms than those accessible to foreign investors. All MSCI indexes are considered free unless a nonfree index is also offered.

Figure 17.5 shows the breakdown in global market capitalization in developed and emerging markets. In the developed market's universe, the U.S., U.K., and Japanese markets are dominant. After the stunning growth during the late 1990s and the bear market of the early 2000s, the U.S. market now represents nearly one-half of the total market capitalization of global equities. The U.K. and Japanese markets are of comparable size and constitute vibrant, broad, and liquid developed markets. Other developed markets, such as Germany, France, Canada, and Switzerland, are much smaller than the leading developed markets. The market value of a handful of leading U.S. companies often rivals, if not exceeds, the market capitalization of several significant emerging and developed markets. This has important implications for investors seeking to add an international dimension to their investment portfolios. Even in developed markets, global investors cannot expect to find a wide range of investment alternatives that have the broad market reach and economic might of the U.S. industrial giants.

Free index
Price performance index of securities that are available to all investors.

Nonfree index
Price performance index of securities that are available on a preferential basis to domestic investors.

FIGURE 17.5   The United States, United Kingdom, and Japan Dominate Developed Markets; Korea, South Africa, and Taiwan Are Major Emerging Markets

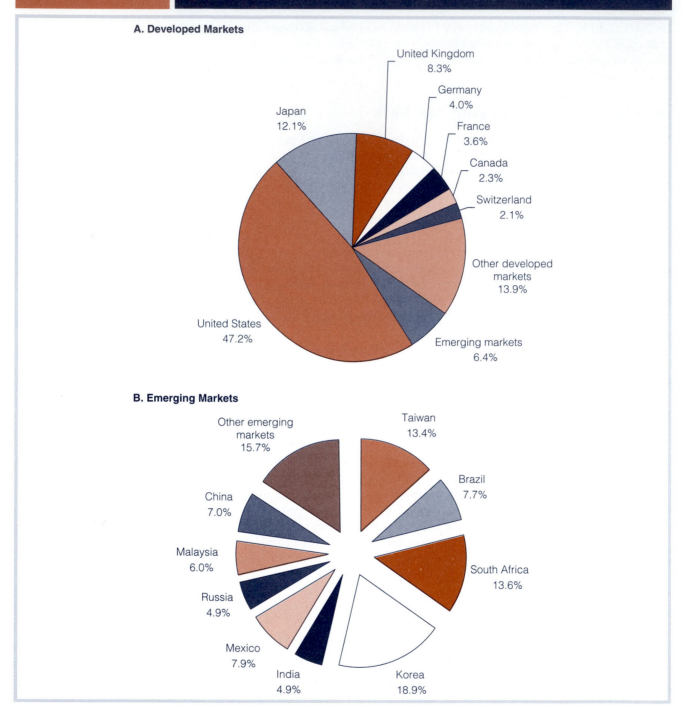

A. Developed Markets

United Kingdom 8.3%
Germany 4.0%
France 3.6%
Canada 2.3%
Switzerland 2.1%
Japan 12.1%
Other developed markets 13.9%
United States 47.2%
Emerging markets 6.4%

B. Emerging Markets

Other emerging markets 15.7%
Taiwan 13.4%
Brazil 7.7%
China 7.0%
South Africa 13.6%
Malaysia 6.0%
Russia 4.9%
Mexico 7.9%
India 4.9%
Korea 18.9%

Source: MSCI Barra, **www.mscibarra.com**. © MSCI. The MSCI data contained herein is the property of Morgan Stanley Capital International Inc. (MSCI). MSCI, its affiliates and information providers make no warranties with respect to any such data. The MSCI data contained herein is used under license and may not be further used, distributed or disseminated without the express written consent of MSCI.

Street Smarts 17.1

Correlations and Crises

The diversification benefits of adding foreign stocks to a domestic portfolio arise because foreign markets do not move in lockstep fashion with the U.S. market. The comovement of markets over time is described by their return correlation. The greatest diversification benefit is derived when asset returns have very low positive correlation, or even negative (or inverse) correlation. If Mexican stocks fell when U.S. stocks rose, for example, then Mexican and U.S. equities would be inversely correlated. A portfolio consisting of Mexican and U.S. equities would then have an annual rate of return that would be more stable than returns on either Mexican or U.S. equities alone. In practice, studies show that the correlation among returns for U.S. stocks and foreign stocks tends to be positive but is less than perfect. Given the prevalence of international trade, prospects for both domestic and foreign equities tend to rise when global economic conditions are favorable.

Over time, the ongoing integration of global capital markets means that the financial market implications of news events and government policy changes are quickly felt all around the globe. In early 2006, for example, Bank of Japan officials began to slowly unwind a policy of easy money that had been a major fixture of the world economy for nearly a decade. For years, Japan's easy-money policy prodded global investors to funnel cash into bonds, currencies, and other speculative investments. Hedge funds and other speculators borrowed money at low Japanese interest rates to invest in higher-yielding assets in the United States and elsewhere. The elimination of this "carry trade" meant higher interest rates on everything from home mortgages in the United States to European government debt. Rising Japanese interest rates also meant greater risks for highly leveraged hedge funds and a sluggish market for global equities in general.

An important by-product of global integration is that benefits from global diversification can fail to materialize during periods of economic crisis. When fear strikes global markets, they all tend to move down together. As a result, all investors must be on the lookout for the contagious implications of global uncertainty.

See Mark Whitehouse and Craig Karmin, "Markets Brace for Japan's Shift on Monetary Policy," *The Wall Street Journal Online*, March 1, 2006 (**http://online.wsj.com**).

Try It!

International and global indexes can easily be located on the Internet. The following sites can be used to view recent index movements, charts, or historical index values:

CNN Money	**http://money.cnn.com/markets/world_markets**
MSN Money	**http://moneycentral.msn.com/investor/market/foreign.asp**
Reuters	**http://today.reuters.com/investing/worldmarkets.aspx**
Yahoo! Finance	**http://finance.yahoo.com**

Visit each site and determine the different indexes and information available among the sites.

Countries versus Sectors

The concept of diversifying a portfolio by owning stocks from many countries has a long history and empirical support. However, economies have changed a great deal over the last several decades. Diversifying across countries made a lot of sense when country economies were segmented, and owning stocks from **segmented markets** was the only way to gain exposure to those areas. Over the past few decades, however, economies have become much more integrated. Now, many companies freely do business in multiple countries.

An alternative to country diversification is global sector diversification. Many countries have one or two dominant industries. Investing in South Africa and Australia, for example, means buying mining stocks. Does investing in both South Africa and Australia provide added diversification, or does their mutual strength in mining mean that both are not needed in a globally diversified portfolio? Many global investors have concluded that sector diversification is as important as, if not more important than, country diversification. For global investors who want to focus on sectors, MSCI developed the All Country Sector Indexes in 2001. Sectors are

Segmented markets
Stock markets in which there are no investment flows between the markets.

determined using the Global Industry Classification Standard (GICS) system developed jointly by MSCI and Standard & Poor's, and the indexes are available for both emerging markets and developed markets. Investors can invest in a broad range of such sectors using exchange-traded funds.

Global Investing Risks

Market Volatility

Until the mid-1990s, there was a growing amount of investor interest in global investment opportunities. This was particularly true of emerging markets. In the United States, there was lots of investor interest in Latin America, where many saw the opportunity to profit from thriving economic cooperation between Canada, the United States, and its Latin neighbors, as typified by the North American Free Trade Agreement (NAFTA). Unfortunately, the severe market correction of 2000–2002 brought enormous losses to global investors.

Recent losses convinced many U.S. investors that global investing, particularly emerging-market investing, is not for them. Thus, it is important to keep in mind that investing in foreign markets, especially emerging foreign markets, generally involves much higher **market volatility** than that associated with U.S. equities. The potential for above-average gains in foreign equity markets comes with the risk of above-average losses in any given year. Foreign stock markets are typically much more volatile than domestic markets.

Table 17.4 shows the volatility of foreign markets as a whole relative to the U.S. market based on annual rates of return. Over the 18-year 1988–2005 period, for example, the average annual rate of return for U.S. equities as captured by the Dow Jones Wilshire 5000 Index was 11.9 percent. Over this time frame, the standard deviation of annual returns on U.S. equities

Market volatility
The level of security price changes, usually measured by standard deviation or variance of returns.

TaBLe 17.4	Annual Returns in Foreign Markets Are More Volatile than Those in the United States		
Year	**DJ Wilshire 5000**	**MSCI EAFE**	**MSCI Emerging Markets**
1988	18.0%	28.6%	34.9%
1989	29.1	10.8	59.2
1990	−6.2	−23.3	−13.8
1991	34.3	12.5	56.0
1992	9.0	−11.8	9.1
1993	11.2	32.9	71.3
1994	−0.1	8.1	−8.7
1995	36.4	11.6	−6.9
1996	21.3	6.4	3.9
1997	31.3	2.1	−13.4
1998	23.4	20.3	−27.5
1999	23.6	25.3	63.7
2000	−10.9	−15.2	−31.8
2001	−11.0	−22.6	−4.9
2002	−20.9	−17.5	−8.0
2003	31.6	35.3	51.6
2004	12.5	17.6	22.5
2005	6.4	10.9	30.3
Mean	**11.9%**	**5.7%**	**10.5%**
Standard deviation	**17.4%**	**18.6%**	**33.4%**

Source: Vanguard, **www.vanguard.com** and MSCI Barra, **www.mscibarra.com**.

was 17.4 percent. These figures compare with average annual rates of return on foreign stocks in developed markets of 5.7 percent per year and a standard deviation of 18.6 percent per year, as captured by MSCI's EAFE Index. Even more volatile are the stocks in emerging markets. As captured by MSCI's Emerging Market Index, their standard deviation was a whopping 33.4 percent, nearly three times riskier than stocks in the U.S. equity market. During recent years, foreign markets have tended to underperform the U.S. market, on average, while displaying higher volatility. No wonder backward-looking U.S. investors prefer to invest in domestic rather than foreign equities.

Liquidity Risk

Liquidity risk is loss potential tied to the fact that a stock can become difficult to buy or sell. This problem is frequently greater in foreign stock markets than in the United States. This is especially true of emerging markets. Foreign markets typically have modest daily trading activity when compared with the United States. In some countries, fewer than 200 stocks trade in quantities sufficient to support the interest of foreign investors. In many emerging markets, trading activity is dominated by a mere handful of investment opportunities. The problem of scarcity in global investment opportunities is exacerbated by the fact that countries with emerging markets often permit foreigners to buy only specific classes of shares for certain companies. Sometimes, quantities of such shares are strictly limited. Under these circumstances, a scarcity of investment opportunities leads to thin trading volume, increased market volatility, and exorbitant prices for sought-after shares.

Thin trading activity in foreign developed and emerging markets often leads to higher **market impact costs**. High bid-ask spreads are the most obvious sign of low liquidity and significant market impact costs. In the United States, bid-ask spreads for highly liquid large-cap stocks listed on the New York Stock Exchange are commonly no more than 10 to 15 basis points (0.1 to 0.15 percent). For smaller and less liquid U.S. equities traded on Nasdaq, bid-ask spreads can easily top 0.5 to 1 percent, or five to eight times higher. In foreign markets, not only do bid-ask spreads tend to be higher than those on Nasdaq, but large buyers and sellers are often not able to deal in quantity at posted prices. Buyers of large blocks of foreign equities, for example, often have to pay a price higher than the quoted ask price to complete a given purchase transaction. Sellers of large blocks of foreign equities often receive only a marked-down price that is lower than the quoted bid price.

Liquidity risks are especially high in emerging markets. Emerging markets are generally small, with few stocks listed and less trading activity than is common in developed countries. Not only can the entire market capitalization of an emerging market be less than that of a single large U.S. company, like Intel, but many companies in emerging markets are closely held family businesses. For example, shares in only a few hundred companies trade on a daily basis in leading European countries such as Italy, Sweden, and Switzerland. Some important emerging markets feature fewer than 100 investment opportunities. This contrasts with the United States, where more than 8,000 companies and roughly 2 billion shares trade on a daily basis. Low trade volumes in emerging markets often mean that institutional investors are not able to get fair and timely trade executions. During financial crises, emerging markets have also been known to close for brief periods; in India, for example, the Bombay Stock Exchange closed for three days in March 1995. Some foreign countries (such as China and Taiwan) also restrict nondomestic investments to certain classes of shares. In Chile, nondomestic investors must wait at least one year to withdraw capital from the market. All such restrictions reduce market liquidity for international investors.

The special liquidity risks associated with investing in developed and emerging markets are accompanied by higher equity transaction costs. **Brokerage commissions**, **exchange fees**, **currency translation costs**, and **custodial fees** tend to be substantially higher in emerging markets than in the developed markets of the United States and Europe. Several foreign governments also levy taxes based on the total value of purchase and sale transactions. For example, brokerage commissions and exchange fees commonly amount to only 5 to 15 basis points (0.05 to 0.15 percent) of the dollar amount of an equity purchase or sale transaction in the

Liquidity risk
Loss potential tied to the fact that a stock can become difficult to buy or sell.

Market impact costs
Costs tied to changing market bid and ask prices.

Brokerage commissions
Sales charges.

Exchange fees
Trading costs imposed by organized trading systems.

Currency translation costs
Expenses of converting host-country currency into the domestic currency of the buyer or seller.

Custodial fees
Bookkeeping charges.

United States. In Brazil, one of the largest and most liquid emerging markets, brokerage commissions, exchange fees, and foreign currency translation costs average 0.60 percent, substantially higher than in the United States. Similarly high transactions costs are incurred by nondomestic equity investors in emerging Asian markets such as Indonesia (0.60 percent), Malaysia (0.55 percent), and the Philippines (0.75 percent). When such fees are combined with meaningful market impact costs, overall transaction costs for buying a basket of emerging-market stocks can easily exceed 2 percent per year. If quoted historical rates of return on benchmark indexes for emerging-market equities do not include such real-world costs, they systematically understate what can become a significant drag on investor returns.

Political Risk

Many global markets are immature, vulnerable to scandal, subject to manipulation and lack strong investor protections. This is especially true of emerging markets in which political events have the potential to threaten the stability of returns. Many countries with emerging markets are vulnerable to **political risk** stemming from coups, assassinations, or civil unrest that increases market volatility and decreases investor returns. Some countries with emerging markets are governed by dictatorships with succession plans shrouded in secrecy and uncertainty. Governments of countries with emerging markets also tend to be moving toward democracy and struggling with long-standing political and social problems. Sudden retreats toward socialism are apt to occur, especially during periods of social unrest.

Economic progress in emerging markets can be stalled by unexpected trade deficits that sometimes undermine currency stability. In 1997–1998, for example, a local currency crisis contributed to severe economic upheaval in Malaysia, where economic controls were quickly put in place to restrict the repatriation of investment funds by foreign investors. **Government policy risk** is an important consideration for global investors. Foreign investors must always be on the lookout for policy changes that could become unfavorable. Such changes could include currency controls, changes in monopoly franchise agreements, and adverse revisions in the taxation of foreign investment. In a worst-case scenario, investors must be on the lookout for the potential expropriation of investments made by international investors. In an era of privatization of formerly public assets, investors also tend to forget the **expropriation risk** that claimed the assets of global investors during the 1960s and 1970s. That's a mistake.

Currency Risk

Currency risk is a pervasive risk that investors face when making global investments. The value of all currencies fluctuates over time. Just like any commodity, the value of the U.S. dollar rises and falls according to the laws of supply and demand. A **strong dollar** signifies an increase in the amount of foreign currency that can be purchased for $1. A **weak dollar** connotes a decrease in the amount of foreign currency that can be purchased for $1. When the dollar is strong, the dollar price of goods and services purchased from abroad falls. When the dollar is weak, the dollar price of goods and services purchased from abroad rises.

Changes in the value of the dollar also have important implications for global investors. If stock prices in Japan rise by 10 percent but the dollar strengthens 3 percent against the Japanese yen, the net return earned by U.S. investors on their Japanese holdings falls to roughly 6.8 percent (= 1.1/1.03). However, if stock prices in Japan rise by 10 percent and the dollar weakens 3 percent against the Japanese yen, the net return earned by U.S. investors on their Japanese holdings jumps by roughly 13.4 percent (= 1.1/0.97).

Figure 17.6 shows the recent depreciation of the U.S. dollar versus both the euro and the U.K. pound sterling. At the end of February 2002, it took only $0.865 to buy 1 euro. Two years later, it took $1.255 to buy 1 euro. The dollar had depreciated against the euro by roughly 45 percent in just two years! The dollar depreciated about 31 percent against the pound during the same period. This recent weakening in the dollar helped U.S. investors with positions in foreign markets. For example, suppose a U.S. investor converted $100 to £70.215 in February 2002 and invested the proceeds in the U.K. equity market. As measured by the FTSE, the U.K.

Political risk

Loss potential tied to government; stems from coups, assassinations, or civil unrest.

Government policy risk

Loss potential tied to changes in government rules and regulations.

Expropriation risk

Loss potential tied to government confiscation of assets.

Currency risk

Loss potential tied to changing relative values of world currencies.

Strong dollar

Increase in the amount of foreign currency that can be purchased for $1.

Weak dollar

Decrease in the amount of foreign currency that can be purchased for $1.

FIGURe 17.6	The Dollar Has Weakened over the Past Five Years

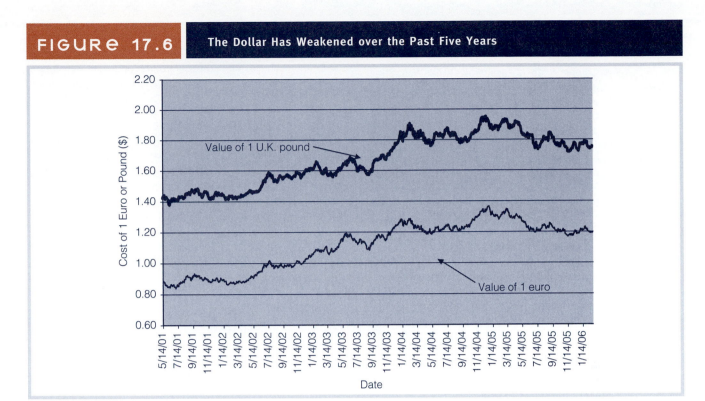

Source: Federal Reserve Economic Data (FRED).

cquitics had declined by −11.63 percent to £62.049 by February 2004. When converting back to dollars, however, the U.S. investor received $115.84. The U.S. investor made a 15.8 percent profit because currency gains overcame losses in the U.K. market. Any such big move in currency exchange rates can dominate the outcomes of international investments. A move this large in a major currency like the U.S. dollar is unusual, but emerging-market currencies are notoriously volatile.

Try It!

An investor with $1,000 can invest in a Japanese stock costing 500 yen (¥) per share. The exchange rate is $1 = ¥111.66. How many shares of the Japanese stock can the investor purchase? In one year, if the Japanese stock has increased to 550 yen and the exchange rate has changed to $1 = ¥119.55, what is the investor's return?

Solution

Convert the U.S. dollars to Japanese yen:	$1,000 × ¥111.66 = ¥111,660
The number of shares purchased is:	¥111,660/¥500 = 223 shares with ¥160 left over
The value (in yen) after one year is:	223 × ¥550 + ¥160 = ¥122,810
This value in US dollars is:	¥122,810/¥119.55 = $1,027.27
The return is:	($1,027.27 − $1,000) / $1,000 = 2.73%

Note that the return on the Japanese stock in yen was 10 percent but the dollar weakened over the year against the yen, so the return to the U.S. investor was only 2.73 percent.

Street Smarts 17.2

Research Perspective

Do Domestic Investors Have an Edge?

The consensus among financial academics and Wall Street professionals has been that domestic investors have an advantage over foreign investors when trading stocks in their home country. A popular explanation for this advantage has been that domestic investors have superior information, given their better familiarity with local products, markets, and customs. It has also been argued that regulators tend to be more tolerant of domestic investors or even biased against foreign investors. The view that domestic investors have an edge over foreign investors has been used to explain various empirical regularities, such as the observed home bias among domestic investors, the volatility of capital flows, and herding among foreign investors.

Hyuk Choe, Bong-Chan Kho, and René M. Stulz shed new light on this topic by considering whether domestic investors have an edge over foreign investors. In a study of the Korean stock exchange, they report that foreign investors suffer a trading disadvantage. Weighting trades by size, the average disadvantage of foreign money managers relative to domestic

money managers is on the order of 21 basis points (0.21 percent) for purchases and 16 basis points for sales. On a round-trip trade, foreign money managers face greater transaction costs on the order of 37 basis points. This is a substantial financial penalty, especially for active traders. A foreign investor who trades three times per year would incur a performance drag in excess of 100 basis points per year. Because the annual performance difference between top-performing and poorly performing mutual funds is typically as little as 65 to 70 basis points per year, the trading disadvantage faced by foreign investors is meaningful.

The trading disadvantage faced by foreign investors cannot be explained by firm characteristics. The key difference between foreign investors and domestic investors appears to be that prices move unfavorably for foreign investors immediately before they trade intensively. This difference may be partly explained by the return-chasing behavior of foreign investors.

See Hyuk Choe, Bong-Chan Kho, and René M. Stulz, "Do Domestic Investors Have an Edge? The Trading Experience of Foreign Investors in Korea," *Review of Financial Studies*, vol. 18, no. 3 (Fall 2005), pp. 795–829.

Investor Protection

Shareholders sometimes need protection against unscrupulous managers seeking to expropriate their wealth. Investor protection comes from the board of directors, auditors, banks, credit agencies, analysts, and regulators. The strength of monitoring varies greatly among countries. Accounting disclosure practices, the legal system, and the quality of regulatory enforcement are all important.

A wide variety of legal environments has created tremendous differences in the structure of corporate governance in public companies across the globe. Among firms in developed markets, companies in Italy have the greatest tendency to stay private. Banks are an important funding and monitoring resource in Germany. Stock ownership is the most widely dispersed in the United States and in the United Kingdom. Public companies in Thailand tend to be majority-owned by individual families. These differences stem from the differences in shareholder rights and protection among countries. For example, accounting disclosure standards in the United States and the United Kingdom are high. By way of comparison, accounting disclosures in Latin America are fairly modest. **Corruption** among government officials is extremely rare in the Scandinavian countries of Denmark, Finland, Norway, and Sweden; it is a cost of doing business in countries such as India, Indonesia, Mexico, and Philippines.

Corruption
Situation in which government officials demand personal payments in order to do business in a country.

Home Bias

Role of Familiarity

Notwithstanding obvious risks, there are benefits to be had through global diversification. Research in finance suggests that portfolio risk can be reduced for a given level of expected return through global diversification. Similarly, global diversification has the potential to enhance returns for a desired level of portfolio risk.

Despite widespread evidence concerning the benefits of global diversification, research in behavioral finance suggests that most investors commit very little of their investment portfolios to global equities. The irrational predisposition of some investors to focus on domestic equities is commonly referred to as **home bias**, as illustrated in Figure 17.7. The figure shows

Home bias
The irrational propensity of investors to predominantly buy domestic securities; an outcome of familiarity bias.

FIGURE 17.7 | Investors Mostly Own Domestic Stocks

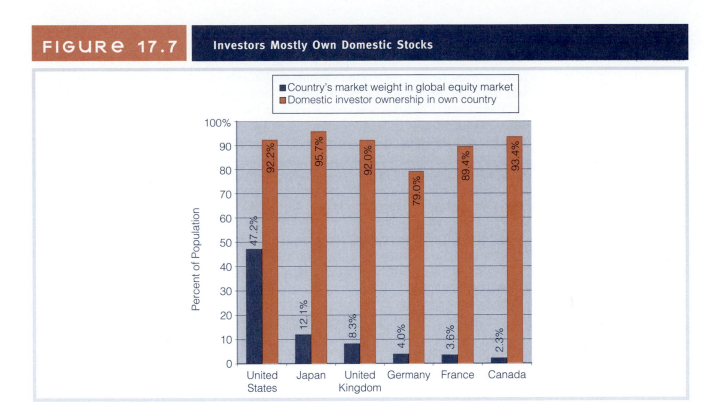

■ Country's market weight in global equity market
■ Domestic investor ownership in own country

the market capitalization of stocks headquartered in the United States, Japan, the United Kingdom, Germany, France, and Canada. The U.S. stock market represents approximately 47 percent of the global market equity. Stock markets in Japan, the United Kingdom, Germany, France, and Canada represent 12, 8, 4, 3.6, and 2.3 percent of the worldwide stock market, respectively. A globally diversified stock portfolio might be expected to allocate 47 percent to U.S. stocks, 12 percent to Japanese stocks, 8 percent to U.K. stocks, and so on.

Figure 17.7 also shows the percentage of domestic investor portfolios that is typically invested among domestic securities. On average, the stock portfolios of U.S. investors are 92 percent invested in U.S.-based companies, not the 47 percent predicted by traditional portfolio theory. That leaves only 8 percent of their portfolios for stocks in foreign-based companies. Japanese investors are nearly 96 percent invested in Japanese stocks. Similarly, U.K. investors, German investors, French investors, and Canadian investors own 92, 79, 89, and 93 percent, respectively, of their own country's stocks. Again, this leaves very little for them to invest in foreign-based companies.

Why do some investors exhibit an irrational home bias? The answer may lie in the behavioral principle of familiarity. Familiarity bias causes investors to believe that things they are familiar with are better than things with which they are not familiar. Investors tend to be less familiar with foreign firms, and some investors may believe that stocks in their own country will have a higher expected return and lower risk than will foreign firms. Investors may need to spend more time studying foreign markets and foreign companies so that they will be more familiar with them and have more confidence in diversifying internationally.

Foreign Bias

Investors also sometimes suffer from an irrational **foreign bias** when investing internationally. That is, investors from one country appear to be biased about which other countries they invest in—they tend to overinvest in some foreign countries and underinvest in others. Traditional portfolio theory recommends that investors seek to own an international market portfolio. The largest capital markets (in order) are the United States, Japan, the United Kingdom, and

Foreign bias

The propensity of investors to overweight investment in familiar countries and underweight investment in others.

France. The average German investor might be expected to make the largest international investment in the United States, the second largest in Japan, and so on. Indeed, Germans invest heavily in the United States, but France is a close second.[2] Japan ranks as only the fifth-largest place to invest for German investors, behind the Netherlands. The Germans have a bias to invest in France over Japan. Singapore investors have a preference for investing in Japan over the United States Austrian investors overweight Germany and underweight Japan and the United Kingdom.

What are the characteristics of the foreign countries that attract international investors? First, international investors tend to invest in countries with well-developed stock markets, such as the United States, Britain, and Japan. Second, investors appear to look for counties that seem familiar. Specifically, they invest more in countries that are geographically close and have the same or similar language and culture. Other factors play a minor role in the allocation of investments in foreign countries. These less influential factors include economic development, existence of capital controls, transaction costs, and investor protection laws.

Investors worldwide do not invest in foreign countries in the same proportion. International investor behavior appears more consistent with behavioral biases like familiarity than with the use of modern portfolio theory.

Global Investment Opportunities

Multinational Investment Strategy

Multinational
Corporation that conducts business in a number of host countries.

An effective way to gain international exposure in an investment portfolio is to buy companies with global business operations. From the United States, **multinational** giants set the pace for technology and innovation in aerospace, autos, telecommunications, computer software and engineering, and related fields. It is fair to say that throughout much of the high-tech sector, U.S. multinationals are at the vanguard in meeting customer needs with new and exciting products.

Global economic integration undoubtedly reduces the penalty attached to any investor tendency toward home bias. For example, while the Coca-Cola Company has its corporate headquarters in Atlanta, Georgia, it has local operations in over 200 countries around the world. Coca-Cola's operating structure includes strategic business units in North America, Africa, Asia, Europe, Eurasia and the Middle East, and Latin America. The North America operating segment accounts for roughly 30 percent of total revenues and operating profits. More than 70 percent of Coca-Cola revenues and operating profits are generated outside North America. From an economic perspective, it is fair to say that more than 70 percent of the value of Coca-Cola is derived from its operations outside North America. Toyota Motor Corporation, based in Tokyo, Japan, boasts about having more than 37,000 employees in North America, and it sells roughly the same number of vehicles in the United States as in Japan (2.5 million units per year). Like Coca-Cola, Toyota and most of the world's largest corporations are truly global in character. Profits derived from non-U.S. operations make up 30 to 45 percent of the profits reported by top U.S. companies. That share is rising fast as global markets become better integrated.

The implication for global investors is obvious. One way to achieve global diversification is to buy stocks in companies with corporate headquarters in foreign lands. Another way to gain global diversification is to buy the stocks of multinational corporations that have globally diverse business operations. Savvy U.S. investors can avoid an irrational emphasis on domestic markets ("home bias") through their participation in the far-flung operations of multinational giants.

---

[2]Kalok Chan, Vicentiu Covrig, and Lilian Ng, "What determines the Domestic Bias and Foreign Bias? Evidence from Mutual Fund Equity Allocations Worldwide," *Journal of Finance*, vol. 60, no. 3 (June 2005).

American Depository Receipts

The United States is the world's largest economy and features the largest capital markets in the world. It also has the most investment capital looking for profitable opportunities. Major foreign companies often want to list their shares on U.S. exchanges to gain access to U.S. investors. They can do this using **American depository receipts (ADRs)**. ADRs are issued by U.S. commercial banks, such as J.P. Morgan, that function as the depository institution. Each ADR traded on a U.S. exchange is backed by a specific number of foreign shares held by a custodian bank. The number of underlying shares represented by each ADR is referred to as the **ADR ratio**. This ratio can be depicted as 1:3, or one ADR per three underlying shares. Each ADR certificate identifies the account number, name(s) of registered owners, transaction or issue date, and number of shares that the certificate represents. ADR certificates are negotiable documents and should be signed only in the event of a sale or transfer of ownership.

ADRs can be listed on the NYSE or American Stock Exchange (Amex) and may be quoted for trading on Nasdaq. The ADR concept has been extended to other geographic markets in the form of global depositary receipts (GDRs), international depositary receipts (IDRs), and European depositary receipts (EDRs) that are traded in one or more global markets. ADRs trade like the stocks of U.S. companies. Shares are bought and sold using U.S. dollars, dividends are paid in dollars, and annual reports are delivered in English. Investors can buy or sell ADRs through any registered broker or dealer. All ADRs must be registered with the Security and Exchange Commission (SEC).

Level I ADRs represent the most basic form of a sponsored ADR program. Level I is used when the issuer is not initially seeking to raise capital in the United States or list its ADRs on an exchange or Nasdaq. Level I ADR programs offer a relatively inexpensive way for issuers to gauge interest in their securities and begin building a presence in U.S. securities markets. Level I ADRs are traded in the OTC market, with bid and ask prices published daily or posted on the OTC bulletin board (OTCBB). **Level II ADRs** are listed on U.S. exchanges or quoted on Nasdaq and feature greater visibility in the U.S. market, active trading, and great liquidity. **Level III ADRs** are the highest-profile form of sponsored ADR programs. In a Level III ADR program, an issuer floats a public offering of ADRs in the United States and obtains listing on a major U.S. exchange or Nasdaq. During recent years, the amount of investment capital raised through Level III ADRs has risen from roughly $5 billion to $15 billion per year. Level II and III ADR programs must comply with the full SEC registration and reporting requirements. Annual reports and interim financial statements must be submitted on a regular basis to the SEC and all registered public shareholders.

In 2005, the NYSE had 459 nondomestic companies from 48 countries with listed ADRs. Nasdaq had 130 ADRs listed. Table 17.5 shows some popular ADRs listed on the NYSE. You may recognize some of the firms. Notice that they come from many different countries and sectors.

Foreign Bonds

Governments and companies throughout the world borrow money in the form of bank loans and bonds. Companies and governments in countries with well-developed capital markets can issue debt called **domestic bonds** to domestic investors. European companies can issue euro-denominated bonds to domestic investors who want to invest in them. It is difficult for small foreign investors to buy and sell these European bonds because they must exchange currency and open a brokerage account that operates in Europe.

Alternatively, many companies from one country issue bonds in another country, which are called **foreign bonds**. The corporate bond market in many countries is mostly nonexistent. Because of the large amount of capital available in the United States, companies from all over the world issue dollar-denominated bonds in the United States, which are called **Yankee bonds**. Bonds issued by AstraZeneca (British firm), Canadian Pacific, Kowloon-Canton Railway (Hong Kong firm), Coca-Cola FEMSA (Mexican firm), Naples (city in Italy), and New Zealand (government) all trade on the NYSE. Because these bonds make interest and principal payments

American depository receipts (ADRs)
Negotiable instruments that represent ownership in the equity securities of a non-U.S. company.

ADR ratio
Number of underlying shares represented by one ADR.

Level I ADRs
ADRs issued when the issuer is not initially seeking to raise capital in the United States or list its ADRs on an exchange or Nasdaq.

Level II ADRs
ADRs issued when a company has no immediate financing needs and listed on U.S. exchanges or quoted on Nasdaq.

Level III ADRs
ADRs issued when an issuer floats a public offering of ADRs in the United States and obtains listing on a major U.S. exchange or Nasdaq.

Domestic bonds
Bonds issued by a local borrower and denominated in local currency.

Foreign bond
Bond issued by a borrower from a different country but denominated in the local currency.

Yankee bond
Foreign bond issued in the United States by a non-U.S. borrower and denominated in dollars.

TABLE 17.5 — Some Popular ADRs Listed on the NYSE

Company Name	Ticker	Ratio	Country	Sector
ABB Ltd.	ABB	1:1	Switzerland	Engineering & construction
Advanced Semiconductor Engineering Inc.	ASX	1:5	Taiwan	Semiconductors
Air France	AKH	1:1	France	Airlines
Allied Irish Banks Plc.	AIB	1:2	Ireland	Banks
Aluminum Corp. of China Ltd.	ACH	1:100	China	Mining
Amvescap Plc.	AVZ	1:2	United Kingdom	Financial services
Bancolombia SA	CIB	1:4	Colombia	Banks
Bank of Ireland	IRE	1:4	Ireland	Banks
BASF Ag.	Bf	1:1	Germany	Chemicals
Brasil Telecom SA	BTM	1:3,000	Brazil	Telecommunications
British Airways Plc.	BAB	1:10	United Kingdom	Airlines
British Sky Broadcasting Plc.	BSY	1:4	United Kingdom	Media
Chilesat Corp. SA	CSA	1:10	Chile	Telecommunications
CNOOC Ltd.	CEO	1:100	Hong Kong	Oil & gas
Deutsche Telekom Ag.	DT	1:1	Germany	Telecommunications
Endesa SA	ELE	1:1	Spain	Electric utility
Gold Fields Ltd.	GFI	1:1	South Africa	Mining
Gruma SA De Cv.	GMK	1:4	Mexico	Food products & services
Hanson Plc.	HAN	1:5	United Kingdom	Building products & materials
Honda Motor Co. Ltd.	HMC	1:0.5	Japan	Auto manufacturers
Koor Industries Ltd.	KOR	1:0.2	Israel	Holding & investment companies
Luxottica Group Spa.	LUX	1:1	Italy	Health care products & services
Madeco SA	MAD	1:100	Chile	Metal fabrication
Matav Rt.	MTA	1:5	Hungary	Telecommunications
Metrogas SA	MGS	1:10	Argentina	Gas production & services
Nokia Oyj.	NOK	1:1	Finland	Telecommunications
Nomura Holdings Inc.	NMR	1:1	Japan	Financial services
Norsk Hydro Asa.	NHY	1:1	Norway	Oil & gas
Novo-Nordisk A/S	NVO	1:1	Denmark	Pharmaceuticals
Philippine Long Distance Telephone	PHI	1:1	Philippines	Telecommunications
Prudential Plc.	PUK	1:2	United Kingdom	Insurance
Repsol Ypf. SA	REP	1:1	Spain	Oil & gas
Schering Ag.	SHR	1:1	Germany	Pharmaceuticals
Sony Corp.	SNE	1:1	Japan	Electronics
Tenaris SA	TS	1:10	Luxembourg	Oil & gas related services
Tenon Ltd.	FFS	1:10	New Zealand	Building products & materials
Tomkins Plc.	TKS	1:4	United Kingdom	Holding & investment companies
Total SA	TOT	1:0.5	France	Oil & gas
Toyota Motor Corp.	TM	1:2	Japan	Auto manufacturers
Turkcell Iletisim Hizmet As.	TKC	1:2,500	Turkey	Telecommunications
Unilever Nv.	UN	1:1	Netherlands	Food products & services
Veolia Environnement	VE	1:1	France	Water products & services
Videsh Sanchar Nigam Ltd.	VSL	1:2	India	Telecommunications
Vimpel-Communications	VIP	1:0.75	Russia	Telecommunications
YPF SA	YPF	1:1	Argentina	Oil & gas

Why Are Cross-Listed Firms Worth More?

In a perfectly efficient global equities market, stock prices give unbiased estimates of firms' future prospects. All useful economic information is embedded in security prices, and market values depend on fundamental criteria only. Against this backdrop, it is interesting to note that market values for large, liquid global corporations appear heavily dependent on more than fundamental economic criteria. They also rely on institutional aspects of global securities markets.

In an award-winning paper, Craig Doidge, Andrew Karolyi, and René Stulz discovered that shares of non-U.S. companies that are cross-listed on U.S. markets enjoy a significant value premium. In a follow-up to their original study, they analyzed over 24,000 public companies in more than 50 developed and emerging markets. Their sample covered more than 96 percent of the market value of the world's publicly traded companies. A cross-listing premium of 10 to 15 percent apparently persists over time, with some modest variation from year to year. The cross-listing premium is statistically significant and robust after controlling for fundamentals like sales growth, industry characteristics, and firm size. The premium is highest for firms cross-

listed on major U.S. exchanges, such as the NYSE and Nasdaq. The average premium for non-cross-listed stocks and cross-listed stocks on major exchanges is a whopping 30 to 35 percent, or more than double the average of all cross-listed stock types.

The cross-listing premium varies across countries. The most consistent valuation premiums are seen for stocks from Canada, France, Germany, Russia, Singapore, Switzerland, and the United Kingdom. The cross-listing premium also varies among sectors and appears greatest for stocks in the mining, transportation, communications, and services sectors.

Nobody knows why the cross-listing premium exists. Conventional wisdom suggests that cross-listing achieves a lower cost of equity capital due to mitigated investment barriers or lower trading costs. On the other hand, some scholars suggest that cross-listing confers benefits on managers and controlling shareholders from "bonding" with U.S. capital markets. Alternatively, premiums for cross-listed shares may simply reflect the fact that global equity markets are not highly efficient.

See Craig Doidge, G. Andrew Karolyi, and René M. Stulz, "The Valuation Premium for Non-U.S. Stocks Listed in U.S. Markets," NYSE Research Paper Series, September 16, 2005 (**www.nyse.com/pdfs/Stulz_091505.pdf**).

---

in U.S. dollars, U.S. investors do not assume currency exchange risk when owning Yankee bonds. Like ADRs, Yankee bonds are registered with and regulated by the SEC. Similarly, foreign firms issue yen-denominated bonds in Japan (called Samurai bonds) and pound-denominated bonds in Britain (called Bulldog bonds).

Global Mutual Funds

U.S. investors have poured nearly $100 billion into international stock funds over the past few years, and the assets of international stock funds approach $500 billion. International stock and bond mutual funds provide small individual investors with a cost-efficient means for participating in foreign securities markets. For small individual investors, investing internationally through mutual funds provides a cost-effective opportunity for better diversification and higher returns. A mutual fund with an international perspective can spread its assets among many securities traded in a number of different countries. Brokerage fees for small foreign stock transactions can be high on a percentage basis, especially when trading activity is minimal. Because mutual fund managers regularly deal with large numbers of buy and sell transactions, they usually have the potential to be more cost-effective than small investors in foreign markets. Of course, mutual funds pay management fees and marketing costs that can offset these cost advantages.

World equity funds invest primarily in the stocks of foreign companies. An **emerging-market fund** invests predominantly in the stocks of companies based in countries with developing economies. Investing in emerging markets is risky because many such countries experience great difficulty in evolving from an agricultural or socialist economy to an industrial free market. Notable examples of countries experiencing birth pains in the 1990s include Argentina, India, Indonesia, and Turkey. Of course, as an offset to their greater risks, emerging-market funds hold the potential for higher rates of economic growth than the rates in more mature markets of the United States, Western Europe, and Japan.

A mutual fund that invests in domestic and foreign stocks is known as a **global equity fund**, or world equity fund. Like international stock funds, global funds typically seek long-term growth. Because global funds can duplicate some U.S. stockholdings for domestic investors with broadly diversified holdings, some investors prefer funds that invest only in foreign

Emerging-market fund
Mutual fund that invests predominantly in the stocks of companies based in countries with developing economies.

Global equity funds
Mutual fund that invests in U.S. and foreign stocks.

International equity fund
Mutual fund that invests in the equity securities of companies located outside the United States.

stocks. A global equity fund invests in equity securities traded on a worldwide basis, including those of U.S. companies. An **international equity fund**, or foreign fund, invests in the equity securities of companies located outside the United States and generally is prohibited from investing in U.S. equities. The most popular and widely held international equity funds invest in the stocks of developed European markets such as the United Kingdom, Germany, and France and various Pacific Rim nations such as Japan, Hong Kong, and Australia. The investment objective of most broadly diversified international stock funds is long-term growth, although some value-oriented funds place modest emphasis on current income.

The investment strategies of international funds vary widely. Some funds emphasize investments in particular countries rather than individual stocks, hoping to capitalize on those countries that will enjoy the highest future economic growth. Other funds use a fundamental investment approach that focuses on the most promising companies, regardless of the countries in which they operate. Indexing is becoming a more popular investment strategy for international stock funds. When adopting an indexing strategy, most mutual funds seek to match the performance of a group of securities that form a recognized global market measure such as the EAFE Index.

Foreign regional fund
International fund that invests in the stocks of a specific global area.

Single-country fund
Mutual fund that invests in a sole foreign country.

An international fund that invests in companies from a particular geographic region, such as Europe or the Pacific Basin, is known as a **foreign regional fund**. By concentrating on a single region, these funds hope to capture the investment benefits derived from explosive economic growth tied to political changes, trade initiatives, or demographic trends. Share prices for regional funds typically fluctuate more than the share prices of broadly diversified international stock funds. Even more volatile is a **single-country fund**, which invests in a single foreign country, such as Hong Kong, Mexico, or Italy. Many single-country funds are closed-end mutual funds that trade on an exchange at sizable discounts or premiums relative to net asset value. Single-country funds can be extremely risky because of their narrow focus.

Most international funds assess a sales commission or sales load on purchases and redemptions. Front-end loads typically vary from 4 to 6 percent on initial purchases and are deducted before the investor's money is invested in the fund. Back-end loads typically range from 2 to 5 percent and are assessed when investors redeem their shares. Loads, operating expenses, and transaction costs all reduce investor returns and must be minimized to achieve a competitive rate of return.

======== **Try It!** ========

Mutual fund information powerhouse Morningstar has a Global Center Web site (**www.morningstar.com/centers/global**). Note that this center offers articles on international mutual funds and fun screens on various applications. Morningstar also reports the average mutual fund performance for funds in many different categories, such as Foreign Large Value, Diversified Pacific/Asia, Europe Stock, and World Stock. Average performance by category is shown for one month to five years. In May 2004, the average Foreign Large Value funds outperformed the Foreign Large Growth funds in every period. What is the performance like now?

International iShares

International iShares
Unit portfolio trusts that track the performance of an underlying international benchmark index.

Barclays Global Investors has been a leader in the development and marketing of index shares (called iShares) that offer investors the broad diversification of an index fund and the trading flexibility of common stocks. Barclays offers **international iShares** that track market movements around the world. Such easy-to-buy exchange-traded funds can effectively add global diversification to domestic portfolios.

The most popular international ETFs are based on well-known MSCI indexes. The objective of international ETFs is to track the performance of a given country's publicly traded equity securities. Barclays offers iShares based on dozens of country and regional MSCI indexes. It also offers iShares based on a variety of regional and global sector indexes created by Standard & Poor's.

Global Titans

Globalization is an investment reality. Once-distinct geographic, economic, and cultural boundaries among countries have been nearly erased. Global Titans, like Microsoft, Nestle, and Coca-Cola, have extended their influence worldwide. For more than a century, Dow Jones has tracked 30 of the most important and influential companies in the United States with the Dow Jones Industrial Average. Today, the DJIA is the best-known and most cited stock market index in the world. In a globally integrated world, however, a global version of the DJIA is needed. Dow Jones & Company created just that in 1992 with its Dow Jones Global Titans 50 Index (DJGT).

The DJGT serves as a benchmark to track the performance of large, multinational corporations as an overall asset class. The index provides exposure to companies headquartered in countries around the world, aiming to reduce risk through country diversification and the inclusion of only the largest and most established blue-chip companies. To select Global Titan companies, Dow Jones ranks all firms on the basis of market capitalization, revenue, and net profits. These three rankings are then combined using a weight of 60 percent on market capitalization, 20 percent on revenue, and 20 percent on profits. The top 50 ranked companies are then selected for the DJGT. Rankings are compiled annually, and changes are made as required to keep the top 50 companies in the index. Only a few firms are changed in any given year, but only 28 percent of the original Global Titans are still in the index today. In 2006, 29 of 50 firms were from the United States. Interestingly, of the 29 U.S. firms, only 18 are presently in the DJIA. The second-largest number of companies comes from Great Britain, which has eight Global Titans.

Investors can participate in the index by buying street-TRACKS Global Titans Index Fund, an ETF that trades on the Amex (ticker, DGT). It remains to be seen if the Global Titans Index will become as popular as the Dow Jones Industrial Average.

See Scott Patterson, "After Global Selloff, a Recovery," *The Wall Street Journal Online*, January 19, 2006 (**http://online.wsj.com**).

As is the case with any foreign market investment, investors in international iShares must be aware that international investing involves not only the normal risks associated with equity investing but also the additional risk of capital loss due to unfavorable fluctuations in the currency markets. Whereas investors buy and sell iShares on the American Stock Exchange in U.S. dollars, the portfolio of assets the ETF invests in is based on foreign currencies. International iShare investors also face exposure to investment losses stemming from economic or political instability in other nations.

Barclays' iShares and other internationally focused ETFs are good options for investors who want to get international exposure in an easy and low-cost way. Investors with an interest in international iShares can learn more at the Barclays Web site, **www.ishares.com**.

Summary

■ There are many opportunities for investors to achieve higher returns investing in foreign countries. In addition, investors can lower total portfolio risk through **global diversification**. When investments in foreign countries have low correlation with U.S. returns, diversification can be achieved by adding them to the domestic portfolio.

■ Each stock market around the world has its own indexes to measure its equity performance over time. It is difficult to compare these indexes with each other because they are constructed differently and are in different currencies. Morgan Stanley Capital International provides standardized indexes for investors. Established equity markets in leading advanced economies are called **developed markets**. Securities markets for countries with rapidly evolving economies are called **emerging markets**. All MSCI equity indexes are calculated by using **full-market-capitalization-weights** (price multiplied by the number of outstanding shares). In some emerging markets, MSCI designates **free indexes** and **nonfree indexes**.

■ Diversifying globally is especially useful when countries have **segmented markets**. It may be less important when international markets become more integrated. Another strategy is to use global sectors to diversify the portfolio.

■ Investing in foreign markets, especially emerging foreign markets, generally involves much higher **market volatility** than that associated with U.S. equities. The potential for above-average gains in foreign equity markets comes with the risk of similarly above-average losses in any given year. **Liquidity risk** refers to the loss potential tied to the fact that a stock can become difficult to buy or sell. Thin trading activity in foreign developed and emerging markets often leads to higher **market impact costs**. Special liquidity risks associated with investing in developed and emerging markets are accompanied by higher global equity transaction costs. **Brokerage commissions**, **exchange fees**, **currency translation costs**, and **custodial fees** tend to be substantially higher in emerging markets than in the developed markets of the United States and Europe.

■ Many countries with emerging markets are vulnerable to **political risk** stemming from coups, assassinations, or civil unrest, which increases market volatility and decreases investor returns. **Government policy risk** is an important consideration for global investors. Foreign investors must always be on the lookout for policy changes that could become unfavorable. In a worst-case scenario, investors must be on the lookout for **expropriation risk**, which claimed the assets of global investors during the 1960s and 1970s. **Currency risk** is a pervasive political risk that investors face when making global investments.

■ A **strong dollar** signifies an increase in the amount of foreign currency that can be purchased for $1. A **weak dollar** connotes a decrease in the amount of foreign currency that can be purchased for $1.

■ Corporate governance, accounting standards, securities laws, and regulatory enforcement differ greatly between countries. Government **corruption** is a problem in some countries. Organizations such as the PSR Group assess country risks for investors.

■ Even though there are many advantages to international investing, some investors may hold few, if any, foreign assets. From a diversification aspect, investors who hold too much of their portfolios in the domestic equity market suffer from **home bias**. Investors also suffer from a **foreign bias** when investing internationally. They tend to overinvest in some foreign countries and underinvest in others.

■ **Multinational** giants set the pace for technology and innovation in aerospace, autos, telecommunications, computer software and engineering, and related fields, and they have revenues and profits coming from foreign countries. When a significant portion of total profit comes from abroad, there is less reason to fear that a company's competitive position in the domestic market is apt to be undermined by global competitors.

■ **American depository receipts (ADRs)** are negotiable instruments that represent ownership in the equity securities of a non-U.S. company. The number of underlying shares represented by one ADR is referred to as the **ADR ratio**. Level I ADRs are used when the issuer is not initially seeking to raise capital in the United States or list its ADRs on an exchange or Nasdaq. **Level II ADRs** are issued when a company has no immediate financing needs and is listed on U.S. exchanges or quoted on Nasdaq. **Level III ADRs** are the highest-profile form of sponsored ADR programs. In a Level III ADR program, an issuer floats a public offering of ADRs in the United States and obtains listing on a major U.S. exchange or Nasdaq. Level II and III ADR programs must comply with full SEC registration and reporting requirements.

■ Investors can buy bonds from international companies by purchasing **domestic bonds** directly in foreign countries. An easier method to achieve international fixed-income diversification is to buy **foreign bonds**, which can be bought locally and whose interest and principal are paid in local currency. Foreign bonds in the United States are called **Yankee bonds**.

■ An **emerging-market fund** invests predominantly in the stocks of companies based in countries with developing economies. A mutual fund that invests in U.S. and foreign stocks is known as a **global equity fund**, or world equity fund. An **international equity fund**, or foreign fund, invests in the equity securities of companies located outside the United States and generally is prohibited from investing in U.S. equities. An international fund that invests in companies from a particular geographic region, such as Europe or the Pacific Basin, is known as a **foreign regional fund**. Share prices for regional funds typically fluctuate more than the share prices of broadly diversified international stock funds. Even more volatile is a **single-country fund**, which invests in a sole foreign country, such as Hong Kong, Mexico, or Italy.

■ **International iShares** are unit portfolio trusts that track the performance of an underlying international benchmark index by holding proportionate interests in component shares. Many of the most popular international iShares follow country-specific MSCI indexes and are traded on the American Stock Exchange. International iShares are available for major developed and emerging markets. The investment objective of international iShares is to offer a cost-effective means for adding an international dimension to domestic investment portfolios.

Self-Test Problems

ST17.1 Use monthly stock prices from April 2000 to May 2005 for the iShares MSCI-Japan (EWJ), iShares MSCI-UK (EWU), and iShares MSCI-Mexico (EWW) to determine the risk and return characteristics of each of these markets. What is their diversification potential?

Solution

First compute monthly returns from the monthly iShare prices. Then use the monthly returns to assess the risk and return characteristics.

◇	A	B	C	D	E	F	G	H
1		Prices				Returns		
2	Date	EWJ	EWU	EWW		EWJ	EWU	EWW
3	Apr-00	$13.97	$16.48	$14.53				
4	May-00	13.17	15.91	13.11		-5.73%	-3.46%	-9.77%
5	Jun-00	13.91	16.12	14.31		5.62%	1.32%	9.15%
6	Jul-00	12.37	16.12	14.25		-11.07%	0.00%	-0.42%
7	Aug-00	13.19	16.27	14.96		6.63%	0.93%	4.98%
8	Sep-00	12.54	15.76	13.57		-4.93%	-3.13%	-9.29%
9	Oct-00	12.01	16.2	14.12		-4.23%	2.79%	4.05%
10	Nov-00	11.12	15.22	12.73		-7.41%	-6.05%	-9.84%
11	Dec-00	11.01	15.56	11.96		-0.99%	2.23%	-6.05%
12	Jan-01	10.95	15.74	13.79		-0.54%	1.16%	15.30%
13	Feb-01	10.48	14.74	12.81		-4.29%	-6.35%	-7.11%
14	Mar-01	10.2	13.85	12.57		-2.67%	-6.04%	-1.87%
15	Apr-01	11.17	14.7	13.48		9.51%	6.14%	7.24%
16	May-01	10.84	14.37	14.7		-2.95%	-2.24%	9.05%
17	Jun-01	10.19	13.91	15.14		-6.00%	-3.20%	2.99%
18	Jul-01	9.36	13.73	14.29		-8.15%	-1.29%	-5.61%
19	Aug-01	9.1	13.63	13.92		-2.78%	-0.73%	-2.59%
20	Sep-01	8.36	12.57	11.17		-8.13%	-7.78%	-19.76%
21	Oct-01	8.35	12.81	11.77		-0.12%	1.91%	5.37%
22	Nov-01	8.34	12.96	12.49		-0.12%	1.17%	6.12%
23	Dec-01	7.68	13.39	13.8		-7.91%	3.32%	10.49%
24	Jan-02	7.11	12.92	15.07		-7.42%	-3.51%	9.20%
25	Feb-02	7.44	12.71	14.69		4.64%	-1.63%	-2.52%
26	Mar-02	8.1	13.37	16.23		8.87%	5.19%	10.48%
27	Apr-02	8.4	13.45	15.77		3.70%	0.60%	-2.83%
28	May-02	8.92	13.18	14.66		6.19%	-2.01%	-7.04%
29	Jun-02	8.39	12.67	13.26		-5.94%	-3.87%	-9.55%
30	Jul-02	7.83	11.94	12		-6.67%	-5.76%	-9.50%
31	Aug-02	7.78	11.73	12.37		-0.64%	-1.76%	3.08%
32	Sep-02	7.3	10.66	11.17		-6.17%	-9.12%	-9.70%
33	Oct-02	6.88	11.18	11.71		-5.75%	4.88%	4.83%
34	Nov-02	7.13	11.68	12.37		3.63%	4.47%	5.64%
35	Dec-02	6.92	11.34	11.77		-2.95%	-2.91%	-4.85%
36	Jan-03	6.74	10.91	11.24		-2.60%	-3.79%	-4.50%
37	Feb-03	6.81	10.39	10.87		1.04%	-4.77%	-3.29%
38	Mar-03	6.43	10.38	11		-5.58%	-0.10%	1.20%
21	Oct-01	8.35	12.81	11.77		-0.12%	1.91%	5.37%
22	Nov-01	8.34	12.96	12.49		-0.12%	1.17%	6.12%
23	Dec-01	7.68	13.39	13.8		-7.91%	3.32%	10.49%
24	Jan-02	7.11	12.92	15.07		-7.42%	-3.51%	9.20%
25	Feb-02	7.44	12.71	14.69		4.64%	-1.63%	-2.52%
26	Mar-02	8.1	13.37	16.23		8.87%	5.19%	10.48%
27	Apr-02	8.4	13.45	15.77		3.70%	0.60%	-2.83%
28	May-02	8.92	13.18	14.66		6.19%	-2.01%	-7.04%
29	Jun-02	8.39	12.67	13.26		-5.94%	-3.87%	-9.55%
30	Jul-02	7.83	11.94	12		-6.67%	-5.76%	-9.50%
31	Aug-02	7.78	11.73	12.37		-0.64%	-1.76%	3.08%
32	Sep-02	7.3	10.66	11.17		-6.17%	-9.12%	-9.70%
33	Oct-02	6.88	11.18	11.71		-5.75%	4.88%	4.83%
34	Nov-02	7.13	11.68	12.37		3.63%	4.47%	5.64%
35	Dec-02	6.92	11.34	11.77		-2.95%	-2.91%	-4.85%
36	Jan-03	6.74	10.91	11.24		-2.60%	-3.79%	-4.50%
37	Feb-03	6.81	10.39	10.87		1.04%	-4.77%	-3.29%
38	Mar-03	6.43	10.38	11		-5.58%	-0.10%	1.20%
39	Apr-03	6.38	11.5	12.78		-0.78%	10.79%	16.18%
40	May-03	6.76	12.2	13.31		5.96%	6.09%	4.15%
41	Jun-03	7.24	12.25	13.67		7.10%	0.41%	2.70%
42	Jul-03	7.57	12.12	14.29		4.56%	-1.06%	4.54%
43	Aug-03	8.26	12.14	14.14		9.11%	0.17%	-1.05%
44	Sep-03	8.72	12.51	14.57		5.57%	3.05%	3.04%
45	Oct-03	9.2	13.5	15.09		5.50%	7.91%	3.57%
46	Nov-03	8.92	13.82	15.42		-3.04%	2.37%	2.19%
47	Dec-03	9.6	15.28	16.89		7.62%	10.56%	9.53%
48	Jan-04	9.62	15.21	18.17		0.21%	-0.46%	7.58%
49	Feb-04	9.67	15.93	19.47		0.52%	4.73%	7.15%
50	Mar-04	10.83	15.55	20.53		12.00%	-2.39%	5.44%
51	Apr-04	10.1	15.29	18.6		-6.74%	-1.67%	-9.40%
52	May-04	9.95	15.6	19.14		-1.49%	2.03%	2.90%
53	Jun-04	10.58	15.84	19.27		6.33%	1.54%	0.68%
54	Jul-04	9.8	15.47	18.83		-7.37%	-2.34%	-2.28%
55	Aug-04	9.94	15.65	19.2		1.43%	1.16%	1.96%
56	Sep-04	9.66	16.02	20.22		-2.82%	2.36%	5.31%
57	Oct-04	9.89	16.48	21.22		2.38%	2.87%	4.95%
58	Nov-04	10.27	17.42	23.06		3.84%	5.70%	8.67%
59	Dec-04	10.92	18.09	25.16		6.33%	3.85%	9.11%
60	Jan-05	10.59	17.65	25.09		-3.02%	-2.43%	-0.28%
61	Feb-05	10.81	18.58	26.86		2.08%	5.27%	7.05%
62	Mar-05	10.49	18.13	24.13		-2.96%	-2.42%	-10.16%
63	Apr-05	10.25	17.91	23.55		-2.29%	-1.21%	-2.40%
64	May-05	10.05	17.74	24.41		-1.95%	-0.95%	3.65%
65								
66	=(B64-B63)/B63			Average =		-0.39%	0.21%	1.11%
67				St. Dev. =		5.49%	4.17%	7.20%
68	=AVERAGE(F4:F64)							
69								
70				=STDEV(F4:F64)				
71								

During this five-year period, the Japan iShares experienced a negative average monthly return of –0.39 percent. The United Kingdom provided a meager 0.21 percent monthly return, while Mexico provided a high return of 1.11 percent. The Mexico market had the highest volatility, followed by Japan and the United Kingdom. The stock market performance of these three countries illustrates just how different the returns and risks can be internationally. The correlation analysis (see Chapter 4) below shows that the Japanese and U.K. markets are not highly correlated. Neither are the Japanese and Mexican markets. However, the U.K. and Mexican markets are highly correlated. This suggests that an investor can diversify by buying these three iShares.

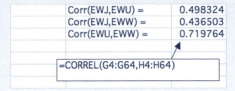

Corr(EWJ,EWU) =	0.498324
Corr(EWJ,EWW) =	0.436503
Corr(EWU,EWW) =	0.719764

=CORREL(G4:G64,H4:H64)

ST17.2 Using the characteristics in ST17.1, compute the expected return and standard deviation of a portfolio consisting of 20 percent iShares Japan, 40 percent iShares U.K., and 40 percent iShares Mexico.

Solution

The expected return for the portfolio, as given in Chapter 4, is

$$E(R_P) = \sum_{i=1}^{N} W_i E(R_i) = 0.2 \times -0.39\% + 0.4 \times 0.21\% + 0.4 \times 1.11\% = 0.45\%$$

The standard deviation is

$$SD(R_P) = \sqrt{\sum_{i=1}^{N} W_i^2 \times VAR(R_i) + \sum_{i=1}^{N}\sum_{j=1}^{N} W_i \times W_j \times COV(R_i R_j)}$$

$$= \sqrt{\sum_{i=1}^{3} W_i^2 \times VAR(R_i) + \sum_{i=1}^{3}\sum_{j=1}^{3} W_i \times W_j \times SD_i \times SD_j \times CORR(R_i, R_j)}$$

$$SD(R_P) = \sqrt{\begin{matrix} 0.2^2 \times 0.0549^2 + 0.4^2 \times 0.0417^2 + 0.4^2 \times 0.0720^2 + 0.2 \times 0.4 \times 0.0549 \times 0.0417 \times 0.498 + \\ 0.2 \times 0.4 \times 0.0549 \times 0.0720 \times 0.437 + 0.4 \times 0.4 \times 0.0417 \times 0.0720 \times 0.720 \end{matrix}}$$

$$= \sqrt{0.0022} = 0.0466 = 4.66\%$$

This portfolio has an expected return of 0.45 percent per month and a risk level indicated by the standard deviation of 4.66 percent. Note that this portfolio doubles the expected return of owning just the iShares U.K. with only slightly more risk.

Questions and Problems

17.1 What is the difference between a weak dollar and a strong dollar, and what are the implications for the balance of trade?

17.2 List three common economic characteristics that tend to be shared by emerging markets.

17.3 What are American Depository Receipts, and how do they simplify foreign stock ownership by U.S. investors?

17.4 U.S. investors can achieve global diversification through stock ownership in large U.S.-based multinationals. Describe four advantages for U.S. investors from the investment in U.S.-based multinationals.

17.5 Explain how different accounting standards among countries can impact valuation techniques.

17.6 Describe some of the benefits of including foreign securities in a portfolio of domestic securities.

17.7 Summarize the risks an investor faces when investing in foreign firms.

17.8 Explain some of the problems in comparing the performance of the Nikkei 225 with that of the FTSE 100.

17.9 Can an investor create a globally diversified portfolio with as little as $15,000? If so, how?

17.10 How much of the following foreign currency could be bought with $500?

Currency	Exchange rate
Euro	€1 /$1.225
British pound	£0.545/$1
Japanese yen	¥110.87/$1

17.11 Characterize the weighting scheme used to calculate MSCI market indexes.

17.12 What is the difference between an MSCI free index and an MSCI nonfree index?

17.13 What is home bias, and how can it affect portfolio returns?

17.14 *The World Fact Book,* published online by the U.S. Central Intelligence Agency at **www.cia.gov/cia/publications/factbook/index.html**, is a wonderful information resource for students, businesses, and government officials. Go to the most recent online version of *The World Fact Book*, and summarize the economic overview provided for China.

17.15 Go to the MSCI Web site (**www.mscibarra.com**). Which MSCI equity index has been the top performer during the last 12 months in local currency and in U.S. dollars? (Click on the Equities link and then on the All Countries link under "Markets.")

17.16 J.P. Morgan maintains adr.com, a free Web site designed to provide comprehensive information to investors about investing opportunities in American depository receipts (ADRs). Go to the adr.com Web Site (**www.adr.com**) and list the 10 most actively traded ADRs during the most recent trading day.

17.17 Go to the Standard & Poor's Market Insight Web site at **www.mhhe.com/ edumarketinsight** and enter the "Company" section. Use the Population menu to examine the companies covered by the site. Pick a company that is an ADR. You can verify that it is an ADR by finding Form 20-F in the "Annual" section of the EDGAR menu. Using this form, determine what country the company is from. What U.S. exchange does it trade on?

STANDARD &POOR'S

17.18 Suppose an investor takes $10,000 and converts it into Australian dollars at the exchange rate of A$1 = $0.718. With Australian dollars, the investor then buys shares of an Aussie company selling for A$25 per share. One year later, the stock is selling for A$30 and the exchange rate has changed to A$1 = $0.726. What is the investor's total return? What part of this return was due to the company return, and what was due to currency fluctuation?

17.19 Calculate the expected return and standard deviation of a portfolio formed by allocating 75 percent to domestic stocks and 25 percent to foreign stocks. Assume the domestic portfolio has an expected return of 11 percent and a standard deviation of 25 percent and the foreign portfolio has an expected return of 14 percent and a standard deviation of 40 percent. The two portfolios have a covariance of 175 percent. (See Chapter 4 for the expected return and risk equations.)

17.20   A U.S. investor who buys Japanese bonds will *most likely* maximize his or her return if interest rates:

a. Fall and the dollar weakens relative to the yen

b. Fall and the yen weakens relative to the dollar

c. Rise and the dollar weakens relative to the yen

d. Rise and the yen weakens relative to the dollar

investment application

The Templeton Touch

Sir John Templeton is one of the 20th century's greatest investors. In the 1950s, long before it became fashionable, Templeton scoured the globe looking for investment opportunities. Templeton's investment strategy is contrarian and value-oriented. He is perhaps most famous for being among the first foreign investors to commit money to Japan.

In the early 1960s, the Tokyo market was selling at 4 times earnings, while in the United States stocks were selling at 16 times earnings. With the Tokyo market at only one-fourth the average P/E ratio of the U.S. market, Templeton spied a bargain. He was able to buy some of the finest Japanese growth companies at only three times earnings. Of course, Templeton's strategy of buying Japanese bargains was criticized by U.S. investors who preferred market bellwether IBM, then a darling of growth-stock investors and selling at a P/E ratio of 33 times earnings. Indeed, at the time, the market capitalization of the entire Japanese market was less than that accorded to IBM. The consensus among professional money managers was that Japanese stocks were risky; IBM was viewed as a safe and secure blue chip. However, Templeton believed that at only one-tenth the P/E of IBM, outstanding Japanese growth stocks offered investors a significant investment opportunity. Templeton was right. Within a few years, the rest of the world caught on to the bargains represented by well-run Japanese companies, and the P/E ratio of a typical Japanese growth stock rose to 33 times earnings. By then, Templeton was off to other world markets seeking more and better bargains.

Today, Templeton is widely regarded as the dean of global investing even though he is no longer involved with active portfolio management. In 1992, Templeton retired after a 50-year career of helping investors manage their money and sold his huge mutual fund complex to Franklin Resources, Inc. Templeton now devotes all his energy to the John Templeton Foundation, a nonprofit organization devoted to the scientific study of world religions. Templeton's investment philosophy lives on with the Templeton Group of funds, a collection of global and world equity funds managed by investment professionals that Templeton hired. Moreover, Templeton is a frequent commentator on investment trends in the print and broadcast media, so investors are able to hear his ongoing advice on a regular basis.

Templeton's investment philosophy is based on four simple bedrock principles. The first of these is that the thrifty will eventually own the spendthrifts. Templeton realized early on that, more than just wanting to be rich, the only sure way to wealth is to save part of what you earn and invest the proceeds in securities that will make you wealthy. As a young couple, Templeton and his wife decided to save a whopping 50 percent of their combined gross income. Even in the investment community, such thriftiness is rare. According to Templeton, few security analysts or Wall Street brokers are thrifty. Although many on Wall Street make amazing incomes, often in the hundreds of thousands of dollars per year, few are sufficiently thrifty to become truly wealthy.

Templeton's second investment principle is that investors should buy at the point of maximum pessimism and sell at the point of maximum optimism. According to Templeton, it is only human nature to be afraid to buy when stories of failure abound. It is also human nature to cast caution to the wind when boastful stories of easy profits are common. The lowest price for any actively traded security can occur only at the point of maximum pessimism. Markets go up in anticipation of good news. It is the beginning of such anticipation, and not the good news itself, that causes prices to rise.

Templeton's third investment principle is that all assets are risky, including cash. When investors say that they are going to play it safe by selling stocks and holding cash, they are merely trading one risky class of assets for another. With inflation common around the globe, cash is losing purchasing power in virtually every nation. Income-producing assets such as common stocks maintain long-run value better than bonds, cash, collectibles, gold, real estate, or virtually any other asset. In every nation, purchasing power fluctuates widely and rapidly for every asset.

Templeton's fourth principle is that outstanding relative performance requires a contrarian attitude. If an investor buys the same securities as everyone else, the exact same investment results will be achieved. Superior investment performance requires investing differently from the crowd. If 10 medical doctors tell a patient to take a certain medicine, the patient is wise to follow their advice. However, if 10 investment advisors tell an investor to buy a given stock, that popularity will already be reflected in a high stock price. The investor would be wise to shun the overwhelming consensus of investment information.

How well has Templeton's commonsense approach to investing performed over the years? A $10,000 investment in the Templeton Growth Fund made in 1954 would now be worth more than $4.5 million. Templeton investors have been well served by the global search for more and better investment bargains.

a. In your opinion, why do few high-income Wall Street professionals manage to accumulate significant personal wealth?

b. In today's investment environment, would it be more difficult to duplicate Templeton's long-term success?

www.mhhe.com/hirschey1e

18

Option Markets and Strategies

In July 2005, online auction house eBay, Inc., reported surprisingly strong earnings and its stock price jumped. Internet service provider Yahoo!, Inc., reported disappointing earnings, and its stock price tumbled. Believing that the market had overreacted to these two announcements, James Stewart, an editor for *Smart Money* magazine and a well-respected author, sold call options on eBay and used the proceeds to buy an equivalent amount of Yahoo! call options. Being short eBay calls meant that Stewart stood to profit if eBay's stock stabilized or declined, and being long Yahoo! calls meant that Stewart also stood to profit if Yahoo!'s stock price jumped; but both stock prices had to move before the options expired in six months. As a service to his readers, Stewart implemented these trades and reported on the result in *The Wall Street Journal*.[1]

Nearly six months later, on Tuesday, January 17, Stewart was feeling smug. Yahoo! had risen in price and eBay had stagnated, just as Stewart had predicted. The Yahoo! and eBay options would expire only three days later, on Friday, January 20, and Stewart anticipated receiving $8 for the Yahoo! calls and paying $1 to repurchase the eBay calls. It looked like a profit of $700 was going to be made on each pair of call-option contracts. Then, just three days before expiration, eBay announced good earnings and Yahoo! announced tepid results. Thus eBay's stock price surged and Yahoo!'s stock price plunged. Yahoo! calls nose-dived from $8 to 15 cents, while eBay calls skyrocketed to $2.50. By expiration, Stewart's option speculation ended with zero profits.

This well-chronicled bit of speculation in the option market illustrates several important lessons. The high degree of leverage implicit in options can cause prices to change dramatically, especially in the period just prior to expiration. Profits can become losses literally overnight. Also, options commonly expire worthless. This all makes profitable speculation in the option market exceptionally difficult for even the most sophisticated speculators. Novice speculators take note.

---

[1]James B. Stewart, "A Lesson from the Options Game: Being Greedy Doesn't Pay Off," *The Wall Street Journal Online*, January 25, 2006 (**http://online.wsj.com**).

CHAPTER OBJECTIVES

- Understand the characteristics of call and put options.
- Know the different types of options.
- Be able to implement covered-call and protective-put strategies.
- Utilize the Black-Scholes option pricing formula.

Option Markets

Origin and Evolution

On April 26, 1973, the **Chicago Board Options Exchange (CBOE)** pioneered the concept of standardized, listed options to be traded on a centralized and regulated marketplace. An **option contract** is the right to buy or to sell a given amount or value of a particular asset at a fixed price until a given expiration date. A **call option** gives the right to buy; a **put option** gives the right to sell. Options are **derivative securities** because their economic value is derived, or stems, from changes in the value of some other asset. Listing call options on just 16 common stocks, the CBOE traded a mere 911 contracts on its first day of business. Put options were introduced in 1977 (see **www.cboe.com**).

Today, almost all actively traded stocks have option contracts available. Trading volume has grown steadily. In 2005, for example, the option industry traded over 1.5 billion contracts—three times the volume in 1999. As shown in Figure 18.1, the majority of option volume comes from options on equity securities, but nonequity option volume is growing. Over the past few years, equity options have become widely accepted as versatile instruments that can be used to help meet a variety of individual investor needs. Options are actively traded on nearly 2,700 underlying equities and more than 100 nonequity securities.

Chicago Board Options Exchange (CBOE)
U.S. options market pioneer.

Option contract
Right to buy or to sell a given amount or value of a particular asset at a fixed price until a given expiration date.

Call option
Right to buy.

Put option
Right to sell.

Derivative securities
Financial instruments with value stemming from changes in the value of some other asset.

FIGURE 18.1   Trading Activity in Equity Option Contracts Has Risen Sharply

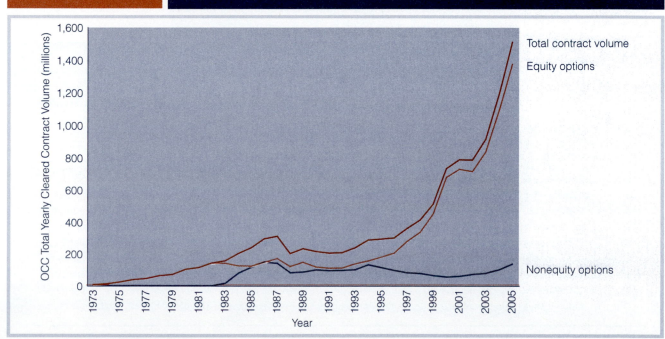

Source: The Options Clearing Corporation.

Characteristics of Exchange-Traded Options

The economic resources and financial integrity provided by major option exchanges contribute the foundation necessary to maintain orderly, efficient, and liquid option markets. In response to rapidly growing investor demand, actively traded exchange-listed options are presently available on four types of underlying assets (or interests): equity securities, stock indexes, government debt securities, and foreign currencies. Each option market selects the underlying assets on which options are traded. Options on other types of underlying assets may become available in the future.

Actively traded options have standardized terms such as the nature and amount of the underlying asset, the expiration date, the exercise price, the option type, and the manner of contract fulfillment (or settlement). Trading activity in the option markets is wholly determined by the forces of supply and demand, and it flexibly expands and contracts as warranted. Composite trading volume is the amount of daily trading activity on the five major option exchanges. The number of outstanding options is commonly referred to as **open interest** and depends on the number of buyers and sellers interested in receiving and conferring these rights. At any point in time, total open interest for equity options stands at roughly 160 million contracts representing 16 billion shares of common stock.

Composite trading volume and open interest tend to be high for stock options tied to volatile common stocks with several institutional and individual shareholders. Activity in stock options tends to be highest for an **exercise price**, or **strike price**, that is near the current market price for the underlying common stock. The exercise price of an option is the price at which the shares of stock can be bought by the buyer of a call option or be sold by the buyer of a put option. Strike prices are set at the time trading is initiated. When the price of the underlying security is equal to the strike price, the option is said to be **at-the-money**. A call option is **in-the-money** if the strike price is less than the market price of the underlying security (see Table 18.1). A put option is in-the-money if the strike price is greater than the market price of the underlying security. A call option is **out-of-the-money** if the strike price is greater than the market price of the underlying security. A put option is out-of-the money if the strike price is less than the market price of the underlying security. Figure 18.2 shows quotes for call and put options for Microsoft. Microsoft stock was trading at $26.93 per share. The most popular options had strike prices of $22.50, $25, $27.50, and $30.

Standardized strike price and expiration month codes are combined with company-specific ticker symbols to give option traders unique symbols for call and put options. The trading symbol for stock options is often a simple combination of the stock ticker symbol, a letter to indi-

---

Open interest
Number of outstanding options.

Exercise price
Purchased (call) or sale (put) price for an exercised option contract.

Strike price
Exercise price.

At-the-money
Option whose strike price equals the current market price of the underlying asset.

In-the-money
Option whose strike price is less (more) than the market price of the underlying security for a call (put).

Out-of-the-money
Option whose strike price is more (less) than the market price of the underlying security for a call (put).

TABLE 18.1

Call and Put Options *Call (put) options are in-the-money when the stock price exceeds (is less than) the strike price; call (put) options are out-of-the-money when the stock price is less than (exceeds) the strike price.*

	Call-Option Strike Price			Put-Option Strike Price		
Stock Price	**$45**	**$50**	**$55**	**$45**	**$50**	**$55**
$45	**At-the-money**	Out-of-the-money	Out-of-the-money	**At-the-money**	In-the-money	In-the-money
$47	In-the-money	Out-of-the-money	Out-of-the-money	Out-of-the-money	In-the-money	In-the-money
$49	In-the-money	Out-of-the-money	Out-of-the-money	Out-of-the-money	In-the-money	In-the-money
$50	In-the-money	**At-the-money**	Out-of-the-money	Out-of-the-money	**At-the-money**	In-the-money
$51	In-the-money	In-the-money	Out-of-the-money	Out-of-the-money	Out-of-the-money	In-the-money
$53	In-the-money	In-the-money	Out-of-the-money	Out-of-the-money	Out-of-the-money	In-the-money
$55	In-the-money	In-the-money	**At-the-money**	Out-of-the-money	Out-of-the-money	**At-the-money**
$57	In-the-money	In-the-money	In-the-money	Out-of-the-money	Out-of-the-money	Out-of-the-money
$59	In-the-money	In-the-money	In-the-money	Out-of-the-money	Out-of-the-money	Out-of-the-money

FIGURE 18.2 Call- and Put-Option Quotes and Volume for Microsoft

MSFT												26.93 −0.04
Mar 05, 2006 @ 18:27 ET (Data 15 Minutes Delayed)							**Bid** 26.93 **Ask** 26.93 **Size** 14 x 146 **Vol** 45234151					

Calls	Last Sale	Net	Bid	Ask	Vol	Open Int	Puts	Last Sale	Net	Bid	Ask	Vol	Open Int
06 Mar 22.50 (MSQ CX-E)	4.60	pc	4.40	4.50	0	667	06 Mar 22.50 (MSQ OX-E)	0.05	pc	0	0.05	0	110
06 Mar 25.00 (MSQ CJ-E)	2.15	+0.10	1.95	2.00	47	14613	06 Mar 25.00 (MSQ OJ-E)	0.05	pc	0	0.05	0	17347
06 Mar 27.50 (MSQ CY-E)	0.10	—	0.05	0.15	2578	79580	06 Mar 27.50 (MSQ OY-E)	0.65	+0.10	0.60	0.70	883	16534
06 Mar 30.00 (MSQ CK-E)	0.05	pc	0	0.05	0	23610	06 Mar 30.00 (MSQ OK-E)	2.90	−0.20	3.00	3.20	2	785
06 Apr 22.50 (MSQ DX-E)	4.60	pc	4.50	4.60	0	13679	06 Apr 22.50 (MSQ PX-E)	0.05	pc	0	0.05	0	35081
06 Apr 25.00 (MSQ DJ-E)	2.15	—	2.10	2.20	30	57696	06 Apr 25.00 (MSQ PJ-E)	0.10	pc	0.05	0.10	0	49933
06 Apr 27.50 (MSQ DY-E)	0.35	−0.05	0.35	0.40	461	147305	06 Apr 27.50 (MSQ PY-E)	0.80	+0.05	0.75	0.85	128	34125
06 Apr 30.00 (MSQ DK-E)	0.05	pc	0	0.05	0	115365	06 Apr 30.00 (MSQ PK-E)	3.08	pc	3.00	3.10	0	670

Source: Chicago Board Options Exchange. © 2006 Chicago Board Options Exchange. Used courtesy of CBOE.

cate the month of the year, and a final letter to indicate strike price. As shown in Table 18.2, the letter *A* is used to indicate a strike price of $5 (or $105, $205, etc.); *B*, a strike price of $10; *C*, a strike price of $15; and so on. A $5 increment in strike prices is most common, but strike price increments of $2.50 are sometimes used for low-priced stocks or for stocks with unusually active option buyer and option seller interest. The table also shows the code for option month expiration. The letter *A* denotes a call option that expires in January. The letter *W* denotes a put option that expires in November. The Microsoft option quotes in Figure 18.2 show these codes. The ticker MSQ CX denotes a Microsoft put option that expires in March and has a strike price of $22.50. The "-E" at the end of the ticker in the figure denotes that this quote comes from the CBOE.

Options that have the same standardized terms but different strike prices constitute an **option series**. The standardization of terms makes it more likely that there will be a secondary market in which **holders**, or buyers, and **writers**, or sellers, of options can close out their positions by offsetting sales and purchase transactions. The length of time between the date that an option contract is established and the date of its expiration is the **contract period**. The market price for an option is the **option premium**. The premium is the amount paid by the buyer to the writer, or seller, of the option. For this amount, the writer of the call option is obligated to deliver the underlying security if the call is exercised. Alternatively, the writer of a put option is required to buy the underlying security if the put is exercised. Writers keep the premium whether or not the option is exercised. It is a nonrefundable payment from the option holder to the option writer for the rights conveyed by the option. Premium amounts are subject to continuous change in response to the economic forces of supply and demand. Premiums are affected by the current value of the underlying asset, exercise price, values of related assets, expected volatility, and so on.

The most actively traded stock options tend to be calls with a short period of time until expiration. Investor interest tends to focus on short-term call options because they are more sensitive than long-term call options to near-term price changes in the underlying stock. In an effort to broaden the potential market for financial derivatives, option exchanges have introduced very long-term stock and index options called *long-term equity anticipation securities* **(LEAPS)**. Like short-term options, LEAPS are available in two types—calls and puts. The distinguishing feature of LEAPS is that they are available with expiration dates up to three years in the future at the time they are initially issued. All LEAPS options expire on the third Friday of January. These options appeal to investors who appreciate the leverage offered by options, but like the long-term investment horizon afforded to equity holders.

Option series
Options that have the same standardized terms but different strike prices.

Holders
Buyers of options.

Writers
Sellers who are obligated to exercise the option at the holder's request.

Contract period
Length of time between the date that an option contract is established and the date of its expiration.

Option premium
Option price.

Long-term equity anticipation securities (LEAPS)
Long-term calls and puts.

TABLE 18.2	Option Ticker Codes

Expiration-Month Code

	Jan	Feb	Mar	Apr	May	Jun	Jul	Aug	Sep	Oct	Nov	Dec
Calls	A	B	C	D	E	F	G	H	I	J	K	L
Puts	M	N	O	P	Q	R	S	T	U	V	W	X

Strike Price Codes

A	B	C	D	E	F	G	H	I	J	K	L	M
5	10	15	20	25	30	35	40	45	50	55	60	65
105	110	115	120	125	130	135	140	145	150	155	160	165
205	210	215	220	225	230	235	240	245	250	255	260	265
305	310	315	320	325	330	335	340	345	350	355	360	365
405	410	415	420	425	430	435	440	445	450	455	460	465
505	510	515	520	525	530	535	540	545	550	555	560	565
605	610	615	620	625	630	635	640	645	650	655	660	665
705	710	715	720	725	730	735	740	745	750	755	760	765

N	O	P	Q	R	S	T	U	V	W	X	Y	Z
70	75	80	85	90	95	100	7.50	12.50	17.50	22.50	27.50	32.50
170	175	180	185	190	195	200	37.50	42.50	47.50	52.50	57.50	62.50
270	275	280	285	290	295	300	67.50	72.50	77.50	82.50	87.50	92.50
370	375	380	385	390	395	400	97.50	102.50	107.50	112.50	117.50	122.50
470	475	480	485	490	495	500	127.50	132.50	137.50	142.50	147.50	152.50
570	575	580	585	590	595	600	157.50	162.50	167.50	172.50	177.50	182.50
670	675	680	685	690	695	700	187.50	192.50	197.50	202.50	207.50	212.50
770	775	780	785	790	795	800	217.50	222.50	227.50	232.50	237.50	242.50

Source: Chicago Board of Trade. © 2006, CBOT. Used with permission.

Option Market Characteristics

In the United States, options are traded on the Chicago Board Options Exchange, American Stock Exchange, Pacific Exchange, and Philadelphia Stock Exchange. In May 2000, the International Securities Exchange (ISE), an electronic exchange, began trading options. Since then, it has steadily increased its share of the total options traded in the United States. Increasingly, options on the same equity securities or equity indexes are traded on more than one option market at the same time. Options traded on U.S. option markets may also be traded on foreign option markets. In early 2006, the ISE was trading more option contracts than the CBOE. The ISE has roughly a 34 percent market share, while the CBOE has roughly a 27 percent market share.

Market makers
Dealers who provide for an orderly market.

Floor brokers
Agents who execute public option orders.

Options Clearing Corporation (OCC)
Issuer of all listed securities options.

Market makers provide liquidity in option trading by risking their own capital for personal trading. They are the backbone of the option trading system. **Floor brokers**, on the other hand, act as agents, executing orders for public or firm accounts. The **Options Clearing Corporation (OCC)** is the sole issuer of all securities options listed on exchanges and with the National Association of Securities Dealers (NASD), Inc. The OCC is a registered clearing agency, and it is the entity through which all option transactions are ultimately cleared. Each U.S. option market is subject to regulation by the Securities and Exchange Commission (SEC) under the Securities Exchange Act of 1934. As the issuer of all exchange-traded options in the United States, the OCC takes the opposite side of every option traded and allows option traders to buy and sell in a secondary market without having to find the original opposite party. The OCC guarantees contract performance and gives buyers and sellers confidence that the option con-

Are Executive Stock Options Fair and Effective?

To ensure proper motivation for top-flight corporate CEOs, companies have come to rely heavily on executive stock options. Executive stock options have many of the same traits as standard call options that trade on organized exchanges. In a typical situation, CEOs are awarded the option to buy hundreds of thousands or millions of shares of stock at a fixed price for an extended time period. At the time of issuance, executive stock option grants are usually good for a 10-year period. The idea is to provide top executives with strong incentives to maximize shareholder value. As an added benefit, until recently, companies were able to avoid showing stock option expenses on their income statements. Not having to show a significant part of employee compensation on the income statement meant that expenses were understated and reported profits got a much-appreciated boost.

Corporate governance scandals during recent years have caused shareholder activists to take a closer look at stock option compensation. Some argue that stock options have led to massive top executive compensation that simply cannot be justified. During the 2000–2005 period, for example, Oracle's Lawrence J. Ellison was paid $867.8 million, UnitedHealth Group paid William W. McGuire $342.3 million, and Lehman Brothers paid Richard S. Fuld Jr. $307.1 million. In defense of these payouts, compensation experts point out that such executives are outstanding performers who have greatly enriched shareholders. Given the long time lag between the date that executive stock options are issued and the date that they are exercised, massive payouts in 2005 also reflect the cumulative effect of decade-long efforts on behalf of shareholders.

Nevertheless, valid criticisms of the executive stock option practices have been raised. When executives are rewarded with 10-year stock options featuring a fixed exercise price, even mediocre performers can reap outsized rewards. Incentive for above-average performance would be created if the strike prices for executive stock options were increased to reflect expected market appreciation. Also, the common practice of repricing options to lower strike prices following a general downturn in the market is difficult to justify. Lastly, while accounting and tax rules allow companies to grant stock options at below-market prices, there is no justification for the undisclosed "back-dating" of executive stock options to unfairly enrich top executives. Top executive abuse of accounting standards and tax regulations with respect to the option granting process is illegal, and deserves to be severely punished.

For interesting information on CEO compensation, see **www.forbes.com**.

---

tracts they enter into will be fulfilled at the agreed-on terms. As such, the OCC substantially reduces the credit risk aspect of trading securities options. Since every option transaction involves both a buyer and a seller, the aggregate rights of option buyers are matched by the aggregate obligations of option sellers. The OCC system is designed so that the performance of all options is between the OCC and a group of clearing member firms that carry the positions of all option buyers and option sellers in their accounts at OCC.

Try It!

Assume the stock of Dell, Inc., is trading for $35 per share. A call option and a put option are available for a given date at a strike price of $30. Which is more valuable, the call or the put?

Solution

The put option is out-of-the-money. The right to sell at $30 is not very useful when the stock price is $35. The call option is in-the-money. It has more value because the right to buy at $30 is worth at least $5 when the stock trades at $35.

Option Basics

Option Concept

The rapid growth of option markets can be explained by two important underlying causes. First, the option concept is an increasingly useful device for transferring investment risk in an interconnected and volatile global marketplace. Without this basic economic value, there would be no investor demand for option trading. Second, the introduction of standardized option contracts provides for orderly, efficient, and liquid option markets. Without the institutional framework provided by the option markets, demand for options would have been stifled.

Hedged position

Use of options to offset the risk inherent in some other investment.

Speculative position

Use of options to profit from the inherent riskiness of some underlying asset.

Because of their unique risk-reward characteristics, options can be used in combination with other financial instruments to create **hedged positions** or **speculative positions**. A hedged position is created when an option contract is used to offset the risk inherent in some other investment. Hedgers use options to limit risk. A speculative position is created when an option contract is used to profit from the inherent volatility of some underlying asset. Speculators assume risk by taking unhedged positions to profit from anticipated price changes. Options have speculative appeal because they often exhibit significant leverage. This leverage stems from the fact that options can often be purchased for a small fraction of the cost of the underlying asset. Of course, leverage not only magnifies the potential benefits from a favorable change in the price of the underlying asset but also magnifies the loss potential following an unfavorable change in price.

Zero-sum game

Transaction in which the buyer's gain is the seller's loss, and vice versa.

Before commissions and other transaction costs, option contracts represent a **zero-sum game** between the buyer and the seller. When the price of the underlying asset rises unexpectedly, the amount earned by the buyer of a call option is exactly equal to the amount lost by the seller. When the price of the underlying asset falls unexpectedly, the amount lost by the buyer of a call option is exactly equal to the amount earned by the seller. The same holds true for put options. Gains and losses for put buyers and sellers are equal in magnitude. A stock option contract is a side bet between the buyer and the seller about the short-term price action in a stock. No money is earned or lost by the company itself. Only option market participants are affected.

Transaction Type and Option Style

An option holder is said to be "long the option position"; the writer of an option position is said to be "short the position." Suppose a given investor buys a single December Ford 50 call at a contract price of $500 during the month of August in an opening transaction. This investor is long the contract. The option writer is considered to be short the contract. By October, assume that the contract price has increased to $800. To realize a $300 profit, the long investor can direct a broker to sell an offsetting December Ford 50 call in a closing transaction. If by October the market price of the option has decreased to $300, the long investor might decide to sell the option in a closing transaction, thereby limiting the amount of loss to $200.

American-style option

Option contract that can be exercised at any time between the date of purchase and the expiration date.

European-style option

Option contract that can be exercised only on the expiration date.

Expiration date

Last day of an American-style option or the single exercise date of a European-style option.

For **American-style options**, the option contract can be exercised at any time between the date of purchase and the expiration date. All company stock options traded in the United States are American-style options. **European-style options** are option contracts that can be exercised only on the **expiration date**. Most index options are European-style options. The expiration date is the last day of an American-style option or the single exercise date of a European-style option.

Settlement

Physical-delivery option

Option that entails the physical delivery of an asset.

Cash-settled option

Option that entails the promise of a cash payment based on the difference between market and exercise prices.

Contract size

Trading unit of an underlying asset.

Some options require physical delivery; others have cash settlement provisions. A **physical-delivery option** gives its owner the right to receive physical delivery of an asset if it is a call, or to make physical delivery of an asset if it is a put, when the option is exercised. In the case of stock options, physical delivery takes the form of a transfer of stock certificates that represent ownership of a specified number of shares. A **cash-settled option** gives the holder the right to receive a cash payment based on the difference between a determined value of the underlying interest at the time the option is exercised and the fixed exercise price of the option. A cash-settled call conveys the right to receive a cash payment if the settlement value exceeds the exercise price. A cash-settled put grants the right to receive a cash payment if the settlement value is less than the exercise price.

The unit of trading, or **contract size**, of a physical-delivery option is the quantity of an underlying asset that is subject to being purchased or sold on the exercise of a single contract. In the case of common stocks, option contracts are generally for 100 shares of stock unless adjusted for a special event, such as a stock split or a stock dividend. As described previously, a Microsoft 27.5 call gives the buyer the right on exercise to buy 100 shares of Microsoft common stock at $27.50 per share. If the option is trading at a market price of, say, $0.10 per share, the total price for a single option contract would be $10, plus commissions and other transaction costs. The contract size of a cash-settled option is determined by a multiplier fixed by the option market on which it is traded. This multiplier determines the aggregate value of each point of difference between the exercise price of the option and the exercise settlement value of the underlying asset. If an option with a multiplier of 100 is trading at a premium of $5, the aggregate premium for a single option contract would be $500.

The cash settlement amount is the amount of cash that the holder of a cash-settled option is entitled to receive on exercise. It is calculated as the difference between the exercise price and the exercise settlement value times the agreed-on multiplier for the option. For example, assume that a cash-settled call on the Nasdaq 100 index with a strike price of 125 is exercised when the exercise settlement value of the index is 130. If the multiplier for Nasdaq 100 index options is 100, the exercising holder would be entitled to receive a cash settlement amount of $500 [= ($130 – $125) × 100].

Equity option buyers have the right to either buy (call) or sell (put) stock at a predetermined price. If they choose to buy or sell at that predetermined price, they are said to **exercise** their right. At that point, the seller, or writer, has the obligation to sell or buy the stock. The seller of an option is said to be **assigned** when the seller is asked to fulfill his or her contract obligation. Typically, this occurs when the option is in-the-money at the time of expiration. Individual investors may be automatically assigned or exercised if they hold options that are ¼ of a point or more in-the-money at the time of expiration. If an option is out-of-the-money at the point of expiration, it expires worthlessly. At that point, the buyer or holder loses the premium paid for the option plus whatever commissions and fees were incurred on that transaction. However, it is worth remembering that the writer of an equity option contract in the United States should anticipate being assigned any time the option becomes in-the-money.

Exercise
Execution of option-holder rights.

Assigned
Execution of option-writer obligations.

The expiration date for stock options is the Saturday immediately following the third Friday of the expiration month. However, brokerage firms typically set an earlier deadline, such as 3 p.m. EST on the third Friday of the month, for notification of an option buyer's intention to exercise.

Option Types

Stock Options

Options share many similarities with common stocks. Both are listed securities. Orders to buy and sell options are handled through brokers in the same way as orders to buy and sell stocks. Listed option orders are executed on the trading floors of national SEC-regulated exchanges, where all trading is conducted in an open and competitive auction market. Like stocks, options trade with buyers making bids and sellers making offers. Option investors, like stock investors, have the ability to follow price movements, trading volume, and other pertinent information day by day or even minute by minute.

Despite these similarities, there are important differences between stock options and common stock. Unlike common stock, an option has a limited life. If an option is not closed out or exercised prior to its expiration date, it ceases to exist as a financial instrument. Unlike stock ownership, which conveys proportional ownership, voting rights, and dividends (if any), option ownership conveys only the potential benefit derived from favorable stock price movements.

While stock options generally cover 100 shares of the underlying security, this number of shares may be adjusted as a result of certain material events. Such material events include a significant stock dividend, stock distribution, stock split, rights offering, reorganization, recapitalization, or merger. As a general rule, no adjustment is made for ordinary cash dividends or distributions. A cash dividend or distribution by most issuers is generally considered ordinary unless it exceeds 10 percent of the aggregate market value of the underlying security.

| TABLE 18.3 | Sample of Index Options, March 4, 2006 |

Index	Index Value	CALL	Last	Volume	Open Interest	PUT	Last	Volume	Open Interest
S&P 100	583.92	Mar 585.0	3.80	3706	6,991	Mar 585.0	5.40	10,109	6,663
Dow Jones Industrial Average	110.22	Mar 110.0	1.05	5,999	24,879	Mar 110.0	0.75	1,843	25,919
Nasdaq 100	1,684.32	Mar 1,700.0	14.10	461	14,208	Mar 1,700.0	15.50	142	9,975
Russell 2000	738.40	Mar 730.0	17.00	1,000	8,566	Mar 730.0	6.30	1,111	8,330

Source: Chicago Board Options Exchange, **www.cboe.com**. © 2006 Chicago Board Options Exchange. Used courtesy of CBOE.

Index Options

All index options are settled by payment of a fixed cash amount, and cash-settled index options do not relate to a particular number of shares. Premiums for index options are expressed in points and fractions of points, where each point represents an amount equal to one U.S. dollar. The size of a cash-settled index option contract is determined by a multiplier and expressed in U.S. dollars. The most actively traded index option in the United Stated is the Standard & Poor's 100 Index (OEX). The OEX is fairly unique among broad-based index options in that American-style OEX options generally may be exercised on any business day before the expiration date. Almost all other broad-based index options traded in the United States are European-style options, meaning that they can be exercised only at the expiration date. Table 18.3 shows several popular index options.

For example, suppose an investor purchases a March 585 OEX call at 3.80. The multiplier for OEX index options is $100, meaning that the dollar value of the call premium for a single contract is $380 (= 3.80 × $100). The $100 multiplier is a convenient basis for index option value calculation and is used for many popular index options, such as those tied to the Dow Jones Industrial Average (DJX) and the Nasdaq 100 Index (NDX).

Debt Options

Price-based options
Rights to purchase or sell a specific debt security.

Yield-based options
Debt options that are cash-settled based on the difference between the exercise price and the value of an underlying yield.

Two kinds of debt options have been approved for trading. Physical-delivery **price-based options** give holders the right to purchase or sell a specific debt security. Cash-settled price-based options give holders the right to receive a cash payment based on the value of an underlying debt security. **Yield-based options** are debt options that are cash-settled based on the difference between the exercise price and the value of an underlying yield. Although price-based debt options have traded in the past, and may be traded in the future, no price-based options are presently traded. Only yield-based options are traded at the present time.

To understand debt options, investors must grasp the relationship between the yield to maturity and the prices for debt securities. Remember that declining interest rates cause prices of outstanding debt securities to increase. Rising interest rates cause the prices of outstanding debt securities to decline. If a 30-year Treasury bond pays a 7 percent coupon rate, the only time prior to maturity that investors will pay a price of 100 (or 100 percent of par value) would be when the prevailing yield on such long-term Treasury bonds is exactly 7 percent. If interest rates move up to 8.5 percent, the price of an outstanding 7 percent 30-year bond would fall to roughly 83⅞ for the bond to yield a competitive 8.5 percent. If rates on such bonds subsequently decline to 6 percent, the price of a 30-year 7 percent coupon bond would rise substantially above par to roughly 113⅓, where it would yield a competitive 6 percent rate of return.

The exercise settlement value of a yield-based option depends on the difference between the value of an underlying yield and the exercise price of the option. Since the underlying

Option Buyers and Sellers

Suppose a small option speculator wanted to bet on a jump in Google's stock price. It would be typical for such a speculator to buy a short-term call on Google. Speculative premiums on options for highly volatile stocks like Google are huge and diminish quickly as the expiration period comes to an end. Sellers of short-term call options are apt to be big institutions seeking to get a piece of the large speculative premium set to expire. A perfect hedge for the seller of Google calls is to be long that same option. Big profits are available only with imperfect hedges, however, so call option sellers might hedge by going long the underlying stock. Alternatively, they may be content to simply short the call as long as Google's stock price remains constant or falls. In such a case, the call-option seller stands to profit as the call premium quickly erodes and the ex-piration period comes to a close. Strengthening the hand of call-option sellers is the fact that they are able to short-sell the stock of companies with actively traded options to push their stock prices down just prior to expiration. Studies show that companies with actively traded options often close at or below popular strike prices on option expiration days.

Of course, trading in the stock market or the option market on the basis of inside information is illegal. Violators who get caught pay large fines and may go to jail. Still, it happens. The next time you want to speculate in the options market, be aware that the "game" you are playing may be stacked against you.

See Mohammed Hadi, "Options Trading of XM Remains Active as Shares Slide," *The Wall Street Journal Online*, February 18, 2006, p. C4 (**http://online.wsj.com**).

---

yields of yield-based options increase as interest rates rise, yield-based calls become more valuable as interest rates rise. Yield-based puts become more valuable as interest rates decline.

The underlying debt instruments of interest rate options are Treasury securities, including short-term Treasury bills, 5- and 10-year Treasury notes, and 30-year Treasury bonds. All are direct obligations of the U.S. government. Treasury bills do not pay interest, and they sell at a discount from par value. The return on T-bills is commonly expressed as a discount rate that represents an annualized yield to maturity based on a 360-day year. T-bonds and notes pay a fixed rate of interest semiannually. All yield-based options are European-style options and feature cash settlement. The underlying yield of these options is the annualized yield to maturity of the most recently issued Treasury security of a designated term to maturity. If the designated debt security is a T-bill, the underlying yield is the annualized discount rate of newly issued Treasury bills. The underlying yield is stated in terms of a yield indicator, which is the annual percentage yield multiplied by 10. For example, if the yield is based on a T-bill having an annualized discount rate of 6.215 percent, the yield indicator would be 62.15.

The aggregate cash settlement amount that the assigned writer of a yield-based option is obligated to pay the exercising option holder is the difference between the exercise price of the option and the exercise settlement value multiplied by the multiplier for the option. Different yield-based options have different multipliers. For example, an exercise price of 63.50 would represent a yield of 6.35 percent. Each point of premium corresponds to 0.1 percent of yield. The dollar value of the premium for a single yield-based option equals the quoted premium multiplied by the dollar value of the option multiplier. Thus, a premium of $3.50 would equal a premium of $350 (= $3.50 × 100) for an option having a multiplier of 100 or a premium of $700 (= $3.50 × 200) for an option having a multiplier of 200.

Option Strategies

Call Strategies

Buying call options is a simple and popular option strategy for bullish investors. Buying calls gives the owner the right, but not the obligation, to purchase the underlying stock at a specified strike price for a limited period of time. The right to buy stock at a fixed price becomes more valuable as the price of the underlying stock increases. Risk for the call buyer is limited to the call premium, or the amount paid for the call, plus commissions. The call buyer's profit potential is unlimited when the underlying stock price rises above the break-even price. The call buyer's break-even point is reached when the market price of the underlying stock rises during the contract period to a level equal to the strike price plus the premium paid for the call plus commissions.

For example, Figure 18.3, Panel A, shows the profit or loss earned by a call buyer who is long one strike price 50 call that was purchased for a call premium of $2 per share, or $200 for a single contract covering 100 shares. For simplicity, this example assumes that the call position is maintained until the time of expiration and that commissions are nil. In reality, call buyers often liquidate their positions prior to expiration, and commission charges for option traders can be substantial.

Notice that the call buyer is in a loss position unless the stock price rises to $52, the strike price of $50 plus the per-share call premium of $2. For stock prices above $52, the call buyer's profit per share will rise dollar for dollar with the stock price. If the stock price is below $52 at the time of expiration, the call buyer will lose money on the call purchase. However, the amount of the call buyer's loss can be no more than $2 per share, or $200 for one call contract. Call buyers have unlimited profit potential with limited loss potential.

FIGURE 18.3 Call Options Are Popular with Bullish Investors

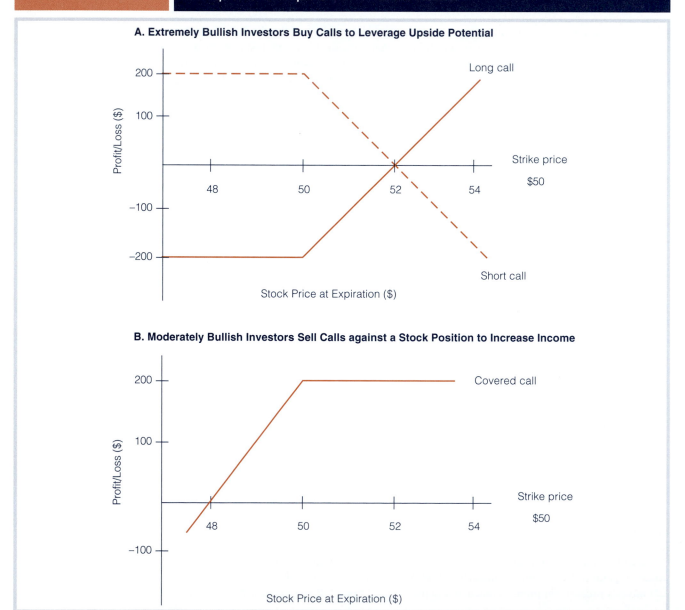

A. Extremely Bullish Investors Buy Calls to Leverage Upside Potential

B. Moderately Bullish Investors Sell Calls against a Stock Position to Increase Income

While an investor who expects a quick rise in the price of a stock might wish to purchase calls, the seller of call options expects to profit from stagnant stock prices. The seller, or writer, of a call option incurs the obligation to sell the underlying stock at a predetermined price if so requested by the buyer of the call option, or the call holder. Option transactions are a zero-sum game, where the call buyer's profit comes at the expense of the call seller. Similarly, any call seller's profit comes at the expense of the call buyer. As shown in Figure 18.3, Panel A, the profit for an investor who sells (or is short) a call option has a payoff pattern that is the mirror image of the payoff pattern for the call buyer. The call seller is in a profit position until the stock price rises above $52, the strike price of $50 plus the per-share call premium of $2. For stock prices above $52, the call seller's loss per share will rise dollar for dollar with the stock price. If the stock price is below $52 at the time of expiration, the call seller will make money on the call sale. The amount of the call seller's profit can be no more than $2 per share, or $200 for one call contract. Call sellers have unlimited loss potential with limited profit potential.

Call buying is a popular option strategy for speculators because stock prices often rise and calls give holders the potential to profit mightily from a steep rise in stock prices. Individual investors also find appealing the fact that calls give the holder the opportunity for large gains with strictly limited losses. However, investors must remember that call buyers profit only when the price of the underlying stock rises far enough and fast enough to exceed the strike price plus the option premium plus commissions prior to the expiration date for the option. Call sellers expect to make a profit too, and the amount charged for call premiums has to be large enough to give call sellers *and* call buyers a profit-making opportunity.

Figure 18.3, Panel B, shows the profit potential for a **covered-call** strategy. A covered call is the sale of a call option on a stock that is owned. Generally, one call option is sold for every 100 shares of stock owned. The covered-call writer receives call premium income in payment for agreeing to sell the underlying stock at the strike price. Because the covered-call writer owns the underlying stock, the investor's option position is hedged against an upside move in the stock price. Risk is limited for the covered-call writer because such an investor can deliver previously purchased shares following an unexpectedly sharp jump in the underlying stock price. A covered-call strategy appeals to investors who are neutral to moderately bullish on a stock or who are bullish about a given company but wary about the overall market. A disadvantage of the covered-call strategy is that it has limited profit potential. High-flying stocks get called away, while underperforming or declining stocks get retained by the covered-call writer. Moreover, high commissions and other transaction costs can dramatically reduce the call premium income generated.

Covered call
Simultaneous purchase of a stock and sale of a call option on that same security.

Put Strategies

Buying put options is a simple and popular option strategy for bearish speculators. Buying puts gives the owner the right, but not the obligation, to sell an underlying stock at the specified strike price for a limited period of time. The right to sell stock at a fixed price becomes more valuable as the price of the underlying stock decreases. Risk for the put buyer is limited to the put premium, or the amount paid for the put, plus commissions. The put buyer's profit potential is limited only by the fact that the price of the underlying stock can fall no lower than zero. The put buyer's break-even point is reached when the market price of the underlying stock falls during the contract period by an amount more than the strike price plus the premium paid for the put plus commissions.

For example, Figure 18.4, Panel A, shows the profit or loss earned by a put buyer who is long one strike price 50 put that was purchased for a put premium of $2 per share, or $200 for a single contract covering 100 shares. For simplicity, this example assumes that the put position is maintained until the time of expiration and that commissions are nil. In reality, put buyers often liquidate their positions prior to expiration, and commission charges for options traders can be substantial.

Notice that the put buyer is in a loss position unless the stock price falls to $48, the strike price of $50 minus the per-share put premium of $2. For stock prices below $48, the put buyer's profit per share will rise dollar for dollar as the underlying stock price falls. If the stock price is above $48 at the time of expiration, the put buyer will lose money on the put purchase.

However, the amount of the put buyer's loss can be no more than $2 per share, or $200 for one put contract. Put buyers have profit potential that is limited only by the fact that the underlying stock price can fall to no less than zero.

While an investor who expects a quick drop in the price of a stock might wish to purchase puts, the seller of put options expects to profit from stagnant or rising stock prices. The seller, or writer, of a put option incurs the obligation to buy the underlying stock at a predetermined price if requested by the buyer of the put option, or the put holder. As in the case of call options, the put buyer's profit comes at the expense of the put seller. Similarly, any put seller's profit comes at the expense of the put buyer. As shown in Figure 18.4, Panel A, the profit for an investor who sells (or is short) a put option has a payoff pattern that is the mirror image of the payoff pattern for the put buyer. The put seller is in a profit position until the stock price drops below $48, the strike price of $50 minus the per-share put premium of $2. For stock prices below $48, the put seller's loss per share will rise dollar for dollar as the underlying share price declines. If the stock price is above $48 at the time of expiration, the put seller

| FIGURE 18.4 | Put Options Are Popular with Bearish Investors |

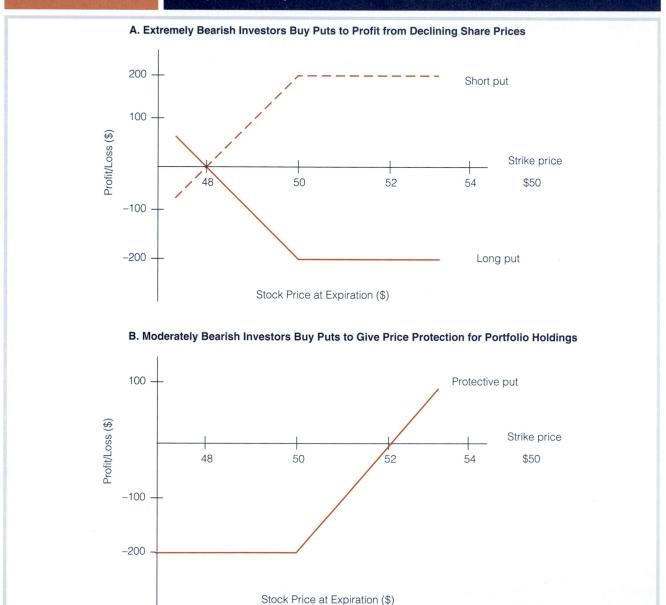

A. Extremely Bearish Investors Buy Puts to Profit from Declining Share Prices

B. Moderately Bearish Investors Buy Puts to Give Price Protection for Portfolio Holdings

will make money on the put sale. However, the amount of the put seller's profit can be no more than $2 per share, or $200 for one put contract. Put sellers have limited profit potential and have loss potential that is limited only by the fact that underlying share prices can fall no lower than zero.

During typically bullish market conditions, put buying is a money-losing proposition. However, investors must remember that selling uncovered puts is far from a risk-free investment strategy. During the stock market crash of 1987 and other sharp breaks in the market, put sellers suffered enormous losses. Despite the potential for small, regular profits from selling uncovered puts, infrequent but enormous losses can undermine the appeal of put selling strategies.

Puts are often used as insurance against a sharp correction in the overall market. Figure 18.4, Panel B, shows the profit potential for a **protective-put** strategy. A protective put is the simultaneous purchase of a stock and purchase of a put option on that same security. Generally, one put option is bought for every 100 shares of stock owned. The buyer of a protective put pays cash for the put but gains piece of mind from the fact that the investor's loss potential on the purchase of the underlying stock has been strictly limited. Risk is limited for the protective-put buyer because the holder has the option of delivering the underlying shares at the put strike price following an unexpectedly sharp drop in the underlying stock price. Because the protective-put buyer owns the underlying stock, the investor has unlimited upside potential following an upward surge in the underlying stock price. Protective-put buying is a conservative option strategy that is sometimes used by pension and index funds that hold large positions of common stocks. Nevertheless, a disadvantage of the protective-put strategy is that this type of portfolio insurance is expensive, especially during turbulent markets.

> **Protective put**
> Simultaneous purchase of a stock and purchase of a put option on that same security.

Compare the covered-call profit picture of Figure 18.3 with the short put position in Figure 18.4. Both profit pictures look similar. Indeed, writing a covered call is very similar to writing a put option. You can create a put-option payoff by buying a call option on a stock that has been shorted; this is called a **synthetic** put position. Also notice that the protective put shown in Figure 18.4 appears similar to the picture for buying a call in Figure 18.3. This is called a synthetic call.

> **Synthetic (option)**
> A payoff derived from holding nonoption securities that is identical with a put or call strategy.

Try It!

An investor owns 200 shares of a stock currently priced at $40 per share. The investor writes two 45 calls, expiring in four months, for a premium of $1.50 each. Ignoring transaction costs, what is the dollar return of this covered-call position if the stock price at expiration is $38, $42, or $47?

Solution

The dollar return comes from both the stock and the option positions.

At stock price of $38: Dollar return = ($38 − $40) × 200 + $1.5 × 100 × 2 = −$400 + $300 = $100

At stock price of $42: Dollar return = ($42 − $40) × 200 + $1.5 × 100 × 2 = $400 + $300 = $700

At stock price of $47: Dollar return = ($47 − $40) × 200 + $1.5 × 100 × 2 − ($47 − $45) × 100 × 2 = $1,400 + $300 − $400 = $1,300.

Combinations

Option strategies that involve positions in more than one option at the same time are called *combinations*. Spreads and straddles are two specific types of combinations. A **spread** involves being both the buyer and the writer of the same type of option (call or put) on the same

> **Spread**
> Purchase and sale of the same type of option (call or put) on the same underlying asset.

Price spread
Simultaneous purchase and sale of options on the same underlying stock but with different exercise prices.

Time spread
Simultaneous purchase and sale of options on the same underlying stock but with different expiration dates.

Bull call spread
Purchase of a low-strike price call and the simultaneous sale of another, high-strike price call on the same underlying equity with the same expiration date.

Bull put spread
Sale of a high-strike price put and the simultaneous purchase of another, low-strike price put on the same underlying equity with the same expiration date.

Straddle
Purchase of a put and sale of a call on the same security.

Intrinsic value
Difference between an in-the-money option's strike price and the current market price of the underlying security.

Time value
Speculative value that diminishes over time.

underlying asset. While the type of option bought and sold is the same, spreads involve taking partially offsetting positions using options. A **price spread** is the simultaneous purchase and sale of options with the same exercise period, on the same underlying stock, but with different exercise prices. A **time spread** is the simultaneous purchase and sale of options with the same exercise price, on the same underlying stock, but with different expiration dates. Spreads can be used to take bullish or bearish positions with respect to a given security, and they can incorporate complex strategies.

Two popular price spread strategies are **bull call spreads** and **bull put spreads**. These are conservative option strategies because the investor's risk exposure is known and limited. They are most appropriate when the investor's outlook is mildly bullish. A bull call spread is the purchase of a low-strike price call and the simultaneous sale of another, high-strike price call on the same underlying equity with the same expiration date. The amount paid for low-strike price calls is always more than the amount received from the short sale of high-strike price calls. A bull put spread is the sale of a high-strike price put and the simultaneous purchase of another, low-strike price put on the same underlying equity with the same expiration date. The amount received from the short sale of high-strike price puts is always more than the amount paid for low-strike price puts.

A **straddle** consists of both purchasing a call and writing a put on the same underlying asset using options that have the same exercise price and expiration date. Straddles are used by speculators who anticipate an uptick in volatility but are not sure if the price move in the underlying stock price will be up or down. For example, suppose a company is about to announce whether it discovered oil during its just-completed massive drilling program. If oil was discovered, the company's stock can be expected to soar. If no oil was found, the company's stock can be expected to plummet. The purchase of a straddle position might result in a profit in such a case.

Option Pricing

Pricing Concepts

Several factors contribute value to an option contract and thereby influence the option premium or price at which the option is traded. The most important of these factors are the price of the underlying stock, time remaining until expiration, volatility of the underlying stock price, cash dividends, and prevailing interest rate.

The difference between an in-the-money option's strike price and the current market price of the underlying security is referred to as the option's **intrinsic value**. Intrinsic value is zero for at-the-money and out-of-the-money options. At the point of expiration, the expiration value of an option equals its intrinsic value. Only in-the-money options have intrinsic value. An option expires worthlessly if it is at-the-money or out-of-the-money at the time of expiration.

For example, if a call option's strike price is $50 and the underlying shares are trading at $65, the option has intrinsic value of $15 because a holder of that option could exercise the option and buy the shares at $50. The buyer could then immediately sell those shares on the stock market for $65, yielding a profit of $15 per share, or $1,500 per option contract.

Prior to expiration, all options are valuable. The fact that out-of-the-money options have no intrinsic value at the present point in time does not mean they are worthless. Unexpired out-of-the-money call and put options are valuable because they might someday have intrinsic value. For example, suppose someone offered you a call option on the Dow Jones Industrial Average with a strike price of 20,000. Given a sufficiently long contract period, say, 10 years or more, the DJIA might indeed rise above 20,000 and this call option would then have intrinsic value. Despite the lack of intrinsic value, all unexpired options have **time value**, or speculative value, because they might someday have intrinsic value.

For in-the-money options, time value is the excess portion of the option premium over its intrinsic value:

$$\text{Call price (option premium)} = \text{intrinsic value} + \text{time value} \qquad (18.1)$$

For at-the-money and out-of-the-money options, time value is the total value of the option premium. Options with greater intrinsic value have higher option prices.

Factors that increase the probability of a favorable exercise at some future point in time give rise to the time value of the option. Primary components of time value include the length of time remaining until expiration (the contract period), volatility in the underlying stock price, amount of cash dividends paid (if any), and prevailing interest rates. The longer the time period remaining until an option's expiration date, the higher the option premium because of the greater possibility of a favorable exercise. Time value drops rapidly in the last few days of an option's life and reaches zero at the point of expiration. Options that expire out-of-the-money are worthless, and the shorter the expiration period, the greater is the likelihood that any given out-of-the-money option will expire worthless. Figure 18.5 shows that the value of a call option comprises time value and intrinsic value. Out-of-the-money and at-the-money call options have no intrinsic value. Their entire value is time value. In-the-money call options have both time value and intrinsic value. As the stock price rises above the exercise price, intrinsic value rises to constitute the bulk of the value of the call. Similar relationships hold for put options.

The intrinsic value and time value components of option value become clear when options with different strike prices and expiration dates are compared. The Microsoft option quotes in Figure 18.2 show that April 25 call options have a bid price of 2.15. With the stock at 26.93, the intrinsic value of April 25 calls is 1.93 (= $26.93 – $25). The remainder of this call option's value is time value. The entire premium paid for out-of-the-money April 30 calls, and any higher strike price calls, is time value and speculative in nature. Also, note that all the June options have a higher premium than the May options of the same strike price. More time to expiration is valuable. The probability of a favorable exercise also increases with heightened price volatility of the underlying security. Price volatility is the propensity of the underlying security's market price to fluctuate either up or down. The higher the volatility of the underlying stock, the higher the time value and option premium because of the greater possibility of a favorable exercise.

Regular cash dividends are paid to stockholders; they are never paid to option holders. High dividend income is typically associated with stocks that display muted rates of capital

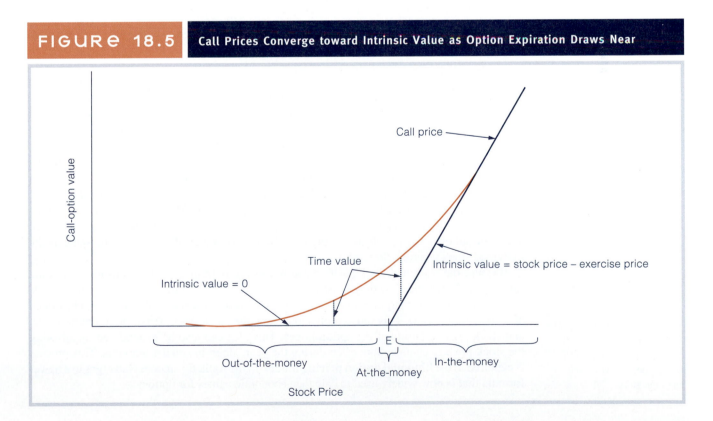

FIGURE 18.5   **Call Prices Converge toward Intrinsic Value as Option Expiration Draws Near**

appreciation over time. In the short run, cash dividends affect option premiums because stock prices typically fall by the amount of the cash dividend in the period surrounding the ex-dividend date. Therefore, higher cash dividends typically imply lower call-option premiums and higher premiums for put options.

Higher interest rates tend to result in higher call premiums and lower put premiums. Lower interest rates tend to result in lower call premiums and higher put premiums because buying calls can be viewed as a substitute for buying the underlying common stock. When interest rates rise, investors might be tempted to use a portion of their funds to buy calls and invest the remainder in interest-bearing instruments. As interest rates rise, the amount of interest income rises and the appeal of buying calls rises. Conversely, when interest rates fall, interest income falls and the value of calls tends to decrease. Put premiums and interest rates tend to move in the opposite direction. A rise in interest rates causes put prices to fall, and a fall in interest rates causes put prices to rise.

Try It!

Suppose GlaxoSmithKline's stock sells for $60 per share. The following four options trade on the CBOE: 55 call at $6.50, 65 call at $0.70, 55 put at $0.60, and 65 put at $6.30. What are the intrinsic value and time premium for each option?

Solution

The 55 call is in-the-money by $5, so $5 is the intrinsic value and $1.50 (= $6.50 − $5) is the time value.

The 65 call is out-of-the-money, so $0 is the intrinsic value and $0.70 (= $0.70 − $0) is the time value.

The 55 call is out-of-the-money, so $0 is the intrinsic value and $0.60 (= $0.60 − $0) is the time value.

The 65 call is in-the-money by $5, so $5 is the intrinsic value and $1.30 (= $6.30 − $5) is the time value.

Consider a simple example in which a $40 stock will either rise to $80 at the end of one year or fall to $20. Suppose the investor is able to partially fund this purchase by borrowing $18.87 at 6 percent interest. At the end of one year, it will cost $20 to repay this $18.87 loan plus $1.13 in interest. At the end of one year, this position will be worth either $60 (= $80 stock value − $20 debt and interest) or $0 (= $20 stock value − $20 debt and interest). Compare this payoff to the payoffs tied to a $60 strike price call option. If the stock increases to $80, the call option will pay $20. If the stock price declines to $20, the call option will be worthless. The payoffs to the $60 strike price call option will be either $20 or $0. To make a $60 strike price call-option position comparable to the margined stock position, an investor must buy three such call options. The payoff to owning three $60 strike price call options is the same as the margined stock position, $60 or $0.

Binomial option pricing model
A model in which a given number of time steps between the valuation date and option expiration are assumed. The underlying stock price can change only to two levels at any time step.

Because the margined stock position and three $60 strike price call options have the same future payoff possibilities, they must have the same current value. The price of three calls equals the cost of the margined stock position, which is $21.13. Each call option will be priced at $7.04 (= $21.13/3). This illustration shows how the stock price, strike price, interest rate, and stock price volatility affect option prices. This idea can also be generalized by allowing the stock price to change more often during the year, albeit in smaller amounts. This process is captured in the **binomial option pricing model**. In the limit, this model converges to a newer formula that is now widely used to calculate economic values for options.

Black-Scholes Option Pricing Model

During the early 1970s, financial economists Fisher Black, Myron Scholes, and Robert Merton developed an option pricing formula that is now referred to as the **Black-Scholes option pricing model**. The binomial option pricing model converges to the Black-Scholes formula. Assuming the ability to continuously and instantaneously rebalance portfolios, no transaction costs, and a risk-free asset, the value of a call option is

Black-Scholes option pricing model
Formula used to calculate economic values for options on the basis of continuous time assumptions and return distributions.

$$
\begin{array}{ccccc}
\text{Call} & = & \text{value of} & - & \text{opportunity cost} \\
\text{price} & & \text{upside potential} & & \text{of invested funds}
\end{array}
\tag{18.2}
$$

$$C = S\big[N(d_1)\big] - \frac{X}{e^{rt}}\big[N(d_2)\big]$$

where C is the current price of a call option, S is the current market price of the underlying common stock (equity), X is the exercise price (strike price) for the call option, e is the natural base $e \approx 2.718$, r is the risk-free rate, and t is the time remaining before expiration (in years). $N(d_1)$ and $N(d_2)$ are the cumulative density functions for d_1 and d_2 as defined below:

$$d_1 = \frac{\ln(S/X) + (r + 0.5\sigma^2)t}{\sigma\sqrt{t}} \tag{18.3}$$

$$d_2 = d_1 - \sigma\sqrt{t} \tag{18.4}$$

In these equations, ln (S/X) is the natural log of (S/X), and σ is the standard deviation of the underlying common stock's annual return. In other words, $N(d)$ is the probability that a random draw from a standard normal distribution will be less than d. This equals the area under the normal curve up to d, as enumerated in Table 18.4.

Valuing call options using the Black-Scholes option valuation formula is quick and easy with a basic hand-held calculator. Only five bits of information are required to determine the price of a call, including the current market price of the underlying equity (S), exercise price (X), risk-free rate (r), time to maturity (t), and volatility as captured by the standard deviation of annual returns on the underlying stock (σ). Notice from Equation 18.2 that call prices rise with a rise in the stock price, risk-free rate, time to maturity, and standard deviation of returns; they fall with a rise in the exercise price.

To illustrate, assume that $S = 50$, $X = 55$, $r = 0.0625$ (or 6.25 percent), $t = 0.5$ year (or 6 months), and $\sigma = 0.4$ (or 40 percent). To solve for d_1, note that

$$
\begin{aligned}
d_1 &= \frac{\ln(50/55) + (0.0625 + 0.5 \times 0.4^2) \times 0.5}{0.4\sqrt{0.5}} \\
&= \frac{-0.0953 + 0.0713}{0.2828} = -0.0851
\end{aligned}
$$

When $d_1 = -0.0851$, $N(d_1) = 0.4661$ from the cumulative probability distributions in Table 18.4. Then, to solve for d_2, note that

$$
\begin{aligned}
d_2 &= -0.0851 - 0.4\sqrt{0.5} \\
&= -0.3679
\end{aligned}
$$

TABLE 18.4 | Standard Normal Cumulative Distribution

d	N(d)	d	N(d)	d	N(d)
−3.00	0.0013	−0.78	0.2177	0.84	0.7995
−2.95	0.0016	−0.76	0.2236	0.86	0.8051
−2.90	0.0019	−0.74	0.2296	0.88	0.8106
−2.85	0.0022	−0.72	0.2358	0.90	0.8159
−2.80	0.0026	−0.70	0.2420	0.92	0.8212
−2.75	0.0030	−0.68	0.2483	0.94	0.8264
−2.70	0.0035	−0.66	0.2546	0.96	0.8315
−2.65	0.0040	−0.64	0.2611	0.98	0.8365
−2.60	0.0047	−0.62	0.2676	1.00	0.8413
−2.55	0.0054	−0.60	0.2743	1.02	0.8461
−2.50	0.0062	−0.58	0.2810	1.04	0.8508
−2.45	0.0071	−0.56	0.2877	1.06	0.8554
−2.40	0.0082	−0.54	0.2946	1.08	0.8599
−2.35	0.0094	−0.52	0.3015	1.10	0.8643
−2.30	0.0107	−0.50	0.3085	1.12	0.8686
−2.25	0.0122	−0.48	0.3156	1.14	0.8729
−2.20	0.0139	−0.46	0.3228	1.16	0.8770
−2.15	0.0158	−0.44	0.3300	1.18	0.8810
−2.10	0.0179	−0.42	0.3372	1.20	0.8849
−2.05	0.0202	−0.40	0.3446	1.22	0.8888
−2.00	0.0228	−0.38	0.3520	1.24	0.8925
−1.98	0.0239	−0.36	0.3594	1.26	0.8962
−1.96	0.0250	−0.34	0.3669	1.28	0.8997
−1.94	0.0262	−0.32	0.3745	1.30	0.9032
−1.92	0.0274	−0.30	0.3821	1.32	0.9066
−1.90	0.0287	−0.28	0.3897	1.34	0.9099
−1.88	0.0301	−0.26	0.3974	1.36	0.9131
−1.86	0.0314	−0.24	0.4052	1.38	0.9162
−1.84	0.0329	−0.22	0.4129	1.40	0.9192
−1.82	0.0344	−0.20	0.4207	1.42	0.9222
−1.80	0.0359	−0.18	0.4286	1.44	0.9251
−1.78	0.0375	−0.16	0.4364	1.46	0.9279
−1.76	0.0392	−0.14	0.4443	1.48	0.9306
−1.74	0.0409	−0.12	0.4522	1.50	0.9332
−1.72	0.0427	−0.10	0.4602	1.52	0.9357
−1.70	0.0446	−0.08	0.4681	1.54	0.9382
−1.68	0.0465	−0.06	0.4761	1.56	0.9406
−1.66	0.0485	−0.04	0.4840	1.58	0.9429
−1.64	0.0505	−0.02	0.4920	1.60	0.9452
−1.62	0.0526	0.00	0.5000	1.62	0.9474
−1.60	0.0548	0.02	0.5080	1.64	0.9495
−1.58	0.0571	0.04	0.5160	1.66	0.9515
−1.56	0.0594	0.06	0.5239	1.68	0.9535
−1.54	0.0618	0.08	0.5319	1.70	0.9554
−1.52	0.0643	0.10	0.5398	1.72	0.9573
−1.50	0.0668	0.12	0.5478	1.74	0.9591
−1.48	0.0694	0.14	0.5557	1.76	0.9608
−1.46	0.0721	0.16	0.5636	1.78	0.9625
−1.44	0.0749	0.18	0.5714	1.80	0.9641

(continued)

TABLE 18.4	Standard Normal Cumulative Distribution (continued)

d	N(d)	d	N(d)	d	N(d)
−1.42	0.0778	0.20	0.5793	1.82	0.9656
−1.40	0.0808	0.22	0.5871	1.84	0.9671
−1.38	0.0838	0.24	0.5948	1.86	0.9686
−1.36	0.0869	0.26	0.6026	1.88	0.9699
−1.34	0.0901	0.28	0.6103	1.90	0.9713
−1.32	0.0934	0.30	0.6179	1.92	0.9726
−1.30	0.0968	0.32	0.6255	1.94	0.9738
−1.28	0.1003	0.34	0.6331	1.96	0.9750
−1.26	0.1038	0.36	0.6406	1.98	0.9761
−1.24	0.1075	0.38	0.6480	2.00	0.9772
−1.22	0.1112	0.40	0.6554	2.05	0.9798
−1.20	0.1151	0.42	0.6628	2.10	0.9821
−1.18	0.1190	0.44	0.6700	2.15	0.9842
−1.16	0.1230	0.46	0.6772	2.20	0.9861
−1.14	0.1271	0.48	0.6844	2.25	0.9878
−1.12	0.1314	0.50	0.6915	2.30	0.9893
−1.10	0.1357	0.52	0.6985	2.35	0.9906
−1.08	0.1401	0.54	0.7054	2.40	0.9918
−1.06	0.1446	0.56	0.7123	2.45	0.9929
−1.04	0.1492	0.58	0.7190	2.50	0.9938
−1.02	0.1539	0.60	0.7257	2.55	0.9946
−1.00	0.1587	0.62	0.7324	2.60	0.9953
−0.98	0.1635	0.64	0.7389	2.65	0.9960
−0.96	0.1685	0.66	0.7454	2.70	0.9965
−0.94	0.1736	0.68	0.7517	2.75	0.9970
−0.92	0.1788	0.70	0.7580	2.80	0.9974
−0.90	0.1841	0.72	0.7642	2.85	0.9978
−0.88	0.1894	0.74	0.7704	2.90	0.9981
−0.86	0.1949	0.76	0.7764	2.95	0.9984
−0.84	0.2005	0.78	0.7823	3.00	0.9987
−0.82	0.2061	0.80	0.7881		
−0.80	0.2119	0.82	0.7939		

When $d_2 = -0.3679$, $N(d_2) = 0.3564$ (from the cumulative probability distributions in Table 18.4. Now the value of this six-month out-of-the-money call can be calculated using Equation 18.2:

$$\text{Call price} = S[N(d_1)] - \frac{X}{e^{rt}}[N(d_2)]$$

$$= 50(0.4661) - \frac{55}{e^{(0.0625)(0.5)}}(0.3564) = \$4.30$$

Thus, the theoretical value of this six-month out-of-the-money call option, according to the Black-Scholes formula, is approximately $4.30. If the current market price of the call option is greater than this theoretical value, the call is overpriced and should not be bought. If the current market price of the call is less than this theoretical value, the call represents a bargain and should be purchased. This presumes that the underlying assumptions of the model are correct and that the specific assumptions made concerning this call option are accurate.

Implied volatility
Estimate of a security's volatility calculated by using market prices and the Black-Scholes option pricing model.

Put-call parity
Relationship that must hold between the price of puts and calls on the same underlying equity.

In practice, it is relatively easy to estimate the current market price of the underlying equity, exercise price, risk-free rate on T-bills, and length of time until expiration. It is impossible to know beforehand the future volatility of the underlying equity σ. Historical volatility is a useful guide to future volatility, but changes in volatility occur, especially during turbulent markets. This makes application of the Black-Scholes model difficult. If the current call price is known, the Black-Scholes model can be used to calculate the level of volatility implicit in this price, called the **implied volatility**. If the assumed level of volatility is too high, then the call is overpriced and should be avoided. If the assumed level of volatility is too low, then the call option is underpriced and should be bought.

The Black-Scholes model can be used to give insight concerning put-option prices because of a concept called **put-call parity**. The put-call parity concept expresses the relationship that must hold between the price of a put option and the price of a call option on the same underlying equity. Remember, the purchase of a call option on a stock that has been shorted gives the investor a synthetic put position, and the price of a synthetic put and a put must be equivalent. The put-call parity relationship is:

$$\text{Put price} = \frac{X}{e^{rt}} - S + C \tag{18.5}$$

where all terms are the same as those in Equation 18.2.

For example, using the same numerical values as those in the call valuation example above, the theoretical put option price is consistent with a call option price of $4.30 if

$$\text{Put price} = \frac{55}{e^{(0.0625)(0.5)}} - 50 + 4.30 = \$7.61$$

CBOE Option Calculator

In practice, it can become tedious to go through the steps outlined above to value call and put options using the Black-Scholes formula. In fast-changing markets, it becomes impossible. Thankfully, there is an easy solution. The CBOE offers an option calculator on its Web site, **www.cboe.com**, on the Learning Center menu. Visit the "Education Tools" section to locate a tool that gives easy access to option prices using the Black-Scholes option pricing model. The CBOE option calculator not only gives precise calculations for call and put option prices but can also be used to derive the amount of implied volatility couched in current option prices. The CBOE option calculator also makes it easy to construct examples that show the dynamic relationships among option prices and underlying economic factors.

Figure 18.6 shows how the option calculator can be used to value an equity option. The price level for an underlying stock and option strike prices can be obtained from *The Wall Street Journal* or from a variety of sites on the Internet, including the CBOE's Web site. Dividend yields for index options can be easily obtained from financial publications such as the *The Wall Street Journal* (Monday edition) or *Barron's*. For stock option pricing, the quarterly dividend amount should be entered along with the next dividend date in the mm/dd/yy format. Most investors use T-bill rates as a good proxy for the current risk-free interest rate. In calculating the number of days remaining until expiration, it is important to include all calendar days, not just business days. Volatility (in percent) must be estimated for the underlying index or common equity.

Given the market price for any given call or put, the option calculator can be used to derive an estimate of implied volatility on the underlying common stock or index. Implied volatility greatly impacts the calculation of an option's theoretical value and tends to vary for each expiration and strike price and for calls versus puts. Professional option traders spend a great deal of time and effort on developing better volatility estimates.

In Figure 18.6, the theoretical call value of $1.41 was calculated for May 45 call options on Wal-Mart (symbol, WMTFL) when the underlying stock closed at $45.27 and there were 73 days left until expiration. The volatility on Wal-Mart is 14 percent per year. At the same time, and assuming the same level of volatility, the theoretical value is $0.92 for May 45 put options on Wal-Mart.

The Long Straddle

Option speculators often seek to profit from changes in volatility, even when they are unable to guess the future direction of prices. One strategy for doing so is called a "long straddle" and involves the purchase of both a call and a put with the same exercise price on a given stock.

Note in the accompanying figure that the payoffs tied to this position "straddle" the exercise price (*E*). The figure is drawn with an exercise price that is slightly higher than the current stock price, so the put premium is slightly higher than the call premium. If the stock price moves by less than the combined amount paid for the call and put options (*C* + *P*), the speculator will lose money. The most that can be lost is the combined premium, so risk is limited. If the stock price moves up or down by more than the combined premium, the long-straddle speculator makes money.

Speculators use a long straddle when a big unpredictable event, such as results from oil well drilling, is in the offing. An interesting example is the recent insider-trading trial of Martha Stewart. Martha Stewart Living Omnimedia (ticker, MSO) was set to tumble with a conviction or soar with vindication. In fact, Stewart was convicted on March 5, 2004, and the stock plunged from $14.03 to $9.55 (–32.0 percent) in just three trading days.

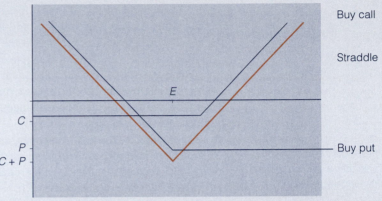

See News Roundup, "Federal Appeals Court Upholds Martha Stewart's Conviction," *The Wall Street Journal*, January 7, 2006, p. B3 (**http://online.wsj.com**).

FIGURE 18.6   **CBOE Option Calculator Can Be Used to Value Equity Options, such as Calls and Puts on Wal-Mart**

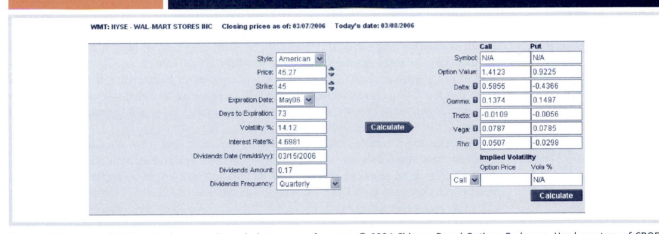

Source: Chicago Board Options Exchange option calculator, **www.cboe.com**. © 2006 Chicago Board Options Exchange. Used courtesy of CBOE.

Option Risk Concepts

The sensitivity of option value to a unit change in the underlying asset price is called **delta**. Delta indicates a percentage change. For example, in the calculations for Wal-Mart call options shown in Figure 18.6, the delta of 0.5855 indicates that the option's theoretical value will change by 58.6 percent of the change in the price of the underlying asset, which is Wal-Mart common stock. Delta is a dynamic concept, and its value changes as the price of the underlying asset changes, so option values can change more or less than the amount indicated by delta. In the option market, delta is reflected in the **hedge ratio**, which shows the number of shares of stock required to offset the price risk of one option contract.

Delta
Percentage change in option price following a $1 change in price of the underlying asset; also called *hedge ratio*.

Hedge ratio
Number of shares of stock required to offset the price risk of one option contract.

In the case of Wal-Mart, the delta of 0.5855 means that a $1 increase in the price of the stock should produce a 58.55-cent change in the price of the option. This implies that a perfectly hedged and riskless position would be established if 0.5855 shares of Wal-Mart common stock were purchased for every call option written. Following the sale of a standard 100-share stock call-option contract, the purchase of 58.55 shares of Wal-Mart stock would establish a perfect hedge. In that case, a $1 increase in the value of Wal-Mart stock would lead to a stock market profit of $58.55 (= $1 × 58.55 shares), which would exactly offset the $58.55 (= 0.5855 × $1 × 100 calls) loss on the call options written. Conversely, a $1 decrease in the value of Wal-Mart stock would lead to a stock market loss of $58.55 (= $1 × 58.55 shares), which would exactly offset the $58.55 (= 0.5855 × $1 ×100 calls) gain on the call options written. A perfectly hedged position leaves total wealth unchanged. Because hedge ratios are less than 1.0, a $1 movement in stock prices causes less than a $1 change in option prices. However, because stock options have a lower price basis than the underlying common stock, the percentage change in option prices tends to be larger than the percentage change in stock prices.

Gamma

Responsiveness of delta to unit changes in the value of the underlying asset.

The sensitivity of delta to unit changes in the value of the underlying asset is called **gamma**. Gamma indicates an absolute change in delta. In the Wal-Mart call-option example, the gamma of 0.137 indicates that delta will increase by 0.137 if the price of Wal-Mart stock were to immediately increase or decrease by $1.

Theta

Sensitivity of option value to a change in time.

The sensitivity of option value to a change in time is called **theta**. Theta indicates an absolute change in option value for a one-unit reduction in time to expiration. The CBOE option calculator assumes one-unit of time is seven days. Thus, a theta of –0.0109 indicates that the option's theoretical value will change by –$0.01 if the number of days to expiration is reduced by seven. In the CBOE option calculator, this seven-day theta changes to a one-day theta when there are seven or fewer calendar days left until expiration.

Vega

Sensitivity of option value to a change in volatility.

Vega indicates the sensitivity of option value to a change in volatility. Vega depicts an absolute change in option value for a 1 percent change in volatility. In Figure 18.6, the vega of 0.0787 signifies an increase in this specific Wal-Mart call option's theoretical value of $0.079 if the volatility percentage is increased by 1 percent. Alternatively, a decrease in this option's value of $0.079 will be noted if the volatility percentage is decreased by 1 percent.

Rho

Sensitivity of option value to changes in interest rates.

And, finally, the sensitivity of option value to changes in interest rates is captured by **rho**. Rho indicates the absolute change in option value for a 1 percent change in the market interest rate. In the case of the Wal-Mart call option depicted in Figure 18.6, the rho of 0.0507 means that the call option's theoretical value will increase by $0.051 if the interest rate is increased by 1 percent. Similarly, the call option's theoretical value will decrease by $0.051 if the interest rate is decreased by 1 percent.

In practice, the numerical values presented for each risk concept in the CBOE option calculator are only approximations. Actual results will vary slightly due to rounding. Perhaps the best way of gaining practical insight about how traders employ these important option risk concepts is to log on to the CBOE Web site and experiment using the CBOE option calculator with some current option market data.

Behavioral Considerations in Option Markets

Overpayment Problem

Daniel Kahneman won the 2002 Nobel Prize in economics for having integrated into economics various insights from psychology concerning human judgment and decision making under uncertainty. Kahneman's Nobel lecture on prospect theory discussed when people want to take risks and when they want to avoid them. In a simple experiment, people were asked whether they would rather have $5 in cash or a 0.001 (or 0.1 percent) chance to win $5,000. In this case, the expected value of the gamble is $5 (= 0.001 × $5,000), the same amount as the $5 cash payment (sure thing). When expressed in this manner, most people want to take the gamble. There is a popular tendency to overpay for the long-shot payoff of a significant amount. State governments know this and have exploited this tendency in the pricing of state lottery tickets. Most state lotteries pay out winnings of no more than 50 percent of the total amount bet. Nevertheless, lottery ticket buyers gladly participate because they richly value the remote chance of a big payoff. Buyers of call options are speculators who display the same overpaying tendencies typical of lottery ticket buyers.

Kahneman's research also shows how people behave when they want to avoid risk. When people are asked to choose between paying $5 or taking a 0.001 (or 0.1 percent) chance of paying $5,000, most people prefer to pay the five bucks! Indeed, people seem willing to overpay in order to avoid a big loss. This tendency is exploited by insurance companies that market "special-risk" life insurance. In Japan, for example, insurance companies make enormous profits selling insurance against dying from cancer. All of us will die someday, but the chance of dying from a specific illness such as cancer is small. Moreover, persons who are concerned about dying from cancer typically take precautionary measures with their lifestyle and diet. As a result, specific-illness life insurance is richly priced and enormously profitable. In the United States, other types of specific-risk insurance are similarly overpriced. At the airport, flight insurance kiosks are sometimes referred to as "two-armed bandits." Slot machines ("one-armed bandits") occasionally pay off; flight insurance kiosks almost never pay off.

Put buyers display some of the same tendencies as buyers of unlikely risk insurance. Stock prices usually progress in bull markets characterized by long periods with rising prices punctuated by short periods of downward price volatility. Regular put buyers are like buyers who regularly overpay for various types of special-risk insurance. Moreover, put buying volume tends to skyrocket in the periods following major market corrections. Just when experience tells us that markets are due to resume their typical long-term rate of progress, put buyers become most risk-averse. Like call option buyers, buyers of put options display a consistent tendency to overpay.

Overconfidence Problem

The most popular option contracts typically have a short time until expiration, often one month or less. Option holders are short-term speculators who must be right about the direction of an anticipated price change and be right about when such a price change will occur. If the price of the underlying asset does not change in the anticipated direction before option expiration, and by an amount sufficient to cover the option premium and transaction costs, the option speculator stands to lose money. The option speculator's short-term predicament contrasts with the situation faced by the patient long-term investor. Patient long-term investors have the time to survive temporarily adverse market conditions. Speculators in the option market do not.

Omaha billionaire investor Warren Buffett is famous for remarking, "In the stock market it's easy to tell *what* will happen, but impossible to tell *when* it will happen." Successful long-term investors like Buffett are prosperous because they have the ability to identify companies with attractive business prospects that are selling at compelling prices. Successful option traders not only have to identify companies with attractive business prospects that are selling at compelling prices but must also be able to predict precisely when the share prices of such companies are apt to rise. That's tough.

Statistics covering over 30 years' experience from the Options Clearing Corporation document that approximately 30 to 40 percent of all option contracts expire worthless, 10 to 15 percent are exercised, and the remaining 45 to 55 percent of option positions are closed prior to expiration (**www.cboe.com/data/AnnualMarketStatistics.aspx**). Precise inferences are not possible, but lots of unprofitable option trading activity is clearly apparent. The prevalence of unprofitable option market speculation is consistent with the suggestion from behavioral finance that many active traders suffer from overconfidence.

Options and the Bubble

Prices of Nasdaq-listed technology stocks skyrocketed in the late 1990s, peaked in March 2000, and then lost more than three-quarters of their value over the next two years. Many of the largest price run-ups and subsequent collapses were associated with Internet stocks. Few of these companies were profitable, and many had only minimal revenues. As a result, many academics and Wall Street professionals believe that a bubble existed during the late 1990s and that Internet stock prices became irrationally high. Under normal circumstances, stock prices are kept within rational bounds because rational investors can sell short overpriced stocks and drive prices back to rational levels.

After a price bubble, researchers look for factors that might have prevented traders from being able to borrow "bubble stocks" and short-sell them at reasonable cost. Even if rational investors found shares to borrow, short selling is a notoriously risky proposition. Well-capitalized, long-term investors can endure adverse price moves by holding on and refusing to sell when prices fall to absurdly low levels. When stocks rise to absurdly high levels, short sellers face a continuing need to meet margin calls with additional capital if prices continue to rise. Many short sellers have limited capital and can find themselves needing to cover their positions at the worst possible time. Moreover, hedge funds and other institutional speculators often face outflows of capital when they lose money over short horizons, and this constrains their ability to endure short-term losses.

In an interesting study, Robert Battalio and Paul Schultz sought evidence that Internet stocks were hard to short by comparing actual stock prices with the prices implied in put and call option prices. Their results suggest that irrational Internet stocks prices were not due to short-selling problems. The fact that rational investors did not take advantage of opportunities to profit from overpriced Internet stocks suggests to Battalio and Schultz that Internet stock overpricing was not as obvious during the bubble as it seems now.

See Robert Battalio and Paul Schultz, "Options and the Bubble," *Journal of Finance*, vol. 6, no. 5 (October 2006).

Summary

■ The **Chicago Board Options Exchange (CBOE)** pioneered the concept of standardized, listed options to be traded in a centralized and regulated marketplace. An **option contract** is the right to buy or sell a given amount or value of a particular asset at a fixed price until a given expiration date. A **call option** gives the right to buy; a **put option** gives the right to sell. Options are **derivative securities** because their economic value is derived, or stems, from changes in the value of some other asset.

■ The number of outstanding options is commonly referred to as **open interest**, and it depends solely on the number of buyers and sellers interested in receiving and conferring these rights. Activity in stock options tends to be highest for an **exercise price**, or **strike price**, that is near the current market price for the underlying common stock. The exercise price, or strike price, of an option is the designated price at which the shares of stock can be bought by the buyer of a call option or sold by the buyer of a put option. When the price of the underlying security is equal to the strike price, the option price is said to be **at-the-money**. A call option is **in-the-money** if the strike price is less than the market price of the underlying security. A put option is in-the-money if the strike price is greater than the market price of the underlying security. A call option is **out-of-the-money** if the strike price is greater than the market price of the underlying security. A put option is out-of-the money if the strike price is less than the market price of the underlying security.

■ Options that have the same standardized terms but different strike prices constitute an **option series**. The standardization of terms makes it more likely that there will be a secondary market in which **holders**, or buyers, and **writers**, or sellers, of options can close out their positions by offsetting sales and purchase transactions. The length of time between the date that an option contract is established and the date of its expiration is the **contract period**. The amount paid for the option is the **option premium**. **Long-term equity anticipation securities (LEAPS)** are long-term call and put options.

■ The **Options Clearing Corporation (OCC)** is the sole issuer of all listed securities options. To ensure contract fulfillment, the OCC requires that buyers and sellers have a clearing member handle their option transactions and that both sides of every option transaction be exactly matched. On the CBOE, **market makers** provide liquidity in option trading by risking their own capital for personal trading. **Floor brokers** act as agents, executing orders for public or firm accounts.

■ A **hedged position** is created when an option contract is purchased or sold to offset the risk inherent in some other investment. Hedgers use options to limit risk. A **speculative position** is created when an option contract is purchased or sold to profit from the inherent riskiness of some underlying asset. Option contracts represent a **zero-sum game** between the buyer and the seller before commissions and other transaction costs.

■ An **American-style option** is an option contract that can be exercised at any time between the date of purchase and the expiration date. In the United States, all stock options and most exchange-traded options are American-style options. **European-style options** are options contracts that can be exercised only on the **expiration date**. The expiration date is the last day of an American-style option or the single exercise date of a European-style option.

■ A **physical-delivery option** gives its owner the right to receive physical delivery of an asset if it is a call, or to make physical delivery of an asset if it is a put, when the option is exercised. A **cash-settled option** gives the holder the right to receive a cash payment based on the difference between a determined value of the underlying interest at the time the option is exercised and the fixed exercise price of the option. The unit of trading, or **contract size**, of a physical-delivery option is the quantity of an underlying asset that is subject to being purchased or sold on the exercise of a single option contract. When and if they choose to buy or sell at the predetermined price, option holders are said to **exercise** their right. The sellers of options are said to be **assigned** when they are asked to fulfill their contract obligation.

■ Physical-delivery **price-based options** give holders the right to purchase or sell a specific debt security. Cash-settled price-based options give holders the right to receive a cash payment based on the value of an underlying debt security. **Yield-based options** are debt options that are cash-settled based on the difference between the exercise price and the value of an underlying yield.

■ A **covered-call** strategy is the simultaneous purchase of a stock and the sale of a call option on that same security. A **protective-put** strategy is the simultaneous purchase of a stock and the purchase of a put option on that same security. The payoffs associated with put and call strategies can often be mimicked through the use of combinations of positions in other securities, called **synthetic** options.

■ Spreads and **straddles** are two specific types of combination positions. A spread involves being both the buyer and the writer of the same type of option (call or put) on the same underlying asset. A **price spread** is the simultaneous purchase and sale of options on the same underlying stock but with different exercise prices. A **time spread** is the simultaneous purchase and sale of options on the same underlying stock but with different expiration dates. A **bull call spread** is the purchase of a low-strike price call and the simultaneous sale of another, high-strike price call on the same underlying equity with the same expiration date. A **bull put spread** is the sale of a high-strike price put and the simultaneous purchase of another, low-strike price put on the same underlying equity with the same expiration date.

■ The difference between an in-the-money option's strike price and the current market price of the underlying security is referred to as the option's **intrinsic value**. Intrinsic value is zero for at-the-money and out-of-the-money options. At the point of expiration, the expiration value of an option equals its intrinsic value. Only in-the-money options have intrinsic value. All unexpired options have **time value**, or speculative value, because they might someday have intrinsic value. Although the **binomial option pricing model** can be used to price a call option, the more common formula used is the **Black-Scholes option pricing model**. Using market call prices, this model can be solved backward to produce the **implied volatility** of the underlying security. The Black-Scholes formula gives insight concerning put option prices because of a concept called **put-call parity**. The put-call parity concept expresses the relationship that must hold between the price of a put option and the price of a call option on the same underlying equity.

■ The sensitivity of option value to a unit change in the underlying asset is called the option's **delta**. In the options market, delta is commonly referred to as the **hedge ratio**. The responsiveness of delta to unit changes in the value of the underlying asset is called **gamma**. The sensitivity of option value to a change in time is called **theta**. **Vega** indicates the sensitivity of option value to a change in volatility. The sensitivity of option value to changes in interest rates is captured by **rho**. The best way for gaining practical insight about how traders employ these important option risk concepts is to log on to the CBOE Web site and experiment using the CBOE option calculator with some current option market data.

www.mhhe.com/hirschey1e

Self-Test Problems

ST18.1   Use a spreadsheet to compute the Black-Scholes option price of a call and put option. The underlying stock has a price of $50 and volatility of 35 percent, and it pays a 1 percent dividend yield. The call option has an exercise price of $55 and will mature in six months. The risk free rate is 6 percent. What is the price of the call and put options?

Solution

The following spreadsheet shows the Black-Scholes option pricing model equations.

◇	A	B	C	D	E	F	G	H	I	J	K
1	**B-S Model Inputs**			**B-S Model Results**							
2											
3	Standard Deviation	0.35		d1 =	-0.1604	=(LN(B5/B7)+(B13-B11+0.5*B3^2)*B9)/(B3*SQRT(B9))					
4											
5	Stock Price	$50.00		d2 =	-0.4078	=E3-B3*SQRT(B9)					
6											
7	Exercise Price	$55.00		N(d1) =	0.4363	=NORMSDIST(E3)					
8											
9	Maturity (in years)	0.5		N(d2) =	0.3417	=NORMSDIST(E5)					
10											
11	Dividend Yield	0.01		Call Price =	$3.577	=B5*E7-(B7*EXP(-1*B13*B9)*E9)					
12											
13	Risk-free Rate	0.06		Put Price =	$6.952	=B7*EXP(-1*B13*B9)-B5+E11					
14											

Note that the call option is out-of-the-money but still has a high option premium of $3.58 per share. The put option is in-the-money by $5, and the put price is $6.95.

ST18.2 Use the spreadsheet in ST18.1 to investigate how the call-option price changes when the inputs vary.

Solution

If the stock price rises by $1 to $51 per share, the call price rises by $0.46 to $4.04. With this $1 stock price increase, the put-option price falls by $0.54. This illustrates that stock price changes and option price changes are not the same. Investors trying to hedge positions using options need to be aware of this dynamic.

When the volatility of the underlying stock decreases from 35 to 25 percent, the call price falls to $2.20. Note that option prices are very sensitive to the volatility input. Increases in volatility increase both call- and put-option prices, while decreases in volatility lower option prices.

Longer-term options are worth more because there is more time, and thus a greater chance, for the stock price to move to become in-the-money. If the call option in ST18.1 were a nine-month option instead of a six-month option, the price would increase $1.39 to $4.97

Option prices are not very sensitive to dividend yield. An increase in yield to 3 percent results in a call price of $3.569, a decrease of only $0.008 when the yield is tripled.

Put and call options react differently to changes in interest rates. When the risk-free rate is changed to 5 percent, the call price declines $0.092 to $3.485 and the put option increases $0.175 to $7.127.

Questions and Problems

18.1 Identify and describe the two main components of option value.

18.2 Determine whether the following options are in-, out-of-, or at-the-money. The underlying stock price is $15 per share.

    a. 12.5 call with premium of $3.60
    b. 12.5 put with premium of $0.80
    c. 15 call with premium of $1.20
    d. 15 put with premium of $1.00
    e. 17.5 call with premium of $0.60
    f. 17.5 put with premium of $3.40

18.3 Using the stock and options listed in Problem 18.2, determine each option's intrinsic value and time value.

18.4 What is the difference between an American-style option and a European-style option?

18.5   Describe why options are a zero-sum game without transaction costs and a negative-sum game with transaction costs. What relevance does this have for the speculator?

18.6   Suppose the Dow Jones Industrial Average closed at 10,250, down 50 for the day. The quotes for the DJIA index options are:

	Last	Change
Jun 103 call	1.90	−0.40
Jun 103 put	2.50	+0.50

How much money does it take to buy each of these options? How much did the value of these options change that day in dollars and in percentage terms?

18.7   What is the option premium?

18.8   Describe the essential difference between a hedged position and a speculative position.

18.9   Holding all else equal, explain how each of the following unexpected events will increase, decrease, or have no effect on the time value and/or minimum expiration value of a given outstanding option:

  a. Rise in interest rates.
  b. Decrease in the underlying common stock's dividend.
  c. Decrease in the underlying common stock's volatility.
  d. Decline in the underlying common stock's price.

18.10 The Chicago Board Options Exchange (CBOE) has an outstanding Web site (**www.cboe.com**). Go to the CBOE site and find the definition of LEAPS. For what type of investor do they hold the greatest appeal?

18.11 An investor writes the call and put options listed below. Graph the profit picture of this straddle position.

95 call priced at $1.50

95 put priced at $3.50

18.12 An investor owns 100 shares of stock selling at $50 per share. The investor also buys a 45 put option for $1.30. Compute and compare the stock-only returns and the protective-put position returns assuming a stock price (at option expiration) of $42 and of $55.

18.13 Using the Black-Scholes option valuation formula, compute the price of a call option with four months to expiration that has a strike price of $45. The current stock price is $48, and the T-bill yield is 4.5 percent. The volatility of the stock is 30 percent.

18.14 Using the information in and solution to Problem 18.13, use put-call parity to compute the value of a put option.

18.15 A call option has delta = 0.709, gamma = 0.038, 7-day theta = −0.103, vega = 0.092, and rho = 0.095. How does the option price change when its valuation parameters change?

18.16 The current price of an asset is 100. An out-of-the-money American put option with an exercise price of 90 is purchased along with the asset. If the break-even point for this hedge is at an asset price of 114 at expiration, then the value of the American put at the time of purchase must have been:

  a. 0
  b. 4
  c. 10
  d. 14

18.17 Joel Franklin is a portfolio manager responsible for derivatives. Franklin observes European-style put options and call options on Abaco Ltd. common stock with the same strike price and time to expiration. Selected information relevant to Abaco Ltd. stock and options is shown in Exhibit 1.

eXHIBIT 1	Abaco Ltd. Securities Selected Data
Closing price of Abaco common stock	$43.00
Put- and call-option exercise price	$45.00
Time to expiration	1 year
Price of the European-style put option	$4.00
Price of the European-style call option, 1-year U.S. Treasury bill rate	5.50%

Samantha Crowe, a colleague of Franklin, believes that Abaco stock is overpriced, and she decides to sell short the stock. However, her broker informs her that an adequate inventory of the stock may not be available to sell short.

Based on a put-call parity, the value of the European-style call option is *closest to:*

a. $0.00
b. $2.00
c. $4.35
d. $4.41

18.18 If the volatility of Abaco's stock price (Problem 18.17) decreases, what is most likely to happen to the values of the related call and put?

a. Both the call and the put will decrease in value.
b. Both the call and the put will increase in value.
c. The value of the call will increase, while the value of the put will decrease.
d. The value of the call will decrease, while the value of the put will increase.

18.19 The chief economist at Franklin's firm is forecasting a substantial decline in interest rates. To help gain from this forecast while assuming limited risk, Franklin should take which of the following actions with regard to the European-style options in Exhibit 1?

a. Buy the call option.
b. Buy the put option.
c. Sell the call option.
d. Sell the put option.

18.20 Franklin considers selling the European-style put option described in Exhibit 1. Ignoring the time value of money and given current prices, the maximum possible loss from this strategy is:

a. $39
b. $41
c. $45
d. Unlimited

INVESTMENT APPLICATION

Taking a Leveraged Bet on Microsoft Corp.

Options are risky. After the fact, it's easy to see what would have happened if one had followed a given option investment strategy. However, before the fact, it's never easy to appropriately assess the risk and returns. For example, on the Sunday before Thanksgiving in 2005, investors were bound to notice the recent climb in the price of Microsoft Corporation (MSFT) stock. In November 2005, *The Wall Street Journal* wrote:

> The real bulls think that the market's recent softness is just a pause before a strong stock rally. Something similar happened a decade ago. In 1994, rising interest rates kept stocks from showing much progress, but once rates began to fall again in 1995, stocks took off. But many investors are reluctant to bank on that happening again this time. In the mid-1990s, the Federal Reserve managed to end its interest-rate-raising campaign without driving the economy into recession. But too often, Fed rate increases have led to recession, or at least to a serious economic slowdown, which is what happened from 2000 through 2002. Investors fear another "hard landing" again now. Partly reflecting those concerns, some of the leaders of the latest stock rally have been "mega-cap" stocks—those of the biggest companies such as Microsoft (MSFT), Intel (INTC) and Wal-Mart Stores (WMT)—which many view as the safest. Microsoft is up 9 percent so far this month. Intel is up nearly 8 percent.[2]

After more than five years of moribund stock price performance, MSFT in particular was the subject of increasing interest:

> Microsoft shares, which have heated up a bit in the past few weeks, going from 25 to 27, have begun to attract attention from investors intrigued about the potential for acceleration in the company's growth rate. Kicking off with the debut of Xbox 360 on Nov. 22, Microsoft is entering a hugely busy year for new products, culminating with the late 2006 debut of Windows Vista. Walter Price considers it a near certainty that the product blitz, which also will include a new version of Office, will boost the company's growth. "There is earnings acceleration coming at Microsoft," he says. "Show me that, and I will show you a stock that acts better." The question, he says, is whether the stock goes to 30—or 40.[3]

Option players were bound to notice the potential for cashing in on options tied to a stock with a stock price poised to surge on the back of raised growth expectations. As of November 19, 2005, the Sunday afternoon prior to the long-anticipated launch of Xbox 360 on November 22, MSFT was priced at $28.07. On November 21, 2005, the January 07 25 calls (VFMAJ) on Microsoft had last traded at $4.50 (bid) and $4.60 (ask). At the same time, the January 08 25 calls (WMFAE) on Microsoft had last traded at $5.60 (bid) and $5.80 (ask).

a. How many call options could $10,000 purchase on November 21, 2005? Determine these amounts for both VSMAJ and WMFAE options and remember that each option is for 100 shares of Microsoft stock.

b. Use the CBOE option price calculator to estimate the implied volatility of each option on November 21, 2005. The prices are given above. The amount of time left to expiration as of November 21, 2005, was 425 days and 790 days for the 2007 and 2008 options, respectively. Microsoft's expected dividend was $0.08 per share (quarterly), and interest rates were 4.9158 percent.

c. On March 1, 2006, Microsoft stock closed at $27.14. Assume both option positions were sold, and compute the value of each call option, and determine the profit or loss from the initial $10,000. Use the implied volatility found in part b, and remember to adjust the time to maturity for both options. By March 1, interest rates had changed to 4.6981 percent, and the expected quarterly dividend was $0.09.

---

[2] E. S. Browning, "For Stocks, a Bummer Year Gets Brighter," *The Wall Street Journal*, November 20, 2005 (**http://online.wsj.com**). Copyright © 2005 Dow Jones Co. Used with permission.

[3] Eric, J. Savitz, "Technology Revival," *Barron's Online,* November 14, 2005 (**http://online.barrons.com**). Copyright © 2005 Dow Jones Co. Used with permission.

19

chapter

Futures Markets

Both fresh and frozen pork bellies are among the most actively traded agricultural commodities. The expression "pork bellies" is a colorful term used to describe the two slabs of bacon obtained from the underside of a hog. Bellies account for about 12 percent of a hog's live weight, but represent a somewhat larger percentage of the total value of realized pork products. Frozen bellies deliverable against futures generally weigh between 12 and 14 pounds each.

The speculative appeal of trading futures on pork bellies was made clear when the low-carb (Atkins) diet was sweeping the nation. Consumers were suddenly buying more meat and cheese and less flour, sugar, and potatoes. That was good for beef, pork, and chicken producers. When a cow in the state of Washington was found to have mad cow disease, futures traders knew what to do! With the demand for meat steadily rising and concerns growing about the safety of U.S. beef, futures traders put their bets on frozen pork bellies. Futures traders bet that low-carb dieters would turn to pork and cause a surge in the demand for bacon. That's exactly what happened. In only five months, frozen pork bellies jumped from 86 cents per pound to $1.25 per pound, a 45 percent increase. A single pork-bellies futures contract is for 40,000 pounds of bacon, so this big price move resulted in $15,600 profit for those long the original $34,400 contract. Those on the short side of the trade lost an identical amount.

Commodity prices depend solely on hard-to-predict changes in demand and supply conditions. The low-carb-diet-inspired jump in pork bellies was due to a temporary increase in demand. When the low-carb diet craze ended, the price of pork bellies quickly slumped to earlier levels. Like unexpected changes in supply, rapidly changing demand conditions make futures market speculation hazardous, at best. While futures markets offer an attractive means for producers and large buyers to hedge their positions, even professional traders find that profits from speculation are often elusive.[1]

---

[1] See Matt Moffett, "In Latin America, Commodities Boom Has Unlikely Fallout," *The Wall Street Journal Online*, March 6, 2006 (**http://online.wsj.com**).

CHAPTER OBJECTIVES

- Understand futures contract characteristics.
- Know how and where futures contracts trade.
- Be able to compute profits and losses on futures positions.
- Recognize the value of futures contracts for hedging purposes.
- Learn the dynamics of futures pricing.

Futures Trading

Market Origin

Futures markets have a long and colorful history. The origin of modern futures markets has been traced to the trading of rice futures in 18th-century Osaka, Japan. In the United States, the history of modern futures trading dates from the mid-19th century and was tied closely to the development of commerce in Chicago and the grain trade in the Midwest. Located on the shores of Lake Michigan, close to the fertile farmlands of the Midwest, Chicago offered a vital link between the producers of agricultural products and major consumer markets in the East. As the early grain trade in Chicago expanded, however, primitive information about changes in supply and demand, transportation, and storage led to a chaotic marketing situation.

At harvest time, midwestern farmers and grain shippers delivered their crops within days of each other, flooding the market with supply and driving down grain prices. Fall price collapses were so violent that after deducting shipping and marketing costs, farmers sometimes figured it was cheaper to burn corn for fuel than to send it to market. By midwinter or spring, most of the stored grain was depleted and prices shot up again. Prices often remained high throughout the summer months, only to plunge again in the autumn, when the annual bust-to-boom cycle for grain prices would resume.

By 1848, telegraph communication had progressed to the point where merchants in Chicago could quickly receive price information from New York, and the **Chicago Board of Trade (CBOT)** was born, as shown in Table 19.1. The CBOT was established by a group of 82 merchants as a centralized marketplace to promote commerce in the city of Chicago by providing a place where buyers and sellers could meet to exchange commodities. In the 1849–1850 period, "to arrive" contracts came into use for future delivery of flour, timothy seed, and hay. By 1851, the earliest **forward contract**, for 3,000 bushels of corn, was recorded. A forward contract is an agreement between two parties to buy or sell a stipulated grade and quantity of a commodity at a specific future time for an agreed-on price. Forward contracts quickly gained popularity among merchants and processors as a means of bringing order to sometimes chaotic grain prices.

During the 1850s, the importance of Chicago as a commercial link between the nation's breadbasket and eastern markets grew rapidly. With the onset of the Civil War, the need for grain storage and price dependability grew rapidly. Grain storage capacity in Chicago skyrocketed, but producers sometimes proved unable or unwilling to deliver promised grains at agreed-on prices. In other instances, buyers vanished when market prices turned lower than the amounts stipulated in forward contracts. Defaults grew and threatened to undermine the market. To remedy the situation, and restore buyer and seller confidence in the grain markets, the CBOT moved to formalize grain trading by developing a standardized agreement called a **futures contract**. Similar to a forward contract, a futures contract is a standardized agreement between two parties that commits one to buy and the other to sell a stipulated quantity and grade of a commodity at a set price on or before a given date in the future.

Chicago Board of Trade
First and largest commodities exchange.

Forward contract
Binding agreement to buy or sell a stipulated grade and quantity of a commodity at a specific future time for an agreed-on price.

Futures contract
Financially secured binding agreement to buy or sell a stipulated grade and quantity of a commodity at a specific future time for an agreed-on price.

TABLE 19.1	Time Line of U.S. Futures Market Development

Date	Event
1848	The Chicago Board of Trade (CBOT) is founded by 82 Chicago merchants.
1851	The earliest forward contract for 3,000 bushels of corn is recorded. Forward contracts gain popularity among merchants and processors.
1856	A group of merchants organize the Kansas City Board of Trade for the purpose of buying and selling wheat.
1865	Forward contracts create confusion for users and subsequent defaults. CBOT formalizes grain trading by developing standardized futures contracts. CBOT begins requiring that margin be posted by buyers and sellers.
1868	MidAmerica Commodity Exchange is founded in Chicago as an open-air market.
1870	New York Cotton Exchange is founded by a group of cotton brokers and merchants.
1872	Manhattan dairy merchants form the Butter and Cheese Exchange of New York, later called the Butter, Cheese and Egg Exchange.
1874	Chicago Produce Exchange is established to provide a market for butter, eggs, poultry, and other farm products in the city of Chicago.
1881	Twenty-one businessmen form the Minneapolis Chamber of Commerce, an organization designed to encourage and promote trade in corn, oats, and wheat.
1882	The Butter, Cheese and Egg Exchange of New York changes its name to the New York Mercantile Exchange.
1882	The Coffee Exchange of the City of New York is created by a group of merchants seeking an orderly process for buying and selling coffee.
1898	The Chicago Butter and Egg Board is formed from a division of the Chicago Produce Exchange.
1916	The Coffee Exchange of the City of New York changes its name to the New York Coffee and Sugar Exchange, Inc.
1919	The Chicago Butter and Egg Board is renamed the Chicago Mercantile Exchange to better reflect its broad purpose.
1922	The federal government establishes the Grain Futures Administration to regulate grain trading.
1925	The New York Cocoa Exchange founded.
1947	The Minneapolis Chamber of Commerce changes its name to the Minneapolis Grain Exchange.
1966	CBOT introduces the industry's first examination for commodity brokers.
1973	The Chicago Board Options Exchange (CBOE) is founded by members of the CBOT.
1974	The Commodity Futures Trading Commission (CFTC) is created by Congress as an independent agency with the mandate to regulate commodity futures and option markets in the U.S.
1975	CBOT launches futures on the Government National Mortgage Association (GNMA) mortgage-backed certificates, the first financial futures instrument.
1979	The Coffee and Sugar Exchange merges with the New York Cocoa Exchange to form the Coffee, Sugar & Cocoa Exchange, Inc.
1982	The Coffee, Sugar & Cocoa Exchange, Inc., introduces options on sugar futures contracts, creating the first U.S. exchange-traded option on a futures contract. CBOT launches options on U.S. Treasury bond futures. The KCBOT introduces futures contracts based on the Value Line Index, the first U.S. stock index used for futures contracts.
1985	The MidAmerica Commodity Exchange acquires the Chicago Rice and Cotton Exchange.
1986	The MidAmerica Commodity Exchange becomes a wholly-owned subsidiary of the CBOT.
1995	CBOT launches MarketPlex, the first futures exchange to open a commercial service on the Internet.
2000	CBOT members become shareholders in two new companies. The first company retains the open-outcry platform of trading and is a closely held, for-profit company. The second company establishes an electronic trading capability.
2002	CBOT launches a number of new products, including $5 minisized electronic Dow futures, 5-year interest rate swap futures, 10-year municipal note index futures, and 10-year and 5-year interest rate swap options. OneChicago joint venture exchange launches, trading over 3,000 contracts (representing more than 300,000 shares of common stock).
2003	CBOT licenses the Liffe Connect technology to power its electronic trading platform, replacing the a/c/e system. CBOT and CME jointly announce signing an agreement for the CME to provide clearing and related services for all CBOT products.
2005	CBOT officially becomes a for-profit nonstock Delaware corporation.

Source: Chicago Board of Trade, **www.cbot.com**. © CBOT, 2006.

To improve on the previously popular but troublesome forward contracts, the CBOT began requiring that performance bonds called **margin** be posted by buyers and sellers of futures. Performance bonds ensure that both buyers and sellers have the economic incentive and financial wherewithal to complete their futures market transactions. Today, futures **mark-to-market** on a daily basis. This means that there is a daily settlement of gains and losses between buyers and sellers. If the **spot price**, or current price, rises, sellers of futures contracts must place additional funds in their margin account to ensure their ability to deliver the now higher-priced commodities. If the spot price falls, buyers of futures contracts must place additional funds in their margin account to ensure their willingness to abide by an earlier agreement to pay higher prices for what are now lower-priced commodities. The CBOT also broadened market acceptance of futures contracts by standardizing the conditions and terms of contract fulfillment. For futures contracts that remain open until trading terminates, the CBOT stipulates mechanisms for either physical delivery or final cash payment (cash settlement).

Margin
Performance bond.

Mark-to-market
Daily reconciliation of futures contract profits and losses based on spot market prices.

Spot price
Current cash price.

Market Development

Futures contracts give farmers and grain merchants a way to lock in predictable prices for agricultural products. An Iowa farmer paying for seed and fertilizer to plant corn in May, for example, can only guess what price will be received for the crop when it is taken to market in October or November. In May, if the farmer sells corn futures contracts for at least a portion of the expected crop, the farmer has the potential to lock in a profit above planning and harvesting costs. The ability to reduce future price risk is an important attraction of the futures market to producers. Similarly, buyers of agricultural products like the ability to lock in future costs. Kellogg's and General Mills, for example, are big players in the grain markets, where they use futures contracts to stabilize their cost of ingredients for ready-to-eat cereals and other products.

Futures markets have a long history of product innovation. In the United States, corn, wheat, and cotton trading dates from the post-Civil War period. Metals trading began in the 1920s, and refined agricultural products, like soybean meal and soybean oil, became available during the 1950s. A new wave of innovation began in the 1960s when futures on livestock, a readily perishable commodity, were introduced. The development of commodity exchanges in New York for coffee, sugar, cocoa, cotton, precious metals, and oil paralleled developments in Chicago's agricultural commodities markets. These futures markets were established and evolved as an efficient means for matching buyers and sellers of standardized commodities with widely fluctuating prices. The obvious economic advantages of agricultural and commodity futures led to commodity futures trading growth. However, the most dramatic growth of the industry was not tied to futures based on agricultural products and other commodities but resulted from the development of financial futures tied to a changing world economy following World War II.

In 1974, currency and interest rate instability caused global investors to flock to gold, and gold futures began to trade. At the same time, an explosion of government-issued debt and spiraling inflation moved the world economy away from a relatively stable interest rate environment into one that was much more volatile. In 1976, three-month Treasury bill futures were introduced. The highly popular 30-year Treasury bond futures were introduced in 1977. Futures on petroleum-based products, like heating oil and gasoline, were another popular introduction in the late 1970s, when OPEC's control over oil prices weakened and oil price volatility skyrocketed.

In 1981, Eurodollar futures became the first futures contract that did not require physical delivery. Instead, the Eurodollar futures contract called for a cash settlement, or a cash payment, on the last trading day of the difference between the cash price and the futures price. The cash-settlement innovation paved the way for new types of futures contracts for which physical delivery would be impossible or prohibitively expensive. Most notable among these are stock index futures, which began trading in 1982.

Today, more than one-third of the financial futures trading volume originates with foreign banks and other foreign institutions. The CBOT's futures contract on U.S. Treasury bonds is the most actively traded futures contract and accounts for roughly two-thirds of that exchange's trading activity.

Futures Characteristics

Asset Specification

Wherever a high degree of price volatility is characteristic of the market for any broadly used good or service, there is potential demand for futures contracts. Active futures markets have grown to encompass dozens of underlying assets from traditional agricultural products to a wide variety of natural resources to a growing list of financial assets, products, and services. Figure 19.1 shows a typical daily listing of futures prices and trading volume as presented in *Barron's*. Notice that futures market activity is naturally clustered according to nine major underlying asset groups: fibers, financial & money, food, foreign currencies, fuels, grains and feed, indexes, livestock & meat, lumber, and metals. Emerging markets are also developing to trade futures contracts on natural disasters, such as hurricanes, for catastrophic insurance and weather futures to hedge against temperature extremes.

All futures contracts represent a standardized agreement between two parties that commits one party to sell and another party to buy a stipulated quantity and grade of a commodity, currency, security, or index or some other specified item at a set price on or before a given date in the future. All futures contracts require the daily settlement of all gains and losses as long as the futures contract remains in force. For futures contracts that remain open until trading terminates, contract specifications provide for physical delivery of the underlying asset or a final cash payment based on the difference between the spot market price and an agreed-on contract price.

The buyer of a futures contract, often referred to as the **long** position, agrees to receive delivery of the underlying asset from the seller of the futures contract, or **short**, who agrees to make delivery. Futures contracts are traded on exchanges either by open outcry in specified trading areas or electronically via a computerized network. In **open-outcry trading**. exchange members stand in **trading pits** making bids and offers, by voice and with hand signals, to other traders. Customer orders are routed to **floor brokers** or **dual traders** who execute them according to order instructions. Brokers and dual traders often assume responsibility for entering complex combinations of buy and sell orders. All futures contracts are marked to market at their end-of-day settlement prices. This means that daily gains and losses are passed through to the gaining and losing accounts. Any futures contracts can be terminated by an **offsetting transaction**. An offsetting trade is an equal but opposite transaction to the one that opened the futures position, and it is executed at any time prior to the expiration of the futures contract. In practice, only 1 to 2 percent of all futures market transactions result in the delivery of the underlying asset. The same or similar futures contracts can be traded on more than one exchange in the United States, although exchanges typically specialize in the trading of certain types of futures contracts.

Contractual Provisions

Standardized futures contracts specify five contractual provisions:

- **Underlying asset:** The commodity, currency, financial instrument index, or other item on which the contract is based must be unambiguously identified.

- **Amount and quality of the underlying asset:** The amount and quality (grade) of the underlying asset covered by the futures contract is precisely identified.

- **Delivery cycle:** Months for which the futures contracts can be traded must be specified.

- **Expiration date:** This date identifies when the futures contract terminates.

- **Settlement mechanism and delivery location (if applicable):** Futures contracts lay out how the physical delivery of the underlying item or a terminal cash payment is to be made. The only unspecified item of a futures contract is the price of the underlying unit. This amount is determined in the trading arena.

Figure 19.2 shows a typical specification for a futures contract. In this case, the commodity is world sugar traded on the New York Board of Trade's Coffee, Sugar & Cocoa Exchange.

Long
Buyer; also used to signify ownership.

Short
Seller; also used to signify sale.

Open-outcry trading
Exchange market dependent on physical communication.

Trading pit
Futures market trading area.

Floor broker
Futures market professional who executes orders for others.

Dual trader
Futures market professional who holds positions and executes orders for others.

Offsetting transaction
Equal but opposite trade.

FIGURE 19.1

Barron's Gives a Weekly Summary of Trading Activity in the Commodities and Financial Futures Markets

Commodities and Financial Futures

Commodities, or futures, contracts originally called for delivery of physical items, such as agricultural products and metals, at a specified price at a specified future date. Increasingly, these contracts have come to apply also to Treasury bills, notes and bonds, certificates of deposit, major market indices and major currencies.

Fibers

Financial & Money

Foreign Currencies

Grains and Feed

Livestock & Meat

Lumber

Source: Commodities and Financial Futures, *Barron's*, March 13, 2006, page M48. Copyright © 2006, Dow Jones Co. Used with permission.

FIGURE 19.2 | Futures Contract Specifications Are Available on the Internet

Futures Contract on Sugar No. 11 (World)

Contract specifications are current as of **January 8 , 2004** and may be subject to change. Verify information with your broker.

Calls for delivery of cane sugar, stowed in bulk, FOB from any twenty-eight foreign countries of origin as well as the United States

Trading Unit
112,000 lbs. (50 Long tons)

Trading Hours
9:00 am to 12:00 pm; closing period commences at 11:58 am

Price Quotation
Cents per pound

Delivery Months
March, May, July, October

Ticker Symbol
SB **Minimum Fluctuation**
1/100 cent/lb., equivalent to $11.20 per contract.

Last Trading Day:
Last business day of the month preceding deliverly month.

Notice Day:
1st business day after the last trading day.

Daily Price Limits:
None

Position Limits/Position Accountability
Spot Month - 5,000 contracts as of the 2nd business day following the expiration of the regular option contract traded on the expiring futures contract. Additionally, Position Accountability rules apply to all futures and options contract months. *Contact the Exchange for more information.*

Grade
Raw centrifugal cane sugar based on 96 degrees average polarization.

Deliverable Growths:
Growths of Argentina, Australia, Barbados, Belize, Brazil, Colombia, Costa Rica, Dominican Republic, El Salvador, Ecuador, Fiji Islands, French Antilles, Guatemala, Honduras, India, Jamaica, Malawi, Mauritius, Mexico, Nicaragua, Peru, Republic of the Philippines, South Africa, Swaziland, Taiwan, Thailand, Trinidad, United States, and Zimbabwe.

Delivery Points:
A port in the country of origin or in the case of landlocked countries, at a berth or anchorage in the customary port of export. Subject to minimum standards established by the Exchange's rules.

Source: New York Board of Trade **www.nybot.com**, © 2006 New York Board of Trade. New York Board of Trade®, NYBOT®, Sugar No. 11SM are registered trademarks/service marks of the Board of Trade of the City of New York, Inc. Used with permission.

Trading unit
Contract size.

Delivery months
Scheduled delivery cycles.

Delivery date
Calendar date by which buyers and sellers of futures contracts are obligated to offset or fulfill their obligations.

Delivery notice
Written advice of delivery intention.

Notice day
Last date on which written advice of an intent to physically deliver commodities may be issued.

The sugar futures contract calls for delivery of cane sugar, stowed in bulk, free on board (FOB) from any of 28 foreign countries of origin as well as the United States. Each such contract represents a **trading unit** of 112,000 pounds, or 50 long tons, of sugar. Prices are quoted in cents, with a minimum price fluctuation of 1/100 cent per pound, equivalent to $11.20 per contract. **Delivery months** for sugar are March, May, July, and October. The **delivery date** is the calendar date by which buyers and sellers of futures contracts are obligated to offset or fulfill their obligations. It occurs on the third Friday of the delivery month. If a seller wishes to satisfy a futures obligation through physical delivery on a particular date, a written **delivery notice** must be given to the buyer. **Notice day** is the last date on which an intent to physically deliver commodities may be issued.

The mechanics of futures trading are simple. Both buyers and sellers deposit funds, called *margin,* with a commodity brokerage firm. Margin can be thought of as a kind of performance bond or good-faith deposit that ensures contract performance. This amount is usually a tiny percentage, often only 5 to 10 percent, of the total value of the item underlying the contract. Thus, a move of as little as 1 percent in the price of the underlying as-

FIGURE 19.3   Futures Contracts Represent a Zero-Sum Game between Buyers and Sellers

A. Payoff for a Long Futures Position

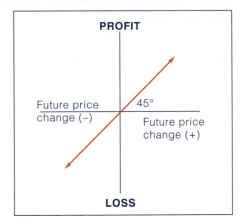

B. Payoff for a Short Futures Position

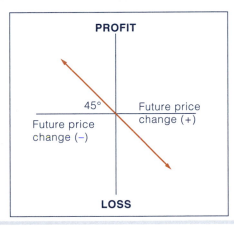

Source: OneChicago © 2006, OneChicago. Used with permission.

set can create a profit or loss of as much as 20 percent for the futures contract buyer or seller. A price move of as little as 5 percent for the underlying asset can double the buyer's or seller's original investment or cause one of them to be wiped out. Because a futures contract represents a legal obligation to buy or sell an agreed-on quantity and quality of the underlying asset at an agreed-on price, the buyer's or seller's actual profit or loss is not constrained by the margin amount. In volatile and fast-moving markets, prices for underlying commodities can sometimes move much more than 5 percent in a single trading day. This means that the minimum required margin can be lost in less than a single trading day, and if it is not quickly replenished, the loss can result in a margin call and forced liquidation. Speculators and hedgers frequently hold more than the minimum margin required in their accounts.

As indicated in Figure 19.3, Panel A, if an investor buys (goes long) a futures contract and the price rises, the investor profits by the amount of the price increase times the contract size. If an investor buys and the price goes down, the investor loses an amount equal to the price decrease times the contract size. Figure 19.3, Panel B, reflects the profit and loss potential of a short futures position. If an investor sells (goes short) a futures contract and the price goes down, the investor profits by the amount of the price decrease times the contract size. If an investor sells and the price goes up, the investor loses an amount equal to the price increase times the contract size. Just like options contracts, futures contracts represent a zero-sum game between the buyer and the seller. Before commissions and other trading costs, the buyer's gain is exactly equal to the seller's loss, and vice versa.

Futures on Stocks

Stock trading became very common in the 1990s. The rise of online brokerage firms, day trading, and deep discount brokerage enabled investors to speculate in stocks. Volume soared and the investment industry flourished. Futures markets also wanted to get some of this new action. One of the recent innovations in the futures market is the introduction of futures contracts on the stock of individual companies by OneChicago. There are currently over 200 single-stock futures (SSFs), such as IBM, Microsoft, and Walt Disney. They are denoted by the company stock's ticker symbol followed by *1C* (i.e., IBM1C for IBM). In addition to the SSFs, there are also futures contracts on the Dow Jones Industrial Average ETFs. Futures on individual stocks made their market debut in 2002, at OneChicago LLC and Nasdaq Liffe markets (visit the market at **www.onechicago.com**).

One single-stock futures contract is an agreement to deliver 100 shares of a specific stock at a designated date in the future. By February 2006, daily trading volume of SSFs averaged 20,800 contracts, or 4.7 million contracts per year. The most popular contracts by volume were on Johnson & Johnson, ConocoPhillips, Altria Group, and Merck. The most popular contracts measured by open interest were on General Electric, with open interest of 171,026 contracts.

Single-stock futures may make speculating and hedging less expensive. To buy shares of stock, investors can pay the full price of the stock or put up 50 percent of the price and borrow the remaining 50 percent as an interest-bearing margin account loan from their brokers. For single-stock futures, traders are typically required to put up only 20 percent of the cash value of the contract as margin equity, and that could be further reduced if the investor also holds certain offsetting positions. The holder of a single-stock futures contract controls a position equivalent to 100 shares of a particular stock with a good-faith deposit of only 20 percent of the position's total value. Of course, the ability to establish a position with only 20 percent margin means that a speculator can become very highly leveraged. High leverage increases the magnitude of potential profits, but enhances the risk of big losses.

Options on Futures

Because futures contracts involve obligations to buy and sell a specific commodity for a given price, both buyers and sellers are exposed to the potential for unlimited losses in the event of adverse market conditions. In contrast, options represent only the right, but not the obligation, to buy or sell a specified item for a preset price during a specific period of time. The loss potential for buyers of call options (rights to buy) and put options (rights to sell) is strictly limited to the amount paid for the option. Because sophisticated option hedging techniques are often beyond the expertise of small investors or prohibitively expensive for them, many small investors shun selling options. For the same reason, many small investors have shunned the futures markets, at least until recently.

Futures option
Right, but not obligation, to buy or sell a contract at a certain price for a limited period of time.

The various futures markets have introduced options on futures to increase the investment appeal of futures contracts among investors who seek financial derivatives with limited loss potential. **Futures options** give the right, but not the obligation, to buy or sell some specific futures contract at a certain price for a limited period of time. As in the case of call and put options on stocks and stock indexes, only the sellers of futures options are obligated to perform according to the terms of the option contract. The loss potential for buyers of futures options, both calls and puts, is limited to the amount of the premium paid for the option. In exchange for the premium received, sellers of futures options are obligated to fulfill the option contract if the buyer so chooses. As in the case of options on stocks and stock indexes, sellers of futures options have unlimited loss potential.

Do You Have a Future in Futures?

Employment opportunities in the U.S. futures industry revolve around the major exchanges. The Chicago Mercantile Exchange (CME) has a staff of more than 800 professionals in full- and part-time positions. In addition, members and clearing firms that conduct the business of trading on the CME floor employ staffs that handle many key duties. Whether it is working with an exchange, a member of a leading exchange, or a clearing firm, there are many different career paths within the futures industry.

Working on the exchange floor, market reporters monitor price changes and input appropriate information to ensure fast and accurate transmission of trading information. Futures exchanges are information-intensive operations that place a high premium on well-trained and highly motivated MIS personnel. Often trained as accountants, staff auditors are responsible for monitoring trading systems and making sure that member firms fall within regulatory guidelines. Exchange auditors are responsible for making sure that member firms comply with capital and other financial requirements. Compliance investigators have the responsibility for monitoring trade practices in exchange markets. They work with arbitration committees appointed by the various exchanges to process and resolve claims between members and customers.

Many key personnel in the futures industry are employed by exchange members or clearing firms. At the center of exchange floor trading activity are floor managers who manage order taking and information processing. Like floor managers, clerks are employed by member firms to communicate trading information from the pits to the phones. Actual trading activity is conducted by option and futures traders, who buy and sell for their own accounts, and brokers, who execute trading orders for public or business customers. Many member firms employ account executives whose responsibility is to develop and serve clients. Account executives are registered with the National Futures Association and earn commissions based on the accounts they open and manage. Clearing firms also employ "back-office" personnel to fulfill basic functions, such as phone receptionists, margin clerks, wire room clerks, and office managers.

Career opportunities with the exchanges or member firms offer the best opportunities in the way of pay and advancement opportunities.

See For further information, contact the exchanges or member firms directly (e.g., **www.cme.com**).

Futures Trading Process

U.S. Futures Exchanges

Futures exchanges serve as a meeting place for exchange members to buy and sell futures contracts on commodities and financial instruments. Futures exchanges are associations of members organized for a single purpose: to provide competitive markets for the trading of futures and options on futures for commodities, natural resources, and financial instruments. As shown in Figure 19.4, U.S. futures and futures option trading is concentrated in major exchanges. Among these futures exchanges, the Chicago Mercantile Exchange (which includes the International Monetary Market), the CBOT, and the New York Mercantile Exchange are commonly regarded as the "big three" and account for well more than 95 percent of U.S. futures and futures options trading activity. While futures and futures options on some popular contracts are listed on more than one U.S. futures exchange, trading on the exchange that first introduced a given product tends to be dominant. As a result, the various U.S. futures exchanges tend to be known by their relative size and by the types of futures contracts with which they are associated.

The CBOT is the world's oldest futures and futures options exchange. More than 3,600 members trade 50 different futures and options products at the CBOT, accounting for annual trading volume of 674 million contracts in 2005, or about 34 percent of total futures and futures option trading in the United States. In addition to the open-outcry floor trading, the CBOT also manages its rapidly growing electronic trading system (called *e-cbot*) powered by Liffe Connect. The CBOT is on the Internet at **www.cbot.com**.

The **Chicago Mercantile Exchange (CME)** is the largest futures exchange in the United States and represents roughly 53.2 percent of total futures market activity, with more than 1,050 million futures and futures options in annual trading volume. It has a diverse product line that includes futures and futures options on agricultural commodities, foreign currencies (a special expertise), interest rates, and stock indexes. As a truly international marketplace, the Chicago Merc enables institutions and businesses to manage financial risks and efficiently allocate assets. On its trading floors, buyers and sellers meet to trade futures contracts and options on futures through

Chicago Mercantile Exchange (CME)
Largest futures exchange in the United States.

FIGURE 19.4   U.S. Futures Exchanges

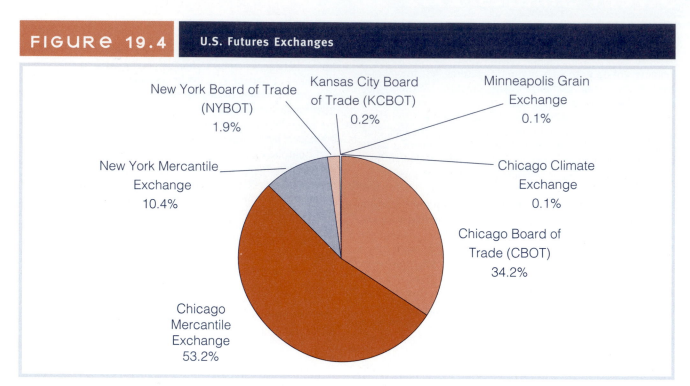

Source: Exchange Web sites.

New York Mercantile Exchange
Third-largest U.S. futures market, and the world's largest physical commodity futures exchange.

New York Board of Trade (NYBOT)
Parent company of the New York Cotton Exchange and the Coffee, Sugar & Cocoa Exchange, Inc.

Kansas City Board of Trade (KCBOT)
Predominant marketplace for hard red winter wheat.

Minneapolis Grain Exchange
U.S. futures exchange specializing in grain contracts.

Chicago Climate Exchange
U.S. futures exchange specializing in greenhouse gas contracts.

Clearinghouses
Institutions that ensure balance in the number of futures and futures option contracts bought and sold and that give fulfillment guarantees.

the open-outcry process. In most contracts, trading continues virtually around the clock on the Globex electronic trading system. Volume has increased on Globex to over 4 million contracts per day. Further information about Chicago Merc products can be obtained at **www.cme.com**.

The **New York Mercantile Exchange** is the third-largest U.S. futures market and the world's largest physical commodity futures exchange, and it specializes in energy and metals contracts. It accounts for trading activity of more than 205 million futures and options contracts per year, or about 10.4 percent of the overall market. The New York Merc is the preeminent trading forum for crude oil, gasoline, heating oil, natural gas, propane, gold, silver, platinum, palladium, and copper (see **www.nymex.com**).

Other important U.S. futures exchanges include the **New York Board of Trade (NYBOT)**, parent company of the New York Cotton Exchange, founded in 1870, and the Coffee, Sugar & Cocoa Exchange, Inc., founded in 1880. The NYBOT offers a wide variety of agricultural, financial, and index products and is responsible for trading volume of more than 38 million futures and futures option contracts per year, or 1.9 percent of the U.S. total. NYBOT is on the Internet at **www.nybot.com**. The **Kansas City Board of Trade (KCBOT)** has been the world's predominant marketplace for hard red winter wheat, the major ingredient in the world's bread. The KCBOT trades more than 4 million futures and futures options contracts per year (see **www.kcbot.com**). The **Minneapolis Grain Exchange** boasts the only authorized market for hard red spring wheat, white wheat, and durum futures and options, trading an average of 20 million bushels daily (**www.mgex.com**). The new **Chicago Climate Exchange** is the world's first greenhouse gas allowance trading system, trading six gasses. By early 2006, the exchange was trading approximately 24,000 contracts (or 600,000 metric tons of carbon dioxide) per month (see **www.chicagoclimatex.com**).

Clearing and Margin Requirements

Each of the various futures exchanges uses **clearinghouses** owned by member firms to ensure the financial integrity of futures and options contracts. Clearinghouses ensure balance in the number of futures and futures option contracts bought and sold, and they give fulfillment guarantees to ensure contract performance. Futures clearinghouses facilitate trade among strangers by eliminating **counterparty risk.** In the United States, each futures exchange has had its own clearinghouse, formed either as a separate entity or as a part of the exchange. Recently, a number of U.S. futures exchanges have begun exploring the possibility of common clearing, as is typical for options on stocks and stock indexes, where the Options Clearing Corporation serves this purpose.

Margin requirements are set by the exchanges at levels sufficient to protect the clearinghouse against one day's maximum price movement in a particular futures or options contract. For most contracts, there is a difference between **initial margin**, the amount of margin exchanges require to commence a trade, and **maintenance margin**, the minimum margin the customer must keep at all times. In volatile markets, additional margin may be collected intraday, with clearing members sometimes required to deposit funds within one hour of a margin call. The mark-to-market process ensures that futures buyer and seller accounts retain sufficient value to guarantee contract fulfillment. If there is a daily profit, this amount can be paid to the customer. If there is a daily loss, the customer must pay this full amount.

Counterparty risk
Chance that a counterparty to a futures contract obligation will not fulfill his or her obligation.

Initial margin
Minimum amount required to initiate a trade.

Maintenance margin
Minimum amount required at all times to sustain a market position.

Try It!

Assume a speculator has a margin account with $2,500 in it and a long position in one gold futures contract. Yesterday, the futures price closed at $395.80 per ounce, and today it closed at $387.50. A gold contract is for 100 troy ounces of gold, and the maintenance margin is $2,025. What happens now?

Solution

The futures price fell by $8.30 (= $395.80 − $387.50) per ounce. In the mark-to-market, the speculator will have $830 (= $8.30 × 100) taken out of the margin account. This money goes to the short position in the contract. The speculator's margin account declines to $1,670 (= $2,500 − $830), which is below the maintenance margin of $2,025. The speculator will receive a margin call and must either get out of the position or contribute cash to the margin account.

Futures Trading Example

In late 2005, *The Wall Street Journal*'s regular "Commodities" column ran an extremely bearish article on sugar titled "Sugar Market Is Set on a Bearish Course." In that article, the *Journal* reported that raw-sugar prices slid as heavy selling from producers in Central and South America and Australia set the market on a bearish course. On Monday, the March contract on New York's Coffee, Sugar & Cocoa Exchange fell 0.14 cent to 5.29 cents per pound, matching the lowest settlement price in eight months. "Clearly, everyone is selling," said a trader at a New York brokerage firm. The market is "very well entrenched into a downtrend." So bearish was the consensus on sugar prices that the *Journal* quoted a leading analyst as saying, "It sort of flummoxes me why the market hasn't fallen more steeply than it has given the fundamentals."

Suppose an investor read the *Journal*'s assessment of the pricing outlook for sugar and decided to sell (or short) 10 sugar futures contracts in the hope of profiting from the expected fall in sugar prices. As indicated in Figure 19.2, each sugar futures contract represents 112,000 pounds of sugar. At a price of 5.29 cents per pound, the total value of one sugar contract is $5,924.80 (= 112,000 × $0.0529), as shown in Table 19.2. The value of 10 sugar contracts at 5.29 cents per pound is simply $59,248 (= 10 × $5,924.80). According to the New York Board of Trade, parent company of the Coffee, Sugar & Cocoa Exchange, where sugar is traded, the minimum initial margin requirement for sugar is $700 per contract, or $7,000 for 10 contracts. The minimum maintenance margin is $500 per sugar futures contract, or $5,000 for 10 contracts. For simplicity, brokerage commissions and other trading costs will be ignored. In practice, these costs are substantial and greatly diminish trading profits and augment trading losses.

TABLE 19.2	Sugar Futures Contract Commodity Trading Example

Contract Specifications

Size of the contract	112,000 lb
Minimum price change	
Of 1 ounce	1/100¢/lb
Of one contract	$11.20
Initial margin level	$700
Maintenance margin level	$500

Day 1

Investor buys 10 sugar futures contracts at 5.29¢/lb (Position value = 10 × 112,000 × $0.0529/lb = $59,248)	
Investor deposits initial margin	$7,000
Price rises to close at 5.32¢/lb.; investor loss of 0.03¢/lb ($33.60 per contract) paid to clearinghouse	−336
Account balance at end of day 1	$6,664

Day 2

Opening account balance (from day 1)	$6,664
Price rises further to close at 5.40¢/lb; investor loss of 0.08¢/lb ($89.60 per contract) paid to clearinghouse	896
Account balance on day 2, after loss is paid to clearinghouse	$5,768

Day 3

Opening account balance (from day 2)	$5,768
Price jumps to 5.52¢/lb; investor loss of 0.12¢/lb ($134.40 per contract) paid to clearinghouse	1,344
Intraday account balance on day 3, after loss is paid to clearinghouse	$4,424
Margin call of $2,576 made to restore the account to the initial margin level ($7,000)	2,576
Account balance at end of day 3, after margin call is met	$7,000

Day 4

Opening account balance (from day 3)	$7,000
Price falls 0.05¢/lb to 5.47¢/lb; investor gain of $56 per contract)	560
Account balance	$7,560
Trader offsets the short futures position at 5.47¢/lb and liquidates the account	$7,560
Account balance at the end of day 4	0

Profit/Loss Summary

Profit/loss = 10 × (contract selling price − contract buying price)
$$= 10 \times \left[112{,}000 \text{ lbs} \left(5.29¢/lb - \$5.47¢/lb\right)\right] = -\$2{,}016 \text{ (loss)}$$

Profit/loss = sum of deposits (−) and receipts (+)

Day 1 Initial margin deposit	−$7,000
Day 3 Margin call deposit	−2,576
Day 4 Account liquidated receipt	+7,560
Net trading loss	−$2,016

On day 1 (Tuesday), sugar actually closes up 0.03 cent at 5.32 cents per pound. This represents a loss of $336 on a 10-contract short position established at 5.29 cents per pound. This $336 amount has to be paid by the investor to the clearinghouse at the end of the trading day, thereby reducing the investor's account balance from an initial $7,000 to $6,664. On day 2 (Wednesday), sugar closes up another 0.08 cent at 5.40 cents per pound. This represents a further loss of $896 on a 10-contract short position. This $896 amount has to be paid by the investor to the clearinghouse at the end of the second trading day, thereby reducing the investor's account balance from the day 1 ending balance of $6,664 to $5,768.

On day 3 (Thursday), the price of sugar jumps another 0.12 cent to 5.52 cents per pound, resulting in a trading loss of $1,344 on a 10-contract short position. This loss also triggers a margin call since it decreases the investor's account value to only $4,424, which is below the $5,000 minimum maintenance margin for a 10-contract short position. Let's assume the affected investor is promptly contacted and is able to wire $2,576 in additional funds to the commodity broker. At the end of day 3, the investor's account balance has thus been restored to its initial margin level of $7,000.

After surging as high as 5.57 cents per pound on day 4 (Friday), sugar settles down to close at 5.47 cents per pound. If the investor closes out the 10-contract short position at the closing price, a daily trading profit of 0.05 cent per pound, or $560 on a 10-contract short position, would be realized. After closing out the short position, the investor would be left with an account balance of $7,560. This reflects a trading loss of $2,016 over the four-day trading period, given the $7,000 in initial margin and $2,576 in additional required margin that was contributed to the account.

This simple illustration shows how an investor could have quickly lost a significant amount of money following reasonable commodity trading advice based on widely publicized sugar market fundamentals. Using actual market prices over a four-day period, a loss of 25 to 30 percent of an investor's original capital could easily have been suffered. To be sure, significant trading profits would have been gained if the investor had taken a directly contrarian approach. The problem is, how does a commodity investor know when to be contrarian or when to "go with the flow"?

Hedging

Hedgers versus Speculators

Historically, futures market participants have been divided into two broad categories. **Hedgers** seek to reduce risks associated with dealing in the underlying commodity or security. **Speculators**, including professional floor traders, seek to profit from price changes. For speculators, the attraction of futures markets include the extraordinary amount of leverage that can be employed and the ease with which long and short positions can be established. Speculators and market makers assume the risk transferred by hedgers and give futures markets a high degree of liquidity. In contrast to hedgers, many speculators never use commodities in any manufacturing capacity. Most speculators trade strictly for the purpose of acquiring profits. By watching the markets closely, speculators can sometimes take advantage of small fluctuations in futures prices.

Most participants in the futures and option markets are commercial or institutional users and hedgers of the commodities traded. The hedger's objective is to lock in a favorable contract price. Hedgers are often willing to give up the possibility of lower spot prices to avoid the detrimental effects of exorbitantly high spot prices. Farmers, mining companies, and oil drillers are examples of hedgers that use futures contracts as a kind of insurance policy for their businesses.

Hedging involves taking a futures position that is opposite that of a cash market position. A corn farmer could hedge by selling corn futures against an expected crop. An importer of Japanese cars might hedge by buying yen futures against an expected yen liability. A precious-metal merchant could hedge by purchasing gold futures against a fixed-price gold sales

Hedgers
Investors who seek to reduce risks associated with dealing in the underlying commodity or security.

Speculators
Individuals who seek to profit from price changes.

contract. A pension fund manager could hedge by selling stock index futures against the fund's portfolio of equities in anticipation of a market decline.

Hedging Concepts

Basis

In the futures market, the difference between a commodity's spot price and the futures price.

Price risk

Chance of adverse change in market prices.

Basis risk

Chance of adverse change in the futures–spot market price relationship.

Hedge ratio

The ratio of underlying asset price volatility divided by the price volatility of the futures contract price.

In the futures market, the difference between a commodity's cash price, or spot price, and the futures price is known as the **basis**, as illustrated in Figure 19.5. While hedging strategies with futures can eliminate **price risk**, hedging strategies cannot eliminate **basis risk**. Price risk is the chance that a security or portfolio will decline in value over time. Basis risk is the chance that the underlying basis will change unpredictably and unfavorably during the lifetime of the hedge. Basis risk derives from the hedger's uncertainty about the basis at the time a hedge may be lifted. Hedging techniques substitute basis risk for price risk.

The cash-futures basis is subject to seasonal factors, weather conditions, temporary gluts or scarcities of commodities, the availability of transport facilities, interest rates, and warehouse fees. In certain financial markets, basis reflects the difference between long-term and short-term interest rates. As shown in Figure 19.5, the cash-futures basis, or difference between spot and futures prices, converges toward zero as futures contracts approach the expiration date. However, prior to expiration, the difference between cash and futures prices can widen or narrow for reasons that are hard to predict. Basis risk tends to be prevalent when traders cross-hedge a risk exposure in one commodity using futures contracts on a different, but closely related, commodity. For example, a trader might use heating oil futures to hedge jet fuel needs or euros to hedge European investments. Prices of two related fuels or two related currencies may have moved closely for significant periods of time in the past, but there is no guarantee that historical price relationships will continue into the future.

As in the option market, the futures market delta (or **hedge ratio**) is the ratio of underlying asset price volatility divided by the price volatility of the hedging instrument. To use futures as a hedge against a long position in an agricultural commodity, natural resource, or financial instrument, hedgers write a certain number of futures contracts. This number is given by the hedge ratio. Suppose a March soybean futures contract representing 5,000 bushels of soybeans has a delta of 0.9. This means that this soybean futures contract's theoretical value should change by 90 percent of the change in the cash price of soybeans. A perfectly hedged and risk-less position would be established if 4,500 bushels of soybeans ($= 0.9 \times 5,000$ bushels) were purchased for every soybean futures contract written. In that case, a 10-cent-per-bushel increase in the cash price of soybeans would lead to a cash market profit of $450 ($= 10¢ \times 4,500$ bushels) that would exactly offset the $450 ($= 0.9 \times 10¢ \times 5,000$-bushel futures contract) loss on the futures contract written. Conversely, a 10-cent-per-bushel decrease in the cash price of

| FIGURE 19.5 | The Difference between Cash and Futures Prices Is the Cash-Futures Basis |

soybeans would lead to a cash market loss of \$450 (= 10¢ × 4,500 bushels) that would exactly offset the \$450 (= 0.9 × 10¢ × 5,000-bushel futures contract) gain on the futures contract written. As in the options market, a perfectly hedged position in the futures market leaves total wealth unchanged. Notice that hedge ratios are less than 1.0: A \$1 movement in underlying asset prices causes less than a \$1 change in futures prices. However, because futures contracts have a lower price basis that the underlying asset, the percentage change in futures prices tends to be larger than the percentage change in spot, or cash, market prices.

A spread position is the simultaneous purchase and sale of two related futures or option positions. Speculators take on spread positions when the prices of related futures or option contracts are considered out of line with historical patterns. An **intramarket spread**, also called a time spread, combines a long position in one contract month and a short position in another month in the same futures contract on the same exchange. An example would be going long March sugar futures and short July sugar futures on the Coffee, Sugar & Cocoa Exchange. The intramarket spread between prices of various futures delivery months reflects supply, demand, and carrying-cost considerations. Warehouse charges and inventory carrying costs generally increase over time, so the commodity futures price for each succeeding delivery month is usually higher than that of the preceding delivery month.

An **intermarket spread** consists of a long position in one market and a short position in another market trading the same or a closely related commodity. An example is the "TED spread" difference between the prices of a U.S. Treasury bill futures contract and a Eurodollar time-deposit futures contract on the Chicago Mercantile Exchange. The TED spread varies with changes in the relationship between short-term interest rates for private and government debt. Another intermarket spread is the "NOB spread," or U.S. Treasury notes over U.S. Treasury bonds on the Chicago Board of Trade. Such spreads reflect differences in interest rates on U.S. Treasury securities of different maturities.

Intramarket spread
In the futures market, the difference between futures prices for different delivery months for the same underlying commodity.

Intermarket spread
Offsetting positions in related commodities.

Try It!

Consider a note-over-bond spread traded on the CBOT. One such spread holds one long five-year T-note and is short one T-bond contract. Both contracts are for \$100,000 par value of notes or bonds, are quoted in terms of bond prices, and move in 32nds of a percent of par value. Each $\frac{1}{32}$ price move represents \$31.25 in the mark-to-market. The five-year T-note closed today at 109-09, up 2. The T-bond closed at 105-25, up 6. Did the spread make money?

Solution

The long five-year T-note contract received a mark-to-market inflow of \$62.50 (= 2 × \$31.25), while the short T-bond contract required a payment of \$187.50 (= 6 × \$31.25). So the net spread caused a loss of \$125 (= \$62.50 − \$187.50). This spread makes money when long-term interest rates increase relative to five-year rates. Since the long-term rate decreased relative to the five-year rate, this spread lost money.

Hedging Example

Suppose Heating Oil Transfer (HOT), Inc., buys heating oil at current wholesale prices from refiners and then markets the oil to large industrial users, school systems, and shopping centers. HOT's customers want to know how much heating oil will cost them during the heating season. To get their business, HOT offers its clients fixed-price contracts. After entering into contracts to deliver heating oil at a fixed price, HOT is exposed to price risk if it doesn't own the oil or have a fixed-price contract to purchase heating oil from a refiner. To hedge its price risk in the futures market, HOT would go long or buy heating oil futures.

Each heating oil futures contract is for 1,000 barrels (42 gallons = 1 barrel) of heating oil. Assume it is now June 1, and HOT enters into a fixed-price contract to deliver 840,000 gallons

TABLE 19.3	A Hypothetical Hedging Example for the Heating Oil Market

	Cash (Spot) Price	(Oct.) Futures
Price/gal., June 1	65¢	60¢
A. Cash and futures prices rise (in tandem), such that:		
	Local Cash	**(Oct.) Futures**
Price/gal., Oct. 1	75¢	70¢
B. Cash and futures prices fall (in tandem), such that:		
Price/gal., Oct 1	60¢	55¢
C. Cash and futures prices remain the same, such that:		
Price/gal., Oct 1	65¢	60¢

of heating oil in early October. Under the circumstances, HOT needs to buy 20 futures contracts to hedge its price risk. To hedge its price risk in the futures market, HOT would go long or buy heating oil futures on June 1 and then liquidate its futures market position on October 1. On October 1, HOT would purchase heating oil in the spot market to fulfill its contractual obligations. Remember, the October heating oil futures contract on the New York Merc expires on the third Friday of the month. HOT could not fulfill its contractual obligations by taking delivery on its October futures contracts. Oil delivered on the October futures contracts would arrive too late for HOT's customers.

Consider the three different oil price scenarios illustrated in Table 19.3. In Scenario A, cash and futures prices rise in tandem by 10 cents per gallon. The cash price for oil rises from 65 to 75 cents per gallon, and the October 1 futures price rises from 60 to 70 cents per gallon. In this case, the heating oil futures contracts that were purchased for 60 cents per gallon in June are sold for 70 cents per gallon in October, for a gain of 10 cents per gallon. What is HOT's effective price per gallon for the heating oil it is delivering to customers? The answer is 65 cents per gallon. Heating oil for delivery in October is purchased on the spot market on October 1 for 75 cents per gallon. HOT's gain on the long futures position of 10 cents per gallon is subtracted from the spot cost of 75 cents per gallon for a net cost of 65 cents per gallon. Under this scenario, HOT's June decision to lock in the June 1 cash price of 65 cents per gallon using the futures market saved the company from having to pay higher heating oil prices that emerged the following October.

In Scenario B, cash and futures prices fall in tandem by 5 cents per gallon. The cash price for oil falls from 65 to 60 cents per gallon, and the October 1 futures price falls from 60 to 55 cents per gallon. In this case, the heating oil futures contracts that were purchased for 60 cents per gallon in June are sold for 55 cents per gallon in October, for a loss of 5 cents per gallon. HOT's effective price per gallon for the heating oil it is delivering is again 65 cents per gallon. Heating oil for delivery in October is purchased on the spot market on October 1 for 60 cents per gallon. HOT's loss on the long futures position of 5 cents per gallon is added to the spot cost of 60 cents per gallon for a net cost of 65 cents per gallon. Under this scenario, HOT's June decision to lock in the June 1 cash price of 65 cents per gallon using the futures market made it impossible for the company to enjoy the benefits from lower heating oil prices that materialized the following October. By locking in prices in the futures market, HOT avoids the risk of higher prices but loses the potential for cost savings from lower prices.

Finally, in Scenario C, cash and futures prices remain constant at 65 cents per gallon (cash price) and 60 cents per gallon (futures price). In this case, the heating oil futures contracts

Street Smarts 19.2

Tips for Futures Traders

To help speculators avoid some of the many pitfalls associated with futures trading, the Chicago Mercantile Exchange (Merc) offers a wealth of investor education. Here are simple, time-tested rules used by successful traders:

- **Start small.** Funds put into a speculative trading account should be completely discretionary. Be able to afford to lose whatever amount is placed in a trading account. Savings for college, retirement, or emergencies should not be included. Do not confuse speculating with investing.
- **Set definite risk parameters.** Before entering into a trade, determine how much you are willing to lose. This can be a dollar figure or a percentage of a trading account. Always keep something in reserve. Do not let emotions dictate trading decisions when the market turns against you.
- **Diversify.** Never expose an entire trading account to a single dominant position in one futures contract. It is always more prudent to take smaller positions in several contracts. At the same time, do not trade too many markets. It is difficult to track positions and follow market fundamentals in a large number of markets.

- **Choose your instruments and trading strategy carefully.** Futures contracts that experience extremely wide daily trading ranges are especially risky. Larger contracts often carry greater risk, although risk also depends on contract the minimum scale of contract price changes (tick size) and the average trading range. Be careful about the excessive use of margin. Being right does you no good if you get stopped out just prior to a big move up in price.
- **Have a workable trading strategy, and stick to it.** Before entering into a futures position, develop a workable trading plan based on the economic fundamentals. Specify a reasonable price target, and decide to sell if your goal is met. How will you know when you are wrong? When is it time to sell?

Successful futures market traders know that their success depends on having a superior grasp of the economic fundamentals of the market and maintaining a strict trading discipline.

See For investor education and trading tips, see the Chicago Mercantile Exchange Web site, **www.cme.com**.

---

locked in the June cash price of 65 cents per gallon, which is exactly the same as the October cash market price of 65 cents per gallon. No gain or loss results from HOT's futures market transactions, and the effective price is 65 cents per gallon, the October spot price, with no futures gain or loss introduced into the calculation.

Program Trading

One of the most popular examples of hedging activity relates to the stock market, and the use of stock index futures and options on stock index futures. The introduction of stock index futures brought a whole new group of investors to the futures markets. As opposed to buying or selling just a handful of stocks, stock index futures give investors the ability to offset security risk through a host of complicated investment strategies, referred to as **index arbitrage**. Index arbitrage is a trading strategy that exploits divergences between actual and theoretical futures prices. For example, buying stock index futures while selling baskets of stocks that underlie the index is a sometimes-effective means for capturing elusive trading profits. Stock index futures also allow traders to make bets on the direction of stock prices as measured by broad market benchmarks.

Index arbitrage
Trading strategy that exploits divergences between actual and theoretical futures prices.

   Program trading of bundles of stocks tied to expiring futures contracts is a type of arbitrage used by institutional investors to exploit price differences between financial derivatives and the underlying securities. While program trading is criticized by some for creating market turmoil, others say it makes for more liquid and efficient markets. In any event, program trading can represent a significant portion of trading activity. For example, program trading in February 2006 accounted for 57.1 percent, or an average 1,030.5 million daily shares, of New York Stock Exchange volume. In these data, program trading is defined as the simultaneous purchase or sale of at least 15 different stocks with a total value of at least $1 million. Of the program total on the Big Board, *The Wall Street Journal* reported that 12.8 percent involved stock index arbitrage. In this strategy, traders dart between stocks and stock index options and futures to capture fleeting price differences.

Futures Pricing

Law of One Price

Financial derivative markets encompass a plethora of tailored financial instruments that are traded by the world's leading financial institutions. **Swaps** are arrangements whereby two companies agree to lend to each other on different terms, such as in different currencies or at different interest rates. Financial institutions sometimes conduct swaps to trade fixed–interest rate obligations for floating–interest rate obligations. **Swaptions** are simply options to engage in a specific interest rate swap on or before a specific date. **Caps** are upper limits on the interest rate paid on floating-rate notes or adjustable-rate mortgages. **Collars** are upper and lower limits on the interest rate paid on floating-rate notes or adjustable-rate mortgages. The fact that financial futures and other financial derivatives are actively traded by savvy financial institutions in active and liquid financial markets ensures that prices are efficiently linked among various financial derivatives.

In perfectly competitive financial markets, the **law of one price** states that identical assets have identical prices. This means that the same asset trading in different markets will have the same price. A stock trading on both the London Stock Exchange and the New York Stock Exchange should trade at the same price, after accounting for currency exchange costs. Similarly, the law of one price implies that strict relations exist between the prices for underlying assets and those for related financial derivatives. This means that the futures price for any agricultural commodity or natural resource equals the spot (or cash market) price plus the cost of carry, including interest and storage costs:

$$\begin{aligned} \text{Commodity futures prices} &= \text{spot price} + \text{cost of carry} \qquad\qquad\qquad \textbf{(19.1)} \\[2mm] &= \text{spot price}\left(1 + \text{risk-free interest rate} + \text{percentage storage cost}\right) \end{aligned}$$

Equation 19.1 shows that the commodity futures price can be viewed as a composite of the spot market price plus the costs necessary to hold agricultural commodities or natural resources until the expiration of the futures contract.

Suppose the spot market price for gold was $300 per ounce and the risk-free interest rate is 6 percent per year. If the gold market anticipated sufficient additional production during the next 12 months, there would be no additional gold storage costs necessary to meet gold futures contract commitments. In such circumstances, the one-year gold futures price would simply be $318 (= $300 × 1.06). If the gold spot market price was $300 and the futures price was above $318, the firm could buy gold in the spot market and sell gold futures and earn risk-free arbitrage profits. If the gold spot market price was $300 per ounce and the futures price was below $318, the firm could buy gold futures and sell gold in the spot market and earn risk-free arbitrage profits. Similarly, if the gold spot market price was above $300 and gold futures were $318, the firm could sell gold in the spot market and buy gold futures and earn risk-free arbitrage profits. If the gold spot market price was below $300 and gold futures were $318, the firm could buy gold in the spot market and sell gold futures and earn risk-free arbitrage profits. Simply put, every spot market price translates into a specific futures price after adjusting for interest and storage costs.

In the case of financial futures, pension funds and other institutional investors use sophisticated hedging strategies to ensure conformance between spot market prices for financial instruments and futures prices. As in the case of futures for agricultural commodities and natural

---

Swaps

Arrangements whereby two companies agree to lend to each other on different terms.

Swaptions

Options to engage in a specific interest rate swap on or before a specific date.

Caps

Upper limits on the interest rate paid on floating-rate notes or adjustable-rate mortgages.

Collars

Upper and lower limits on the interest rate paid on floating-rate notes or adjustable-rate mortgages.

Law of one price

Concept that identical assets have identical prices.

resources, arbitrage between the spot and futures markets ensures efficiency in the pricing of financial futures:

$$\begin{array}{l} \dfrac{\text{Financial}}{\text{futures price}} = \dfrac{\text{spot price for}}{\text{financial instrument}} + \dfrac{\text{borrowing costs}}{\text{of carry}} - \dfrac{\text{dividend yield}}{\text{or interest income}} \qquad \textbf{(19.2)} \\[2em] = \dfrac{\text{Spot}}{\text{price}}\left(1+ \dfrac{\text{Risk-free}}{\text{interest rate}} - \dfrac{\text{Percentage income on}}{\text{financial instrument}}\right) \end{array}$$

Equation 19.2 shows that the financial futures price depends on the spot market price and the borrowing costs necessary to hold instruments until the expiration of the futures contract minus the amount of dividend or interest income that would be generated by the underlying financial instrument.

For example, if the risk-free interest rate is 6 percent per year and the dividend yield on an underlying stock index is 2 percent per year, the net cost of carry is only 4 percent (= 6% − 2%) per year. If the spot market price for the underlying index is $1,500, a one-year futures contract would have a price of $1,560 (= $1,500 × 1.04). If the index spot price was $1,500 and the futures price was above $1,560, investors could buy in the spot market and sell in the futures market and earn risk-free arbitrage profits. If the index spot price was $1,500 and the futures price was below $1,560, investors could sell in the spot market and buy in the futures market and earn risk-free arbitrage profits. Similarly, if the index spot price was below $1,500 and the futures price was $1,560, investors could buy in the spot market and sell in the futures market and earn risk-free arbitrage profits. If the index spot price was above $1,500 and the futures price was $1,560, investors could sell in the spot market and buy in the futures market and earn risk-free arbitrage profits.

As shown in Figure 19.6, Panel A, a carrying-charge, or **contango,** futures market is one in which futures prices are higher in distant delivery months. An inverted market, or one in **backwardation,** as shown in Figure 19.6, Panel B, features lower futures prices in distant delivery months. Inverted markets sometimes occur when demand for the cash commodity is unusually strong relative to current supply. Inverted markets also occur when the income derived from holding a cash position exceeds the costs of carrying the position. Backwardation can occur in U.S. Treasury bond futures when long-term interest rates exceed short-term rates, and, therefore, the underlying bond yield is greater than the cost of financing the cash bond portfolio.

Contango
Futures market with higher prices in distant delivery months.

Backwardation
Inverted market in which futures prices are lower in distant delivery months.

Try It!

Suppose the closing price of gold futures contracts yesterday was $388.40 for the June contract, $390.70 for the October contract, and $392.00 for the December contract. Why is the price higher for later delivery dates?

Solution

Futures prices rely on the arbitrage between buying the gold in the future month with the futures contract or buying the gold now and holding it until the future month. Buying the gold now and holding it incurs carrying costs. As seen in Equation 19.1, the longer the period of time until contract maturity, the longer the gold holder must pay the risk-free rate and the holding costs.

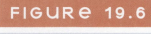

FIGURE 19.6   Intramarket Spreads Reflect Influences of Supply, Demand, and Carrying Costs

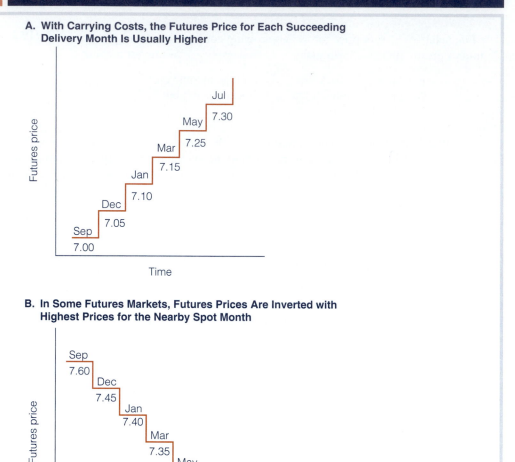

Investor Risk Considerations

Social benefits of futures markets lie in their price discovery and risk-shifting roles. Financial institutions and individual investors look to the futures markets to help determine the best current market prices. That's because futures markets provide a forum that is somewhat independent from cash markets for buyers and sellers who want to trade. Futures markets give buyers and sellers an alternative means for collecting bids and offers and bringing them together in an open-outcry auction market. Another major function of futures markets is to transfer risk. If you were a cattle rancher, your objective might be to raise and sell cattle at a price that would give the most profit. A major risk would stem from declining cattle prices. You could transfer this risk by selling cattle futures. If cattle prices plunge, you could buy back the futures contracts at a lower price and offset your cash loss. Hence, the risk of lower prices is transferred to a buyer who may be a speculator or commercial user, such as a beef processor. Those who accept a transfer of risk through futures markets hope to generate profits.

It is worth keeping in mind that mundane examples like the cattle rancher and the beef processor account for little of the actual trading activity in futures markets. In practice, only 1

The Cognitive Reflection Test

People with higher cognitive ability (or "IQ") have lots of advantages. On average, they live longer, earn more, have larger working memories, and have faster reaction times. Unfortunately, they also tend to be more susceptible to visual illusions—and that can get them into trouble when it comes to trading.

A common adage among commodity traders is to trust your first instinct, but the most successful traders tend to be those who go beyond their initial impulse and ask themselves if the planned course of action really makes sense. Shane Frederick, MIT Sloan Professor, has developed a simple 60-second test that measures people's ability to resist their first instinct. The test, called the Cognitive Reflection Test, consists of three simple questions: (1) A bat and ball cost $1.10 in total. The bat costs $1 more than the ball. How much does the ball cost? (2) If it takes five machines five minutes to make five widgets, how long would it take 100 machines to make 100 widgets? (3) In a lake, there is a patch of lily pads. Every day the patch doubles in size. If it takes 48 days for the lily pads to cover the entire lake, how long would it take the lily pads to cover one-half of the lake?

Each of these questions has a wrong intuitive response. Because most people need a bit of reflection to get the correct answers, the questions test a type of intelligence known as "cognitive reflection." Apparently, that's a rare form of intelligence. The average student taking the test gets only 1.24 answers correct. Those who score highest in cognitive reflection tend to be good at evaluating risky investment opportunities that involve complex calculations involving probabilities and the time value of money. Frederick has also found that those who do well on the CRT like to gamble.

How did you do? [Correct answers: (1) five cents, (2) five minutes, and (3) 47 days. Intuitive but incorrect answers are (1) 10 cents, (2) 100 minutes, and (3) 24 days.]

See Shane Frederick, "Cognitive Reflection and Decision Making," *Journal of Economic Perspectives*, vol. 19, no. 4 (Fall 2005), pp. 25–42.

to 2 percent of futures contracts ever result in the delivery of an actual commodity. Futures markets are not intended as an alternative to gambling casinos, but that's what they are for many individual speculators. For most individual speculators, futures represent a high-risk gamble and a losing proposition. In the best of times, individual futures market speculators have less than an even chance of making money because of high trading costs and informational disadvantages. Individuals often find themselves trading against huge grain-trading companies or financial institutions. Not only do the pros have nearly instant access to market-moving information, but their own multimillion-dollar trades can send futures prices soaring or skidding in seconds. Before speculating on the trend in oil prices, ask yourself a simple question: What's the chance of beating the ExxonMobil Corporation on oil? In the grain markets, what's the chance that you know more than Kraft Foods, Inc.?

The Wall Street Journal estimates that no more than 5 percent of all commodity traders end a single trading year without losing money. The National Futures Association, an industry trade group, estimates that 60 to 90 percent of all individual speculators lose money in the futures markets. For many, the best futures trading advice is simple: Forget it.

Futures Market Regulation

Commodity Futures Trading Commission

While federal and state regulation has governed the futures industry since 1924, the scope of oversight increased dramatically during the early 1970s when a series of economic events brought dramatic change to the U.S. futures industry. Global demand for agricultural products grew, while supplies dwindled. Wild price fluctuations on agricultural futures contracts and the emergence of new futures contracts on metals, lumber, and currencies attracted new, and largely unregulated, participants to the industry. Customer losses due to firm insolvencies and unethical business practices increased, and the industry's reputation was threatened.

Recognizing the need for additional regulation, Congress enacted the Commodity Exchange Act in 1974 and established the **Commodity Futures Trading Commission (CFTC)**, an independent federal regulatory agency with jurisdiction over futures trading. The CFTC strives to protect market participants against manipulation, abusive trade practices, and fraud. Through effective oversight and regulation, the CFTC enables the markets to better serve their important functions in the nation's economy—providing a mechanism for price discovery and

Commodity Futures Trading Commission (CFTC)
Independent federal regulatory agency with jurisdiction over futures trading.

Information Cascades

Imagine you are driving home late one night in the left lane of a divided highway. Traffic is heavy and visibility is limited. Suddenly, you notice that all of the cars in your left lane of traffic begin to brake and switch into the right lane. What should you do? Well, most drivers would also begin to brake and switch to the right lane. They assume that distant drivers with better information are making the rational decision to avoid future congestion by switching to the right lane. There must be an accident up ahead, or some other obstruction in the left lane of traffic.

Anyone with similar experience has familiarity with the concept of an "information cascade." Information cascades can arise in technology adoption, medical treatment, and response to the environmental hazards. Perhaps the best-known examples of information cascades occur in financial markets. Investors with imperfect information about the true state of financial markets sometimes ignore fundamental information and make decisions based on what they believe to be more informative public signals. Because investment decisions are made sequentially, information cascades can cause bubbles or crashes.

Evidence on the financial market implications of information cascades is limited because there is often no direct link between the theoretical concept of herding and statistical tests. Laboratory experiments have also been criticized because professional behavior in the field can differ from student behavior in the laboratory. In an interesting study of information cascades, Alevy, Haigh, and List compared the behavior of market professionals from the Chicago Board of Trade (CBOT) with that of college students in an experimental setting. A key finding is that experienced professionals rely more heavily on private information and the quality of public signals than do students. Professionals are involved in fewer overall cascades and significantly fewer *reverse cascades* (cascades that lead to inferior outcomes). Student behavior is consistent with the notion that losses loom larger than gains, but market professionals appear unaffected by such considerations.

See Jonathan E. Alevy, Michael S. Haigh, and John A. List, "Information Cascades: Evidence from a Field Experiment with Financial Market Professionals," *Journal of Finance*, February, 2007.

---

a means for offsetting price risk. Other government bodies with an important interest in futures market regulation include the House Committee on Agriculture, Securities and Exchange Commission, Senate Committee on Agriculture, Nutrition and Forestry, U.S. Department of Agriculture, and the Federal Trade Commission.

Major policy decisions and CFTC actions occur in such areas as approval of exchange designations, adoption of agency rules and regulations, and authorization of enforcement actions. Most CFTC meetings are open to the public, and CFTC rules and regulations can be obtained from the commission's Office of Public Affairs or the CFTC's home page on the Internet, **www.cftc.gov**.

National Futures Association

National Futures Association (NFA)
Futures industry self-regulatory organization.

The Commodity Exchange Act authorized the creation of registered futures associations to give the industry an opportunity to develop self-regulatory organizations that might work in conjunction with government oversight. As a result, the **National Futures Association (NFA)** was created; it officially began operations in 1982. Today, any company or individual that handles customer funds or gives trading advice in the futures market must apply for registration through the NFA. Like the National Association of Securities Dealers (NASD), whose actions are approved by the SEC, the NFA is a self-regulatory organization. In the case of the NFA, its actions must be approved by the CFTC. Together with the NFA, the CFTC seeks to protect customers by requiring that brokers and dealers disclose market risks and past-performance information to prospective customers. To guard against customer loss from trading firm insolvency, customer funds must also be kept in separate accounts from those maintained by futures trading firms. To guard against trading firm losses from customer insolvency, the CFTC requires that customer accounts be adjusted to reflect current market value at the close of trading each day. In addition, the CFTC monitors registrant supervision, internal controls, and sales practice compliance programs.

Rule-making actions of the NFA and the various futures and option exchanges complement federal regulation. Such rules covet the clearance of trades, trade records, position limits, price limits, disciplinary actions, floor trading practices, and standards of business conduct. Any new or amended exchange rule may be implemented only on approval by the CFTC. On its own, the CFTC may direct the exchanges to change their rules or practices.

Summary

■ The **Chicago Board of Trade (CBOT)** is the first and largest commodities exchange. Like a **forward contract**, a **futures contract** is an agreement between two parties to buy or sell a stipulated grade and quantity of a commodity at a specific future time for an agreed-on price. **Margin** ensures that buyers and sellers have the economic incentive and financial wherewithal to complete their futures contract agreements. Futures contracts **mark-to-market** on a daily basis; there is a daily settlement of gains and losses between buyers and sellers. Changes in the **spot price**, or current price, require additional margin to ensure buyer or seller willingness to abide by futures contract agreements.

■ The buyer of a futures contract, often referred to as the **long**, agrees to receive delivery of the underlying asset from the seller of the futures contract, or **short**, who agrees to make delivery. Futures contracts are traded on exchanges either by open outcry in specified trading areas, called **trading pits** or rings, or electronically via a computerized network. In **open-outcry trading**, exchange members stand in pits making bids and offers, by voice and with hand signals, to other traders. Customer orders are transmitted to **floor brokers** or **dual traders** who execute them. Any futures contracts can be terminated by an **offsetting transaction**, or an equal but opposite trade.

■ Each contract represents a **trading unit** of some underlying commodity. **Delivery months** are regularly scheduled delivery cycles. The **delivery date** is the calendar date by which buyers and sellers of futures contracts are obligated to offset or fulfill their obligations. If a given seller wishes to satisfy his or her futures obligation through physical delivery, a written **delivery notice** must be given by the **notice day**, the last date on which written advice of an intent to physically deliver commodities pertaining to a specified delivery month may be issued. **Futures options** give the right, but not the obligation, to buy or sell some specific futures contract at a certain price for a limited period of time.

■ The CBOT is the world's oldest futures and futures option exchange and is responsible for about 34 percent of total futures and futures option trading in the United States. The **New York Mercantile Exchange** is the third-largest U.S. futures market and the world's largest physical commodity futures exchange. It accounts for about 10.4 percent of the overall market. The **Chicago Mercantile Exchange (CME)** is the largest futures exchange in the United States and represents roughly 53.2 percent of total futures market activity. The **New York Board of Trade (NYBOT)** is parent company of the New York Cotton Exchange and the Coffee, Sugar & Cocoa Exchange, Inc., and is responsible for about 1.9 percent of U.S. futures market activity. The **Kansas City Board of Trade (KCBOT)** is the world's predominant marketplace for hard red winter wheat. The KCBOT accounts for less than one-quarter of 1 percent of U.S. futures and futures option trading activity. The **Minneapolis Grain Exchange** trades roughly 0.1 percent of U.S. futures and futures options. The **Chicago Climate Exchange** trades greenhouse gas emission contracts.

■ **Clearinghouses** ensure balance in the number of futures and futures option contracts bought and sold, and they give fulfillment guarantees to ensure contract performance. Clearinghouses facilitate trade among strangers by eliminating **counterparty risk**. For most futures contracts, there is a difference between **initial margin**, the amount of margin exchanges require to initiate a trade, and **maintenance margin**, the minimum amount of margin the customer must keep at all times.

■ **Hedgers** seek to reduce risks associated with dealing in the underlying commodity or security. **Speculators**, including professional floor traders, seek to profit from price changes. In the futures market, the difference between a commodity's spot price and the futures price is known as the **basis**. While hedging strategies with futures can eliminate **price risk**, hedging strategies cannot eliminate **basis risk**. The **hedge ratio** is the ratio of underlying asset price volatility divided by the price volatility of the hedging instrument and tells how many contracts should be used to hedge a position. An **intramarket spread** combines a long position in one contract month against a short position in another contract month in the same futures contract on the same exchange. An **intermarket spread** consists of a long position in one market and a short position in another market trading the same or a closely related commodity.

■ Stock index futures give investors the ability to offset security risk through a host of complicated investment strategies, referred to as **index arbitrage**. Program trading of index arbitrage is an investment strategy of using a mix of index futures, leveraged stock portfolios, and stock options in such a manner as to profit from mispricing between these securities.

■ Financial derivative markets encompass a plethora of tailored financial instruments, such as swaps, swaptions, caps, and collars, that are traded by the world's leading financial institutions. **Swaps** are arrangements whereby two companies agree to lend to each other on different terms, such as in different currencies or at different interest rates. **Swaptions** are simply options to engage in a specific interest rate swap on or before a specific date. **Caps** are upper limits on the interest rate paid on floating-rate notes or adjustable-rate mortgages. **Collars** are upper and lower

www.mhhe.com/hirschey1e

limits on the interest rate paid on floating-rate notes or adjustable-rate mortgages. In perfectly competitive financial markets, the **law of one price** states that identical assets have the same prices.

■ A carrying-charge, or **contango**, futures market is one in which futures prices are higher in distant delivery months. An inverted market, or one in **backwardation**, features lower futures prices in distant delivery months. Inverted markets sometimes occur when demand for the cash commodity is unusually strong relative to current supply. Inverted markets also occur when the income derived from holding a cash position exceeds the costs of carrying the position.

■ Recognizing a need for additional regulation, Congress enacted The Commodity Exchange Act in 1974 and established the **Commodity Futures Trading Commission (CFTC)**, an independent federal regulatory agency with jurisdiction over futures trading. A futures brokerage firm also must be a member of the **National Futures Association (NFA)**, an industrywide self-regulatory organization.

Self-Test Problems

ST19.1 Assume a speculator buys a Dow $10 futures contract at the end of April 11, 2005. The contract requires an initial margin of $4,875 and a maintenance margin of $3,900. Given the daily prices realized to May 23, 2005, compute the daily cash flow and margin account balance of the investor.

Solution

Using the daily settle price, first compute the change from the previous day. The Dow $10 futures contract requires a mark-to-market cash flow of $10 times the change in settle price. The following spreadsheet shows the daily cash flow and margin account balance.

	A	B	C	D	E	F	G	H	I
1	Date	Dow Futures Price	Change		Cash Flow		Margin Account Balance		
2	11-Apr-05	10482.51					$4,875.00		
3	12-Apr-05	10541.07	58.56		$585.60		$5,460.60		4875
4	13-Apr-05	10436.18	-104.89		-$1,048.90		$4,411.70		
5	14-Apr-05	10310.15	-126.03		-$1,260.30		$3,151.40		
6	15-Apr-05	10118.06	-192.09		-$1,920.90		$1,230.50		
7	18-Apr-05	10100.95	-17.11		-$171.10		$1,059.40		=10*C5
8	19-Apr-05	10156.26	55.31		$553.10		$1,612.50		
9	20-Apr-05	10040.36	-115.90		-$1,159.00		$453.50		
10	21-Apr-05	10245.75	205.39		$2,053.90		$2,507.40		
11	22-Apr-05	10184.01	-61.74		-$617.40		$1,890.00		=G10+E11
12	25-Apr-05	10267.92	83.91		$839.10		$2,729.10		
13	26-Apr-05	10175.73	-92.19		-$921.90		$1,807.20		
14	27-Apr-05	10222.55	46.82		$468.20		$2,275.40		
15	28-Apr-05	10093.27	-129.28		-$1,292.80		$982.60		
16	29-Apr-05	10214.56	121.29		$1,212.90		$2,195.50		
17	2-May-05	10272.90	58.34		$583.40		$2,778.90		
18	3-May-05	10277.30	4.40		$44.00		$2,822.90		
19	4-May-05	10404.14	126.84		$1,268.40		$4,091.30		
20	5-May-05	10359.03	-45.11		-$451.10		$3,640.20		
21	6-May-05	10363.20	4.17		$41.70		$3,681.90		
22	9-May-05	10401.29	38.09		$380.90		$4,062.80		
23	10-May-05	10297.21	-104.08		-$1,040.80		$3,022.00		
24	11-May-05	10315.50	18.29		$182.90		$3,204.90		
25	12-May-05	10203.88	-111.62		-$1,116.20		$2,088.70		
26	13-May-05	10153.67	-50.21		-$502.10		$1,586.60		
27	16-May-05	10264.99	111.32		$1,113.20		$2,699.80		
28	17-May-05	10343.73	78.74		$787.40		$3,487.20		
29	18-May-05	10475.45	131.72		$1,317.20		$4,804.40		
30	19-May-05	10503.34	27.89		$278.90		$5,083.30		
31	20-May-05	10481.21	-22.13		-$221.30		$4,862.00		
32	23-May-05	10532.01	50.80		$508.00		$5,370.00		

The market eventually moved in the direction the speculator predicted. However, before the stock market increased, it decreased a substantial amount. This caused the margin account to dip below the maintenance margin level. The investor would have had to make a cash deposit into the margin account on April 14 to maintain the position. If the speculator decided to get out of the contract at that time, a substantial loss would have resulted.

ST19.2 In order to maintain the position shown in ST19.1, more money will have to be contributed. How much money, and when will it need to be contributed? What was the overall profit and return?

Solution

When the margin account comes under the maintenance margin of $3,900, the speculator must add enough cash to get back to the initial margin of $4,875.

◇	A	D	E	F	G	H	I
1	Date		Cash Flow		Margin Account Balance	New Cash Added	
2	11-Apr-05				$4,875.00		
3	12-Apr-05		$585.60		$5,460.60	=4875-G5	
4	13-Apr-05		-$1,048.90		$4,411.70		
5	14-Apr-05		-$1,260.30		$3,151.40	$1,723.60	
6	15-Apr-05		-$1,920.90		$2,954.10	$1,920.90	
7	18-Apr-05		-$171.10		$4,703.90		
8	19-Apr-05		$553.10		$5,257.00		
9	20-Apr-05		-$1,159.00		$4,098.00	=G5+E6+H5	
10	21-Apr-05		$2,053.90		$6,151.90		
11	22-Apr-05		-$617.40		$5,534.50		
12	25-Apr-05		$839.10		$6,373.60		
13	26-Apr-05		-$921.90		$5,451.70		
14	27-Apr-05		$468.20		$5,919.90		
15	28-Apr-05		-$1,292.80		$4,627.10		
16	29-Apr-05		$1,212.90		$5,840.00		
17	2-May-05		$583.40		$6,423.40		
18	3-May-05		$44.00		$6,467.40		
19	4-May-05		$1,268.40		$7,735.80		
20	5-May-05		-$451.10		$7,284.70		
21	6-May-05		$41.70		$7,326.40		
22	9-May-05		$380.90		$7,707.30		
23	10-May-05		-$1,040.80		$6,666.50		
24	11-May-05		$182.90		$6,849.40		
25	12-May-05		-$1,116.20		$5,733.20		
26	13-May-05		-$502.10		$5,231.10		
27	16-May-05		$1,113.20		$6,344.30		
28	17-May-05		$787.40		$7,131.70		
29	18-May-05		$1,317.20		$8,448.90		
30	19-May-05		$278.90		$8,727.80	=G2+H5+H6	
31	20-May-05		-$221.30		$8,506.50		
32	23-May-05		$508.00		$9,014.50		
33					Total Money In =	$8,519.50	
34				=G32-H33	Profit =	$495.00	
35					Return =	5.81%	
36					=H34/H33		
37							

In this case, the Dow had three large down days in a row, which caused the speculator to twice add more cash to the margin account ($1,723.60 and $1,920.90). After getting two margin calls in a row, many investors will simply get out of the position and take the loss. Subsequently, the Dow recovered and the speculator made a nearly $500 profit. Because the speculator had to provide additional cash to the position, the contract earned a 5.81 percent return.

Questions and Problems

19.1 Standardized futures contracts specify a common set of five contractual provisions. What are they?

19.2 Describe three ways in which a futures contract can be terminated.

19.3 What is the difference between hedging and speculating in futures contracts?

www.mhhe.com/hirschey1e

19.4 Suppose a speculator determined that the S&P 500 Index future is overpriced relative to the spot S&P 500 Index. What positions would the speculator establish to arbitrage this suspected mispricing?

19.5 If you believe that the interest rate yield curve will become less steep (that is, the difference between long interest rates and short-term rates will decrease), how can you profit from this?

19.6 Suppose a farmer has a crop of wheat that will be ready to deliver in two months. The current spot price of wheat is $3.75 per bushel. The farmer wants to lock in this price and shorts a wheat futures contract with a delivery date in two months and a futures price of 384 (cents per bushel). In two months, the spot and futures prices have both settled at $3.79 per bushel. What cash flow occurred because of the futures contract, and what was the impact of the basis?

19.7 The spot price for a T-note is 105-23. The annual risk-free rate is 4 percent and the T-note's yield is 6 percent per year. The future's delivery month is in three months. Calculate the futures price.

19.8 You can hedge or speculate in cross-currency exchange rates by using two futures contracts. For example, by being long in a dollar-to-British-pound contract and short in a dollar-to-Japanese-yen contract, you can take positions to profit from change between pounds and yen. Suppose the pound contract is for £62,500, and the futures price closed at $1.8087, up $0.0201. The yen contract is for ¥12,500,000, and the futures price closed at $0.008950, up $0.000078. What happened to the cross-currency position?

19.9 The mini-Dow futures contract uses a $5 multiplier. If the DJIA futures price increased 70 points to 10,255, what was the mark-to-market? Who gains and loses?

19.10 An investment manager holds a large portfolio of technology-oriented stocks. The manager is concerned that the stock market is in a precarious position, and she is willing to insulate the portfolio from all stock market fluctuations. What futures position might the manager take?

19.11 An orange grower might short orange juice futures to hedge price risk while the oranges are still growing on the tree. If orange prices increase over time, what concerns might the hedged grower have?

19.12 There is a single stock futures contract for 100 shares of Caterpillar stock. The stock price is $74.65, up $0.65, and the futures price closed at $74.55, up $0.42. If you owned 100 shares of the stock, what would have been your dollar and percentage returns? If instead you had been long one futures contract with $2,000 on margin, what would be your dollar and percentage returns?

19.13 The Chicago Board of Trade (CBOT) has an excellent Web site for traders, students, educators, and others interested in futures markets. Go to the CBOT Web site (**www.cbot.com**) and get a quote for the shortest-term Dow $10 futures contract. What was the mark-to-market settle price? Who pays, and how much do they pay?

19.14 The Chicago Mercantile Exchange (CME) is known for its currency exchange futures contracts. Go to the CME Web site (**www.cme.com**) and find the CME Euro FX futures contract. What are the specifications of this contract? What is a recent quote and mark-to-market?

19.15 The National Futures Association (NFA) is the industrywide, self-regulatory organization for the U.S. futures industry. Go to the NFA Web site (**www.nfa.futures.org**). What kinds of fraud is the NFA warning investors about?

19.16 A speculator shorts a 100-ounces-of-gold futures contract at the closing price on April 14, 2005. The contract requires an initial margin of $1,013 and a maintenance margin of $750. Given the following daily prices realized (see next page), compute the daily cash flow and margin account balance of the speculator.

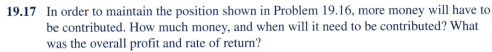

◇	A	B
1	Date	Gold Futures Price
2	14-Apr-05	$423.45
3	15-Apr-05	$424.60
4	18-Apr-05	$425.75
5	19-Apr-05	$427.45
6	20-Apr-05	$433.20
7	21-Apr-05	$433.20
8	22-Apr-05	$433.20
9	25-Apr-05	$432.90
10	26-Apr-05	$432.90
11	27-Apr-05	$434.35
12	28-Apr-05	$432.50
13	29-Apr-05	$435.70
14	3-May-05	$427.90
15	4-May-05	$428.80
16	5-May-05	$429.15
17	6-May-05	$425.15
18	9-May-05	$425.50
19	10-May-05	$427.40
20	11-May-05	$426.10
21	12-May-05	$424.25
22	13-May-05	$420.00
23	16-May-05	$419.25
24	17-May-05	$420.00
25	18-May-05	$419.75
26	19-May-05	$420.80
27	20-May-05	$418.00
28	23-May-05	$418.00

19.17 In order to maintain the position shown in Problem 19.16, more money will have to be contributed. How much money, and when will it need to be contributed? What was the overall profit and rate of return?

19.18 In futures trading, the minimum level to which an equity position may fall before additional margin is required is the:

   a. Initial margin
   b. Variation margin
   c. Cash flow margin
   d. Maintenance margin

19.19 A silver futures contract requires the seller to deliver 5,000 troy ounces of silver. An investor sells one July silver futures contract at a price of $8 per ounce, posting a $2,025 initial margin. If the required maintenance margin is $1,500, the price per ounce at which the investor would first receive a maintenance margin call is *closest to*:

   a. $5.92
   b. $7.89
   c. $8.11
   d. $10.80

19.20. Sandra Kapple asks Maria VanHusen about using futures contracts to protect the value of the Star Hospital Pension Plan's bond portfolio if interest rates rise as Kapple expects. VanHusen states:

- "Selling a bond futures contract will generate positive cash flow in a rising interest rate environment prior to the maturity of the futures contract."
- "The cost of carry causes bond futures contracts to trade for a higher price than the spot price of the underlying bond prior to the maturity of the futures contract."

Indicate whether *each* of VanHusen's two statements is accurate or inaccurate. Support *each* of your responses with *one* reason.

INVESTMENT APPLICATION

Weather Futures

Estimates suggest that nearly 20 percent of the U.S. economy is directly affected by the weather. Business profits can be adversely impacted by summers that are hotter than normal or winters that are colder than anticipated. Utility profits can suffer from temperate summers with less need for air conditioning or mild winters with less residential heating demand.

On the Chicago Mercantile Exchange and other futures markets, weather derivatives have been created to enable businesses that could be adversely affected by unanticipated temperature swings to transfer this risk. Just as professionals regularly use futures and options to hedge their risk in interest rates, equities, and foreign exchange, now there are tools available for the management of risk from extreme temperatures. This sector of hedging and risk management products represents one of today's fastest-growing derivative markets.

The Chicago Merc Heating Degree Day (HDD) and Cooling Degree Day (CDD) futures and options on futures were the first exchange-traded, temperature-related weather derivatives. These contracts are designed to help businesses protect their revenues during times of depressed demand or excessive costs because of unexpected weather conditions. The Chicago Merc offers HDD and CDD futures and options on futures for select population centers and energy hubs with significant weather-related risks throughout the United States. Cities are chosen based on population, the variability in their seasonal temperatures, and the activity seen in over-the-counter trade in HDD/CDD derivatives.

In the weather derivatives market, an important concept is a degree day. A degree day is the measure of how much a day's average temperature deviates from 65° Fahrenheit. Years ago, the utility industry adopted 65° Fahrenheit as a temperature baseline because that was the temperature at which furnaces tend to be switched on. It is used with the assumption that for each degree below 65°, consumers will use more energy to heat their homes. For each degree above 65°, more energy will be consumed to run air conditioners. An HDD measures the coldness of the daily temperature compared to the 65° Fahrenheit standard. An average daily temperature of 40° Fahrenheit gives a daily HDD of 25. If the average temperature is 67° Fahrenheit, it is assumed that no energy would be used to heat homes, and the daily HDD would be zero. The Chicago Merc HDD Index is an accumulation of daily HDDs over a calendar month, with $100 attached to each HDD for final cash settlement.

For example, assume the average daily HDD for a city in the month of November is 25 (= 65° Fahrenheit – 40° Fahrenheit). With 30 days in the month of November, the HDD Index would be 750 (= 25 daily HDDs × 30 days). With an HDD Index of 750 for November, the nominal value of a futures contract on that city would be $75,000 (= 750 HDD Index × $100). To illustrate, suppose a trader was to go short, or sell, the November 2008 HDD futures on the city of Chicago at a price of 750 on January 10, 2008. If, on October 11, 2008, the trader bought the futures contract back at a price of 625, closing out the position, the trader would show a gain of $12,500 (= $100 × 125 HDD Index points) on the position taken in January.

The CDD concept works in a similar manner. A CDD measures the warmth of the daily temperature compared to a standard of 65° Fahrenheit. An average daily temperature of 75° Fahrenheit gives a daily CDD of 10. If the average temperature is 58° Fahrenheit, it is assumed that no energy would be used to cool homes, and the daily CDD would be zero. Like the HDD Index, the Chicago Merc CDD Index is an accumulation of daily CDDs over a calendar month, with $100 attached to each CDD for final cash settlement. For example, assume the average daily CDD for a city in the month of June is 10 (= 75° Fahrenheit – 65° Fahrenheit). With 30 days in the month of June, the CDD Index could be 300 (= 10 daily CDDs × 30 days). With a CDD Index of 300 for June, the nominal value of a futures contract on that city would be $30,000 (= 300 CDD Index × $100).

These weather futures contracts can be used to hedge the risk a utility or a power provider may face as the result of a warmer-than-expected winter or a summer that does not get too hot. Utilities have long used derivative instruments to hedge the price of fossil fuels or electricity.

They can now use weather derivatives to hedge against revenue losses when HDDs and CDDs are unseasonably low.

The strong relation that exists between power usage and temperature shows the practical usefulness of weather futures instruments. People use more power when it is both cold and hot outside and less power when the temperature is moderate. To illustrate, suppose the Windy City Power (WCP) Co. sells electricity in the Chicago area. Assume the retail price charged in the winter months is locked in at $0.08 per kilowatt hour. With a normal winter, the power sales quantity is forecasted as 1 billion kilowatt-hours (kWh). This gives projected revenue for a normal winter of $80 million (= 1 billion kWh × $0.08/kWh). However, WCP worries that the coming winter could be relatively mild and the sales quantity would be reduced. The research department at WCP finds that power sales are positively correlated with the Chicago Merc HDD Index with a weather risk sensitivity of 0.9. This means that a 1 percent decrease in the Chicago Merc HDD index results in a 0.9 percent (= 0.9 × 1%) reduction in sales quantities. Chicago HDD Index futures can be used as a cross-hedge for WCP's revenue fluctuations.

To stabilize its winter revenue, WCP considers selling the Chicago HDD Index January 2008 futures valued at 1,250. It is important to note that a seasonal hedge would typically involve the sale of a series of HDD contracts, for example, October 2007 through March 2008. For the sake of keeping this illustration simple, assume the entire hedge is placed in the January contract, which is typically the coldest month of the year in Chicago. To discover the number of HDD contracts to sell, or what is referred to as the hedge ratio, WCP reviews statistical research. It knows that a 1 percent decline in the HDD Index corresponds to a 0.9 percent fall in revenue. At current price levels, a 1 percent decline in the HDD Index would be worth $1,250 (= 0.01 × 1,250 HDD price × $100/HDD tick). A 0.9 percent decline in revenue is worth $720,000 (= 0.009 × $80,000,000 projected revenue). To fully protect against weather-related fluctuations in its winter revenues, WCP would have to sell 576 weather futures contracts, since

$$\text{Hedge ratio} = \text{change in revenue} / \text{change in contract value}$$

$$576 \text{ contracts} = \$720,000 / \$1,250$$

Assume that on October 1, 2007, WCP shorts 576 of the January 2008 HDD futures at a price of 1,250.

a. Suppose the winter weather is truly mild and the January 2008 Chicago HDD contract settles at 1,150. Calculate WCP's sales quantity reduction, customer revenue reduction, and futures position gain.

b. Suppose the winter weather is especially severe and the January 2008 Chicago HDD contract settles at 1,400. Calculate WCP's sales quantity gain, customer revenue gain, and futures position loss.

20

chapter

Real Estate and Tangible Assets

Real estate developer Donald Trump is renowned for building large skyscrapers and renovating landmark buildings in Manhattan and in upscale vacation locales, like West Palm Beach, Florida. Far from shy, Trump names acquired properties after himself, and he often gets premium rents for such "signature" properties. As a talented deal-maker in the 1980s, Trump was able to secure loans with little collateral and created a real estate empire. Trump also became a celebrity. Trump wrote best-selling books on real estate investing and became a prominent television celebrity. Most recently, Trump has become widely known for his role on the popular TV reality show, *The Apprentice*.

Trump also illustrates the ups and downs that often occur in the real estate business. After he built a real estate empire in the 1980s, the recession of 1990 left Trump unable to meet loan obligations. Several of Trump's businesses filed for bankruptcy, and Trump himself was on the brink of personal bankruptcy. Stockholders, bondholders, and banks lost hundreds of millions of dollars when they bet on Trump. Trump relinquished a number of money-losing businesses, such as the Trump Shuttle (a small airline), but managed to retain the Trump Tower in New York City and control of three casinos in Atlantic City. Ten years later, "The Donald" is back. Trump now owns and operates buildings, apartments, condos, hotels, golf courses, and casinos all over the United States. In New York, flagship properties include the Trump Tower along the East River and the Trump Place apartment complex on the Hudson River. Also noteworthy is the Trump International Golf Club in West Palm Beach. Trump recently announced the creation of an on-line business school called—you guessed it—Trump University. Despite being burned repeatedly, public investors remain willing to bet on "The Donald." Trump Hotels & Casino Resorts owns the Trump Taj Mahal and two other Atlantic City casinos. The Casino Resorts has just emerged from bankruptcy and been renamed Trump Entertainment Resorts. Perhaps it should be named Caveat Emptor! (Buyer beware!)[1]

---

[1]See Troy McMullen, "Trump: The Art of the Delay," *The Wall Street Journal Online*, March 3, 2006 (**http://online.wsj**)

CHAPTER
OBJECTIVES
- Understand the investment characteristics of owning real property.
- Know the risks of income property.
- Be able to appraise real estate value.
- Utilize real estate securities in a portfolio.
- Learn how to invest in gold.

Real Property

The field of investments primarily deals with **financial assets**—like stocks, bonds, mutual funds, options, and futures contracts. Such assets consist of legal claims on specific cash flows and entitlements. Some investors prefer tangible assets, things they can touch. Many investors complement a portfolio of financial assets with investments in **real property**. Popular tangible investment assets include various forms of real estate, precious metals, art, and collectibles.

The real estate business encompasses the construction of buildings and development of subdivisions, the management and leasing of commercial and residential real estate, the buying and selling of property, and the selling of materials and equipment to support these activities. While it might not take a great deal of expertise to rent out the other half of the duplex one owns and lives in, it takes lots of expertise to oversee the design, construction, and sale of 100 beachfront condos. Savvy investors start with smaller real estate projects to gain experience and confidence. Great fortunes have been earned and lost developing real estate.

To what extent do people own real estate? As owning a home is a primary goal of most households, nearly every investor will own at least some real estate. Table 20.1 shows the amount of assets owned by U.S. households at the end of 2005. In aggregate, households own over $25 trillion in tangible assets. This represents 41 percent of all assets owned. Most of these tangible assets are real estate, $22.5 trillion. For many, real estate investments consist solely of their homes. Many others own vacation property, land, and rental property. Another

Financial assets
Investment instruments, issued by corporations, governments, or other organizations, that offer legal rights to debt or equity cash flow.

Real property
Land and the buildings or other objects permanently affixed to the land.

TABLE 20.1	U.S. Household Assets	
	Year-End 2004 (billions)	Percent of Total Assets
Tangible assets	$25,340.9	41.1
Real Estate	21,579.7	35.0
Consumer durable goods	3,761.2	6.1
Financial assets	$29,564.1	48.0
Deposits	5,887.6	9.6
Bonds	2,733.4	4.4
Stocks and mutual funds	10,296.4	16.7
Pension funds	10,646.7	17.3
Equity in noncorporate business	$ 6,677.1	10.8
Total assets	$61,582.1	100.0

Source: Federal Reserve, Flow of Funds Accounts of the United States, March 9, 2006, table B100.

tangible-asset category is consumer durable goods, or goods that provide a stream of services over more than one year. While ownership in art and gold would be included in this category, most of the $3.7 trillion value in durable goods comprises home furnishings, cars, trucks, recreation vehicles, and so on.

In comparison, households own nearly $30 trillion in financial assets. This represents 48 percent of the total value of assets owned by U.S. households. These financial assets primarily consist of stocks, mutual funds, and pension funds. Bank deposits and bond investments also make up an important part of the household portfolio. The other asset category shown in the table primarily consists of agricultural land but also includes small businesses like restaurants, convenience stores, and so on. The 11 percent average ownership of other assets for U.S. households is somewhat misleading in the sense that most households have no business equity. For those households that own a small business, equity in that business often represents the overwhelming share of household assets. As Table 20.1 makes clear, tangible assets are a large and important part of total household wealth in the United States.

Real Estate

Real Estate Characteristics

Real estate
Real property and closely related businesses.

The term **real estate** is commonly used to identify investments in land and buildings. It is also used to denote the ownership of various rights associated with using the land, like forestry harvest privileges, mining and drilling rights, and so on. Lastly, the real estate business also refers to the industry that has grown up surrounding the development and operations of property involving land and buildings.

Income property
Real estate bought for the purposes of generating rental income.

Raw land
Unimproved land.

Investors commonly take a position in the real estate market by purchasing **income property** or **raw land**. Income property can include single-family residences, apartment buildings, commercial, and retail property. The profits from rental property come in the form of rental income derived from current tenants and in the form of capital appreciation of the rental property. Raw land is property that has not yet been developed with buildings or other improvements necessary to support income-generating activities, such as recreation. Investment profits from raw land come in the form of appreciation.

Real estate investment characteristics are usually quite different from the characteristics of many financial assets. Real property tends to be heterogeneous, immobile, local, indivisible, and illiquid. Property is heterogeneous in that each real estate parcel tends to have important unique characteristics. Each piece of land has a different size, shape, and local economic environment. Even within a given area, real estate **improvements** tend to feature construction quality that differs with respect to design, age, materials, and level of upkeep. In many local real estate markets, it is difficult to obtain pricing information based on a realistic study of close comparables. By way of contrast, there are often several close comparables for common stocks and bonds. Given the wide availability of standardized information concerning stocks and bonds, a broad market of potential investors is often available to buy or sell specific issues. In contrast, the lack of standardized data concerning real property means that information barriers limit the potential number of buyers and sellers. In many instances, real estate markets tend to be local or regional in character given the general lack of familiarity with risks and opportunities tied to differences in local government zoning policies, traffic flow patterns, strength of the local economy, and so on.

Improvements
Buildings and structures.

Real estate investments also tend to be "lumpy," and can involve minimum investment thresholds of $100,000, $500,000 or $1 million that can be insurmountable for the small investor. This contrasts with the situation faced by the common stock investor, where the typical large company has tens of millions of shares available for purchase at a price that commonly falls in the $20 to $40 price range. In mid-2006, for example, an investor could buy 100 shares of Microsoft Corporation (ticker, MSFT) for less than $2,800. Debt issues are commonly marketed in $1,000 increments in bonds, and mutual fund minimums can range as low as $25 for fractional shares. Because real estate investments tend to be lumpy, and often re-

Bubbles in San Francisco Bay?

Low interest rates and strong demand helped push 2005 prices for single-family homes to unheard-of levels in Marin County ($850,000 median price, up 19.9 percent from January 2004), San Francisco ($713,000, up 22.9 percent), and San Mateo ($698,000, up 16.3 percent). These prices represented stupendous gains for San Francisco Bay Area residents, where the median single-family home price for nine Bay Area counties had risen from $380,000 in 2002 to $556,000 by 2005. By early 2006, signs of a market top were beginning to emerge. Home prices were leveling off in Marin County ($750,000 median price, down 11.8 percent from January 2005), San Francisco ($712,000, down 0.1 percent), and San Mateo ($720,000, up 3.2 percent). The median single-family home price for nine Bay Area counties rose to $586,500 by early 2006, a moderate rise of 5.5 percent.

The Bay Area surge in real estate prices has far outstripped local income and population growth. It has the classic signs of a real estate bubble. Rents are less than one-half of typical mortgage payments, and the only way many new buyers can qualify is by using adjustable interest-only loans. New buyers will face a big hit as interest rates on adjustable-rate mortgages (ARMs) get revised upward. Equally ominous, more than 300,000 jobs have been lost from the Bay Area since the dot-com bubble popped. That's the worst local job-loss percentage in the last 60 years—worse than the job loss experienced due to Detroit's car problems or Houston's oil bust. Local incomes are less than one-half of what they need to be to sustain current house prices.

Comfortable houses that would cost $700,000 to buy can be rented for as little as $1,800 per month. Ownership costs much more. With tax-deductible interest costs of $3,500 (at 6 percent) and property taxes of $729 (at 1.25 percent) per month, basic after-tax carrying costs are $2,537 per month (assuming a 40 percent marginal tax rate). Insurance and minimal maintenance costs push the after-tax cost of owning to more than $3,000 per month. Owning right now is a very poor choice.

Nobody knows when this bubble will pop, but one thing is certain: If the Bay Area housing market can't get any better, it's bound to get worse.

Data on Bay Area housing can be obtained from the San Francisco Chronicle at www.sfgate.com.

quire that buyers qualify for the use of substantial leverage, investing in real property tends to be difficult for many small investors.

Another important characteristic of real estate markets is that real property tends to be an **illiquid market** with high transaction costs and can involve substantial delays. Buying and selling real estate is typically a cumbersome process that involves brokers, lenders, lawyers, accountants, and title firms. The **real estate agent** is responsible for attracting interested and qualified buyers and typically charges a whopping 6 percent of the eventual selling price. Given the general lack of liquidity in the real estate market, the selling process commonly takes anywhere from several weeks to several months to complete. Imagine selling $100,000 worth of Google common stock, paying a $6,000 commission, and having to wait six months or more to get the net proceeds from the sale! Not many common stock investors would sign up for such a "bargain." Investors must carefully consider the special risk characteristics, high transaction costs, and general lack of liquidity involved with real estate before taking the plunge into this asset class.

Illiquid market
Slow market with high transaction costs.

Real estate agent
Licensed salesperson or real estate broker.

Home Ownership

For most investors, buying their homes is the largest single investment decision that they ever make. More than just a place to live, a home is an important investment because it gives a stream of vital shelter services over time. Because expansion and improvement in the nation's housing stock is an important social goal, a variety of tax breaks and other advantages to home ownership have been conferred by the U.S. Congress. This makes home ownership one of the very best investment opportunities facing the individual investor.

To benchmark changes in housing values for a given region or the nation as a whole, the U.S. Office of Federal Housing Enterprise Oversight (OFHEO) computes and distributes a **House Price Index (HPI)**. Unlike most price indexes based on hypothetical transactions, the OFHEO Housing Price Index is based on actual real estate transactions over time. The HPI uses transaction prices derived from mortgage-lending data provided by mortgage giants Fannie Mae and Freddie Mac. These data allow OFHEO to track price changes for local neighborhoods and even individual properties over time. Anytime a home is purchased or a mortgage is refinanced by Fannie Mae and Freddie Mac, OFHEO is alerted and able to incorporate new transaction prices

House Price Index (HPI)
A timely indicator of house price trends at various geographic levels.

| FIGURE 20.1 | Some Markets for Homes Are Hotter than Others |

Source: U.S. Office of Federal Housing Enterprise Oversight, **www.ofheo.gov**.

or new assessed valuations into its database. City, state, and national HPIs are available from **www.ofheo.gov**. Figure 20.1 shows how home prices have changed over the last 30 years in several locations. The HPI's were standardized to 100 in 1975.

In general, home prices have risen over the past three decades. On average, U.S. home prices increased from an index level of 100 in 1975 to 606 in 2005. This represents a 6.2 percent rate of increase per year for the 30-year period. An old adage in the real estate business says that the three most important factors in the valuation of a property are location, location, and location. This usually refers to the neighborhood, street, or specific location of a property, but it is also applicable to city and state location. During recent years, property values on both the East and the West Coasts have increased at a much higher rate than have values of homes in the heartland. Figure 20.1 shows that property in California increased an average of 9.0 percent per year while property in Kansas increased at only a 4.4 percent annual rate. Homes in the San Francisco/San Mateo area increased in value by 9.4 percent per year, while Cleveland homes rose only 5.0 percent per year during the period.

Figure 20.1 also shows that home prices do not always go up. Home prices actually declined in many areas over the five-year period beginning in 1989. This was an especially difficult time for people who wanted to sell their homes and found that the current market price was lower than their mortgage balances. Lately, home prices have increased at a very rapid pace in many areas. The figure shows that California homes have increased by over 16.8 percent per year during the last five years. The pace of change in housing prices can be very different from what the national average of 6 percent might suggest.

Still, it is important to recognize that despite some ups and downs over the past three decades, there has been a substantial general increase in home prices. At the same time, U.S. home ownership has steadily increased. In 1900, only 46.7 percent of U.S. households owned their own homes. This number increased to 55.0 percent in 1950 and 67.4 percent in 2000. The U.S. Census Bureau reports that home ownership increased to 69.1 percent in 2005. This means that most American households have seen their wealth increase because of their ownership of real property. For most small investors, there is simply "no place like home" for investing.

Income Property

Beyond the amount invested in a single-family residence, the most common entry-level investment in real estate is rental property. Many small real estate investors find that a modest investment in a duplex or small apartment building is a good place to start. Some large real estate investors develop a large portfolio of such small individual properties over time. Investing in income property is mostly focused on the amount of positive cash flow that can be generated. With generous cash flow, there is no need to ever sell a property, and rental property income can fund a comfortable retirement. Aggressive real estate investors may seek only sufficient cash flow to pay mortgage expenses, taxes, maintenance, and other carrying costs. After breaking even on a cash basis, such aggressive real estate investors are in a position to enjoy positive capital appreciation over time. Whether real estate property is acquired to generate current income, capital appreciation, or both, careful cash flow analysis is essential.

Table 20.2 shows a simple cash flow worksheet for a straightforward real estate investment example. Revenue is estimated on the basis that the property is fully rented and every tenant pays in full. Then, vacancy and collection losses are subtracted. Any other income, such as rental income from garage or storage space, is also added.

The total costs of operating residential rental property typically include expenses associated with employees (property manager, maintenance personnel), maintenance, and so on. Maintenance expenditures are the costs of making repairs, painting, replacing worn-out fixtures (like carpeting), updating plumbing fixtures, and so on. Periodically, significant capital expenditures become necessary, such as roof replacement. Depending on the landlord's agreement with tenants, either the owner or the renters must pay for water, electric, and gas utilities. Insurance is another important cost. Casualty insurance protects the value of land and improvements in the event of fire, flood, or other natural disasters. Liability insurance protects owner assets from the risk of litigation tied to ownership of the property. Finally, real estate investors must pay real estate taxes on an annual basis. Real estate taxes are determined by the local **tax rate** and the property's **assessed value**. The assessed value is determined by the county tax assessor, who assigns

Tax rate
Percentage of the property value paid to support government services.

Assessed value
Property value determined for purposes of taxation.

TABLE 20.2	Cash Flow Determinants of Income Property
Revenue:	
Ideal rental income	IRI
Vacancy and collection losses	−VC
Miscellaneous income	+MI
Gross income	GI
Costs:	
Operating expenses	OE
Maintenance expenditures	ME
Utilities	U
Insurance	I
Property taxes	PT
Total costs	TC
Net operating income (GI−TC)	NOI
Financing:	
Mortgage payment	MP
Cash flow (GI−TC−MP)	CF

an appraised or assessed value as a percentage of market value. In some areas, property is assessed at 100 percent of market value; in other areas, residential, industrial, commercial, and agricultural properties are assessed at various rates of market values. In many instances, market values are determined by the sales prices at the point of sale. In other cases, local tax assessors periodically estimate new market values over time. Local taxing authorities have powerful incentives to estimate higher market values over time in order to justify ever-increasing local property taxes.

Income generated by a residential real estate investment is denoted as net operating income. When income property is purchased using debt financing, a monthly amortized payment of mortgage interest and principal is required. To buy income property, real estate investors often contribute 20 percent of the purchase price in equity and borrow 80 percent in the form of a mortgage. A common mortgage on residential property is a fixed-rate loan amortized over 30 years, but variable-rate mortgages have become very popular during recent years. Mortgage payments during the early part of a 30-year amortization period consist primarily of interest payments; payments toward principal become larger later in the life of the mortgage. Of course, whenever all the mortgage principal and interest payments have been paid in full, the property is no longer encumbered.

Try It!

Suppose an investor purchases a duplex for $120,000 with 20 percent down and a 30-year mortgage at an interest rate of 8 percent. What is the monthly mortgage payment? What is the annual payment? If the county assesses property at 85 percent of market value and bills a 2.2 percent tax rate, what is the property tax liability?

Solution

Use a financial calculator and the following data:

Number of periods	360 (= 30 × 12)
Interest rate	0.667 (= 8%/12)
Present value	$96,000 (= 0.80 × $120,000)
Future value	0

The monthly payment is $704.41. This is $8,452.97 annually.
The assessed value of the property will be $102,000 (= 0.85 × $120,000). Given the 2.2 percent tax rate, the tax liability will be $2,244 (= 0.022 × 102,000).

Owner cash flow is gross income less total costs and mortgage payment. Savvy real estate investors look for property that they can buy with positive cash flow. Over time, some of the expenses tied to operating income property will increase. Landlords hope to compensate for such rising costs by increasing rental rates. In fact, landlords hope to increase rents at a faster pace than the rate of change in costs and thereby enjoy rising positive cash flow over time. In addition to gaining value tied to rising positive cash flow, real estate investors hope to build equity through an increase in the value of the property and by paying down the mortgage.

While the income and capital gains potential of residential real estate can be attractive, there are also risks that must be considered. Table 20.3 shows a variety of significant risks to an investor's property value and profits over time. For example, local governments have the power to make laws and policies that limit landowners' ability to use their land and profitably exploit its long-term potential. Zoning codes can change in unpredictable ways that can prevent or severely restrict permissible construction. Maintenance costs can also increase unexpectedly as buildings age and local building codes change. The rate of occupancy and market rental rates can be adversely impacted by new properties that compete

TABLE 20.3	Profit Risks in Owning Income Property

Profit Impact of Risk	Sources of Risk
Uses	Government regulations and policies can change and limit the use of land.
Maintenance costs	Aging buildings need more maintenance. Vandalism and harsh weather can also cause damage.
Occupancy rates	Occupancy rates can vary over time due to local economic conditions and the supply of similar properties.
Rental rates	Rental rates can vary over time due to local economic conditions and the supply of similar properties.
Rental revenue	Tenants may fail to pay rent.
Profits	Hazardous substances on the property increase the liability of the owner.
Property value	Uninsurable losses due to earthquakes, terrorist acts, nuclear accidents, floods, etc., damage the property.
Selling value	The illiquidity of the market may cause a reduced sales price or require that the seller help finance the purchase for the buyer.

for the same tenants or by changing traffic flow patterns. Needless to say, unpredictable and uninsurable events like earthquakes, floods, or terrorist attacks add to the risks involved with real estate income property.

Real Estate Valuation

Discounted Cash Flow

How much should an investor pay for a given property? Is a certain property a good deal at the market's asking price, or is that price too high to be justified on an economic basis? The process of estimating real estate value is called the **appraisal** process. Two different but comparable techniques are commonly used: discounted cash flow analysis and the use of comparable transactions. The **discounted cash flow approach** to valuing real estate investment property converts the expected income generated by the property and expected appreciation into a present-value calculation. For investors, the value of an income property is derived from the cash flows the property is expected to generate. As with stocks and bonds, valuing real estate involves estimating annual cash flows, the proper discount rate for an appropriate holding period, and terminal cash flows.

An estimate of annual cash flow is illustrated in Table 20.2 as **net operating income (NOI)**. Each entry for annual NOI is discounted to a present value in the discounted cash flow approach to valuing real estate. In the first year, NOI is also used in a quick valuation method referred to as **direct capitalization**. In the direct capitalization method, the **capitalization rate**, R, is estimated as

$$R = \frac{NOI}{V} \qquad (20.1)$$

where V is the property sales price. In words, to value a given property, investors first compute the capitalization rate implicit in the prices paid for similar properties. This capitalization rate is used in the same way that a P/E ratio is used to value stocks. Similar companies are expected to have similar P/E ratios, and similar real estate investment properties should have similar capitalization rates. Given the capitalization rate for similar properties and the NOI of the property being appraised, the direct capitalization method uses Equation 20.1 to quickly and simply estimate property value.

Appraisal
Professional opinion of market value.

Discounted cash flow approach
Real estate valuation based on present-value calculations.

Net operating income (NOI)
Income after deducting operating expenses but before deducting income taxes or financing costs.

Direct capitalization
Process for estimating property value by dividing NOI by a capitalization rate.

Capitalization rate
Income yield computed as property income divided by property value.

Try It!

An investor is valuing a four-unit apartment building as a potential investment. Three similar properties have recently sold. The NOI and sales price for property A were $14,400 and $130,900, respectively. For property B, the NOI and sales price were $12,300 and $117,200, and for property C, they were $15,700 and $157,000. The NOI of the property being considered is estimated to be $13,100. Use the direct capitalization method to estimate the value of the property.

Solution

First, compute the going capitalization rate of the three similar properties:

R_A = $14,400/$130,900 = 0.110, or 11%
R_B = $12,300/$117,200 = 0.105, or 10.5%
R_C = $15,700/$157,000 = 0.100, or 10%

Use the range of capitalization rates found to estimate a range of property values:

V = $13,100/0.10 = $131,000
V = $13,100/0.11 = $119,091

Note that the range between these two estimates is quite high, nearly $12,000. The average value is $125,045.

The real estate property capitalization rate is analogous to a stock's dividend yield or a bond's current yield. It is not total return or the required rate of return. To value a stock, cash flows are discounted using the required rate of return. This discount rate can be estimated as the dividend yield plus the expected growth rate of the stock's price (capital appreciation). The discount rate used to value a bond is the yield to maturity, which combines the current yield of the interest payments with the return generated from any capital gain (or loss) in the bond's price. For real estate, the required rate of return or discount rate is estimated in a similar manner, as

$$k = R + g \qquad (20.2)$$

where k is the discount rate, R is the capitalization rate, and g is the expected rate of annual appreciation in the property's price. Therefore, the discount rate used in the discounted cash flow valuation method is the capitalization rate plus the expected pace of property price appreciation.

Whereas the direct capitalization method uses the first year NOI only, NOI is apt to change from year to year with changes in revenues and costs. Over time, if the landlord is able to increase rental rates faster than operating expenses without increasing vacancy rates, gross income will increase over time. If the landlord is not able to increase rental rates faster than operating expenses without increasing vacancy rates, gross income will decrease over time. In a conventional analysis of a given property, prospective buyers must estimate the NOI for each year in the anticipated holding period.

For example, consider an investment property with ideal annual rental income of $39,000 and with the vacancy rate and collection loss projected to be 15 percent. Operating expenses and maintenance expenses are estimated at $2,000 and $3,500, respectively. Utilities paid by the owner will be $1,680, and insurance and taxes are predicted to be $5,200. Table 20.4 shows the first-year NOI computation of $20,770. To compute the NOI for later years, certain assumptions need to be made. Assume that the rental income can be increased by 5 percent per year, operating and maintenance expenses grow at 4 percent, and utilities, insurance, and taxes increase by 3 percent per year. The table shows how an Excel spreadsheet can be used to compute the NOI over time. Notice that costs increase every year but that rental revenue is increasing at a faster rate. As a result, NOI increases every year.

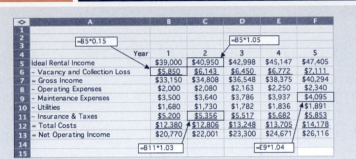

	TABLE 20.4	Computing Net Operating Income over Time.
		Assumptions: Rental income increases by 5 percent per year, operating and maintenance expenses grow at 4 percent, and utilities, insurance, and taxes increase at 3 percent.

	A	B	C	D	E	F
2	=B5*0.15			=B5*1.05		
4	Year	1	2	3	4	5
5	Ideal Rental Income	$39,000	$40,950	$42,998	$45,147	$47,405
6	– Vacancy and Collection Loss	$5,850	$6,143	$6,450	$6,772	$7,111
7	= Gross Income	$33,150	$34,808	$36,548	$38,375	$40,294
8	– Operating Expenses	$2,000	$2,080	$2,163	$2,250	$2,340
9	– Maintenance Expenses	$3,500	$3,640	$3,786	$3,937	$4,095
10	– Utilities	$1,680	$1,730	$1,782	$1,836	$1,891
11	– Insurance & Taxes	$5,200	$5,356	$5,517	$5,682	$5,853
12	= Total Costs	$12,380	$12,806	$13,248	$13,705	$14,178
13	= Net Operating Income	$20,770	$22,001	$23,300	$24,671	$26,116
14	=B11*1.03			=E9*1.04		

The terminal-value cash flow in year n is the sales price of property at the end of the holding period minus expected selling expenses. To estimate the future sales price, the direct capitalization model from Equation 20.1 is used. Terminal value is the estimated NOI in the selling year divided by the capitalization rate:

$$TV = \frac{NOI_T}{R} \qquad (20.3)$$

If the capitalization rate is expected to change between now and year T, the expected future rate should be used. If the capitalization rate is not expected to change, then the current rate, R, should be used. Once the annual NOI, the discount rate, k, and the terminal value are estimated, the value of the property can be estimated by discounting the cash flows using the present-value formula:

$$V = \sum_{t=1}^{n} \frac{NOI_t}{(1+k)^t} + \frac{TV}{(1+k)^T} \qquad (20.4)$$

The present value V is the estimated economic value of the property being appraised. A prospective real estate investor can compare this economic value with the list price to make an informed judgment as to whether a property is fairly priced, overvalued, or undervalued (a bargain).

Try It!

An investor with a five-year holding period estimates the NOI each year as shown in Table 20.3. The capitalization rate for similar properties was computed to be 10.5 percent. If real estate is expected to appreciate at 4 percent per year, what is the discounted cash flow value of the property?

Solution

First, compute the discount rate:

$k = R + g = 10.5\% + 4\% = 14.5\%$

Second, compute the terminal value. Remember that selling a property involves a 6 percent commission:

$TV = (NOI_5/R) \times (1 - 0.06) = (\$26,115/0.105) \times (1 - 0.06) = \$233,791$

(continued)

Lastly, compute the discounted cash flow value:

$$V = \sum_{t=1}^{n} \frac{NOI_t}{(1+k)^t} + \frac{TV}{(1+k)^T}$$

$$V = \frac{\$20,770}{1.145} + \frac{\$22,002}{1.145^2} + \frac{\$23,300}{1.145^3} + \frac{\$24,670}{1.145^4} + \frac{\$26,115}{1.145^5} + \frac{\$233,791}{1.145^6}$$

$$= \$18,140 + \$16,782 + \$15,522 + \$14,353 + \$13,270 + \$118,796 = \$196,863$$

The discounted cash flow approach computes an investment value of $196,863. If the property is listed for less, it is undervalued and would be a good value to purchase.

Comparable Transactions

In some instances, the discounted cash flow method is not useful. A good example is the case of seeking a fair market value appraisal of a single-family residence to be used as a home. In such instances, there is the obvious problem of estimating various noncash benefits to owning versus renting, and useful appraisals typically depend on a consideration of comparable transactions. While it might have been many years since a specific home was sold, transaction prices for similar properties can be used to estimate the market value of the subject property. Since no two properties are identical, adjustments must be made. The **comparable-transactions approach** to valuing real estate involves three steps: (1) Find recent prices for comparable properties, (2) compute and adjust prices for comparable transactions, and (3) estimate the indicated value.

Sales prices for recent real estate transactions can be found in several places. The local tax assessor has records of sales prices, addresses, and property attributes, and these public records are available to everyone. Information on real estate property values can also be obtained with the help of a real estate agent using the **multiple listing service (MLS)** database of recent sales prices and property attributes. Comparable transactions are similar in type, quality, and location to the property being appraised. If the property to be appraised is an attached townhouse, comparable sales should be for other attached townhouses in similar locations.

The second part of this process is to make appropriate adjustments to the sales prices of comparable transactions (see Table 20.5). First, there may be adjustments for differences in transaction terms; sale conditions refer to adjustments due to unusual buyer or seller characteristics. For example, some comparable transactions might involve a family member with prices at less than market prices. Other transactions might involve unusually motivated buyers or sellers. Adjustments may also need to be made because of unusual financing terms. Buyers might qualify for government-sponsored low-income program with below-market interest rate, or sellers might be motivated to provide buyer financing at below-market rates. A final adjustment to the terms of comparable transactions comes from general differences in market conditions. The appraisal process attempts to estimate current market values, so appraisers must make adjustments if real estate prices have increased or decreased since the time of comparable transactions.

Another set of adjustments that may need to be made to comparable transactions stems from differences in the properties being compared. The first property-related adjustment is for the location of the comparable transactions. One property might have a better view, while another may be in a less desirable neighborhood. Because location is one of the most important factors in real estate valuation, properly selected comparable transactions must have locations similar to that of the property being appraised. In a careful comparable-transactions analysis, few location adjustments should need to be made. Most property-related adjustments are made for differences in the physical characteristics. The subject home may have three bedrooms while a comparable home has four bedrooms. In this case, some money should be subtracted from the comparable home's sales price to make that home similar to the subject home. Differences in lot sizes, floor plans,

Comparable-transactions approach
Real estate valuation based upon transactions involving similar properties.

Multiple listing service (MLS)
Proprietary database of available real estate.

TABLE 20.5	Adjusting the Sale Price of a Comparable Property

Transaction Price of Comparable

    +/– Sale conditions
    +/– Financing terms
    +/– Market conditions

    = Market-Adjusted Value of Comparable

        +/– Location
        +/– Physical characteristics
        +/– Other

        = Final Adjusted Comparable Price

architectural styles, and conditions are also important—as are the presence of a fireplace, swimming pool, patio, built-in appliances, and so on. Important differences in commercial property depend on access to freeways and airports, zoning, warehouse size, and so on.

A natural question that arises in the adjustment process relates to how much money should be used to adjust each item. How much is an extra bedroom worth? What is the worth of an extra quarter of an acre in lot size? These answers depend on the location of the property. In a neighborhood where homes sell for $350,000, a bedroom may be worth much more than one in a neighborhood where homes sell for $100,000. Appropriate market value adjustments for location and physical differences can be derived from qualitative methods and experience or from quantitative models such as multiple regression analysis.

Try It!

Consider the following subject home to be appraised and two comparable transactions.

Element of Comparison	Subject Home	Comparable 1	Comparable 2
Sales price	—	$178,100	$168,900
Sale conditions	—	Typical	Typical
Financing terms	—	Conventional	Conventional
Date of sale	—	1 month ago	2 months ago
Neighborhood	Sunnyside Basin	Sunnyside Basin	Sunnyside Basin
Lot size	0.33 acre	0.40 acre	0.33 acre
Home age	5 years	9 years	7 years
Living area	2,060 sq. ft.	2,110 sq. ft.	1,990 sq. ft.
Baths	2	2.5	2
Bedrooms	3	4	3
Fence	Yes (100 feet)	None	None
Garage spaces	2	2	2

If the following guidelines are used to make adjustments, what are the final adjusted prices of each comparable property?

Attribute	Adjustment
Market conditions	Rise of 0.3 per month
Lot size	$80,000 per acre
Living area	$55 per square foot
Bath	$3,500
Bedroom	$4,000
Fence	$9 per foot

(continued)

Solution

The final adjusted comparable prices are shown below.

Element of Comparison	Comparable 1	Comparable 2
Transaction price	$178,100	$168,900
Sale conditions	0	0
Financing terms	0	0
Market conditions	534	1,520
Market adjusted price	$178,634	$170,420
Location	0	0
Site	−5,600	0
Effective age	6,000	3,000
Living area	−2,750	3,850
Baths	−1,750	0
Fence	900	900
Final adjusted price	$171,434	$178,170

The last step in the comparable-transactions method is the reconciliation of adjusted comparable prices to form an estimate of the market value of the property being appraised. A typical reconciliation involves simply averaging comparison prices, but a weighted-average approach may be used if some comparable properties are deemed highly similar. Greater weights are assigned to the more similar properties. For example, in the Try It! above, if comparable 2 is more similar to the subject home, a weighted average of 60-40 might be used. If so, the estimated market value of the subject home would be $174,128 (= 0.6 × $178,170 + 0.4 × 171,434).

Real Estate Securities

Real Estate Investment Trusts

Real estate investment trust (REIT)
Publicly traded company that manages property and/or mortgage loans.

Buying, building, and managing real estate properties take an enormous amount of time, expertise, and capital. One of the easiest and most promising ways for investors with limited time and expertise to effectively invest in real estate is through publicly traded **real estate investment trusts (REITs)**. Over $300 billion of real estate equity and debt is held through REITs. Real estate investment trusts can be thought of as being similar to exchange-traded funds (ETFs) except that REITs focus on real estate investments rather than common stocks. In the case of REITs, the investment portfolio comprises a pool of real estate assets. To qualify as a REIT, the trust must distribute at least 90 percent of its taxable income to shareholders annually in the form of dividends. An example is Camden Property Trust (**www.camdenliving.com**), a real estate company engaged in the ownership, development, acquisition, management, and disposition of multifamily apartment communities. It trades on the New York Stock Exchange under the ticker symbol CPT. As of June 2005, it owned interests in or operated 191 multifamily properties containing 65,992 apartment units located in the Sunbelt and midwestern markets from Florida to California. A big advantage that REITs have over direct real estate ownership is liquidity. They can be easily and quickly bought and sold with minimal transaction costs, just like stocks. For example, on March 9, 2006, 428,300 shares of Camden Property Trust traded at over $65 per share.

The price performance of REITs over time also gives a good benchmark to judge the performance of real estate investing. The National Association of Real Estate Investment Trusts (NAREIT) is the REIT industry's association (see **www.nareit.com**). Members are REITs and other businesses that own, operate, and finance income-producing real estate. The association develops and follows REIT indexes. Table 20.6 shows that a comparable total return has been earned for the All REITs Index and the S&P 500 Index over time.

TABLE 20.6	REIT and Common Stock Return Characteristics	
	All REITs Index	**S&P 500 Index**
1972	11.19%	18.98%
1973	−27.22	−14.66
1974	−42.23	−26.47
1975	36.34	37.20
1976	48.97	23.84
1977	19.08	−7.18
1978	−1.64	6.56
1979	30.53	18.44
1980	28.02	32.42
1981	8.58	−4.91
1982	31.64	21.41
1983	25.47	22.51
1984	14.82	6.27
1985	5.92	32.16
1986	19.18	18.47
1987	−10.67	5.23
1988	11.36	16.81
1989	−1.81	31.49
1990	−17.35	−3.17
1991	35.68	30.55
1992	12.18	7.67
1993	18.55	9.99
1994	0.81	1.31
1995	18.31	37.43
1996	35.75	23.07
1997	18.86	33.36
1998	−18.82	28.58
1999	−6.48	21.04
2000	25.89	−9.10
2001	15.50	−11.90
2002	5.22	−22.10
2003	38.47	28.70
2004	30.41	10.90
2005	8.29	4.91
Arithmetic average	12.61%	12.64%
Median	15.16%	17.63%
Standard deviation	20.21%	17.47%
Coefficient of variation	1.60	1.38
Correlation	0.507	

Source: National Association of Real Estate Investment Trusts, **www.nareit.com**.

Nevertheless, Table 20.6 shows that the annual return on REITs has been quite volatile. In 1974, the index plunged a disappointing −42.2 percent. However, in 1976, REITs earned a spectacular 49.0 percent return. Over the entire period, REITs have earned an average 12.6 percent, which is the same as the average return earned in the stock market. The higher volatility in the REIT index (standard deviation of 20 percent versus 17 percent) makes the risk-reward relationship slightly better in the stock market. This is shown by a lower coefficient of variation (standard deviation divided by average return) for common stocks (1.4) compared to REITs

FIGURE 20.2 | REIT Sector Value in Billions of Dollars (number of REITS in category shown in parentheses)

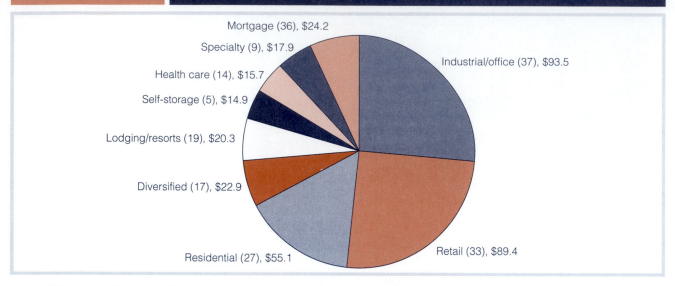

Source: National Association of Real Estate Investment Trusts, **www.nareit.com**, February 28, 2006.

(1.6). Knowledgeable investors know that the relatively low level of correlation of 0.51 between these two asset classes means that some risk reduction can be achieved in a portfolio that combines REITs and stocks

As shown in Figure 20.2, REITs own and operate everything from golf courses and casinos to self-storage units and hospital buildings. REITs are commonly categorized by the type of real estate assets owned and by their focus on equity or debt instruments. **Equity REITS** own real properties, and their value is determined by the value of their real estate holdings and the cash flow generated. Over 90 percent of publicly traded REITs are equity REITs. **Mortgage REITs** lend money to owners and developers of real estate and purchase existing mortgages or mortgage-backed securities. The price of mortgage REITS is determined by the net interest generated and the credit quality of their loan portfolios. **Hybrid REITs** combine the investment strategies of equity REITs and mortgage REITs by investing in both properties and mortgages.

Equity REITs and mortgage REITs have very different return characteristics. Table 20.7 shows that equity REITs have earned an average 14.7 percent annual return during the period 1972–2005 while mortgage REITs have returned only 11.0 percent, on average. Mortgage REITs have earned lower returns with a much higher volatility. This helps explain why equity REITs have dominated mortgage REITs over the last 30 years. As might be expected, hybrid REITs have return and risk characteristics that fall between the characteristics of equity and mortgage REITs. Because all

Equity REIT
REIT with an ownership position in real estate.

Mortgage REIT
REIT that invests in real estate–oriented debt.

Hybrid REIT
REIT that generates income from real estate debt and equity.

TABLE 20.7 | Return Characteristics of REIT Categories, 1972–2005

	Equity REITs	Mortgage REITs	Hybrid REITs
Average annual return	14.66%	10.95%	12.06%
Standard deviation	16.72	30.43	26.84
Minimum	−21.40	−45.32	−52.22
Median	17.18	13.36	16.92
Maximum	47.59	77.34	56.19

Source: National Association of Real Estate Investment Trusts, **www.nareit.com**.

Are Realtor Practices Anticompetitive?

Brokerage commissions for trading stocks have plummeted on the Internet. Commissions on airline tickets and hotel accommodations have also plunged. On the Internet, investors can buy and sell as much as $500,000 worth of common stock for as little as $10 in brokerage commissions. Many travelers now avoid travel agent commission costs altogether by booking their travel using popular sites like **www.expedia.com** or **www.orbitz.com**. Against this backdrop, it is reasonable to ask, Why do real estate commissions remain so high?

The biggest single commission cost people will ever pay is the traditional 6 percent cost for selling a home. This means that selling a $200,000 home through a typical real estate agent costs a whopping $12,000 in commissions. Many thought the growing popularity of shopping on the Internet would drive down real estate commission costs, but so far that has not happened. Condensed versions of real estate listings are indeed posted online, thus enabling consumers to do more market research on their own. However, most real estate agents still charge full 6 percent commissions on real estate transactions, even when much of the "legwork" is done on the Internet.

The National Association of Realtors is a powerful trade association for the nation's real estate agents and controls what is known as the *Multiple Listing Service (MLS)*. MLS is a central source for all local real estate listings and is made available on the Internet to member realtors and potential homebuyers (**www.mls.com**/). Any home buyer wanting to know about all real estate listings in the local area can access relevant information on the web, but must retain a realtor before making a purchase offer. For years, the National Association of Realtors has pursued policies that have effectively blocked discount-oriented real estate firms from using MLS information to make offers to buy or sell homes at discounted commission rates.

The U.S. Department of Justice and the Federal Trade Commission have been warning the National Association of Realtors and state affiliates against creating policies that limit competition in the real estate market. Time will tell if such efforts will begin to help home sellers.

See Greg Ip, "Some Indicators Hint Housing Has Stabilized, *The Wall Street Journal Online*, March 2, 2006 (**http://online.wsj**).

REITs must distribute 90 percent of taxable income, REITs typically offer dividend yields that are two or three times higher than that provided by the S&P 500 Index.

Real Estate Stocks and Mutual Funds

Investors also get some real estate exposure in their portfolios through common stock ownership. Consider the real estate holdings of Hilton Hotels Corporation (ticker, HLT). Hilton engages in the ownership, management, and development of hotels, resorts, and timeshare properties. With $4 billion in properties, Hilton's value is closely tied to the real estate industry. Similarly, Starwood Hotels & Resorts Worldwide, Inc. (ticker, HOT; known as Sheraton Hotels), and Marriott International, Inc. (ticker, MAR), can be thought of as real estate companies.

While Hilton is similar to an equity REIT, the government-sponsored enterprises known as Fannie Mae (ticker, FNM) and Freddie Mac (ticker, FRE) are similar to mortgage REITs. Fannie and Freddie provide loans for the acquisition or refinancing of homes and multifamily apartment buildings. These companies focus on increasing the supply of funds that mortgage lenders can make available to home buyers and multifamily investors. They primarily buy mortgages from lenders, create pools of such mortgages, and then sell these mortgage-backed securities to investors. In addition, Fannie and Freddie hold a $1 trillion mortgage portfolio of their own.

In addition to investing in REITs and real estate–oriented companies, investors can also invest in mutual funds that have a real estate emphasis. Morningstar reports that there are some 200 real estate mutual funds available. These funds invest in a portfolio of REITs and real estate–oriented companies. While an investor can easily and quickly obtain a diversified real estate portfolio through mutual funds, the investor pays a cost in the form of management fees and loads.

Investors can also get a diversified exposure to real estate investment opportunities using ETFs with a real estate focus. The iShares Cohen & Steers Realty Majors Index Fund (ticker, ICF) attempts to emulate the Cohen & Steers Realty Majors Index, which is broadly diversified by both geographic region and property type through 30 REITS. The iShares Dow Jones U.S. Real Estate Index Fund (IYR) tracks the Dow Jones REIT Composite Index. The streetTRACKS Wilshire REIT Index Fund (RWR) follows the Wilshire REIT Index, and the Vanguard REIT VIPERS (VNQ) follows the Morgan Stanley REIT Index. The performance characteristics of these four exchange traded funds are similar.

Precious Metals

Investing in Gold

People have had a fascination with gold for thousands of years. Archaeologists have discovered gold jewelry in southern Iraq dating to 3000 BC and gold ornaments in Peru dating to 1200 BC. Of course, the ancient Egyptians were masters in the use of gold for jewelry, ornaments, and economic exchange. By 1000 BC, squares of gold were a legal form of money in China. The Romans issued a popular gold coin called the Aureus. By 1100 AD, gold coins had been issued by several European countries. Gold has been a highly sought-after asset all over the world, and it has retained at least some economic value over thousands of years.

The United States has had a very chaotic history with gold. In 1792 the newly created United States passed the Coinage Act, which put the U.S. dollar on a silver-gold standard. At that time, the U.S. dollar was defined as equal to 24.75 grains of fine gold and 371.25 grains of fine silver. Americans sought to "strike it rich" through gold rushes in North Carolina (early 1800s), California and Nevada (mid-1800s), and Alaska (late 1800s). Later, with the nation struggling in the Great Depression, President Franklin D. Roosevelt banned the export of gold and halted the convertibility of dollar bills into gold. Roosevelt also ordered U.S. citizens to hand in all the gold they possessed, and a daily price for gold was established. It was not until 1973 that the United States took the dollar off the **gold standard**; it was not until the end of 1974 that the ban on gold ownership by U.S. citizens was lifted. By 1986, the U.S. government's attitude on gold ownership had completely turned around, as evidenced by the resumption of the U.S. Mint's production of gold coins imprinted with the American Eagle image.

Prior to 1974, the U.S. dollar was on the gold standard. This effectively means that the price of gold was fixed in U.S. dollars. It was not until after the dollar was taken off the gold standard that gold could be used as a modern investment. Consequently, American investors have just over 30 years of gold investing experience. Figure 20.3 shows how the price of gold per troy ounce has changed since 1974. The figure's end-of-December prices do not illustrate the

Gold standard
Monetary system that backs currency with gold.

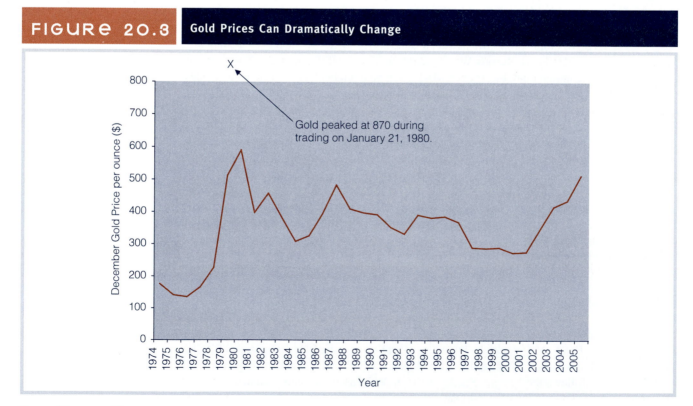

FIGURE 20.3   **Gold Prices Can Dramatically Change**

Gold peaked at 870 during trading on January 21, 1980.

Source: Kitco, **www.kitco.com**.

true magnitude of the bubble in gold prices that occurred in 1980. The price of gold increased from $512 at the end of 1979 to $870 on January 21, 1980. That increase of $358 per ounce (69.9 percent) occurred during only three weeks. The subsequent crash in the price of gold was just as spectacular. One year after the peak, gold had declined by 34 percent. Two years after the peak, the gold price had fallen 57 percent to $376. Clearly, the price of gold has been driven by the same type of irrational investor sentiment that caused the tech-stock bubble.

The return characteristics of gold are shown in Table 20.8 and are compared to the S&P 500 Index. The average annual return on gold was 6.2 percent since the ban on owning gold was lifted. This does not compare favorably to the 14.6 percent achieved in the stock market. In addition, gold prices have been much more volatile. While gold rose in price by over 126 percent in 1979, it also fell by more than 32 percent in 1981. In comparison, the high and low returns for the S&P 500 Index were only 37 percent (1995) and –22 percent (2002). Since gold earned

TABLE 20.8	Gold Returns Are Uncorrelated with Stock Returns	
Year	**Annual Gold Return**	**Annual S&P500 Return**
1975	–19.86%	37.2%
1976	–4.10	23.8
1977	22.64	–7.2
1978	37.01	6.6
1979	126.55	18.4
1980	15.19	32.4
1981	–32.60	–4.9
1982	14.94	21.4
1983	–16.31	22.5
1984	–19.19	6.3
1985	5.68	32.2
1986	21.31	18.5
1987	22.21	5.2
1988	–15.26	16.8
1989	–2.84	31.5
1990	–1.47	–3.2
1991	–10.07	30.6
1992	–5.75	7.7
1993	17.68	10.0
1994	–2.17	1.3
1995	0.98	37.4
1996	–4.59	23.1
1997	–21.41	33.4
1998	–0.83	28.6
1999	0.85	21.0
2000	–5.44	–9.1
2001	0.75	–11.9
2002	25.57	–22.1
2003	19.89	28.7
2004	4.65	10.9
2005	17.77	4.9
Average	**6.2%**	**14.6%**
Standard deviation	**27.60%**	**15.96%**
Coefficient of variation	**4.46**	**1.09**
Correlation	**–0.089**	

Source: Kitco, **www.kitco.com**, and Standard & Poor's, **www2.standardandpoors.com**.

a relatively low return with a high volatility, the coefficient of variation was poor in comparison to the stock market (4.46 versus 1.09).

The poor investment performance of gold suggests that most investors should avoid gold, but some investors may be attracted by the fact that investment returns on gold and common stocks in general are relatively uncorrelated. This means that investors can lower risk by adding some gold to a common stock portfolio. The three most common forms of gold ownership are through gold coins or bullion, gold-mining stocks, and gold-focused mutual funds. Each has advantages and disadvantages.

Gold Coins and Bullion

Gold coins are popular with investors who are sometimes derisively referred to as "gold bugs." Unlike the case with jewelry, investors know exactly the amount and purity of the gold in each coin. In addition, gold coins are traded at local pawnshops, coin shops, gold brokers, and national dealers. These characteristics make for a fairly liquid market, but transaction costs can be huge, especially in local markets. The most popular gold coins used for wealth preservation and investing purposes are shown in Figure 20.4. Panel A shows the recently manufactured coins with 1 troy ounce of gold. The American Eagle and Canadian Maple Leaf are particularly popular in North America. All the gold bullion coins shown are commonly owned by investors and speculators around the world. Panel B shows coins with other amounts of gold.

Spot price
Price of gold for immediate delivery.

Bullion coins have no particular appeal for coin collectors and are priced using the **spot price** of gold. The spot gold market trades very close to 24 hours a day. Most of the trading

FIGURE 20.4 **Gold Investors Buy Gold Coins from All Over the World**

A. One-Ounce Gold Coins

American Eagle   Australian Kangaroo   Austrian Philharmonic

Canadian Maple Leaf   Chinese Panda   South African Krugerrand

B. Other Gold Coins

Mexican Peso
(1.206 troy oz.)

Denmark 20 Kroner
(0.259 troy oz.)

British Sovereign
(0.235 troy oz.)

French Rooster
(0.187 troy oz.)

See: USAGOLD-Centennial Precious Metals, Inc., © **www.usagold.com/gold-coins.html**.

activity takes place on commodity exchanges in New York, London, Sydney, Hong Kong, Tokyo, and Zurich. By convention, the daily change in the price of gold is the difference between the current price and the price at 1:30 p.m. New York time. The cost of gold coins is determined by the following factors:

$$\text{Coin price} = \text{value of gold} + \text{numismatic value} + \text{dealer spread} \qquad \textbf{(20.5)}$$

The value of gold in a coin depends on the current market price of gold and the amount of gold in the coin. **Numismatic value** is the amount of premium attributed to collector appeal stemming from scarcity and appearance quality (fine, extra fine, proof, etc.). Numismatic value is difficult to assess. While coin collectors seek rare coins with high numismatic value, many gold investors prefer common gold coins with no numismatic value.

Numismatic value
Worth to collectors.

Try It!

On June 2, 2005, gold was trading for $423.90 per troy ounce. Goldline International (see **www.goldline.com**) offered Krugerrands for $8.95 over the spot price. What is the cost to buy and sell Krugerrands through Goldline?

Solution

The Krugerrand is a common gold coin bought by gold investors. It has no numismatic value. Therefore, each 1-troy-ounce coin can be purchased through Goldline for $432.85 (= $423.90 + $8.95) and sold for $423.90. Note that the price of gold must increase by 2.11 percent (= $8.95/$423.90) for the investor to recover the dealer spread cost.

In addition to investing in gold coins, investors who deal in large quantities might purchase gold bars that vary in size from 1 ounce to 400 ounces to 1,000 grams. When a 1-ounce bar is available for $434.40, the 400-ounce and 1,000-gram bars will cost $173,760.00 and $13,757.30, respectively. Another popular method for investing in gold is to buy stock in gold-mining companies. Table 20.9 shows several popular gold-mining stocks. Barrick Gold and Agnico Eagle Mines are Canadian firms, and AngloGold Ashanti and Gold Fields are South African firms. Many large mining firms have operations in countries all over the world.

Instead of buying stock in gold-mining firms, investors can buy shares in gold-focused portfolios through mutual funds that focus on precious-metal investments. These mutual funds hold gold-mining stocks and sometimes own gold directly. In addition, an EFT called the iShares COMEX Gold Trust (ticker, AIU) began trading on January 28, 2005. The fund's net assets consist primarily of gold held by a custodian on behalf of the trust, and price changes reflect changes in the price of gold after trust expenses.

Other Precious Metals

Periodically, investors have been interested in other precious metals. While gold rules the precious-metal market, platinum and silver are also popular and can be used to diversify precious-metal holdings. People who want to invest in silver or platinum can purchase either coins or bars of each metal. Because silver is usually valued at a much lower price than gold (the price of silver reached a high of $11 per ounce in early 2006), investors buy bags of silver coins instead of individual silver coins. Platinum, with a price that is about twice that of gold, can be bought in coins and bars.

Whom Do Real Estate Agents Represent?

Effective real estate agents help sellers by quickly locating prospective buyers and by using their superior knowledge of the market to suggest the best asking price. In return for their services, agents typically receive 6 percent of the transaction price as commission. Big money is involved. According to the Federal Trade Commission, real estate agents participate in the sale of more than 80 percent of all single-family dwellings in the United States. In 2005, the median price of the more than 7 million single-family homes sold in the United States was $207,300. That implies a total sales volume of about *$1.5 trillion*.

The relationship between a home seller and a real estate agent is what economists Rutherford, Springer, and Yavas call a perfect example of the *principal-agent problem*. As agents, real estate professionals have a fiduciary responsibility to represent principals (home sellers) to the best of their ability. Real estate agents should represent sellers in the same way that they themselves would like to be represented. However, agency problems are created because the economic interests of the real estate agent do not perfectly coincide with the interests of home sellers. For example, a typical listing involves projected gross real estate commissions of $12,438 [= $207,300 × 0.06]. This amount is equally split between the listing and selling real estate agents, who, in turn, share their portion of gross commissions with their employers. Agents typically receive one-half of the gross commissions generated, so a selling broker might expect to personally receive 1.5 percent of the sales price, or $3,109.50 [= $207,300 × 0.06 × 0.5 × 0.5] for a typical single-family residence. As a result, home sellers would take a big hit from a $5,000 price reduction, but the selling agent stands to lose only $75 dollars in commission income.

Given the incentives involved, it's no wonder that agents are typically eager to cut prices for a quick sale. The percentage commission system creates an agency problem because it induces real state agents to expend too little effort on behalf of the client.

See R. C. Rutherford, T. M. Springer, and A. Yavas, "Conflicts between Principals and Agents: Evidence from Residential Brokerage," *Journal of Financial Economics*, vol. 76, no. 3 (June 2005), pp. 627–665.

TABLE 20.9 Popular Gold-Mining Stocks (quotes from March 9, 2006)

Symbol	Name	Last Trade	Market Cap ($ billions)	Volume
ABX	Barrick Gold Cp.	25.65	21.9	5,626,300
AEM	Agnico Eagle Mines	24.28	2.4	1,534,000
AU	AngloGold Ashanti Lt.	47.83	13.0	1,328,000
FCX	Freeport McMoran B	48.35	8.9	3,844,800
GG	Goldcorp Inc.	25.64	8.7	4,589,100
GFI	Gold Fields Ltd. Ads.	18.71	9.2	4,129,600
GLG	Glamis Gold Lmt.	26.21	3.5	1,375,600
HMY	Harmony Gold Mng. A	12.90	5.1	2,653,400
KGC	Kinross Gold Corp.	8.99	3.2	2,074,300
NEM	Newmont Min. Cp. (Hldg.)	47.79	22.2	9,145,900
PAAS	Pan Amer. Silver Co.	22.24	1.5	1,344,124

Source: Yahoo! Finance, **finance.yahoo.com**. Reproduced with permission of Yahoo! Inc. © 2006 by Yahoo! Inc. Yahoo and the Yahoo! logo are trademarks of Yahoo! Inc.

Alternative Investments

Art and Collectibles

The investment values of works of art and other collectibles are based on the artist's reputation, training, education, and sales record. Exhibition history and the origin of the artist are also of vital importance. For example, *Self Portrait* and other works by Vincent van Gogh, the famous postimpressionist master, have brought astounding prices at auction. Van Gogh's reputation, background, and prolific painting career have combined to produce works of great value for van Gogh collectors. At the other end of the price spectrum, collectors have long expressed an interest in antiques, stamps, rare coins, oriental rugs, sports memorabilia, and a rich variety of other items. Like art, collectibles are difficult to value because of the significant time commitment required to become a knowledgeable collector.

In general, the investment value of art and other collectibles is determined by the simple interplay of supply and demand. In the case of dead artists, the supply of authentic art is fixed. Rembrandt and van Gogh are no longer painting. While the artist's reputation and the quality of a specific work or object are of paramount importance, a host of other minor factors can also influence investment value. Whether the work has been restored, and by whom, can be important. Who has previously owned the work and where it has been displayed previously can also impact demand. Art and other collectibles usually carry more value if the artist studied and worked under a master painter or sculptor. The reputation and skill of famous teachers often translates into greater value for the creations of their less-than-famous pupils.

Across all categories of art and collectibles, assessment of investment value is made difficult by hard-to-characterize differences in character and quality. For example, paintings can be described by their medium as drawings, oil, or watercolors. They can also be classified as landscapes, portraits, or caricatures. They are also grouped according to schools, movements, and styles. Art historians describe these painting styles as characteristic of the Renaissance period, impressionists, symbolists, cubism, minimalism, abstract expressionism, modernism, and dozens more. Sculptures and other forms of art have their own descriptions.

Perhaps the most famous painting in art history is Leonardo da Vinci's *Mona Lisa*. Painted in 1503, the *Mona Lisa* hangs in the Louvre Museum (Musée du Louvre) in Paris, France. It was removed from the Louvre and hidden during several wars over the past five hundred years. Napoleon even hung it in his bedroom. The painting was stolen on August 22, 1911, by a Louvre employee when Vincenzo Peruggia walked out the door with it hidden under his coat. Considered a cultural symbol, the French were outraged by the theft. It was masterminded by a con-man who had commissioned a French art forger to make copies of the painting so that he could sell them to wealthy, private collectors as the missing original. He did not need the original for his con, and so he never contacted Peruggia to collect it. After having kept the painting in his apartment for two years, Peruggia was finally caught when he attempted to sell it to a Florence art dealer. It was exhibited all over Italy and finally returned to the Louvre in 1913. In 1956, the lower part of the painting was severely damaged after a patron tossed acid on it. Several months later someone threw a stone at it. It is now displayed in a climate-controlled enclosure behind unbreakable, nonreflective glass.

Nobody knows the current commercial value of the *Mona Lisa*. To be sure, it was created by a famous artist and has a remarkable history. In 1962, the *Mona Lisa* had an insured value of $100 million. With inflation, that would be over $600 million in 2006 if the *Mona Lisa*'s recent rate of price appreciation has kept pace with the overall rate of inflation. In the absence of any recent market transactions, it is impossible to guess the current values of the *Mona Lisa*, Vincent van Gogh's *Field of Irises*, Claude Monet's *Sunflowers,* or other such "priceless" works of art.

Auctions

The market for art and collectibles is dominated by **auctions**. The world's two largest auction houses are Christie's (**www.christies.com**) and Sotheby's (**www.sothebys.com**). Both conduct auctions all over the world on a daily basis. Table 20.10 shows just a few of the auctions conducted by Christie's in April 2006. Note the incredible variety of art and collectibles sold. Impressionist and modern art sold for nearly $143 million on one day in New York. Wine and cigars sold for nearly $1 million in Geneva. Over $6 million in sporting art sold in London.

Auctions are risky and costly for buyers and sellers alike. Seller commission costs typically start with a 10 percent fee on the first $100,000, 8 percent on the next $150,000, 7 percent on the next $250,000, 5 percent on the next $500,000, and so on. Buyers also pay commission costs. A **buyer's premium** of 20 percent is commonly added to the auction price to cover local sales taxes plus an additional commission for the auction house. These are *minimum* transaction costs for an authenticated work of art by an established artist with broad appeal. Suppose you bought or inherited a piece of art by a renowned artist but the piece has not been involved in a market transaction for several years. In such a case, it would not be unusual to

Auction
Public sale through open bidding.

Buyer's premium
Added commission paid by buyer.

Street Smarts 20.4

Antiques and Collectibles

The *Antiques Roadshow* on PBS owes its amazing success to an "addictive mix of suspense, history, and dramatic revelations—in bite-sized segments." The magic ingredient that keeps viewers coming back is the promise that they can turn trash into treasure. Unfortunately, appraisals on the *Antiques Roadshow* are merely professional judgments of what various items might command when offered for sale to informed and motivated buyers, before steep appraisal fees, sales commissions, and other marketing costs are deducted. Nobody on the *Antiques Roadshow* is promised anything in cold, hard cash.

A practical problem faced by investors is that there is no universal agreement concerning what constitutes an antique or collectible. The term *antiques* generally refers to older objects valued because of their aesthetic or historical significance. In Europe, the word could describe an antiquity from ancient Rome or Greece. In the United States, the word *antique* could describe an object made as recently as during the Civil War period. When seeking to impose duties on imported items, the U.S. Customs Office defines an antique as something made over 100 years ago. From a collector's perspective, the beauty of the U.S. Customs Office definition is that it is flexible. As the years go forward, so too does the cutoff date that defines an antique.

Collectibles include artistic and historical items that are less than 100 years old, like Tiffany lamps. They may be mass-produced and not have any individual artistic merit, like Beanie Babies, Hummel statues, and Pokémon cards. Sometimes, producers of collectibles seek to artificially inflate prices by producing "limited editions" that cap the number of objects being sold. Another type of collectible is any object that gains value because of its associations. The drum set used by the Beatles on the Ed Sullivan Show has been reproduced in a valuable "collector's edition," for example.

Unfortunately, investing in antiques and collectibles is a betting game. Baby boomers love Barbie, the Beatles, Marilyn Monroe, and Mickey Mantle memorabilia. Who knows if anybody will care about any of them in 100 years?

See Karen Mazurkewich, "Sticking with Stamps, Collecting Postage Memorabilia Can Yield Big Gains," *The Wall Street Journal Online*, February 24, 2006 (**http://online.wsj**).

TABLE 20.10	Sample of Completed Auctions at Christie's, April 2006	
Sale Date	**Items for Sale**	**Sale Location**
4 Apr	The Hermitage Antiques Collection	South Kensington
4 Apr	Intérieurs	Paris
4 Apr	Art of the Islamic and Indian Worlds	King Street
5 Apr	Impressionist and Modern Art	South Kensington
6 Apr	Important Old Master Paintings	Rockefeller Center
6 Apr	Post-War and Contemporary Art	South Kensington
6 Apr	Oriental Rugs and Carpets	King Street
7 Apr	English Furniture	Rockefeller Center
8 Apr	Fine and Rare Wines	Rockefeller Center
11 Apr	Magnificent Jewels	Rockefeller Center
11 Apr	Art Nouveau and Art Deco	South Kensington
12 Apr	Watches	Rockefeller Center
13 Apr	British and Continental Ceramics	South Kensington
19 Apr	19th Century European Art	Rockefeller Center
20 Apr	Fine Wines and Vintage Port	King Street
21 Apr	19th Century Furniture	Rockefeller Center
24 Apr	Russian Works of Art	Rockefeller Center
24 Apr	Silver	Rockefeller Center
25 Apr	Photographs	Rockefeller Center
26 Apr	Asian Art	South Kensington

Source: Christie's, **www.christies.com**.

pay an additional $10,000 to $50,000 to have the piece restored and authenticated by Christie's or Sotheby's. Even then, how can you be sure to receive a fair price at auction? History is replete with examples of rigged auctions by art dealers who had previously been thought to be reputable. Even in the best of circumstances, the value of art and other collectibles may have to increase for several years before transaction costs are covered.

During recent years, a variety of Internet auction sites have sprung up to provide a low-cost alternative to the traditional Christie's or Sotheby's auctions. The leader in Internet auctions is eBay, Inc. Founded in 1995, eBay (**www.ebay.com**) has grown to be a powerful and popular trading platform that lists millions of items for sale on a daily basis. In 2005, $44.3 billion of sales occurred. One reason for eBay's popularity is the low trading fees. Sellers pay a fee of less than $5 to have their items listed for auction plus a final value fee if an item sells. The final value fee is a graduated percentage of the selling price: 5.25 percent on the first $25, plus 2.75 percent on the next $975, plus 1.5 percent on any remaining value. This is a real bargain when compared with the standard fees charged by Christie's and Sotheby's.

While profits can be made investing in art and other collectibles, novice investors must be aware of the fact that the art world is subject to trends, fads, and fraud. Highly sought-after and highly prized works of art in one decade can be all but ignored in another. High costs of storage, maintenance, and insurance add to daunting transaction costs to make investing in art and collectibles problematic for all but the most sophisticated and most experienced investors.

Summary

- **Financial assets**, like stocks, bonds, mutual funds, options, and futures contracts, consist of paper that has the legal claim to specific cash flows and entitlements. Some investors complement a portfolio of financial assets with **real property**. Popular tangible investment assets include real estate, precious metals, art, and collectibles.

- **Income property** includes single-family residences and apartment buildings. It also includes land with other **improvements**, like warehouses, factories, or restaurants leased to others to operate their own business. The profits of rental property come from both the appreciation of the property's value and the positive cash flows from renting. **Raw land** is unimproved land held for capital appreciation.

- Real property tends to be heterogeneous, immobile, local, indivisible, and illiquid. In an **illiquid market**, transaction costs are high and it takes a long time to execute transactions. Buying and selling land is a cumbersome process that could involve brokers, lawyers, and title firms. Most investment property is sold through a **real estate agent**, who brings interested and qualified buyers to the seller. The agent's services typically cost the seller 6 percent of the selling price. The selling process may take from a few weeks to many months.

- In general, home prices have risen over the last three decades. Measured by the **House Price Index (HPI)**, U.S. home prices have increased at a 6 percent pace, on average, during recent years. Property values on both the East and West Coasts have increased at a much higher rate than those of homes in the heartland, but home prices do not always go up. They declined over the five-year period beginning in 1989, for example, in many areas.

- Investing in income property is focused on the amount of positive cash flow that can be generated. A prospective buyer must carefully identify the potential annual revenue and costs of operating the property. Taxes are determined by the local **tax rate** and the property's **assessed value**. While the income potential of real estate can be tremendous, there are also great risks.

- The process of estimating real estate value is called an **appraisal**. Different techniques are commonly used to appraise property values: discounted cash flow and the use of comparable transactions. The **discounted cash flow approach** to valuing investment property converts the income the property generates and any price appreciation into a present value. An estimate of the annual cash flow is the **net operating income (NOI)**. The first-year NOI is also used in a quick valuation method referred to as **direct capitalization**. In the direct capitalization method, the **capitalization rate** is used in the same way that a P/E ratio is used for stocks. Given the capitalization rate of similar properties and the NOI of the property being appraised, the direct capitalization method can quickly estimate property value.

- The **comparable-transactions approach** to valuing real estate involves three steps: (1) Find sales transactions of comparable properties, (2) compute the final adjusted comparable price for each transaction, and (3) reconcile the final adjusted prices to estimate the indicated value. Details for comparable transactions can be found at the local property tax assessor's office and through the **multiple listing service (MLS)**. The last step in the comparable-transactions method is the reconciliation of the final adjusted comparable prices to form the estimate of the market value of the property being appraised.

- Some of the most promising instruments for investing in real estate are publicly traded **real estate investment trusts (REITs)**. Real estate investment trusts are similar to exchange-traded mutual funds in that REITs represent ownership in a pool of real estate assets. They are commonly categorized by the type of real estate assets owned, equity or debt. **Equity REITS** own property. Over 90 percent of publicly traded REITs are equity REITs. **Mortgage REITs** deal in mortgages. Lastly, **hybrid REITs** combine the investment strategies of equity REITs and mortgage REITs. Investors can also get some real estate exposure in their portfolios through stock ownership in regular companies with a high degree of real estate ownership or real estate–focused mutual funds.

■ Gold has been a highly sought-after asset for thousands of years. The United States took the dollar off the **gold standard** in 1973 and ended the ban on U.S. citizens owning gold in 1974. In 1986, the U.S. Mint began production of American Eagle gold coins. The value of a gold coin depends on the amount of gold in the coin, the **spot price** of

gold, and **numismatic value**. In addition to investing in gold coins, some investors buy gold bars, the stock of gold-mining companies, gold mutual funds, and gold-indexed exchange-traded funds.

■ Art derives its value from the demand of people who want to own it. Important factors that impact demand are the reputation of the artist, quality and condition of the work, whether the work has been restored and by whom, who has previously owned the work, and where it has been displayed. The market for art and collectibles is mainly conducted through **auctions**. Auctions are very costly markets for both buyers and sellers. The seller pays a commission, and a **buyer's premium** is typically added to the auction price to pay local sales taxes and additional commissions.

Self-Test Problems

ST20.1   Suppose an investor is examining a rental property listed for sale. The investor is mostly concerned about the cash flow of the property. The property has five apartments that can each be rented for $750 per month. A 10 percent vacancy and collection loss rate is expected. Operating expenses and maintenance expenses are estimated to be $3,000 and $3,800, respectively. Utilities paid by the owner will be $2,600, and insurance and taxes are predicted to be $7,100. If the investor can put 20 percent down on the $250,000 and obtain a 30-year mortgage at 7.5 percent, what is the cash flow of the property?

Solution

The annual mortgage payment can be computed with a financial calculator. Use the following data:

- Number of periods $360 (= 30 \times 12)$
- Interest rate $0.625 (= 7.5\%/12)$
- Present value $200,000 (= 0.80 \times \$250,000)$
- Future value   0

The monthly payment $1,398. This is $16,781 annually.
The cash flow of the property is therefore

	Cash Flow	Computation
Revenue:		
Ideal rental income	$45,000	$750 × 5 ×12
Vacancy and collection loss	−4,500	$45,000 × 0.10
Gross income	$40,500	
Costs:		
Operating expenses	$ 3,000	
Maintenance expenses	3,800	
Utilities	2,600	
Insurance & taxes	7,100	
Total costs	$16,500	
Net operating income	$24,000	(GI − NOI)
Mortgage payment	−16,781	
Cash flow	$7,219	

The property will generate $7,219 of positive cash flow if the assumptions hold true.

ST20.2 Annual gold and bond returns are shown from 1975 to 2005. What are the diversification characteristics of gold compared with long-term Treasury bonds?

Year	Annual Gold Return	Long-Term Treasury Bonds
1975	−19.86%	9.20%
1976	−4.10	16.75
1977	22.64	−0.69
1978	37.01	−1.18
1979	126.55	−1.23
1980	15.19	−3.95
1981	−32.60	1.86
1982	14.94	40.36
1983	−16.31	0.65
1984	−19.19	15.48
1985	5.68	30.97
1986	21.31	24.53
1987	22.21	−2.71
1988	−15.26	9.67
1989	−2.84	18.11
1990	−1.47	6.18
1991	−10.07	19.30
1992	−5.75	8.05
1993	17.68	18.24
1994	−2.17	−7.77
1995	0.98	31.67
1996	−4.59	−0.93
1997	−21.41	15.08
1998	−0.83	13.52
1999	0.85	−8.74
2000	−5.44	20.11
2001	0.75	4.56
2002	25.57	17.17
2003	19.89	2.06
2004	4.65	7.70
2005	17.77	3.05

Solution

The Excel computations are:

	A		C	D	E	F	G
1			Annual	Long-term			
2	Year		Gold Return	Treasury Bonds			
3		1974					
4		1975	-19.86%	9.20%			
5		1976	-4.10%	16.75%			
6		1977	22.64%	-0.69%			
7		1978	37.01%	-1.18%			
8		1979	126.55%	-1.23%			
9		1980	15.19%	-3.95%			
10		1981	-32.60%	1.86%			
11		1982	14.94%	40.36%			
12		1983	-16.31%	0.65%			
13		1984	-19.19%	15.48%			
14		1985	5.68%	30.97%			
15		1986	21.31%	24.53%			
16		1987	22.21%	-2.71%			
17		1988	-15.26%	9.67%			
18		1989	-2.84%	18.11%			
19		1990	-1.47%	6.18%			
20		1991	-10.07%	19.30%			
21		1992	-5.75%	8.05%			
22		1993	17.68%	18.24%			
23		1994	-2.17%	-7.77%			
24		1995	0.98%	31.67%			
25		1996	-4.59%	-0.93%			
26		1997	-21.41%	15.08%			
27		1998	-0.83%	13.52%			
28		1999	0.85%	-8.74%			
29		2000	-5.44%	20.11%			
30		2001	0.75%	4.56%			
31		2002	25.57%	17.17%			
32		2003	19.89%	2.06%			
33		2004	4.65%	7.70%			
34		2005	17.77%	3.05%			
35			Gold Return	Treasury Bonds			
36	Average =		6.2%	9.9%	=AVERAGE(D4:D34)		
37	Standard deviation =		27.60%	12.05%	=STDEV(D4:D34)		
38	Coefficient of variation =		4.46	1.22			
39					=D37/D36		
40	Correlation =		-0.151				
41				=CORREL(C4:C34,D4:D34)			
42							

Notice that long-term bonds have experienced a better risk-return relationship than gold. Gold has experienced a lower average return and a higher volatility than bonds. Thus, the Treasury bond coefficient of variation is much better than that of gold. However, a bond investor should still consider adding gold to the portfolio because it provides a good diversification opportunity, as shown with a correlation between the two of –0.151.

Questions and Problems

20.1 Explain the characteristic differences between financial assets and real property.

20.2 What are the risks of owning income property?

20.3 An investor is valuing a small office building. The NOI of the building is estimated to be $60,000. Two similar buildings were recently sold. The first, office X, sold for $895,000 and has an estimated NOI of $85,000. Office Y sold for $705,000 and has an NOI of $70,000. Use the direct capitalization method to determine the capitalization rate and estimate the market value of the office building.

20.4 A real estate investor is computing the discount rate to be used for discounting the cash flows of a retail-space building. Capitalization rates of similar properties are estimated to be 9.0, 8.7, and 9.4 percent. If the historical property value appreciation rate has been 5.3 percent per year, what discount rate should be used?

20.5 A landowner expects to sell a property in five years. The expected NOI in five years is $41,000, and the capitalization rate is expected to be 12 percent. If selling commissions are expected to be 5.5 percent, what is the expected terminal value?

20.6 A real estate investor has estimated the annual NOIs of a property over a six-year holding period to be (beginning in year 1): $29,100, $30,050, $31,200, $33,000, $33,200, and $33,900. If the terminal value is $325,000 and the discount rate is 13.5 percent, what is the value of the property?

20.7 An investor purchases an investment property for $185,000 with 10 percent down and a 30-year mortgage at an interest rate of 7.5 percent. What is the monthly mortgage payment?

20.8 A property is purchased for $185,000. If the county assesses property at 80 percent of market value and bills a 2.5 percent tax rate, what is the property tax liability?

 20.9 Investigate the tools available on Yahoo! Real Estate (**realestate.yahoo.com**). Click on the What's My Home Worth link. Enter an address for a house, and report what comparable transactions are available.

20.10 Given the seller's commission schedule discussed in the "Auction" section and a buyer's premium of 20 percent, compute the transaction costs of a $780,000 sale.

 20.11 Kitco Bullion Dealers provides a good Web site for following gold prices and for buying and selling gold (see **www.kitco.com**). At what prices is Kitco willing to buy and sell the 1-ounce American Eagle and Canadian Maple Leaf gold coins? What is the bid-ask spread?

 20.12 Go to the Morningstar Web site (**www.morningstar.com**) and use the mutual fund screener to find the funds that focus on precious-metal investing. How many are there? Pick one fund and report its top five holdings.

20.13 The iShares COMEX Gold Trust began trading on January 28, 2005. Shares represent ownership in a portfolio of gold. How closely does the stock price mimic gold prices?

◇	A	B	C	D	E	F
1	Date	AIU Closing Price	COMEX Spot Price	Date	AIU Closing Price	COMEX Spot Price
2	1/28/05	$42.69	$425.80	4/1/05	$42.63	$425.90
3	1/31/05	$42.27	$421.80	4/4/05	$42.42	$423.90
4	2/1/05	$42.13	$420.80	4/5/05	$42.48	$424.50
5	2/2/05	$42.23	$421.10	4/6/05	$42.68	$427.10
6	2/3/05	$41.72	$416.60	4/7/05	$42.59	$426.50
7	2/4/05	$41.50	$414.00	4/8/05	$42.68	$426.90
8	2/7/05	$41.35	$413.60	4/11/05	$42.80	$428.60
9	2/8/05	$41.30	$412.60	4/12/05	$42.80	$427.60
10	2/9/05	$41.34	$412.90	4/13/05	$42.92	$429.30
11	2/10/05	$41.81	$417.20	4/14/05	$42.38	$424.00
12	2/11/05	$42.12	$420.50	4/15/05	$42.47	$424.90
13	2/14/05	$42.62	$425.80	4/18/05	$42.72	$427.50
14	2/15/05	$42.59	$425.90	4/19/05	$43.29	$432.90
15	2/16/05	$42.56	$425.50	4/20/05	$43.46	$435.30
16	2/17/05	$42.74	$427.30	4/21/05	$43.18	$433.00
17	2/18/05	$42.84	$427.10	4/22/05	$43.47	$434.30
18	2/22/05	$43.60	$434.50	4/25/05	$43.45	$434.60
19	2/23/05	$43.48	$434.90	4/26/05	$43.71	$437.90
20	2/24/05	$43.43	$434.50	4/27/05	$43.23	$433.00
21	2/25/05	$43.54	$434.90	4/28/05	$43.06	$431.30
22	2/28/05	$43.61	$436.50	4/29/05	$43.43	$435.00
23	3/1/05	$43.25	$432.90	5/2/05	$42.97	$429.50
24	3/2/05	$43.32	$432.80	5/3/05	$42.80	$426.70
25	3/3/05	$43.06	$429.90	5/4/05	$42.94	$429.00
26	3/4/05	$43.43	$434.20	5/5/05	$43.00	$429.80
27	3/7/05	$43.48	$435.00	5/6/05	$42.59	$426.10
28	3/8/05	$44.05	$440.30	5/9/05	$42.62	$426.20
29	3/9/05	$44.08	$442.10	5/10/05	$42.63	$427.20
30	3/10/05	$44.23	$442.80	5/11/05	$42.74	$427.20
31	3/11/05	$44.50	$446.20	5/12/05	$42.19	$421.60
32	3/14/05	$44.06	$441.10	5/13/05	$41.94	$420.20
33	3/15/05	$44.08	$440.90	5/16/05	$41.88	$418.90
34	3/16/05	$44.34	$443.70	5/17/05	$41.89	$419.40
35	3/17/05	$43.87	$438.70	5/18/05	$42.09	$421.50
36	3/18/05	$43.95	$439.30	5/19/05	$42.03	$420.50
37	3/21/05	$43.10	$431.10	5/20/05	$41.70	$417.40
38	3/22/05	$42.70	$431.30	5/23/05	$41.66	$416.60
39	3/23/05	$42.47	$425.20	5/24/05	$41.73	$417.50
40	3/24/05	$42.47	$424.70	5/25/05	$41.89	$418.80
41	3/28/05	$42.58	$425.90	5/26/05	$41.69	$418.00
42	3/29/05	$42.62	$426.00	5/27/05	$41.97	$419.80
43	3/30/05	$42.65	$426.90	5/31/05	$41.69	$416.30
44	3/31/05	$42.87	$428.70	6/1/05	$41.55	$415.30

20.14 Both equity REITs and mortgage REITs securitize real estate instruments to be sold in the stock market. In this regard they seem very similar. However, equity REITs deal with the equity, or ownership, side of real estate, while mortgage REITs deal with the mortgage, or debt, side. In this regard they seem very different. Assess the annual returns of the two types of REITs, and determine whether their characteristics are similar or different.

◇	A	C	E
1		Equity REITs	Mortgage REITs
3	1972	8.01%	12.17%
4	1973	-15.52%	-36.26%
5	1974	-21.40%	-45.32%
6	1975	19.30%	40.79%
7	1976	47.59%	51.71%
8	1977	22.42%	17.82%
9	1978	10.34%	-9.97%
10	1979	35.86%	16.56%
11	1980	24.37%	16.80%
12	1981	6.00%	7.07%
13	1982	21.60%	48.64%
14	1983	30.64%	16.90%
15	1984	20.93%	7.26%
16	1985	19.10%	-5.20%
17	1986	19.16%	19.21%
18	1987	-3.64%	-15.67%
19	1988	13.49%	7.30%
20	1989	8.84%	-15.90%
21	1990	-15.35%	-18.37%
22	1991	35.70%	31.83%
23	1992	14.59%	1.92%
24	1993	19.65%	14.55%
25	1994	3.17%	-24.30%
26	1995	15.27%	63.42%
27	1996	35.27%	50.86%
28	1997	20.26%	3.82%
29	1998	-17.50%	-29.22%
30	1999	-4.62%	-33.22%
31	2000	26.37%	15.96%
32	2001	13.93%	77.34%
33	2002	3.82%	31.08%
34	2003	37.13%	57.39%
35	2004	31.58%	18.43%

20.15 Access the Office of Federal Housing Enterprise Oversight Web site at **www.ofheo.gov**. Obtain the Housing Price Index (HPI) for the city of Atlanta, Georgia. What is the beginning HPI value? What is the most recent value? What has the average annual return been for Atlanta houses?

20.16 Consider the following subject home to be appraised and two comparable transactions.

Element of Comparison	Subject Home	Comparable A	Comparable B
Sales price	—	$315,000	$285,000
Date of sale	—	2 months ago	3 months ago
Lot size	0.45 acre	0.50 acre	0.45 acre
Home age	4 years	3 years	5 years
Living area	2,650 sq. ft.	3,050 sq. ft.	2,700 sq. ft.
Baths	3	4	3.5
Bedrooms	4	5	4
Garage spaces	2	3	2

If the following guidelines are used to make adjustments, what are the final adjusted prices of each comparable property?

Attribute	Adjustment
Market conditions	Rise of 0.2 per month
Lot size	$100,000 per acre
Age	$2,500 per year
Living area	$50 per square foot
Bath	$4,000
Bedroom	$6,000
Garage	$5,000 per bay

20.17 The ideal annual rental income of an investment property is $27,000. However, the vacancy rate and collection loss are expected to total 12 percent. Operating expenses and maintenance expenses are estimated to be $1,500 and $2,500, respectively. Utilities paid by the owner will be $1,000, and insurance and taxes are predicted to be $3,800. Compute the NOI for the first year. Also, assume that the rental income can be increased by 4 percent per year, operating and maintenance expenses grow at 3.5 percent, and utilities, insurance, and taxes increase at 3 percent per year. Compute the NOI for an additional three years after the first year.

20.18 Using the data below and the direct capitalization approach, an analyst estimated the market value of an income-producing property to be $2,750,000.

Annual gross potential rental income	$400,000
Annual property operating expenses	$100,000
Annual vacancy and collection losses	$50,000

Which of the following capitalization rates is *closest* to the rate the analyst used to calculate the market value of the property?

a. 9.1 percent
b. 10.9 percent
c. 12.7 percent
d. 14.6 percent

20.19 Robin Quon is reviewing two indexes that measure real estate investment performance. One index is composed of equity real estate investment trusts (the EREIT Index), and the other is composed of commingled real estate funds (the CREF Index). Both indexes are broadly diversified and hold similar types of properties from the same geographic areas in roughly comparable amounts. Quon has noted, however, that the performances of the two indexes have been noticeably different. In discussing the possible reasons for the differences, he states, "With CREFs, there are transaction barriers, in that the minimum investment in a CREF may be too large for some investors."

Identify and discuss *two other* reasons that might account for the differences in the performances of the two indexes.

20.20 Gerald Becker, a domestic real estate portfolio manager, currently owns several office buildings in the eastern region of his country. To further diversify his real estate portfolio, he is planning to invest in office buildings in the northern, southern, and western regions of his country. He states, "I want a more diversified real estate portfolio, and by holding properties in all four geographical regions of the country, I should obtain higher risk-adjusted returns."

a. Explain *one* advantage and *one* disadvantage of Becker's approach to attaining real estate portfolio diversification.
b. Recommend and describe one other domestic real estate diversification strategy that Becker might use to obtain higher risk-adjusted returns.

INVESTMENT APPLICATION

Is Gold an Inflation Hedge?

When inflation picks up, stocks tend to perform poorly. The conventional wisdom is that investors can use gold as a hedge against the effects of a high inflation rate. This wisdom is prevalent in both the industry and the media. For example, in 2005, *Forbes* magazine advised:

> With the stock market in negative territory this year and inflation perking up (consumer prices climbed 3.1 percent in the 12 months ending March), you wouldn't be called crazy to want a modest hedge in the form of commodities.... You could buy, say, 500 1-ounce American Eagle gold coins for $214,000 and stow them in a safe-deposit box.[2]

Many investors heed this advice. Indeed, even institutional investors like the California Public Employees' Retirement System (CalPERS), with $185 billion in assets, has an interest in gold: "CalPERS officials are investigating an initial investment in the asset class [gold] to protect against inflation."[3] CalPERS has a diversified portfolio consisting of 68 percent equities, 25 percent fixed income, 6 percent real estate, and 1 percent cash. An investment in gold would further diversify the portfolio. However, CalPERS' stated purpose for wanting to buy gold is to protect against inflation.

How could gold protect against inflation? For gold to be a hedge against inflation, its price would have to increase during periods of high inflation. The gains in a portfolio including gold could offset declines in other asset classes (such as stocks and bonds) that often occur during periods of rapidly rising inflation. In other words, for gold to provide an effective inflation hedge, gold prices and an inflation index should be highly correlated.

Figure 20.5 shows the end-of-year prices of gold between 1974 and 2005. Also shown for the period is the Consumer Price Index reported by the Federal Reserve. The inset shows the correlation between gold prices and the CPI over various time periods.

a. Does gold appear to be a good inflation hedge? Explain.

b. Why do advisors, the media, and others in the investment industry believe gold is an inflation hedge?

FIGURE 20.5 — The Price of Gold and Inflation over Time

Correlation	
1974 – 2005	0.326
1974 – 1979	0.868
1979 – 2005	–0.380
1990 – 2005	0.240

Source: Kitco, **www.kitco.com,** and U.S. Federal Reserve, **http://research.stlouisfed.org/fred2**.

---

[2]Mark Tatge, "Rare Commodity," *Forbes*, June 6, 2005, p. 130.

[3]Arleen Jacobius, "Institutions Hope to Find Gold Mine with Commodities," *Pensions & Investments*, May 30, 2005, p. 1.

APPENDIX A

The Time Value of Money

Future Value

A simple way of thinking about the investment process is to think about the difference between present sums and future values. Investing is simply the means of converting present sums into future values. Whenever you calculate the future value of a present sum, you must consider the dollar amount of the investment, the rate of interest, the number of time periods, and the method of compounding.

The future value of a present sum using once-a-year, or annual, compounding is

$$\text{Future value} = \text{present sum} \times (1 + \text{interest rate})^t \tag{A.1}$$

where t is the number of years (or time periods) involved.

For example, the future value of a \$5,000 investment earning 8 percent interest over a period of 15 years is roughly \$15,861 because

$$
\begin{aligned}
\text{Future value} &= \text{present sum} \times (1 + \text{interest rate})^t \\
&= \$5,000 \times (1 + 0.08)^{15} \\
&= \$15,861
\end{aligned}
\tag{A.2}
$$

Present Value

An alternative way of looking at the process of investment is to look at present-day dollars rather than future dollars. Notice that in Equation A.1, the future value of a present sum is expressed. If instead one wishes to express the present value of a future sum, an analogous technique called *present-value analysis* is used. In present-value analysis, the time-value-of-money concept is used to discount the value of future dollars back to their present-day equivalent. Instead of growing current dollars into future dollars, present-value analysis shrinks future dollars into their present-day equivalent. The present value of a future sum is given by the expression

$$\text{Present value} = \frac{\text{future sum}}{(1 + \text{interest rate})^t} \tag{A.3}$$

where t is again the number of years (or time periods) involved.

For example, the present value of \$15,860 to be received in 15 years when an 8 percent rate of return can be earned on investments is, as before, \$5,000 because

$$
\begin{aligned}
\text{Present value} &= \frac{\text{future sum}}{(1 + \text{interest rate})^t} \\
&= \frac{\$15,860}{(1 + 0.08)^{15}} \\
&= \$5,000
\end{aligned}
\tag{A.4}
$$

Notice the similarity of the present-value equation with the prior future-value equation. Calculating the future value of a present sum is the other side of the coin from calculating the present value of a future sum. Both approaches can be used to evaluate investment opportunities. The concept of present value is important for investors. The value of a potential investment is dependent on the benefits to be received in the future. For stocks, the benefits are the dividends and the future sales price of the stock. Bondholders receive interest payments. The value of a stock or bond is the present value of these future benefits.

Try It!

What is the present value (or worth) of a stock that you expect to sell for $50 per share in five years if you demand an annual 10 percent return? (The stock is not expected to pay a dividend.)

Solution

$$\text{Present value} = \frac{\text{future sum}}{(1 + \text{interest rate})^t}$$

$$= \frac{\$50}{(1 + 0.10)^5}$$

$$= \$31.05 \text{ per share}$$

Frequent Compounding

Interest on Interest

Many investments pay benefits to the holder more frequently than once per year. For example, many corporate bonds make interest payments every six months. When you receive the first interest payment after six months, you can reinvest that cash immediately instead of waiting until the end of the year. Reinvesting the payment during the year allows you to earn a little more return. You are compounding your interest more frequently than annual compounding. The future- and present-value equations are easily modified to account for more frequent compounding. Two adjustments are needed. First, be sure to use an interest rate that fits the length of the period used. If six-month periods are needed, divide the annual return by 2 because there are two six-month periods in one year. Second, use the number of periods, not the number of years. In the preceding example, $5,000 grew into $15,860 over a period of 15 years with once-a-year, or annual, compounding at 8 percent. If semiannual compounding is needed, then use an interest rate of 4 percent (= 8%/2) per period for a total of 30 periods (= 15 years × 2 periods per year). Compounding semiannually causes the $5,000 to grow to $16,217. Note that this amount is much higher than that with annual compounding.

Since stock dividends are paid quarterly, it may be necessary to use quarterly compounding in computing future and present values. Simply use quarterly interest rates and the total number of quarters in Equations A.1 and A.3.

You could compound by the week, day, or even minute. The greatest level of compounding is called continuous compounding. With continuous compounding, the most "interest on interest" is earned compared to less frequent compounding.

A simple expression for the continuous-compounding method of showing interest is

$$\text{Future value} = \text{present sum} \times e^{rt} \tag{A.5}$$

where e is the so-called Napierian constant (and approximated by 2.7182818 ...), r is the interest rate, and t is the number of years (or time periods) involved. With continuous compounding, more interest on interest is earned. This means, for example, that with continuous compounding at 8 percent over a 15-year period, $5,000 grows into $16,600 because

$$\text{Future value} = \text{present sum} \times e^{rt} \tag{A.6}$$

$$= \$5,000 \times e^{0.08 \times 15}$$

$$= \$16,600$$

where t is the number of years (or time periods) involved.

In the event of continuous compounding, $16,600 to be received in 15 years has a present value of $5,000 because

$$\text{Present value} = \frac{\text{future sum}}{e^{rt}} \tag{A.7}$$

$$= \frac{\$16,600}{e^{0.08 \times 15}}$$

$$= \$5,000$$

Using continuous compounding at 8 percent interest, $5,000 is the present-value equivalent of $16,600 to be received in 15 years.

The annual, semiannual, or even continuous methods of compounding interest are merely different ways of characterizing the growth in investment value over time. They are used successfully to distinguish between superior and inferior investment alternatives. Although it matters little which approach is used to rank investment choices, it is essential to focus on only one method of compounding interest when making an "apples to apples" comparison of investment alternatives.

Try It!

What is the future value of a $1,000 investment three years from now if it receives a 9 percent annual return compounded (a) annually, (b) quarterly, and (c) continuously?

Solution

a. Future value = $1,000 $\times$ (1 + 0.09)^3 = $1,295
b. Future value = $1,000 $\times$ (1 + 0.0225)^{12} = $1,306
c. Future value = $1,000 $\times$ $e^{0.09 \times 3}$ = $1,310

Rule of 72

One of the most useful simple rules that any investor uses to evaluate investment is the Rule of 72. The Rule of 72 is a rule of thumb. Any rule of thumb is a simple technique used to make a complex subject easier to apply in real-life situations. The Rule of 72 says to simply divide the number 72 by any interest rate percentage, and the resulting number is the number of years it will take to double your investment. For example, the number 9 divided into 72 equals 8, and it takes eight years at a 9 percent return to double your investment. Similarly, if you invest and earn 6 percent, the number 6 divided into 72 yields 12. This means at a 6 percent interest rate on an investment, money will double in 12 years.

Table A.1 shows some comparisons between continuous compounding, annual compounding, and the Rule of 72. What interest rate is needed to double your money if you are receiving continuous compounding versus annual compounding? What interest rate does the Rule of

72 suggest you need? Table A.1 shows that a lower return is needed when interest is compounded continuously. Also note that the Rule of 72 provides a very accurate estimate of the return needed to double your money after only two years.

TABLE A.1	**The Rule of 72** *Divide the number 72 by any interest rate percentage. The result is the number of years it takes to double your investment (e.g., at 9 percent, an investment doubles in eight years).*

	What Interest Rate Will Double Your Money?		
How Many Years Will It Take?	Continuous Compounding	Annual Compounding	Rule of 72
1	69.3%	100.0%	72.0%
2	34.7	41.4	36.0
3	23.1	26.0	24.0
4	17.3	18.9	18.0
5	13.9	14.9	14.4
6	11.6	12.2	12.0
7	9.9	10.4	10.3
8	8.7	9.1	9.0
9	7.7	8.0	8.0
10	6.9	7.2	7.2
11	6.3	6.5	6.5
12	5.8	5.9	6.0
13	5.3	5.5	5.5
14	5.0	5.1	5.1
15	4.6	4.7	4.8
20	3.5	3.5	3.6
25	2.8	2.8	2.9
30	2.3	2.3	2.4

Try It!

How long will it take to double your money when earning 6, 9, and 12 percent returns?

Solution

At 6 percent, you double your money in 72/6 = 12 years.

At 9 percent, you double your money in 72/9 = 8 years.

At 12 percent, you double your money in 72/12 = 6 years.

Using a Financial Calculator

The future-value and present-value calculations are programmed into modern financial (or business) calculators. Although there are different brand names and levels of sophistication, all financial calculators take the same approach to solving common time-value-of-money applications. The basic financial calculator uses five buttons that represent the inputs to time-value computations. For example, the Texas Instruments BA II Plus uses the notations N, I/Y, PV, PMT, and FV:

- N denotes the number of periods in the computation. It is taken as the compound frequency interval. This could be the number of years, quarters, months, or any other interval of periods in the problem.

- I/Y represents the interest rate for the period. For a 12 percent annual interest rate, the value of 12 would be used for annual compounding, 6 for semiannual compounding, and 1 for monthly compounding.

- PV and FV are the present value and future value, respectively.

- PMT denotes a recurring payment made every period. For example, most employee retirement plans consists of consistent monthly contributions to the portfolio.

To use the calculator, enter the value in the calculator and then press the applicable time-value button. Enter a zero in a button that is not used. For the solution, press the unknown button. You may need to press the CPT or COMP button first on some calculator types. Most financial calculators are sold with settings developed for someone who will always use monthly compounding (like a loan broker). Since investors need to compute values using various compounding intervals, it is recommended that the presetting be changed. In the TI BA II Plus calculator, the change is accomplished by pressing the [2nd] button and then [P/Y]. The calculator may display {P/Y= 12.00}. If so, press 1 and then [ENTER] to change the setting. The financial calculator solution to the problem in Equation A.2 is

N	I/Y	PV	PMT	FV
15	8	−5,000	0	|

CPT FV = $15,860.85

Notice that a negative sign is used for the present sum. These calculators use a negative number for a cash flow an investor pays and a positive number for a cash flow received by the investor. In this case, the investor *pays* $5,000 for an investment yielding 8 percent for 15 years in order to *receive* the future value of $15,860.85. If this investment used semiannual compounding, then the solution would be

N	I/Y	PV	PMT	FV
30	4	−5,000	0	|

CPT FV = $16,216.99

Payments

Future Value of Recurring Payments

An investor who contributes to a 401(k) retirement plan will do so on a monthly basis. How much will the investor have at retirement? The answer to this question requires the future value of an annuity equation:

$$\text{Future value} = \text{Payment} \times \frac{(1 + \text{interest rate})^t - 1}{\text{interest rate}} \qquad \text{(A.8)}$$

Payment is the cash flow invested every period. Consider that over the next 30 years of employment, an employee contributes $300 per month to an investment expected to earn 9 percent per year. Note that this problem requires monthly compounding, so use an interest rate of 0.0075 (= 0.09/12). Also note that there will be 360 (= 30 × 12) months. After 30 years, the employee will have

$$\text{Future value} = \$300 \times \frac{(1 + 0.0075)^{360} - 1}{0.0075} \qquad \text{(A.9)}$$

$$= \$300 \times 1,830.7435 = \$549,223$$

A financial calculator can also easily compute the future value:

N	I/Y	PV	PMT	FV
360	0.75	0	−300	|

CPT FV = $549,223.04

Present Value of Recurring Payments

There are also cases where investors use a present sum of money and invest it for income. What level of retirement nest egg is needed for retirement? The answer to this question uses the present value of an annuity equation:

$$\text{Present value} = \text{Payment} \times \frac{(1+\text{interest rate})^t - 1}{\text{interest rate} \times (1+\text{interest rate})^t} \qquad \textbf{(A.10)}$$

An investor expects to be retired for 25 years. In addition to other sources of income in retirement (like Social Security), a monthly income of $3,000 is desired. If the nest egg is expected to earn a conservative 6 percent per year, what nest egg value is needed to fund this income? Use an interest rate of 0.005 (= 0.06/12) and 300 (= 25 ×12) months. The nest egg needs to be

$$\text{Present value} = \$3,000 \times \frac{(1+0.005)^{300} - 1}{0.005 \times (1+0.005)^{300}} \qquad \textbf{(A.11)}$$

$$= \$3,000 \times 155.2082 = \$465,621$$

A financial calculator can also easily compute the present value:

N	I/Y	PV	PMT	FV
300	0.5	|	3,000	0

CPT PV = −$465,620.59

Solving for Payments and Interest Rates

Other applications of the time-value formula include solving for the payment in the annuity formula and solving for the interest rate earned on an investment. For example, an investor who has just retired already knows the level of the nest egg saved. The new retiree wants to know how much money can be withdrawn from the nest egg. Rearranging Equation A.10 to solve for the payment gives

$$\text{Payment} = \text{Present value} \times \frac{\text{interest rate} \times (1+\text{interest rate})^t}{(1+\text{interest rate})^t - 1} \qquad \textbf{(A.12)}$$

For the investor in Equation A.9 who saved a nest egg of $549,223, what monthly income can be generated if a 9 percent return is achieved over a 35-year retirement horizon?

$$\text{Payment} = \$549,223 \times \frac{0.0075 \times (1+0.0075)^{420}}{(1+0.0075)^{420} - 1} \qquad \textbf{(A.13)}$$

$$= \$549,223 \times 1,830.7435 = \$4,306$$

A financial calculator can also easily compute the payment:

N	I/Y	PV	PMT	FV
420	0.75	−549,223 |		0

CPT PMT = $4,305.87

However, this new retiree is a little nervous about investing so aggressively during the retirement years in the attempt to earn the 9 percent return. If the retiree is willing to withdraw only $3,000 per month, what interest rate does the investor need to achieve so that the nest egg will last the planned 35 years? Interest rate problems are usually easiest to solve using the financial calculator. In this case, the solution is

N	I/Y	PV	PMT	FV
420	|	−549,223	3,000	0

CPT I/Y = 0.47

The answer of 0.47 percent is a monthly return. The annual interest rate needed is 5.64 percent (= 0.47% × 12).

The time-value-of-money equations are important tools in any investor's tool box. Using them to value stocks and bonds and to compute investment returns is a common occurrence.

APPENDIX B

Each end-of-chapter CFA question is reprinted with permission from the CFA Institute, Charlottesville, Virginia.[1] Following is a list of the CFA questions in the end-of-chapter material and the exams and study guides from which they were taken and updated.

CHAPTER 1
18. CFA Level I Sample Examination for 2002 Candidates, ©2002
19. CFA Level I Sample Examination for 2002 Candidates, ©2002
20. CFA Level I Sample Examination for 2002 Candidates, ©2002

CHAPTER 2
19. CFA Level I Sample Examination for 2002 Candidates, ©2002
20. CFA Level I Sample Examination for 2002 Candidates, ©2002

CHAPTER 3
18. CFA Level I Sample Examination for 2002 Candidates, ©2002
19. CFA Level I Sample Examination for 2002 Candidates, ©2002
20. CFA Level I Sample Examination for 2002 Candidates, ©2002

CHAPTER 4
16. CFA Level I Sample Examination for 2002 Candidates, ©2002
17. CFA Level I Sample Examination for 2002 Candidates, ©2002
18. CFA Level I Sample Examination for 2002 Candidates, ©2002
19. CFA Level I Sample Examination for 2002 Candidates, ©2002
20. CFA Level I Sample Examination for 2002 Candidates, ©2002

CHAPTER 5
17. CFA Level I Sample Examination for 2002 Candidates, ©2002
18. CFA Level I Sample Examination for 2002 Candidates, ©2002
19. CFA Level I Sample Examination for 2002 Candidates, ©2002
20. 2004 CFA Level III Examination, Morning Session, ©2004

CHAPTER 6
19. CFA Level I Sample Examination for 2002 Candidates, ©2002
20. CFA Level I Sample Examination for 2002 Candidates, ©2002

CHAPTER 7
19. CFA Level I Sample Examination for 2002 Candidates, ©2002
20. CFA Level I Sample Examination for 2002 Candidates, ©2002

CHAPTER 8
19. 2004 CFA Level III Examination, Morning Session, ©2004
20. 1997 CFA Level III Examination, Morning Section, ©1997

CHAPTER 9
18. CFA Level I Sample Examination for 2002 Candidates, ©2002
19. CFA Level I Sample Examination for 2002 Candidates, ©2002
20. CFA Level I Sample Examination for 2002 Candidates, ©2002

CHAPTER 10
17. CFA Level I Sample Examination for 2002 Candidates, ©2002
18. CFA Level I Sample Examination for 2002 Candidates, ©2002
19. CFA Level I Sample Examination for 2002 Candidates, ©2002

[1]The CFA Institute does not endorse, promote, review, or warrant the accuracy of the product or services offered by The McGraw-Hill Companies.

glossary

1/_n_ heuristic   Employees contribute equal amounts into each investment option offered in a pension plan.

10K report   Annual accounting information filed with the SEC.

10Q report   Quarterly accounting information filed with the SEC.

12b-1 fees   Marketing expenses.

13D   Filings made to the SEC within 10 days of an entity's attaining a 5 percent or more position in any class of a company's securities.

200-day moving average   Average stock price over 200 trading days (roughly one year).

50-day moving average   Average stock price over the previous 50 trading days (roughly two calendar months).

ADR ratio   Number of underlying shares represented by one ADR.

Accounting restatements   Changes to balance sheet, income statement, and cash flow statement numbers published previously.

Administrator   Person who oversees the services provided by other firms.

Advance-decline line   Ongoing sum of the number of advancing stocks minus the number of declining stocks.

Advance-decline ratio   The number of firms that advanced in price divided by the number that declined on a given trading day.

Affinity fraud   Investment scams that prey on members of identifiable groups, such as religious or ethnic communities, the elderly, or professional groups.

Agency auction market   Market in which brokers represent buyers and sellers and prices are determined by supply and demand.

All or none   Buy or sell instruction that must be filled exactly or not at all.

All-or-none offering   Security offering in which a complete sale is required.

Alpha   Abnormal return measured from the CAPM required rate of return.

American Depositary Receipts (ADR)   Coupons that signify ownership of foreign stocks; negotiable instruments that represent ownership in the equity securities of a non-U.S. company.

American Stock Exchange (Amex)   Nation's second-largest stock exchange.

American-style option   Option contract that can be exercised at any time between the date of purchase and the expiration date.

Anchoring   A strong mental attachment to a particular price.

Announcement date   News publication date.

Announcement period   Time frame during which an economic event occurs.

Antitrust policy   Laws and rules designed to promote competition.

Appraisal   Professional opinion of market value.

Arbitrage   The simultaneous buying and selling of the same asset at different prices to capture a mispricing.

Arbitrage pricing theory (APT)   Multifactor asset pricing model that allows market betas to represent only one of the firm's many risk factors.

Arithmetic average return   Sum of investment returns divided by number of periods or securities.

Ask   Lowest price an investor will accept to sell.

Ask size   Number of shares offered by current sellers.

Assessed value   Property value determined for purposes of taxation.

Asset allocation   Process of diversifying an investment portfolio across various asset categories, such as stocks, bonds, and cash.

Assigned execution   Option-writer obligations.

At-the-money   Option whose strike price equals the current market price of the underlying asset.

Auction   Public sale through open bidding.

Auditors   Accountants hired by the board to validate the firm's financial statements.

Average life   Typical period before refunding.

Baby-boom generation   People born between 1946 and 1964.

Back-end load   Commissions paid when a fund is sold.

Back testing   Backward-looking analysis.

Backwardation   Inverted market in which futures prices are lower in distant delivery months.

Balance sheet   "Snapshot" information about a company's financial well-being at a specific point in time.

Bankers' acceptances   Time drafts drawn on and accepted by banking institutions.

Barbell strategy   Bond portfolio concentration at both the short and the long ends of the maturity spectrum.

Basic earnings per share   Firm's earnings divided by number of shares outstanding.

Basis   In the futures market, the difference between a commodity's spot price and the futures price.

Basis points   1/100th of 1 percent (e.g., 0.5 percent is 50 basis points).

Basis risk   Chance of adverse change in the futures–spot market price relationship.

Bear trap   Temporary increase in prices followed by a further sharp decline in the market.

Bearer bonds   Bonds with ownership defined by possession.

Beginning-of-day effect   Tendency of stock prices to rise during the first 45 minutes of the trading day.

Behavioral finance   A study of cognitive errors and emotions in financial decisions.

Behavioral portfolios The formation of a portfolio through the funding of individual goals.

Below-investment-grade bonds Junk bonds.

Benchmark A diversified portfolio of similar risk or investment style used as a comparison.

Benchmark interest rate Interest rate standard.

Best-efforts underwriting Security offering in which the investment banker simply agrees to make its best effort at selling the agreed-on amount of debt and equity securities.

Beta The sensitivity of a security's returns to the systematic market risk factor.

Bid Highest price an investor is willing to pay.

Bid-ask spread Gap between the bid and ask prices that represents a cost to the investor.

Bid size Number of shares sought by current buyers.

Bid test SEC criterion that allows a short sale to occur if the current bid price is higher than the previous bid price.

Binomial option pricing model A model in which a given number of time steps between the valuation date and option expiration are assumed. The underlying stock price can change only to two levels at any time step.

Black-Scholes option pricing model Formula used to calculate economic values for options on the basis of continuous time assumptions and return distributions.

Block trades Trades of 10,000 shares or more.

Block transactions Transactions of at least 10,000 shares usually matched outside the auction process and then cleared through the exchange.

Blow off Spike in volume when prices have stalled.

Board of directors People elected by shareholders to hire management and monitor the firm.

Bond coupon rate Bond interest rate expressed as a percentage of par value.

Bond dealers Securities firms and banks that act as financial intermediaries between bond issuers and investors.

Bond funds Funds that buy debt instruments.

Bond investors Individuals and institutions that purchase bonds for interest income and long-term capital gains.

Bond issuers Entities that supply new bonds (supply source).

Bond rating Measure of credit quality.

Bond redemption value Amount to be received from the issuer on the maturity date.

Bond swap Simultaneous sale and purchase of fixed-income securities to achieve some investment purpose.

Bond tender offer Offer to buy an entire outstanding class of securities.

Bonds Interest-bearing debt obligations.

Book-entry form Electronic record of bond ownership.

Break-even time Number of years over which the conversion premium can be recovered by the increased income of the senior security over the junior security.

Broker call rate Interest rate charged to investors using margin debt.

Brokerage account credit balance indicators Gauges of buying power that resides in the account balances of Wall Street brokerage customers.

Brokerage commissions Sales charges.

Bull call spread Purchase of a low-strike price call and the simultaneous sale of another, high-strike price call on the same underlying equity with the same expiration date.

Bull put spread Sale of a high-strike price put and the simultaneous purchase of another, low-strike price put on the same underlying equity with the same expiration date.

Business cycle Rhythmic pattern of contraction and expansion in the overall economy.

Buy stop order Buy order that is to be held until the market price rises to a specified stop price.

Buy-side analysts Analysts who work for mutual funds and other institutions managing portfolios.

Buyer's premium Added commission paid by buyer.

CUSIP Unique code used to identify financial securities.

Call option Right to buy.

Call premium The dollar amount over the par value of a callable bond that is paid to holders when the bond is called by the issuer.

Call protection Amount of time before a newly issued bond is callable.

Call provisions Contractual authority that allows the issuer to redeem bonds prior to scheduled maturity.

Capital asset pricing model (CAPM) Method for predicting how investment returns are determined in an efficient capital market.

Capital gains distribution Payment of realized capital gains.

Capital market line (CML) Linear risk-return trade-off for all investment portfolios.

Capital spending When firms buy assets to increase efficiency or expand operations.

Capitalization rate Income yield computed as property income divided by property value.

Caps Upper limits on the interest rate paid on floating-rate notes or adjustable-rate mortgages.

Cash flow statement Report that shows change in the company's cash position over a period of time.

Cash reserves Short-term money market instruments.

Cash-settled option Option that entails the promise of a cash payment based on the difference between market and exercise prices.

Certified Financial Planner (CFP) Finance professional who helps individuals identify and meet financial needs.

Channel Area between resistance and support lines.

Charting Use of two-dimensional price and volume graphs to analyze market behavior and anticipate future price movements.

Chartists Another name for technicians.

Chicago Board of Trade First and largest commodities exchange.

Chicago Board Options Exchange (CBOE) U.S. options market pioneer.

Chicago Climate Exchange U.S. futures exchange specializing in greenhouse gas contracts.

Chicago Mercantile Exchange (CME) Largest futures exchange in the United States.

Choice overload hypothesis Theory that excessive options can limit participation because decision makers generally prefer a manageable number of decision alternatives.

Churning Illegal broker-initiated trading in client accounts to generate commission income.

Circuit breakers Rules for halting securities trading in volatile markets.

Clearinghouses Institutions that ensure balance in the number of futures and futures option contracts bought and sold and that give fulfillment guarantees.

Closed-end funds Investment companies that issue a fixed number of shares at a given point in time.

Coefficient of variation A common risk-reward measure.

Cognitive dissonance The mental discord that arises when the memory of an event conflicts with a positive self-perception.

Coin-flipping contest Investment metaphor for gambling.

Cold calls Unrequested telephone solicitations.

Collars Upper and lower limits on the interest rate paid on floating-rate notes or adjustable-rate mortgages.

Commercial paper Money market instruments issued by private entities.

Commodity Futures Trading Commission (CFTC) Independent federal regulatory agency with jurisdiction over futures trading.

Common stock A proportionate ownership stake in a corporation.

Common stock equivalent value Worth of a bond as common stock if converted at the present time.

Comparable-transactions approach Real estate valuation based upon transactions involving similar properties.

Competitive advantage Unique ability to create, distribute, or service products.

Computer stock screen A computerized sort of companies according to financial characteristics.

Concentration ratios (CRs) Percentage market share held by a group of leading firms.

Confidence Index Indicator of investor mood based on bond yields.

Conservatism A slow updating of opinions when new information is available.

Constant-growth model Stock valuation method based on constantly growing future dividends and risk considerations.

Contango Futures market with higher prices in distant delivery months.

Continuation pattern Persistence of the underlying bullish or bearish trend signal.

Contract period Length of time between the date that an option contract is established and the date of its expiration.

Contract size Trading unit of an underlying asset.

Contraction A sustained period of declining economic activity.

Contrarian investment philosophy Investment strategy based on the premise that investors can profit by betting against the overly emotional crowd; strategy to select unpopular stocks.

Contrary indicator A measure that assesses what others are doing and suggests you should do the opposite.

Conversion price Amount per unit of the junior security that the company is willing to accept in trade per bond.

Conversion ratio Number of junior securities per bond after conversion.

Conversion value Worth of a bond as a junior security if converted at the present time.

Convertible bond Debt that can be exchanged into more junior securities.

Convexity Sensitivity of modified duration to changes in yield to maturity.

Cooling-off period Period of time during which the SEC is examining the registration materials and the investment bankers are conducting marketing activities.

Corporate governance Control system that helps corporations effectively administer economic resources.

Correlation A measure of comovement that varies between −1 and +1.

Corruption Situation in which government officials demand personal payments in order to do business in a country.

Cost of capital The cost to the firm that is required by debt and equity holders.

Counterparty risk Chance that a counterparty to a futures contract obligation will not fulfill his or her obligation.

Coupon bonds Bonds with tangible interest vouchers.

Coupons Interest vouchers.

Covariance An absolute measure of comovement that varies between plus and minus infinity, $+\infty$ and $-\infty$.

Cover the short Return borrowed shares.

Covered call Simultaneous purchase of a stock and sale of a call option on that same security.

Credit risk Chance of loss due to issuer default.

Credit-quality risk Chance of loss due to the inability of a bond issuer to make timely interest and principal payments.

Credit-rating agencies Companies that grade the quality of debt issues.

Cumulative abnormal returns The sum of abnormal returns over some event-interval period, typically of one, two, or three days.

Currency risk Loss potential tied to changing relative values of world currencies.

Currency translation costs Expenses of converting host-country currency into the domestic currency of the buyer or seller.

Current cost Amount that must be paid under prevailing market conditions.

Current ratio Liquidity measured by current assets divided by current liabilities.

Current yield Bond's promised interest payment divided by its current purchase price.

Custodial fees Bookkeeping charges.

Custodian Bank that holds portfolio securities.

Customer loyalty risk Chance of losing customers to established competitors or new entrants.

Customer order flow Customer buy and sell activity.

DIAMONDS ETFs that track the price performance and dividend yield of the Dow Jones Industrial Average.

DJIA divisor Adjustment factor used to account for stock splits.

Data-snooping problem Reliance on chance observations in historical data as a guide to investment decision making.

Day order Instruction to buy or sell during the present trading session.

Day-count basis Method for calculating interest rates, usually 30 days per month and 360 days per year.

Dealer's agreement Contractual obligation of syndicate members.

Debenture Unsecured debt.

Debt-to-asset ratio Long-term debt divided by total assets.

Default risk Chance of nonpayment of interest or principal.

Deficiency letter Disapproval notice issued by the SEC.

Defined-benefit retirement plan Employer-funded retirement program in which the employer promises to pay the employee a fixed retirement income that depends on salary history and time employed.

Defined-contribution retirement plan Employee-funded retirement program in which employees direct and contribute to their own retirement plans. Retirement income is dependent on employee success in investing.

Delivery date Calendar date by which buyers and sellers of futures contracts are obligated to offset or fulfill their obligations.

Delivery months Scheduled delivery cycles.

Delivery notice Written advice of delivery intention.

Delta Percentage change in option price following a $1 change in price of the underlying asset; also called *hedge ratio*.

Derivative securities Financial instruments with value stemming from changes in the value of some other asset.

Developed markets Securities markets in countries with advanced economies.

Diluted earnings per share Net income divided by the number of shares outstanding after consideration of the possible conversion of stock options and convertible securities.

Direct capitalization Process for estimating property value by dividing NOI by a capitalization rate.

Discount Percentage by which the market price per share for a closed-end fund is less than net asset value.

Discount rate Interest rate charged by the Federal Reserve to member banks.

Discount to par Markdown from par value.

Discounted cash flow approach Real estate valuation based on present-value calculations.

Dispersion Variation from the average.

Disposition effect The predisposition to sell winners and hold losers.

Disutility Psychic loss.

Divergence A momentum reversal within a continuing price trend.

Diversifiable risk Another term for unsystematic risk.

Divest Sell a part of the business or a product line.

Dividend discount model Stock valuation approach based on expected dividend income and risk considerations.

Dividend payout ratio Percentage of income paid out in the form of dividends.

Dividend yield Dividend income expressed as a percentage of the amount paid for a stock.

Dividend-growth investors Investors who place primary emphasis on the potential for dividend growth in their stock selection strategy.

Dollar-cost averaging Strategy of investing a fixed dollar amount in a security at regular intervals.

Domestic bonds Bonds issued by a local borrower and denominated in local currency.

Dow Jones Industrial Average (DJIA) Price-weighted index of 30 large, industry-leading stocks.

Dow Jones Wilshire 4500 Completion Index Mid-cap index of Dow Jones Wilshire (5000) Index companies minus the S&P 500.

Dow Jones Wilshire 5000 Composite Index Total dollar value of the U.S. equity market (in billions of dollars).

Dow Theory Idea that market movements can be predicted by studying trends in the DJIA and DJTA.

Downtick trade Trade at a lower price than the previous trade.

Dual trader Futures market professional who holds positions and executes orders for others.

Due diligence Required analysis of the security issuer by the underwriter.

Duration Economic life of a bond measured by the weighted-average time to receipt of interest and principal payments.

EBITDA Earnings before interest, taxes, depreciation and amortization.

EDGAR Electronic Retrieval Analysis System for SEC filings.

EPS growth Growth in earnings per share; achieved by increasing earnings and/or decreasing the number of shares outstanding.

Earnings per share Net income divided by the number of shares outstanding

Earnings surprise Earnings that differ from expected earnings.

Earnings yield Earnings-price, or E/P, ratio.

Economic event Change in the underlying perceptions of investors.

Economic indicators Data series that successfully describe the pattern of projected, current, or past economic activity.

Economic value Value determined by business prospects.

Economic value added (EVA) A measure of residual wealth calculated by deducting the cost of capital from operating profit.

Effective date Date securities are offered to institutional investors and the general public.

Efficient frontier Collection of all efficient portfolios.

Efficient market Stock market in which the price for any given stock effectively represents the expected net present value of all future profits.

Efficient portfolio Portfolio with maximum expected return for a given level of risk or with minimum risk for a given expected return.

Efficient-Market Hypothesis (EMH) Theory stating that security prices fully reflect all available information; idea that every security is correctly priced, not overvalued or undervalued.

Emerging markets Securities markets in countries with rapidly evolving economies.

Emerging-market fund Mutual fund that invests predominantly in the stocks of companies based in countries with developing economies.

End-of-day effect Tendency of stock prices to rise near the close of the trading day.

Equipment trust certificate Debt backed by a specific equipment lien.

Equity benchmark Performance standard to be evaluated against.

Equity REIT REIT with an ownership position in real estate.

Equity-income investors Investors who stress income first and long-term capital growth second.

Eurodollar Dollar deposit in a European bank.

Europe, Australasia, Far East (EAFE) Index Leading global stock index of stocks from 21 countries.

European-style option Option contract that can be exercised only on the expiration date.

Event studies Studies that measure abnormal returns surrounding significant news items that may have important economic consequences for the firm.

Excess return A security or portfolio return less the risk-free rate

Exchange fee Charge assessed when an investor exchanges shares from one fund to another within the same fund family; trading cost imposed by organized trading systems.

Exchange-traded funds (ETFs) Tradeable shares that represent proportional ownership in baskets of stocks.

Executive stock options A compensation plan that pays the executive increasingly more as the price of the stock rises.

Exercise Execution of option-holder rights.

Exercise price Purchase (call) or sale (put) price for an exercised option contract.

Expansion A sustained period of rising economic activity.

Expected return Future return anticipated after analyzing the financial asset; anticipated profit over some relevant holding period.

Expected values Anticipated amounts.

Expiration date Last day of an American-style option or the single exercise date of a European-style option.

Export The amount of domestic goods and services sold internationally.

Expropriation risk Loss potential tied to government confiscation of assets.

Ex-split date Date on which the stock begins trading at the new postsplit price.

FTSE-100 Capitalization-weighted index of the 100 top companies on the London Stock Exchange.

Face amount Stated bond principal obligation (also par value).

Fair game Even bet, or 50-50 chance.

Familiarity bias A mental shortcut that treats familiar things as better than less familiar things.

Federal funds rate Overnight bank lending rate.

Filing date Date the investment bank submits a registration statement with the SEC.

Fill or kill All-or-none order that must be immediately filled or canceled.

Final prospectus Final statement of offering.

Financial analyst bias Tendency of Wall Street analysts to issue favorable recommendations.

Financial assets Investment instruments, issued by corporations, governments, or other organizations, that offer legal rights to debt or equity cash flow.

Financial engineering Sophisticated manipulation of the balance sheet through use of exotic forms of debt and equity financing.

Financial leverage The amount of debt used. Its use magnifies the size of profits and losses, thus increasing the firm's risk.

Firm-commitment underwriting Security offering in which the investment banker underwrites or purchases the entire issue from the corporation and reoffers the securities to the general public.

Firm-specific risk Chance that problems with an individual company will reduce the value of investment.

Fixed-income securities A group of securities that include preferred stocks and bonds.

Flip An IPO purchase in the primary market quickly followed by a sale on the stock exchange.

Floor broker Futures market professional who executes orders for others.

Footnotes Additional disclosures and details of the firm's business activities.

Foreign bias The propensity of investors to overweight investment in familiar countries and underweight investment in others.

Foreign bond Bond issued by a borrower from a different country but denominated in the local currency.

Foreign regional fund International fund that invests in the stocks of a specific global area.

Form 144 Filings submitted to the SEC by holders of restricted stock who intend to sell shares.

Forward contract Binding agreement to buy or sell a stipulated grade and quantity of a commodity at a specific future time for an agreed-on price.

Forward P/E ratio Current stock price divided by expected next year's earnings per share.

Free cash flow The cash that a company is able to generate after the expenses required to maintain or expand its asset base; earnings before depreciation, interest, taxes, and amortization, minus necessary capital expenditures.

Free index Price performance index of securities that are available to all investors.

Front-end loads Commissions paid at the time of a fund purchase.

Full-market-capitalization weight Price multiplied by the number of outstanding shares.

Fund family A mutual fund firm that offers many portfolio choices.

Fundamental value Underlying value based on the firm's assets and profit potential.

Futures contract Financially secured binding agreement to buy or sell a stipulated grade and quantity of a commodity at a specific future time for an agreed-on price.

Futures option Right, but not obligation, to buy or sell a contract at a certain price for a limited period of time.

Gambler's fallacy The belief that a short-term deviation from a "fair" gamble changes the odds of the next gamble; the erroneous belief that there is a self-correcting process in a set of fair gambles.

Gamma Responsiveness of delta to unit changes in the value of the underlying asset.

General-obligation bonds Municipal bonds backed by the full faith and credit of the issuer.

Geometric mean return Compound rate of return earned on investment.

Global diversification The addition of foreign investment assets to a portfolio, thereby decreasing the total risk.

Global equity funds Mutual fund that invests in U.S. and foreign stocks.

Gold standard Monetary system that backs currency with gold.

Good 'til canceled order A limit order that is open until executed or canceled by the investor.

Government policy risk Loss potential tied to changes in government rules and regulations.

Government-sponsored enterprises Private corporations with a public purpose.

Graham and Dodd Coauthors of *Security Analysis*, the value investor's bible.

Growth-and-income investors Investors who seek a relative balance between the goals of high and stable income and long-term capital growth.

Growth-at-a-reasonable-price (GARP) investors Disciplined growth-stock investors who seldom buy growth stocks with PEG ratios greater than 1.

Growth stock investing Investment approach that focuses on companies expected to have above-average rates of growth in sales and earnings.

Hang Seng Index Market-cap-weighted measure of Hong Kong stocks.

Head and shoulders Popular price chart pattern that signals a reversal to a bear market trend.

Hedge funds Investment partnerships that employ speculative investment techniques, such as leverage and short selling, that are very risky and commonly prohibited for mutual funds.

Hedge ratio Number of shares of stock required to offset the price risk of one option contract; the ratio of underlying asset price volatility divided by the price volatility of the futures contract price.

Hedged position Use of options to offset the risk inherent in some other investment.

Hedgers Investors who seek to reduce risks associated with dealing in the underlying commodity or security.

Herfindahl Hirschmann Index (HHI) Measure of size inequality among competitors.

Heuristic simplification Mental shortcuts used by the brain to make quicker decisions and choices with uncertain outcomes.

High-yield bonds Below-investment-grade bonds.

Historical cost Actual cash cost for the asset.

Holders Buyers of options.

Holding-period risk Chance of loss during periods of adverse changes in bond prices.

Holiday effects Regularity of unusually good performance for stocks on the day prior to market-closing holidays.

Home bias The irrational propensity of investors to predominantly buy domestic securities; an outcome of familiarity bias.

Hot IPO IPO with limited shares and high demand.

House money effect The propensity to take risky gambles after winning some money; failure to mentally integrate new winnings as personal wealth.

House Price Index (HPI) A timely indicator of house price trends at various geographic levels.

Hybrid REIT REIT that generates income from real estate debt and equity.

Illiquid market Slow market with high transaction costs.

Illusion of control The belief that people have influence over the outcome of uncontrollable events.

Illusion of knowledge The illusion that more information creates more knowledge and better predictions.

Implied volatility Estimate of a security's volatility calculated by using market prices and the Black-Scholes option pricing model.

Import The amount of foreign goods and services purchased domestically.

Improvements Buildings and structures.

In-the-money Option whose strike price is less (more) than the market price of the underlying security for a call (put).

Incentive pay Compensation according to measurable performance.

Incentives Financial reasons for inciting an action.

Income bonds Bonds with interest that must be paid only in the event of positive earnings.

Income distribution Payment of interest and dividends.

Income property Real estate bought for the purposes of generating rental income.

Income statement Report of business inflows and outflows during a given period.

Indenture agreement Bond contract.

Indenture Legal stipulation of bond agreement.

Independent directors Board directors with no business ties to the investment advisor.

Independent public accountant Person or firm that audits the mutual fund's financial statements.

Index arbitrage Trading strategy that exploits divergences between actual and theoretical futures prices.

Index effect Tendency of stocks to jump when Standard & Poor's announces that they are about to be added to the S&P 500.

Index fund Mutual fund strategy designed to mimic the performance of some broad market benchmark.

Industrial revenue bonds Bonds used to develop industrial and/or commercial property for the benefit of private users.

Inflation Increase in the cost of goods and services over time.

Initial margin Minimum amount required to initiate a trade.

Initial public offering (IPO) Newly issued common stock in the primary market.

Inside equity Common stock held by management and other employees.

Inside market Highest bid and lowest offer prices.

Insider information Proprietary data within the firm.

Institutional equity Common stock ownership by pension funds, mutual funds, and other large independent shareholders.

Institutional investors Mutual funds, pension funds, insurance companies, etc.

Interest coverage A measure of the firm's ability to pay interest charges.

Interest rate risk Chance of loss in the value of fixed-income investments following a rise in interest rates.

Interest reinvestment risk Chance of lost income on reinvested interest payments.

Intermarket spread Offsetting positions in related commodities.

Intermarket Surveillance Group Coordinated effort to detect cross-market manipulative trading.

Internally sustainable growth Rate at which a firm can grow without obtaining more capital.

International equity fund Mutual fund that invests in the equity securities of companies located outside the United States.

International iShares Unit portfolio trusts that track the performance of an underlying international benchmark index.

Intramarket spread In the futures market, the difference between futures prices for different delivery months for the same underlying commodity.

Intrinsic value Difference between an in-the-money option's strike price and the current market price of the underlying security; real economic value.

Inventory turnover A measure of the amount of inventory needed to achieve the firm's sales.

Investment advisor Firm that manages the fund's portfolio and policies.

Investment bank Financial firm that helps other firms raise capital by selling securities to investors in the primary market; bank that helps companies acquire capital through the issuance of securities.

Investment banker Finance professional who helps companies and government organizations acquire capital through the issuance of financial assets.

Investment benchmark Investment standard to which portfolio performance is compared.

Investment clubs A group formed to learn and invest. Members contribute money and investment ideas.

Investment horizon Holding period.

Investment newsletters Subscription services that deliver periodic investing advice.

Investment portfolio Collection of securities that together provide an investor with an attractive trade-off between risk and return.

Investment rule of thumb Simple guide to investment valuation that has served the test of time; simple procedures created in advance to help investors make good decisions.

Investor confidence The level of the investing public's trust in corporate information and investment industry advice.

Investor herding The movement of large groups of investors into or out of a stock or industry of companies.

Investor mood Level of optimism or pessimism by investors; also called *sentiment*.

Investor psychology The reasons, emotions, and perceptions of the human brain as they pertain to investments.

Investor sentiment Investor mood of optimism or pessimism.

Irrational bubbles Extreme changes in financial asset values that cannot be tied to changes in economic fundamentals.

iShares Index shares (ETFs) created by Barclays Global Investors.

January effect Phenomenon of unusually large positive rates of return for stocks during the first few trading days of the year.

Joint test problem Situation in which anomalies can indicate market inefficiency or market model inaccuracy.

Junk bonds Highly speculative debt securities.

Kansas City Board of Trade (KCBOT) Predominant marketplace for hard red winter wheat.

Kondratieff wave Long, 60-year economic cycle.

Laddering Portfolio allocation into bonds with a steplike sequence of maturity dates.

Lagging indicators An economic index that changes after the economy has already begun to follow a particular trend.

Law of one price Concept that identical assets have identical prices.

Leading indicators An economic index that changes before the economy begins to follow a particular trend.

Level I ADRs ADRs issued when the issuer is not initially seeking to raise capital in the United States or list its ADRs on an exchange or Nasdaq.

Level II ADRs ADRs issued when a company has no immediate financing needs and listed on U.S. exchanges or quoted on Nasdaq.

Level III ADRs ADRs issued when an issuer floats a public offering of ADRs in the United States and obtains listing on a major U.S. exchange or Nasdaq.

Leverage Total assets divided by stockholders' equity. It reflects the extent to which debt and preferred stock are used in addition to common stock financing.

Limit order Instruction to buy or sell at a specified price.

Liquidation value Company worth measured in terms of scrap value.

Liquidity preference hypothesis Theory that rising yield curves give long-term bond investors a holding-period risk premium.

Liquidity risk Loss potential tied to the fact that a stock can become difficult to buy or sell.

Load charges Sales commissions.

London Interbank Offered Rates (LIBOR) London federal funds rate.

Long Buyer; also used to signify ownership.

Long-term equity anticipation securities (LEAPS) Long-term calls and puts.

Low-load funds Funds that charge sales fees ranging from 1 to 3 percent.

Macroeconomics Study of aggregate measures of economic activity

Maintenance fees Bookeeping charges.

Maintenance margin Minimum amount required at all times to sustain a market position.

Margin Performance bond.

Margin account Account that holds securities purchased with a combination of cash and borrowed funds.

Margin call Broker's demand for additional collateral when the equity has declined below the maintenance margin level.

Margin debt Amount borrowed to buy or maintain a security investment.

Margin of safety Positive difference between price and appraised value.

Mark-to-market Daily reconciliation of futures contract profits and losses based on spot market prices.

Market breadth Measure of how many issues are rising relative to the number of issues that are declining.

Market bubble A significant overvaluation of economic fundamentals in the stock market.

Market cap Market value of the firm.

Market correction Temporary decline in an ongoing bull market.

Market cycles Observable tendency of prices to rotate.

Market depth Number of active buyers and sellers.

Market impact costs Costs tied to changing market bid and ask prices.

Market index bias Distortion to beta estimates caused by the fact that market indexes are only imperfect proxies for the overall market.

Market interest rate Prevailing rate of interest on essentially identical securities.

Market maker spread Difference between bid and ask prices.

Market makers Member firms that use their own capital to trade and hold an inventory of NASD stocks; dealers who provide for an orderly market.

Market niche Market segment that can be successfully exploited through the special capabilities of a given firm.

Market order Instruction to buy or sell at the current market price.

Market peak Price high point.

Market portfolio The current value of all assets.

Market risk General fluctuation in stock and bond prices.

Market structure Competitive environment.

Market timing Investment style that attempts to buy into the stock market before a bull market move and sell before a bear market move.

Market trough Price low point.

Market volatility The level of security price changes, usually measured by standard deviation or variance of returns.

Market-adjusted abnormal returns Returns different from the market return.

Market-model abnormal returns Returns that cannot be explained by the CAPM.

Maturity Time at which bond principal and all interest will be paid in full.

Maturity date Date on which the security expires, or ceases to accrue interest.

Mean-adjusted abnormal returns Returns different from the average return.

Mental accounting Thinking about money and investing using individual categories instead of a unified perspective.

Merger risk Economic loss stemming from failure to achieve merger benefits.

Microcap stocks Companies with very small stock market capitalizations.

Microeconomics Study of economic data at the industry, firm, plant, or product level.

Minneapolis Grain Exchange U.S. futures exchange specializing in grain contracts.

Misattribution bias Tendency to attribute an unrelated feeling to the decision at hand.

Model specification bias Distortion to beta estimates because the SCL fails to include other important systematic influences on stock market volatility.

Modified duration Percentage change in bond price for each percentage-point change in market interest rates.

Momentum indicators Measures of momentum. Popular indicators are the rate of change, MACD, and Relative Strength Index.

Momentum The rate of change, or velocity, of a price change. Also, the belief that stocks with high prior returns will continue to achieve high returns in the future. Stocks with low prior returns are believed to continue earning low returns.

Monday effect Regularity of Monday being the only day of the week that averages a negative rate of return.

Money flow The relative buying and selling pressure each day on share prices.

Money market mutual funds Funds that invest in cash reserves, or short-term IOUs.

Monopoly A single seller or producer in the industry.

Mortgage REIT REIT that invests in real estate–oriented debt.

Mortgage bond Debt backed by a specific property lien.

Mortgage securitization Process of creating diversified loan portfolios and selling proportionate shares to investors.

Multifactor CAPM Asset pricing model that assumes portfolio risk is tied to market risk and other factors, such as firm size and P/B ratios.

Multinational Corporation that conducts business in a number of host countries.

Multiple listing service (MLS) Proprietary database of available real estate.

Municipal bonds Debt issued by state or local governments.

Mutual fund Open-end investment company.

Mutual fund flow indicators Mutual fund inflows, outflows, and credit balance information.

Mutual fund shareholders Investors in the mutual fund portfolio.

Mutual fund tournament Incentive-created behavior where funds increase portfolio risk to increase potential performance.

Myopic Short-term focus.

Myopic loss aversion Irrational focus on trying to avoid short-term losses.

Nasdaq 100 Index Market-capitalization-weighted index of Nasdaq's largest companies.

Nasdaq Composite Index Market value-weighted index of all 5,000+ stocks listed on the Nasdaq Stock Market.

Nasdaq SmallCap Market Market for smaller companies that trade prior to full listing on the Nasdaq national market.

Nasdaq Stock Market Largest organized equities market by trading volume and number of listed companies.

National Association of Securities Dealers (NASD), Inc. A self-regulatory organization of the securities industry.

National Futures Association (NFA) Futures industry self-regulatory organization.

Negative abnormal returns Below-average returns that cannot be explained by below-market risk.

Negotiable certificates of deposit Time deposits at commercial banks.

Negotiated market Price determination through bargaining.

Net asset value Per-share value of a mutual fund's stock, bond, and cash reserve holdings.

Net income Difference between revenues and expenses, often expressed on an after-tax basis.

Net operating income (NOI) Income after deducting operating expenses but before deducting income taxes or financing costs.

Net profit margin Profit earned per dollar of sales.

New York Board of Trade (NYBOT) Parent company of the New York Cotton Exchange and the Coffee, Sugar & Cocoa Exchange, Inc.

New York Mercantile Exchange (NYME) Third-largest U.S. futures market, and the world's largest physical commodity futures exchange.

New York Stock Exchange (NYSE) Largest stock market in terms of market capitalization.

Nikkei 225 Index Leading measure of the Japanese stock market.

No-load funds Funds sold on a commission-free basis.

Noise traders Investors who make systematic errors when they assess the characteristics of companies and expected stock returns.

Nominal return Gross investment profit expressed as a percentage.

Nominal risk-free rate Monetary reward for postponing consumption (T-bill return).

Nondiversifiable risk Another term for systematic risk.

Nonfree index Price performance index of securities that are available on a preferential basis to domestic investors.

Nonpublic information Proprietary data.

Nonstationary beta problem Difficulty tied to the fact that betas are inherently unstable.

Normal distribution Bell-shaped probability curve.

Normative A description of what people should do

North American Industry Classification System (NAICS) Method for categorizing establishments according to the economic activity in which they are engaged.

Notice day Last date on which written advice of an intent to physically deliver commodities may be issued.

Numismatic value Worth to collectors.

OTC Bulletin Board (OTCBB) Regulated quotation service for very small over-the-counter equity securities.

Odd-lot indicators Gauges of small-investor buying and selling.

Offering circular Document filed with the SEC that describes a private placement.

Offsetting transaction Equal but opposite trade.

Oligopoly Few sellers in an industry.

Open interest Number of outstanding options.

Open order A limit order that has yet to be executed.

Open-end funds Mutual funds that continuously offer to sell and buy shares.

Open-outcry trading Exchange market dependent on physical communication.

Operating expense ratio Operating expenses expressed as a percentage of fund assets.

Operating leverage A measure of business risk taken through the use of fixed-cost production.

Optimal portfolio Collection of securities that provides an investor with the highest level of expected utility.

Option contract Right to buy or to sell a given amount or value of a particular asset at a fixed price until a given expiration date.

Option premium Option price.

Option series Options that have the same standardized terms but different strike prices.

Options Clearing Corporation (OCC) Issuer of all listed securities options.

Out-of-the-money Option whose strike price is more (less) than the market price of the underlying security for a call (put).

Overbought Insufficient future demand at market top.

Overconfidence People overestimate their knowledge and ability.

Oversold Insufficient future supply at market bottom.

PEG ratio P/E divided by the expected EPS growth rate.

Par value Face amount, usually $1,000.

Pay date Date on which a split becomes effective.

Penny stocks Stocks that trade at prices below $5.

Physical-delivery option Option that entails the physical delivery of an asset.

Pink sheets A listing of price quotes for microcap stocks that trade in the over-the-counter market.

Political risk Loss potential tied to government; stems from coups, assassinations, or civil unrest.

Political-cycle effect Pattern of abnormally high annual returns during the third and last years of a presidential administration.

Ponzi scheme Fraud in which new-investor money is used to make payments to earlier investors to give the false illusion of profitability (like a chain letter).

Pools Diversified loan portfolios.

Portfolio Diversified collection of stocks, bonds, and other assets.

Portfolio manager Finance professional in charge of making buy, sell, and hold decisions for a portfolio.

Portfolio rebalancing Adjusting a portfolio to a target asset allocation.

Portfolio theory Concept of making security choices based on portfolio expected returns and risks.

Positive A description of what people actually do.

Positive abnormal returns Above-average returns that cannot be explained as compensation for added risk.

Post-earnings announcement drift Stock price movements tied to earnings announcements that continue after the announcement.

Postannouncement drift Predictable returns for a period after an announcement.

Preferred stock A class of stock with fixed dividends.

Preliminary prospectus Preliminary statement of offering characteristics.

Premium Percentage by which the market price per share for a closed-end fund exceeds net asset value.

Premium to conversion Percentage over conversion value at which a convertible bond trades.

Premium to par Excess of market price over face amount.

Price risk Chance of overpaying for attractive companies; chance of adverse change in market prices.

Price spread Simultaneous purchase and sale of options on the same underlying stock but with different exercise prices.

Price to cash flow (P/CF) Current stock price dividend by annual cash flow.

Price to sales (P/S) Current stock price dividend by annual sales, or revenue.

Price-based options Rights to purchase or sell a specific debt security.

Price-book (P/B) ratio Stock price divided by accounting net worth.

Price-earnings (P/E) ratio Stock price divided by earnings per share.

Primary bond market Market for new bonds; the issuer-to-investor market.

Primary dealers Investment bankers that buy new Treasury securities.

Primary market Market for new securities sold to investors for the first time to raise capital for the issuer.

Primary trends Bull and bear markets that last anywhere from less than one year up to several years.

Principal amount Face amount or par value.

Principal underwriter Firm that sells the fund shares to the public.

Private placement Sale to a small group of investors, generally under exemption of SEC and state securities registration requirements.

Probability distribution Apportionment of likely occurrences.

Productivity growth The change in output of a worker, a machine, or an entire national economy in the creation of goods and services.

Prospect theory A positive description of how people frame and value a decision involving uncertainty.

Prospectus Offering circular.

Protective put Simultaneous purchase of a stock and purchase of a put option on that same security.

Proxy statement Annual meeting announcement and shareholder voting information.

Psychological biases Predictable tendencies caused by cognitive errors.

Public float Common stock held by unaffiliated institutional and individual investors.

Public information Freely shared knowledge.

Pump-and-dump scheme Manipulation conspiracy in which promoters artificially inflate a stock price so that they can sell their own inventories to unwitting investors.

Put option Right to sell.

Put provisions Contractual authority that allows investors to sell bonds back to the issuer prior to scheduled maturity.

Put-call parity Relationship that must hold between the price of puts and calls on the same underlying equity.

Put-call ratio A ratio of the trading volume of put options to call options.

QQQQs ETFs that track the price performance and dividend yield of the Nasdaq 100 Index.

Quality-at-a-reasonable-price investors Investors who seldom buy value stocks with VRE ratios less than 1.

Quick ratio Cash and near-cash assets relative to current liabilities.

Random walk Irregular pattern of numbers that defies prediction.

Random walk theory Concept that stock price movements do not follow any patterns or trends.

Random walk with drift Slight upward bias to inherently unpredictable daily stock prices.

Rational bubbles Extreme changes in financial asset values tied to changing economic fundamentals.

Raw land Unimproved land.

Real estate Real property and closely related businesses.

Real estate agent Licensed salesperson or real estate broker.

Real estate investment trust (REIT) Publicly traded company that manages property and/or mortgage loans.

Real property Land and the buildings or other objects permanently affixed to the land.

Real return Investment return after inflation.

Real risk-free rate of return Return without chance of default or volatility.

Real time Up-to-the-minute, current stock quote.

Receivables turnover A measure that implies the speed at which receivables are collected.

Recession Severe economic contraction.

Record date Date on which a shareholder must be a registered owner in order to receive the benefit of a stock split (or other stockholder benefit).

Red herring Nickname for the preliminary prospectus.

Reference points Prices that investors remember and use for comparison with the current price.

Refunding Retirement of seasoned securities with proceeds from a new issue.

Registered bonds Bonds sold in book-entry form.

Registration statement SEC document that describes an offering.

Regression to the mean Tendency of profit rates to return toward long-term industry and economywide averages; the concept that both past outperformers and past underperformers tend to become average in the future.

Regret of commission Disappointment from taking an action that had a bad result.

Regret of omission Disappointment from not taking an action that would have had a good result.

Regulation risk Chance of investor loss due to burdensome government rules and regulations.

Regulation Government control or influence.

Relative P/E ratio Firm's P/E ratio divided by an index P/E ratio.

Representativeness bias A mental shortcut by which some known characteristics represent what is to be expected for other, unknown characteristics; a perception that historical data will be repeated in the future.

Required risk premium Necessary compensation for risk taking.

Resistance line Graphical depiction of price points at which selling pressure (supply) has emerged in the recent past.

Retention rate Share of earnings retained to fund investment.

Return anomaly An inexplicable pattern of abnormal stock market returns.

Return on assets (ROA) Net income divided by the book value of total assets.

Return on equity Accounting net income divided by stockholders' equity, or book value per share.

Return on stockholders' equity (ROE) Net income divided by the book value of stockholders' equity.

Revenue bonds Bonds payable from the earnings of revenue-producing government agencies or public enterprises.

Reversal pattern Change in trend signal.

Reverse stock split Stock split that reduces the number of shares outstanding.

Reversion to the mean Tendency of stock and bond returns to return toward long-term averages.

Rho Sensitivity of option value to changes in interest rates.

Risk Chance of a loss of wealth or a failure to meet investment goals;

return dispersion; usually measured by the standard deviation of returns.

Risk averse   Desire to avoid risk.

Risk immunization   Elimination of interest rate risk by matching the durations of financial assets and liabilities.

Risk-adjusted discount rate   Investor's required return.

Road show   Series of investment banker presentations to promote company securities being sold.

Roll-up   Company that grows through constant acquisition.

Round lot   100 shares; in the bond market, $1 million of par value.

Russell 1000 Index   Market capitalization index for the 1,000 largest U.S. companies (90 percent of U.S. market cap).

Russell 2000 Growth Index   Small-cap benchmark for growth stocks with relatively high price-book ratios and high forecasted growth.

Russell 2000 Index   Small-company stock price index for the 2,000 smallest companies in the Russell 3000 Index.

Russell 2000 Value Index   Small-cap benchmark for value stocks with relatively low price-book ratios and low forecasted growth.

Russell 3000 Growth Index   Large-cap benchmark for growth stocks with relatively high price-book ratios and high forecasted growth.

Russell 3000 Index   Market capitalization index for the 3,000 largest U.S. companies (98 percent of U.S. market cap).

Russell 3000 Value Index   Large-cap benchmark for value stocks with relatively low price-book ratios and low forecasted growth.

S&P 500 Index   Popular value-weighted market index.

S&P MidCap 400 Index   Market cap index for 400 medium-sized domestic stocks.

S&P Pure Style benchmark indices   Performance standards for growth and value stocks precisely identified using S&P criteria.

S&P SmallCap 600 Index   Market-cap-weighted index of 600 small domestic stocks.

S&P Style benchmark indices   Performance standards for growth and value stock components of popular S&P Indices.

Sarbanes-Oxley Act   Law instituting public accounting reforms and investor protections.

Seasoned bonds   Bonds traded from one investor to another.

Seasoned issue   Issuance of a security to raise additional capital for which there is already an existing public market.

Secondary bond market   Market for previously issued bonds; an investor-to-investor market.

Secondary market   Stock exchange where investors trade stocks with each other.

Secondary offerings   Public sale of previously issued securities held by large investors, corporations, or institutional investors.

Secondary trends   Short-term moves in the market that run contrary to the primary trend and usually last from three weeks to three months.

Securities and Exchange Commission (SEC)   Federal regulatory body charged with monitoring corporations and the investment industry.

Securities arbitration   Private form of dispute resolution with binding outcomes.

Security analyst   Finance professional who analyzes and makes recommendations regarding stocks and other financial assets.

Security characteristic line (SCL)   Linear relation between the return on individual securities and the overall market at every point in time.

Security market line (SML)   Linear risk-return trade-off for individual stocks.

Segmented markets   Stock markets in which there are no investment flows between the markets.

Segmented-market hypothesis   Theory that yield curves reflect the hedging and maturity needs of institutional investors.

Select sector SPDRs   ETFs that track the price performance and dividend yield of particular industry groups.

Selectivity   Ability to pick stocks that outperform the overall stock market.

Self-regulatory organizations (SROs)   Industry group with oversight authority granted by the SEC.

Sell-side analysts   Analysts who work for brokerage firms or investments banks.

Semiannual interest   Interest paid in two equal installments per year.

Semistrong-form hypothesis   Premise that stock prices reflect all public information.

Senior bond   Debt with prior claim to other, junior securities in the event of default.

Sensitivity analysis   Computation of fundamental values in which small changes are made to the model's input data to determine how sensitive the results are to those variables.

Sentiment   General level of optimism or pessimism.

Serial bonds   A series of bonds to be retired in sequence.

Settlement date   Date on which the buyer takes effective possession of a security.

Sharpe Ratio   Risk premium earned relative to total risk.

Short   Seller; also used to signify sale.

Short interest   Number of shares sold short.

Short interest ratio   Short interest expressed in terms of an average day's trading volume.

Short sale   Sale of borrowed stock used to profit from a falling stock price.

Short squeeze   Pressure on short sellers through margin calls caused by rapidly appreciating stock prices.

Single-country fund   Mutual fund that invests in a sole foreign country.

Small-cap effect   Tendency for outperformance by small-capitalization stocks.

Social norms   The informal opinions, rules, and procedures of a group.

Specialist   Employee of a NYSE firm who manages the market for an individual stock.

Speculative position   Use of options to profit from the inherent riskiness of some underlying asset.

Speculators   Individuals who seek to profit from price changes.

Spin-off anomaly   Tendency of spin-offs of smaller companies from larger organizations to lead to favorable stock market performance.

Split ratio   Rate of increase in stock outstanding.

Spot price   Current cash price.

Spread   Purchase and sale of the same type of option (call or put) on the same underlying asset.

Standard & Poor's Depository Receipts (SPDR)s   ETFs that track the price performance and dividend yield of the S&P 500 Index.

Standard deviation   A common risk measure.

Status quo   The tendency to do nothing.

Stock funds   Funds that make equity investments.

Stock market information   Stock price and trading volume information.

Stock market investment   Process of buying and holding stock for dividend income and long-term capital appreciation.

Stock market speculation   Purchase or sale of securities on the expectation of short-term trading profits from share price fluctuations tied to temporary good fortune.

Stock market volatility   Large increases and decreases in prices over time.

Stock-price trend   Propensity for a stock that is rising in price to continue to rise or for one falling in price to continue to fall until some new demand or supply force takes effect.

Stock quotes   Offers to buy and sell shares at specific prices.

Stock Watch   Computerized system that flags unusual volume or price changes.

Stockbroker   Financial agent who assists investors with buying and selling financial assets.

Stop order   Market order to buy or sell a certain quantity of a security if a specified price is reached or passed.

Stop-limit order   Order to buy or sell a certain quantity of a security at a specified price or better, but only after a specified price has been reached.

Stop-loss order   Stop order to sell a long position at a specified price that is below the current market price.

Stopped out   Position that is liquidated by the execution of a stop order.

Straddle   Purchase of a put and sale of a call on the same security.

Strike price   Exercise price.

Strong dollar   Increase in the amount of foreign currency that can be purchased for $1.

Strong-form hypothesis   Premise that stock prices reflect all public information and nonpublic information.

Style box   Means of characterizing portfolio risk according to market capitalization and value-growth orientation. Morningstar classifies fund portfolio holdings into nine categories based on these characteristics.

Subordinated   Ranked as less important.

Support line   Graphical depiction of price points at which additional demand for the stock has emerged in the past.

Swaps   Arrangements whereby two companies agree to lend to each other on different terms.

Swaptions   Options to engage in a specific interest rate swap on or before a specific date.

Syndicate manager   Lead investment bank in a syndicate.

Synthetic (option)   A payoff derived from holding nonoption securities that is identical with a put or call strategy.

Systematic risk   Return volatility tied to the overall market.

T-bills   Treasury bills (mature in less than one year).

T-bonds   Treasury bonds (mature in 10 to 30 years).

T-notes   Treasury notes (mature in 1 to 10 years).

TRIN (*trading in*dex) ratio   Common indicator of market imbalance.

TSE-35   Market basket of 35 blue-chip Canadian companies.

Tax rate   Percentage of the property value paid to support government services.

Technical analysis   Study of historical price and volume information to forecast future prices

Technicians   Technical analysts.

Technology stocks   Shares in companies at the vanguard of important new innovations.

Term structure of interest rates   Interest rate relation among bonds with the same credit quality but different maturities.

Tertiary trends   Very short-term stock market trends that reflect minor price moves.

Theta   Sensitivity of option value to a change in time.

Ticker symbol   Unique one-, two-, three-, or four-letter code for any company.

Ticker symbols   Unique stock identifier with one to five letters.

Time interval bias   Beta estimation problem derived from the fact that beta estimates depend on the data interval studied.

Time series   Data points over time.

Time spread   Simultaneous purchase and sale of options on the same underlying stock but with different expiration dates.

Time value   Speculative value that diminishes over time.

Tombstone ad   Advertisement announcing details of an upcoming security offering.

Top-line growth   Growth in revenue (the top line of the income statement).

Total asset turnover   Sales revenue divided by the book value of total assets.

Total return   The sum of dividends, interest income, and capital gains or capital losses.

Trade deficit   Excess value of imports over exports.

Trading pit   Futures market trading area.

Trading unit   Contract size.

Transfer agent   Person or firm who executes shareholder transactions, maintains records, and issues account statements.

Treasury bills   Treasury obligations with maturities of one year or less.

Treasury bonds   Treasury obligations with maturities of 10 years or more.

Treasury Inflation Protected Securities (TIPS)   Treasury bonds whose par value is adjusted semi-annually for inflation, as measured by the CPI.

Treasury notes   Treasury obligations with maturities of more than 1 year but less than 10 years.

Treynor Index   Risk premium earned relative to systematic risk.

Turnover rate   A common measure of a mutual fund's trading activity.

Undervalued   A stock priced below its true economic value.

Underwriter   Investment bank that endorses and sponsors a company's new securities.

Underwriter's allotment   Investment banker's allocation of the new shares.

Underwriting syndicate   Group of underwriters who agree to participate in selling an issue.

Unrealized capital gains   Increase in fund value caused by a rise in the value of fund investments.

Unsecured corporate bond   Debt backed only by the reputation, credit record, and financial stability of the corporation.

Unsystematic risk   Return volatility specific to an individual company.

Up-down ratio   Value of uptick trades relative to value of downtick trades.

Uptick trade   Trade at a higher price than the previous trade.

Utility   Positive benefit.

Valuation risk   Chance of loss due to relatively high stock prices.

Value effect   Tendency for outperformance by value stocks.

Value investing   Investment approach that concentrates on securities considered to be temporarily undervalued or unpopular.

Value investors   Investors who seek out-of-favor stocks selling at a discount to the overall market.

Value of ROE   ROE percentage divided by the P/E ratio.

Variable growth rate   Model used when short-term growth rates are not expected to persist in the long run.

Vega   Sensitivity of option value to a change in volatility.

Weak dollar   Decrease in the amount of foreign currency that can be purchased for $1.

Weak-form hypothesis   Premise that current prices reflect all stock market information.

Writers   Sellers who are obligated to exercise the option at the holder's request.

Yankee bond   Foreign bond issued in the United States by a non-U.S. borrower and denominated in dollars.

Yield curve   Line connecting the yields offered on similar-risk bonds of different maturities.

Yield spread   Difference in yield for bonds with the same term to maturity but different credit risks.

Yield to call   Investor return over the period from the settlement day to the security's repurchase by the issuer.

Yield to maturity   Investor return over the period from the settlement day to the security's expiration.

Yield-based options   Debt options that are cash-settled based on the difference between the exercise price and the value of an underlying yield.

Zero-coupon bonds ("zeros")   Discount bonds that pay no coupon interest.

Zero-risk portfolio   A constant-return portfolio.

Zero-sum game   Transaction in which the buyer's gain is the seller's loss, and vice versa.

Index